1985

The Theory
and Practice
of Reliable
System Design

The Theory and Practice of Reliable System Design

DANIEL P. SIEWIOREK

ROBERT S. SWARZ

DIGITAL PRESS

Printed in U.S.A.
10 9 8 7 6 5 4 3 2

Documentation number EY-AX016-DP
ISBN 0-932376-13-4

Library of Congress Cataloging in Publication Data

Siewiorek, Daniel P.
  The theory and practice of reliable system design.

  Bibliography: p.
  Includes index.
  1. Electronic digital computers—Reliability.
2. Fault-tolerant computing.   I. Swarz, Robert.
II. Title.
QA76.5.S538   001.64   81-9696
ISBN 0-932376-13-4   AACR2

Trademarks appear on p. 749.

CREDITS

Figures 5–12, 5–13, 5–14, 5–15

Jacob A. Abraham and Daniel P. Siewiorek, "An Algorithm for the Accurate Reliability Evaluation of Triple Modular Redundancy Networks," IEEE TRANSACTIONS ON COMPUTERS (July 1974). Copyright © 1974 IEEE. Reprinted by permission.

Figure 3–68

D.G. Armstrong, "A General Method of Applying Error Correction to Synchronous Digital Systems," THE BELL SYSTEM TECHNICAL JOURNAL, vol. 40, p. 580. Copyright © 1961, American Telephone and Telegraph Company. Reprinted by permission.

Credits are continued on p. 751 and are considered part of the copyright page.

To Karon and Lonnie

Contents

Preface

System reliability has been a major concern since the beginning of the electronic digital computer age. The earliest computers were constructed of components such as relays and vacuum tubes that would fail to operate correctly as often as once every hundred thousand or million cycles. This error rate was far too large to ensure correct completion of even modest calculations requiring tens of millions of operating cycles. The Bell relay computer (c. 1944) performed a computation twice and compared results; it also employed error-detecting codes. The first commercial computer, the UNIVAC I (c. 1951), utilized extensive parity checking and two arithmetic logic units (ALUs) in a match-and-compare mode. Today, interest in reliability pervades the computer industry, from large mainframe manufacturers to semiconductor fabricators, who produce not only reliability-specific chips (such as for error-correcting codes) but also entire systems (such as the Intel 432).

Computer designers have to be students of reliability, and so do computer system users. Our dependence on computing systems has grown so great that it is becoming difficult or impossible to return to less sophisticated mechanisms. When an airline seat selection computer "crashes," for example, the airline can no longer revert to assigning seats from a manual checklist; since the addition of roundtrip check-in service, there is no way of telling which seats have been assigned to passengers who have not yet checked in without consulting the computer. The last resort is a free-for-all rush for seats. The computer system user must be able to understand the advantages and limitations of the state-of-the-art in reliability design; determine the impact of those advantages and limitations upon the application or computation at hand; and specify the requirements for the system's reliability so that the application or computation can be successfully completed.

The literature on reliability has been slow to evolve. During the 1950s reliability was the domain of industry, and the quality of the design often depended on the cleverness of an individual engineer. Notable exceptions are the work of Shannon [1948] and Hamming [1950] on communication through noisy (hence error-inducing) channels, and of Moore and Shannon [1956] and von Neumann [1956] on redundancy that survives component failures. Shannon and Hamming inaugurated the field of coding theory, a cornerstone in contemporary systems design. Moore, Shannon, and von Neumann laid the foundation for development and mathematical evaluation of redundancy techniques.

During the 1960s the design of reliable systems received systematic treatment in industry. Bell Telephone Laboratories designed and built an Electronic Switching System (ESS), with a goal of only two hours down-time in 40 years [Downing, Nowak, and Tuomenoksa, 1964]. The IBM System/360 computer family had extensive serviceability features [Carter et al., 1964]. Reliable design also found increasing use in the aerospace industry, and a triplicated computer helped man land on the moon [Cooper and Chow, 1976; Dickinson, Jackson, and Randa, 1964]. The volume of literature also increased. In 1962 a Symposium on Redundancy

Table P–1.   Proposed structure for undergraduate course.

Chapters	Remarks
1 Fundamental Concepts	
2 Faults and Their Manifestations	
3 Reliability and Availability Techniques	A suitable subset such as one branch of the taxonomy (i.e., fault avoidance, fault detection, masking redundancy, dynamic redundancy)
4 Maintainability and Testing Techniques	
5 Evaluation Criteria	Through to, but not including, Markov models
6 Financial Considerations	
7 C.vmp	As time permits, augment by other examples
18 Intel 432	

Techniques held in Washington, D.C. led to the first comprehensive book on the topic [Wilcox and Mann, 1962]. Later, Pierce [1965] published a book generalizing and analyzing the Quadded Redundancy technique proposed by Tryon and reported in Wilcox and Mann [1962]. A community of reliability theoreticians and practitioners was developing.

During the 1970s interest in system reliability expanded explosively. Companies were formed whose major product was a reliable system (such as Tandem). Due to the effort of Algirdas Avizienis and other pioneers, a Technical Committee on Fault Tolerant Computing (TCFTC) was formulated within the Institute of Electrical and Electronic Engineers (IEEE). Every year since 1971, the TCFTC has held an International Symposium on Fault-Tolerant Computing. The time is ripe for a book on the design of reliable computing structures.

This book has three audiences. The first is the advanced undergraduate student interested in reliable design; as prerequisites, this student should have had courses in introductory programming, computer organization, digital design, and probability. Part I of the book, selected chapters of Part II, and end-of-chapter problems are sufficient for a quarter- or semester-length course like that suggested in Table P-1.

The second audience is the graduate student seeking a second course in reliable design, perhaps as a prelude to engaging in research. The more advanced portions

Table P–2.   Proposed structure for graduate course.

Chapters	Augmentation
1 Fundamental Concepts	
2 Faults and Their Manifestations	Ross [1972] and/or Shooman [1968] for random variables, statistical parameter estimation ARINC [1964] for data collection and analysis
3 Reliability and Availability Techniques	Appendix A, Peterson and Weldon [1972] for coding theory Sellers, Hsiao, and Bearnson [1968b] for error detection techniques Proceedings of Annual IEEE International Symposium on Fault-Tolerant Computing Special issues of the *IEEE Transactions on Computers* on Fault-Tolerant Computing (e.g., Nov 1971, March 1973, July 1974, May 1975, June 1976, June 1980, July 1982) Special issues of *Computer* on Fault-Tolerant Computing (e.g., March 1980)
4 Maintainability and Testing Techniques	Breuer and Friedman [1976] for testing Proceedings of Cherry Hill Test Conference Special issues of *Computer* on Testing (e.g., Oct. 1979) ARINC [1964] for maintenance analysis
5 Evaluation Criteria	Ross [1972], Howard [1971], Shooman [1968], Craig [1964] for Markov models and their solutions
6 Financial Considerations	Phister [1979]
Part II	Oct. 1978 special issue of the Proceedings of the IEEE.

of Part I and the system examples of Part II should be augmented by other books and current research literature as suggested in Table P-2. A project, such as design of a dual system with a factor of 20 greater Mean-Time-To-Failure, while minimizing Life-Cycle Costs, would help to crystallize the material for students. An extensive bibliography provides access to the literature.

The third audience is the practicing engineer. A major goal of this book is to provide enough concepts to enable the practicing engineer to incorporate comprehensive reliability techniques into his or her next design. Part I provides a taxonomy of reliability techniques and the mathematical models to evaluate them. Design techniques are illustrated through the series of articles in Part II, which describe actual implementations of reliable computers. These articles were written by the system designers. The final chapter provides a methodology for reliable system design and illustrates how this methodology can be applied in an actual design situation (the Intel 432).

The book is divided into two parts. Part I deals with the theory and Part II with the practice of reliable design. The appendixes provide detailed information on coding theory, design for testability, and the MIL-HDBK-217 component reliability model.

The authors wish to express deep gratitude to many colleagues in the fault-tolerant computing community. Without their contributions and assistance this book could not have been written. We are especially grateful to the authors of the papers who shared their design insights with us. Special thanks go to Sudhir Bhagwani and Justin Rattner for assistance with Chapter 18. John Shebell provided material and insight for Chapter 6.

Xavier Castillo and Vittal Kini provided material on mathematical modeling and computer aids, respectively. Ashok Ingle assisted in an earlier draft and provided several problems at the end of chapters. Comments from several reviewers and students were particularly helpful.

Special thanks are due to colleagues at both Carnegie-Mellon University and Digital Equipment Corporation (DEC) for providing an environment conducive to generating and testing ideas. The entire staff of Digital Press provided excellent support for a timely production.

This book would not have been possible without the patience and diligence of Mrs. Dorothy Josephson, who typed and retyped the many drafts of the manuscript.

Dan Siewiorek
Bob Swarz

REFERENCES*

ARINC [1964]; Breuer and Friedman [1967]; Carter et al. [1964]; Cooper and Chow [1976]; Craig [1964]; Dickinson, Jackson, and Randa, [1964]; Downing, Nowak, and Tuomenoksa [1964]; Hamming [1950]; Howard [1971]; Moore and Shannon [1956]; Peterson and Weldon [1972]; Phister [1979]; Pierce [1965]; Ross [1972]; Sellers, Hsiao, and Bearnson [1968b]; Shannon [1948]; Shooman [1968]; von Neumann [1956]; Wilcox and Mann [1962].

---

* For full citations of the shortened references at the end of each chapter, see References at the back of the book.

THE THEORY OF RELIABLE SYSTEM DESIGN

PART

I

Part I of this book presents the many disciplines required to construct a reliable computing system. Chapter 1 explains the motivation for reliable systems and provides the theoretical framework for their design, fabrication, and maintenance. First we consider the motivation for interest in fault-tolerant systems. Next we present the hierarchical levels into which a computer system is customarily divided to enable the engineer to deal with it efficiently and effectively; we also explain the reasons for introducing divisions into the life cycle of a computer system. After defining several terms and metrics important to fault-tolerant computing, Chapter 1 provides a detailed discussion of two stages in a system's life: manufacturing and operation. Last, the chapter explains some of the mathematical models used in the design of a computer system and specifies the parameters that are under the engineer's control.

Chapter 2 discusses faults in a computer system: failure mechanisms, fault manifestations at several levels in the structural hierarchy (physical, logical, and system), fault prediction, and fault measurement. A review of applicable probability theory is presented as an aid to understanding the mathematics of the various fault distributions. Common techniques for matching empirical data to fault distributions, such as the maximum likelihood estimator, linear regression, and the chi-square goodness-of-fit test are discussed.

Chapter 2 introduces methods for estimating permanent failure rates, including the MIL-HDBK-217 procedure, a widely used mathematical model of permanent faults in electronic equipment, and the life-cycle testing and data analysis approaches. It then addresses the problem of finding an appropriate distribution for transient errors by analyzing field data from four mainframe time-sharing computers operated by Carnegie-Mellon University.

Chapter 3 deals with reliability techniques, that is, ways to improve the mean time to failures. A comprehensive taxonomy of reliability and availability techniques is presented. There is also a catalog of techniques, along with evaluation criteria.

Chapter 4 deals with maintainability techniques, that is, ways to improve the mean time to repair of a failed computer system. It provides a taxonomy of testing and maintenance techniques and describes ways to detect and correct sources of errors at each stage of a computer's life cycle. Specific strategies are discussed for testing during the manufacturing phase. Several logic-level acceptance tests are explained, such as exclusive-OR testing, signature analysis, Boolean difference, path sensitization, and the D-algorithm. The chapter also introduces a discipline, called design for testability, which attempts to define properties of easy-to-test systems.

1

How can a reliable or maintainable design be mathematically evaluated? That is, if a system is supposed to be down no more than two hours in 40 years, how can one avoid waiting that long to confirm success? Chapter 5 defines a host of evaluation criteria, establishes the underlying mathematics, and presents deterministic models and simulation techniques. Simple series-parallel models are introduced as a method for evaluating the reliability of nonredundant systems and systems with standby sparing. Next, several types of combinatorial (failure-to-exhaustion) models are described. The chapter also introduces ways of reducing nonseries, nonparallel models to more tractable forms.

Chapter 5 continues with Markov models, which define various system states and express the probability of going from one state to another. In these models, the probability depends only on the present state and is independent of how the present state was reached. After describing several other simulation and modeling techniques, the chapter culminates in a case study of an effort to make a more reliable version of the PDP-8/e, using the techniques defined in Chapter 3.

Finally, Chapter 6 is concerned with the financial considerations inherent in the design, purchase, and operation of a computer system. The discussion adopts two major viewpoints: that of the maintenance provider and that of the system's owner/operator. An explanation of the various sources of maintenance costs, such as labor and material, is followed by an overview of the field service business. Several maintenance cost models are suggested, along with a method for assessing the value of maintainability features. The chapter describes two of the many ways of modeling the life-cycle costs of owning and operating a computer system; these cost models are essential to the system designer in understanding the financial motivations of the customer.

Fundamental Concepts

THE IMPORTANCE OF RELIABILITY

1

Historically, reliable computers have been limited to military, industrial, aerospace, and communications applications in which the consequence of computer failure is significant economic impact and/or loss of life. Reliability is of critical importance wherever a computer malfunction could have catastrophic results, as in the space shuttle, aircraft flight-control systems, hospital patient monitors, and power system control. Reliability techniques have become of increasing interest to general purpose computer systems because of several recent trends, a few of which are listed below:

Harsher Environments. With the advent of microprocessors, computer systems have moved from the clean environments of computer rooms to industrial environments. The cooling air contains more particulate matter. Temperature and humidity vary widely and are frequently subject to spontaneous changes. The primary power supply fluctuates, and there is electromagnetic interference.

Novice Users. As computers proliferate, the typical user knows less about proper operation of the system. Consequently, the system has to be able to tolerate more inadvertent user abuse.

Increasing Repair Costs. As hardware costs continue to decline and labor costs escalate, a user cannot afford frequent calls for field service. Figure 1-1 depicts the relation between cost of ownership and the addition of reliability, maintainability, and availability features. Note that as hardware costs increase, service costs decrease due to fewer and shorter field service calls.

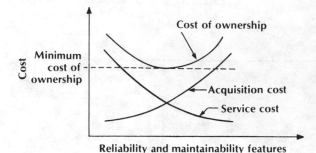

Figure 1–1. Cost of ownership as a function of reliability and maintainability.

Larger Systems. As systems become larger, there are more components that can fail. Because the overall failure rate is directly related to the sum of the failure rates of individual components, fault-tolerant designs may be required to keep the overall system failure rate at an acceptable level.

The increased interest in fault tolerance has already had an impact on the industrial world. Manufacturers of large mainframe computers, such as IBM, Univac, and Amdahl, use redundancy both for improving reliability and for assisting field service personnel in fault isolation. Minicomputer manufacturers have also been incorporating fault-tolerant features, such as Hamming error-correcting codes in memory. Special Large Scale Integration (LSI) chips have been introduced to perform cyclic redundancy coding and decoding. Some companies, such as Tandem, have been formed solely to market fault-tolerant computers.

LEVELS IN A DIGITAL SYSTEM*

Digital computer systems are enormously complex. To make them more comprehensible it is necessary to divide the system into several levels.

* This discussion is adapted from D. Siewiorek, G. Bell, and A. Newell, *Computer Structures: Principles and Examples*, (New York, McGraw-Hill, 1981).

One can then proceed upward from the most primitive level to the highest conceptual level through a series of abstractions. Each abstraction contains only information important to its level and suppresses unnecessary information about lower ones. Because system designers utilize the hierarchical concept to manage the complexity of a digital system, the levels frequently coincide with the system's physical boundaries. Table 1-1 describes a typical set of levels for a digital computer.

Table 1–1. Levels of abstraction for digital computers.

Level	Sublevel	Components
PMS		Processors
		Memories
		Switches
		Controllers
		Transducers
		Data operators
		Links
Program	High-level language	Software
	ISP	Memory state
		Processor state
		Effective address calculation
		Instruction decode
		Instruction execution
Logic	Register transfer	Data paths
		Registers
		Data operators
		Control
		Hardwired
		Sequential logic machines
		Microprogramming
		Microsequencer
		Microstore

(Table continues on next page)

Table 1–1—*Continued*

Level	Sublevel	Components
	Switching circuit	Sequential
		Flip-flops
		Latches
		Delays
		Combinatorial
		Gates
		Encoders/Decoders
		Data operators
Circuit		Resistors
		Capacitors
		Inductors
		Power sources
		Diodes
		Transistors

Circuit Level. The circuit level consists of such components as resistors, capacitors, inductors, and power sources. The metrics of system behavior include voltage, current, flux, and charge. The circuit level is not the lowest possible level at which to describe a digital system. Various electromagnetic and quantum mechanical phenomena underlie circuit theory, and the operation of electromechanical system devices (such as disks) requires more than circuit theory to model their operation.

Logic Level. The logic level is unique to digital systems. The switching-circuit sublevel is composed of such things as gates and data operators built out of gates. The logic level is further subdivided into combinatorial and sequential logic circuits, the fundamental difference being the absence of memory elements in combinatorial circuits.

A register is a digital device that remembers the state of a set of binary digits. The Register Transfer (RT) sublevel deals with the next higher level of abstraction, namely, registers and functional transfers of information among registers. RT sublevels frequently are further subdivided into a data part and a control part. The data part is composed of registers, operators, and data paths. The control part provides the time-dependent stimuli that cause transfers between registers to take place.

In some computers, the control part is implemented as a hard-wired state-machine. With the availability of low-cost Read-Only Memories (ROMs), microprogramming is now a more popular way to implement the control function.

Program Level. The program level is unique to digital computers. At this level a sequence of instructions in the device is interpreted and causes action upon a data structure. This is the Instruction Set Processor (ISP) sublevel. The ISP description is used in turn to create software components that are easily manipulated by programmers—the high-level-language sublevel. The result is software, such as operating systems, run-time systems, application programs, and application systems.

PMS Level. Finally, the various elements—input/output devices, memories, mass storage, communications, and processors—are interconnected to form a complete system.

STAGES IN SYSTEM LIFE

Not only are system levels important for describing a digital computer; a time dimension is also required. At what point a technique or methodology is applied during the life cycle of a system may be more important than at what physical level.

From a user's viewpoint, a digital system can be treated as a "black box" that produces outputs in response to input stimuli. Table 1-2 lists the numerous stages in the life of the box as it progresses from concept to final implementation. These stages include specification of input/output relationships, logic design, prototype debug-

Table 1–2.   Stages in the development of a system.

Stage	Error Sources	Error Detection Techniques
Specification and design	Algorithm design	Simulation
	Formal specifications	Consistency checks
Prototype	Algorithm design	Stimulus/ response testing
	Wiring and assembly	
	Timing	
	Component failure	
Manufacture	Wiring and assembly	System testing
	Component failure	Diagnostics
Installation	Assembly	System testing
	Component failure	Diagnostics
Operational life	Component failure	Diagnostics
	Operator errors	
	Environmental fluctuations	

ging, manufacturing, installation, and field operation. Deviations from intended behavior, or errors, can occur at any stage as a result of incomplete specifications, incorrect implementation of a specification into a logic design, and assembly mistakes during prototyping or manufacturing.

During the system's operational life, errors can result from change in the physical state or damage to hardware. Physical changes may be triggered by environmental factors such as fluctuations in temperature or power supply voltage, static discharge, and even alpha particle emissions. Inconsistent states can also be caused by operator errors and by design errors in hardware or software.

Design errors, whether in hardware or software, are those caused by improper translation of a concept into an operational realization. Closely tied to the human creative process, design errors are difficult to predict. Gathering statistical information about the phenomenon is difficult because each design error occurs only once per system. The rapid rate of development in hardware technology constantly changes the set of design trade-offs, further complicating the study of hardware design errors. In the last five years there has been some progress in the use of redundancy—using additional resources beyond the minimum required to perform the task successfully—to control software design errors.

Any source of error can appear at any stage; however, it is usually assumed that certain sources of error predominate at particular stages. Furthermore, error-detection techniques can be tailored to the manifestation of fault sources. Thus, at each stage of system life there is a primary methodology for detecting errors. In the following discussion, the student of systems reliability must keep in mind the question, "At what level and at what stage of the system development does the subject matter apply?" The two dimensions of physical level and temporal stage serve as a framework to relate otherwise mutually exclusive factors. Later a third dimension, cost, will be considered.

ATTRIBUTES OF FAULT-TOLERANT COMPUTING AND THEIR DEFINITIONS

Fault-tolerant computing is the correct execution of a specified algorithm in the presence of defects. The effect of defects can be overcome by the use of redundancy. This redundancy can be either temporal (repeated executions) or physical (replicated hardware or software).

As in all systems design, system specifications constrain the design space and thus the design techniques that can be used. At the highest level of specification, fault-tolerant systems are categorized as either highly available or highly reliable.

Availability

The availability of a system as a function of time, $A(t)$, is the probability that the system is operational at the instant of time, t. If the limit of this function exists as t goes to infinity, it expresses the expected fraction of time that the system is available to perform useful computations. Activities such as preventive maintenance and repair reduce the time that the system is available to the user. Availability is typically used as a figure of merit in systems in which service can be delayed or denied for short periods without serious consequences.

Reliability

The reliability of a system as a function of time, $R(t)$, is the conditional probability that the system has survived the interval $[0, t]$, given that it was operational at time $t = 0$. Reliability is used to describe systems in which repair cannot take place (as in satellite computers) or in which the computer is serving a critical function and cannot be lost even for the duration of a repair (as in flight computers on aircraft) or in which the repair is prohibitively expensive. In general, it is more difficult to build a highly reliable computing system than a highly available one because of the more stringent requirements imposed by the reliability definition. An even more stringent definition than $R(t)$, sometimes used in aerospace applications, is the maximum number of failures anywhere in the system that the system can tolerate and still function correctly.

Two important stages in the development of a system will be discussed next: the manufacturing stage and the operational life stage. A third important stage, design, is the subject of the remaining chapters in Part I.

THE MANUFACTURING STAGE

A careless manufacturing process can make even the most careful design useless. The manufacturing stage begins with the final portion of the prototype stage in a process called Design Maturity Testing.

Design Maturity Testing

A Design Maturity Test (DMT) estimates the Mean Time To Failure (MTTF) for a new product before it is committed to volume manufacturing. The DMT is conducted to isolate and correct repetitive systemic problems that, if left in the design, would result in higher service costs and customer dissatisfaction.

The DMT is accomplished by operating a set of sample devices for a prolonged time (typically six to eight units for two to four months) to simulate actual field operation. In cases in which the duty cycle of the equipment is less than 100 percent, the duty cycle under test may be increased to 100 percent to accelerate testing. As failures are observed and recorded, they are classified according to such factors as failure mode, time, or environmental cause. Similar failures are then ranked in groups by decreasing frequency of occurrence.

This procedure establishes priorities for eliminating the causes. After the fundamental cause of the failure is found and corrective design action is taken, the operation of the modified or repaired test samples provides a closed-loop evaluation of the efficacy of the change. Repeating the procedure improves the design of the test samples until their estimated MTTF meets the

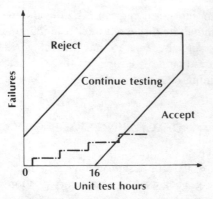

Figure 1–2. Reliability Demonstration Chart for monitoring the progress of a Design Maturity Test.

specifications with a certain statistical confidence.

The progress of the test can be monitored with a chart prepared in advance for the product under test, shown in Figure 1-2 [von Alven, 1964], which provides an objective criterion for judging the MTTF of a product with a predetermined statistical risk. The construction of the chart is determined by four parameters:

- Specified MTTF, Θ_0
- Minimum acceptable MTTF, Θ_1
- Consumer's risk, α. This is the probability that a product with an MTTF lower than Θ_0 will be accepted.
- Producer's risk, β. This is the probability that a product with an MTTF higher than Θ_0 will be rejected.

A ratio of Θ_0 to Θ_1 between 1.5 and 2 to 1 is typically used. Consumers' and producers' risks are commonly taken to be 20 percent. Operating time in unit hours is the abscissa, and number of failures is the ordinate. The resultant performance line is a staircase that moves up and to the right as test experience accumulates. The chart is divided into three areas: accept, reject, or continue testing. When the performance line crosses into the accept region, the test samples' MTTF is at least equal to the minimum acceptable MTTF (with the predetermined risk of error), and the design should be accepted.

If the performance line crosses into the reject region, the MTTF of the design is probably lower than the acceptable minimum with its corresponding probability of error; testing should be suspended until the design has been sufficiently improved and it can reasonably be expected to pass the test.

Incoming Inspection

Figure 1-3 depicts typical steps in the volume manufacturing process. Note the alternating pattern of test/inspect and fabrication [Foley, 1979].

Incoming inspection is an attempt to cull weak or defective components prior to assembly into subsystems. All semiconductor processes yield a certain number of defective devices. Even after the semiconductor manufacturer has detected and removed these defective devices, failures will continue to occur for a time known as the "infant mortality period." This period is typically 20 weeks or less, during which the rate of failures continues to decline. At the end of this period, failures tend to stabilize at a constant rate for a long time, sometimes 25 years or more. Ultimately the failure rate begins to rise again, in a period known as wear-out. This variation in failure rate as a function of time is illustrated by the bathtub-shaped curve shown in Figure 1-4.

Over the years, with the accumulation of experience in the manufacture of semiconductor components, the failure rate per logic device has steadily declined. Figure 1-5 depicts the number of failures per million hours for bipolar technology as a function of the number of gates on a chip. The curves Mil Model 217A were derived from 1965 data. The curves Mil Model 217B (see Appendix D) and Mil Model 217C (see Appendix E) were generated from a 1974 reliability prediction model. Actual failure data are also plotted to calibrate the 217B and 217C models. The curve Field data was derived from a yearlong reliability study of a sample of video terminals [Harrahy, 1977]. The curve Life cycle data was derived from elevated temperature testing of

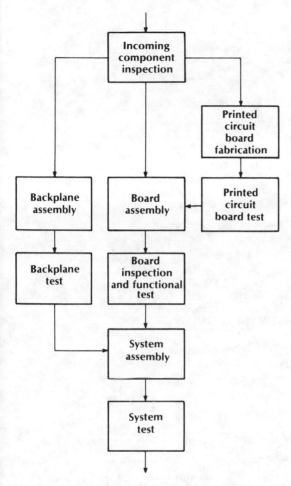

Figure 1–3. Typical steps in the manufacture of a digital system. (© 1979 IEEE.)

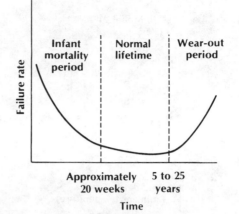

Figure 1–4. Bathtub curve depicting component failure rate as a function of time.

chips, followed by application of a mathematical model that translated the failure rates to ambient temperatures [Siewiorek et al., 1978b]. Finally, the improvement in the 3,000-gate Motorola MC6800 is plotted [Queyssac, 1979].

Two trends are noteworthy. First, there is more than an order of magnitude decrease in failure rate per gate. Plots of failure per bit of bipolar random access memory indicate that the failure rates per gate and per bit are comparable for comparable levels of integration.

Obviously, the chip failure rate is a function of chip complexity and is not a constant. Failure rate per function (gate or bit) decreases by one order of magnitude over two orders of magnitude of gate complexity and two to three orders of magnitude of memory complexity. The failure rate decreases in direct proportion to increases in complexity.

The second trend is that the MIL-HDBK-217B model predicted an increase in failure rate per function beyond about 200-gate complexity, presumably because of the immaturity of the fabrication process at that scale of integration at that time.[*]

Now consider a system composed of a constant number of semiconductor chips. Because the chips double in density every one to two years, the number of functions, f, in the system is proportional to changes in time, Δt:

$$f \propto 2^{\Delta t}$$

where t is time in years. The failure rate per function, from Figure 1-5, is proportional to the

---

[*] The switch from a polynomial to an exponential function in number of gates occurs at 100 in 217B and 1,000 in 217C. This reflects the improvements in the fabrication process over time. See Appendixes D and E.

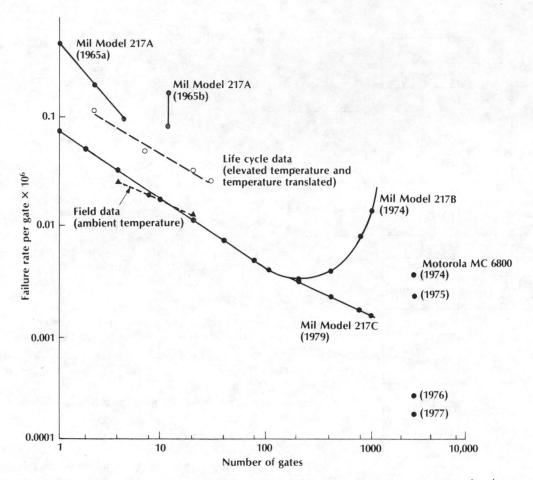

Figure 1–5. Failure rate per gate as a function of chip complexity for bipolar technology.

square root of the number of functions per chip:

$$r \propto f^{1/2}$$

Hence

$$r \propto 2^{\Delta t/2}$$

and the Mean Time To Failure (MTTF) is

$$\text{MTTF} \propto \frac{1}{r} \propto \frac{1}{2^{(\Delta t/2)}}$$

This implies that over a 10-year period a system with the same number of semiconductor chips has increased its logic complexity by a factor of 1,024 and decreased its MTTF by a factor of 32. Hence, system reliability has not kept pace with system complexity. Complex, high-performance machines are on the verge of becoming virtually unusable. For example, when the Los Alamos Scientific Laboratory evaluated the reliability of its CRAY-1 over a 6-month period, the mean time to failure was found to be four hours [Keller, 1976]. The average repair time was only about 25 minutes, due to the skilled on-site maintenance crew. Even so, this represented the loss of about 100 billion potential machine operations [Avizienis, 1978]. Gains in system reliability cannot be attained from improved component reliability alone. Redundancy must be introduced. Redundancy techniques are the subject of Chapter 3.*

The cost of component failure depends upon the level at which the failure is detected: the higher the level, the more expensive the repair. Fault detection at the semiconductor component level minimizes cost. Fault detection at the next highest level, the board, has been estimated at $5; at the system test level, $50; and at the field service level, $500 [Russel, 1980]. The level at which a computer manufacturer detects initial and infant mortality failures is a function of the incoming test program chosen.

Even relatively low semiconductor failure rates can cause substantial board yield problems, aggravated by the density of the board. Consider a board with forty semiconductor devices that have an initial failure rate of 1 percent:

$$\text{Probability board not defective} = (0.99)^{40}$$
$$= 0.669$$

The benefits of an incoming inspection program can be easily quantified. The value of culling bad semiconductor components before they are inserted into the board is the most easily measured benefit. Board/system test savings, inventory reduction, and service personnel savings depend on the particular strategy used. To calculate the

value of removing defective components at incoming inspection, multiply the number of bad parts found by the cost of detecting, isolating, and repairing failures at higher levels of integration. The following formula estimates the total savings:

$$D = 5B + 50S + 500F$$

where

D = dollar savings,
B = number of failures at board test level,
S = number of failures at system test level, and
F = number of failures in the field.

This formula can be translated into annual savings by considering total component volume and mean failure rate data:

Potential annual savings

= annual component volume ×

[(% initial failures)

(% failures detected at board level × $5

+ % failures detected at system level × $50)

+(% infancy failures)

(% failures detected at system level × $50

+ % failures detected in the field × $500)]

Typical savings for 100 percent incoming inspection can be estimated and compared with the cost of the Automatic Test Equipment (ATE) required to carry out such testing. Figure 1-6 (from [Russell, 1980]) shows the potential annual savings as a function of annual component volumes. A family of curves is shown for overall failure rates of 0.8, 1.2, 2.0, and 4.0 percent.

Process Maturity Testing

The term *process* includes all manufacturing steps to acquire parts, assemble, fabricate, in-

* The same semiconductor evolution that has led to increased reliability per gate or bit has also introduced new failure modes. The smaller dimensions of semiconductor devices have decreased the amount of energy required to change the state of a memory bit.

The loss of memory information caused by the decay of radioactive trace elements in packaging material has been documented. Studies show that even in sheltered environments such as well-conditioned computer rooms, soft errors are 20 to 50 times more prevalent than hard failures. Soft errors also exhibit clustering (a high probability that, once one error has occurred, another will occur soon), workload dependence (the heavier the system workload, the more likely an error), and common failure modes (more than one system, or portion of a system, affected simultaneously). Semiconductor failure rates and failure modes are discussed in detail in Chapter 2.

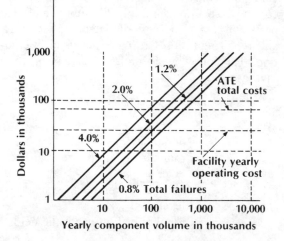

Figure 1–6. Savings from screening and testing as a function of defective component rate and annual device volume.

spect, and test a product during volume production. The rationale for Process Maturity Testing (PMT) is that newly manufactured products contain some latent defects built in by the process that produced them.

A large number of units, about the first 120 off the production line, are operated for 96 hours, often in lot sizes convenient to the particular production process. They are operated (burned in) in a manner that simulates the normal production process environment as closely as possible. If the burn-in and production process environments differ significantly, appropriate test results must be adjusted accordingly.

Infant mortality characteristics may fluctuate significantly throughout the test lot. The composite of these individual failure characteristics is considered the "normal infancy" for the device.

The end of the burn-in period for production equipment is determined by the normal infancy curve thus derived from the PMT. The objective is to ship products of consistently good quality and acceptable MTTF after a minimum burn-in period. Typical production burn-in times are 20 to 40 hours.

PMT is used to identify several classes of failures. Infancy failures are problems generally caused by parts that were defective from the time they were received. In largely solid-state devices, component problems will remain in this category until identified and controlled by either incoming inspection or changes implemented by the component vendor.

Manufacturing/inspection failures are generally failures repaired by readjustments or retouching, such as a part damaged by the assembly process or defects that bypassed the normal incoming test procedures.

Engineering failures are recurrent problems in the design that have not yet been corrected or new problems not yet resolved because of lack of experience.

Residual failures are problems that have not yet recurred and for which there is no corrective action except to repair when they occur. These are the truly random failures.

Experience has shown that the three major recurring problems usually account for 75 percent of all failures. It is reasonable to expect that the correction of the top four to six recurring problems will yield a tenfold improvement in MTTF.

THE OPERATIONAL LIFE STAGE

Maintenance and repair during the field operational stage are the customer's primary contacts with system reliability. In the early days of computers, repairing a downed system was an art. Diagnostics that were halted or trapped when executing certain instructions did give clues to the location of the failure but did not pinpoint the failing Field Replaceable Unit (FRU). To identify the failing FRU, technicians swapped circuit boards one by one with "known good boards" in the hope of eventually restoring the system to proper operation. In time, diagnostic techniques became better able to identify the specific failed FRU before swapping any boards;

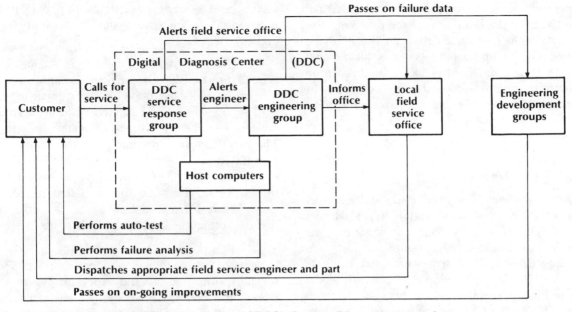

Figure 1–7. Overview of DEC's Remote Diagnosis Network.

then the failed board could rapidly be replaced with a good one.

Unfortunately, as on-site repair time is decreased by better diagnosis, travel time to the site becomes a limiting factor. At today's labor and transportation rates, the cost of travel time frequently exceeds the cost of the actual repair. Return trips, because the failed FRU was identified but the field service engineer had no replacement along, are very cost inefficient. Alternative service strategies have developed in response to these factors, such as customer carry-in service for small computers and service vans that carry enough sets of spare parts to permit long absences from the branch field service office.

A good example of a current field service approach is Digital Equipment Corporation's Digital Diagnosis Center (DDC). An overview of the network operation is shown in Figure 1-7. When customers detect or suspect a computer malfunction, they call a special telephone response line that is attended 24 hours a day, seven days a week. The heart of the DDC is a dual

PDP-11/70 configuration with auto-dial equipment. Once attached to the customer's failing computer (typically within 15 minutes), the DDC host system directs the diagnosis process based on results produced by the system under test. A configuration file is kept on each system supported. The DDC host executes the appropriate diagnostic "scripts," which simulate the thought processes of an on-site field service engineer. Each script executes a diagnostic sequence that can be modified according to the error responses generated by the computer being tested.

At the same time, the remote diagnosis specialist puts the local field service office on alert for a probable call. When initial diagnostic results are available, an engineer in the DDC reviews them and may then initiate further automatic tests or take direct control of the system under test.

When the analysis is complete, the problem will be described to the local field service branch office, which then dispatches the right person with the right part to the site. The on-site field engineer replaces the predetermined failed part and verifies the resolution of the problem. Final results of the corrective action are transmitted to the DDC to update the system's maintenance log. Information about problem areas in various computer systems is passed on to the engineering development groups for improvements in the future.

COST OF OWNERSHIP

The third dimension of the reliability framework, in addition to physical and temporal stage is cost. The cost of a computer system is not limited to initial purchase; significant costs recur during the life of a system. As a result, computer owners frequently develop mathematical models that enable them to make optimal decisions, minimizing the total cost of ownership.* Following is a description of some of the more significant costs:

Purchase Price.   The purchase price of a computer, though significant, can represent less than half the cost of ownership, computed on the basis of net present value. The purchase price usually includes system hardware, documentation, software license fees, training, and installation. The potential owner of a computer always has renting and leasing alternatives to consider, which can sometimes be advantageous in terms of cash flow or net present value.

Site Preparation.   Many computers require special operating environments. This may include special air conditioning, with closely controlled temperature, humidity, and airborne particulate matter size and density. A large computer may also require a raised floor for cabling. The main power supply may require a separate transformer with three-phase service and Radio Frequency Interference (RFI) filters. In some instal-

lations, an Uninterruptible Power Supply (UPS) is essential to increase system availability or prevent loss of data.

Maintenance.   All computers require some degree of preventive and corrective maintenance. The user usually has the option of purchasing a field service contract at a fixed price or paying for field service on a time-and-materials basis. The maintenance can come from the computer manufacturer, Original Equipment Manufacturer (OEM), a third party, or may be performed by the customer. The trade-offs inherent in decisions about when and how often to perform preventive maintenance also affect cost of ownership.

Supplies.   A computer system requires paper for the printers, disks and tapes for the mass storage devices, and other periodically replaced material. Very significant, too, is the power required to run the computer. With ever-escalating energy costs, supplying power to a computer for its operational lifetime can be one of the most significant expenses associated with ownership.

Cost of Downtime.   Depending on the application of the system, the cost of downtime can be trivial or crucial. In a system that acquires revenue, for example, the cost of downtime can far exceed the actual purchase price. This parameter requires careful evaluation by the potential customer.

Consider a system that has only an initial cost, I, and a failure rate λ. The cost, C, of owning this system for n years can be expressed as:

$$C = I + \sum_{i=1}^{n} \frac{S_i P_i}{(1 + D)^i}$$

where

S_i = the cost of one corrective maintenance call in year i
P_i = the expected number of failures during year i, and
D = the discount rate.

* These financial considerations are discussed in detail in Chapter 6.

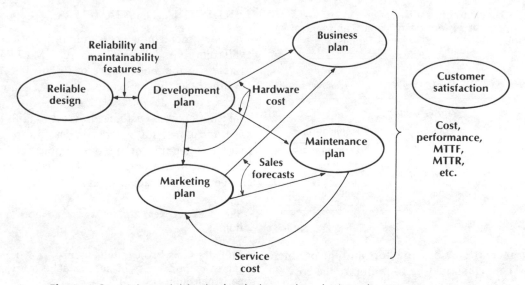

Figure 1–8.   Major activities in the design and marketing of a computer system.

The discount rate expresses the value of money in terms of time. For example, if you need $100 in two years and can get 10 percent annual interest in a savings account, you need to put away only $100/1.1^2 = \$82.65$ today. Here 10 percent represents the discount rate.

Assume that the failure rate is constant over the period in question. Then

$$C = I + P \sum_{i=1}^{n} \frac{S_i}{(1 + D)^i}$$

Further assume that the system has a five-year life, that a service call costs $300, and that the discount rate is 20 percent. Expressing λ in failures per million hours and noting the fact that there are 8,760 hours in a year results in:

$$C = I + (300)\frac{8760\lambda}{10^6} \sum_{i=1}^{5} \frac{1}{(1.2)^i}$$

$$= I + 7.86\lambda$$

Consider a system that costs $21,000 and has a failure rate of 6,500 per million hours (equivalent to a Mean Time To Failure of 154 hours). Its cost of ownership, using the assumptions above, is $72,090. Now consider another system that

costs more to purchase, $27,500, but is more reliable. Its failure rate is 4,400, or an MTTF of 227 hours. Its cost of ownership is $62,084. Although the second system is 31 percent more expensive to purchase, its 47 percent increase in reliability results in a 14 percent reduction in five-year cost of ownership.

UNIVERSE OF MODELS

Figure 1-8 depicts the major activities in the design and marketing of a computer system. Each activity has a model that can be used for predictive and evaluation purposes. The goal of all these activities is to produce a system which fulfills its intended use, thereby satisfying the customer. Customer satisfaction is a complex function of system cost, performance, reliability, and maintainability.

Once the need for a system is established, usually by technological or market pressures, a design is developed. Enhanced reliability usually involves some degree of hardware redundancy, and maintainability improvements usually involve the addition of self-testing circuits, both of

Table 1–3. Parameters a designer can control, their impact on system design goals, and typical techniques used to achieve these goals.

Designable Parameters	Goals	Example Techniques
	Hard Failures	
MTTF	Tolerate	Replication
MTTR	Isolate	Detection
	Transient Faults	
MTTC	Tolerate	Detection/Retry

which increase the design effort and the product cost. The goal should be to minimize the cost of ownership.

Ideally, sales forecasts are expressed as a function of selling price. Thus, the cost of hardware affects the sales forecasts and the business plan. Reliability (MTTF) and maintainability (MTTR) influence the field service plan. The sales forecasts affect both the field service and business plans. Coupled with the MTTF, MTTR, and sales forecasts, the field service plan produces the service costs, which further affect the business plan. Finally, the business plan determines the marketing, manufacturing, and field service strategies. Thus, all the components interact with and influence one another, and a modeling process underlies each component. Because financial plans vary greatly according to markets, and indeed between companies in the same market, this book focuses on evaluating reliability (see Chapter 5).

THE DESIGNABLE PARAMETERS

The designer influences reliability (MTTF), availability, and maintainability (MTTR) parameters in the model space of Figure 1-8. Table 1-3 illustrates the implication of these parameters on the system design.

With increased customer interest in fault tolerance and constantly decreasing hardware costs, there is a significant trend to implement more fault tolerance in hardware. Hardware error tolerance has many advantages:

· Simplifies recovery for software and user applications
· Saves time
· Provides transparency to the user
· Increases probability of successful recovery, given early detection
· Decreases MTTR
· Increases MTTF, MTTE (Mean Time To Error), and MTTC (Mean Time To Crash)
· Simplifies software recovery and reduces dependence on implementation
· Error detection logic can help isolate design errors so that future implementations are even more reliable.

The goal of this book is to provide methodologies for designing and evaluating the use of MTTF, MTTE, MTTC, and MTTR improvement techniques in computer systems.

REFERENCES

Avizienis [1978]; Foley [1979]; Harrahy [1977]; Keller [1976]; Queyssac [1979]; Russel [1980]; Siewiorek et al. [1978b]; Siewiorek, Bell, and Newell [1982]; von Alven [1964].

Faults and Their Manifestations

INTRODUCTION

Designing a fault-tolerant system requires finding a way to prevent the logical fault that arises from a physical failure from causing an error. Figure 2-1 depicts the possible sources of an error. The following apply [Avizienis, 1975]:

- *Failure.* Physical change in hardware.
- *Fault.* Erroneous state of hardware or software resulting from failures of components, physical inteference from the environment, operator error, or incorrect design.
- *Error.* Manifestation of a fault within a program or data structure. The error may occur some distance from the fault site.
- *Permanent.* Describes a failure, fault, or error that is continuous and stable. In hardware, permanent failure reflects an irreversible physical change. The word *hard* is used interchangeably with *permanent*.
- *Intermittent.* Describes a fault or error that is only occasionally present due to unstable hardware or varying hardware or software states (for example, as a function of load or activity).
- *Transient.* Describes a fault or error resulting from temporary environmental conditions. The word *soft* is used interchangeably with *transient*.

A fault can be caused by a physical failure, an inadequacy in the design of the system, an environmental influence, or the operator of the system. A permanent failure may lead to a permanent fault. Intermittent faults can be caused by unstable, marginally stable, or incorrect designs. Environmental conditions can lead to transient faults. All these faults can cause errors. Incorrect designs and operator mistakes can lead directly to errors.

The distinction between intermittent and transient faults is not always made in the literature [Kamal, 1975; Tasar and Tasar, 1977]. The di-

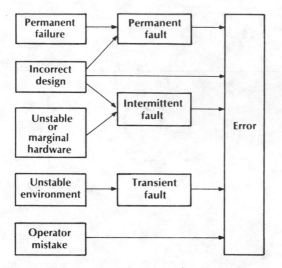

Figure 2–1. Sources of errors.

viding line is the applicability of repair [Breuer, 1973; Kamal and Page, 1974; Losq, 1978; Savir, 1978]. Faults resulting from physical conditions of the hardware, incorrect hardware or software design, or unstable but repeated environmental conditions are potentially detectable and repairable by replacement or redesign; faults due to temporary environmental conditions, however, are incapable of repair because the hardware is physically undamaged. It is this attribute of transient faults that magnifies their importance. Even in the absence of all physical defects,

including those manifested as intermittent faults, errors will still occur.

Transient and intermittent faults are already a major source of errors in systems. An early study for the U.S. Air Force [Roth et al., 1967a] showed that 80 percent of the electronic failures in computers are intermittent. Another study by IBM [Ball and Hardie, 1967] indicated that "intermittents comprised over 90% of field failures." Table 2-1 depicts the ratio of measured Mean Time Between Errors (MTBE) to Mean Time To Failure (MTTF) for several systems [Siewiorek et al., 1978a; Morganti, 1978; McConnel, Siewiorek, and Tsao, 1979]. The last row of this table is the estimate of permanent and transient failure rates for a one-megaword, 37-bit memory composed of 4K MOS RAMs [Geilhufe, 1979; Ohm, 1979]. In this case, transient errors are caused by alpha particles emitted by the decay of trace radioactive particles in the semiconductor packaging materials. As they pass through the semiconductor material, alpha particles create sufficient hole-electron pairs to add charge to or remove charge from bit cells. By exposing MOS RAMs to artificial alpha particle sources, the operational life error rate can be determined as a function of RAM density (Figure 2-2), voltage, and cycle time [Brodsky, 1980].

Transient errors have also been observed in microprocessor chips [Brodsky, 1980]. Transient

Table 2–1. Ratios of transient to permanent errors.

System/Technology	Mechanism	Processor MTBE	Processor MTTF	MTBE/ MTTF
CMUA PDP–10, ECL	Parity	44 hrs.	800–1,600 hrs.	0.03–0.06
Cm* LSI-11, NMOS	Diagnostics	128 hrs.	4,200 hrs.	0.03
C.vmp TMR LSI-11	Crash	97–328 hrs.	4,900 hrs.	0.02–0.07
Telettra, TTL	Mismatch	80–170 hrs.	1,300 hrs.	0.06–0.13
1M × 37 RAM, MOS	(Parity)	106 hrs.	1,450 hrs.	0.07

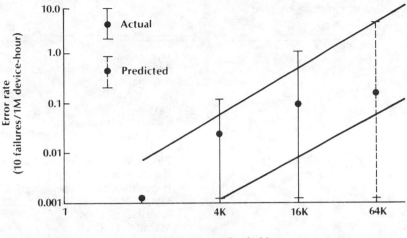

Figure 2–2. Measured soft error rates vs. dynamic RAM densities. (© 1979 IEEE.)

errors will become even more of a problem in the future with shrinking device dimensions, lower energy levels for indicating logical values, and higher-speed operation.

To design and evaluate the reliability and availability of systems requires a fault model. How do faults manifest themselves as errors? Do the arrival times of faults (or errors) fit a probability distribution? If so, what are the parameters of that distribution? This chapter attempts to answer these questions.

FAULT MANIFESTATIONS

Physical Defects

Physical defects are the lowest level in the hierarchy of failures. There are numerous ways in which a semiconductor chip can fail. Some failures result from defects in the manufacturing process. Others are due to stress during normal operation. The Reliability Analysis Center (RAC) of the Rome Air Development Center

(RADC) collects reliability data from government and industry on all phases of component development, assembly, testing, and field operation. The data are summarized in publications dealing with digital ICs, hybrid circuits, linear/interface devices, memory/LSI, discrete transistors/diodes, and nonelectronic parts.

Summary data are provided on device fall-out rates (the percent that fail initial screening), accelerated life testing (performed at high temperatures), and field operation. Analysis indicates the effect of package type, logic family, complexity, temperature, environment, and screening class on failure rates. Detailed information, listed in Table 2-2, is also given on each individual test of a device.

Tables 2-3 through 2-7 illustrate some failures observed in the RAC data as a function of technology [Rickers, 1976; Klein, 1976]. Many of the defects are related to manufacture and assembly; others develop as a result of aging. To eliminate as many of these defects as possible before board insertion, various screening tests are employed to stress devices and promote early

Table 2–2. Typical data reported in RAC detailed test information.

Device function

Test type
    Life
    Environmental/screening

Technology
    Bipolar
    MOS
    MOS, silicon gate
    CMOS

Device complexity

Manufacturer/part number

Package material/type
    Ceramic
    Ceramic-metal
    Epoxy
    Silicone
    Phenolic
    CAN
    DIP
    Flat-pack

Number of pins

Screening class
    MIL-STD-883 class B
    MIL-STD-883 class C
    Selected screening
    Previously subjected to burn-in
    Previously subjected to environmental test
    Commercial off-the-shelf

Rated operational temperature

Ending date of test

Source of data
    Part-level environmental test
    Equipment-level reliability demonstration test
    Equipment-level checkout and burn-in
    Part-level burn-in
    Part-level life test

Test type
    Accelerated life (operating)
    Autoclave
    Bond strength
    Burn-in
    Constant acceleration
    Electrical parameter measurement
    Leak
    Electrical measurement (functional)
    High pressure
    Humidity life (nonoperating)
    Intermittent life
    Lead fatigue
    Mechanical shock
    Moisture resistance
    Dynamic operation life
    Operating life (equipment-level)
    Power cycle
    Reverse bias life
    Humidity life with reverse bias
    Salt atmosphere
    Solderability
    Electrical measurement (static parameters)
    Storage life
    Temperature, vibration, and power cycle
    Temperature cycle
    Thermal shock
    Varied frequency vibration
    Visual inspection
    Wearout life test
    X-ray

Stress level
    Ambient temperature
    Number of cycles
    Minimum and maximum stresses

Number of devices tested

Total number of device hours

Number of failed devices

Description of failures

Table 2–3. Die-related malfunction summary for LSI device technologies.

Failure Classification	Bipolar No. Devices	%	MOS No. Devices	%	CMOS No. Devices	%
Surface	29	29.00%	78	45.09%	1	20.00%
Contamination	1	1.00	41	23.70	1	20.00
Inversion/channeling	15	15.00	1	.58		
Leakage	13	13.00	36	20.81		
Oxide defects	14	14.00	43	24.86	2	40.00
Pinholes						
Gate oxide			32	18.50	2	40.00
Field oxide	12	12.00	1	.58		
NOC						
Oxide fault/ breakdown	2	2.00	10	5.78		
Diffusion defects	1	1.00	17	9.83		
Diffusion anomaly			3	1.74		
Diffusion spike						
Masking fault	1	1.00	14	8.09		
Metalization defects	21	21.00	3	1.74		
Open	3	3.00	1	.58		
Short	16	16.00	1	.58		
Pitted/corroded			1	.58		
Smeared/scratched	2	2.00				
NOC						
Bond defects	5	5.00	7	4.05		
Misplaced						
Multiple bond						
Smeared/overbonded						
Lifted	4	4.00	7	4.05		
Broken	1	1.00				
Intermetallic compound						
Interconnection defects	29	29.00	7	4.05		
Open			6	3.47		
Short	28	28.00	1	.58		
Missing						

(Table continues on next page)

Table 2–3—*Continued*

Failure Classification	Bipolar		MOS		CMOS	
	No. Devices	%	No. Devices	%	No. Devices	%
Broken wire	1	1.00				
Die (mechanical)			3	1.74	2	40.00
Cracked/chipped			1	.58		
Die attach bond defect			2	1.16	2	40.00
Degraded input cktry	1	1.00	15	8.64		
Excessive leakage	1	1.00	13	7.48		
Short			2	1.16		

Table 2–4. Die-related failure modes: SSI, MSI, LSI CMOS.

Failure Classification	SSI CMOS		MSI CMOS		LSI CMOS	
	No. Devices	%	No. Devices	%	No. Devices	%
Surface defects	26	37%	31	37%	8	50%
Contamination	22	31	22	27	8	50
Foreign material/stray particles	2	2	2	2		
Inversion/channeling	2	3	5	6		
Surface leakage			2	2		
Bulk defects	2	3	10	12	0	0
Crystal imperfections	1	2	9	11		
Cracked, chipped die	1	2	1	1		
Oxide defects	27	39	21	25	6	38
Gate oxide pinholes	8	11	2	2	5	31
Field oxide pinholes						
Oxide fault			1	1	1	6

(*Table continues on next page*)

Table 2–4—*Continued*

Failure Classification	SSI CMOS		MSI CMOS		LSI CMOS	
	No. Devices	%	No. Devices	%	No. Devices	%
Oxide short/ breakdown	17	24	17	21		
Glassivation defect	2	2	1	1		
Diffusion defects	8	11	2	2	0	0
Diffusion anomaly						
Diffusion spike/ piped junct.						
Isolation defect						
Mask fault	8	11	2	2		
Metalization defects	4	7	8	10	2	12
Open at oxide step	2	3				
Open at contact window						
Open/not specified	1	2	4	5	2	13
Short/interlevel metal						
Short/not specified			1	1		
Pitted/corroded						
Smeared/scratched	1	2	3	4		
Electromigration						
Input output circuit defects	3	4	12	14	0	0
Excessive input leakage			8	10		
Input circuit short	3	4	2	2		
Excessive output leakage						
Output circuit short			2	2		
Total	70		84		16	

Table 2–5. Die-related defect summary: SSI, MSI, LSI CMOS.

General Defect Classification	No. Malfunctions	Relative Percent
Surface	65	38%
Bulk	12	7
Oxide	54	32
Diffusion	10	6
Metalization	14	8
Input/output circuit	15	9

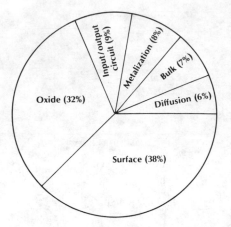

Table 2–6. Die-related failure modes: SSI, MSI, LSI standard TTL.

Failure Classification	SSI STD TTL No. Devices	%	MSI STD TTL No. Devices	%	LSI STD TTL No. Devices	%
Surface defects	51	20%	10	11%	5	8%
Contamination	29	11	5	6	2	3
Foreign material/ stray particles	7	3	4	5	1	2
Inversion/channeling	11	4	1	1	2	3
Surface leakage	4	2				
Bulk defects	24	9	5	6	0	0
Crystal imperfections	2	1	3	3		
Cracked, chipped die	22	8	2	2		
Oxide defects	27	10	10	11	22	33
Gate oxide pinholes						
Field oxide pinholes	8	3	6	7	12	18
Oxide fault	19	7	3	3	3	4
Oxide short/ breakdown					5	8
Passivation defect			1	0	2	3
Diffusion defects	19	7	13	15	0	0
Diffusion anomaly	4	2	9	10		
Diffusion spike/ piped junction	3	1	2	2		
Isolation defect	1	0				

(Table continues on next page)

Table 2–6—Continued

Failure Classification	SSI STD TTL		MSI STD TTL		LSI STD TTL	
	No. Devices	%	No. Devices	%	No. Devices	%
Mask fault	11	4	2	2		
Metalization defects	136	52	38	43	39	59
Open at oxide step						
Open at contact window	85	33	4	5		
Open/not specified	13	5	10	11	11	17
Short/interlayer metal	8	3	7	8	9	13
Short/not specified	22	8	15	17	17	26
Pitted/corroded	5	2				
Smeared/scratched	3	1	2	2	2	3
Electromigration						
Input/output circuit defects	5	2	12	14	0	0
Excessive input leakage	1	0	6	7		
Input circuit short	2	1	4	5		
Excessive output leakage			1	1		
Output circuit short	2	1	1	1		
Total	262		88		66	

Table 2–7. Die-related defect summary: SSI, MSI, LSI standard TTL.

General Defect Classification	No. Malfunctions	Relative Percent
Surface	66	16%
Bulk	29	7
Oxide	59	14
Diffusion	32	8
Metalization	213	51
Input/output circuit	17	4

1/5, 257

failure. The majority of the test types in Table 2-2 are electrical, mechanical, or environmental screens. Table 2-8 illustrates how tests can be constructed to uncover multiple defect types. Because screening consumes time, money, and resources, how much screening is used is a major decision. The optimum amount is a function of screening costs, device costs, fall-out rate, and cost of device failure in an assembled system.

Logic-Level Fault Classes

To determine the effect of failures on logic functions, physical data such as those given in the previous section must be used to generate circuit-level fault classes, which in turn are used to formulate logic-level fault classes. The abstraction process prevents proliferation of details. The following logic-level fault models have been used successfully as abstractions of the physical defect mechanisms:

- *Stuck-at.* Logical values in lines, gates, pins, and the like are permanently constrained to a value of 1 (s-a-1) or 0 (s-a-0).
- *Bridging.* Two or more adjacent signal lines are physically shorted together. In some logic families this introduces an additional "wired-AND" or "wired-OR" function.
- *Short or Open.* These correspond to missing (open) or additional (short) connections.
- *Unidirectional.* Due to the geometric nature of circuits, some single failures can effect multiple signal lines. An open circuit in a memory-select line may cause a word to be incorrectly read as all 1s. The multiple bits in error are all in the same logical direction (that is, correct 0s have been transformed into incorrect 1s).

Faults have two other important properties: extent and value. The extent of a fault may be an independent occurrence (local) affecting a single logical variable, or correlated with other simultaneous occurrences (related) because of the density of logic elements or the failure of a common element. The fault value may be determinate (such as s-a-1) or indeterminate (for example, varies between logical 0 and 1).

System-Level Abstractions

The manifestations of intermittent and transient faults and of incorrect hardware and software design are much harder to determine than permanent faults. The permanent fault models often can be applied to intermittents; however, because the fault is present only temporarily and because most contemporary computer systems do not have substantial on-line error detection, the normal manifestations of an intermittent are at the system level (such as system crash or I/O channel retry). Transient faults and incorrect designs do not have a well-defined, bounded, basic fault model. Transients are a combination of local phenomena (such as ground loops, static electricity discharges, power lines, and thermal distributions) and universal phenomena (such as cosmic rays, alpha particles, power supply characterics, and mechanical design). Even if models could be developed for transients and incorrect designs, they would quickly become obsolete because of the rapid changes in technology.

Consider now the types of system-level manifestations that might be expected from intermittent faults, transient faults, and incorrect design. The experience reported below, derived from an extensive study of system crashes on C.mmp, a multiprocessor in which 16 processors converse with 16 memories through a crosspoint switch, indicate that system-level fault behavior is complex. There is a large gap between logic-level fault models and system-level manifestations. Much work remains to be done before an acceptable system level model can be developed.[*]

Memory parity failures have, with rare exception, been the most common failure mode, accounting for 50-100 percent of the system crashes. Most are transient, but permanent errors occur with regularity. Often the memory failure rate had largely determined the Mean-Time-To-Crash (MTTC).

---

[*] The remainder of this section is excerpted and adapted from Siewiorek et al., 1978a.

Table 2-8. Screening test summary.

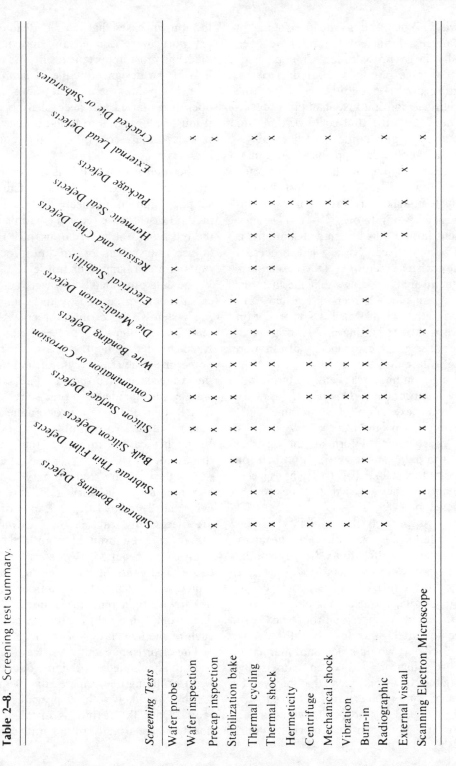

Screening Tests	Substrate Bonding Defects	Substrate Thin Film Defects	Bulk Silicon Defects	Silicon Surface Defects	Contamination or Corrosion	Wire Bonding Defects	Die Metalization Defects	Electrical Stability	Resistor and Chip Defects	Hermetic Seal Defects	Package Defects	External Lead Defects	Cracked Die or Substrates
Wafer probe		×				×	×	×					
Wafer inspection				×		×						×	
Precap inspection	×		×	×	×	×						×	
Stabilization bake		×	×	×	×	×	×						
Thermal cycling	×		×	×	×	×		×	×	×		×	
Thermal shock	×		×	×	×	×		×	×	×		×	
Hermeticity										×			
Centrifuge	×			×	×					×			
Mechanical shock	×			×	×					×		×	
Vibration	×			×	×					×			
Burn-in		×	×	×		×	×						
Radiographic	×				×				×	×		×	
External visual			×						×	×	×		
Scanning Electron Microscope				×		×						×	

It is always difficult to locate the source of transient failures. Transient failures have been an especially large problem on C.mmp, since there are few trace points in most data paths. Not including powerful debugging aids in the logical design has continuously hampered development. There was little that could be done for the processors, but aids could have been incorporated in all the custom-built logic. A similar weakness became evident in the software: often information about a failure was lost by the operating system, making recording of the conditions for transients unreliable.

A transient failure that has eluded solutions is the problem of "false NXMs." The processor reports a nonexistent memory (NXM) exception, but subsequent analysis shows that the memory is responding, and the instruction, registers, and index words are well-formed. No exception should have resulted. Timing problems are suspected, but there is insufficient information available to isolate the failure.

Other long-standing transient failures are stack operation problems. This usually appears as an incorrect execution of subroutine call/return instructions or interrupt entry/exit mistakes. The most common form of the error is having one too many (or few) words pushed (or popped) from the stack. The transient is relatively rare, and no method of recovering from it has been developed.

A pleasant surprise is the reliability of the crosspoint switch; however, an early problem required considerable effort to fix. Certain conditions, characterized by a memory access not completed by the UNIBUS master, could cause the switch to deadlock, due to lack of a time-out circuit in the memory port control logic. Any other processor attempting to access the deadlocked memory port would block until manually cleared. This situation was often caused by poorly designed I/O controllers that recovered from errors by simply aborting the current access, with no regard for proper termination of UNIBUS or crosspoint switch protocols. While

the known cases that caused deadlocked memory ports were isolated and individually remedied, the most important result was an appreciation of the design principle of *mutual suspicion.* The crosspoint switch should never trust that an operation started will necessarily be completed; it must be prepared to time-out, clear itself, and report a failure condition to the requesting processor.

The interprocessor bus is as unreliable as the crosspoint switch is trustworthy. The reliability is so poor that, if a cheap and highly effective method of software recovery hadn't been found, the bus would be nearly unusable. The mode of failure is transient loss of interprocessor interrupts and changing interrupt level.

The data presented below were culled from the crash reports produced by the C.mmp's operating system's suspect/monitor crash logging system. These dumps must often be manually analyzed to determine the reason for the crash. Sometimes, the reason cannot be found; always, the analysis is error-prone. The crash records were never intended as a precise reliability measure. Rather, they are a programmer's and engineer's tool to isolate trouble spots in the system. With this caveat in mind, the data may be discussed.

A failure causing a crash may be the result of either hardware or software failure. Of the five symptoms listed in Table 2-9, only parity failures are necessarily caused by hardware. All the others may be brought about by either, and analysis is required to determine the actual cause. The cause of most failures can be determined, but a substantial number of crashes of unknown origin remain. Figure 2-3 restates the data from Table 2-9 to show the contribution of each of the five classes of errors.

The error frequency of software-related errors is strongly related to the introduction of new features. Being new and relatively untested, new features are likely to have previously undetected faults. Once the feature is installed, any errors due to it are usually found and corrected very

Table 2–9. A summary of eight months of C.mmp crash data.

Date	July (1) 1977	Aug. (2) 1977	Sept. (3) 1977	Oct. (4) 1977	Nov. (5) 1977	Dec. (6) 1977	Jan. (7) 1978	Feb. (8) 1978
Uptime (hrs.)	516.6	610.5	513.8	701.9	538.8	595.6	600.2	478.5
MTBF (hrs.)	5.9	7.6	2.9	9.4	8.7	16.5	15.4	7.3
Crashes								
User	32	55	38	27	34	18	15	30
Nonuser	87	80	175	75	62	36	39	66
Crash Type								
Software	20	7	35	33	34	11	7	16
Unknown	32	40	14	4	9	7	8	3
Hardware	35	33	126	38	18	18	24	47
Crash Symptom								
System error	24	10	47	46	31	11	9	15
IllInst**	1	0	3	3	0	2	0	0
No response	13	33	34	3	4	4	10	10
NXM	14	13	32	4	9	5	2	14
Parity	32	24	57	17	18	14	18	21

* MTBF = (Uptime)/(nonuser crashes)

** IllInst = Illegal Instruction

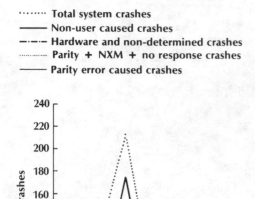

······· Total system crashes
—— Non-user caused crashes
—·—·— Hardware and non-determined crashes
········· Parity + NXM + no response crashes
—— Parity error caused crashes

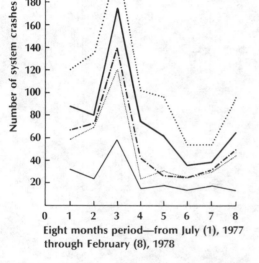

Figure 2–3. C.mmp reliability: distribution of crashes.

quickly. Therefore, the trend is bursts of errors, with any particular error becoming less frequent as time passes. The four months with high software error counts all follow this trend, even though new faults kept the counts high for several consecutive months.

FAULT DISTRIBUTIONS

Probability Review

Before asking whether the arrival times of faults fit a probability distribution, we must review some probability theory. Central to the study of probability is the notion of *randomness*. A phenomenon is considered random if its future behavior is not exactly predictable. Tossing a pair of dice or measuring the time between alpha particle emissions by a radioactive sample are experiments that involve random phenomena. In many cases it is more interesting to know the value of a number associated with the experiment under observation rather than the actual outcome. Thus, there must be a function that associates a number with every possible outcome of an experiment. Such a function is called a *random variable*. The time between any two failures of an electronic component, the number of jobs processed by a computer center in one day, or the time to the next crash of a time-sharing system are examples of random variables.

For each random variable, X, its *Cumulative Distribution Function* (CDF), $F(x)$, is defined as

$$F(x) = P[X \leqslant x] \qquad (1)$$

That is, $F(x)$ is the probability that the event X is less than or equal to x. If X is a discrete random variable, all its possible values $\{x_1, x_2, x_3, \ldots\}$ can be put into one-to-one correspondence with the positive integers. The *probability mass function* (pmf), $f(x)$, is then defined as

$$f(x) = P[X = x] \qquad (2)$$

If X is a continuous random variable, its *probability density function* (pdf), $f(x)$, is defined as

$$f(x) = \frac{dF}{dx} \qquad (3)$$

such that, in general

$$P[a \leqslant x \leqslant b] = \int_a^b f(x)\,dx \qquad (4)$$

The two most important parameters used to describe or summarize the properties of a random variable, X, are the *mean* or *expected value* $E\{X\}$ and the variance σ_X^2. If X is discrete

$$E\{X\} = \sum_{x_i} x_i f(x_i) = x_1 f(x_1) \\ + x_2 f(x_2) + \cdots \qquad (5)$$

while if X is continuous

$$E\{X\} = \int_{-\infty}^{\infty} xf(x)\,dx \qquad (6)$$

The variance is defined as

$$\sigma_X^2 = E\{(x - E\{x\})^2\} \qquad (7)$$

The mean acts as a kind of summary of what we expect from a random variable, and the variance measures the deviations of a random variable from its mean. The *standard deviation* σ_X (the square root of the variance) is also used to measure the variability of a random variable about its mean.

Two more functions are of particular interest in reliability theory. If the random variable under study is the time, T, to the next failure of a system or component the *Reliability Function*, $R(t)$, is defined as

$$R(t) = 1 - F(t) \qquad (8)$$
$$= P[T > t] \qquad (9)$$

$R(t)$ is thus the probability of not observing any failure before time t.

Finally, the hazard function, $z(t)$, is defined as

$$z(t) = \frac{f(t)}{1 - F(t)} \qquad (10)$$

With renewal processes techniques it can be shown that $z(t - \tau)\Delta t$ is the conditional probability that the nth failure occurs in the infinitesimal interval $[t, t + \Delta t)$ given that the $(n - 1)$st point occurs at time τ [Snyder, 1975]. Hence, the units of $z(t)$ are failures/unit time, and $z(t)$ provides a description of how the instantaneous probability of failure evolves in time.

Exponential Distribution

The exponential distribution is the one most commonly encountered in reliability models. The probability density function (pdf), Cumulative Distribution Function (CDF), reliability function, and hazard (failure rate) function of the exponential distribution are shown in Equations 11 through 14 (for $\lambda > 0$):

$$\text{pdf} = f(t) = \lambda e^{-\lambda t} \qquad (11)$$
$$\text{CDF} = F(t) = 1 - e^{-\lambda t} \qquad (12)$$
$$\text{Reliability} = R(t) = e^{-\lambda t} \qquad (13)$$
$$\text{Hazard function} = z(t) = \lambda \qquad (14)$$

The parameter λ is sometimes referred to as the *failure rate* because (in reliability theory) it describes the rate at which failures occur in time.

The failure rate, λ, is usually assumed to be a constant. In reality, λ is usually a function of time as depicted in the bathtub-shaped curve in Figure 1-4. During early life there is a higher failure rate, called infant mortality, due to the failure of weaker components. Often these infant mortalities result from a defect or stress introduced in the manufacturing process. Once the infant mortalities are eliminated, the system settles into operational life, in which the failure rate is approximately constant. The system then approaches wearout, in which time and use (such as mechanical stress due to temperature cycling, ion or metal migration) cause the failure rate to increase. For most cases we will assume a constant failure rate. For the exponential distribution, the mean is $1/\lambda$ and the standard deviation is $1/\lambda$.

Weibull Distribution

The Weibull distribution has two parameters: α (the shape parameter) and λ (the scale parameter). The probability density function, cumulative distribution function, reliability function, and hazard (failure rate) function of the Weibull distribution are shown in Equations 15 through 18 (for $\alpha > 0$, $\lambda > 0$):

$$\text{pdf} = f(t) = \alpha\lambda(\lambda t)^{\alpha-1} e^{-(\lambda t)^{\alpha}} \qquad (15)$$
$$\text{CDF} = F(t) = 1 - e^{-(\lambda t)^{\alpha}} \qquad (16)$$
$$\text{Reliability} = R(t) = e^{-(\lambda t)^{\alpha}} \qquad (17)$$

Hazard function $= z(t) = \alpha\lambda(\lambda t)^{\alpha-1}$ (18)

Note that the values of all these functions depend on time only through the product of the scale factor and time, λt.

Because the failure rate is given by $(\lambda t)^{\alpha}$, the shape parameter directly influences the failure rate:

- if $\alpha < 1$, the failure rate is decreasing with time;
- if $\alpha = 1$, the failure rate is constant with time, resulting in an exponential distribution; and
- if $\alpha > 1$, the failure rate is increasing with time. ($\alpha = 2$ is the special case of a linearly increasing failure rate, known as the Rayleigh distribution.)

For the Weibull distribution, the mean (denoted by μ where $\mu = E\{x\}$) and standard deviation (denoted by σ where $\sigma = \sigma_x$) are defined as follows in terms of α and λ:

$$\mu = \Gamma((\alpha + 1)/\alpha)/\lambda \quad (19)$$

$$\sigma = [\Gamma((\alpha + 2)/\alpha) - \Gamma^2((\alpha + 1)/\alpha)]^{1/2}/\lambda \quad (20)$$

where the gamma function, $\Gamma(\omega)$, is given by

$$\int_0^{\infty} \rho^{\omega-1} \exp(-\rho)\, d\rho.$$

The influence of the Weibull parameters on the mean of the distribution is illustrated in Figure 2-4. The maximum likelihood estimates of the Weibull parameters for the recorded data are indicated in the graph (see the section Distributions for Transients and System Errors below). With only the mean and standard deviation available, the Weibull failure rate can be determined to be decreasing, constant, or increasing as follows:

- if $\mu < \sigma$, the failure rate is decreasing;
- if $\mu = \sigma$, the failure rate is constant;
- if $u > \sigma$, the failure rate is increasing.

Geometric Distribution

If t takes only the discrete times 0, 1, 2, . . . , then replacing $\exp[-\lambda]$ by q and t by n obtains the discrete time geometric distribution corresponding to the continuous time exponential distribu-

tion. The probability mass function, (pmf), cumulative distribution function, and reliability function of the geometric distribution are shown in Equations 21 through 23 (for $0 < q < 1$):

$$\text{pmf} = f(n) = q^n - q^{(n+1)} = q^n(1 - q) \quad (21)$$

$$\text{CDF} = F(n) = 1 - q^n \quad (22)$$

$$\text{Reliability} = R(n) = q^n \quad (23)$$

The mean, μ, and standard deviation, σ, of the geometric distribution are defined as follows in terms of q:

$$\mu = 1/(1 - q) \quad (24)$$

$$\sigma = q^{1/2}/(1 - q) \quad (25)$$

Discrete Weibull Distribution

Like the geometric distribution deriving from the exponential distribution, the discrete Weibull distribution is obtained from the Weibull distribution by substituting q for $\exp[-\lambda^{\alpha}]$ and n for t [Nakagawa and Osaki, 1975]. The probability mass function, cumulative distribution function, reliability function, and hazard function of the discrete Weibull distribution are shown in Equations 26 through 29 (for $0 < q < 1$):

$$\text{pmf} = f(n) = q^{n^{\alpha}}(1 - q^{(n+1)^{\alpha}-n^{\alpha}}) \quad (26)$$

$$\text{CDF} = F(n) = 1 - q^{n^{\alpha}} \quad (27)$$

$$\text{Reliability} = R(n) = q^{n^{\alpha}} \quad (28)$$

$$\text{Hazard function} = z(n) = 1 - q^{(n+1)^{\alpha}-n^{\alpha}} \quad (29)$$

The mean, μ, of the discrete Weibull function is given by

$$\sum_{k=0}^{\infty} q^{k^{\alpha}} \quad (30)$$

It is very difficult to derive a closed-form formula for this sum for any q and α. In this book, the geometric distribution and the discrete Weibull distribution are used only to approximate the exponential and Weibull distributions, respectively.

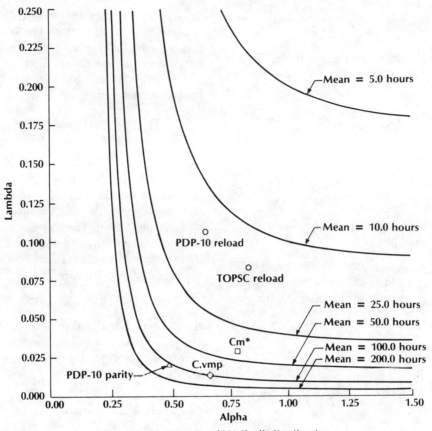

Figure 2–4.   Means of Weibull distributions.

MATCHING SAMPLED DATA TO MATH DISTRIBUTIONS

Maximum Likelihood Estimators

After the decision to characterize the failures of a given system or component with a particular distribution, the problem is to determine (estimate) the values of the parameters of the distribution from experimental data. One of the simplest methods of estimation is that of maximum likelihood [Melsa and Cohen, 1978]. Let $\bar{x}_n$ be a vector of observed data and let $\bar{\theta}$ be a vector of unknown parameters. If $P(\bar{x}_n|\bar{\theta})$ is the probability of observing $\bar{x}_n$ given the parameters $\bar{\theta}$, the *maximum likelihood* estimation of $\bar{\theta}$, $\bar{\theta}_{ML}$, is the value of $\bar{\theta}$ for which $P(\bar{x}_n|\bar{\theta})$ is maximum, that is

$$P(\bar{x}_n|\bar{\theta}_{ML}) \geqslant P(\bar{x}_n|\bar{\theta}) \qquad (31)$$

for any value of $\bar{\theta}$.

Assume, for example, that the time to failure is described by an exponential distribution. The vector $\bar{\tau} = (\tau_1, \tau_2, \ldots, \tau_N)$ is a collection of observed times to failure and is needed to compute the maximum likelihood value of λ in the exponential distribution. The function $P(\bar{\tau}|\lambda)$ is given by

$$P(\bar{\tau}|\lambda) = \lambda e^{-\lambda\tau_1} \times \lambda e^{-\lambda\tau_2} \times \cdots \times \lambda e^{\lambda\tau_N} \qquad (32)$$

$$= e^{\displaystyle -\lambda \sum_{i=1}^{N} \tau_i + N \ln \lambda} \qquad (33)$$

The function in Equation 33 will be at a maximum for $\lambda = \lambda_{ML}$. Maximizing the above function is equivalent to minimizing the function

$$f(\lambda) = \lambda \sum_{i=1}^{N} \tau_i - N \, ln \, \lambda$$

Differentiating with respect to λ and setting the derivative equal to zero obtains the following value of λ:

$$\lambda_{ML} = \frac{N}{\sum_{i=1}^{N} \tau_i}$$

which is equal to the inverse of the sample mean time to failure.

Maximum Likelihood Estimation of Weibull Parameters

The Maximum Likelihood Estimators (MLE) α_{ML} and λ_{ML} for the Weibull distribution satisfy the following equations [Thoman, Bain, and Antle, 1969]:

$$(N/\alpha_{ML}) + \sum_{j=1}^{N} ln \, (X_{ML})$$

$$= N \times \left(\sum_{j=1}^{N} X_j^{\alpha_{ML}} \times ln \, (X_j) \right) \bigg/ \left(\sum_{j=1}^{N} X_j^{\alpha_{ML}} \right) \tag{34}$$

$$(\lambda_{ML})^{\alpha_{ML}} = N \bigg/ \sum_{j=1}^{N} X_j^{\alpha_{ML}} \tag{35}$$

Once the value of the shape parameter is known, Equation 35 can be used to calculate the scale parameter λ_{ML}. Equation 34 can be used to derive a difference equation in the form

$$\alpha_{ML_{i+1}} = \text{Function} \, (\alpha_{ML_i}, \overline{X}_N)$$

A quickly converging solution can be found by using the Newton-Raphson method [Thoman, Bain, and Antle, 1969]. The linear estimate of α_{ML} found by the linear regression analysis described below is useful as an initial value for the iterative solution process.

Linear Regression Analysis

Due to the computational complexity of obtaining the MLE values, graphical linear regression analysis of the cumulative distribution function is often used to fit data to the Weibull function [Berger and Lawrence, 1974]. This technique is based on the transformation of the Weibull cumulative distribution function (Equation 16) into a linear function of $ln \, (t)$:

$$ln \, \{ ln \, [1/(1 - F(t))] \} = \alpha \, ln \, (t) + \alpha \, ln \, (\lambda) \tag{36}$$

If the data are from a Weibull distribution, the plot should approximate a straight line. The line is fitted to the data by applying the method of least squares to the transformed points [Miller and Freund, 1965]. The slope of the straight line is an estimate of α, and the Y-intercept divided by the slope is an estimate of $ln \, (\lambda)$. The value of the function $F(t)$ is estimated by

$$F(t_j) = (j - 0.5)/N \tag{37}$$

If nothing else, the results of linear regression analysis are useful as an indication of the desirability of performing the more involved analyses.

Confidence Intervals

Point estimates such as those obtained by linear regression or maximum likelihood estimation are only approximations and rarely match the values they are intended to estimate. Because of this, interval estimates are often desirable. These are intervals that can be asserted with some certainty to contain the actual value of the parameter under consideration. The most common application of this idea is expressed in "confidence intervals." For $0 < p < 1$, a p-level confidence interval is a range within which the actual value of the estimated parameter would fall with probability p, if the experiment were repeated many times. That is, to say that a certain range of values is a 0.90 confidence interval for a parameter is to say that in repeated sampling, 90 percent of the confidence intervals so constructed would contain the actual parameter values [Miller and Freund, 1965].

Goodness-of-Fit Tests

After a distribution has been chosen to describe the probabilistic behavior of failures of some system and its parameters have been estimated, a Goodness-of-Fit Test can give quantitative information about the likelihood that the system is actually following that distribution.

In a *Chi-Square Goodness-of-Fit* Test, each observed value of a random variable is assigned to one of k categories, $C_1, \ldots, C_k$. Given the total number of observed values, the expected number of observations in each category is computed according to the hypothetical distribution. Let O_i and E_i be respectively the number of observed and expected observations in category i. The χ^2 (chi-square) statistic is given by

$$\chi^2 = \sum_{i=1}^{k} \frac{(O_i - E_i)^2}{E_i}$$

The number of degrees of freedom of this χ^2 statistic is $m = k - n - 1$, where n is the number of parameters that have been estimated from the same experimental data that are being used in the test. A level of significance, α, must be chosen such that the probability that a chi-square random variable with m degrees of freedom will exceed χ^2_α is α. (The values of χ^2_α can be found in such tables as Pear, 1954.) If $\chi^2 \geq \chi^2_\alpha$, the hypothesis that the failures are properly characterized by the hypothetical distribution must be rejected. Otherwise, the hypothesis is accepted. Finally, it should be noted that all the E_i must be equal to at least 5. To make each $E_i \geq 5$, it may be necessary to pool categories. A reasonable level of confidence is 0.05.

Example 1

Data are collected from the file system of a time-sharing system about the times between transient errors in eight disk drives in an effort to discover whether the time between transient errors follows an exponential distribution. The estimated value of λ is 0.1344 (time units in minutes)

corresponding to a MTBF of about seven minutes.

The total number of observed errors is 877 in a five-day interval. Table 2-10 shows both the data's division into categories and the expected number of errors in each category according to an exponential distribution. For instance, the first row in the table means that 548 errors were observed with times between errors of 0–5 minutes, while an exponential distribution with $\lambda = 0.1344$ gives the expected number of errors in that range as 429.20 (given that the total number of failures is 877). The remaining categories have to be pooled until no E_i is smaller than 5. The result of this operation is shown in Table 2-11.

The number of degrees of freedom is $m = 8 - 1 - 1 = 6$ because there are eight different

Table 2–10. Data from transient errors in a time-sharing file system.

Category	O_i	E_i
0–5	548	429.20
5–10	148	219.15
10–15	63	111.89
15–20	35	57.13
20–25	28	29.17
25–30	18	14.89
30–35	12	7.60
35–40	6	3.88
40–45	3	1.98
45–50	1	1.01
50–55	3	0.5178
55–60	2	0.2639
60–65	1	0.1347
65–70	1	0.06881
70–75	1	0.03514
75–80	1	0.01794
80–85	1	0.009160
85–90	1	0.004690
90–95	1	0.002395
95–100	1	0.001215
100–105	1	0.000627

Table 2–11. Combining categories from Table 2–10.

Category	O_i	E_i	$(O_i - E_i)^2/E_i$
0–5	548	429.20	32.88
5–10	148	219.15	23.10
10–15	63	111.89	21.36
15–20	35	57.13	8.57
20–25	28	29.17	0.04
25–30	18	14.89	0.64
30–35	12	7.60	2.53
35–∞	25	7.93	36.74
		Total $\chi^2 =$	125.86

categories and one parameter (λ) has been estimated from the data. For six degrees of freedom, $\chi^2_{0.05} = 12.592$. Since $\chi^2 > \chi^2_{0.05}$, the hypothesis that the time between errors has an exponential distribution must be rejected.

Example 2

The times between crashes of a time-sharing system (see Table 2-12) have been recorded for one month of system operation. The goal is to find whether the distribution of time between crashes follows a Weibull distribution. The maximum likelihood estimates of the Weibull parameters are $\lambda = 0.0888$, and $\alpha = 0.98$ (time units in hours) corresponding to a time between crashes of about 11 hours. Table 2-12 gives the observed counts in several ranges of time between crashes.

After the pooling of categories so that no E_i is smaller than 5, Table 2-13 is obtained.

The number of degrees of freedom is $m = 9 - 2 - 1 = 6$. For a χ^2 random variable with six degrees of freedom, $\chi^2_{0.05} = 12.592$. Because $\chi^2 < \chi^2_{0.05}$, the hypothesis that the distribution of the time to crash is a Weibull is accepted.

Another Goodness-of-Fit statistical test is the Kolmogorov-Smirnov. The Kolmogorov-Smir-

Table 2–12. Time between crashes for a time-sharing system during one month of operation.

Category (hours)	O_i
0–1	6
1–2	3
2–3	5
3–4	2
4–5	7
5–6	5
6–7	1
7–8	1
8–9	3
9–10	4
10–11	2
11–12	1
12–14	2
14–15	2
15–16	1
16–17	1
17–18	3
18–21	1
21–24	4
24–29	1
29–38	3
38–75	2

Table 2–13. Combining categories from Table 2–12.

Category (hours)	O_i	E_i	$(O_i - E_i)^2/E_i$
0–2	9	9.97	0.09
2–4	7	8.17	0.16
4–6	12	6.79	3.97
6–8	2	5.67	2.37
8–11	9	6.80	0.70
11–15	5	6.66	0.41
15–20	5	5.61	0.06
20–28	6	5.14	0.14
28–∞	5	5.13	0.003
		Total $\chi^2 =$	7.95

nov test has been developed for known parameters or for exponential distribution [Lilliefors, 1969]. If the parameters of the distribution are estimated from the experimental data or the distribution is not exponential, the Kolmogorov-Smirnov test may give extremely conservative results.

DISTRIBUTIONS FOR PERMANENT FAULTS: THE MIL-HDBK-217 MODEL[*]

The Reliability Analysis Center has extensively studied statistics on electronic component failures. The data have led to development of a widely used reliability model of chip failures, the MIL-HDBK-217. A more detailed explanation of the model is found in Appendixes D and E.

For MIL-HDBK-217B, the reliability function is assumed to be an exponential with the failure rate for a single chip taking the form:

$$\lambda = \pi_L \pi_Q (C_1 \pi_T + C_2 \pi_E) \pi_P$$

where

π_L = a *learning factor* based on the maturity of the fabrication process; it assumes a value of 1 or 10;

π_Q = a *quality factor* based on incoming screening of components; values range from 1 to 150;

π_T = a *temperature factor* based on the ambient operating temperature and the type of semiconductor process; values range from 0.1 to 1000;

π_E = an *environmental factor* based on the operating environment; values range from 0.2 to 10; and

$C_1, C_2 \pi_P$ = *complexity factors*, based on the number of gates (for random logic) or bits (for memory) in the component, and the number of pins.

[*] This section was adapted from Siewiorek et al., 1978a.

With the rapid rate of technological advance, new component types are continually being introduced. In addition, because the learning curve for any component type changes as field experience accumulates, there is some question of the accuracy of MIL-HDBK-217B, particularly with regard to newer technologies such as MOS RAMs and ROMs.

Typical component failure rates are in the range of 0.1–1.0 per million hours. Thus, tens of millions of component hours are required to gain statistically significant results. Two separate approaches can be used to gather sufficient data for comparison with the MIL-HDBK-217B model: life-cycle testing of components, and analyzing field repair information. The following subsections summarize typical results from each of these approaches.

Life-Cycle Testing and Field Data

Life-cycle testing involves a small number of components in a controlled environment. Frequently, temperature is elevated to accelerate failure mechanisms. A translation factor is then used to equate one hour at elevated temperature to a number of hours at ambient. The translation factor is usually derived from the Arrhenius equation:

$$R = Ae^{-E_a/kT}$$

where

R = reaction rate constant,

A = a constant,

E_a = activation energy in electron-volts,

K = Boltzmann's constant, and

T = absolute temperature.

These accelerating factors are often extrapolated into regions (such as ambient temperature operations) where there are very few corroborating data. Because of the exponential in the Arrhenius equation, accelerating factors can become quite large.

In addition, there is little consensus on the appropriate activation energy. Activation energies of 0.23–1.92 *eV* have been used. The temperature factor of MIL-HDBK-217B assumes an activation energy of 0.41 *eV*, whereas MIL-STD-883A (used to qualify components for procurement) assumes 1.02 *eV*.

Consider conversion from 125°C to 50°C. The ratio of the MIL-STD-883A acceleration factor to the MIL-HDBK-217B acceleration factor is 62. This means a factor of 62 difference in predicted failure rate, λ, from the same life-cycle test data. Figure 2-5 depicts the various acceleration factor models.

Furthermore, the Arrhenius equation assumes only one activation energy, and the acceleration factor is assumed to be a uniform function of temperature. Assuming a straight line (on a semilog scale) can result in substantial errors. Figure 2-6, from Signetics, illustrates the nonlinear behavior.

Consider three test points, 150°C, 125°C, and 85°C. Drawing a best-fit straight line through these points in Figure 2-6 on the 1970 curve yields a rate of about 0.0002 at 25°C, whereas the 25°C observed point is 0.0013, too low by a factor of 7. The same three points on the 1975 curve suggest a failure rate of 0.06 instead of 0.0017, too high by a factor of 35.

With the MIL-HDBK-217B model, high temperature testing calibrates only the temperature portion. The environmental effects of aging and mechanical stress are not measured, even though these effects can range from 10 percent (at high temperature) to 70 percent (at low temperature) of the predicted failure rate.

One last problem with using high-temperature life-cycle testing is that semiconductor manufacturers usually lump test data by process (bipolar, MOS), thus hindering comparison with the MIL-HDBK-217B complexity factors.

Given the problems listed above, data from several field sources were combined, using certain assumptions to establish commonality. First, data for chips with a low-level complexity (that

is, SSI, MSI) will be discussed. These data represent over 3 billion hours of operation (of which 137 million were at high temperatures). The data sources were:

- *RADC*:   A list of life-cycle test data as a function of device complexity. Most were from high-temperature testing. Some data about test temperatures were missing.
- *Signetics*:   High-temperature testing with data lumped by process; some individual test data by component number, but usually a small number of component-hours. An activation energy of 0.41 *eV* is assumed and calibrated by experiment for bipolar component temperature translation.
- *Sanders Associates*:   Analysis of field data.

Figure 2-7 was made using a transistor junction temperature of 50°C, a temperature-accelerating factor corresponding to 0.41 *eV* activation energy, and adding in the MIL-HDBK-217B predicted environmental portion. The RADC data are raw and were not temperature translated because a significant percentage did not have a test temperature recorded. The two anomalous points in the RADC data (at 20 and 58 gates) should be treated as suspect because they had the least number of test hours—less than a million.

The temperature-translated data in Figure 2-7 track the MIL-HDBK-217B model generally within a factor of 2; the Sanders Associates data were in close agreement.

The Reliability Analysis Center (RAC) of the Rome Air Development Center (RADC) has also collected field failure rate data. Figure 2-8 depicts 50 collections of field data representing SSI and MSI complexity devices from various screening classes and operating in various environments [Nicholls, 1979]. Altogether 0.921 $\times 10^9$ device operating hours and 328 failures are represented. For most of the data collections, no failures were observed; hence only an upper 80 percent confidence limit can be plotted. For those data sets with observed failures, both the upper 80 percent and lower 20 percent confi-

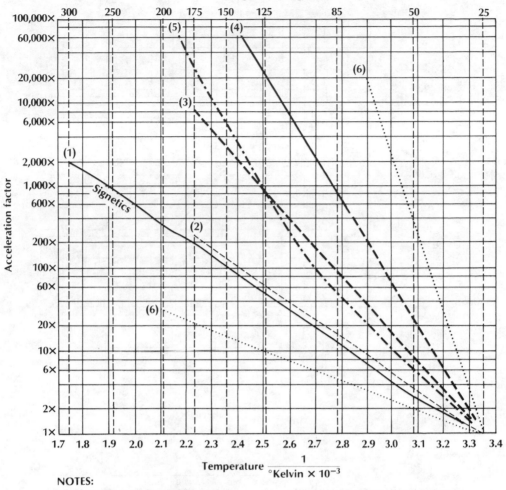

Degrees Centigrade

NOTES:

1. Calculated from the Signetics Failure Rate vs. Temperature Graph in [Signetics, 1975]. Signetics uses acceleration factors of 15 (for +85°C), 100 (for +150°C), 200 (for 175°C), 350 (for +200°C), 970 (for +250°C) and 2100 (for +300°C) to relate to +25°C equivalent ambient temperature. The +25°C to +125°C segment of the graph is based primarily on operating life data. The segment of the graph above +125°C is based on high temperature storage data. The graph equates to an "activation energy" E_a = 0.41eV.

2. Calculated from MIL-HDBK-217B, 20 September, 1974. Table 2.1.5.4. for πT_j vs T_j values. The graph equates to an "activation energy" E_a = 0.41eV and is applicable to all bipolar digital (except ECL) in the normal mode of operation.

3. Calculated from MIL-HDBK-217B, 20 September, 1974. Table 2.1.5.4. for πT_j vs. T_j values. The graph equates to an "activation energy" E_a = 0.70eV and is applicable to all MOS, all linear,

and bipolar ECL devices in the normal modes of operation.

4. Calculated from MIL-STD-883A, 15 November 1974. Figures 1005-4 and 1015-1 by extrapolating the time temperature regression graph from +78°C back to +25°C. The MIL-STD-883A graph is the Bell Telephone Laboratories graph (Specification A-8-689143, 16 January 1974, etc) and as such applies to storage and operating T_j values and primarily surface inversion failure mechanisms. The graph equates to an "activation energy" E_a = 1.02eV.

5. This curved graph is the result of plotting the "rule of thumb" that failure rates (hence acceleration factors) double for every + Δ 10°C.

6. All competitor data (available to Signetics) produced graphs falling within these two boundaries. The two boundaries equate to "activation energies" E_a = 0.23eV (for lower graph) and E_a = 1.92eV (for the top graph).

Figure 2–5.   Failure rate acceleration factor vs. temperature graphs: Signetics and others.

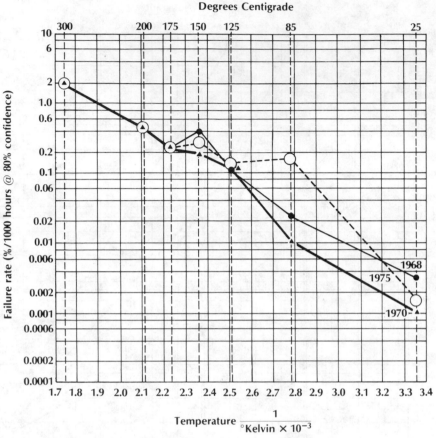

		1968		1970		1975	
		Cat.	Both (●)	Cat.	Both (▲)	Cat.	Both (○)
HTSL	300°C	2.1	2.1	2.1	2.1	2.1	2.1
HTSL	200°C	0.22	0.48	0.20	0.46	0.2	0.46
HTSL	175°C	0.21	0.29	0.20	0.28	0.2	0.28
HTSL	150°C	0.32	0.40	0.182	0.20	0.155	0.24
HTSL & HTOL	125°C	0.088	0.117	0.101	0.125	0.110	0.147
HTOL	85°C	0.022	0.022	0.013	0.013	0.104	0.160
HTOL	25°C	0.0029	0.0038	0.0011	0.0013	0.0013	0.0017

NOTE:

1. The graphs were constructed to aid in the analysis and dramatization of the effect of the constituent parts of the failure rate equation. All tabulated failure rates were obtained from [Signetics, 1975] by combining life test data for like temperatures. Note that life test results of various die process technologies were indiscriminately summed together for this study.

Figure 2–6.   Assessed failure rate vs. temperature graphs from 1963 to 1975 for catastrophic plus degradational failures.

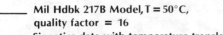

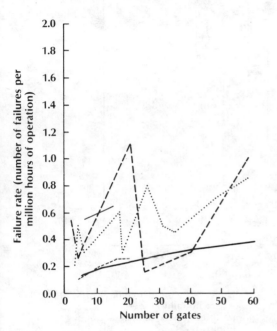

Figure 2–7. Data from life-cycle testing. (© 1978 IEEE.)

percent) had a predicted failure rate greater than that observed, and 2 (12 percent) a predicted failure rate less than that observed. Even given the difficulty in gathering enough data to generate statistically meaningful comparisons, the MIL-HDBK-217B model for older technologies, such as TTL, SSI, and MSI, appears relatively accurate in absolute terms (i.e., within a factor of two of observed data). For comparisons between designs, then, the MIL model is more than adequate for established technologies.

Now consider chips of LSI complexity, especially RAMs, and ROMs. The RAM and ROM data, which are less extensive, are reproduced in Table 2-14 along with a few points of MOS data. The Signetics data were temperature-translated to 50°C. The total failure rate and temperature-dependent portion are listed separately to permit comparison with high-temperature translated test data. The Signetics data with a < symbol are upper bounds in cases in which no failures were observed.

For bipolar RAMs and ROMs, the MIL-HDBK-217B model for total failure rate tracks within a factor of two and is generally pessimistic. The temperature portion tracks less precisely. It should be noted that the majority of these data are from one source (Signetics).

For MOS RAMs, ROMs, and random logic there are even fewer data, but they clearly indicate that the MIL-HDBK-217B model is a factor of 16–64 pessimistic. Because the MIL-HDBK-217B model, published in 1974, was probably developed on 1972 data, MOS technology was probably insufficiently mature when the model was developed.

Many parameters can be altered in MIL-HDBK-217B to take into account process maturity. For example, the complexity factor could be modified with time because, as the process matures, more complex components are feasible. A general rule is that memory doubles in complexity every 1–1.5 years. To make the state-of-the-art portion of the curve in 1977 correspond to that in 1972, the complexity axis (number of bits)

dence limits were calculated. The MIL-HDBK-217B calculated values in general made assumptions leading to optimistic predictions; for example, data from multiple sources operating in the 26–50°C junction temperature range were treated as one source operating at 26°C. Hence the region where the predicted failure rate is greater than the observed failure rate has been exaggerated. Of the 50 data collections, 17 (34 percent) have predicted failure rates greater than observed, 7 (14 percent) have predicted failure rates equal to observed, and 26 (52 percent) have predicted failure rates less than observed. Of the 17 data collections with observed failures, 8 (47

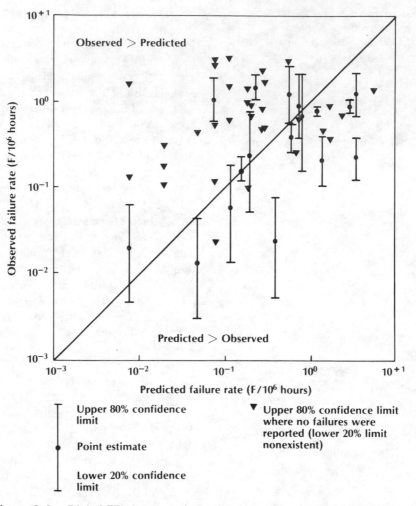

Figure 2–8. Digital-TTL integrated circuit observed vs. MIL-HDBK-217B predicted failure rates of SSI (1-10 gates) and MSI (11-25 gates) complexity.

should be divided by $2^4 = 16$ (that is, a complexity derating factor of 16). This modified MIL-HDBK-217B model is shown in the last column of Table 2-14. The modified MIL-HDBK-217B model does poorly on bipolar components but is within a factor of three on MOS components.

Figure 2-9 compares 32 collections of field data on RAM failures with the failure rate predicted by the MIL-HDBK-217C model [Klein, 1979]. Of the 23 data collections with

observed failures, 17 (74 percent) have a predicted failure rate greater than observed, 5 (22 percent) have predicted failure rates equal to observed, and only 1 (4 percent) has a predicted failure rate less than observed. Thirteen (57 percent) of the data collections have observed failure rates more than a factor of 10 less than predicted. Eleven of the 13 data sets are 1K and 4K MOS RAMs. The 217B/217C models are extremely pessimistic on predicting LSI—especially MOS LSI—failure rates.

Table 2–14. ROM, RAM, and LSI life-cycle test data.

Part Description	Source	Failure Rate Observed per Million Hours		Failure Rate from MIL Std 217B per Million Hours		Failure Rate from MIL Std 217B per Million Hours Reduced by a Factor of 16 in Bits		Failure Rate from MIL Std 217B per Million Hours Reduced by a Factor of 64 in Bits
		Temperature portion	Total	Temperature portion	Total	Temperature portion	Total	Total
Bipolar RAMs								
256 bits	Sanders Associates	—	1.28	—	0.635	—	0.113	———
256 bits	*Signetics	0.078	0.398	0.313	0.635	0.059	0.113	——
576 bits	*Signetics	<0.544	<0.797	0.511	1.000	0.096	0.173	——
1K bits	*Signetics	0.068	0.852	0.723	1.51	0.267	0.136	—
Bipolar ROMs								
256 bits	*Signetics	<0.44	<0.668	0.179	0.363	0.034	0.064	——
1K bits	*Signetics	0.211	0.659	0.414	0.865	0.078	0.153	——
2K bits	*Signetics	1.75	2.45	0.629	1.33	0.118	0.236	——
4K bits	*Signetics	0.053	1.173	0.955	2.06	0.179	0.364	—
Schottky PROMs								
256 bits	**RAC	0.073	0.265	0.179	0.363	0.034	0.064	—
1K bits	**RAC	1.14	1.588	0.414	0.865	0.078	0.153	—
MOS RAMs								
1K bits	Sanders Associates	—	0.194	—	2.504	—	0.454	0.193
MOS ROMs								
1K bits	Sanders Associates	—	0.078	—	1.433	—	0.26	0.111
MOS Random Logic								
8080 Micro-processor	**RAC	—	0.418	—	—	—	0.616	0.293

* Temperature translation to 50°C
** Reliability Analysis Center, RADC

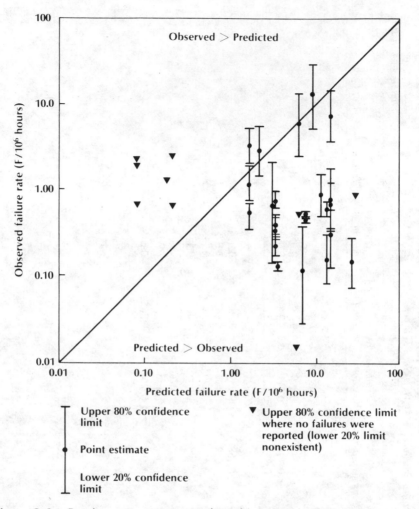

Figure 2–9. Random access memory (RAM) observed failure rates vs. MIL-HDBK-217C predicted failure rates.

Analysis of Permanent Failure Data: Estimating the Distribution and Its Parameters

Information about total systems can be analyzed and then broken down into failure rate by components. The major difficulties in this approach are lack of control over the environments of the systems and incomplete data. Various systems have different configurations and are subjected to different operating environments, temperatures, and duty cycles. In addition, current repair practices do not lend themselves to component-level data analysis. Typically, a field engineer will fix a system by board replacement. The boards are then sent to a repair depot, where they lose their identities and where repair actions are often not recorded. Furthermore, the repair activity may induce additional or future failures when the boards return to the field.

With careful planning and documentation, however, these difficulties can be overcome. In one case, permanent failure data from the Cm* multiprocessor were collected and the Mean

Time To Failure (MTTF) was calculated assuming that failures were independent [Bellis, 1978]. The MTTF was obtained by dividing the total time by the total errors. Because of the small number of failures per module, a concept called "module time" was introduced. Module time allows data from all modules to be combined. If there are k modules running during a period of time, then

$$\text{module time} = \sum_{i=1}^{k} t_i$$

where t_i is the amount of time the ith module was working. Assuming that all modules of a type are identical, then the failures that were recorded in real time can be transferred to a "typical" module in module time. Table 2-15 depicts the module time data for Cm*. The complexity in chips referenced in the table is a measure of the actual utilization of chips per module. In the DEC LSI-11, the actual number of chip sockets used is 76, of which 72 contain digital ICs. The number of chips used is recorded as 68, which implies that the unused functions add up to 4 chips.

The next step was to determine the failure distribution from the data. There are two basic approaches. The first is to determine the instan-taneous failure rate or hazard function, which indicates the failure distribution. The second method is to use statistical tests to differentiate between distributions.

The following equation is used for plotting a piecewise linear graph of the hazard function:

$$z(t) = \frac{(n(t) - n(t + \Delta t))/n(t)}{\Delta t}$$

The number of survivors at any time is given by $n(t)$. The choice of Δt is not specified and is occasionally chosen to end just after each failure. Another method of choosing the size of Δt, that smooths out the curve, is to divide the total time into equal intervals. The number of intervals is given by the following equation [Sturges, 1926]:

$$k = 1 + 3.3 \log_{10} M$$

where k is the number of intervals and M is the number of failures. This latter method was used for plotting data on the modules.

Data for these hazard calculations are commonly obtained through life tests. The data obtained from Cm* differed from those of a life test in that, when a failure was detected in a module, the module was repaired and put back into operation. Thus, some components in the

Table 2–15. Failure data on Cm*.

Module	Complexity (Chips)	# of Modules	Total Time (Hours)	Total Failure	MTTF (Hours)
K.bus	138	3	36696	8	4587
P.map	106	3	37416	12	3118
M.micro	116	6	68328	4	17082
M.data	142	3	37080	2	18540
L.inc	116	3	22608	0	—
LSI-11	68	14	163200	10	16320
S.local	126	10	120720	5	24144
4K memory	56	21	260568	5	52003.6
16K memory	104	10	122280	5	24456
Slu	28	17	223248	5	44649.6
Power board	6	16	195456	3	65152
Refresh	14	16	162912	0	—

Source: [Siewiorek et al., 1978a].

module were starting their operational life, whereas others were in intermediate stages. A second difference is that various modules had different amounts of operating time. Due to the few failures detected and the small number of modules being tested, all the failure data must be used. To accommodate the data on Cm*, a replacement assumption is necessary.

The replacement assumption postulates that a repaired module can be considered new. The concept of module time described above is then used along with this assumption to make effective use of the small amount of data available. For example, consider the case of some set of modules, $\{M_i\}$. Each time some M_i fails, it is repaired and considered new in accordance with the replacement assumption. The ith incarnation of M_i can be considered a new "virtual" module, $M_{i,j}$, which has a lifetime of $t_{i,j}$ until it fails and is in turn reincarnated as the new virtual module $M_{i,j+1}$. Thus, at any given time, the set of virtual modules $\{M_{i,j}\}$ is such that each member of the set either has suffered an incapacitating failure or has not failed at all. Module time for this set is then given by:

$$t_m = \sum_{i,j} t_{i,j}$$

A "typical" virtual module of the set $\{M_i\}$ is then assumed to have been in use for time t_m and to have suffered the same number of failures as the set $\{M_i\}$, taken as a whole. The hazard function expression previously mentioned is then redefined as follows:

$$z(t) = \frac{F(t, t + \Delta t)/n(t)}{\Delta t}$$

where $F(t, t + \Delta t)$ is the number of failures between time t and time $t + \Delta t$. For these cases, $n(t)$ is always equal to one, that is, the "typical" module.

There were only enough data on the modules to construct four rough hazard functions. Figure 2-10 shows the modules known as the P.map, K.bus, LSI-11, and the total system.

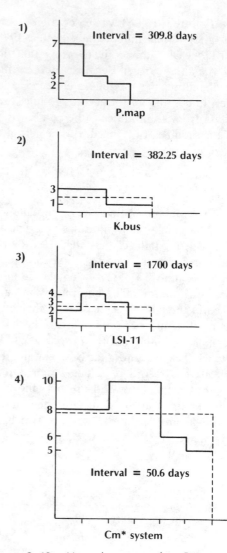

Figure 2–10. Hazard curves for P.map, K.bus, LSI-11, and the Cm* system. (© 1978 IEEE.)

The graph of the P.map exhibits a decreasing hazard function. This indicates a problem with infant mortality; 9 of the 12 failures on the P.map were attributed to one chip type, the 74373. The K.bus displays a constant or slightly decreasing hazard function. Assuming it to be constant, its value would be around two failures per 382.25 days, which corresponds to an MTTF of about 191 days. The LSI-11 curve indicates a constant hazard function of 2.5 failures per 1,700 days, or an MTTF of 680 days. The final hazard function depicted is that of the system using all the modules. It is plotted using the first 304 days after commissioning all modules. Over this period, an MTTF of 155.2 hours is indicated.

The MTTFs presented in Table 2-15 were calculated by dividing the total time by the number of failures. In the case of a constant hazard rate, the MTTF was calculated by dividing the length of an interval by the average number of failures per interval. That these two calculations are equivalent can be seen from:

MTTF for constant hazard rate

= (length of interval)/(average

   failures per interval)

= (length of interval)/(total

   failures)/(number of intervals)

= (total time)/(total failures)

= MTTF from Table 2-15

The results presented have been inconclusive in predicting the failure distribution. An exponential distribution is plausible, but a better test for the data is needed. To accomplish this, the data should be refitted to a generalized distribution that has the exponential as a special case, such as the Weibull. Table 2-16 presents the maximum likelihood estimate for α and the 95 percent and 68 percent confidence intervals on α for the various modules.

The data in Table 2-16 indicate a wide spread in the maximum likelihood estimates of α, but in all but two cases, $\alpha = 1$ is enclosed in the 95 percent confidence interval. The 68 percent confidence interval is able to enclose $\alpha = 1$ for only half the modules. This means that, although an exponential failure distribution is plausible, actual data present enough variation that the impact of an exponential failure assumption on the system should be examined. It should be emphasized that the parameters above were estimated using a small number of data points.

Table 2-17 gives the Maximum Likelihood Estimator (MLE) of λ and its 50 percent confidence interval assuming the failure distributions are exponential. Again, it should be emphasized that this analysis has been based on a small number of failures.

Table 2–16. Estimated parameters of the Weibull from failure data.

Module	α	95% Confidence Interval on $\alpha(\alpha \pm 1.96 \sqrt{\sigma^2(\alpha)})$	68% Confidence Interval on $\alpha(\alpha \pm \sqrt{\sigma^2(\alpha)})$
K.bus	0.721	0.30 : 1.15	0.50 : 0.94
P.map	0.537	0.29 : 0.79	0.41 : 0.66
M.micro	1.264	0.23 : 2.30	0.73 : 1.79
M.data	0.344	0.0 : 0.79	0.12 : 0.57
LSI-11	0.915	0.41 : 1.42	0.66 : 1.17
S.local	0.584	0.1 : 1.07	0.34 : 0.83
4K memory	1.320	0.28 : 2.36	0.79 : 1.85
16K memory	1.945	0.40 : 3.50	1.15 : 2.74
Slu	1.348	0.25 : 3.08	0.79 : 1.91
Power board	1.295	0.0 : 2.67	0.59 : 2.00

Source: [Siewiorek et al., 1978a].

Table 2–17. Calculated failure rates from data on Cm*.

Module	λ (Fail/10^6Hr)	MTTF (Hours)	50% Confidence Interval (on MTTF)
K.bus	218	4587	3397.8 : 6167.4
P.map	320.7	3118	2461.6 : 3938.5
M.micro	58.5	17082	10932.5 : 26953.9
M.data	53.9	18540	9459.2 : 38625.0
L.inc	—	—	—
LSI-11	61.3	16320	12553.9 : 21058.1
S.local	41.4	24144	16313.5 : 35822.0
4K memory	19.2	52113.6	35211.9 : 77319.9
16K memory	40.9	24456	16524.3 : 36284.9
Slu	22.4	44649.6	30168.7 : 66245.7
Power board	15.3	65152	38324.7 : 113307.8
Refresh	—	—	—

Source: [Siewiorek et al., 1978a].

Four variants of the MIL-HDBK-217B model were selected for comparison with actual data: quality factors of 16 and 150, and LSI chip complexity deratings of 1 and 16. The predicted failure rates are shown in Table 2-18. The results of comparing the data with various parameter changes are shown in Table 2-19. They consist of the observed failure rate, the best-fitting variant of the MIL-HDBK-217B model examined, and its associated failure rate prediction. This table indicates that the modules tend toward a derating of the complexity of MOS chips by a factor of 16. This result coincides with the conclusion from life-cycle test data mentioned earlier.

Table 2–18. Predicted failure rates for Cm* components.

Module	Complexity (Chips)	Quality Factor/Derating Factor			
		16/16	16/1	150/1	150/16
K.bus	138	44.1	53.3	499.3	413
P.map	106	35.6	39.6	371.7	333.7
M.micro	116	26.6	128.3	1203	249.2
M.data	142	35.4	146.5	1373.8	332.4
L.inc	116	35.5	75.1	704.6	332.8
LSI-11	68	29.9	379350.8	35568289.0	280.3
S.local	126	27.4	31.8	298.4	256.8
4K memory	56	23.1	99.8	936	216.9
16K memory	104	74.1	380.9	3571.1	694.7
Slu	28	4.7	8.7	81.6	43.9
Power board	6	0.97	0.97	9.1	9.1
Refresh	14	2.6	2.6	24.9	24.9

Source: [Siewiorek et al., 1978a].

Table 2–19. Results of maximum likelihood ratio
test.

Module	Failure Rate	Best Fit	Predicted Failure Rate
K.bus	218	$Q = 150/16$	413
P.map	320.7	$Q = 150/16$	333.7
M.micro	58.5	$Q = 16/16$	26.6
M.data	53.9	$Q = 16/16$	35.4
L.inc	—		
LSI-11	61.3	$Q = 16/16$	29.9
S.local	41.4	$Q = 16/1$	31.8
4K memory	19.2	$Q = 16/16$	23.1
16K memory	40.9	$Q = 16/16$	74.1
Slu	22.4	$Q = 150/16$	43.9
Power board	15.3	$Q = 150/16$	9.1
Refresh	—		

Source: [Siewiorek et al., 1978a].

The data on the P.map indicate a quality
factor of 150, with a derating factor of 16. As
was noted above, 9 of the 12 failures were
attributed to a single chip type. There are seven
of these chips in each of the three P.maps. The
MIL-HDBK-217B model predicts that 6.7 percent of failures for the P.map will be due to this
chip. The failure rate observed for the 74373s in
the P.map was 9 failures in 37,416 hours, or 240.5
failures per million hours (fpmh). This corresponds to a quality factor for the 74373s of 516,
which suggests a possible bad batch of chips.
Using only the other failures to calculate a
failure rate results in 80.2 fpmh. This corresponds to a quality factor of 36, which is indeed
between 150 and 16.

The S.local module is best fit by a quality
factor of 16. If a derating of 16 is assumed, then
the quality factor for the S.local lies between 150
and 16. In fact, all but the memory boards (just
under 16) and the power boards (just over 150)
lie within the range of 16 to 150. In general,
industrially produced components indicate a
quality factor close to 16.

The expected failure rate for a system composed of all the modules using their best fit
prediction from Table 2-19 is 5360.5 fpmh. This
is equivalent to an MTTF of 186.5 hours, which
may be compared to the MTTF of 155.2 hours
derived from the hazard curve in Figure 2-10.

MIL-HDBK-217 is constantly being updated,
and a version called MIL-HDBK-217C is now
available. It is described in more detail in Appendix E.

AUTOMATED FAILURE RATE CALCULATION

Two computer programs, AUTOFAIL and
FAIL (for MIL-HDBK-217B and MIL-
HDBK-217C, respectively), have been written
[Elkind, 1980a] that simplify the procedure of
computing a system's failure rate. A system may
be described to the programs in the form of a list
of chips and/or subsystems, which can be likewise recursively nested. Table 2-20 is the input
description of the DEC LSI-11 microcomputer.
Parameters such as the various MIL-HDBK-217
factors can be modified to obtain a sensitivity
analysis. The format of this file is:

[Module name

Body]

where Body is a listing of all the component
chips and submodules. A chip is identified by an
integer specifying the number of chips of this
type used or by an integer followed by an F,
specifying the number of functions (such as
NAND-gates) of this chip type that were used.
This is then followed by a comma and the name
of the chip. Submodules are constructed on the
same format as modules.

Table 2-21 is a listing of the output for the
LSI-11 produced by AUTOFAIL. The top line
presents the values of the various derating factors used. The model parameters are on the
following line. The failure rates for the LSI-11

Table 2–20. LSI-11 input file for AUTOFAIL, FAIL.

```
[LSI=11                                    [CONTROL.CHIP
  [SPECIAL.FUNCTIONS                         1 ,CP1621B]
    2F,DM8641                              [BUS.DRIVERS.AND.RECEIVERS
    3F,7474                                 4 ,74257
    1 ,7442                                 4 ,DM8641
    5F,7404                                 1F,DM8641
    1F,7400]                                4F,7411
  [BUS.ARBITRATION.LOGIC                     2F,7405]
    1F,7400                               [MEMORY
    1F,DM8837                               16,MK4096]
    3F,7474                               [BUS.I/O.CONTROL.LOGIC
    1F,DM8641]                              1F,7497
  [INTERRUPT.CONTROL.AND.RESET.LOGIC        7F,7400
    4F,7404                                 7F,7404
    4F,7474                                 2F,7411
    2F,DM8641                               4F,7474
    2F,7400                                 5F,7410
    5F,DM8837                               5F,DM8641
    1F,7405                                 1F,DM8837]
    1F,74174]                            [I/O.BUS.MEM.READ.DATA.MUX
  [CLOCK.PULSE.GENERATOR                     4F,7475
    1F,7400                                 2F,74257
    1F,74140                                3F,7410
    2F,7474                                 3F,7400
    1F,74139                                2F,74140
    6F,7404                                 2F,7405
    4F,MH0026]                              2F,74107]
  [ROM.CHIPS                             [FAST.DIN.MUX
    3 ,CP1631B]                             1F,74257
  [DATA.CHIP                                1F,7400
    1 ,CP1611B]                             1F,7404]]
```

Source: [Siewiorek et al., 1978a].

Table 2–21. Output from AUTOFAIL for LSI-11.

```
lsi11.rel(x330ds73)  LSI=   16.000  ROM=   16.000   RAM=   16.000

E =    1.000 Q=   16.000 L =    1.000 T =   25.000
```

MODULE	FAILURE RATE	PERCENTAGE
LSI11	29.893	100.000
SPECIAL.FUNCTIONS	.669	2.237
BUS.ARBITRATION.LOGIC	.350	1.172
INTERRUPT.CONTROL.AND.RESET.LOGIC	.776	2.596
CLOCK.PULSE.GENERATOR	.851	2.847
ROM.CHIPS	3.413	11.416
DATA.CHIP	1.160	3.880
CONTROL.CHIP	1.160	3.880
BUS.DRIVERS.AND.RECEIVERS	1.588	5.314
MEMORY	16.991	56.837
BUS.I/O.CONTROL.LOGIC	1.500	5.019
I/O.BUS.MEM.READ.DATA.MUX	1.195	3.999
FAST.DIN.MUX	.241	.805

```
# of chips =    68.917  # of gates =   7145.083  # of bits = 99328.000
```

TYPE	# OF CHIPS	FAILURE RATES	PERCENTAGE
SSI	37.250	4.899	16.387
MSI	10.667	2.272	7.600
LSI	2.000	2.320	7.760
ROM	3.000	3.413	11.416
RAM	16.000	16.991	56.837
MOS	21.000	22.723	76.013
BIP	47.917	7.171	23.987

Source: [Siewiorek et al., 1978a].

and the submodules are shown with the percentage of the failure rate for each module that is attributed to each submodule. In the case of partially used chips, AUTOFAIL prorates the chip failure rate by the fraction of the total number of functions used. It is sometimes desirable to examine the behavior of a particular chip or chip type. The lower table provides this ability by listing the number of chips, failure rates, and percentages for the different chip types.

The parameters of the MIL-HDBK-217 model can be varied by subsystem or even chip type, so that variations in ambient temperature (such as a board near a power supply) or technology (such as a new chip for which all parameters are not known) can be modeled. At the chip level, it is also possible to modify the number of devices on a chip to gauge the effect of the size of the new chip type on the design. Furthermore, individual chip type or entire chip class (RAM, MOS, LSI) can be arbitrarily assigned any complexity derating factors in order to test the sensitivity of the system failure rate as a function of the unknown parameter.

DISTRIBUTIONS FOR TRANSIENTS AND SYSTEM ERRORS

Data Collection

PDP-10

The main source of transient data error for this study [McConnel, 1980] is a set of four mainframe time-sharing computers operated by Carnegie-Mellon University. One is a large DECsystem-10 (PDP-10) that supports research in the Computer Science Department. The other three are DECSYSTEM-20s used by the university's Computation Center for administrative and educational needs. Memory sizes on these machines range from 256 Kwords to 1 Mword, and disk

storage capacity ranges between 528 and 1,600 Mbytes.

The core of the PDP-10 error-reporting system is the on-line error log file maintained by the TOPS-10 and TOPS-20 operating systems. Entries are made in this file for a variety of reasons, most notably system reloads and memory and I/O errors [DEC, 1978]. Each entry contains the date and time at which the error occurred, the processor serial number, and the type of error or other condition being reported.

To facilitate statistical analysis of transient errors on PDP-10s, a program named SEADS (Statistical Error Analysis Data Summary) has been written. It derives interarrival times and time-of-day distributions from the system error log files. The outputs generated include the following:

- Lower-bound estimates of system availabilities, in total and for each file processed;
- Graphs of the time-of-day distribution of entries, divided into 48 half-hour segments;
- Graphs of the distributions of interarrival times for all entries in total, for each entry individually, and for arbitrary sets of entries; and
- Data files containing the time-of-day distributions and the lists of interarrival times and error types.

Examples of the first three types of outputs are shown in Table 2-22 and Figures 2-11 and 2-12.

LSI-11

In addition to the PDP-10 system error log files, data were also collected from Cm* and C.vmp, an experimental triplicated microprocessor. The data for Cm* were collected by recording transient errors detected by failures in one of the several diagnostic programs executed continuously on idle processors. The data for C.vmp were collected by recording all crashes not traced to hard failures. Both these systems are described fully in the literature [Siewiorek, Canepa, and Clark, 1977; Siewiorek et al., 1978a; Swan, Fuller, and Siewiorek, 1977].

Table 2–22.   Sample file/availability output from SEADS.

```
SEADS VERSION 3A(100) ERROR FILE ANALYSIS


COUNT OF BAD TIME ERRORS:   0

TOTAL NUMBER OF ENTRIES FOR ALL INPUT FILES:  16445
TIME SPAN:    1542 HRS., FROM: 17-Feb-79  5:03:11    TO: 18-May-79 11:30:59
APPROXIMATE SYSTEM AVAILABILITY:  0.877


SYSTEM #2149   NUMBER OF ENTRIES:    344
TIME SPAN:     170 HRS., FROM: 17-Feb-79  5:03:11    TO: 18-Feb-79 7:30:06
APPROXIMATE SYSTEM AVAILABILITY:  0.987


SYSTEM #2227   NUMBER OF ENTRIES:    2045
TIME SPAN:     150 HRS., FROM: 24-Feb-79  22:22:08   TO:  3-Mar-79 5:09:59
APPROXIMATE SYSTEM AVAILABILITY:  0.947


SYSTEM #2326   NUMBER OF ENTRIES:    1149
TIME SPAN:     140 HRS., FROM: 3-Mar-79   5:43:04    TO: 9-Mar-79  1:55:27
APPROXIMATE SYSTEM AVAILABILITY:  0.894


SYSTEM #1080   NUMBER OF ENTRIES:    12907
TIME SPAN:    1081 HRS., FROM: 3-Apr-79   10:01:24   TO: 18-May-79 11:30:59
APPROXIMATE SYSTEM AVAILABILITY:  0.847
```

Source: [McConnel, Siewiorek, Tsao, 1979].

Events recorded	TOPS20 bughlt-bugchk
	Massbus device error
System reloaded	Front end device report
Non-reload monitor error	Front end reloaded
CPU NXM error	Processor parity trap
Data channel error	Processor parity interrupt
Disk unit error	NETCON started
Magtape statistics	Network down-line load
KL10 data parity interrupt	Network up-line dump
KL10 data parity trap	Network line stats
TOPS20 system reloaded	DN64 statistics

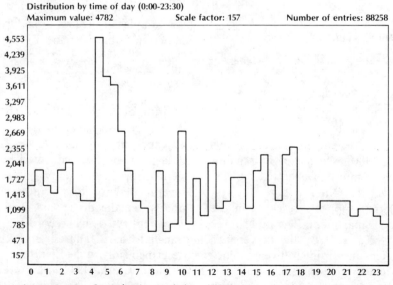

Distribution by time of day (0:00-23:30)

Maximum value: 4782   Scale factor: 157   Number of entries: 88258

Figure 2–11.   Sample time-of-day distribution output from SEADS.

Source: [McConnel, Siewiorek, Tsao, 1979].

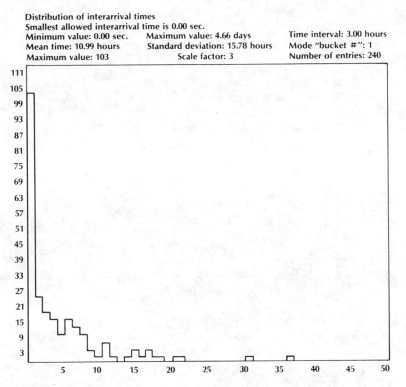

Distribution of interarrival times
Smallest allowed interarrival time is 0.00 sec.

Minimum value: 0.00 sec.	Maximum value: 4.66 days	Time interval: 3.00 hours
Mean time: 10.99 hours	Standard deviation: 15.78 hours	Mode "bucket #": 1
Maximum value: 103	Scale factor: 3	Number of entries: 240

Figure 2–12. Sample interarrival time distribution output from SEADS.

Graphical Data Analysis[*]

The interarrival data can be plotted as a histogram to form an approximation of the probability density function of transient errors. This is useful in deciding initially on which distributions to study. The obvious skew toward the low end for all the data collected on these systems indicate that the Weibull distribution should be used.

System reloads were chosen as being likely due to transient errors, because reloads are commonly caused by crashes, and in systems with stable hardware and matured software, the most frequent cause of crashes appears to be transient errors.

The data generated by SEADS make it clear that the PDP-10 systems frequently recorded

several errors for one fault. To mask out the effects of this, error entries within five minutes of a previous entry were counted as a part of the previous fault. The software allowed any choice for the threshold, facilitating examination of the sensitivity of the data to threshold values. (Threshold values of one minute and ten minutes were also tried without changing the results presented here.)

Two groups of system reload data are presented, one from the individual system (TOPSC) that had the most complete data, the second from all four systems. Figures 2-13 and 2-14 show histograms of the distributions of the interarrival times for system reloads on TOPSC and for all four systems, overlaid with the MLE Weibull probability density function. Figures 2-15 and 2-16 show the plots of the TOPSC and overall PDP-10 reload data using the transformation of the Weibull into a linear distribution given by Equation 36.

[*] This section is adapted from McConnel, Siewiorek, and Tsao, 1979.

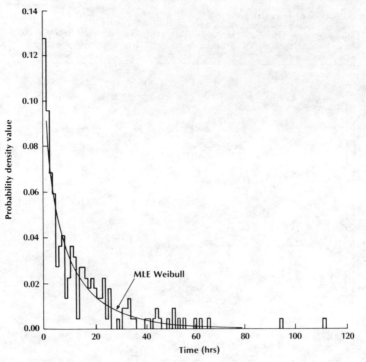

Figure 2–13. Distribution of TOPSC system reloads.

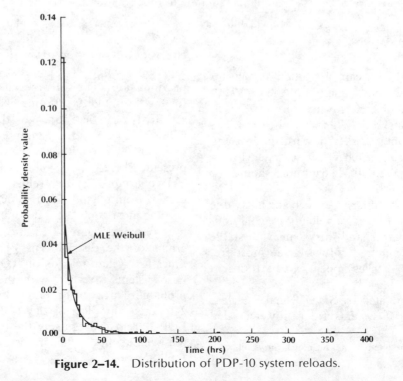

Figure 2–14. Distribution of PDP-10 system reloads.

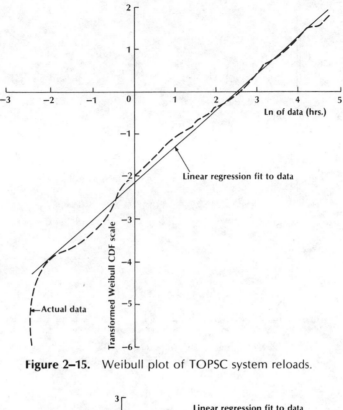

Figure 2–15. Weibull plot of TOPSC system reloads.

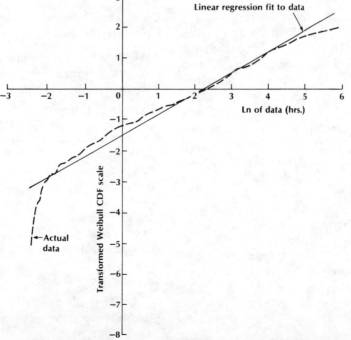

Figure 2–16. Weibull plot of PDP-10 system reloads.

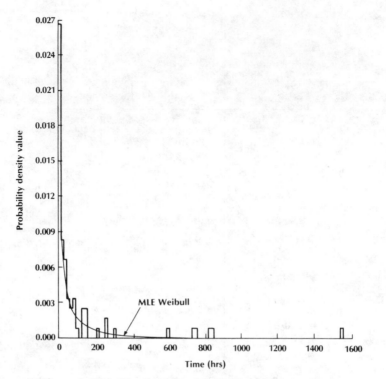

Figure 2–17.   Distribution of PDP-10 parity interrupts.

The second class of events likely to reflect transient errors in the PDP-10 data was the memory parity error interrupt. Except in the case of failing devices that cause intermittent, and finally permanent, faults, these are always the result of transient faults in the memory system. Figures 2-17 and 2-18 show the interarrival distribution and the Weibull plot of the data. In this case, because too few data points were collected from any one of the four systems to be statistically significant, only the total data for all four systems are shown.

Figures 2-19 and 2-20 show the adjusted histograms of the interarrivals for Cm* and C.vmp, respectively. Figures 2-21 and 2-22 are plots of the interarrival data for each system's transient errors, drawn according to the linearizing transformation of Equation 36. The linearity of the data shows that the samples follow a Weibull distribution.

Confidence Intervals for the Parameters

Table 2-23 lists some general statistics about the interarrival times for the five sets of data: TOPSC reloads, PDP-10 reloads, PDP-10 parity errors, C.vmp crashes, and Cm* transient errors. In all cases, the mean is less than the standard deviation, indicating a decreasing failure rate.

Confidence intervals of 90 percent for α and λ were generated for the last three sets using methods developed in Thoman, Bain, and Antle [1969]. The values are listed in Table 2-24. Note that the range of values for α does not include 1.0 (the exponential distribution) for any of the three sets of data.

Goodness-of-Fit Tests

To confirm the impression from the Weibull plots that the data collected on transient errors

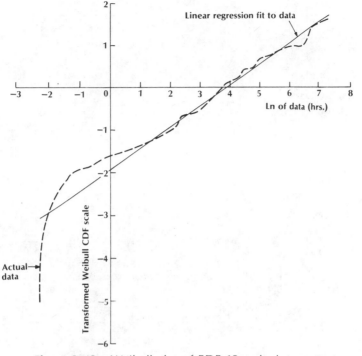

Figure 2–18.   Weibull plot of PDP-10 parity interrupts.

for the various systems are in fact Weibull, a chi-square goodness-of-fit test was performed on each of the five sets of data. The results are given in Table 2-25. The high *P*-levels for each set of data show very good fits to the Weibull distribution.

To complete the testing procedure, a chi-square test was done for each of the five sets of data, assuming an exponential distribution. The comparison of these results is shown in Table 2-26. Although the exponential hypothesis fits the data fairly well in a few cases, the Weibull fits better in every case.

SUMMARY

Sources of errors were traced to their origins in hardware, software, environment, design, and human mistakes. The predominance of transient and intermittent faults was demonstrated. Error manifestations were discussed at both the component and the system level. The mathematics governing the two major statistical fault distributions (exponential and Weibull) were introduced, along with maximum likelihood, regression, confidence interval, and goodness-of-fit tests.

Permanent faults were shown to follow an exponential distribution with the failure rate parameter, λ, predictable by the MIL-HDBK-217 model. Some pitfalls in accelerated temperature testing were illustrated.

Transients and system-level error manifestations (observed over 17,700 hours) follow a Weibull distribution across a wide range of system size and redundancy.

The mathematical techniques introduced in the analysis of permanent and transient faults can be used by the interested reader to confirm fault distributions and/or estimate parameters of the fault distributions for more accurate reliability evaluation.

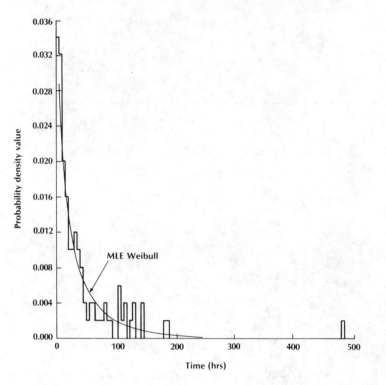

Figure 2–19.   Distribution of Cm* transient errors.

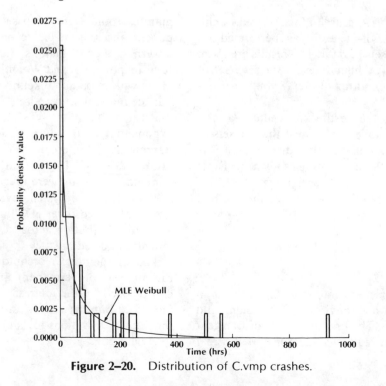

Figure 2–20.   Distribution of C.vmp crashes.

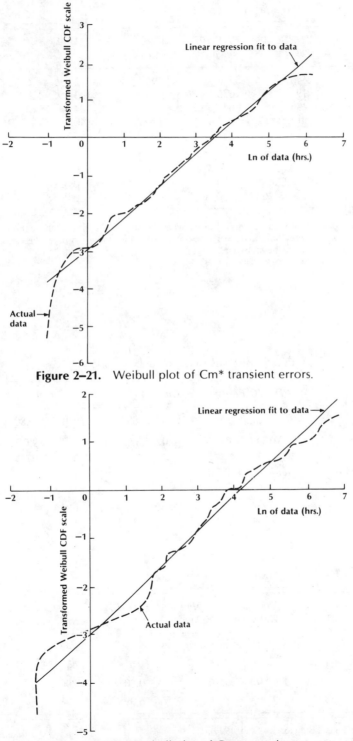

Figure 2–21.   Weibull plot of Cm* transient errors.

Figure 2–22.   Weibull plot of C.vmp crashes.

Table 2–23. Statistics for transient errors.

	TOPSC Reload	PDP-10 Reload	PDP-10 Parity	Cm*	C.vmp*
Time (hrs)	2646	8576	8596	4222	4921
Errors	195	636	74	103	50
Interarrivals	196	640	78	104	51
μ	13.5	13.4	110.2	40.6	96.5 (328)
σ	16.5	24.6	244.9	59.8	167.8 (471)
α (Linear)	0.864	0.684	0.500	0.834	0.711
α (MLE)	0.826	0.639	0.481	0.779	0.654
λ (Linear)	0.0843	0.109	0.0206	0.0294	0.0149
λ (MLE)	0.0826	0.106	0.0203	0.0288	0.0146

* Note that the pessimistic value discussed in [Siewiorek et al., 1978a] is used throughout for C.vmp because there were too few interarrivals in the optimistic value (shown in parentheses for the mean and standard deviation) to be statistically significant.
Source: [McConnel, Siewiorek, Tsao, 1979].

Table 2–24. 90% confidence intervals for alpha and lambda.

	PDP-10 Parity	Cm*	C.vmp
$[\alpha_{low}, \alpha_{high}]$	[0.421,0.566]	[0.693,0.893]	[0.558,0.806]
$[\lambda_{low}, \lambda_{high}]$	[0.0134,0.0307]	[0.0231,0.0359]	[0.0099,0.0214]

Source: [McConnel, Siewiorek, Tsao, 1979].

Table 2–25. Chi-square goodness-of-fit test statistics.

	TOPSC Reload	PDP-10 Reload	PDP-10 Parity	Cm*	C.vmp
Q	23.36	6.40	6.72	9.46	3.71
Degrees of freedom d	34	5	11	17	7
P-level	0.90	0.25	0.80	0.90	0.80
$\chi^2_{p,d}$	23.95	6.63	6.99	10.08	3.82

Source: [McConnel, Siewiorek, Tsao, 1979].

Table 2–26. Chi-square test of exponential distribution.

	TOPSC Reload	PDP-10 Reload	PDP-10 Parity	Cm*	C.vmp
Q	30.61	252.55	79.95	15.14	18.35
Degrees of freedom d	30	6	12	13	7
Level of significance p	0.40	0.00	0.00	0.25	0.01
$\chi^2_{p,d}$	31.32	∞	∞	15.98	18.48

Source: [McConnel, Siewiorek, Tsao, 1979].

REFERENCES

Ball and Hardie [1967]; Bellis [1978]; Berger and Lawrence [1974]; Breuer [1973]; Brodsky [1980]; DEC [1978]; Elkind [1980a]; Geilhufe [1979]; Kamal [1975]; Kamal and Page [1974]; Klein [1976]; Lilliefors [1969]; Losq [1978]; McConnel [1980]; McConnel, Siewiorek, and Tsao [1979]; Melsa and Cohen [1978]; Miller and Freund [1965]; Morganti [1978]; Morganti, Coppadoro, and Ceru [1978]; Nakagawa and Osaki [1975]; Nicholls [1979]; Ohm [1979]; Pear [1954]; Rickers [1976]; Roth et al. [1967a]; Savir [1978]; Siewiorek, Canepa, and Clark [1977]; Siewiorek et al. [1978a]; Signetics [1975]; Snyder [1975]; Sturges [1926]; Swan, Fuller, and Siewiorek [1977]; Tasar and Tasar [1977]; Thoman, Bain, and Antle [1969].

PROBLEMS

1. The reliability function, $R(t)$, describes the probability of not observing any failure before time t. Another reliability metric sometimes used to compare the reliabilities of two alternate designs is the Mission Time Improvement (MTI). It is the ratio of the times at which the two system reliability functions decay below some specified value, say 0.9. Compute MTI (λ_a, λ_b) for a.) an exponential distribution, and b.) a Weibull distribution with a constant shape parameter.

2. Using the data in Table 2-10, make the transformation suggested in Equation 36 and estimate the Weibull parameters, λ and α, by making a least-squares fit to the transformed data. Test the hypothesis that the data follow this distribution. Assume that failures occur at the end point of each interval.

3. Consider an MOS RAM, with $\pi_L = 1$, $\pi_Q = 16$, $\pi_T = 25$, and $\pi_E = 1$. Plot the failure rate, λ, as a function of number of bits according to MIL-HDBK-217B. (See Appendix D.)

Reliability and Availability Techniques

Steven A. Elkind

This chapter presents a spectrum of techniques available to the designer of reliable digital systems. The spectrum spans the range of techniques derived to deal with the problem of building computers from unreliable components. Although the emphasis is on techniques that deal with hard (component) failures, most of the techniques are also effective against transient and intermittent faults.*

There are two approaches to increased reliability: fault avoidance (fault intolerance) and fault tolerance. Fault avoidance results from conservative design practices such as the use of high-reliability components, component burn-in, and careful signal path routing. The goal of fault avoidance is to reduce the possibility of a failure. Even with the most careful fault avoidance, however, failures will eventually occur and result in system failure (hence the name fault intolerance). In fault-tolerant designs redundancy is used to provide the information needed to negate the effects of failures. The redundancy is manifested in one of two ways: extra time or extra components. One form of time redundancy involves extra executions of the same calculation, perhaps by different methods. Comparisons or other operations on the multiple results (identical when no errors are present) provide the basis for subsequent action. Time redundancy is usually provided by software and thus is not within the scope of this chapter. Component redundancy is the use of extra gates, memory cells, bus lines,

---

* In the reliability and fault tolerance literature, the terms *fault* and *failure* are sometimes used interchangeably. In coding theory literature, *failure* and *error* are used interchangeably. These practices are followed in parts of this chapter, in deference to common usage.

functional modules, and the like to supply the extra information needed to guard against the effect of failures.

A redundant system may go through as many as 10 stages in response to the occurrence of a failure. These stages—fault confinement, fault detection, fault masking, retry, diagnosis, reconfiguration, recovery, restart, repair, and reintegration—are explained in the following text. Designing a redundant system involves the selection of a coordinated failure response that combines some or all of these steps. The ordering above corresponds roughly to the normal chronology of the steps, although the actual timing may be different in some instances.

- *Fault confinement.* When faults occur, it is desirable to limit the scope of their effects. Fault confinement is the step of limiting the spread of fault effects to one area of the system, thereby preventing contamination of other areas. Fault confinement can be achieved through liberal use of fault-detection circuits, consistency checks before performing a function ("mutual suspicion"), and multiple requests/confirmations before performing a function. These techniques may be applied in both hardware and software.
- *Fault detection.* Most failures eventually result in logical faults. Many techniques are available to detect faults, such as parity, consistency checking, and protocol violation. Unfortunately these techniques cannot be perfect, and an arbitrary period of time may pass before detection occurs. This time is called fault latency. Fault-detection techniques are of two major classes: off-line detection and on-line detection. With off-line detection, the device is not able to perform useful work while under test. Diagnostic programs, for example, run in a stand-alone fashion even if executed on idle devices or multiplexed with the operations software. Thus, off-line detection assures integrity before and possibly at intervals during operation, but not during the entire time of operation. On-line detection, on the other hand, provides a real-time detection capability, for it is performed concurrently with useful work. On-line techniques include parity detection and duplication.
- *Fault masking.* Fault-masking techniques hide the effects of failures. In a sense, the redundant information outweighs the incorrect information. In its pure form, masking provides no detection. However, many fault-masking techniques can be extended to provide on-line detection as well. Otherwise, off-line detection techniques are needed to discover failures. Majority voting is an example of fault masking.
- *Retry.* In many cases a second attempt at an operation may be successful. This is particularly true of a transient fault that causes no physical damage.
- *Diagnosis.* If the fault detection technique does not provide information about the failure location and/or properties, a diagnostic step may be required.
- *Reconfiguration.* If a fault is detected and a permanent failure located, the system may be able to reconfigure its components to replace the failed component or to isolate it from the rest of the system. The component may be replaced by backup spares. Alternatively, it may simply be switched off and the system capability degraded; this process is called graceful degradation.
- *Recovery.* After detection and (if necessary) reconfiguration, the effects of errors must be eliminated. Normally the system operation is backed up to some point in its processing that preceded the fault detection, and operation recommences from this point. This form of recovery, often called rollback, usually entails strategies using backup files, checkpointing, and journalling. In recovery, error latency becomes an important issue because the rollback must go far enough to avoid the effects of undetected errors that occurred before the detected one.
- *Restart.* Recovery may not be possible if too much information is damaged by an error, or if the system is not designed for recovery. A "hot" restart, a resumption of all operations from the point of fault detection, is possible only if no damage has occurred. A "warm" restart implies that only some of the processes can be resumed without loss. A "cold" restart corresponds to a complete reload of the system, with no processes surviving.
- *Repair.* The component diagnosed as failed is replaced. As with detection, repair can be either on-line or off-line. In off-line repair, either the failed component is not necessary for system operation, or the entire system must be brought down to perform the diagnosis and repair. In on-line repair, the component may be replaced immediately by a back-up spare in a procedure equivalent to reconfiguration or operation may continue without the component, as is the case with masking redundancy or graceful degradation. In either case of on-line repair, the failed component may be physically replaced or repaired without interrupting system operation.
- *Reintegration.* After the physical replacement of a component the repaired module must be reintegrated into the system. For on-line repair, reintegration must be accomplished without interrupting system operation.

Figure 3-1 depicts one scenario that illustrates some of the concepts above. The time line illustrates the stages in fault handling for a nonfault-tolerant system, whereas fault-tolerant systems automate one or more of these stages. Upon detection, the system is brought down, diagnosed, and manually reconfigured to allow a restart. Before operation recommences, the software process must first be rolled back to a point before the errors occurred, and then restarted. Finally, after the failed module is repaired and put back on line, the system is halted temporarily to allow the module to be reintegrated into the system. Figure 3-1 also illustrates some of the reliability measurement concepts discussed in Chapter 5: the Mean Time To Failure (MTTF), Mean Time To Detection (MTTD, sometimes called error latency), Mean Time To Repair (MTTR), and Availability.

Taking these system-failure response stages into account, the spectrum of fault-tolerance techniques can be divided into three major classes: fault detection, masking redundancy, and dynamic redundancy. Figure 3-2 proposes a taxonomy of system-failure response strategies. Fault detection provides no tolerance to faults, but gives warning when they occur. It is used in many small systems such as micro- and mini-computers, some of which may incorporate simple on-line detection mechanisms. This branch does not represent fault tolerance in the strictest sense: even though faults are detected they cannot be tolerated (except for retry upon transient faults).

Masking redundancy, also called static redundancy, tolerates failures but gives no warning of them. It is used in such systems as computers with error-correcting code memories, or with majority-voted redundancy in a fixed configuration (that is, the logical connections between circuit elements remain constant).

The rightmost branch of the figure covers those systems whose configuration can be dynamically changed in response to a fault, or in which masking redundancy, supplemented by on-line fault detection, allows on-line repair. Examples are multiprocessor systems which can degrade gracefully in response to processing element failures, and triplicated systems which include disagreement detection in the voter and are designed for on-line repair.

The range in cost of fault-tolerant techniques is almost a continuum in terms of percentage of redundancy. Figure 3-3 depicts three regions of hardware redundancy, each corresponding to one of the three major areas of the fault-toler-

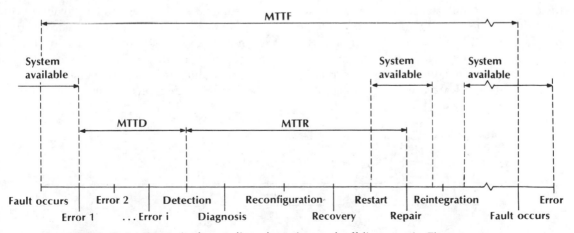

Figure 3–1. Scenario for on-line detection and off-line repair. The measures MTTF, MTTD, and MTTR are the average times to failure, to detection, and to repair.

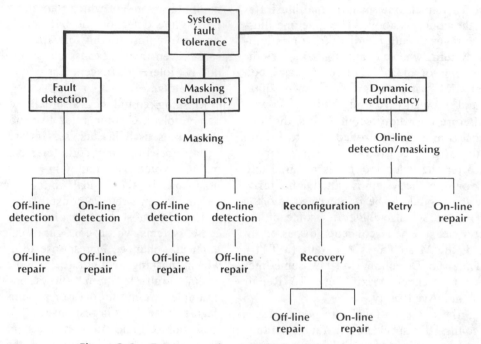

Figure 3–2. Taxonomy of system fault-tolerance strategies.

ance technique spectrum. Even though most techniques in each area fit within these regions, individual techniques may fall well outside them.

Because it is mainly a straightforward application of conservative design practices, fault avoidance is only covered briefly in this chapter. However, it is important to note that most successful designs use a balanced combination of both fault avoidance and fault tolerance. The final design is the result of trade-offs among cost, performance, and reliability. Cost, performance, and reliability goals are usually incompatible to

some degree, and their relative importance depends upon the ultimate application of the final product. For example, some fault-tolerance techniques may find little application in cost-sensitive commercial computing systems but may be required for long-term space missions.

A summary of the techniques covered in this chapter is shown in Table 3-1. The reliability techniques spectrum is broken up into four major regions: fault avoidance, fault detection, masking redundancy, and dynamic redundancy. The last three divisions derive from Figure 3-2.

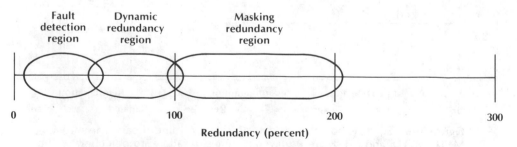

Figure 3–3. Cost range of fault-tolerance techniques (in terms of the redundancy required).

Table 3–1. Classification of reliability techniques.

Region	Technique
Fault avoidance	Environment modification
	Quality changes
	Component integration level
Fault detection	Duplication
	Error detection codes
	M-of-*N* codes
	Parity
	Checksums
	Arithmetic codes
	Cyclic codes
	Self-checking and fail-safe logic
	Watch-dog timers and timeouts
	Consistency and capability checks
Masking redundancy	NMR/voting
	Error correcting codes
	Hamming SEC/DED
	Other codes
	Masking logic
	Interwoven logic
	Coded-state machines
Dynamic redundancy	Reconfigurable duplication
	Reconfigurable NMR
	Backup sparing
	Graceful degradation
	Reconfiguration
	Recovery

This division is not exact. Some basic techniques have properties pertaining to more than one region and some, while they should be considered basic techniques in their own right, require concurrent use of other techniques (for example, failure detection is needed to invoke replacement of a broken module with a spare). Nevertheless, the discussion of each technique below treats each as a basic entity. Whenever possible, a measure of the technique's effectiveness is provided (such as coverage and/or reliability formula). The application of the technique to different areas of digital design is illustrated, often with examples from specific systems. The illustrations cannot be comprehensive due to lack of space; often the techniques have been applied to design areas other than those mentioned.

Table 3-1 is not complete but covers most of the major techniques now in use. In many cases the technique set forth is only a representative from a class of similar techniques; space limitations preclude covering them all. In this event, references are given for other techniques in the same class.

FAULT-AVOIDANCE TECHNIQUES

One method of increasing computer reliability is to lessen the possibility of failures. This method is called fault avoidance. If fault avoidance alone cannot economically meet system design goals, fault-detection and/or fault-tolerance techniques must be used. Some fault-avoidance techniques are intended to decrease the possibility of transient faults. Careful signal routing, shielding, cabinet grounding, and input-line static filters are examples of techniques that effectively increase the signal-to-noise ratio. Other techniques are useful against both hard and transient faults. A design rule that limits the fanout of gates to a small number, for example, decreases power dissipation (decreasing thermal effects, and thus hard failures). Fanout limitation also increases the effective noise margin at the inputs of subsequent gates and thus decreases the possibility of a transient fault. Another concern is the avoidance of human errors through such measures as labeling and documentation. In addition, the possibility of assembly errors should be minimized. For example, many manufacturers produce printed circuit boards and connectors that are shaped in such a way that they cannot be plugged in backward or into the wrong slots.

$$\lambda = \pi_L \pi_Q (C_1 \pi_T + C_2 \pi_E)$$
$$\lambda = \text{failure rate, failures per million hours}$$
$$\text{(fpmh)}$$
$$\pi_L = \text{learning curve factor}$$
$$\pi_Q = \text{quality factor}$$
$$C_1, C_2 = \text{complexity factors}$$
$$\pi_T = \text{temperature factor}$$
$$\pi_E = \text{environment factor}$$

Figure 3–4. MIL-HDBK-217B failure rate calculation for integrated circuits.

This section presents three techniques for avoiding hard failures. The goal is to obtain a smaller system failure rate as determined by one of the MIL-217 models (Chapter 2). Figure 3-4 shows the formula for the failure rate of an integrated circuit in the MIL-217B model. Fault avoidance can be obtained by manipulating factors that affect the failure rate. The subsections below cover possible changes in environment, quality, and complexity factors.

Environmental Changes

Two of the parameters in the formula of Figure 3-4 are related to the operating environment. The first is π_E, which is specified for general classes of environmental conditions. Table 3-2 gives some examples of the MIL-217B environment factor. Ground benign environment implies air-conditioned computer rooms; ground fixed implies office or factory floor installations. Conditions (and π_E values) between the extremes provided by MIL-217B can be estimated. For the full set of standard π_E values, see Appendix D. Usually the operating environment is beyond the designer's control and thus is not a means of affecting system reliability.

The other parameter affected by the environment is π_T, which is a function of junction temperature. The junction temperature is a result of several factors: ambient air temperature, heat transfer from chip to package and package to air, and the heat created by the power consumed on the chip. Junction temperature can be modified

Table 3–2. Examples of π_E, environment parameter.

Environment	π_E	Description
Ground benign	0.2	Nearly zero environmental stress with optimum engineering operation and maintenance.
Space, flight	0.2	Earth orbital....[No] access for maintenance....
Ground fixed	1.0	Conditions less than ideal to include installation in permanent racks with adequate cooling air, maintenance by military personnel, and possible installation in unheated buildings.
Airborne inhabited	4.0	Typical cockpit conditions without environmental extremes of pressure, temperature, and vibration.
Missile, launch	10.0	Severe conditions . . . related to missile launch and . . . space vehicle boost into orbit . . . reentry and landing....

Source: MIL-HDBK-217B [U. S. Department of Defense, 1976]

by changing power dissipation, heat sinking of boards and chips, and controlling air temperature and air flow. Power dissipation is controllable to some extent by fan-out limitation. In gate array and master slice technologies, power dissipation can be controlled during chip design. Heat sinking may be necessary for selected devices, and is sometimes even used for all ICs in a given design.

Complex, expensive fluid cooling systems (such as Freon cooling) have occasionally found use in systems that require high power dissipation ECL logic and high component densities. In these systems, such as high-speed scientific computers, the cooling design is as much of a challenge as the logic design. The CRAY-1 com-

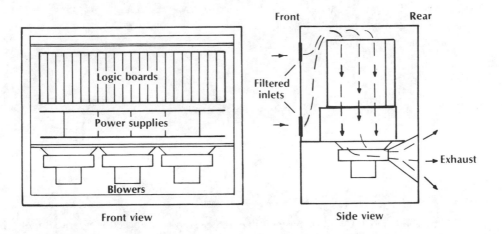

Figure 3–5. Cooling system design for the DEC VAX-11/780 cabinet.

puter, for example, has heat-conductive surfaces integral to each module and uses Freon to keep the machine running at reasonable temperatures [Russel, 1978].

In most cases, a cabinet ventilation system is sufficient. Fans can be installed to increase air flow through the cabinet and lower cabinet air temperature. Fans also increase air flow across the circuit boards, improving heat transfer from the component packages to the air. Careful design of the cabinet itself is also important in improving air flow and heat transfer.

One problem often encountered is "hot spots" on circuit boards. These result when heat-producing components reside on the lee side (or airflow shadow) of other components. Hot spots can be designed out of a system. For example, the Texas Instruments ASC (Advanced Scientific Computer) uses air cooling, unlike most high-performance machines. Its designers carefully studied the properties of cooling air flow and found that empty spaces on the PC board increased board-level air turbulence. The turbulence caused nonuniform heat transfer, and hot spots resulted. The outcome of this research was the addition of dummy packages in spaces where no actual ICs were used.

The VAX-11/780 provides a good example of cabinet design for improved cooling (Figure 3-5). To minimize the air temperature near the circuit boards, the power supplies are placed at the bottom of the cabinet, away from the logic boards. The blower system provides filtered air drawn from outside the cabinet. The air is routed down across the circuit boards in such a way that it passes over only one board before being exhausted to the outside.

The cost of potential ventilation schemes must be weighed against potential gains in reliability. A PDP-8/e computer will be used to provide an example of the range of improvement available through temperature modification. Figure 3-6 shows an AUTOFAIL failure rate analysis of the PDP-8/e design assuming an expected ambient (package) temperature of 50° C.* This assumption is reasonable with normal room temperatures and no ventilation other than convection

---

* In this chapter, AUTOFAIL analyses use the complexity factor modification discussed in Chapter 2. For LSI, RAM, and ROM devices, the gate (bit) count is divided by 16 before calculating the MIL-217B complexity factors (C_1 and C_2 in Figure 3-4).

```
PDP8E.REL    LSI=   16.000    ROM=   16.000    RAM=   16.000

E =    1.000    Q =   16.000    L =    1.000    T =    50.000

MK4096    Q =    16.000
MODULE                                 FAILURE RATE              PERCENTAGE

PDP8E                                          281.261                  100.000
    PROCESSOR                            36.559                   12.998
        DATA.PART                        16.989                   46.471
            REGISTERS                     7.119                   41.903
            ADDER.ETC.                    2.065                   12.153
            PATH.SHUNTING                 7.805                   45.944
        BUS.CONNECT.OPEN.COLL             1.048                    2.867
        CONTROL.LOGIC                    18.522                   50.663
    KM8.MEM.EXT.TIM.SHR                   9.546                    3.394
    16K.MEMORY                          235.156                   83.608
        MEMORY.CHIPS                    232.487                   98.865
        CONTROL                           2.276                     .968
        BUS.CONN.OC                        .393                     .167

 # of chips =    285.083    # of gates =    2830.000    # of bits = 196608.000
```

Figure 3–6. AUTOFAIL analysis of PDP-8/e system with no cooling; in-cabinet temperature of 50°C.

```
PDP8E.REL    LSI=   16.000    ROM=   16.000    RAM=   16.000
E =    1.000    Q =   16.000    L =    1.000    T =    40.000

MK4096    Q =    16.000
MODULE                                 FAILURE RATE              PERCENTAGE

PDP8E                                          107.218                  100.000
    PROCESSOR                            32.111                   19.203
        DATA.PART                        14.592                   45.443
            REGISTERS                     5.903                   40.454
            ADDER.ETC.                    1.756                   12.034
            PATH.SHUNTING                 6.933                   47.511
        BUS.CONNECT.OPEN.COLL              .966                    3.007
        CONTROL.LOGIC                    16.553                   51.549
    KM8.MEM.EXT.TIM.SHR                   8.509                    5.089
    16K.MEMORY                          126.598                   75.708
        MEMORY.CHIPS                    124.186                   98.095
        CONTROL                           2.050                    1.619
        BUS.CONN.OC                        .362                     .286

 # of chips =    285.083    # of gates =    2830.000    # of bits = 196608.000
```

Figure 3–7. AUTOFAIL analysis of PDP-8/e system with fans installed in cabinet; in-cabinet temperature of 40°C.

```
PDP8E.REL    LSI=   16.000    ROM=   16.000    RAM=   16.000

E =    1.000    Q =   16.000    L =    1.000    T =    30.000

MK4096    Q =    16.000
MODULE                                 FAILURE RATE              PERCENTAGE

PDP8E                                          106.742                  100.000
    PROCESSOR                            29.064                   27.228
        DATA.PART                        12.944                   44.537
            REGISTERS                     5.055                   39.054
            ADDER.ETC.                    1.543                   11.917
            PATH.SHUNTING                 6.346                   49.029
        BUS.CONNECT.OPEN.COLL              .910                    3.132
        CONTROL.LOGIC                    15.209                   52.331
    KM8.MEM.EXT.TIM.SHR                   7.802                    7.310
    16K.MEMORY                           69.876                   65.462
        MEMORY.CHIPS                     67.637                   96.796
        CONTROL                           1.898                    2.716
        BUS.CONN.OC                        .341                     .489

 # of chips =    285.083    # of gates =    2830.000    # of bits = 196608.000
```

Figure 3–8. AUTOFAIL analysis of PDP-8/e system with cabinet ventilation system; in-cabinet temperature of 30°C.

currents within the cabinet. The system failure rate is 281 failures per million hours (fpmh), which is equivalent to a Mean Time To Failure (MTTF) of 3,555 hours.

Figure 3-7 shows the effect of placing a few small fans in the cabinet. If the increased circulation can lower the cabinet temperature by 10 degrees, the failure rate drops to 167 fpmh, a decrease of 41 percent. The MTTF increases to 5,980 hours, an increase of 68 percent.* Figure 3-8 shows the effect of using a better ventilating system, perhaps including ducting, blowers, and filters, which is capable of a 20-degree reduction in temperature. This modification more than doubles the MTTF of the system. The failure rate analyses have ignored the cooling system (fan) failure rates because there are usually multiple fans, and the failure of only one fan will not cause immediate system failure.

Thus, it is possible to obtain reliability improvement through an effective ventilation system and changes in cabinet design. Noisy fans may be considered undesirable in certain environments such as an office. A quieter (and more expensive) system is possible but cooling is often left to convection, and the MTTF loss is absorbed in exchange for a more saleable product.

Quality Changes

Using higher-quality components is an obvious strategy for improving reliability. The simplest implementation is to buy high-reliability ("hi-rel") components directly from the manufacturer. However, such components may be expensive (usually twice as much as commercial grade) and/or may have long procurement lead times. There are two possible solutions to these problems. The first is in-house screening and burn-in. The second is specification of hi-rel components for only those areas of a design where they are most economically effective.

The use of higher quality components is re-flected in the parameter π_Q (quality factor) of Figure 3-4. Table 3-3 lists some of the standard quality factors for integrated circuits in MIL-217B. A complete list is in Appendix D.

The quality level of a component is determined partly by packaging method and materials, such as a hermetically vs. nonhermetically sealed package and ceramic vs. plastic package material. Another major factor for determining the quality level is the screening done during and after component manufacture. Not all the properties required of military-grade components make sense in a commercial environment. For example, hermetic package seals are often required for MIL-spec components, so that when the device is unpowered moisture will not condense inside the component. Many commercial systems are left on all the time or operate in low-humidity environments, eliminating the need for perfectly hermetic packages. MIL-spec components also undergo high-G acceleration screening in centrifuges. Most commercial systems will not be subject to G-stresses such as acceleration and impact.

Table 3–3. Examples of π_Q, quality factor.

Class	π_Q	Description
C	16	Procured in full accordance with MIL-M-38510, Class C requirements. [Parts falling in this or higher classifications are commonly referred to as "mil-spec" or "hi-rel" components.]
D-1	150	Commercial (or non-mil standard) part, hermetically sealed, with no screening beyond the manufacturer's regular quality assurance practices.
D-2	300	Commercial (or nonmil standard) part, packaged or sealed with organic materials, (e.g., epoxy, silicone, or phenolic).

Source: **MIL-HDBK-217B** [U.S. Department of Defense 1976]

---

* Note that this example does not quite fit the old rule of thumb that a 10-degree temperature drop increases the MTTF by a factor of 2.

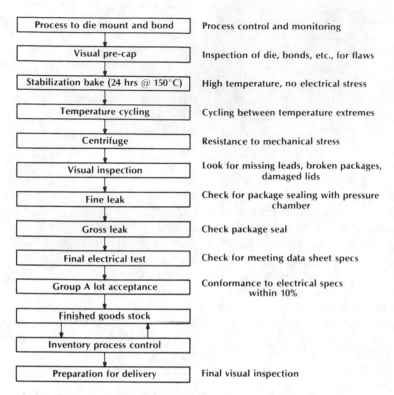

Process to die mount and bond	Process control and monitoring
Visual pre-cap	Inspection of die, bonds, etc., for flaws
Stabilization bake (24 hrs @ 150°C)	High temperature, no electrical stress
Temperature cycling	Cycling between temperature extremes
Centrifuge	Resistance to mechanical stress
Visual inspection	Look for missing leads, broken packages, damaged lids
Fine leak	Check for package sealing with pressure chamber
Gross leak	Check package seal
Final electrical test	Check for meeting data sheet specs
Group A lot acceptance	Conformance to electrical specs within 10%
Finished goods stock	
Inventory process control	
Preparation for delivery	Final visual inspection

Figure 3–9.   Texas Instruments MACH-IV procurement specification for class C level component processing.

Some component users may wish to do their own screening, avoiding some of the harsher military environmental tests that the component manufacturer must perform (and charge for) on MIL-rated devices. Figure 3-9 diagrams the Texas Instruments Class C qualification process for integrated circuits [Texas Instruments, 1976]. Table 2-8 lists a set of the possible screening tests. Some of these tests are discussed below; others were considered in Chapter 2.

In manufacture, visual inspection of the wafer is possible before it is cut into dies. The manufacturer can also visually inspect the chip and bonds before sealing the package. The component buyer can do the same by opening and inspecting sample components. Electrical tests can be performed. Each wafer often has a special test pattern or transistor upon which probes can be placed to test the values of various character-

istic parameters. Individual circuits on the wafer may also be tested. Electrical testing after packaging checks both the silicon circuit and the pin bonding. Stress testing may also be employed. Overvoltage, vibration, heat, humidity, and other stresses are applied to the component, followed by electrical tests to determine resistance to the stresses.

The manufacturer often performs additional processing on components subsequent to manufacture and testing. The most common is component burn-in. This is accomplished by continual simulated operation of all the components, possibly at higher-than-normal temperatures. Slight overvoltages are sometimes applied at signal and power inputs. The purpose of burn-in is to eliminate weak components. The beginning, or infant mortality, phase of the bathtub curve of Figure 1-4 is traversed during burn-in. Finally, entire assemblies or systems can be burned-in before shipment. This last procedure has the advantage of eliminating incompatibilities between components that have passed testing, but whose parameters combine to result in poor or improper operation (often a cause of intermittent faults).

The final value of π_Q is determined by the types and frequency of testing and processing. Tests can be performed with varying thoroughness: for each component, for sample components from each manufacturing lot, or for periodic samples every few lots. Additional tests may be performed if higher-quality components are needed for special applications. Lower quality-factor components (i.e., higher π_Q) are the result of less stringent testing and processing, or are components that failed testing for higher standards but still meet lower-quality grade specifications.

Research at Carnegie-Mellon University has shown that an average component π_Q of 16 is not unusual for a manufacturer of commercial systems [Siewiorek et al., 1978b]. The components in the study were primarily plastic package DIPs. This π_Q is obtained through in-house screening and burn-in of components and systems. DEC, for example, rejects 2.5 percent of its incoming components, with the result that only 0.04 percent of the screened components fail during subsequent system manufacturing steps [DEC, 1975c]. In addition, some IC manufacturers offer class C-grade components in their standard product lines.

Another benefit of screening beyond functional testing is the reduction of manufacture and warranty costs. Replacement costs for a component increase by about an order of magnitude for each step during the manufacture and warranty periods. Craig [1980] reports that the typical cost for screening out a bad IC is 50¢. Repair of the board resulting from a bad chip costs about $5 on the plant floor; diagnosis and repair of the same failure in an assembled system costs $50. During the warranty period, when the system is in the field where sophisticated, special test set-ups are not available, the same repair costs the manufacturer $500 (and might cost the customer $5,000 in lost revenue and time). If only 0.5 percent of the components used are bad or weak, a system with 1,000 components has a $(1 - 0.995^{1000})$ or 99.3 percent chance that repair will be necessary during the assembly process (so-called rework) or the warranty period because of a component that could have been screened out. Alternatively, an average of five such repair incidents could be expected for each system in addition to incidents resulting from normal failures (those due to components that would survive screening). This is because the expected number of weak components in a system is 1000×0.005.

The manufacturer of the Vidar/TRW 2900B subscriber billing system incorporates testing and screening for increased component reliability [McDonald, 1976]. The testing and inspection flow in use in 1976 is shown in Figure 3-10. The component sampling consisted of a DC parametric test followed by a test for intermittent lead bonding failures. If more than 5 percent of an incoming lot of ICs failed the DC test or more than 0.1 percent failed the bonding test, the lot was rejected. This form of component acceptance is called Acceptable Quality Level testing (AQL). Next, a 100 percent DC parametric test screened all components. In the burn-in phase, an assembled board had to operate for at least 24 error-free hours at 50° C before it was removed from the test. In 1977 the screening tests for the 2900B changed, partly because of changes in chip technologies [McDonald and McCracken, 1977]. The testing and inspection flow remained the same, but component burn-in was added. The data in Table 3-4, gathered during this later period, show the effectiveness of the component burn-in after incoming AQL testing.

Reconsider the PDP-8/e analysis in Figure 3-7, in which the quality factor for all components is 16. The AUTOFAIL analysis shows that

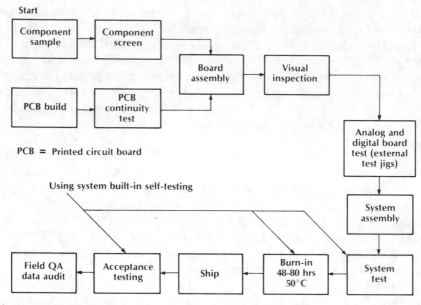

Figure 3–10. Reliability enhancement in Vidar/TRW 2900B subscriber billing system. (© 1976 IEEE.)

the 4K-bit memory chips have a total failure rate of 124 fpmh, accounting for 74 percent of the system failure rate (76 percent of the PDP-8 failure rate is in the memory, and 98 percent of that is due to the RAM chips). An improvement

in the quality of this component alone should result in a major increase in overall reliability. If 4K-bit memory chips with a π_Q of 10 can be obtained (MIL-STD quality class B-2), either by purchase or by in-house screening and burn-in, the system failure rate drops to 121 fpmh, a 28 percent improvement in the system's failure rate and a 39 percent increase in MTTF. Figure 3-11 shows the AUTOFAIL analysis of this modified design.

Finally, consider the possibility of burning-in all PDP-8/e systems before shipment. The burn-in time is made long enough to improve the quality factor of all components by, say, 2 points ($\Delta\pi_Q = -2$). The π_Q of the hi-rel RAMs is assumed not to be affected, since additional burn-in of these will have little effect. As shown by the AUTOFAIL analysis in Figure 3-12, the system failure rate drops to 115 fpmh, a net improvement in system failure rate of 31 percent and in MTTF of 45 percent over the design of Figure 3-7 (for which $\pi_Q = 16$ for all components, including the RAM chips).

Table 3–4. Vidar/TRW 2900B burn-in test results.

Device	Quantity Processed	Quantity Defective	Percent Defective
Linear	123,212	5,011	4.07%
TTL standard	316,909	3,735	1.18
TTL low power	379,959	4,982	1.31
Schottky	7,058	130	1.84
Low power Schottky	86,244	1,670	1.94
CMOS	56,293	1,240	2.20
Misc.	63,666	1,833	2.88
Total	*1,033,341*	*18,601*	*1.80*

Source: McDonald and McCracken, 1977

```
PDP8E.REL     LSI=    16.000     ROM=   16.000     RAM=   16.000

E =    1.000    Q =    16.000    L =    1.000    T =    40.000

MK4096    Q =    10.000
```

MODULE	FAILURE RATE	PERCENTAGE
PDP8E	120.648	100.000
PROCESSOR	32.111	26.615
DATA.PART	14.592	45.443
REGISTERS	5.903	40.454
ADDER.ETC.	1.756	12.034
PATH.SHUNTING	6.933	47.511
BUS.CONNECT.OPEN.COLL	.966	3.007
CONTROL.LOGIC	16.553	51.549
KM8.MEM.EXT.TIM.SHR	8.509	7.053
16K.MEMORY	80.028	66.332
MEMORY.CHIPS	77.616	96.986
CONTROL	2.050	2.561
BUS.CONN.OC	.362	.452

```
# of chips =    285.083    # of gates =    2830.000    # of bits =  196608.000
```

Figure 3–11. AUTOFAIL analysis of PDP-8/e system with hi-rel RAM chips in memory.

```
PDP8E.REL     LSI=    16.000     ROM=   16.000     RAM=   16.000

E =    1.000    Q =    14.000    L =    1.000    T =    40.000

MK4096    Q =    10.000
```

MODULE	FAILURE RATE	PERCENTAGE
PDP8E	115.279	100.000
PROCESSOR	28.097	24.375
DATA.PART	12.768	45.443
REGISTERS	5.165	40.454
ADDER.ETC.	1.537	12.034
PATH.SHUNTING	6.066	47.511
BUS.CONNECT.OPEN.COLL	.845	3.007
CONTROL.LOGIC	14.484	51.549
KM8.MEM.EXT.TIM.SHR	7.446	6.459
16K.MEMORY	79.727	69.166
MEMORY.CHIPS	77.616	97.353
CONTROL	1.794	2.250
BUS.CONN.OC	.317	.397

```
# of chips =    285.083    # of gates =    2830.000    # of bits =  196608.000
```

Figure 3–12. AUTOFAIL analysis of PDP-8/e system with hi-rel RAM chips and preshipment burn-in.

Component Integration Level

LSI component technology possesses many well-known advantages. The cost of a single chip is usually less than that of the set of standard SSI/MSI components needed to implement the same function. Fewer chips means fewer solder joints, less board space, and thus lower costs in board manufacture and assembly. Normally, power consumption is lower and performance benefits from shorter signal paths. In sum, more functionality can fit into less space, consume less power, operate at least as fast, and cost little or no more.

Higher integration levels yield another benefit: increased reliability. In the MIL-217B model, the failure rate of a component does not increase linearly with its complexity (measured in gates or bits on the chip). The complexity factors C1 and C2 (Figure 3-4) follow a power-law relationship with the number of gates. This relationship is reflected in Figure 1-5, which plots the failure rate as a function of gates. The individual gate failure rate decreases as the gate count per package goes up. As a result, total system failure rate decreases as the level of integration increases. Thus reliability becomes an additional factor in the decision to use LSI components where possible. Figure 3-13 demonstrates the effect of larger-scale integration. Each module in the AUTOFAIL analysis contains 256 gates. Changes in integration level from 4 to 256 gates per package result in module failure rates ranging from 7.3 fpmh to 0.4 fpmh, or a range of 18 to 1.

Standard LSI circuits are often not available in the exact functionality a design requires. There are alternative solutions to adapt the design to fit the available components. One of these is to fabricate a custom LSI chip. An increasing number of systems manufacturers are developing in-house LSI circuit design and production capabilities. Large volume requirements may make outside design and manufacture worthwhile. Conversely, if only a small volume of custom ICs is required, the manufacturing process may not have the opportunity to stabilize and traverse the learning curve. The result is that the custom chip may be more unreliable than the equivalent SSI/MSI circuit (π_L is 10 instead of 1). The learning curve problem is avoided in the gate array and transistor array approaches to customized LSI circuits. These and other technologies are programmable either in manufacture (such as by a final metalization step) or in the field (such as electrically alterable ROMs and FPLAs).

Another solution to the custom LSI problem is to design a microcoded machine. Microcoded design brings many different benefits, including flexibility (ease of modification), design regularity, and debugging ease. ROMs, a relatively inexpensive form of custom LSI, can replace large amounts of random SSI/MSI circuitry. Microcoded designs bring potential reliability benefits other than lower component failure rates. Their regularity of structure makes microcoded ma-

```
      INTDEM.REL    LSI =    16.000    ROM=    16.000    RAM=    16.000

      E =    1.000    Q =    16.000    L =    1.000    T =    30.000


      MODULE                                   FAILURE RATE              PERCENTAGE


      MODULES.OF.256.GATES                         20.516                 100.000
         CHIP.4.GATES                               7.282                  35.494
         CHIP.8.GATES                               4.785                  23.324
         CHIP.16.GATES                              3.161                  15.407
         CHIP.32.GATES                              2.479                  12.084
         CHIP.64.GATES                              1.709                   8.328
         CHIP.128.GATES                              .701                   3.417
         CHIP.256.GATES                              .399                   1.947

      # of chips =    127.000    # of gates =    1792.000    # of bits =    .000
```

Figure 3–13. AUTOFAIL analysis of modules containing 256 gates. Each module is made with ICs having identical gate counts. The first (CHIP.4.GATES) is made with SSI circuits with 4 gates per chip. The last (CHIP.256.GATES) is made with one LSI circuit containing all 256 gates. The number in the module name denotes the gate count for each chip used in the module.

chines particularly amenable to many of the reliability techniques presented in later sections.

Consider a PDP-8 design based on the AMD-2901 bit-slice microprocessor chip [Siewiorek, Bell, and Newell, 1982]. This design is only a partial one: I/O and Omnibus facilities are not included. Nevertheless, it provides an indication of the potential savings resulting from increased integration levels via the microcode ROMs. The failure rate for this design is 136 fpmh (Figure 3-14), only 81 percent of the design of Figure 3-7. System MTTF is 7,358 hours, up 23 percent from 5,980 hours. The LSI processor MTTF is about 107,000 hours; the SSI/MSI processor and KM8 memory extension unit that it replaces have a total MTTF of about 25,000 hours, an improvement of more than 325 percent.

Table 3-5 summarizes all the PDP-8/e examples used in the discussion of fault-avoidance techniques, showing the effect of the various approaches (temperature, quality, and integration). The table also includes a few designs not discussed earlier that demonstrate the combination of more than one approach. Note that a 5.5 to 1 MTTF improvement is attained solely through fault-intolerant techniques.

FAULT-DETECTION TECHNIQUES

Fault-avoidance techniques attempt to decrease the possibility of failures. Fault detection, discussed in this section, and the techniques discussed in subsequent sections deal with the inevitability of failures. The key to these techniques is redundancy: extra information or resources beyond those needed during normal system operation.

Most of this section is devoted to techniques useful in detecting failures, or more exactly, detecting the faults and errors that are caused by failures. Action following such detection can range from ignoring the failure, to retries, to switching in replacement parts. In some real-time applications, for example, occasional erroneous results can be ignored (that is, not used). In many cases a retry can be successful, particularly with transient or intermittent faults. Finally, attempts at correction or reconfiguration and rollback are possible. Some of those possibilities

```
8BS.REL        LSI=   16.000     ROM=   16.000     RAM=   16.000

E =    1.000    Q =   16.000    L =   1.000    T =   40.000

MK4096    Q =   16.000
```

```
MODULE                                 FAILURE RATE              PERCENTAGE

PDP8.BIT.SLICED                             135.908                 100.000
   PROCESSOR                                  9.310                   6.850
      MICROSTORE                              4.259                  45.741
      MICROSEQUENCER                          1.009                  10.839
      DATA.PATHS                              3.452                  37.077
         LINK.BIT                              .604                  17.484
         COND.CODE.MUX                         .689                  19.957
         SKIP.GENERATE                         .483                  13.987
         CONSTANT.MASK                         .082                   2.363
      MISC.                                    .590                   6.342
   16K.MEMORY                               126.598                  93.150
      MEMORY.CHIPS                          124.186                  98.095
      CONTROL                                 2.050                   1.619
      BUS.CONN.OC                             .362                    .286

# of chips =   97.000     # of gates =  2545.500    # of bits =  202880.000
```

Figure 3–14. AUTOFAIL analysis of PDP-8/e with AMD2901/2910 chip set.

Table 3–5. Summary of PDP-8/e fault-avoidance designs.

Analysis Figure	Temp. (°C)	π_Q	RAM π_Q	λ (fpmh)	MTTF (hours)	Notes
3-6	50	16	16	281.26	3,555	Base design, no cooling
3-7	40	16	16	167.22	5,980	Fans installed
3-8	30	16	16	106.74	9,369	Cabinet ventilation system
3-11	40	16	10	120.65	8,288	Fans installed, hi-rel RAM chips
3-12	40	14	10	115.28	8,675	Fans installed, hi-rel RAM chips, system burn-in
N/A	30	14	10	76.49	13,074	Cabinet ventilation system, hi-rel RAM chips, system burn-in
3-14	40	16	16	135.91	7,358	Fans installed, LSI bit-slice chips and ROMS used in CPU
N/A	30	14	10	51.15	19,550	Cabinet ventillation system, LSI bit-slice chips and ROMS used in CPU, hi-rel RAM chips, system burn-in

are considered in the section on Dynamic Redundancy.

Reliability functions, $R(t)$, and the measures derived from them are not very useful in considerations of the effectiveness of failure-detection and fail-safe techniques. The redundant hardware actually contributes to a reduced $R(t)$ when corrective action does not follow detection. The concept of coverage, however, provides the view of reliability required when discussing detection techniques. This section uses two measurements of coverage.* The first, called general coverage, is more qualitative. Usually general coverage specifies the classes of failures that are detectable, and may include failure detection percentages for different classes of failures. The second form of coverage is more explicit. It is the probability that a failure (any failure) is detected, and is denoted by C. C can be determined from the general coverage specifications by using

the average of the coverages for all possible classes of failures, weighted by the probability of occurrence of each fault class. Thus C is more difficult to obtain, since the relative probabilities are implementation-dependent and indeed may not be known. In many instances, simplifying assumptions are employed for the possible failure modes and probabilities. For these reasons, the technique discussions below will always have the general coverage measure, and when possible, the explicit coverage C.

Cost and performance effects of reliability techniques are also important. Dollar costs are impossible to give here. Even explicit costs in numbers of chips will often be hard to predict without knowing details of specific implementations. The same is true of performance effects, as shown by the single error-correcting-code memory example in Chapter 5. Diagnosability is yet another important issue when considering fault-detection and fail-safe techniques. Diagnosability is usually considered in terms of diagnostic resolution, that is, the size of the region to which

---

* The issues involving coverage measurement are discussed in detail in Chapter 5.

the fault can be isolated. In many systems diagnostic resolution to the Field-Replacable Unit (FRU) is considered necessary. When fault detection techniques are used in conjunction with fault-tolerant techniques (see the section on Dynamic Redundancy), the diagnostic resolution may become crucially important. Diagnostic resolution is a function of implementation and is difficult to determine accurately without specific details. Thus, while cost, performance, and diagnosability are considered in the discussions below, the information given will often be vague.

Duplication

Conceptually, duplication is the simplest fault detection technique. Two identical copies are employed. When a failure occurs, the two copies are no longer identical and a simple comparison detects the fault. The simplicity, low cost, and low performance impact of the comparison technique are particularly attractive. Duplication is applicable to all areas and levels of computer design and thus is widely used.

Duplication successfully detects all single faults except that of the comparison element. In some cases, particularly for memories or multiple line output circuits, failures in both copies are detected as long as at least one failure results in a nonoverlapping failure. An example of nonoverlapping failure is a duplicated eight-bit word. If the first copy has a failure in bit position 0 and the second copy has failures in bit positions 0 and 5, the failures in bit position 0 will not be detected if they result in identical errors. The bit position 5 failure, however, is nonoverlapping and will be detected. Identical faults from the identical modules are not detectable because both copies are in agreement. Thus, in many cases physical division and/or separation of the modules is a necessity.

There are many variants on duplication. Some combine duplication with other techniques, resulting in increased coverage over some classes of faults, or in fault tolerance (such as reconfiguration, error correction). Several such combinations are covered in the section on Dynamic Redundancy.

One method for increasing coverage is the "swap-and-compare" technique used on the C.mmp multiprocessor [Siewiorek et al., 1978a]. Initially used for important data structures in memory, the technique can also be applied to other areas of a computer. Figure 3-15 illustrates the concept. There are two copies of a word, but one copy has its two bytes reversed. Error checking involves swapping the bytes of one copy prior to comparison. In addition to covering all single, nonoverlapping failures, swap-and-compare provides coverage of most identical failures affecting both copies (such as bit-plane failure).

In duplication, both copies may be subject to identical failures (common-mode failures), particularly if both have an identical design error or if both reside on the same IC chip. Sedmak and Liebergot [1980] propose the use of complementary functions to solve this problem for VLSI IC chips (Figure 3-16). This approach is similar in concept to dual-diversity reception of radio signals, in which the same signal is received by two different antennae and receivers. One copy of the logic is the logical dual of the other copy. Common failure modes would probably cause different error effects, resulting in detection and thus coverage of these modes. A similar solution is to use both "on-set" and "off-set" realizations

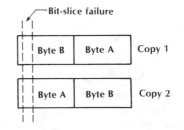

Figure 3–15. Swap-and-compare check scheme for critical data structures in C.mmp.

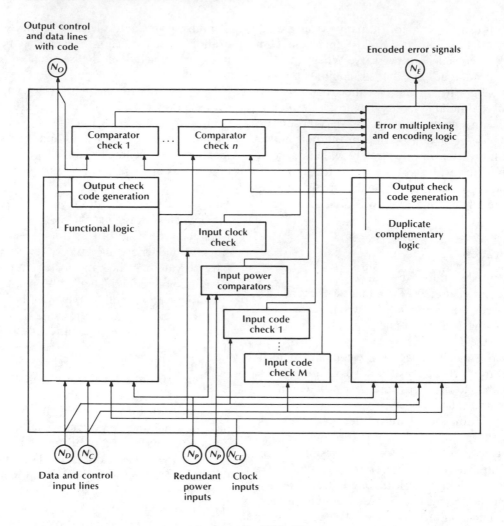

a. Generalized VLSI chip.

Figure 3–16. Proposed use of duplicate circuits on one VLSI chip. Complementary implementations improve resistance to common mode failures. (© 1980 IEEE.)

for the two copies [Tohma and Aoyagi, 1971]. The on-set is the set of input and state variables that result in logical one outputs. The off-set results in logical zero outputs.

Duplicate information may already be present in a circuit so that the amount of additional redundancy needed may be small. An example is a possible internal modification to the Advanced

Micro Devices Am2901 bit-slice ALU chip. In the chip are functional units that compute $A + B$, AB, and $A \oplus B$ (this last is part of the adder). Because $A \oplus B = (A + B) \oplus (AB)$, the two sets of signals can be used to check each other. In this case, the only additional elements needed to utilize the duplicate information would be two XOR gates (one to form one of the

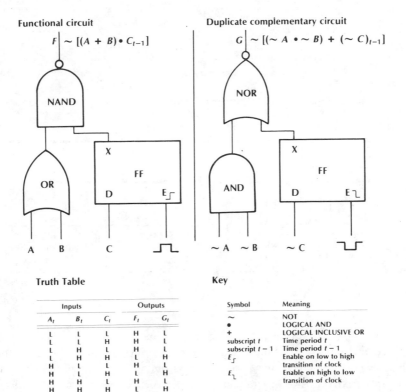

Functional circuit

$$F \mid \sim [(A + B) \bullet C_{t-1}]$$

Duplicate complementary circuit

$$G \mid \sim [(\sim A \bullet \sim B) + (\sim C)_{t-1}]$$

Truth Table

Inputs			Outputs	
A_t	B_t	C_t	F_t	G_t
L	L	L	H	L
L	L	H	H	L
L	H	L	H	L
L	H	H	L	H
H	L	L	H	L
H	L	H	L	H
H	H	L	H	L
H	H	H	L	H

Key

Symbol	Meaning
~	NOT
•	LOGICAL AND
+	LOGICAL INCLUSIVE OR
subscript t	Time period t
subscript $t-1$	Time period $t-1$
E_Γ	Enable on low to high transition of clock
$E_\lrcorner$	Enable on high to low transition of clock

b. **Example of functional versus duplicate complementary circuits.**

Figure 3–16 —*Continued*

duplicate signals, the other to compare the two signals).

Duplication can also be carried out at the bus level. The Sperry Univac 1100/60 (see Chapter 10) uses comparison at the bus level for its instruction processors [Boone, Liebergot, and Sedmak, 1980]. The processor is split into two 36-bit subprocessors. Each subprocessor is duplicated, and only one of the two duplicates drives the master data bus during any one microcycle. The other drives the duplicate data bus (Figure 3-17). Both copies operate in the same way upon the same data. At the end of the microcycle the results are compared. A disagreement causes interruption of operations. Univac's implementation of this scheme produced a performance increase as a result of splitting driven loads between the two subprocessors.

Comparing module outputs is not the only way to apply duplication. The Bell ESS-1 processor demonstrates duplication at the system level, but comparison is performed at the register-transfer level [Toy, 1978]. Certain key values within each of the dual central control units (CCs) are compared by matchers residing within each CC. Only one CC is on line at a time; the other is running in microcycle lockstep. The oscillator in the on-line CC drives the clock circuits in both. The matcher immediately detects any divergence in operation. This level of duplication decreases error latency, increases coverage, and has the side effect of making system diagnosis easier and quicker. Each of the matching circuits compares 24 bits from each CC during the 5.5 μsec machine cycle. Each CC has two matchers, and each matcher has access to six

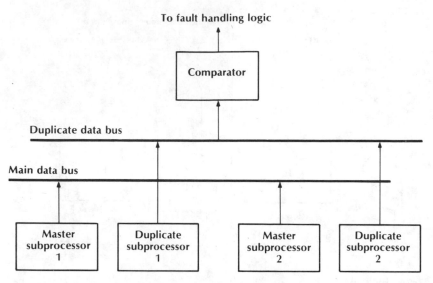

Figure 3–17.   Duplication at bus level in Sperry/Univac 1100/60.

24-bit sets of internal nodes (Figure 3-18). The processing performed during the machine cycle determines which set is checked, and a mismatch generates an interrupt. A diagnostic program is run to locate the faulty CC, which is then removed from service for repair.

The cost of duplication is twice that of an equivalent simplex system, plus the cost of the comparison element. Performance degradation can result from at least two sources. The first is lack of synchronization between the compared signals, which could be remedied by either a common clock or a delay period before comparison. Some delay would result in any event from the inevitable variance in propagation times and other parameters in the circuits of both copies. The other source of degradation is the propagation and decision time required by the comparison element. Normally, the performance loss due to these factors is small enough not to detract from the benefits of duplication.

At a cost in performance, expenses can be halved by using the same hardware to perform duplicate operations, one following the other in time. This time redundancy at least doubles execution time. It also is more susceptible to nondetection of faults because the same hardware, with the same problem, is used for both operations. Transient faults would not be a problem, but hard failures would be. Hard-failure coverage could be increased somewhat by carrying out the operation with a different ordering or algorithm, using as many different resources as possible. Although a single failed ALU would probably give bad results both times, the results would differ for most failures and still result in a mismatch and failure detection. For example, a string of additions could be performed twice in different order, or could be done the second time by forming and adding the two's complements and negating the result.

One frequently perceived problem of duplication (and some other redundancy techniques) is incomplete use of resources. A duplicated computer, for example, is actually two processors performing the same task in parallel, with a loss of half the available computing power. As a result, in some designs only part of the processing is done in parallel by both copies, and checking is performed for only the portion of

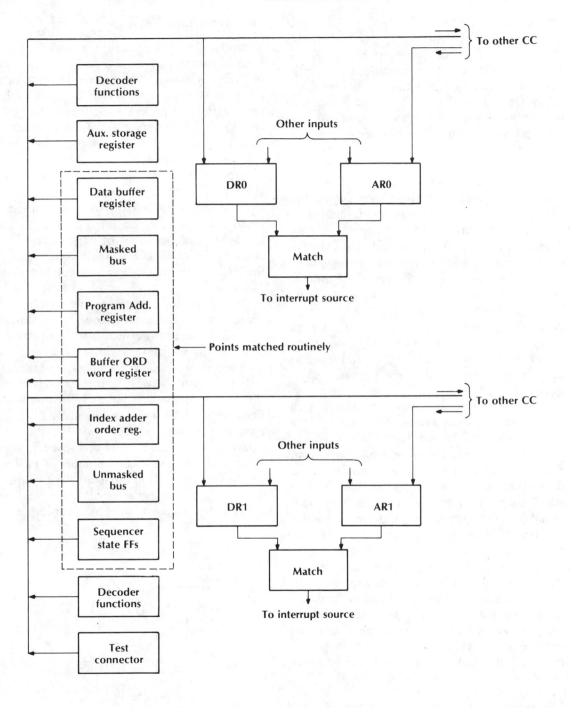

Figure 3–18.   Bell ESS-1 CC match access.

processing still performed in duplicate. All other processing is performed on only one processor or the other. In this case, duplication is usually at the task level and the comparison is performed between the intermediate and/or final results of the two task instantiations. The yield is increased utilization of the hardware; the disadvantages are decreased coverage and increased error latency. Careful design, however, can minimize these disadvantages, and in many instances the remaining coverage is more than sufficient.

Another source of performance degradation with processors duplicated in this fashion is the bus bandwidth consumed by interprocess communication. While this is an expected overhead in multiprocessing architectures, the problem is increased by the bandwidth needed for duplication. One possible solution can be found in the Tandem Computer.* The Tandem design attacks this problem with its Dynabus, a high-speed interprocessor bus used solely for interprocessor communication. All I/O and memory accesses are handled through a more conventional bus.

Duplication, like all other reliability techniques, involves the classic dilemma of "who shall watch over the guardians?" In the case of duplication, failure in the matching equipment results either in no error-detection or in an occasional or permanent false indication of error. This problem can be alleviated with additional cost, complexity, and/or performance degradation, as the matching circuit is made more reliable using some of the techniques in the following sections. The problem, however, can never be completely solved. There are decreasing returns to adding more and more redundancy. Eventually the redundancy becomes a liability too large to accept in cost, performance, or even reduced net system reliability. This point is demonstrated in Chapter 5, which contains an example of an extensive PDP-8/e redesign.

* The Tandem computer does not use duplication as a means of error detection. However, the Dynabus design could prove useful in a system where duplication is used.

Error-Detection Codes

Error-detection codes are systematic applications of redundancy to information. The concept of codes is simple: for the set of all possible combinations of symbols, only a subset of them represents valid information (Figure 3-19). The valid set is called the set of code words. In essence, many redundancy techniques can be considered coding techniques. Duplication, for example, can be considered a code whose valid elements are words consisting of two identical symbols. Error detection with codes consists of determining whether an input is a valid code word. Most of the codes of concern to a computer system designer are binary codes, in which the code words are made from a combination of 1s and 0s.

One of the key concepts in determining code properties is Hamming distance. The Hamming distance between two words is the number of bit positions in which they differ. The minimum distance, d, of a code is the minimum Hamming distance found between any two code words. Figure 3-20 shows the space of three-bit words. Each edge of the cube represents a distance-1 transition between adjacent words in the space. Consider a code taken from this space, in which all code words have an odd number of 1s. These are the boxed words in the figure. The minimum distance between code words is 2, and any distance-1 transition results in a noncode word.

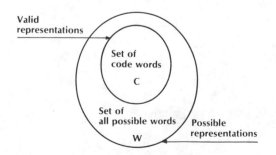

Figure 3–19. An example code space. The set of invalid representations (noncode words) is W−C.

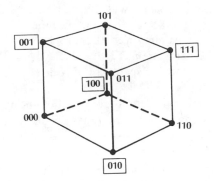

Figure 3–20. The 3-bit word space.

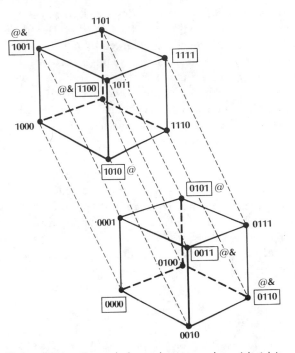

Figure 3–21. Expanded word space cube with 1 bit added to the word size. Boxed words are even-parity words, @ marks a code word in a 2/4 *m*-of-*n* code, and & marks code words from the complemented duplication code used as an example in the text. The unmarked words are odd-parity code words.

The distance-1 transitions from code words represent single-bit errors. Thus, for this code (called odd parity) any single error is detectable. The nonboxed points of this set form another code (even parity) with the same coverage of single failures. For both codes, any distance-2 transition (double error) results in another code word, and is thus a nondetectable error.

Another code is formed by joining a 2-bit value with its complement. This code is called the CD code because the second half is the complemented duplicate of the first half. The set of valid code words is $D = \{0011, 0110, 1001, 1100\}$. This code has a minimum distance of 2. Detection for this code consists of a check to see whether the 4-bit input is an element of D, or equivalently, not an element of D'.

Figure 3-21 illustrates the 4-bit word space containing this code. The CD code words are marked by &. Each arc in the figure is a distance-1 transition, that is, a single bit flip. Between 1100 and 1001 at least 2 bit flips (errors) must occur. Between 1100 and 0011 4 bit flips must occur to produce the wrong code word. Some of the intermediate paths consist entirely of noncode words. Thus, the code will detect any single-bit error, but some double errors will go undetected because they result in another code word (the wrong one). Herein lies a key to code performance: the use of a code with a minimum distance, d, allows detection of any t errors,

where $t < d$. Duplication can be considered a code with $d = 2$, triplication (three copies) a code with $d = 3$, and, in general, replication with n copies a code with $d = n$.

Minimum distance is not the only characteristic needed to evaluate a code's performance. The CD code of Figure 3-21, for example, is a variation on duplication in which the extra copy is the complement of the original. This design gives protection against all multiple adjacent unidirectional faults. For example, if the code is used for a register that resides on one IC chip, a failure of the chip that results in the grounding of some or all outputs would be detected. Simple duplication provides no protection against unidirectional faults. In both cases, however, the minimum distance for the code is 2.

Two other distance-2 codes are shown in Figure 3-21. The first, called the 2/4 (2-of-4) code, consists of all the words (marked by @) containing exactly two 1s. This code requires slightly less redundancy than the CD code because it allows six code words out of the code space instead of the CD code's four. Although the 2/4 code detects all adjacent unidirectional errors it detects fewer distance-2 errors than the CD code. The other code is an even-parity code (boxed words). This code has the least redundancy, for it allows eight code words out of the code space. However, it has no coverage of distance-2 errors and will detect only some multiple adjacent unidirectional errors. In particular, it will not detect a unidirectional failure affecting all bits. The odd-parity code (all the unmarked points in Figure 3-21) has the same drawbacks as even parity, except that it will detect both the all-0s failure mode and the all-1s failure mode.

Table 3-6 summarizes the properties of the four codes shown in Figure 3-21. These four codes constitute the spectrum of code choices for a 4-bit code word.

Other error-detection codes, though not as simple as replication, are generally better in at least some respects. Most require less redundancy to achieve the same minimum distance. For many codes, decoding is eased because the code word consists of two parts: the original value, and the code bits that are simply appended to make it a code word. Such a code is called a separable code. In linear separable codes, each check bit is calculated as a linear combination of some of the data bits. Parity-check codes are linear separable codes for which each check bit

Table 3–6. Properties of the codes shown in Figure 3–21.

Code	Bits in Word	Code Words	Distance	Coverage
CD	4	4	2	Any single bit error
				66% of double-bit errors
				Any multiple adjacent unidirectional error
2/4	4	6	2	Any single-bit error
				33% of double-bit errors
				Any multiple adjacent unidirectional error
Even parity	4	8	2	Any single-bit error
				No double-bit error
				Not all multiple adjacent unidirectional errors
				Not all-0s or all-1s errors
Odd parity	4	8	2	Any single-bit error
				No double-bit errors
				Not all multiple adjacent unidirectional errors
				All-0s and all-1s errors

can be calculated as the parity bit (sum modulo-2) of some subset of the data bits. Parity-check codes can be encoded and decoded using parity generation and parity-check matrices (for details, see Appendix A by Tang and Chien.)

In discussion of codes the term (n, k) code is often used. In this expression n is the number of bits in the entire code word, while k is the number of data bits. Thus in an (n, k) separable code there are $(n - k)$ bits concatenated with the data bits to form the code words.

Some codes can be modified, extended, or combined with other codes or redundancy techniques to increase coverage. For example, a distance-d code can be modified by a further restriction on the valid code words, such as using a subset of code words which contains a high percentage with a minimum distance greater than d. Often, however, increased effectiveness may not be reflected in the minimum distance, as in the examples of Figure 3-21, where the CD code is a subset of the 2/4 code, and the 2/4 code is in turn a subset of the even-parity code.

If some fault classes are more probable than others, the code choice is affected. The CD code example of Figure 3-21 detects not only single faults but also all adjacent unidirectional faults up to and including the entire word.

In addition to the minimum distance and error-detection properties of a code, the cost of the extra information needed (the redundancy) must be considered. Another factor is the difficulty of error detection and decoding. The actual value to be communicated is first encoded, or transformed into a valid code word. Upon receipt it must be checked for validity. For nonseparable codes the received quantity must also be decoded, or transformed back into its original form, before it can be used.

A final issue is the intended application of the code. Most codes, for example, will not be invariant or closed with respect to data operations. In the simple addition of code words the result may or may not be another code word, or may not be the correct code word. Conversely, there are codes that are invariant with respect to some set of operations, or for which there exist

simple algorithms for generating the code word that should result from the operation (short of the process of decode, operate, encode). Furthermore, some codes can be decoded efficiently in a serial fashion, bit by bit in a shift register, but may be difficult to decode in a parallel fashion. These serial-decodable codes are used in applications that employ serial data streams.

Codes can also be used for failure detection in random logic. In such an application all internal logic states or signals must be represented as members of a code. This topic is treated below in the section Self-Checking, Fault-Secure, and Fail-Safe Logic.

This subsection presents a representative sample of the more common error-detection codes. The references [Tang and Chien, 1969;* Peterson and Weldon, 1972; Rao, 1974; MacWilliams and Sloane, 1978] provide more complete treatment of the subject.

M-of-N Codes

An m-of-n code (m/n code) consists of n-bit code words in which m (and only m) bits are ones. Thus, there are $_nC_m$ code words.** For example, the 2/4 code has $_4C_2$, or six possible code words. The set of code words for the 2/4 code is $\{1100, 1010, 1001, 0101, 0011, 0110\}$. This code detects all single and unidirectional faults. The basic concept for the m-of-n codes is simple, but they have several disadvantages. One is that circuitry for parallel detection and decoding is complex, whereas a serial decoder can be made by simply using a counter for the one-bits. Another problem is that they often require a large amount of redundancy. For example, in the case of k data bits with all 2^k values possible, then at least k extra coding bits are needed if the code is to be separable, as in the example of Figure 3-22 (that is, detection is necessary, de-

***

* The paper by Tang and Chien is included as Appendix A.

** $_nC_m$ is a shorthand expression for the number of unique combinations of n things taken m at a time. A verbal shorthand for this term is "n choose m."

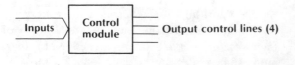

Valid output control line signal sets:

1010	1110
1100	1011
1001	0111
0011	1101

Figure 3–22. Four-output control module and valid output line states.

coding is not). Less redundancy can be used at the cost of adding a decoder and encoder. For example, if there are four data bits ($k = 4$) a 3/6 code could be used in place of a separable 4/8 code, since only 16 code words are needed. The 3/6 code has 20 code words and less redundancy than a 4/8 code, which has 70 code words. If there are $_nC_m$ code words and only $q < {_nC_m}$ of them are to be allowed , there is less coverage of multiple faults unless the erroneous code words are also detected. In the 3/6 code example there are four unused code words that could pass undetected as errors, and in the 4/8 code there

would be 54 undetectable unused code words.

One common use for m/n codes is in control circuitry. To produce a separable m/n coding, extra lines are used in addition to the output control lines. The redundancy lies in extra logic for encoding (determining the value of the extra lines) and in the detection logic. In some cases extra lines are not needed or can be reduced in number. For instance, the number of set lines may be less than or equal to some maximum number. Consider a control module with four output lines whose possible output states are shown in Figure 3-22. Either two or three lines are set at any one time, and the addition of a single line can produce a 3/5 separably coded output. Figure 3-23 shows the implementation of this scheme, including a TTL error detector. Because the control line states (0110, 0101) are not valid, the demultiplexer (demux) outputs for 5 and 6 are not included in the circuit even though such a code word is a valid 3/5 code word. The logic that generates the redundant signal provides fault detection only for signals from which it is independent. Thus, the logic for the fifth line would normally not use the other

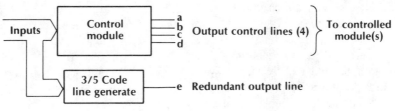

a. 3/5 Code control line generation

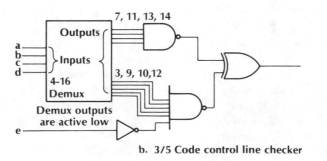

b. 3/5 Code control line checker

Figure 3–23. 3/5 code used to check control module output lines and function.

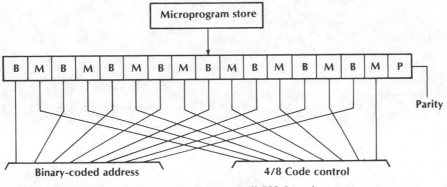

Figure 3–24.   4/8 coding in Bell ESS-3A microstore.

four module outputs as its inputs. Otherwise, the only coverage afforded is over corruption of the signals on the wires, not over the logic that generates them.

The Bell ESS-3a uses an *m*-of-*n* code in its microstore. The TO and FROM control fields in the microword are each encoded in a 4/8 code and are interlaced with the address field (Figure 3-24). This arrangement gives coverage of multiple adjacent unidirectional errors and all even numbers of bit failures in the address field as well. This would not be the case if the address were kept separated, for it is covered only by a single-parity bit. More complete details of the scheme, including decoding/detection implementation, are given in Toy [1978] (Chapter 12). In a paper written about the microstore alone, Cook et al. [1973] present a detailed examination of its design.

Parity Codes

If a given group of bits has an even number of 1s, it is defined as having even parity. If the number of 1s is odd, the group has odd parity. Parity codes involve the addition of an extra bit to each group of bits so that the resulting word has even parity or odd parity, depending on the implementation. Parity codes are linear separable codes and give on-line detection of errors.

For a *b*-bit group of bits, the (even) parity can be generated by using a *b*-input XOR gate.

Because large XOR gates are not available as standard logic functions, the parity can be generated using a *b*-input tree of 2-input XOR gates or one of the standard parity-generation chips (such as the 74190, which encodes an 8-bit input, decodes a 9-bit input, and can be used in a modular fashion for longer words). Parity codes are suitable for serial detection and encoding, needing only a single memory cell and a single XOR gate to perform the modulo-2 addition of the bits in the word. The choice between even and odd parity depends upon the prevalent failure mode. Even parity gives detection of the all-1s failure mode if the parity group (data bits and parity bit) is an odd number of bits long, but not for an even number of bits. Even parity does not detect the all-0s failure mode. Odd parity detects the all-0s failure mode for parity groups of all lengths, and the all-1s failure for parity groups an even number of bits long. Several variants of parity encoding are discussed below; Figure 3-25 illustrates some of these.

With bit-per-word parity, one parity bit is appended to the entire data word. It is one of the least expensive forms of error detection, because it requires a minimum of redundancy in terms of information transferred, and one parity tree can be used for both encoding and detection if information is both transmitted and received. In addition to the extra bits and parity tree, other hardware is needed for such uses as setting parity error detection status bits and allowing wrong

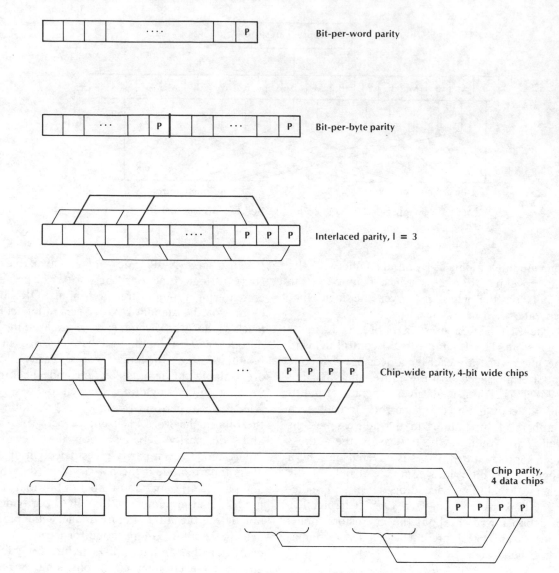

Figure 3–25. Five parity schemes.

parity to be written for maintenance (testing) purposes. Bit-per-word parity codes detect all single-bit errors and all errors that involve an odd number of bits. The all-1s and all-0s failure coverage is as discussed above, with the entire code word becoming the parity group. The costs of bit-per-word parity for a b bit word are $1/b$ redundancy in data, a b-bit parity tree encoder, a $(b + 1)$-bit parity tree decoder (in some cases a

single encoder/decoder tree is possible), and a logic delay of approximately $\lceil \log_2(b + 1) \rceil$* gate levels in the encoding and detection operations.

In bit-per-byte parity, an extra bit is added to each byte of data. Alternating even and odd parity in the bytes of the data word gives im-

---

* The ceiling symbol, $\lceil\ \rceil$, means round the value up to the next highest integer.

proved coverage, since both wordwide stuck-at-1 and wordwide stuck-at-0 failure modes are covered. The wordwide failure mode is a common result of timing and select-line errors. Also, the bit-per-byte code detects all single- or odd-number errors in each byte. Thus, as long as at least one byte contains an odd number of failures, many more kinds of multiple errors in a word are detectable. The diagnostic resolution is also improved over bit-per-word parity, because fewer data bits are covered by each parity bit. Encoding and detection are faster because the parity trees have fewer inputs and thus fewer gate levels of delay. The extra costs are more parity trees and a redundancy of $1/m$ where there are m bits per byte. The C.mmp multiprocessor used this technique for its shared memory [Siewiorek et al., 1978a].

In interlaced parity, i parity bits are appended to the data word. Each parity bit is associated with a group of (b/i) bits, and is generated by forming the parity over every ith bit, starting in a different bit position for each parity bit. The encoded word thus has i separate parity groups. Interlaced parity covers single bit errors in each group, as well as all multiple errors in which at least one group has an odd number of errors. If the parity sense (odd/even) is alternated from group to group, the code covers a large number of unidirectional failures. Thus interlaced parity would be particularly useful for buses, where the shorting-together of signal lines is a common failure mode, as well as for whole-chip failures of memory and bus transceiver chips. These failures are sure to be detected relatively quickly. The diagnostic resolution of interlaced parity is to the parity group in error. As for bit-per-byte parity, the speed of detection and encoding is increased as a result of the smaller parity tree sizes. The costs are an i/b redundancy, and i parity trees of $(\lceil b/i \rceil + 1)$ bits for detection.

Chip-wide parity, proposed for memories in which each word is spread over $(\lceil b/w \rceil)w$-bit wide chips [McKevitt, 1972], is actually a special case of interlaced parity. There are w parity bits appended to each data word, and they reside on

their own w-bit wide memory chip. Each parity bit is the parity over the same bit position on all the other chips. When single-bit wide chips are used, chip-wide parity is the same as duplication. The coverage is the same as for interlaced parity, with the additional property that any single-chip failure is detectable (as long as at least one bit is in error). This technique is also applicable to many other areas of digital system design in which blocks of signals (control, data) are to be protected.

Another way of detecting single-chip failures is to use a parity bit for each chip. The chip parity bits are stored separately from the chips they cover. The advantage of this technique, called chip parity, is that a parity error detection immediately locates the failed chip. Chip parity thus has a more useful diagnostic resolution than chip-wide parity. However, if data bit values are uniformly distributed and the 0-to-1 and 1-to-0 failure modes are equally likely, chip parity has only a 0.5 probability of detecting failure of an entire chip (for a given data word). This is because there is a 0.5 probability that the parity bit is the correct one for the erroneous data on the chip. Chip-wide parity, on the other hand, has a $(1 - (0.5)^w)$ probability of detection in the same situation, given w-bit wide chips. The cost of chip parity is (b/w) extra bits per word and $(\lceil b/w \rceil)(w + 1)$-bit parity trees.

Table 3-7 summarizes the properties of the five basic parity techniques described above.

The same single-chip failure coverage and diagnostic resolution that chip parity provides can be obtained with less redundancy by using a variant of the Hamming single-error correcting (SEC) codes (discussed in the following section on Error-Correcting Codes). Assume there are m w-bit wide chips for a data word, and that c_i $(i = 1, 2, \ldots, m)$ is the parity of the ith chip. The addition of n parity bits, where

$$2^n > m + n$$

can be used to give detection of any single-chip failure and diagnostic resolution to the failed chip or parity bit. The parity check bits are

Table 3–7.   Properties of the basic parity techniques.

Technique	Bit Redundancy	Parity Trees			Coverage
		Number	Size	Delay	
Bit-per-word	$1/b$	1	$a = b + 1$	$\lceil \log_2 a \rceil$	All single-bit errors All odd-bit errors
Bit-per-byte	$1/m$	b/m	$a = m + 1$	$\lceil \log_2 a \rceil$	All single-bit errors All errors with an odd number in at least one byte
Interlaced	i/b	i	$a = \lceil b/i \rceil + 1$	$\lceil \log_2 a \rceil$	All single-bit errors All errors with an odd number in at least one parity group Large number of adjacent multiple unidirectional errors
Chip-wide	w/b	w	$a = \lceil b/w \rceil + 1$	$\lceil \log_2 a \rceil$	All single-bit errors All errors with an odd number in at least one parity group Large number of adjacent multiple unidirectional errors Any single chip failure
Chip	$1/w$	$\lceil b/w \rceil$	$a = w + 1$	$\lceil \log_2 a \rceil$	All single-bit errors All errors with an odd number on at least one chip 50 percent of single-chip failures Points to failed chip for single errors

formed similarly to the Hamming SEC code bits. The difference is that the check bits are formed from the c_i's (chip parities) instead of from individual data bits as in the SEC code. The full technique will not be given here, and an example used instead. This example is a 32-bit-wide microstore made from four 8-bit-wide chips. Three parity bits are used, and are computed as:

$$p_1 = c_1 \oplus c_2 \oplus c_4$$
$$p_2 = c_1 \oplus c_3 \oplus c_4$$
$$p_3 = c_2 \oplus c_3 \oplus c_4$$

After a microword has been read, the parity check bits are computed and XORed with the stored parity bits. If any of the resultant bits are nonzero, the three bits ($p_3 p_2 p_1$) form an indica-tion (called the syndrome) that is uniquely asso-ciated with a particular chip or parity bit in error (001, 010, 100 for parity bits 1, 2, and 3, respec-tively, and 011, 101, 110, 111 for data chips 1, 2, 3, and 4, respectively). The cost for this scheme is n extra bits per word, n parity trees with ($\lceil \log_2(m + n) \rceil$) inputs, and m parity trees with w inputs if w-bit wide chips are used. The coding/decoding circuitry is greater than for chip parity, but the decrease in redundant bits can be significant, especially for large memories. On the other hand, coverage of multiple chip failures is much lower, and in the case of multi-ple chip failures the syndrome may point to a nonfaulty chip if it is nonzero.

Parity techniques have been used in many systems, most often for main memory and less often for buses. The UNIBUS on PDP-11s, for example, does not have parity but defines two extra signal wires for reporting memory or peripheral device parity errors. One wire carries the parity error signal; the other is a parity enabling signal, necessary because not all bus devices and memories use parity checking. The PDP-11/60 has parity on its writable control store (WCS), main memory, and cache. The WCS has 3 parity bits in each word, one for each 16-bit segment of the 48-bit word. The cache has 3 parity bits, one for the tag field and one for each of the data bytes. Starting with the 1108, all of the Univac 1100-series systems use parity. The 1108 had parity in main memory and on the processor general registers. As the 1100 series matured, parity was expanded to more parts of the systems (see Chapter 10). Finally, the VAX-11 systems, detailed in Chapter 8, make extensive use of parity.

Standard LSI chips are being used increasingly in systems design. However, they are not usually designed for the external application of error-detection codes to check for proper chip operation. Data transformations occur internally for which codes are not invariant. In some cases, however, partial checking can be accomplished

without resorting to duplication, as in the DEC-system 2020 processor. A parity code is used on the bus that feeds an Am2901 bit-sliced ALU. As the data are gated into the 2901 the bus monitor checks them for proper parity. If the data are merely being read into the 2901 register file, their parity bit is simultaneously stored in an external register (Figure 3-26). The external register has two bits associated with each register in the 2901: the parity bit, and a "parity valid" bit, which remains set as long as no data transformations are performed on the contents of the corresponding internal register. The parity-valid bit value is determined by the control signals for the 2901. When the data are brought out to the bus from the 2901, their parity is generated before they are placed on the bus. If the parity-valid bit is still set, the stored parity is used to verify that the data have no errors. This scheme provides fault detection for the 2901 register file, internal data paths, and the parts of the ALU used to move data internally without transformation.

Even though parity (and other) codes are not invariant with respect to data transformations, it is possible to use parity as a check on the data operation. This is possible when, given the inputs to the operation, the parity of the result of the

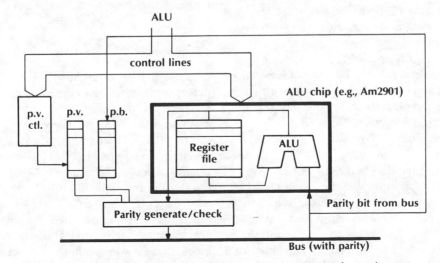

Figure 3-26. Use of parity to detect errors during nontransformation operations in LSI ALU chips in the DEC 2020.

transformation can be predicted. Chinal [1977] proposes a high-speed parity prediction circuit for binary adders. Khodadad-Mostashiry [1979] presents a general method for predicting the parity of any transformation, and in particular, bit-sliced functional circuits. The resulting prediction circuit, however, is often much more complex than the circuit it checks.

Parity can be used to detect addressing faults in a memory by storing the parity of the address and data with the memory word. On access, the stored parity is compared with that of the data and address used. If the parity is wrong, either the word retrieved is incorrect, the word retrieved was stored in the wrong place, or the wrong word was retrieved. In this way all single-bit addressing errors as well as data errors are detected.

In many applications of redundancy techniques the redundancy needed may already be partially or wholly present. The 3/5-coded control module mentioned in the previous section is an example. An example concerning parity is a host-to-LSI-11 network for a system containing several LSI-11s. This network allows direct host communication with the individual LSI-11s. The bus for the network has a data field and a 3-bit opcode field (Figure 3-27). There are two unused opcodes (011 and 111). If an opcode starting in 01 is used for data writes and in 11 for data reads, the third bit could carry the parity of the data field. Since it is predicted that 90 percent of the bus transactions will be data reads and writes, this scheme would give bit-per-word parity protection on 90 percent of the bus activity without any extra bus wires.

Finally, in a design analysis for the use of parity on a processor-memory bus, three alternatives were considered. The first was simple (17, 16) parity. The second was the same (17, 16) parity with a modification that performs a cumulative parity check of the entire two-way bus transaction. The address sent to the memory has an appended parity bit. The parity appended to the returned data word is formed as the mod-

Bus⟨1:8⟩	Data	
Bus⟨9:11⟩	Function	
	000	Write address
	001	Write network CSR
	010	Write data
	011	Unused
	100	Read device characteristics (polling)
	101	Read CSR
	110	Read data
	111	Unused
Bus⟨12⟩	Strobe	
Bus⟨13⟩	Acknowledge	

Figure 3–27. Network bus signals for host-to-LSI-11 command bus.

ulo-2 sum of the received address parity bit, the computed parity of the received address, and the parity of the memory word itself. This scheme provides detection of a failure in the memory parity checker. The third alternative was an interlaced $(18, 16)$ parity $(i = 2)$ with alternated parity senses, modified as above to provide a cumulative parity check on the bus transaction. Table 3-8 shows the coverage of several different failure classes for this scheme. From the table it can be determined that the cumulative $(17, 16)$ parity is better than the simple $(17, 16)$ parity because it detects a large number of memory unit parity generate/check errors, and that the $(18, 16)$ cumulative parity provides the best coverage of the three.

Checksums

One of the least expensive methods of fault detection is checksumming. The checksum for a block of s words is formed by adding together all of the words in the block modulo-n, where n is arbitrary. The block of s words and its checksum together constitute a code word in a linear separable code. The number of bits in the sum is usually limited. This quantity is then compared with the checksum formed and stored when the block was last transmitted. In memories, the checksum must be stored along with the data block. If any word within the block is modified, the checksum must also be modified at the same

Table 3–8. Percentage of coverage of processor-memory bus failures.

Error Type	Coverage		
	(17,16) Parity	(17,16) Cumulative	(18,16) Cumulative
Hard failure:			
Bus all 1	50%	50%	100%
Bus all 0	50	50	100
Bus half 1	0	0	Near 100
Bus half 0	0	0	Near 100
Wire-or:			
2 wires	100	100	100
3 wires	0	0	88
4 wires	0	0	100
5 wires	0	0	0
Single bit*	100	100	100
Double bit			
Adjacent	0	0	100
Random	0	0	Near 100
Triple bit	100	100	100
Quadruple bit			
Two pairs adjacent	0	0	0
Two adjacent	0	0	Near 100
Three adjacent	0	0	100
Four adjacent	0	0	50
Random	0	0	0
Parity generate and check			
Stuck-at-ok	0	100	100
Stuck-at-1	50	50	Near 100
Stuck-at-0	50	50	Near 100

*One bit value, not a failed wire

time. The stored checksum is normally kept physically separate from the data block to limit the effect of a catastrophic failure on the fault-detecting capability.

Although checksumming is inexpensive in terms of excess information, it has three disadvantages. First, it is best suited to applications in which data are handled in large, contiguous blocks, such as buses that carry data in blocks, sequential storage, and block-transfer peripherals.

Second, checksumming in memories takes a long time to detect faults even when reading a single word, for s words must be read and added,

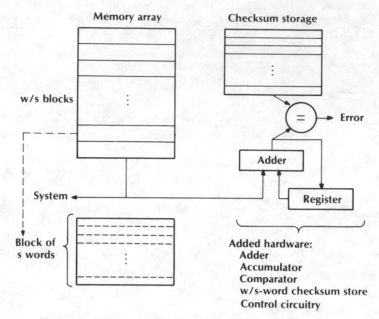

Figure 3-28.   Memory with checksum error detection.

and the sum compared with the stored value. Thus, checksumming is not suited to on-line checking when reading from memories. If the technique is used in a writable store, the checksum must be updated on each write by reading the old data and checksum, subtracting the old data, adding the new data, and finally storing both the data and the updated checksum.

This cumbersome procedure, however, may not be a problem when writing is infrequent or when updating is performed in parallel with subsequent system operations not involving the memory. The memory checksum (and checksum update on writes) may be performed by dedicated hardware without interference to the rest of the system (Figure 3-28). The checksum can also be performed by the ALU or other system component, which will cause a degradation of the system's throughput. The Xerox Alto, for example, uses the processor ALU to perform the checksums for its disk, thus allowing the disk controller to be less complex. In this case, if it takes t_c seconds to perform a checksum for one block, and on the average a block of memory is checked every T_c seconds, the system perfor-

mance is degraded by (t_c/T_c). The additional degradation due to a checksum update time of t_w when writes are performed every T_w seconds is, on the average, (t_w/T_w).

Though cumbersome for random access writable stores, checksumming is very applicable to read-only memory, which can be checked by a background process. The Pluribus system (see Chapter 13) uses checksum error detection on both shared-code storage and local-code storage [Ornstein et al., 1975]. Another application would be microstore checks performed by dedicated hardware or console processors. Finally, critical data structures and program code could occasionally be verified through software-implemented checksumming.

The third disadvantage of checksumming is low diagnostic resolution. In memories, the detected fault could be in the block of s words, the stored checksum, or the checking circuitry. In data transmission, the fault could be in the data source, the transmission medium, or the checking circuitry.

Four checksumming techniques are presented below. The first is a single-precision checksum.

Table 3–9. Probability of detection for different errors with single-precision checksum.

Error Types	Coverage Ratio	Condition
Single device-multiple word		
-Single column	1	$i < z - \log_2 s$
	$(1 - 2^{-s})$	$i = z - \log_2 s$
	$(1 - 2^{-s}(1 + {}_sC_{s/2}))$	$i = z - (\log_2 s) + 1$
	$(1 - 2^{-(z-i)} + 2^{-s})$	Otherwise
-Multiple adjacent columns	1	$i \leqslant z - (\log_2 s) - c$
	$(1 - 2^{-(z-i)} + 2^{-cs})$	Otherwise
Multiple device		
-Single word	1	
-Multiple word adjacent columns	$(1 - 2^{-cs})$	$i \leqslant z - (\log_2 s) - c$
	$(1 - 2^{-(z-i)})$	Otherwise

The second is an extended-precision (extended-word-length) checksum. The third, called the Honeywell checksum, is a modified double-precision technique. More complete information on these can be found in Jack et al. [1975], from which much of the discussion below was abstracted. The last technique is called a low-cost residue code, which gives better coverage than the single-precision checksum for about the same cost.

In single-precision checksumming the memory is divided into blocks of s words. Each word has z bits. The checksum is a z-bit word that is the modulo-(2^z) sum of the s words in the block. The memory redundancy for this system is $(1/(s + 1))$. Errors in any one column will cause either the corresponding checksum bit or the carry to the adjacent column to be in error. Thus, for the most significant column the error coverage afforded by the information contained in the carry is lost. The bit positions nearby pose the same problem in lesser degrees, depending on their distance from the most significant bit. Thus, error coverage varies for each bit position, with the best coverage available for errors in the least significant bit. As the size of the block that the checksum guards increases, coverage decreases. Thus, coverage is a function of the block size and the column(s) in error.

Table 3-9 summarizes the results for different error conditions. The derivations can be found in Jack et al. [1975]. In the table, c is the number of columns in error, i is the lowest-order column that has an error, s is the number of words that a checksum guards, and z is the number of bits in the checksum (the least significant bit is column 0). Unidirectional errors were assumed in the derivation. It is also assumed that multiple-word failures extend over all words in the memory block (such as one entire column). If this is not the case, s should be replaced by the number of words in the block with failures. The formulas for multiple adjacent-column faults and multiple device*–multiple word faults also hold approximately for nonadjacent failures in their carry range; that is, the carry from the column of the least significant bit faults will affect the result of the column holding the other failure. The coverage improves if the faults are not within carry range. Note that in the case of

---

* Multiple device faults can be either a single fault affecting multiple devices (such as a stuck address line) or multiple independent faults on several devices.

multiple column failures, i is the number of the least significant failed column.

If the checksum being formed is A bits longer than the memory word length, the coverage is greater than that afforded by the single-precision checksum. This form of checksum is called the extended-precision checksum. In particular, if $s < 2^A$, then the coverage for all columns is the same as for the lowest-order column in the single-precision checksum, because there can be no overflow and thus no loss of information in the carry bits from the higher-order columns. The probability of detecting any type of error is thus 100 percent.

The Honeywell checksum is a modified double-precision checksum technique in which successive pairs of memory words in a block are concatenated. The checksum is formed by combining double-length quantities to form a double-length word. Thus any single-column error in memory will affect two columns in the checksum being formed. Overflow can still cause loss of carry-bit information. Provided that $s < 2^{(z+1)}$, the coverage formulas in Table 3-10 apply to the Honeywell checksum.

Table 3-11 shows an example using the formulas from Table 3-9. An analysis is made of a 32-word $\times$ 16-bit read-only memory made from 32-$\times$ 4-bit ROM chips. The probability of successful error detection is calculated for each column (or chip), assuming that column (chip) is failed. These intermediate results are combined to provide the coverage for a single column (chip) failure anywhere in the memory.

A modification of the single-precision checksum with an end-around carry adder is termed a low-cost residue code. The end-around carry retains the information normally lost with the most significant carry bit; it results in modulo-m addition where $m = 2^b - 1$ for a b-bit adder. This technique [Usas, 1978] provides about the same single-word coverage as the single-precision checksum. The coverage for double-bit errors is slightly better, and is much better for unidirectional errors in one column or two adja-

cent columns. The number of possible undetectable 2- and 3-bit errors is:

$$U_2 = sb(s - 1) \qquad \text{for } b > 2 \text{ and}$$
$$U_3 = s^2 b(s - 1) \qquad \text{for } b > 3$$

where s is the block length.

When one column or two adjacent columns have unidirectional errors, the total number of possible undetectable errors is:

$$U_{1col} = bU \text{ and } U_{2col} = (b - 1)(2N - 2U)$$

where

$$U = 2 \sum_{1 \leqslant k \leqslant P} {}_s C_{(k(2b-1))},$$

$$N = \sum_{1 \leqslant i \leqslant Q} \sum_{0 \leqslant k \leqslant R_i} (-1)^k {}_s C_k \; {}_{T_i} C_{s-1},$$

$$T_i = i(2^b - 1) + s - 4i - 1,$$

$$P = s/(2^b - 1),$$

$$Q = 3s/(2^b - 1), \text{ and}$$

$$R_i = i(2^b - 1)/4.$$

With these formulas, Usas showed the low-cost residue code to be superior to the single-precision checksum.

Arithmetic Codes

An arithmetic code, A, has the property that $A(b * c) = A(b) * A(c)$ where b and c are noncoded operands, $*$ is one of a set of arithmetic operations (such as addition and multiplication), and $A(x)$ is the arithmetic code word for x. Thus, the set of code words in A is closed with respect to a specific set of arithmetic operations. Such a code can be used to detect or correct errors and to check the results of arithmetic operations.* Some operations (such as logical operations),

---

* Other codes are not invariant with respect to arithmetic operations. For some separable linear codes other than arithmetic codes, the check symbol portion of the result can be produced by a prediction circuit. Usually such circuits are complex. Wakerly [1978] details check symbol prediction for parity-check codes and checksum codes.

Table 3–10. Probability of detection of errors through Honeywell checksum.

Error Types	Coverage Ratio	Condition
Single word	1	
Multiple word		
Single column	1	$i < z - \log_2(s/2)$
	$(1 - 2^{-(s+1)})$	$i = z - \log_2(s/2)$
	$(1 - 2^{-s}(1 + {}_{s/2}C_{s/4}))$	$i = z - (\log_2(s/2)) + 1$
	$(1 - 2^{-(z-i+(s/2))} + 2^{-s})$	Otherwise
Multiple column	1	$1 \leqslant z - (\log_2(s/2)) - c$
	$(1 - 2^{-(z-i+(cs/2))} + 2^{-cs})$	Otherwise

Table 3–11. Sample calculation using the formulas of Table 3–9 in an analysis of a 32-word × 16-bit ROM made of 32 × 4-bit chips.

Type of Failure	Column	Probability of Error Detection, Each Column	Net Probability of Error Detection
Single column	0,1,2,...10	1	11/16
	11	≈ 1	1/16
	12	0.860	0.860/16
	13	0.875	0.875/16
	14	0.75	0.75/16
	15	0.5	0.5/16
			0.937
One whole chip	0,4	1	2/4
	8	0.996	0.996/4
	12	0.938	0.938/4
			0.983

however, cannot be checked by arithmetic codes and must be performed on unencoded operands. The discussion below is just an introduction to the topic of arithmetic codes; Appendix B, a paper by Avizienis [1971], examines in detail the three classes of arithmetic codes presented briefly here: AN, residue-m, and inverse residue-m arithmetic codes. Other references on arithmetic codes are Rao [1974]; Sellers, Hsiao, and Bearnson [1968b]; and Avizienis [1973].

The simplest arithmetic codes are the AN codes. These codes are formed by multiplying the data word by a number that is not a power of the radix of the representation (such as two for binary). The redundancy is determined by the multiplier chosen, called the modulus. AN codes are invariant with respect to unsigned arithmetic. If the code chosen has $A = 2^a - 1$ and a length that is a multiple of a bits, it is also invariant (using one's-complement algorithms)

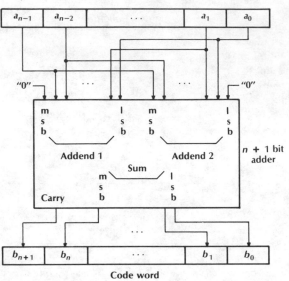

Figure 3–29. Simple encoder for 3N single-error-detecting arithmetic code.

with respect to the operations of addition and left and right arithmetic shifting. Additionally, complementation and sign detection are the same [Avizienis, 1973]. An example of a single-error detecting AN code is the 3N code. An n-bit word is encoded simply by multiplying by 3. This adds at most 2 bits of redundancy and can be encoded quickly and inexpensively in parallel with an $(n + 1)$-bit adder (Figure 3-29). Error checking is performed by confirming that the received word is evenly divisible by 3, and can be

accomplished with a relatively simple combinational logic decoder. Although there is one more bit than in bit-per-word parity for roughly the same coverage, the operation of other system functions (such as ALU and address calculations) can be checked. The hardware cost is a $(2/n) \times 100$ percent memory element increase, an $(n + 1)$-bit adder for encoding, a combinational decoding circuit, and extra control circuitry. The delay on reads results from a small number of gate delays, and on writes from the delay of the adder. Avizienis [1973] presents algorithms for operations involving AN codes, and discusses in detail the design of a 15N code arithmetic processing unit used in an early version of the JPL STAR computer (see Chapter 14).

Residue codes are a class of separable arithmetic codes. The residue of a data word N is defined as $R(N) = N \bmod m$. The code word is formed by concatenating N with $R(N)$ to produce $N|R$ (the vertical bar denotes concatenation). The received word $N'|R'$ is checked by comparing $R(N')$ with R'. If they are equal, no error has occurred. Figure 3-30 is a block diagram of a residue-code arithmetic unit. A variant of the residue-m code is the inverse residue-m code. The separate check quantity, Q, is formed as $Q = m - (N \bmod m)$. The inverse residue code has greater coverage of repeated-use faults than does the residue code. A repeated-use fault occurs when a chain of operations is performed sequentially on the same faulty hardware before

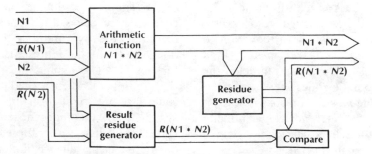

Figure 3–30. Block diagram of an arithmetic unit using a separable residue arithmetic code.

checking is performed. For example, iterative operations such as multiplication and division are subject to repeated-use faults. Both the residue-m and inverse residue-m codes can be used with either one's-complement or two's-complement arithmetic. The JPL STAR computer, discussed in Chapter 14 [Avizienis et al., 1971], uses an inverse residue-15 code. Elsewhere, Avizienis [1973] describes the adaptation of two's-complement arithmetic for use with an inverse residue code.

In both the AN and residue codes, the detection operations can be complex, except when the check moduli (A for AN codes, m for residue-m codes) are of the form $2^a - 1$. The check operation in this case can be performed using an a-bit adder with end-around carry, serially adding a-bit bytes of the data word (or code word for AN codes) [Avizienis, 1971, 1973]. In effect, this operation performs the division of the word by the check modulus. The operation can also be implemented in a faster, parallel fashion. Arithmetic codes with check moduli of this form are called low-cost arithmetic codes.

Cyclic Codes

In cyclic codes, any cyclic (end-around) shift of a code word produces another code word. Cyclic codes are easily implemented using linear-feedback shift registers, which are made from XOR gates and memory elements. These codes find frequent (though not exclusive) use in serial applications such as sequential-access devices (tapes, bubble memories, and disks) as well as data links. Sometimes encoding is performed independently and in parallel over several serial-bit streams, as for the multiple-wire buses shown in Figure 3-31. The bits of each byte are transmitted simultaneously. The CRC (Cyclic Redundancy Check) check bits for each bit stream are generated for the duration of the block transmission and are appended to the end of the block.

The (n, k) cyclic codes can detect all single errors in a code word, all burst errors (multiple adjacent faults) of length $b \leqslant (n - k)$, and many other patterns of errors, depending on the particular code. A cyclic code is uniquely and completely characterized by its generator polynomial $G(X)$, a polynomial of degree $(n - k)$ or greater, with the coefficients either 0 or 1 for a binary code. Appendix A provides a complete discussion of cyclic codes and other polynomial-based codes.

Given the check polynomial $G(X)$ for an (n, k) separable code, a linear-feedback shift register encoder/decoder can be easily derived.* The block check register (BCR) will contain the check bits at the end of the encoding process,

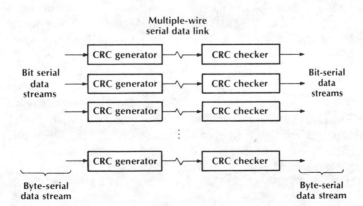

Figure 3–31. Use of cyclic codes for byte-serial bus data transfers (i.e., the bits of each byte are transmitted simultaneously). The CRC check bits are generated for each bit stream during the block transmission and are appended at the end of the block.

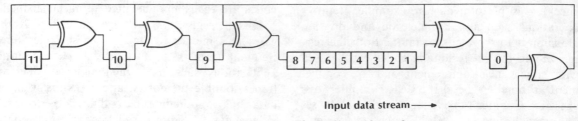

Generator polynomial $G(X) = X^{12} + X^{11} + X^3 + X^2 + X + 1$

Figure 3–32. Block Check Register (BCR) for CRC-12 cyclic code.

during which the data bits have been simultaneously transmitted and fed to the input of the BCR. The BCR is an r-bit shift register, where $r = (n - k)$, the degree of $G(x)$. In Figure 3-32, the register shifts to the right, and its memory cells are labeled $(r - 1)$, $(r - 2)$, ..., 1, 0, from left to right. The shift register is broken to the right of each cell i, where $i = (r - j)$ and j is the degree of a nonzero term in $G(X)$. At each of these points an XOR gate is inserted, and the gate output connected to the input of the cell on the right side of the break. The output of the gate to the right of cell 0 is connected to the input of the leftmost memory cell (cell $r - 1$) and to one of the inputs of each of the other gates. The remaining input of each gate is connected to the output of the memory cell to the left. The second input of the rightmost gate is connected to the serial data input. The result is a feedback path, whose value is the XOR of BCR bit 0 and the current data bit. Figure 3-32 shows the BCR for a cyclic code with

$$G(X) = X^{12} + X^{11} + X^3 + X^2 + X + 1.$$

This code, called CRC-12, is often used with 6-bit bytes of data because the check bits fit evenly into two 6-bit bytes. The XOR gates are placed to the right of the five shift register cells, $\{(12 - 12), (12 - 11), (12 - 3), (12 - 2), (12 - 1)\}$

---

*The following discussion is based in part on the CRC chapter in McNamara [1977]. The shift registers described here vary slightly in form from those in Appendix A.

or $\{0, 1, 9, 10, 11\}$. The output of the rightmost XOR gate is fed back into the register via the other XOR gates.

In operation the BCR is preloaded with an initial value (normally all 0s). The data are simultaneously transmitted and fed to the data input of the BCR. When the output of the data-input XOR gate has stabilized, the shift register is clocked. Once the last data bit has been transmitted, the BCR contains the check bits of the code word. The contents of the BCR are then transmitted starting with the rightmost bit, but without feedback.

Figure 3-33 shows a CRC-12 BCR operation with a 12-bit data word. The same BCR is used at the receiving end. The input stream is fed to the BCR input in the same way, with the data bits going to both the BCR and the destination. The BCR is preloaded with the same value as that used in the transmitting BCR. The received check bits are input to the BCR following the data bits. When preloading involves all 0s, the result in the receiver BCR should be 0.

CRC-12 is a $(12 + k, k)$ code that provides error detection of all burst errors of length 12 or less. The data length is arbitrary. Thus, redundancy and coverage probability change with the data length. CRC-16 is a $(16 + k, k)$ code based on the generator polynomial

$$G(X) = X^{16} + X^{15} + X^2 + 1.$$

CRC-CCITT is another $(16 + k, k)$ code, with

$$G(X) = X^{16} + X^{12} + X^5 + 1.$$

Shift clock	BCR contents	Input data bit	Feedback (input XOR bit 0)
0	0000 0000000	0	
		1	1
1	1111 0000000	1	
		0	1
2	1000 1000000	1	
		0	1
3	1011 0100000	1	
		1	0
4	0101 1010000	0	
		0	0
5	0010 1101000	0	
		0	0
6	0001 0110100	0	
		0	0
7	0000 1011010	0	
		0	0
8	0000 0101101	0	
		0	0
9	0000 0010110	1	
		0	1
10	1111 0001011	1	
		0	1
11	1000 1000101	0	
		1	1
12	1011 0100010	0	

Transmitted data bits: 100000001001 (right-most bit first)
Transmitted check bits: 101101000100 (right-most bit first)

Figure 3–33. BCR calculation of check bits for CRC-12 and a 12-bit data word.

Both CRC-16 and CRC-CCITT provide detection for all burst errors 16 bits long or less, and 99 percent of bursts greater than 16 bits. CRC-16 is used by the DDCMP and Bisync protocols, while CRC-CCITT is used by the ANSI X.25, HDLC, and SDLC protocols. These $(16 + k, k)$ codes are normally used when the data are in 8-bit bytes because the check bits consume exactly 2 bytes; however, k can be any arbitrary length. Figure 3-34 shows a BCR for CRC-CCITT.

IBM's SDLC (Synchronous Data Link Control) data communications protocol uses the CRC-CCITT cyclic code with a small variation: the BCR is preloaded with all 1s instead of all 0s. At the end of the data transmission the BCR contents are complemented (logical complement) before being transmitted. This scheme allows detection of extra or missing 0s at the beginning and end of the data fields, which are of variable length. At the receiver, the BCR result must equal $F0B8_{16}$.

CRC encoders/decoders are available as integrated circuit chips. An example is the Fairchild F6856 Synchronous Protocol Communications Controller chip, which provides communications protocol handling for microprocessor systems [Kole, 1980]. Embedded on the chip is a CRC encoder/decoder. The chip is designed to handle CRC-12, CRC-16, CRC-CCITT, and several other CRC codes. In addition, the internal BCR can be preset optionally with all 0s or all 1s. Another available integrated circuit is the Signetics 2653 intelligent bus monitor, analyzed in depth in Weissberger [1980]. In addition to its other functions, the circuit provides CRC checking and generation.

CRC checks are often performed in software to detect errors in critical data structures and programs. An algorithm for doing this, shown in Figure 3-35, is essentially a software implementation of a linear feedback shift register. A processor register is used as a shift register, and the XOR feedback gates are replaced by a CRC constant, which is XORed with the register. The CRC constant is formed by finding the numbers, i, for which $i = ((r - 1) - j)$, where j is the degree of a nonzero term in $G(X)$ (except for the X^r term). The bits i of the CRC constant are 1s, and the rest are 0s. The bits are labeled $(r - 1)$ for the leftmost (most significant) bit, to 0 for the least significant bit. The constant for CRC-CCITT is 8408_{16}, and is $0F01_{16}$ for CRC-12. This algorithm would be useful, for example, when a separate maintenance or console processor performs occasional checking for microstore corruption via a CRC check.

The Interdata 8/32 uses the algorithm of Figure 3-35 in its microcoded CRC instruction [Interdata, 1975]. The Interdata 8/32 CRC instruction works for either CRC-12 or CRC-16, with any arbitrary preloading of the check character. Each invocation of the CRC instruction adds only one data byte to the CRC check character, so that it must be invoked for each

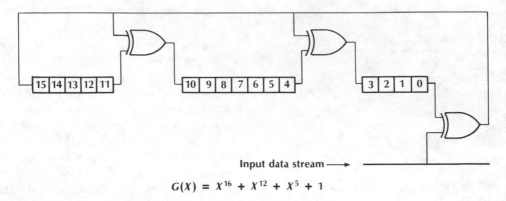

$$G(X) = X^{16} + X^{12} + X^5 + 1$$

Figure 3–34.   BCR for CRC-CCITT cyclic code.

byte in the data field. The Interdata 8/32 Auto-driver Channel, used for direct memory-peripheral I/O, can be commanded to perform this operation automatically on incoming or outgoing blocks of data. The VAX-11/780 has a CRC instruction that performs CRC checking or encoding for up to 64K 8-bit bytes in memory. $G(X)$ can be any check generator polynomial of degree 32 or less [DEC, 1977]. The VAX uses the algorithm and constants as described above.

Cyclic codes can also be encoded and decoded in parallel for nonserial applications. Like other linear codes, they can be processed with matrix techniques. An example of parity-check matrices can be found in the section on Hamming codes. For more details on forming the parity-check and parity-generation matrices for cyclic codes, see Appendix A.

Self-Checking, Fault-Secure, and Fail-Safe Logic

Although duplication and codes are general solutions to fault detection, both techniques are vulnerable to single-point failures in the comparison element (duplication) or the decoder/detector element (codes). These single points of failure can be eliminated through self-checking, fault-secure, and fail-safe logic design. These logic design techniques can be used for general-purpose logic design as well as for comparators and checkers. Due to space limitations the following discussion can only serve as an introduction to the topic of self-checking and fail-safe logic. The field is large and many different approaches have been used. Wakerly [1978] has written an excellent text on self-checking logic. Several papers on various aspects of self-checking and fail-safe logic design are listed at the end of this section for further reference.

Self-checking circuit design is based on the premise that the circuit inputs are already encoded in some code, and that the circuit outputs are also to be encoded. The inputs and outputs are not necessarily in the same code. The following definitions from Anderson [1971] and Anderson and Metze [1973] are based on this premise.

Self-Testing Property.   A circuit is self-testing if, for every fault from a prescribed set, the circuit produces a noncode output for at least one code input.

Fault-Secure Property.   A circuit is fault-secure if, for every fault from a prescribed set, the circuit never produces an incorrect code output for code inputs.

Totally Self-Checking (TSC) Property.   A circuit is totally self-checking if it is both self-testing and fault-secure.

Thus, to be self-testing, the circuit must experience a set of inputs during normal operation

```
register temp <(r-1):0> ;              !rth degree G(X) ;
variable bcr <(r-1):0> ;               !will hold block check character ;
variable flag <0> ;
variable input <(b-1):0> ;             !input data byte ;
integer variable counter ;
logical variable new.code.word ;
constant bcr.preload <(r-1):0>=00..0₁₆ ;    !would be FFFF₁₆ for SDLC ;

constant crc.constant <(r-1):0> = XX..XX₁₆ ;   ! 8408₁₆ for CRC-CCITT

                                         0F01₁₆ for CRC-12 ;

begin                                  ! this algorithm updates the block check character
                                       for a new data byte. new.code.word is TRUE only if
                                       a new CRC computation is to be commenced, i.e., if
                                       this is the first byte in a CRC code word. ;

    if new.code.word then bcr ← bcr.preload ;
    temp ← 0 ;
    temp <(b-1):0> ← input ;
    temp ← temp XOR bcr ;
    for counter ← 0 to (r-1) do
        begin
                flag ← temp <0> ;
                shift.right (temp) ;       ! shift temp right one, shifting 0 into temp <r-1> ;
                if (flag = 1) then temp ← temp XOR crc.constant ;
        end ;

    bcr ← temp ;                         ! bcr now contains current check characters ;
end ;
```

Figure 3–35. An algorithm for computation of CRC check bits using processor registers.

that tests for all faults in the prescribed set. If such a set of inputs is not assured, the circuit is self-testing only for the faults that are tested. This same restriction applies to TSC circuits.

These three properties are illustrated by a TSC comparison element (derived from the TSC comparison element in Wakerly [1978]). A dual-rail signal is a coded signal whose two bits are always complementary. This is equivalent to the $1/2$ code. The comparison element checks for the equality of the two dual-rail signals at its inputs, and outputs a dual-rail signal (01 or 10) only if the inputs are both equal and properly encoded; otherwise it outputs a noncode word, either 00 or 11. In addition, the comparison element is self-testing for any internal single fault, and is thus TSC as long as all four possible sets of code inputs appear during normal operation. Figure 3-36 shows the logic circuit for the comparison element, while Table 3-12 shows an analysis of the possible single stuck-at-faults and the inputs that test for them. An input signal tests a fault in

the circuit if the output is a noncode word. To test for all faults in the set (m, n, o, p: stuck-at-1), all four possible input signal sets must appear. As a result, all four signal sets must appear at the circuit input during normal operation. Conversely, it can be seen that there is no stuck-at fault which is not tested by at least one of these signals. Thus, the comparator is self-testing (given a guarantee of all four signal sets appearing). Finally, further examination of Table 3-12 shows that under stuck-at faults at a, b, c, or d, the outputs are either noncode words or the correct code word (i.e., the code word that would appear in normal operation). Since these stuck-at faults produce a condition equivalent to having noncode inputs, the circuit is shown to be fault secure as well. Since the circuit is both fault secure and self-testing, it is TSC. Note that since stuck-at faults of signals a, b, c, and d are equivalent to faults in the input signals, these conditions show the response of a nonfaulty comparator to faulty (noncode) inputs.

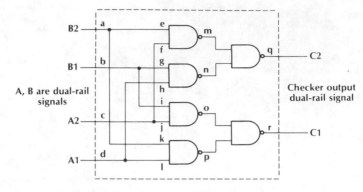

Figure 3–36. Logic circuit of basic TSC comparison element.

Some operations are not amenable to the use of codes, and full duplication is the least redundant form of checking that can be used. To check the logical operations AND and OR, for example, duplication can be used with a TSC comparator. Wakerly [1974] has proposed partially self-checking logic as a less expensive alternative:

Partially Self-Checking (PSC) Property. A circuit is partially self-checking if it is self-testing for a set N of normal inputs and a set F_t of faults, and is fault-secure for a set I (a nonnull subset of N) and a set F_s.

In normal operation of a PSC circuit, all faults from F_t are tested. In addition, for a subset I of the normal inputs, no incorrect code output can be produced by a fault in the set F_s. Thus, PSC logic provides eventual detection of a fault at the cost of introducing fault latency (undetected faults produced prior to fault detection). The benefit is a redundancy cost lower than that of duplication.

Fail-safe techniques, on the other hand, are not concerned with the detection of faults per se. Thus, they can result in an even lower redundancy cost.

Fail-Safe Property. A circuit is fail-safe if, for every fault from a prescribed set, any input produces a "safe" output, that is, one of a preferred set of erroneous outputs.

A traffic light with a fail-safe output of stuck-

Table 3–12. TSC dual-rail comparator responses to stuck-at-faults.

Inputs B2B1 A2A1	Normal Output	Outputs C2C1 Resulting from Single Stuck-at-1 Faults																
		a	b	c	d	e	f	g	h	i	j	k	l	m	n	o	p	q	r
01 01	10	11	10	11	10	10	10	10	10	10	11	11	10	10	00	10	10	10	11
01 10	01	11	01	01	11	11	01	01	11	01	01	01	01	01	01	00	01	11	01
10 01	01	01	11	11	01	01	11	11	01	01	01	01	01	01	01	01	00	11	01
10 10	10	10	11	10	11	10	10	10	10	11	10	10	11	00	10	10	10	10	11

Inputs B2B1 A2A1	Normal Output	Outputs C2C1 Resulting from Single Stuck-at-0 Faults																
		a	b	c	d	e	f	g	h	i	j	k	l	m	n	o	p	q	r
01 01	10	10	00	10	00	10	10	00	00	10	10	10	10	10	10	11	11	00	10
01 10	01	01	00	00	01	01	01	01	01	00	00	01	01	11	11	01	01	01	00
10 01	01	00	01	01	00	01	01	01	01	01	01	00	00	11	11	01	01	01	00
10 10	10	00	10	00	10	00	00	10	10	10	10	10	10	10	10	11	11	00	10

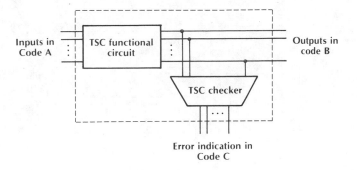

Figure 3–37. A TSC network made from TSC elements.

at-red on all sides is a good example of a fail-safe system [Mine and Koga, 1967]. Stuck-at-red is the most desirable failed state because all drivers approaching the intersection must stop, and may proceed only after realizing the light is broken. This state causes the least possible harm, for any driver will enter the intersection with extreme caution and at a low speed.

In the remainder of this section general models will be presented for TSC and PSC networks. Some specific examples of TSC and PSC networks are included. The examples cover only a subset of the possibilities of these techniques, and references for more are given at the end of the section. Fail-safe techniques will not be treated any further although several references are included at the end of the section.

Figure 3-37 shows a general model for a TSC network proposed by Anderson [1971], consisting of both a TSC functional circuit and a TSC checker. The advantage of this network over the TSC functional circuit alone is that a correct checker output from the network guarantees that the network functional output is correct.

Conceptually, the simplest form of a TSC functional circuit is duplication, in which two copies of the function are used. Together, their total inputs and outputs are coded (duplication). As stated before, for some functions duplication may be the least redundant coding alternative for achieving TSC. The only other component of a duplication-based TSC network is the TSC comparator, which performs the checking of the functional outputs. The most economical form of

checker complements one set of the functional unit outputs before routing it to the comparison element [Anderson, 1971]. In this case a checker for an arbitrary number of inputs can use the two-signal input dual-rail comparator of Figure 3-36 as the basic element. These elements are assembled in tree fashion, as shown in Figure 3-38, using $\log_2 n$ two–input dual-rail signal comparators. Figure 3-39 shows the entire TSC duplication network scheme. To qualify for the self-testing property each checker basic module must receive the four input signals mentioned above. It is not necessary, however, to apply all possible combinations of dual-rail signals to the entire checker to test it completely. Anderson [1971] has shown that for every size comparator built as

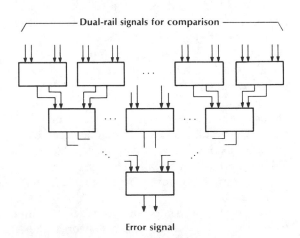

Figure 3–38. Assembly of *n*-input dual-rail signal comparison checker from basic two-input elements.

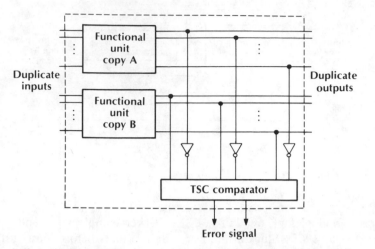

Figure 3–39. TSC network based on duplication as a code.

a tree of the basic dual-rail checker modules, at least one set of four tree input signals will ensure complete self-testing for any single fault in the checker. If the four signal sets are assured of appearing during normal operation, the network is TSC.

The same comparison checker can be used to make a TSC separable-code error detector [Ashjaee and Reddy, 1976; Wakerly, 1978]. The inputs to the checker are the received check character and a locally generated check character, as shown in Figure 3-40. Wakerly [1978] provides the proof of the TSC property for this detector. As in the duplication scheme, the self-test property of the comparison checker must be assured by having the check characters that appear include a set of four characters that tests for all possible faults in the checker. For (n, k) codes in which all $2^{(n-k)}$ possible combinations of the check bits appear, this is no problem. Other codes, however, may present more difficulty. The residue-3 arithmetic code check character, for example, has only three possible values (00, 01, and 10); thus, all four signals necessary for self-testing do not appear and the checker cannot be TSC.

Wakerly [1974] has proposed models for three types of partially self-checking networks, shown in Figure 3-41. All three have two modes of operation: secure or insecure. In the secure

mode, used during operation with code inputs that map into code outputs, the network is TSC. The insecure mode, invoked by fixing the error outputs to a nonerror indication, is used when a noncode output from the functional circuit is the correct function of the inputs. An example would be the AND and OR functions of an ALU operating on residue-m-coded inputs. In the insecure mode the PSC network is neither self-testing nor fault secure.

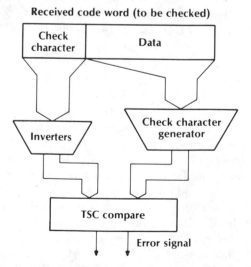

Figure 3–40. TSC detector for separable codes, based on a TSC comparator.

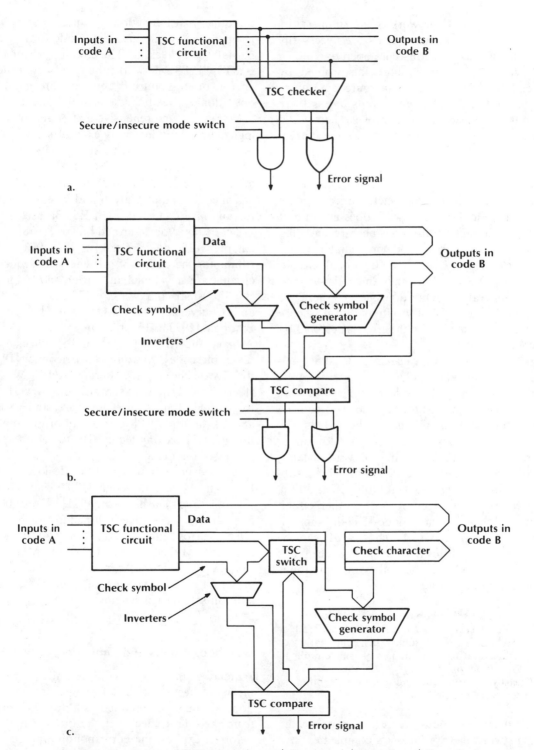

Figure 3–41. Types of PSC networks. a.) Type 1. b.) Type 2. c.) Type 3.

The Type 1 PSC network is the simplest. Its disadvantage is that the outputs are necessarily noncode outputs in the insecure operating mode. The Type 2 PSC network solves this problem by reencoding outputs during insecure operation; thus, all outputs are coded outputs unless there are faults in the encoder. However, there is no guarantee that the code outputs are the correct outputs during insecure operation. A Type 3 PSC network causes less delay than a Type 2 network on secure mode outputs, by using a bus switch for the check character. During secure operations, the Type 2 network does not output the check character until it has been regenerated locally; the Type 3 network immediately gates the check symbol from the functional circuit. Both Types 2 and 3 have the same delay during insecure operations. One drawback of the Type 3 scheme is that a faulty output during secure mode may be used before the error is detected by the checker.

Figure 3-42 shows an example of a PSC network due to Wakerly [1974]. It shows an ALU made with 4-bit 74181 adder chips, and with inputs coded in the distance-2 residue-15 code. A single stuck-at fault in one of the 74181s will produce a detectable error during addition or subtraction. Hence, this ALU network is fault-secure for the operations of addition and subtraction for all single stuck-at faults. In addition, the circuit is fault secure for the other circuit functions for which the residue-15 code is invariant: A, B, A', B', 0, and 1. The 74181 can be shown to be self-testing for all single faults provided that all of the following operations occur during normal use:

1. Addition and subtraction (tests carry logic)
2. The set of operations A XOR B and $(A$ XOR $B)'$ or the set A, B, A', B', or some other combination of operations that tests for all possible single faults in the logic function circuitry
3. At least one arithmetic and one logic function, to test the carry enable logic

If all these operations are assured to occur, the ALU network is TSC for one's-complement addition and subtraction, A, B, A', B', 0, and 1. If

the other 74181 functions are used, the network is operating in an insecure mode and is only partially self-checking. The circuit in Figure 3-42 is a Type 2 PSC network: the necessary reencoder for outputs during the insecure mode of operation is already present in the TSC checker.

Wakerly's comprehensive text on self-checking logic [1978] contains many examples, including a paper design of a self-checking processor. Algorithms for the design of TSC m/n code checkers are developed in Anderson and Metze [1973] for $m/2m$ codes and in Marouf and Friedman [1977] for any m/n code. The Bell ESS-3a uses a TSC 4/8 code detector described in Toy [1978] (or see Chapter 12) and in Cook et al. [1973]. Algorithms for the design of self-checking sequential circuits are developed in Carter and Schneider [1968], Osman and Weiss [1973], Diaz, Geffroy, and Courvoisier [1974], Ozgunner [1977], and Pradhan [1978a, 1978b]. Other references are Ashjaee and Reddy [1976] on TSC checkers for separable codes, Marouf and Friedman [1978b] for TSC checkers for Berger codes, Wakerly [1974] for PSC networks, Smith and Metze [1978] for strongly fault-secure networks, and Crouzet and Landrault [1980] for a study of the application of self-checking techniques to a 4-bit microprocessor on a chip.

A good introduction to fail-safe logic can be found in Mine and Koga [1967] and Tokura, Kasami, and Hashimoto [1971]. Fail-safe sequential machines are developed in Sawin [1975], Diaz, Geffroy, and Courvoisier [1974], Patterson and Metze [1974], Tohma [1974], and Mukai and Tohma [1974]. Diaz, Azema, and Ayache [1979] present a unified overview of both self-checking and fail-safe design schemes.

Watchdog Timers and Timeouts

Watchdog timers are a simple and inexpensive means of keeping track of proper process function. A timer is maintained as a process separate from the one it checks. If the timer is not reset before it expires, the corresponding process has probably failed in some way; the assumption is

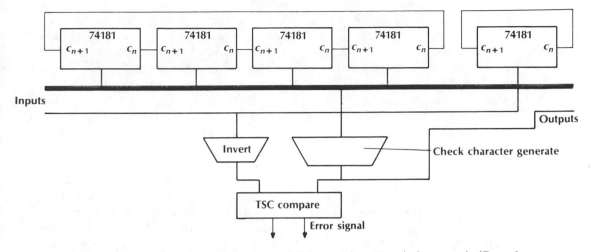

Figure 3–42. Partially self-checking ALU for residue-15 coded operands (Type 2 PSC network).

that any failure or corruption of the checked process will cause it to miss resetting its watchdog. On the other hand, coverage is limited because data and results are not checked. All the timer provides is an indication of possible process failure. The process may be only partially failed and produce errors, yet still be able to reset its timer. The coverage may be improved if the checked process has to exercise a large proportion of its internal components in order to reset its watchdog.

The watchdog timer concept can be implemented in software or hardware. The process it guards can be a software or hardware process. In fact, the computing process and the timer could be running on the same hardware. In this and most other cases, at least one other process monitors the timer, or is interruptible by it, to handle possible failure situations.

Pluribus [Ornstein et al., 1975] (or see Chapter 13), a reliable multiprocessor designed primarily for use as a switching node for the ARPANET, makes extensive use of both hardware and software watchdog timers. These timers have time spans of from 5 μsec to 2 minutes. Subsystems that are monitored by timers go through a cycle of a known length. Part of each cycle is a complete self-consistency check. Failure to reset

the timer is seen as an indication that the subsystem has failed in such a way that it cannot recover by itself. Message buffers, for example, have 2-minute watchdog timers that are reset each time the buffer is returned to the free list of unused buffers. If the timer runs out, the buffer is forced back to the free list by the process which the timer alerts upon expiring. Another timer in each processor interrupts the processor every 1/15 second if not reset. This timer prevents subsystems from waiting forever for a resource that is erroneously allocated and thus will not be released. A final example of the timer is the bus arbiter. If there is no bus activity for 1 second, the bus arbiter resets all the processors. This is useful, for example, when all processors execute a spurious halt command that somehow gets planted in the common program store. In this case, the 60-Hz processor timers cannot help because a halted processor will not respond to interrupts. PLURIBUS also has several other timers not mentioned above.

The VAX-11/780 is a more commercially-oriented system that makes use of a watchdog timer. The console processor monitors the micro-machine activity. If the micromachine does not strobe an interrupt line to the LSI-11 console processor at least every 200 μsec, the console processor will try to determine the reason for the failure.

Bus timeouts are also based on the principle that some operations should take no more than a certain maximum time to complete. Time limits are set for certain responses required by the bus protocol. Thus, when one device (e.g., master) requires a response from another device (e.g., slave), a failure to respond in time indicates a possible failure. Timeouts are different from watchdog timers in that they provide a finer check of control flow.

Timeout detection is provided on the buses of most computers, including the PDP-11 UNI-BUS. During the interrupt request/bus grant sequence a timeout is generated if the requesting device does not respond to the bus grant signal in 5–10 μsec. Similarly, during data transfers a 10–20 μsec timeout detection occurs if the slave device does not respond to the bus master's synchronization signal. The UNIBUS bus specifications [DEC, 1979] does not specify the exact response to these timeout detections; the response depends on the particular PDP-11 model. Generally, however, the processor response is a trap to a bus timeout handling routine.

Consistency and Capability Checking

Consistency checking is a simple fault-detection technique that often requires minimal hardware redundancy. A consistency check is performed by verifying that the intermediate or final results are reasonable, either on an absolute basis (fixed test) or as a simple function of the inputs used to derive the result. One form of consistency check is a range check: confirming that a computed value is in a valid range. For example, a computed probability must lie between 0 and 1. The range can be narrowed further if a priori probabilities are known. Weekly paychecks should have positive denominations and should not exceed some maximum value (such as a function of normal and overtime pay rates and the 168

hours in the week). Similarly, commercial aircraft altitude sensors should indicate elevations between Death Valley and 45,000 feet.

Most computers use some form of consistency checking. Address checking, opcode checking, and arithmetic operation checking are the most common. In its usual form, address checking consists of verifying that the address to be accessed exists. DEC PDP-11s provide an NXM (nonexistent memory) trap for this purpose. Further coverage may be provided by assuring that the address for a write is actually a RAM and not a ROM location, and that an I/O address is consistent with the operation to be performed. Checking for a valid opcode occurs before instruction execution commences. Without this check it is possible to perform undefined and (usually) undesirable operation sequences in the CPU. For example, programmers of some microprocessors occasionally utilize undocumented opcodes with unique actions. This use of undefined processor features is undesirable because of possible unknown side effects. Underflow and overflow checking of binary arithmetic, a form of range checking, is provided in most computers, either in hardware or in program run-time systems.

Another form of consistency checking is to utilize a memory in which the parity bit on any word can be arbitrarily set for either parity sense (odd or even). In practice, data words would use odd parity and instruction words even parity. In addition to parity errors, addressing errors and programming errors are likely to be discovered. Examples are data words accidentally accessed during instruction fetch and program code erroneously overwritten with data. When an addressing and a parity error occur simultaneously, however, there is a chance that they will complement each other with no error detection resulting.

Capability checking is also a form of fault detection. Usually it is part of the operating system, although it may be realized as a hardware mechanism. In this concept, access to objects is limited to users with the proper authorization. Objects include memory segments and I/O devices; users might be processes or even independent physical processors in a system. Further functionality is provided by allowing multiple levels of access privileges for different user/object combinations, such as execute only, read only, and read/write privilege levels in a disk system. One common means of checking access privileges is through the memory-mapping mechanism of virtual address machines. An example is the virtual address generation mechanism for Cm*, shown in Figure 3-43 [Swan, Fuller, and Siewiorek, 1977a]. A *Capability* in Cm* consists of a 3-bit field specifying access rights and a 16-bit field containing the segment name. During the address translation, the access rights are checked against the operation to be performed. If the operation is not permitted, an error trap is forced.

Capability checking provides more than fault detection: it also provides some fault isolation by locking out corrupted users. For example, it should prevent a bad process from erroneously overwriting portions of memory to which it has no legal access. More information on capability checking can be found in texts on operating systems design.

Another method of capability checking is the use of passwords. The Pluribus system (see Chapter 13) incorporates password protection. A processor that does not reset its watchdog timer will be restarted by an outside process. To prevent spurious resets, the resetting process must give the proper password before it can initiate a reset. A Boeing duplicated processor system used password protection for a similar purpose in its reconfiguration hardware; the goal was to prevent spurious reconfiguration of the system [Wachter, 1975].

MASKING REDUNDANCY

Fault-detection techniques supply warnings of faulty results. They may also provide diagnostic capabilities, with a resolution of some finite number of possible failure locations (such as a device or set of devices causing the fault). However, the use of fault-detection techniques alone does not provide actual tolerance of faults. Fault masking, on the other hand, employs redundancy which provides fault tolerance by either isolating or correcting fault effects before they reach module outputs. Fault masking is a "static" form of redundancy [Short, 1968; Avizienis, 1977]: the logical interconnection of the circuit elements remains fixed, and no intervention occurs from elements outside the module. Thus, when the masking redundancy is exhausted by faults in the module, any further faults will cause errors at the output.

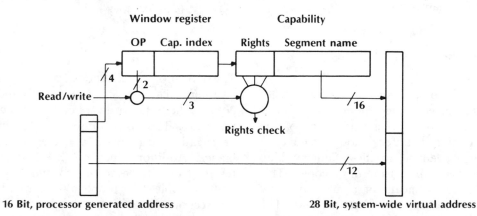

Figure 3–43. Virtual address calculation with capability checking in Cm*.

Notification of fault occurrence is implicit in fault detection. In its pure form, fault masking does not provide fault detection: the effects of faults are automatically neutralized without notification of their occurrence. Pure fault masking thus gives no warning of a deteriorating hardware state until enough faults have accumulated to cause an error. As a result, most fault-masking techniques are extended to provide fault detection as well. The additional redundancy needed for this purpose is usually minor. In the case of a few fault-masking techniques, however, fault detection is either impossible or too costly. The following presentations of fault-masking techniques discuss fault-detection extensions where applicable.

Like fault detection, fault masking can be used in combination with other techniques in a dynamic redundancy scheme. For example, fault masking may be used until its redundancy is exhausted, after which spares may be switched in to renew the redundancy. This possibility and others are the subject of the section on Dynamic Redundancy.

Because fault masking provides fault tolerance, the reliability function becomes a meaningful measurement of technique effectiveness. This section provides simple reliability models for the techniques it presents. More detailed models are usually possible, and provide more accurate information. More detailed reliability models are the subject of Chapter 5.

N-Modular Redundancy with Voting

Duplication with output comparison was considered as a fault-detection technique in the section on Duplication above. If a third copy of th functional circuit is added, enough redundant information is available to allow fault masking of a failure in any one of the three copies. This is accomplished by means of a majority (two-out-of-three) vote on the circuit outputs. The groundwork for the triple modular redundancy (TMR) technique was first laid by von Neumann

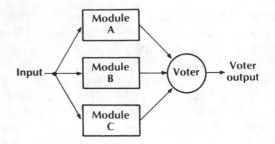

Figure 3–44. Basic Triple Modular Redundancy (TMR) configuration.

[1956]. He proposed a configuration employing independently computed copies of a signal, with "restoring organs" placed between logical operations.

Figure 3-44 illustrates the basic concept. The reliability of the configuration shown is

$$
\begin{aligned}
R &= R_v \cdot (R_m^3 + 3R_m^2(1 - R_m)) \\
&= R_v \cdot (3R_m^2 - 2R_m^3)
\end{aligned} \tag{1}
$$

where R_v and R_m are the reliabilities of the voter and a single copy of the triplicated module, respectively. The concept can be extended to include N copies with majority voting at the outputs. The resulting technique is called N-modular redundancy, or NMR. Normally N is made an odd number to avoid the uncertain state in which the output vote is a tie. The reliability of an NMR configuration similar to that of Figure 3-44 is

$$
R = R_v \cdot \sum_{i=0}^{\lfloor N/2 \rfloor} {}_N C_i \cdot R_m^{(N-i)} \cdot (1 - R_m)^i \tag{2}
$$

The derivations of equations 1 and 2 are given in Chapter 5. The cost of N-modular redundancy is N times the basic hardware cost, plus the cost of the voter. The voter causes a delay in signal propagation, leading to a decrease in performance. Additional performance-cost overhead results from the necessity to synchronize the multiple copies (this problem is discussed later in this section).

The two reliability formulas above are the simplest models possible. In most cases they will

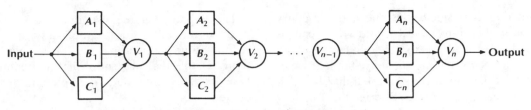

Figure 3–45. Cascading of TMR modules.

be pessimistic; that is, some failures in two or more copies may occur in such a way that an error is avoided. Such failures are called compensating failures. For example, consider a module output failed stuck-at-1 in a TMR network. If the same line fails on another copy, there is no error caused if it fails stuck-at-0. In this case, whichever value the remaining nonfaulty line takes on, it has another to match it and the correct voted output results. Another possibility is nonoverlapping failures, such as a failure in memory location 123 on one memory module and a failure in memory location 67 on another. Although these failures are on two different copies, they do not act together in the voting process to cause an error. Models of TMR systems that take compensating failures into account are discussed in detail in Chapter 5.

A complex system can be partitioned into smaller subsystems, each of which can be transformed into an NMR configuration. Figure 3-45 shows a system transformed into a cascaded series of TMR modules. The reliability of this configuration is

$$\prod_{i=1}^{n} R_{v_i} \cdot (3R_{m_i}^2 - 2R_{m_i}^3)$$

The advantage of partitioning is that the resulting design can withstand more failures than the equivalent configuration with only one large triplicated module. However, subdivision cannot be extended to arbitrarily small modules, because voter unreliability ultimately overrides any potential reliability gains.

The TMR configurations shown so far have single points of failure: the voters. In the circuit of Figure 3-44 the only solution is to make the voter more reliable through a fault-avoidance and/or fault-tolerance technique. In the circuit of Figure 3-45, however, all but one of the single points of failure can be removed by triplicating the voters themselves, as illustrated in Figure 3-46. If a triplicated output is desired, all single points of failure are removed. The reliability of the configuration shown in Figure 3-46 is

$$R_{v_n} \cdot (3R_{m_1}^2 - 2R_{m_1}^3)$$

$$\cdot \prod_{i=2}^{n} \{3(R_{m_i}R_{v_{i-1}})^2 - 2(R_{m_i}R_{v_{i-1}})^3\}$$

If the last voter is also triplicated, R_{v_n} in the above formula is replaced by

$$3R_{v_n}^2 - 2R_{v_n}^3.$$

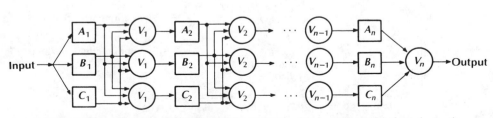

Figure 3–46. The use of TMR voters to remove single points of failure from the network of Figure 3-45.

If functional considerations allow, the circuitry can be broken into modules, and voters can be located so as to maximize reliability. Gurzi [1965] has shown that for nonredundant voter configurations (Figure 3-45), reliability is maximized when $R_{m_i} = R$; that is, when the functional modules have identical reliabilities. If all the voters have reliability R_v, the maximum system reliability is attained when the functional breakdown is such that

$$R_v = \frac{1}{(3 - 2R)R^\alpha},$$

where $\alpha = \dfrac{2R}{3 - 2R}$ **(3)**

The upper limit of reliability gain in this case is

$$\frac{\text{TMR network reliability}}{\text{Nonredundant network reliability}}$$

$$= \frac{(3R^2 - 2R^3)^n R_v^n}{R^n} \leqslant (9/8)^n R_v^n$$

The graph of Figure 3-47 can be used to arrive at the optimum partitions graphically. If R_v and R fall within the parabola, the TMR network is more reliable than the equivalent nonredundant network. The solid line is the optimum decision curve of Equation 3.

Figure 3-48 shows the decision boundaries for configurations similar to Figure 3-46, with triplicated voters. In this case, $R_{m_i} = R$ ($i = 2,$ $3, \ldots, n$), and $R_{m_1} = R \cdot R_v$. The two solid lines indicate a trade-off between R and R_v. The optimum falls between the two lines. In this case, the maximum reliability improvement is also

$$\frac{R_\text{TMR}}{R_\text{nonredundant}} \leqslant (9/8)^n R_v^n$$

Finally, the nonredundant voter scheme is better than the TMR voter scheme if

$$R < \frac{3}{2(1 + R_v)}$$

More complex TMR networks are possible.

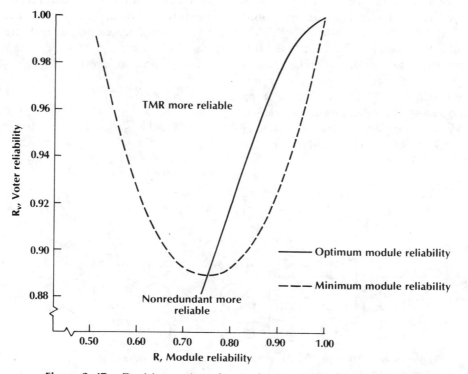

Figure 3–47.   Decision regions for single voter TMR. (© 1965 IEEE.)

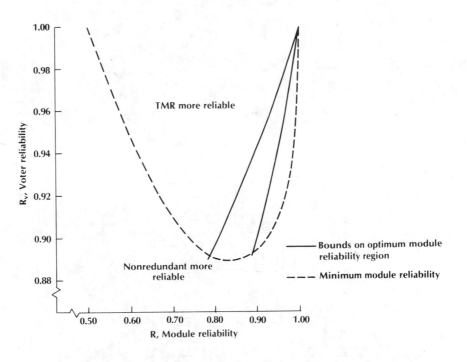

Figure 3–48. Decision regions for triplicated voter TMR. (© 1965 IEEE.)

Figure 3-49 shows a nonredundant network and a TMR equivalent. The reliability of such networks is more difficult to determine accurately; Chapter 5 discusses reliability evaluation of complex TMR structures.

In digital systems, majority voting is normally performed on a bit-by-bit basis. The majority function for a single-bit line can be performed by a 1-bit adder. The triplicated outputs are fed into the adder data and carry-in inputs; the carry-out output is the majority-voted result (see Figure 3-50). For a module with n output lines, the TMR implementation has three modules and n single-bit voters. Threshold logic [Hampel and Winder, 1971] has also been used for voting. In threshold logic, the output is 1 only if at least a minimum number (the threshold) of inputs are 1.

While voting can be applied at any level in the digital system hierarchy, the voter is almost always made up of single-bit majority elements. Although it has been proposed [Brown, Tierney, and Wasserman, 1961], majority voting at the gate level has had little actual use. At the module level, many designs have incorporated triple modular redundancy. The Saturn IB and Saturn V on-board computers both incorporated TMR modules [Cooper and Chow, 1976]. The Saturn V computer logic was divided into seven modules, each with approximately ten voted outputs. Triplicated voters were used between the modules in this design [Dickinson, Jackson, and Randa, 1964]. The Test and Repair Processor (TARP) of the JPL-STAR (see Chapter 14) is an ultrareliable hard core that controls system configuration. The TARP is triplicated with a majority vote at its outputs. (The TARP is actually hybrid redundant. See the section below on hybrid redundancy and other dynamic redundancy variants of N-modular redundancy.) The Fault Tolerant Spaceborn Computer (FTSC) [Stiffler, 1976; Avizienis, 1978] is another aerospace computer. Its Configuration Control Unit (CCU) is triplicated.

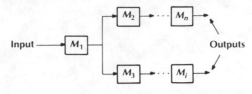

a. Nonredundant network

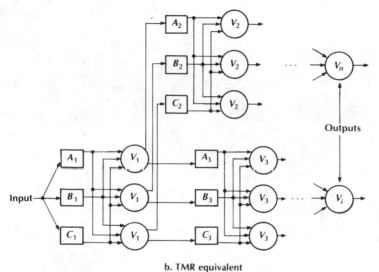

b. TMR equivalent

Figure 3–49. TMR applied to more complex networks.

Unlike the STAR's TARP, however, the CCU output voting is performed locally at each destination.

Voting is also possible at the bus level. C.vmp (Computer-voted multiprocessor) is implemented with off-the-shelf DEC LSI-11 components [Siewiorek, Canepa, and Clark, 1977a]. A single voter module divides the LSI-11 bus in two and employs special bidirectional voters on the bidirectional bus lines. As Figure 3-51 shows, the three processors and three memories reside on different sides of the voter. Triplicated floppy disk drives reside on the memory side of the voter. Chapter 7 analyzes the design of C.vmp in detail. FTMP (Fault Tolerant Multiprocessor) uses triplication with voting [Smith and Hopkins, 1978; Hopkins, Smith, and Lala, 1978; and Chapter 17]. Its processors and memories are configured in groups of three to form bus triads and memory triads. Each module in a triad operates in synchronization with the other two, and voting is used to mask the effects of a failed module.

Finally, voting can be applied at the software level. For example, a single processor could be

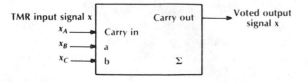

Figure 3–50. Logic signal voting with a one-bit adder.

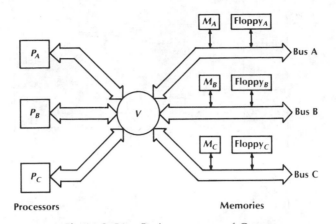

Figure 3–51.   Basic structure of C.vmp.

made less susceptible to transient and/or programming errors by performing a task three times and voting on the result. Making the algorithm different for each execution producing the results to be voted on may result in some protection against hard failures. Chen and Avizienis [1978] formalized this concept and gave it the name *N*-version programming. The SIFT (Software Implemented Fault Tolerance) computer uses software voting in a different way (see Chapter 16): each processor uses a two-out-of-three vote on data from other processors executing the same task to obtain a correct version for further operations.

As with duplication, synchronization of the multiple copies in *N* modular redundancy is necessary to prevent false outputs. Figure 3-52 illustrates one of the problems that can result without proper synchronization. The signal line in question carries pulses of fixed duration and is used in a master-slave protocol. The first set of pulses occurs soon enough for the simple voter of Figure 3-50 to provide a valid signal. The second set of signals caused a voted output that may be too short for proper operation of the slave logic. The slave may never respond, resulting in a timeout at the master. If the slave device is triplicated, the different copies may respond differently to the runt pulse, resulting in divergent slave behavior, and ultimately, loss of slave synchronization. In the third set of pulses, even though the voted master request pulse is valid, the lagging master may not be ready to receive the reply when it is transmitted. In this case the operation of the lagging processor may diverge from that of the other two, leading to a loss of master synchronization.

The problem of synchronization is often solved by using a common clock. Unless the clock is fault tolerant, however, a single point of failure exists. Another solution is the synchronizing voter shown in Figure 3-53a. Incoming re-

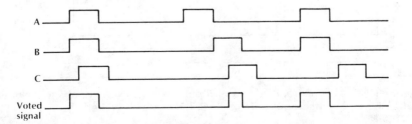

Figure 3–52.   Triplicated request line using a pulse signalling convention.

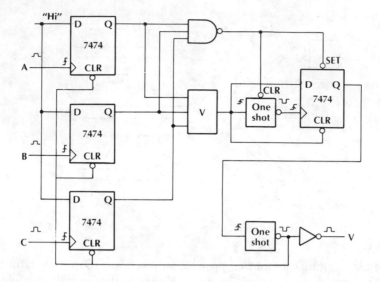

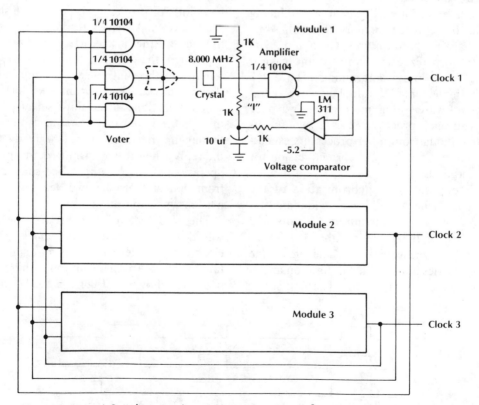

Figure 3–53. a.) Synchronized voter for pulse signals [McConnel and Siewiorek 1981]. b.) Fully synchronized TMR clock [Davies and Wakerly 1978]. (© 1981, 1978 IEEE.)

quest pulses are latched. If pulses are received from two lines, the voter waits for a time for the lagging master to catch up. If the third pulse comes before the waiting period is over, the voted pulse is sent out immediately, minimizing delay. The one-shot at the output ensures a voted pulse signal of the proper duration. The problems and solutions of synchronization in C.vmp are discussed at length in Chapter 7. More detailed consideration of the problems of synchronization and voting can be found in Davies and Wakerly [1978] and McConnel and Siewiorek [1981]. Davies and Wakerly also discuss the design of a fully synchronized TMR clock, in which synchronization is achieved by inserting a voter into the feedback path of each of the three crystal oscillators (Figure 3-53b).

Fault detection in N-modular redundancy can be provided by a disagreement detector that usually operates in parallel with the voter. The disagreement detector is an important element in NMR systems that are reconfigurable. Even in nonreconfigurable systems they act as an aid in diagnosis and can be used to warn of a deteriorating hardware state as the redundancy is exhausted. C.vmp, JPL-STAR, and FTMP are among the systems that use disagreement detectors.

In the earlier consideration of software triplication, it was mentioned that using three different implementations of the same process provides protection from software design errors as well as hard failures. A scheme based on a similar principle has been proposed for protection against both hardware design errors and inadequacies in component screening [Platteter, 1980]. Because only a tiny fraction of a microprocessor's possible states can be tested in the few seconds normally allowed in electrical screening tests, complete confidence in a complex LSI chip is almost impossible. Three microprocessors are employed in a TMR configuration; each is from a different source but implements the same architecture (such as 8080As from three different manufacturers). All three share the same clock and inputs, and thus oper-

ate synchronously in lockstep. When employed with a disagreement detector to report faults in any of the chips, this strategy can also be used for more thorough testing of components over a long test period.

As mentioned earlier in the section on Duplication, when a computing element is replicated for voting only a fraction of the available computing power is utilized because all copies are performing the same task. As with duplication, the solution is to use the multiple processors for independent tasks and invoke the voting mode only when necessary. Voting might occur periodically for critical tasks to ensure that all processors are running properly and/or when there is some indication of a possible malfunction (such as power supply flicker, processor self-test warning, or memory parity error). System performance benefits from such a scheme, at the cost of increased susceptibility to uncorrected (and undetected) errors during operation in independent mode. C.vmp is an example of a TMR system that can trade off performance for reliability. C.vmp can switch between voting and independent modes under program control, permitting use as a three-processor multiple processor in independent mode. Although this feature has not been used in C.vmp in an actual application, it has been used in SIFT, which also has this capability.

One problem with triplication is the occasional occurrence of common-mode transient faults. One possible solution is to deliberately skew the synchronization of the programs running in the three processors, but the data on common-mode phenomena are incomplete. C.vmp is currently being used to gather statistics on transient faults, to help determine what provisions are needed to tolerate transient faults.

Finally, voting on analog signals is a particularly important topic to designers of control and data collection systems that require ultrareliable sensors. Using multiple analog-to-digital converters and performing bit-by-bit voting on their digital outputs is not satisfactory, because the least significant bits are almost certain not to

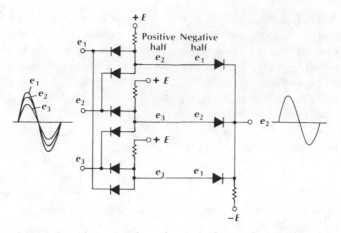

Figure 3–54.   Pseudo voting by selection of a median analog signal.

agree even when everything is working properly. The normal approach is to perform "voting" in the analog domain instead. One possibility is to take the mean instantaneous value (average the three signals); averaging is the method used for the redundant sensor inputs in the NASA Airborne Advanced Reconfigurable Computer Systems [McCluskey and Ogus, 1977]. The average could also be weighted by a priori probabilities of sensor reliability and accuracy. Another possibility is to take the mean of the two most similar signals [Klaassen and Van Peppen, 1977a]. Figure 3-54 illustrates yet another scheme, called pseudo voting [Dennis, 1974], which chooses the median of the three signals. Thus, if the three sensors had outputs of 1.0, 2.5, and 2.8 volts at a given instant, the median 2.5 volt value would be used. This approach has the advantage of being simple to implement. More complete treatment of analog voting, including methods and accuracy analysis, can be found in Dennis [1974], and Klaassen and Van Peppen [1977a, 1977b].

Error-Correcting Codes

Error-correcting codes (ECC codes) are the most commonly used means of masking redundancy. In particular, a large proportion of current pri-

mary memory designs use Hamming single-error-correcting (SEC) codes. There are several reasons for the popularity of SEC coded memories. First, they are inexpensive in terms of both cost and performance overhead. The redundancy of SEC codes is only 10 to 40 percent, depending on the design. Decoding and encoding delays are relatively minuscule. Second, the increasingly dense RAM chips in use are more prone to soft (transient) faults, such as memory-cell charge loss caused by alpha-particles and cosmic-rays. Third, random access memories constitute an increasingly larger part of digital systems and currently contribute as much as 60 to 70 percent of system failure rates. Finally, LSI SEC code correction/detection chips have become available, reducing both the dollar and performance costs of employing SEC codes.

Other error-correction codes with different characteristics are available. Some provide multiple-error correction but may prove economical only in special applications, because the redundancy and decoding delay of multiple error correcting codes increase dramatically with error-correcting ability. Some error codes are well suited for specific applications in which the code properties can be used to advantage and the code limitations make little or no difference. Serial decoding, for example, is usually much less expensive than parallel decoding. Serial decoding can be used when data are transmitted serially or when performance is not as critical. In such an application an efficient multiple-error-correcting code can be employed that requires less redundancy but whose complexity would be prohibitive in a parallel decoder. In other situations, limitations on possible failure modes may be used to advantage. For example, in many applications multiple errors will almost always appear closely grouped in space or time (so-called burst errors). In these cases, special codes called burst-error-correction codes may be employed. Finally, there are error-correcting codes that are invariant with respect to certain arithmetic operations, and hence are suitable for use in checking arithmetic processors. Some of these codes are an extension of the arithmetic error-detection codes mentioned previously.

The concepts introduced in the section on Error-Detection Codes also apply to error-correction codes. The minimum distance of a code determines its error-correction/detection abilities. For example, the code C=(0010, 0101) is contained in the space of 4-bit words illustrated in Figure 3-21 and has a minimum distance of 3. This code can detect any single or double error. It can instead be used to correct any single error, since a word with a single error will be closer to the code word it derives from than to the other code word. In general, a code with distance d can correct any pattern of up to t errors, where $(2t + 1) \leq d$.* All ECC codes can be used to provide error detection, error correction, or both correction and detection. There is, however, a trade-off between detection and correction capabilities. In general, a distance-d code can correct up to t errors and detect an additional p errors, where $(2t + p + 1) \leq d$.

The most important class of error-correcting codes is the linear error-correction codes. Linear error-correction codes can be described in terms of their parity-check matrices (PCMs). The PCM for an (n, k) linear code is an $(n - k)$ by n matrix whose elements are 0s and 1s (for binary codes). Each column corresponds to a bit in the code word, and each row corresponds to a check bit. If the n-element column vector $\mathbf{r}$ represents the received code word, and the parity check matrix is $\mathbf{H}$, the decoding operation is represented by the matrix operation

$$\mathbf{H} \cdot \mathbf{r} = \mathbf{s}$$

$\mathbf{s}$ is an $(n - k)$-element row vector called the syndrome. Most codes are formed by the n-element column vectors with 0 syndromes, or expressed more rigorously, the code is the null space of $\mathbf{H}$. Note that the all-0s word is always a code word when the null space of the PCM forms the code. Codes that are formed by the null space of a PCM are often called parity-check codes. If the PCM is binary, the syndrome can be calculated using $(n - k)$ binary trees. Each tree corresponds to a different row of the PCM, with its inputs specified by the bit positions in the row that are 1s.

Now consider the set of n column vectors $\mathbf{e}_i$ ($i = 1, 2, \ldots, n$), where the vector has a single 1 located in position i. If $\mathbf{f}$ is the code word transmitted, a received word with a single error in position i can be represented by

$$\mathbf{r} = \mathbf{f} + \mathbf{e}_i$$

If m errors are present in the bit locations specified by the set E, the received word can be represented by

$$\mathbf{r} = \mathbf{f} + \sum_{i \varepsilon E} \mathbf{e}_i$$

The decoding operation for $\mathbf{r}$ is thus

$$\mathbf{H} \cdot \mathbf{r} = \mathbf{H} \cdot \mathbf{f} + \mathbf{H} \cdot (\sum_{i \varepsilon E} \mathbf{e}_i) = \mathbf{H} \cdot (\sum_{i \varepsilon E} \mathbf{e}_i) = \mathbf{s}'$$

Note that

$$\sum_{i \varepsilon E} \mathbf{e}_i$$

is the same as the all-0s code word with m errors.

* N modular redundancy can be considered an application of an $(N, 1)$ distance-N code.

For t-error correcting codes, the syndrome s' is unique for each pattern of t or fewer errors, and can thus be used to correct the errors present if $m \leqslant t$. If $t < m < d$ (for a distance-d code), the syndrome indicates that an uncorrectable error has occurred. The actual correction operation based on s varies for different codes, particularly if the code is used for special error classes (such as b-bit burst errors, where $b \leqslant (n - k)/2$). Thus, the explanation of the correction operation is best left to the references cited later. The correction operations for the Hamming SEC codes and the orthogonal Latin square codes, however, are relatively simple and are explained below.

As for error-detection codes, distance is not the only consideration in the properties of error-correction codes. In many applications, tolerance of special classes of failures is often important, and codes have been derived to tolerate unidirectional errors, burst errors, and multiple adjacent unidirectional errors. In addition, the properties of the error sources in a given situation may be used to advantage. For example, in most communications channels, errors occur in a completely random fashion. In digital circuits, however, once a bit value is in error, there is a high probability that errors will continue to occur in that bit (such as hard or intermittent failures of memory cells, sense amps, and bus lines). This form of error (sometimes called an erasure) can be put to use if a history of error locations is kept [Ingle and Siewiorek, 1973a]. Consider a bus with a single-parity bit in which a particular bit line is known to be failed. If the possibility of additional failures and transient faults can be ignored, any parity error that occurs must be caused by the bad bit line. Thus, the error location is known and the error can be corrected. In memories a history may be unnecessary, because erasures caused by failed bits in a memory word can be found by writing and reading an arbitrary word and its complement into the memory location. XORing of the two retrieved values determines the position of stuck-at failures.

An algorithm which allows correction of up to $(d - 2)$ errors using a distance-d code is given in Figure 3-55 [Ingle and Siewiorek, 1973a]. This algorithm assumes that only one new error can occur before it is discovered (that is, for a received word with a errors in it, $a - 1$ of them are in already known erasure positions), and that at most $(d - 2)$ erasures exist. The algorithm uses the code itself to correct only single errors at a time. During a given iteration, the algorithm

```
k = number of known failures (<d-2) ;
i = 0 ;
r = received word ;
s = syndrome ;
for i = 0 to k do
    begin
        for j = 1 to kCi do
            begin
                pick a new permutation of i of the known failure locations
                    and change the corresponding bits of r ;
                form s ;
                if s ≠ 0 then
                    begin
                        temp = r corrected using s (change only one bit location);
                        reform s using temp ;
                        if s = 0 then ; ! errors corrected successfully ;
                            begin
                                update history of failed bit locations if there is
                                    a new failure location indicated ;
                                EXIT ;
                            end ;
                    end ;
            end ;
    end;
    signal (uncorrectable error) ; ! a nonzero s could not be found using the
                                      known failure locations ;
```

Figure 3–55. Proposed algorithm to correct up to $d-2$ errors in a distance-d code, using knowledge of erasures present.

changes the bit values in locations specified by some subset of the known erasures, forms a new single error correction syndrome, and then performs the single-bit correction specified by the syndrome. Next it forms a new syndrome from the corrected word to determine if the correction just performed (the combination of erasure positions and single error correction) was valid. Thus, if a $(d-1)$st error occurs during use of this algorithm, it is mistakenly corrected to a code word that is at a distance d from the correct word and only distance-1 from the received word. Figure 3-56 shows a table-lookup implementation of this scheme. Note that the erasure-correction algorithm of Figure 3-55 can be greatly simplified when used with a distance-3 (single-error-correcting) or distance-4 (single-error-correcting/double-error-detecting) code.

Presumably, the $(d-1)$st error can be corrected if, when there are $(d-2)$ erasures, it is assumed at the beginning of the correction process that at least one error exists in an erasure position. The algorithm of Figure 3-55 is changed by incrementing i from 1 instead of 0 when $k = d - 1$. This modification means, however, that a single error occurring in a nonerasure position will cause an error if $d - 1$ erasures are known, even if it is the only bit in error. Stiffler [1978] proposed a corrector design based on an algorithm similar to Figure 3-55. The design can be varied to correct up to any e errors, $e < d$, and detect an additional p errors, $e < (e + p) < d$.

With the addition of erasure correction, consideration must include the possibility of transient and soft errors and the ways in which they affect the validity of the schemes just presented. If an error history is being maintained, there is the problem of ensuring that the recorded erasure locations are due to hard failures instead of transient errors; otherwise, the storage space may quickly become saturated with spurious erasure locations.

The following subsections present samples of several kinds of ECC codes. Except for the Hamming codes, this coverage is neither detailed nor complete. Peterson and Weldon [1972], Berlekamp [1968], MacWilliams and Sloane [1978],

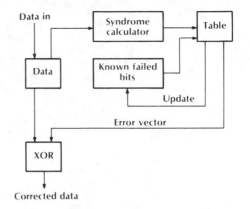

Figure 3–56. Proposed table look-up implementation of the error correction algorithm of Figure 3-55.

and Lin [1970] are excellent general references on coding theory as it applies to digital systems. A paper by Tang and Chien [1969], reproduced in Appendix A, provides a good introduction to coding theory, and should be read in conjunction with this section. An article by Pradhan and Stiffler [1980] is a general discussion of error codes: their properties, applications, limitations, and possible ways to overcome these limitations. The article also contains an extensive bibliography on codes and code applications. A book by Rao [1974] is a complete treatment of arithmetic error codes. Finally, new codes, modifications of old ones, and more efficient ways of employing codes are constantly being introduced. The *IEEE Transactions on Computers*, the *IBM Journal of Research and Development*, and the proceedings of the annual Fault Tolerant Computing Symposiums (published by the IEEE) are good sources for papers on coding theory and applications.

Hamming SEC Codes

As mentioned before, Hamming SEC codes are the most commonly encountered codes in computer systems. For k data bits, an (n, k) Hamming code requires c additional check bits, where

$$2^c \geq c + k + 1$$

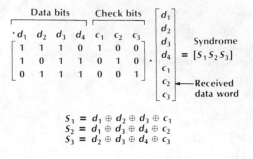

$$S_1 = d_1 \oplus d_2 \oplus d_3 \oplus c_1$$
$$S_2 = d_1 \oplus d_3 \oplus d_4 \oplus c_2$$
$$S_3 = d_2 \oplus d_3 \oplus d_4 \oplus c_3$$

a. Parity-check matrix and syndrome formation for a (7,4) Hamming SEC code.

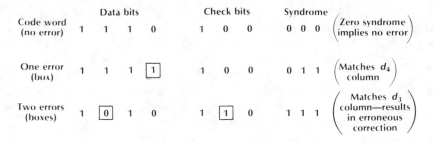

b. Received code words and their syndromes for zero, one, and two errors.

$$
\begin{array}{ccccccc}
c_1 & c_2 & d_1 & c_3 & d_2 & d_3 & d_4 \\
\left[\begin{array}{ccccccc}
1 & 0 & 1 & 0 & 1 & 0 & 1 \\
0 & 1 & 1 & 0 & 0 & 1 & 1 \\
0 & 0 & 0 & 1 & 1 & 1 & 1
\end{array}\right]
\end{array}
$$

c. Parity-check matrix for (7,4) Hamming code for which syndrome is the binary-coded position of the bit in error.

Figure 3–57.   Hamming SEC code examples.

Thus, $n = c + k$. These codes are separable. They are best described in terms of their parity-check matrices. Figure 3-57a shows the parity-check matrix for a (7,4) Hamming SEC code. A received code word is decoded by forming the dot product of the matrix and the code word column vector as shown, using modulo-2 addition. The result is a c-bit vector called the syndrome. If the syndrome is all 0s, no correctable error is present. If a single error occurs, the syndrome matches the column in the check matrix corresponding to the bit in error. A multiple error results in a false syndrome that is indistinguishable from the syndrome for one or no errors; thus, Hamming SEC codes have a minimum distance of 3. Figure 3-57b shows a

$$\begin{array}{c} \begin{array}{cccccccc} d_1 & d_2 & d_3 & d_4 & c_1 & c_2 & c_3 & c_4 \end{array} \\ \begin{bmatrix} 1 & 1 & 1 & 1 & 1 & 1 & 1 & 1 \\ 1 & 1 & 1 & 0 & 0 & 1 & 0 & 0 \\ 1 & 0 & 1 & 1 & 0 & 0 & 1 & 0 \\ 0 & 1 & 1 & 1 & 0 & 0 & 0 & 1 \end{bmatrix} \end{array} \cdot \begin{bmatrix} d_1 \\ d_2 \\ d_3 \\ d_4 \\ c_1 \\ c_2 \\ c_3 \\ c_4 \end{bmatrix} = [S_1 S_2 S_3 S_4]$$

a. Parity-check matrix for (8,4) Hamming SEC/DED code.

Number of errors	Received data bits				Received check bits				Syndrome			
	d_1	d_2	d_3	d_4	c_1	c_2	c_3	c_4	S_1	S_2	S_3	S_4
Zero	1	1	1	0	0	1	0	0	0	0	0	0
One	1	0	1	0	0	1	0	0	1	1	0	1
Two	1	0	1	0	0	1	1	0	0	1	1	1

b. Received words and their syndromes.

Figure 3–58.   Hamming SEC/DED code examples.

code word and its syndrome for 0, 1, and 2 errors.

As stated previously, a syndrome generator for this code can be made using c parity trees, with the inputs for each tree the code-word bits with 1s in the row corresponding to the syndrome bit. Encoding for this code uses the same set of parity trees, with the check-bit inputs corresponding to the check bit being generated held at 0. This matrix is not unique for a (7,4) Hamming SEC code; any 4 by 7 matrix will work as long as no two columns are alike, none is all 0s, and, for easier encoding, the columns corresponding to the c check bits contain only a single 1 in each.

The most common form of parity-check matrix is of the form shown in Figure 3-57c, originally proposed by Hamming [1950]. Each column of this matrix contains the binary-coded representation of the column number containing it (columns are numbered starting with 1). The check bits are located in bit positions $2^i (i = 0, 1, 2, \ldots, (n - k - 1))$. Thus, the syndrome in the event of an error is actually the binary-coded number of the bit position in error. This may allow a simpler design for the circuitry that uses the syndrome to perform the correction.

Because a nonzero syndrome is an indication of an error, a small amount of extra circuitry will provide a means of error notification, and thus, error detection. In addition, a small increase in the size of the code word can result in improved error-detection capabilities. Most implementations of the Hamming codes use an extra check bit, which allows detection of all double errors. This check bit is usually the parity of all the other check and data bits in the code word (even parity sense). The check matrix is changed by adding both an extra check-bit column with a single 1 and a row of all 1s that corresponds to the extra overall parity bit. A PCM for an (8,4) Hamming SEC/DED (single-error-correcting/double-error-detecting) code is shown in Figure 3-58a. A nonzero syndrome not matching any column indicates a double (or greater) error. In the case of this (8,4) code, the last three syndrome bits point to the column number in error (numbered starting with 0) as long as the first bit is 1. If the first bit is a 0 and any of the others nonzero, a double or greater error has occurred. If all the bits are 0, there is no error. This is demonstrated in Figure 3-58b, which shows the syndromes for a received word with 0, 1, and 2 errors.

These codes do not detect the all-0s failure mode, for the all-0s word is a code word. In the many hardware designs prone to an all-0s failure mode (such as through a power failure in a memory array or a failure in a select circuit), this problem can be overcome by a modified Hamming code. The code of Figure 3-58, for example, could be modified by using the odd instead of even parity sense for the overall parity-check bit. Pradhan and Stiffler [1980] give an example of a modified Hamming code that detects multiple unidirectional failures short of the all-1s or all-0s failure.

It is possible to obtain a Hamming code with a lower amount of redundancy, by concatenating several data words and coding the resultant longer word. The (8,4) code above used for a 4-bit data word has 100 percent redundancy. If eight data words are concatenated, the resulting 32 bits of data can be protected by using a (39,32) Hamming SEC/DED code with only 22 percent redundancy. There is a greater possibility of a fatal error because the single-bit-correction ability is now distributed over five times as many bits. Also, the parity trees needed for decoding have more gate levels and thus a longer delay. Finally, if this is a RAM, on writes the old code word must be retrieved, the old data byte replaced by the new one, and the new code word formed and stored. These increases, however, are often balanced by the much lower redundancy (and cost) needed. An example of this approach is the SEC/DED memory option for the PDP-11/60, whose 16-bit data words are stored in 39-bit code words.

Some subsets of Hamming codes have useful special properties. Hsiao [1970] describes a set of SEC/DED codes that are equivalent to conventional Hamming codes, in that they require the same number of check bits. These codes, called optimal odd-weight column codes, use a parity-check matrix in which the number of 1s is minimal. Each column has an odd number of 1s, and the number of 1s in each row is as close to the average number per row as possible. The result is a minimum number of inputs to the syndrome generation parity trees, which means the syndrome generator has fewer components and fewer gate-level delays. The conventional Hamming SEC/DED codes, in contrast, require an n-input tree for the overall parity check. Thus, the codes described by Hsiao result in better cost, reliability, and performance.

There are other possibilities for improving the implementation of Hamming SEC/DED codes. Carter, Duke, and Jessep [1973] propose an efficient method of decoding called lookaside correction. In this scheme, the SEC/DED code word is translated to a byte-parity encoded word. The code employed is a special subset of SEC/DED codes called rotational codes. These codes also have a minimum number of 1s in the check matrix. Carter, Duke, and Jessep show that a received code word with a correctable error translates to a byte-parity encoded word with a detectable parity error. Thus, detection of byte-parity errors indicates that error correction is necessary with the received code word; otherwise, the data is ready for transmission on a byte-parity encoded bus. With no error present, the translation-and-check operation is faster than the decoding and recoding (into byte-parity code) operation required in a conventional Hamming code implementation.

In the earlier section on parity codes, a memory design was suggested wherein the parity bit stored with the memory word was the parity of the combined data word and address. The Intel 432 (see Chapter 18) employs a similar scheme based on the Hamming codes. The check bits stored are for the concatenation of the data and address, and thus provide protection against both data and addressing faults.

An erasure correction technique similar to that of Figure 3-55 is used in a prototype memory described by Carter and McCarthy [1976]. This design uses a subset of Hamming SEC/DED distance-4 codes called maintenance codes, in which the data word W and its bit-wise complement W' have identical check bits. The memory also utilizes the fact that hard stuck-at-α failures can be discovered by writing and reading back both a word and its complement, then XORing the results to learn the location of the failures (pointed to by set bits in the result). (Stuck-at-α means a bit is stuck at either 1 or 0.) As shown before, this information can be used to correct up to $d - 2$ errors in a word, or in this case, two errors. The memory can detect permanent triple faults and recover from all permanent double faults. Black, Sundberg, and Walker [1977] describe a spacecraft computer memory that can correct single errors and erasures.

In the final variation of the Hamming SEC/DED code given here, any single-byte error can be corrected and any double-byte error detected. This is accomplished (assuming 8-bit bytes) by using 8 Hamming codes in parallel in the same fashion as for interlaced parity (described in the section on Parity Codes above.)* Thus, for a 64-bit data word with 8-bit bytes, each Hamming syndrome is formed using every eighth bit. In essence, 8 13-bit Hamming code words are being evaluated in parallel. The redundancy is 63 percent. If 16-bit bytes are used, the number of parallel code words is 4 (22 bits each), with a 38 percent redundancy. Even though this scheme is easy to implement using readily available standard-support ICs (discussed below), other codes to be discussed later provide similar fault-masking capability but require lower redundancy.

---

* In fact, assuming b-bit bytes, this scheme can correct any pattern of errors spanning at most b adjacent bits, even if the pattern transcends a byte boundary. Such a pattern is known as a b-bit burst error.

If a Hamming code is employed purely for masking purposes (that is, there is no error notification if the error is correctable), deterioration of the hardware may be present but unknown to the system maintainer. Furthermore, it is desirable to be able to test the encoding/decoding hardware. Thus, most implementations of Hamming-coded memory systems include the ability to write noncode words and to read memory words without the correction being performed. This provision aids in the diagnosis of memory problems.

Reliability and performance modeling of Hamming (and other) SEC codes is deferred to Chapter 5, where the topic is covered in depth.

A great many commercial computers, over a large range of sizes and performance, use Hamming SEC codes for main memory. Among these are several models of the IBM 360/370 series, the PDP-11/60 (as an option), the VAX-11/780 and VAX-11/750, some models of the PDP-10 and DECsystem 20, the Univac 1100/60, the Xerox Alto, and the Bell ESS-1. In addition, many manufacturers of plug-compatible aftermarket memories offer SEC add-on memory for various computers. Hamming SEC codes see usage in other areas of computer design, particularly buses. The IBM STRETCH, for example, used SEC/DED codes on both its memory and processor-memory bus, with encoding/decoding performed on the processor end of the bus. Finally, several semiconductor manufacturers are now supplying LSI support chips for SEC code memories. Among these are the Advanced Micro Devices Am2960 and AmZ8160, the Motorola MC68540, and the Fujitsu MB1412A. Most of these use modified Hamming SEC/DED codes. The MB1412A, for example, is an 8-bit (data) slice that can also be stacked for data words of 2, 4, or 8 bytes. The Am2960 and AmZ8160 are 16 bits wide but can be used for data words of 2, 4, or 8 bytes. The MC68540 is a 16-bit wide unit to be used for data words of 1, 2, or 4 bytes and also detects the all-0s and all-1s failure mode.

Other Error-Correction Codes

Although Hamming SEC/DED codes are the most commonly used codes in computers, there are several others, many of which are effective against particular classes of errors. For example, Tang and Chien [1969] (see Appendix A) discuss classes of cyclic codes for correcting single errors, burst errors, multiple independent errors, and multiple-character (i.e., byte) errors. This section briefly presents a few other codes as an indication of the abundant possibilities that codes offer.

Burst-error-correction codes are uniquely suited to some applications in digital systems. A b-bit burst error is an error pattern that spans b bits in a word. Another form of multiple error is a b-adjacent error, in which the errors occur within specific b-bit boundaries, such as byte boundaries. b-adjacent error correction is particularly useful in designs organized as several parallel byte-wide modules, as in Figure 3-59. In such designs, a single failure can affect an entire block of signal lines. In a memory of $(h \times b)$-bit words organized as h b-bit-wide memory chips, for example, a failure of the addressing logic in one chip would cause the simultaneous failure of b adjacent bits. The interlaced multiple Hamming code of the previous subsection can correct b-adjacent errors. Other codes provide similar protection with less redundancy, such as those formed from binary-coded characters instead of individual bits. Thus, for characters of b bits, there are 2^b possible characters. The PCM elements are b-bit characters instead of 0s and 1s and the parity-check summations are performed over the characters in the code word, modulo-2^b. Thus, the error detection/correction characteristics are in terms of b-bit characters, and the codes are effective against b-adjacent errors. Since b-adjacent errors are a subset of b-bit burst errors, burst error codes are also effective. Examples of this class of codes are the Reed-Solomon cyclic codes [Peterson and Weldon, 1972; Tang and Chien, 1969]. Also, codes specifically for b-adjacent errors can be derived from burst error

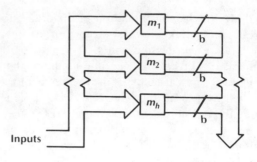

Figure 3–59. Circuit design of parallel byte-wide modules.

codes. In addition to the general references cited earlier, other papers on b-adjacent error correction are Bossen [1970], Reddy [1978], Srinivasan [1971b], Bhatt and Kinney [1978], Hong and Patel [1972], Fujiwara and Kawakami [1977], Carter and Wadia [1980], and Kaneda and Fujiwara [1980].

Unidirectional errors are a common hazard in digital systems. In this type of error, the signal lines in error have all made the same transition, that is, 0-to-1 or 1-to-0, but not both. These errors may or may not be adjacent. On an open collector bus, for example, a gating circuit failed in the on state can cause multiple signals to be gated onto the bus. The signal lines affected will carry the wire-or of the desired and spurious signals, resulting in unidirectional 0-to-1 errors. Other possible causes of unidirectional failures are power failures, shorts, and loss of charge in memory cells. The all-0s and all-1s failure modes mentioned previously are a case of multiple adjacent unidirectional failures. If multiple unidirectional errors are likely to occur in an application requiring an error-correcting code, the best code to use is one that at least detects such failures. Pradhan [1980] has developed a class of separable random-error-correcting codes that also detect any number of unidirectional errors.

When k data bits are needed, there is often no (n, k) code with the desired properties. Thus, many of the codes used instead are shortened versions, such as an (n, k') code shortened to an $(n - i, k' - i)$ code, where $k' = k + i$. This can be accomplished by assuming that i of the data bits are always 0. The resultant PCM is that of the (n, k') code, with the i columns corresponding to the always-0 data bits deleted. Often the columns to be deleted can be chosen to minimize the decoder complexity. Most implementations of Hamming codes are examples of shortened codes. Consider a (21,16) Hamming SEC code. According to the criteria for Hamming codes, the 5 check bits will provide SEC protection for up to 26 data bits. Thus, any (21,16) Hamming code is actually a shortened (31,26) Hamming code.

Hsiao, Bossen, and Chien [1970] state that usually, the less redundancy a code has relative to its error-correction ability, the greater are the complexity, delay, and cost of the decoder. From this principle they derive a class of codes in which a systematic addition of redundancy adds error-correction ability. In particular, their orthogonal Latin square codes are $(m^2 + 2tm, m^2)$ codes that can correct any t errors ($t \leqslant (m + 1)/2$). Thus, the code length grows linearly with t for a given data length. These codes are decodable quickly in parallel using simple majority logic-decoding [Peterson and Weldon, 1972; Tang and Chien, 1969]. The parity-check matrices are easy to construct. The high redundancies result in parity-check matrices with few 1s, resulting in simple (minimal) decoding circuitry. Finally, the systematic nature of the matrix allows modular additions to the decoder for increased error-correction ability. Needed for each bit are t modules, each containing 2 m-bit parity trees, and a $(2t + 1)$-bit majority voter. Figure 3-60 shows the PCMs and one of the bit-correction slices for the (15,9) and (21,9) single- and double-error-correcting Latin square codes. For 9 data bits, double-error correction is the maximum attainable with this class of codes.

Product codes are the result of the simultaneous application of two codes in a particular fashion. (Tang and Chien [1969] refer to these codes as N-dimensional codes; see Appendix A.) Figure 3-61 illustrates the concept. If the two codes used have minimum distance d_1 and d_2, the product code formed by them has weight $d_1 d_2$. This concept can be extended to N dimensions (N codes applied simultaneously). One product code, often used on tapes and other serial devices, is the result of using single-bit parity along both the horizontal and vertical axes. Because parity is a distance-2 code, the result is a distance-4 code. In practice, a single error produces a parity error detected by both vertical and horizontal parity. The intersection of these two parity errors points to the bit in error (see Figure 3-62). Furthermore, it can be seen that any double error is detectable. This code is applicable to random-access memories as well as to serial applications, and can result in less redundancy than a comparable Hamming SEC/DED code. The section on Single-Error-Correcting Memory Models in Chapter 5 examines the use of the code in detail and compares its reliability, cost, and performance with the Hamming SEC/DED code.

AN arithmetic error-detection codes were discussed earlier. With a sufficiently large modulus A, an AN code is capable of error correction. Table 3-13, from Kautz [1962], lists the check modulus, maximum data length, and code word length for a number of possible single-error-correcting AN codes. In practice, these codes are decoded like the error-detection AN codes: division by the check modulus. If the remainder of the division (the residue) is 0, there is no error. A single-bit error in the rth bit position results in a residue of ($\pm 2^r$ modulo A). Kautz suggests that the correction be performed by table lookup using the residue. Because none of the AN codes of Table 3-13 are low-cost check moduli (see the previous section on Arithmetic Codes), the division operation to obtain the residue is complex. Rao [1972] presents a modification of AN codes that allows for more efficient decoding. There are other arithmetic error-correcting codes. Error correction using residue-number-system (RNS) codes is the subject of several papers [Watson

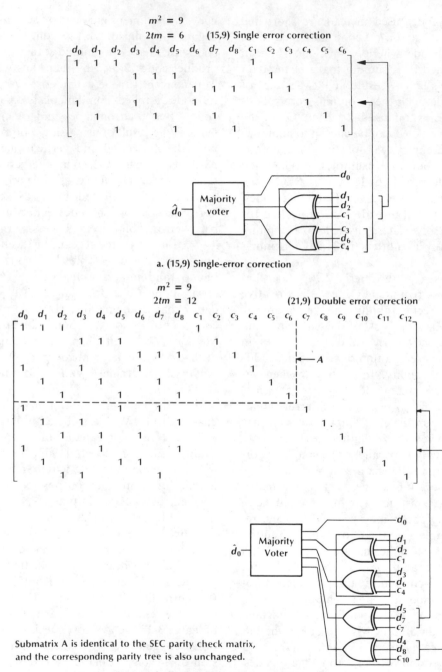

Figure 3–60. Latin square code parity-check matrix with one bit-slice of decoder for nine data bits. Decoding is performed by a majority vote among the received value of a data bit and two values calculated for it from the other received bits. a.) Single-error correction. b.) Double-error correction.

$$\begin{bmatrix} \text{Data bits} & \begin{array}{c} \text{Row} \\ \text{check} \\ \text{bits} \end{array} \\ \hline \begin{array}{c} \text{Column check} \\ \text{bits} \end{array} & \begin{array}{c} \text{Checks on} \\ \text{check bits} \end{array} \end{bmatrix}$$

Figure 3–61. Product code resulting from combination of two linear codes. The check bits in the lower right-hand corner may be formed either as row checks on the column check bits or vice versa. Either way, they will be consistent.

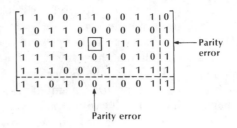

Figure 3–62. Product code using two even-parity codes.

and Hastings, 1966; Mandelbaum, 1972a; Barsi and Maestrini, 1973, 1974]. The paper by Watson and Hastings also describes the design of a microprogrammed general-purpose computer that utilizes RNS coding. A paper by Rao [1970] discusses biresidue error-correcting codes, a class of separable codes. Neumann and Rao [1975] explore the application of arithmetic codes to byte-sliced arithmetic processors. Finally, Rao [1974] has written a textbook on arithmetic error coding.

Table 3–13. Single-error-correcting AN codes.

Check Modulus A	Maximum Data Length k	Code Word Length n
13	2	6
19	4	9
23	6	11
29	9	14
37	12	18
47	17	23
53	20	26
59	23	29
61	24	30
67	26	33
71	28	35
79	32	39
83	34	41
101	42	50
103	43	51

Source: Kautz [1962]

Reliability models for a code depend upon the frequency and types of errors that occur, as well as on the properties of the code. Thus, no general model can be presented here. However, a model is given for an (n, k) t-random-error correcting code, when single errors occur randomly (in random locations, and not in bursts). The reliability of a single code word, given bit reliability R_b, is:

$$R_{word} = \sum_{i=0}^{t} {}_nC_i R_b^{n-i}(1 - R_b)^i$$

More detailed modeling is the subject of Chapter 5.

Masking Logic

Discussion of the two previous masking techniques did not include fault masking at the gate level of digital design. NMR with voting is used almost exclusively for modules or for functional partitions of designs. Coding is normally applied when some regular strucure is present, as in memories or buses. Thus, in both NMR and coding applications a single restoring organ (voter, decoder/corrector) normally protects a set of hardware that is much more complex and error prone than the restoring organ itself. In fact, the increased regularity of control logic obtained through the use of PLAs and microcode techniques means that error-coding techniques can have an important impact on system reliability. However, some random logic always remains that cannot be protected through the straightforward application of error codes.

This section discusses techniques other than module replication that have been devised for random logic. These techniques perform restoration at the gate level or, for sequential machines, at the state level, usually with a massive use of redundant gates. Because of their high cost, few of the techniques have seen actual use. The discussion is divided into two parts: the first concerns gate-level masking; the second deals with the application of error codes to the states of finite-state machines.

Interwoven Logic

Several techniques have been proposed for gate-level fault masking. All employ redundant inputs to each gate. Among these are von Neumann's original work on circuits with interspersed restoring organs, quadded logic [Tryon, 1962; Jensen, 1963], and radial logic [Klaschka, 1969]. Pierce [1965] combined these variant schemes into a general theory of what he termed interwoven logic. Some of the basic precepts of interwoven logic are briefly presented here, based largely upon Pierce [1965]. Armstrong [1961] proposed an entirely different technique for fault-tolerant combinational logic, presented in the next section.

Faults in logic circuitry are considered to be limited to stuck-at-α (where $\alpha = 0, 1$) faults on gate outputs, gate inputs, or input lines to the network. The effect on the logic depends on the value of the fault and the type of gate whose inputs are affected. Consider a NAND gate. If one of its inputs is stuck-at-0, its output is forced to be 1 regardless of the gate's other inputs. On the other hand, a stuck-at-1 input does not force the output to 0 unless the other inputs are also 1. Thus, two types of faults exist; critical faults, which by themselves force a certain gate output, and subcritical faults, which alone will not cause a gate output error. Table 3-14 lists some com-

Table 3–14. Critical and subcritical input faults for some common logic gates.

Gate Type	Critical Faults	Subcritical Faults
AND	$1 \to 0$	$0 \to 1$
OR	$0 \to 1$	$1 \to 0$
NOT	$0 \to 1, 1 \to 0$	None
NAND	$1 \to 0$	$0 \to 1$
Majority	None	$0 \to 1, 1 \to 0$

mon gates and their critical and subcritical input faults. In a network of AND gates a critical fault is propagated through the network: a critical input fault on a gate in one layer forces an output error that is critical to the subsequent layers of AND gates. If, however, the network is composed of alternating layers of AND and OR gates, a critical fault may be stopped within two layers: a critical input fault to one layer results in an output error that is a subcritical input fault in the following layer. Similarly, an all-NAND (or all-NOR) gate network may stop a critical fault within two layers. Finally, majority-logic faults may be stopped after only one layer because there are no possible critical faults.

Interwoven logic makes use of the properties of subcritical and critical faults by assuring that the effects of up to t faults in any layer are masked by subsequent layers; t is design-dependent, and the circuit so designed is called t-fault tolerant. Fault tolerance is accomplished by using redundant gates with redundant inputs. The interconnections between logic layers are *interwoven* so that critical faults at one stage are masked out in subsequent stages, through the mixing of faulty and good replicated signals. Figure 3-63 illustrates this masking action and a necessary condition: the interweaving pattern must vary from layer to layer. Without this variation, the fault will propagate.*

---

* The inputs to the interwoven logic circuit must also be independently replicated if the circuit is to tolerate input faults.

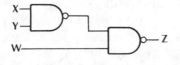

a.   Nonredundant circuit

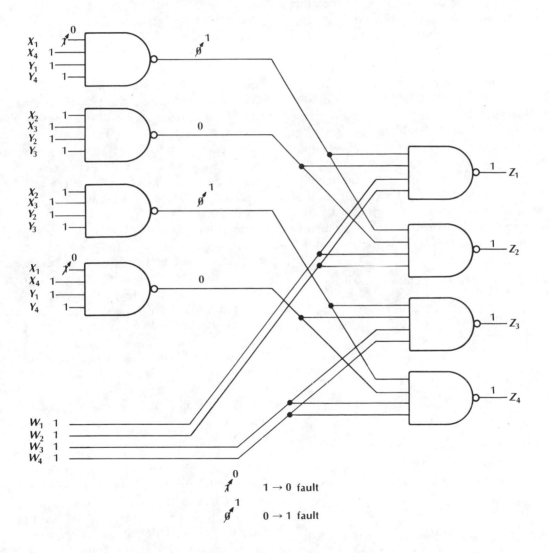

b. Fault-tolerent interwoven circuit

Figure 3–63.   Fault tolerance via interwoven logic.

Using the principles of critical and subcritical faults, interweaving, and weave-pattern variation, Pierce developed a general theory of implementing interwoven logic. To correct any t critical errors, the redundancy in gates must be $R = (t + 1)^2 = B^2$, and each gate must have B times the inputs needed for the corresponding gate in the nonredundant realization. At least three different interweaving patterns are needed if the circuit has feedback (such as flip-flops or loops). A pattern consists of B groupings. If the redundant copies of a gate are numbered from 1 to R, each of the B groupings contains a unique set of B different numbers; there are no overlaps between groups. Finally, each group in a pattern must have elements drawn from at least B different groups in any of the other patterns, as Table · 3-15 shows for $t = 1, 2,$ and 3. In the table, a grouping, such as (a, b, c) for $t = 2$, implies that the output from a gate, a, is connected to an input on each of the gates a, b, and c in the next layer; the same applies for the outputs of gates b

Table 3–15. Groupings (g_i) for interweaving patterns for $t = 1, 2,$ and 3.

Single-Fault Tolerant
$t = 1, B = 2, R = 4$

$g_1 = (1, 2)(3, 4)$

$g_2 = (1, 4)(2, 3)$

$g_3 = (1, 3)(2, 4)$

Double-Fault Tolerant
$t = 2, B = 3, R = 9$

$g_1 = (1, 2, 3)(4, 5, 6)(7, 8, 9)$

$g_2 = (1, 4, 7)(2, 5, 8)(3, 6, 9)$

$g_3 = (1, 6, 8)(5, 7, 3)(9, 2, 4)$

Triple-Fault Tolerant
$t = 3, B = 4, R = 16$

$g_1 = (1, 2, 3, 4)(5, 6, 7, 8)(9, 10, 11, 12)(13, 14, 15, 16)$

$g_2 = (1, 5, 9, 13)(2, 6, 10, 14)(3, 7, 11, 15)$
$(4, 8, 12, 16)$

$g_3 = (1, 6, 12, 15)(2, 5, 11, 16)(3, 8, 9, 14)$
$(4, 7, 10, 12)$

Source: Pierce [1965]

and c. In Figure 3-63, the grouping g_2 of the single-fault tolerant groupings was used for the X inputs, while the grouping g_1 was used for the inputs to the second level of gates. A critical 0-to-1 input fault to one layer is masked out by the next layer; thus, the input fault in signal X does not cause an error in output Z. If the same interweaving pattern had been used in both layers, the fault would have been propagated.

The need for a shorthand notation of interwoven logic is demonstrated in Figure 3-63, in which a simple nonredundant two-gate logic function is transformed into a complex tangle of gates and interconnections. Figure 3-64 illustrates the notation to be used. A symbol for replicated gates is formed by using a double line for the gate symbol edge. The term g_i inside the symbol indicates the weaving pattern that is to be used in connecting the replicated gates to the previous layer.

The gate in Figure 3-64 is a gate used in *quadded logic*, where $t = 1, B = 2,$ and $R = 4$; however, the notation can also be generalized to higher redundancy. Quadded logic was first introduced by Tryon [1962] for use with AND, OR, and NOT logic. There are two problems with the use of this family of logic gates if two-level correction is to be assured at all times. First, the AND and OR logic levels must be strictly alternated. Second, because the NOT gate (inverter) has only one input and no subcritical faults, it does not provide any fault masking. Also, when a NOT is placed between AND and OR layers, the effect is to make the two layers it joins identical, since what would normally be a subcritical output fault is inverted into a critical input error. The two difficulties can be overcome in part by rearrangement of the logic function, and in part by the insertion of identity-AND or -OR gates (one leg fixed at 1 and 0, respectively) where appropriate. Figure 3-66b demonstrates this approach with a quadded logic implementation of Figure 3-65b. Requiring alternating AND/OR gate levels is not a problem when NOR [Jensen, 1963] gates or NAND gates are used in implementing quadded

a. Symbol for quadded gate with inputs woven with pattern g_i.

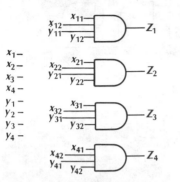

b. Expansion of quadded gate into four physical gates, with inputs x_{jk} and y_{jk}.

jk \ g_i	g_1	g_2	g_3
11	1	1	1
12	2	4	3
21	1	2	2
22	2	3	4
31	3	2	1
32	4	3	3
41	3	1	2
42	4	4	4

c. Table of interweaving patterns g_i, and the relation for each pattern between the inputs to gate $j(x_{jk}$ and $y_{jk})$ and the output gate number (k) of the previous stage.

Figure 3–64. Weaving notation.

logic. Figures 3-65a and 3-66a show NAND and quadded NAND gate realizations of the same circuit. Finally, the principles of two-layer masking also apply to single-layer fault-correcting technologies such as majority gate logic.

Radial logic [Klaschka, 1969] is a variation of interwoven logic that offers single-fault tolerance with a gate redundancy factor of only 2. This is possible if the gates used fail in a nonsymmetric (fail-safe) manner. In particular, for radial logic based on NOR gates, the gates used must be

unlikely to experience 0-to-1 failures at their outputs. In other words, it is assumed that critical input faults cannot occur. If this is the case, the fault is corrected at the next duplicated stage. Klaschka gave RTL implementations of NOR gates that are unlikely to have 0-to-1 output failures.

More recently, Freeman and Metze [1972] proposed a form of interwoven logic called *dotted logic*, derived from the use of dotted outputs of NAND and/or NOR gates (such as utilizing the wire-or that results from connecting the outputs of TTL logic open-collector gates). Although gates are implicit at the dotted connections, the actual gate count as well as the number of interconnections is greatly reduced.

Finally, Pradhan and Reddy [1974a] propose a design method using two-level AND and OR logic that can tolerate subcritical faults both on its inputs and due to internal failures. As in radial logic, gates with asymmetric failure modes are required. In this scheme, the inputs that result in a logical one output are coded in a distance-d code. At most, then, duplication of the inputs is required. Further reductions in complexity can be achieved through the use of don't-care output conditions for some input combinations. The resulting design tolerates up to $(d - 1)$ internal subcritical faults, given a distance-d coded input. Alternatively, a total of t faults (combined internal and external) can be tolerated, where $(2t + 1 \leqslant d)$.

Reliability modeling of interwoven logic can be extremely complex, and no models will be given here. Pierce [1965] developed a complex method of obtaining a lower limit on the reliability. Jensen [1963] developed a cut-set model for quadded logic (Chapter 5 discusses reliability modeling with the use of cut sets). Abraham [1975] developed a combinatorial procedure for modeling interwoven logic, as well as an easily calculable formula for providing a tight lower limit on the network reliability.

In addition to reliability, there is another factor to be considered in the employment of interwoven logic. By the very nature of internal

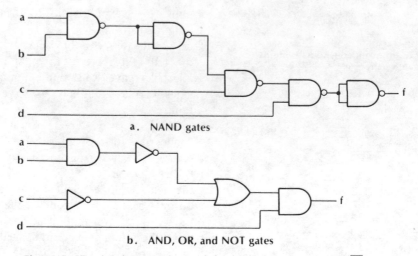

a. NAND gates

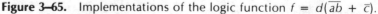

b. AND, OR, and NOT gates

Figure 3–65. Implementations of the logic function $f = d(\overline{ab} + \overline{c})$.

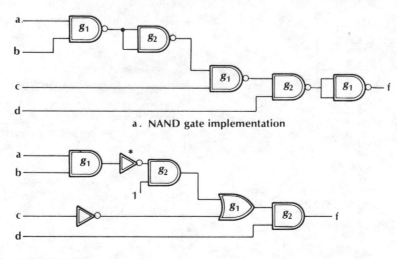

a. NAND gate implementation

b. AND, OR, NOT gates implementation (note the extra inverter, marked by an asterisk).

Figure 3–66. Quadded implementations of the circuit of Figure 3-65.

fault masking, the logic network that results is difficult or impossible to diagnose. When a fault occurs, no notice is given unless the outputs are in error. Even with outputs in error, diagnosis is difficult without probing the internal signals. Tryon [1962] suggested a possible solution: removing the power from some of the redundant gates, thereby forcing their outputs to values that

effectively eliminate them from the network. At the same time, some of the redundant inputs must be neutralized.

Coded State Machines

The interwoven logic techniques of the previous section can be used to implement sequential

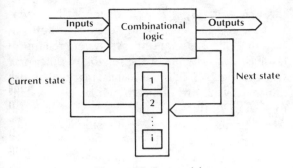

Figure 3–67. Generic design for a sequential circuit. In asynchronous circuits the memory elements are replaced by delays.

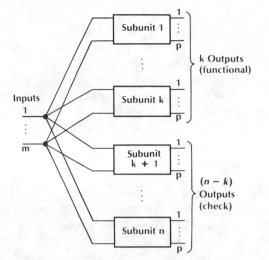

Figure 3–68. Division of logic network into subunits for outputs in k independent sets.

(synchronous or asynchronous) logic. However, there are other techniques that could result in lower redundancy and simpler designs. The basic concept, first proposed by Armstrong [1961], is that the state of the machine, represented by its state variables, can be encoded in an error-correction code. Thus, any fault can be masked if it causes a correctable error in the state of the machine.*

Figure 3-67 shows a generic form for a finite state machine. If input errors are ignored, there are two sources of error in the machine: the combinational logic and the memory elements. Figure 3-68 demonstrates Armstrong's solution to faults in the combinational logic. The logic network is split into k independent units, each devoted to producing a subset of p of the output signals. An additional $(n - k)$ subunits produce independently generated sets of error-code check bits for the k functional outputs. Thus, the net output of this circuit is p parallel (n, k) coded

signals. If $p = 1$ the result is a single set of output signals that forms an (n, k) code word. Conceptually, the check-bit units are not difficult to design, for the check-bit functions can be derived as the XOR of the appropriate output-bit functions.

Combinational logic of the type illustrated in Figure 3-68 is used to provide both coded output signals and coded feedback (next-state) signals for the machine. The decoder/corrector for the state signals is placed between the memory elements and the current state inputs to the combinational logic. In this way, faults in both the combinational logic and the memory elements can be tolerated. In a companion paper to Armstrong's, Ray-Chaudhuri [1961] developed a class of minimally redundant codes tailored to this application.

Armstrong showed that, when coupled with maintenance (faulty component replacement), a state machine implemented in this fashion has a greatly improved reliability over that of the equivalent nonredundant version. He also stated that for some large systems this technique yields a redundancy at least as great as for triplication, but that for others it may be considerably less.

---

* The following discussion primarily concerns synchronous machines. In asynchronous machines, state assignment problems occur because of the possibility of races, hazards, and the like. However, Pradhan and Reddy [1974b] have extended these principles to asynchronous machines, and Pradhan [1978b] described a method of realizing fault-tolerant asynchronous coded-state machines using read-only memories.

The actual redundancy can be determined only by a detailed design.

Others have worked on this concept since Armstrong's paper. Frank and Yau [1966] proposed designing sequential machines using error-code state assignments. Mandelbaum [1972b] suggested a scheme in which, given a sequential machine M, a simpler machine M' is derived into which the states of M can be mapped. M' is operated independently of M, but with the same inputs, and supplies the check bits for the state encoding. Meyer [1971] discussed state assignment and design realization for tolerance of memory-cell faults. Russo [1965] proposed fault-tolerant counters with distance-3 coded states. Reed and Chiang [1970] discussed error-coded state counters and also offered a synthesis procedure for fault-tolerant sequential circuits. Larsen and Reed [1972] presented a synthesis procedure for fault-tolerant sequential machines. Using an analysis based on this procedure, they demonstrated that for a given ability to tolerate faults, replication is more reliable as well as simpler to implement. Conversely, they found that for a fixed complexity (gate count, cost), schemes that use orthogonal (majority-logic decodable) codes are more reliable. Osman and Weiss [1973] developed a technique that can be used to reduce the redundancy in fault-tolerant logic. In Figure 3-68 it can be seen that considerable redundancy is incurred by separate generation of the outputs; their technique allows some of the circuitry to be shared between modules generating the output functions. If this sharing is performed properly the reliability is not affected and there are considerable savings. Osman and Weiss applied this technique to triplication and to parity-check codes.

DYNAMIC REDUNDANCY

Fault-detection techniques provide a means of flagging the potential presence of errors emanating from a digital system. In addition, fault detection offers an increase in system availability through more rapid failure diagnosis. However, because it does not provide tolerance, fault detection alone does not improve system reliability (at least not in terms of the reliability function). On the other hand, fault-masking techniques improve system reliability by allowing a system to operate correctly in the presence of failures. Also, minor amounts of extra redundancy can add the benefits of fault detection (error flagging and rapid diagnosis) to a fault-masking design. Fault masking in turn is limited by its static configuration: a system employing a fault-masking technique cannot heal itself, but only hide its failures. Eventually, the accumulation of failures is large enough to saturate the fault-masking ability, and the entire system fails. In a TMR system, for example, the failure of a second of the three modules causes system failure: even though a good module is still available, the two failed ones outvote it.

Another approach to increased reliability utilizes redundancy in a dynamic way. Dynamic redundancy techniques involve the *reconfiguration* of system components in response to failures. The reconfiguration prevents failures from contributing their effects to the system operation. In many instances reconfiguration amounts to disconnecting the damaged units from the system. If fault masking is used as part of the dynamic redundancy scheme, the removal of failed components may be postponed until enough failures have accumulated to threaten an impending nonmaskable failure.

Reconfiguration is triggered either by internal detection of faults in the damaged subunit or by detection of errors in its output.* Thus, fault-detection techniques (with or without masking) form the basis of dynamic redundancy. A system's chance of a successful reconfiguration is

---

* Reconfiguration can be performed either automatically by the system itself (on-line repair) or manually by operations or maintenance personnel (off-line repair). In the first case, the system experiences a temporary pause before operation continues; in the second, the halt is longer and may require complete reinitialization. Hence, on-line repair improves both reliability and availability, whereas off-line repair usually only increases the availability. The emphasis in this section is upon on-line repair.

greatly dependent on its fault detection ability. Three issues are involved in the employment of fault detection in a reconfigurable system. The first is the confinement of fault effects before unrecoverable damage occurs; the second is fault detection; and the third is correct diagnosis of the failure location, so that the faulty unit— and only the faulty unit—is marked for remedial action (removal and/or replacement). Thus the two fault-detection criteria of coverage and diagnosability (see the earlier section on Fault-Detection Techniques) are important factors in the choice of a detection technique. Detection coverage in particular is commonly used in deriving the reliability formula of a dynamically redundant system. In modeling dynamically redundant systems, coverage is often generalized to mean the probability of a successful reconfiguration; successful fault detection then becomes only one of the factors in determining coverage along with the probabilities of successful error confinement and resource switching.

The following subsections present several dynamic redundancy techniques that utilize a combination of fault detection, fault masking, and reconfiguration. The first subsection discusses methods that use duplication for detection as well as for fault tolerance; the second treats N-modular redundancy-based designs. Duplication and N-modular redundancy-based reconfiguration requires massive amounts of redundancy solely for error detection (and/or correction). Other, less redundant forms of fault detection (correction) can also provide a basis for dynamic redundancy. The more hardware-efficient detection techniques (such as parity, ECC codes, timers) can be used to monitor the health of individual modules. Such detectors can be located either inside or outside the modules they monitor. They can exist either in hardware or software. The subsections on Backup Sparing, Graceful Degradation, and Reconfiguration present reconfiguration techniques that are usually based on the less redundant detection methods. Backup sparing is the provision of spare units that remain unused until an active unit fails. In graceful degradation, the functionality and/or performance is allowed to degrade as parts of the system fail and are removed without replacement. The subsection on reconfiguration presents miscellaneous dynamic redundancy techniques that do not fit into the categories provided by the other sections.

The effect of transient errors on the various reconfiguration techniques is not discussed below. If there is no specific mechanism for determining that an error is due to a transient, perfectly good modules may be switched out when a transient occurs. Fortunately, there exists a technique which is common to most of the reconfiguration methods discussed below. This technique, called retry, returns the module initially diagnosed as failed to the system for another chance. Detection of an error immediately after the module is returned to service is a good indication that the module is in fact defective.

The final subsection on dynamic redundancy discusses recovery, the actions taken after reconfiguration to erase failure effects and restore the state of the system and the process(es) it was executing before the failure. Recovery is usually performed by special software, but often requires some support by hardware mechanisms.

Reconfigurable Duplication

Fault detection by duplication and comparison was discussed earlier in this chapter. In a static configuration, a duplicated system does not provide fault tolerance, for only disagreement can be determined in the presence of a fault. Two enhancements to the duplicated system can, however, produce fault tolerance.* The first enhancement needed is the ability to determine which of the two modules is faulty if a disagreement is detected. The second is the ability to

---

*In this discussion duplication is considered only as the basis for fault detection. This form of duplication should not be confused with "duplication," in which an extra copy is presented as a standby spare, and is not used for fault detection by comparison. The latter form is discussed in subsequent subsections.

disconnect the faulty module and at the same time disable the comparison element. Thus, upon fault detection (mismatch), diagnosis determines the faulty copy, which is then removed from service. The resulting simplex system continues to function.

Figure 3-69 illustrates the concept of reconfigurable duplication. In the figure, only one of the duplicated units (the active unit) is connected to the system outputs. The other (standby) unit is functioning in parallel with the active unit but is not connected to the outputs. In practice, the duplicate modules are often resident on the same bus (or buses), and the switching function is performed by the bus interface unit in each module.

When a fault is detected by a mismatch, there are several means of determining the faulty copy and switching it out. Four methods are discussed here. The first is to run a diagnostic program. In the Bell ESS-2 (Chapter 12), for example, the active processor runs a self-diagnostic program.

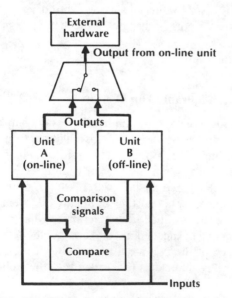

Figure 3–69. Reconfigurable duplication. A detected mismatch during comparison of characteristic signals triggers reconfiguration.

If the diagnostic is failed, control is passed to the standby processor. The faulty processor is taken off line to run maintenance programs that facilitate its rapid repair. Figure 3-70 shows a block diagram of the ESS-2 organization.

Another means of identifying the faulty copy is to include self-checking capabilities in each module. The joint occurrence of an internally detected fault and a mismatch provides immediate determination of the faulty copy. The use of comparison in addition to self-checking provides more coverage than self-checking alone. The UDET 7116 telephone switching system control [Morganti, Coppadoro, and Ceru, 1978], for example, uses a set of internal hardware checkers (such as parity or timers) to automatically switch a faulty CPU out of service. The primary detection mechanism in the UDET 7116, however, is duplication. When a mismatch occurs with no internal alarm indication, both CPUs are taken off line and forced to run diagnostics. The first to successfully complete its self-diagnosis becomes the active CPU. The Bell ESS-1, -1A, and -2 processors also use internal self-checking in conjunction with duplication. Finally, the internal detection mechanisms can also be used in conjunction with diagnostic software.

A third approach to determining the faulty processor is to use a watchdog timer. In the Bell ESS-2, for example, the active processor must reset a timer periodically. If it fails to do so, the timer automatically invokes a change of control to the standby processor. Thus, the timer protects the system when the active processor becomes stuck while attempting to perform the diagnostic after a mismatch has occurred. Timers are used in another fashion in the Bell ESS-1A. When the current configuration does not function, a set of timers is used to force a sequence of reconfigurations until a working configuration is found.

The last method of configuration selection is to use an outside arbiter to control the configuration. In the COMTRAC railroad traffic control

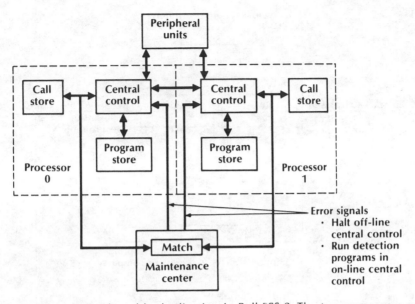

Figure 3–70. Reconfigurable duplication in Bell ESS-2. The two processors run synchronously; comparison of the call store input registers is performed constantly.

computer [Ihara et al., 1978], a mismatch forces both processors to run identical test programs. The test program exercises the entire processor in the course of calculating a single constant. If a failure is present, there is a high probability that the calculation will result in a wrong answer. The results from the two processors are compared with a stored constant by a special controller (called the Dual System Controller, or DSC), as shown in Figure 3-71a. Based on the results of the test, the DSC performs the proper configuration action. Designers at Boeing Aerospace used a similar concept in a duplication-based design of a prototype aerospace computer [Wachter, 1975]. In the Boeing design, the reconfiguration control logic can be accessed only by a "good" machine, that is, one that can successfully construct two levels of key words. The key construction process is designed to make successful key construction by a faulty processor unlikely.

The problems of synchronization with repli-cated processes has been discussed previously (see the subsections on Duplication and N-Modular Redundancy with Voting). Three examples of different synchronization methods that can be applied to reconfigurable duplication systems are presented here. In the first, the duplicated modules perform in lockstep to a common clock, synchronized at the microcycle level. This method is used on the Bell ESS-1, -1A, and -2 processors, as well as the UDET 7116. Comparisons in these telephone-switching control processors are performed at the end of each clock period.

The AXE telephone switching control [Ossfeldt and Jonsson, 1980] uses a different method of synchronization. Each of its two processors is formed of asynchronous functional units (e.g., microinstruction generator, ALU) that communicate via an internal bus (CPB), as shown in Figure 3-72. One of these units is the update and match unit (UPM), which performs the detection function. On most microinstructions, data from

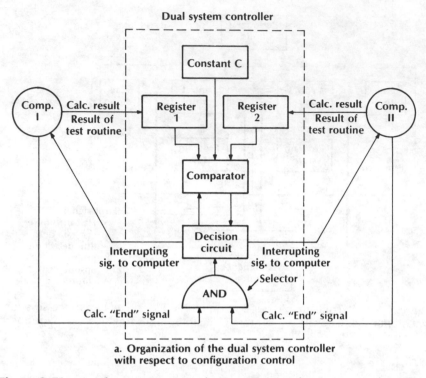

Dual system controller

a. Organization of the dual system controller
with respect to configuration control

Figure 3–71. Synchronization, matching, and reconfiguration in the COM-TRAC computer. Synchronization and matching are performed at the task level, [Ihara et al., 1978]. (© IEEE 1978.)

the active processor CPB is input to a buffer in the standby processor's UPM. The data are held in the buffer to await comparison with the data on the standby processor's CPB. Synchronization of the two processors is performed by the UPMs, which keep a count of the bus cycles. The UPM on the faster side periodically brings its processor back into synchronization by simulating a busy signal on the control lines of its own CPB.

A third method of synchronization is used by the COMTRAC system. Synchronization is maintained at the program task level. The Dual System Controller (DSC) is used to ensure that both processors are performing the same calculations. When both computers have finished the calculation, the DSC compares the two results. If a mismatch occurs, the DSC then invokes the

diagnosis mode discussed earlier. Figure 3-71b illustrates the procedure.

A simple reliability model for a reconfigurable duplication system with individual module reliability R_m is:

$$R_{sys} = (R_m^2 + CR_m(1 - R_m))R_k \qquad (4)$$

In Equation 4, R_k is the reliability of the control, switching, and matching circuitry. C is the coverage factor, and represents the combined probability of successful fault detection and reconfiguration. A system with reconfigurable duplication can achieve increased reliability and availability if a faulty module can be repaired while the rest of the system remains on line. In such a case the model of Equation 4 is pessimistic. The more complex modeling techniques of Chapter 5

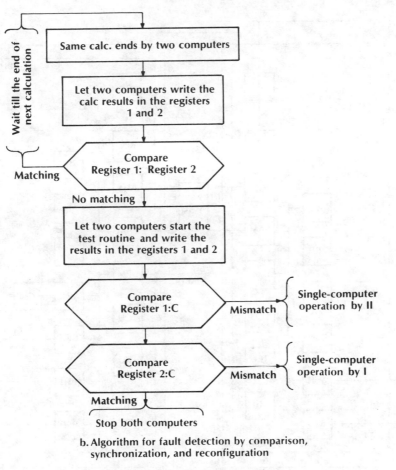

b. Algorithm for fault detection by comparison,
synchronization, and reconfiguration

Figure 3-71—*Continued*

(such as Markov modeling) are needed to properly evaluate a system with repair.

Reconfigurable NMR

One of the drawbacks of N-modular redundancy with voting (NMR) is that fault masking ability deteriorates as more copies fail. The faulty modules eventually outvote the good modules. However, an NMR system could continue to function if the known bad modules could be discounted in the vote. Two methods of reconfiguration based on NMR realize this potential. The first, hybrid redundancy, replaces failed modules with previously unused spares. The second is to modify the voting process dynamically as the system deteriorates. The latter method actually encompasses a variety of techniques, which can be loosely classified under the term adaptive voting. Both hybrid redundancy and adaptive voting depend upon detection of disagreements and the ability to determine the identity of the module(s) not agreeing with the majority.

Hybrid Redundancy

Hybrid redundancy obtains its name from the fact that it is the wedding of two redundancy

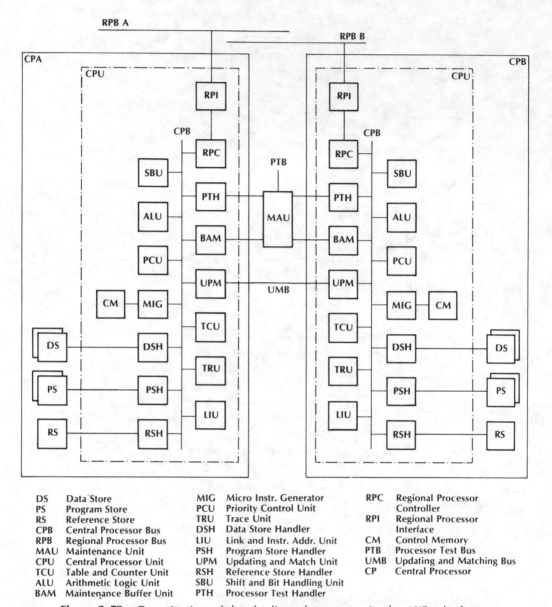

Figure 3–72. Organization of the duplicated processor in the AXE telephone-switching control processor. (© 1980 IEEE.)

DS	Data Store	MIG	Micro Instr. Generator	RPC	Regional Processor
PS	Program Store	PCU	Priority Control Unit		Controller
RS	Reference Store	TRU	Trace Unit	RPI	Regional Processor
CPB	Central Processor Bus	DSH	Data Store Handler		Interface
RPB	Regional Processor Bus	LIU	Link and Instr. Addr. Unit	CM	Control Memory
MAU	Maintenance Unit	PSH	Program Store Handler	PTB	Processor Test Bus
CPU	Central Processor Unit	UPM	Updating and Match Unit	UMB	Updating and Matching Bus
TCU	Table and Counter Unit	RSH	Reference Store Handler	CP	Central Processor
ALU	Arithmetic Logic Unit	SBU	Shift and Bit Handling Unit		
BAM	Maintenance Buffer Unit	PTH	Processor Test Handler		

techniques: N-modular redundancy with voting (discussed earlier) and backup sparing (discussed below). Figure 3-73 illustrates the basic concept. A "core" of N identical modules is in use at any one time, with their outputs voted upon to produce the system output. When a disagreement is detected, the module or modules in the minority are considered to be failed and are replaced by the equivalent number of spare modules. Initially the system contains a total of $(N + S)$ modules. As long as there are never more than $t = \lfloor N/2 \rfloor$ failed modules in the core before reconfiguration can take place, the system can tolerate the failure of $P = (t + S)$ of its

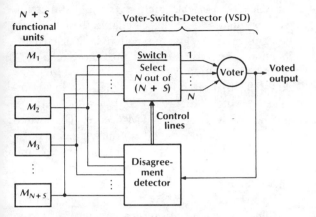

Figure 3–73. Basic organization of a hybrid-redundant system.

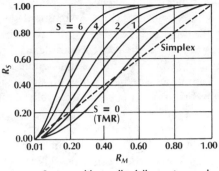

a. System with standby failure rate equal to on-line failure rate

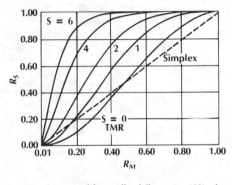

b. System with standby failure rate 10% of on-line failure rate.

Figure 3–74. Plots of hybrid TMR system reliability (R_s) vs. individual module reliability (R_m). S is the number of spares. (© 1970 IEEE.)

modules. Thus, assuming the reliability of the modules on standby is the same as for those on-line, the system reliability is:

$$R_{sys} = R_{vsd} \sum_{i=O}^{P} {}_{n+s}C_i \, R_m^{(N+S-i)} (1 - R_m)^i . \quad (5)$$

R_m is the individual module reliability, and R_{vsd} is the reliability of the unit comprised of the voter, switch, and disagreement detector (VSD unit). Equation 5 is a simple model. It assumes that, as long as there are spares remaining, reconfiguration occurs before there are enough failed modules in the core to outvote the good modules. The model also does not take compensating failures into acccount. One final factor not considered is that the standby units may be unpowered until they are switched in. A module in an unpowered state will probably have a lower failure rate; if so, Equation 5 will provide a pessimistic estimation of the system reliability.

Mathur and Avizienis [1970] derived a reliability model for hybrid redundant systems that takes the standby failure rates into account. They then used the model to examine the trade-offs between N, S, and R_m. The VSD unit is assumed to be perfect ($R_{vsd} = 1$). Figure 3-74 demonstrates the use of the model for a hybrid TMR system with up to six spare modules. In Figure 3-74a, the standby failure rate is assumed equal to the active state failure rate, with the

result that a system with one spare is more reliable than a simplex system if $R_m > 0.23$. Figure 3-74b assumes that the standby failure rate is only 10 percent of the active failure rate. The crossover point has shifted, and a system with one spare is more reliable than the simplex system if $R_m > 0.17$. Another result of the model is that for a system with one spare, a TMR system ($N = 3$) is more reliable than an NMR system ($N > 3$) if $R_m < 0.55$. For a system with two spares, a TMR system is better than an NMR system if $R_m < 0.62$.

Examination of Equation 5 shows that hybrid system reliability is greatly dependent on the switch complexity. If every spare can be connected with every voter (total assignment), it can be seen that as the core size (N) and the number of spares (S) grow, the switch complexity grows even more rapidly. Eventually, the switch unreliability dominates the reliability of the system, and the hybrid system becomes less reliable than a simplex system. Siewiorek and McCluskey [1973a] demonstrated that total assignment is not necessary. Assuming a perfect switch, the same reliability is achieved even if only ($\lceil N/2 \rceil + 1$) of the voter inputs can be connected to every spare module. (Note that for $N = 3$, this is the same as total assignment.) Because no switch can in

practice be perfect, such a partial connection strategy tends to be more reliable than the total assignment strategy; the switch for partial connection is less complex and thus more reliable.

In a companion paper, Siewiorek and McCluskey [1973b] presented a design for a low-complexity switch. Figure 3-75 shows the iterative cell array switch for a TMR core. The switch works in the following fashion. A clock pulse causes the outputs of the modules to appear, and the outputs of the N core modules are gated to the voter inputs. The same clock pulse, suitably delayed in accordance with the VSD unit propagation delays, loads disagreement signals into the

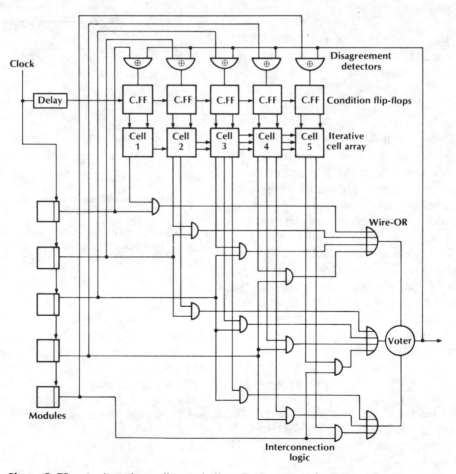

Figure 3-75. An iterative cell switch for a TMR core and two standby spares.

condition flip-flops. Based on the condition of its corresponding module (agree/disagree with the voted output) and the condition of the iterative cells to its left (0, 1, 2, or [3 or more] good modules present), each iterative cell decides whether to connect its module to the voter, and if so, to which voter input. Table 3-16 contains the cell state and output tables for the iterative cells used in the design of Figure 3-75.

One of the problems with an iterative cell switch of the form of Figure 3-75 is the propagation delay through the chain of iterative cells, particularly for large N and S. Siewiorek and McCluskey proposed three different solutions to the problem: carry bypass, carry lookahead, and redesign of the cell. The first two solutions are similar to those found in fast adders. The last

solution, cell redesign, was shown to be the fastest for $(N + S) < 12$, while the carry bypass method was shown to be the least complex.

Finally, the iterative cell switch (or any other hybrid redundancy switch) was shown to be simpler if a threshold voter with $(N + S)$ inputs is used. The threshold is set at $((N + 1)/2)$, and the switching function is realized merely by using AND gates to connect modules to the voter inputs.

Siewiorek and McCluskey [1973b] modeled the cost and complexity of several different approaches to designing switches for hybrid redundancy, and found the iterative cell switch to be generally superior. Ingle and Siewiorek [1973b, 1976] proposed reliability models for various switch designs. Assuming that switch complexity grows linearly with N and S (the iterative cell method approaches this growth), they found that there is a number of spares for which reliability is maximized, and beyond which the reliability decreases. In addition, they found that maximum reliability for most hybrid TMR systems is reached with one or two spares. Finally, it was found that hybrid TMR systems may have lower mission times than simple TMR systems. Ogus [1973, 1974] obtained similar results in another analysis of iterative cell switch reliability.*

Table 3-16. Cell state and output tables for the iterative cell switch network of Figure 3-75.

Current State	C_i	
(*number of previous* *cells functional*)	*Failed* 0	*Functional* 1
A (zero)	A	B
B (one)	B	C
C (two)	C	D
D (three +)	D	D

Next State

(a) Cell state table

	C_i	
Current State	*Failed* 0	*Functional* 1
A (zero)	000	100
B (one)	000	010
C (two)	000	001
D (three +)	000	000

$$V_1^i \, V_2^i \, V_3^i$$

V_j^i: Connect module i to voter input j.

(b) Output table

Source: Siewiorek and McCluskey [1973b].

Adaptive Voting

Adaptive voting is a technique in which, for modules i, the voter inputs n_i are weighted by the factors a_i. In the pure form of adaptive voting the decision is based on the sum $\sum a_i n_i$, using a threshold detector. The a_i are modified over time by the accumulated history of disagreements and fault detection. In practical digital systems the a_i are usually zero or one, and the voting may or may not be performed by a threshold voter.

---

* A derivation of complexity and reliability models for hybrid redundancy is presented in Chapter 5.

Thus, hybrid redundancy can be considered a form of adaptive voting, with the a_i determined by the switch. Discussed here are two other proposed forms of adaptive voting techniques: NMR/simplex and self-purging redundancy.

In NMR/simplex systems [Mathur, 1971a; Mathur and DeSousa, 1975], the initial configuration is conventional NMR. When one module fails, it and one other module are removed from the system, leaving an $(N - 2)$ modular redundancy system. The removal of two modules preserves the property that all votes are unambiguous; no tie is possible. Eventually, the system deteriorates to a simplex system. C.vmp (see Chapter 7) or any other TMR system capable of independent (nonvoting) mode operation has the potential of being a TMR/simplex system with only minor modifications. Upon detection of a failure, a TMR/simplex version of C.vmp would go into independent mode operation, with the on-line processor selected from the two remaining processors. The NMR/simplex concept can be extended to allow the intermediate step of duplicate operation (detection with a standby spare) before the final step of simplex operation is necessary.

Figure 3-76 illustrates self-purging redundancy [Losq, 1976].* A comparison of Figures 3-75 and 3-76 shows a similarity between self-purging redundancy and hybrid redundancy implemented with an iterative cell switch. This is particularly true if the hybrid redundant design incorporates the threshold voter simplifications mentioned previously. In self-purging redundancy, all P modules are initially connected to the voter, and are removed only when they disagree with the voted output. The delayed clock line avoids spurious resets caused by delay in the voter. Module retry (in case of transient errors) and

---

* The switching circuitry in Figure 3-76 is altered from Losq's design by the addition of the delayed clock line and the attached AND gates. This is necessary to avoid spurious flipflop resets due to the propagation delay of the voter. The AND gates can be eliminated if clocked SR flipflops are used.

system initialization are accomplished via the retry line. For hybrid redundancy with a TMR core, the iterative cell switch for each module requires 8 gates and a flip-flop, including the AND gate for gating the module output to the voter input. (This is for a threshold voter only. The majority voter iterative cell switch requires even more gates.) The self-purging switch, on the other hand, requires only 3 gates and a flipflop for each module, regardless of the number of redundant modules in the system. The decreased complexity of the self-purging redundancy switch is one reason for its being more reliable than the hybrid redundancy switch. The other factor is that a single failure in the self-purging redundancy switch element attached to one module will not affect the other switch elements and modules. In contrast, a failure in an iterative cell may cause an error that will propagate to other switch cells via the carry lines.

The threshold for a P-module self-purging system voter can be as low as 1 if 0-to-1 errors cannot occur, and as high as $(P - 1)$ if 1-to-0 failures are impossible. If 0-to-1 errors do occur, the threshold must be higher than 1. This is particularly true if stuck-at-1 failures can occur in a switch output. Losq found that in general, the optimum threshold for a self-purging system is equivalent to half the number of remaining good modules. The variable threshold can be obtained by using a threshold voter with P weight-2 inputs and P weight-1 inputs (or a threshold voter with $3P$ weight-1 inputs). The weights of the inputs are the weights used when summing inputs to determine whether the threshold is reached (weighted sum); thus, a weight-2 input counts twice as much as a weight-1 input. The Q' output of each condition flipflop, shown unconnected in Figure 3-76b, is connected to a weight-1 input; the gated module output is connected to a weight-2 input (or two weight-1 inputs).

After deriving an accurate and simple reliability model for self-purging redundancy, Losq demonstrated that if the standby failure rate is

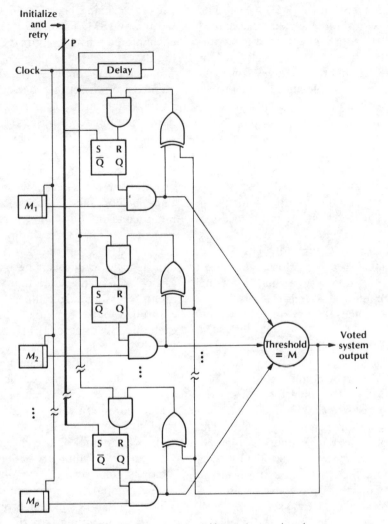

Figure 3–76.   System using self-purging redundancy.

equal to the active failure rate, the self-purging design is potentially more reliable than the equivalent hybrid redundant design. Unfortunately, threshold gates are analog circuit elements; large threshold gates are not available as standard integrated circuits. As a result, either threshold voters must be implemented from discrete components or from standard logic gates and they become prohibitively complex for even moderate numbers of inputs. Though not consid-

ered in the analysis above, this practical limitation on threshold voters must be taken into account when considering the use of self-purging redundancy or any other technique that includes a threshold voter. For a large number (P) of redundant modules, a self-purging system requires a complex (thus, less reliable) and expensive threshold voter. In a hybrid system with the same number of redundant modules, however, the threshold voter complexity is limited because it has only N inputs, not the $(N + S) = P$ inputs required for the self-purging system; the hybrid system may thus be more reliable and less complex than the self-purging system. Table 3-17, in the section on Reconfiguration, gives some examples of the relative complexities of the restoring organs for hybrid and self-purging redundancies.

Four examples of actual systems employing reconfigurable N-modular redundancy techniques are the JPL STAR, the Space Shuttle computer, FTMP, and SIFT. All except the Space Shuttle computer are described in detail in later chapters. The test and repair processor (TARP) in the JPL STAR spacecraft computer (Chapter 14) is hybrid redundant. The TARP must be ultrareliable, because it forms the "hard core"—the part of the system that must be functioning to enable the system to be reconfigured. The TARP design uses hybrid TMR with a threshold voter.

The Space Shuttle computer [Sklaroff, 1976; AWST, 1981] uses four of its five computers as a redundant set during critical mission phases, in a fashion similar to NMR/simplex; the fifth performs noncritical tasks in simplex mode and acts as a simplex backup for the primary system. The control outputs of the four primary computers are voted on at the control actuators. In addition, each computer listens to the outputs of the three other computers and compares those signals with its own via special software. If a computer detects a disagreement, it signals the disagreeing computer. The received disagreement detection signals are voted on in the redundancy management circuitry of each computer; if the vote is positive, the redundancy management unit removes its computer from service. Up to two computer failures can be tolerated in voting mode operation. After the second failure, the system converts to a duplex system that can survive one additonal computer failure by using comparison and self-test methods. The fifth computer contains a backup flight software package written by Rockwell International, while the

package running on the primary computers was written by IBM. This is in case program bugs are encountered in the primary software during flight.

The FTMP computer (Chapter 17) is implemented from a set of processor/cache, memory, and I/O modules, all interconnected by redundant common serial buses (Figure 3-77a). Computations are performed by triads: three processor/caches* and three memories performing the same operation in voting mode and synchronized at the clock level. Voting is performed in each memory and each processor/cache at its interface to the bus. Thus, because most processing utilizes the cache, voting is not necessarily performed at every clock cycle, but whenever data is transferred over the bus. Multiple triads can operate at the same time, thereby affording multiprocessing capabilities. Configuration is controlled by a redundant "bus guardian" in each module that controls access to the bus. Upon detection of a module failure, once the affected triad has completed its current operation another triad forces reconfiguration of the affected triad. If sufficient spares are available, the failed module is replaced. Otherwise, the triad is broken up and the good modules are added to the pool of spares.

The SIFT computer (Chapter 16), on the other hand, is implemented from a set of self-contained computers and redundant buses (Figure 3-77b).** Each computer broadcasts its results, and software voting is performed in each computer at intermediate points in each NMR task. Synchronization and reconfiguration are also

---

* The term *cache* used in this context is misleading, for the memory unit attached to the processor does not perform quite the same function that a cache in a high-performance computer does. A better term would be *local* or *scratchpad* memory.

** The bus shown in Figure 3-77b is consistent with the SIFT design in Chapter 16. The current implementation of SIFT, however, does not use redundant buses. Instead, a totally connected scheme is used, in which a pair of unidirectional serial links connects each pair of computers (one link in each direction).

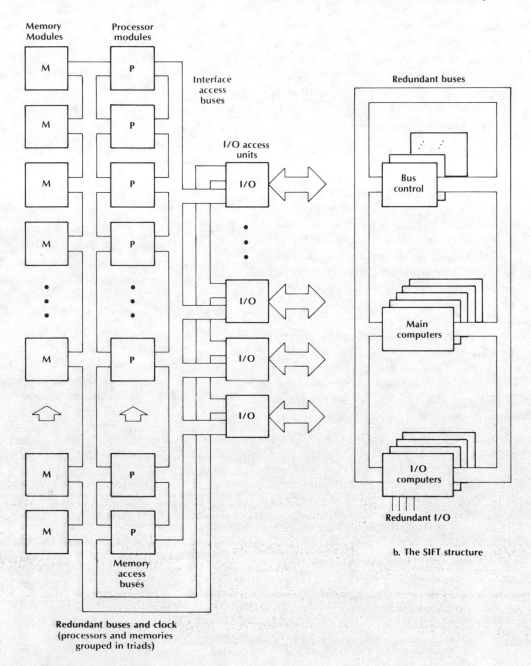

Figure 3–77. Block diagrams of the FTMP and SIFT flight control computers [Rennels, 1980]. (© 1980 IEEE.)

performed by software. Reconfiguration occurs through ignoring the broadcasts of known bad computers and reallocating tasks to nonfaulty computers. Critical tasks are performed in an NMR fashion (the redundancy N is variable, depending on the criticality); noncritical tasks can be executed by single computers.

Backup Sparing

In hybrid redundancy there is a core of N modules operating in parallel, with a voter determining the system output. In addition, there is initially a set, S, of backup spare modules that can be switched in to replace failed modules in the core. The concept of backup spares can also be combined with redundancy techniques other than N-modular redundancy. In general, some means of failure detection is used to trigger the replacement of a failed on-line unit with a spare. The detection means can be internal (either through self-test or the use of self-checking circuitry), external (such as timer, parity check, reasonability check), or some combination of internal and external checks. As with hybrid redundancy, the switch complexity is an important factor. Another concern is the effectiveness of the failure detection techniques used. In Chapter 5, a few simple models of standby sparing reliability are derived. A more general reliability model of a system with standby sparing is [Bouricius et al., 1971]:

$$R(t; s, c, q, \lambda, \mu) = R(t; (s - 1), c, q, \lambda, \mu)$$
$$+ \int_0^t \frac{\partial[-R(u; (s-1), 1, q, \lambda, \mu)]}{\partial u} \quad (6)$$
$$\cdot (c^s e^{-\mu u} e^{-q\lambda(t-u)} du)$$

where

$q =$ the number of on-line modules required

$s =$ the initial number of spare modules

$(q + s) =$ the total number of modules in the system

$c =$ the probability of successful replacement by a spare (coverage)

$\lambda =$ failure rate of an on-line module

$\mu =$ failure rate of a standby module*

The recursive form of Equation 6 can be transformed by induction on s:

$$R(t; s, c, q, \lambda, \mu) = e^{-q\lambda t}[\sum_{k=0}^s {}_aC_k c^k (1 - e^{-\mu t})^k]$$

where $a = (q\lambda/\mu) + k - 1$. This model does not explicitly include the reliability of the switch, detection elements, and control circuitry (SDC unit). If any failure in the SDC unit is assumed to cause a system failure, the reliability of the system is:

$$R_{SDC}(t) \cdot R(t; s, c, q, \lambda, \mu). \quad (7)$$

If, however, compensating failures can occur (as with some switch failures; see Chapter 5 for discussion of modeling compensating failures), modeling a spares-switching system becomes difficult. Sometimes the coverage factor (c) is modified to include the effect of some or all failures in the SDC unit, thereby retaining the simplicity of the model of Equation 7. The increased ease of modeling is gained at the cost of decreased accuracy.

One widely used application of spares switching is in systems that are bit- or byte-sliced (such as Figure 3-78). Possibilities include memories physically assembled from a set of bit planes, and ALUs made from ALU byte slices (such as the Am2903). Figure 3-79 shows a possible implementation of a byte-sliced system containing a single spare slice (M4). Initially, all the input

* Spare modules that are unpowered (cold spares) may have a lower failure rate than on-line modules or powered-up spare modules (hot spares).

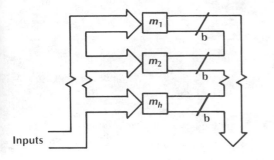

Inputs

h · b **output lines**

Figure 3–78. Circuit design of parallel byte-wide modules.

MUXes are set to connect their right leg inputs to the modules, and the output MUXes are set to connect their left leg inputs to the system outputs. The MUXes could be replaced by pairs of open-collector AND gates with outputs tied together. When a slice fails, the MUXes are reset so that a bad slice is bypassed in both input and output data paths. If, for example, module M2 has failed, M2 can be bypassed and M4 switched in by resetting input MUX 2 to connect its left leg input to M3, while output MUXes 2 and 3 are reset to select their right leg inputs. Figure 3-79 shows the states of the MUX control lines during normal operation, and when module M2 is failed. The addition of more spares to the circuit of Figure 3-79 requires more complex arrangements. For example, the addition of a second spare requires replacement of the two-to-one MUXes by three-to-one MUXes, as well as more interconnections.

In addition to the inclusion of more spares, other concerns may affect the design of a spares switch. The arrangement in Figure 3-79, for example, will not work for memories in which the information stored in the nonfailed modules must remain in the same relational order both before and after the spare is switched in. In the example of a failure of module M2, bytes 0 and

1 are in their correct locations, but byte slice 3 now contains the byte slice 2 data, and byte slice 2 is blank. The recovery procedure for this situation involves restoring the contents of *two* byte slices. For this reason, an order-preserving switch would be better. An order-preserving switch allows a reconfiguration that preserves the logical order of the entire system except for the placement of the failed module and its replacement. Order-preserving switches, however, are more complex than nonorder-preserving switches. For more complex arrangements (such as order-preserving switches with a large number of spares) an iterative cell-switching network such as that proposed in Levitt, Green, and Goldberg [1968] could be used. The section below on Reconfiguration includes a brief discussion of such switching networks and methods of making the networks themselves fault tolerant.

Bit-slice spares switching is often used for memories. The data and program stores in the AXE telephone exchange control computer [Ossfeldt and Jonsson, 1980], for example, incorporate both a spare bit plane and a parity bit. Other designs have combined spares switching with error-correcting codes. For example, a design by Carter and McCarthy [1976] combines a (22,16) single-error-correcting (SEC/DED) code, erasure correction, and a spare bit plane. A Boeing aerospace computer [Wachter, 1975], designed for extended missions without maintenance, uses a (35,28) SEC code and four spare bit planes, with two of the spares hot and two cold. The DEC MF20 memory (for the DECSYSTEM-20) uses a (44,36) SEC/DED code. In addition, the memory has a single spare bit for each 8K words of memory. The spare bit can be switched in to replace any bit in the 8K words that the system software has determined to contain a hard failure.

The Saturn V launch vehicle computer [Dickinson, Jackson, and Randa, 1964], which uses TMR for its functional modules, uses a backup sparing technique for its memory. The Saturn V memory operates in a duplex mode. The duplicate copy, however, is not used for error detec-

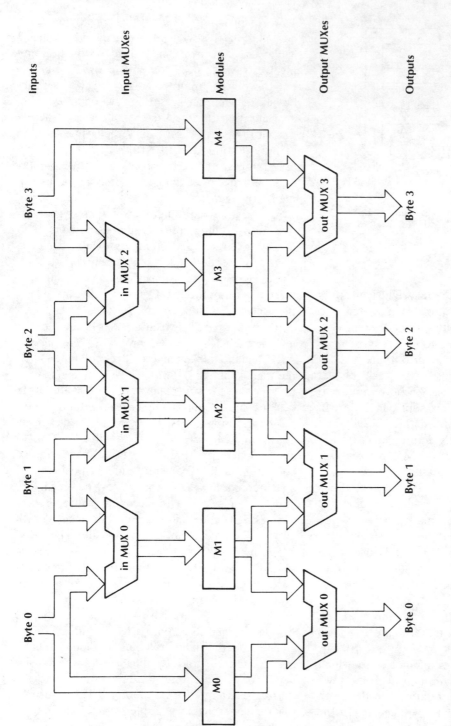

Control input to MUX: 0 (left leg), 1 (right leg)

Normal control line state: (in MUX 0, in MUX 1, in MUX 2) = (1, 1, 1)
(out MUX 0, out MUX 1, out MUX 2, out MUX 3) = (0, 0, 0, 0)

Control line state if M2 failed: in MUX = (1,X,0)
out MUX = (0,0,1,1)
X = don't care

Figure 3–79. Possible implementation of a system made from four byte-slice modules, with a fifth module added as a spare.

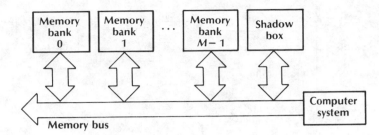

Figure 3–80. The shadow box memory backup technique proposed by Arulpragasm and Swarz.

tion. Error detection is accomplished by the parity bit in each memory word and by monitoring of memory-access-line drive current. If an error is detected in the on-line memory, operation is transferred to the standby memory without interruption of service or loss of data.

Arulpragasm and Swarz [1980] proposed another spare-switching memory architecture that is able to preserve data through a failure occurrence. The concept, illustrated in Figure 3-80, is an extension of the principle of product codes (discussed earlier.) The spare memory box (called the shadow box) is identical to the other m memory boxes. However, a word stored at address i in the shadow box is actually the XOR of the words stored in the locations i in the on-line memory boxes. The contents of the shadow box must be updated every time a word is written into the memory. In other words, if $M_s[i]$ denotes the contents of location i of the shadow box, $M_j[i]$ the current contents of the same location in box j, and $M_j'[i]$ the new contents, then at every write into location i in memory box j, the following operation is simultaneously executed in the shadow box:

$$M_s[i] = M_j[i] \oplus M_j'[i] \oplus M_s[i]$$

The details of the similar update action required in a block-code memory are discussed in Chapter 5. If one of the active memory boxes fails, the shadow box replaces it. The contents of the lost box can be resurrected by XORing the contents of the remaining memory boxes with those of the

shadow box. In other words, if memory box k fails, the following operation is performed:

$$M_s[i] = M_s[i] \oplus \sum_{j=0}^{k-1} M_j[i] \oplus \sum_{j=k+1}^{m-1} M_j[i].$$

In its simplest form, the shadow box method requires a parity bit in each memory word for failure detection. Arulpragasm and Swarz also examined the extension of the shadow box concept with the use of error-correction codes and multiple spares. Finally, they projected the effects of the shadow box on system performance and cost, and found them to be relatively small.

In other applications, the JPL STAR (Chapter 14) uses backup sparing extensively; the configuration is controlled by the hybrid-redundant TARP (test and repair processor). The MECRA computer [Maison, 1971] uses backup spares for its counters and registers. MECRA has 8 Hamming-coded registers and 4 spare registers. Any of the spares can easily be used to replace any of the active registers, since both the active and spare registers are connected to the same internal bus. The spares switching for the MECRA counters is implemented in the same manner. In another application of standby sparing, Lewis [1979] proposed a design for a fault-tolerant clock for a TMR system, shown in Figure 3-81. There are two oscillators, one of which is in standby mode. When on-line oscillator failure is detected, the spare replaces it. In addition to the use of standby sparing for the oscillator, the additional clock circuitry (such as failure detection, control, and shaping) is triplicated, with

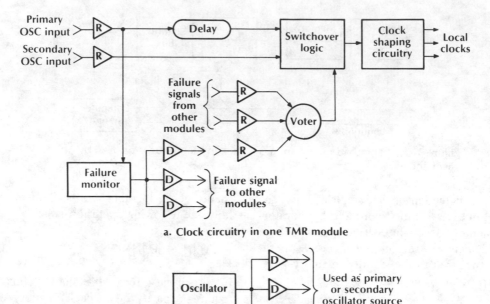

a. Clock circuitry in one TMR module

b. One of two oscillators, with a separate output for driving clock circuitry on each TMR module.

Figure 3–81.   Fault-tolerant clock for TMR system using standby sparing. © IEEE 1979.

each copy of the clock circuitry residing in one functional module. The unique feature of the clock system is that careful consideration is given to the avoidance of glitches, runt pulses, pulse width variation, and missing clock pulses during the switchover. The goal is to prevent any anomaly in the clock output that might cause desynchronization of the TMR system using the clock.

In the final reference, Losq [1975a] proposed a model for spare-switching systems using Markov chain techniques (see Chapter 5) and examined the effects of fault-detection coverage on system reliability. He found that for short mission times a single spare results in the best reliability; for longer mission times, the optimum number of spares increases with mission time. The addition of spares beyond the optimum number decreases the chances of mission success (mission reliability). Losq also derived a method of determining the optimum number of spares.

Graceful Degradation

The dynamic redundancy techniques discussed so far have one thing in common: redundant units are used for error detection, correction, and/or replacement of failed units. They can perform no useful work until they have replaced a failed on-line unit. Graceful degradation techniques, on the other hand, use the redundant hardware as part of the system's normal resources at all times. There are two similar but distinct graceful degradation perspectives. In the first, system resources needed to attain a specified performance are designed so that continued (though degraded) operation is possible in the event of failures: degraded operation is preferable to no operation at all. In the second, extra resources are added to a system to ensure that, with a high probability of success, a minimum performance level can be maintained in the presence of failures. The extra resources are also used to boost performance above the minimum requirements; the augmented performance continues as long as the extra hardware is not used in overcoming failure effects. The major purpose of both perspectives is to allow system performance to degrade gracefully while compensating for failures. The distinction between the two perspectives usually lies in the motivations for including fault tolerance. The motivation for the first perspective is the priority of a certain cost/performance goal, along with some ability to continue operation in the presence of failures without regard to performance. A computer intended primarily for time sharing is an example of such a system. With the second perspective, the motivation is that any performance below a certain level is not acceptable; the latter is exemplified by real-time control processors for critical applications (such as aircraft control). In many gracefully degrading designs, it may be impossible to classify the design goals according to one or the other perspective.

The first form of graceful degradation occurs in a wide variety of commercial uniprocessor systems.* In many computers, portions of memory can be removed from the address space if they contain failures. This is often accomplished through virtual address mapping facilities in the hardware and/or operating system software. In many disk memory subsystems, portions of individual disks can be deallocated if they contain permanent errors. The Univac 1100 operating systems, for example, make a record of bad tracks on a disk as soon as they are discovered, and avoid using bad tracks when writing files onto disk. The DEC VAX-11/780 performs a similar function on its disk memory (Chapter 8). In systems with multiple disk drives, the loss of one, two, or more drives can be tolerated as long as the data lost are not essential to system operation.

---

* Many commercial systems contain only some of the aspects of graceful degradation. The chief missing factor is the ability to tolerate failures; although the systems can operate in a degraded fashion, they must be manually reconfigured (that is, the operating system is reinitialized after throwing a few switches) after the failure causes a system crash.

Cache memories added to a system to improve performance can be bypassed in the event of failure. In the VAX-11/780, set-associative-two mapping in the cache allows the disabling of one set of the cache when a cache failure is detected (effectively turning off one half of the cache, and using the other half as a directly-mapped cache.) Because the cache is a write-through cache, there is no data loss involved in turning off half the cache. The VAX-11/750 has a set-associative-one cache; thus, it must shut down its entire cache if a cache failure occurs, and the performance degradation is greater than for the VAX-11/780. The Univac 1100/60 also has the ability to shut down portions of its cache (Chapter 10).

The Cm* and C.mmp multiprocessor systems [Siewiorek et al., 1978a, 1978b] are systems for which it is not possible to specify which of the graceful degradation perspectives is relevant. Both Cm* and C.mmp were designed to exploit the high performance possible with multiprocessors. Both machines, however, were also designed to benefit from the high reliability that results when a multiprocessor system is capable of degrading gracefully with failures. Cm* and C.mmp are both capable of withstanding multiple processor and memory failures, and tasks can be reassigned to other modules. The key to the performance/reliability properties in multiprocessors like Cm* and C.mmp lies more in the systems and application software than in the hardware. In other words, the software must be written to take advantage of the "hooks" that exist in the hardware to provide graceful degradation possibilities.

The Pluribus multiprocessor (Chapter 13), designed as a modularly expandable interface message processor (IMP) for the ARPANET, utilizes the second perspective of graceful degradation. Redundant Pluribus systems contain only one extra processor, which is used to provide extra throughput. If any processor fails, only the excess capacity is lost; although the Pluribus system throughput is degraded, the system can still supply the required performance. Likewise, the SIFT, FTMP, and Tandem computers (Chapters

16, 17, and 11) are initially capable of exceeding performance requirements but will allow graceful degradation of capacity as portions of the system fail. All these systems have a high probability of maintaining at least a minimum level of functionality until the end of a mission (SIFT, FTMP) or until repairs can be effected (Tandem).

Borgerson and Freitas [1975] developed a reliability model for systems using both backup spares and graceful degradation. The model is based on four different fault classes: solitary faults, space domain faults (e.g., simultaneous failure of multiple pieces of hardware), time domain faults (e.g., a second fault occurring before the first is recovered from), and resource exhaustion (running out of extra modules). In using the model to analyze the PRIME gracefully degrading computer system [Baskin, Borgerson, and Roberts, 1972], it was found that solitary and space domain multiple faults were much more of a factor in system reliability than were time domain multiple faults or resource exhaustion.

Evaluation of systems with graceful degradation involves more factors than does evaluation of systems using other redundancy techniques. In gracefully degrading systems, performance varies widely over time as failures are accumulated but the systems continue to operate. Thus, the total amount of work done (computation performed) over a time interval is as important as a go/no-go reliability determination. Measures of combined performance and reliability properties are therefore attracting increasing attention. Proposed measures include probability distributions of capacity at time T, mean computation before failure, and the probability of a successful completion of a task started at time T. Computing resource availability is not the only factor in such measures; consideration must be given to additional degradation resulting from recovery and/or restart of processes executing when a failure occurs. Performance-related reliability measures are discussed in Chapter 5.

Additionally, recent work on performance/reliability modeling is reported in papers by Losq [1977], Troy [1977], Beaudry [1978], Meyer [1978], Gay and Ketelson [1979], Mine and Hatayama [1979], and Castillo and Siewiorek [1980]. In another paper, Meyer, Furchgort, and Wu [1980] evaluated the performance and reliability of the SIFT computer in the air transport application for which it is designed.

Reconfiguration

The four previous sections presented four classes of dynamic redundancy techniques: reconfigurable duplication, reconfigurable NMR, backup sparing, and graceful degradation. These classes include the majority of reconfiguration techniques. Many other dynamic redundancy schemes, however, do not fit neatly into the four categories discussed. This section presents a sampling of some of these miscellaneous techniques.

The first technique is sift-out redundancy [DeSousa and Mathur, 1978], proposed as an alternative to hybrid and self-purging redundancy techniques. With N redundant modules in the initial configuration, sift-out redundancy can tolerate up to $(N - 2)$ module failures. This is comparable to the fault tolerance of hybrid redundancy with a TMR core and to self-purging redundancy (voter threshold = 2). The major difference in sift-out redundancy is that there is no actual voting element; the bad module outputs are eliminated as described below. As a result, the restoring organ for sift-out redundancy is potentially simpler than that for hybrid and self-purging redundancies. Figure 3-82 shows the basic configuration for a system with sift-out redundancy. The comparator, used to detect disagreements between all possible pairs of the functional modules, contains $_NC_2$ XOR gates. Using $_NC_2$ signal lines, the comparator signals the detector which pairs are not in agreement. The detector uses these signals to identify the faulty module. Included in the detector are N

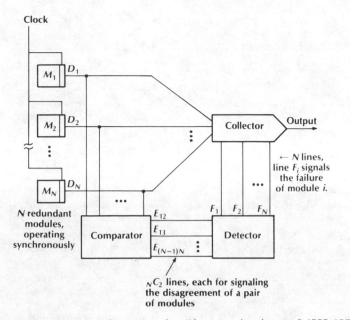

Figure 3–82.   Basic configuration for sift-out redundancy. © IEEE 1978.

memory cells; the ith cell is set when it is determined that the ith module has failed. The detector contains N flip-flops and $(_N C_2 + N)$ NOR gates. Finally, the collector uses the N detector outputs, each one signaling the state of a single module (failed/nonfailed), to determine which module outputs to ignore, or sift out. The collector requires $(N + 1)$ NOR gates. Figure 3-83 shows the design of a sift-out restoring organ, with $N = 4$.

If XOR gate implementation requires X elemental (e.g., NOR) gates, the total complexity of the sift-out restoring organ is:

$$(X + 1)_N C_2 + 2N + 1$$

NOR gates and N flip-flops. If $X = 1$, as assumed previously when comparing iterative cell-switch hybrid redundancy with self-purging redundancy, the total number of gates required is:

$$N^2 + N + 1.$$

Table 3-17 compares the restoring organ com-

plexities for self-purging redundancy (voter threshold = 2), hybrid TMR redundancy (with a threshold gate voter), and sift-out redundancy for several amounts of redundancy. All the designs are able to tolerate up to $(N - 2)$ module failures. If the complexity of the threshold voters (the number of standard logic gates needed to implement one) is taken into account, it can be seen that sift-out redundancy requires less total restoring organ complexity than does hybrid redundancy for the range of N considered. Furthermore, sift-out redundancy and self-purging redundancy are roughly equal in terms of restoring organ complexity;[*] the major difference between the two techniques is that the self-purging redundancy scheme is vulnerable to some multiple stuck-at-1 failures, while the collector for sift-out redundancy (as shown in Figure 3-83) is

---

[*] Note that if each XOR gate requires four simpler gates to implement, sift-out redundancy is much less attractive because of its heavy use of XOR gates in the comparator.

Table 3–17. Comparison of restoring organ complexity for hybrid TMR, self-purging, and sift-out redundancy techniques.

N	Hybrid				Self-purging				Sift-out	
	Gates	*T.V.** Gates*	*Total Gates*	*ff**	*Gates*	*T.V.** Gates*	*Total Gates*	*ff**	*Total Gates*	*ff**
4	36	10	46	4	12	10	22	4	21	4
5	45	16	59	5	15	16	31	5	31	5
6	54	23	83	6	18	23	41	6	43	6

* ff = flip-flops
**T.V. gates = approximate number of gates needed to implement N-input threshold voter with threshold of 2.

Assumptions:
Iterative cell hybrid redundancy, TMR core:
  $9N$ gates, N flip-flops, N-input threshold gate
    (threshold = 2)

Self-purging redundancy:
  $2N$ gates, N flip-flops, N-input threshold gate
    (threshold = 2)

Sift-out redundancy:
  $N^2 + N + 1$ gates, N flipflops
    (threshold = 2)

vulnerable to some multiple stuck-at-0 failures. Unlike the self-purging restoring organ, however, the collector for sift-out redundancy can be designed (with little change in complexity) to be vulnerable to the form of stuck-at failures that are less likely to occur; that is, if stuck-at-0 failures are less likely than stuck-at-1 failures for the modules being used, then the collector design shown in Figure 3-83 should be used. The two possible collector designs are logical duals of each other.

Another dynamic redundancy technique is the memory reconfiguration approach proposed by Hsiao and Bossen [1975]. Assume a bit-sliced memory using an SEC/DED code. In the usual straightforward design, the memory can tolerate any single-bit failure in a given memory word but fails if any word contains two or more bit failures. If, however, the memory cell addressing function can be performed independently on each bit slice, reconfiguration of the memory is possible without using a spare bit slice. This is accomplished by skewing the address mapping when a double failure is detected, so that the new configuration contains at most a single failure in any word. In other words, the address mapping

is changed so that the same address now maps into a different bit location on each module. Figure 3-84 illustrates the concept. To get the maximum reconfiguration ability possible with this approach, the properties of orthogonal Latin squares are utilized.* However, if there are 2^k memory words (with k large), using orthogonal Latin squares of order 2^k requires considerable complexity. Latin squares of a smaller size can be used instead, with the address skewing performed on blocks of memory cells in the bit plane. When using order-m Latin squares, the skewing is performed using only ($\log_2 m$) bits of the address. Thus, using order-4 Latin squares as in Figure 3-84 and skewing by the two most significant bits in an address results in addresses skewed in contiguous blocks of $2^{(k-2)}$ words.

* Definition [Hsiao and Bossen, 1975]: "A Latin square of order (size) m is an $m \times m$ square array of the digits 0, 1, ..., ($m - 1$), with each row and column a permutation of the [m digits]. Two Latin squares are orthogonal if, when [one] is superimposed on the other, every ordered pair of elements appears only once." The four matrices in Figure 3-84 are the four possible orthogonal Latin squares of order 4. Figure 3-85 demonstrates the result of superimposing the first two Latin squares in Figure 3-84.

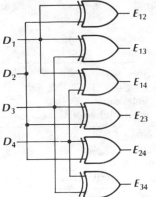

a. Comparator

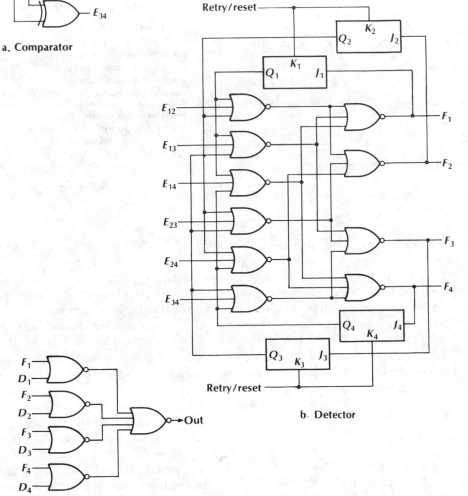

b. Detector

c. Collector

Figure 3–83. Design of restoring organ elements for sift-out redundancy scheme (Figure 3-82) using four redundant modules, with a fault tolerance of two module failures. © IEEE 1978.

	Bit planes				Bit location on plane mapped into address
Address	0	1	2	3	SEC code memory
0	0	0	0	0	Initial configuration: two
1	1	1	(1)	[1]	single-bit failures (boxes) and
2	2	2	2	2	a third failure (circle) cause
3	3	3	3	[3]	a double (noncorrectable) error
0	0	(1)	2	[3]	Second configuration:
1	1	0	3	2	with three tolerable
2	2	3	0	[1]	single-bit failures, a fourth,
3	3	2	[1]	0	noncorrectable failure occurs (circle).
0	0	2	3	[1]	Third configuration:
1	1	3	2	0	the fourth failure is
2	2	0	[1]	[3]	no longer aligned with
3	3	(1)	0	2	any other failure; however, another configuration is needed because two old failures are aligned.
0	0	3	[1]	2	Fourth configuration:
1	1	2	0	[3]	no double failures
2	2	[1]	3	0	exist, but any additional
3	3	0	2	[1]	failure is unrecoverable.

Figure 3–84. Orthogonal Latin squares–based memory address skewing used to reconfigure a bit-sliced SEC code memory.

Hsiao and Bossen suggested a simple implementation based on linear feedback shift registers that allows the use of identical modules for each bit plane. Each module contains a memory bit slice and its associated addressing circuitry. The overall design of the Latin squares memory is less complex and costly than a memory with a spare bit plane. Finally, Hsiao and Bossen demonstrated the power of the technique by simulation of an 8-megabyte memory using order-8 Latin squares for address skewing. In a popula-

0, 0	0, 1	0, 2	0, 3
1, 1	1, 0	1, 3	1, 2
2, 2	2, 3	2, 0	2, 1
3, 3	3, 2	3, 1	3, 0

Figure 3–85. The superimposition of the upper two order-4 Latin squares of Figure 3-84.

tion of 1,000 memories, 500 failures were assumed to occur over a period of five years. The simulation found that a successful reconfiguration was possible for 66 percent of the failures that caused multiple errors.

Through another technique for memory fault tolerance, the Univac 1100/60 (Chapter 10) is able to tolerate single-bit stuck-at-α failures in its microstore. When a parity error is detected in the microstore, the system maintenance processor attempts to correct the error by rewriting the microstore. If the error is due to a failure the rewriting will not correct the problem, and the maintenance processor makes one final attempt at repair. It writes the logical complement of the microstore contents into the microstore and sets a special designator to indicate that microwords must be inverted before use. Complementing the microstore contents allows toleration of multiple failures as long as all failures cause a bit to be stuck at its inverted value. The 1100/60 uses another technique for tolerating transient errors. Whenever an error is detected in the processor, the machine pauses until a special timer expires. During the pause, any transient phenomenon (such as static discharge, power fluctuation) that may have caused the error should die out without further interference, because the machine is not operating. The timer is variable for periods of up to 5 seconds, allowing for adjustment to a variety of computing environments.

The microstore inversion method could be extended so that each microstore location has an extra bit indicating whether the word is inverted before use. Such an extension would speed up reconfiguration because only a failed word would have to be rewritten. The fault tolerance is also increased, because the chance that multiple failed bits in a microstore would all be stuck at the same values is small.

Another microstore technique is to use an extra bit in each word to denote that the contents are bad. A few blank microstore locations are included at the end of the memory, and each word in the main part of the microstore maps into one (and only one) of the locations using a fixed mapping. When a word fails, the "remapped" indicator bit is set and a new copy of the affected word is written into its backup location (providing it is not already occupied). If the microstore is not writable, ROM could be used for all of the microstore except the indicator bits and the backup locations.

The MECRA computer [Maison, 1971] uses its main store for microstore as well. A special bit in each memory word denotes whether the location is being used for microcode. Recovery from failure in the microstore consists of simply rewriting the microcode in another part of memory. This approach is similar to the graceful degradation of main memory by memory block deallocation, discussed in the previous subsection. In addition, storing the microcode in main memory means that it can be easily modified.

MECRA utilizes this feature to perform system reconfiguration, which is done by changing the microprogram. For example, there is a separate hardware element for each of the logical operations AND, OR, XOR, and complementation. If one of the four logic elements fails, it can be replaced by any of a variety of combinations of operations using the remaining logical operators. The failure of, say, the XOR operator can be tolerated by employing the AND, OR, and inversion operators using the relation:

$$A \oplus B = AB' + A'B$$

The reconfiguration that permits replacement of the XOR operator is expensive to provide for if hardwired into the hardware, but is readily accommodated by MECRA's easy-to-change microcode.

Another technique has applications in fault-tolerant interconnection networks. Interconnection networks between component modules are needed by many spare-switching and gracefully degrading systems. The complexity of the switching network can cause reliability problems. Levitt, Green, and Goldberg [1968] have proposed some methods for realizing fault-tolerant switching networks. Consider the situation depicted in Figure 3-86, in which there are two types of elements, processors and memories.* The system can be made gracefully degradable because each processor can be connected to any memory through the crossbar switch. Thus, the network is totally connected; that is, any of the N inputs can be connected to any of the N outputs (one at a time). The network also allows all processors and memories to be utilized simultaneously, without waiting for a signal path to become free.

---

* The fault-tolerant switching networks discussed here are equally employable in other applications needing crossbar or other types of switching networks, such as multiprocessors and telephone systems. For example, the C.mmp multiprocessor system [Siewiorek et al., 1978a, 1978b] uses a 16×16 crossbar switch to interconnect processor and memories.

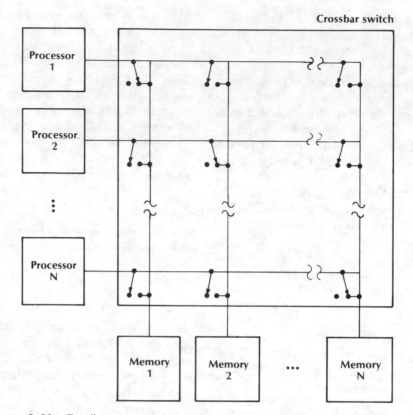

Figure 3–86. Totally connected design, in which any processor can be connected to any memory. Shown with each processor *i* connected to memory *i*.

Networks of this type are termed CPCU(N) [Complete Permutation–Complete Utilization, $N \times N$) networks. CPCU(N) networks can be realized with a crossbar switch, as shown in Figure 3-86. However, the complexity of the network increases as N^2. For large N the design complexity of the network is tremendous, especially when it also takes into account control and fan-out problems. Fortunately, a switching network such as that in Figure 3-86 can be implemented economically from basic 2×2 crossbar switching cells, in a fasion which trades increased complexity for decreased performance. Each of the cell's two inputs (I_1, I_2) can be connected to each of the two outputs (O_1, O_2). The cell thus has two operating modes: crossing and bending (Figure 3-87a and b). Figure 3-88 demonstrates

the use of the basic cell in a CPCU(8) network. The most efficient procedure for implementing CPCU(N) networks, based on an iterative implementation of the network, requires

$$N\lceil \log_2 N \rceil - 2^{\log N} + 1$$

cells. The methods of employing the two-mode cells for economical and/or high performance realization of switching networks are discussed in Levitt, Green, and Goldberg [1968], Kautz, Levitt, and Waksman [1968], and Waksman [1968]; many other references are available, in part because switching networks are important in telephone systems.

Figure 3-87c shows a possible implementation of the basic cell in which the crossing mode is attained by pulsing control input R high with

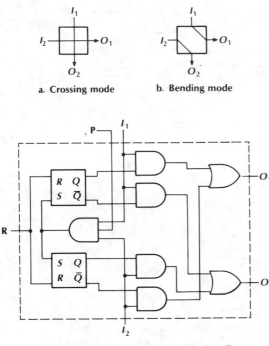

a. Crossing mode   b. Bending mode

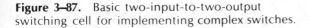

c. Redundant implementation of basic cell

Figure 3–87. Basic two-input-to-two-output switching cell for implementing complex switches.

control input P kept low, thereby resetting the flip-flops. The bending mode is invoked by pulsing P high, with inputs I_1 and I_2 kept high and R low. The cell of Figure 3-87c could be built with fewer components, but the circuit shown has one of the following two fail-safe responses to a single gate or flip-flop failure:

- *Stuck-Functions.* The cell is stuck either in bending mode or crossing mode, with the outputs valid for that mode.
- *Bad-Output.* One and only one of the output lines may contain faulty data.

These fail-safe responses can be used to make fault-tolerant networks. A CPCU(N) network that can compensate for any single stuck-at fault can be implemented from two cascaded networks, as shown in Figure 3-89. For example, both subnetworks could be CPCU(N) networks.

A fault in one subnetwork could be compensated for in the other network, with the good network performing the entire switching function. In this case, the faulty network is basically performing a null function: all its gates except the faulty one are being wasted. There are more efficient methods of making a single fault-tolerant network. One uses the same layout of Figure 3-89. In place of the CPCU(N) network for subnetwork A, a less complex subnetwork suffices. A stuck-at fault in subnetwork B results in an interchange of the signals on two of the output leads. It is possible to compensate for it by designing subnetwork A to be capable of interchanging the signals on any two input leads; such a network is less complex than a CPCU(N) network. Figure 3-90 shows a network that performs this function for $N = 8$. The structure, which can be generalized to different N, is called a "double tree" (TDT(N)) network. A TDT(N) network in general requires $(3N/2)$ switch cells. Note that a stuck-at fault in subnetwork A can be compensated for by subnetwork B, because it is CPCU(N).*

Levitt, Green, and Goldberg [1968] examined several more techniques for making switching networks fault tolerant. Among these are single stuck-at fault-tolerant CPCU(N) networks, which are slightly more efficient (in terms of the number of gates needed) than a combination of nonredundant CPCU(N) and TDT(N) networks. They also described networks that can tolerate bad-output faults, and fault-tolerant networks of the following types (in addition to CPCU(N) networks):

- Complete permutation–incomplete utilization
- Incomplete permutation–order preserving
- Incomplete permutation–nonorder preserving

---

* Note that only data paths have been discussed here. The issues of error detection and configuration control logic have been totally ignored. The circuitry for performing such functions can be quite complex, especially if the paths in use at the time of reconfiguration must be left untouched. Telephone exchanges, though admittedly more complex than computer interconnection networks, require computers to control the switching configuration (such as Bell ESS-1a).

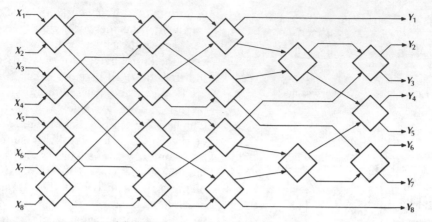

Figure 3–88. CPCU(8) switching network implemented from basic cells of Figure 3-87.

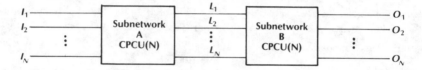

Figure 3–89. A fault-tolerant network, in which the damage due to a single stuck-at fault in one subnetwork can be compensated for by the other subnetwork.

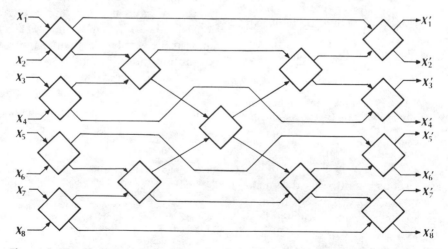

Figure 3–90. Compensation network used as subnetwork A (Figure 3-89) for a CPCU(8) single stuck function fault-tolerant network.

- "Shorting" (connecting outputs of stage *i* to inputs of stage (*i* + 1), or bypassing (shorting around) stage (*i* + 1))

Finally, Shen and Hayes [1980] examined the fault tolerance of several types of networks that can be implemented by means of the basic 2×2 crossbar cells.

The final reconfiguration technique to be mentioned is a memory reconfiguration approach, in which the memory chips are arranged in a self-healing network. The technique requires that an integral switch be built into each memory chip [Goldberg, Levitt, and Wensley, 1974].

Recovery

Fault masking techniques such as TMR and error-correcting codes permit uninterrupted system operation as long as the masking redundancy is not exhausted. Faults occur but do not become errors. When only detection is employed, perhaps combined with reconfiguration, faults become errors unless some kind of error-correction ability is added. A duplicated memory, for example, can continue operation following error detection only if:

- both memory copies have been performing the same operations in parallel, so that an error-free copy of the information is available in one of the memories; and
- it is possible to determine which copy contains the erroneous information.

If these criteria are met, restoration of the memory state merely requires reconfiguration. In many systems, however, the correction ability either does not exist or cannot compensate for more than a limited number of failures at a time. When the correction capability is exceeded, the system state is irretrievably in error. As an example, consider a Hamming SEC/DED-coded memory with a spare bit slice; the bit plane is switched in only after a double error is detected. The memory is capable of successful operation after a double failure occurs, but the information

it contained is corrupted beyond the hope of self-correction. As long as the initial data, program code, and the information acquired by the process prior to a data-corrupting failure are still available (such as from backup copies), the process can be restarted from scratch after the spare bit plane is switched in. The only loss is the (possibly costly) time expended during the first, unsuccessful, execution of the process. If, however, the initial data are corrupted and no backup copy exists, or if the information acquired during the first execution is irretrievably lost (such as real-time sampled data), the process cannot be successfully restarted from scratch.

Recovery techniques can restore enough of the system state to allow process execution to recommence without a complete restart, and with little or no loss of acquired information. Recovery techniques are usually implemented in software, but may have some hardware basis as well. The techniques considered here are all backward error recovery techniques [Randell, 1975], in which process execution is restarted at (rolled back to) some point before the occurrence of the error. Forward error recovery techniques, in contrast, attempt to continue operation with the system state at hand, even though it may be faulty. Forward error correction is usually highly application-dependent, as in the case of a real-time control system in which an occasional missed response to a sensor input is tolerable. Because loss of sensor information due to a failure is not critical, the system can recover by skipping its response to the lost sensor input sample. After reconfiguration, the process proceeds immediately to deal with the following sensor input samples. Forward error recovery is not discussed further here; Randell, Lee, and Treleaven [1978] consider the topic briefly.

All forms of backward error recovery require some redundant process-state information to be recorded as the protected process executes. The information is used to roll back an interrupted process to a point for which correct state information is known. Three forms of backward error recovery are considered, ordered by the length of rollback required: retry techniques, checkpoint techniques, and journaling techniques.

Retry techniques are the fastest form of error recovery, and conceptually the simplest. They depend upon detection of an error as soon as it occurs. Immediately after the error is detected, the necessary repairs are effected. If the error is transient, repair consists in pausing long enough for the transient to die away. If there is a hard failure, the system is reconfigured. The operation affected by the error is then retried, which necessitates knowing what the system state was immediately before the operation was first attempted. If the interrupted operation had already irrevocably modified some data the retry will be unsuccessful, especially if the failure itself caused a spurious (and undiscovered) modification. Retry techniques are most commonly employed as a means of tolerating transient errors. One retry application common to many commercial computers is I/O operation retry. Disk-read errors, for example, are common occurrences and are usually due to transients. Without disk-read retry capabilities, system and/or job failures would occur with distressing frequency. In most modern disk drives, retry on disk-read error detection is built into the disk controller itself, removing the burden of the retry operation from the host system. Other common retry applications are retry on memory read errors and bus transaction retry (for both data and protocol errors).

The Univac 1100/60 (Chapter 10) provides retry for macroinstructions after a failure. After a pause that permits transients to die away, a microroutine is invoked that examines the fault effects and determines whether the instruction is retryable. If a retry is possible, the retry microroutine restores the contents of the operand and addressing registers from a special retry memory provided for the purpose (the retry memory is updated every time a register is read). The macroinstruction is then refetched and its execution attempted. If the retry is not possible or if it fails, the microroutine attempts to transplant the process on another processor (assuming a multiprocessor configuration is being used). The IBM System/360 (Chapter 9) also provides extensive retry capability, performing retries for both CPU and I/O operations.

Alternate-Data Retry (ADR), proposed by Shedletsky [1978a], is a variation of the retry approach that offers tolerance of hard failures as well as of transients. The hardware is designed to be able to perform the same function using different data representations. Upon error detection, the same operation is retried using an alternate data representation; the use of a different form for the data is an attempt to ensure that the same error will not recur even if there is a hard failure. In particular, Shedletsky explored the use of C-morphic representations, in which there are two possible data representations. Each representation is the bitwise complement of the other. The design of C-morphic systems that are capable of ADR combines the elements of error-detection codes, complemented duplication, and self-checking circuitry. Shedletsky also applied ADR principles to the design of a simplified processor. The net hardware cost was slightly over that of a duplex processor system with only normal retry capability.

Retry techniques require immediate error detection to be successful and usually require substantial dedicated hardware. In contrast, checkpoint techniques allow some error latency, for the process is backed up to an earlier point in its execution. Checkpointing is most often implemented in software and requires little or no extra hardware. These techniques result from a combination of checkpointing and rollback. In checkpointing, some subset of the system state is saved at specific points (the checkpoints) during process execution. The information to be stored is the subset of system state (data, programs, machine state) that is necessary to the continued successful execution and completion of the process past the checkpoint, and which is not backed up by other means. Rollback is part of the actual recovery process and occurs after the repair (e.g., by reconfiguration) of the physical damage which caused the detected error (or after the transient causing the error dies out). The

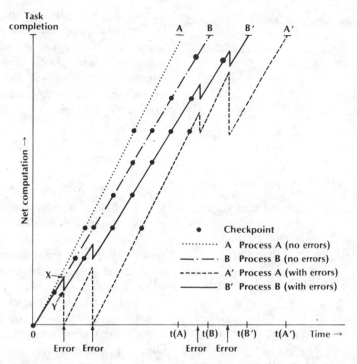

Figure 3–91. Scenario of two processes, identical except for checkpoint frequency.

rollback consists of resetting the system and process state to the state stored at the latest checkpoint. Hence the only loss is the computation time between the checkpoint and the rollback, plus any data received during that interval that cannot be recreated.

Figure 3-91 illustrates graphically some of the issues involved in checkpointing. First, consider lines B and B'. Line B shows the progress process B would make if no errors occurred. Line B' shows the actual progress of process B as a result of the error occurrence scenario shown. During process B execution, checkpoints are reached at regular intervals (regular in terms of amount of computation, not time). Point X on line B' corresponds to an error event. The vertical line segment XY is the rollback performed upon error detection. Point Y is the point in the process immediately following the checkpoint, at which execution restarts. Although the actual process execution time $t(B')$ is longer than the

ideal time $t(B)$, the process does not have to start from the beginning four times, as it must without checkpointing. Line A represents the progress of process A in the absence of errors. Process A is identical to process B except that in order to achieve faster execution, only one-third the number of checkpoints are used. The use of fewer checkpoints lowers the overhead required for saving system states and allows process A to run, say, 20 percent faster than process B. The actual performance of process A is actually lower, however, as shown by line A'. The reason is that the rollbacks were longer for process A than for process B, and the computation time lost for this error scenario outweighed process A's speed advantage. Thus, it is clear that the correct choice of checkpoint locations is important. If the checkpoints are too infrequent for the error rate encountered, much computation time can be lost to rollbacks. On the other hand, too frequent checkpointing results in an unnecessary increase

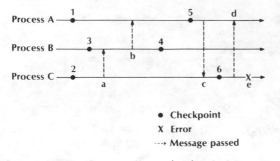

- Checkpoint
X Error
---> Message passed

Figure 3–92. Cooperating checkpointing processes. A failure at point e forces process C to roll back to checkpoint 6. Because of a message sent by process C, process A must then be rolled back to checkpoint 5. Rolling back of the processes in this fashion eventually requires all three processes to be rolled back to their initial checkpoints.

in computation time due to the overhead of saving-system states.

There are other issues in checkpointing design. One is the selection of checkpoints to minimize the amount of state information that must be saved at each checkpoint. A second is deciding which information must be backed up for proper assurance of successful rollback. A third situation arises when multiple concurrent processes communicate with each other. If one process is rolled back, any other process receiving data from it since the checkpoint must also be rolled back at least that far. This can give rise to a "domino effect" [Randell, 1975], illustrated in Figure 3-92, which causes multiple rollbacks throughout a multiprocess system. Another consideration is avoiding error latency situations in which the validity of the state saved at the checkpoint is jeopardized by the possibility of a previous, undetected error. More detailed examination of these and other issues is left to other sources. Chandy and Ramamoorthy [1972] proposed checkpointing strategies that dynamically insert checkpoints when the expected loss of computation reaches a certain value. Troy [1978] proposed a model for interacting processes operating concurrently. The model, based on Petri net-like representations, allows a determination of the rollback actions needed when an error

occurs in one of the processes. Shedletsky [1978b] dealt with the problem of error latency when imperfect error detection is present. He presented a method for determining a rollback length concomitant with the desired probability of successful recovery, and demonstrated the procedure by analyzing an imperfectly self-checking ALU.

The Tandem computer (Chapter 11) uses checkpointing extensively. User processes can be replicated, with the extra copies used for backup (usually only duplication is used). The operating system has a checkpointing facility through which the active process can checkpoint its state to a backup process. The Fault-Tolerant Spaceborne Computer (FTSC) employs a checkpointing scheme in which the only information needed to roll back a process is the program counter contents stored at its last checkpoint [DeAngelis and Lauro, 1976; O'Brien, 1976; Stiffler, 1976]. The COPRA computer [Meraud, Browaeys, and Germain, 1976; Meraud et al., 1979] uses checkpoints automatically inserted by its assembler; rollback is microprogrammed and is automatically invoked by detection of an error. Finally, the JPL STAR (Chapter 14) operating system also employs checkpointing.

Randell [1975] described an approach to the design of complex hardware/software systems using recovery blocks, which combine elements of checkpointing and backup spares to provide tolerance of software design faults as well as recovery from hard failures and transient errors. Figure 3-93 shows a sample recovery block at the user level. Recovery blocks are similar in nature to blocks in ALGOL. The recovery block shown executes a search for a key in a data structure and returns the index of the array element that matches the key. Checkpointing a variable global to the block occurs only if it is altered within the block, and is performed automatically just before the alteration actually takes place. This backup procedure not only minimizes the amount of state information backed up, but also releases the programmer from determining which variables should be checkpointed, and

```
variable locations.searched ;
logical variable errorflag ;
locations.searched := 0   ;
errorflag :=  false  ;

ensure
    (keystructure [pointer] = key) or errorflag     ! start of recovery block
    by tree.search (pointer, key)                   ! acceptance test
    elseby binary.search (pointer, key)             ! primary alternate
    elseby linear.search (pointer, key)             ! second alternate
    elseby                                          ! third alternate
        begin                                       ! final alternate
        print ("Not able to find key")  ;
        pointer := nil  ;
        errorflag := true  ;
        end
    else error  ;
```

Figure 3–93. Recovery block as seen at program level.

when. Assume that all the search algorithms use the global variable *locations.searched* as a counter during the search, and that upon completion *locations.searched* contains the number of locations searched by the algorithm. The first time the variable is accessed, its old value (0) is written into the cache. Upon entry to the block, the primary alternate—a tree search algorithm in the case of Figure 3-93—first attempts the desired computation. Once the primary alternate completes its function, the acceptance test is used to detect any errors in the result. If the test is passed, the block is exited. If the test is failed, or if the primary alternate fails to complete the computation, the contents of the recovery cache pertaining to this recovery block are automatically reinstated (in the case of Figure 3-93, *locations.searched* is reset to zero) and the second alternate is initiated. The cycle of execution, test, rollback, and initiation of the next alternate continues until either an alternate completes the computation successfully or there are no more alternates. If the block runs out of alternates, an error is signaled to the context containing the recovery block. Usually, the first alternate is the most desirable (more efficient, more powerful) and the desirability of the subsequent alternates decreases at each level. In Figure 3-93 the binary search takes longer than the tree search but, being less complex, may have a lower probability of failure; the linear search takes even longer (it

is assumed that the data structure is universal; that is, it supports all three search algorithms.) The last alternate does not execute the desired task, but instead prints an error message and returns an obviously faulty value for the index.

A graphical representation of recovery blocks is shown in Figure 3-94a; the representation is used here to briefly illustrate some of the extensions to the recovery block idea that can be found in Randell [1975]. Figure 3-94b shows that it is possible to nest recovery blocks. Failure by exhaustion of alternates in a lower level recovery block causes the recovery block containing it to invoke the next alternate. Figure 3-94c shows the extension of recovery blocks to parallel processes, with some restrictions on the times at which messages can be passed between processes. Recovery blocks can be used at different levels of abstraction in a hierarchical system (in the same way that there can be a physical computer as well as multiple levels of virtual machines) as long as proper care is taken when designing the interfaces between the levels.

The strength of the acceptance test is important to the successful detection of errors. Thus, if weaker alternates which return false or dummy results are used, the acceptance test must be weakened to allow the recovery block to be exited when they complete. Shrivastava and Akinpelu [1978] proposed a method of avoiding this trouble by the use of assertion statements in a

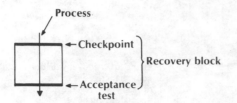

a. Graphic notation for a recovery block

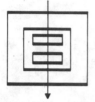

b. Nesting of recovery blocks

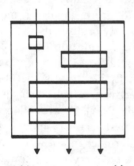

c. Multiprocess recovery blocks

Figure 3–94. Use of Randell's graphical notation to demonstrate extensions beyond the simple recovery block.

recovery block. Anderson and Lee [1979] considered means of improving the fault tolerance of hardware/software interfaces, making them more recoverable by adding extra levels of abstraction. Russell and Tiedeman [1979] examined message passing among multiple processes within the same recovery block (a "conversation"), and its requirements on the degree of coupling between cooperating processes.

A possible practical implementation of recovery blocks would utilize a form of cache mechanism to store the current values of checkpoint variables about to be altered and to keep track of the nesting depth of the current recovery block. Shrivastava and Akinpelu [1978] evaluated the performance of recovery cache scheme, and found that the overhead involved was not high. Lee, Ghani, and Heron [1980] have described an experimental design of an add-on cache for a PDP-11 that divides the Unibus between the processor and memory, and requires no modifications to the system other than cutting the bus. Because the cache cannot access the registers in the processor without modifying the processor hardware, it can checkpoint only variables stored in the memory. The projected performance degradation is about the same as in C.vmp (Chapter 7). C.vmp, however, will survive hard processor failures, whereas the recovery cache PDP-11 will not. The recovery cache system is about as complex as a C.vmp-type configuration, but with full use of recovery blocks it will survive transient errors and most software design errors.

Of the three backward error recovery techniques discussed here, journaling is the simplest and least efficient; it requires the longest time to recover the state attained before an error. In journaling, a copy of the initial data (database, disk, file) is stored as the process begins. As the process executes, it makes a record of all transactions that affect the data. Thus, if the process fails, its effect can be recreated by running a copy of the backup data through the transactions a second time (after any failures have been repaired). The recovery takes the same amount of time as the initial attempt. Journaling is better than completely restarting because it eliminates the loss of information involved in a restart. The Bravo editor on the Xerox Alto personal computer uses journaling to recover an editing session during which an error causes the computer to crash [Lampson, 1979]. A special program called Bravobug is run when the system is restarted and can be stopped at any point (up to the point where the error occurred) to recreate any intermediate states of the edited file. Typically, a three-hour editing session takes substantially less time to recreate because there are no human delays involved the second time.

SUMMARY

The presentation of reliability and availability techniques in this chapter followed the organization of Table 3-1, which provides a logical progression of techniques from the simplest methods of fault avoidance to the most complex methods of dynamic redundancy. However, there are two elements missing from this development. First, the major emphasis is on *techniques*, and not on the *functionality* of the system elements they are used on. This chapter could also have been organized on the basis of function: memories, processors, ALUs, operating systems, and so on. Organization by function would highlight which techniques work best in each area of system design and how those techniques can be best implemented for that design area. However, organization by technique has the important advantage of stressing the universality of techniques. Most techniques can be incorporated into several, if not all, areas of design. Thus, rather than improving the reliability of isolated pieces of a system at a time, the designer can choose to apply a single technique over several areas. For example, parity error detection can be applied to a memory, register set, ALU (with parity prediction), and the connecting data paths. A single parity checker on each data path, monitoring each transaction, is sufficient to monitor system health. By using a single technique for all the pieces, the need for multiple translators, checkers, and encoders of several different types has been eliminated.

The other element missing from the organization of this chapter is the simultaneous use of multiple techniques. The development followed required treating each technique as a separate entity. Often, two or more reliability improvement techniques can be synergistically combined to provide vastly improved protection. Examples of a few such combinations have been briefly mentioned, such as the shadow box memory. Many other combinations are possible; their suitability depends on the application. For this reason, the evaluation methods and criteria de-

veloped in the following chapters are necessary to ensure successful use of the techniques presented in this chapter.

REFERENCES

Abraham [1975]; Anderson [1971]; Anderson and Lee [1979]; Anderson and Metze [1973]; Ashjaee and Reddy [1976]; Armstrong [1961]; Avizienis [1971, 1973, 1977, 1978]; Avizienis et al. [1971]; Avrulpragasm and Swarz [1980]; AWST [1981]; Barsi and Maestrini [1973, 1974]; Baskin, Borgerson, and Roberts [1972]; Beaudry [1978]; Berlekamp [1968]; Bhatt and Kinney [1978]; Black, Sundberg, and Walker [1977]; Boone, Liebergot, and Sedmak [1980]; Borgerson and Freitas [1975]; Bossen [1970]; Bouricius et al. [1971]; Brown, Tierney, and Wasserman [1961]; Carter, Duke, and Jessup [1973]; Carter and McCarthy [1976]; Carter and Schneider [1968]; Carter and Wadia [1980]; Castillo and Siewiorek [1980]; Chandy and Ramamoorthy [1972]; Chen and Avizienis [1978]; Chinal [1977]; Cook et al. [1973]; Cooper and Chow [1976]; Craig [1980]; Crouzet and Landrault [1980]; Davies and Wakerly [1978]; DeAngelis and Lauro [1976]; Dennis [1974]; DeSousa and Mathur [1978]; Diaz, Geffroy, and Courvoisier [1974]; Diaz, Azema, and Ayache [1979]; Dickinson, Jackson, and Randa [1964]; DEC [1975, 1977, 1979]; Frank and Yau [1966]; Freeman and Metze [1972]; Fujiwara and Kawakami [1977]; Gay and Ketelson [1979]; Goldberg, Levitt, and Wensley [1974]; Gurzi [1965]; Hamming [1950]; Hampel and Winder [1971]; Hong and Patel [1972]; Hopkins, Smith, and Lala [1978]; Hsiao [1970]; Hsiao and Bossen [1975]; Hsiao, Bossen, and Chien [1970]; Ihara et al. [1978]; Ingle and Siewiorek [1973a, 1973b, 1976]; Interdata [1975]; Jack et al. [1975]; Jensen [1963]; Kaneda and Fujiwara [1980]; Kautz [1962]; Kautz, Levitt, and Waksman [1968]; Khodadad-Mostashiry [1979]; Klaassen and Van Peppen [1977a, 1977b]; Klaschka [1969]; Kole [1980]; Lampson [1979]; Larsen and Reed [1972]; Lee, Ghani, and Heron [1980]; Levitt, Green, and Goldberg [1968]; Lewis [1979]; Lin [1970]; Losq [1975a, 1975b, 1978]; MacWilliams and Sloane [1978]; Maison [1971]; Mandelbaum [1972a, 1972b]; Marouf and Friedman [1977, 1978]; Mathur [1971a]; Mathur and Avizienis [1970]; Mathur and DeSousa [1975]; McCluskey and Ogus [1977]; McConnel and Siewiorek [1981]; McDonald [1976]; McDonald and

McCracken [1977]; McKevitt [1972]; McNamara [1977]; Meraud, Browaeys, and Germain [1976]; Meraud et al. [1979]; Meyer [1971, 1978]; Meyer, Furchgott, and Wu [1980]; Mine and Koga [1967]; Mine and Hatayama [1979]; Morganti, Coppadoro, and Ceru [1978]; Mukai and Thoma [1974]; Neumann and Rao [1975]; O'Brien [1976]; Ogus [1973, 1974]; Ornstein et al. [1975]; Osman and Weiss [1973]; Ossfeldt and Jonsson [1980]; Ozgunner [1977]; Patterson and Metze [1974]; Peterson and Weldon [1972]; Pierce [1965]; Platteter [1980]; Pradhan [1978a, 1978b]; Pradhan and Reddy [1974a, 1974b]; Pradhan and Stiffler [1980]; Randell [1975]; Randell, Lee, and Treleaven [1978]; Rao [1970, 1972, 1974]; Ray-Chaudhuri [1961]; Reddy [1978]; Reed and Chiang [1970]; Russel [1978]; Russel and Tiedeman [1979]; Russo [1965]; Sawin [1975]; Sedmak and Liebergot [1980]; Sellers, Hsiao, and Bearnson [1968b]; Shedletsky [1978a, 1978b]; Shen and Hayes [1980]; Short [1968]; Shrivastava and Akinpelu [1978]; Siewiorek, Canepa, and Clark [1977a]; Siewiorek and McCluskey [1973a, 1973b]; Siewiorek, Bell, and Newell [1982]; Siewiorek et al. [1978a, 1978b]; Sklaroff [1976]; Smith and Hopkins [1978]; Smith and Metze [1978]; Srinivasan [1971b]; Stiffler [1976, 1978]; Swan, Fuller, and Siewiorek [1977a]; Tang and Chien [1969]; Tohma and Aoyagi [1971]; Tohma [1974]; Tokura, Kasami, and Hashimoto [1971]; Torng [1972]; Toy [1978]; Troy [1977, 1978]; Tryon [1962]; Usas [1978]; von Neumann [1956]; Wachter [1975]; Wakerly [1974, 1978]; Waksman [1968]; Watson and Hastings [1966]; Weissberger [1980].

PROBLEMS

1. There are 32 data lines on a bus protected by four interlaced parity bits. Parity bits 1 and 3 are odd parity and parity bits 2 and 4 are even parity.
   a. Sketch the data bus and indicate which lines are covered by which parity bits.
   b. List all fault sets that are detected in one bus transfer. Illustrate one fault from each set on your diagram.
2. Assuming that only transient errors lasting exactly one operation cycle of the system can occur, the triple modular redundancy is equivalent to (choose one)
   a. a Hamming single-error-correcting, double-error-detecting code
   b. a simple parity code (odd parity)
   c. a repetition code with a complete decoding algorithm
   d. a repetition code with an incomplete decoding algorithm.
3. A Hamming single-error-correcting code has the parity-check matrix

$$H = \begin{bmatrix} 0 & 0 & 1 & 1 & 1 & 0 & 1 \\ 0 & 1 & 0 & 0 & 1 & 1 & 1 \\ 1 & 0 & 0 & 1 & 1 & 1 & 0 \end{bmatrix}$$

A word [0111011] was received. The word sent must be (choose one)
   a. [0110011]
   b. [0111001]
   c. [0111010]
   d. [0001011].
4. Below is a parity matrix for a Hamming code.

$$\begin{array}{c} \\ c_1 \\ c_2 \\ c_3 \end{array} \begin{array}{ccccccc} d_1 & c_1 & d_2 & c_2 & d_3 & c_3 & d_4 \\ \begin{bmatrix} 0 & 1 & 1 & 1 & 0 & 1 & 0 \\ 1 & 0 & 0 & 1 & 0 & 1 & 1 \\ 1 & 1 & 0 & 0 & 1 & 1 & 0 \end{bmatrix} \end{array}$$

   a. Write the parity equations for the three check bits.
   b. Using these parity equations, encode the data word $d_1 d_2 d_3 d_4 = 0110$.
   c. The encoded word 1100001 ($d_1 c_1 d_2 c_2 d_3 c_3 d_4$) has a single-bit error. Which bit is in error?
   d. Assuming that bit failures are independent and the probability of failure is p, what is the probability that the encoded data is not decoded correctly?
   e. If the receiver and support electronics has a reliability of $k/(1 - p)$, where k is a constant, what value of p maximizes the reliability of the system?
5. A binary transmission channel is said to be an erasure channel if a received bit may be neither a one nor a zero. Such an error is called an *erasure*. To correct up to e erasures, the minimum distance between any two code words must be (choose one)
   a. e
   b. $e + 1$
   c. $2e$
   d. $2e + 1$.
6. Which of the following cannot be a code word in a linear single-error-correcting Hamming code?
   a. 0010110
   b. 1101100

c. 1110110

d. 0110000

e. 1010111

7. A 3-of-6 code was modified by adding two check bits that indicated how many ones the 6 information bits have. The number of all possible erroneous words that go undetected is (choose one)

a. 20

b. 22

c. 32

d. 42

e. 41.

8. The arithmetic distance between the two codewords [100001] and [010011] is (choose one)

a. 1

b. 2

c. 3

d. 4.

9. In a $25N + 15$ single-error-correcting arithmetic code, a word [10010011] was received from the ALU. Therefore, the corrected output of the ALU is (choose one)

a. 0001011

b. 1011011

c. 0111011

d. 1001100

e. 1110011.

10. A biresidue code forms residues modulo 3 and modulo 7. An erroneous word is ([01111], 2, 0). Assuming that the check bits are correct, the corrected information bits are (choose one)

a. [10000]

b. [10001]

c. [01110]

d. [01101].

11. In a computing system, memory is one of the chief sources of failures. When a high degree of data integrity is desired, the overhead for encoding and decoding may be tolerated. To correct a single-bit error (Hamming error) in an 8-bit byte, speed is to be sacrificed in favor of minimizing the total storage required for a task. The problem is thus to maximize the number of code words. Find a single-error-correcting code of block length eight with a maximum number of code words. (Hint: A linear code of block length eight has 16 code words. A code that is made up of a number of cyclic spaces has 20 code words but is not the code that maximizes the number of code words.)

12. For the double-error-correcting code with the parity-check matrix

$$H = \begin{bmatrix} 0 & 0 & 1 & 1 & 1 & 0 & 1 \\ 0 & 1 & 0 & 0 & 1 & 1 & 1 \\ 1 & 0 & 0 & 1 & 1 & 1 & 0 \\ 0 & 0 & 1 & 1 & 0 & 1 & 1 \\ 0 & 1 & 0 & 1 & 1 & 0 & 1 \\ 1 & 1 & 1 & 0 & 0 & 0 & 1 \end{bmatrix}$$

the syndrome formed was [101110]. This implied (choose one)

a. no error

b. single error

c. double error

d. more than two errors.

13. With the same parity-check matrix, if the bits are numbered 1 through 7 from left to right, a syndrome [100111] implies (choose one)

a. a single error in position 3

b. two bit errors in positions 1 and 4

c. two bit errors in positions 1 and 5

d. more than two bit errors.

14. For a double-error-correcting code of block length 32, the least upper bound on the number of information bits is (choose one)

a. 24

b. 25

c. 26

d. 27

e. 28.

15. Given the polynomials $h(x) = X^2 + 1$ and $g(x) = x^4 + x + 1$, the circuit

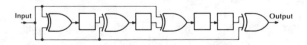

can be used (with proper initial conditions) to obtain from the incoming polynomial $f(x)$ the output (choose one)

a. f/gh

b. fh/g

c. fg/h

d. fgh

e. $f(g + h)$.

16. With the input polynomial $x^7 + 1$ and the circuit

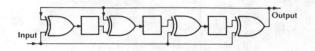

the output polynomial will be (choose one)
a. $x + 1$
b. $x^2 + 1$
c. $x^{14} + 1$
d. $x^7 + x^6 + x^5 + x^4 + x + 1$.

17. A new disk storage unit is to be added to a PDP-10 system. Because the performance of the system deteriorates considerably as a result of disk failures, the new disk should be as reliable as possible. The field was narrowed to two disks, DSKRAW and DSKCRC. Both store up to 200 million bytes (eight-bit wide), run at a rate of 3,600 rpm with a byte transfer frequency of 1.25 MHz. Both cost approximately the same. The difference lies in redundancy techniques. DSKRAW uses a Read-After-Write (RAW) to detect (and correct) errors in transfer, while DSKCRC uses a cyclic redundancy code (CRC). The CRC generates a 16-bit check word using a generator polynomial

$$x^{16} + x^{12} + x^5 + 1$$

on an information frame of any size. Carry out a reliability analysis on the two disks and make recommendations.

18. The design goal is an SEC memory for a 16-bit minicomputer with memory mapping. The memory is to be a 128K-word memory, built with 1K-bit MOS RAMs. Assume that the ambient temperature is 30° C, components are of quality class C,

the environment is ground fixed, and single-bit failures are the dominant mode of memory-chip failures.

a. To save on memory chips, a 39-bit SEC/DED Hamming code is to be used (its parity-check matrix is given below). Design the correction/detection/encoding tree, holding register, correction circuit, and other data path elements shown in the block diagram in Figure 5-16. Use 7400 series TTL and do not bother with pin numbers (this is a rough design). Assume control circuitry of 10 SSI chips ($\approx$ 8 gates per chip) and 5 MSI chips ($\approx$ 15 gates each). Evaluate this design using the MIL-217 model and techniques discussed in this chapter.

b. Design a block-coded memory with a better MTTF. Assess the difference in cost in number of chips (if any). Assume 10 MSI and 15 SSI chips for auxiliary circuitry, and design the data-path elements shown in the block-code memory diagram in Figure 5-17. Justify your choice of block size.

c. Discuss the relative performance (not reliability) of the two designs, both with and without errors present. Can the vertical parity words be kept in a separate memory so that they can be accessed in parallel with the data on writes? How does this affect the performance? Discuss the conditions under which you would choose each design.

19. a. The 8080 microprocessor chip has approximately 1000 gates. Calculate the failure rates of this architecture assuming SSI, MSI, and LSI implementation (40°C ambient).

b. What is the effect of changing π_q for the three implementations above? Changing the ambient

Parity-check matrix for 39-bit SEC/DED Hamming code.

1	1	1	1	1	1	1	1	1	1	1	1	1	1	1	1	1	1	1	1	1	1	1	1	1	1	1	1	1	1	1	1	1	1	1	1	1	1	1
0	0	0	0	0	0	0	0	0	0	0	0	0	0	0	0	0	0	0	0	0	0	0	0	0	0	0	0	0	0	0	1	1	1	1	1	1	1	0
0	0	0	0	0	0	0	0	0	0	0	0	0	0	0	1	1	1	1	1	1	1	1	1	1	1	1	1	1	1	1	0	0	0	0	0	0	0	0
0	0	0	0	0	0	1	1	1	1	1	1	1	1	1	0	0	0	0	0	0	0	0	1	1	1	1	1	1	1	1	0	0	0	0	0	0	0	0
0	0	0	1	1	1	1	0	0	0	0	1	1	1	1	0	0	0	0	1	1	1	1	0	0	0	0	1	1	1	1	0	0	0	0	1	1	1	0
0	1	1	0	0	1	1	0	0	1	1	0	0	1	1	0	0	1	1	0	0	1	1	0	0	1	1	0	0	1	1	0	0	1	1	0	0	1	0
1	0	1	0	1	0	1	0	1	0	1	0	1	0	1	0	1	0	1	0	1	0	1	0	1	0	1	0	1	0	1	0	1	0	1	0	1	0	0

temperature from 40°C to 30°C? Compare these effects over the three different implementations.

c. Assume SSI chips cost 20 cents, MSI chips 50 cents, and LSI chips $10; and that screening weeds out all but 0.2 percent of the weak components. Also assume that the average diagnosis and repair cost due to a bad chip is $5 plus the chip cost through the warranty period. Compare the expected repair costs for the SSI, MSI, and LSI implementations of the 8080 architecture.

20. a. In a memory made with 1K-bit by four-bit-wide chips, there are 16 data bits and 2K words. Zero and one bit values are equally likely. Assume chip failure modes are single-bit cell (50 percent), single-row all zeros (20 percent), single-column all zeros (20 percent), and whole-chip all zeros (10 percent). Calculate single error detection coverage for this scheme when the following detection techniques are used:
   i. interlaced parity ($i = 4$)
   ii. chip parity
   iii. chip-wide parity
   iv. duplication
   v. single-precision checksum (assume checksum is stored separately, one sum for the entire memory)
   vi. low-cost residue code (checksum stored separately).

b. Estimate costs (chip counts) for the memories above, including check circuitry. Comment on relative performance overheads.

21. What is the CRC constant for the CRC code used by AUTODIN II, with $G(x) = x^{32} + x^{26} + x^{23} + x^{16} + x^{12} + x^{11} + x^{10} + x^8 + x^7 + x^5 + x^4 + x^2 + x + 1$? Design a BCR for this code.

22. In the multiplexer for parity-coded operands shown at the top of the next column [Wakerly, 1978], $\langle S_1 S_0 \rangle = \langle 01 \rangle$ transfers bus A to bus T, while $\langle 10 \rangle$ transfers bus B to bus T.

a. Demonstrate that this circuit is totally self-checking.

b. Design a totally self-checking multiplexer network around this TSC multiplexer; that is, the network serves as a multiplexer with a TSC error-detection indicator.

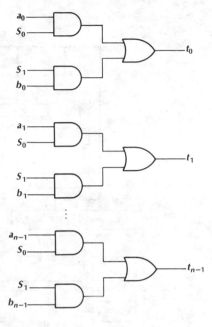

23. a. A digital system block diagram is shown on the next page. Discuss which fault-detection techniques can be used to prevent undetected errors in this system.

b. Discuss the application of TMR with voting to this system. Consider replication at various architectural levels.

c. Discuss the application of error-correcting codes to this system in at least five different segments of the design.

24. a. Using the next-state and output-function table below, design a single-error-correcting coded-state machine. Compare its cost and reliability with a TMR implementation of the same machine. The machine is synchronous, with an external clock signal.

		Input		
State	01	11	10	00
a	a/1	c/0	h/0	e/1 next state/output
b	c/1	a/1	d/1	f/0
c	b/1	g/0	e/1	f/1
d	g/0	c/0	d/1	e/1
e	a/1	b/0	c/0	e/0
f	b/0	b/1	g/1	h/0
g	h/0	h/1	b/0	g/1
h	e/1	c/1	d/1	a/1

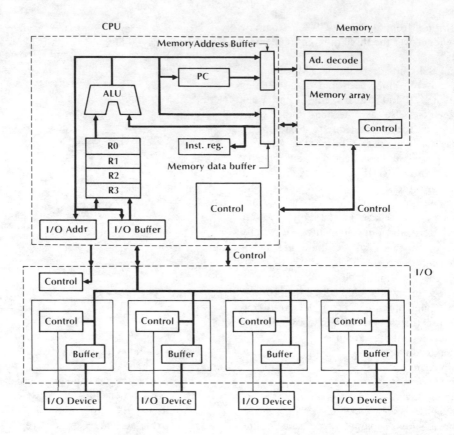

b. Implement the next-state function in quadded logic. Compare the cost with a TMR implementation. Compare maximum clocking speeds.

25. a. Design restoring organs for a redundant module with two output lines and a redundancy factor of 5 (five identical modules) using the following techniques:
   i. NMR/simplex ($N = 5$)
   ii. hybrid TMR
   iii. duplication with spares switching (assume an external diagnostic circuit can correctly determine which of the two modules is faulty with probability 0.95, and takes 10 ms to do so)
   iv. self-purging redundancy
   v. sift-out redundancy

   Use standard TTL logic (designs down to pin number detail are not necessary).

b. Assume new data are produced synchronously every 500 ns, that gate complexities for the function modules are 2,000 gates each, and that the duplication diagnostic circuit uses 300 gates. Compare the five designs for complexity, cost, performance, and reliability.

26. Discuss the issues involved in making a multiprocessor system such as the Intel 432 (Chapter 18) gracefully degradable (cost, extra circuitry, performance, computation overhead, detection and diagnostic capability); assume that
   a. no modification can be made to the hardware
   b. simple alterations can be made to the hardware

28. Redesign the error-correcting code memory of Problem 18 to allow it to switch in two spare bit planes. Evaluate the effect on the memory system cost, performance, and reliability.

29. Select a computer system for which processor and operating system documentation is available to you. Analyze the fault tolerance, fault detection, and recovery techniques and abilities of the hardware/software system. Propose some low-cost improvements that might be made.

30. a. Pick a technique from each of the subsections in Chapter 3 dealing with error detection, fault masking, and dynamic redundancy. Use each independently in the design of the same (logically) microstore. Rank the designs in terms of cost, performance, and reliability.

    b. Combine the techniques chosen above in groups of two (using each technique in only one pair) and apply them to the same microstore above. Rank the designs in terms of cost, performance, and reliability.

    c. Select four of the techniques above to make the best possible microstore design. Evaluate the cost, performance, and reliability of this design.

Maintainability and Testing Techniques

A significant proportion of maintenance involves some form of testing, not only to isolate the failed component but also to ensure that the repair operation was successful. This chapter examines maintainability from the perspective of testing.

Testing can be characterized as a "black box" experiment. Each black box has an associated set of input and output terminals. The correct functioning of the black box must be determined by applying stimuli to the input terminals and observing responses on the output terminals, called terminal characteristics. The terminal characteristics may be electrical (such as a straight-line relationship between voltage and current for a resistor), combinational (such as an AND gate), sequential (such as a counter), or even complex systems (such as a microprocessor on a chip). As the functions of the component become more complex the testing problem becomes critical, for there is less direct control and less direct observability of internal behavior. Manipulation of external inputs must establish a certain condition in a component deep in the recesses of the black box, and the outputs of that component must be propagated to the output terminals. With increasing system complexity, not only are there more components, but each component is also harder to test.

Testing covers multiple activities, not just maintenance, during the life of a digital system. Table 4-1, reproduced from Chapter 1, depicts the stages in the life of a system. During the specification and design phase the faults of most concern are logic errors in the algorithms. During prototype development there can be any number of failures. Logical design errors, wiring mistakes, or incorrect timing can lead to different functional behavior. Failed components can also cause altered functional behavior. The former, designated as a logical fault, can be signifi-

Table 4–1.   Stages in the development of a system.

Stage	Error Sources	Error Detection Techniques
Specification and design	Algorithm design	Simulation
	Formal specification	Consistency checks
Prototype	Algorithm design	Stimulus/ response testing
	Wiring and assembly	
	Timing	
	Component failure	
Manufacture	Wiring and assembly	System testing
	Component failure	Diagnostics
Installation	Assembly	System testing
	Component failure	Diagnostics
Operational field	Component failure	Diagnostics
	Operator errors	
	Environmental factors	

cantly more difficult to test than the latter, termed a structural fault. With logical faults, the proper algorithm must be ultimately distinguished from any arbitrary algorithm. Here testing involves many similarities to proving programs correct; however, given a correct design, there are many fewer faulty behaviors due to a malfunction. The component interconnections limit the number of realizable faulty behaviors.

In prototype development, the final errors in the design and proposed implementation are sought by testing. Physical connectivity may cause timing errors and coupling between multiple signal lines. Subjecting a small number of systems to design maturity testing (described in Chapter 1) establishes baseline failure manifestations and MTTF.

During manufacturing and installation the main goal is acceptance testing. At this stage, problems of design have been resolved, and testing focuses on mass-produced black boxes. The faults are primarily structural, but there may be any number of them resulting from the assembly process.

When an installed system malfunctions, maintenance testing is used to isolate and repair faults. This is perhaps the easiest form of testing, for at this stage there are usually few structural faults. Frequently, maintenance tests are run during system idle time to detect failures and increase confidence in the correct functioning of the system. As mentioned in Chapter 1, there is a significant trend toward remote diagnosis, either to pinpoint failures before dispatching field service personnel or to issue instructions for customer repair.

At any of the stages of system life, testing can occur at each level in the system hierarchy defined in Chapter 1 (circuit, logical, program, and system). Figure 4-1 classifies the types of testing typically performed at each stage. The figure has been simplified by combining the design/prototype and installation/operational stages and the logical/instruction set levels.

It is extremely important to understand at what level and stage a testing technique is aimed. Chapter 1 briefly discussed system-level testing at all three stages presented in Figure 4-1. This chapter focuses on logic-level testing at the production and operational stages. Maintainability techniques for discovering faults during field operation can frequently also be used to isolate defects during the production stage.

PRODUCTION

As pointed out in Chapter 1, defects should be located and eliminated at the earliest possible stage of production; the cost of a defect increases by a factor of 10 with each inspection stage that fails to identify it [Hotchkiss, 1979;

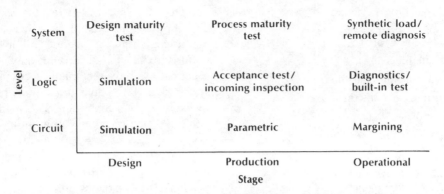

Figure 4–1. Testing as a function of system level and time.

Craig, 1980]. Figure 4-2, reproduced here from Chapter 1, shows the typical steps in the manufacturing process.

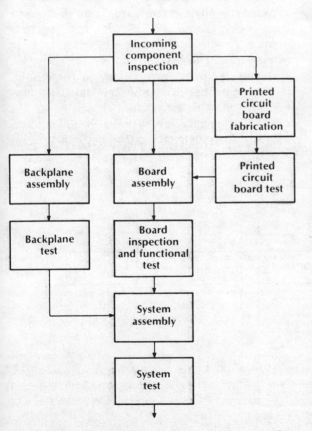

Figure 4–2. Typical steps in the manufacture of a digital system. (© 1979 IEEE.)

Parametric Testing

At the circuit level, incoming inspection may vary from simple electrical parametric and functional tests to stress-tests that force infant mortalities. Stress testing can include vibration, overvoltage, burn-in, and thermal shock (see Chapter 2). The more extensive the testing, the more costly the incoming inspection. For mass-produced, low-cost systems, incoming inspection is often less than 100 percent because only randomly selected lots are tested.

Table 4-2 lists some typical parametric tests used to determine whether components meet vendors' electrical specifications. Figure 4-3 illustrates a computer-driven test station for driving and measuring electrical parameters [Howard and Nahourai, 1978]. A relay matrix is used to configure the sources and measuring instruments to the pin configuration of the unit under test. Parametric testing is most often done by the IC manufacturer or by a system house when it initially qualifies an IC vendor's process.

Acceptance Testing

The largest body of theory has been developed for logic-level acceptance testing. Usually single structural stuck-at-logical-0/1 faults are assumed. A means must be provided for generating stimulus and checking responses in the Unit Under Test (UUT). Table 4-3 categorizes the varied approaches to testing. In general, any

Table 4–2. Typical MOS parametric tests.

Gate-oxide breakdown voltage

Drain-to-substrate breakdown voltage

Drain-to-source punchthrough voltage

Gate-to-source threshold voltage

Drain current at 0 gate voltage

Drain current at specified operating voltage

Gate-to-source leakage current

Drain-to-substrate leakage current

Transconductance at specified operating voltage

Drain-source resistance

stimulus generation approach could be used with any response checking approach; however, certain stimulus/response approach pairs have been more widely adopted than others.

The stimulus/response can be generated off-chip or on-chip. If off-chip, they may be dynamically generated or precomputed and stored. Table 4-3 provides the framework for discussion of the various testing approaches developed.

The simplest form of response checking is to compare the outputs of the UUT with those of a known good component (exclusive OR testing). The input stimuli could be generated by incrementing a counter to produce all possible combinations (exhaustive testing). Exhaustive testing is practical for only the smallest circuits. Williams and Parker [1979] give an example of an exhaustive test of an LSI circuit with n inputs and m latches, which requires a minimum of 2^{n+m} tests. For $n = 25$ and $m = 50$ there are $2^{75} = 3.8 \times 10^{22}$ patterns. At 1 microsecond per pattern the test would require over a billion years.

Alternatively, the stimuli could be generated randomly (probabilistic testing). In probabilistic testing, a predetermined number of inputs are generated and properties of the output observed. The output properties are then compared with stored characteristics of the good circuit. This response checking is termed compact testing because responses are not stored or checked in detail; only summary statistics are checked. Summary statistics include counting the number of 1s produced and/or the number of transitions. If the count exceeds a predetermined threshold, the component is declared functional. The number, arrived at statistically, is chosen to yield a specific confidence level [Williams and Parker,

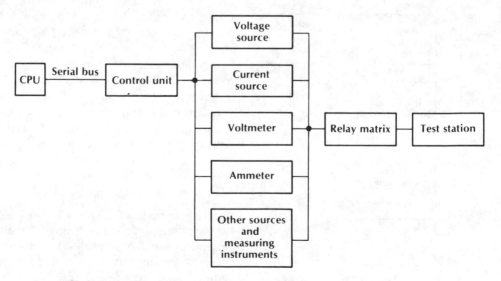

Figure 4–3. Block diagram of an automated parametric test system.

Table 4–3. Approaches to stimulus generation and response checking.

Stimulus Generation	Response Checking
Exhaustive	Exclusive OR
Random	Stored
	Compact testing
	Transition counting
	Signature analysis
Stored	
Simulation	Predicted response
Deductive	
Parallel	Fault dictionary
Concurrent	
Algorithmically generated	
Algebraic	
Boolean difference	
Path sensitization	
D-algorithm	
On-chip	On-chip

1979]. A variation of compact testing is signature analysis [Nadig, 1977]. In signature analysis, a set of known inputs is dynamically applied to the UUT. The outputs are either displayed for visual comparison with a known good pattern or sensed by computer for comparison with a stored pattern. If the patterns produced by the most likely failures are stored, signature analysis can also be used for fault diagnosis. Often output patterns are summarized by feeding the sequence of outputs into Feedback Shift Registers (FSR), such as those used in the generation and checking of serial codes (see Chapter 3). The FSR output is a function of all the response bits, no matter how long the test sequence may be. Although theoretically appealing, compact testing in practice usually provides low fault coverage. In any event, the fault coverage is extremely hard to

estimate. Consequently, effort has focused on the systematic generation of input stimuli.

Systematic test-set generation starts with a list of all faults of concern. The fault set usually consists of all single stuck-at-logical 0/1 faults. A test for each fault is generated in turn. Once a fault list and set of tests have been generated, it is possible to select a minimal set of tests to detect all faults or to determine which fault is present [Kautz, 1968].

Tests can be generated by simulation, algebraic methods, and path sensitization. In simulation, faults are inserted into the simulation of the circuit. Both the faulty and the good circuit are simulated until their outputs differ [Seshu and Freeman, 1962]. This is primarily a trial-and-error approach. Faulty behavior may be deduced from a logic simulator by comparing the simulated output of each component with the faulted output. Alternatively, the nonfaulty and several faulty circuits could be simulated and compared in parallel. In concurrent simulation, circuit components are copied and simulated every time the faulty output differs from the good circuit [Grason and Nagle, 1980].

For each test, the predicted output is stored for use in response checking. If the responses of faulty and good circuits are tabulated into a fault dictionary, field service personnel can use the dictionary to diagnose to the field replaceable unit. Chang, Smith, and Walford [1974] describe the LAMP system used to create fault dictionaries for the computers used in the Bell System.

An alternative to simulation is algorithmic generation of the stimulus. One algorithmic approach is based upon an algebra of differences. Sellers, Hsiao, and Bearnson [1968a] and Susskind [1972] describe an algebraic approach called the Boolean Difference. Figure 4-4 illustrates a circuit and a minimal test set for all single stuck-at faults (see Appendix C). Each line has a separate identification number and can be stuck-at either logical 0 or 1. The abstract model makes no assumption about electrical connectivity; thus, a stuck-at fault on line 5 does not imply

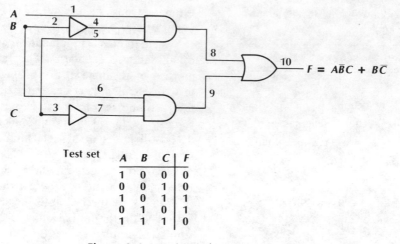

Test set

A	B	C	F
1	0	0	0
0	0	1	0
1	0	1	1
0	1	0	1
1	1	1	0

Figure 4–4. A circuit for test generation.

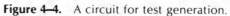

Table 4–4. The D-algorithm definition of elementary gate functions in terms of the symbol D.

	AND				OR	
Input 1	Input 2	Output		Input 1	Input 2	Output
1	1	1		1	1	1
1	0	0		1	0	1
0	1	0		0	1	1
0	0	0		0	0	0
1	D	D		1	D	1
D	1	D		D	1	1
1	$\overline{D}$	$\overline{D}$		1	$\overline{D}$	1
$\overline{D}$	1	$\overline{D}$		$\overline{D}$	1	1
0	D	0		0	D	D
D	0	0		D	0	D
0	$\overline{D}$	0		0	$\overline{D}$	$\overline{D}$
$\overline{D}$	0	0		$\overline{D}$	0	$\overline{D}$
D	D	D		D	D	D
$\overline{D}$	$\overline{D}$	$\overline{D}$		$\overline{D}$	$\overline{D}$	$\overline{D}$
$\overline{D}$	D	0		$\overline{D}$	D	1
D	$\overline{D}$	0		D	$\overline{D}$	1

Inverter

Input	Output
1	0
0	1
D	$\overline{D}$
$\overline{D}$	D

anything about line 3. In practice, certain faults, such as an open metalization, will comply with this abstraction while others, such as a short-to-ground, may cause several lines to be in error.

A test for a fault is one in which the faulty circuit's output differs from that of the good circuit. Consider line 5 stuck-at-1 in Figure 4-4. The first test, 100, should produce an output of 0. With line 5 stuck-at-1, the output is 1. Hence, 100 is a test for line 5 stuck-at-1 (as well as for other faults).

The Boolean Difference for a line, i, is defined as the exclusive-OR of the function with line i taking on the values of both 1 and 0:

$$\frac{dF}{dx_i} \triangleq F(x_1, x_2, \ldots, x_{i-1}, 1, x_{i+1}, \ldots, x_n)$$

$$\oplus F(x_1, x_2, \ldots, x_{i-1}, 0, x_{i+1}, \ldots x_n)$$

The Boolean Difference generates all tests such that a change in the value of x_i results in a change in the value of F. For the example in Figure 4-4,

$$\frac{dF}{dx_5} = (x_1 x_4 + x_6 x_7) \oplus x_6 x_7$$

Setting $dF/dx_5 = 1$ yields all the tests for line 5.

$$1 = (x_1 x_4 + x_6 x_7) \oplus x_6 x_7$$
$$= (\bar{x}_1 + \bar{x}_4)(\bar{x}_6 + \bar{x}_7) x_6 x_7$$
$$+ (x_1 x_4 + x_6 x_7)(\bar{x}_6 + \bar{x}_7)$$
$$= x_1 x_4 \bar{x}_6 + x_1 x_4 \bar{x}_7$$

For $x_1 x_4 \bar{x}_6 = 110$, $F = x_5$, and for $x_1 x_4 \bar{x}_7 = 110$, $F = x_5$. The corresponding input tests are:

$$ABC = 100 \text{ for } x_5 \text{ stuck-at-1 and}$$

$$ABC = 101 \text{ for } x_5 \text{ stuck-at-0.}$$

Path sensitization techniques are essentially an intelligent form of simulation. In path sensitization, all components along a path from the fault to an output are placed in a state such that the output changes value only as a function of the value of the faulty component. To complete the test, the conditions to sensitize the path are driven back, by means of consistency checks, to corresponding conditions on the network inputs. In all these methods, once a test has been generated, a post process determines which other faults in the fault list have also been detected and eliminates them from the list. In Figure 4-4, in order to propagate x_5 to the output, lines 1 and 4 have to be 1 and line 9 has to be 0. Driving these values back toward the circuit inputs implies that $A = 1$, $B = 0$.

The path sensitization approach has been formalized in the D-algorithm [Roth, 1966; Roth, Bouricius, and Schneider, 1967]. A symbol, D, is defined to be equal to 1 in the good circuit and to 0 in a bad circuit ($\bar{D}$ is 0 in the good circuit and 1 in a bad circuit). Each elementary gate has its function redefined in terms of the symbol D, as shown in Table 4-4. First D is placed on the line for which a test is to be generated, and then propagated to circuit outputs one step at a time. An implication step sets values on other circuit lines required to realize the state specified by the propagation step. The propagation/implication cycle is repeated until either D or $\bar{D}$ is propagated to the circuit outputs. If at least one test exists, the D-algorithm is guaranteed to find one.

Starting with $\bar{D}$ on line 5 (line 5 stuck-at-1) of Figure 4-4, the three propagation steps from line 5 to line 8 to line 10 could be tabulated as shown in Figure 4-5. The D is propagated through each elementary gate in turn without regard to the state of other gates. The implication steps assign values to other circuit lines. For example, in order for line 8 to take a value $\bar{D}$, lines 1 and 4 must be 1. Line 4 being 1 implies line 2 being 0. Contradictions (such as a line taking on both a 0 and a 1 value) signal the nonexistence of a test.

In any algorithmic test-generation technique, once a test for a fault has been found, the list of faults the test has detected is compared with the original fault list. Tested faults are thus removed and the fault list shortened. Significant work has been done to reduce the length of the original

Step	Line									
	1	2	3	4	5	6	7	8	9	10
Initial test on Line 5	x	x	x	x	$\bar{D}$	x	x	x	x	x
Implication on other gate inputs	x	x	$\bar{D}$	x	$\bar{D}$	x	x	x	x	x
Propagate to Line 8	x	x	$\bar{D}$	x	$\bar{D}$	x	x	D	x	x
Implication on other gate inputs	1	0	$\bar{D}$	1	$\bar{D}$	x	x	$\bar{D}$	x	x
Propagate to Line 10	1	0	$\bar{D}$	1	$\bar{D}$	x	x	$\bar{D}$	x	D
Implication on other gate inputs	1	0	$\bar{D}$	1	$\bar{D}$	0	0	$\bar{D}$	0	D

a. Forward propagation and implication

$$
\begin{array}{ccc|c}
A & B & C & F \\
1 & 0 & \bar{D} & \bar{D}
\end{array}
$$

b. Test

Figure 4–5. The D-algorithm applied to Line 5 stuck-at-1 in Figure 4-4.

fault list by grouping faults into equivalence classes (that is, members of the class are indistinguishable) [McCluskey and Clegg, 1971].

Figure 4-6 shows the relationships among six faults for a two-input AND gate and their respective test sets. The test set for lines 1, 2, and 3 stuck-at-0 is the same. Hence, these are equivalent faults and it is sufficient to generate a test for only one of them. Another relationship between faults is that of dominance. Because the test set for line 3 stuck-at-1 includes the tests for lines 1 and 2 stuck-at-1, line 3 stuck-at-1 dominates those two faults. The dominating fault is automatically tested for if all the dominated faults are tested. Thus, instead of six faults on the original fault list for this two-input AND gate, only three are required: line 3 s-a-0, line 1 s-a-1, and line 2 s-a-1. In general, for elementary gates of N inputs, only $N + 1$ faults need to be on the original fault list instead of the $2(N + 1)$ single faults, provided the single-fault assumption is being used. The reduction of fault lists for multiple faults has also been addressed [Bossen and Hong, 1971]. Circuits exist, however, for which a test set for all single structural faults will not detect certain multiple faults. Fault models other than s-a-0, s-a-1 have also been used. The

bridging fault, frequently caused by a solder bridge, is a common fault type in digital system fabrication [Mei, 1974].

Special fault models developed for memories look for sensitivity to multiple-bit patterns. Table 4-5 lists some of these tests and their complexity as a function of the number of bits.

Test-set generation algorithms based on gate level and the stuck-at fault model are not applicable to VLSI complexity. Williams and Parker [1979] have observed that the computer run time to perform test generation and fault simulation is related to the number of logic gates by a cubic law:

$$T = kn^3$$

Hence, there have been efforts to test systems at higher levels of functionality [Breuer and Friedman, 1980; Thatte and Abraham, 1978]. The purpose of functional testing is to validate the correct functional operation of a digital system with respect to its functional specification. Ideally the tests developed are based solely on the specification and are capable of validating any implementation that is alleged to perform the specified function. Functional testing not only

	Fault	Test
Equivalent { 1	s-a-0	11
2	s-a-0	11
3	s-a-0	11
Dominated { 1	s-a-1	01
2	s-a-1	10
Dominating { 3	s-a-1	01,10,00

Figure 4–6. Equivalence and dominance relations among faults.

reduces test-generation complexity, but also, being free of implementation details, allows one test set to serve for implementations produced by multiple vendors. Indeed, manufacturers of LSI chips will not release the implementation details of their chips lest they be copied. Thus, the user of LSI chips who by necessity deals with multiple sources has no recourse but functional testing.

The literature abounds with surveys on test-set generation: Breuer and Friedman [1976], Chang, Manning, and Metze [1970], Friedman and Menon [1971], Hennie [1968], and Bennetts and Lewin [1971] are examples. More recent research has focused on generating tests and checking responses directly on the semiconductor chip, so that chips could test themselves without reliance on external support. Such self-testing chips could alleviate both production and operational testing. One approach [Bozorgui-Nesbat and McCluskey, 1980] partitions the logic into small

Table 4–5. Tests for pattern sensitivities in memory chips. (The test complexity is given in terms of the number of memory bits.)

Test	Complexity
Checkerboard pattern of 1s and 0s	N
Walking pattern	$N^{3/2}$
Galloping 1s and 0s (dynamic test)	N^2
Ping pong	N^2

groups for exhaustive testing. A counter on the group inputs generates all possible input combinations. An FSR on the group's output is compared with a hard-wired constant to provide the matching function.

Design for Testability

The discussion so far has focused on the problem of "Given a circuit, derive a test set for it." It has long been recognized that it is easier to derive test sets for some circuits than for others. Attempting to define easy-to-test properties has led to a new discipline called design for testability. Table 4-6 lists four stages of testability design. Each stage has an increasing effect upon the original design until ultimately a totally new design is created. Bennetts and Scott [1976] (see Appendix C) and Grason and Nagle [1980] discuss in detail techniques for each of these stages. Only a cursory review will be provided here.

The first stage in testability is developing test sets for an existing design. The faults assumed are usually of the single stuck-at structural variety. The Boolean Difference and *D*-algorithm are among the approaches used for combinational circuits. Sequential circuits are more difficult to test because of feedback. Approaches for combinational circuits have been extended to sequential circuits by replicating logic and treating the sequential circuit as a cascade of combinational circuits. Figure 4-7a depicts a typical sequential circuit. In Figure 4-7b the combinational logic has been replicated three times, representing three transitions in the state of the original circuit. The inputs in Figure 4-7b actually correspond to a sequence of three inputs to the original sequential circuit. Note that a single fault in the original circuit (such as a stuck-at-1 on a next-state line) would correspond to a multiple fault (a stuck-at-1 on all three copies of the next-state line) in the expanded circuit. Furthermore, there is no guarantee that the combinational logic test generation algorithms can find a test in three state transitions. The whole proc-

Table 4–6. Stages in design for testability.

Stage	Combinational	Sequential
Test set for unmodified circuit	Structural faults	Extension of combinational approaches for structural faults
		Functional faults
Minimum modification to existing circuit	Add a small number of test points	Add synchronizing sequence
		Add distinguishing sequence
		Break selected feedback
Extensive modification to existing circuit	Improve controllability	Make combinational LSSD
	Improve observability	
New design	Reed-Muller expansion	Fail-safe design
	Totally self-checking circuits	

ess may have to be repeated for multiple-state transitions until a test, if any, can be found. The increased number of faults to be considered and the additional complexity of the replicated logic make sequential circuit testing much more complicated than combinational circuit testing.

Another approach to sequential testing is based on a fault model that is different from the structural model. The sequential circuit is represented as a functional state-table, regardless of its implementation. Faults are simply changes in the next state or the output for an entry in the state table. Single structural faults may exist that are not representable by a single functional fault, and vice versa. The testing approach is to derive a sequence that ensures that each state, and each transition between states, exist. By assuming that faults cannot introduce new states, a test sequence (on the order of N^3 symbols, where N is the number of states) is generated such that no sequential machine of fewer states could respond correctly [Hennie, 1964].

The next stage in testability adds a small amount of logic to the existing circuit. For combinational logic this usually takes the form of insertion of a test point or control point. Test

points are added at critical positions (such as flip-flop outputs, sources of large fan-out, buses, deeply buried components) to increase observability. Control points (flip-flop inputs, large fan-in points, buses, deeply buried information paths) are added to increase control.

For sequential circuits, extra pins or logic may be added to produce synchronizing (set circuit to a known state) or distinguishing sequences. In addition, feedback lines may be broken by the insertion of independently controlled blocking gates.

The third stage starts with the original circuit but adds extensive modifications; any amount is possible, but 5 to 20 percent is typical. If sufficient logic is added, only three tests would be required for combinational logic circuits [Bennetts and Scott, 1976]. Often, however, it is not possible to make the extensive modifications, and a more practical approach is required. Table 4-7, from Grason and Nagle [1980], summarizes the types of added logic that can assist testing of printed circuit boards.

Test points can utilize pins at the edge of boards, sockets accessible to plug-in of automatic test equipment, internal posts accessible by

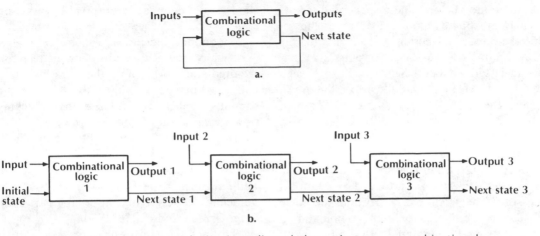

Figure 4–7. A sequential circuit replicated three times as a combinational circuit.

clips, tristate drivers to break or connect a line, and signal clips placed over an integrated circuit. Pull-up resistors can be used to isolate power supplies, providing constant logical values that allow the line to be forced to the opposite logical value.

Table 4–7. Design for testability-added hardware types.

Test points
    Edge connectors
    Dual In-line Package (DIP) sockets
    Terminal posts
    Tristate drivers
    IC clips
Pull-up resistors
Pin amplification
    Input demultiplexers
    Output multiplexers
    Parity trees
Blocking gates
Control and observation switching
Disconnection structures
    Edge connectors
    DIP sockets
    Tristate drivers
    Blocking gates
Test-state register
Power-up reset
Scan-in/scan-out shift registers

A major problem is to provide enough pins for observing/controlling the circuit. A small number of output pins can be driven by a multiplexer so that a large number of internal points can be sequentially observed. Likewise, a demultiplexer on a set of inputs can be used to drive a large set of controllability points. Parity trees can be used to summarize the state of a large number of points (like the on-board data reduction used in signature analysis). Blocking gates can be used to break feedback in sequential circuits or to partition a combinational circuit. Lines that are difficult to control/observe can be multiplexed with an easily controlled/observed line. In test mode, the easily controlled/observed line is tied directly to the difficult line.

Often circuits are easier to test if they are partitioned into smaller ones. Techniques similar to test-point addition can be used to partition (disconnect) the circuit. Circuit test-mode control information (such as the control of blocking gates, tristate drivers, multiplexers) may be more extensive than the number of test points that can be added. Test-mode information is relatively static and can often be derived from an on-board test-state register. Finally, a power-up signal can often be used to set a predetermined state into the sequential logic.

As mentioned before, many sequential testing strategies are based upon transforming the sequential circuit into a combinational circuit. One such technique uses scan-in/scan-out shift registers and is termed Level Sensitive Scan Design (LSSD) by IBM. Figure 4-8 illustrates the use of LSSD in the IBM 4341 [Frechette and Tanner, 1979]. Every latch is replaced by a latch pair. During normal operation the second latch is invisible. During test mode, the latch pairs are tied together into a shift register controlled by a separate clock (in this case provided by a support processor). The latch pairs partition the logic into sections composed only of combinational logic. In test-mode operation the test mode is set, test input data are shifted in, the normal mode is set, one system clock pulse is applied, the test mode is set again, and the result of the test is shifted out for analysis. LSSD makes the system

state almost completely observable and controllable. Test set generation is the same as for combinational logic, for which there already exist many practical results. Few extra pins are required and IBM reports the extra logic cost to be 5 to 20 percent. A major disadvantage is that stimulus application and response checking is slow. A variation of LSSD is the Visibility Bus, which provides observability only in the VAX-11/780 and VAX-11/750 (see Chapter 8).

Table 4-8 contains suggestions on where to add hardware while Table 4-9 gives some design guidelines for testability. Both tables are adapted from Grason and Nagle [1980].

The final stage in design for testability is to develop new designs with unique properties. These designs should have a small test-set size that is easy to generate. Bennetts and Scott [1976] (see Appendix C) describe the Reed-

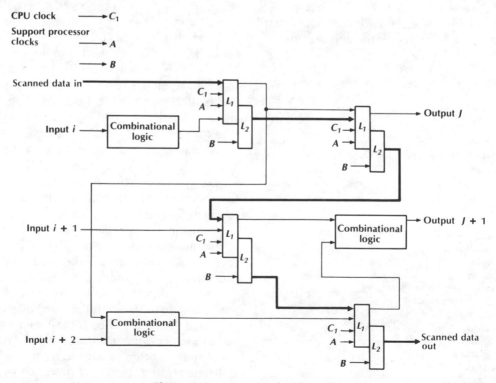

Figure 4–8.   An example of LSSD.

Table 4–8.   Design for testability-added hardware location suggestions.

1. Make sequential circuit components such as counters, shift registers, and control flip-flops initializable. Some ways of providing initializability are to wire control signals or testpoints to component clear or preset inputs, or to provide direct-load capabilities. Do not tie both the set and preset inputs of flip-flops to a common permanent logic signal.

2. Make counter chains controllable and observable in a reasonably short test sequence. For example, break long counter chains during test mode by inserting testpoints in the carry-propagate/count-control lines. This is especially important in the case of clock countdown circuits that are used to provide control inputs for the rest of the circuit. In the latter case it may even be wise to provide testpoints to bypass the counters entirely during portions of the test.

3. On-board clock oscillators should be made disconnectable during test. This can be done by disconnecting their output with a testpoint or by socketing them for removal during test.

4. If one-shots are used, control and observe their outputs with testpoints.

5. Try to break global feedback loops during test mode. Blocking gates can be used for this, rather than more costly testpoints.

6. Use added hardware to partition the circuit into functionally independent subcircuits for testing. This is especially important for separating digital and analog subcircuits. One method is to place testpoints between subcircuits.

7. Break reconvergent fan-out paths when they interfere with testability.

8. Place testpoints at locations of high fan-out or high fan-in.

9. Route logic drives of lamps and displays to testpoints so that the tester can check for correct operation. Make keyboard and switch outputs accessible to the test machine by breaking with testpoints.

10. In circuits containing microprocessors and other LSI devices, use testpoints to enhance controllability and observability of address buses and data buses, important control signals such as the reset and hold inputs to the microprocessor, and bus tristate control. In particular, the address and data terminals of RAMs and ROMs should be easily accessible.

Muller expansion for realizing combinational circuits. This test-set size and contents are derived by inspection.

Some of the techniques described in Chapter 3 can be used for on-line testing. In particular, Carter, Wadia, and Jessep [1972] introduce an algebra for totally self-checking circuits and an algorithm for producing them from the regular Boolean description. The physical realization of these circuits is usually twice as complex as nonself-checking circuits (roughly comparable to dual-rail logic or duplication). However, there are important classes of these checkers that are only about as complex as the nonredundant Boolean realization. Anderson and Metze [1973] explore such a class of check circuits for data encoded in m-of-n codes (see Chapter 3).

For sequential machines, it is possible to en-

Table 4–9.   Design for testability suggestions not requiring added hardware.

1. Avoid the use of asynchronous sequential circuits. Edge-triggered D-type flip-flops are preferable to other types of flip-flops. These are synchronous, and behave merely as clocked data delays during testing.

2. Avoid one-shots when possible.

3. Avoid unnecessary wired-OR or wired-AND connections. When these must be used, try to employ gates from the same IC package to enhance fault locations.

4. Use elements in the same IC package when designing a series of inverters.

5. Try to assign gates in a feedback loop to the same IC package.

code states such that the machine does not make a mistake. There are two general approaches. The first constructs the sequential machine such that any error drives the machine into an error state from which it cannot escape. Thus, the machine remains in essentially a do-nothing state and no further outputs are issued. The second approach is the so-called fail-safe [Tohma, Ohyama, and Sake, 1971] sequential machine. One of the two possible outputs is designated as fail-safe, and the occurrence of that output is used in such a way that no damage is done if that output is wrong. The other output value can always be assumed correct, even in the presence of a fault. Consider the example of a traffic light, mentioned in Chapter 3 in the section on fail-safe logic design. Whenever green appears it is correct, even if there are internal failures. When red appears it is either correct or the result of an internal failure.

Several theoretical models have been developed for the application of tests to isolate a faulty subsystem. The goal of these models is to isolate the faulty component as quickly as possible [Brule, Johnson, and Kletsky, 1960; Chang, 1965, 1968]. If subsystems are given the capability of diagnosing each other, then it becomes possible to construct a system that could diagnose (and perhaps reconfigure) itself automatically; but the application of test sets requires the setting of inputs and observation of outputs. In systems with parallel data paths, the "hooks" necessary to set and observe results are many bits wide and costly to implement; the number of these hooks should be kept to a minimum.

Preparata, Metze, and Chien [1967] treat the case of subsystem interconnection for diagnosis when each subsystem is completely capable of testing another subsystem. Kime [1970], combining the work of Kautz [1968] and Preparata, Metze, Chien, extends the possible outcomes of a test (passed, failed) to include the incomplete test—a test whose output is indeterminate under the influence of a fault (that is, it is unknown whether the test will pass or fail when the fault is present). This corresponds to a don't-know condition. Procedures for determining the diagnostic resolution of a set of tests are developed. Subsequent work by Kime and others treats the cases in which subsystems are not identical.

FIELD OPERATION

The final phase of system life is in the field. Field service must respond to both real and customer-perceived failures. Due to the complex nature of systems, it is not unusual for the false-alarm rate to be two to four times higher than the actual fault rate. Therefore, one goal of design for maintainability is to decrease the rate of false alarm.

Another problem is illustrated by the typical Time-To-Repair (TTR) distribution in Figure 4-9. It is not unusual for 5 percent of calls to consume 35 percent of the time spent in repair. This Time-To-Repair "tail" is very costly. Hard failures are easy to diagnose and repair; more subtle errors are often due to interactions between systems components and are also a function of system load. Diagnostics are unable to reproduce the events leading up to the error.

When the Time-To-Repair a system has gone beyond a threshold (typically, 4 hours), a second person, usually a more experienced troubleshooter, can be dispatched to assist in the repair process. Subsequently, a third and even a fourth person might be dispatched in an attempt to limit customer downtime. A more realistic view of the cost of repair is the number of labor hours involved in repair; for example, two people for 1 hour yields 2 labor hours. Figure 4-10 depicts a typical labor-hour-to-repair (LH) distribution corresponding to the TTR distribution in Figure 4-9. The tail on the LH due to problem systems is even more pronounced than the TTR tail. Hence, the second goal of design for maintainability is to decrease the tails on the TTR (affecting customer downtime) and LH (affecting cost of maintenance) distributions.

The maintenance philosophy is a function of the total set of design decisions, including design choices for fault tolerance and design for testa-

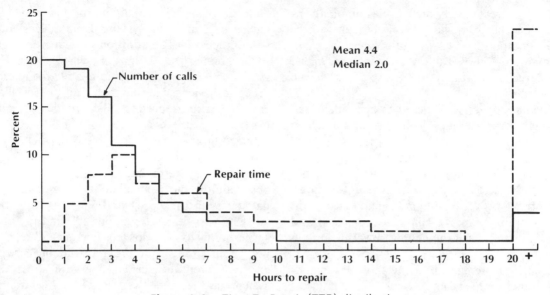

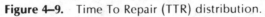

Figure 4–9.   Time To Repair (TTR) distribution.

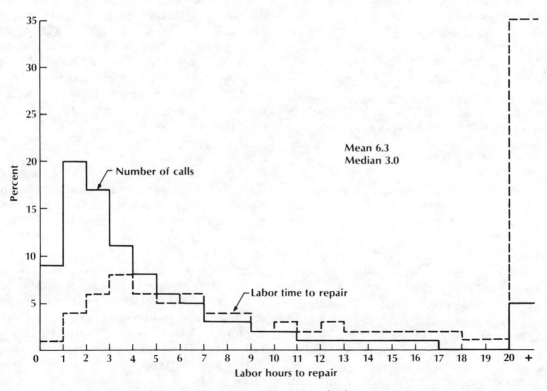

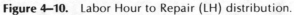

Figure 4–10.   Labor Hour to Repair (LH) distribution.

bility. The great variety of possible combinations of design choices makes it very difficult to provide a comprehensive set of guidelines for design for maintainability. Table 4-10 is an incomplete, unordered list that may be used to stimulate the generation of ideas.

Once a suspect subsystem has been identified (through error detection logic, periodic diagnostics, error reports, and the like), the first consideration is to determine whether a fault is actually present. Verification should start with the smallest set of logic that can perform useful functions. In a processor, the minimum functionality might be execution of move constant, compare, and branch instructions. Functions are verified incrementally.

Each subsystem should be testable as a standalone environment. For example, communications devices should have a test mode that wraps the sending port around to a receiving port. The sending and receiving logic can be tested without the aid of other subsystems.

Table 4–10. Suggestions on design for maintainability.

---

1. Start small. Verify subsystem operation step by step, from the minimal logic configuration through the addition of each incremental function.

2. Provide isolated environments so that each subsystem is completely exercised without requiring other subsystems.

3. Provide subsystem self tests, including tests of error-detection circuitry.

4. Provide internal observability and controllability in subsystems.

5. Provide error reporting and logging.

6. Minimize the need for external test equipment such as logic state analyzers and probes.

7. Provide a cabinet structure that facilitates repair.

8. Base repair strategies on component replacement, not on component swap.

9. Provide a support processor and remote access for diagnosis.

Because of the availability of low-cost LSI technology, most subsystems have at least one microprocessor. The addition of a microprocessor simplifies the design of self-tests for the subsystem. These tests should include the microprocessor (checksumming its memory) as well as error detection/reporting circuitry that is normally not exercised.

Suggestions 4 and 5 in Table 4-10 attempt to provide information that will eliminate lengthy repairs. The fourth suggestion is to increase observability and controllability of internal signals (as with the LSSD and Visibility Bus discussed under design for testability) and the fifth suggestion is to provide error logging and reporting. Often a diagnostic program cannot recreate an error event because it does not stress the system in the same way that the operational program does. Indeed, often the operational program is the best diagnostic. Error logging captures information about the state of the system at the time of the error, thus providing clues to the source of the error. Error logging makes it possible to perform automatic trend analysis. A program can periodically scan the error log looking for patterns (such as multiple-read retries to one head of a disk). Trend analysis can be used in all systems, whether they contain little or extensive error-detection logic.

Suggestions 6 through 8 are aimed at the repair process itself. The use of external test equipment should be minimized or eliminated. Such test equipment is difficult to transport, time-consuming to hook up, and may perturb the system to the point of masking the fault. Even options such as a diagnostics control store should be avoided, because its installation changes the system configuration (perhaps even necessitating removal of a board to make room). A very important factor in maintenance is the selection of a Field-Replaceable Unit (FRU). Typically FRUs are printed circuit boards or LSI chips. The physical layout of the system should provide for easy access and replacement of the FRUs. If the maintenance strategy calls for verification with the cabinet open or the FRU on an extender board, the subsystem should operate correctly under these conditions (power should still be applied and timing margins still met). If on-line repair is mandated, care should be taken to minimize human error, such as the switching off of the wrong power supply. Telettra builds telephone switching equipment that supports on-line repair [Morganti, 1978]. The power pins on each card are slightly longer than the signal pins. Furthermore, there is enough mechanical resistance in card insertion to allow enough time for capacitors to charge up and electrical equilibrium to be reached prior to logic-signal contact with the rest of the system. On removal, the logic signals are disconnected prior to power disruption. The cards are keyed to prevent incorrect orientation or insertion into the incorrect slot; thus, there are never any ill-formed logic signals in the system due to the insertion/removal of a card. In addition, the processor is logically notified when a card is not present.

Above all, the repair strategy should be one of replacement rather than swap. In replacement the faulty FRU is uniquely identified. FRU swapping, sometimes called the "shotgun" approach, removes and substitutes several components at a time. Mostly on the basis of guesswork, components are substituted, sometimes en masse, until the system again functions properly. Swapping increases TTR/LH averages and spare-inventory costs. More spare FRUs are required because all removed FRUs are suspect. The workload on repair facilities is also increased. The swapping strategy was popular in the early days of computing, but it is no longer economically justifiable with today's more complex systems.

The final suggestion in the list is to provide a support processor to serve as a hub for maintenance activities. When provided with remote access, the support processor can help eliminate tails on the TTR and LH distributions and decrease both. Given an average transit time of one hour from a field service office to a customer site and a TTR of two hours, an average field service engineer can make two repairs per day. Even if the TTR were halved there would still be only two repairs per day because of the constraint of an eight-hour work day. Thus, savings can be realized by reducing transit time and eliminating false alarms through use of remote diagnosis (RD). As described in Chapter 1, consider a PDP-11/70 system with an RD option. When a customer perceives a failure, the data disk is dismounted, a diagnostic disk is mounted, the RD option is switched to remote and the customer telephones the PDP-11/70 diagnostic center, which dials up the target PDP-11/70. The RD option gives the engineer visibility to the implementation registers, microsequencer, backplane bus, and other internal components. The engineer can then run and interpret diagnostics as if on-site. The RD option greatly reduces false alarms. The experience of the RD center personnel tends to ensure that the field engineer is dispatched with the appropriate repair kit and expertise. Multiple trips for additional spare parts or additional expertise are greatly reduced. The RD center can also run extensive diagnostics under control of an RD computer when the customer is not using his computer. For remote diagnosis to be most effective, the system should be designed with RD in mind.

The IBM 4341 also uses a support processor to perform on-line analysis of errors [Frechette and Tanner, 1979]. The maintenance and support processor logs environmental factors such as power-line transients, electrostatic discharge, and internal machine temperatures. The 4341 processor is implemented using the Level Sensitive Scan Design (LSSD) technique. There are approximately 5,000 latch pairs in the CPU, 300 of which are used solely to aid fault diagnosis. In the diagnostic mode, the data latch is transferred to the scan latch, capturing the state of the machine for the support processor. The latch pairs are linked together to form shift registers called scan rings. The support processor subsequently can serially shift out the scan latch data. Thus, when the checking circuitry detects an error dynamically (such as with parity or duplication), the state of the machine is captured. There is no need to recreate the failure.

When error notification occurs, the support processor reads the scan latches, determines the error type, attempts recovery via retry for transient errors, records failure information in an error log on a diskette, and, in the case of hard faults, invokes error-log analysis microcode, whose 17,000 bytes analyze the error logs to identify the faulty FRU.

REFERENCES

Anderson and Metze [1973]; Bennetts and Lewin [1971]; Bennetts and Scott [1976]; Bossen and Hong [1971]; Bozorgui-Nesbat and McCluskey [1980]; Breuer and Friedman [1976, 1980]; Brule, Johnson, and Kletsky [1960]; Carter, Wadia, and Jessep [1972]; Chang [1965, 1968]; Chang, Manning, and Metze [1970]; Chang, Smith, and Walford [1974]; Craig [1980]; Frechette and Tanner [1979]; Friedman and Menon [1971]; Grason and Nagle [1980]; Hennie [1964, 1968]; Hotchkiss [1979]; Howard and Nahourai [1978]; Kautz [1968]; Kime [1970]; Lesser and Shedletsky [1980]; McCluskey and Clegg [1971]; Mei [1974]; Morganti [1978]; Nadig [1977]; Preparata, Metze, and Chien [1967]; Roth [1966]; Roth, Bouricius, and Schneider [1967]; Sellers, Hsiao, and Bearnson [1968a]; Seshu and Freeman [1962]; Susskind [1972]; Thatte and Abraham [1978]; Tohma, Ohyama, and Sake [1971]; Williams and Parker [1979]

PROBLEMS

1. Assume incoming components have a defective rate of 0.01.
   a. Without incoming screening, what is the probability that a 500-chip system will be defective after assembly?
   b. What fraction of the defective components would have to be removed by incoming screening if the probability that the 500-chip system will not be defective is 0.8?

c. If the cost of screening incoming chips is one-tenth the cost of loading a defective chip in the assembled system, at what defect rate (assuming screening is 100 percent effective) is incoming screening more cost effective than no screening?

2. Use the Boolean Difference to find all the tests in the circuit below for:
   Line 2 stuck-at-0
   Line 6 stuck-at-0

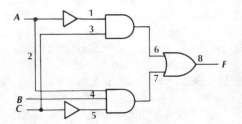

3. Use the D-algorithm to find a test for:
   A stuck-at-1
   Line 7 stuck-at-1
   in the circuit of Question 2. What other faults do these tests also detect?

4. Find a minimal test set for the circuit in Question 2. (Hint: This is a minimal cover problem; see Kautz [1968] for further information if required.)

5. Create the Reed-Muller implementation for the circuit in Question 2.

6. Create a controllable version of the circuit (Appendix C) and list the five required tests (including control points) for the circuit in Question 2.

7. For the circuit pictured below, generate a test for:
   a. Line 8 stuck-at-0
   b. Line 1 stuck-at-0
   Explain your approach in each case.

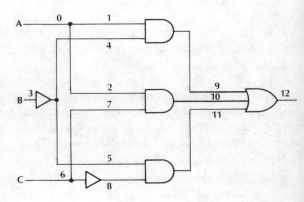

Evaluation Criteria

Stephen McConnel   Daniel P. Siewiorek

5

Comparing redundancy techniques and making subsequent design trade-offs require a method of evaluation. Evaluation criteria are often loosely referred to as reliability. Reliability, however, can mean many things. The difficulty arises in the measurement and interpretation of reliability. To a businessman, a computer is reliable when paychecks are printed on time and contain no errors. To a scientist, the computer is reliable if it has enough computing power available to process experimental numerical data. A space scientist considers a spacecraft's on-board computer reliable when the mission (perhaps years in length) is successfully completed. Finally, an airline on-board control computer is considered reliable if it makes no decisions with fatal consequences. The major difference among these users is the application-dependent interpretation of what a reliable system does. The great variety of applications has engendered a large number of reliability measures, both quantitative and qualitative. Often several measures are required to describe a system adequately.

This chapter introduces several criteria for evaluating the dependability of computing structures. The chapter also develops techniques for modeling such structures in order to obtain reasonable predictions for those criteria. These models typically divide a computer into various substructures that are easier to study than the whole system. There are certain levels at which it is customary to model systems.

The highest level of modeling is the *system* level, at which the entire system is considered as a black box. After statistics are gathered about events such as failures of a certain kind, a model can be suggested to fit the data as closely as possible. Modeling at this level requires an enormous amount of data.

At the next level, the *module* level, the system is subdivided into several modules that have mutually independent failures. The system model is obtained by a composite of the models for the modules.

The next lowest level is the *gate* level. It is seldom necessary to model a system below the gate level. However, if the redundancy is introduced at a lower level, the *component* level of modeling is required, where components are such items as transistors, diodes, and resistors. The failure rate and reliability functions of individual components were discussed in Chapter 2.

Modeling is most often performed at the module level. Redundant systems are then modeled in terms of their nonredundant subsystems.

Table 5–1. Evaluation criteria for system reliability.

Deterministic
  Survive at least k component failures

Probabilistic functions
  Hazard (failure rate) function—$z(t)$
  Reliability—$R(t)$
  Mission Time—$MT(r)$
  Repair rate—μ
  Availability—$A(t)$

Single parameters (probabilistic)
  Mean Time To Failure—MTTF
  Mean Time To Repair—MTTR
  Mean Time Between Failures—MTBF
  Coverage

Comparative measures (probabilistic)
  Reliability difference $R_2(t) - R_1(t)$
  Reliability gain $R_2(t)/R_1(t)$
  Mission Time Improvement $MT_2(r)/MT_1(r)$

SURVEY OF EVALUATION CRITERIA

Hardware Evaluation

Deterministic Model

Table 5-1 lists several evaluation criteria for system reliability. The simplest is the deterministic model. In this model, the minimum number of component failures that can be tolerated without system failure is taken as the figure of merit for the system. Deterministic modeling can result in wasted resources and unbalanced system design because highly reliable components must be replicated as many times as the low-reliability components. The only common use of the deterministic model in practice is to specify that no *single* component failure should cause the system to fail.

Probabilistic Models

Probabilistic Functions. Thus probabilistic modeling, based on relative component failure and repair rates, is the most often used. Failure rates of electronic devices vary with time, as shown in Figure 1-4. (The theory behind hardware component failure rates was discussed in Chapter 2.) This time-dependent failure rate is called a *hazard function*, denoted as $z(t)$. The hazard function is sometimes called the hazard rate or the force of mortality, and is usually measured in failures per million hours. For a known distribution,

$$z(t) \triangleq \frac{pdf}{1 - CDF}$$

For electronic components on the normal-life portion of the bathtub curve, the failure rate is assumed to be constant. This means that the exponential hazard function is applicable:

$$z(t) = \lambda$$

For the periods of infant mortality and component wearout, the Weibull hazard function is often used:

$$z(t) = \alpha\lambda(\lambda t)^{\alpha - 1}$$

(As noted in Chapter 2, the exponential function is equivalent to the Weibull function with α equal to one.) The Weibull shape parameter α and the scale parameter λ (used in both hazard functions), are constants specific to a particular component.

For the nonredundant constant-failure-rate model, the system hazard function is the sum of the component failure rates. For the combination of Weibull processes and for redundant systems with either model, the relationship is much more complex.

The hazard function is easy to measure in ascertaining the operational reliability of physical systems, because it can be calculated from a histogram of times between failures.

In keeping with the probabilistic nature of the concepts of failure rate and hazard function, the failure of electronic components is assumed to follow a general Poisson distribution:

- Probability of one failure during an interval Δt is approximately $z(t)\Delta t$.
- Probability of two or more failures during an interval Δt is negligible.
- Failures are independent.

Defining $m(t) = \int_0^t z(x)\,dx$, Ross [1972] has shown that the probability of k failures in time [0,t] is given by

$$\frac{e^{-m(t)}[m(t)]^k}{k!}$$

The expected value (or mean) of the number of failures in time [0, t] is

$$E[k] = \sum_{k=0}^{\infty} k \frac{e^{-m(t)}[m(t)]^k}{k!} = m(t)$$

The variance is

$$\text{Var}\,[k] = E[k^2] - (E[k])^2 = m(t) = E[k]$$

For a constant failure rate λ, $m(t) = \lambda t$. Thus,

$$\text{Pr}\,\{k \text{ failures in time } [0, t]\} = \frac{e^{-\lambda t}(\lambda t)^k}{k!}$$

$$E[k] = \text{Var}\,[k] = \lambda t$$

For the Weibull hazard function $z(t) = \alpha\lambda(\lambda t)^{\alpha-1}$, $m(t) = (\lambda t)^{\alpha}$. Therefore,

$$\text{Pr}\,\{k \text{ failures in time } [0, t]\} = \frac{e^{-(\lambda t)^{\alpha}}(\lambda t)^{k\alpha}}{k!}$$

$$E[k] = \text{Var}\,[k] = (\lambda t)^{\alpha}$$

The reliability function $R(t)$ of a system is mathematically defined as the probability that the system will perform satisfactorily from time zero to time t, given that operation commences successfully at time zero. It is a monotonically decreasing function whose initial value is one. The reliability function can be used to derive many of the other reliability measures detailed below.

Given the general Poisson distribution developed above, the reliability function for a single component becomes:

$$R(t) \stackrel{\Delta}{=} \text{Pr}\,\{0 \text{ failures in time } [0, t]\}$$

$$= e^{-m(t)}$$

For a constant failure rate, substitute λt for $m(t)$. Then,

$$R(t) = e^{-\lambda t}$$

If a system does not contain any redundancy—that is, if every component must function properly for the system to work—and if component failures are statistically independent, then the system reliability is the product of the component reliabilities and is thus also exponential. Furthermore, the failure rate of the system is the sum of the failure rates of the individual components. Therefore,

$$R_{\text{sys}}(t) = \prod_{i=1}^{n} R_i(t) = \prod_{i=1}^{n} e^{-\lambda_i t} = e^{-\left(\sum_{i=1}^{n} \lambda_i\right)t}$$

where there are n components.

For the Weibull hazard function, substitute $(\lambda t)^{\alpha}$ for $m(t)$:

$$R(t) = e^{-(\lambda t)^{\alpha}}$$

The Weibull model is more flexible but less

tractable than the exponential when large groups of components are involved. The reliability function for a group of components is:

$$R_{sys}(t) = e^{-\left[\sum_{i=1}^{n} (\lambda_i t)^{\alpha_i}\right]}$$

The sum must be performed for each new value of t, resulting in lengthy calculations. It is also difficult, if not impossible, to integrate analytically, which affects the other reliability measures discussed below.

For the general hazard function, recall that $m(t) = \int_0^t z(x)\,dx$. Thus,

$$R(t) = e^{-\int_0^t z(x)\,dx}$$

$$R_{sys}(t) = e^{-\left[\sum_{i=1}^{n} (\int_0^t z_i(x)\,dx)\right]}$$

As noted earlier, the Weibull function is more accurate than the exponential function for components subject to wear and aging (increasing failure rates) or those that improve with time, as the weaker members of the population are culled out (decreasing failure rates). When extremely accurate reliability predictions are needed, sample components are tested to find the underlying distribution (Weibull or otherwise) and the value of pertinent parameters. This is necessary because different kinds of components experience different distributions, as do similar components from different manufacturing lots or manufacturers.

For systems with stringent reliability requirements, a different but related measure is sometimes used. The mission time function $MT(r)$ gives the time at which system reliability falls below the level r. The mission time function is particularly well suited for applications with a minimum lifetime requirement due either to impossible or prohibitively expensive repair or to fixed intervals between maintenance. Such applications include spacecraft computers, undersea cable repeaters, and commercial airliner avionics systems.

The relationship between $R(t)$ and $MT(r)$ is given by

$$R[MT(r)] = r$$
$$MT[R(t)] = t$$

For a constant failure rate ($z(t) = \lambda$), the component mission time function is easily shown to be

$$MT(r) = \frac{-\ln r}{\lambda}$$

A nonredundant system with n components therefore has

$$MT(r) = \frac{-\ln r}{\sum_{i=1}^{n} \lambda_i}$$

For a more complex hazard function or for a redundant system, the mission time function is much more difficult to compute.

In most cases it is possible to repair or replace failed components, and accurate models of system reliability should take this into consideration. Repair activity, however, is not as easily modeled analytically as failure mechanisms. Many factors affect the rate at which repair occurs, including human ability, travel time, diagnostic capabilities, and parts availability. Despite the lack of strong theoretical backing, probabilistic models usually assume a repair rate analogous to the failure rate discussed already. For the purposes of this text, the repair rate function is treated similarly to the hazard (failure rate) function and generally denoted $z_r(t)$. The form and parameter values of this function can be measured for existing systems or estimated from experience with comparable situations. For a Weibull repair rate function, μ is used for the scale parameter ($= \lambda$ in the failure rate function) and β for the shape parameter ($= \alpha$ in the failure rate function). The solution of a reliability model with both failure and repair rates requires the use of Markov models, discussed later in this chapter. These models usually assume that repair of a failed system restores it such that the failure rate of the repaired system is the same as if no failure had occurred. In the case of the exponential model (constant hazard rate) process, this is completely true. The assumption is less valid for the Weibull process, but is usually made in order to provide analytic solutions.

For systems that can be repaired, a new measure of reliability is often used: the probability that the system is operational at any given time. This measure, called *availability*, is expressed symbolically as $A(t)$. Availability $A(t)$ differs from reliability $R(t)$ in that any number of system failures can have occurred prior to time t, but the system is available *if all those failures have been repaired*. Recall that with reliability $R(t)$, the system is considered reliable only if *no* system failures have occurred prior to that time. As a result, the availability function has a non-zero constant (steady-state) term. For a constant failure rate λ and a constant repair rate μ, the steady-state availability can be expressed as

$$A_{ss} = \frac{\mu}{\lambda + \mu}$$

The exact form of the availability function requires the solution of the appropriate Markov model which will be derived later in the chapter.

Single-Parameter Models. Reliability and availability equations, even for simple systems with repair, are often too complex to comprehend except (perhaps) in graphic form. Therefore, single-parameter metrics have been proposed to summarize these continuous-time equations.

Mean Time To Failure (MTTF). Measuring the Mean Time To Failure (MTTF) for components was discussed in Chapter 2. As for components, the MTTF of a system is the expected time of the first system failure in a population of identical systems given successful startup at time zero. It assumes a new (perfect) system at time zero. For the reliability functions used here, the MTTF is defined as:

$$MTTF = \int_0^\infty R(t)\, dt$$

Reliability functions of complex redundant systems require numeric integration techniques, as do the Weibull reliability functions because of their nonintegrability. However, the MTTF is still relatively easy to determine by means of numerical integration of the reliability function on a computer. Although the MTTF, in theory, applies only to a large population of systems, it is also useful as a measure for a given design (population of one).

For an example of MTTF calculation, consider a nonredundant system with n components, each with individual constant failure rate λ_i:

$$MTTF = \int_0^\infty R(t)\, dt = \int_0^\infty e^{-\left(\sum_{i=1}^n \lambda_i\right)t}\, dt$$

Hence

$$MTTF = \frac{1}{\sum_{i=1}^n \lambda_i}$$

This direct relationship between MTTF and the system failure rate is one reason the constant-failure-rate assumption is often made even when supporting data are scanty.

Mean Time To Repair (MTTR). The Mean Time To Repair (MTTR) is often used to measure the repairability of a system. It is the expected time for repair of a failed system or subsystem. MTTR is related to the repair rate discussed above much as MTTF is related to the failure rate. As with the repair rate, MTTR is not easily modeled analytically, and must usually be measured or estimated.

As indicated for exponential distributions, $MTTF = 1/\lambda$ and $MTTR = 1/\mu$. The steady-state availability, A_{ss}, defined earlier can be rewritten in terms of these parameters:

$$A_{ss} = \frac{MTTF}{MTTR + MTTF}$$

Mean Time Between Failures (MTBF). The term Mean Time Between Failures (MTBF) is often mistakenly used in place of Mean Time To Failure (MTTF). The MTBF is the mean time between failures in a system with repair, and is thus derived from a combination of repair and failure processes. The easiest approximation for MTBF is

$$MTBF = MTTF + MTTR$$

This expression should be exact for nonredundant systems, but is only approximate for redundant systems because the interplay of multiple failures usually causes the repair rate to change.

Coverage. Coverage is a concept serving diverse purposes, with two major meanings: quantitative and qualitative. The quantitative meaning is used most often in reliability modeling of redundant systems. In its quantitative sense, coverage is the probability that the system successfully recovers from a specific type of failure. Quite often, coverage is the probability that a particular class of fault is successfully detected before a complete system corruption occurs. Other typical uses include the probability of successful takeover by backup systems and noncorruption of checkpoint (restart) variables.

The qualitative meaning of coverage specifies the types of errors against which a particular redundancy scheme guards. For example, the coverage of Hamming single error-correcting–double-error-detecting code is correction for all single-bit errors in a code word and detection of all double bit errors and some multiple bit errors. Jack et al. [1975] develop this measure of coverage for a variety of both error-detection and corrrection techniques.

Comparative Measures. A major use of the evaluation criteria discussed so far is to compare different systems or different models of the same system. Such comparisons generally involve arithmetic differences of the measures or ratios between the measures. Three common comparative measures are

- Reliability difference $R_{new}(t) - R_{old}(t)$
- Reliability gain $R_{new}(t)/R_{old}(t)$
- Mission time improvement, $MT_{new}(r)/MT_{old}(r)$

where Mission Time (MT) is the time the system is above the reliability, r.

The use of these and similar measures is illustrated later in the section "Design Example: The PDP-8/e."

Software Evaluation

Software reliability assessment is part of the more general area of software quality assessment [Mohanly, 1973]. Effective mechanisms for measuring software quality are required because of the high cost of software development and maintenance. Forecasts indicate that by 1985 over 90 percent of the total computing dollars spent annually will be for software [Horowitz, 1975]. The development of techniques for measuring software reliability has been motivated mainly by project managers, who need not only ways of estimating the manpower needed to develop a software system with a given level of performance but also techniques to determine when this level of performance has been reached. Most software reliability models presented to date are still far from satisfying these two needs in a general context.

Most models assume that the software failure rate will be proportional to the number of bugs or design errors present in the system, without taking into account that different kinds of errors may contribute differently to the total failure rate. Eliminating one significant design error may double the mean time to failure, whereas eliminating ten minor implementation errors (bugs) may have no noticeable effect.

Even assuming that the failure rate is proportional to the number of bugs and design errors in the system, no model considers the fact that the failure rate will then be related to the workload of the system. For example, doubling the workload without changing the distribution of input data to the system may double the failure rate.

Software reliability models can be roughly grouped in four categories: time domain, data domain, axiomatic, and other.

Time Domain Models

Models formulated in the time domain attempt to relate software reliability (characterized, for instance, by an MTTF figure under typical workload conditions) to the number of bugs present in the software at a given time during its development. Typical of this approach are the models presented in Shooman [1973], Musa [1975], and Jelinsky and Moranda [1973]. Removal of implementation errors should increase MTTF, and correlation of bug-removal history with the time evolution of the MTTF value may allow the prediction of when a given MTTF value will be reached. The main disadvantages of time domain models are that bug correction can generate more bugs, and that software unreliability can be due not only to implementation errors but also to design (specification) errors, characterization, and simulation during testing of the typical workload.

The Shooman model [Shooman 1973] attempts to estimate the software reliability—that is, the probability that no software failure will occur during an operation time interval $[0, t]$—from an estimate of the number of errors per machine-language instruction present in a software system after T months of debugging. The model assumes that at system integration there are E_i errors present in the system and that the system is operated continuously by an exerciser that emulates its real use. The hazard function after T months of debugging is assumed to be proportional to the remaining errors in the system. The reliability of the software system is then assumed to be

$$R(t) = e^{-C E(r,T)}$$

where $E(r, T)$ is the remaining number of errors in the system after T months of debugging, and C is a proportionality constant. The model provides equations for estimating C and $E(r, T)$ from the results of the exerciser and the number of errors corrected.

The Jelinsky-Moranda model [Jelinsky and Moranda, 1973] is a special case of the Shooman model. The additional assumption is made that

each error discovered is immediately removed, decreasing the remaining number of errors by one. Assuming that the amount of debugging time between error occurrences has an exponential distribution, the density function of the time of discovery of the ith error, measured from the time of discovery of the $i - 1$th error, is

$$p(t_i) = \lambda(i)e^{-\lambda(i)t_i}$$

where $\lambda(i) = f(N - i + 1)$ and N is the number of errors originally present. The model gives the maximum likelihood estimates for N and f.

An extension of the Jelinsky-Moranda model has been given by Wolverton and Schick [1974]. It assumes that the error rate is proportional not only to the number of errors but also to the time spent in debugging, so that the chance of discovery increases as time goes on.

Another extension is given in Thayer, Lipow, and Nelson [1978], in which more than one error can be detected in a time interval, with no correction being made after the end of this interval. The new maximum likelihood estimators of N and f are also given.

All the models presented so far attempt to predict the reliability of a software system after a period of testing and debugging. In a good example of an application of this type of model, Miyamoto [1975] describes the development of an on-line realtime system for which a requirement is that the Mean Time Between Software Errors (MTBSE) has to be longer than 30 days. The system will operate on a day-by-day basis, 13 hours a day. (It will be loaded every morning and reset every evening.) The requirement is formulated such that the value of the reliability function, $R(t)$, for $t = 13$ hours has to be greater than $e^{[-13/\text{MTBSE}]} = 0.9672$.

Miyamota also gives the variations in time of the MTBSE as a function of the debugging time. The MTBSE remained at a very low value for most of the debugging period, jumping to an acceptable level only at the end. The correlation coefficient between the remaining number of errors in the program and the failure rate was 0.77, but the scatter plot shown is disappointing and suggests that the correlation coefficient between the failure rate and any other system variable could have given the same value. In the same paper Miyamoto describes in detail how the system was tested.

None of the models above takes into account that in the process of fixing a bug, new errors may be introduced in the system. The final number given is usually the Mean Time Between Software Errors, but only Miyamoto points out that this number is valid only for a specific set of workload conditions.

Other models to study the improvement in reliability of a software item during its development phase exist, such as Littlewood [1975], where the execution of a program is simulated with continuous-time Markov switching among smaller programs. This model also demonstrates that under certain conditions in the software system structure, the failure process will be asymptotically Poisson. Another Markov model is given in Trivedi and Shooman [1975], where the most probable number of errors that will have been corrected at any time t is based on preliminary modeling of the error occurrence and repair rates. The model also provides predictions of the availability and reliability of the system at time t. Schneidewind [1975] describes a model that assumes that the failure process is described by a nonhomogeneous Poisson process. The rate of error detection in a time interval is assumed to be proportional to the number of errors present during that interval. This leads to a Poisson distribution with a decreasing hazard rate.

Data Domain Models

Another approach to software reliability modeling is to study the data domain. The first model of this kind is described in Nelson [1973]. In principle, if sets of all input data values upon which a computer program can operate are identified, an estimate of the reliability of the program can be obtained by running the program for a subset of input data values. A more detailed description of data domain techniques is given in Thayer, Lipow, and Nelson [1978]. In Schick and Wolverton [1978] the time domain and data domain models are compared. However, different applications will tend to use different subsets of all possible input data values, yielding different reliability values for the same software system. This fact is formally taken into account in Cheung [1980], where software reliability is estimated from a Markov model whose transition probabilities depend on a user profile. Techniques for evaluating the transition probabilities for a given profile are given in Cheung and Ramamoorthy [1975].

In the Nelson model [1973], a computer program is defined as a computable function, F, defined on the set $E = \{E_i, i = 1, \ldots, N\}$. E includes all possible combinations of input data values, each E_i being a sample of data values needed to make a run of the program. Execution of a program produces, for a given value of E_i, the function value $F(E_i)$.

In the presence of bugs or design errors, a program actually implements F'. Let E_e be the set of input data values such that $F'(E_e)$ produces an execution failure (execution terminates prematurely, fails to terminate, or the results produced are not acceptable). If N_e is the number of E_i in E_e, then

$$p = \frac{N_e}{N}$$

is the probability that a run of the program will result in an execution failure. Nelson defines the reliability, R, as the probability of no failures, or:

$$R = 1 - p$$

$$= 1 - \frac{N_e}{N}$$

This model, then, takes into account that the inputs to a program are not selected from E with equal a priori probability, but are selected according to some operational requirement. This requirement may be characterized by a probability distribution $\{P_i : i = 1, \ldots, N\}$, P_i being the probability that the selected input is E_i. If we define the auxiliary variables Y_i to have the value zero if a run with E_i is successful, and one otherwise,

$$p = \sum_{i=1}^{N} P_i Y_i$$

where p is again the probability that a run of the program will result in an execution failure. A mathematical definition of the reliability of a computer program is given as the probability of no execution failures after n runs.

$$R(n) = R^n = (1 - p)^n$$

The model elaborates on how to choose input data values at random from E according to the distribution P_i to obtain an unbiased estimator of $R(n)$. In addition, if the execution time for each E_i is also known, the reliability function can be expressed in terms of the more conventional probability of no failure in a time interval, $[0, t]$.

Chapter 6 in Thayer, Lipow, and Nelson [1978] extends the previous models to take into account how the testing input data sets should be partitioned. Also discussed are the uncertainty in predicting reliability values, the effect of software errors removal, and the effect of program structure.

Axiomatic Models

The third category includes models in which software reliability (and software quality in general) is postulated to obey certain universal laws [Ferdinand, 1974; Fitzsimmons and Love, 1978]. Although such models have generated great interest, their general validity has never been proven and, at most, they only give an estimate for the number of bugs present in a program.

The best-known axiomatic model is the so called Software Science developed by Halstead [Fitzsimmons and Love, 1978]. Halstead used an approach very similar to that of thermodynamics to provide quantitative measures of program level, language level, algorithm purity, program

clarity, effect of modularization, programming effort, and programming time. In particular, the estimated number of bugs in a program is given by the expression

$$B = K\left(\frac{V}{EO}\right)$$

where K is a proportionality constant, V is the volume of the implementation of an algorithm, and EO is the mean number of mental discriminations between errors made by the programmer. V is given by

$$V = N \log_2 (n)$$

where N is the program length and n the size of the vocabulary defined by the language used. More specifically,

$$N = N1 + N2$$
$$n = n1 + n2$$

where:

$n1 =$ number of distinct operators appearing in a program

$n2 =$ number of distinct operands appearing in a program

$N1 =$ total number of occurrences of the operators in a program

$N2 =$ total number of occurrences of the operands in a program

EO has been empirically estimated to have a value around 3000.

Many publications have either supported or contradicted the results proposed by the Software Science, including a special issue of the *IEEE Transactions on Software Engineering* [Halstead, 1979].

Though unconventional, the measures proposed by the Software Science are easy to compute, and in any case it is an alternative for estimating the number of bugs in a software system. Table 5-2 shows the correlation coefficient between the real number of bugs found in a software project and the predicted number according to software science theory for several experiments. There are significant correlations

Table 5–2.   Correlation of actual experience to software bug prediction by axiomatic models.

Reference	Correlation Coefficient Between Predicted and Real Number of Bugs	
[Funami and Halstead, 1975]	0.98 - 0.83 - 0.92	
[Cornell and Halstead, 1976]	0.99	
[Fitzsimmons and Love, 1978]	System A	0.81
	System B	0.75
	System C	0.75
	Total	0.76

with error occurrences in the programs, although the data reported by Fitzsimmons and Love (obtained from three General Electric software development projects totaling 166,280 statements) show weaker correlation than the original values reported by Halstead.

Other Models

The model presented in Costes, Landrault, and Laprie [1978] is based on the fact that for well-debugged programs the occurrence of a software error results from conditions on both the input's set of data and the logical paths encountered. These events, then, can be considered random and independent of the past behavior of the system, that is, with constant failure rate. Also, because of their rarity, design errors or bugs may have the same effect as transient hardware faults.

The model is built on the following assumptions:

1. The system initially possesses N design errors or bugs that can be totally corrected by N interventions of the maintenance team.
2. The software failure rate is constant for a given number of design errors present in the system.
3. The system starts and continues operation until a fault is detected, then passes to a repair state. If the fault is due to a hardware transient, the system is put into operation again after a period of time for

which the probability density function is assumed to be known. If the fault is due to a software failure, maintenance takes place, during which the error may be removed, more errors may be introduced, or no modifications may be made to the software.

The model computes the availability of the system as a function of time by use of semi-Markovian theory. That is, the system will make state transitions according to the transition probabilities matrix, and the time spent in each state is a random variable whose probability-density function is either assumed to be known or is measurable.

The main result presented in Costes, Landrault, and Laprie [1978] is how the availability of the system tends towards the asymptotic availability (availability of the system when all the design errors have been removed) as the design errors are being removed under some restrictive conditions.

The minimum availability is shown to depend only on the software failure rate at system integration, and not on the order of occurrence of the different types of errors. The presence of different types of design errors only extends the time necessary to approach the asymptotic availability.

The mathematics involved for the model are complex, requiring numerical computation of inverse Laplace transforms for the transition probabilities matrix, and it is not clear that the parameters needed to simulate a real system accurately can be easily measured from a real system.

Finally, there have been some attempts to model fault-tolerant software through module duplication [Hecht, 1976] and warnings about how not to measure software reliability [Littlewood, 1979].

None of the models above characterizes system behavior accurately enough to give the user a figure of guaranteed level of performance under general workload conditions. They estimate the number of bugs present in a program but do not provide any accurate method to characterize and measure operational system unreliability due to software. There is a large gulf between the variables that can be easily measured in a running system and the number of bugs in its software. Instead, a cost-effective analysis should allow precise evaluation of software unreliability from variables easily measurable in an operational system, without knowing the details of how the software has been written.

MODELING TECHNIQUES

Redundant systems can be modeled under various operational assumptions, such as failure to exhaustion and failure with repair. Redundancy with failure to exhaustion is a simplistic and pessimistic model which assumes that all redundant modules fail before any repair. Failure with repair, on the other hand, models two separate but concurrent processes: the failure process and the repair process. Failure to exhaustion can be modeled by simple combinatorial probability, the first topic in this section. Failure with repair, which requires solutions of sets of differential equations, is the second main topic. Next, the impact on system availability of different assumptions concerning repair strategy is explored, followed by models built on the assumption that failures affect the performance of redundant systems.

Combinatorial Modeling

In combinatorial modeling, the system is divided into nonoverlapping modules. Each module is assigned either a probability of working, P_i, or a probability as a function of time, $R_i(t)$. The goal is to derive the probability, P_{sys}, or function, $R_{sys}(t)$, of correct system operation. The following assumptions are made:

1. Module failures are independent.
2. Once a module has failed, it is assumed always to yield incorrect results.
3. The system is considered failed if it does not satisfy the minimal set of functioning modules.

4. Once the system enters a failed state, subsequent failures cannot return the system to a functional state. This property, called coherency, is mathematically defined by Esary and Proschan [1962] in terms of a structure function $\varphi(x)$. x is a vector composed of elements $x_1, x_2, \ldots, x_n$, where each x_i is 1 if module i is functional, and 0 if module i is failed. A coherent system satisfies the following properties:
   a. $\varphi(1, 1, \ldots, 1) = 1$, when all modules function, the system must function;
   b. $\varphi(0, 0, \ldots, 0) = 0$, when all modules fail, the system fails; and
   c. $\varphi(x) \geq \varphi(y)$ whenever $x_i \geq y_i \ \forall i, i = 1, 2, \ldots, n$

Failure to exhaustion models typically enumerate all the states of the system (where a state is a pattern of failed and working modules) that meet or exceed the requirements of the minimal module set. Combinatorial counting techniques are used to simplify this enumeration. The following three subsections treat commonly used modeling techniques for series/parallel systems, M-of-N systems, and complex systems.

Series/Parallel Systems

Most frequently, reliability evaluation involves a series or parallel combination of independent systems. Figure 5-1 illustrates a serial string of modules, all of which must function for the system to function correctly. The modules could be resistors, fuel valves, computers, or any other components. If $R_i(t)$ is the reliability of module i and if the modules are assumed independent, then the overall system reliability is:

$$R_{\text{series}}(t) = \prod_{i=1}^{n} R_i(t) \tag{1}$$

Hence, the failure probability, denoted by Q, of a series system can be written as:

$$Q_{\text{series}}(t) = 1 - R_{\text{series}}(t) = 1 - \prod_{i=1}^{n} R_i(t)$$

$$= 1 - \prod_{i=1}^{n} (1 - Q_i(t)) \tag{2}$$

Figure 5–1. A series connection of *n* modules.

The parallel configuration in Figure 5-2 fails only if all the systems fail. The probability of failure is:

$$Q_{\text{parallel}}(t) = \prod_{i=1}^{n} Q_i(t) \qquad (3)$$

The system reliability is:

$$R_{\text{parallel}}(t) = 1 - Q_{\text{parallel}}(t) = 1 - \prod_{i=1}^{n} Q_i(t)$$
$$= 1 - \prod_{i=1}^{n} (1 - R_i(t)) \qquad (4)$$

Note the duality between R, Q; Equations 1 and 3; and Equations 2 and 4. For some systems it may be easier to work with failure probability than with reliability. Equations 1 through 4 can be applied recursively to complex series/parallel configurations to arrive at an overall reliability function. Figure 5-3 depicts two different interconnections of four components. These configurations have been used in aerospace systems for providing redundant transmission paths between terminals t_1 and t_2 where each working path has to contain at least one good component. The modules may be resistors or diodes (such as the component quadding used in OAO, the Orbital Astronomical Observatory) or valves controlling fuel flow to a rocket motor. The configuration in

Figure 5-3a tolerates more patterns of shorted components (such as shorted resistors/diodes or stuck-at-open fuel valves) than does configuration (b). Both configurations tolerate all single shorts and double shorts (ac, bd). Configuration (a) also tolerates double shorts (ad, bc). In a dual manner, configuration (b) tolerates more patterns of open components (such as open resistors/diodes or stuck-at-closed fuel valves). In particular, configuration (b) tolerates the double-open failures of (ad, bc) for which configuration (a) fails.

Now consider the case where blocks (a, c) are processors and (b, d) are memories. For the system to operate, at least one processor-memory pair is required. Configuration (a) represents a

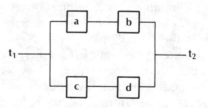

Shorts tolerated: a, b, c, d, ac, ad, bc, bd

Opens tolerated: a, b, c, d, ab, cd

a.

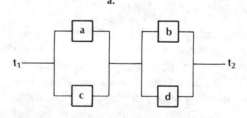

Shorts tolerated: a, b, c, d, ac, bd

Opens tolerated: a, b, c, d, ab, ad, bc, cd

b.

Figure 5–3. Two forms of series/parallel interconnection designed to tolerate a.) short and b.) open failures.

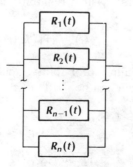

Figure 5–2. A parallel connection of *n* modules.

computer with a standby spare. Figure 5-4a illustrates the application of the series reliability equation. Now, applying the parallel reliability equation:

$$R_{short}(t) = 1 - (1 - R_a R_b)(1 - R_c R_d) \quad (5)$$

Note that the R_i's may be either a single such as a probability of success, or a function of time. In this text the function notation $R_i(t)$ is reserved for special cases. The reader may interpret R_i as either a single numbered probability or a function. Applying the parallel reliability equation to configuration (b) (Figure 5-4b) results in:

$$R_{open} = (1 - (1 - R_a)(1 - R_c))$$
$$\times (1 - (1 - R_b)(1 - R_d))$$

Letting $R_a = R_b = R_c = R_d = R_m$ yields

$$R_{short} = 2 R_m^2 - R_m^4 \quad (6)$$

and

$$R_{open} = 4 R_m^2 - 4 R_m^3 + R_m^4$$

Because there are more combinations of working systems in configuration (b), it is obvious that

$$R_{open} > R_{short}$$

for all $t > 0$. Now consider the case of n modules in parallel, only one of which is required to function. The other $n - 1$ modules represent

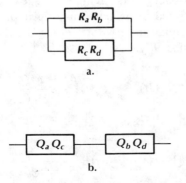

a.

b.

Figure 5–4. Applying a.) the series and b.) the parallel unreliability formula to Figure 5-3b.

spares. The spares can be operating in parallel or, as is more usually the case, standing by to replace the operating module when it fails. The form of Equation 3 suggests that as n grows large, $Q_{parallel}$ becomes close to perfection. For example, for $R_{parallel}$ to be within ϵ of 1.0, choose n such that:

$$n = \frac{ln\,\epsilon}{ln\,Q} \quad (7)$$

for $\epsilon = 10^{-6}$ and $Q_m = 0.1$, $n = 6$.

Equations 3 and 4, however, assume that the detection of the failed operating module and the switchover of a standby spare occur flawlessly. This is not a valid asumption in complex systems, in which even failure detection is far from perfect (a typical diagnostic program, for example, may detect only 80–90 percent of possible faults). As a result, the concept of coverage [Wyle and Burnett, 1967; Bouricius, Carter, and Schneider, 1969a, 1969b] has been introduced. In this context, coverage is defined as the conditional probability that a system recovers, given there has been a failure. What constitutes proper recovery is a strong function of the intended application. It may mean merely establishing a workable hardware system configuration (such as telephone switching processors) or it may demand that no data are lost or corrupted (such as in transaction processing computers, used in banks). Let coverage be denoted by c. Then, for a system with two modules:

$$R_{sys} = R_1 + cR_2(1 - R_1) \quad (8)$$

The first term is the probability that the first module survives. The second term is the probability that the first module fails, the second is still functioning, and a successful switchover was accomplished. Note that if $c = 1$ and $R_1 = R_2 = R_m$, $R_{sys} = 2 R_m - R_m^2 = 1 - (1 - R_m)^2$. If the modules are identical, then Equation 8 can be generalized to:

$$R_{sys} = R_m \sum_{i=0}^{n-1} c^i(1 - R_m)^i \quad (9)$$

This geometric progression can be evaluated by noting that:

$$\sum_{i=0}^{n} x^i = \frac{1 - x^{n+1}}{1 - x}$$

For $0 < x < 1$
Hence:

$$R_{sys} = R_m \left(\frac{1 - c^n(1 - R_m)^n}{1 - c(1 - R_m)} \right)$$

$$= R_m \left(\frac{1 - c^n Q_m^n}{1 - cQ_m} \right)$$

For R_{sys} to be within ϵ of 1.0, choose n such that:

$$n = \frac{ln\left[1 - \frac{(1 - \epsilon)(1 - cQ_m)}{R_m} \right]}{ln(cQ_m)} \quad (10)$$

Returning to the example where $R_{sys} = 1 - \epsilon$ for $\epsilon = 10^{-6}$, $R_m = 0.9$, and $c = 1.0$, it was shown that $n = 6$ was sufficient. Now assume a nonperfect, but still high coverage of $c = 0.99$. Even for $n = \infty$, R_{sys} from Equation 9 is only 0.99889. For a more conservative coverage of $c = 0.9$, the maximum value for R_{sys} with $n = \infty$ is 0.989.

Table 5-3 lists the values of system reliability expressed by Equation 9 as a function of module reliability (R_m), coverage (c), and number of modules (n). Two things should be noted from this table. First, as in all redundancy techniques, the initial application of redundancy produces a major decrease in system unreliability. Factors of 10 or more are not uncommon. In a comparison of R_m with R_{sys} for $n = 2$, the ratios of unreliability vary from a high of 9.09 to a low of 1.67. However, once n is increased to 4, the great majority of the system reliability improvement has been realized. Second, the single most important parameter is coverage. For high values of coverage (such as 0.99) and a moderate number of modules (say, four to six), system reliability is almost independent of module reliability over a wide range. Although coverage is a mathematically concise concept, it is often impossible to measure (or indeed even estimate) in practice because so many factors influence the final value of c.

The MTTF of a standby sparing system can be derived by integrating Equation 9.

MTTF (n modules)

$$= \int_0^\infty R_m \sum_{i=0}^{n-1} c^i(1 - R_m)^i \, dt$$

which can be rewritten for exponential reliability as:

MTTF (n modules) = MTTF ($n - 1$ modules)

$$+ \int_0^\infty R_m c^{n-1}$$

$$\times (1 - R_m)^{n-1} \, dt$$

$$= \text{MTTF } (n - 1 \text{ modules})$$

$$+ \int_0^\infty e^{-\lambda t} c^{n-1}$$

$$\times (1 - e^{-\lambda t})^{n-1} \, dt \quad (11)$$

$$= \text{MTTF } (n - 1 \text{ modules})$$

$$+ \frac{c^{n-1}}{n\lambda}$$

$$= \frac{1}{\lambda c} \sum_{i=1}^{n} \frac{c^i}{i}$$

The nth spare's contribution to MTTF is c^{n-1}/n times that of a single module. If c is not very close to 1.0, the added spare's contribution to MTTF is negligible.

The impact of improving coverage can also be demonstrated using mission time improvement. Setting Equation 4, with t replaced by It, equal to Equation 9, yields:

$$1 - Q_m(It)^n = R_m(t) \left(\frac{1 - c^n Q_m(t)^n}{1 - cQ_m(t)} \right)$$

Solving for I gives:

$$I = \frac{1}{\lambda t} ln[1 - \{1 - R_m(t) \left(\frac{1 - c^n Q_m(t)^n}{1 - cQ_m(t)} \right)\}] \quad (12)$$

Equation 12 is tabulated in Table 5-4 and plotted in Figure 5-5 for the value of $R_m(t) = 0.9$. Both

Table 5–3. Standby system reliability for various values of module reliability, coverage, and number of spares.

R_m \ n	Coverage 0.99			Coverage 0.9			Coverage 0.8		
	2	4	∞	2	4	∞	2	4	∞
0.9	0.9891	0.9988	0.9989	0.9810	0.9889	0.9890	0.9720	0.9782	0.9783
0.8	0.9584	0.9960	0.9975	0.9440	0.9746	0.9756	0.9280	0.9518	0.9524
0.7	0.9079	0.9880	0.9957	0.8890	0.9538	0.9589	0.8680	0.9180	0.9211
0.6	0.8376	0.9689	0.9934	0.8160	0.9218	0.9375	0.7920	0.8731	0.8824
0.5	0.7475	0.9307	0.9901	0.7250	0.8718	0.9091	0.7000	0.8120	0.8333

illustrate the high sensitivity to the coverage parameter c.

M-of-N Systems

M-of-N systems are a generalization of the parallel model. However, instead of requiring only one of the N modules for the system to function, M modules are required. Consider triple modular redundancy (TMR), in which two of three must function in order for the system to function. Thus for module reliability R_m:

$$R_{TMR} = R_m^3 + \binom{3}{2} R_m^2 (1 - R_m) \quad (13)$$

Equation 13 enumerates all the working states. The R_m^3 term represents the state in which all three modules function. The $\binom{3}{2} R_m^2 (1 - R_m)$

term represents the three states in which one module is failed and two are functional. Because the modules are assumed to be identical, all three states need not be enumerated. Any combination of two of the three modules is enumerated by the 3-take-2 combinatorial coefficient, denoted by $\binom{3}{2}$ where

$$\binom{N}{M} = \frac{N!}{(N-M)! \, M!}.$$

Table 5–4. Mission time improvement derived from increasing coverage from the indicated value to 1.0.

C	n = 2	n = 4
0.8	1.738	4.601
0.85	1.579	4.208
0.9	1.408	3.720
0.95	1.218	3.034
0.99	1.047	1.957

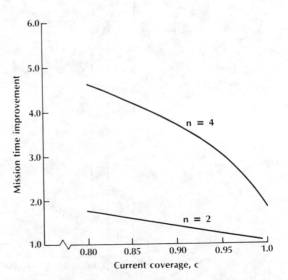

Figure 5–5. Potential mission time improvement with coverage increase from C to 1.0.

The *M*-of-*N* model can be generalized as: If there are *N* identical modules with the reliability of each module R_m (R_m may be a single number, such as a probability of success, or may be a function of time), and if a task requires *k* modules, the system can tolerate up to $N - k$ failures, and the reliability of such a system is:

$$R = \sum_{i=0}^{N-k} \binom{N}{i} R_m^{N-i} (1 - R_m)^i$$

We will use the *M*-of-*N* model to make several further points about system modeling, including incorrect conclusions drawn from single parameter summaries and the effect on redundant system reliability of extra logic (e.g., voters), more detailed modeling, more accurate modeling, and nonredundant components.

Single and Multiple Parameters. To compare different redundant systems, it is often desirable to summarize their models by a single parameter. The reliability may be an arbitrarily complex function of time and the selection of the wrong summary parameter could lead to incorrect conclusions. Consider, for example, TMR and MTTF. For the nonredundant system:

$$R_{\text{simplex}} = e^{-\lambda t}$$

$$\text{MTTF}_{\text{simplex}} = \frac{1}{\lambda}$$

For TMR with an exponential reliability function:

$$R_{\text{TMR}} = (e^{-\lambda t})^3 + \binom{3}{1} (e^{-\lambda t})^2 (1 - e^{-\lambda t})$$

$$= 3e^{-2\lambda t} - 2e^{-3\lambda t}$$

$$\text{MTTF}_{\text{TMR}} = \frac{3}{2\lambda} - \frac{2}{3\lambda}$$

$$= \frac{5}{6\lambda} < \frac{1}{\lambda} = \text{MTTF}_{\text{simplex}}$$

Thus, by the MTTF summary, TMR is worse than a simplex system.

Figure 5-6 plots the reliability functions for a simplex PDP-8 and a redundant PDP-8 (TMR

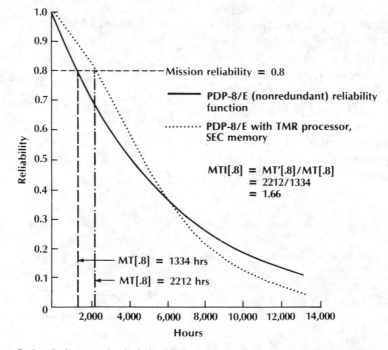

Figure 5–6. Relation of reliability function, mission time, and mission reliability.

processor and Hamming coded memory). Even though there is more area under the nonredundant curve (e.g., MTTF), the redundant system maintains a higher reliability for the first 6,000 hours of system life. Hence, comparison functions such as Mission Time Improvement (MTI) have been utilized to compare redundant systems in subregions of their operational life. The redundant PDP-8 in Figure 5-6 operates at or above a probability of success of 0.8, 66 percent longer than the simplex PDP-8. The S-shaped curve is typical of redundant systems; usually there is a well-defined knee. Above the knee, the redundant system has spare components that tolerate failures and keep the probability of system success high. Once the system has exhausted its redundancy, however, there is merely more hardware to fail (voters, switches, and other elements that support the redundancy) than in the nonredundant system. Thus, there is a sharper decrease in the redundant system's reliability function.

When modeling redundant systems with repair, single parameters such as MTTF may again be appropriate since the repair process replenishes the redundancy. There is no exhaustion phenomenon. This topic is discussed later in the chapter.

The Effect of Extra Logic in Redundant Systems.*

In adding redundancy to a system, care must be taken that the extra logic to control the redundancy does not actually decrease the overall system reliability. Ingle and Siewiorek [1976] model various switches proposed for hybrid redundancy and show that the switch is a significant factor in determining the overall system reliability. A hybrid redundancy scheme with a TMR core may have a maximum attainable reliability for only one or two spares. Adding spares complicates the switch enough to cause the system reliability actually to decrease. There are conditions under which the switch becomes so complex that simple TMR would yield a better solution.

* This section is based on Ingle and Siewiorek [1976].

Consider the hybrid redundancy with a TMR voter described in Chapter 3. If only one of the three TMR core modules (those currently being voted on) is assumed to fail at a time, the system fails only if all the modules fail or if all but one module fails. The reliability of the hybrid system with a TMR core and $n - 3$ spares is:

$$R_{\text{hybrid}} = R_v \times R_{sw}$$
$$\times \{1 - nR_m(1 - R_m)^{n-1} - (1 - R_m)^n\}$$

where R_v and R_{sw} are the voter and switch reliabilities, respectively. Subtracting the system reliability for n modules from that for $n + 1$ modules:

$$R_{sw} \times (1 - (n + 1) \times R_m(1 - R_m)^n - (1 - R_m)^{n+1})$$

$$-R_{sw} \times (1 - nR_m(1 - R_m)^{n-1} - (1 - R_m)^n)$$

$$= R_{sw} \times nR_m^2(1 - R_m)^{n-1}$$

This expression is positive for any $0 < R_m < 1$ and $n \geq 1$. Therefore, under the assumption that R_{sw} is independent of n, adding modules increases the system reliability. The switch typically becomes more complex as more modules are added, although the dependence of the switch complexity on n will be a function of the particular design. A reasonable assumption, however, is that switch complexity grows nearly linearly with n; that is, the addition of each module to the system increases switch complexity by a constant amount [Siewiorek and McCluskey, 1973]. Consequently, as a more realistic assumption we will consider the R_{sw} to be p^n, where p is the reliability of the switch component that must be added when a module is added. Further, let $p = R_m^\alpha$, where α is used to relate the relative complexities of the incremental switch component to the basic module. Hence, the system reliability is:

$$R_{\text{hybrid}} = R_m^{n\alpha}\{1 - nR_m(1 - R_m)^{n-1}$$
$$- (1 - R_m)^n\}$$

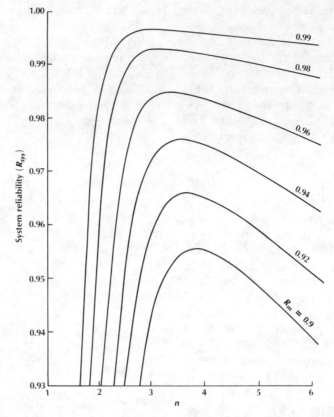

Figure 5–7. R_{sys} as a function of n and module reliability R for hybrid redundancy, $\alpha = 0.1$. (© 1976 IEEE.)

Figure 5-7 shows the variation of R_{hybrid} as a function of n, R_m (basic module reliability), and α. All curves exhibit a definite maximum. The optimum value, $n_{\max}$, of the number of modules for maximum R_{sys}, is higher for lower R_m or lower α. Differentiating R_{hybrid} with respect to n and equating the resultant expression to zero yields:

$$\alpha ln R_m = Q^{n-1} \times \{R_m + (\alpha \ln R_m + \ln Q_m) \\ \times (nR_m + Q_m)\}$$

where $Q_m = 1 - R_m$.

This equation may be numerically solved for $n_{\max}$. Values of $n_{\max}$ for hybrid redundancy are plotted in Figure 5-8, which shows that $n_{\max}$ is about 4 to 6 for most practical cases. This means that only one to three spares should be used. In

Figure 5-8, $n_{\max}$ exceeds 6 only for $\alpha \le 10^{-3}$. Given that α is the complexity of the switch component compared with that of the module, more than three modules need be used only when the module is more than 1,000 times as complex as the switch. For the iterative cell switch component that consists of 22 equivalent gates [Siewiorek and McCluskey, 1973b], the module will contain about 22,000 gates. A central processor of a computer has this complexity. Figures 5-9 and 5-10 illustrate similar trends for variations of the hybrid scheme:

· Hybrid redundancy (H.simplex)
· Checker redundancy scheme [Ramamoorthy and Han, 1973] (CRS)
· TMR switch with single voter (H.tmr.sv)
· TMR switch with triplicate voter (H.tmr.tv)
· Switch with Hamming coded states [Ogus, 1973] (H.hc)

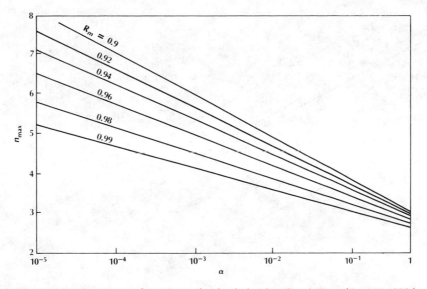

Figure 5–8. n_{max} as a function of α for hybrid redundancy. (© 1976 IEEE.)

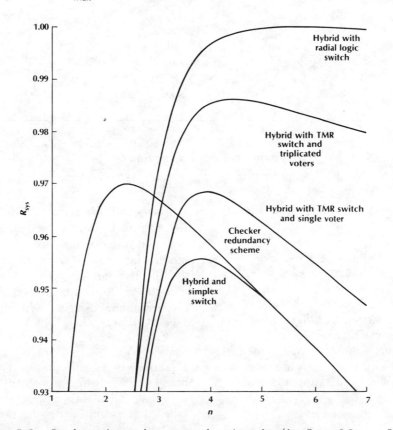

Figure 5–9. R_{sys} for various schemes as a function of m (for $R_m = 0.9$, $\alpha = 0.1$).
(© 1976 IEEE.)

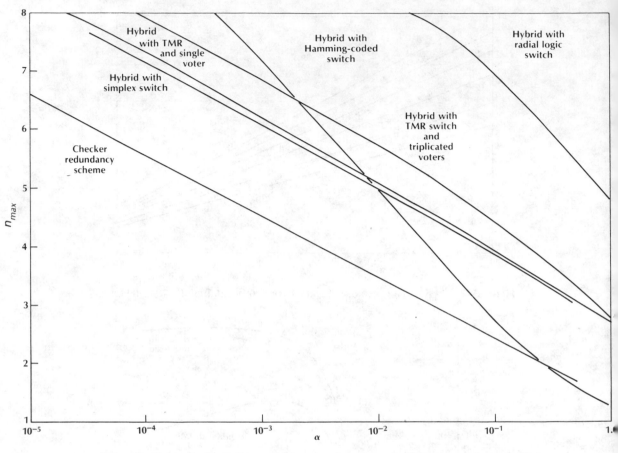

Figure 5–10. n_{max} for various schemes as a function of α (for $R_m = 0.9, \alpha = 1.0$).
(© 1976 IEEE.)

· Switch implemented with radial logic [Klaschka, 1969] (H.rl)

H.hc does not appear on Figure 5-9 because its maximum reliability (at $m = 3$ for $R = 0.9$) is only 0.75.

The Effect of More Detailed Modeling.*
Equation 13 is the classical model for TMR. The effect of nonperfect voters can readily be incorporated into Equation 13 if voters are assigned to module inputs [von Neumann, 1956; Brown,

---

* This section is based on Siewiorek [1975].

Tierney, and Wasserman, 1961; Teoste, 1962]. Because each voter drives exactly one module input, a voter failure has the same effect as a module failure. If R_v is the voter reliability, then the effective module reliability (for a two input module) in Equation 13 becomes $R_v^2 R_m$. The classical model can be rewritten as:

$$R_{\text{TMR}} = R_v^6 R_m^3 + 3 R_v^4 R_m^2 (1 - R_v^2 R_m) \quad \textbf{(14)}$$

Equation 14 is still pessimistic, for there are many cases in which a majority of the modules may have failed and yet the system would not be failed. For example, consider two failed modules

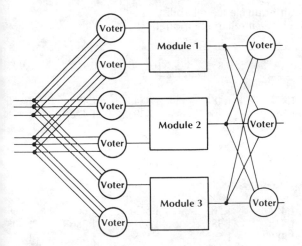

Figure 5–11. Classical triple-modular redundancy. (© 1975 IEEE.)

for the system shown in Figure 5-11. Assuming that module 1 has a permanent logical one on its output and module 3 has a permanent logical zero output, the network will still realize its designed function. Such multiple module failures that do not lead to system failures are called compensating module failures.

Taking into account these double, and even triple, module failure cases can often lead to a substantially higher predicted reliability than the classical reliability model. With a better reliability model some systems may be found to be overdesigned for their specific mission because an inadequate reliability model was used.

Siewiorek [1975] develops a model based on stuck-at interconnection failures. For TMR, the model takes the form:

$$R_{\mathrm{TMR}} = R_m^3 + 3R_m^2(1 - R_m) + R_m f_2 + f_3 \ \textbf{(15)}$$

where f_2 and f_3 are complex expressions for double and triple module failures.

An exact model is based on the concept of functionally equivalent faults [McCluskey and Clegg, 1971; Schertz and Metze, 1972]. A less complex and less accurate alternative is based on fault dominance [Mei, 1970]. Table 5-5 summa-

rizes the results. The fault-equivalence model increases the predicted mission time by at least 40 percent over the classical model for even simple systems. The fault-dominance model shows up to a 75 percent improvement for slightly more complex networks.

The Effect of More Accurate Modeling.* Figure 5-11 shows TMR in its simplest configuration: triplicated modules followed by triplicated voters. Systems whose nonredundant form may be represented by a serial cascade of modules are referred to as serial TMR.

Reliability modeling becomes more complex when fan-in and fan-out are considered and when not all module inputs are driven by voters. Several investigators have addressed the problem of modeling the reliability of TMR and multiple-line systems. There have been two basic approaches. The first is to approximate the system by a serial TMR system, modeling the system as a cascade of single-input single-output modules, adding extra voters if required. [Brown, Tierney, and Wasserman, 1961; Teoste, 1962; Rhodes, 1964; Longden, Page, and Scantlebury, 1966; Lyons and Vanderkulk, 1962; Gurzi, 1965].

A variation of this first approach [Rubin, 1967] models systems as serial cells and inserts fictitious module trios where required to make all the cells serial cells, then alters the standard serial voter-module reliability formula to approximate the effect of these added fictitious modules.

The second basic approach is to develop a bound on the system reliabilty by treating TMR as a coherent system. (The concept of coherent systems defined above was introduced by Essary and Proschan [1962].) One property of coherent systems is that, having once failed, the system or component cannot work properly again. A system cut is defined as a set of components whose failure causes system failure. A minimal cut is a cut from which no members can be deleted without the set losing the property of being a

* This section is adapted from Abraham and Siewiorek [1974].

Table 5–5. Mission time improvement (MTI) of the fault-equivalence reliability model and fault dominance reliability model over the classical reliability model for various modules.

Module Type	R_m	0.75	0.8	0.85	0.9	0.95	0.99
Single-NAND gate							
Equivalence Model		1.476	1.477	1.481	1.484	1.491	1.496
Dominance Model		1.358	1.382	1.405	1.439	1.472	1.491
Two NAND gates							
Equivalence Model		1.494	1.497	1.510	1.515	1.526	1.539
Dominance Model		1.355	1.384	1.414	1.452	1.492	1.531
Four-Level Full							
Binary Tree							
Dominance Model		1.405	1.451	1.505	1.575	1.663	1.766
Multiple-Fault Model		1.300	1.318	1.389	1.361	1.386	1.408
Dominance plus Multiple		1.442	1.485	1.535	1.598	1.692	1.771
Exclusive-OR							
Dominance Model		1.196	1.207	1.214	1.232	1.246	1.259
Priority Encoder							
Dominance Model		1.228	1.244	1.263	1.283	1.304	1.324

system cut. The value obtained by taking the product, over all minimal cuts, of the probability that the cut does not occur is a lower bound on coherent system reliability.

Jensen [1964] uses matrix manipulation to establish the minimal cuts of a system. However, if there are n modules in the nonredundant system, Jensen's method in the worst case requires on the order of n^3 operations and on the order of n^2 storage locations just to set up the matrices for determining the minimal cuts.

Another approach is to use an algorithm that divides the system into independent cells; that is, any nonfatal pattern of failures in a cell that leaves a cell operational does not interact with a nonfatal pattern of failures in another cell to cause system failures. The system reliability is then the product of the reliability of the independent cells. Figure 5-12 illustrates the partitioning of a complex system into cells (voters are represented by circles and modules by squares). Voter 1 has to be in the same cell as voter 2. If the indicated voters were in different cells, voters 1 and 2 would be nonfatal cell failures, yet the

system would fail because modules 3 and 4 receive potentially faulty inputs. The cell reliability is calculated by:

$$R_{cell} = \sum_{i=0}^{N_v} \sum_{j=0}^{N_m} F(i,j) R_v^{3N_v - i} (1 - R_v)^i R_m^{3N_m - j}$$
$$\times (1 - R_m)^j$$

where N_v and N_m are the number of voters and modules, respectively, in the cell, $F(i,j)$ is a complicated function of the cell structure, and

$$R_{sys} = \prod_{i=1}^{k} R_{cell_i}$$

The algorithm in Abraham and Siewiorek [1974] calculates the exact classical reliability of TMR networks (that is, the reliability of a coherent system as defined in Essary and Proschan [1962]). The results of this algorithm can be compared with the previously defined approaches: serial cell, and minimal cut set.

Consider a 16-register multiplexed data bus system in which the contents of a data register can be supplied to any one of 16 general-purpose

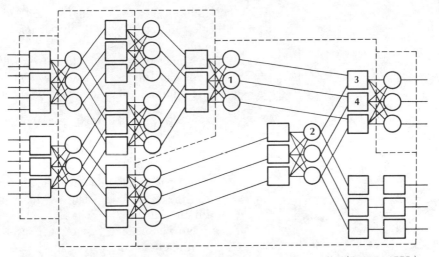

Figure 5–12. Partitioning a TMR system network into cells. (© 1974 IEEE.)

registers. Figure 5-13 shows a TMR configuration of the data register to register transfer along one path.

In the serial cell reliability model, the reliability of a serial cell is given by Equation 13. For nonperfect voters, Equation 13 becomes:

$$R_{\text{cell}} = 3(R_m R_v)^2 - 2(R_m R_v)^3 \quad \textbf{(16)}$$

where R_v is the voter reliability.

Figure 5-13 is more complicated than a cascade of serial cells. One approach to include fan-in/-out in the serial cell reliability model is to assign the voters to the modules they drive [Roth et al., 1967], because a voter failure affects only the module it drives. Cell 2 of Figure 5-13 shows one way to assign voters to the driven modules. Now the serial cell reliability model for the network of Figure 5-13 can be developed.

The reliability of a module "end cell" such as cell 1 can be derived from Equation 16 by letting $R_v = 1$. Similarly, setting $R_m = 1$ in Equation 16 yields the reliability of voter end cells such as cell 3. Next assume $R_m = R_v$. This simplification is not crucial and similar results are obtainable when R_v and R_m retain their separate identities. The end cell reliability is thus $3R_m^2 - 2R_m^3$. The serial cell reliability model for the system of

Figure 5-13 would consist of 17 end cells (16 voter and 1 module), and 16 serial cells like cell 2, each of which share the one voter trio. The system reliability is thus modeled by:

$$R_{\text{serial}} = (3R_m^2 - 2R_m^3)^{17}(3R_m^4 - 2R_m^6)^{16} \quad \textbf{(17)}$$

For the case of fan-in there are still 17 end cells (16 module and 1 voter). The fan-in portion would consist of 16 overlapping serial cells. Thus, Equation 17 represents the serial cell model for both fan-in and fan-out.

For the minimal cut set reliability model the lower bound on system reliability is given by Essary and Proschan [1962]:

$$R_{\text{sys}} \geqslant \prod_{\forall i \in I} (1 - Q_{\text{cut}_i})$$

such that i is a minimal cut where Q_{cut_i} is the probability that the minimal cut does not occur (that is, all the components composing the minimal cut do not fail). Consider Figure 5-13. A minimal cut is a set of modules whose failure causes the system to fail. All minimal cuts consist of either two voters ($Q_{\text{cut}} = Q_v^2$), two modules ($Q_{\text{cut}} = Q_m^2$), or one voter and one module ($Q_{\text{cut}} = Q_v Q_m$). Note that $Q_v = 1 - R_v$ and $Q_m = 1 - R_m$. There are three ways in which two modules can fail in the module end cell and

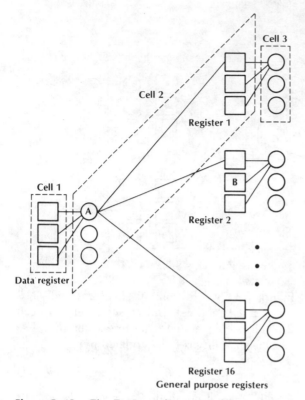

Cell 3

Cell 2

Register 1

Cell 1

Register 2

Data register

B

A

•
•
•

Register 16
General purpose registers

Figure 5–13. The TMR configuration for one bit of the data register to register fan-out block. Only one TMR path is shown. (© 1974 IEEE.)

16×3 ways in which two voters can cause system failure in the voter end cells. In the fan-out portion there are three double-voter failures, 3×16 double-module failures, and $3 \times 2 \times 16$ single-voter and single-module failures (such as voter A and module B) whose failure would cause system failure. Hence, the minimal cut reliability model for fan-out is:

$$R_{mcs} = (1 - Q_v^2)^{51}(1 - Q_m^2)^{51}(1 - Q_v Q_m)^{96}$$
$$= (1 - (1 - R_m)^2)^{198} \qquad \textbf{(18)}$$

Now consider the case of fan-in. There are 16×3 ways in which two modules can cause system failure in the 16 module end cells and three ways for two voters in the voter end cell. In the fan-in portion there are three double-module

failures, $3 \times 16 \times 2$ single-voter and single-module failures, 3×16 double-voter failures in the same voter trio, and $3 \times 2 \times \Sigma_{i=1}^{15} i$ or 720 ways in which two-voter failures from different voter trios can interact to cause system failure. Thus, the minimal cut reliability model for fan-in is:

$$R_{mcs} = (1 - Q_v^2)^{771}(1 - Q_m^2)^{51}(1 - Q_v Q_m)^{96}$$
$$= (1 - (1 - R_m)^2)^{918} \qquad \textbf{(19)}$$

The system reliability for the three approaches for the system in Figure 5-13 is plotted as a function of module reliability in Figure 5-14.

Now consider a case of 16:1 fan-in, such as an Arithmetic and Logic Unit (ALU) multiplexer that takes data from one of 16 registers as an input to an ALU. The three models for this fan-in network are also depicted in Figure 5-14. The minimal cut lower bound is a rather poor predictor of system reliability, whereas the serial cell approach predicts the same system reliability for both fan-in and fan-out systems.

Figure 5-15 shows a plot of mission time improvement when I is the ratio of the exact model to the serial cell model. It can be seen that a mission time improvement of 50 percent for the 1:16 fan-out system can be obtained with the more accurate reliability model. If the serial cell model is used, the resultant system is overdesigned by 50 percent, for it could meet its mission time specification with less reliable components. In the case of 16:1 fan-in, the system has only 50 percent of designed mission time.

The Effect of Nonredundant Components.*
As noted before, the first application of a redundancy technique produces the largest improvement in reliability. Furthermore, the application of redundancy to one portion of a system may significantly change the distribution of unreliability. In particular, a portion of the system that formerly had only a small contribution to unre-

---

* This section is adapted from Elkind and Siewiorek [1978]. Also available in Elkind and Siewiorek [1980].

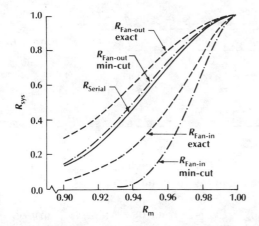

Figure 5–14. System reliability as a function of module reliability for the fan-out network of Figure 5-13 and a 16:1 fan-in network. The serial cell approximation to both networks is identical and plotted as the solid line. (© 1974 IEEE.)

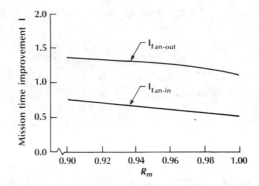

Figure 5–15. Mission time improvement over serial cell approach with exact reliability model for 1:16 fan-out and 16:1 fan-in networks. (© 1974 IEEE.)

liability may become the dominant contributor. This shift in balance is illustrated by the modeling of memory and error-correcting codes.

Current digital systems design is dominated by use of memory chips in the form of microstores, register files, caches, and main memories. Thus, improvement in memory reliability will greatly affect overall system reliability.

The use of Single-Error-Correcting (SEC) codes, such as Hamming and block, SEC codes [Peterson and Weldon, 1972] is a primary method of increasing memory system reliability. These techniques result in tolerance of single bit-faults in each memory code word. The decision to use SEC is a function of system cost, complexity, performance, serviceability, and reliability. The last two factors determine field repair costs. Before modeling memory systems with SEC, a fault model for memory chips must be proposed.

Memory-Chip Failure Modes. There are few data on semiconductor memory-chip failure modes during operating life. Most semiconductor manufacturers are more interested in the physical failure mechanisms than in the functional characteristics of a failure. What data are

available come mostly from screening, burn-in, and, to a lesser extent, high-temperature accelerated-life tests. Table 5-6 summarizes some of the data.

Not surprisingly, the data show that memory-chip failure modes are dependent on technology, process, and device design and thus may vary widely. Failure mode distributions also change with time for a given device as the fabrication process matures.*

Nevertheless, there is good evidence that the whole-chip failure mode (complete inability to store and/or retrieve data) is not the dominant failure mode for most chips. Rather, single-bit, row, and column failure modes seem to be the effect of the majority of chip failures. This fact motivates the formulation of the error-correcting-code (ECC) memory models presented below.

Memory Organization and Reliability Models. Wang and Lovelace [1977] present a model for main-memory reliability, based on the use of 4,096 bit chips in a 16-bit word memory system

---

* The Texas Instruments (TI) data indicate that 92 percent of the failures observed were single-bit failures. This proportion has since declined as a result of process improvements; however, the dominant portion of all failures for these chips is still due to partial-array failures.

Table 5–6. Chip failure mode data summary, in percentages.

Source	Devices	Whole Chip	Single Bit	Row/Column	Not Known
[Texas Instruments, n.d.]	4K MOS RAM	—	92%	—	8%
[Pascoe, 1975]	4K MOS RAM	11.8%	35.3	29.4%	23.5
[Rickers, 1975–76]	varied PROMs	17.9	53.9	15.3	12.9
[Gear, 1976]	8K MOS EPROM	—	100.00	—	—

using a Hamming single-error-correcting/double-error-detecting code The model allows a combination of different chip failure modes. Another model, by Levine and Meyers [1976], is used to prepare numerical charts and tables to allow a designer to predict the Mean Time To Failure (MTTF) of Hamming coded memories. The model is based on the whole-chip failure mode. Neither model allows for the effect of the nonredundant memory controller on the total memory system MTTF. The following models cover any single-error-correction scheme for any size memory, and are developed in such a way that the reliability of all the control, correction, and interface circuitry for the memory system is included, thus modeling the reliability of the entire memory system. A formula is derived that can be used to calculate Mean Time To Failure (MTTF) efficiently under any of the various failure mode assumptions. A modification of the model allows inclusion of the effect of failures already present.

This section presents three models for error-correcting-code (ECC) memory reliability, based on a different assumption of dominant memory-chip failure mode. Two of the models provide upper and lower bounds for the reliability of an ECC memory. The third, presented for comparison, is a model for a nonredundant memory. All the models assume that component failures in the memory-support circuitry cannot be survived. Many current commercial memory designs prove the validity of this assumption. Two error-correcting schemes, Hamming codes and block codes, illustrate the applicability of the general model. The measures used are mean time

to failure (MTTF), the hazard function $z(t)$, and the reliability function $R(t)$.

Single-Error-Correcting Memory Properties. The ECC memory reliability models depend on the properties of the single-error-correcting schemes used. In the Hamming and block code ECC schemes, two types of memory words are considered. The first, called a logical word, is the word that the system using the memory requires. The second, called a physical word, is made up of one or more logical words in addition to whatever coding bits are required.

For Hamming codes a k-bit word has c coding bits (which may or may not include the extra bit for double-error detection) added to it. The total number of bits is $n = (k + c)$. Several logical words may be combined into a larger physical word for error encoding, thus decreasing the number of coding bits in the memory. If j logical words occupy a physical word that includes e coding bits, the physical word size becomes $n = (kj + e)$, and the number of physical words in an x-logical word memory is $w = (x/j)$. For a complete explanation of Hamming codes, see Peterson and Weldon [1972].

Block codes are widely used for sequential-access memory systems but have seen little or no use in other types of memories. In this scheme, each word has a parity bit appended (horizontal parity bit) and j words of k bits are grouped to form a block. Each block has an extra word associated with it, each of whose $(k + 1)$ bits is the parity bit for the appropriate bit slice of the block (vertical parity bits). The total number of bits in the physical word is $n = (k + 1) \times$

$(j + 1)$, and for an x-logical word memory there are $w = (x/j)$ physical words. In the case of a single error, a horizontal parity error is found and the vertical parity word reconstructed. The intersection of the horizontal parity error and vertical parity error pinpoint the bit to be corrected. This method also detects double errors not in the same logical word.

Both the Hamming-coded and block-coded memories contain n-bit physical words and w physical words in the memory. The only difference between these two or any other SEC schemes as far as the model is concerned is that n and w vary. In each case, the memory can tolerate no more than one failure in the n bits of a given word in a w-word memory. This common property is the one upon which the following development is based.

Single-Error-Correcting Memory Models. The first ECC memory model assumes that single-memory bit-cell failures dominate, and provides an upper bound on system reliability by assuming that individual bit failures are independent. In this case, up to one failure per word, or w total failures, can be tolerated. The second model assumes that the dominant failure mode is complete functional failure of memory chips. It provides a lower bound on system reliability, since bit failures are not assumed to be independent but to occur d at a time, where d is the number of bits on a chip. Only w/d total failures* of this type can be tolerated. Between these two extremes lie row and column failures in the arrays internal to the chips, and combinations of whole-chip, single-cell, and row/column failures. A third model for ECC memory reliability assumes that the row (column) failure mode is the dominant failure mode.

Single-Bit-Failure Mode (SBFM) Model. Single-bit failures are assumed to be independent events, with each cell following the exponential

---

* Assuming a $d \times 1$-bit memory chip, one bit per physical word per chip.

failure law with failure rate λ_b and reliability function R_b. Each n-bit word can tolerate the failure of a single bit. Thus, the reliability R_g of a given word is:

$$R_g(t) = R_b^n + n(1 - R_b)R_b^{(n-1)}$$

For a w word memory the array reliability is:

$$R_{asb}(t) = (nR_b^{(n-1)} - (n-1)R_b^n)^w$$

Fault-free operation of the memory requires that the selection, control, and decoding circuitry be functioning correctly. It is assumed that these also follow exponential failure processes, with total failure rate λ_s. The reliability of the complete memory is then expressed as:

$$R_{msb}(t) = e^{-\lambda_s t}(ne^{-(n-1)\lambda_b t} - (n-1)e^{-n\lambda_b t})^w$$

The mean time to failure of the memory is:

$$\text{MTTF}_{sb} = \int_0^\infty e^{-\lambda_s t}(ne^{-(n-1)\lambda_b t} - (n-1)e^{-n\lambda_b t})^w dt$$

The integral is evaluated as:

$$\text{MTTF}_{sb} = \int_0^\infty e^{-\lambda_s t}e^{-\lambda_b(n-1)w} \times (n - (n-1)e^{-\lambda_b t})^w dt$$

Next, make the substitutions

$$x = e^{-\lambda_b t}, \qquad dx = -\lambda_b e^{-\lambda_b t} dt,$$

$$x|_{t\to\infty} = 0, \text{ and } x|_{t=0} = 1.$$

To further simplify the integral, let

$$m = (n-1)w + \lambda_s/\lambda_b - 1$$

and

$$v = -(n-1)$$

The integral becomes

$$\text{MTTF}_{sb} = -\frac{1}{\lambda_b}\int_1^0 x^m(n + vx)^w dx$$

which has the recursive solution

$$\text{MTTF}_{sb} = -\frac{1}{\lambda_b} \left\{ \frac{x^{(m+1)}(n + vx)^w}{m + w + 1} \right.$$

$$\left. + \frac{nw}{m + w + 1} \int x^m (n + vx)^{(w-1)} dx \right\} \Big|_1^0$$

After one more recursion, the equation becomes

$$\text{MTTF}_{sb} = \frac{1}{\lambda_b} \left\{ \frac{x^{(m+1)}(n + vx)^w}{m + w + 1} \right.$$

$$+ \frac{nw}{m + w + 1} \left[\frac{x^{(m+1)}(n + vx)^{(w-1)}}{m + w} \right.$$

$$\left. \left. + \frac{n(w - 1)}{m + w} \int x^m(n + vx)^{(w-2)} dx \right] \right\} \Big|_1^0$$

More simplifications are now possible. Let

$$f_i = (m + w + 1) - i = wn + \lambda_s/\lambda_b - i,$$

$$g_i = w - i + 1,$$

and

$$y = n + vx.$$

With some rearranging the MTTF_{sb} equation reduces to

$$\text{MTTF}_{sb} = -\frac{1}{\lambda_b} \left\{ \frac{x^{(m+1)} y^{g_1}}{f_o} \right.$$

$$\left. + \frac{ng_1}{f_0} \left[\frac{x^{(m+1)} y^{g_2}}{f_1} + \frac{ng_2}{f_1} \int x^m y^{g_3} dx \right] \right\} \Big|_1^0$$

The final term in the recursion is:

$$ng_w \int x^m y^{g_{(w+1)}} dx = \frac{ng_w x^{(m+1)}}{f_w}$$

Thus, $x^{(m+1)}$ can be factored out, giving

$$\text{MTTF}_{sb} = \frac{x^{(m+1)}}{\lambda_b f_0} \left\{ y^{g_1} + \frac{ng_1}{f_1} \right.$$

$$\left. \times \left[y^{g_2} + \frac{ng_2}{f_2} \times \left(\cdots \frac{ng_w}{f_w} \cdots \right) \right] \right\} \Big|_1^0$$

When $x = 0$, $x^{(m+1)} = 0$, while at $x = 1$, $x^{(m+1)} = 1$ and

$$y^{g_i} = (n - (n - 1))^{g_i} = 1,$$

yielding

$$\text{MTTF}_{sb} = \frac{1}{\lambda_b f_0} \left\{ 1 + \frac{ng_1}{f_1} \right.$$

$$\left. \times \left[1 + \frac{ng_2}{f_2} \left(\cdots \frac{ng_w}{f_w} \cdots \right) \right] \right\}$$

A final reorganization yields an iterative formula:

$$\text{MTTF}_{sb} = \frac{1}{\lambda_b} \left(\frac{1}{f_0} + \frac{ng_1}{f_0 f_1} + \cdots + \frac{n^w g_1 \cdots g_w}{f_0 f_1 \cdots f_w} \right) \tag{20}$$

The choice of this form of solution is due to its easy and direct iterative implementation on a computer or calculator. Usually only the first few terms need to be computed, for the value of successive terms quickly drops to zero and the number of terms is bounded by w.

The MTTF of the memory array alone is obtained by setting $\lambda_s/\lambda_b = 0$. Equation 20 offers a quicker means of calculating ECC memory MTTF than the earlier methods of numerical integration or Monte Carlo simulation. Equation 20 also lends itself well to exploring reliability properties of ECC memories. This topic is discussed later.

It is important to note that in solving the integral, m is assumed to be an integer, which in turn constrains λ_s/λ_b to also be an integer. In almost all cases this constraint is not a problem, because normally $\lambda_s \gg \lambda_b$.

The hazard function $z(t)$ expresses the instantaneous failure rate of a population. At a given time it measures the ratio of the instantaneous rate of change in reliability to the current reliability. A constant hazard function implies that the percentage change in reliability is constant through time. The corresponding reliability function is exponential. An increasing hazard function implies that the percentage change in reliability grows larger with time, and can be thought of as accelerating (rather than just increasing) unreliability. An increasing hazard function is inherent in redundant systems. Intuitively, as a redundant system approaches the limit of its tolerance to failures it becomes more unreliable than it was when new. The hazard function for the SBFM model can be shown to be

$$z_{sb}(t) = \lambda_s + \lambda_b wn(n-1)\frac{(1 - e^{-\lambda_b t})}{(n - (n-1)e^{-\lambda_b t})}$$

The Whole-Chip Failure Mode (WCFM) and Row Failure Mode (RFM) Models. The whole-chip and row (or column) failure mode models have the same form as the SBFM model. These models depend on the additional assumption. An SEC memory architecture is intolerant of multiple-bit failures in a single physical word. A memory design must utilize this fact. If the whole-chip failure mode is dominant, the design must apportion no more than one bit per chip per physical word. A similar restriction applies in the case of a dominant-row (or column) failure mode. The models here assume these restrictions.

In the WCFM model, the parameter h replaces the parameter w of the SBFM model. For a w-word memory of n-bit physical words implemented with d-bit chips, $h = w/d$. In effect the memory is organized into rows of n chips each, every row containing d words; h is then the number of such rows. λ_c, the memory-chip failure rate, takes the place of λ_b, the bit-failure rate. These substitutions apply in the reliability, MTTF, and hazard formulas.

The RFM model also derives from the SBFM model. For a w-word memory of n-bit physical words implemented with d-bit memory chips having q bits per row (column), w of the SBFM model is replaced by $p = w \times q/d$, which is the number of one-word-wide sets of rows (columns) in the memory architecture. λ_b is replaced by λ_r, the row (column) failure rate.

MTTF Calculation with Failures Present. A variation of the MTTF formula above should be useful in maintenance planning. Assume that β failures are present at time zero. These failures are of the type assumed to be dominant (single-

bit, whole-chip, or row (column)). The expression for the MTTF of an SBFM model is:

$$\text{MTTF}_{sb\cdot\beta} = \frac{1}{\lambda_b}\left(\frac{1}{f_0} + \frac{ng_1}{f_0 f_1} + \cdots + \frac{n^\alpha g_1 \cdots g_\alpha}{f_0 \cdots f_\alpha}\right)$$

where

$$f_i = nw - \beta + (\lambda_s/\lambda_b) - i,$$

$$g_i = w - \beta - i + 1,$$

and

$$\alpha = w - \beta.$$

The forms for the WCFM and RFM models follow using the previously defined substitutions.

Nonredundant Memory Model. The model for nonredundant memory is based on the assumptions that components have exponential failure processes and that any component failure results in complete memory failure. The support and storage array circuitry have failure rates λ_{enr} and λ_a, respectively. The reliability of the entire memory is then expressed by

$$R_{mnr} = e^{-(\lambda_{enr} + \lambda_a)t}$$

The MTTF of the memory is:

$$\text{MTTF}_{nr} = \frac{1}{\lambda_{enr} + \lambda_a}$$

The nonredundant memory has the constant hazard function

$$z_{nr}(t) = \lambda_{enr} + \lambda_a$$

ECC Memory Reliability Exploration via the Models. The Single-Bit Failure Mode (SBFM), Whole-Chip Failure Mode (WCFM), and Non-Redundant (NR) memory models will be compared for two SEC schemes, Hamming and block coding. The comparison measures are the MTTF, the hazard function $z(t)$, and the reliability function $R(t)$. Where specific values for memory-chip reliability are used, they are based on the failure rates for 4,096-bit chips found in Table 5-7. The ranges in Table 5-7 cover ob-

Table 5–7. Memory-chip failure rates for 4096 bit memory chips in failures per million hours.

Chip λ_c	Bit λ_b
0.005	0.0000122
0.2	0.0000488
0.5	0.000122
3.0	0.000732
5.0	0.00122

served failure rates for state-of-the-art chips. The reliabilities of control circuitry for error-correcting and nonredundant memories are derived from the models depicted in Figures 5-16 and 5-17, assuming the use of standard SSI/MSI logic. These memories are assumed to be "barebones" memories of relatively simple design. Assume a nonredundant k-bit per word memory of w words. Hamming single-error-correcting capabilities are added to it as shown in Figure 5-16 by increasing the array size to include the coding bits. Extra control and data manipulation facilities (MUXes, parity trees, XORs, registers) are added to perform error correction and detection, as well as error coding when writing into the

memory. When j logical words are combined into a larger physical word to limit the increase in array size, extra logic in the form of wider data paths, more complex coding/decoding circuitry, and a final one-of-j switch is needed.

In the block-coded memory shown in Figure 5-17 the control circuitry is more complex than for the Hamming code. The total support circuitry required is less, however, because the coding/decoding logic for block codes is less complex than for a Hamming code. For example, only one parity tree is needed whereas the Hamming-coded memory needs several. The block code also requires fewer redundant bits than the Hamming code. The block code decoder works in the following manner. When a word is read and XORed with zeros being fed into the other leg of the XOR array (zero is the XOR identity operator), the parity tree calculates the parity. If there is an error, the vertical parity for the block is calculated by successively XORing words from the memory block with what is already in the register. The results of the new vertical parity point to the bit in error. If more than one horizontal or vertical parity bit in the block indicates an error, a multiple-bit failure

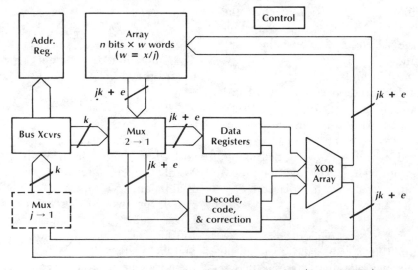

Figure 5–16. Hamming-coded memory model. (© 1980 IEEE.)

has occurred and the error is unrecoverable. In the case of a write, the horizontal parity is calculated and the vertical parity updated simply by XORing the new and old data words with the old vertical-parity word. Because writes to memory occur only 10–30 percent of the time, degradation due to vertical parity update is small. However, the block code is particularly effective for read-only memory because the extra complication on writes is not necessary. The vertical parity word could be stored in a separate memory array, thus allowing the update of the vertical parity word to proceed in parallel with the data write.

Block coding of small memories presents some problems because of the relatively large physical word size and the small number of physical words in the memory. Tolerance of whole-chip failure modes requires an allocation of no more than one bit per block per chip. When whole-chip failure modes are dominant, block codes are efficient only for large memories. For a small memory, the number of memory chips is fixed by the number of bits in a block. A large number of

chips with relatively few bits on each must be used. The same disadvantage applies less stringently for row/column failure modes. For single-bit failure modes there is no such problem.

The comparisons that follow use support reliabilities calculated from these model memory designs of Figures 5-16 and 5-17.

MTTF. In comparisons of the SBFM and WCFM models, a normalized MTTF is used in order to avoid dependence on specific reliabilities of the current or any other technology. The normalized measure is obtained by multiplying the MTTF formulas by λ_b. When this is done the MTTF becomes a function of the ratio λ_s/λ_b instead of being a function of λ_s and λ_b. $\mathrm{MTTF}_{\mathrm{wc.norm}}$ is still dependent on the number of bits per chip.

It is possible to normalize the nonredundant memory MTTF in the same way, assuming that the ratio $r = \lambda_{enr}/\lambda_s$ is known. The normalized MTTF for the nonredundant memory becomes

$$\mathrm{MTTF}_{\mathrm{nr.norm}} = \frac{1}{r(\lambda_s/\lambda_n) + wn}$$

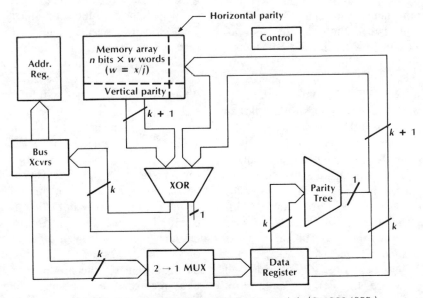

Figure 5–17. Block-coded RAM model. (© 1980 IEEE.)

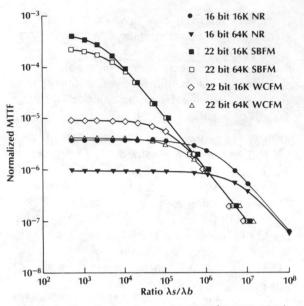

Figure 5–18.   Comparison of MTTF. (© 1980 IEEE.)

Figure 5-18 shows the normalized MTTF curves plotted against the ratio λ_s/λ_b. These curves are for 16-bit logical word memories of 16K and 64K words in the SBFM and WCFM (assuming 4,096 bits per chip) ECC models and the nonredundant memory model.

Figure 5-18 illustrates a factor of 20–30 superiority in MTTF predicted for the SBFM over the WCFM model for small values of λ_s/λ_b, with the size memories modeled. As λ_s/λ_b increases, the ECC memory MTTF becomes essentially that of the support circuitry (which would plot as a line with unity negative slope). Thus, the limiting factor on the memory reliability is the support-circuitry reliability. The plot also shows that the ratio λ_s/λ_b at which the array reliability can be ignored in computing MTTF is lower for the SBFM than for the WCFM model. This difference becomes greater for larger chip size. For λ_s in the range from 1 to 100 failures per million hours this corresponds to a λ_s/λ_b of 10^4 to 10^6 for the λ_b values in Table 5-7. This is well into the range where the SBFM assumption shows that the memory reliability can be modeled as simply as that of the support circuitry, and just at or below that range for the WCFM

assumption. To interpret Figure 5-18 in terms of a specific memory-chip technology, divide the vertical scale by λ_b.

The normalized MTTF for the nonredundant memory (assuming $r = \lambda_{enr}/\lambda_s = 0.1$) shows the same behavior as the ECC memories: the MTTF is limited by the support circuitry MTTF, although at a higher value of λ_s/λ_b. It also illustrates the fact that by the time

$$\lambda_s/\lambda_b \geqslant \frac{wk}{(1-r)},$$

the nonredundant memory becomes more reliable than ECC memory, and that for large λ_s/λ_b, its MTTF is greater by the factor $1/r$. Thus, the formulas and derived curves such as Figure 5-18 can be used to select the appropriate memory organization as a function of λ_s/λ_b and the failure mode assumptions.

Hazard Function. Based on the calculated support failure rates, the hazard functions for 32-bit logical word memories of 16K and 64K words were calculated for the SBFM and WCFM models and the nonredundant memory model. Figure 5-19 plots the results. The assumed bit failure rate is $\lambda_b = 0.000122$ failures per million hours.

For the SBFM model the hazard is nearly constant for the 80 years shown, and the two different-size memories exhibit an almost total hazard function dominance by the support circuitry's constant hazard function $z(t) = \lambda_s$. The WCFM model exhibits very different behavior for this ratio of λ_s/λ_b. For both sizes of memory the hazard functions increase throughout the 80 years, with a rapid rise in the first 10 to 20 years as the memory array hazard function grows and eventually dwarfs the contribution of the support circuitry's constant hazard function. At the end of 15 to 25 years the WCFM models have larger hazards than do the models for the nonredundant memories of the same (logical) size. The nonredundant memories exhibit constant hazard functions dominated by the greater constant hazard of the memory array alone ($\lambda_a \gg \lambda_{enr}$).

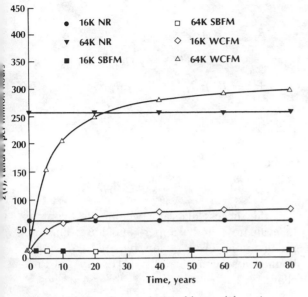

Figure 5–19. Comparison of hazard function. (© 1980 IEEE.)

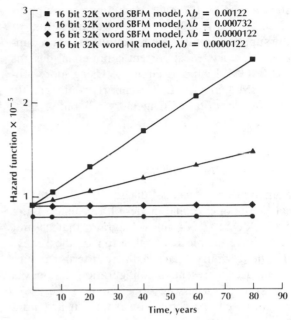

Figure 5–20. Sensitivity of the hazard function to λ_b.

Figure 5-20 demonstrates the effect of varying λ_b while holding λ_s constant (i.e., more reliable memory for the same support technology, thus increasing λ_s/λ_b). The memory modeled is a 16-bit logical-word memory of 32K words. For larger λ_b the memory array hazard function becomes more important and the SBFM model begins to exhibit the same qualities as the WCFM model in Figure 5-19. Below some λ_b the nonredundant memory model has a consistently lower hazard function. Its hazard function never gets as large as the Hamming code hazard function.

A block-coded memory of 64K logical words, with 16 words per block, was compared against a Hamming SEC-coded memory of the same (logical) size, but having one logical word per physical word [Elkind and Siewiorek, 1980]. The SBFM model was used for both memories. The Hamming-coded memory had a hazard function that was approximately constant at 9 failures per million hours over 80 years. The block-coded memory, on the other hand, had a hazard function that increased from 4.5 to 7.5 failures per million hours over 80 years. The block code's

greater departure from a constant hazard function was due to its larger, and hence less reliable, code word size. This was more than compensated for by the less complicated support circuitry: over the entire period modeled, the block code memory hazard function remained lower than the Hamming code hazard function. Thus, the block code memory design is more reliable, and requires fewer memory chips than the Hamming code memory design.

ECC Summary. The way in which memory chips fail affects the reliability of single-error-correcting memories. It also dictates the choice of models for memory system reliability. When the dominant failure mode, chip failure rate, and control failure rate are known, the models presented above can be used in making trade-off analyses in memory system design.

ECC memories are not inherently more reliable than nonredundant memories. With very reliable memory chips the limiting factor is the reliability of the support circuitry. When using standard SSI/MSI logic, Hamming code support circuitry has a failure rate several times that of the support circuitry for an equivalent nonredundant memory. Most current commercial designs use SSI/MSI support circuitry. Using more reliable LSI logic for ECC support would greatly improve the total ECC memory reliability.

Reduction of the Nonseries/Nonparallel Case

Sometimes a "success" diagram is used to describe the operational modes of a system. Figure 5-21a depicts a success diagram that is not directly reducible by application of the series/parallel formulas. Each path from terminal x to terminal y represents a configuration that leaves the system successfully operational. The exact reliability can be derived by expanding around a single module:

$$R_{sys} = R_m \times P(\text{system works} \mid m \text{ works})$$

$$\text{(21)}$$

$$+ (1 - R_m) \times P(\text{system works} \mid m \text{ fails})$$

where the notation $P(s|m)$ denotes the conditional probability "s given m has occurred."

Selecting module B to expand around, Equation 21 yields the two reduced diagrams in Figure 5-21b. In one, module B is replaced by a "short" (module B works); in the other, module B is replaced by an "open" (module B is failed and not available). Using the series/parallel reductions on the case where B is failed yields:

$$R_{sys} = R_B \times P(\text{system works} \mid B \text{ works})$$

$$+ (1 - R_B)(R_D[1 - (1 - R_A R_E) \quad \text{(22)}$$

$$\times (1 - R_F R_C)])$$

The case for module B working has to be further reduced. Expanding around module C yields:

$$P(\text{system works} \mid B \text{ works})$$

$$= R_C[R_D(1 - (1 - R_A)(1 - R_F))]$$

$$+ (1 - R_C)[R_A R_D R_E]$$

Thus:

$$R_{sys} = R_B[R_C R_D (R_A + R_F - R_A R_F)$$

$$+ (1 - R_C) R_A R_D R_E]$$

$$+ (1 - R_B)[R_D(R_A R_E + R_F R_C$$

$$- R_A R_C R_E R_F)]$$

Letting

$$R_A = R_B = R_C = R_D = R_E = R_F = R_m:$$

$$R_{sys} = R_m^6 - 3R_m^5 + R_m^4 + 2R_m^3$$

If the success diagram becomes too complex to evaluate exactly, upper- and lower-limit approximations on R_{sys} can be used. An upperbound on system reliability is [Essary and Proschan, 1962]:

$$R_{sys} \leqslant 1 - \Pi(1 - R_{\text{path } i}) \qquad \text{(23)}$$

where $R_{\text{path } i}$ is the serial reliability of path i. Equation 23 calculates the system reliability as if all paths were in parallel. Placing the paths in parallel yields a Reliability Block Diagram (RBD). Figure 5-22 shows the RBD of Figure 5-21. Equation 23 is an upperbound because the paths are not independent; that is, the failure of a single module affects more than one path. Equation 23 is a close approximation when $R_{\text{path } i}$ is small.

Hence:

$$R_{sys} \leqslant 1 - (1 - R_A R_B R_C R_D)(1 - R_A R_E R_D)$$

$$\times (1 - R_F R_C R_D) \qquad \text{(24)}$$

Letting

$$R_A = R_B = R_C = R_D = R_E = R_F = R_m:$$

$$R_{sys} \leqslant 2R_m^3 + R_m^4 - R_m^6 - 2R_m^7 + R_m^{10}$$

The RBD method can be altered to yield an exact result.

Because the paths are not independent, perform the multiplication in Equation 23 by re-

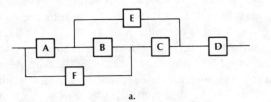

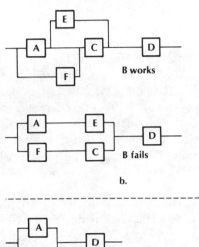

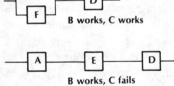

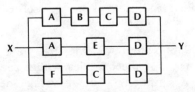

Figure 5–21. A system success diagram. a.) Reduced diagram replacing module B by a "short" (working) and an "open" (failed) b.) and further reduction with module B "shorted" (working) and module C replaced by an "open" and a "short" c.).

placing R_m^i with R_m; that is, an individual module can only have its reliability raised to the first power.

$$R_{sys} = R_A R_B R_C R_D + R_A R_E R_D$$
$$- R_A R_B R_C R_D R_E$$
$$+ R_C R_D R_F - R_A R_C R_D R_E R_F$$
$$- R_A R_B R_C R_D R_F$$
$$+ R_A R_B R_C R_D R_E R_F$$

Letting

$$R_A = R_B = R_C = R_D = R_E = R_F = R_m:$$
$$R_{sys} = R_m^6 - 3R_m^5 + R_m^4 + 2R_m^3$$

which is the same result obtained from Equation 22. Setting all R_i's to R_m has to occur after the multiplication; otherwise, individual R_i's would be raised to higher than the first power and the result would be a lower bound. For obtaining exact reliability, the **RBD** approach is more suitable to noncomputerized calculations, because simplifying assumptions (such as $R_i = R_m$ for all i) can be made before algebraic expansion.

Essary and Proschan [1962] also define a lower bound in terms of the minimal cut sets of the system. Given that a minimal cut set is a list of components such that removal of any component from the list (by changing the component from operational to failed) will cause the system to change from operational to failed, a lower bound is given by:

$$R_{sys} \geqslant \Pi R_{\text{cut } i} \qquad (25)$$

where $R_{\text{cut } i}$ is the reliability of minimal cut set i. The minimal cut sets for Figure 5-21a are D, AC, AF, CE, and BEF. Hence:

$$R_{sys} \geqslant R_A^2 R_B R_C^2 R_D R_E^2 R_F^2$$

For

$$R_A = R_B = R_C = R_D = R_E = R_F = R_m:$$
$$R_{sys} \geqslant R_m^{10}.$$

Figure 5–22. Reliability block diagram (RBD) of Figure 5-21.

Reliability Calculation Aids

Existing algorithms and programs for calculating computer system reliability may be roughly cast into one of two classes based on the form of the input data and type of problem being considered.

The first class of algorithms and programs accepts the graph of the physical (or logical) interconnections of system components and calculates fairly simple measures of reliability for the system. Typically the system is a computer communication network, and the vertices of the interconnection graph denote the computers while the arcs denote the communication links. Either arcs or vertices or both are assumed to fail stochastically. Typically, all failing elements are considered homogeneous, with identical probabilities of failure. Two common reliability measures computed for such a system are

- The probability that some specific pair of vertices will have at least one communication path between them at all times
- The probability that the operative arcs always contain a spanning of the network

Frank and Frisch [1970] and Wilkov [1972] are good tutorial papers on the subject. These types of network reliability calculation problems have been shown to be NP-hard in the case of general networks [Rosenthal 1977; Ball, 1980].

The second class of algorithms and programs accepts as input some intermediate representation that encodes the reliability behavior of the system under consideration. This representation, from which the system reliability is computed, is expected to be derived by human computation from the system interconnection structure and functionality requirements before being input to the program. Reliability Graphs and Fault Trees are the most commonly used intermediate representations. The system interconnection graph may or may not be isomorphic to the derived intermediate representation. Fault Trees are used as aids in Failure Modes Effects and Criticality Analysis (FMECA). Reliability Graphs are more often used to compute numerical values of reliability (also termed network reliability analysis in the literature). Shooman [1970] shows that these two intermediate representations are equivalent. The kinds of problems addressed here are far more general than the simple networks of the first class. Generalization is made possible by the fact that Reliability Graphs and Fault Trees are hand derived from a knowledge of the system. Lapp and Powers [1977] describes recent work toward automating synthesis of Fault Trees for chemical engineering systems. The literature on the analysis of Reliability Graphs and, in particular, Fault Trees is vast; the references here serve as a bare introduction [Misra, 1970; Gandhi, Knove, and Henley, 1972; Satyanarayana and Prabhaker, 1978; Aggarwal and Rai, 1978; Bennetts, 1975].

CARE II.

CARE II (Computer-Aided Reliability Estimation II), developed at the Raytheon Company under contract to NASA [Raytheon 1974, 1976], implements a very general combinatorial model for systems consisting of one or more subsystems or stages. Each stage contains a number of identical modules configured as a set of active devices with spares. CARE II handles hard and transient faults, reconfiguration with degraded performance, and coverage. Two operating modes are allowed for each stage: fully operational and degraded but partially operational. The coverage model depends on three conditional probabilities:

1. D = the probability that a fault is detected, given that one occurs;
2. I = the probability that a fault is correctly isolated, given that it is detected; and
3. R = the probability that the system recovers from a fault, given that it was properly isolated and that sufficient spares still exist.

The inputs to CARE II are the reliability parameters for the modules within each stage, and a description of the coverage detection/

isolation/recovery mechanisms. The output includes coverage specification and contributions, system reliability and unreliability (both tables and plots), MTTF, mission time, and several other measures. CARE II is a very versatile program, limited largely by its combinatorial approach, which precludes repair.

ADVISER. Recent work by Kini [1981] has advanced the state of the art with respect to computation of computer system reliability at the Processor-Memory-Switch (PMS) [Bell and Newell, 1971] level of design. Kini describes a program named ADVISER (ADVanced Interactive Symbolic Evaluator of Reliability), which computes the symbolic system reliability expression given:

1. The interconnection graph (PMS diagram) of the system,
2. The reliability of each *class* of identical system components, and
3. A simple statement of system functionality requirements.

The program assumes that the arbitrary system PMS diagram is represented as a nondirected graph whose vertices are labeled with the corresponding system component names. However, the organization of the program does not preclude a directed graph model. Component behavior is lumped into the vertices, which are subject to stochastic failures, whereas the edges of the graph are perfect and represent only the topology of the interconnection. Hence, the failure of a component implies the removal from the graph of the corresponding vertex and all arcs incident on it. Components are assumed to be binary-state entities. The communication axiom, fundamental to the reliability calculation paradigm of ADVISER, states roughly that functioning components belonging to the component classes distinguished by the statement of functionality requirements must at all times be able to communicate in order for the system to be functional. Only hard-failure reliability is com-

PMS DIAGRAM:

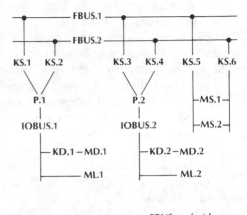

Key: P = processor,   FBUS = fast bus,
   KS = fast bus interface,   MS = shared memory,
   IOBUS = processor bus,   ML = local memory,
   MD = disk memory,   KD = disk controller.

REQUIREMENTS EXPRESSION:
  1 of P and 1 of ML and 1 of MD and 1 of MS

Figure 5–23. Sample PMS and requirements expression input to ADVISER.

puted, and the effects of coverage are not modeled in the present version of the program. An example illustrates the operation of ADVISER.

Figure 5-23 shows a simple dual-processor system with a duplicated fast interprocessor bus that also allows access to shared dual-ported memories. Each processor also has its own I/O bus with a disk and local memory. The Boolean requirements expression in the figure distinguishes four of the component classes (processor, local memory, disk, and shared memory) and states that *at least* one component from each of the four classes must be functioning at all times if the system is to be functional. A requirements expression may also contain a disjunction, such as

1 of *P* and 1 of *MD* and (1 of *MS* or 1 of *ML*).

During the course of the reliability computation ADVISER takes into account all component classes not mentioned in the requirements expression, whose members must be functional in the various system success states.

ADVISER begins its analysis by detecting symmetries in the interconnection graph. Two subgraphs will be symmetric if they are isomorphic, and corresponding vertices of the subgraphs represent components drawn from the same class of identical system components. Any symmetries found will enable the calculations for one member of a group of symmetric subgraphs to be used as templates for the results concerning the other members of the group. The graph is then segmented into subgraphs for which special reliability calculation techniques are known. When these known subgraphs are removed from the original interconnection graph, the remaining vertices and edges form a subgraph, called the kernel, for which special techniques are not known, and which is therefore treated with simple pathfinding algorithms to compute reliability. Currently the only subgraphs for which special techniques have been devised are *Pendant Tree Subgraphs*. These are rooted tree subgraphs whose root vertices are articulation vertices of the interconnection graph; the path between any two vertices in the subgraph is the only such path between those two vertices in the interconnection graph. Pendant tree subgraphs were a natural starting point in the search for special techniques because they occur so frequently in typical PMS structures. The design of ADVISER, however, allows inclusion of other types of subgraphs in the scheme as and when special reliability calculation techniques are devised for them.

Figure 5-24 shows the example PMS segmented into symmetric Pendant Tree Subgraphs and a Kernel. The interface vertices, in this case P.1 and P.2, are considered only once during reliability calculation although for convenience they appear both in the Kernel and in the Pendant Tree Subgraphs of which they are roots. At this time ADVISER fragments the requirements expression into its atoms and analyzes cases in

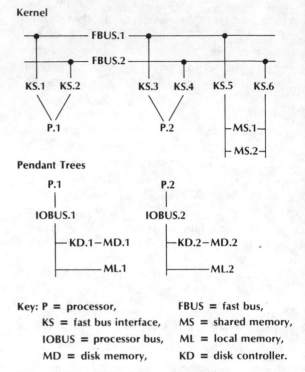

Figure 5–24. PMS of Figure 5-23 after segmentation.

which the system satisfies each of those atomic requirements. Assume, for example, that one of the atomic requirements is "5 of M.shared" and the interconnection graph is divided into three segments. Then any one of the different ways in which five M.shared components could feasibly be chosen from the three graph segments would satisfy the atomic requirement "5 of M.shared." For each of these cases a symbolic expression would be produced representing the probability of having five functional M.shared components scattered in a different way among the three segments. In our example the atomic requirement "1 of ML" can be satisfied by the functioning either of ML.1 in one Pendant Tree Subgraph or of ML.2 in the other, but no components of class ML are available in the

Kernel. In the case that ML.1 is functioning, then, to be useful, it must be available to the rest of the system in the other segments. This implies that IOBUS.1 and P.1 must be functional. The symbolic probability expression for this is $R_{P.1} R_{IOBUS.1} R_{ML.1}$. The probability expression in the case of ML.2 functioning in the other (symmetric) Pendant Tree Subgraph is identical in form. Each satisfaction of an atomic requirement produces such a symbolic probability expression. The atomic requirements "1 of P," "1 of ML," and "1 of MD" are each satisfied by two of the three segments of the graph. The atomic requirement "1 of MS" is satisfied only by the Kernel. Thus, there is a total of eight cases in which the system is functional.

ADVISER contains algorithms that accept symbolic probabilities of events, such as are generated for the cases above, and produces other symbolic probabilities for the conjunction or disjunction of those events. By using these algorithms it is possible to assemble the probabilities of the analyzed functional cases to obtain the reliability of the system. The symbolic probabilities and the eventual symbolic system-reliability function are maintained in sum-of-products canonical form within ADVISER.

The output of ADVISER consists of the text of a FORTRAN function that computes the symbolic reliability function assembled by the program. Optionally, a procedure in the SAIL language can also be output. Figure 5-25 shows the FORTRAN output from ADVISER for the PMS of Figure 5-23. The block of comments preceding the function definition of RSYS (the name is user-assignable) is simply a reproduction of the salient input data for the problem. The type definitions identify the classes of identical components in the PMS structure and give the parameters for the reliability of a representative member of each class. Currently, components may be described as having exponential, Weibull, constant, and external reliability functions. In the last case, ADVISER inserts a user-supplied function that computes the component

reliability. Failure rates (or the scale parameter, in the Weibull case) are under the LAMBDA column and are in units of per-million-hours. The numbers in this example were arbitrarily chosen.

The definition of the function itself initializes variables to the value of component class reliabilities at the time, which is given as the function parameter. Some expressions are computed and assigned to temporary variables. These expressions represent the templates for the various symbolic probabilities derived for symmetric subgraphs of the interconnection graph. Finally, the expression that gives the system reliability is computed and the resultant floating-point number is returned as the value of the function. Continuation lines are preceded by a dollar-sign in column six, and the variable MODREL is especially useful when printing of the reliability function requires more continuation lines than are allowed by the FORTRAN compiler.

Redundancy to Enhance Chip Yield

As pointed out in Chapter 2, semiconductor technology continues to produce increased densities and chip sizes. As chip size increases and defect density remains constant, however, the chip yield diminishes. Redundancy on the chip has been suggested as an effective means to increase yield [Tamman and Angell, 1967]. Indeed, several semiconductor manufacturers already provide spare bits and control electronics on 16- and 64K-bit memory parts [Posa, 1980]. The redundancy is configured after wafer probe but before final assembly. Polysilicon fuses or a second layer of metallization provide the means for handwiring the configuration. The redundancy may vary from as little as 1 percent to over 25 percent. The redundancy requires additional chip area, raising the question of how much improvement of chip yield redundancy will actually provide. This section uses combinatorial

```
C-------------------------------------------------------------------------------
C ** FORTRAN Module for Reliability Function evaluation
C **        produced by ADVISER on Sunday, 18 Jan 81 at 17:32:37 for [4,1367]
C-------------------------------------------------------------------------------
C ** Task Title: EXPMS.PMS -- An example PMS to demonstrate ADVISER.
C
C ** Requirements on the Structure were:
C
C          (1-OF-P AND 1-OF-ML AND 1-OF-MS AND 1-OF-MD)
C
C ** Component-Type definitions for this task:
C
C    INDEX  TYPENAME    PRINTNAME   REL.FN.  PARAMS
C    -----  --------    ---------   -------  ------
C      0    FASTBUS     FBUS        Expon.   Lambda= .00010000
C      1    K.FBUS      KS          Expon.   Lambda=6.00000000
C      2    M.SHARED    MS          Expon.   Lambda=10.00000000
C      3    M.LOCAL     ML          Expon.   Lambda=10.00000000
C      4    CPU         P           Weibull  Lambda=8.00000000
C                                            Alpha= .95000001
C      5    IOBUS       IOBUS       Expon.   Lambda= .00010000
C      6    DISK        MD          Expon.   Lambda=10.00000000
C      7    K.DISK      KD          Expon.   Lambda=6.00000000
C
C ** PMS Structure Definitions for this task:
C
C    INDEX  NAME      TYPE        NNEIG   NEIGHBORS
C    -----  ----      ----        -----   ---------
C      0    FBUS.1    FASTBUS       3     (KS.1, KS.3, KS.5)
C      1    FBUS.2    FASTBUS       3     (KS.2, KS.4, KS.6)
C      2    KS.1      K.FBUS        2     (FBUS.1, P.1)
C      3    KS.2      K.FBUS        2     (FBUS.2, P.1)
C      4    KS.3      K.FBUS        2     (FBUS.1, P.2)
C      5    KS.4      K.FBUS        2     (FBUS.2, P.2)
C      6    KS.5      K.FBUS        3     (FBUS.1, MS.1, MS.2)
C      7    KS.6      K.FBUS        3     (FBUS.2, MS.1, MS.2)
C      8    P.1       CPU           3     (KS.1, KS.2, IOBUS.1)
C      9    P.2       CPU           3     (KS.3, KS.4, IOBUS.2)
C     10    IOBUS.1   IOBUS         3     (P.1, KD.1, ML.1)
C     11    IOBUS.2   IOBUS         3     (P.2, KD.2, ML.2)
C     12    ML.1      M.LOCAL       1     (IOBUS.1)
C     13    ML.2      M.LOCAL       1     (IOBUS.2)
C     14    KD.1      K.DISK        2     (MD.1, IOBUS.1)
C     15    KD.2      K.DISK        2     (MD.2, IOBUS.2)
C     16    MD.1      DISK          1     (KD.1)
C     17    MD.2      DISK          1     (KD.2)
C     18    MS.1      M.SHARED      2     (KS.5, KS.6)
C     19    MS.2      M.SHARED      2     (KS.5, KS.6)
C
C-------------------------------------------------------------------------------
C
C *** Begin Reliability Function evaluation code;
      REAL FUNCTION RSYS (T);
      IMPLICIT REAL (A-Z)

      WEIBUL(LAMBDA,ALPHA,TIME)=EXP(-(LAMBDA*1E-6*TIME)**ALPHA)

      FBUS = EXP(-0.000100 * 1E-6 * T)
      KS = EXP(-6.000000 * 1E-6 * T)
      MS = EXP(-10.000000 * 1E-6 * T)
      ML = EXP(-10.000000 * 1E-6 * T)
      P = WEIBUL( 8.000000 , 0.950000 , T )
      IOBUS = EXP(-0.000100 * 1E-6 * T)
      MD = EXP(-10.000000 * 1E-6 * T)
      KD = EXP(-6.000000 * 1E-6 * T)
C ** End of expressions for calculating individual reliabilities;
```

Figure 5–25. FORTRAN output from Adviser.

```
        XXX0 = ML * P * IOBUS
        XXX2 = P * IOBUS * MD * KD
        XXX4 = ML * P * IOBUS * MD * KD
C ** End of template evaluating expressions;

        MODREL = 0

        MODREL = 8.0 * FBUS * KS**2 * MS * XXX4  +  8.0 * FBUS * KS**3
$ * MS * XXX0 * XXX2  -  4.0 * FBUS * KS**2 * MS**2 * XXX4 -
$8.0 * FBUS * KS**3 * MS * XXX0 * XXX4  -  8.0 * FBUS * KS**3 *
$MS * XXX4 * XXX2  +  4.0 * FBUS * KS**3 * MS * XXX4**2  -  4.0
$ * FBUS * KS**3 * MS**2 * XXX0 * XXX2  +  4.0 * FBUS * KS**3 *
$MS**2 * XXX0 * XXX4 + 4.0 * FBUS * KS**3 * MS**2 * XXX4 * XXX2
$  -  2.0 * FBUS * KS**3 * MS**2 * XXX4**2  -  4.0 * FBUS**2 *
$KS**4 * MS * XXX4  -  4.0 * FBUS**2 * KS**4 * MS * XXX4**2  +
$2.0 * FBUS**2 * KS**4 * MS**2 * XXX4  -  4.0 * FBUS**2 * KS**6
$ * MS * XXX0 * XXX2  +  2.0 * FBUS**2 * KS**4 * MS**2 * XXX4**2
$  +  8.0 * FBUS**2 * KS**5 * MS * XXX4**2  +  4.0 * FBUS**2 *
$KS**6 * MS * XXX0 * XXX4  +  4.0 * FBUS**2 * KS**6 * MS * XXX4
$ * XXX2  -  6.0 * FBUS**2 * KS**6 * MS * XXX4**2  +  2.0 * FBUS
$**2 * KS**6 * MS**2 * XXX0 * XXX2  -  2.0 * FBUS**2 * KS**6 *
$MS**2 * XXX0 * XXX4  -  2.0 * FBUS**2 * KS**6 * MS**2 * XXX4 *
$XXX2  +  3.0 * FBUS**2 * KS**6 * MS**2 * XXX4**2  -  4.0 * FBUS
$**2 * KS**5 * MS**2 * XXX4**2
C **  End of System Reliability computation;


        RSYS = MODREL
        RETURN
        END
```

Figure 5–25 —*Continued*

---

modeling techniques to evaluate duplication as a means of yield improvement.

In the absence of redundancy, one or more defects in a chip cause it to be discarded. There are three basic types of defects [Murphy, 1964]:

1. Area defects caused by such faults as diffusion or masking errors, surface layer inversion and general contamination. They affect whole slices or areas larger than the chip size.
2. Line defects caused by scratches during the handling of a chip.
3. Highly localized spot defects, the most common defects, caused by imperfections during the diffusion or masking process.

As the predominant cause for discarding the chip, the last category affects the yield most.

In several attempts to predict chip yield, the assumptions for defect density range from a simple Poisson distribution to a compound (or mixed) Poisson distribution [Murphy, 1964; Stapper, 1973; Warner, 1974; Gupta, Porter, and Lathrop, 1974]. Using the simple Poisson distribution to illustrate the usefulness of redundancy on a chip, let D be the defect density measured in number of spot defects per unit area. Assuming that the defect centers obey the Poisson probability distribution and are independent, then, if the effective circuit area is A, the probability that the device is good is:

$$p = e^{-DA} \qquad (26)$$

The defect density D itself is not constant. Let $f(D)$ be the normalized distribution function of D. Then the overall yield, Y, is:

$$Y = \int_0^\infty e^{-DA} f(D)\, dD \qquad (27)$$

On the basis of experiences in the field, Murphy [1964] has claimed that the distribution function, $f(D)$, may be assumed to be the bell-shaped curve shown in Figure 5-26. The curve can be further approximated by a δ-function, a rectangular step function, or a triangular func-

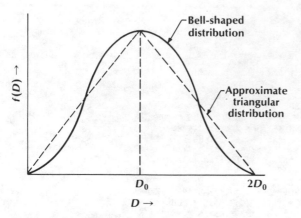

Figure 5–26. Normalized distribution function of chips in defect densities.

tion. For our purposes, the bell-shaped curve is approximated by:

$$f(D) = D/D_0^2 \qquad \text{for } 0 \leqslant D \leqslant D_0 \qquad \textbf{(28)}$$
$$= (2D_0 - D)/D_0^2 \qquad \text{for } D_0 \leqslant D \leqslant 2D_0$$

Evaluating the integral in Equation 27, using $f(D)$ from Equation 28, produces:

$$y = \left(\frac{1 - e^{-D_0 A}}{D_0 A} \right) \qquad \textbf{(29)}$$

Figure 5-27 shows the yield as a function of $D_0 A$.

Now consider replication as a means of improving yield. A circuit is logically divided into n sections of identical complexity, as shown in Figure 5-28. Each section is then duplicated, and simple switching circuitry is added to each pair of sections to allow selection of a good section after testing for spot defects. Assuming that the area required for a circuit is directly proportional to its complexity, let the complexity of the logic added to each section be α times the complexity of the section. The parameter α includes the additional circuitry required to control the functions of the chip (such as a shift register to control which duplicate sections are being used).

The probability that there is at least one good section to use is:

$$e^{-D\alpha A/n}(2e^{-DA/n} - e^{-2DA/n})$$

Because there are n such sections, the probability that the chip is good is:

$$p = e^{-D\alpha A}(2e^{-Da/n} - e^{-2DA/n})^n \qquad \textbf{(30)}$$

Again, using the expression for yield:

$$Y_r = \int pf(D)\,dD \qquad \textbf{(31)}$$

we can determine Y_r, the yield of a chip with redundancy.

The integration of terms in Equation 30 presents difficulties. The solution is obtained by first expanding the bracketed terms using the binomial theorem. The expression can then be integrated with comparative ease.

$$Y_r = \sum_{i=0}^{n} \binom{n}{i} 2^{n-i}(-1)^i \left(\frac{1 - e^{D_0 b}}{D_0 b} \right)^2 \qquad \textbf{(32)}$$

where $b = A[1 + \alpha + (1/n)]$.

The expression for Y_r remains very complex. It is best evaluated numerically, and then compared with Y. Figure 5-29 shows the yield of a redundant chip as a function of $D_0 A$ for $n = 2$. The yield of a nonredundant chip with the same $D_0 A$ is also depicted with the curves for $\alpha = 1.0$, $\alpha = 0.5$, $\alpha = 0.1$, and $\alpha = 0$. As expected, the Y_r for the worst case of $\alpha = 1.0$ (the selection and switch circuitry comparable to the original circuits) is less than that of the nonredundant chip. Significant increases in Y_r are observed as α reduces to 0.5, and further to 0.1. Any further gains, however, are marginal, for there is only a slight increase in Y_r as α is allowed to approach zero. For a typical LSI microprocessor circuit (0.2 in. $\times$ 0.2 in.) with mean defect density D_0 about 6.4 defects per sq. cm. [Muehldorf, 1975], the yield of a nonredundant chip as predicted by Equation 28 is 24 percent. With duplication after dividing the circuit into two sections ($n = 2$) and with $\alpha = 0.1$, the yield will increase to 42

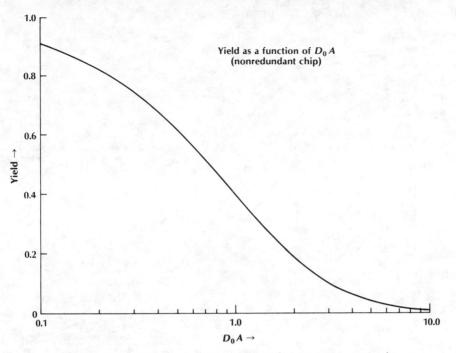

Figure 5–27. Yield as a function of D_0A (nonredundant chip).

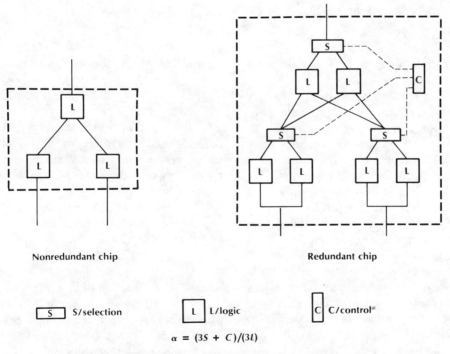

Nonredundant chip   Redundant chip

$\boxed{S}$ S/selection $\boxed{L}$ L/logic $\boxed{C}$ C/control

$$\alpha = (3S + C)/(3L)$$

Figure 5–28. Proposed redundancy to enhance yield.

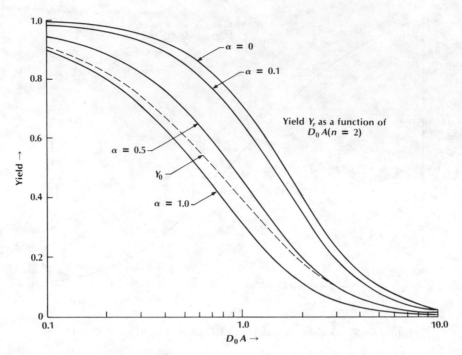

Figure 5–29.   Yield Y_r as a function of $D_0 A(n = 2)$.

percent, a factor of 1.75 increase in yield for a small increase in complexity.

In Figure 5-30 Y is plotted allowing n to vary with $\alpha = 0.5$. Again, the yield of the nonredundant chip is also depicted for comparison. Although the yield increases with n, the maximum increase is at low values of n (two and four), larger numbers of divisions providing diminishing returns. This fact is also obvious in Figure 5-31, where Y_r is depicted as a function of n for $D_0 A = 1.5$. Once again, for $\alpha = 1.0$ the yield is less than that of a nonredundant chip.

Alternatively, redundancy can be used to enhance logic complexity while maintaining a given level of yield (the production point established for maximizing return). The equations above can be used to estimate the degree to which logic complexity can be increased while maintaining a constant yield.

If there are N possibles on a wafer, for the nonredundant case the number of good possibles is

$$NY_0 \tag{33}$$

where Y_0 is the nonredundant yield. For the redundant case there are $N Y_r / [2(1 + \epsilon) + \alpha]$ possibles, where ϵ represents an increase in logic complexity over the nonredundant circuit and Y_r is the redundant yield.

If the redundant and nonredundant number of possibles are equated, we have:

$$Y_0 = \frac{Y_r}{(2 + \alpha + 2\epsilon)} \tag{34}$$

where Y_r is a function of ϵ.

The second column of Table 5-8 lists the value of $D_0 A$ beyond which redundancy is better than nonredundancy as a function of the number of sections, n. For larger values of $D_0 A$, redundancy yields more possibles. When these are only

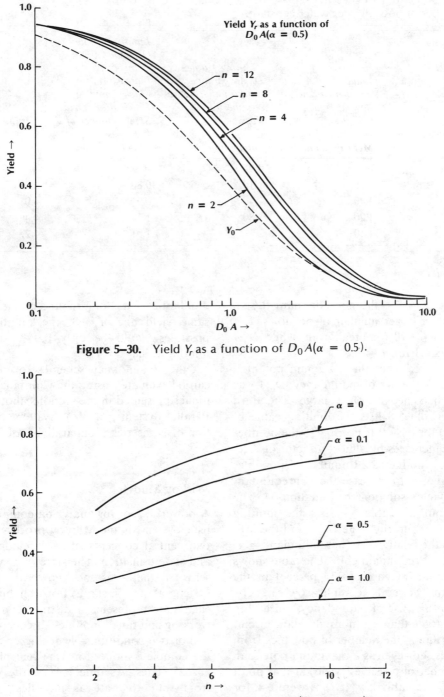

Figure 5–30. Yield Y_r as a function of $D_0 A(\alpha = 0.5)$.

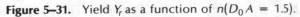

Figure 5–31. Yield Y_r as a function of $n(D_0 A = 1.5)$.

Table 5–8. Use of redundancy to increase nonredundant circuit complexity, holding number of possibles per wafer constant.

Number of Sections in Chip, n	Value of $D_0 A$ (number of defects) Beyond Which Complete Duplication Yields More Possibles	Limiting Value (as $D_0 A$ approaches infinity) of Relative Number of Possibiles Complete Duplication	Limiting Value of Original Circuit Complexity Increase (ε) for which Compete Duplication Yields Same Number of Possibles Wafer	Chip Size of Resultant Redundant Chip Relative to Nonredundant Chip
2	None	0.94	—	—
3	1.78	1.17	0.86	3.90
4	1.40	1.40	0.91	4.01
6	1.20	1.80	1.14	4.49
8	1.10	2.18	1.01	4.22

two sections ($n = 2$), the nonredundant design always yields a larger number of possibles. For $n = 3$, $D_0 A = 1.78$ for break-even, while $D_0 A$ is as small as 1.1 for $n = 8$.

In order to see what the maximum potential gain is through the use of redundancy, $D_0 A$ was allowed to become arbitrarily large. The third column of Table 5-8 lists the limiting value of $Y_r/Y_0(2 + \alpha)$ for $\alpha = 0.1$. For $n = 8$ the number of possibles increases by almost a factor of 2.2.

Converting the increased number of possibles from redundancy to increase the nonredundant circuit size yields solutions to Equation 34. The fourth column of Table 5-8 lists the limiting value of ϵ for arbitrarily large $D_0 A$, and the fifth column lists the relative size (nonredundant = 1) of the resultant redundant chip. The table shows that a potential increase of 114 percent in the nonredundant circuit complexity can be achieved through use of redundancy and a chip 4.49 times larger than the nonredundant circuit without sacrificing the number of possibles from a wafer. This, however, is a maximum potential, and the number of possibles (yield) at that point might be unacceptably low. If $D_0 A$ were 2.4, for example, the yield would be 0.143 for the nonre-

dundant circuit. For a redundant circuit with the same yield and $n = 3$, the number of extra possibles would be only 0.04 instead of the limiting value of 0.17.

Other redundancy schemes to enhance yield can be evaluated using the Combinatorial Techniques presented in the sections above on Series/Parallel Systems, M-of-N Systems, and Reduction of Nonseries/Nonparallel Cases.

Markov Models

A powerful tool for analyzing complex probabilistic systems is the Markov process model. The two central concepts of such models are state and state transition. The state of a system represents all that must be known to describe the system at any instant. For reliability models, each state represents a distinct combination of working and failed modules. If each module is in one of two conditions—working or failed—then the complete model for a system of n modules has 2^n states. As time passes, the system goes from state to state as modules fail and are repaired. These changes of state are called state transitions. Discrete-time models require all state transitions to occur at fixed intervals and assign probabilities to each possible transition. Continuous-time models allow state transitions to occur at varying, random intervals, with transition rates assigned to possible transitions. For reliability models, the transition rates are the module hazard functions and repair-rate functions, possibly modified by coverage factors.

Time-Invariant Markov Models

The basic assumption underlying Markov models is that the probability of a given state transition depends only on the current state. For continuous-time Markov processes, the length of time already spent in a state does not influence either the probability distribution of the next state or the probability distribution of remaining time in the same state before the next transition. These very strong assumptions imply that the waiting time spent in any one state is geometrically distributed in the discrete-time case, or exponentially distributed in the continuous-time case [Howard, 1971]. Thus, the Markov model naturally fits with the standard assumption that failure rates are constant, leading to exponentially distributed interarrival times of failures and Poisson arrivals of failures.

Figure 5-32 is a graphic representation of the two-state discrete-time Markov model. The labeled nodes correspond to the states of the modeled systems, and the labeled, directed arcs represent the possible state transitions. The information conveyed by the model graph is often summarized in a square matrix P, whose elements p_{ij} are the probabilities of a transition from state i to state j. The probabilistic nature of the matrix requires that each row of the matrix must sum to one, and that all elements of the matrix must be nonnegative. The transition probability matrix for the model of Figure 5-32 is

$$\begin{array}{cc} \text{Current} & \text{New} \\ \text{State} & \text{State} \end{array}$$

$$\begin{array}{c} \\ 0 \\ 1 \end{array} \begin{array}{cc} 0 & 1 \end{array} \\ \left[\begin{array}{cc} 1 - q_e & q_e \\ q_r & 1 - q_r \end{array} \right] = P$$

The discrete-time model is solved by a set of linear equations based on the transition probability matrix. In vector notation, these equations are defined as:

$$\vec{P}(k + 1) = \vec{P}(k) \times P$$

In more explicit form, the equations for the model of Figure 5-32 are:

$$[p_0(k + 1), p_1(k + 1)] = [p_0(k), p_1(k)]$$

$$\times \left[\begin{array}{cc} 1 - q_e & q_e \\ q_r & 1 - q_r \end{array} \right]$$

Multiplying into separate equations yields:

$$p_0(k + 1) = (1 - q_e)p_0(k) + q_r p_1(k)$$
$$p_1(k + 1) = q_e p_0(k) + (1 - q_r)p_1(k)$$

The n-step transition probability matrix that contains the probabilities of transitions from one state to another in exactly n transition intervals is given by P^n. In general, to find the probability distribution of a transition from one state to another in no more than k steps, $f_{ij}(k)$, state j can be made a "trapping" state, with p_{jj} set equal to one, and the analysis is straightforward.

The continuous-time Markov model can be derived from the discrete-time model by taking

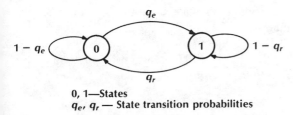

0, 1—States
q_e, q_r — State transition probabilities

Figure 5–32. Two-state discrete-time Markov model.

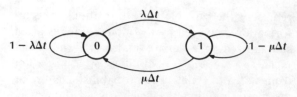

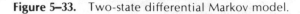

λΔt, μΔt—State transition probabilities
λ, μ—State transition rates

Figure 5–33. Two-state differential Markov model.

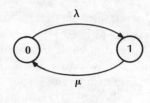

λ—Failure rate
μ—Repair rate

Figure 5–34. Two-state continuous-time Markov model.

the limit as the time-step interval approaches zero. Consider a single system with constant failure rate λ that can be repaired with constant repair rate μ. Let $p_0(t)$ and $p_1(t)$ be the probabilities of being in the nonfailed state and the repair state, respectively. The transactions between states can be represented as in Figure 5-33. From the figure we can write the following transition matrix:

$$P = \begin{bmatrix} 1 - \lambda\Delta t & \lambda\Delta t \\ \mu\Delta t & 1 - \mu\Delta t \end{bmatrix}$$

The probability of being in state 0 or 1 at time $t + \Delta t$ can be formulated by multiplying the probability at time t by the transition matrix:

$$[p_0(t + \Delta t), p_1(t + \Delta t)] = [p_0(t), p_1(t)]$$
$$\times \begin{bmatrix} 1 - \lambda\Delta t & \lambda\Delta t \\ \mu\Delta t & 1 - \mu\Delta t \end{bmatrix}$$

Performing the indicated multiplication yields a system of equations

$$p_0(t + \Delta t) = (1 - \lambda\Delta t)p_0(t) + \mu\Delta t p_1(t)$$
$$p_1(t + \Delta t) = \lambda\Delta t p_0(t) + (1 - \mu\Delta t)p_1(t)$$

Rearranging and dividing by Δt produces:

$$\frac{p_0(t + \Delta t) - p_0(t)}{\Delta t} = -\lambda p_0(t) + \mu p_1(t)$$
$$\frac{p_1(t + \Delta t) - p_1(t)}{\Delta t} = \lambda p_0(t) - \mu p_1(t)$$

Taking the limit as Δt approaches zero generates

a set of simultaneous differential equations (the Chapman-Kolmogorov equations):

$$\frac{dp_0(t)}{dt} = \dot{p}_0(t) = -\lambda p_0(t) + \mu p_1(t)$$
$$\frac{dp_1(t)}{dt} = \dot{p}_1(t) = \lambda p_0(t) - \mu p_1(t) \tag{35}$$

In matrix form

$$[\dot{p}_0(t), \dot{p}_1(t)] = [p_0(t), p_1(t)] \times \begin{bmatrix} -\lambda & \lambda \\ \mu & -\mu \end{bmatrix}$$

or

$$\vec{P}(t) = \vec{P}(t) \times T \tag{36}$$

The set of equations (continuous time Chapman-Kolmogorov equations) can be written by inspection of a transition diagram without self-loops or Δt's. Consider Figure 5-34. The change in state 0 is minus the flow out of state 0 times the probability of being in state 0 at time t plus the flow into state 0 from state 1 times the probability of being in state 1. The equation for the change in state 1 is derived in a similar manner.

The set of equations in 35 can be solved by use of the LaPlace Transform of a time domain function, given by:

$$L\{f(t)\} = f^x(s) = \int_0^\infty f(t)e^{-st} dt$$

The LaPlace Transform reduces ordinary, constant-coefficient linear differential equations to

Table 5–9. Common LaPlace Transforms.

$f(t)$	$f^x(s)$
1. k	$\dfrac{k}{s}$
2. $\delta(t)$ [Unit Impulse]	1
3. e^{-at}	$\dfrac{1}{s+a}$
4. $\dfrac{t^{n-1}}{(n-1)!}e^{-at}$	$\dfrac{1}{(s+a)^n}$
5. $kf(t)$	$kf^x(s)$
6. $f(t)+g(t)$	$f^x(s)+g^x(s)$
7. $\dot{f}(t)$	$sf^x(s)-f(0)$
8. $tf(t)$	$-\dot{f}^x(s)$
9. $\int_0^t f(\tau)\,d\tau$	$(1/s)f^x(s)$
10. $\dfrac{1}{t}f(t)$	$\int_s^\infty f(\sigma)\,d\sigma$
11. e^{At}, A = matrix	$[sI-A]^{-1}$

Note: $f(0)$ denotes the value of $f(t)$ at time $t = 0$.

algebraic equations in s. The algebraic equations are solved and transformed back into the time domain.

Taking the LaPlace Transform of Equation 35 using Table 5-9 gives:

$$sp_0^x(s) - p_0(0) = -\lambda p_0^x(s) + \mu p_1^x(s)$$

$$sp_1^x(s) - p_1(0) = \lambda p_0^x(s) - \mu p_1^x(s)$$

(37)

where $p_0(0)$ is the value of $p_0(t)$ at $t = 0$. The algebraic equations in Equation 37 can be solved by any linear equation-solving technique such as Kramer's rule or Gaussian elimination. Using matrix algebra, Equation 37 can be written as:

$$[p_0(0), p_1(0)] = [p_0^x(s), p_1^x(s)] \times \begin{bmatrix} s+\lambda & -\lambda \\ -\mu & s+\mu \end{bmatrix}$$

or

$$\vec{P}(0) = \vec{P}^x(s) \times [sI - T] = \vec{P}^x(s) \times A$$

where I is the identity matrix and T is the differential matrix derived earlier. Thus:

$$\vec{P}^x(s) = \vec{P}(0) \times [sI - T]^{-1} = \vec{P}(0) \times A^{-1}$$

To derive A^{-1} from A, recall that element a'_{ij} of A^{-1} can be calculated as:

$$a'_{ij} = \frac{\text{cofactor}_{ji}(A)}{\det A}$$

where cofactor$_{ji}(A)$ is defined as:

cofactor$_{ji}(A) \triangleq (-1)^{i+j} \times$ determinant of matrix formed by removing row j and column i from A

and $\det A$ is the determinant of A. For our example,

$$A = \begin{bmatrix} s+\lambda & -\lambda \\ -\mu & s+\mu \end{bmatrix}$$

$$\det A = s^2 + \lambda s + \mu s$$

$$A^{-1} = \frac{\begin{bmatrix} s+\mu & \lambda \\ \mu & s+\lambda \end{bmatrix}}{s^2 + \lambda s + \mu s}$$

Assuming that the system starts out in the operational state, then $\vec{P}(0) = [1, 0]$. So:

$$\vec{P}^x(s) = [1, 0]$$

$$\times \begin{bmatrix} \dfrac{s+\mu}{s^2+\lambda s+\mu s} & \dfrac{\lambda}{s^2+\lambda s+\mu s} \\ \dfrac{\mu}{s^2+\lambda s+\mu s} & \dfrac{s+\lambda}{s^2+\lambda s+\mu s} \end{bmatrix}$$

or

$$p_0^x(s) = \frac{s+\mu}{s^2+\lambda s+\mu s}$$

$$p_1^x(s) = \frac{\lambda}{s^2+\lambda s+\mu s}$$

The general form of the transforms calculated by this stage in the solution process is that of a rational fraction in s, which is a ratio of two polynomials in s:

$$f^x(s) = \frac{N(s)}{D(s)}$$

The inverse transform of a rational fractional is obtained by the following process.

1. If the degree of the numerator is greater than or equal to the degree of the denominator, divide the denominator into the numerator until the degree of the remainder is one less than that of the denominator. The result is:

$$f^x(s) = N_q(s) + \frac{N_r(s)}{D(s)}$$

The inverse transform of $N_q(s)$ can be found by using relationships 2 and 7 from Table 5-9 and added to the remaining solution because of relationship 6. (For our example, this step is unnecessary, as indeed is usually the case. Even when required, the degree of $N_q(s)$ is almost never higher than one or two.)

2. The roots of the denominator polynomial $D(s)$ must be found. In general, the roots may be either real or complex, and there may be multiple occurrences of distinct roots. For our example, we shall assume that all roots are real and distinct. This is usually the case, and other cases can be found using similar techniques. If $D(s)$ is a second degree polynomial, the two roots can be found by direct use of the quadratic formula. Otherwise, the roots can be extracted using such techniques as Horner's method or Lin's method.

3. After finding the roots $-a_1, -a_2, \ldots, -a_r$ of $D(s)$, the rational fraction $N_r(s)/D(s)$ must be expanded into

$$\frac{N_r(s)}{D(s)} = \frac{N_r(s)}{(s + a_1)(s + a_2) \cdots (s + a_r)}$$

$$= \frac{k_1}{s + a_1} + \frac{k_2}{s + a_2} + \cdots + \frac{k_r}{s + a_r}$$

where r is the degree of $D(s)$ and k_i is a constant associated with the ith root. This expansion is called the partial fraction expansion of the rational fraction. The easiest way to find each constant k_i is

to cancel the $(s + a_i)$ factor in $D(s)$ and evaluate the modified fraction for $s = -a_i$:

$$k_i = [N_r(-a_i)]/[(a_1 - a_i)$$
$$\times (a_2 - a_i) \cdots (a_{i-1} - a_i)$$
$$\times (a_{i+1} - a_i) \cdots (a_r - a_i)]$$

After obtaining the partial fraction expansion, the inverse transform is found by applying relationships 3 through 6 from Table 5-9.

Returning to our example, after following the steps above, we find the partial fraction expansions of the transforms:

$$p_0^x(s) = \frac{\dfrac{\mu}{\lambda + \mu}}{s} + \frac{\dfrac{\lambda}{\lambda + \mu}}{s + \lambda + \mu}$$

$$p_1^x(s) = \frac{\dfrac{\lambda}{\lambda + \mu}}{s} - \frac{\dfrac{\lambda}{\lambda + \mu}}{s + \lambda + \mu}$$

Taking the inverse transforms:

$$p_0(t) = \frac{\mu}{\lambda + \mu} + \frac{\lambda}{\lambda + \mu} e^{-(\lambda + \mu)t}$$

$$p_1(t) = \frac{\lambda}{\lambda + \mu} - \frac{\lambda}{\lambda + \mu} e^{-(\lambda + \mu)t}$$

(38)

$p_0(t)$ is the time-dependent probability that the system is in the operational state, defined earlier as the availability function $A(t)$. The availability consists of a steady-state term and an exponentially decaying transient term. As noted earlier, for a nonredundant system with failure rate λ and repair rate μ, the steady-state availability is $\mu/(\lambda + \mu)$. Figure 5-35 plots $A(t)$ for an MTTF of 1,000 hours ($\lambda = 0.001$) and an MTTR of 10 hours ($\mu = 0.1$). The steady-state value is reached in a very short time.

If only the steady-state solution is sought, the required computation is substantially less than that for the time-dependent solution. The differential equations in 35 are changed to algebraic equations by replacing $\dot{p}_0(t)$ and $\dot{p}_1(t)$ by zero, $p_0(t)$ by p_0, and $p_1(t)$ by p_1. That is, there is no

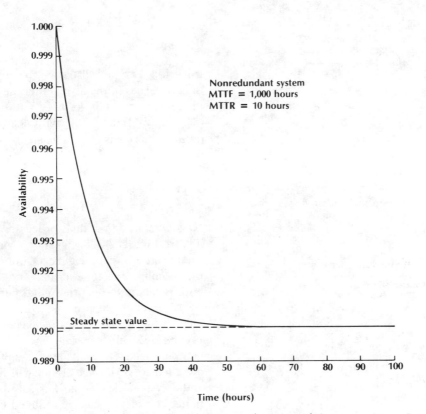

Figure 5–35.   Availability as a function of time.

rate of change in steady state, and the state probabilities have reached their equilibrium values. p_0 is then the steady-state probability of proper system operation, if a solution exists. Applying these changes to Equation 35 yields:

$$0 = -\lambda p_0 + \mu p_1$$

$$0 = \lambda p_0 - \mu p_1$$

or

$$p_1 = \frac{\lambda}{\mu} p_0 \qquad (39)$$

The condition that $p_0 + p_1 = 1$ is required to solve Equation 39. Thus:

$$p_0 + \frac{\lambda}{\mu} p_0 = 1$$

or

$$p_0 = \frac{1}{1 + \dfrac{\lambda}{\mu}} = \frac{\mu}{\lambda + \mu}$$

which is the result obtained earlier.

The reliability function can also be represented as a Markov model by making the system-failed state a trapping state; that is, once the failed state is entered, the probability of exiting is zero. Figure 5-36 depicts the transition probabilities for the single-system model. The differential equations become:

$$\dot{p}_0(t) = -\lambda p_0(t)$$

$$\dot{p}_1(t) = \lambda p_0(t) \qquad (40)$$

a. Discrete-time (differential) model

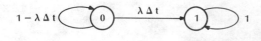

b. Continuous-time model

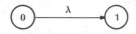

Figure 5–36. Markov model for single system without repair.

The T matrix can be written by inspection:

$$T = \begin{bmatrix} -\lambda & \lambda \\ 0 & 0 \end{bmatrix}$$

$$\vec{P}(0) = \vec{P}^x(s) \times [s\mathbf{I} - T] = \vec{P}^x(s) \times A$$

$$\vec{P}(0) = \vec{P}^x(s) \times \begin{bmatrix} s+\lambda & -\lambda \\ 0 & s \end{bmatrix}$$

$$\vec{P}^x(s) = \vec{P}(0) \times A^{-1}$$

Letting $\vec{P}(0) = [1,0]$:

$$\vec{P}^x(s) = [1,0] \times \frac{\begin{bmatrix} s & \lambda \\ 0 & s+\lambda \end{bmatrix}}{s^2 + \lambda s}$$

$$p_0^x(s) = \frac{s}{s^2 + \lambda s}$$

$$p_1^x(s) = \frac{\lambda}{s^2 + \lambda s}$$

Simplifying and performing partial fraction expansion yields:

$$p_0^x(s) = \frac{1}{s+\lambda}$$

$$p_1^x(s) = \frac{1}{s} - \frac{1}{s+\lambda}$$

Taking the inverse transform gives the final solutions:

$$p_0(t) = e^{-\lambda t}$$
$$p_1(t) = 1 - e^{-\lambda t} \tag{41}$$

Equation 41 could also have been derived from the properties of the exponential distribution and the fact that $p_0 + p_1 = 1$. In addition, Equation 41 is simply Equation 38 with μ set equal to zero (an infinite repair rate). The steady-state solution to Equation 40 yields:

$$p_0 = 0$$
$$p_1 = 1 - p_0 = 1$$

Now consider a dual-processor system with repair. Figure 5-37a gives the Markov model. There are four states, corresponding to both functioning, one functioning and one not, and both failed. Two repairmen and perfect coverage are assumed. If the processors and repairmen are identical, the model can be collapsed as in Figure 5-37b. In general, if there are n components in a system that may be either functional or failed, the Markov model will have 2^n states and a system of 2^n equations to solve. Computational complexity can be reduced by using symmetry to coalesce states. Furthermore, solutions may be limited to finding only the probability of occupying one state of interest (the all-failed state) instead of the probabilities of all states.

To solve the model in Figure 5-37c, which assumes a single repairman (and perfect coverage), by inspection:

$$T = \begin{bmatrix} -2\lambda & 2\lambda & 0 \\ \mu & -\lambda-\mu & \lambda \\ 0 & \mu & -\mu \end{bmatrix}$$

Therefore:

$$A = \begin{bmatrix} s+2\lambda & -2\lambda & 0 \\ -\mu & s+\lambda+\mu & -\lambda \\ 0 & -\mu & s+\mu \end{bmatrix}$$

The solution requires finding the inverse of this matrix, which also requires finding the determinant (at top of next page):

$$\det A = s^3 + (3\lambda + 2\mu)s^2 + (2\lambda^2 + 2\lambda\mu + \mu)s$$

$$A^{-1} = \frac{\begin{bmatrix} \det\begin{bmatrix} s + \lambda + \mu & -\lambda \\ -\mu & s + \mu \end{bmatrix} & -\det\begin{bmatrix} -2\lambda & 0 \\ -\mu & s + \mu \end{bmatrix} & \det\begin{bmatrix} -2\lambda & 0 \\ s + \lambda + \mu & -\lambda \end{bmatrix} \\ -\det\begin{bmatrix} -\mu & -\lambda \\ 0 & s + \mu \end{bmatrix} & \det\begin{bmatrix} s + 2\lambda & 0 \\ 0 & s + \mu \end{bmatrix} & -\det\begin{bmatrix} s + 2\lambda & 0 \\ -\mu & -\lambda \end{bmatrix} \\ \det\begin{bmatrix} -\mu & s + \lambda + \mu \\ 0 & -\mu \end{bmatrix} & -\det\begin{bmatrix} s + 2\lambda & -2\lambda \\ 0 & -\mu \end{bmatrix} & \det\begin{bmatrix} s + 2\lambda & -2\lambda \\ -\mu & s + \lambda + \mu \end{bmatrix} \end{bmatrix}}{\det A}$$

$$A^{-1} = \frac{\begin{bmatrix} s^2 + (\lambda + 2\mu)s + \mu^2 & 2\lambda s + 2\lambda\mu & 2\lambda^2 \\ \mu s + \mu^2 & s^2 + (2\lambda + \mu)s + 2\lambda\mu & \lambda s + 2\lambda^2 \\ \mu^2 & \mu s + 2\lambda\mu & s^2 + (3\lambda + \mu)s + 2\lambda^2 \end{bmatrix}}{s^3 + (3\lambda + 2\mu)s^2 + (2\lambda^2 + 2\lambda\mu + \mu)s}$$

If we assume that $\vec{P}(0) = [1, 0, 0]$, then

$$p_2^y(s) = \frac{2\lambda^2}{s^3 + (3\lambda + 2\mu)s^2 + (2\lambda^2 + 2\lambda\mu + \mu)s} \tag{42}$$

(If the initial state is known with certainty, and only one state probability is of interest, then only one element of A^{-1} needs to be calculated, a potentially large savings in effort.) $p_2(t)$ is the probability of the system's being in the failed state at time t. The availability function $A(t)$ is therefore equal to $1 - p_2(t)$. Alternatively, $A(t)$ could be calculated by solving for $p_0(t) + p_1(t)$, which increases the amount of computation required.

Since the degree of the numerator (0) is obviously less than the degree of the denominator (3), the next step in the solution is to find the roots of the denominator. Using the quadratic formula, after noticing that one root is zero:

$$-a_1 = 0$$

$$-a_2 = -\frac{1}{2}(3\lambda + 2\mu) - \frac{1}{2}\sqrt{\lambda^2 + 4\lambda\mu}$$

$$-a_3 = -\frac{1}{2}(3\lambda + 2\mu) + \frac{1}{2}\sqrt{\lambda^2 + 4\lambda\mu}$$

a. Full four-state model

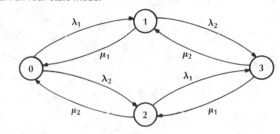

b. Collapsed three-state model ($\lambda_1 = \lambda_2, \mu_1 = \mu_2$)

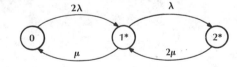

c. Single repairman model

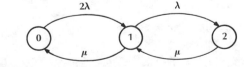

d. Reliability model

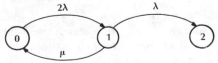

Figure 5–37. Markov models for dual system with repair.

Next, finding the partial fraction expansion:

$$p_2^x(s) = \frac{k_1}{s} + \frac{k_2}{s + a_2} + \frac{k_3}{s + a_3}$$

where

$$k_1 = \frac{2\lambda^2}{a_2 a_3} = \frac{2\lambda^2}{2\lambda^2 + 2\lambda\mu + \mu^2}$$

$$k_2 = \frac{2\lambda^2}{-a_2(a_3 - a_2)}$$

$$= \frac{4\lambda^2}{\lambda^2 + 4\lambda\mu + (3\lambda + 2\mu)\sqrt{\lambda^2 + 4\lambda\mu}}$$

$$k_3 = \frac{2\lambda^2}{-a_3(a_2 - a_3)}$$

$$= \frac{4\lambda^2}{\lambda^2 + 4\lambda\mu - (3\lambda + 2\mu)\sqrt{\lambda^2 + 4\lambda\mu}}$$

and taking the inverse transform:

$$p_2(t) = k_1 + k_2 e^{-a_2 t} + k_3 e^{-a_3 t}$$

As noted earlier, $A(t) = 1 - p_2(t)$. Therefore:

$$A(t) = 1 - k_1 - k_2 e^{-a_2 t} - k_3 e^{-a_3 t}$$

$$A(t) = \frac{2\lambda\mu + \mu^2}{2\lambda^2 + 2\lambda\mu + \mu^2}$$

$$- \frac{4\lambda^2 e^{-\frac{1}{2}[(3\lambda+2\mu)+\sqrt{\lambda^2+4\lambda\mu}]t}}{\lambda^2 + 4\lambda\mu + (3\lambda + 2\mu)\sqrt{\lambda^2 + 4\lambda\mu}}$$

$$- \frac{4\lambda^2 e^{-\frac{1}{2}[(3\lambda+2\mu)-\sqrt{\lambda^2+4\lambda\mu}]t}}{\lambda^2 + 4\lambda\mu - (3\lambda + 2\mu)\sqrt{\lambda^2 + 4\lambda\mu}}$$

The steady-state availability is:

$$A_{ss} = 1 - k_1 = \frac{2\lambda\mu + \mu^2}{2\lambda^2 + 2\lambda\mu + \mu^2} \qquad \textbf{(43)}$$

As discussed earlier, the steady-state availability alone can be found more easily by substituting zero for $\dot{\vec{P}}(t)$ and $\vec{P}$ for $\vec{P}(t)$ in Equation 36.

The availability model in Figure 5-37c can be transformed into a reliability model by making state 2 a trapping state (see Figure 5-37d). Then the solution proceeds as follows:

$$T = \begin{bmatrix} -2\lambda & 2\lambda & 0 \\ \mu & -\lambda - \mu & \lambda \\ 0 & 0 & 0 \end{bmatrix}$$

$$A = \begin{bmatrix} s + 2\lambda & -2\lambda & 0 \\ -\mu & s + \lambda + \mu & -\lambda \\ 0 & 0 & s \end{bmatrix}$$

$$\vec{P}^x(s) = \vec{P}(0) \times A^{-1}$$

For $\vec{P}(0) = [1, 0, 0]$, we need to calculate only a'_{13} in order to find $R(t) = 1 - p_2(t)$.

$$p_2^x(s) = a'_{13} = \frac{\text{cofactor}_{31}(A)}{\det A}$$

$$p_2^x(s) = \frac{\det \begin{bmatrix} -2\lambda & 0 \\ s + \lambda + \mu & -\lambda \end{bmatrix}}{(s + 2\lambda)(s + \lambda + \mu)s - 2\lambda\mu s}$$

$$p_2^x(s) = \frac{2\lambda^2}{s^3 + (3\lambda + \mu)s^2 + 2\lambda^2 s}$$

$$p_2^x(s) = \frac{2\lambda^2}{s(s + a_2)(s + a_3)}$$

$$(a_1 = 0, \text{ by inspection})$$

where the roots are

$$-a_2 = -\frac{1}{2}(3\lambda + \mu) + \frac{1}{2}\sqrt{\lambda^2 + 6\lambda\mu + \mu^2}$$

$$-a_3 = -\frac{1}{2}(3\lambda + \mu) - \frac{1}{2}\sqrt{\lambda^2 + 6\lambda\mu + \mu^2}$$

Expanding the partial fractions:

$$p_2^x = \frac{k_1}{s} + \frac{k_2}{s + a_2} + \frac{k_3}{s + a_3}$$

where

$$k_1 = \frac{2\lambda^2}{a_2 a_3} = 1$$

$$k_2 = \frac{2\lambda^2}{-a_2(a_3 - a_2)}$$

$$= \frac{4\lambda^2}{\lambda^2 + 6\lambda\mu + \mu^2 - (3\lambda + \mu)\sqrt{\lambda^2 + 6\lambda\mu + \mu^2}}$$

$$k_3 = \frac{2\lambda^2}{-a_3(a_2 - a_3)}$$

$$= \frac{4\lambda^2}{\lambda^2 + 6\lambda\mu + \mu^2 + (3\lambda + \mu)\sqrt{\lambda^2 + 6\lambda\mu + \mu^2}}$$

the desired reliability function is

$$R(t) = 1 - p_2(t)$$

Therefore, taking the inverse of the LaPlace Transform;

$$R(t) = -k_2 e^{-a_2 t} - k_3 e^{-a_3 t}$$

$$R(t) =$$

$$\frac{4\lambda^2 e^{-\frac{1}{2}(3\lambda + \mu - \sqrt{\lambda^2 + 6\lambda\mu + \mu^2})t}}{(3\lambda + \mu)\sqrt{\lambda^2 + 6\lambda\mu + \mu^2} - \lambda^2 - 6\lambda\mu - \mu^2}$$

$$- \frac{4\lambda^2 e^{-\frac{1}{2}(3\lambda + \mu + \sqrt{\lambda^2 + 6\lambda\mu + \mu^2})t}}{(3\lambda + \mu)\sqrt{\lambda^2 + 6\lambda\mu + \mu^2} + \lambda^2 + 6\lambda\mu + \mu^2}$$

In review, continuous-time Markov models are solved using the Chapman-Kolmogorov differential equations

$$\vec{P}(t) = \vec{P}(t) \times T$$

where

$\vec{P}(t)$ is the vector of state probability functions

$\vec{\dot{P}}(t) = \dfrac{d\vec{P}(t)}{dt}$

T is the differential state transition rate matrix

The elements of T are easily derived from the graph of the Markov model. For $i \neq j$, t_{ij} is the state transition rate (possibly zero) from state i to state j. Each diagonal element t_{ii} is minus the sum of all transition rates leaving state i. Thus, the rows of T all add up to zero, making it a differential matrix.

Using LaPlace transforms, the differential equations are changed into algebraic equations:

$$\vec{P}^x(s) = \vec{P}(0) \times A^{-1}$$

where

$$A = [sI - T]$$

After solving the set of linear algebraic equations, the final solutions are obtained by applying the inverse LaPlace transform.

Time-Varying Markov Models

A useful generalization of the Markov process for reliability modeling is to allow state-transition probabilities to change over time. This causes difficulties in analysis, since it generally makes the use of transform analysis impossible. Nevertheless, if failure rates (or repair rates) are functions of time, the techniques discussed in this section can be used.

Discrete-Time Equations. Define $q_{ij}(m, n)$ as the probability that the system is in state j at time n given that it was in state i at time m ($m \leqslant n$). For consistency, $Q(m, m) = I$. With this notation, in matrix form the Chapman-Kolmogorov equation is:

$$Q(m, n) = Q(m, k)Q(k, n) \qquad m \leqslant k \leqslant n$$

Letting $k = n - 1$:

$$Q(m, n) = Q(m, n - 1)Q(n - 1, n)$$

Defining $P(n) = Q(n, n + 1)$:

$$Q(m, n) = Q(m, n - 1)P(n - 1) \qquad (44)$$

This equation can be expanded recursively:

$$\mathbf{Q}(m, n) = \mathbf{Q}(m, n - 2)\mathbf{P}(n - 2)\mathbf{P}(n - 1)$$

$$\mathbf{Q}(m, n) = \mathbf{Q}(m, n - 3)\mathbf{P}(n - 3)\mathbf{P}(n - 2)$$
$$\times \mathbf{P}(n - 1)$$
$$\cdots$$

yielding the final solution:

$$\mathbf{Q}(m, n) = \prod_{i=m}^{n-1} \mathbf{P}(i) \qquad (45)$$

For $m = 0$ and all $\mathbf{P}(i) = \mathbf{P}$, this becomes $\mathbf{P}^n$, as given earlier.

Continuous-Time Equations.   Define the difference operator as:

$$\Delta_n f(n) = f(n + 1) - f(n)$$

Then:

$$\Delta_n \mathbf{Q}(m, n - 1) = \mathbf{Q}(m, n) - \mathbf{Q}(m, n - 1)$$

From Equation 44:

$$\Delta_n \mathbf{Q}(m, n - 1) = \mathbf{Q}(m, n - 1)\mathbf{P}(n - 1)$$
$$- \mathbf{Q}(m, n - 1) \qquad (46)$$
$$\Delta_n \mathbf{Q}(m, n - 1) = \mathbf{Q}(m, n - 1)[\mathbf{P}(n - 1) - \mathbf{I}]$$

Defining the differential matrix

$$\mathbf{T}(n) = \mathbf{P}(n) - \mathbf{I}$$

Equation 46 is rewritten:

$$\Delta n \mathbf{Q}(m, n - 1) = \mathbf{Q}(m, n - 1) \times \mathbf{T}(n - 1) \quad (47)$$

Equation 47 is the difference-equation form of the Chapman-Kolmogorov equation for discrete-time Markov processes. The continuous-time Chapman-Kolmogorov equations are directly derived from this equation. Defining $\mathbf{Q}(\tau, t)$ as the continuous-time interval transition probability matrix analogous to the discrete-time multi-step translation probability matrix $\mathbf{Q}(m, n)$ defined earlier, the matrix form of the Chapman-Kolmogorov equation is:

$$\mathbf{Q}(\tau, t) = \mathbf{Q}(\tau, \rho)\mathbf{Q}(\rho, t)$$

In differential equation form, this becomes:

$$\dot{\mathbf{Q}}(\tau, t) = \mathbf{Q}(\tau, t) \times \mathbf{T}(t) \qquad (48)$$

Equation 48 is a more general form of Equation 36. If $\tau = 0$, Equation 36 is obtained by summing

$$p_j(t) = \sum_{i=1}^{N} q_{ij}(0, t)p_i(0)$$

The solution to Equation 47 comes from basic differential equation theory:

$$\mathbf{Q}(\tau, t) = e^{\left[\int_{\tau}^{t} \mathbf{T}(\rho)\, d\rho\right]} \qquad (49)$$

Obtaining explicit solutions from this may be quite difficult. If $\tau = 0$ and $\mathbf{T}(t) = \mathbf{T}$ for all values of t, Equation 49 becomes:

$$\mathbf{Q}(t) = e^{\mathbf{T}t}$$

which is a reformulation of the solution using LaPlace Transforms that was discussed in the section on time-invariant Markov models.

Numerical integration techniques are used to solve Equation 49 because of its complexity [Stiffler, Bryant, and Guccione, 1979]. An alternative method is to approximate the continuous-time process with discrete-time equivalents. Because numerical integration involves some degree of approximation anyway, this is frequently a good choice. The major difficulty is that many transition rates that are effectively zero in the continuous-time differential transition rate matrix assume small but nonzero probabilities in the discrete-time transition probability matrix. Consider the model of Figure 5-37c solved in the previous section. A discrete-time approximation has to consider the probability of two failures during the same interval. This cross-coupled transition probability can be ignored for continuous-time models because of the infinitesimal time-steps involved.

For converting from continuous-time hazard functions (failure and repair rate functions) to discrete-time hazard functions, a discrete-time probability distribution must be found that corresponds to the continuous-time distribution de-

a. Continuous time model

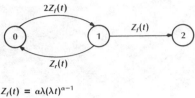

$$Z_f(t) = \alpha\lambda(\lambda t)^{\alpha-1}$$
$$Z_r(t) = \beta\mu(\mu t)^{\beta-1}$$

b. Discrete time model

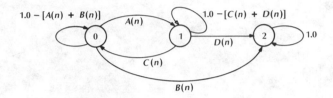

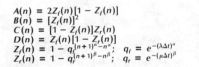

$$A(n) = 2Z_f(n)[1 - Z_f(n)]$$
$$B(n) = [Z_f(n)]^2$$
$$C(n) = [1 - Z_f(n)]Z_r(n)$$
$$D(n) = Z_f(n)[1 - Z_r(n)]$$
$$Z_f(n) = 1 - q_f^{(n+1)^\alpha - n^\alpha}; \quad q_f = e^{-(\lambda\Delta t)^\alpha}$$
$$Z_r(n) = 1 - q_r^{(n+1)^\beta - n^\beta}; \quad q_r = e^{-(\mu\Delta t)^\beta}$$

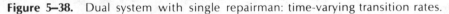

Figure 5–38. Dual system with single repairman: time-varying transition rates.

fined by that hazard function. The corresponding parameters can then be calculated for the desired time-step Δt. For the Weibull distribution function mentioned earlier:

$$pdf = f(t) = \alpha\lambda(\lambda t)^{\alpha-1}e^{-(\lambda t)^\alpha}$$

Recall that a corresponding discrete Weibull function exists (see Chapter 2):

$$pmf = f(k) = q^{k^\alpha} - q^{(k+1)^\alpha}$$

Given that $f(k)$ is defined as the probability of an event (failure) occurring between time Δt and time $(k + 1)\Delta t$ for some chosen interval size Δt, this probability mass function can be expressed as:

$$f(k) = Pr[\text{no event by } k\Delta t]$$
$$- Pr[\text{no event by } (k + 1)\Delta t]$$
$$f(k) = R(k) - R(k + 1)$$

where $R(k)$ is the reliability function. Substituting the continuous-time equivalents:

$$f(k) = R(k\Delta t) - R((k + 1)\Delta t)$$
$$f(k) = e^{-(\lambda k \Delta t)^\alpha} - e^{-(\lambda(k+1)\Delta t)^\alpha}$$

and rearranging terms:

$$f(k) = \left(e^{-(\lambda\Delta t)^\alpha}\right)^{k^\alpha} - \left(e^{-(\lambda\Delta t)}\right)^{(k+1)^\alpha}$$

which makes it obvious that

$$q = e^{-(\lambda\Delta t)^\alpha}$$

and that α does not change between the continuous-time distribution and the discrete-time equivalent. The transition probabilities are now given by:

$$z(n) = 1 - q^{(n+1)^\alpha - n^\alpha}$$

Consider the reliability model of Figure 5-38a,

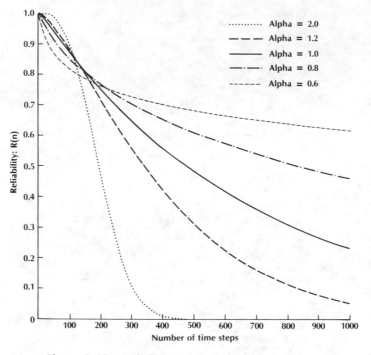

Figure 5–39. Reliability of dual redundant systems.

which is the same as that shown in Figure 5-37c except that the failure and repair rates have been replaced with Weibull hazard functions. In the equivalent discrete-time model displayed in Figure 5-37b the complexity of terms is greater, particularly due to the joint probabilities of state transitions.

After deriving the transition probability matrix function $P(n)$ from the model graph, Figure 5-39 plots the solution of Equation 45 for representative values of α with $\beta = 1$.

For purposes of comparison, failure processes of equal means are used throughout. The values of λ are changed along with the values of α to maintain a constant value for the mean of each process. The reliability curves plotted in Figure 5-39 are based on a module MTTF of 100 time-steps and a module MTTR of 10 time-steps. Table 5-10 lists discrete Weibull parameter values.

The differences in reliability caused by changing the value of α_f (and adjusting other parameters to maintain a constant module MTTF) are

highlighted in Figure 5-40, which plots the reliability difference using $\alpha_f = 1.0$ as the baseline system. Two features are generally discernible from these curves. First, for values of α_f less than one, the system reliability is less than that for α_f equal to one for some period. This is followed by a much longer period during which the reliability of systems with α_f less than one is greater than the reliability of systems with α_f equal to one. (Similar but opposite effects are evident for systems with α_f greater than one.) The second feature is that as α_f gets farther from 1.0, the magnitude of deviation in the curves becomes

Table 5–10. Discrete Weibull parameter values.

α	q_f	β	q_r
0.6	0.922319	1.0	0.90
0.8	0.972515	1.0	0.90
1.0	0.990000	1.0	0.90
1.2	0.996285	1.0	0.90
2.0	0.999921	1.0	0.90

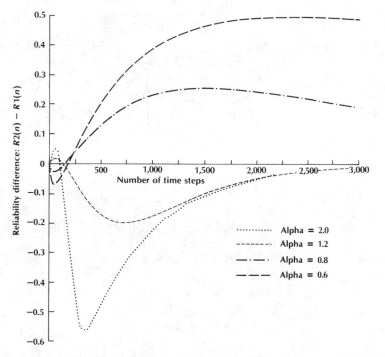

Figure 5—40. Reliability differences between exponential and Weibull for a dual redundant system.

larger. Significant deviations in reliability occur even for relatively small deviations in α_f.

These examples of Markov analysis have been given to illustrate the analysis procedure. The interested reader is referred to more comprehensive analysis such as Howard [1971] and Shooman [1968] for additional solution techniques and examples.

Monte Carlo Simulation

The techniques considered so far are insufficient to obtain results for even quite minor changes in the modeling assumptions. In the issue of failure process renewal, for example, it seems obvious that a repaired module should be "as good as new," but that is *not* the assumption behind the model of Figure 5-38. In that model, the failure processes $z_f(t)$ (or $z_f(n)$) are not reset to time $t = 0$ ($n = 0$) when a module is repaired. This fact can make a dramatic difference in the failure rates. In the Weibull hazard function, for α less

than one, the failure rate asymptotically approaches zero; for α greater than one, it grows without limit. Thus, the failure rate immediately following a repair can vary tremendously under the two modeling assumptions (of course, for constant failure rates there is no difference in effect between the two assumptions.) Consider the discrete Weibull hazard function:

$$z(n) = 1 - q^{(n+1)^\alpha - n^\alpha}$$

If this failure process is reset (renewed) whenever a repair occurs, then the conditional hazard function of the process given the renewal time N_r is:

$$z(n) = 1 - q^{(n - N_R + 1)^\alpha - (n - N_R)^\alpha}$$

In general, the hazard function of the failure process with renewal is given by:

$$z(n) = 1 - \sum_{k=0}^{n} (q^{(n-k+1)^\alpha - (n-k)^\alpha}) Pr\{N_R = k|n\}$$

The second factor in the summation is the conditional probability that the renewal time has

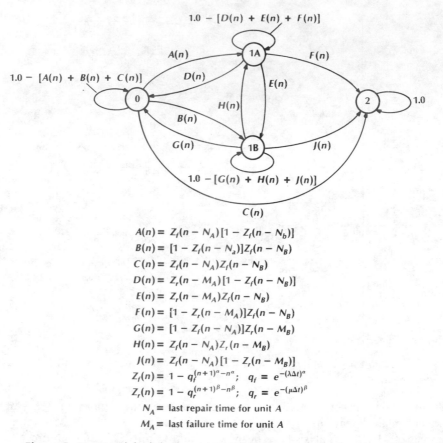

$$A(n) = Z_f(n - N_A)[1 - Z_f(n - N_b)]$$
$$B(n) = [1 - Z_f(n - N_a)]Z_f(n - N_B)$$
$$C(n) = Z_f(n - N_A)Z_f(n - N_B)$$
$$D(n) = Z_r(n - M_A)[1 - Z_f(n - N_B)]$$
$$E(n) = Z_r(n - M_A)Z_f(n - N_B)$$
$$F(n) = [1 - Z_r(n - M_A)]Z_f(n - N_B)$$
$$G(n) = [1 - Z_f(n - N_A)]Z_r(n - M_B)$$
$$H(n) = Z_f(n - N_A)Z_r(n - M_B)$$
$$J(n) = Z_f(n - N_A)[1 - Z_r(n - M_B)]$$
$$Z_f(n) = 1 - q_f^{(n+1)^\alpha - n^\alpha}; \quad q_f = e^{-(\lambda \Delta t)^\alpha}$$
$$Z_r(n) = 1 - q_r^{(n+1)^\beta - n^\beta}; \quad q_r = e^{-(\mu \Delta t)^\beta}$$
$$N_A = \text{last repair time for unit } A$$
$$M_A = \text{last failure time for unit } A$$

Figure 5–41. Model of dual system with failure and repair process renewals.

any particular value given the current time. Calculation of this value depends on the entire past history of the system, which makes it intractable to compute in practice. Therefore, a new technique to attack the problem of reliability modeling is needed.

A standard method of studying the reliability of systems that are too complex to model analytically is to simulate their performance and examine the results [Almassy, 1979; Yakowitz, 1977]. The basis of such "Monte Carlo" simulation schemes is a pseudo-random number generator that produces a sequence of numbers between 0 and 1. This sequence approximately follows the uniform distribution. For good results, simulations should be run on two or more independent pseudo-random number generators, and the gen-

erators used should be thoroughly tested [Knuth, vol. 2, 1969].

Figure 5-41 shows the reliability model of a dual redundant system. Because of the need to distinguish between failures and repairs of the individual modules, a full four-state model is necessary. Otherwise, this models the same system as Figures 5-37d and 5-38b. From the model graph, the transition probability matrix function $P(n; N_A, N_B, M_A, M_B)$ is defined. Each simulation run follows this algorithm:

1. Global initialization
   i = current state = 0
   $N_A = N_B = M_A = M_B$ = renewal times = 0
   n = current time = −1

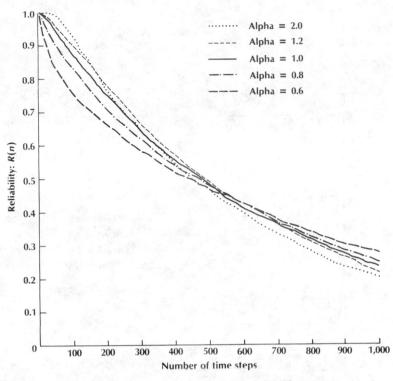

Figure 5–42.   Simulated reliability of dual system.

2. Set loop variables

   $n = n + 1$

   j = next state = -1

   x = cumulative probability = 0

   R = next pseudo-random number in sequence

3. Test for next state

   a) $j = j + 1$

   b) $x = x + p_{ij}(n; N_A, N_B, M_A, M_B)$

   c) if $R > x$ then go to step 3a

4. Next state found

   a) if $i \neq j$ then set one of $\{N_A, N_B, M_A, M_B\}$ to

      $n + 1$

   b) $i = j$

   c) if $i \neq$ a trapping (failed) state then go to step 2

5. Output value of n for this simulation run

For each value of α used in the preceding example of time-varying Markov processes (0.6, 0.8, 1.0, 1.2, 2.0), 3,000 simulations were performed, using three pseudo-random number gen-

erators for 1,000 simulations apiece. Figure 5-42 plots the empirical reliability curves for a dual redundant system with independent failure and repair process renewals, using the same parameter values $(q_f, \alpha, q_r, \beta)$ as for Figure 5-39; only the modeling assumption concerning process renewals was changed. Figure 5-43 plots the corresponding reliability difference curves. The reliabilities of systems with α_f not equal to one diverge quite sharply under the two different modeling assumptions. The general shapes of the curves remain much the same, but the magnitude of the deviation is much smaller in the second time period (underestimation for α_f less than one and overestimation for α_f greater than one) for the systems with error process renewals (although comparable in the earlier time frame). Also, the crossover points are significantly delayed for the systems with error process renewals, compared to the systems without renewals.

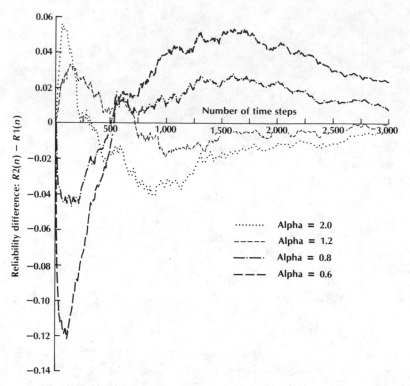

Figure 5–43. Simulated reliability differences between exponential and Weibull for a dual redundant system.

If the exponential (constant error rate) assumption is used for reliability modeling, significant deviations between predicted and experimental reliability will occur whenever the data indicate that failures follow a nonconstant error rate. The extent of deviation from exponential model results depends both on the explicit form of the failure rate (hazard) function and on whether the failure process is renewed whenever a repair occurs.

Modeling a TMR System

This section applies Markov modeling techniques and assumptions to a common structure, a simple TMR (Triple Modular Redundant) system. In TMR correct operation continues as long as two of the three modules are working properly. A second module failure causes the system to fail.

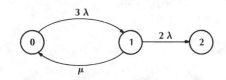

Figure 5–44. Markov model for TMR system reliability.

Constant Failure Rates: Markov Model. A repair strategy of calling in a repairman whenever a module fails produces a Markov model like that shown in Figure 5-44. By inspection, the differential transition rate matrix is:

$$T = \begin{bmatrix} -3\lambda & 3\lambda & 0 \\ \mu & -2\lambda-\mu & 2\lambda \\ 0 & 0 & 0 \end{bmatrix}$$

where λ is the module failure rate and μ is the repair rate. From this, the LaPlace transform $p_2(s)$ is calculated (assuming that $\vec{P}(0) = [1,0,0]$):

$$p_2(s) = \frac{6\lambda^2}{s\left(s + \frac{1}{2}(5\lambda + \mu - \sqrt{\lambda^2 + 10\lambda\mu + \mu^2})\right)\left(s + \frac{1}{2}(5\lambda + \mu + \sqrt{\lambda^2 + 10\lambda\mu + \mu^2})\right)}$$

Expanding the partial fractions, taking the inverse of the LaPlace Transform, and subtracting from one produces the reliability function:

$$R(t) =$$

$$\frac{5\lambda + \mu + \sqrt{\lambda^2 + 10\lambda\mu + \mu^2}}{2\sqrt{\lambda^2 + 10\lambda\mu + \mu^2}} e^{-\frac{1}{2}(5\lambda + \mu - \sqrt{\lambda^2 + 10\lambda\mu + \mu^2})t}$$

$$\frac{5\lambda + \mu - \sqrt{\lambda^2 + 10\lambda\mu + \mu^2}}{2\sqrt{\lambda^2 + 10\lambda\mu + \mu^2}} e^{-\frac{1}{2}(5\lambda + \mu + \sqrt{\lambda^2 + 10\lambda\mu + \mu^2})t}$$

Integrating this function to find the MTTF produces:

$$\text{MTTF} =$$

$$\frac{5\lambda + \mu + \sqrt{\lambda^2 + 10\lambda\mu + \mu^2}}{(5\lambda + \mu)\sqrt{\lambda^2 + 10\lambda\mu + \mu^2} - \lambda^2 - 10\lambda\mu - \mu^2}$$

$$- \frac{5\lambda + \mu - \sqrt{\lambda^2 + 10\lambda\mu + \mu^2}}{(5\lambda + \mu)\sqrt{\lambda^2 + 10\lambda\mu + \mu^2} + \lambda^2 + 10\lambda\mu + \mu^2}$$

Adding together and simplifying:

$$\text{MTTF} = \frac{5\lambda + \mu}{6\lambda^2}$$

Rearranging this expression yields:

$$\text{MTTF} = \frac{5}{6\lambda} + \frac{\mu}{6\lambda^2}$$

Thus, the MTTF of a TMR system with repair is equal to the MTTF of a TMR system without repair *plus* an additional term due to the repair activity.

Consider the effect of redundancy and repair on the reliability of a module with a failure rate of one per 1,000 hours ($\lambda = 0.001$) and a repair rate of one per 10 hours ($\mu = 0.1$.) Figure 5-45 plots the reliability curves of a nonredundant

system, a TMR system without repair, and a TMR system with repair for these parameter values. The MTTF calculations show the following results:

$$\text{Nonredundant MTTF} = \frac{1}{\lambda} = 1000 \text{ hours}$$

$$\text{TMR without repair MTTF} = \frac{5}{6\lambda} = 833 \text{ hours}$$

$$\text{TMR with repair MTTF} = (5/6\lambda) + (\mu/6\lambda^2)$$

$$= 17,500 \text{ hours.}$$

Thus, although redundancy alone reduces the MTTF by about 17 percent, the strategy of on-line repair allows the system MTTF to increase by a factor of 17. This strongly suggests that redundant systems should be designed to allow on-line repair whenever possible.

Time-Varying Failure Rates: Time-Varying Markov Model. If the failure and repair processes vary with time according to the Weibull distribution, a model such as that shown in Figure 5-46 applies. Solving this model for the same parameter values as used earlier in the dual redundant system model (Table 5-10), that is, a module MTTF of 100 time-steps and an MTTR of 10 time-steps, generates the family of reliability curves shown in Figure 5-47. Figure 5-48 plots the difference between the reliability of systems with α not equal to one and systems with α equal to one (constant failure rates). The same patterns are evident in these plots as appeared in the dual redundant system reliability plots in Figures 5-39 and 5-40.

Another comparative measure mentioned previously in this chapter is the mission time improvement. Instead of comparing the system reliabilities at fixed intervals, mission time improvement compares the amount of time different systems require to fall to fixed levels of

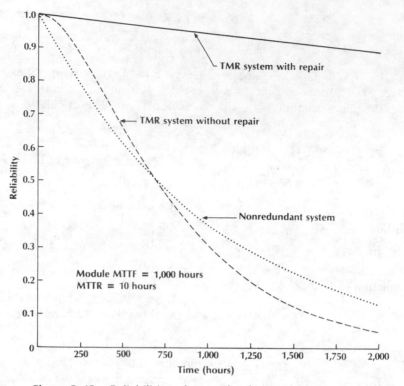

Figure 5–45.   Reliabilities of nonredundant and TMR systems.

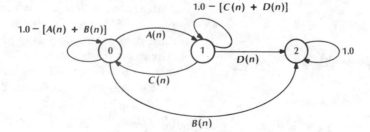

$$A(n) = 3Z_f(n)[1 - Z_f(n)]^2$$
$$B(n) = 3[Z_f(n)]^2[1 - Z_f(n)] + [Z_f(n)]^3$$
$$\quad\;\; = 3[Z_f(n)]^2 - 2[Z_f(n)]^3$$
$$C(n) = [1 - Z_f(n)]^2 Z_r(n)$$
$$D(n) = 2Z_f(n)[1 - Z_f(n)][1 - Z_r(n)] + [Z_f(n)]^2$$
$$Z_f(n) = 1 - q_f^{(n+1)^\alpha - n^\alpha}; \quad q_f = e^{-(\lambda \Delta t)^\alpha}$$
$$Z_r(n) = 1 - q_r^{(n+1)^\beta - n^\beta}; \quad q_r = e^{-(\mu \Delta t)^\beta}$$

Figure 5–46.   TMR model with time-varying failure and repair rates.

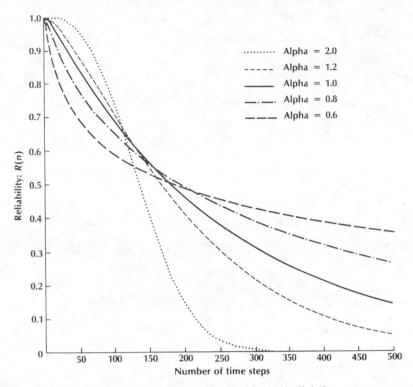

Figure 5–47. Reliabilities of TMR system with Weibull failure processes.

reliability. The calculations are performed by taking the ratio between the mission time of the system under study and the mission time of some baseline system. For our purposes, the baseline system is the nonredundant system with the same parameters as the TMR system under consideration. This is the usual way of using mission time improvement to evaluate different redundant system designs. Table 5-11 lists the mission time improvement factors at several reliability levels. Two patterns are broadly discernible: first, an increasing value for α results in a decreasing value of the mission time improvement. Second, whereas the mission time improvement values decrease monotonically for α greater than or equal to one, they hit a minimum point and start increasing again for the values of α less than one.

Failure Process Renewals: Monte Carlo Simulation. If the individual failure processes are renewed (reset to time zero) whenever a corresponding repair occurs, then a simulation model is needed like the one developed earlier for a

Table 5–11. Mission time improvement factors for TMR systems.

		Reliability		
α	0.90	0.80	0.70	0.60
0.6	4.50	2.88	3.13	3.62
0.8	3.33	3.14	3.12	3.23
1.0	3.30	2.82	2.74	2.70
1.2	2.93	2.55	2.34	2.27
2.0	1.97	1.73	1.61	1.53

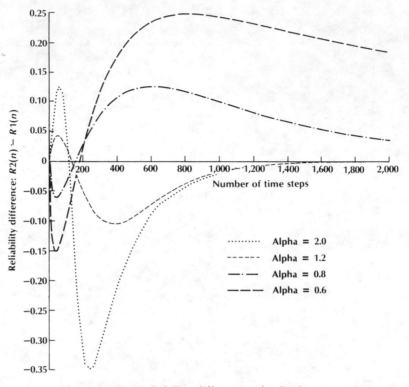

Figure 5–48. Reliability differences for TMR system.

dual redundant system. Figure 5-49 shows the model for the simple TMR system under discussion. The simulation process is similar to that discussed for the previous model with 1,000 runs from each of three pseudo-random number generators for five different values of α. A rough check on the validity of the simulation results is provided by comparing the mission times for several levels of reliability of the analytic solution and the simulation solution for α equal to one. The values should be in close agreement, because the constant failure rate (exponential) process is memoryless, as Table 5-12 confirms. Figure 5-50 shows the empirical reliability curves for the simulated systems; Figure 5-51 plots the empirical reliability difference curves. The same patterns are evident in these plots as in the

earlier dual redundant system and TMR system reliability and reliability difference plots. The degree of convergence for system reliabilities under the assumption of failure process renewals is even greater for the TMR systems than for the dual redundant systems.

Although Figures 5-40 and 5-43, the reliability difference plots for the dual redundant system, show a superficially different pattern from those for the TMR system (Figures 5-48 and 5-51), the changes from the analytical time-varying Markov model to the Monte Carlo simulation models are actually quite similar. In both cases, the magnitudes of deviation for the initial period of overestimation for α less than one (underestimation for α greater than one) increase slightly with the assumption of error process renewals. After

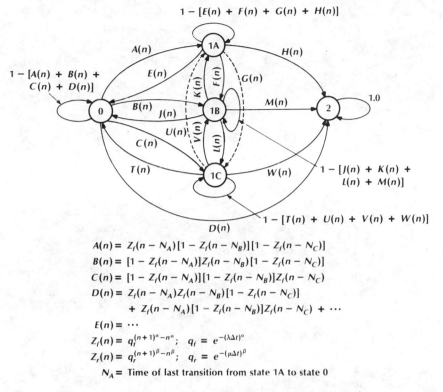

$$1 - [E(n) + F(n) + G(n) + H(n)]$$

$$1 - [A(n) + B(n) + C(n) + D(n)]$$

$$A(n) = Z_f(n - N_A)[1 - Z_f(n - N_B)][1 - Z_f(n - N_C)]$$
$$B(n) = [1 - Z_f(n - N_A)]Z_f(n - N_B)[1 - Z_f(n - N_C)]$$
$$C(n) = [1 - Z_f(n - N_A)][1 - Z_f(n - N_B)]Z_f(n - N_C)$$
$$D(n) = Z_f(n - N_A)Z_f(n - N_B)[1 - Z_f(n - N_C)]$$
$$\quad + Z_f(n - N_A)[1 - Z_f(n - N_B)]Z_f(n - N_C) + \cdots$$

$$E(n) = \cdots$$
$$Z_f(n) = q_f^{(n+1)^\alpha - n^\alpha}; \quad q_f = e^{-(\lambda \Delta t)^\alpha}$$
$$Z_r(n) = q_r^{(n+1)^\beta - n^\beta}; \quad q_r = e^{-(\mu \Delta t)^\beta}$$

N_A = Time of last transition from state 1A to state 0

Figure 5–49. TMR model with failure process renewals.

the initial period of error, the magnitudes after the crossover points are much smaller. These crossover points are also delayed for the models assuming error process renewals, in contrast with the simpler models.

Table 5-13 lists the mission time improvement factors for TMR systems with failure process renewals, calculated in the same way as those in the previous section. The first trend noted above, that an increasing value of α results in a decreasing value for the mission time improvement, is not so evident. The second trend is almost reversed: for α greater than one, the mission time improvement hits a minimum point and starts increasing again, whereas for α less than one, the decline in mission time improvement values is almost monotonic.

The deviation of the mission time improvement for $\alpha = 0.8$ compared with $\alpha = 1.0$ is of interest because some data collected on transient errors have yielded experimental values in that range (see Chapter 2 and McConnel, Siewiorek, and Tsao [1979]). The TMR model without failure process renewal shows a ratio increasing from just over 1.0 to almost 1.4. With failure process renewals, there is no steady increase in the ratio. The ratio between the mission time improvement for $\alpha = 0.8$ to that for $\alpha = 1.0$ ranges from between 1.1 and 1.2 for the TMR model with failure process renewals. If the calculations had been made assuming α equal to one in the baseline system, the deviations shown by these ratios would be even greater.

These examples show that even in models of

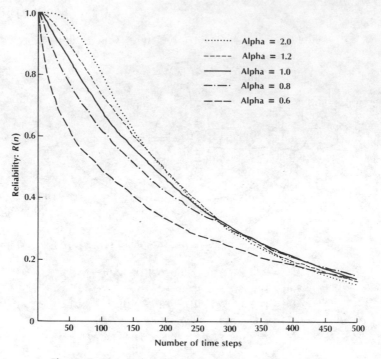

Figure 5–50. Reliabilities of simulated TMR system.

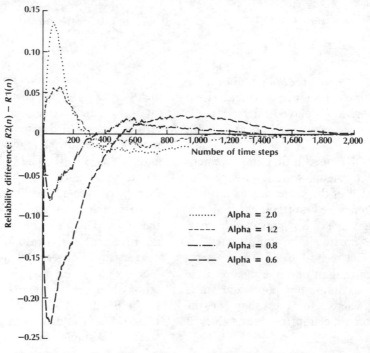

Figure 5–51. Reliability differences for simulated TMR system.

Table 5–12. Comparison of mission times for analytic and Monte Carlo solutions.

	Times	
Reliability	Analytic	Monte Carlo
0.99	7	7
0.90	34	34
0.80	63	63
0.70	97	94
0.60	136	130
0.50	182	179
0.40	238	234
0.30	310	304
0.20	412	412
0.10	587	581

Table 5–13. Mission time improvement factors for TMR systems with failure process renewals.

	Reliabilities			
α	0.90	0.80	0.70	0.60
0.6	6.00	2.80	2.33	2.52
0.8	3.60	3.33	3.18	3.11
1.0	3.30	2.81	2.66	2.48
1.2	2.81	2.63	2.49	2.53
2.0	2.00	1.87	1.82	1.88

simple structures serious differences exist between exponential models and models based on Weibull processes with nonconstant hazard functions.

Hybrid Models Using Measured Statistics

The measures traditionally used to compare systems do not take into account the performance of the system whose reliability is being measured. Table 5-14 lists the results obtained from seven different experiments whose specific goal was to gain experience on systems reliability. Data for the first system [Yourdon, 1972] were from a summary of failure statistics on a Burroughs 5500 over a 15-month period starting in April 1969. Limited information is available about the cause of each failure. One category, for example, includes system failures resulting from unexpected I/O interrupts. These failures are recorded whenever the software responds to an interrupt signifying that some I/O action has taken place but discovers that it has no record of having initiated such action. Thus, there is an indication of some form of hardware or software error, but the particular cause for the failure (hardware or software) remains unknown. The data for the second system, reported in Lynch, Wagner, and

Schwartz [1975] come from the first 13 months of operation of a system called Chi/OS developed by the Chi Corporation for the Univac 1108 between 1970 and 1973. There is no explanation of how such an accurate distinction between hardware and software failures was obtained. Reynolds and Kinsberger [1975] reports data obtained over three years from a dual IBM 370/165 installed at Hughes Aircraft Company to handle a mixed batch and time-sharing load. The fourth system is at the Stanford Linear Accelerator Center (SLAC), where the main workload is processed as a multistream background batch. The system consists of a foreground host (IBM 370/168) and two background batch servers (IBM 370/168 and IBM 360/91) and is designed to be highly available and reconfigurable. The CMU-10A is an ECL PDP-10 used in the Computer Science Department at Carnegie-Mellon University. The data for the CRAY-1 were reported in Keller [1976]; those for the three generic UNIVAC systems in Siewiorek and Rennels [1980].

Table 5-14 gives, when available, a Mean Time to reStart (MTTS) value in hours (that is, the Mean Time to System Failure), a Mean Number of Instructions to Restart (MNIR), which is an estimate of the mean number of instructions executed from system start up until system failure; and the percentages of system failures caused by hardware faults, software faults, and whose cause could not be resolved. The information about execution rates needed to

Table 5–14. Reliability experience of several commercial systems.

System	MTTS (hours)	MNIR	Percent Hardware Faults	Percent Software Faults	Percent Unknown
B 5500	14.7	2.6×10^{10}	39.3%	8.1%	52.6%
Chi/05 (Univac 1108)	17	6.7×10^{10}	45	55	—
Dual 370/165	8.86	2.8×10^{11}	65	32	3
SLAC	20.2	2.3×10^{11}	73.3	21.6	5.1
CMU-10A	10	4.3×10^{10}	—	—	—
CRAY-1	4	1.9×10^{12}	—	—	—
UNIVAC (large)	—	—	51	42	7
UNIVAC (medium)	—	—	57	41	2
UNIVAC (small)	—	—	88	9	3

compute the MNIR value was obtained from Phister [1979].

Obviously, the numbers in Table 5-14 do not convey much information. A MTTS figure alone does not reveal the impact of unreliability on system use. Compare, for example, the CRAY-1 [Russel, 1978] with the CMUA [Bell et al., 1978]. Although the CRAY-1 crashes twice as often as the CMUA, it can operate continuously at rates above 138 Million Instructions Per Second (MIPS), whereas the CMUA operates at 1.2 MIPS. Hence, the CMUA executes $\approx 10^{10}$ instructions between crashes, whereas the CRAY-1 executes $\approx 10^{12}$ instructions between crashes. Inconsistencies like this suggest that reliability modeling and measuring should be closely related with the characterization of the performance of the system under study. Integrated performance-reliability models have already started to appear in the literature. In Meyer, Furchtgot, and Wu [1979], a performance measure called performability gives the probability that a system performs at different levels of "accomplishment." Gay and Ketelsen [1979] models systems with Markov processes to estimate the probability of their being in one of several capacity states. This approach is similar to the one pre-

viously taken in Beaudry [1978], who introduced the concept of "computation reliability" as a measure that takes into account the computation capacity of a system in each possible operational state. Finally, Chou and Abraham [1980] provides a performance availability model for gracefully degrading systems with critically shared resources.

Consider now Figure 5-52, which shows the expected elapsed time required to execute a program for a time-sharing system at three different times of day. The curves were obtained as follows. From April 3, 1979 to July 2, 1979 a CPU bound program (basically a loop that computes several FFTs with no I/O involved and small memory requirements) was executed three times daily. The program required 10 seconds of run-time (Tmin = 10 secs.), and the actual elapsed time for each execution was recorded in the histogram of Tuse at each of these three times of day.

The mean time to system crash was measured for the same period. This value of mean time to crash was substituted as $1/\lambda$ in the model given in Castillo and Siewiorek [1980]. The $1/\lambda$ value was measured at noon (mean time to crash $1/\lambda = 9.6$ hours), 4:00 p.m. ($1/\lambda = 11$ hours),

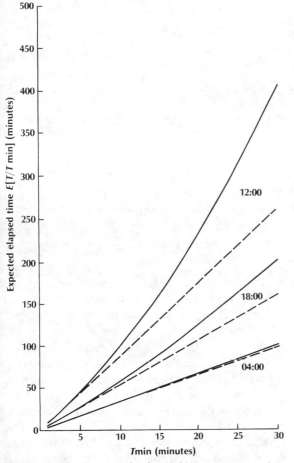

Figure 5–52. Expected elapsed time versus the minimum time required to execute a program. (© 1980 IEEE.)

and 4:00 a.m. ($1/\lambda = 33$ hours). A down-time value of five minutes was assumed in all cases. These three values of the mean time to fatal failure were computed by assigning two-hour time slots around each of the three times of day and counting the number of system restarts in each of the slots during the same three months for which the histograms of Tuse was computed.

Figure 5-52 plots the value of the expected elapsed time required to execute a program at these three times of day for different values of the minimum CPU time required to execute the program (Tmin). The expected elapsed time in-

cludes the effect of workload and unreliability, for it takes into account the time wasted by a system restart due to software or hardware transient errors.

For each curve, the dashed straight line represents the values of the expected elapsed time due only to workload (the expected elapsed time in the absence of errors), and the solid line represents the total expected elapsed time. The figure shows that at 12:00 noon the contribution due to restarts for a program requiring 30 minutes of CPU time amounts to over 40 percent of the total elapsed time.

The curves have been obtained assuming that the time to system crash can be characterized with an exponentially distributed random variable with constant λ. But for the same curves different values of λ are used at different times of day. This suggests that in models for time-sharing systems the failure rate is a periodic function of time.

A workload-dependent model presented in Butner and Iyer [1980] assumes a linear dependency between failure rate and workload. The workload is characterized by a periodic function of time. The pdf becomes an exponential "modulated" by a periodic function

$$P_p(t < \tau) = 1 - e^{-K_p \tau} e^{-F_p U_p(\tau)}$$

where F_p is defined as the load-induced failure rate and $U_p(\tau)$ denotes the instantaneous load value. This model, referred to as the *periodic model*, assumes a periodic utilization function $u(t) = m(t)$. It further assumes that the instantaneous value of the system failure rate is a linear function of this utilization function; that is:

$$\lambda_p(t) = s_p m(t) + c_p$$

Castillo [1980] shows that under this assumption the pdf of the time to system crash is given by

$$P(t < \tau) = 1 - e^{-(s_p m + c_p)\tau} e^{\ln \phi(\tau)}$$

where $\phi(\tau)$ is a periodic function of time.

A closer study of the utilization functions of

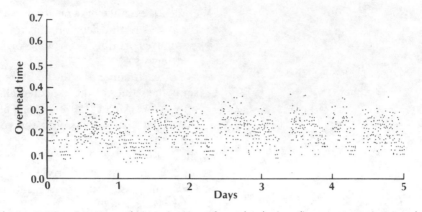

Figure 5–53. Fraction of time in Kernel mode during five consecutive weekdays.

critical resources in time-sharing systems reveals, however, that it is an oversimplification to assume that they can be approximated by a purely periodic function.

Figure 5-53 shows the sampled values of the fraction of time the operating system spends in Kernel mode for five consecutive weekdays in a time-sharing computing system. There are reasons to assume that the instantaneous value of the system failure rate should follow the variations of the fraction of time in Kernel mode.

First, assume a constant failure rate for the primary memory of a digital computing system operating in a stable environment under a time-sharing policy. That the transient failure rate in a memory is constant is a reasonable assumption. There is also justification for thinking that certain complex devices may follow an exponential failure law [Barlow and Proschan, 1965, pp. 18–22]. Because the physical characteristics of the memory ICs do not change with time (at least during the effective life cycle of modern digital computing systems), the origin of these transients must lie either in external sources, such as radiation, the presence of noise (possibly impulsive) in the power supply, or in the limitations of the manufacturing process. In fact, Geilhufe [1979] has reported that MOS memory devices exhibit nonrecurring bit failures caused by alpha particles emitted from small amounts of radioactive elements present in IC packaging material. The failure rate for this kind of failures is, of course, constant. Now assume that a transient memory failure has higher probability of leading to a system crash when the central processor is executing in Kernel mode than when it is executing in user mode. A memory failure when the CPU is executing in user mode may affect a user process but will not crash the system. The *system* failure rate due to transient memory failures will then depend on the ratio of the number of memory references while in Kernel mode to the total number of memory references per unit time. Because it is well known that operating system overhead increases with workload, the previous ratio will also be a nondecreasing function of the system workload, increasing in turn the observed system failure rate. The result is that the observed system failure rate due to transient memory failures should be equal to the sum of a component following the operating system overhead variations in time (or, indirectly, workload variations in time) plus a constant, workload-independent component (even if the system is idle, there may still be memory errors that corrupt, say, the clock interrupt subroutine).

Even if the fact that a computing system is not

always equally sensitive to the presence of hardware errors, there are still arguments to support the idea that the apparent system failure rate should depend on the workload. In practice, in most computing systems a component failure will be noticed only if the component is used. A time-sharing system with no load, spending most of its time in a wait state and only a fraction of the time executing the clock interrupt routine may sustain several failures and still not report any errors if the minimal hardware configuration required to execute these basic functions is not affected. The idea here is not that failures will be caused by increased utilization (although in some cases this situation is certainly possible), but that they will be detected by an increase in system utilization. This effect has also been referred to as error latency [Shedletsky and McCluskey, 1973].

Analogous arguments lead to the expectation that the rate of system failures due to software unreliability will depend on how much the software is used. System software failures result from either of two conditions: the (static) input data to a program module present some peculiarities that the program is not able to handle, or the software is not capable of handling some time-dependent (dynamic) sequence in the input data stream. In a time-sharing system, the only software capable of provoking a system failure is the Kernel of the Operating System. This software executes in a privileged processor state, and a software error that corrupts some critical information in the Kernel data structures may lead to a system crash. However, because nobody knows a priori what these errors are, it is less likely that the system finds one of these combinations in its input stream under low load than in a high load situation (that is, small amounts of input data to process per unit time probably exercises software that has been more thoroughly debugged). Again, the observed system failure rate has to depend on the system load. Furthermore, upon correct system operation, a user program is prevented from accessing any resource for which it has not been given explicit permission by the

Kernel. Consequently it is not necessary to consider the effects of user programs.

Assuming that the failure rate is workload related, and given the workload measured in Figure 5-53, a utilization function of the form

$$u(t) = m(t) + z(t),$$

where $m(t)$ is a periodic function of time and $z(t)$ is a zero-mean stationary Gaussian process, is thus appropriate for modeling a time-sharing system. Castillo [1980] shows that, under the assumption

$$\lambda_i(t) = s_i[m(t) + z(t)] + c_i$$

the following expression is obtained for the pdf of the time to system failure:

$$P(t < \tau) = 1$$
$$- e^{\left(-(\alpha_c + \sigma_{c1} + \sigma_{c2})\tau - (\sigma_{c1}/\beta_1)[1 - e^{-\beta_1\tau}] - (\sigma_{c2}/\beta_2)[1 - e^{-\beta_2\tau}] + \ln \phi(\tau)\right)}$$

where $\phi(\tau)$ is a periodic function of time depending only on $m(t)$, and the additional assumption is that the autocorrelation function of $z(t)$ is of the form

$$R_{zz}(t) = \alpha_1 e^{-\beta_1 t} + \alpha_2 e^{-\beta_2 t}$$

This model is termed cyclostationary because it is obtained from a cyclostationary utilization function (that is, the utilization function $u(t)$ is a stochastic process with periodic mean and autocorrelation functions).

Table 5-15 summarizes the reliability functions and hazard functions of the two models above (periodic and cyclostationary) along with the exponential and Weibull distributions. The fifth distribution in Table 5-15 is a simplified version of the distribution obtained with the cyclostationary model, considering only one exponential in the hazard function and neglecting the periodic component $\phi(\tau)$. This last distribution is particularly important because it has a known LaPlace Transform that makes it suitable for Markov modeling (neither the Weibull distribution nor the distributions obtained from the periodic and cyclostationary models have known

Table 5–15. Reliability and hazard function of five failure models.

Exponential

$$R_e(\tau) = e^{-\lambda_e \tau}$$

$$h_e(\tau) = \lambda_e$$

Weibull

$$R_w(\tau) = e^{-(\lambda_w \tau)^{\alpha_w}}$$

$$h_w(\tau) = \frac{\alpha_w \lambda_w}{(\lambda_w t)^{1-\alpha_w}}$$

Periodic

$$R_p(\tau) = e^{-\lambda_p \tau_e} e^{-F_p u(\tau)}$$

$$h_p(\tau) = \left[\lambda_p + F_p \frac{\partial u(\tau)}{\partial \tau t}\right]$$

Cyclostationary

$$R_c(\tau) = e^x$$

where

$$x = \{-(\lambda_c + \sigma_{c1} + \sigma_{c2})\tau - (\sigma_{c1}/\beta_1)[1 - e^{-\beta_1 \tau}]$$

$$-(\sigma_{c2}/\beta_2)[1 - e^{-\beta_2 \tau}] + \ln \phi(t)\}$$

$$h_c(\tau) = \lambda_c - \sigma_{c1}[1 - e^{-\beta_1 \tau}]$$

$$-\sigma_{c2}[1 - e^{-\beta_2 \tau}] + \frac{1}{\phi(t)} \frac{\partial \phi(t)}{\partial t}$$

Simplified Cyclostationary

$$R_m(\tau) = e^{-(\alpha_m - \gamma_m)\tau - (\gamma_m/\beta_m)[1 - e^{-\beta_m \tau}]}$$

$$h_m(\tau) = \alpha_m - \gamma_m[1 - e^{-\beta_m \tau}]$$

LaPlace Transforms). Castillo [1980] has shown that both the cyclostationary and simplified cyclostationary models have substantially better statistical fits to measured data than the exponential, Weibull, and periodic models.

Automated Markov Analysis Programs

As with combinatorial modeling, programs have been written using Markov modeling to assist in evaluating general classes of system structures. Two of these programs deserve special mention.

ARIES. ARIES (Automated Reliability Interactive Estimation System), developed at UCLA by Ng and Avižienis [1980], implements a general time invariant Markov model for systems similar to those covered by CARE II. The structures handled consist of a series of one or more independent subsystems or stages, each containing a number of identical modules that are either active or serve as spares. Systems can be reconfigured by adding, deleting, or replacing stages, or by modifying the values of some parameters. The inputs to ARIES include the following:

1. The initial numbers of active and spare modules;
2. The number of repair facilities for each stage;
3. The failure rates for active and spare modules, and the repair rates for the repair facilities;
4. The coverage factors for recovery from failed spares;
5. The number and sequence for allowed degradations, and the coverage factors for degraded configurations.

The program outputs several measures, including MTTF, mission time, and reliability plots or tables. ARIES is very general in the type of redundant structures it can model, limited primarily by the assumption of distinct eigenvalues for the Markov differential transition matrix.

CARE III. CARE III (Computer-Aided Reliability Estimation III), developed at Raytheon [Stiffler, Bryant, and Guccione, 1979], implements a time-varying Markov model for ultrareliable redundant systems. The system structures handled by CARE III are like those handled by CARE II and ARIES. Two new assumptions are made, one more restrictive than ARIES and one more general. The first assumption is that the user is interested only in extremely reliable (system failure rates less than 10^{-10} per hour) systems with short mission times (no longer than 10 hours) and no repair during missions. Typical target systems are flight-critical avionics computers for future aircraft. The second, more general assumption is that failures follow a Weibull distribution. CARE III handles not only hard failures but also intermittent and transient faults. It also implements an extensive coverage model based on that of CARE II. The inputs to CARE III include the module-failure parameters (both α and λ for the Weibull function) for each stage, and the coverage parameters. The output includes both tables and plots of the system reliability and unreliability. The generality of CARE III is limited both by the assumption of extremely high mission reliability and by the assumption of no repair during a mission.

System Availability Models

In general, modeling the availability of systems with repair requires the use of Markov models. If certain restrictions are made, however, special techniques can be used that are easier to apply. This section presents two such methods. The first permits calculation of the system availability function $A_{sys}(t)$, given the module availability functions $A_i(t)$ for any arbitrary structure, provided that the module availabilities are independent. The second uses queuing theory to obtain the steady-state availability for a structure composed of identical modules with constant failure rates. Both of these restricted models (as well as

the general Markov model) assume that redundant structures are designed for on-line repair.

Combinatorial Modeling of Systems Availability

The reliability function $R(t)$ and the availability function $A(t)$ are both probability functions, although of different asymptotic behavior. Because they are both probabilities, the combinatorial modeling techniques developed earlier in this chapter for system reliability calculations apply equally well to calculating system availability if three basic assumptions are met. The first, natural assumption is that the system design is coherent—that a module failure never causes the system to have increased availability. The second assumption is that individual modules are always in one of two states—working or failed. The last necessary condition is that the individual module availabilities must be statistically independent. For this condition to hold, there is only one allowable repair strategy: one repairman called for each failed module, and repair proceeding on failed modules while the remainder of the system continues to function (on-line repair). This also dictates the size of the subdivision into modules that are used in the model. Separate repairmen may be a reasonable assumption for minicomputer-sized modules but probably not for individual memory or I/O cards, and certainly not for individual memory or logic chips.

To illustrate the application of combinatorial modeling to system availability, consider the Markov model of Figure 5-54. The differential

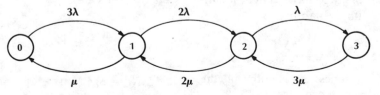

Figure 5–54. Markov model of system with three modules.

transition rate matrix defined by this model graph is

$$T = \begin{bmatrix} -3\lambda & 3\lambda & 0 & 0 \\ \mu & -2\lambda - \mu & 2\lambda & 0 \\ 0 & 2\mu & -2\mu - \lambda & \lambda \\ 0 & 0 & 3\mu & -3\mu \end{bmatrix}$$

Solving this for an initial state vector of $\vec{P}(0) = [1, 0, 0, 0]$, using the Markov model solution techniques developed earlier, produces the following state probability functions:

$$p_0(t) = \frac{\mu^3 + 3\lambda\mu^2 e^{-(\lambda+\mu)t} + 3\lambda^2\mu e^{-2(\lambda+\mu)t} + \lambda^3 e^{-3(\lambda+\mu)t}}{(\lambda + \mu)^3}$$

$$p_1(t) = \frac{3\lambda\mu^2 + 3\lambda\mu(2\lambda - \mu)e^{-(\lambda+\mu)t} + 3\lambda^2(\lambda - 2\mu)e^{-2(\lambda+\mu)t} - 3\lambda^3 e^{-3(\lambda+\mu)t}}{(\lambda + \mu)^3}$$

$$p_2(t) = \frac{3\lambda^2\mu + 3\lambda^2(\lambda - 2\mu)e^{-(\lambda+\mu)t} - 3\lambda^2(2\lambda - \mu)e^{-2(\lambda+\mu)t} + 3\lambda^3 e^{-3(\lambda+\mu)t}}{(\lambda + \mu)^3}$$

$$p_3(t) = \frac{\lambda^3 - 3\lambda^3 e^{-(\lambda+\mu)t} + 3\lambda^3 e^{-2(\lambda+\mu)t} - \lambda^3 e^{-3(\lambda+\mu)t}}{(\lambda + \mu)^3}$$

The Markov model can be interpreted in any of three ways. First, it may represent a system that requires all three modules in order to work properly. For this case, the availability function is

$$A(t) = p_0(t)$$

The alternative way to derive this function (derived earlier in Equation 38 as the solution for the two-state Markov model with initial state vector $\vec{P}(0) = [1, 0]$) is to consider the system as a series connection of three independent identical modules, each with availability

$$A_m(t) = \frac{\mu}{\lambda + \mu} + \frac{\lambda}{\lambda + \mu} e^{-(\lambda+\mu)t}$$

The equation for series connection of the availability block diagram produces:

$$A_{sys}(t) = \prod_{i=1}^{3} A_i(t) = [A_m(t)]^3$$

$$A_{sys}(t) = \left(\frac{u + \lambda e^{-(\lambda+\mu)t}}{\lambda + \mu} \right)^3$$

$$A_{sys}(t) = [\mu^3 + 3\lambda\mu^2 e^{-(\lambda+\mu)t} + 3\lambda^2\mu e^{-2(\lambda+\mu)t} + \lambda^3 e^{-3(\lambda+\mu)t}] / [(\lambda + \mu)^3]$$

which is the same result as obtained by solving the Markov model.

The second interpretation of the Markov model is that it represents a simple TMR system such as the one modeled for reliability earlier (see Figure 5-44).

For the two-of-three model, the availability defined by the Markov model solution is

$$A(t) = p_0(t) + p_1(t)$$

The combinatorial solution proceeds as follows:

$$A_{sys}(t) = \sum_{i=0}^{1} \binom{3}{i} [A_m(t)]^{3-i} [1 - A_m(t)]^i$$

$$A_{sys}(t) = \binom{3}{0} [A_m(t)]^3$$

$$+ \binom{3}{1} [A_m(t)]^2 [1 - A_m(t)]$$

$$A_{sys}(t) = 3[A_m(t)]^2 - 2[A_m(t)]^3$$

$$A_{sys}(t) = \frac{3(\mu + \lambda e^{-(\lambda+\mu)t})^2}{(\lambda + \mu)^2} - \frac{2(\mu + \lambda e^{-(\lambda+\mu)t})^3}{(\lambda + \mu)^3}$$

$$A_{sys}(t) = \frac{3(\lambda + \mu)(\mu + \lambda e^{-(\lambda+\mu)t})^2 - 2(\mu + \lambda e^{-(\lambda+\mu)t})^3}{(\lambda + \mu)^3}$$

$$A_{sys}(t) = \frac{\mu^3 + 3\lambda\mu^2 + 6\lambda^2\mu e^{-(\lambda+\mu)t} + 3\lambda^2(\lambda - \mu)e^{-2(\lambda+\mu)t} - 2\lambda^3 e^{-3(\lambda+\mu)t}}{(\lambda + \mu)^3}$$

Careful examination shows that this combinatorial solution for $A_{sys}(t)$ is indeed equal to that derived from the Markov model.

The remaining system modeled by Figure 5-54 is a module with two spares, which is otherwise expressed as a parallel structure in the availability block diagram. The availability function derived from the Markov model is:

$$A(t) = p_0(t) + p_1(t) + p_2(t) = 1 - p_3(t)$$

The solution as a parallel system with three modules is as follows:

$$A_{sys}(t) = 1 - \prod_{i=1}^{3}(1 - A_i(t))$$

$$= 1 - [1 - A_m(t)]^3$$

$$= 1 - \left(\frac{\lambda}{\lambda + \mu} - \frac{\lambda}{\lambda + \mu}e^{-(\lambda+\mu)t}\right)^3$$

$$= 1 - [\lambda^3 - 3\lambda^3 e^{-(\lambda+\mu)t} + 3\lambda^3 e^{-2(\lambda+\mu)t}$$

$$- \lambda^3 e^{-3(\lambda+\mu)t}]/[(\lambda + \mu)^3]$$

Again, the results obtained from the combinatorial and Markov model solutions match.

The combinatorial M-of-N formula assumes that all modules have identical availability. This is *not* necessary for the series-parallel approach. Also, the methods discussed obviously apply equally to calculating steady-state availability, which is the next topic of discussion.

Modeling Steady-State System Availability: Queuing Theory Applications

Several of the Markov models in Figure 5-55 have already been discussed in this chapter. All are members of an important class of Markov process models known as birth-and-death processes. The defining characteristics of birth-and-death processes are:

1. State transitions occur only between "adjacent" states: that is, for state N (not an end state), transitions occur only to state $N - 1$ or $N + 1$.
2. Both "birth" transitions (N to $N + 1$) and "death" transitions (N to $N - 1$) follow a Poisson process.
3. The probability of both a "birth" and a "death" occurring simultaneously is negligible.

Figure 5-56a shows the general infinite birth-and-death process, Figure 5-56b the general finite birth-and-death process.

A very fruitful application of birth-and-death processes has been the study of waiting-line behavior, or queuing theory. Queues, or waiting lines, are common in daily life: the checkout line at the grocery store, the line of customers waiting to be seated at a restaurant, the innumerable lines of students at college registration. The queue involved here consists of a finite population of modules that fail randomly, entering a waiting line to be repaired by a finite (possibly smaller) number of repair personnel. This queuing model is known as the Machine-Repair, Multiple-Repairmen model, and is named the M/M/c/K/K Queuing System. This cryptic nomenclature is decoded as follows:

1. The first letter describes the interarrival time distribution for failures ("birth"). M (which stands for Markov, or the memoryless property of the exponential distribution) means that failures follow an exponential distribution.
2. The second letter gives the distribution for service (repair) time, again exponential for this model.
3. The third term is the maximum number of repairmen (servers).
4. The fourth term is the maximum number of failed modules that can be serviced, either immediately or after waiting for the next available repairman.
5. The last term (which is always equal to the fourth term in this model) is the population size, that is, the total number of modules in the system.

a. Two modules, one repairman

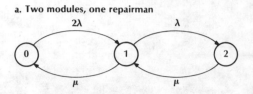

b. Two modules, two repairmen

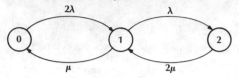

c. Three modules, one repairman

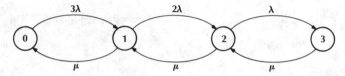

d. Three modules, two repairmen

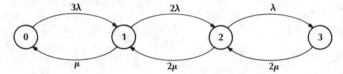

e. Three modules, three repairmen

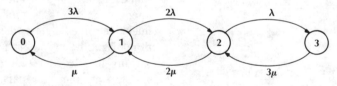

Figure 5–55. Markov models for two and three module systems for different numbers of repairmen.

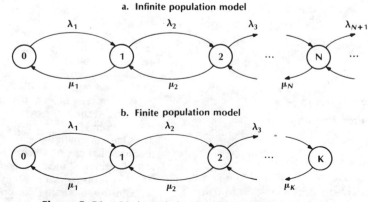

a. Infinite population model

b. Finite population model

Figure 5–56. Birth-and-death process Markov models.

Figure 5-57 shows the general form of the Markov model that fits the M/M/c/K/K queuing system. All modules are assumed to have the same (constant) failure rate λ, and all repairmen work at the same (constant) rate μ.

For the model shown in Figure 5-57, the limiting (steady-state) state probabilities p_n are defined by the following recurrence equation:

$$p_n = \left(\frac{\lambda_n}{\mu_n}\right) p_{n-1}; \quad n = 1, 2, 3, \ldots, K \quad (50)$$

with

$$p_0 = 1 - \sum_{n=1}^{K} p_n$$

The specific adaptation of Equation 50 to the M/M/c/K/K queue of Figure 5-57 is:

$$p_n = \left(\frac{K-n+1}{n}\right)\left(\frac{\lambda}{\mu}\right) p_{n-1};$$

$$n = 1, 2, 3, \ldots, c$$

$$p_n = \left(\frac{K-n+1}{c}\right)\left(\frac{\lambda}{\mu}\right) p_{n-1};$$

$$n = c+1, \ldots, K$$

$$(51)$$

Solving these in terms of p_0:

$$p_n = \binom{K}{n}\left(\frac{\lambda}{\mu}\right)^n p_0, \quad n = 1, 2, \ldots, c$$

$$p_n = \frac{n!}{c!\,c^{n-c}}\binom{K}{n}\left(\frac{\lambda}{\mu}\right)^n p_0;$$

$$n = c+1, \ldots, K$$

$$(52)$$

and

$$p_0 = 1 - \left[\sum_{n=1}^{c} \binom{K}{n}\left(\frac{\lambda}{\mu}\right)^n p_0 \right.$$

$$\left. + \sum_{n=c+1}^{K} \frac{n!}{c!\,c^{n-c}}\binom{K}{n}\left(\frac{\lambda}{\mu}\right)^n p_0 \right]$$

$$(53)$$

$$p_0 = \frac{1}{\displaystyle\sum_{n=0}^{c} \binom{K}{n}\left(\frac{\lambda}{\mu}\right)^n + \sum_{n=c+1}^{K} \frac{n!}{c!\,c^{n-c}}\binom{K}{n}\left(\frac{\lambda}{\mu}\right)^n}$$

The limiting state probabilities p_n ($n = 0, 1, \ldots, K$) are used to calculate the steady-state availa-

bility A_{sys}. For an M-of-N system structure, the equation for A_{sys} is

$$A_{\text{sys}} = \sum_{n=0}^{N-M} p_n = 1 - \sum_{n=N-M+1}^{N} p_n \quad (54)$$

The first model of Figure 5-55 (two modules, one repairman) was solved in the section on Time-Invariant Markov Models above. Applying Equation 53 to this M/M/1/2/2 queue:

$$p_0 = \frac{1}{1 + \binom{2}{1}\left(\frac{\lambda}{\mu}\right) + \frac{2!}{1!}\binom{2}{2}\left(\frac{\lambda}{\mu}\right)^2}$$

$$= \frac{\mu^2}{\mu^2 + 2\lambda\mu + 2\lambda^2}$$

Using Equation 51 yields:

$$p_1 = 2\left(\frac{\lambda}{\mu}\right) p_0 = \frac{2\lambda\mu}{\mu^2 + 2\lambda\mu + 2\lambda^2}$$

$$p_2 = \left(\frac{\lambda}{\mu}\right) p_1 = \frac{2\lambda^2}{\mu^2 + 2\lambda\mu + 2\lambda^2}$$

If Figure 5-55 represents a dual redundant system, then

$$A_{\text{sys}} = p_0 + p_1$$

$$A_{\text{sys}} = \frac{\mu^2 + 2\lambda\mu}{\mu^2 + 2\lambda\mu + 2\lambda^2}$$

which is the result obtained in the section on Time-Invariant Markov Models, Equation 43 above.

If the repair strategy is changed to call a second repairman when a second module fails, the model of Figure 5-55b results, a M/M/2/2/2 queue. For this model:

$$p_0 = \frac{1}{1 + \binom{2}{1}\left(\frac{\lambda}{\mu}\right) + \binom{2}{2}\left(\frac{\lambda}{\mu}\right)^2}$$

$$= \frac{\mu^2}{\mu^2 + 2\lambda\mu + \lambda^2}$$

$$p_1 = 2\left(\frac{\lambda}{\mu}\right) p_0 = \frac{2\lambda\mu}{\mu^2 + 2\lambda\mu + \lambda^2}$$

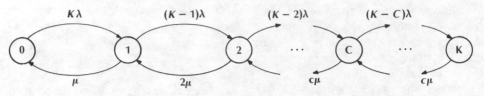

Figure 5–57. Model for M/M/K/K queuing system.

$$p_2 = \frac{1}{2}\left(\frac{\lambda}{\mu}\right)p_1 = \frac{\lambda^2}{\mu^2 + 2\lambda\mu + \lambda^2}.$$

The system availability for a dual redundant structure now becomes:

$$A_{\text{sys}} = \frac{\mu^2 + 2\lambda\mu}{\mu^2 + 2\lambda\mu + \lambda^2}$$

This new availability is greater than that of the previous model because of the smaller λ^2 term in the denominator; that is, access to more repairmen improves the availability.

Figure 5-55d shows an example of an M/M/2/3/3 queue, where the number of repairmen is greater than one but less than the number of modules.

$$p_0 =$$

$$\frac{1}{1 + \binom{3}{1}\left(\frac{\lambda}{\mu}\right) + \binom{3}{2}\left(\frac{\lambda}{\mu}\right)^2 + \frac{3!}{2!\,2}\binom{3}{3}\left(\frac{\lambda}{\mu}\right)^3}$$

$$= \frac{\mu^3}{\mu^3 + 3\lambda\mu^2 + 3\lambda^2\mu + 1.5\,\lambda^3}$$

$$p_1 = 3\left(\frac{\lambda}{\mu}\right)p_0 = \frac{3\lambda\mu^2}{\mu^3 + 3\lambda\mu^2 + 3\lambda^2\mu + 1.5\,\lambda^3}$$

$$p_2 = \left(\frac{\lambda}{\mu}\right)p_1 = \frac{3\lambda^2\mu}{\mu^3 + 3\lambda\mu^2 + 3\lambda^2\mu + 1.5\,\lambda^3}$$

$$p_3 = \frac{1}{2}\left(\frac{\lambda}{\mu}\right)p_2 = \frac{1.5\,\lambda^3}{\mu^3 + 3\lambda\mu^2 + 3\lambda^2\mu + 1.5\,\lambda^3}$$

Using this to model a system with two spares (one-of-three), the steady-state system availability is:

$$A_{\text{sys}} = p_0 + p_1 + p_2$$

$$A_{\text{sys}} = \frac{\mu^3 + 3\lambda\mu^2 + 3\lambda^2\mu}{\mu^3 + 3\lambda\mu^2 + 3\lambda^2\mu + 1.5\,\lambda^3}$$

Considering the system modeled by Figure 5-55c to be a TMR structure, the resulting steady-state availability should be the same as the constant terms in the example solved using combinatorial techniques. For the M/M/3/3/3 queue:

$$p_0 = \frac{1}{1 + \binom{3}{1}\left(\frac{\lambda}{\mu}\right) + \binom{3}{2}\left(\frac{\lambda}{\mu}\right)^2 + \binom{3}{3}\left(\frac{\lambda}{\mu}\right)^3}$$

$$= \frac{\mu^3}{\mu^3 + 3\lambda\mu^2 + 3\lambda^2\mu + \lambda^3}$$

$$p_1 = 3\left(\frac{\lambda}{\mu}\right)p_0 = \frac{3\lambda\mu^2}{\mu^3 + 3\lambda\mu^2 + 3\lambda^2\mu + \lambda^3}$$

$$p_2 = \left(\frac{\lambda}{\mu}\right)p_1 = \frac{3\lambda^2\mu}{\mu^3 + 3\lambda\mu^2 + 3\lambda^2\mu + \lambda^3}$$

$$p_3 = \frac{1}{3}\left(\frac{\lambda}{\mu}\right)p_2 = \frac{\lambda^3}{\mu^3 + 3\lambda\mu^2 + 3\lambda^2\mu + \lambda^3}$$

$$A_{\text{sys}} = p_0 + p_1 = \frac{\mu^3 + 3\lambda\mu^2}{\mu^3 + 3\lambda\mu^2 + 3\lambda^2\mu + \lambda^3}$$

$$= \frac{\mu^3 + 3\lambda\mu^2}{(\mu + \lambda)^3}$$

This is indeed the constant term from the solution derived earlier.

Modeling Performance Impact of Redundancy

Adding redundancy to a system often affects performance. A triplication-with-voting scheme such as C.vmp (see Chapter 7), for example, incurs the gating delay of the voter. Such gate delays are easy to measure and model. Main-memory cycle time degradation, due to the addition of error checking logic, is easy to calculate. The system degradation is usually small because the processor-memory bandwidth is normally not fully utilized. Parallel operations and relative frequency of use, however, generally make performance degradation modeling more difficult.

Another difficulty is determining the effect on performance when there are (covered) failures present in a functioning redundant system. In some cases (as in backup systems) there is no additional degradation beyond the time required for system reconfiguration. In others, performance becomes degraded (such as extra time required for correction, or fewer resources left to accomplish tasks).

The impact of single-error-correcting codes for main memory or microstore on system reliability was discussed above. The effect such ECC memories have on system performance serves as an example of performance-degradation modeling. Chapter 7 provides additional examples.

Because most error checking can be carried out in parallel with the use of data, there is usually no performance change in an error-free state. This is the case if no irreversible actions (such as an overwriting of information needed to restart the current operation) occur before the error checking has been completed, and if the hardware has stall/restart capabilities. Most processor/main memory systems and vertically coded microemulators belong in this class. Most register-transfer level results are not latched until the end of a microcycle, leaving enough time for error checking in most designs. On the other hand, a horizontally microcoded machine with a short microcycle and a very large word width

would not allow retry, because the propagation time through the several XOR levels required for ECC checking would be greater than the microcycle time. This should not very often be the case, however. This section focuses on the effect of recoverable memory errors on system performance.

Main-Memory Performance in the Presence of Errors

Assume that the access frequency is not uniform throughout the memory, so that some memory segments, such as those containing parts of the operating system kernel, are more likely to be accessed than others. Suppose that each location i has access probability P_i, and that there are n errors in a w word memory. The expected memory access time can be expressed as a function of the cycle time c and the cycle time degradation due to an error, ϵc:

$$\sum_{i=1}^{w} P_i(1 - \frac{n}{w})c + \sum_{i=1}^{w} P_i(\frac{n}{w})(c + \epsilon c)$$

$$= c(1 + \frac{n\epsilon}{w})$$

(55)

since $\sum P_i = 1$. Thus, the expected degradation of the memory access time is $n\epsilon/w$.

Figure 5-58 illustrates the effects of errors on memory access time for several values of n and w. Two types of ECC memory are represented: a Hamming code memory with an ϵ of one (one full extra memory cycle to correct an error) and a block-coded memory with an ϵ of 64 (reading all words in the block to determine the vertical parity). The performance degradation is negligible (less than 1 percent) for the Hamming code, whereas the degradation becomes significant for the block code only when n becomes large.

The degradation of system performance depends on how often the memory is accessed. A system with a low memory bandwidth utilization will exhibit less degradation than one whose bandwidth is almost saturated. Table 5-16 com-

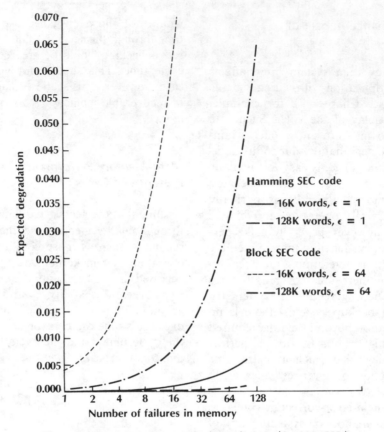

Figure 5–58. Memory access degradation. (© 1980 IEEE.)

pares the degradation in three different PDP-11 systems. The data in the first two columns, drawn from Snow and Siewiorek [1978], are the result of dynamic measurements of PDP-11 programs. Another result from the same source is that an average of 2.16 memory references occur for each instruction. If T_m is the memory access time, T_I the average instruction execution time, and D_m the expected memory access time degradation, the expected system degradation D_s is:

$$D_s = \frac{D_m T_m (2.16)}{T_I} \quad (56)$$

Based on this formula, the third column of Table 5-16 lists the proportion of memory degradation that comes through as system degradation. The system performance degradation is less than the memory performance degradation in all cases. For the LSI-11 and the PDP-11/10, a large memory degradation must occur before its effects are noticeable. The system degradation effects are more noticeable on the PDP-11/34, which comes close to saturating the processor-memory bandwidth. Therefore, even though the memory performance degradation is more serious for block codes than Hamming codes, as shown in Figure 5-58, overall system performance is comparable over wide ranges of failure situations. Using Equations 55 and 56, the data in the last column of Table 5-16 were calculated assuming four failures in a 16K word block code memory with 64 word blocks. The degradation is negligible (1 percent) even in the PDP-11/34.

Table 5–16. Timing data and resulting degradation for PDP-11 computer systems.

| System | Time in Microseconds for: | | System Degradation: | |
	Memory Access	Average Instruction Execution	D_s (% of D_m)	D_s for m = 4, ε = 64, w = 16K
LSI-11	0.400	5.883	14.7%	0.0023
PDP-11/40	0.600	4.096	31.6	0.0049
PDP-11/34	0.940	3.129	64.9	0.0101

Microstore Performance in the Presence of Errors

Microstore reliability is becoming more important as the use of microcoded system design increases. The growing size of microstores being used and the subsequent effect on system reliability make error-coding techniques more attractive. Unlike main memory, in which degraded segments can be left unallocated, degraded sections of microcode are permanently allocated and will continue to affect system performance until repaired.

Table 5-17 summarizes the characteristics of a microcoded machine. It is assumed that all F fetch and S (interrupt) service microwords are executed during each macrocycle. The expected

Table 5–17. Microstore model: allocation and access frequency.

Purpose	Size	P [access]	# of Occurrences in Microstore
Fetch	F	1	1
Interrupt service	S	1	1
Addressing mode	A_j	P_j	a
Instruction	I_k	P_k	i
Total memory	$w = F + S + \sum\limits_{j=1}^{a} A_j + \sum\limits_{k=1}^{i} I_k$		

macrocycle time M_0 with no errors present can be shown to be:

$$E[M_0] = (F + S + \overline{A} + \overline{I})m$$

where m is the microcycle time, $\overline{A}$ is the average number of microwords needed to access the operands, and $\overline{I}$ is the average number of microwords to execute the instruction.

Formulating the performance degradation model entails two additional assumptions: first, the probability distribution of errors is uniform over all memory words; second, an error code with one logical word per physical word is being used. If the number of microcycles needed to correct a word with an error is ε and there are n errors in the memory, the expected macrocycle time is

$$E[M_n] = E[M_0](1 + \frac{n\varepsilon}{w}). \qquad (57)$$

The derivation is similar to that of Equation 55. Thus, the expected performance degradation is $n\varepsilon/w$, as with main memory. This result has been shown to hold for block codes also.

Consider three computers with microstores of 256, 1,024, and 4,096 words, with ε = 1 (Hamming code) and ε = 16 (block code, 16 words per block), and with three failures. The expected degradation can be calculated as in Elkind and Siewiorek [1978]. Degradation is negligible for the Hamming code (1.7 percent for w = 256; 0.3 percent for w = 1,024; and 0.1 percent for w = 4,096). In the block-code design, degradation is

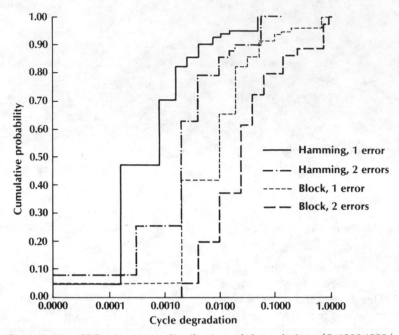

Figure 5–59.   SEC microstore distribution of degradation. (© 1980 IEEE.)

negligible when the block size is small in relation to the memory size (1.2 percent for $w=4,096$). In the other cases it is more noticeable (4.7 percent for $w=1,024$; 18.8 percent for $w=256$).

Given a machine like the one outlined in Table 5-17, the probability distribution of the performance degradation with n errors present can be computed. Figure 5-59 shows this distribution for two slightly different machines; Table 5-18 lists their characteristics. Addressing mode and instruction frequencies were drawn from a study of PDP-11 program traces [Snow and Siewiorek, 1978]. The microstore is divided into sections for F, S, and each of the addressing modes and instructions. A vector, $\vec{f}$, represents a given error pattern, with an element for each of the microstore divisions. The expected degradation was calculated for each $\vec{f}$ possible in Elkind and Siewiorek [1978, 1980].

For the Hamming coded machine, the probability of negligible (less than 1 percent) degradation is 93 percent. The probability that the

degradation is less than the expected degradation (0.0039) from Figure 5-59 is 86 percent. The probability of noticeable degradation (more than 5 percent), is only 5 percent, whereas severe degradation does not occur.

A second curve in Figure 5-59 details the probability distribution for the machine when two errors are present. Although there is a possibility of severe degradation (more than 10 percent), the probability is small (0.24 percent)

Table 5–18.   Microstore specifications.

Hamming Code	Block Code
$F = 3$	$F = 4$
$S = 10$	$S = 12$
$A_j = 3$	$A_j = 4$ for all j
$I_k = 3$	$I_k = 4$ for all k
$a = 16$	$a = 16$
$i = 65$	$i = 65$
$w = 256$	$w = 336$
	16 words per block

while there is an 86 percent probability that the degradation will be less than 1 percent.

The other two curves in Figure 5-59 are for the block-coded microstore. Its performance degradation is more severe than that of the Hamming coded microstore. With one error present, the probability of severe degradation (more than 10 percent) is about 8 percent, whereas the probability of negligible degradation (1 percent or less) is only 65 percent. When two errors are present, the chance of a severe performance loss is 17 percent, and that of a benign failure drops to 40 percent.

Summary of ECC Memory Models

When data are used in parallel with error checking, error-correcting memories can have performance similar to nonredundant memories if no failures are present. In the majority of cases, error-correcting-code memories experience negligible performance degradation in the presence of failures. The results above can be used to predict such degradation. These results, coupled with the failure-present MTTF predictor developed earlier in the section on the Effect of Nonredundant Components, should be useful in planning memory system maintenance.

Block-coded memories have several desirable properties. When SSI/MSI support circuitry is used, they can be more reliable than Hamming code memories. The memory redundancy required is less than that for Hamming codes. Even though large Hamming words (many logical words per physical word) could be used, the decoding/encoding for such large code sizes would be complex and slow. The block code, however, does have disadvantages that limit applicability. Writing into a block-coded RAM takes longer (although Hamming codes with multiple words per physical word have a similar problem). This would be offset somewhat if serial memory DMA devices are used. The stored data are already encoded, for DMA devices usually

perform block transfers; thus, reading from tape or disk would have no degradation. Block-code error correction also takes longer, but the resultant degradation is negligible. Another limitation is that some double errors (those in the same logical word) cannot be detected. Finally, although some chip (or row/column) failure modes are to be tolerated, the block coding scheme is board-space efficient only for large memories. Even with these limitations, the block code is still suitable for many RAM and ROM applications.

TRADE-OFF ANALYSIS IN SYSTEM DESIGN

An incremental improvement method is often used to design a cost effective system. This technique gives rise to the two related problems of choosing which part of the system design to improve and deciding how best to improve that section in accord with the design goals. The MIL-HDBK-217B parts-count model provides one way to pinpoint hard-failure problem areas in a nonredundant system. The least reliable module (or functional area) will necessarily have the largest module failure rate. However, the most effective target for improvement is not always the one with the highest failure rate. The control logic of the PDP-8/e, for example, which contributes to about 30 percent of the non-memory failure rate, is exceedingly difficult to add redundancy to without complete redesign. The techniques that work for random logic, such as quadded logic [Tryon, 1962] and triplication with voting (TMR), unfortunately involve massive amounts of redundancy. Quadded logic uses four times the normal number of gates; TMR requires three times that number. TMR also requires a majority voter on each of the output lines, a significant disadvantage if there are a large number of output lines. Thus, regularity of structure is an important factor in the choice of fault-tolerance techniques.

The failure-rate analysis method becomes at

least partially invalid with redundancy, because the reliability function is no longer a simple exponential. Approximations are feasible in practice. Often, the redundant portion of a system can be assumed to be perfect with respect to other portions of the system.

Design Example: The PDP-8/e

This section illustrates a possible iterative improvement method utilizing the PDP-8 and only two redundancy techniques. Chapter 8 will illustrate the type of analysis that can be performed during the design of a system, specifically the VAX-11/750.

The evaluation criteria for the example are cost and MTTF (Mean Time To Failure). Manufacturing cost, in terms of chip count, is the easiest property to model. In early design stages it is usually taken to be just the materials cost of a design. Quite often the design is optimized for minimal materials cost alone. Other costs can also be used. Total manufacturing costs or user purchase price are important. Repair, spare parts, and operating costs can also be important. Attempts to predict these and other costs over the lifetime of a system, or life-cycle cost (LCC) models, usually predict present value, total, or annual costs of combinations of purchase, financing, repair, inflation, and all other possible costs and factors. The number of different models is staggering (IEEE [1977] provides some examples). No single LCC model applies to all problems and viewpoints. Chapter 6 discusses economic criteria in more detail. Chip count will be used as the cost function in this example.

The PDP-8, an early minicomputer, has a one-address architecture with 12-bit words. The PDP-8/e is an SSI/MSI TTL implementation of the PDP-8 [DEC, 1971, 1972]. This design exercise will employ a simple algorithm for making design changes. The two techniques in the algorithm's catalogue are Single-Error-Correcting/ Double-Error-Detecting (SEC/DED) codes and Triple Modular Redundancy (TMR) with vot-

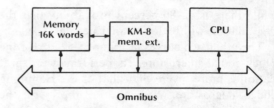

Figure 5–60. Simple PDP-8/e system.

ing, the two most commonly used fault-tolerance techniques. The site chosen for applying a redundancy technique is the module with the largest percentage failure rate, determined by the AUTOFAIL program (discussed in Chapter 2.) The site choice can be done in a recursive fashion; the subarea having the largest failure rate within the area having the largest failure rate, and so on, until a suitable site is found for applying one of the techniques. Finally, if the MTTF shows a decline from the previous step, the algorithm requires the designer to return to the previous step and try again. This algorithm uses only MTTF and failure rate as evaluations; it ignores other factors such as cost and performance.

Figure 5-60 shows the PDP-8/e system discussed here. It consists of a PDP-8/e processor, 16K words of MOS memory, and the KM-8 memory extension and time sharing board.* This system model is used as the basic design prior to reliability improvement.

Initial Improvement: Adding SEC/DED Encoding to the Memory

Evaluating the initial design is the first step in reliability enhancement. This is accomplished by preparing the parts list for the PDP-8/e system, categorized by function, then running the list through AUTOFAIL. Figure 5-61 shows the

---

* The KM-8 is needed to extend the PDP-8 memory space beyond the 4K word range directly addressable by its 12-bit addresses.

```
Plain PDP-8/e


PDP8e.REL     LSI=    16.000    ROM=    16.000    RAM=    16.000

E =    1.000    Q =    16.000    L =    1.000    T =    40.000


MODULE                                 FAILURE RATE              PERCENTAGE

PDP8e                                     167.218                 100.000
   Processor                              32.111                   19.203
      data.part                           14.592                   45.443
         registers                5.903                   40.454
            MB300.A.MQ.MB.PC.MA   5.808                   98.387
            MB310.LINKBIT          .095                    1.613
         adder                    1.146                    7.854
         true.compl.one.zero       .610                    4.180
         path.shunt.in            2.651                   18.167
         path.shunt.out           4.282                   29.344
      bus.connect.open.coll                 .966                    3.007
         MB300                     .724                   75.000
         MB310                     .241                   25.000
      bus.loads.MB320                       .121                     .376
      control.logic                       16.432                   51.173
         MB300                     .543                    3.303
         MB310                    6.868                   41.798
         MB330                    9.021                   54.899
   KM8.Mem.ext.tim.shr                      8.509                    5.089
   16k.memory                             126.598                   75.708
      memory.chips                        124.186                   98.095
      control                              2.050                    1.619
      bus.conn.oc                           .362                     .286

# of chips =    285.083    # of gates =   2830.000    # of bits =  196608.000

              MISSION
      Reliability    Time

      .9999          0.57
      .999           6.0
      .995           30.0        MTTF = 5984
      .99            60.1
      .98            121         total chips = 285
      .95            307
      .9             630
      .8             1334
      .7             2133
```

Figure 5–61. Basic PDP-8/e.

results. The system has a total failure rate of 167.2 failures per million hours (fpmh) and an MTTF of 5,984 hours. The percentage column shows that the memory contributes 76 percent of the failure rate, making it the most logical place for initial improvement. The strategy chosen is to use a Hamming SEC/DED code for the memory words. Each 12-bit memory word is encoded into an 18-bit code word. The extra circuitry (control, encoding/decoding, and so forth) is designed assuming a special 18-bit Hamming encoding/ decoding tree chip. The approximate model in

Elkind and Siewiorek [1978] is used to generate the parts list. The 18-bit encoding/decoding chip replaces the parity chip trees in the model to accomplish a considerable reduction in chips. The standard 22-bit SEC chips now becoming available could also be used, with four data-bit inputs held at fixed values.

The resulting design is checked by AUTO-FAIL for the nonredundant part of the system (everything except the memory array). Figure 5-62 shows the resultant failure rate to be 49.6 fpmh, less than a third of the original. However,

```
PDP-8/e, ECC memory

8ECC.REL    LSI=    16.000    ROM=    16.000    RAM=    16.000

E =    1.000    Q =    16.000    L =    1.000    T =    40.000


MODULE                                    FAILURE RATE          PERCENTAGE


PDP8e                                         49.624              100.000
  Processor                              32.111                 64.708
    data.part                    14.592                    45.443
      registers              5.903                     40.454
        MB300.A.MQ.MB.PC.MA    5.808               98.387
        MB310.LINKBIT          .095                 1.613
      adder                    1.146                     7.854
      true.compl.one.zero       .610                     4.180
      path.shunt.in            2.651                    18.167
      path.shunt.out           4.282                    29.344
    bus.connect.open.coll            .966                  3.007
      MB300                     .724                75.000
      MB310                     .241                25.000
    bus.loads.MB320                  .121                   .376
    control logic             16.432                    51.173
      MB300                     .543                 3.303
      MB310                    6.868                41.798
      MB330                    9.021                54.899
  KM8.Mem.ext.tim.shr                          8.509               17.147
  16k.ecc.memory                               9.004               18.145
    control                   2.050                    22.764
    bus.conn.oc                .362                     4.022
    extra.support             6.592                    73.215

# of chips =    264.083    # of gates =    3365.500    # of bits =    .000

                MISSION
        Reliability    Time

        .9999          2.0
        .999          20.2
        .995          101              MTTF =   20,136
        .99           203
        .98           407              total chips =    336
        .95          1034
        .9           2123
        .8           4496
        .7           7187
```

Figure 5—62.   PDP-8/e with SEC memory.

examining the failure process of the entire design, including the memory array, is necessary to ensure an accurate appraisal. To perform this examination, the program SEC* is employed with the 18-bit ECC memory parameters, using 49.6 fpmh as the nonredundant "control" portion failure rate. The SEC program predicts an

MTTF of 20,136 hours (assuming a dominant single-bit failure mode in the memory chips)—a 237 percent improvement over the basic PDP-8/e. The MTTF of the nonredundant portion alone is 20,161 hours. Thus, as demonstrated in the section on the Effect of Nonredundant Components, the SEC code memory array can essentially be ignored as a contributor to the system failure rate.

The original (nonredundant) design used 285 ICs; the 18-bit ECC memory version uses 336. The difference results from the extra support

* The program SEC (Single Error Correcting) uses the models of the section on the Effect of Nonredundant Components to calculate the MTTF of a single-error-correcting code memory.

circuitry and the memory chips for the redundant code bits. The AUTOFAIL chip count does not include the chips in the redundant portions of the design. The result is a total increase in cost of around 18 percent.

The code word size can be increased (and extra memory bits for coding decreased) by combining two 12-bit memory words into a 30-bit SEC/DED code word. This represents a savings of 12 memory chips over the 18-bit ECC version. However, the control and coding/decoding functions become more complex. The net cost savings over the 18-bit code memory are nil. The MTTF is also adversely affected (down to 14,948 hours). The memory cycle time on reads increases over the 18-bit code because there are more levels in the decoding trees. On writes, the 30-bit word must first be read, decoded, and then re-encoded and rewritten with the new word replacing half the code word; this process takes almost twice as long as a nonredundant memory. Thus, the 18-bit SEC/DED code is the best improvement to make for the size of memory involved. (For a 64K-word memory, the 30-bit code would use 48 chips less than the 18-bit code. This results in more attractive cost savings and perhaps a different decision would be made if cost were an important factor.)

Triplication of the Processor

The AUTOFAIL output from the previous step (see Figure 5-62) shows that the processor has the largest failure rate, contributing 65 percent of the nonredundant portion's failure rate. Because the processor outputs are limited in number and easily identifiable (as the OMNIBUS), the next attempt at improvement is to triplicate the processor and vote on its OMNIBUS outputs. Triplication requires 78 voters. Of these, four lines carry the major clock phase signals. To force synchronization of all three copies of the processor, synchronizing voters [McConnel and Siewiorek, 1981] will be employed on the four clock phase lines. The synchronizing voter is more

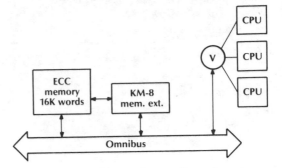

Figure 5–63.   PDP-8/e with triplicated processor.

complex than the ordinary voter used on the other 74 lines. Figure 5-63 is a block diagram of the resulting modified system.

Figure 5-64 shows the evaluation results. The overall reliability of this design is more difficult to assess. Its complex reliability formula is developed in Elkind [1980b]. The nonredundant portion's failure rate has dropped to 28.9 fpmh, a reduction of 42 percent. Numerical integration of the reliability formula, however, yields an MTTF of 16,952 hours, a 16 percent decline. Thus, by the rules of the algorithm, a return to the previous design is required.

Triplication of the Timing Board

The AUTOFAIL listing (Figure 5-62) shows that the control logic contributes the largest proportion of the processor failure rate. Most of the control logic, however, is well integrated into the structure of the rest of the processor. Its triplication would require a large number of voters at the interface between the control logic and the rest of the processor. However, the timing board (MB330), which contributes to over half of the failure rate of the pieces of the control logic, has only 13 outputs at its interface with the rest of the processor. Thus, the timing board is chosen as the site for the next improvement. Triplication of the board requires installation of synchronizing voters on the four output lines carrying the major clock phase signals; the other nine will

```
PDP-8/e, TMR processor, ECC memory

8TPROC.REL     LSI=   16.000    ROM=   16.000    RAM=   16.000

E =    1.000    Q =    16.000    L =    1.000    T =    40.000
```

MODULE	FAILURE RATE	PERCENTAGE
PDP8E.tripproc.ecc.mem	28.865	100.000
Processor	11.351	39.325
omnibus.voters.78	10.265	90.430
synch.voters.4	.777	7.568
normal.voters	9.488	92.432
bus.connect.open.coll	.966	8.507
MB300	.724	75.000
MB310	.241	25.000
bus.loads.MB320	.121	1.063
KM8.Mem.ext.tim.shr	8.509	29.480
16k.ecc.memory	9.004	31.195
control	2.050	22.764
bus.conn.oc	.362	4.022
extra.support	6.592	73.215

```
# of chips =   146.333    # of gates =   2149.500    # of bits =    .000

           MISSION
     Reliability    Time
     .9999          3.4
     .999           34.5
     .995           171          MTTF = 16,952
     .99            337
     .98            658          total chips = 696
     .95            1553
     .9             2911
     .8             5420
     .7             7889
```

Figure 5–64. PDP-8/e with SEC memory, TMR processor.

```
PDP-8/e, TMR timing, ECC memory

8TRIP6.REL     LSI=   16.000    ROM=   16.000    RAM=   16.000

E =    1.000    Q =    16.000    L =    1.000    T =    40.000
```

MODULE	FAILURE RATE	PERCENTAGE
PDP8e	42.534	100.000
Processor	25.020	58.824
data.part	14.592	58.322
registers	5.903	40.454
MB300.A.MQ.MB.PC.MA	5.808	98.387
MB310.LINKBIT	.095	1.613
adder	1.146	7.854
true.compl.one.zero	.610	4.180
path.shunt.in	2.651	18.167
path.shunt.out	4.282	29.344
bus.connect.open.coll	.966	3.859
MB300	.724	75.000
MB310	.241	25.000
bus.loads.MB320	.121	.482
control.logic	9.342	37.337
MB300	.543	5.810
MB310	6.868	73.523
MB330.trip.voter	1.931	20.668
synced.lines	.777	40.233
nonsynced.lines	1.154	59.767
KM8.Mem.ext.tim.shr	8.509	20.006
16k.ecc.memory	9.004	21.170
control	2.050	22.764
bus.conn.oc	.362	4.022
extra.support	6.592	73.215

```
# of chips =   221.917    # of gates =   2950.500    # of bits =    .000

           MISSION
     Reliability    Time
     .9999          2.4
     .999           23.5
     .995           118          MTTF = 20,774
     .99            236
     .98            474          total chips = 446
     .95            1198
     .9             2444
     .8             5107
     .7             8052
```

Figure 5–65. PDP-8/e with SEC memory, TMR timing board.

employ regular voters. The reliability formula for this design is developed in Elkind [1980b].

Figure 5-65 shows the evaluation results. The nonredundant portion's failure rate has dropped by 14 percent from the SEC design (Figure 5-62). More important, the MTTF has increased to 20,774 hours, up 3 percent. According to the algorithm, then, this is a successful step in the design improvement.

Triplication of the Data Area

The processor failure rate still dominates for the nonredundant portion of the system, but the data area now accounts for the largest share. Figure 5-66, a simplified block diagram of the PDP-8/e data paths, shows two sets of 12 output lines. An SEC code would not work in this case, because there are data transformations inside the data area. The small number of output lines also makes triplication the technique of choice for the data area.

Elkind [1980b] develops the reliability function for the resulting configuration (SEC memory, TMR timing board, and TMR data area). Figure 5-67 shows the reliability evaluation re-

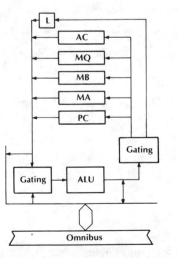

Figure 5–66. Original PDP-8/e data paths.

sults. The nonredundant failure rate has dropped by 27 percent. The MTTF, however, has increased by only 0.6 percent, to 20,898 hours.

Analyses of the Example

This treatment of the PDP-8/e follows only one of the possible routes through the design space. Figure 5-68 shows other routes, for which each of the design points was evaluated. In the following discussion, each point is specified by the combination of path and step indexes from the figure. For example, the PDP-8/e with ECC memory added is denoted equivalently by A1, B1, and C1, since it belongs in all three paths. The PDP-8/e with a TMR processor and ECC memory is denoted by the index A2. The subsections below examine the path through the design space followed by the simple redesign algorithm, analyze its performance, and compare it with other possible paths.

The Path of the Simple Algorithm

Path B of Figure 5-68 portrays the path of the simple algorithm through the design space. The sole aim of the algorithm is MTTF improvement through reduction of the nonredundant portion's failure rate. The net improvement in MTTF in the example was 249 percent, of which 237 percent occurred in the first step, adding the SEC memory. Thus, the algorithm attained the MTTF improvement goal.

It is necessary to evaluate the performance of the algorithm in relation both to the MTTF improvement and to the cost of that improvement. One possible measure is:

$$I_n = \frac{\text{MTTF}_n - \text{MTTF}_{(n-1)}}{(c_n - c_{(n-1)})}$$

MTTF_n is the MTTF of the design resulting from the nth successful step, and c_n is the cost of the design (in this example, the number of inte-

```
PDP-8/e, TMR timing & data part, ECC memory

8SETT.REL    LSI=    16.000    ROM=    16.000    RAM=    16.000

E =    1.000    Q =    16.000    L =    1.000    T =    40.000
```

MODULE	FAILURE RATE	PERCENTAGE
PDP8e	31.019	100.000
Processor	13.505	43.539
trip.data.part	3.077	22.785
24.voters	3.077	100.000
bus.connect.open.coll	.966	7.150
MB300	.724	75.000
MB310	.241	25.000
bus.loads.MB320	.121	.894
control.logic	9.342	69.171
MB300	.543	5.810
MB310	6.868	73.523
MB330.trip.voter	1.931	20.668
synced.lines	.777	40.233
nonsynced.lines	1.154	59.767
KM8.Mem.ext.tim.shr	8.509	27.433
16k.ecc.memory	9.004	29.028
control	2.050	22.764
bus.conn.oc	.362	4.022
extra.support	6.592	73.215

```
# of chips =    181.167    # of gates =    1969.500    # of bits =    .000
```

MISSION		
Reliability	Time	
.9999	3.2	
.999	32.2	
.995	161	MTTF = 20,898
.99	321	
.98	640	total chips = 565
.95	1585	
.9	3134	
.8	6220	
.7	9399	

Figure 5–67. PDP-8/e with SEC memory, TMR timing board, and data part.

Figure 5–68. Design space for fault tolerant PDP-8/e.

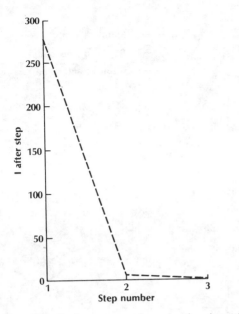

Figure 5–69. Performance of a simple algorithm for design improvement.

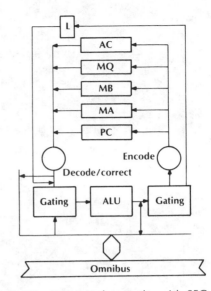

Figure 5–70. PDP-8/e data paths with SEC register modification.

grated circuits). The graph of Figure 5-69 shows the performance evaluation of the example. The plot is monotonic decreasing, which indicates that each step is the most cost effective of those performed. In this sense, then, the algorithm performs well.

Other Paths through the Design Space

The path followed by the algorithm is not necessarily optimal. In fact, another path attempted works better in terms of total cost of the final design and the MTTF attained. Path C of Figure 5-68 portrays an early attempt based on intuition and guided by AUTOFAIL. The second step of path C was taken because of the better performance of SEC codes over TMR in improving MTTF. Although the registers have a smaller failure rate than the timing board and are in the data area, which has a smaller failure rate than the control area, the choice was obvious. Figure 5-70 shows the resultant modification. The final design has an MTTF of 21,903 hours, a 266

percent improvement on the original PDP-8/e design. The final cost is 457 chips. In contrast, the algorithmic path resulted in only a 249 percent increase in MTTF, with a cost of 565 chips. Figure 5-71 compares the performance measurements of the two algorithms. Not only does the intuitive algorithm yield a better end result, but I_n has a steadier decline, implying a more consistent performance.

It is also interesting to look at the design paths followed in terms of mission time improvement, even though neither algorithm had this as a goal. The simple algorithm guided primarily by failure rates and not suitability of technique to improvement site. Thus, the simple approach tends to choose TMR more often because it works for many sites (such as random logic) for which SEC/DED codes will not. TMR tends to improve MT[R] for large R, often with the result of lower MTTF. The final design of the simple algorithm has an MT[.95] of 1,585 hours, versus the 1,280-hour MT[.95] for the intuitive approach. The MTI[.95] is 5.16 and 4.17 for the simple and intuitive approaches, respectively. Figure 5-72 plots a modified performance mea-

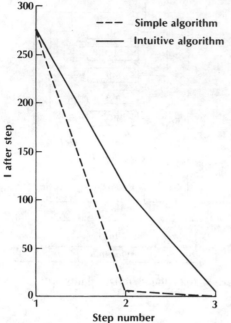

Figure 5–71. Performance comparison of the simple and intuitive approaches.

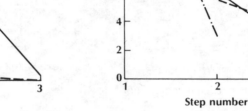

Figure 5–72. Performance of improvement with respect to MT[.95].

surement, I'_n, with the MTTF_n replaced by MT_n [.95], for the two approaches. Both approaches performed well in this respect, although the simple algorithm's heavier use of TMR caused it to do better.

If MT[.95] had been the goal instead of MTTF, both approaches would do equally well. Both would follow path A of Figure 5-68 to design A2. In the case of the simple algorithm, the second step to a TMR processor would have been deemed successful because the resulting MT[.95] is 1,553 hours, up 406 percent. Previously, the same step was unsuccessful because it resulted in a decline in MTTF. Neither approach, however, reaches the best design in terms of MT[.95]. Design B3 has a slightly better MT[.95] of 1,585 hours for 131 fewer chips. Design A2, however, has better MTs for values of R equal to or greater than 0.98.

Path D, though not actually followed, is depicted in Figure 5-68 for the sake of complete-

ness. Figures 5-73 and 5-74 show the MTTF and MT[.95] for each point in the design space as a function of chip count.

Finally, Figure 5-68 portrays in path E an attempt to ascertain the results of a redesign using a different design style, created by Tsao [1982]. Although it is not a complete implementation of Figure 5-60, the design demonstrates potential improvement resulting from a change in design style. The MTTF of design E1, a bit-slice PDP-8 with SEC code memory, is 54,000 hours, more than twice as high as the best design previously, and with many times fewer chips. Thus, even allowing for the added complexity of a complete implementation, the potential improvement is considerable.

This exploration of design space minimized the number of design trade-offs (such as redundancy techniques) in order to illustrate the methodology. Inclusion of additional redundancy or fault-intolerant techniques (such as changing en-

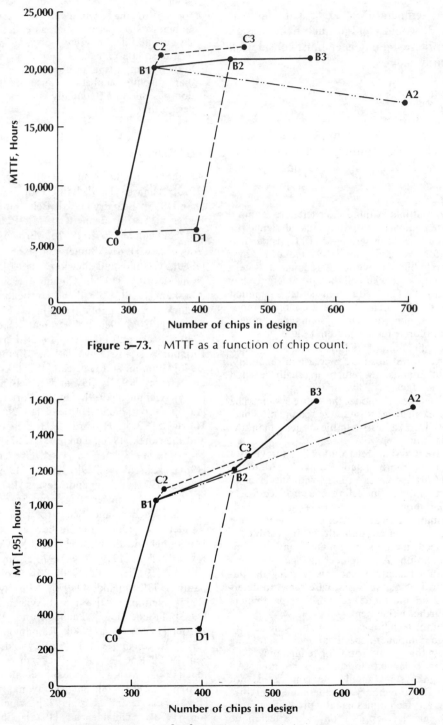

Figure 5–73. MTTF as a function of chip count.

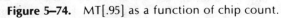

Figure 5–74. MT[.95] as a function of chip count.

vironmental, temperature, and quality factors; see Chapter 3) would yield a much richer design space. The practicing engineer must consider all these alternatives.

SUMMARY

This chapter introduced a number of evaluation criteria for reliable computing structures. Several essential considerations in evaluating systems are:

- Frequently, multiple evaluation criteria are required for adequate comparison of alternative designs. The most frequently used criterion—MTTF—is particularly poor for evaluating massively redundant systems. The reliability curve for a redundant system exhibits a sharp knee when all the fault tolerance has been exhausted. The redundant system is much more likely to fail, because there are more components than in a nonredundant system, and the next component failure causes a system failure.
- The first application of redundancy to a system produces the largest absolute increase in reliability. The point of diminishing returns is usually reached by redundancy factors of five or less.
- Care must be taken to model the entire system. The addition of extra logic to manage redundancy may actually result in a less reliable system than the nonredundant one.
- Often, apparent system reliability will improve as a result of using more detailed models. Although modeling effort increases rapidly with the level of detail, more effort in modeling can produce a less overdesigned, more cost effective system.
- Values for mathematically concise parameters (such as coverage) are often difficult or impossible to predict. Indeed, the gross parameters may oversimplify the situation. An engineering "guesstimate," coupled with a sensitivity analysis (varying the parameter over a best case, worst case range to determine effects on the model) can isolate parameters that need further refinement.
- Fault-intolerant techniques should not be neglected. Extra care in component specification and screening may cost less than many forms of redundancy.
- Above all, a balanced approach is required. All portions of a system should be considered, not simply the CPU or memory. Furthermore, a mixture of fault-tolerant techniques usually produces a more effective design than application of one technique throughout the system. Each technique should be

applied to the portion of the system that best matches its properties (such as codes to portions of systems that deal in vectors of data—memory, registers, bus, data paths).
- System comparison techniques are stressed rather than absolute numbers because the reliability function of a module frequently is not known at system design time.

REFERENCES

Abraham and Siewiorek [1974]; Aggarwal and Rai [1978]; Almassy [1979]; Ball [1980]; Barlow and Proschan [1965]; Beaudry [1978]; Bell and Newell [1971]; Bell et al. [1978]; Bennetts [1975]; Bouricius, Carter, and Schneider [1969a, 1969b]; Brown, Tierney, and Wasserman [1961]; Butner and Iyer [1980]; Castillo [1980]; Castillo and Siewiorek [1980]; Cheung and Ramamoorthy [1975]; Cheung [1980]; Chou and Abraham [1980]; Cornell and Halstead [1976]; Costes, Landrault, and Laprie [1978]; DEC [1971, 1972]; Elkind [1980a, 1980b]; Elkind and Siewiorek [1978, 1980]; Essary and Proschan [1962]; Ferdinand [1974]; Fitzsimmons and Love [1978]; Frank and Frisch [1970]; Funami and Halstead [1975]; Gandhi, Knove, and Henley [1972]; Gay and Ketelsen [1979]; Gear [1976]; Geilhufe [1979]; Gupta, Porter, and Lathrop [1974]; Gurzi [1965]; Halstead [1979]; Hecht [1976]; Horowitz [1975]; Howard [1971]; IEEE [1977]; Ingle and Siewiorek [1976]; Jack et al. [1975]; Jelinsky and Moranda [1973]; Jensen [1964]; Keller [1976]; Kini [1981]; Klaschka [1969]; Knuth [1969]; Lapp and Powers [1977]; Levine and Meyers [1976]; Littlewood [1975, 1979]; Longden, Page, and Scantlebury [1966]; Lynch, Wagner, and Schwartz [1975]; Lyons and Vanderkulk [1962]; McCluskey and Clegg [1971]; McConnel and Siewiorek [1981]; McConnel, Siewiorek, and Tsao [1979]; Mei [1970]; Meyer, Furchtgot, and Wu [1979]; Misra [1970]; Miyamoto [1975]; Mohanly [1973]; Muehldorf [1975]; Murphy [1964]; Musa [1975]; Nelson [1973]; Ng and Avižienis [1980]; Ogus [1973]; Pascoe [1975]; Peterson and Weldon [1972]; Phister [1979]; Posa [1980]; Ramamoorthy and Han [1973]; Raytheon [1974, 1976]; Reynolds and Kinsbergen [1975]; Rhodes [1964]; Rickers [1975–76]; Rosenthal [1977]; Ross [1972]; Roth et al. [1967]; Rubin [1967]; Russel [1978]; Satyanarayana and Prabhakar [1978]; Schertz and Metze [1972]; Schick and Wolverton [1978]; Schneidewind [1975]; Shedletsky and McCluskey [1973]; Shooman [1968, 1970, 1973]; Sie-

wiorek and McCluskey [1973b]; Siewiorek [1975];
Siewiorek and Rennels [1980]; Snow and Siewiorek
[1978]; Stapper [1973]; Stiffler, Bryant, and Guccione
[1979]; Tammaru and Angell [1967]; Teoste [1962];
Texas Instruments [n.d.]; Thayer, Lipow, and Nelson
[1978]; Trivedi and Shooman [1975]; Tryon [1962];
Tsao [1982]; von Neumann [1956]; Wang and Lovelace [1977]; Warner [1974]; Wilkov [1972]; Wolverton
and Shick [1974]; Wyle and Burnett [1967]; Yakowitz
[1977]; Yourdon [1972].

PROBLEMS

1. Assume that the failures of three computers, A, B,
   and C, are independent, exponentially distributed
   random variables with failure rates $\lambda_A = 1/800$,
   $\lambda_B = 1/1,300$, and $\lambda_C = 1/1,300$ failures per
   hour, respectively.
   a. What is the probability that at least one system
      fails in a four-week period?
   b. What is the probability that all three systems
      fail in a four-week period?

2. Calculate the reliability of the structure below
   between points A and B. Assume all modules have
   a reliability of R.

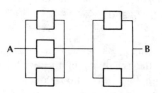

3. Consider the system success diagram below.

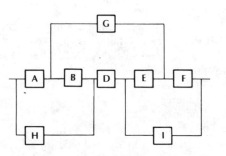

   a. List all possible working paths in the form of a
      "Reliability Block Diagram" (RBD).

b. Derive the upperbound for system reliability
   given by:

$$R_{sys} \leqslant 1 - \prod_{i=1}^{j} (1 - R_{path_j})$$

c. Derive the lowerbound for system reliability
   from the minimal cut set

$$R_{sys} \geqslant \prod_{i=1}^{k} (1 - Q_{cut_i})$$

d. Derive the exact reliability formula.
e. Simplify the results above if all modules exhibit
   the same reliability R.

4. Given the probabilities f_0 (probability of a relay or
   MOS transistor failure in open position) and f_s
   (probability of a failure in short position), and that
   the system can tolerate a short between points A
   and B (that is, a short failure is acceptable but an
   open failure is not), the reliability of
   is given by (choose one)

   a. $1 - f_0$
   b. $(1 - f_0)^2$
   c. $1 - 2f_0$
   d. $1 - f_0^2$.

5. With f_0 and f_s as in question 4, and given that a
   short between A and B may be tolerated, the
   reliability of
   is given by (choose one)

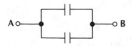

   a. $1 - f_0$
   b. $(1 - f_0)^2$
   c. $1 - 2f_0$
   d. $1 - f_0^2$.

6. Given that $f_0 = f_s$, that a short between A and B
   is tolerated, and that Y is known to have failed
   already, the reliability of

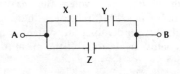

is given by (choose one)

a. $1 - (f_0/2)$
b. $1 - ((f_0 + f_s)/2)$
c. $0.5(2 - f_0)(1 - f_0)$
d. $0.5(1 - f_0)^2$
e. $1 - 0.5 f_0 - 0.5 f_0^2$.

7. The connection between points A and B is to be controlled. The circuit below is used instead of a single relay or MOS transistor in order to achieve highly reliable control.

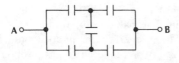

The probability of failing in an open position is f_0, and the probability of a failure in a short position is f_s. Assume that statistically, the reliabilities of the relay/transistors are mutually independent. What is the reliability of this network? Find the conditions under which this network is more reliable than a single relay/transistor between A and B.

8. If the reliability of a module is R_m, and if a perfect arbiter chooses between the outputs of a pair of identical independent modules, the reliability of a system is (choose one)

a. R_m^2
b. $R_m^2 + 0.5 R_m$
c. $R_m^2 + 0.5 R_m(1 - R_m)$
d. R_m.

9. The reliability of a nonredundant system ranges between (0.2,1); that is, below 0.2 the system is considered failed. To achieve unconditional improvements in reliability through triple modular redundancy, the system is divided into m modules of identical reliability. If voters are perfect, the minimum value of m is (choose one)

a. 2
b. 3
c. 4
d. 5.

10. With an imperfect voter, the maximum system reliability in a TMR scheme with triplicated voters resulted from dividing the system into eight modules before triplication. If the mean time to failure

(MTTF) for the original system was 800 hours, the MTTF for a voter must have been (choose one)

a. 100 hours
b. 800 hours
c. 3,200 hours
d. 6,400 hours.

11. With a perfect voter and a perfect switch, the reliability of a TMR scheme with two spares at the time when the reliability of a single module is 0.5 is (choose one)

a. 0.5
b. 0.1875
c. 0.8125
d. 1.0.

12. With a perfect switch but an imperfect voter, a TMR scheme with S spares would show a maximum reliability (at the time when module reliability is 0.7) at S equal to (choose one)

a. 1
b. 2
c. 3
d. 4.

13. The inputs of an AND gate may be stuck-at-0 or stuck-at-1 with probabilities f_0 and f_s, respectively. If $f_s = 0$ and if the inputs are totally random, the reliability of the output is (choose one)

a. $1 - f_0$
b. $(1 - f_0)^2$
c. $1 - 0.5f_0 + 0.25f_0^2$
d. $1 - 1.5f_0 + 0.75f_0^2$.

14. With f_0 and f_s as defined in Problem 13, and if $f_0 = 0$, the reliability of the output of an AND gate (with $f_s \neq 0$) is (choose one)

a. $1 - f_s$
b. $(1 - f_s)^2$
c. $1 - 0.5f_s + 0.25f_s^2$
d. $1 - 1.5f_s + .075f_s^2$.

15. The failures in a system are known to alternate; that is, a stuck-at-0 failure is followed by a stuck-at-1 failure, and so on. A 7MR scheme can then tolerate (choose one)

a. 3 failures
b. 4 failures
c. 5 failures
d. 6 failures.

16. A variation of a hybrid redundancy scheme associates a spare with a specific module; that is, a spare, S_i, can replace only the module M_i and no

other. For a TMR system with three such spares, the difference between the reliabilities of the variant system and of the hybrid system (with reliability of a module $= R_m$, $Q_m = 1 - R_m$) is (choose one)

a. 0
b. 1
c. $3R_m^3 Q_m^3 + 3R_m^4 Q_m^2$
d. $3R_m^2 Q_m^4$
e. $6R_m^3 Q_m^3 + 12R_m^2 Q_m^4$.

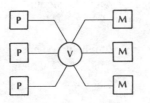

17. The following reliability model has been proposed for the system above:

$$R_{sys} = R_v(3R_p^2 - 2R_p^3)(3R_m^2 - 2R_m^3)$$

where R_v, R_p, and R_m are the voter, processor, and memory reliability, respectively. Several factors are ignored in this model. Ignoring each factor makes the model either pessimistic or optimistic. List at least four of these factors and explain their effect on the model.

18. Consider a TMRed register file composed of eight 16-bit words.

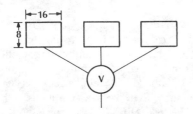

a. Assuming only single-bit failures, write the system reliability function, R_{TMR}, in terms of the bit reliability, R_b, and the voter reliability, R_v.
b. Now assume that the register file is protected by a 21-bit (16 data bits and five check bits) single-error-correcting Hamming code. Write

the system reliability function, R_{SEC}, in terms of the bit reliability, R_b, and the encoder/decoder reliability, R_e.

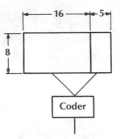

c. Assume $R_v = R_e = 1$. Pick a value of R_b for which $R_{TMR} > R_{SEC}$. Also pick a value of R_b for which $R_{SEC} > R_{TMR}$. Which scheme, TMR or SEC, would you recommend using and why? (Hint: The functions are well behaved and intersect only at one value of R_b.)

19. a. Derive the expression given in Chapter 5 for the reliability of a hybrid redundant system with a TMR core.
    b. Generalize this expression to hybrid redundancy with an NMR core.
    c. What is the effect of including coverage? Consider two cases: TMR with one spare and TMR with $m - 3$ spares.

20. a. As an alternative to the conventional hybrid system with a TMR core and a single spare, the following organization is proposed.

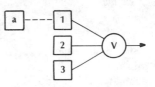

In this scheme the spare, a, can replace only module 1 and no other. If the voter and the switching circuits are perfect, show that the reliability of the system is:

$$R_m^4 + 4R_m^3(1 - R_m) + 3R_m^2(1 - R_m)^2$$

where R_m is the reliability of a module. (Hint: With the three original modules denoted by numbers 1, 2, 3 and the spare by a, a failure tree showing all permutations for the system above is

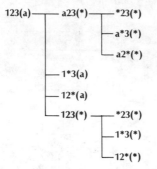

b. Using the tree approach (or otherwise), what is the reliability of the system below?

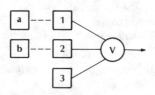

(This is an alternative to a hybrid scheme with a TMR core and two spares. The spares are once again dedicated, spare a to module 1 and spare b to module 2.)

21. If we denote the expression in Problem 20 by R_d (i.e., $R_d = R_m^4 + 4R_m^3(1 - R_m) + 3R_m^2(1 - R_m)^2$) and the reliability of the switching circuits by R_{swd}, then we may model the system reliability as:

$$R_{sysd} = R_{swd} \cdot R_m$$

We may also model the reliability of a hybrid scheme with one spare, R_{hyb}, as a product of the switch reliability, R_{swh}, and the probability of having two or more good modules in the core of the system. Assume that all modules are identical and that the reliability is $R_m (= e^{-\lambda t})$. The ratio of the circuit complexity of the switch in the hybrid scheme to the complexity of a single module is denoted by α. Assuming that failure rates are directly dependent on the complexity, we may write $R_{swh} = R_m^\alpha$. Realizing that the switching circuits in a dedicated spare system need to attain only half the number of states required by switch-

ing circuits in a hybrid system with a single spare, we estimate the complexity ratio to be half also; that is, $R_{swd} = R_{swh}^{0.5}$. For $\alpha = 0.1$, plot the mission time improvement (MTI) of R_{swh} over R_{swd} as a function of R_m. (Use $R_{swd}(R_m)$ as R_{sysmin}, the minimum required system reliability that defines the mission time.) For the plots, use logarithmic scale for R_m if you prefer. From the plot, determine the range of R_m during which R_{swd} is better than R_{swh}. Repeat for $\alpha = 0.01$. (Note: $\alpha = 0.01$ implies that the basic modules are 100 times as complex as the switch in the hybrid system. If the switch had 10 gates, the module would have 1,000 gates. Compared with the LSI-11, how big is the module?)

22. Consider two redundant systems based on voting:

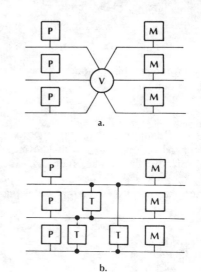

System (a) does bus-level voting on every P-M transfer. System (b) is a multiprocessor that votes after each subtask by mutual communications over interfaces (T). Develop a reliability model for each system. State your assumptions. Which system is better? (Hint: This is purposely left as an open-ended problem. At the highest level of modeling the systems appear identical. Drive the modeling to a low enough level to illustrate the differences in the systems.)

23. Figures (a) and (b) on the next page depict two computer structures, C.mmp and Cm*. Besides being multiprocessor systems, the two structures

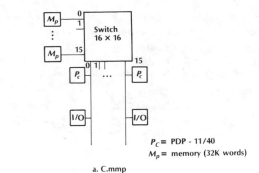

P_C = PDP - 11/40
M_p = memory (32K words)

a. C.mmp

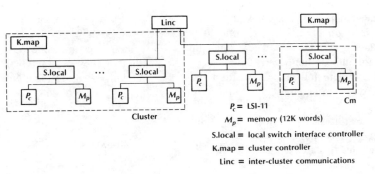

P_c = LSI-11
M_p = memory (12K words)
S.local = local switch interface controller
K.map = cluster controller
Linc = inter-cluster communications

b. Computer module system (Cm*) with two clusters.

may also be viewed as fault-tolerant structures with redundant processing power. Consider the 16-processor, 16-memory C.mmp, and a two-cluster, 8-processor-per-cluster Cm* organization. For a task that requires at least four processors and at least 48K words of memory, compare the reliabilities of C.mmp and Cm* using various modeling techniques. Assume that the recovery processes are imperfect and the probability of recovery given a failure is a function of the size of the system. Suggest a model for the probability of recovery. A parts-count model of the components of the two systems yields the failure rates shown in the table opposite. Make reasonable assumptions where necessary, such as assuming that the failure rate of K.map includes that of the inter-Cm bus. (Note: Although a single-memory port of 64K words of C.mmp seems sufficient for the task, a single-port with multiple processors is a highly unbalanced system and not only slows down the system, but also is extremely susceptible to transient failures. Therefore, assume that at least as many memory ports as the number of processors are required for reliable operation of C.mmp.)

Component	Failure Rate (failure per 10^6 hrs.)
C.mmp	
PDP-11/40	56.9
Processor associated circuitry (RELOC box, processor interface)	20.3
Memory box (32K words)	159.6
Memory associated circuitry/port (Priority decode, etc.)	9.8
Switch	507.6
Cm*	
LSI-11 processor	29.9
Memory (12K words; semiconductor)	69.4
K.map	131.0
Linc	34.8
S.local	24.0

24. Consider a dual redundant system that normally operates with both units running. Error detection is achieved by comparing the outputs of the two units. If either unit fails, the probability that the failure is isolated correctly so that the remaining unit (and system) continues to run properly is c (coverage $= c$). The system can therefore fail in two ways: both units fail (exhaustion of spares) or one unit fails in a bad way (coverage failure). Assume that each unit exhibits failure rate λ and repair rate μ.

(Note: Whenever a coverage failure occurs, both units are considered to have failed, and repair— with rate μ—starts on each. The first one to be repaired brings the system as a whole back up, while repair continues on the other.)

a. Draw the complete four-state transition diagram for the system and give the corresponding T matrix.

b. Reduce the transition diagram to three states and give the corresponding T matrix.

c. Derive the steady-state availability for the three-state model.

25. Consider the dual redundant system discussed in Chapter 5. Assume now that when both systems have failed, two repairmen are called in, one for each system. Furthermore, assume that the dual system is configured as a main unit with a backup. Whenever the main unit fails, there is only the probability c (coverage $= c$) that the backup comes on-line successfully to keep the system going. Whenever the backup fails, the system will continue to operate if the main unit is working, or will fail if the main unit has already failed without yet being repaired. Both the main unit and the backup unit exhibit failure rate λ and repair rate μ.

(Note: Whenever the main unit fails the backup does not come on-line—coverage failure, both units are considered to have failed, and repair— with rate μ—starts on both. The first one to be repaired brings the system as a whole back up, while repair continues on the other.)

a. Draw the complete four-state transition diagram.

b. Draw the three-state transition diagram obtained by merging the states with a single failed unit.

c. Derive the availability function $A(t)$ for the three-state model.

d. Derive the reliability function $R(t)$, first drawing the modified three-state transition diagram.

26. Tandem Computers, Inc. introduced a multiple computer system in 1975 for critical applications, characterized by a high cost for loss of computer power. A prime example is electronic funds transfer wherein interest is charged by the hour and one company estimated a $300,000 revenue loss per hour of computer down time. The structure of a dual processor Tandem Non-Stop system is shown below.

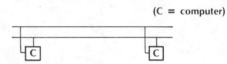

(C = computer)

The computers communicate via the intercomputer Dynabus. The system is considered failed only if both computers are down at the same time (assume the Dynabus never fails).

a. Assume that the failure rate is exponential with $\lambda = 1/1000$ failures per hour. Also assume that computer repair is exponential, with μ repairs per hour. Develop the Markov model for the system with λ, μ as parameters. What is the probability that the system is failed for $\mu = 1/48$? Draw a graph of probability of failure versus μ.

b. What is the expected time to failure for the system?

27. Reformulate the analysis in the Redundancy to Enhance Chip Yield section for a RAM chip employing the redundancy technique of your choice.

Financial Considerations

INTRODUCTION AND FUNDAMENTAL CONCEPTS

This chapter discusses several fundamental financial considerations in the development, acquisition, and operation of a computer system and explains why knowledge of these costs is important to the designer of a computer system or component. These concepts can also guide the owner or operator of a computer system in assessing the effects of a system's reliability and maintainability on the cost of ownership.

Several fundamental terms and concepts will be defined and used as parameters in mathematical models. Of primary interest are discounted cash-flow cost of ownership models, maintenance cost models, life-cycle cost models, and maintainability feature–decision analysis techniques.

Definitions

Maintenance cost is the cost associated with keeping a computer system functioning according to operational specifications. This very complex topic should not be trivialized by the designer; maintenance cost constitutes a significant proportion of the cost of owning a computer, and it is under at least indirect control of the designer.

From the point of view of the maintenance provider, an important factor in the calculation of maintenance cost is the *installed base*. This is the number of systems (as a function of time) that the manufacturer is required to service. Some customers may elect self-maintenance or third-party service (by someone other than the manufacturer); these are not included in the installed base. (The fact that some customers may have fixed-price contracts and that others pay for each service call is potentially significant in terms of field service revenue but has no real importance to the designer.) The installed base can be estimated from three basic parameters: the shipment rate, contract penetration rate, and contract renewal rate.

The *shipment rate* is simply the number of units sold, shipped, and installed in the field, as a function of time. Typically, the value of the frequency distribution is low at the beginning and end of product life, and very high in the middle. The *contract penetration rate* is the percentage of customers who elect to have the manufacturer service their system. It does not include those who either self-maintain or go to a third party. This discussion makes no distinction between per-call (parts and labor) and fixed-price contract customers. Contract penetration is normally quite high for medium- to large-scale systems, ranging from 85 to 95 percent. The last important parameter in determining installed base is the *contract renewal rate*. This factor takes into account the fact that not all customers renew their commitment to service from the manufacturer.

Table 6-1 is an example of an installed base calculation with an assumed three-year shipment rate (in quarters), a 75 percent contract penetration rate, and a 90 percent renewal rate. Seventy-

five percent of the customers receiving systems take out a contract. Thus, 45 of the 60 systems shipped in the first quarter become part of the installed base, 150 of the 200 shipped in the second quarter, and so on. The last column shows the accumulation of these contracts in the installed base.

By the fifth quarter, 90 percent of the 45 contracts coming up for renewal are actually renewed, resulting in the attrition of approximately five contracts. The last column in the fifth quarter shows the addition of 1,050 contracts (from new shipments) to the installed base, minus the attrition of five.

In the ninth quarter, the attrition is 10 percent of the fifth quarter's new contracts (105), plus 10 percent of the 40 remaining contracts opened in the first quarter. Figure 6-1 restates Table 6-1 graphically.

Sources of Maintenance Costs

Labor Expense

The largest expenditure for computer servicing is for labor. Even the most efficient field service organizations have an average round-trip travel time to and from the customer's site (that is, totally unproductive time) on the order of 1.5

Table 6–1. Example of installed base calculation.

Quarter	Shipments	New Contracts	Contract Attrition	Total Contracts
1	60	45	0	45
2	200	150	0	195
3	1,000	750	0	945
4	1,400	1,050	0	1,995
5	1,400	1,050	5	3,040
6	1,400	1,050	15	4,075
7	1,400	1,050	75	5,050
8	1,200	900	105	5,845
9	600	450	109	6,186
10	300	225	119	6,292
11	0	0	173	6,119
12	0	0	185	5,934

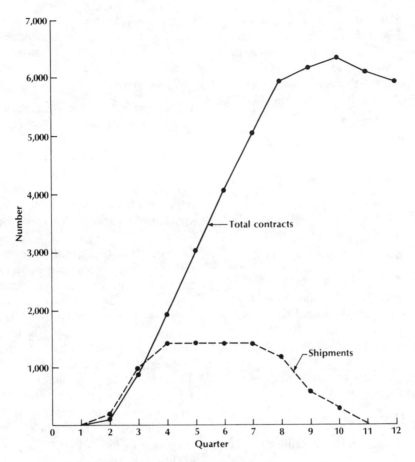

Figure 6–1.   Example of installed base curve.

hours. At $50 or more per hour, fully burdened, a service call costs the service provider $75 before any work is performed. Labor expense depends on Mean Time Between Failures, Mean Time To Repair, Preventive Maintenance (PM) interval, Mean Time to PM, travel times, average labor cost, and support ratio (a measurement of the amount of assistance needed on a particular service call). The formula below is a rough estimate of the annual labor expense involved in servicing a computer system.

$$ALE = \{CPH\}\{8760\}$$
$$\times \{(MTTR + TTR)/MTBF$$
$$+ (MTPM + TTPM)/MTBP\}$$

where:

ALE	= annual labor expense,
CPH	= cost per hour for labor,
8760	= number of hours in a year,
MTTR	= mean time to repair,
TTR	= travel time for a repair call,
MTBF	= mean time between failures,
MTPM	= mean time to perform preventive maintenance,
TTPM	= travel time for a preventive maintenance call, and
MTBP	= mean time between preventive maintenance.

Assume that the labor cost per hour is $50, the MTTR is 2.5 hours, and the MTPM is 4.5 hours.

Further assume a travel time of 1.5 hours for a repair and 0.5 hours for a PM (it is usually assumed that because several simultaneous PMs can be scheduled in advance, the cost of travel time can be apportioned among several devices). For an MTBF of 4,000 hours and an MTBP of 5,000 hours, the annual labor expense is:

$$ALE = \{50\}\{8760\}\{(2.5 + 1.5)/(4000)$$
$$+(4.5 + .5)/5000\}$$
$$= \{50\}\{8760\}\{(.001) + (.001)\}$$
$$= \$876.$$

Material Expense

The next largest expense is the cost of the Field Replaceable Unit (FRU). The choice between a logical and physical partitioning of the system is crucial for a system designer, for it directly affects both the maintainability and cost of ownership of the system. The cost impact can be estimated from the cost and reliability of each FRU as follows:

$$Total\ Cost = \Sigma\{(FRU\ cost)_i$$
$$\times (FRU\ failure\ rate)_i\}$$

This formula, however, estimates only the cost of replacing failed hardware. For the service provider, there are also other costs.

Inventory Costs.   Inventory costs are the costs associated with keeping a supply of spare parts; they consist of all the costs of maintaining a supply depot, including order processing costs and the fully burdened cost per square foot of the building.

Level of Service.   An important consideration in determining inventory costs is the level of service. In this context, level of service is the conditional probability that a part is in stock, given a failure of that part. If the MTBF of each part and its field population are known, a relatively straightforward statistical calculation can determine how much of each part to have in stock to attain a given level of service.

Other Expenses

Training Costs.   The persons who service the computer must be trained. Whether the owner self-maintains the system or purchases field service externally, this cost is ultimately borne by the system owner. Because training and course development can be a significant expense, it is important to design a system that minimizes the amount of special training necessary.

Depreciation of Capital Equipment.   If special test equipment is required to service the computer system, the cost of that equipment may be significant and must be taken into account by both the system purchaser and the designer. For example, such equipment is frequently written off during a period of 5 years, using the double-declining balance method. This method expenses the cost of the equipment at a rate double that of a linear method, but it applies this rate to the remaining balance instead of to the original amount. Thus, a straight-line depreciation over 5 years would be 20 percent per year. A double-declining balance would write off 40 percent in the first year, 40 percent of the remainder (40 percent of 60 percent, or 24 percent) the next year, and 40 percent of the remainder (40 percent of 36 percent, or 14.4 percent) the third year. Because this series is infinite, it is customary to divide the remainder evenly between the last 2 years; thus, 10.8 percent of the original cost is written off in each of the last 2 years.

Cost of Customer Ownership

Cost of ownership is the true total cost of owning a computer system, not just the acquisition cost. It includes a multitude of factors, such as purchase cost; maintenance cost; and costs of downtime, site preparation, storage media and supplies, power, environmental conditioning, and operating personnel. Maintenance cost alone can easily equal the purchase price after just 5 years of operation.

The other costs of operation can render the purchase cost relatively insignificant. Consider especially the cost of downtime. Presumably, all computer systems are purchased in order to increase productivity and efficiency. If a computer system is properly utilized (consistently loaded at or near full capacity), an interruption in service will inevitably lead to a loss of money or time, which normally equates to loss of revenue.

It is difficult to present a generalized model of the cost of downtime because it varies greatly with the application. In some systems it is negligible; in others, it far outweighs any other financial considerations. Finally, in some applications its value cannot be computed because the survival of priceless things (such as a human life) depends upon the computer's continuous operation. Below are some examples of systems in which the cost of downtime is high.

On-Line Billing System. In an on-line billing system used, say, by a telephone company for recording charges on long distance calls, the lost revenue when the system is down is practically unrecoverable, and typically substantial. In this case, a "lost-revenue-per-hour" figure should be arrived at by the system's financial analysts and factored into the cost of ownership.

Airline Reservation System. It is more difficult to establish a quantitative measure of lost bookings due to this system's failure, but it can obviously be significant.

Electronic Funds Transfer. When money is being transmitted electronically, there is a great danger that system failure (including loss of data integrity) can lead to large losses.

Life-Support Systems. In systems such as those for monitoring hospital intensive care patients, system failure at an inopportune time can lead to loss of life. With the increasing use of computers

in medical care and biomedical engineering, the incidence of loss of life due to computer failures is bound to increase. The cost is, of course, impossible to assess. Systems that deal with transportation (such as flight control systems) and building management (such as fire alarm and containment systems) also belong in this category.

National Defense Systems. Computers now form the backbone of the defense of entire countries. A recent minicomputer failure resulted in an indication that a Russian missile attack on the United States was taking place. The system was designed to fail "safely," that is, to indicate an attack when it failed. (The premise adopted is that it is better to indicate an attack when none is occurring than not to indicate an attack when one is occurring.) Fortunately, an adequate system of cross-checks was necessary before counteroffensive measures were taken, the failure was discovered before any potentially devastating actions occurred.

Net Present Value

A simplified economic model of the cost of computer ownership assumes an initial cash purchase, followed by periodic maintenance payments. It is possible to compute the true cost of ownership as the present value of these outlays. Present value is a financial concept that takes the time value of money into account; that is, if you receive $10 today and put it into a savings account for a year at a 10 percent effective annual interest rate, in a year you will have $11. Conversely, if I promise to give you $11 one year from today, its present value is only $10.

The rate used to calculate present value is known as the discount rate. Assuming a discount rate of 10 percent, the present value of a dollar received or expended one year from now is:

$$\frac{1}{(1 + 0.10)}$$

The present value of a dollar received or expended two years from now has a present-value factor of:

$$\frac{1}{(1 + 0.10)^2}$$

and so on.

Assume an initial cost of $1 million, an annual maintenance cost of $100,000, an income tax rate of 50 percent, a write-off over 5 years using the double-declining balance method, and a discount rate of 10 percent. Table 6-2 lists the cost of ownership.

The amount in column 3 is the depreciation on the capital outlay according to the double-declining balance method. Column 4 is the difference between columns 2 and 3, or the net expense. Column 5 shows the after-tax cash flow (50 percent is deductible from the company's income tax). Column 6 shows the present-value factors. Column 7 is the product of columns 5 and 6.

After subtracting the sum of column 7 from the initial outlay of $1 million, the cost of ownership is $784,050.

Alternatives to Net Present Value

There are several alternatives to assessing cost of ownership by the net present value method used above. The first is the payback method, which assumes no time value of money and thus simply adds (or subtracts) the yearly net values to the initial investment. The payback period is then defined as the time at which the cumulative cash flows reach zero.

A better alternative is Internal Rate of Return (IRR). To determine the internal rate of return, the discount value is assumed to be unknown, and an iterative procedure is performed to discover the discount rate at which the net present value equals zero. The company establishes a minimum IRR, and if the IRR is greater than this minimum, it is a desirable investment.

FIELD SERVICE OVERVIEW AND COST MODELS

In many computer companies, field service (hardware and software) is a business unit with independent responsibility for profit and loss. The expense the company incurs when repairing equipment under warranty accumulates in the field service department. Because each company's financial structure varies, it is impossible to generalize about the field service business units, but it is important to realize that field service revenues can be a significant proportion of corporate revenues, in some cases approaching 30 percent. For a large end-user minicomputer com-

Table 6–2. Example of cost of ownership calculation (in thousands of dollars).

(1) Year	(2) Maintenance Cost	(3) Depreciation	(4) Net	(5) After Tax Cash Flow	(6) Present Value Factor	(7) Discounted Cash Flow
1	100	400	−300	−150	0.909	−136.36
2	100	240	−140	−70	0.826	−57.85
3	100	144	−44	−22	0.751	−16.53
4	100	108	−8	−4	0.683	−2.73
5	100	108	−8	−4	0.621	−2.48
					Total	−215.95

pany or mainframe manufacturer, field service personnel typically account for 20–30 percent of the total personnel.

Field service is a labor intensive business, with travel time also a very significant part of the expense. The cost of field service is determined primarily by product traits (reliability, diagnosability, and the like). The business can be further characterized by a potentially lengthy and strong commitment to the customer. There are inherent risks in charging fixed contract prices: loss of profits if the price is set too low, and loss of business to third-party maintenance organizations if the price is too high.

There is also a growing set of legal considerations about which to worry. What if a client company loses substantial revenue because of the failure of a computer? What if property damage results from a computer malfunction? What if personal injury occurs as the result of an unsafe design? In one case, a small data processing company was located near a fire station. Electromagnetic emissions from some of the computer equipment were interfering with the fire department's radio communications. The problem was remedied before any damage was done, but the consequences of a computer's interfering with the reporting of a major fire could have been critical. The number of individual litigations, class action suits, and government regulations is likely to increase as computers and the consequences of their malfunctions proliferate.

Maintenance Cost Models

Maintenance cost models estimate the variable costs associated with servicing a particular system or part of a system. A variable cost is one that varies in direct proportion to the number of service calls received, as distinct from a fixed cost, which is incurred independently of the number of calls received. Typically, a variable

cost is the cost of a particular replacement part for a broken computer system. An example of a fixed cost is the cost of a piece of test equipment, which is required whether or not anything ever actually breaks.

Typical parameters in a maintenance cost model are:

- Mean time between failures
- Mean time to repair
- Travel time associated with the service call, perhaps computed at some average rate
- Material consumed, such as replacement parts and lubricants
- Preventive maintenance performed, either on a regular basis or in conjunction with a repair action
- Cost of labor

The results of such a calculation would provide a rough estimate of the cost per unit time of maintaining a system or part of a system. This type of model ignores fixed (front-end) costs and can be expected to estimate only variable costs.

A comprehensive model that includes these fixed costs, as well as items such as salvage value, has been developed by Xerox and reported in Pierce [1977]. Alternative designs can easily be analyzed, as the histograms in Figure 6-2 demonstrate. This case involved comparison of three alternative packaging schemes. The overall life costs were shown to be less for one large, relatively expensive board than for a system partitioned into smaller boards; the smaller boards had decreased reliability resulting from the increase in number of connectors.

Sensitivity analyses evaluate the effect of various parameters on profitability. Figure 6-3 shows an example.

Other trade-off studies performed with this model include:

- Should the diagnostic hardware for the system be included as part of the system hardware or carried by the field engineer?
- Should a unit replaced in the field be repaired and recirculated or discarded?

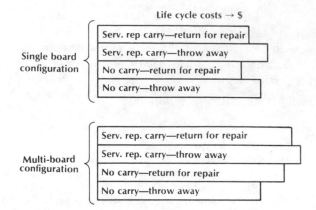

Figure 6–2. Life-cycle costs of alternative configurations.

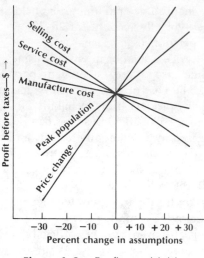

Figure 6–3. Profit sensitivities.

• Should a given availability goal for a subassembly be achieved by improving its reliability or its maintainability?
• At what level (region, district, branch, individual person) should a spare part be stocked?

Table 6-3 lists the model sensitivity to primary categories of input and output data [Pierce 1977].

Maintenance Cost Model with Risks

Risk factors could be added to the above model, in the form of probability distributions expected for each of the parameters. Adding risk factors would take into account the fundamentally random nature of failures. The model parameters could be established to give minimum cost (with appropriate confidence levels), average cost, and so on.

The outputs would be a probability distribution of the expected maintenance costs instead of a point estimate. This type of model facilitates a simple sensitivity analysis, answering questions such as:

• What happens to the cost of maintenance if the MTBF is 10 percent higher than the estimate?
• What happens to the cost of maintenance if the MTTR is decreased by 15 minutes?

Feature Failure-Mode Matrix

A feature failure-mode matrix is a technique to evaluate a series of maintainability features for their effect on the cost of maintaining a given system or device. For example, for a hypothetical digital tape unit, engineering can generate a list of potential maintainability features such as data path loop-around, error simulation, internal parity, speed check, skew check, and power check. Field service can provide a list of failure modes (projected from experience with previous similar designs) such as permanent/intermittent data path errors, faulty controller, faulty error logic, faulty head preamplifier, faulty servos, and faulty power supply. These features and modes are then put in matrix form, as shown in Table 6-4.

Next to each maintainability feature is the estimated percent of failures resulting from each of the defined failure modes. At each intersection of a feature and a failure mode is an estimate of the time that would be saved when repairing this failure, were the feature present. A projection of the total time saved by each maintainability feature can then be obtained by taking column-wide weighted averages.

Table 6–3. Input and output parameters for a maintenance cost model.

Primary data inputs are listed by category as follows:	*Primary data outputs obtained are listed as follows:*
Part data	1. Increase in number of service personnel by year
1. Unit cost	2. Number of spares replaced per year
2. Repair cost	3. Average cost of a spare item
3. Repair transportation cost	4. Mean corrective maintenance time
4. Power-on hours	5. Number of spares returned from the field per year
5. Repair turnaround time	6. Number of additional spares needed per year
6. Repair attrition	7. Number of spares shipped to the field per year
7. Part population	8. Number of nonrepairable parts
8. Erroneous replacements	9. Number of parts in field inventory
9. Replacement rates (MTBF)	10. Number of parts returned from the repair facility
10. Reliability growth	11. Initial cost of parts per year
11. On-site time to repair	12. Initial parts depreciation/tax recovery per year
12. Salvage value	13. Cost of replaced spare parts per year
	14. Tax recovery from replaced parts per year
Business economic factors	15. Cost of service labor per year
1. Life-cycle period	16. Shipping cost of failed parts per year
2. Corporation-selected depreciation	17. Cost of vendor repair of failed parts per year
3. Corporate tax rate	18. Shipping cost of spares per year
4. Service Personnel labor rate	19. Salvage value of nonrepair parts
5. Part cost improvement	
6. Machine placements	
7. Machine workload per service personnel	
Program option controls	
1. Detailed or summarized output	
2. Supplemental quarterly output	
3. Unit cost vs. reliability indifference routine	
4. Part repair or discard evaluation	
5. Service rep carry part or no-carry evaluation	
6. Computations without present value, depreciation, and tax influences	

The decision about whether to include a particular feature in the final design would proceed as follows: From an estimate of the base parameters of the design (MTBF, MTTR, MTPM), calculate the projected decrease in MTTR due to the feature. Using an appropriate cost model with sales projections, calculate the present value of incorporating this feature. Compare this result with the cost of including this feature in the design, including development cost and the cost of the hardware for all the units to be shipped, expressed in present value. Incorporate the feature if the difference between the life-cycle cost savings and the feature's cost is positive.

Life-Cycle Cost (LCC) Models

Life-cycle cost models take into account the total product business profile: the cost of purchase of the computer system, maintenance, supplies, environmental controls, power, and so on. Every expense associated with owning a computer is considered.

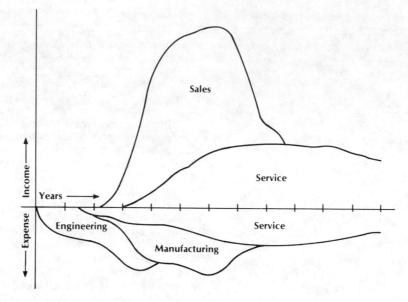

Figure 6–4.   Cost and income distribution over the life of a system.

Table 6–4.   A feature failure-mode matrix.

	Percent of System Failures	Data Path Loop-Around	Error Simulation	Internal Parity	Speed Check	Skew Check	Power Check	Reel LEDs
Permanent data path	11%	74	24	74				
Intermittent data path	2			168				
Controller	6							
Error logic	6	24	54	24				
Head preamp	10	84		84				
Servos	25				390	210		66
Power supply	5						90	
Minutes saved		18	6	21	97.5	52.5	4.5	16.5

Such a model enables an organization to evaluate design alternatives with regard to effects on life-cycle cost and to make a choice that minimizes that cost. Figure 6-4 shows how revenues and expenses (the difference of which is defined as income) might vary over time. Engineering expenses dominate the first years, and manufacturing and service expenses begin to take over as sales revenues increase. Even after manufacturing has ceased, service expenses and revenues continue for a long time, with (it is hoped) a net positive income.

Typical inputs to an LCC model might be:

- Shipment forecasts over the planned life of the product
- Contract penetration (the percentage of customers electing to purchase service contracts) and renewal (percentage renewing each year) rates

- List price of the system
- Warranty period
- Spares requirements (number of spare parts kits required per system, cost per kit)
- Installation expenses (labor and material expense per installation), expenses incurred due to DOA (dead-on-arrival) parts, and other installation difficulties
- MTTR, varying over time as experience with repairing the system increases
- Labor costs per corrective and preventive maintenance action
- MTBF, several values for a sensitivity analysis
- Travel time
- An estimate of average material cost per failure
- Training costs
- Capital equipment costs
- Spare parts inventory carrying expense

The result of such an analysis would be a tabulation of maintenance cost as a function of MTBF (or other independent variables), profit

Table 6–5. Cost of manufacturing three systems as a function of time with different MTBFs (base: 6 months, alternative 1: 8.5 months, alternative 2: 10 months) in thousands of dollars.

Quarter	Shipments	Base ($K)	Alternative 1 ($K)	Alternative 2 ($K)
1	1	11	11.3	11.8
2	4	44	45.2	47.2
3	73	803	824.9	861.4
4	354	3,894	4,000.2	4,177.2
5	612	6,732	6,915.6	7,221.6
6	820	9,020	9,266.0	9,676.0
7	990	10,890	11,187.0	11,682.0
8	1,000	11,000	11,300.0	11,800.0
9	1,000	11,000	11,300.0	11,800.0
10	1,000	11,000	11,300.0	11,800.0
11	1,000	11,000	11,300.0	11,800.0
12	1,000	11,000	11,300.0	11,800.0
13	1,000	11,000	11,300.0	11,800.0
14	1,000	11,000	11,300.0	11,800.0
15	1,000	11,000	11,300.0	11,800.0
16	1,000	11,000	11,300.0	11,800.0
17	650	7,150	7,345.0	7,670.0
18	447	4,917	5,051.1	5,274.6
19	320	3,520	3,616.0	3,776.0
20	229	2,519	2,587.7	2,702.2

and loss information, and warranty expense estimates, all with discounted cash flows.

Table 6-5 lists the five-year expense forecasts for manufacturing costs of a hypothetical piece of equipment under a base case (6 months MTBF) and two alternatives (8.5 and 10 months MTBF). The basic assumption is that increased reliability requires a higher manufacturing cost and results in a higher field MTBF and lower field MTTR. This example assumes that the system manufacturing cost was $11,000 in the base case, $300 more for the first alternative, and $800 more for the second alternative.

Table 6-6 lists the service costs for the base case and the two alternatives over the five-year planned shipments of the product. There is a decrease in service costs due to increased MTBFs and an asociated increase in manufacturing costs. From a life-cycle cost point of view, which alternative is preferable?

Tables 6-7, 6-8, and 6-9 list the discounted expenses (manufacturing ' and service ') over the shipment life of the product. At the bottom of the primed columns is the discounted present value of service and manufacturing costs and their total for the base case and two alternatives. In summary:

- The total discounted present value for the base case (6 months MTBF and $11,000 manufacturing cost) is $109,277,600.
- The total discounted present value for Alternative 1 (8.5 months MTBF and $11,300 manufacturing cost) is $108,152,300.
- The total discounted present value for Alternative 2 (10 months MTBF and $11,800 manufacturing cost) is $110,849,300.

This analysis shows that Alternative 1 has the best financial profile, because it has the lowest total life-cycle cost, and Alternative 2 has the lowest service cost (about 2 percent less than Alternative 1). Is it worth the investment?

Table 6-6. Cost of maintaining three systems with different MTBFs (base: 6 months, alternative 1: 8.5 months, alternative 2: 10 months) (in thousands of dollars).

Quarter	Base ($K)	Alternative 1 ($K)	Alternative 2 ($K)
0	17	17	17
1	425	425	425
2	196	177	170
3	554	493	462
4	847	757	709
5	909	818	773
6	1,179	1,045	992
7	1,243	1,075	1,007
8	1,576	1,309	1,239
9	1,777	1,481	1,361
10	1,852	1,527	1,401
11	2,042	1,673	1,521
12	2,194	1,776	1,609
13	2,336	1,876	1,693
14	2,484	1,981	1,782
15	2,626	2,081	1,866
16	2,609	2,044	1,831
17	2,448	1,866	1,651
18	2,345	1,767	1,542
19	2,265	1,677	1,464
20	2,224	1,633	1,419

LCC Model with Generalized Data Elements

Common LCC models require detailed and precise analysis of the system's characteristics and its operating environment. It is a difficult task to compare alternative designs, for much information must be collected and entered in the model for each alternative. Eames and Spann [1977] have developed a method that uses cursory system descriptions to produce timely and comprehensive LCC data to support design decisions.

Implied Characteristics

The system is first classified according to the following implied characteristics:

Table 6–7. Discounted cost of manufacturing and service for the base system (in thousands of dollars).

Quarter	Manufacturing ($K)	Manufacturing' ($K)	Service ($K)	Service' ($K)
0			17	17.0
1	11	10.5	425	406.1
2	44	40.2	196	178.9
3	803	700.4	554	483.2
4	3,894	3,245.4	847	705.9
5	6,732	5,360.9	909	723.9
6	9,020	6,863.1	1,179	897.1
7	10,890	7,917.0	1,243	903.7
8	11,000	7,640.9	1,576	1,094.7
9	11,000	7,300.7	1,777	1,179.4
10	11,000	6,975.7	1,852	1,174.4
11	11,000	6,665.1	2,042	1,237.3
12	11,000	6,368.3	2,194	1,270.2
13	11,000	6,084.8	2,336	1,292.2
14	11,000	5,813.8	2,484	1,312.9
15	11,000	5,555.0	2,626	1,326.1
16	11,000	5,307.6	2,609	1,258.9
17	7,150	3,296.4	2,448	1,128.6
18	4,917	2,165.9	2,345	1,033.0
19	3,520	1,481.5	2,265	953.3
20	2,519	1,013.0	2,224	894.4

Present values................... 89,806.4 ....19,471.2

Total present value = $109,277.6

Table 6–8. Discounted cost of manufacturing and service for the first alternative with a 42 percent improvement in MTBF (in thousands of dollars).

Quarter	Manufacturing Cost ($K)	Manufacturing Cost' ($K)	Service ($K)	Service' ($K)
0			17	17.0
1	11.3	10.8	425	406.1
2	45.2	41.3	177	161.6
3	824.9	719.5	493	430.0
4	4,000.2	3,333.9	757	630.9
5	6,915.6	5,507.1	818	651.4
6	9,266.0	7,050.3	1,045	795.1
7	11,187.0	8,133.0	1,075	781.5
8	11,300.0	7,849.3	1,309	909.3
9	11,300.0	7,499.8	1,481	982.9
10	11,300.0	7,165.9	1,527	968.3

Table 6–8 –*Continued*

Quarter	Manufacturing Cost ($K)	Manufacturing Cost' ($K)	Service ($K)	Service' ($K)
11	11,300.0	6,846.8	1,673	1,013.7
12	11,300.0	6,542.0	1,776	1,028.2
13	11,300.0	6,250.7	1,876	1,037.7
14	11,300.0	5,972.4	1,981	1,047.0
15	11,300.0	5,706.5	2,081	1,050.9
16	11,300.0	5,452.4	2,044	986.3
17	7,345.0	3,386.3	1,866	860.3
18	5,051.1	2,225.0	1,767	775.7
19	3,616.0	1,521.9	1,677	705.8
20	2,587.7	1,040.6	1,633	656.7

Present values.................... 92,255.7 .... 15,896.6

Total present value = $108,152.3

Table 6–9. Discounted cost of manufacturing and service for the second alternative with a 67 percent improvement in MTBF (in thousands of dollars).

Quarter	Manufacturing Cost ($K)	Manufacturing Cost' ($K)	Service ($K)	Service' ($K)
0			17	17.0
1	11.8	11.3	425	406.1
2	47.2	43.1	170	155.2
3	861.4	751.4	462	403.0
4	4,177.2	3,481.5	709	590.9
5	7,221.6	5,750.8	773	615.6
6	9,676.0	7,362.3	992	754.8
7	11,682.0	8,492.8	1,007	732.1
8	11,800.0	8,196.6	1,239	860.6
9	11,800.0	7,831.7	1,361	903.3
10	11,800.0	7,483.0	1,401	888.4
11	11,800.0	7,149.8	1,521	921.6
12	11,800.0	6,831.5	1,609	931.5
13	11,800.0	6,527.3	1,693	936.5
14	11,800.0	6,236.7	1,782	941.8
15	11,800.0	5,958.9	1,866	942.3
16	11,800.0	5,693.6	1,831	883.5
17	7,670.0	3,536.1	1,651	761.2
18	5,274.6	2,323.5	1,542	679.3
19	3,776.0	1,589.3	1,464	616.2
20	2,702.2	1,086.7	1,419	570.6

Present values.................... 96,337.8 .... 14,511.5

Total present value = $110,849.3

- Reliability—developed from a parts stress analysis, from past engineering data and estimates, or from a parts-count reliability prediction model.
- Maintainability—determined from maintainability scores described in MIL-HDBK-472, Procedure III.
- Availability—the availability of a nonredundant functional entity related to its reliability and maintainability by:

$$A_e = \frac{\text{MTTF}}{(\text{MTTF} + \text{MTTR})}$$

The system availability can then be estimated by taking the product of the availabilities of each functional entity, provided that system operation is dependent upon concurrent and continuous functioning of each entity and that the functional entities are independent in terms of failures and repairs.

Cost Categories

These data are then incorporated in an LCC estimate that includes the following cost categories:

- Research and development costs
- Investment costs
  - Acquisition
  - Initial installation
  - Initial and replaceable spares
  - Support equipment
  - Personnel training
  - Management and technical data
  - New facilities
- Operating and support costs
  - Organizational level maintenance
  - Intermediate and depot level maintenance
  - Inventory management

Table 6-10 lists a description of the variables used and the resulting equations, with suggested typical values for the constants.

A method of quantifying revenue loss resulting from system downtime is: determine the optimum simplex system, and divide the total LCC by the number of hours in the system design life. The optimum simplex system is defined as a system with no redundancy, but with maintainability and fault-intolerant features optimized for minimum life-cycle cost. Eames and Spann [1977] cite an example of a system whose design life is 10 years, with a total LCC of $10 million.

If the system is being used 24 hours a day, the user of the system is paying:

$$\frac{\$10M}{87,600} = \frac{\$114.16}{\text{hour}}$$

for the use of the system. Therefore it must be worth at least this amount to keep the system running.

Consider a large computer-aided instruction (CAI) system[*], consisting of keyboards, video terminals, tape units, line printers, software, and various controllers and display generation equipment. Each of these system components is first assigned to one of two categories: electromechanical and large electronic assemblies, and printed circuit boards and small electronic assemblies. LCC analyses are performed with the parameters described above. The system is first considered in its optimum simplex form; Table 6-11 shows the results for three different part quality grades.

Next, the effects of various kinds and degrees of redundancy are considered. Table 6-12 compares the results. Column A restates the results of the optimum simplex analysis. Column B shows three variations of a 9-out-of-10 redundancy scheme: 11 percent of the system with 9-out-of-10 redundancy, the rest simplex; 63 percent with 9-out-of-10 redundancy, the rest simplex; and 100 percent with 9-out-of-10 redundancy. Columns C and D show similar analyses with 4-out-of-5 and 1-out-of-2 redundancies in various portions of the system.

The ratio of LCC change to the change in system downtime yields the value of avoiding downtime for each of these approaches. Figure 6-5 shows these values graphically.

CONCLUSIONS

It is for a financial reason of one sort or another that any fault-tolerant system is designed and

---

[*] This example is adapted from Eames and Spann [1977].

Table 6–10. A simple life-cycle cost model and its parameters.

Description of Variables:

NUM	Number of equipment items	Input	*These are assumed to be constant:*		
HOURS	Total life cycle operating hours per equipment item	Input	FIXILQ	Fraction of failures repaired at intermediate level (IL) branch office by quantity	0.20
LABOR	Average labor rate $/MH	50.00			
RPPTIP	Ratio of system purchase price to sum of PRICE(I)	0.40	FIXDLQ	Fraction of failures repaired at depot level (DL) by quantity	0.20, 0.50
DEVELS	Cost of development	Input	AILRS	Average IL repair material cost percent of PRICE	0.05
INSTAS	Cost of initial installation material and equipment, $	Input	AILRT	Average IL repair time, mh	5.0
MTTF	Mean Time To Failure for the whole system	Input	ADLRS	Average DL repair material cost percent of PRICE	0.10
TQUANT	Total quantity of systems to be made to amortize development costs	Input	ADLRT	Average DL repair time, mh	5.0
			AOLRT	Average organizational level (OL) factory repair time, mh	5.0
All the following are arrays of size 'NUM'					
PRICE	Initial price	Input			
TFAIL	Failure rate for total quantity of equipment item(I), F/MHR	Input	AOLRTS	Average OL repair material cost percent of PRICE	0.20
QUANT	Total quantity of equipment item(I)	Input	TRIP	Cost to make service trip	100

Equations:

Acquisition $= RPPTIP \times \sum [PRICE\,(I) \times QUANT\,(I)]$

Development $= DEVELS/TQUANT$

Initial Installation $= INSTAS$

Initial and replaceable spares $=$
$(0.05 + HOURS \times 6.0E\text{-}6) \times Acquisition$

Organizational level maintenance $=$
$int\,(HOURS/MTTF) \times (\sum [TFAIL\,(I) \times MTTF \times 1.0E\text{-}6 \times \{1.0 - FIXDLQ - FIXILQ\} \times X(I)] + TRIP)$
Where $X\,(I) = AOLRTS \times PRICE\,(I) + AOLRT \times LABOR$

Intermediate and depot level maintenance $=$
$int\,(HOURS/MTTF) \times (\sum [TFAIL\,(I) \times MTTF \times 1.0E\text{-}6 \times \{FIXILQ \times V\,(I) + FIXDLQ \times W\,(I)\}] + TRIP)$
Where $V\,(I) = AILRS \times PRICE\,(I) + AILRT \times LABOR$
and $W\,(I) = ADLRS \times PRICE\,(I) + ADLRT \times LABOR$

Inventory management $= 4.0 \times Initial\ Installation$

Support Equipment $= 0$

Personnel Training $= 0$

Management and Technical Data $= 0$

New Facilities $= 0$

Source: Note this model is a modified version of one proposed in *Life Cycle Analysis Utilizing Generalized Data*   *Elements* by Susan Eames and Al Spann of GTE Sylvania Incorporated.

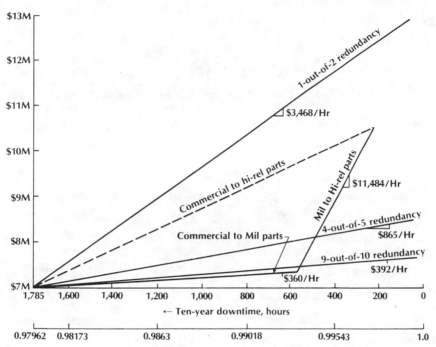

Figure 6–5. Cost-to-reduce downtime.

Table 6–11. Example of effects of component quality levels on LCC.

Parts Quality Grade:	Commercial	MIL	HI-REL
Total LRUs:	1,600	1,600	1,600
Availability:	0.979624	0.993635	0.997444
Mean Uptime:	24 Hrs.	78 Hrs.	195 Hrs.
Acquisition	$ 2,560,000	$ 2,900,244	$ 4,400,516
Development	207,999	207,999	207,999
Initial installation	84,979	84,979	84,979
Initial and replacement spares	2,880,000	3,262,804	4,950,596
Organization level maintenance	125,974	122,017	120,968
Branch and depot level maintenance	430,346	147,256	84,849
Inventory management	309,287	309,287	309,287
Support equipment	185,000	185,000	185,000
Personnel training	0	0	0
Management and technical data	200,804	196,638	195,530
New facilities	0	0	0
Life-cycle cost	$ 6,984,389	$ 7,416,224	$ 10,539,720
		Cost to Avoid Downtime $360/Hr.	Cost to Avoid Downtime $11,484/Hr.

Table 6–12. Example of effects on LCC of reliability improvement via redundancy.

Configuration:	A	B 9-out-of-10 Redundancy		
	Series	11% Redundancy	63% Redundancy	100% Redundancy
Total LRUs:	1600	1617	1706	1777
Availability:	0.979624	0.981619	0.991583	0.999540
Mean uptime:	24 Hrs.	26 Hrs.	58 Hrs.	1,085 Hrs.
Acquisition	$ 2,560,000	$ 2,588,423	$ 2,730,836	$ 2,844,423
Development	207,099	216,412	225,545	235,674
Initial installation	84,979	85,086	85,619	86,046
Initial and replacement spares	2,880,000	2,908,423	3,050,636	3,164,423
Organization level maintenance	125,974	127,374	134,372	139,970
Branch and depot level maintenance	430,346	435,125	459,034	478,163
Inventory management	309,287	309,287	309,287	309,287
Support equipment	185,000	185,000	185,000	185,000
Personnel training	0	0	0	0
Management and technical data	200,804	202,291	209,710	215,649
New facilities	0	0	0	0
Life-cycle cost	$ 6,984,389	$ 7,057,421	$ 7,389,939	$ 7,658,635

◄——————— Cost to avoid downtime $392/Hr.————————►

built. Calculating the costs and/or benefits of a given high reliability, maintainability, or availability design is a complex task. This chapter has explained important financial concepts related to the purchase, operation, and servicing of a computer system. Also explained were several mathematical techniques, including discounted cash-flow cost-of-ownership calculations, maintenance cost and life-cycle cost models, and a method to assess the cost effectiveness of maintainability features.

This chapter should give the design engineer an adequate understanding of the principles necessary for a rudimentary analysis of the financial considerations for a given system. More sophisticated problems can be handled by financial analysts and management scientists.

REFERENCES

Eames and Spann [1977]; Pierce [1977].

C 4-out-of-5 Redundancy			D 1-out-of-2 Redundancy		
12% Redun-dancy	65% Redun-dancy	100% Redun-dancy	18% Redun-dancy	75% Redun-dancy	100% Redun-dancy
1640	1839	2000	1760	2560	3200
0.981619	0.991562	0.999484	0.981616	0.991453	0.999186
26 Hrs.	58 Hrs.	967 Hrs.	26 Hrs.	58 Hrs.	613 Hrs.
$ 2,624,000	$ 2,943,906	$ 3,199,903	$ 2,816,000	$ 4,095,896	$ 5,119,392
216,527	226,437	237,812	217,151	231,049	249,533
85,219	86,419	87,379	85,939	90,739	94,579
2,944,000	3,263,906	3,519,903	3,136,000	4,415,898	5,439,892
129,122	144,869	157,466	138,571	201,557	251,946
441,110	494,905	537,931	473,384	688,559	860,683
309,287	309,287	309,287	309,287	309,287	309,287
185,000	185,000	185,000	185,000	185,000	185,000
0	0	0	0	0	0
204,143	220,845	234,209	214,167	280,971	334,412
0	0	0	0	0	0
$ 7,138,408	$ 7,875,624	$ 8,468,890	$ 7,575,499	$10,498,950	$12,845,220

←——Cost to avoid downtime $865/Hr. ——→ ←——Cost to avoid downtime $3,468/Hr. ——→

PROBLEMS

1. Suppose that you are issuing maintenance contracts on a new system with the following shipment schedule:

Quarter	Shipments
1	50
2	250
3	1250
4	4000
5	5000
6	5000
7	5000
8	2000
9	1000
10	500
11	0
12	0

If the contract penetration rate is 50 percent and the annual contract renewal rate is 75 percent, calculate the resulting number of contracts in each quarter.

2. What is the cost of owning a system purchased for $500,000, with an annual cost of maintenance of $40,000? Assume a discount rate of 15 percent and a tax rate of 50 percent, with the system depreciated over 4 years, using the double-declining balance method.

3. Consider the feature failure-mode matrix (Table 6-4). Suppose that the development costs associated with each feature are as follows:

Data Path Loop-Around	$1000.
Error Simulation	$8500.
Internal Parity	$1500.

Speed Check	$2000.
Skew Check	$5000.
Power Check	$7400.
Reel LEDs	$9000.

Assume that the MTBF of the device remains at a constant 5,000 hours, and that a minute of repair time saved is worth $1. Ignoring the time value of money, which features should be incorporated into the device if you are going to ship a total of 100 units? 1000 units? 10,000 units? Assume the manufacturing cost per unit is $1000 and the system lifetime is 5 years.

THE PRACTICE OF RELIABLE SYSTEM DESIGN

The ultimate system goals affect design philosophy and design trade-offs. The costs of fault tolerance must be weighted against the cost of error. Error costs include downtime as well as incorrect computation. Some system goals that affect design philosophy are listed in Table II-1. Is the system to be highly reliable or highly available? Do all outputs have to be correct, or only data committed to long-term storage? How familiar must the user be with the architecture and software redundancy? Is the system dedicated so that attributes of the application can be used to simplify fault-tolerant techniques? Is the system constrained to use existing components? Even if the design is new, what is the cost and/or performance penalty to the user who does not require fault tolerance? Is the design stand-alone, or are there other processors that can be called upon to assist in times of failure?

Rennels [1980] has identified five different application types to which fault tolerance has been applied:

1. *High Availability*. High availability systems share resources when the occasional loss of a single user is acceptable but a systemwide outage or common data base destruction is unacceptable. These systems are most frequently oriented toward general-purpose computing, executing a variety of user programs whose demands cannot be anticipated. Because they are targeted for the cost-sensitive commercial marketplace these systems use minimal modifications to existing designs. Hamming-coded memory, bus parity, timeout counters, diagnostics, and software reasonability checks are the primary redundancy techniques. Thus, coverage is low. In multiple-processor systems, however, the fault can be isolated once it is identified, and the system can continue operation, perhaps in degraded mode. Examples of high-availability systems include Tandem (see Chapter 11) and Pluribus (see Chapter 13).

2. *Long Life*. Long-life systems, such as unmanned spacecraft, cannot be manually maintained over the system operating life (frequently five or more years). Often, as in spacecraft monitoring of planets, the peak computational requirement comes at the end of system life. These systems are highly redundant, equipped with enough spares to survive the mission with the required computational power. Redundancy management may be performed automatically (on the spacecraft) or remotely (from ground stations). STAR (see Chapter 14) and Voyager (see Chapter 15) are examples of long-life spacecraft systems.

3. *Postponed Maintenance*. Closely related to long-life systems are systems designed to survive faults until periodic maintenance can be performed. For small systems like spacecraft, maintenance could be postponed for the entire

Table II–1.   System goals determine design philosophy.

- Reliability versus availability
- Grain of correctness
  - Correct data output
  - No loss of data
- Transparency to user
- Dedicated or general purpose
- New design or add-on
  - Penalty to nonreliability user
- Stand-alone or multiple processor

system life. For other systems in which on-site repair is difficult, redundancy is more cost effective than unscheduled maintenance. There are many mobile systems that depart from a central facility for a period of time and return. Stocking spares and maintenance expertise are most cost effective if maintenance can be postponed until the mobile unit returns to the central facility. Such systems include mass transit, ships, airplanes, and tanks.

4. *High-Performance Computing*.   High-performance computing systems (such as signal processing) are very susceptible to transient errors (due to close timing margins) and permanent faults (due to complexity). As performance demands increase, fault tolerance may be the only way of building systems with sufficient Mean Time To Error (MTTE) to allow useful computation. Occasional errors that disrupt processing for several seconds are tolerable as long as automatic recovery follows. Table II-2 lists some high performance general-purpose computing systems, their Mean Time to Crash (MTTC), and Mean Number of Instructions Executed (MNIE) between crashes.

Table II–2.   Number of instructions executed between system crashes for several mainframe systems.

System	Mean Time To Crash MTTC (hours)	Mean Number Instructions Executed MNIE ($\times 10^{10}$)
B5500 [Yourdon, 1972]	14.7	2.6
Chi/05 (Univac 1108) [Lynch, Wagner, and Schwartz, 1975]	17.0	6.7
Dual 370/165 [Reynolds and Kinsberger, 1975]	8.86	28.0
SLAC	20.2	23.0
PDP-10 [Castillo, 1980]	10.0	4.3
CRAY-1 [Keller, 1976]	4.0	190.0

5. *Critical Computations.* The most stringent requirement for fault tolerance is in realtime control systems in which faulty computations can jeopardize human life or have high economic impact. Not only must computations be correct, but also recovery time from faults must be minimized. Specially designed hardware operates with concurrent error detection so that incorrect data never leave the faulty module. SIFT (see Chapter 16) and FTMP (see Chapter 17) are examples of avionic computers designed to control dynamically unstable aircraft. Their design goal is a failure probability of less than 10^{-9} for a 10-hour mission.

Part I presented the techniques used in fault-tolerant computer design. It remains to the system designer to combine these techniques into a coherent architecture and to evaluate the resultant architecture. The remaining 12 chapters present a cross-section of existing fault-tolerant architectures; every system has been built. Chapter 7 traces the evolution of a simple redundancy technique (TMR) into a working system. The remaining chapters are roughly arranged in order of increasingly stringent reliability requirements. Chapters 8 through 10 discuss commercial computing systems. Chapters 11 through 13 treat high-availability systems. Chapters 14 through 17 describe spacecraft and avionics systems. Finally, Chapter 18 presents a design methodology for fault-tolerant systems and traces the use of this design process in a commercially available system.

C.VMP

C.vmp is a triplicated microprocessor system designed for realtime control environments. There are two major reasons for studying this system. First, it illustrates the process by which a simple technique (triplication) is translated into a working system. Numerous problems require solution before even simple techniques are reduced to practice. Auxiliary functions such as error status information, enabling/disabling of the redundancy, and initialization must support the technique. From the detailed C.vmp implementation the reader may be able to extrapolate the higher-level descriptions of more complex systems into plausible implementations. Space does not permit a detailed discussion of every design.

The second reason for considering C.vmp is to explore the consequences of redundancy on system performance. Chapter 7 presents several methods of predicting and measuring performance.

COMMERCIAL COMPUTERS

DEC

The RAMP (Reliability, Availability, and Maintainability Program) features in the VAX-11/780 and VAX-11/750 minicomputers are representative of contemporary design. Some RAMP features are defined in the system architecture and must appear in every implementation. Other features are implementation specific. Chapter 8 compares the architecture-defined and implementation-specific RAMP features of the VAX-11/780 and VAX-11/750, and describes the typical hardware required to support system maintainability. This hardware includes registers for status, control, and error-monitor maintenance, as well as a special visibility bus for examining internal signals that are usually not accessible. Discussion of the VAX-11/750 also considers the early design trade-off studies that led to the final RAMP package.

IBM

Table II-3 presents the evolution of IBM's maintenance strategy. Techniques are listed for a representative machine from each major era. The techniques can be loosely grouped in three major categories: internal hardware error-detection circuits, diagnostics (including software and microcode), and display (such as lights, error logs, tracing). The IBM strategy has evolved from "failure recreate" to "failure capture." Prior to the S/370, IBM customer engineers attempted to recreate the failure by rerunning diagnostics, sometimes in conjunction with varying voltage and clock frequency, until the failure recurred. The system was placed in a tight programmed loop to produce a continuous failure condition for analysis. In failure capture, hardware circuits detect errors, and information about the current status of the machine state is logged for subsequent analysis.

Table II-4 lists the features in the IBM 4300 series. The hardware error-detection, error-correction, and monitoring circuits described in Table II-4 are used in the following maintenance scenario. The support processor displays a diagnostic code. A customer engineer is called to the site and examines the error information on the system diskette, executes diagnostics from the system diskette, and uses the support processor to monitor results. For additional information the customer engineer can telephone a central data base (called RETAIN) for the latest service aids and failure data from other sites. A Field Technical Support Center specialist can use the telephone link to monitor remotely and/or control diagnostics on the 4341.

Chapter 9 describes in detail the Reliability, Availability, and Serviceability (RAS) features of the IBM System/360–System/370. The goal is high availability with minimized impact of failures. Four stages of corrective action are identified, each with successively larger impact on users: transparent recovery, one user affected, multiple users affected, and down. The successively higher-severity stage recovery structure is common in systems with high-availability goals or in realtime data processing environments in which temporary loss of data is tolerable.

UNIVAC

Chapter 10 describes the ARM (Availability, Reliability, and Maintainability) features in the Univac 1100/60. ARM at Univac emphsizes on-line error

Table II–3. Evolution of IBM maintenance strategy.

Machine	Era	Techniques
650	Late 1950s	Six internal checkers
		Stand-alone diagnostics on punched cards
		Light and switch panel
1401	Early 1960s	20 internal checkers
		Stand-alone diagnostics
		Light and switch panel
S/360-50	Mid-1960s	75 internal checkers
		OLTEP—On-Line Test Executive Program
		Microdiagnostics
		Log fault data to main memory. EREP—Error Recording and Edit Program for outputting logged data
		Maintenance panel
370/168 Mod 3	Early 1970s	Error-detection circuits
		OLTEP
		Microdiagnostics for fault isolation
		Service processor, including trace unit—trace up to 199 fixed and 8 movable logic points over 32 machine cycles for intermittent or environmental faults
303X	Mid-1970s	Error-detection circuits
		OLTS—On-Line Functional Tests
		Console and processor microdiagnostics
		EREP
		Scope loops
		Support processor, including trace and remote (telephone) access to log data and trace information
4341	Late 1970s	Error-detection circuits
		25,000 shadow latches
		Support processor—error logging and environmental monitoring

Table II—4.   IBM 4300 series RAS (Reliability, Availability, Serviceability).

Error-detection/correction circuits
  - Single-bit error correction/double-bit error detection in main memory
  - Data-path parity
  - Store-and-fetch memory access protection
  - Instruction retry (4341 only). On an error, processor performs a retry and, if
    successful, loads the machine check interrupt. Options include hardstop on error,
    no retry (but logout), disable error report, and stop after logout. During
    instruction execution, data in certain machine facilities is saved. Prior to
    instruction re-execution this data is restored.
  - Disk error correction
  - I/O retry at both processor and disk controller level
  - Peripheral unit power-off signal (4341 only)
  - Disk self-test
  - Voltage margin under program control
  - Relocatable control storage
  - Level Sensitive Scan Design (LSSD)
  - Microdiagnostic location to Field Replaceable Unit 80 percent of time
  - Halt or trace on address or data match comparisons can be made on any reference,
    I/O reference, data store, or instruction fetch

Support Processor
  - Separately powered
  - Separate system diskette for microcde loading, system error logging, and storage of
    microdiagnostics
  - Sensors for monitoring power variances, temperature fluctuations, and electrostatic
    discharge (4341 only)
  - For both retriable and unretriable errors, the support processor performs an internal
    logout. Each logout has an identifer that specifies the number of logouts to date.
  - Support-processor-generated eight digit reference code guide to failing unit.
    Reference code logged on diskette and display console.
  - Display console and data link functions for Remote Support Facility (RSF)

Remote support facility
  - Remote monitoring (especially of error registers) and control
  - Remote initiation of diagnostics
  - Remote examination of error log on system diskette
  - Distribute microcode updates

detection. As Table II-5 indicates, parity on multibit logic and duplication of random logic are primary error-detection techniques employed in the 1100/60. Based upon the assumption that most errors are transients, recovery consists primarily of retry (Table II-6). Instead of attempting a number of retries immediately after an error is detected, the 1100/60 pauses so that the source of a transient (such as power supply instability) dies out. The pause can be from five milliseconds to five seconds in one-millisecond increments. The pause value is set to cope with site-dependent conditions. Hard failures are tolerated in main memory through ECC, in cache through performance degradation, and in the control store by inverting the bits in the microinstruction, if required for a bit to match a stuck-at value.

An integral part of the 1100/60 ARM philosophy is the System Support Processor (SSP). The SSP combines many features of the IBM 4341 Support Processor and the VAX-11/780 Console Processor. With the advent of low-cost microprocessors, it became cost effective to concentrate in a support processor the functionality traditionally provided by front console switches and maintenance panels. Once the basic functionality was provided for system control, expansion to ARM functionality followed naturally. A support processor typically consists of a 50K–100K instruction-per-second processor, a small amount of nonvolatile ROM (such as 4K words), RAM (up to 256K words), secondary storage (floppy disk), remote access port, and interfaces to buses and control signals internal to the CPU. Table II-7 lists some of the functionality associated with support processors [Kunshier and Mueller, 1980].

Table II–5. Error-detection hardware in the UNIVAC 1100/60.

Memory
    Double-error-detecting code on memory data
    Parity on address and control information
Cache
    Parity on data, address, and control information
I/O Unit
    Parity on data and control
CPU
    Parity on data paths
    Parity on control store
    Duplication and comparison of control logic

Table II–6. Error recovery in the UNIVAC 1100/60.

Memory
    Single-error-correction code on data
    Retry on address or control information parity error
Cache
    Retry on address or control information parity error
    Disable portions of cache on data parity errors
I/O unit
    Retry on data or control parity errors
CPU
    Retry on control store parity error
    Invert sense of control store
    Macroinstruction retry

Table II–7.   Uses of support processors.

- System console
- System boot
- System quick test of boot path
- Error logger
- Diagnostic tool
    - Microdiagnostics
    - Scan/set/compare internal state
    - Fault injection
    - Remote diagnosis
- Error recovery
    - Writable control store reload
    - Transplant state to another processor
    - Reconfiguration

HIGH-AVAILABILITY SYSTEMS

Tandem

Tandem Computers, Inc., was founded in 1976 for the purpose of building high-availability computer systems for commercial transaction processing. The Tandem 16, discussed in Chapter 11, is the first commercially available, modularly expandable system designed specifically for high availability. Design objectives for the system included:

- "Nonstop" operation wherein failures are detected, components reconfigured out of service, and repaired components configured back into the system without stopping the other system components.
- No single hardware failure can compromise data integrity of the system.
- Modular system expansion through adding more processing power, memory, and peripherals without impacting applications software.

Tandem is composed of up to 16 computers interconnected by two message-oriented Dynabuses. A loosely coupled architecture was selected instead of a tightly coupled, shared-memory architecture because it was felt that the former allowed for more complete fault containment. Built-in hardware includes:

- Checksums on Dynabus messages
- Parity on data paths
- Error-correcting-code memory
- Watchdog timers

All I/O device controllers are dual ported for access by an alternate path in case of processor or I/O failure. Upon this hardware structure the software builds a process-oriented system with all communications handled as messages. This abstraction allows the blurring of the physical boundaries between processors and peripherals. Any I/O device or resource in the system can be accessed by a process, no matter where the resource and process reside.

Data integrity is maintained through the mechanisms of I/O "process-pairs": one I/O process is designated as primary, the other as backup. All file modification messages are delivered to the primary I/O process. The primary sends a message with checkpoint information to the backup so that it can take over if the primary's processor or access path to the I/O device fails. Files can also be duplicated on physically distinct devices controlled by an I/O process-pair on physically distinct processors. All file modification messages are delivered to both I/O processes. Thus, in the event of physical failure or isolation of the primary, the backup file is up-to-date and available.

User applications can also use the process-pair mechanism. Consider a nonstop application program, A, in Figure II-1. A starts a backup process, $A1$, in another processor. There are also duplicate file images, one designated primary and the other backup. Program A periodically (at user-specified points) sends checkpoint information to $A1$. $A1$ is the same program as A but knows that it is a backup program. $A1$ reads checkpoint messages to update its data area, file status, and program counter. $A1$ loads and executes if the system reports that A's processor is down (error messages sent from A's operating system image or A's processor fails to respond to a periodic "I'm alive" message). All file activity by A is performed on both the primary and backup file copies. When $A1$ starts to execute from the last checkpoint, it may attempt to repeat I/O operations successfully completed by A. The system file handler will recognize this and send $A1$ a successfully completed I/O message. A periodically asks the operating system if a backup process exists. Since one no longer does, it can request the

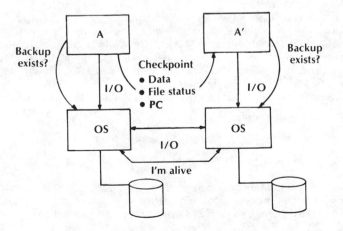

Figure II–1.   Shadow processor in Tandem.

creation and initialization of a copy of both the process and file structure. More information on the operating system and the programming of nonstop applications can be found in Bartlett [1978].

Networking software exists that allows interconnection of up to 255 geographically dispersed Tandem systems. Tandem applications include order entry, hospital records, bank transactions, and library transactions.

ESS Processors

The Electronic Switching Systems (ESS) developed by Bell Laboratories over the last two decades are the most numerous fault-tolerant digital systems. They are discussed in Chapter 12. The ESSs handle routing of telephone calls through central offices. They have an aggressive availability goal: two hours down time in 40 years (three minutes per year).

Telephone switching has many properties in common with the Pluribus (see Chapter 13) ARPAnet IMP application's realtime routing of information. There is some natural redundancy in the network and in the data; that is, telephone users will redial if they get a wrong number or are disconnected. However, there is a user aggravation level that must be avoided: users will redial so long as errors do not happen too frequently. User aggravation thresholds are different for failure to establish a call (moderately high) and disconnection of an established call (very low). Thus an ESS follows a staged failure recovery process, presented in Table II-8.

A substantial portion of the complexity of an ESS system is in the peripheral hardware. Because the telephone-switching application results in a substantially different organization from that of general-purpose computers, the following extract is included to describe briefly the hardware of the No. 4 ESS system.*

> Figure II-2 contains an overall system diagram of a No. 4 ESS office, broken down by major functional blocks. Essentially it consists of a digital time division network which switches digitally encoded 4-wire long distance telephone traffic. This is controlled by a stored program processor abetted by a group of autonomous signalling units (signal processors and terminals). The major functional blocks of Figure II-2 can be further segregated into four major areas: 1A processor, network, signal processors, and transmission interface.
>
> Each area is reviewed below with a brief functional description of its component subsystems.

1A Processor

- Central Control (CC): Main processor performing logic and data manipulation associated with calling processing, administrative tasks, and a recovery task.
- Program Store (PS): Memory complex storing executable instructions.

* J. J. Kulzer, "Systems Reliability: A Case Study of No. 4 ESS," in *System Security and Reliability, Infotech State of the Art Report*, Maidenhead, England, 1977, pp. 186–188.

Table II–8.   Levels of recovery in an ESS system.

Phase	Recovery Action	Effect
1	Initialize specific transient memory.	Temporary storage affected. No calls lost.
2	Reconfigure peripheral hardware. Initialize all transient memory.	Lose calls being established. Calls in progress not lost.
3	Verify memory operation, establish a workable processor configuration, verify program, configure peripheral hardware, initialize all transient memory.	Lose calls being established. Calls in progress not affected.
4	Established a workable processor configuration, configure peripheral hardware, initialize all memory.	All calls lost.

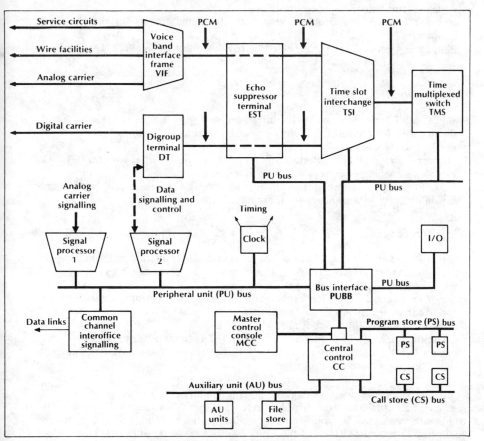

Figure II–2.   No. 4 ESS system diagram.

- Call Store (CS): Memory complex storing transient information related to the processing of telephone calls as well as data describing office equipment and routing (referred to as translations).
- File Store (FS): Disk System used to store backup program copies, seldom used maintenance programs, and other miscellaneous types of data.
- Auxiliary Units (AU): Additional units used to reference magnetic tape storage media which retain basic restart programs, new input data and support maintenance. Also possible future use for data link features.
- Input/Output (I/O): Interface hardware used to reference input and output terminal devices.
- Bus Systems (AU, PS, CS, PU): Bus systems used to interconnect the various functional units with the Central Control.
- Master Control Console (MCC): Control and display console to permit limited manual control of system and provide performance information.

Network

- Time Slot Interchange (TSI): First and fourth stage of the 4-stage time-shared switching network. Performs time division portion of the time-space-time switching function (described in later paragraphs).
- Time Multiplexed Switch (TMS): Provides second and third stage of 4-stage switching (time-shared space portion).
- Network Clock (NC): Provides very accurate timing signals for the switching network.
- Peripheral Unit Bus Interface (PUBI): Provides interface between 1A processor and the peripheral units.

Transmission Interface

- Voiceband Interface Frame (VIF): Interfaces analogue transmission facilities with the network for converting analogue voiceband channels into digitally encoded Pulse-Code Modulated (PCM) signals.
- Digroup Terminal (DT): Interface digital transmission facilities with the network. Provides signalling interfaces with these facilities.
- Echo Suppressor Terminal (EST): Provides digital 4-wire Echo Suppression capability for long distance trunks, both analogue and digital.

Signal Processors

- Signal Processor 1 (SP1): Provides scanning and signal distributing functions for analogue carrier, metallic trunk, and service circuits. Also can provide miscellaneous control points for other peripheral units.
- Signal Processor 2 (SP2): Performs scanning and signal distributing functions for digital carrier trunks terminated on DTs. Can also provide miscellaneous scan and signal distribution functions similar to the SP1.
- Common Channel Interoffice Signalling (CCIS) Terminal: Terminates the Interoffice CCIS data links serving as the interface between these data links and the signal processors and 1A Processor.

Briefly, No. 4 ESS operates in the following manner. Various types of transmission channels, analogue and digital carriers, and both 2-wire and 4-wire metallic trunks are connected to voice-frequency terminal units. The 4-wire outputs are connected to subunits (VIUs) of the Voice band Interface Unit (VIF). These VIUs sample, multiplex, and digitally encode analogue signals in one direction, reversing the process for the other. The digital output, a 128 time-slot digital bus, carries 8-bit Pulse Code Modulated (PCM) signals in each time slot to the Time Slot Interchange (TSI). The TSI, among other functions, provides a stage of switching PCM signals to different time slots on the bus. The output of the TSI goes to the Time Multiplexed Switch (TMS), which permits switching of the PCM signals during a particular time slot from any bus to any other. The output of the TMS goes to the TSI where PCM signals may be interchanged to another time slot and back to a VIU for reconversion to analogue space-divided signals. The VIU does no switching. A similar scenario exists for digital lines (T1 carrier) which terminate on subunits of the Digroup Terminals, called DTUs. However, the DTU also handles synchronization and signal extraction/insertion for these facilities, eliminating any need for conventional scan and signal distribute interfaces to channel banks in the transmission area.

Four-wire echo suppression can be provided optionally by the Echo Suppressor.

The EST has subunits, ESUs which reside on the digital bus between the VIF/DT and the TSI. These subunits process the digital PCM signals passing in both directions of each 4-wire trunk and digitally suppress detected echos. Coordinated timing for all of the above functions is critical and is provided by the network clock. The wired logic Signal Processor (SP) is used to provide scanning and signal distribution functions relieving the central processor of any need to perform these duties. Similar functions are provided for digital trunks by the SP2. The Common Channel Interoffice Signaling (CCIS) terminal provides a separate data link for signalling as an alternative to in-band signalling over trunk facilities. The separate signalling system handles digital signals in a special format over a 2-way data channel between switching machines. This system handles both supervisory and address signals for a group of trunks. The CCIS terminal interfaces to the system processor over the peripheral bus.

The entire complement of peripheral hardware described above is controlled by the 1A Processor using parallel AC-coupled buses. The processor interfaces with the periphery through the Peripheral Unit Bus Interface and has been designed to be separable for use in other applications such as No. 1A ESS.

The 1A Processor provides overall system control, administration, and call processing support. Complete self-contained system maintenance is also provided through the 1A Processor. Elements of this include automatic isolation of faulty units, defensive software strategies, and system supported rapid repair.

Chapter 12 sketches the evolution of ESS processors, summarized in Table II-9.

Pluribus

Pluribus was conceived as a modular, highly available multiprocessor for the ARPAnet task. Chapter 13 describes the architecture as well as the fault-tolerant techniques employed.

Most of the Pluribus fault tolerance is achieved at the software task level. A relatively long period between fault occurrence and fault detection was acceptable because of the nature of the IMP task. The several levels of protocol in the ARPAnet, each with its own error detection and recovery, relieve the Pluribus from concentrating on data integrity: if a failure occurred, all messages in progress would be buffered at other ARPAnet nodes until positively acknowledged, and eventually rerouted past the failed Pluribus. Even if the subnet

Table II–9. Summary of installed ESS systems.

System	Number of Lines	Year Intro- duced	Number Installed	Processor	Comments
ESS-1	5,000-65,000	1965	1,000	No. 1	First processor with separate control and data memories.
ESS-2	1,000-10,000	1969	500	No. 2	
ESS-1A	100,000	1976		No. 1A	Four to eight times faster than No. 1
ESS-2B	1,000-20,000	1975	500	No. 3	Combined control and data store. Microcoded, emulates No. 2.
ESS-3	500-5,000	1976		No. 3	

protocol failed to complete the message transmission reliably, the host-to-host protocol would retry the entire message transmission. Thus, the application required only that the Pluribus recover gracefully from a failure. This goal can be achieved by quick system reinitialization with omission of questionable components.

The Pluribus IMP (Interface Message Processor) software utilizes:

· Periodic software checks including diagnostics
· Redundancy in data structures
· Watchdog timers that must constantly be reset by software

The multiprocessor structure allows for maximum performance when there are no failures (that is, the periodic checks are estimated to degrade performance by only 1 percent) and maximum assistance when there are failures (by focusing all resources on reaching a consensus on a failure-free configuration).

The network structure allows for remote diagnostics from the Network Control Center (NCC). Even in the case of total destruction of memory contents, the Pluribus can request the code be transmitted from the NCC or other Pluribuses in the network. Any transitory messages lost will be restored via the retransmission mechanism in the various levels of protocol.

It is well known that the best system diagnostic is the normal execution of programs. Frequently, normal execution will stress the system in ways not reproduced by diagnostics (especially for I/O or timing sensitive problems). The "friendly" environment provided by the IMP application allows the Pluribus to rotate hardware into use. Any problematic hardware will appear as only a transient to the system because the offender will be quickly configured out.

The Pluribus represents a cost effective fault-tolerant architecture that takes fullest advantage of the characteristics of its application environment (realtime applications in which data loss and brief outages are tolerable). The Pluribus is operational in the ARPAnet and has achieved a measured factor improvement of five in unavailability (0.32 percent) over the previous generation IMPs (1.64 percent) [Kleinrock and Naylor, 1974].

SPACECRAFT AND AVIONIC SYSTEMS

Spacecraft are the primary example of systems requiring long periods of unattended operation. Unlike most other applications, spacecraft must control their environment (such as electrical power, temperature, and stability) directly. Thus one must treat all aspects of a spacecraft (e.g., structural, propulsion, power, analog, and digital) when designing for reliability.

Spacecraft missions range from simple (such as weather satellites in low earth orbit) to sophisticated (such as deep-space planetary probes through uncharted environments). Within this range are low earth-orbit sensing, low earth-orbit communication or navigation, low earth-orbit scientific, synchronous orbit communication, and deep-space scientific.

A typical spacecraft can be divided into five subsystems:

Propulsion. The propulsion system controls the stability and orientation of the spacecraft. Multiple, often redundant, chemical or pressurized-gas thrusters are most frequently used. Occasionally spacecraft employ a spin for stability instead of the active control provided by thrusters.

Power. The generation and storage of electrical energy must be closely monitored and controlled because all other spacecraft systems operate on electricity. Most often, spacecraft electrical systems consist of solar cells and battery storage. The batteries carry the system through loss of sun or loss of orientation periods. Control of solar cell orientation, battery charging, power transients, and temperature is the most time-consuming task for the spacecraft computers.

Data Communications. Data communications are divided into three, often physically distinct, channels. The first is commands from the ground to the spacecraft via the uplink. It is even possible to reprogram a spacecraft computer by means of the uplink. The other two channels are from the spacecraft to the ground (downlinks). One downlink carries data from the satellite payload; the second carries telemetry data about the spacecraft subsystems (temperature, power supply state, thruster events).

Attitude Control. A dedicated computer is often used to sense and control the orientation and stability of the spacecraft.

Command/Control/Payload. All aspects of spacecraft control are usually centered in a single command/control computer. This computer is also the focus for recovery from error events. Recovery may be automatic or controlled from the ground via uplink commands.

Typically, each subsystem is composed of a string of elements. As an example, Table II-10 lists seven stages in a representative power subsystem. Solar panels are physically oriented by tracking motors. Power is delivered to the spacecraft via slip rings. A charge controller automatically keeps the batteries at full potential. A power regulator smooths out voltage fluctuations while a power distributor controls the load connected to the power subsystems. At each stage, redundancy is used to tolerate anticipated fault modes. To reduce complexity, usually only the output of a string is reported via telemetry.

A typical maintenance procedure would be as follows. When a failure has been detected, the spacecraft automatically enters a "safe" or "hold" mode. All nonessential loads on the power subsystem are shed. Normal mission sequencing and solar array tracking are stopped. The spacecraft is oriented to obtain maximum solar power. Meanwhile, ground personnel must infer which failures could cause the output behavior of each of the strings. A possible failure scenario is selected as most likely and a reconfiguration (termed a "work-around") of the spacecraft subsystems devised. A command sequence implementing the work-around is sent to the satellite. Depending on the severity of the failure, this procedure may take days, or even weeks, to complete.

Spacecraft fault responses vary from automatic in hardware for critical faults (such as power, clocks, and computer), to on-board software for serious faults (such as attitude and command subsystems), to ground intervention for noncritical faults. Faults can be detected by one of several means:

- *Self-tests.* Subsystems fail self-test, such as checksums on computer memories.
- *Cross-checking between units.* Either physical or functional redundancy may be used. When a unit is physically duplicated, one is designated as on-line and the other as monitor. The monitor checks all outputs of the on-line unit. Alternatively, there may be disjoint units capable of performing the same function. For example, there is usually a set of sensors and actuators for precision attitude control. Attitude may also be less precisely sensed by instruments with other primary functions. The less precise calculation can be used as a sanity check on the more precise units.
- *Ground-initiated special tests.* Used to diagnose and isolate failures.
- *Ground trend analysis.* Routine processing and analysis of telemetry detects long-term trends in units that degrade or wear out.

Table II-11 lists the major features of each spacecraft subsystem for RCA's Defense Meteorological Satellite Program (DMSP) and JPL's Voyager. DMSP relays weather photographs from a polar orbit. Voyager is a deep-space probe used in the Jupiter and Saturn planetary fly-bys (see Chapter 15).

Figure II-3 illustrates the interconnections of the major subsystems in the DMSP spacecraft. Standby redundancy is used in all but the sensor payload. The standby spares are cross-strapped so that either unit can be switched in to communicate with other units. This form of standby redundancy is called block redundancy because redundancy is provided at the subsystem level rather than internally to each subsystem. The C-MOS command and control computer has 52 instructions and a 4.68-microsecond Add time. There are four addressing modes: direct, indirect, indexed, and relative to the program counter. The memory is composed of 16K, 16-bit words protected by parity. Internally

Table II–10. Typical power subsystem.

Element	Tracking solar array	Solar array drive	Slip ring assembly	Charge controller	Batteries	Power regulation	Power distribution
Redundancy	Extra capacity. Series/parallel connections of individual solar cells allows for graceful degradation	Redundant drive elements and motors	Parallel rings for power transfer	Automatic monitoring and control of battery charge state	Series/parallel connections. Diode protection	Redundant spares	Automatic load shedding

Table II–11. Attributes of DMSP and Voyager spacecraft.

Spacecraft	System Characteristics	Propulsion	Power	Data Communications	Attitude Control	Command and Payload
Defense Meteorological Satellite Program (DMSP)	Meteorological 3-axis stabilized sun-synchronous, polar orbit. Mission life: 2 years	Pressurized N$_2$ and hydrazine thrusters	Sun-tracking solar array. Cd Battery 300W minimum average power	Telemetry downlink: 2 or 10 Kbps. Payload data downlink: 3 links at 1–2.7 Mbps. Uplink: 1 Kbps command or 100 Kbps. 6 antennae (1 per link)	Star, earth, and sun sensors. Four reaction wheels. Magnetic torque ring coils. Redundant processors	Command rate: 1 Kbps. Redundant, ground programmable computers, 16K 16-bit words each. Downlink data encrypted
Voyager	Planetary probe 3-axis stabilized. Mission life: 7 years	Hydrazine thrusters	3 radioactive thermal generators. 430W at Jupiter	2 downlinks. 1 uplink. 2 antennae (high gain and low gain)	Redundant sun sensors and Canopus trackers	Command rate: 16 bps. Redundant computers, 4K words each. Data storage on board

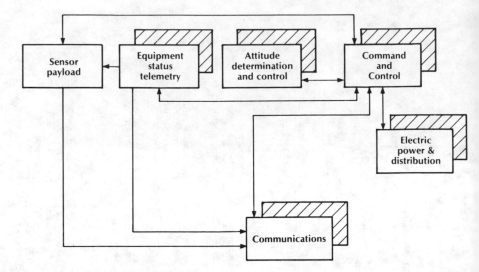

Figure II–3. Interconnection of major subsystems in RCA's Defense Meteorological Satellite Program (DMSP) block 5D-1 spacecraft.

detected error conditions include memory parity, memory address, arithmetic overflow, and illegal transfer. DMSP uses block redundancy, cross-checking on attitude control, routine self-testing, automatic load shedding upon undervoltage detection, and block switching under ground control.

Figure II-4 displays the interconnection of subsystems on the Voyager spacecraft. Again, block redundancy is the primary fault-tolerant mechanism. The Attitude Control Subsystem (ACS) is composed of redundant computers; one is an unpowered standby spare. The Command and Control Subsystem (CCS) is also a redundant computer, but the standby is powered and monitors the on-line unit. Cross-strapping and switching allow reconfiguration around failed components. The CCS executes self-testing routines prior to issuing commands to other subsystems. Tables II-12, II-13 list the error detection mechanisms in the Voyager Attitude Control and Command/Control Subsystems. Memory is only 4K words. The tape recorders are used for storage of scientific data only. New programs for memory must be loaded from the ground.

A list of typical redundancy techniques used in contemporary spacecraft is:

- Propulsion
  Redundant thrusters
  Multiple valves for propellant flow control
  Automatic switchover based on excessive attitude change rates
  Multiple commands required to initiate any firing sequence
- Power
  Redundant solar cell strings, batteries, power buses
  Automatic load shedding

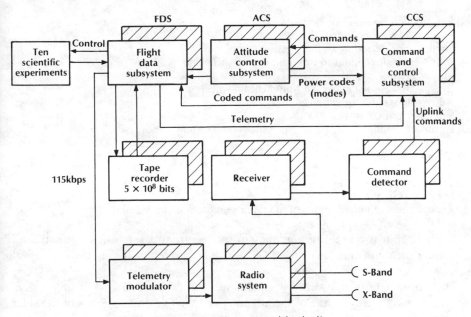

Figure II–4. Voyager system block diagram.

Table II–12. Error detection in Voyager attitude control subsystem.

- CCS fails to receive "I'm healthy" report every 2 seconds
- Loss of celestial (sun and Canopus) reference
- Power supply failure
- Fail to rewrite memory every 10 hours
- Spacecraft takes longer to turn than expected (thruster failure)
- Gyro failure
- Parity error on commands from CCS
- Command sequence incorrect
- Failure to respond to command from CCS

Table II–13. Error detection in Voyager command and control subsystem.

Hardware
- Low Voltage
- Primary command received before previous one processed
- Attempt to write into protected memory without override
- Processor sequencer reached an illegal state

Software
- Primary output unit unavailable for more than 14 seconds
- Self-test routine not successfully completed
- Output buffer overflow

- Data communications
   Redundant transponders
   Digital error detection and correction techniques
   Switch from directional to omni antennae for backup
- Attitude control
   Redundant sensors, gyros, and momentum wheels
   Automatic star reacquisition modes
- Command and control
   Hardware testing of parity, illegal instructions, memory addresses
   Sanity checks
   Memory checksums
   Task completion timed
   Watchdog timers
   Memory write protection
   Reassemble and reload memory to map around the memory failures

Table II-14 lists typical redundancy in spacecraft subsystems as a function of mission. For nondemanding missions, reduced complexity of design is a way of meeting system reliability goals.

The Voyager missions were lower-cost substitutes for a Grand Tour mission, which was to take advantage of the alignment of the five outer planets of the solar system. In support of the grand tour mission, the Jet Propulsion Laboratory (JPL) designed and breadboarded a Self-Test And Repair (STAR) computer. Chapter 14 presents the architecture of this unique computer. STAR primarily used hardware-subsystem fault-tolerant techniques, such as functional unit redundancy, voting, power-spare switching, coding, and self-checks. Task-level rollback was also incorporated in the design, which represented the most advanced fault-tolerant techniques in the 1960's decade.

Another fault-tolerant uniprocessor designed as a satellite computer is the Fault Tolerant Spaceborne Computer (FTSC) [FTSC, 1976]. FTSC is a 32-bit, general-purpose computer with a 60K-word memory and five-microsecond average instruction execution time. Error-detection/correction codes and bit-sliced sparing are extensively used to tolerate failures.

With the advent of microprocessors, emphasis has shifted to multiple-computer spacecraft. The Fault Tolerant Building Block Computer (FTBBC) is an experimental set of VLSI chips that allow construction of reliable multiprocessors with standard microprocessor and memory LSI chips. The new chips provide ECC circuitry for memory and duplication/comparison for processors [Rennels, 1980].

FTMP and SIFT

SIFT (Software Implemented Fault Tolerance), designed by SRI International (see Chapter 16), and FTMP (Fault Tolerant Multiprocessor), designed by C. S. Draper Labs (see Chapter 17), are intended for realtime control of aircraft. Due to concerns about fuel efficiency and performance, aircraft in the future will be dynamically unstable, and loss of computer control for even a few milliseconds could lead to disaster. Thus, these experimental systems are designed for a failure

Table II-14. Typical redundancy in spacecraft subsystems as a function of mission.

Mission Subsystem	Low Earth Orbit Sensing	Low Earth Orbit Navigation or Communication	Low Earth Orbit Scientific	Synchronous Orbit Communications	Deep Space Scientific
Propulsion		Station keeping maneuvers via ground commands → Redundant thrusters and leak detection →			Backup system; Leak detection and automatic switching
Power	Redundant batteries → Low-voltage detection and load shedding →			Overload protection; Low-voltage dropout →	Overload protection
Data communication	Redundant links →			Low-rate telemetry and commands	Redundant data and command channels; Omni antennae for backup
Attitude control	Safe hold and ground fix →			Automatic	Automatic
Command and payload		Multiple repeaters	Fault-tolerant on-board data processing	Multiple repeaters and graceful degradation	High reliability design

probability of 10^{-9} during a 10-hour mission. With this reliability goal, verification that the systems meet their design specification becomes a major problem: 10^{-10} failures per hour translates into 1.14 million operating years before failure.

REFERENCES

Bartlett [1977]; Castillo [1980]; FTSC [1976]; Keller [1976]; Kleinrock and Naylor [1974]; Kulzer [1977]; Kunshier and Mueller [1980]; Lynch, Wagner, and Schwartz [1975]; Rennels [1980]; Reynolds and Kinsberger [1975]; Yourdon [1972].

C.vmp: A Voted Multiprocessor

Daniel P. Siewiorek   Vittal Kini   Henry Mashburn
Stephen McConnel   Michael Tsao

DESIGN GOALS

A design study was initiated in the summer of 1975 to examine fault-tolerant architectures in industrial environments. Major attributes of this environment were electromagnetic noise, less knowledgeable users, and nonstop operation. From these attributes the following design goals were established.

1. *Permanent and Transient Fault Survival.* The system should have the capability to continue correct operation in the presence of a permanent hardware failure, i.e., a component or subsystem failure, and in the presence of transient errors, i.e., a component or subsystem is lost for a period of time due to the superposition of noise on the correct signal.
2. *Software Transparency to the User.* The user should not know that he is programming a fault-tolerant computer, with all fault tolerance being achieved in the hardware. This would allow the user to rely on established software libraries, increasing the reliability of the software itself.
3. *Capable of Real-Time Operation.* A fault should be detected and corrected within a short period from the time the fault actually occurs.
4. *Modular Design to Reduce Down Time.* The hardware should be able to operate without certain sections activated. Hence maintenance could be performed without having to halt the machine. Modularity includes the design of separate power distribution networks to be able to deactivate selected sections of the machine. The use of modules in the design also has the virtue of allowing the user to upgrade from a nonredundant, to a fully fault-tolerant computer, in steps.

5. *Off-the-Shelf Components.* To decrease the amount of custom-designed hardware, to be able to rely on an established software library, and to allow systematic upgrading to a fault tolerant system, the computer should primarily employ off-the-shelf components. Further, as illustrated in a companion paper [Siewiorek, et al., 1978b], advantage can be taken of the greater reliability of high production volume components.

6. *Dynamic Performance/Reliability Tradeoffs.* The fault-tolerant computer should have the capability, under operator or program control, to dynamically trade performance for reliability.

SYSTEM ARCHITECTURE

Actual System Configuration

To be consistent with the design goals of modularity and software transparency, bus level voting was selected as the major fault tolerance mechanism. (See [Siewiorek, Canepa, and Clark, 1976] for a more detailed discussion leading up to the selection of voting.) That is, voting occurs every time the processors access the bus to either send or retrieve information. There are three processor-memory pairs, each pair connected via a bus as depicted in Figure 7-1. A more precise definition of C.vmp (for Computer, Voted Multi-Processor) would therefore be: a multiprocessor system capable of fault-tolerant operation. C.vmp is in fact composed of three separate machines capable of operating in independent mode executing three separate programs. Under the control of an external event or under the control of one of the processors, C.vmp can synchronize its redundant hardware, and start executing the critical section of code.

With the voter active, the three buses are voted upon and the result of the vote is sent out. Any disagreements among the processors will, therefore, not propagate to the memories and vice versa. Since voting is a simple act of comparison, the voter is memoryless. Disagreements are caught and corrected before they have a chance to propagate. The nonredundant portion of the voter does not represent a system reliability "bottleneck," as will be shown later. However, the voter may be totally triplicated if desired. With voter triplication even the voter can have

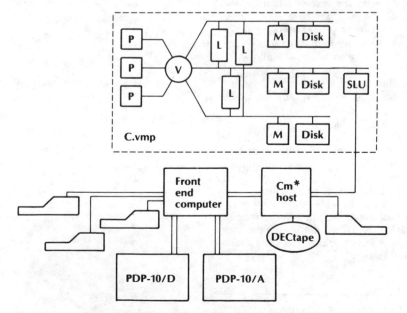

Figure 7–1. C.vmp configuration and connection to C-MU facilities.

either a transient or a hard failure and the computer will remain operational. In addition, provided that the processor is the only device capable of becoming bus master,* only one bidirectional voter is needed regardless of how much memory or how many I/O modules are on the bus. Voting is done in parallel on a bit by bit basis. A computer can have a failure on a certain bit in one bus, and, provided that the other two buses have the correct information for that bit, operation will continue. There are cases, therefore, where failures in all three buses can occur simultaneously and the computer would still be functioning correctly.

Bus level voting** works only if information passes through the voter. Usually the processor registers reside on the processor board and so do not get voted upon. The PDP-11, for example, has six general purpose registers, one stack pointer, and one program counter. However, after tracing over 5.3 million instructions over 41 programs written by five different programmers and using five different compilers, the following average program behavior was discovered [Lunde, 1977]:

1. On the average a register gets loaded or stored to memory every 24 instructions.
2. A subroutine call is executed, on the average, every 40 instructions, thus saving the program counter on the stack.
3. The only register that normally is not saved or

written into is the stack pointer. To maintain fault tolerance the system must periodically save and reload the pointer.

Thus normal program behavior can be counted on to keep the registers circulating through the voter.

To present a detailed description of the voter, a brief digression to explain the DEC LSI-11 Qbus is necessary [DEC 1975b]. The 36-signal bus uses a hybrid of synchronous and asynchronous protocols.

Every bus cycle begins synchronously with the processor placing an address on the time multiplexed Data/Address Lines (DAL).

1. SYNC goes high and all the devices on the bus latch the address from the DAL lines. The address is then removed by the processor. This terminates the synchronous portion of the bus cycle.
2. In the event of an input cycle (DATI shown in Figure 7-2) the processor activates DIN on the bus.
3. The addressed slave responds by placing a data word on the DAL lines and asserting REPLY.
4. The processor latches the data word and terminates DIN and SYNC.
5. In the event of an output cycle (DATO), after removing the address the processor places a data word on the bus and activates DOUT.
6. When the slave device has read the word it activates REPLY.
7. The processor responds by terminating DOUT and SYNC.

* Note that this restriction prohibits the use of Direct Memory Access (DMA) devices. If such devices were only allowed to communicate with the processors and the memory (not other I/O devices), a second voter between the memory and the I/O devices on the bus would be sufficient to retain fault tolerance.

** This bus level voting scheme can be contrasted with the Draper Laboratory Symmetric Fault Tolerant Multiprocessor [Hopkins and Smith, 1975] (see also Chapter 17). In SFTMP, memory and processor triads are interconnected by a triplicated serial bus. Program tasks are read from a memory triad into local memory in a processor triad where execution takes place. After execution the results are transferred back to memory triads. The major architectural differences from C.vmp are as follows. Serial bus rather than parallel bus, thus degrading performance. Voting only

takes place on transfers from and to memory triads. Errors in the processors may accumulate to the point that their results are not comparable. Programmer has to partition problems into tasks and provide for transfer to processor triads. SFTMP has up to 14 processors that can be dynamically assigned to four triads (two are spares). When a processor fails it can be replaced in its triad by another processor. However, processors cannot operate independently of triads to improve throughput. Another voting design is described by Wakerly, [1976]. The described system is based on an Intel 8080 microprocessor and has an output address and data bus and an input (from memory to processor) data bus. The major difference from C.vmp is that only a unidirectional voter is employed, on the input data bus. Thus only information flow from memory to processor is voted upon. There is no consideration of I/O, apart from an assertion that each I/O device on the bus requires a separate voter.

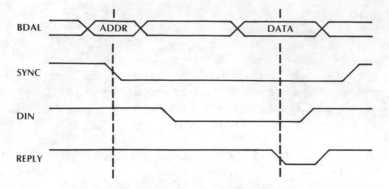

Figure 7–2. DATI cycle for LSI-11 computer.

Voter Modes of Operation

The multiplexed paths through the voter are shown in Figure 7-3. Figure 7-3a shows the case for the (unidirectional) control lines. Signals generated by the processor are routed from bus receivers to multiplexers which allow either signals from all three buses, or signals only from bus A, to pass to the voting circuit. The output of the voting circuit always feeds a bus driver on external bus A, but is multiplexed with the initially received signals on buses B and C. This arrangement allows all three processor signals to be voted on and sent to all three external buses; the signal from only processor A to be "broadcast" to all three external buses; and the independent processor signals to be sent to the separate external buses, albeit with extra delay on bus A.

1. *Voting Mode.* The transmitting portion of each of the three buses is routed into the voter, and the result of the vote is then routed out to the receiving portion of all three buses. In addition to the voting elements the voter has a set of disagreement detectors. These detectors, one for each bus, activate whenever that bus has "lost" a vote. By monitoring these disagreement detectors, one can learn about the kinds of failures the machine is having.

2. *Broadcast Mode.* Only the transmitting portion of bus A is sampled, and its contents are broadcast to the receiving portions of all three buses. This mode of operation allows selective triplication and nontriplication of I/O devices, depending on the particular requirements of the user. The voter has no idea which devices are triplicated and which are not. The only requirement is that all nontriplicated devices be placed on bus A. To handle nontriplicated devices two extra lines are added to bus A. One is a special copy of REPLY for use by nontriplicated devices instead of the standard bus A REPLY, and the other is a special copy of the Interrupt ReQuest Line (IRQ).

3. *Independent Mode.* Buses B and C are routed around the voting hardware. Bus A is routed to feed its signals to all three inputs of the voting elements. In this mode C.vmp is a loosely coupled mulitprocessor. Switching between independent and voting modes allows the user to perform a performance/reliability tradeoff.

The unidirectional control signals generated by devices on the external buses are handled the same way as processor signals, except that the direction (external-processor) has been changed.

Figure 7-3b shows the more complex case of the bidirectional data/address lines. Two sets of

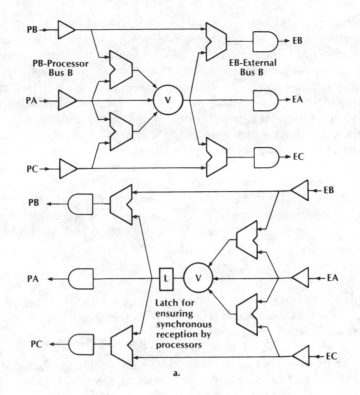

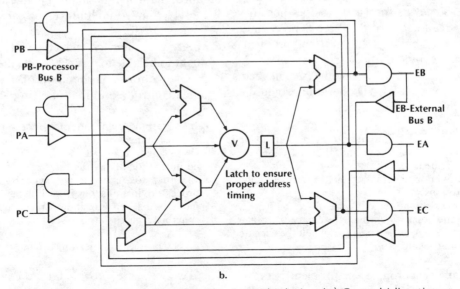

Figure 7–3. a.) C.vmp unidirectional voter multiplexing. b.) C.vmp bidirectional voter multiplexing.

bus transceivers replace the sets of receivers and transmitters used before, and another level of multiplexing has been added. The received signals from both sets of transceivers are fed into a set of multiplexers that choose which direction the signals are flowing. After passing through the set of multiplexers and the voter circuit, the voted signal goes through a latch which ensures that bus timing specifications are met. From there the signals pass onto the opposite bus from which they were initially received. (Note that the drivers on the receiving bus are disabled to avoid both sinking and sourcing the same signal.)

Peripheral Devices

In most cases, triplicating a device just means plugging standard boards into the backplane, as is the case with memory. In some cases, however, the solution is not quite so simple. An example of a device that has to be somewhat modified is the RX01 floppy disk drive. The three floppies run asynchronously. Therefore, there can be as much as a 360-degree phase difference in the diskettes. Since the information does not arrive under the read heads of the three floppies simultaneously, the obvious solution to this problem is to construct a buffer whose size is large enough to accommodate the size of the sectors being transferred. A disk READ operation would then occur as follows [DEC 1975c]:

1. The track and sector number to be read are loaded into the three interfaces and the "READ" command is issued.
2. The three floppies load their respective buffers asynchronously.
3. The processors wait until the three buffers are loaded and then synchronously empty the buffers into memory. A write operation would be executed in a similar fashion.

The main synchronization problem is to find out when all three floppies have completed their task or when one of the floppies is so out of

specification that it can be considered failed. Once this is determined the "DONE" signals are transmitted to the three buses simultaneously.

When in independent mode, the three processors must be able to commmunicate to each other. For this reason there are three full duplex single word transfer fully interlocked parallel interfaces in the system (labeled L in Figure 7-1). These interfaces provide data transfer between the separate processors (in independent mode) at rates up to 180K bytes per second [DEC 1975b]. These interfaces are used for software synchronization of the processors prior to reestablishment of voting mode, in addition to straight data transfers.

ISSUES OF PROCESSOR SYNCHRONIZATION

Dynamic Voting Control

A major goal in the design of C.vmp was to allow dynamic tradeoff between reliability and performance. Ideally, when reliabilty is of less importance, the machine should be able to split into a loosely coupled multiprocessor capable of much greater performance. Conversely, when reliability becomes crucial, the three processors ought to be able to resynchronize themselves and resume voting. Consideration of dynamic voting mode control led to the following features.

- In transiting from voting to independent mode, a simple change in the multiplexing control signals causes the next instruction to be fetched and executed independently by the three processors;
- In order to insure proper synchronization of all processors in transiting from independent to voting mode, a delayed transition forces an interrupt, presumably after each processor has had ample time to execute a "WAIT" instruction. ("WAIT" halts the processor until an interrupt occurs.)

Two bits are provided in the voter control register for voter mode control. The first, a read-only bit, monitors the state, returning "0" if voting, and "1" if not. The other, a read/write bit, chooses the desired mode. Each processor has a copy of the voter control register, and a vote is taken on the mode control bit. This control register is accessed like any I/O device register, as a specific memory location (in this case, 167770).

Dynamic voting mode control has been demonstrated by a test program. When in voting mode, setting the appropriate bit in the control register causes the three processors to split apart and begin executing separately. To resynchronize the processors, a simple handshaking protocol is used, in which each processor waits for both of the others to signal permission before clearing the control bit. (A more sophisticated protocol would provide for a timeout if one of the processors has failed, with efforts to recover from such a situation.) After clearing its copy of the control bit, each processor releases control of its bus and ceases execution via a "WAIT" instruction. The ensuing interrupt generated by the voter then serves to resynchronize the three processors, and the first instruction of the interrupt service routine is the first instruction executed in voting (fault-tolerant) mode.

Bus Control Signal Synchronization

There are two levels of synchronization used in C.vmp to keep the three processors in step: bus signal synchronization and processor clock synchronization. The first type of synchronization deals with the bus control signals. The voter uses RPLY to synchronize the three buses, as it is asserted by an external device (memory and I/O devices) once every bus cycle. Thus processors can stay in step if they receive RPLY concurrently. A set of possible voting circuits is shown in Figure 7-4. (The boxes labeled V are voters, and the boxes labeled T are delays.) The first voter is the one used for the data/address lines. The other voters attempt to maintain synchroni-

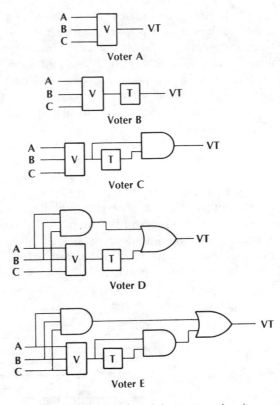

Figure 7–4.   Synchronizing voter circuits.

zation of five critical control lines (SYNC, DIN, DOUT, IAK, and RPLY)* by waiting an appropriate period of time for a lagging control signal. (The delay is not only selected long enough that a lagging device is far enough out of specification to be suspect, but also short enough not to degrade performance severely. For maintaining processor synchronization, a value for T of at least one microcycle—400 ns—is desirable, as processors are most likely to slip just one microcycle in the five to ten microcycles between bus cycles rather than to become several microcycles out of synchronization.)

---

* SYNC is used to clock the address lines, and is left asserted for the remainder of the bus cycle; DIN indicates a read cycle; DOUT indicates a write cycle; IAK is used to acknowledge receipt of an interrupt request; and RPLY is asserted to indicate that the device has responded to the request indicated by the previous four signals.

The first circuit considered for synchronizing the five control lines was voter A in Figure 7-4. This was rejected because it provides no synchronization at all: if a signal fails high, the voter passes the first of the other two to be asserted without regard to the second. Thus, if the two remaining processors get at all out of step, the voting process fails.

The second circuit, voter B in Figure 7-4, provides a measure of synchronization by waiting a time T for the third signal after two have been asserted. However, performance is degraded because this delay occurs even when all three processors are working and synchronized. Also, control signals will continue to be asserted after they should be in relation to the data on the bus, failing to meet bus specifications. (RPLY is asserted after DATA is invalid; see Figure 7-5.)

The third circuit, voter C in Figure 7-4, fixes the problem of meeting bus specifications by having a slow-rising, fast-falling delay after the voter. However, performance is still degraded by the presence of the delay even when all is well.

The fourth circuit, voter D in Figure 7-4, addressed the performance problem by providing a second path through the voter for when all three processors are working. However, the delay used after the voter to provide synchronization still causes the signal to fail bus specifications, and also causes some amount of unavoidable performance degradation. (RPLY is asserted after DATA is invalid; see Figure 7-5.)

The last circuit, and the one used (voter E in Figure 7-4), combines the features of the pre-

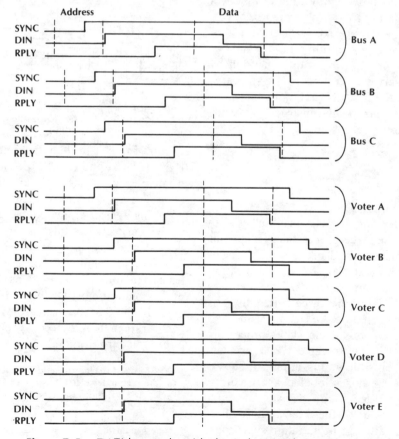

Figure 7–5. DATI bus cycle with desynchronized processors.

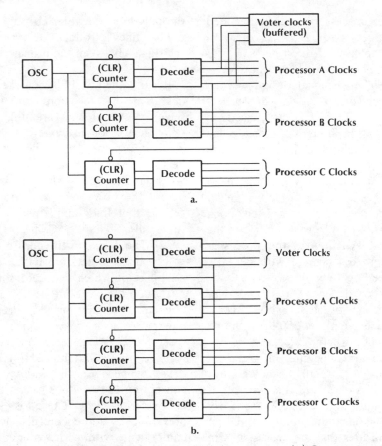

Figure 7–6. a.) Original processor clock synchronization. b.) Current processor clock synchronization.

vious two. Thus, a slow-rising, fast-falling delay is used in order to meet bus specifications; and a second path through the voter is provided for optimal performance when all is well. Note that the fast-falling feature of the delay not only allows bus specifications to be met, but also removes any performance degradation due to the voting process when all three signals are in step. This circuit was used for SYNC, DIN, DOUT, IAK, and RPLY in C.vmp. The value for T is about 400–500 ns for SYNC, DIN, DOUT, and IAK, and about 75–100 ns for RPLY. This method allows the three processors to receive RPLY within 5 ns of each other, and thus to stay synchronized.

System Clock

Perhaps the most critical timing problem encountered in the design of C.vmp was the synchronization of the four phase processor clocks, and also the memory refresh* timing oscillators. This part of the design was left untriplicated in C.vmp due to its very small size, hence high reliability, relative to the rest of the machine. The original design, shown in Figure 7-6a, used the oscillators on processor A to drive the clock

---

* Note that the LSI-11 uses dynamic MOS RAM memory, which requires continual refreshing. This is normally done by processor microcode at regular intervals of about 1.67 ms.

circuits on all three processors, and the decoded clock signals of processor A to feed the voter and to synchronize the phases of the other two processors by forcing phase one when processor A was in phase one. This original design worked fairly well, as processors B and C were closely synchronized, but the extra loading placed on the clocks of processor A caused them to lag several nanoseconds behind, a significant figure for pulses of less than 100 ns duration. This resulted in sufficient unreliability that the mean time between crashes in voting mode was never more than five minutes. Therefore, a new clock circuit, shown in Figure 7-6b, was installed in the voter to drive and synchronize the processor clocks. All three processors were wired exactly the same way, needing only three wires to be changed on each board. Since this change was made, the mean time between software discernible disagreement has been over 250 hr, with one run of more than 900 hr before crashing.

Initial measurements using the disagreement detection circuit attached to all the bus control lines showed no errors on any of the three buses over periods ranging between eight to forty hours. (Note that data/address lines were not included.) This indicates that the processors are well synchronized by the current design.

PERFORMANCE MEASUREMENTS

Processor Execution/Memory Fetch Time

An important parameter in the design of fault-tolerant computers is the amount of performance degradation suffered to obtain greater reliability. In a triplicated architecture such as C.vmp, the obvious loss of two-thirds of the available computing power is unavoidable. This was the reason why C.vmp was made flexible enough to switch between voting (fault-tolerant) mode and independent (high performance) mode. However, this fundamental loss due to triplication is not the only loss: the voter cutting and buffering all the bus lines introduces delays of 80 to 140 ns in the signals between the processors and the memories.

Because the LSI-11 is a clocked machine, these delays are not too significant in and of themselves. However, the latching of RPLY from slave devices on the external buses in order to preserve processor synchronization turns out to be the more dominant degradation factor. The voter latches RPLY one clock phase (100 ns) before the processors to allow sufficient latch settling time for minimizing the probability of a runt pulse [Chaney, Ornstein, and Littlefield, 1972]. The delays in the control lines due to the voter cause the external RPLY to return during the phase on which the processors sample RPLY but *after* the voted RPLY has already been latched. Thus, the voted processors must wait one more clock cycle (four phases/400 ns) to receive their RPLY after asserting SYNC than would a nonredundant LSI-11. The same sort of delay happens on the falling edge of RPLY, causing up to two clock cycles to be lost in one complete bus cycle. These losses could likely be prevented by more careful selection of timing components within the voter, and more important, by choosing different timing on the memory boards.

Measurements were taken on the various bus cycles to learn what amount of degradation actually was occurring. These measurements, and all others presented later, were taken on the voted processor (C.vmp) and on either processor B (PBB) or C (PCC) in independent mode. (Note that in independent mode, bus A passes through the entire voter via the broadcast multiplexing, while both buses B and C pass only through a bus receiver/driver pair. Comparison tests with other LSI-11's showed that processors B and C operated fully as fast in independent mode as a standard LSI-11.) The degradation within bus cycles introduced by the voter ranges from 27 percent to 67 percent, with 40 percent degradation for the most common (read) cycles.

Table 7–1. Normalized instruction phases.

Phase	C.vmp	PCC	C.vmp/PCC
Fetch	7.00	6.00	1.167
Source	2.69	2.09	1.287
Destination	3.68	3.22	1.143
Execution	3.53	3.53	1.000
Total	16.90	14.84	1.139
Time (μsec)	6.760	5.936	

As the LSI-11 does not saturate its bus, the above figures are worse than the overall processor degradation. A second step in measuring degradation was to check the different phases of instruction execution. Tests were made using the MOV, TST, and BR instructions* as typical double operand, single operand, and zero operand instructions. From this data, a prediction can be made of performance degradation by using instruction frequency data provided by Snow and Siewiorek [1978]. Table 7-1 summarizes the calculations, showing that the voting process should degrade instruction execution peformance by roughly 14 percent.

The third stage for measuring performance was to run a set of test programs with representative mixes of instructions and addressing modes to test the validity of the above model. Table 7-2 compares the triplicated processor with a single LSI-11, both without faults and with certain induced faults. These faults were in the two most critical bus control signals, SYNC and RPLY, and represent worst case failures. Each signal was forced to be either always asserted (hi) or never asserted (lo) on one of the three buses.

As illustrated by Table 7-2, a degradation in performance of about 16-19 percent can be expected, as compared to a standard LSI-11. This figure is somewhat larger than predicted by the

* MOV loads the destination from the source, TST examines the destination for various conditions, and BR causes an unconditional transfer of control.

above model, which can be attributed to the greater degree of degradation in such functions as memory refresh, which is done by the processor microcode (18.5 percent), and also to normal deviations of programs from the "standard" instruction mix.

The measurements involving the four failure modes show that only certain failures will cause further degradation: those which cause the processor's synchronizing signals (e.g., SYNC, DIN, and DOUT) never to be asserted. Even in these extreme cases, only another 12–14 percent slowdown is experienced. Most faults, however, would not degrade the speed at all, but just the future reliability. For instance, the loss of power to a bus would force all signals to ground, which is the active assertion level (hi) on the LSI-11 bus. Only lo failures in the five bus control signals which require synchronization will cause any degradation. (Recall that there are a total of 36 bus lines.)

Disk Access Time

The last performance measurements involved the floppy disks used for mass storage on C.vmp. Access time to a particular position on a rotating memory is assumed to be directly proportional to the initial position of the disk. Since the hardware makes no attempt to synchronize disk rotation, access to the triplicated disks will take the maximum of the three times. In general, for n disks, the access time is given by:

$$T_n = \text{MAX}\,(t_1, t_2, \ldots, t_n).$$

Assuming that each access time t is uniformly distributed over the normalized range [0, 1], the expected value for access time is:

$$T_n = n/(n + 1).$$

This means that for a single disk ($n = 1$), we can expect to wait 0.5 rotations; for the triplicated disk ($n = 3$), 0.75 rotations. This gives a 50 percent degradation in access time for the tripli-

Table 7–2. Sample Program Execution Times*

Unit	DVKAA	DZKMA	QSORT
	ms	min	s
LSI-11	18.51	7:03	11.9
C.vmp (normal)	21.4	8:23	14.0
C.vmp (RPLY hi)	21.4	8:23	14.0
C.vmp (RPLY lo)	21.4	8:23	14.0
C.vmp (SYNC hi)	21.4	8:23	14.1
C.vmp (SYNC lo)	23.6	9:20	15.6
C.vmp/LSI-11	1.157	1.189	1.176
C.vmp/LSI-11	1.324	1.276	1.311 (SYNC lo)

*DVKAA is the basic instruction diagnostic, testing all instructions and addressing modes. DZKMA is the memory diagnostic, and would tend to make more memory references than average. QSORT is an example of compiler-produced code, being an integer sorting program coded in BLISS-11.

cated disks over the nontriplicated disk for random accesses. This figure was verified to an extent by experimental data. In reading 50 sectors in a random pattern from the same physical track, the triplicated machine experienced about 51 percent degradation, a very close confirmation. However, if the track was also chosen at random for each of the 50 sectors, the triplicated machine was only 18 percent slower than the single disk system. The model failed to consider that, although sector access time is affected by the diskettes' being out of phase, track access time is the same regardless of triplication.

Another shortcoming of the disk performance model based only on consideration of the diskettes being out of phase with each other is the impact of the resulting slowdown on nonrandom disk access patterns. The impact of this can be much more severe (or much less severe) than predicted, depending on the pattern of nonrandom disk accesses. For instance, the RT-11 floppy disk software uses a 2:1 interleaving of sectors in order to minimize access time for sequential file storage.* The extra delay due to

* 2:1 interleaving means that only every other sector on a track is read when reading sectors sequentially. As some amount of time is necessary to read the data into memory after it has been fetched from the diskette, this allows all 26 sectors of a track to be read in just two revolutions rather than in 26 revolutions.

voting causes this interleaving to be insufficient for achieving much speedup in accesses, as illustrated by Figure 7-7. Waiting for all three drives to read a sector can cause the first two drives to overrun the next sector in sequence before the third drive has read the initial sector. This causes part of an additional revolution to be required on the next sector read. For the example shown, a nontriplicated disk drive requires only 0.375 revolutions to read sectors 1 and 3, while the triplicated drive needs 1.75 revolutions. The specific values depend on the number of sectors per revolution, the access pattern (and interleaving scheme), and the degree to which the three disks of the triplicated drive are out of phase.

Table 7-3 summarizes timing data collected by a program which was written to test different interleaving schemes. A number of consecutive logical sectors were read, which mapped into the same number of physical sectors in the pattern dictated by the desired interleaving. In addition, a test program was assembled under RT-11, using its 2:1 interleaving, to examine the impact of increased disk latency on typical operations. Figure 7-8 plots access time versus interleaving factor for reading 1000 sectors sequentially. The data indicate that perhaps the best sequential file access could be achieved for triplicated disks using 8:1 interleaving. The point to be made about replicated disk access time is that it is very

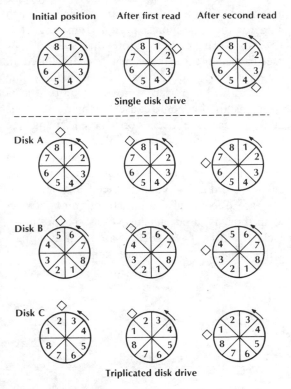

Initial position   **After first read**   **After second read**

Single disk drive

Disk A

Disk B

Disk C

Triplicated disk drive

Figure 7–7. Effects of disk triplication on sequential access (2:1 interleaving).

pattern sensitive: very little degradation due to replication occurs in sequential accesses without interleaving, but great degradation is seen when interleaving is used. Instead of the factor of ten speedup available with 2:1 interleaving on a single disk, only a factor of roughly 1.5 is possible (using 8:1 interleaving) on a triplicated disk.

OPERATIONAL EXPERIENCES

Operating History

Implementation of C.vmp has been completed, and stable performance achieved. The software is a standard, unmodified single-user diskette-based real-time operating system (RT-11). The system has been utilized under actual load conditions with students doing projects in an introductory real-time programming course. The students were supplied with an RT-11 software manual and a short paper on C.vmp specific data (i.e., location of the power switches, reminder to load three diskettes, etc.). To these users, C.vmp successfully appeared as a standard LSI-11 uniprocessor running standard software.

C.vmp System Reliability

C.vmp has repeatedly demonstrated hard-failure survival by bus power switching and board removal (see comments later about on-line maintenance). Another aspect of fault tolerance is transient-fault survival. The only transients which should cause C.vmp to crash are those occurring simultaneously in more than one module. According to the data from Cm* presented in Siewiorek, et al., [1978a], such transients make up 17 percent of the total, occurring roughly every 1,000 hr. The mean time to crash should equal or exceed this figure. Indeed, as the hardware situation has been stabilizing, C.vmp's reliability has been increasing toward this order of

Table 7–3. Disk timing tests (in seconds).

Sectors	Interleave	C.vmp	PBB	C.vmp/PBB
10	1:1	1.69	1.66	1.021
10	2:1	1.55	0.17	9.218
50	1:1	8.51	8.06	1.055
50	2:1	7.66	0.81	9.403
1,000	1:1	171.2	159.9	1.071
1,000	2:1	153.9	14.6	10.540
Assembly	2:1	109.6	15.8	6.937

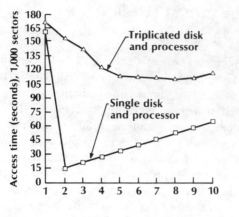

Figure 7–8. Disk access time versus interleaving factor.

magnitude. Table 7-4 summarizes C.vmp crash data for the nine-month period from August 1, 1977 to April 30, 1978. Note that software- or user-caused crashes have not been included in the data. Also, repeated crashes (ones due to the same cause) have been removed. Due to uncertainty as to the exact causes of many crashes, dual tables have been constructed giving the "best case" and "worst case" figures. Crashes which may have been software or user caused are included in the worst-case but not in the best-case data. The voter-induced transient failures are due mainly to construction. The wire-wrap boards used in the voter are prone to socket failures. These sockets are being systematically replaced, with a consequent improvement

Table 7–4. C.vmp crash data (in hours).

	Worst Case				
Month	Mean	Std. Dev.	Median	Number	Uptime
August	64.8	91.9	28.0	5	323.8
September	108.7	139.6	35.6	4	434.9
October	35.5	51.1	19.8	16	568.3
November	49.3	33.0	52.0	10	492.9
December	204.8	191.6	113.1	3	614.5
January	95.4	104.3	70.5	7	667.7
February	258.8	78.6	258.8	2	517.6
March	298.3	276.4	298.3	2	596.7
April	352.4	114.2	352.4	2	704.7
Total	96.5	167.8	30.6	51	4921.1
	Best Case				
Month	Mean	Std. Dev.	Median	Number	Uptime
August	81.0	96.1	34.6	4	323.8
September	217.4	132.4	217.4	2	434.9
October	142.1	44.5	125.7	4	568.3
November	246.5	167.3	246.5	2	492.9
December	614.5	0.0	614.5	1	614.5
January	—	—	—	0	667.7
February	517.6	0.0	517.6	1	517.6
March	—	—	—	0	596.7
April	704.7	0.0	704.7	1	704.7
Total	328.1	470.8	114.3	15	4921.1

Note: Std. Dev. is the standard deviation.

in mean time to crash (MTTC). With permanent construction techniques (e.g., printed circuit boards) the voter should be removed as a source of system crashes.

One measure of transient fault survival lies in the severity of the methods necessary for recovery. Five levels of recovery exist:

1. CONTINUE execution at the same location without any change to processor registers or memory;
2. RESTART the program in memory, which will also reset the I/O devices and processor registers;
3. RELOAD the program into memory, also resetting the I/O devices and processor registers;
4. RESET the processors and reload the program; and
5. DEBUG the hardware to whatever extent is required to restore stable operation.

Table 7-5 summarizes this data in correspondence to the entries of Table 7-4.

It is interesting to note that the majority of crashes required relatively little effort to recover from. Only a few required the processor to be actually reset, and several required only the resident monitor to be restarted. All the cases of debugging involved socket failures in the voter boards and seem to be getting less frequent.

On-Line Maintenance

The success of the voting mechanism has been established by experiments with powering down buses and removing components, while still having the system as a whole continue operating.

Table 7–5.   C.vmp crash recovery data.

	Worst Case				
Month	Continue	Restart	Reload	Reset	Debug
August	0	1	3	0	1
September	0	0	2	0	2
October	0	5	7	1	3
November	0	1	7	1	1
December	0	0	2	0	1
January	0	7	0	0	0
February	0	1	0	0	1
March	0	2	0	0	0
April	0	2	0	0	0
Total	0	19	21	2	9
	Best Case				
Month	Continue	Restart	Reload	Reset	Debug
August	0	0	3	0	1
September	0	0	0	0	2
October	0	0	1	0	3
November	0	0	0	1	1
December	0	0	0	0	1
January	0	0	0	0	0
February	0	0	0	0	1
March	0	0	0	0	0
April	0	1	0	0	0
Total	0	1	4	1	9

With a bus powered down, the associated processor and memory are, of course, lost, but the system keeps working. Defective components (if such exist) can be replaced, and the bus powered back up. Contents of the newly restored memory can be brought into agreement with the other copies by providing a read/write memory background job. Normal operation suffices to resynchronize the processor, as it starts executing code randomly until it gets in execution phase with the other two processors.

Actual experiments have included removing memory boards from one, two, or even all three buses (different 4K banks of memory from different buses). Also, a processor was removed, and the machine kept running. Even with one of the processors missing and a different 4K bank of memory removed from each bus, the machine continued in operation.

The only problem encountered with these experiments was that restoring power to a bus sometimes causes a crash. All three buses, and even the voter itself, draw power from the same +5 V supply. The transients on the power lines associated with turning on an LSI-11 processor, 12K of memory, and assorted I/O interfaces are the cause of the crashes. (These transients arise from the sudden demand for 7–10 A current for the various components on each bus.) Independent power supplies, as would be desirable in any case for a fault-tolerant computer, are necessary to correct this problem.

The ability described above to power down selective sections of C.vmp in order to remove or replace defective modules is certainly a strength of the system as regards being a highly available machine.

REFERENCES

Chaney, Ornstein, and Littlefield [1972]; DEC [1975b, 1975c]; Hopkins and Smith [1974]; Lunde [1977]; Siewiorek et al. [1978a, 1978b]; Siewiorek, Canepa, and Clark [1976]; Snow and Siewiorek [1978]; Wakerly [1976].

RAMP in the VAX Family: VAX-11/780 and VAX-11/750

The VAX-11 (Virtual Address Extension) is an expansion upon the architectural principles incorporated in the PDP-11. At the time of the inception of the VAX-11 architecture, concerns for RAMP were gaining momentum. This chapter focuses on the RAMP features in two different implementations of the VAX-11 architecture: the VAX-11/780 (ca. 1977) and VAX-11/750 (ca. 1980). This chapter discusses the VAX-11 from two viewpoints: architecture* and implementation. The first section deals with the VAX architecture and architectural-level RAMP (Reliability, Availability, and Maintainability Program) features. The next presents an archetypical implementation and describes the common RAMP implementation features, followed by two sections on the detailed RAMP features of the VAX-11/780 and VAX-11/750. A summary of the VAX-11/780 and VAX-11/750 RAMP features concludes the chapter.

THE VAX ARCHITECTURE

Compatibility between members of a computer family is essential. The need for compatibility at the architectural level is the most pronounced, but there are also substantial benefits from similarities between implementations. Similarities can reduce costs of training, documentation, and repair. The original VAX architecture paper [Strecker, 1978] reveals the enormous pressure for compatibility:

> VAX-11 is the Virtual Address extension of PDP-11 architecture [Bell et al., 1970; Bell and

---

* The term *architecture* describes the attributes of a system from the viewpoint of the programmer.

Strecker, 1976]. The most distinctive feature of VAX-11 is the extension of the virtual address from 16 bits as provided on the PDP-11 to 32 bits. With the 8-bit byte the basic addressable unit, the extension provides a virtual address space of about 4.3 gigabytes which, even given rapid improvement in memory technology, should be adequate far into the future.

Since maximal PDP-11 compatibility was a strong goal, early VAX-11 design efforts focused on literally extending the PDP-11: preserving the existing instruction formats and instruction set and fitting the virtual address extension around them. The objective here was to permit, to the extent possible, the running of existing programs in the extended virtual address environment. While realizing this objective was possible (there were three distinct designs), it was felt that the extended architecture designs were overly compromised in the areas of efficiency, functionality, and programming ease.

Consequently, it was decided to drop the constraint of the PDP-11 instruction format in designing the extended virtual address space or *native mode* of the VAX-11 architecture. However, in order to run existing PDP-11 programs, VAX-11 includes a PDP-11 *compatibility mode*. Compatibility mode provides the basic PDP-11 instruction set less only privileged instructions (such as HALT) and floating point instructions (which are optional on most PDP-11 processors and not required by most PDP-11 software).

In addition to compatibility mode, a number of other features to preserve PDP-11 investment have been provided in the VAX-11 architecture, the VAX-11 operating system VAX/VMS, and the VAX-11/780 implementation of the VAX-11 architecture. These features include:

1. The equivalent native mode data types and formats are identical to those on the PDP-11. Also, while extended, the VAX-11 native mode instruction set and addressing modes are very close to those on the PDP-11. As a consequence VAX-11 native mode assembly language programming is quite similar to PDP-11 assembly language programming.
2. The VAX-11/780 uses the same peripheral buses (Unibus and Massbus) as the PDP-11 and uses the same peripherals.
3. The VAX/VMS operating system is an evolution of the PDP-11 RSX-11M and IAS operating systems, offers a similar although extended set of system services, and uses the same command

languages. Additionally, VAX/VMS supports most of the RSX-11M/IAS system service requests issued by programs executing in compatibility mode.
4. The VAX/VMS file system supports the RSX-11M/IAS operating systems permitting interchange of files and volumes. The file access methods as implemented by the RMS record manager are also the same.
5. VAX-11 high level language compilers accept the same source languages as the equivalent PDP-11 compilers and execution of compiled programs gives the same results.

The VAX-11 architecture defines the following data types: byte, word, longword, quadword, floating, double-floating, packed decimal, character string, and bit field. In addition to the basic data manipulation and program flow control instructions, there are instructions to accelerate the performance of special operating system functions and to perform high-level language constructs. For example, the FORTRAN-computed GOTO and CALL instructions and loop control each translate into a single VAX instruction. Nine addressing modes use the 16 32-bit general registers to identify operand locations.

The architecture defines two ways to invoke execution of software outside the explicit flow of control. The first, resulting from internal events (usually related to the current instruction under execution), is called an exception. The second, resulting from external events, is called an interrupt. The VAX-11 architecture specifies three types of exceptions: aborts, faults, and traps.

Aborts are the most severe form of exception. When an instruction is aborted, the machine registers and memory may be left in an indeterminate state. Because system state is destroyed, the instruction cannot be correctly restarted, completed, simulated, or undone.

Faults, on the other hand, leave the machine registers and memory in a consistent state. Once the fault is eliminated, the instruction may be restarted and the correct results obtained. Faults

Table 8–1. Arithmetic exceptions.

Exception	Type
Integer overflow	Trap
Integer divide by zero	Trap
Floating overflow	Trap
Floating/decimal divide by zero	Trap
Floating underflow	Trap
Decimal overflow	Trap
Subscript range	Trap
Floating overflow	Fault
Floating divide by zero	Fault
Floating underflow	Fault

Table 8–2. Exception and interrupt vectors.

Name	Type	Notes
Machine check	Abort/trap	Length parameter and error-specific data pushed onto the stack, if possible.
Kernel stack not valid	Abort	No parameters
Power fail	Interrupt	No parameters
Reserved or privileged instruction	Fault	No parameters
Customer reserved instruction	Fault	No parameters
Reserved operand	Fault/abort	No parameters
Reserved addressing mode	Fault	No parameters
Access control violation	Fault	Virtual address causing the fault is pushed onto the kernel stack.
Translation not valid	Fault	Virtual address causing the fault is pushed onto the kernel stack.
Trace pending	Fault	No parameters
Breakpoint instruction	Fault	No parameters
Compatibility mode	Fault/abort	Type code pushed onto stack
Arithmetic	Trap/fault	Type code pushed onto stack
Corrected memory read data	Interrupt	No parameters
Memory write timeout	Interrupt	No parameters
Interval timer	Interrupt	No parameters
Console terminal receive	Interrupt	No parameters
Console Storage device	Interrupt	VAX-11/750 only
SBI SILO compare	Interrupt	VAX-11/780 only
SBI alert	Interrupt	VAX-11/780 only
SBI fault	Interrupt	VAX-11/780 only

restore only enough state to allow restarting. The state of the process may not be the same as before the fault occurred.

Finally, a trap occurring at the end of the instruction causing the exception. The machine registers and memory are consistent and the address of the next instruction to execute is stored on the machine stack. The process can be restarted with the same state as before the trap occurred.

Several arithmetic exceptions are architecturally defined. These exceptions deal primarily with overflow/underflow and illegal operations. Table 8-1 summarizes the arithmetic exceptions. The floating point faults differ from the traps in that the faults do not affect the destination operand.

Table 8-2 lists the defined exception and interrupt vectors. Each vector represents a unique memory location where an address is stored. The address points to the start of a software routine unique to the corresponding exception or interrupt. Exceptions may store information about their type on the system stack to help guide the software in restarting the system. Some exceptions are triggered by consistency checks and detect primarily software errors. Other exceptions are detected by hardware and represent hardware or environmentally induced errors. The next few paragraphs provide more details for the entries in Table 8-2.

The machine check is the most damaging exception. It is triggered when internal CPU error-checking circuitry detects an exceptional condition. The processor may be restartable if the exception is related to redundant logic whose sole purpose is to improve machine performance (such as an instruction cache or instruction look-ahead buffer).

The VAX-11 has four defined modes of access: Kernel, Executive, Supervisor, and User. These modes are used to grant or deny privileges, such as access to portions of memory or execution of specific instructions. An exception occurs if an access to the kernel, or most privileged stack, encounters a memory-access violation (such as no access or attempted write to a read-only page) or if the translation from virtual address to physical address is not valid.

Power failure causes an interrupt so that machine state can be saved for a clean power-up sequence.

Execution of reserved or privileged (such as improper system state) instructions triggers faults. Faults may be caused by attempted use of a reserved operand format or reserved addressing mode (that is, ill-formed instruction and addressing mode).

The VAX-11 architecture defines an extensive virtual-to-physical address translation. Associated with each memory page is a protection code. The system mode and address request must match the code, or a Translation Not Valid fault results. Table 8-3 lists the various allowable system modes and access rights.

When the Trace bit is enabled, the system faults after every instruction execution. Tracing is used for performance evaluation or debugging.

The breakpoint fault is also associated with debugging. The breakpoint instruction can be placed anywhere in the software flow and is designed to restore control to the user for examining the state of the program.

Table 8–3. Address protection.

Protection Code	System Mode			
	Kernel	Executive	Supervisor	User
0000	No	No	No	No
0001		Unpredictable		
0010	R/W	No	No	No
0011	RO	No	No	No
0100	R/W	R/W	R/W	R/W
0101	R/W	R/W	No	No
0110	R/W	RO	No	No
0111	RO	RO	No	No
1000	R/W	R/W	R/W	No
1001	R/W	R/W	RO	No
1010	R/W	RO	RO	No
1011	RO	RO	RO	No
1100	R/W	R/W	R/W	RO
1101	R/W	R/W	RO	RO
1110	R/W	RO	RO	RO
1111	RO	RO	RO	RO

Key: No—No Access
R/W—Read/write access
RO—Read only access

When executing in PDP-11 compatibility mode, errors (those defined in the PDP-11 architecture) are reported via the compatibility fault/abort.

Two interrupts report memory-related problems: an error on read-from-memory was corrected by an error-correcting code, and no memory responded to a write request (such as NonExisting Memory).

Three interrupts are specific to the VAX-11/780 and deal with the bus between processor and memory (the Synchronous Backplane Interconnect, or SBI).

In addition to exceptions, the architecture also defines several processor registers, listed in Table 8-4. Most of the registers deal with the software structure. The Translation Buffer is similar to a data cache except that it caches virtual addresses that have already been translated.

Of the architecturally defined registers, the 10 registers detailed in Table 8-5 are related to RAMP functionality. The numbers in brackets

Table 8–4. VAX architecturally defined processor registers.

Name	Type	Scope	Initialized?
Kernel Stack Pointer	R/W	Process	—
Executive Stack Pointer	R/W	Process	—
Supervisor Stack Pointer	R/W	Process	—
User Stack Pointer	R/W	Process	—
Interrupt Stack Pointer	R/W	CPU	—
P0 Base Register	R/W	Process	—
P0 Length Register	R/W	Process	—
P1 Base Register	R/W	Process	—
P1 Length Register	R/W	Process	—
System Base Register	R/W	CPU	—
System Length Register	R/W	CPU	—
Process Control Block Base	R/W	Process	—
System Control Block Base	R/W	CPU	—
Interrupt Priority Level	R/W	CPU	Yes
Asynchronous System Trap Level	R/W	Process	Yes
Software Interrupt Request	W	CPU	—
Software Interrupt Summary	R/W	CPU	Yes
Interval Clock Control	R/W	CPU	Yes
Next Interval Count	W	CPU	—
Interval Count	R	CPU	—
Time of Year	R/W	CPU	No
Console Receiver Control and Status	R/W	CPU	Yes
Console Receiver Data Buffer	R	CPU	—
Console Transmit Control and Status	R/W	CPU	Yes
Console Transmit Data Buffer	W	CPU	—
Memory Management Enable	R/W	CPU	—
Translation Buffer Invalidate All	W	CPU	—
Translation Buffer Invalidate Single	W	CPU	—
Performance Monitor Enable	R/W	Process	Yes
System Identification	R	CPU	No
Processor Status Register	R/W	Process	—

Table 8–5. Details of RAMP-related VAX architecturally defined processor registers.

Name	Subfields	Comments
Interval Counter ⟨31:0⟩		1-microsecond resolution
Next Interval Counter ⟨31:0⟩		Loaded into Interval Counter when counter overflows
Interval Clock Control and Status	Error	Second overflow occurs before first serviced
	Interrupt Request	Set on counter overflow
	Interrupt Enable Single CLK	Advances counter one step
	Transfer	Loads counter from next Interval Counter
	Run	Increments counter
Time of Year ⟨31:0⟩		
Console Subsystem Receiver Control and Status	Ready, Interrupt Enable	
Console Receiver Data Buffer	Data ⟨31:0⟩	
Console Subsystem Transmit Control and Status	Done, Interrupt Enable	
Console Subsystem Transmit Data Buffer	Data ⟨31:0⟩	
System ID	System Type ⟨7:0⟩ ECO Level ⟨7:0⟩ Manufacturing Plant ⟨3:0⟩ System Serial Number ⟨11:0⟩	
Processor Status Word	Compatibility Mode	CPU executing PDP-11 instructions
	Trace Pending	Initiates trace trap at end of current instruction
	First Part Done	Set by microcode on certain instructions to indicate instruction may be restarted from that point if instruction is interrupted
	Current Mode ⟨1:0⟩	User, Supervisor, Executive, Kernel
	Previous Mode ⟨1:0⟩	
	Interrupt Priority Level of CPU ⟨4:0⟩	
	Enable decimal overflow exceptions	
	Enable floating underflow exceptions	
	Enable integer overflow exceptions	
	T	Trace
	N	Negative condition code
	Z	Zero condition code
	V	Overflow condition code
	C	Carry condition code

indicate the number of bits in each field. The interval counter has a one-microsecond resolution and can be used by diagnostics for timing critical functions. The Time-Of-Year Clock is used to put a time stamp on software objects, such as entries of error information into a file (error log), for post error analysis.

A console terminal is defined via Data and Control/Status register pairs for the Transmit/Receive functions. A System ID register provides information that can be used to isolate failures to the manufacturing process. Finally, the Processor Status Word contains control for enabling tracing and various arithmetic exceptions.

ARCHETYPICAL VAX-11 IMPLEMENTATION

Figure 8-1 illustrates an archetypical implementation of a VAX-11. The CPU is interconnected to memory and I/O devices by a backplane bus. I/O devices reside on either the Unibus or Massbus. The latter is a high-speed block-transfer bus used primarily for block-oriented mass storage devices such as disks and tapes. Bus adapters convert Unibus or Massbus protocols to the backpanel bus protocol.

The backpanel bus is optimized for bandwidth rather than for minimum response time. Thus, the various ports to the backplane (Unibus, Massbus, CPU, and memory) are provided with buffers. The buffers can support one of two purposes: they can smooth data flow between buses or devices with different data rates, or they can reduce bus accesses by holding frequently used data items.

Two standard options are the Floating Point Accelerator (FPA) and the Writable Control Store (WCS). Although the CPU microcode implements the full floating-point instruction set, the FPA provides data paths specifically tailored to executing floating-point operations. The FPA is logically invisible to software and affects only the instruction execution rate. The Writable Control Store supports microcode changes and additions. The WCS can also be used for microdiagnostics.

The Console Subsystem serves as a system console. The system console terminal provides control (halt, restart, initialize, and so on) over the CPU, as well as access to internal system registers. The Console Subsystem also has a mass storage device containing the main system bootstrap code and some diagnostics. Finally, a port is provided for Remote Diagnosis (RD). The RD port provides all the functionality of the Console Subsystem to a remote site.

Table 8-6 gives a brief summary comparison of the VAX-11/750 and VAX-11/780 implementations. The Control Store (CS) of each CPU has associated parity bits. Each CPU has three buffers: instruction lookahead, cache, and address translation. The Instruction Buffer (IB) serves two purposes. First, it decomposes the highly variable instruction format into its basic components; second, it constantly fetches ahead of

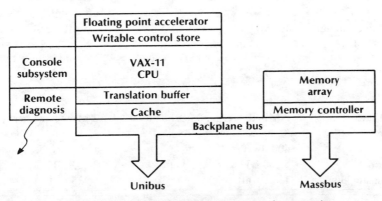

Figure 8–1. Archetypical VAX-11 implementation.

Table 8–6. Comparison of VAX-11/750 and -11/780 implementations.

Component	VAX-11/750	VAX-11/780
Processor		
Relative performance	0.6	1.0
Relative cost	0.4	1.0
Control store		
Word length	78 bits + 2 parity	96 bits + 3 parity
Number of words	6K ROM + 1K RAM	4K ROM + 1K RAM
Microcycle time	320 nsec	100 nsec
Data path width	32 bits	32 bits
Instruction lookahead buffer	8 bytes	8 bytes
Cache		
Size and organization	4 Kbyte direct-mapped	8 Kbyte, 2-way set associative
Cycle time	320 nsec	290 nsec
Typical hit ratio	.9	.95
Effective main memory cycle time	400 nsec/32 bits	1800 nsec/64 bits
Address Translation Buffer		
Size (number of entries)	512	128
Typical hit ratio	.98–.99	.97
Main Memory		
Physical address bits	24	30
Physical size (words)	2 Mbyte in 256-Kbyte increments	8 Mbyte in 256-Kbyte increments
Battery backup option	10 minutes for 2 Mbytes	10 minutes for 4 Mbytes
Cycle time		
Read	800 nsec/32 bits	800 nsec/64 bits 1,300 nsec with single-bit errors
Write	640 nsec/32 bit	1400 nsec/64 bit
ECC	7-bit ECC per 32-bit word	8-bit ECC per 64-bit word
Interleaving factor	1	2 with 2 independent memory controllers
I/O		
Max system I/O rate	5 Mbyte/sec	13.3 Mbyte/sec with 2 memory controllers
Unibus		
Number	1	up to 4
Maximum I/O rate through buffered data paths	1.5 Mbyte/sec	1.5 Mbyte/sec
Number of buffered data paths	3 total, 4-byte buffer in each	15 total, 8-byte buffer in each
Massbus		
Number	up to 3	up to 4
Maximum I/O rate	2 Mbyte/sec per Massbus total	2 Mbyte/sec per Massbus
Buffer size	32 bytes/Massbus	32 bytes/Massbus
Weight	400 lbs.	1,100 lbs.
Max. heat dissipation	5,800 BTU/hr.	21,230 BTU
Max. AC power consumption	1,700 watts	6,225 watts

CPU execution to reduce delays in obtaining the instruction components. The cache stores away frequently used data so that subsequent accesses to a datum do not incur the memory-fetch delay. The virtual-to-physical address translation specified in the VAX architecture requires several table lookups and memory fetches. The Address Translation Buffer (TB) is a cache of recent virtual to physical address translations.

The main memory is protected by Error-Correcting Code (ECC) and has a battery backup option that preserves the contents of memory over short-term power failures.

I/O consists of Unibus and Massbus adapters. The adapters contain buffers that smooth data flow between the slower data rate Unibus/Massbus and the higher data rate Backplane Interconnect, and also serve as assembly/disassembly stations for differences in data path widths; for example, the Unibus and Massbus deal in 16-bit words while the main memory has either 32-bit words for the /750 or 64-bit words for the /780. The adapters also contain tables for mapping Unibus/Massbus physical addresses into Backplane Interconnect physical addresses.

Remote Diagnosis is an integral part of the VAX-11 maintenance philosophy. In a typical VAX-11 maintenance scenario, disk-resident, user mode diagnostics periodically execute under the VMS operating system to exercise and detect functional errors in memory, Massbus Adapters (MBA), Unibus Adapters (UBA), device controllers, and device drives. Errors reported by User Mode diagnostics or hardware check circuits prompt a customer call to the Diagnostic Center (DC). The customer replaces the removable disk media with a diagnostic and scratch disk, turns a key on the front console to "remote," and calls the DC; unauthorized access is not possible. The DC engineer calls the customer's processor, logs onto the system, and begins to execute a script of diagnostics. Micro- and macrodiagnostics can be loaded from the diagnostic disk and executed, the error log can be examined, memory locations deposited or examined, and so on. If the diagnostic disk is not operable, the diagnostics can be loaded from the Console Subsystem mass storage device or down-line loaded over a telephone line. The DC will attempt to isolate the failure to a subsystem. If the CPU is faulty, the diagnostic on the Console Subsystem mass storage device is executed to verify the CPU status.

The DC advises the local Field Service office of the failing subsystem. At the customer's site, Field Service replaces the faulty board and re-verifies the system. If the failing subsystem is the CPU, microdiagnostics are loaded into the writable control store.

Remote diagnosis has at least three major advantages:

- Faster MTTR, especially when the problem is of a trivial nature and can be resolved over the remote diagnostic link;
- Faster resolution of difficult problems, because the person at the DC is an expert in VAX system fault determination; and
- Much greater certainty that the repairman arrives with the correct part.

All diagnostics can be run either at the site or remotely. In a building-block approach, the Console Subsystem first verifies its own operation; then the system hard core (CPU, Backplane Interconnect, and memory controller) is checked by loading microdiagnostics into the writable control store. Macro level tests on the I/O bus adapters and peripheral controllers are run next, followed by the peripheral device diagnostics.

Functional level tests—that is, isolation to the failing major unit—can generally be performed on-line with the operating system. Faulty field-replaceable units can then be identified by stand-alone fault-isolation diagnostics.

Automatic on-line error logging is an integral part of every VAX system. A snapshot of the system is taken upon occurrence of a CPU, memory, I/O, or software error, with two exceptions. First, if a long time has elapsed with no errors, only the time of day is logged. Second, if the number of errors from the ECC memory exceeds a certain threshold (due to a permanent correctable failure in a frequently accessed location), no more entries are made for a period of time. The operating system has a special utility routine that converts the log into a readily analyzed form.

The next two sections discuss the VAX-11/780 and VAX-11/750 implementations in more detail, focusing on the RAMP-related features.

THE VAX-11/780 IMPLEMENTATION

The VAX-11/780 is the first implementation of the VAX-11 architecture. Random logic is implemented in standard, low-power Schottky SSI/MSI; memory consists of standard MOS LSI memory chips. A committee was formed to establish RAMP goals, with members representing Diagnostic Engineering, Documentation, Field Service, Hardware Development, Manufacturing, Marketing, Software Development, Software Support, and Software Quality Management.

Figure 8-2 shows the major functional blocks in the VAX-11/780 implementation. The main memory array is protected by ECC; the Data Cache, Translation Buffer, Control Store, and Writable Control Store memory arrays are protected by multiple parity bits for error detection. Several special-purpose buses interconnect the various functional blocks.

The Synchronous Backplane Interconnect (SBI) joins the CPU, memory, and I/O subsystems. As its name implies, the SBI is a synchronous bus with a minor cycle time of 200 nanoseconds. The data path is 32 bits wide. During each 200-nsec minor cycle, either 32 bits of data or 30 bits of physical address can be transferred. Because read or write operations require the transmission of both address and data, two SBI minor cycles are required to complete the transaction. The SBI protocol also provides for 64-bit operations in three minor cycles, one address and two data. The CPU and I/O devices use the 64-bit mode whenever possible.

Each minor cycle is checked by two parity bits. One covers the 32 address/data lines; the other covers 12 control information lines. During each minor cycle the receiver checks and confirms parity. Each SBI interface checks bus arbitration and SBI protocol. Any irregularities are reported to the CPU. The CPU also maintains a history of the last 16 SBI cycles. Any SBI error condition preserves the history for diagnostic purposes.

To reduce accesses to the SBI, the CPU contains an 8K-byte write-through cache. The cache is two-way set associative, as depicted in Figure 8-3. A portion of the address is used to index two arrays. If the tag field of the address matches either of the stored tags, the data are resident in cache (cache hit) and an SBI/memory cycle can be avoided. The cache uses a random replacement policy on a read miss. On a write hit, the location is updated in the cache as well as main memory. On a write miss, the location is not stored in the cache. The typical hit rate is 95 percent resulting in a 290-nsec effective address-operand access time.

The CPU also contains a two-way, set-associative Translation Buffer (TB). The TB is a cache of recent virtual-to-physical address translations.

The VAX-11/780 maintenance philosophy centers on the Console Subsystem. Two important RAMP-related buses, the ID (Internal Data) and V (Visibility) Buses are tied into the Console Subsystem. The Console Subsystem is composed of an LSI-11 microcomputer with 16K bytes of RAM and 8K bytes of ROM, a hard copy terminal, a floppy disk, and a remote diagnostic port. The LSI-11 performs a self-test on power-up. The LSI-11 can examine and deposit values in internal processor registers via the ID bus. Registers accessible to the ID include configuration control, error summary, error data, and maintenance registers. The V Bus makes almost 600 internal logic signal values visible to the microdiagnostics.

The VAX-11/780 maintenance philosophy can be understood by examining the registers associated with each hardware error-detection or -correction element. In general, each element can be associated with up to four types of registers:

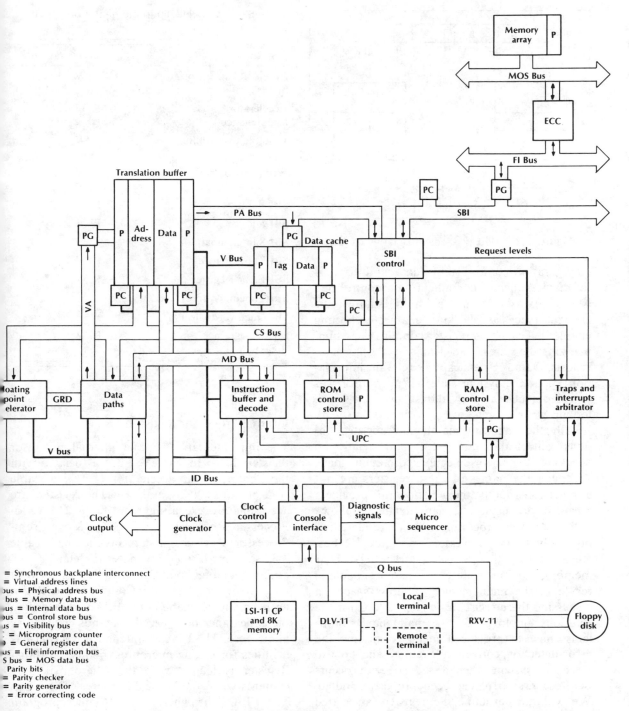

Figure 8–2. VAX-11/780 data paths and error checking.

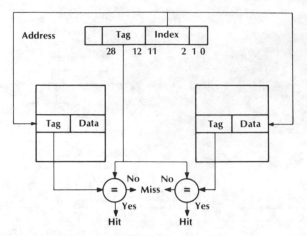

Figure 8–3. Two-way, set-associative cache.

configuration/control, status, data, and diagnostic/maintenance. The configuration/control register contains information on the state of the element (such as checking enabled, reporting enabled). The status register contains flags summarizing the state of the element, including error reports. Data registers capture relevant information about the system state when an error was detected (such as the address used on cache lookup when a cache parity error was detected). Finally, the diagnostic/maintenance register contains control and status information relative to checking the error-detection/correction logic. Although the names of these registers are not applied consistently, the generic terms provide a means of organizing the many details to follow.

Registers for processor elements reside either internally to the processor or on the ID bus. Registers for other ports on the SBI (such as memory, Unibus adapters, Massbus adapters) reside in the main memory address space. In discussing these registers we should look for the solutions employed to two maintenance problems: how to provide a means of testing the error-detection/correction circuitry and how to alert the system when a second error occurs before a first error has been properly handled. We will now examine the registers associated with each of these areas.

Table 8–7. VAX-11/780 implementation-specific processor registers.

Register	Access Permitted
Accelerator Control/ Status	R/W
Accelerator Maintenance	R/W
Writable Control Store Address	R/W
Writable Control Store Data	R/W
SBI Fault/Status	R/W
SBI Silo	R
SBI Silo Comparator	R/W
SBI Maintenance	R/W
SBI Error Register	R/W
SBI Timeout Address	R
SBI Quadword Clear	W
Microprogram Breakpoint	R/W

Internal Processor Registers

The implementation-specific internal processor registers listed in Table 8-7 are associated with the floating point accelerator (FPA), writable control store (WCS), and SBI. The registers are accessible by executing the MTPR (Move-to-Processor Register) and MFPR (Move-From-Processor Register) macro instructions. Table 8-8 lists some of their attributes in detail.

The Floating Point Accelerator has its own microprocessor. The FPA Control Status Register has a bit for enabling the FPA and recording the appearance of reserved operands encoded as minus zero. The FPA Maintenance Register has facilities for setting microbreakpoints. A Match Register is loaded with the Microbreak$\langle 8{:}0 \rangle$ contents when the Write Microbreak Bit is set. The FPA halts when the FPA microprogram counter is equal to the Match Register. An FPA

Table 8–8. Details of RAMP-related VAX-11/780 implementation-specific processor registers.

Register	Subfields	Comments
Floating Point Accelerator Control Status	Reserved Operand	Minus zero error
	Accelerator Enable	
	Accelerator Type $\langle 3:0 \rangle$	
Floating Point Accelerator Maintenance	Write Trap Address	
	Trap Address $\langle 7:0 \rangle$	Forms FPA ROM address on trap
	Write Microbreak	
	Match	Indicates a match has occurred
	Microbreak/Current Microaddress $\langle 8:0 \rangle$	Load micromatch register with this subfield. FPA halts when microprogram counter matches the register value. Used for setting breakpoints. Reading yields current value of microprogram counter.
Write Control Store (WCS) Address/Control	Invert parity	When set, inverts writable control store parity
	Counter $\langle 1:0 \rangle$	Modulo-3 counter points to 32-bit quantity to write
	Address $\langle 12:0 \rangle$	Microstore word to be written
WCS Data	Data $\langle 31:0 \rangle$	When written, causes 32-bit write into WCS. When read, indicates number of WCS boards available (up to 8).
SBI Fault Status	Parity Fault on SBI	
	Unexpected Read Response	
	Multiple Transmitter	
	SBI Fault	Fault on SBI confirmation lines
	Fault Interrupt Enable	Allows interrupts on receipt of SBI Fault Signal
	Error First Pass	Set by microcode during first pass through fault-handling code; detects double errors.
	Transmitter During Fault	Set if device was the transmitter during the fault.
	Fault Silo Lock	Indicates Silo is locked due to SBI fault

(Table continues on next page)

Table 8–8 —*Continued*

Register	Subfields	Comments
Silo	First entry after fault	16 locations storing data from the 16 most recent SBI cycles; cleared to indicate first SBI cycle after a fault.
	Stored SBI fields: Interlock $\langle 0 \rangle$ ID $\langle 4:0 \rangle$ Tag $\langle 2:0 \rangle$ CNF $\langle 1:0 \rangle$ Arbitration $\langle 15:0 \rangle$ Mask $\langle 3:0 \rangle$ or Data $\langle 31:28 \rangle$	Data bits written when tag has value "command address"; otherwise mask written.
Silo Comparator	Compare Silo Lock	Set when certain conditions, other than faults, have been met
	Silo Lock Interrupt Enable	
	Lock Unconditional	Locks when Silo is full (counter $= F_{16}$)
	Conditional Lock $\langle 1:0 \rangle$	Locks Silo when certain conditions exist. Comparator examines SBI; when there is a match, Silo counter can increment until counter $= F_{16}$. Unlocks by writing F_{16} into counter.
	Command/Mask for Comparison $\langle 3:0 \rangle$	
	Tag for Comparison $\langle 2:0 \rangle$	
	Count Field $\langle 3:0 \rangle$	
SBI Error	Interrupt Enable on Read Data Substitute (RDS)	Interrupts when memory has detected an uncorrectable data error
	CPU Corrected Read Data (CRD) received from memory	Memory-corrected data
	CPU RDS	Read Data Substitute received from memory
	CPU Processor Timeout Status $\langle 2:0 \rangle$	No device response; device busy, waiting for read data
	CPU SBI Error Confirmation	Set when Processor initiated request is responded to by an Error code on the SBI confirmation lines
	Instruction Buffer (IB) RDS	Read Data Substitute received from memory
	IB Timeout Status $\langle 2:0 \rangle$	No device response: device busy, waiting for read data

(*Table continues on next page*)

Table 8–8 —*Continued*

Register	Subfields	Comments
	IB SBI Error Confirmation	Set when Instruction Buffer initiated request is responded to by an Error code on the SBI confirmation lines
	Multiple CP Error	Set when a second error occurs before the first is serviced
	SBI Not Busy	
SBI Timeout Address	Mode	Kernel, executive, supervisor, user
	Physical address $\langle 27:0 \rangle$	Address latched when SBI time-outs
	Cache Match $\langle 1:0 \rangle$	Indicates group that had a cache hit
	Force Timeout	Forces read timeouts
SBI Maintenance	Force P0 Reversal on SBI	Forces appearance that base register P0 has an illegal value
	Force Write Sequence Fault	
	Force Unexpected Read Data Fault	Transmits Read Data command with maintenance ID, undefined data, with good parity
	Maintenance ID $\langle 4:0 \rangle$	ID for forced Unexpected Read Data
	Force SBI Invalidate	Writes by CPU on SBI forced to invalid cache entries
	Enable SBI Invalidate	Allows CPU writes to forced invalid cache entries
	Reverse Cache Parity $\langle 3:0 \rangle$	Designates which of 14 parity bits to flip; 2 groups of 3 address bytes and 4 data bytes.
	Force Cache Miss $\langle 1:0 \rangle$	No miss, group 1 miss, group 0 miss, both group 1 and 0 miss
	Cache Replacement $\langle 1:0 \rangle$	Random, group 0 always, group 1 always. Allows for disabling cache halves on permanent error.
	Disable SBI	When set, no SBI cycles will be started.
	Force P1 Reversal on SBI	Forces appearance that base register P1 has an illegal value
Ubreak $\langle 12:0 \rangle$		Data used to compare microprogram counter for stopping system clock or oscilloscope sync

trap can be vectored to different microcode locations as a function of the FPA trap address. Setting the Write Trap Address Bit loads the Trap Address Register from the Trap Address subfield.

The Writable Control Store has Address/Control and Data registers. When the Data Register $\langle 31:0 \rangle$ is written, the contents are loaded into the control store word designated by Address $\langle 12:0 \rangle$, and the word location pointed to by Counter $\langle 1:0 \rangle$ in the WCS Address/Control Register. The Invert Parity Bit causes the parity generated by the Data $\langle 31:0 \rangle$ word to be placed in the WCS in a complemented form. Thus, the Control Store Bus (see Figure 8-2) parity checker and CPU Error Status Register (see the section on ID Bus Registers below) can be tested by use of this bit. The WCS can be loaded with microdiagnostics to assist in fault isolation.

Every port on the SBI has a register that summarizes errors detected on the SBI. The SBI Fault Status Register records these errors as seen by the processor. One bit records parity errors. Two bits record SBI protocol errors: the Unexpected Read Response Bit is set if data are placed on the bus in response to a read command not seen by the CPU; the Multiple Transmitter Bit is set if more than one transmitter was seen. The SBI Fault Bit is set if the CPU sees a fault signal asserted by an SBI port, that is, if the SBI port detected an SBI parity error. Setting the Fault-Interrupt Enable Bit allows an SBI fault to interrupt the CPU. The Transmitter During Fault Bit is set if the CPU was transmitting when an error was detected. This bit allows the software to isolate the error. The Error First Pass Bit is used to detect the occurrence of a second SBI fault prior to complete handling of the first fault.

The Silo is a history of a selected 32 bits from each of the last 16 SBI cycles. The Silo is frozen (locked) whenever a fault is signalled on the SBI confirmation lines or when a condition defined by the Silo Comparator Register has been met. The Silo can be used in postfault analysis of subtle problems such as intermittents.

The Silo Comparator Register allows the definition of predetermined conditions to trigger loading of the SBI Silo. The Silo can be loaded unconditionally or upon matches in SBI subfields: port ID, ID and Tag, ID and Tag and Mask. When the Silo is full it is frozen (locked), a bit set, and an interrupt generated if the interrupt enable bit is set.

The SBI Error Register contains further SBI status information. Bits indicate whether the memory corrected a single-bit error (Corrected Read Data: CRD) or detected a double error (Read Data Substitute: RDS). RDS errors can cause an interrupt to the processor. Also recorded are SBI timeouts and parity errors detected on cycles requested by the CPU (SBI Error Confirmation). The SBI Error Register distinguishes whether the SBI error was triggered by a regular CPU request or an instruction prefetch request made by the Instruction Buffer (IB). The IB requests are for performance reasons only, and errors can be tolerated by simply flushing the IB. Errors associated with other performance-related buffers such as Translation Buffer and Cache, are easily tolerated because they cause no change in system state; that is, they are logically transparent to the system.

The SBI Maintenance Register contains bits for forcing error conditions in various CPU subsystems. The various error-detection circuits can be tested by these forced-error conditions. Force P0/P1 reversal performs bounds checking on the system base registers. SBI errors are simulated by forcing Write Sequence, Unexpected Read Data, and Timeouts. Cache operation can be checked by observing the Cache Match field while invalidating cache entries and forcing cache misses. Permanent failures in cache can be configured out by disabling Cache halves or disabling the Cache altogether. Cache disabling is achieved by specifying where new entries are to be placed upon a Cache miss (that is, Cache Replacement $\langle 1:0 \rangle$).

Finally, the microbreak register can be used to stop the microsequencer in specific regions of microcode.

ID Bus Registers

The internal processor registers and other registers listed in Table 8-9 are accessible to the Console Subsystem over the ID bus. These registers may be read or written during local or remote diagnosis even if the CPU is halted. Key implementation registers such as the Instruction Buffer and D/Q (used as register extensions in multiple precision operations) are accessible.

There are status error registers for the CPU and cache. The CPU Error Status Register holds the control store parity-error summary (that is, which third of the control store caused a parity error). In conjunction with the microbreak register, the CPU Error Status Register can be used to identify the faulty Control Store chip. The value of internal condition codes is made available to facilitate checking of condition code operations. Finally, the arithmetic trap code is captured to aid software recovery from arithmetic errors.

Table 8–9. Details of RAMP-related VAX-11/780 registers available on the ID bus.

Register	Subfields	Comments
Instruction Buffer $\langle 31:0 \rangle$		
D/Q Register	Read D $\langle 31:0 \rangle$ or write Q $\langle 31:0 \rangle$ register in system data paths	
CPU Error Status	Control Store Parity Error Summary	OR of Control Store Parity Error Bits
	Control Store Parity Error Bits $\langle 2:0 \rangle$	1 bit for every 32 bits of control store
	ALU N	Negative condition from ALU
	Exponent N	Negative condition from Exponent Unit
	ALU Z	Zero condition from ALU
	Exponent Z	Zero condition from Exponent Unit
	ALU C31	Carry bit from ALU
	Arithmetic Trap Codes	Decimal divide by zero Decimal overflow Floating underflow Floating divide by zero Integer divide by zero Integer overflow
Cache Parity Error	Any error	Logical OR of all error indications
	CP/IB Error	Designates whether CPU or IB caused error
	Data Parity OK $\langle 7:0 \rangle$	Indicates which of 8 data bytes indicates parity error (2 groups of 4 bits)
	Address Parity OK $\langle 5:0 \rangle$	Indicates which of 6 address bytes indicates parity error (2 groups of 3 bits)

(Table continues on next page)

Table 8–9 —*Continued*

Register	Subfields	Comments
Translation Buffer (TB) Data	Valid	TB allows matches
	Protection Code ⟨3:0⟩	See Table 8–3.
	Modify	Page has been modified
	Page Frame Number ⟨20:0⟩	Page Frame of Physical Address after translation
	TB Hit ⟨1:0⟩	Indicates which group had a TB hit
	Force TB Parity Error ⟨3:0⟩	Allows parity error to be generated independently on each of three data bytes or three address bytes in either group 0 or group 1
	Enable Memory Management	
Translate Buffer Register 1	TB Parity Error Status ⟨11:0⟩	Indicates which of possible 12 parity errors: group (2), data byte (3 per group), or address byte (3 per group)
	TB Parity Error	Indicates TB microtrap was requested due to error during CPU access
	Last TB Write	Indicates which TB group was last written
Translation Buffer Register 0	Force Replace ⟨2:0⟩	Forces TB writes to define groups: both, group 1, or group 2
	Force Miss ⟨1:0⟩	Forces TB miss on group 0 or 1.
USTACK ⟨15:0⟩		Reading pops top address from microsequencer stack. Writing pushes address onto microsequencer stack.
Others		26 scratch-pad registers used as temporaries by the microcode in implementing the VAX instruction set

The Cache Parity Error Register contains the parity bit values of the cache data and tag fields. Another bit assists recovery software by indicating whether the CPU or IB caused the cache parity error.

Three registers are associated with Control, Status, and Data of the Translation Buffer (TB). Translation Buffer Register 0 can disable TB halves (that is, Force Replace). The Force Miss and TB Hit Fields (in Translation Buffer Data Register) can be used by diagnostics to check TB functionality; the Force TB Parity Error (in Translation Buffer Data Register) coupled with the TB Parity Error Status bits (in Translation Buffer Register 1) can be used to test the TB parity checkers. Finally, the Translation Buffer Data Register captures relevant information about a virtual address that caused a protection violation.

Because the ID Bus is not accessible to the VAX-11/780 instruction set, an error log format has been defined that places several key registers

Table 8–10. VAX-11/780 machine-check error information logged onto machine stack.

Information

Byte Count of Error Log
Error Summary (see below)
CPU Error Status
Trapped Microprogram Counter
Virtual Address
D Register
Translation Buffer Error Register 0
Translation Buffer Error Register 1
SBI Timeout Address
Cache Parity
SBI Error
Program Counter
Program Status Longword

Error Summary

CP/IB Read Timeout or Error Confirmation
CP/IB Translation Buffer Parity Error
CP/IB Read Data Substitute Fault
CP/IB Cache Parity Error
Control Store Parity-Error Abort
Microcode "not supposed to get here" Abort

on the kernel stack when an error occurs. Table 8-10 details the information placed on the kernel stack. ID Bus registers include the CPU Error Status, D register, and Translation Buffer Error Registers 0 and 1. SBI-related processor registers include SBI Error, SBI Timeout Address, and Cache Parity registers. The virtual address, program counter, and microprogram counters are also stored. Finally, an Error Summary, also listed in Table 8-10, indicates the type of error that caused the machine check.

Machine checks force the microsequencer to trap. The error-handling microcode first copies the registers to be logged into temporary registers accessible on the ID Bus. Subsequently the registers are logged onto the machine stack. If the error-handling microcode finds the Error-First-Pass bit set in the SBI Fault Status Register, the CPU is halted. Data related to the first error are found in the ID temporary registers; those related to the second error are found in the corresponding error/status registers. Both sets of data are readable by the Console Subsystem.

Main Memory Registers

Registers related to errors in SBI ports—the memory, Unibus Adapter, and Massbus Adapter registers—are in the main memory address space.

Table 8-11 lists the three main memory registers. Register A contains the memory port's fault status of the SBI. This field is identical to the corresponding fields in the CPU SBI Fault Status Register. Similar fields reside in the UBA and MBA registers. The remaining Register A fields deal with memory configuration and power status.

Register B contains additional memory configuration (such as Memory Starting Address), status (such as ascertaining whether battery backup allowed the memory to ride through a power loss), and maintenance fields. The memory controller is buffered and can have up to four reads and four writes in progress. The File Pointer fields can be used to check the functionality of these buffers. ECC check logic can be tested by forcing the ECC bits to be replaced by the contents of the Substitute ECC Bits $\langle 7:0 \rangle$ field.

Register C has two fields that capture the address and syndrome of the memory word in error. Both fields are locked until the error is serviced. The Error Log Request Bit identifies the memory controller in error for the error-handling subroutine. A set High Error Rate Bit indicates that a second error occurred before the first was serviced. Finally, error correction on reads can be disabled by the Inhibit CRD Bit.

Table 8-12 lists six registers associated with the Unibus Adapter (UBA). The Configuration Register records the standard SBI Fault Status. The Control Register contains interrupt enable bits for reporting Unibus errors to the CPU.

The Unibus Status Register records several situations. The Read Data and Command Transmit timeouts are checks on the Unibus timeout circuitry. The bits are set if the SBI has not responded within 100 microseconds and the Unibus timeout of 10 microseconds has failed to cancel the request. The Read Data Substitute Bit

Table 8–11. VAX-11/780 memory configuration registers.

Main Memory Register	Subfields	Comments
Register A	SBI Fault Status ⟨4:0⟩	
	Bus Parity Error	
	Write Data Sequence Fault	
	Memory was Transmitter During a Fault	
	Multiple Transmitters on Bus	
	Interlock Sequence Fault	
	Power Up/Down Status ⟨1:0⟩	
	Power Up Alert	
	Power Down Alert	
	Memory Size ⟨6:0⟩	
	Memory Type ⟨1:0⟩	
	4K chips	
	16K chips	
	Interleave ⟨3:0⟩	
	Interleave Factor	No interleaving or 2-way interleaving
	Interleaving Enable	
Register B	File Output Pointer ⟨1:0⟩	Points to which of 4 address buffers is next to command the memory to read
	File Input Pointer ⟨1:0⟩	Points to which of 4 buffers will receive next write address and data
	Memory Starting Address ⟨12:0⟩	
	Enable Write to Memory Starting Address Subfield	
	Memory Initialization Status ⟨1:0⟩	Memory data valid or invalid following power loss
	Force ERR	When set, replaces ECC bits with substitute ECC bits
	Substitute ECC Bits ⟨7:0⟩	Bits to be substituted for ECC bits in memory; checks ECC logic.
	Bypass ECC	Disables ECC generation, checking

(Table continues on next page)

Table 8–11—*Continued*

Main Memory Register	Subfields	Comments
Register C	Inhibit CRD	Enables/disables reporting of corrected read data
	High Error Rate	Bit set if error occurs between time of generating first-error message and time of invoking error service subroutine.
	Error Log Request	Indicates whether memory controller has recorded an error. When set, subsequent corrected Read Data events are not reported.
	Error Address $\langle 19:0 \rangle$	Indicates address generating read error. Field changed only after first error serviced.
	Error Syndrome $\langle 7:0 \rangle$	Value of error syndrome. Field changed only after first error serviced.

is set if a Unibus request ends in an uncorrectable error: no data are transmitted to the Unibus, the Unibus times out, and a Unibus nonexisting-memory error is recorded. The Command Transmit Error Bit is set when the SBI cycle causes an error on the Confirmation lines. Finally, parity errors on the internal UBA data paths or in the address translation memory are recorded. Data associated with errors are captured in the Failed Map Entry and Failed Unibus Address registers. Subsequent errors do not overwrite the Failed Map Entry Register until the first error has been cleared.

The Diagnostic Control Register has bits to inhibit parity on the data and map registers. If data with an even number of ones are used, the odd-parity checking circuitry is tested. The Microsequencer OK bit is used to detect when the microsequencer is caught in a loop.

Table 8-13 lists the four registers of the Massbus Adapter (MBA). The Configuration/Status Register records the standard SBI Fault Status. The Control Register has a Maintenance Mode Bit that allows for testing the Massbus without any devices attached. An Interrupt Enable Bit allows reporting of Massbus errors to the CPU.

The Status Register records SBI, device, and Massbus parity errors. The Diagnostic Register allows exercising of MBA parity-check circuits and testing of the Massbus by reading and writing of selected Massbus fields.

Console Subsystem

Table 8-14 lists several of the RAMP-related console commands available to probe and test the CPU. The Examine/Deposit command allows reading and setting of most of the CPU registers. In addition to the ID Bus Error registers, almost 600 internal logic signals are observable over the Visibility Bus (V-Bus).

The V-Bus is composed of seven channels. Table 8-15 lists the logic associated with each channel. Figure 8-4 depicts the operation of a V-Bus channel. When requested, the internal logic signals are entered in a shift register, which is emptied into a register for examination and display. To illustrate the type of information associated with the V-Bus, Table 8-16 lists the signals available on Channel 4. The V-Bus test points for Channel 4 are superimposed on logic

Table 8–12.   RAMP-related VAX-11/780 Unibus adapter registers.

UBA Registers	Subfields	Comments
Configuration	SBI Status $\langle 4:0 \rangle$	Records errors detected in SBI operation, including parity, write data sequence, unexpected read data, interlock sequence, multiple transmitter, and transmitting
Control	SBI to Unibus Error Interrupt Enable	Enables interrupts when Unibus times out
	Unibus to SBI Error Interrupt Enable	Enables interrupts on errors reported in Unibus status register
Unibus Status	Read Data Timeout	Set when SBI memory has not responded
	Command Transmit Timeout	Set when SBI has not responded to command
	Read Data Substitute	Set if SBI read has an uncorrectable error
	Command Transmit Error	Set when error confirmation returned on SBI cycle initiated by Unibus adapter
	Data Path Parity Error	Set when parity error detected on data path internal to Unibus Adapter
	Map Register Parity Failure	Set when address mapping registers have incorrect parity when selected
	Lost Error Bit	Set if one of the above error bits has been set and another error occurs before it is cleared
Failed Map Entry	Map Register Number $\langle 8:0 \rangle$	Provides number of the map register being used during one of the error conditions reported in the Unibus Status Register
Failed Unibus Address	Unibus Address Bits $\langle 15:0 \rangle$	Captures address that caused a Unibus timeout
Diagnostic Control	Defeat Map Parity	When set, inhibits parity bits from the map registers from entering the parity checkers
	Defeat Data Path Parity	When set, inhibits parity bits of data path RAM from entering parity checkers
	Microsequencer OK	Set when microsequencer is idle

Table 8–13. RAMP-related VAX-11/780 Massbus adapter registers.

Register	Subfields	Comments
Configuration/Status	SBI Status $\langle 4:0 \rangle$	Records errors detected in SBI operation, including parity, write-data sequence, unexpected read data, multiple transmitter, and transmitting
Control	Maintenance Mode	When set, software can exercise Massbus without any attached devices. All Massbus devices detach from the bus.
	Interrupt Enable	When set, causes an interrupt in CPU on the occurrence of any errors reported in the status register
Status	No Response	Set if SBI returns a no-response confirmation. Causes retry of command.
	Nonexistent Drive	Set if drive fails to respond within a specified time
	Data Late	
	Miss Transfer Error	
	Massbus Data Parity Error	Error in parity check of bus data field
	Massbus Control Parity Error	Error in parity check of bus control field
	Page Frame Map Parity Error	Parity error in memory where page map information is stored
	Error Confirmation	Set when SBI returns an error confirmation on a transaction
	Read Data Substitute	Set when SBI indicates an uncorrectable error
	Read Timeout	
Diagnostic	Invert Parity $\langle 2:0 \rangle$	Inverts the sense of the bus data, bus control, and map register file parity generator
	Simulate asynchronous control lines $\langle 3:0 \rangle$	Allows setting, clearing of various Massbus signals when in Maintenance Mode
	Read Signals $\langle 20:0 \rangle$	Allows reading of selected Massbus fields

Table 8–14. Subset of console VAX-11/780 commands.

Command	Comments
Examine⟨address⟩ /Deposit⟨address⟩ ⟨data⟩	Memory: using physical or virtual address
	Internal Registers
	General Registers
	V-Bus Channels (read only)
	ID Bus Registers
Examine IR	Instruction Register
Start⟨address⟩/ Continue/Halt/Boot/ Initialize	Action performed on CPU
Show	Displays CPU and Console state
Show Version	Displays version of microcode and console
Test	Runs microdiagnostics
Test/Com	Calls microdiagnostic monitor, awaits commands
Unjam	Unjams SBI
Set Step	Enables single time state, bus cycle, or instruction mode
Clear Step	Enables normal mode
Next⟨number⟩	Steps until ⟨number⟩ cycles are done. Step type depends on last Set Step Command.
QClear⟨address⟩	Clears 64 bits at ⟨address⟩ as well as ECC errors
Set/Clear SCMM	Sets/Clears "stop on microbreak match" enable
Set Clock Slow/Fast/ Normal	Sets CPU clock frequency
Load⟨Filename⟩	Loads file to memory or WCS
Q⟨Filename⟩	Processes a file of console commands
Repeat⟨any-console-command⟩	Repeat any console command until stopped by control C
REBOOT	Reloads console software
BOOT	Boots CPU
DIAGNOSE	Boots Diagnostic Supervisor
HALT	

Table 8–15. V-bus channels and associated logic.

Channel	Logic	Signals
0	Microsequencer	101
1	Data Paths, Arithmetic Section	60
2	Data Paths, Data and Exponent Section	92
3	Instruction Decode, Instruction Buffer, Translation Buffer Data Matrix	85
4	Cache and Translation Buffer Address Matrix, Cache Data Matrix	103
5	SBI Control	93
6	Floating Point Accelerator: Control, Exponent Processor, and Fraction Adder	43

diagrams for the Cache Address Matrix, shown in Figure 8-5; for the Translation Buffer Address Matrix, shown in Figure 8-6; and for the Cache Data Matrix, shown in Figure 8-7.

Other Console commands enable execution of micro- and macrodiagnostics; single-stepping a state, a bus cycle, or an instruction at a time; setting microbreaks; and CPU clock margining.

Micro- and Macrodiagnostics

The microdiagnostics are stored on floppy disks accessible to the LSI-11 console processor, which can load them into the Writable Control Store (WCS). The field service engineer gives the console a TEST command. The first portion of the microdiagnostics sizes the system and prints out system configuration information. Upon completion, it prompts the engineer to load a new floppy disk. Table 8-17 lists a sample of the commands available to the engineer. The microdiagnostics consist of a series of "go-chains." Detection of a disagreement initiates a fault tree analysis, which uses the V-Bus to isolate the

Table 8–16. Signals available on V-Bus, channel 4.

Cache Address Matrix

CAML Group 0, Byte Parity Odd ⟨2:0⟩

CAML Group 0, Byte Parity Even ⟨2:0⟩

CAMK Group 0 Match

CAMK Group 1 Match

CAML Group 1, Byte Parity Odd ⟨2:0⟩

CAML Group 1, Byte Parity Even ⟨2:0⟩

CAMM CPT Clock ⟨3:0⟩

CAMB Physical Address Latch Valid

CAMB Physical Address Latch ⟨28:12⟩

CAMB Tag Parity Even ⟨2:0⟩

SBHF Force Read Parity Errors ⟨3:0⟩H, ⟨3⟩L

SBHF Force Miss Group 0 from Maintenance Register

SBHN Force Miss Group 1 from Maintenance Register

SBLN Miss Data Replacement G0

SBLN Miss Data Replacement G1

Translation Buffer Address Matrix

CAMS Group 0 Address Parity Odd ⟨2:0⟩

CAMS Group 1 Address Parity Odd ⟨2:0⟩

CAMU TB Parity ⟨1:0⟩

CAMV Receiver Parity

TBMX Force Parity Error ⟨3:0⟩

TBMD Enable CDM Data

Cache Data Matrix

CDMR Group 0 Data Parity Odd ⟨3:0⟩

CDMR Group 0 Data Parity Even ⟨3:0⟩

CDMS Group 1 Data Parity Odd ⟨3:0⟩

CDMS Group 1 Data Parity Even ⟨3:0⟩

CDMA Mask ⟨3:0⟩

CDMH Address Latch ⟨11:2⟩

CDMU Clock CPT2-H; CPT1-L

CAMP Group 0 Write Enable

CAMP Group 1 Write Enable

SBHF Force Read Parity Errors ⟨3:0⟩ L

Table 8–17. Sample of microdiagnostic monitor commands.

Command	Action
HALT	Halts CPU
INIT	Initializes
UNJAM	Clears SBI
LOAD ⟨CODE⟩	Loads a macrodiagnostic
RUN ⟨CODE⟩	Executes a macrodiagnostic
Diagnose/Test : 2F/ PASS : 2	Executes microdiagnostic test 2F twice in succession.
SET/CLEAR SCMM : ⟨ADDRESS⟩	Sets/clears micromatch; loads address into micromatch register.
SET STEP STATE/ BUS/INSTRUCTION	Enables single-stepping
SET CLOCK FAST/ SLOW/NORMAL/ EXTERNAL	Selects CPU clock speed and source
EXAMINE	
ID : ⟨ADDRESS⟩	Registers on ID bus
VBus : ⟨CHANNEL⟩	Displays contents of specified V-Bus channel
RA/RC	Scratch-pad registers
LA/LC	Latches
DR/QR/SC/FE/VA	Registers
PC	Program counter
DEPOSIT	A corresponding deposit command exists for all except the V-Bus and PC. There is a deposit for the PA (physical address) register.

failure. The V-Bus is read only (thus requiring the machine to be in a known state before applying the next test) and is normally used only by the microdiagnostics.

The Diagnostic Supervisor allows the engineer to control and run macrodiagnostic programs through a command line interpreter in either stand-alone or user (on-line) mode. At the beginning of each diagnostic program, the Diagnostic Supervisor requests information from the engineer, such as the unit to be tested. Table 8-18

Table 8–18. Sample of macrodiagnostic supervisor commands.

Command	Action
LOAD ⟨File⟩	Loads specified file when in user mode
START	Starts execution of program in memory. Supervisor enters dialogue with user to set values of diagnostic switches (such as unit to test).
RESTART	Reexecutes the previous program with the same switch values as established by the START dialogue
SUMMARY	Prints statistics of tests to date
HALT	Halts on detected error
LOOP	Enters predetermined scope loop when a subtest detects an error
QUICK	Enters quick-verify mode
TRACE	Reports execution of each test
LOCK	Disables program relocation. Self-relocating programs are thus locked into their current physical memory space.
SET BREAKPOINT ⟨address⟩	Diagnostic supervisor assumes control when program accesses the specified location.
CLEAR BREAKPOINT ⟨address⟩	
EXAMINE/DEPOSIT ⟨address⟩	Examines or deposits the specified memory address.

lists a subset of the Macrodiagnostic Supervisor command available to the engineer. A User Environment Test Package (UETP) can be employed for on-line diagnostics. A scratch tape or disk is mounted on the peripheral device to be tested. The UETP simulates a user load on the selected device. The number of simulated users is a function of the peripheral device type and the amount of memory in the system.

The Error Log is another tool available to the engineer. Information about exceptions is automatically captured by the hardware and entered into a disk file. The engineer can select printouts of the error log by device and error class. Error classes include hardware (such as machine checks, corrected read data, read data substitute, SBI alerts, and SBI faults), configuration changes (such as mount and dismount of peripherals), and system information (such as system startup time, crashes, software bug checks). The engineer can select one of five report formats:

- Rollup: a summary of the number of errors by each device;
- Brief: brief description of each error entry, including device, type of error, and time;
- Cryptic: contents of associated registers for hardware and device errors;
- Standard: complete information on each error; and
- Unknown: full information on unknown, invalid, and undefined errors.

THE VAX-11/750 IMPLEMENTATION

The VAX-11/750 is the second implementation of the VAX architecture. Although the VAX-11/780 implementation influenced the design team, the VAX-11/750 differs from its predecessor in several major respects. This section first discusses the evolution of the VAX-11/750 design with special focus on the RAMP-related decisions. This discussion should provide insights on how the material in the first six chapters can be applied in practice. Next, the section discusses the details of the VAX-11/750 RAMP features.

Design Evolution

Several global design goals were set even before the design team was established. These global design goals placed constraints on implementation and RAMP design trade-offs.

The targeted market determined the cost and

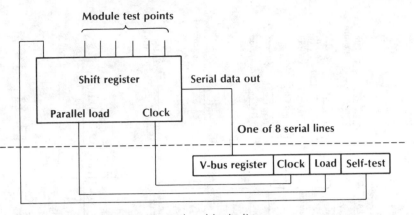

Figure 8–4. V-bus block diagram.

performance goals: one-third to one-half the cost and 60–70 percent of the native mode performance of the VAX-11/780. The 11/750 should have at least 50 percent of the 11/780 performance to achieve a performance/cost ratio improvement so that three years' difference in technology would be aggressively utilized.

The improved performance/cost ratio dictated the use of dense circuitry to decrease signal delays and decrease area, which is directly related to cost. The design specified the extended hex board (12″ × 15″) used on the VAX-11/780. To achieve a density increase over the 11/780, a new random logic technology was selected. Custom-designed 48-pin gate arrays (400 bipolar gates plus 44 transceivers per chip) were to be used. Each hex board could hold up to 50 gate array chips. The projected cost of the hex board/gate array combination required a three-board basic processor if the cost goal was to be met.

To take advantage of mass production and standardization, several 11/780 features were adopted, including use of the same operating system, functional diagnostics, Unibus/Massbus I/O, and—as nearly as possible—the same maintenance/repair procedure.

Also, to reduce cost, the 11/750 was specified as a bounded system with limited expansion capacity. In contrast with the 11/780, which can be configured with multipled cabinets, the 11/750 CPU/Memory/IO adapters were to be contained in a single cabinet. Figure 8-8 shows a preliminary system diagram (devised about four months after the design team was formed). The synchronous backplane bus was dubbed CMI (Comet Memory Interconnect). Primarily for performance reasons, the CMI was limited to eight ports and a length of six inches. The CPU, memory controller, one Unibus Adapter, Writable Control Store (WCS), and the Remote Diagnostic Module (RDM) were dedicated ports. The other three ports could be allocated to Massbus and/or Unibus Adapters, multiport memory, or directly interfaced DMA (Direct Memory Access) devices. The memory controller could handle up to eight memory array cards of 128 Kbytes or 256 Kbytes each for a maximum system memory of 2 Mbytes.

The three-board goal resulted in a straightforward functional partitioning: Data Path Module (DPM), Microsequencer and Control Store (MCS), and Memory Interface (MI). An optional Floating Point Accelerator (FPA) was also envisioned. Figure 8-9 illustrates this initial partitioning. Custom gate array, RAM, and ROM chips were used extensively to keep board densities high. To minimize the number of custom gate array designs, a bit-sliced approach was adopted. Depending on logic complexity, each gate array handled 4, 8, or 16 bits of data.

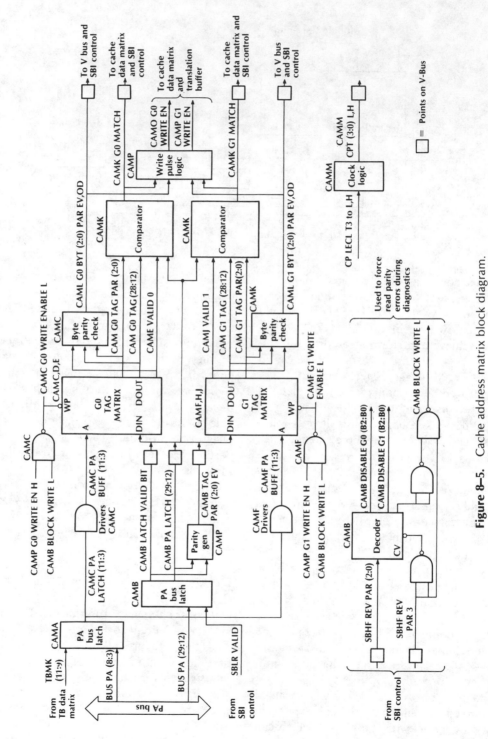

Figure 8–5. Cache address matrix block diagram.

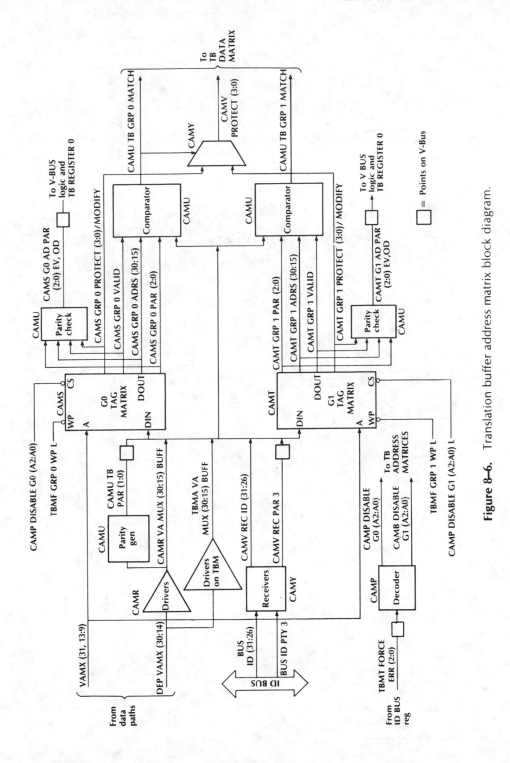

Figure 8–6.   Translation buffer address matrix block diagram.

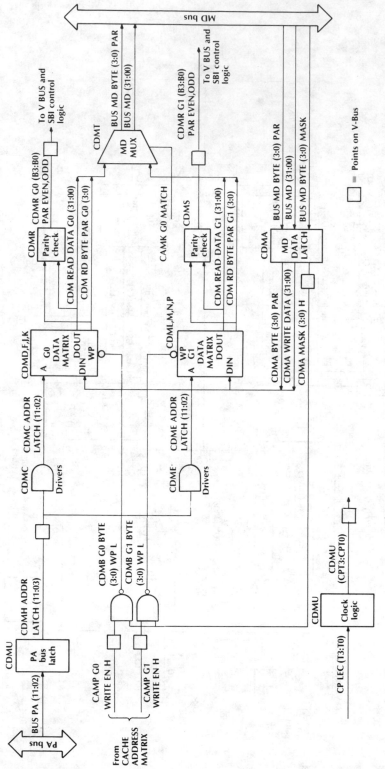

Figure 8-7. Cache data matrix block diagram.

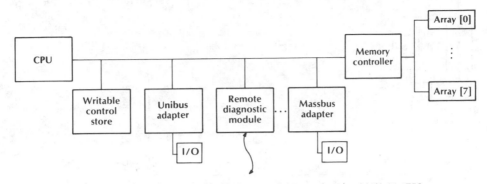

Figure 8–8. Backplane interconnect structure for the VAX-11/750.

The DPM consisted of a bit-sliced ALU fed by two RAM/ROM files. The ROMs supplied frequently used constant operands. All the complex rotate, mask, and extract functions implied by the VAX instruction set were handled by the Rotate/Mask bit slice, which was driven by a 10-bit select code.

The microsequencer occupied two chips. One gate array (Instruction Register Decode—IRD) and four PROMs accomplished opcode decoding for the microsequencer. The control store was 8K words by 56 bits per word, composed of 56 2K × 4-bit chips.

The Memory Interface accomplished address translation and alignment of data to/from memory (a VAX instruction stream is composed of a string of bytes, without any word-boundary alignment restrictions). A translated address cache and data cache improve system performance. The Unibus Adapter was standard with all processors, providing a minimal I/O and diagnostic load path.

The Floating Point Accelerator was a set of 64-bit data paths controlled by a 16-bit extension of the microword to 72 bits.

Even a preliminary design provides enough detail to make a first order reliability model. The preliminary design was dominated by LSI, RAM, and ROM chips. Almost 95 percent of the chips were of LSI complexity, and over 45 percent represented a new technology—the gate arrays. As indicated in Chapter 2, the MIL-HDBK-217B model was not accurate in predicting failure rates for LSI components. The first

RAMP-related problem was to devise better estimates of component failure rates. Better estimates were essential because of the effect of MTTF predictions on maintenance and repair strategies.

The failure rate of RAM chips could be estimated from the failure rates observed by Memory Engineering during their high-temperature, accelerated-life testing of memory chips from potential vendors. Although accelerated-life testing has shortcomings, as discussed in Chapter 2, it provided the most up-to-date data available; data complied by RADC are a few years old by the time they are published and hence give little information on the newest components. To be competitive, components are designed into systems even prior to general availability. As components become more reliable as a result of an accumulated learning curve, systems produced with these components will experience a general reliability improvement throughout their life.

The gate array failure rate was even more difficult to estimate. There was no similar technology inside Digital Equipment Corporation (DEC). Even data on random logic LSI were difficult to acquire. The major random logic LSI chip used by DEC at that time was the LSI-11 NMOS chip set. One potential source of information was DEC's Field Service Labor Activity Reporting System (LARS). Each field service call is recorded according to system identity, time to repair, type of call (such as installation, preventive maintenance, repair), and module failure action (such as adjust, repair, replace, trouble-

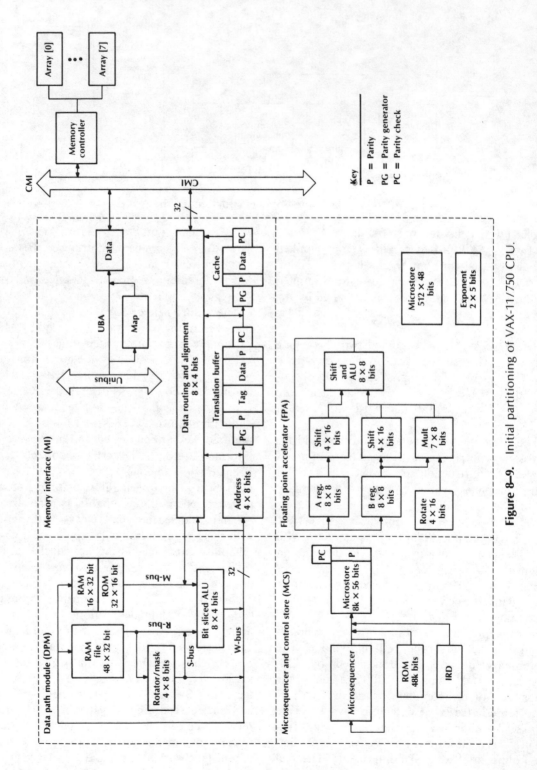

Figure 8–9. Initial partitioning of VAX-11/750 CPU.

shoot). The total number of DEC systems reported in LARS is not known. A second system, Regional Customer Obligation File (RCOF), is composed of systems under contract whose configurations were known. With LARS and RCOF, MTTR and Mean Time Between Calls (MTBC) can be estimated. Because the system duty cycle is not known, MTTF calculations are "guesstimates" at best. Furthermore, because of the small size of systems employing them, LSI-11s rarely appear in RCOF or even LARS. One solution was to obtain data from a controlled environment. Carnegie-Mellon University and DEC had entered into cooperative research in multiprocessors based on LSI-11s. The LSI-11 data presented in Chapter 2 were collected and compared for consistency with data on RAM chip MTTFs culled from several sources. Complexity derating for LSI was developed (see Chapter 2) and applied to the preliminary design.

Table 8-19 lists estimates for the chip and board failure rates. Even though the design evolved, the relative failure rates did not change significantly. The major changes in the relative board failure rates resulted from repartitioning the logic functions as some boards became overcrowded.* The absolute failure rate for the CPU changed less than 5 percent in two years. In fact, during Design Maturity Testing the basic CPU was tested to 90 percent of its initially predicted failure rate at a 90 percent confidence level. Thus, fairly accurate failure rate predictions can be made using even preliminary designs. The relative failure rate predictions are accurate enough to make RAMP design trade-off decisions.

* The basic machine evolved to a four-board design partitioned into a Data Path Module (DPM), Microsequencer and Unibus Adapter (UBA), Memory Interface (MIC) and PROM Control Store (CCS). Although the partitioning changed, the design depicted in Figure 8-9 did not substantially change. Minor design changes include removal of the ROM array feeding the ALU (constants are generated directly from the microstore), a 6K- by 78- (plus two parity) bit control store (arranged as 120 1K- by 4-bit chips), and the FPA now has its own microsequencer and control store.

Table 8–19. Reliability analysis of preliminary VAX-11/750 design.*

Chip Type	Number	Percent of Failure Rate
Gate Array	97	41%
4K ROMs	16	9
8K ROMs	56	47
64-bit RAMs	32	2
512-bit ROM	1	0
SSI/MSI	12	1
	214	100

Board	Percent of Failure Rate (initial)	(after two years)
DPM	7%	10.4%
MCS	57	43.6
MI	15	29.0
FPA	21	16.9
	100	99.9

*See Figure 8-10 for analysis of final design.

One of the first RAMP design studies was the sensitivity of system failure rate to the junction temperature of the gate array transistors. Whereas the gate arrays were designed for up to two watts of power dissipation, the actual transistor junction temperature was unknown. Indeed, no gate array chip had been fabricated at that time and the semiconductor process was just being defined. Table 8-20 lists the results of the temperature-sensitivity study. The sensitivity to high junction temperatures reinforced and economically justified the addition of heat sinks for the gate array chips.

The following conclusions were drawn from the initial reliability study.

- For a 2-Mbyte system, main memory chips would account for 71 percent of the system failure rate. The application of Hamming code (which to a first-order approximation removes the memory chips as a source of error—see Chapter 5) improved CPU/Memory MTTF (under a failure-to-exhaustion model) by a factor of almost 3.5.
- The Control Store board represented 57 percent of the CPU failure rate. Of that total, 82 percent was

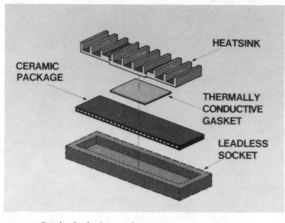

Exploded view of gate array assembly.

Two complete gate array assemblies.

microstore; thus, a total of 47 percent of the CPU failure rate was attributable to the microstore.

• Fifty-six percent of the three-board CPU failure rate and 51 percent of the CPU/Memory control failure rate consisted of RAM and ROM failures.

A series of fault-tolerant techniques was proposed for the RAMs/ROMs in the CPU. Figure 8-10 shows an AUTOFAIL analysis of the standard VAX-11/750 processor as finally implemented (the failure rate groupings thus correspond to the final partitioning, not to the board partitioning depicted in Figure 8-9). The control store (now 80 bits wide) accounts for 55 percent of the RAM/ROM failure rate and 33 percent of the total failure rate. Table 8-21 lists the expected improvements after applications of a series of error-correcting codes to the RAM/ROM arrays in the three-board CPU plus memory controller. With these modifications, a factor of two improvements in MTTF was predicted for a cost of 11 gate array chips.* A point of diminishing returns was reached after applications of ECC to

---

* A gate level design for a Block-Code Corrector chip (see Chapter 3) was the basis for this chip estimate. No performance degradation was anticipated in the case of no failures. The overall parity detection was fast enough to freeze the processor and perform microinstruction retry after correction in all cases except the multiply and divide microoperations, which used a double frequency 160 nsec cycle clock to produce two results every microcycle time.

the Control Store, Translation Buffer, and Data Cache.

Full Hamming coding was too expensive in terms of board area for the Control Store. Block-code correctors are susceptible to multiple-bit failures. Because the Control Store was to be implemented by four-bit-wide chips, the relative failure rate of multiple bits was an additional unknown in establishing the effectiveness of a Block-Code Corrector. It was therefore decided to disperse the resource commitment to RAMP throughout the CPU. In particular, a Visibility Bus was implemented to improve MTTR and to support chip-level repair (see below). In the Control Store, the number of parity bits was increased from one to two to improve the diagnostic resolution of the chip in error. Field Service would have at most 10 suspect ROM chips instead of 20 (hardware captures the mi-

Table 8–20. Sensitivity of CPU failure rate to gate array junction temperature.

Gate Array Junction Temperature	Relative Failure Rate of CPU
50° C	1.00
60° C	1.05
70° C	1.15
80° C	1.30

```
              LSI=    16.000    ROM=    16.000    RAM=    16.000
    E =    1.000    Q =    16.000    L =    1.000    T =    40.000

    MODULE                                                      PERCENTAGE
    COMET.CPU.PLUS.MEMORY.CONTROL                                   100.000
        Data.Path.Module                                         16.187
            Misc                                          42.643
            ROM.AND.RAM                                   27.007
            GATE.ARRAY                                    30.271
        Memory.Interface.Cache                                   25.038
            Misc                                          30.003
            ROM.AND.RAM                                   48.648
            GATE.ARRAY                                    21.349
        Unibus.Interface                                         14.158
            Misc                                          58.633
            ROM.AND.RAM                                   20.905
            GATE.ARRAY                                    20.462
        Control.Store                                            29.908
            Misc                                           5.657
            ROM.AND.RAM                                   94.343
        Memory.Controller                                        14.717
            Misc                                          64.169
            ROM.AND.RAM                                   25.237
            GATE.ARRAY                                    10.594

    # of chips =    662.000    # of gates =    33361.000    # of bits =    732416.000
```

- -

```
            SUMMARY ROLLUP BY COMPONENT TYPE

    TYPE              # of CHIPS                       PERCENTAGE

    SSI               180.000                          10.824
    MSI               142.000                          22.809
    LSI                67.000                          14.914
    ROM               150.000                          35.179
    RAM               123.000                          16.274
    MOS                  .000                             .000
    BIP               662.000                         100.000
```

Figure 8–10. Relative failure rates in 11/750 three board CPU and memory controller.

Table 8–21. Projected improvements in applying ECC to the RAM/ROM arrays in the three-board 11/750 CPU and memory controller.

	Percent Change in Failure Rate	Relative Failure Rate	Extra Chips Required
Stock 11/750	—	1.00	—
ECC Control Store	28%	0.72	4
ECC Memory Interface/Cache	12	0.58	4
ECC Data Path	4		
ECC Unibus	3	0.49	3
Interface	3		
ECC Memory Controller	3		

croaddress that triggered the parity error as well as to which half of the Control Store the error occurred in).

Parity was provided on the Cache and each half of the Translation Buffer. Upon error detection, the appropriate Translation Buffer half could be disabled, thus providing a form of fault tolerance in exchange for performance degradation.

RAMP Features

Figure 8-11 depicts the final implementation of the VAX-11/750. The eight CMI ports are occupied by the CPU, memory controller, floating point accelerator, three Massbus Adapters, Writable Control Store, and Remote Diagnostics Module (RDM). A Unibus Adapter and small cassette tape (TU 58)—for logging, bootstrap-

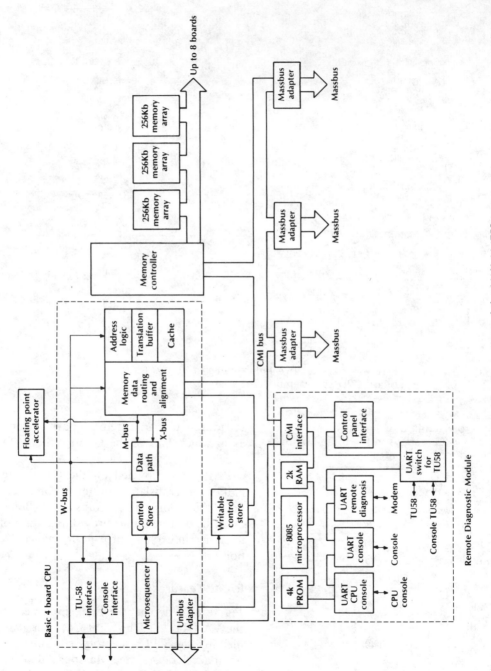

Figure 8–11. Final configuration of the VAX-11/750 system.

ping, and software distribution—are provided as part of the CPU.

The VAX-11/750 does differ from the VAX-11/780 in two major ways that affect the RAMP philosophy: it has gate-array custom LSI chips and a bounded, single cabinet environment. Table 8-22 lists the characteristics and utilization of the gate array chips. The extensive use of gate arrays, the decreased visibility of logic signals because of LSI gate densities, and the higher board costs result in a repair strategy based on microdiagnostics, a Visibility Bus, sockets for the gate array chips, and chip-level repair. The bounded, single-cabinet environment results in reduced complexity and the use of fault intolerant techniques. To reduce complexity, the same microsequencer that implements the VAX architecture also services the Console Subsystem. Because of the limited, controlled environment the six-inch CMI is less likely than the intercabinet SBI to pick up noise. Errors are less likely to occur and substantial complexity can be saved by not implementing parity on the CMI.

Processor Registers

Because there is no separate console processor in the VAX-11/750, there is no equivalent to the ID Bus. All registers are located in either the processor (accessible by the special Move-To/From-Processor Register instructions) or the main memory address space.

Table 8-23 lists the implementation-specific VAX-11/750 processor registers. Four registers are associated with the control of the TU-58, the Console Subsystem mass storage device. These registers are absent from the VAX-11/780 because its separate LSI-11 console processor directly manages the Console Subsystem's floppy disk. Another consequence of lack of a separate console processor is that in the 11/750 the registers associated with error detection in the processor (such as machine check, cache, and translation buffer) are found as processor registers, whereas in the 11/780 they were available only on the ID Bus.

Table 8-22. VAX-11/750 gate array techology.

Gate Array Characteristics

Technology—Low-power bipolar Schottky

Die Size—.215 inch × .244 inch

Package—48 pins

Circuitry—400 identical 4-input NAND gates
44 I/O transceiver gates

Speed per gate—5 to 10 nanoseconds

Gate Array Utilization	Total Used	Unique Types
CPU and Memory Controller	55	27
Floating Point Accelerator	28	7
Massbus Adapter	12	5

As mentioned above, no parity or error checking was deemed necessary on the CMI due to its sheltered environment and implementation similarity to other data paths in the CPU. Hence, there are no registers to control or report CMI errors in the CPU or, for that matter, any CMI port.

Table 8-24 lists details of the RAMP-related processor registers. The Machine Check Error Summary Register records the region of the machine where the error was reported: CMI, Translation Buffer, or Unibus. It also records whether the error occurred on a CPU fetch or an Instruction Buffer (IB) prefetch. Transient errors associated with the IB prefetch can be recovered from by simply flushing the IB.

The Machine Check Status Register gives detailed information about bus and Translation Buffer errors. The CMI can be disabled. Memory errors that are logged include nonresponding memory, ECC corrected read data, and uncorrectable ECC errors. A Lost Error Bit is set if a second error occurs before the first error is serviced. Translation Buffer (TB) errors include the parity bit in error as well as the status (hit or miss) of the last translation.

The Translation Buffer Disable Register controls the replacement strategy on a TB miss.

Table 8–23. VAX-11/750 implementation-specific processor registers.

Register	Access Permitted
Console Storage Receive Status	R/W
Console Storage Receive Data	R
Console Storage Transmit Status	R/W
Console Storage Transmit Data	W
Machine Check Error Summary	R/W
Machine Check Status	R/W
Translation Buffer Disable	R/W
Translation Buffer	R/W
Cache Disable	R/W
Cache Error	R/W
I/O Reset	R/W
Memory Management Enable	R/W

Replacement can be random or forced to one half of the TB. The latter case can be used to disable half of the TB and allows reconfiguration around a permanent failure. The Force Miss Bits, coupled with the TB Hit/Miss Bit (in the Machine Check Status Register) can be used by diagnostics to check the TB's functionality. Finally, the Translation Buffer Register records the address that caused the last protection violation. This datum can be used by system software to repair or isolate software errors.

Because the cache is direct-mapped, the Cache Disable Register controls only turning the cache on or off. The Cache Error Register records whether the Tag or Data recorded the parity error. The Lost Error Bit indicates that a second cache error occurred before the first one was serviced. As in the TB, the Cache Hit/Miss Bit indicates the status of the last reference.

When an internal error is detected, status information is automatically placed on the ma-

chine stack for software analysis and error logging. Table 8-25 lists the error status registers and other information that is placed on the stack. An error summary code pinpoints the region of the system where the error occurred.

Main Memory Registers

There are registers in main memory associated with each CMI port type: memory, Unibus Adapter, and Massbus Adapter.

Table 8-26 details the three registers associated with the ECC main memory. Control and Status Register 0 (CSR 0) contains the address and syndrome of the last detected error. Two bits record whether an error was correctable or uncorrectable. The address and syndrome of an uncorrectable error overwrites the address and syndrome of a correctable error. The Uncorrectable Error, Information Lost Bit records the occurrence of a second uncorrectable error before the first was serviced. The address and syndrome of this second error will not overwrite the address and syndrome of the first error.

CSR 1 contains control and maintenance bits. Single correctable errors can be ignored by setting the Inhibit Reporting Correctable Errors Bit. The Page Mode Address bits specify the memory page affected by the other maintenance-mode bits. The Page Mode Bit controls whether the whole memory is involved or just the specified page. The Check Bits are used to replace or make accessible the ECC bits associated with a word in main memory. The Diagnostic Check Mode allows for substitution on a memory read of the Check Bits field for the ECC bits stored in memory, providing a means of testing the ECC check logic. During writes, the newly generated ECC bits are stored in both memory and Check Bits$\langle 6:0 \rangle$. The Diagnostic Check Mode can operate only on a single page whose address is specified by the Page Address field. While in Diagnostic Check Mode, read errors in other memory pages will not be logged into CSR 0. The Error Disable Mode turns off error detection, correction, and logging. ECC can be dis-

Table 8–24. Details of VAX-11/750 implementation-specific processor registers.

Registers	Subfields	Comments
Machine Check Error Summary	Bus Error	CPU or instruction prefetch caused error
	Translation Buffer Error	
	Unaligned Unibus Reference	
	Operand Fetch/Execution Buffer Fetch	
Machine Check Status	Enable/Disable Buffer	
	Translation Buffer Group 1 Tag Parity Error	
	Translation Buffer Group 0 Tag Parity Error	
	Translation Buffer Group 1 Data Parity Error	
	Translation Buffer Group 0 Data Parity Error	
	Translation Buffer Hit/Miss	Indicates status of last address translation
	Nonexistent Memory Timeout	
	Uncorrectable Data Error	
	Lost Error	Second error occurred before first serviced
Translation Buffer Disable	Replace	Replaces entries at random or forced
	Force G0/G1	Forces replacement to group G0 or G1
	Force Miss G1	If set, forces a miss on group G1
	Force Miss G0	If set, forces a miss on group G0
Translation Buffer	Valid Protection Code $\langle 3:0 \rangle$	Value of address translation that caused last error
	Modify Page Frame Number $\langle 20:0 \rangle$	
Cache Disable	Cache on/off	

(*Table continues on next page*)

Table 8–24 —*Continued*

Registers	Subfields	Comments
Cache Error	Tag Error	
	Data Error	
	Lost Error	
	Hit/Miss	Indicates status of last reference
Unibus Initialize	Initialize	
Memory Management Enable	Enable/Disable	

Table 8–25. VAX-11/750 machine check error logout onto machine stack.

Information

Byte Count (length of information on stack)

Error Summary Code (see below)

Virtual Address Register (operand address)

Program Counter

Memory Data Register

Saved Mode Register (CPU mode during fault)

Read Lock Timeout Register

Translation Buffer Group Parity (subfield of Machine-Check Status Register)

Cache Error Register

Bus Error Register (subfield of Machine-Check Status Register)

Machine-Check Error Summary Register

Backup Program Counter (address of instruction)

Program Status Word

Error Summary Code

Control Store Parity Error

Cache Parity Error

Memory Error

Corrected Memory Data

Write Bus Error

Bad Instruction Register Decode

abled for the entire memory or a single page, depending on the value of the Page Mode Bit.

CSR 2 contains memory configuration information such as the starting address of memory, the validity of memory contents after a power failure, and the presence of memory array boards.

The Unibus Adapter has only one RAMP related-register, the Buffered Data Path Control and Status Register detailed in Table 8-27. Only nonexisting memory and uncorrectable ECC errors are recorded.

The Massbus Adapter has three RAMP-related registers, detailed in Table 8-28. The Control Register has a Maintenance Mode Bit that allows exercising the Massbus without requiring an attached peripheral. When the bit is set, all Massbus devices detach from the bus. The Interrupt Enable Bit allows reporting of Massbus-related errors to the CPU.

The MBA Status Register has three groups of signals. The first group records errors associated with the CMI portion of the access: corrected ECC, no response, and error. The second group deals with Massbus-related errors: control bus hung, nonexistent drive, data late, miss transfer, Massbus parity, and programming. A programming error is logged if a second MBA operation is attempted before completion of the first. The third group logs errors associated with logic in

Table 8–26. VAX-11/750 memory control and status registers.

Register	Subfields	Comments
CSR 0	Page Address ⟨14:0⟩	Address of the 512-byte page in which the error occurred
	Error Syndrome ⟨6:0⟩	
	Correctable Error	Set when a correctable error occurs during a read. Correctable errors during a byte write do not affect this bit.
	Uncorrectable-Error	Set when an even number of errors occurs in a word, or an odd number of errors that generates an invalid syndrome
	Uncorrectable-Error, Information-Lost	Set when an uncorrectable error has occurred after the setting of the Uncorrectable-Error bit
CSR 1	Inhibit Reporting Correctable Errors	When set, single errors will be corrected but not reported to the CPU nor error-related information logged in CSR 0.
	Page Mode Address ⟨14:0⟩	
	Page Mode	When set, the ECC Disable or Diagnostic Check Modes operate on the page specified in Page Mode Address ⟨14:0⟩.
	Check Bits ⟨6:0⟩	Substituted for the Check Bits in Diagnostic Check Mode. In ECC Disable Mode, a read replaces these bits by the Check Bits in the memory array.
	Diagnostic Check Mode	When set, during a read the Check Bits ⟨6:0⟩ are substituted for the ECC bits stored in memory.
	Error Disable Mode	When set, no error detection, correction, logging, or reporting is done.
CSR 2	Starting Address ⟨6:0⟩	Starting address of memory
	Battery Backup Failure	Set when battery backup power has been exhausted
	Memory Present Map ⟨15:0⟩	Bits represent amount and location of memory in the backplane. There are 8 possible locations for memory array boards. Each board, when inserted, sets 2 adjacent bits in this register.

Table 8–27.   RAMP-related VAX-11/750 Unibus adapter register.

Register	Subfields	Comments
Buffered Data Path Control and Status	Error	Logical OR of error bits
	Nonexistent Memory	Set when NXM received from memory
	Uncorrectable Error	Set when memory has uncorrectable error

the MBA: page map and data-path parity errors.

The MBA Diagnostic Register allows setting of incorrect parity on the Massbus, page map, or MBA data path, and reading or writing of selected Massbus fields.

Diagnostics and Repair

Table 8-29 lists the five levels of diagnostics employed in the VAX-11/750, ranging from User Mode Macrodiagnostics, which execute concurrently with user software, to microdiagnostics, which require dedicated use of hardware. A Micro-Verify routine resident in the PROM control store is executed upon system initialization.

The Remote Diagnostics Module (RDM) plays a critical role in the 11/750 RAMP philosophy. Because the 11/750 console interface is provided by microcode executed in the main microsequencer, a CPU failure would bring the system completely down. A large percentage of the CPU hardware would have to be functioning correctly in order to respond to console commands such as examine registers, deposit values, and single step. The RDM has a separate microprocessor that can read the W-bus in Figure 8-11 (for access to the CPU registers) and single-step (either single clock or single instruction) the CPU. It can also write via DMA over the CMI. The RDM contains a small 64-word Writable Control Store (WCS) for executing microdiagnostics stored on a TU-58 cassette. It can also force arbitrary microaddresses, thus using CPU control store to provide more microdiagnostics. A typical scenario would be to set up the

CPU registers by DMA write into memory, execute some CPU microcode through forced microaddresses and clock control, set up a microtest via the forced microaddress and clock control, and observe results via the W-bus.

Another key philosophy is chip-level repair. A board-swap repair strategy usually ties up as many boards in Field Service repair kits and in transit to/from repair depots as there are in functioning CPUs. Because of the high cost of large, LSI-intense boards, a board-swap strategy would have required too large an investment in inventory. Given that the gate array chips represented a complexity comparable to that of an early 1970s SSI printed circuit board and that those earlier diagnostics were targeted at a board-level resolution (that is, the FRU was a board), chip-level repair was deemed practical. Even if only 20 percent of failures were repaired by chip replacement in the field, the reduced inventory costs for boards would offset the chip socket cost. To facilitate field repair, a special leadless chip socket was used. Because sockets potentially increase costs and also increase CPU failure rate, the question of socket failure rate had to be adequately resolved with the socket vendor to insure that more problems were not introduced than were solved. A special Visibility Bus (like that in the 11/780) chains together the outputs of the gate array chips. The goal is resolution to a path containing three to five gate arrays and other MSI chips in 98 percent of the cases. When chip replacement fails, the board will be swapped.

In a typical maintenance scenario on the VAX-11/750, disk-resident, User Mode diagnos-

Table 8–28.   RAMP-related VAX-11/750 Massbus adapter registers.

Register	Subfields	Comments
Control	Maintenance Mode	When set, software can exercise the Massbus without any attached devices.
	Interrupt Enable	When set, causes an interrupt in CPU on the occurrence of any errors reported in the status register.
Status	Corrected Read Data	Set when CMI indicates a correction was made on data
	No response	Set if CMI returns a no response confirmation
	Error Confirmation	Set when CMI returns an error confirmation on a transaction
	Control Bus Hung	Set if MBA Register access times out
	Nonexistent Drive	Set if drive fails to respond within a specified time
	Data Late	
	Miss Transfer Error	
	Massbus Data Parity Error	Indicates error in parity checking of bus data field
	Massbus Control Parity Error	Indicates error in parity checking of bus control field
	Programming Error	Set if software tries to initiate a data transfer while MBA is currently performing one
	Page Frame Map Parity Error	Indicates parity error in memory where page map information is stored
	Silo Parity Error	Set when there is a parity error in data transfer buffer
Diagnostic	Invert Parity ⟨3:0⟩	Inverts the sense of the bus data, bus control, map, and Silo parity generator
	Simulate Asynchronous Control Lines ⟨4:0⟩	Allows setting, clearing of various Massbus signals when in maintenance mode
	Read Signals ⟨20:0⟩	Allows reading of selected Massbus fields

Table 8–29.   VAX-11/750 diagnostics.

Level	Action
Level 1	User Mode Macrodiagnostics run under the VMS (Virtual Memory System) operating system, such as line printer, card reader, terminal, tape, disk, instruction set.
Level 2	Macrodiagnostics executed under Diagnostic Supervisor while VMS is still operational. Used in acceptance tests.
Level 3	Macrodiagnostics executed under the Diagnostic Supervisor with the CPU operating in a stand-alone mode. Used in Unibus diagnostics.
Level 4	Macrodiagnostics executing stand-alone without the Diagnostic Supervisor. Used in instruction set diagnostics.
Level 5	Microdiagnostics executing in a stand-alone mode.
Micro-Verify	PROM resident microdiagnostics executed upon system initialization. A sanity check of the Data Path and Memory Interconnect Modules.

tics periodically execute under VMS (Virtual Memory System), to execise and detect functional errors in memory, MBA, UBA, device controllers, and device drives. Errors reported by User Mode diagnostics or hardware check circuits prompt a customer call to the Digital Diagnostic Center (DDC). The customer replaces the removable disk media with a diagnostic and scratch disk. The DDC engineer calls the customer's processor and loads macrodiagnostics from the diagnostic disk. If the disk is not operable, the diagnostics can be loaded from the TU-58 or down-line loaded over the telephone. The DDC attempts to isolate the failure to a subsystem. If the CPU is faulty, the diagnostic

on the TU-58 is executed to verify the CPU status.

The DDC advises the local Field Service Office of the failing subsystem. At the customer's site, Field Service performs a board-swap and reverifies the system. If the failing subsystem is the CPU, microdiagnostics are loaded into the 64-word WCS on board the RDM. Multiple TU-58 cassettes are used to accommodate the extended length of the microdiagnostics (the VAX-11/780 microdiagnostics occupy five floppy disks). Length is also the reason that microdiagnostics are not down-line loaded from the DDC to attempt CPU failure isolation at the board or chip level. The 64-word WCS is loaded to set up data paths, registers, and the like, then overlaid with a series of tests. Each test exercises a single gate-array function. Results of tests are observed on the W-bus or Visibility Bus. The RDM also monitors output of the control store. In the case of control store failure, parity pinpoints the failure to 10 chips. A microstore image stored on the TU-58 is used for comparison when the RDM accesses the faulty microstore word.

The microdiagnostics isolate the failure to between three and five gate array chips. If the malfunction persits after chip replacement, the board is swapped. The board is also swapped if one of the nonsocketed SSI/MSI chips fails.

SUMMARY

Table 8-30 lists the RAMP features common to the VAX-11/750 and VAX-11/780 implementations. In addition to describing the benefit of each feature, the table indicates whether the feature improves MTTF and/or MTTR.

Table 8-31 lists the RAMP-related features that vary in the two implementations.

REFERENCES

Bell et al. [1970]; Bell and Strecker [1976]; Strecker [1978].

Table 8–30. Common VAX RAMP features.

Feature	Example	Benefit	Aids MTTF	Aids MTTR
Processor consistency checking	Arithmetic traps, memory-address protection, limit checking, reserved opcodes	Limits damage due to hardware or software errors	Yes	Yes
Interval timer	1-microsecond resolution	Used by diagnostics to test time-dependent functions	No	Yes
Disk error correcting codes	RP05, RP06, and RK06 detect all errors up to 11 bits and correct single burst up to 11 bits	Tolerates transient and media related faults	Yes	Yes
Peripheral write-verify checking hardware	Read after write followed by comparison	Detects error	No	Yes
Track offset retry hardware	Upon error, disk retries read. If retry fails, disk head is offset for retry.		Yes	Yes
Bad block handling	VMS operating system removes bad disk blocks from use.		Yes	Yes
On-line error logging	Records exceptional conditions in an error log, including time and system state	Aids permanent and intermittent fault isolation	No	Yes

Table 8-31. Comparison of VAX-11/750 and VAX-11/780 features.

Feature	VAX-11/750	VAX-11/780	Benefit	Aid MTTF	Aid MTTR
Fault Intolerance					
Air flow	Blowers	Blowers	Lowers chip junction temperature	Yes	No
LSI	Memory chips, 90% of CPU Logic functions implemented as custom gate array	Memory Chips	Fewer chips result in fewer boards, more reliable per function over SSI/MSI, lower power consumption, hence, cooler junction temperatures	Yes	Yes
Cabling	Card cage fixed mounted and not on slides. No internal cables. Connections through backplane, no cables to cards.		Fewer pluggable connectors to fail	Yes	Yes
Physically bounded system	Yes	No	Limited number of system configurations; CPU and memory in one cabinet results in greater control of environmental factors such as temperature and electromagnetic interference.	Yes	Yes
Sensors and indicators	Power loss, temperature, air flow	Power loss	Protects system from damage resulting from emergency conditions	Yes	Yes
Modular power supply	Yes	Yes	Easy replacement	No	Yes
Fault Tolerance					
Main memory	7-bit ECC per 32-bit word	8-bit ECC per 64-bit word	Tolerates transient and permanent failures. Logging of error information allows quick fault isolation.	Yes	Yes

Component	Error detection	Description		
Control store	2 parity bits: 1 even parity, 1 odd parity, over disjoint subfields of the 78-bit-wide control store	3 parity bits. 1 per 32 bits of control store	Provides tolerance of transient errors as well as partial isolation to the failing chip	No	Yes
	Micro-verify		Control store resident check of data paths, registers, and other portions of the system boot path. Ensures proper boot of system if passed.	No	Yes
Translation buffer	2-way set-associative. 4 parity bits for each set: 1 over 15-bit tag and valid bit; 3 over disjoint subfields of 15-bit page frame number, 4-bit protection, and modify bit	2-way set-associative. 6 parity bits for each set: 3 over 16-bit tag, valid, modify, and 4-bit protection: 3 over 21 bits of page-frame number	Provides faulty chip isolation. Tolerates transients by recalculating TB contents. Tolerates permanent failures by disabling one set.	Yes	Yes
Cache	Direct-mapped cache: 5 parity bits, 1 over 12-bit tag and valid bit: 4 over 32 data bits (byte parity)	2-way set-associative. 7 parity bits per set: 3 over 12-bit tag and valid bit: 4 over 32 data bits (byte parity)	Provides faulty chip isolation. Tolerates transients by refetching cache contents. Tolerates permanent failures by disabling cache (11/750) or one set (11/780).	Yes	Yes
Synchronous Backplane Interconnect (SBI)	None	2 parity bits: 1 over 32-bit data/address field. 1 over 12 bits of control information	Detects errors and isolates to faulty bus port. Transients tolerated by bus level retry.	No	Yes
		Silo captures last 16 bus cycles	Isolates faulty chips	No	Yes
Unibus Adapter	None	Parity on data paths and Unibus Map	Provides faulty chip isolation. Transients tolerated by retry.	No	Yes
Massbus	Data and Control Bus lines parity. Data buffer parity.	Data and Control Bus lines parity	Provides faulty chip isolation. Transients tolerated by retry.	No	Yes
Watchdog timer	None	In LSI-11 console processor	Detects hung machine and allows automatic restart	No	No

(Table continues on next page)

Table 8-31 —*Continued*

Feature	VAX-11/750	VAX-11/780	Benefit	Aid MTTF	Aid MTTR
Clock margining	None	Change clock speed	Aids isolation of timing problems	No	Yes
Maintenance registers	Machine Check Error Summary Cache Error Machine Check Status	SBI Fault/Status SBI Silo Comparator SBI Error SBI Timeout Address SBI Maintenance Buffer Translation Parity	Aids fault isolation	No	Yes
Visibility Bus	Internal signals made available to microdiagnostics	Internal signals made available to the console or microdiagnostics	Aids fault isolation	No	Yes
Chip Sockets	Gate array	None	Allows replacement of individual gate array chips	No	Yes
Remote diagnostic module	Load/examine critical machine registers Monitor control store output for control store verification Error status registers readable over W-bus Monitor Memory Data Register (MDR) to verify memory-CPU transfers and opcode undergoing execution Visibility of cache and translation buffer contents to insure correct functionality Access to V-Bus. On-board 64-word writable control store for microdiagnostics.	Load/examine critical machine registers Single-step sequencer Clock margining Error status registers readable over ID Bus Access to V-Bus Microdiagnostics loadable into writable control store	Provides remote, expert troubleshooting	No	Yes

Recovery through Programming System/360—System/370

Donald L. Droulette

INTRODUCTION

Recovery Management can be defined as the operational control of those system facilities (both program and machine) which strive to effectively deal with detected machine malfunctions within an operating system. Its primary concern is to maintain total system operation with minimum impact upon the availability of system resources.

Recovery Management, defined above and treated in this report, refers to recovery from an unscheduled system interruption resulting from a machine malfunction. As such, Recovery Management can be viewed as a consideration which leads to a higher degree of total system reliability, serviceability, and availability.

Effective Recovery Management is not a luxury; on the contrary, it may, in a given system, be a necessity. Without it, what need only be a minor problem becomes a major problem, possibly a catastrophe.

Recovery Management facilities service unscheduled system interruptions originating within an I/O device/unit, channel, processor storage unit, or central processing unit. The presence of such an interruption is indicated by a device/unit, channel, or machine-check condition. No

Droulette, D., "Recovery Through Programming System/360–System/370," *Proceedings of the Spring Joint Computer Conference*, 1971, pp. 467–476.

individual Recovery Management facility services all machine malfunctions.

Recovery Management facilities attempt recovery at different levels; these levels differ with respect to the consequences imposed upon the system during the recovery process. Not all of the Recovery Management facilities have the capability of effecting recovery at each level. Recovery Management facilities are optional, and as such, must be specified by the user at system generation time. Considering that Recovery Management facilities are directed at specific types of failures, only after the thorough analysis of an installation's applications and requirements should a Recovery Management package be structured.

THE RECOVERY MANAGEMENT OBJECTIVE

The objective of Recovery Management is to provide the user with a higher degree of system availability (more time for more jobs) by minimizing the impact of machine malfunctions upon the user's operations. This objective is realized with the successful achievement of the following goals:

- Reduce the number of unscheduled system interruptions resulting from machine malfunctions.
- Minimize the impact of such interruptions in the event they do occur.

Through Programming, interruptions to the user can be reduced, their impact minimized and their causes isolated. There are a number of functions which can be performed to achieve these objectives of Recovery Management. Some of these are:

- *Instruction Retry*.   The concept of instruction retry is not new. It is something IBM has been doing for years, particularly in the I/O area. Instruction retry has been standard procedure whenever an error was encountered in reading or writing a tape. It is possible to extend this retry capability and to employ it when a CPU or main storage malfunction occurs. A relatively large number of malfunctions are intermittent in nature, rather than being solid

failures; therefore, there is a high probability of success of execution and recovery if an instruction retry can be attempted.
- *Refreshing Main Storage*.   If instruction retry cannot be accomplished, one function which could be of value would be the ability to refresh main storage. Through this damage which either caused or was caused by a malfunction could be repaired. This function could be accomplished by loading a new copy of the affected module or "Csect" into main storage or by a process known as check summing.
- *Selective Termination*.   This function would enable the system to examine the failing environment, determine what problem program was executing and then proceed to terminate this program while entering all other jobs which were executing at the time of the malfunction. This is really a type of job which "frees" the resources of the system allocated to the job and makes them available for future use. This process results in the loss of a specific job but it keeps the system alive.
- *I/O Recovery*.   The above functions have been directed mainly to errors which occur in the CPU or main storage. From an examination of system incidents, it is evident that a certain portion of errors occur in the I/O area. Recovery could be accomplished by I/O retry which is available through the error recovery procedures for the different I/O devices. Another group of I/O errors—channel control checks, channel data checks, and interface control checks—may be analyzed and under certain conditions a retry can be attempted. The I/O device or medium can malfunction and if retry is not successful the ability to switch data sets may be provided and then retry the operation on the new drive. Another is to try alternate routes to the same device, that is by addressing a device through a different channel or control unit.
- *Operator Awareness*.   A group of system incidents is due to procedural and operator errors. Several things can be done to decrease these errors such as better trained personnel, minimal control information and clear and concise operator messages.

All of these functions are aimed at continuing the operation of the system. This is not always possible to accomplish. Therefore, the next best thing is to minimize the effect of the malfunction. This can be done by attempting to preserve information concerning the malfunction and to make it available to assist personnel to determine what caused the error and what can be done to correct it. Recording, therefore, is a major part of recovery management.

Recovery Management support has provided a number of these functions in the operating systems. RMS has provided a hierarchy of recovery which involves four levels of error recovery.

1. *Functional Recovery*.   Retry the interrupted operation.
2. *System Recovery*.   Terminate the affected task.
3. *System-Supported Restart*.   Prepare for Re-IPL.
4. *System Repair*.   Require stop for repair.

Functional Recovery

Functional recovery is achieved when an interrupted operation is successfully retried. Such recovery is extremely desirable from a system point of view, because it makes the entire incident transparent to the user.

System Recovery

System recovery is achieved when system operation is maintained although an interrupted operation has not been retried. This effort involves: an analysis of the failure's environment, a repair of the damage associated with the malfunction to prevent further interruptions, and/or an attempt to associate the malfunction with a particular task in order to allow selective termination of the affected job and continued processing of the unaffected jobs.

System-Supported Restart

System-supported restart is achieved when a stop for repair is not required and system operation is restarted using an Initial Program Load (IPL) procedure supported by System Restart facilities. (System Restart facilities aid the IPL procedure by preserving and using system job and data queues.)

System Repair

System repair, the lowest but most critical level of error recovery, consists of stopping the system and repairing a malfunction which cannot be serviced by the particular recovery facility at any of the previous levels. Recovery Management facilities aid maintenance personnel by providing them with detailed error analysis records. There is always, however, the possibility that system damage will be severe enough to preclude retrieval of the error records. In those cases, personnel will have to make use of the System/360 diagnostics available to them.

The levels of error recovery applicable to IBM Operating Systems operations are illustrated in Figure 9-1; the outcome of recovery procedures 1, 2, or 3 determines the level at which recovery will be effected. The bracketed information on a given flowline indicates the consequences of recovery at that level.

USER PERSONNEL INVOLVEMENT

The successful operation of a Recovery Management package is directly proportional to the planning for and use of specific facilities in a given operating system.

Once a user has determined what his needs and requirements are, the amount of specification required to tailor his Recovery Management package is minimal. The selection of some recovery facilities is made during the system generation process. Modifications can be made during the IPL/NIP process.

The programmer's responsibility varies greatly with respect to the Recovery Management options available to him:

- He may code actual error recovery routines which will receive control through macros specifying user exits (see *Optional User-written Routines*).
- He need not involve himself at all with regard to certain Recovery Management facilities.

Once the system has been set up and is running, it is the operator's responsibility to be aware of and responsive to the parameters required by, and the messages and wait-state codes issued by particular Recovery Management facilities.

Maintenance personnel should acquaint themselves with the scope and operation of those

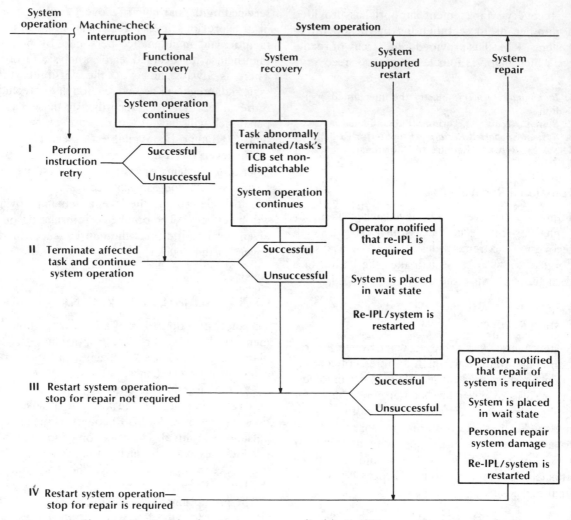

Figure 9–1. Levels of error recovery applicable to IBM operating systems.

Recovery Management facilities incorporated into the systems for which they have responsibility. They must be familiar with the messages and wait-state codes issued, and the error records produced, if they are to make effective use of the information available to them.

SUMMARY DESCRIPTION OF FACILITIES

This section briefly describes the available Recovery Management facilities. Included are discussions of the Machine-Check Handler (MCH),

the Channel Check-Handler (CCH), and I/O Recovery Management-Support (I/O RMS). The individual recovery facilities are discussed as they apply to specific types of failures, or to specific recovery functions. The topics of discussion are:

- I/O Device/Unit Recovery Facilities
- Channel Recovery Facilities
- I/O Recovery Management Facilities
- CPU/Processor Storage Recovery Facilities
- System Associated Recovery Facilities
- Error Record Retrieval Facilities

The following points are made to clarify the function and scope of those recovery facilities which cross the bounds of two or more failure types:

• The *Optional User Routines* receive control from the IBM supplied Error Recovery Procedures (ERPS) on permanent I/O device/unit errors in order to determine whether their associated tasks are to be terminated.
• The *System Environment Recording Routines (SER0, SER1) and the Machine-Check Handler (MCH) program* can perform recording functions for channel and machine-check conditions. However, the limited SER1 and extensive MCH recovery capabilities deal only with machine-check conditions. Therefore, if one desires channel recovery, he must also make use of the *Channel-Check Handler (CCH)*. CCH may be used in conjunction with MCH, SER0, or SER1.
• The *System Environment Recording Editing and Printing (SEREP) program* may be used to record, edit, and print I/O device/unit, channel, CPU, and processor storage conditions. SEREP will be used when no automatic recording facility has been invoked, the facility invoked has failed in its operation, or the recorded records cannot be retrieved by the *Environmental Record Editing and Printing (EREP) program*. EREP is a utility which edits and prints those error analysis records placed on the SYS1.LOGREC data set. This data set resides on the system residence device and is reserved for the exclusive use of all those recovery facilities which generate error analysis records.

I/O DEVICE/UNIT RECOVERY FACILITIES

The problem of malfunctions occurring within I/O device/units has been a concern for quite some time. The facilities available for the servicing and detection of these failures are:

• IBM Standard Error Recovery Procedures
• Optional User Written Routines
• On-Line Test System

IBM Standard Error Recovery Procedures

Standard error recovery procedures (ERPs) exist for I/O devices/units in order to maintain device performance and to provide uniform recovery procedures for all failures. The three types of IBM-supplied error routines are:

• Device-dependent routines
• Common routines
• I/O Recording routines

The device-dependent routines attempt functional recovery for particular device types by retrying operations a specific number of times. If functional recovery is not possible, control is passed to an optional user-written routine for further determination. Device-dependent routines exist for:

• Teleprocessing Devices
• Unit Record Devices
• Tape Devices
• Direct Access Devices
• Graphic Devices

The common routines are used by the device-dependent routines to analyze the type of error, to issue console messages, and to update the statistics table.

The I/O recording routines are the outboard recorder (OBR) and the statistical data recorder/channel-check recorder (SDR/CCR). OBR produces records for permanent I/O device failures on the SYS1.LOGREC data set. SDR/CCR updates the statistic counters on the SYS1.LOGREC data set whenever one of the error statistics counters in the statistics table overflows, and places I/O inboard records produced by the optional Channel-Check Handler (CCH) on the SYS1.LOGREC data set. The records placed on the SYS1.LOGREC aid maintenance personnel at the System Repair level.

Optional User-Written Routines

Should an installation determine that available Recovery Management facilities do not fill a need unique to the installation's requirements, user-written routines may be added to the system. When in the system, user-written routines are given control through the DCB macro instruction (SYNAD and EROPT). The user routine can determine on certain I/O device conditions if its associated task should be terminated.

On-Line Test System

The purpose of the On-Line Test System is to test the functioning of I/O devices in a controlled environment with minimum interference to the operating system. The On-Line Test System consists of an executive program, a series of tests for I/O devices/units, and a special SVC to perform functions required in the OS nucleus. The executive program serves as an interface between the operating system and the unit tests. It schedules and controls the running of the tests and provides communication with the operator. The use of the On-Line Test System serves to insure the integrity of the system's I/O devices. It might be considered preventive Recovery Management since its use should lead to the repair of faulty equipment prior to failure during system operation.

CHANNEL-CHECK HANDLER (CCH)

The Channel-Check Handler is designed to increase machine availability by minimizing the effects of channel malfunctions for 2860/2870/2880 and System/370 Model 155 channels. Without CCH, such malfunctions would be system incidents. The Channel-Check Handler will (1) determine the effect on the system of particular conditions that may have occurred, (2) set error indicators in the Error Recovery Procedure Interface Bytes (ERPIB) for the Error Recovery Procedure (ERP), and (3) create a record of the channel-error condition.

Unlike MCH, which is model dependent, CCH is only channel dependent because the Channel I/O Logout area is the analysis material used by the CCH program.

CCH includes the Dynamic Loading feature, which enables the main part of CCH (channel

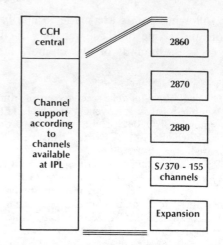

Figure 9–2.   CCH dynamic loading.

and model independent) to link to the various channel-dependent analysis routines. (See Figure 9-2.) Dynamic Loading also allows dynamic configuration for the specific channels on-line at NIP time, even if more channels were specified at SYSGEN time.

The Channel-Check Handler receives control from the I/O Supervisor (IOS) after detection of a channel control check, channel data check or an interface control check. CCH then completes its analysis of the error condition by setting up the ERPIB for the ERP or by indicating that immediate retry or termination is necessary. If termination is indicated, the error is recorded on the SYS1.LOGREC data set and a wait-state condition is set. If immediate retry is indicated, control is then returned to IOS who performs the retry and passes control to the next processing program on a successful retry. This retry is for special I/O operations such as SENSE. If an ERPIB has been created, IOS schedules the appropriate device ERP which operates in the Error Transient Area and receives a pointer to the ERPIB. (See Figure 9-3.) Based on the ERPIB information, the device ERP can determine whether a retry of the failing operation can be attempted or if the operation must be considered a permanent error.

For permanent error conditions, a message to the operator is printed (WTO Error MSG), the statistical data counters (STAT Update) for the devices are updated, a record of the permanent error condition is made on the SYS1.LOGREC data set by the Outboard Recording Routine (OBR), and an exit is taken. For errors marked as retryable, a retry is attempted and, if successful, control is passed to STAT Update to update the statistical data counters and then to OBR, which records the successful Channel-check recovery.

Functional Recovery is achieved on channel errors that can be successfully retried by CCH or the device ERP. CCH enhances the performance of OS/360 by reducing the number of system incidents resulting from channel malfunctions.

I/O RECOVERY MANAGEMENT SUPPORT

I/O Recovery Management Support (I/O RMS) is an extension to existing functions of the Operating System that address the availability and reliability needs of IBM customers that may not be realized due to channel, control unit, device, and medium failures.

Initially, these functions encompassed only the Device Dependent Error Recovery Procedures

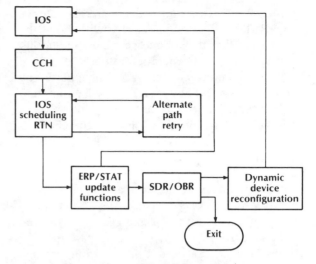

Figure 9–4. APR/DDR processing.

(ERP's), which were designed to effect a retry of a device failure on a particular path after a unit-check condition. Subsequently, with the implementation of the Channel-Check Handler (CCH), the utility of the ERP's was extended to effect a retry of channel failures (channel checks). In order to meet the continuing need for higher availability and reliability, I/O RMS provides two additional optional system functions that may be used to address the problem of I/O errors: Alternate Path Retry (APR) on the channel level and Dynamic Device Reconfiguration (DDR). (See Figure 9-4.)

Without these functions, when an ERP is unable to successfully retry an I/O operation, permanent error is indicated. When a program encounters a permanent I/O error, it either accepts the error and continues, or ABENDS. If a critical supervisor function encounters a permanent I/O error, the system terminates.

APR

I/O RMS extends recovery from an I/O error with APR by ensuring that a different channel will be tried (if one exists) during error recovery on a channel-detected error. If a permanent error

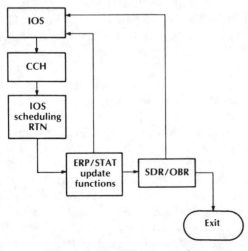

Figure 9–3. CCH processing.

exists on a device with a demountable volume, I/O RMS will extend recovery with DDR by requesting that the volume be moved to another device and the I/O operation retried.

The maximum number of paths supported by any one device will be four. APR will ensure that a different channel will be tried (if one exists, is on-line, and ready) only on retry of channel-detected errors, Retry on other errors will be handled as in the past. APR does not support tape.

In addition, APR provides an operator Command-VARY PATH. Through this command an operator can select a specific channel path and remove it from the system. Also, a path that has been removed can be put back on line through this command.

Alternate Path Retry is an extension of the Channel-Check Handler.

DDR

DDR extends I/O recovery when a permanent error develops on a device with a demountable volume by causing the system to request that the volume be moved.

The operator may also request DDR during normal execution to allow a volume to be moved from one device to another. A DDR can be operator-requested for volume cleaning, etc.

DDR can also be requested by the operator during "intervention required" conditions on readers, printers, and punches.

DDR will support the 2400 tape series, the 2420-7 tape, the 2311 and 2314 disks, the 2321 data cell drive, and readers, punches, and printers.

DDR can be requested by the operator anytime during execution, or by the system after a permanent error for all 2400 (including 2420-7), 2311, 2314, and 2321 devices. DDR can be requested only by the operator for readers, printers, and punches during "intervention required" conditions. "Intervention required" is either indicated by the system or may be caused by the operator. (The operator may cause an "interven-

tion required" condition by making the unit "not ready.")

DDR's support of the 2314 allows the operator to move a volume to a drive on another 2314. It also allows the operator to move all data cells from the failing 2321 to another 2321. DDR will *not* allow the swapping of data cells on one device.

If the SYSRES option is selected, the SYSRES volume may be moved from one device to another at the request of the system or of the operator. The system will not request SYSRES swap unless a critical I/O operation is involved. (A critical I/O operation is one which involves the SVC library.)

If high availability is important to the installations, a duplicate SYSRES volume would be advisable. In order to use such a volume, writing on SYSRES would have to be prohibited except for the SYS1.LOGREC data set. Therefore, no libraries on SYSRES could be updated, no work data sets could be allocated on the SYSRES device, and SYS1.SYSJOBQE would have to be on a volume other than SYSRES. If the installation had such a duplicate volume, as well as an additional available SYSRES device, it would be possible to recover from both a device error and a media error.

SYSRES Option: Since some users do not have a demountable SYSRES device, DDR support of SYSRES will be an option at SYSGEN time. Thus, the resident code necessary for SYSRES DDR is included only when the option is taken.

Dynamic Device Reconfiguration is an extension of IOS as it applies as much to device errors as channel errors.

With I/O RMS, a device encountering an error-prone channel path may be able to continue operating on a different channel path. A volume on an error-prone device may be used effectively on a different device. Specifically, bus-out checks and data checks, along with other error types, will have a higher degree of recovery, since a path to the volume may be made available that excludes the source of error.

I/O RMS is not model dependent.

In summary, I/O RMS will extend device performance in areas that may have previously rendered a job or the system inoperative.

CPU/PROCESSOR STORAGE RECOVERY FACILITIES

Machine-check conditions which arise within the CPU or processor storage are serviced by the mutually exclusive recovery facilities MCH, SER0, and SER1. If none of these are chosen at SYSGEN time, the default condition is a wait state. That is, when a machine check is encountered, the machine goes into a wait state. If such a wait state condition occurs or should a facility fail in its recovery attempt, SEREP may be used to access the CPU logout. (MCH is mandatory in the System/360 Model 85 and System/370 Models 155 and 165.)

Machine-Check Handler (MCH)

The primary function of the Machine-Check Handler is to attempt recovery from main storage or CPU failures which ECC or HIR has not previously corrected. An important additional function is to record each failure. The goal of MCH is total recovery, achieved when the interrupted program is enabled to continue processing at the point where the interruption occurred. When total recovery is not possible, MCH attempts to terminate the effected task without halting the entire system. If, however, a stop in system processing cannot be avoided, the error records produced by MCH aid manual repair.

MCH processing is inseparable from the operations of the machine recovery facilities, ECC and HIR. Upon detection of a hardware failure, either ECC or HIR (depending on the type of error) receives control. Only after these circuits make their recovery attempt does a machine-check interruption occur. MCH receives control at the interruption by means of the machine-check new PSW which contains the address of

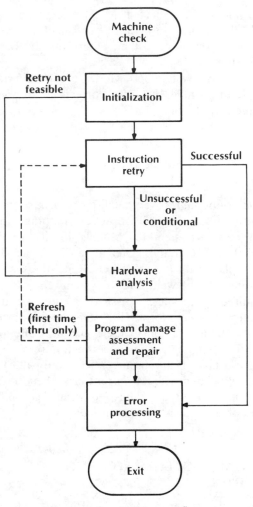

Figure 9–5. MCH gross flow.

the MCH Resident Nucleus. Figure 9-5 illustrates the sequences of operations performed by MCH.

The path followed by MCH processing depends on whether or not the machine facilities were successful in their recovery attempt. If so, MCH only records the error, after which control is returned to the system. If the recovery attempt was unsuccessful, MCH analyzes the error and attempts recovery. If recovery is achieved, MCH records the error, notifies the operator, and returns control to the system. However, should recovery not be effected, MCH attempts to record the error, informs the operator of the condition of the system, then enters the disabled-wait state.

Note: In System/360 Model 65, Instruction retry and single bit error correction are performed by the program.

System Environment Recording (SER0 and SER1)

These optional recovery facilities record machine malfunctions of the CPU, processor storage, and channels in System/360 Models 40, 50, 65, 75, and 91 (SER1 only). After an error record has been placed on the SYS1.LOGREC, the system is placed in the wait state. If system repair is not required, a message is issued to the operator requesting him to re-IPL (System-Supported Restart). In addition to the recording function, SER1 attempts to associate the failure with a specific task. If the failure affects only the job step associated with the current task, the job step can be terminated without requiring a complete stop of the system (System Recovery).

SYSTEM ASSOCIATED RECOVERY FACILITIES

While the following facilities do not actually record or analyze errors, they are an integral part of the Recovery Management scheme in that they further reduce the time involved in recovering from a malfunction which has caused an interruption in system operation:

• System Restart
• Checkpoint/Restart

System Restart

The system restart facilities aid the IPL procedures by allowing the system to resume opera-

tion without having to reenter jobs that have been enqueued. This is especially time-saving in the case of those malfunctions which require a halt of system operation without a stop for repair. Information concerning input work queues, output work queues, and jobs in interpretation, execution, or termination is preserved for use when the system is reloaded. When the system is restarted, a message is written to the operator describing the status of each job in the system.

Checkpoint/Restart

The checkpoint/restart facility provides the capability of restarting program processing subsequent to an I/O device/unit error, machine check, channel check, intentional operator intervention, or similar event. Job step information is recorded at user designated checkpoints in a problem program; if restart becomes necessary, it can be initiated from an available checkpoint. Checkpoint/restart can be invoked subsequent to system restart or subsequent to the abnormal termination of an effected job by one of the recovery facilities.

Use of this facility minimizes time lost in reprocessing a job step that has been terminated. It is used to best advantage in programs of long duration, or with programs where restarting from the beginning would be difficult.

ERROR RECORD RETRIEVAL FACILITIES

Although automatic recovery procedures are extremely desirable, such recovery is sometimes impossible, and human intervention on the part of the maintenance personnel is required. The following facilities are part of the Recovery Management scheme, in that they facilitate system repair by providing a means of accessing failure data:

- Environment Record Editing and Printing (EREP) utility
- System Environment Recording Editing and Printing (SEREP) program

Environment Record Editing and Printing Utility

EREP, running under the operating system, edits and prints error records generated by OBR, SDR/CCR, CCH, SER0, SER1, and MCH and recorded on the SYS1.LOGREC data set.

The EREP utility program can edit and print:

- Combinations of the above records
- Records that were generated within a specific period of calendar time
- I/O outboard or statistical count records, or both, related to a specific channel or unit
- I/O outboard or statistical count records, or both, related to a specific I/O device type

EREP normally clears each selected record to zeros in the SYS1.LOGREC data set when processing of that record is complete. However, an option can be specified to prevent the clearing of selected records. Thus, a log of specific error conditions can be retained in the data set.

EREP output provides information for interpretation by the people performing the repair function.

A standard operating procedure in a Computer Center using MCH and/or CCH should be to execute EREP on a regular basis and then the information would be available to repair personnel as an aid or indicator to anticipate serious trouble. Upon review, if a particular pattern appears indicating possible degradation, preventative maintenance may be performed before the occurrence of a serious incident.

System Environment Recording, Editing and Printing Program

SEREP is used to access failure information when:

- No automatic error recording facility (SER0, SER1, CCH, MCH, OBR, SDR/CCR) has been invoked
- An automatic error recording facility has failed in the performance of its function
- The SYS1.LOGREC data set cannot be accessed to obtain the error analysis records

SEREP is manually loaded using the standard IPL procedure. The program prints the information regarding the failure's environment on an online printing device. The SEREP procedure is aimed at improving the overall performance by minimizing unscheduled downtime. The program allows maintenance personnel to take full advantage of the machine diagnostic capabilities of the system in analyzing and correcting the following types of machine malfunctions:

- I/O Channel Failure
- I/O Device Failure
- I/O Test Channel Failure
- I/O Device Not Operational
- I/O Machine Check Failure

RMS/65 RELATIONSHIP TO THE OPERATING SYSTEM

The RMS/65 package is comprised of two components, the Machine Check Handler (MCH) and the Channel Check Handler (CCH). For System/360 Model 65, both components are optional and a user at SYSGEN time may choose (1) CCH only, (2) MCH only, or (3) both MCH and CCH, depending on the needs of the installation. For System/360 Model 85 and System/370 Models 155 and 165, the MCH and CCH are an integral part of the Control System and, therefore, are not an option.

When selected at SYSGEN time, the components of RMS are included as part of the resident OS Nucleus. See Figure 9-6.

SYSTEM/370 CONSIDERATIONS

The current program status word (PSW) bit 13 has taken on more significance in System/370. In

OS nucleus

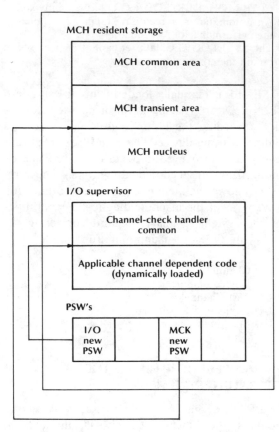

Figure 9–6.   RMS relationship to OS.

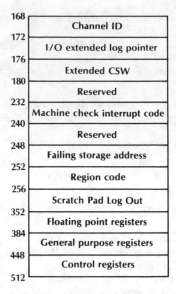

168	Channel ID
172	I/O extended log pointer
176	Extended CSW
180	Reserved
232	Machine check interrupt code
240	Reserved
248	Failing storage address
252	Region code
256	Scratch Pad Log Out
352	Floating point registers
384	General purpose registers
448	Control registers
512	

Figure 9–7.   Permanently allocated storage locations.

System/360, bit 13 had sole control of Recovery Management functions. In System/370 there are recovery submasks in the control registers area which function in conjunction with bit 13 of the current PSW. Therefore, if bit 13 of the PSW is one submask and the subclass mask bit in the control register is another, the associated condition will initiate a machine-check interruption. If either bit is zero, an interruption would not be initiated. Some subclass condition masks are system damage, timer damage, system recovery, etc.

Permanently allocated storage locations have been extended in System/370 for machine-check handling. Storage locations 168 thru 512 contain the added information for handling machine checks. (See Figure 9-7.) This information is supplied to assist in performing the recovery function. Such information consists of Channel ID, I/O extended by log-out pointer, limited channel log-out, I/O address, machine-check interruption code (discussed below), failing storage address, floating point, general and control registers as well as model dependent areas.

The Machine-Check Interruption Code is a double word starting at location 232. It contains such information as the time of interruption occurrence, machine-check intended log-out length, and subclasses. A subclass identifies the machine-check condition which caused the interruption. Some subclass conditions that can be indicated are system damage, instruction processing damage, timer damage, external damage, automatic configuration (when performed by hardware) and storage error type (whether corrected or uncorrected).

CONCLUSION

I believe that effective error recovery is a partnership between engineering and programming and these two must form a partnership and attack the problem together in order to provide a satisfactory solution. Recovery Management Support is a step in the direction which Error Recovery must take if the requirements of computer technology are to be met in this area. Every sign indicates that this is being accomplished.

It appears that some meaningful steps are being taken toward the goal of reducing the number of interruptions to which a user is exposed and to minimizing the impact of these interruptions when they do occur.

REFERENCE MATERIALS

IBM System/360 Operating System—System Reference Library

Concepts and facilities	GC28-6535
Operator's reference	GC28-6691
MFT guide	GC27-6939
MVT guide	GC28-6720

IBM System/360 Operating System—Program Logic Manuals

I/O supervisor	GY28-6616
MVT job management	GY28-6660
MCH for model 65	GY27-7155
MCH for model 85	GY27-7184

IBM System 360 Operating System

Machine check handler for	GY27-7198
the IBM System/370	
Models 155 and 165, systems logic	

Availability, Reliability, and Maintainability Aspects of the SPERRY UNIVAC 1100/60

L. A. Boone   H. L. Liebergot   R. M. Sedmak

Abstract

This paper describes the fault tolerant capabilities of the SPERRY UNIVAC 1100/60 Information Processing System, a recently announced medium scale general purpose computer system. In the 1100/60, a variety of techniques is employed for the detection/correction and isolation of, and recovery from, most single-bit hardware faults as well as many multiple-bit faults. An approach for checking fault detection circuits is implemented using a comprehensive fault injection system. A four level maintenance philosophy based around the built-in fault handling logic, scan network, and intelligent support processor and console provides for rapid location and repair of the failing logic.

During development, substantial resources were devoted to assure the quality of the 1100/60 design, recognizing that fault tolerance strongly complements, but is not a substitute for, design quality and correctness. An evaluation of the various fault handling features was carried out to provide measures of system availability, reliability, and maintainability.

INTRODUCTION

At Sperry Univac, the acronym ARM stands for Availability, Reliability, and Maintainability. ARM concepts include the organizational procedures used to develop systems; the tools and techniques used during design, development, and manufacturing; and the logic, firmware, and software that are included to minimize the effects of a failure. The latter ARM features include many of the fault tolerant features developed over the years.

Several important trends in the computer industry have strongly influenced decisions with regard to ARM at Sperry Univac. The evolution of computer applications from primarily a batch processing orientation to a stronger emphasis on demand and real time processing has resulted in greater dependence on computers and thus in increased sensitivity to their availability and reliability.

The second major trend relates to hardware technology. The increase in gate densities in LSI and VLSI chips has effectively brought the cost of hardware down, to the extent that it is becoming more practical and cost effective to incorporate fault tolerance in the computer [Sedmak and Liebergot, 1978].

A third trend lies in the area of field maintenance. The costs of labor for maintenance activities are increasing at a rate close to that of inflation. In addition, as systems become more complex, it becomes increasingly more difficult for customer engineers to master the detailed workings of the entire system.

The reaction to these industry trends is to deemphasize manual field diagnosis procedures and to stress the incorporation of built-in automatic fault detection, correction and recovery capabilities. The SPERRY UNIVAC 1100/60 Information Processing System reflects this increased emphasis on fault tolerance in commercial computers.

ARM PHILOSOPHY FOR 1100/60

ARM in Previous SPERRY UNIVAC 1100 Series Systems

The SPERRY UNIVAC 1108 [Borgerson, Hanson, and Hartley, 1978; Borgerson et al., 1979], introduced in 1965, was the first SPERRY UNIVAC 1100 Series computer to offer both a multiprogramming operating system and multiprocessing configurations. These two capabilities

reflect a general ARM approach that has been carried forward in other Sperry Univac systems—the attempt to isolate a problem to either a particular job in the system or to a particular unit in the configuration.

The success of this approach is determined largely by the error detection attributes of the system. For a typical 1108 system, error detection consists of parity in the main storage and processor general registers. For the successor 1100/10 and 1100/20 systems, this coverage was enhanced to include parity on the I/O channels and in some of the mass storage control units, while the main storage utilized an error detection/correction code instead of parity. Maintenance on the central complex (instruction processor, input/output unit, and main storage) is performed using a built-in maintenance panel and diagnostic programs.

The 1100/40 system has all of the previous error detection capabilities, and in addition, a maintenance controller as an adjunct to the maintenance panel. The controller incorporates a scan compare capability that allows operations in the processor to be examined after each clock cycle and compared to known correct data from a magnetic tape. Any difference can be used to indicate the location of the problem area. This was the first automation of the maintenance task for 1100 series systems.

In the 1100/80, additional error detection was provided for the input/output unit, and a cache memory with parity was added. The maintenance controller was replaced with a maintenance processor—an intelligent unit that can write several of the registers in the central complex and read almost all of them. The customer engineer's interface to the system is via CRT rather than a maintenance panel, and the maintenance processor can function even if most of the central complex is disabled.

ARM in the 1100/60—General Approach

A fundamental requirement for the 1100/60 was to produce a system whose ARM attributes matched the processing modes of the future with the technology of today. The price/performance goals allowed the selection of proven ECL technology for the instruction processor (IP) and cache, TTL for the input/output unit, and 16K MOS chips for the main storage. In addition, the IP is microprogrammed and uses four-bit-slice microprocessors to achieve a reduction in component count. Established design rules allow adequate temperature, voltage, and timing margins. The basic unit processor and most expansion features are packaged in one cabinet and air-cooled. A block diagram of the 1100/60 system is shown in Figure 10-1.

Error detection has been given increased emphasis in the 1100/60 relative to previous systems. This provides protection from incorrect results, aids in system recovery and reconfiguration, and helps to isolate a failure to a replaceable unit. The 1100/60 uses duplication, coding techniques, and parity to provide error detection throughout the system.

The main storage and the IP's microcode control storage have error correction capabilities to allow error recovery to be transparent to the user. The cache memory architecture allows recovery from an error by automatically disabling an area of the cache and retrieving desired data from the main storage. Other solid faults are handled by reconfiguration. Extensive retry capabilities are provided to recover from transient or intermittent faults in the central complex.

DETAILED ARM IMPLEMENTATION

System Characteristics

The 1100/60 instruction processor is microprogrammed and is based on a high usage of LSI microprocessors. The amount of hardware required for the IP has been kept low by implementing a large portion of the control functions in microcode. The net effect of such an approach is to replace the traditional mass of SSI/MSI gates with high-density LSI arithmetic and storage components. The high throughput of the 1100/60 is achieved by the use of multiple microprocessors, overlap at the microinstruction level, prefetch of instructions and operands, and other design techniques [Datamation, 1979].

Figure 10-2 is a block diagram of the main data paths of the IP. Each 1100/60 macroinstruction and interrupt is performed by executing a series of microinstructions. The execution of each microinstruction consists of bringing data from the general register set, main storage, or

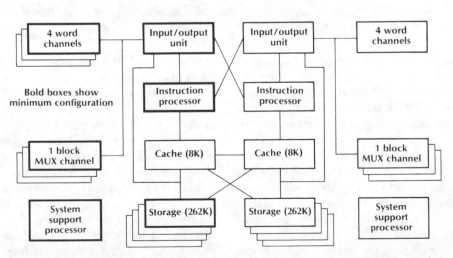

Figure 10–1. System block diagram (two processor, two I/O configuration).

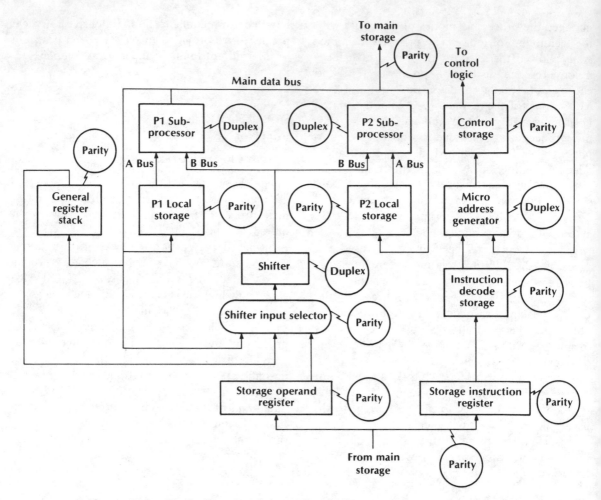

Figure 10-2. Block diagram of the 1100/60 microexecution section, showing sample applications of fault detection techniques.

other source through the shifter into the subprocessors. Here, using multiple microprocessor chips, an arithmetic or logical operation is performed, combining the data from the shifter with data from the local storages or the accumulators, and placing the results in the accumulators internal to the microprocessor chips. At this point, the data may be placed onto the main data bus and written into local storage, the general register set, or main storage. These data movements are controlled by a microinstruction that partitions the work between microprocessors, selects the various resources (registers, local storage,

etc.) to be used, and initiates selection of the next microinstruction.

The 1100/60 central complex contains, in addition to the IP, an input/output unit (IOU), an optional cache or storage interface unit (SIU), main storage unit (MSU), and a system support processor (SSP). The functions of each of these units are well known except for the SSP, a freestanding, intelligent processor that employs a CRT and keyboard and serves as the system maintenance and operator consoles. In addition, this unit carries out the function of system partitioning, control storage loading, fault injection, and some assorted system support tasks. The system software and the IP microcode and hardware communicate with the SSP through interrupt mechanisms.

Fault Detection

The philosophy in the 1100/60 is to detect 100 percent of all single-bit faults in the data path, and many single faults in control logic. The rationale for such a philosophy is based on the principle of minimizing the probability that a user's data could be corrupted without the system detecting or correcting the erroneous operation and signaling the operator. As a general rule, faults are detected in storage elements by the use of parity codes, while redundancy is used for arithmetic and control circuitry. The various detection circuits are strategically placed in an effort to achieve a high coverage in hardware such as storages, which have the highest failure rate, and in areas such as the main data path, which has a high usage and where a large impact on the system might be experienced if a failure occurred.

An overview of the fault detection techniques used in various portions of the 1100/60 IP is given in Figure 10-2. The general register set, local storages, and the shifter input selector employ conventional parity; the shifter and, as discussed previously, the subprocessors (including the main data bus) are duplicated and compared. In addition, parity checks are used on control storage, while duplication is used on the control storage address generation and logic function generation circuitry.

An example of fault detection through redundancy is shown in Figure 10-3. Each of the two 36-bit master subprocessors is paired with a duplicate subprocessor that performs the same function on the same data as the master subprocessor. During each microcycle, only one of the master subprocessors can drive the main data bus; and when one of them is chosen to drive it, its duplicate drives a duplicate bus. At the end of the cycle, a comparison is made between the data on the two buses; any discrepancy will cause the operation to be interrupted.

During the development of the 1100/60, an observation was made that is contrary to most claims about fault detection and its associated performance impact. Many sections of the data path are duplicated and compared to achieve fault detection. However, the duplicated logic

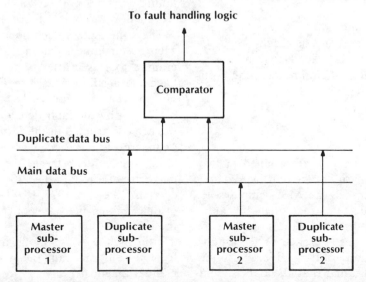

Figure 10–3. Example of fault detection through duplication in the 1100/60 IP.

serves another purpose: it provides additional output drive capability (i.e., loading) for the functional circuits. For example, if a functional circuit has 8 unit loads on its outputs, the addition of a duplicate circuit could reduce that number to 4 by splitting the loads between the functional and duplicate circuits. This allows a reduction in the propagation delay time of the output stage of the functional circuit. In fact, as additional portions of the data path were duplicated to detect faults, it was discovered that the combined effect could be an increase in performance compared to a strictly simplex design. This result points out the fact that fault detection need not have an adverse effect on performance.

Several factors have contributed to keeping costs low for the fault detection features:

- Design approach of incorporating fault detection mostly in high-usage and high-failure-rate sections of the logic.
- Incorporation of most of the control functions in microcode, which is stored in LSI storage components where fault detection is very economical.
- Heavy use of microprocessors, which are well-ordered, bus-oriented logic structures that lend themselves to conventional fault detection techniques.
- The philosophy of designing fault detection circuitry at the same time as functional logic, and designing functional logic that lends itself to fault detection.

As a result of these and other factors, the extensive fault detection mechanisms require about 15 percent of the total CPU logic. This translates to less than 15 percent of the manufacturing costs attributable to the detection logic.

Error Correction

Error correction techniques are applied in two primary areas: the main storage unit (MSU) and the IP's control storage. The MSU employs an error correction code to correct single-bit faults and detect double-bit faults in the storage array chips during every read reference. When a·double-bit fault occurs, an error signal is sent to the requesting unit indicating that the data should not be used.

Error correction is also utilized in the microprocessors' control storage, although a different approach is taken than in the main storage. When a single-bit fault occurs, the parity code stored with each microinstruction will permit the detection of a fault. If a fault is detected, a macroinstruction retry is attempted. Should the retry fail, an interrupt then allows a correction procedure to be initiated by the system support processor. The procedure involves rewriting the failed portion of control storage. After each attempt at rewriting, the SSP will read the data from the failed portion of the control storage to verify the proper correction. When proper correction is achieved, the SSP signals the IP to restart execution.

Fault Isolation

There are two major techniques used for fault isolation in the 1100/60. One technique relies on the high level of coverage provided by the fault detection capabilities in the processor. For example, referring to Figure 10-2, it can be seen that because of the application of the duplication and comparison technique to both the shifter and the two subprocessors, it is possible to isolate a failure in that portion of the microexecution section down to one of those three logic sections.

The other major technique employed in the 1100/60 for fault isolation is the diagnostic program, a tool used after symptoms of the failure have surfaced. This approach is usually employed when the failure has not been isolated sufficently by the fault detection logic. Diagnostics are constructed in the form of microroutines or macroroutines, which are run on the failing unit. Frequently, these diagnostic programs make use of a tool in the 1100/60 known as scan compare [Stewart, 1977, 1978], which is a method of determining the states of major test points in the IP.

Utilizing the two methods, the capability exists to isolate automatically (i.e., without the need for manual diagnosis) any failure in the main data path to one or two printed-circuit cards. The obvious values of such a feature are to reduce the time to repair the central complex (and hence reduce field support costs) and dramatically improve the availability of the system to the user.

Error Recovery

The basic requirement in the development of an integrated error recovery procedure is that the computer system must deal with both solid and transient faults. When a solid fault occurs, any operation affected will continue to produce incorrect results. Detection and isolation of such a fault is relatively easy, but recovery from it without manual intervention and repair is frequently difficult unless some type of error correction or masking capability exists in the system.

In contrast, a transient fault is more difficult to detect and isolate due to its lack of persistence during diagnosis. However, recovery from transient faults in many areas can frequently be achieved in a more economical way than for solid faults. To accomplish this, the main items required are the ability to detect the error close to the time of occurrence, a mechanism to stop processing upon error detection, and the capability to reset the operation to a valid state which existed prior to the error, utilizing information that was saved during execution.

The error recovery procedure in the 1100/60 IP is designed to deal with both solid and transient faults. An overall picture of the recovery procedure is shown in Figure 10-4. The procedure uses a combination of hardware and

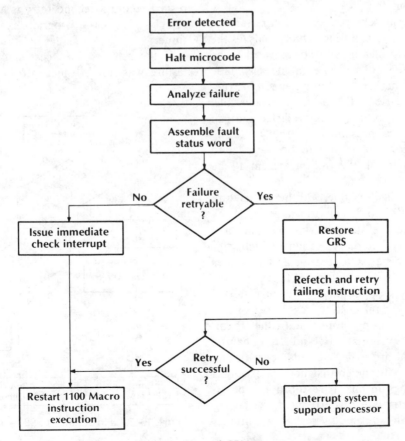

Figure 10—4.   Flowchart of CPU error recovery.

firmware to implement fault detection, abort the operation in progress, analyze the fault, and initiate retry. This approach allows the recovery procedure to utilize the same microexecution resources as the macroinstruction set utilizes, resulting in a cost savings and a sharing of fault detection capabilities.

When a fault is detected by any of the detection circuitry discussed in the section on fault detection, microexecution is halted via hardware by forcing the control store to execute continuously a no-operation microinstruction and by blocking the loading of internal registers and storages. Execution is suspended until a hardware timer expires, during which time no execution or change of machine state occurs. This allows time for transient failures to die out. The period of the timer may be adjusted for different program environments.

When the period expires, execution restarts in a fault recovery microroutine, which analyzes the failure and assembles a fault status word to be presented to the software. Then a check is made to determine whether the failing macroinstruction can be retried. If no retry is possible, macroinstruction execution is restarted and an error interrupt is presented to the operating software to allow the failure to be logged and software recovery of the failing system to be attempted.

If the failure is retryable, another procedure occurs. The 1100/60 IP incorporates a "save" storage for machine state restoration. The save storage is a small memory element which captures general register set operands and addresses during GRS reads. The fault recovery microcode can restore original operands to the correct GRS location. Thus, even if GRS writes are performed by a macroinstruction before it fails, the IP can be restored to its original state and a retry can be attempted. This approach permits retry of the vast majority of the macroinstructions executed in a normal program mix. If restoration is possible so that a retry can be performed, the failing macroinstruction is retried by restoring it into its

original storage location and then refetching and reexecuting it. If the retry is successful, program execution continues from the point of the failure and a subsequent interrupt is presented to the operating system for logging purposes.

If the retry or the fault recovery microroutine fails, execution in the IP is halted and the system support processor is interrupted. Figure 10-5 shows the SSP fault recovery sequence. The IP is scanned to determine the machine state. If the failure is in the control storage, correction is attempted by rewriting the storage to its original values. If this is unsuccessful, control storage is rewritten using complemented values, and a designator is set which causes each control word to be reinverted before use. This allows both soft failures and single cell solid failures to be corrected. If the correction is successful, the IP is restarted and a second retry is attempted. If this retry is successful, program execution can continue.

If the retry is unsuccessful or if the original failure was not in the control store, the failure

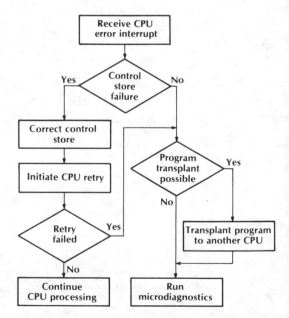

Figure 10–5. Flowchart of SSP recovery procedure.

may still be recovered in a multiprocessor configuration by "program transplant." Utilizing this procedure, the SSP reads the program environment and GRS contents from the failing IP and transmits them to the operating system for use by another IP in the configuration. The failing instruction sequence can then be restarted in the other IP. Effectively, a failure in one IP can be retried in another IP. Following program transplant, or if no transplant is possible, the internal storages in the failing IP are reinitialized by the SSP, and a microdiagnostic program is invoked. If the execution completes successfully, the failing IP can be reintroduced to the system. If the microdiagnostics fail, the operator is notified and the maintenance techniques discussed in the section on maintenance are used to isolate and repair the failure. No manual intervention is needed in the recovery procedure until recovery is as complete as possible and the SSP has determined that a solid unrecoverable failure exists in the IP.

Fault Injection

In the 1100/60 processing system, a capability has been included that uses hardware and software to verify that the fault detection, isolation, and recovery mechanisms are operational. The capability is provided through fault injection, which is the process of deliberately causing a fault to occur in a system by inserting erroneous data or control signals in a portion of logic covered by a fault detection capability. The need for such a feature arises because the error handling portion of the design is not frequently exercised under normal operation of the system, so it could fail with no indication to the software. Without periodic verification of the integrity of the error handling logic, one could not be confident of its ability to function when needed. This capability is also needed during prototype testing to verify the design of the hardware and software fault-handling capabilities.

The 1100/60 system incorporates fault injection for fault detection circuits in the processor, input/output unit, storage interface unit, and main storage unit. In the case of the control storage or the small storage used for instruction decoding in the IP, the fault injection is under control of the SSP. For example, the SSP can inject a control storage parity error by writing incorrect parity directly into the desired address location in order to stimulate one of the associated parity checkers. Injection of other IP faults is initiated by the presence of certain processor state bits and a predetermined micro-control store bit. During normal system operation, the state bits are set via a special 1100 macroinstruction which is periodically executed during system idle time. This instruction causes injection of a fault and then monitors for detection of that same fault.

After the fault is detected, the system is purged of the fault, and the instruction is retried without an injected fault. Successful completion of these steps indicates that the particular fault detection and retry hardware exercised is operating correctly.

In the input/output unit, injection is also under the control of the SSP. For example, a fault can be injected in the channel control word storage registers by setting and clearing flip-flops that specify the type of fault desired and the device operation during which the fault should occur. After the proper logic has been primed for the injection, the chosen fault will be triggered the next time the preselected device operation takes place.

In the 1100/60 cache (SIU) and main storage unit (MSU), the injection process is controlled by an IP instruction routine. Forced faults internal to the SIU are specified by the unit requesting or sending data, and that requester then expects a certain type of fault at a predetermined point in the operation. In the MSU, the routine provides the capability to insert an invalid ECC code or bad parity on read data. On the access cycle of the MSU, the fault should be detected and an interrupt signaled.

Maintenance

The maintenance philosophy for the 1100/60 incorporates four methods of dealing with a failure in the system. In the order of priority of use, they are:

1. Automatic error log
2. Macrodiagnostic tests
3. Scan compare tests
4. Manual troubleshooting

The automatic error log represents a record kept by the system of any fault handled by the built-in fault detection/correction, isolation, and recovery mechanisms. In the majority of cases, the log should provide sufficient information for the customer engineer to determine the source of the problem.

In those cases when the problem has not been completely identified by the error log information, macrodiagnostic tests are employed. These tests are written on a macroinstruction level; they serve to exercise most portions of the system establishing either a high level of confidence that the system is operating correctly, or determining the general area in which it has failed.

If the previous two techniques have not identified the trouble area or if a finer resolution of the failure is needed, the scan-compare tests are run. These routines are tests run under the control of the SSP. They make use of the previously mentioned scan network (built into the processor), permitting access to the state of all major storage elements in the IP. The tests will exercise the processor and compare the results to a table of predetermined correct results to establish the nature and source of the problem. A similar process is applied to the IOU, which is a hardwired unit. I/O instructions are executed and the scan network is employed under control of the SSP without the use of the IP.

Accessible through the scan network is a built-in logic analyzer which is available in each 1100/60 as an additional diagnostic tool for the customer engineer. This feature permits automatic storage of 1,024 consecutive states of any

16 logic points sampled twice during each microinstruction cycle. The logic analyzer is helpful in the diagnosis of a particularly difficult failure mode, such as might exist in the presence of an intermittent fault.

Should none of the three methods above locate the failure, the customer engineer will resort to manual troubleshooting techniques. These manual efforts, however, are greatly enhanced by the features available in the SSP. For example, the scan network will permit the troubleshooter to capture and display on the CRT a substantial amount of internal test-point information that in the past would only have been available by using such tools as oscilloscopes and logic probes. In addition, the SSP has a communications capability that allows a linkage with a remote maintenance facility staffed with a team of diagnostic experts. This feature provides the ability to collect from a remote location any error information (for example, the contents of the logic analyzer) that is normally gathered and analyzed onsite. In addition, this interface can be used for remote control of diagnostic execution and troubleshooting procedures.

As a means of verifying the tolerance of the system to reasonable voltage variations during operation, the 1100/60 IP incorporates power supplies with output levels that can be varied by programmable margins under control of the SSP. This allows customer engineering personnel at the computer site, or at the remote maintenance facility, to alter the output voltages easily and to observe the IP behavior. Hence, this margin testing tool provides one means of identifying marginally stable components before they have degraded to the level where a system fault may occur.

ARM EVALUATION

To measure how the design goals were being met with respect to the ARM characteristics of the IP, an evaluation method was developed that facilitates a quantitative prediction of the ARM behavior of the central complex. Using this method, an estimation was made of the fault detection/recovery coverage, the system stability or mean time between stops (MTBS), the mean down-time (MDT), the mean time to repair (MTTR), and the availability of the central complex.

The use of the evaluation method requires an initial examination of the various elements of the system and their anticipated contributions to the overall stability and availability of the central complex. After such an examination the two major ARM measures can be analyzed: MTBS and availability. MTBS is a measure of system stability and is calculated by evaluating its two components: hardware MTBS (MTBSH) and software MTBS (MTBSS).

The hardware stability is determined from component failure rates, the coverage of the fault detection mechanisms, and the recoverability of the system from each of the faults detected that do not lead to a system stop. The failure rates are obtained by studying vendor, government, and internal failure data for each of the integrated circuits and components used in the units. Coverage is analyzed by examining the current detailed hardware documentation for the system and determining which fault detection circuits will capture which faults, and in which chips. The recoverability factor is determined by studying what percentage of detected faults can be recovered from by each recovery mechanism and by analyzing the probability of success of that recovery.

The software stability is calculated by examining the inherent characteristics of the modules, such as size and complexity; considering the quality assurance during development; and evaluating the environment in which the software will be used based on our experience with the stability of similar software systems in the past.

The other major ARM factor, system availability, is predicted by considering the MTBFs and MTTRs of the various units in the central complex, the amount of redundancy of units in the system, and the recovery time necessary following a system stop. The application of the evaluation method described above proved to be a valuable tool for management and design personnel in gaining visibility of the unfolding ARM characteristics of the 1100/60 CPU versus the established goals for development. It has been encouraging to observe that preliminary data gathered from approximately one hundred initial installations reflect a very favorable comparison with the predicted values.

SUMMARY

As the applications of computers become more complex and sophisticated, and as new electronic technologies emerge in the industry, the demand, as well as the potential, for increased availability, reliability, and maintainability appears to be growing. The Sperry Univac 1100/60 Information Processing System reflects the results of a coherent development effort that takes advantage of the current state of the art in achieving a high level of inherent quality of design and a dramatic increase in the fault tolerant attributes of the commercial computer system.

REFERENCES

Borgerson, Hanson, and Hartley [1978]; Borgerson et al. [1979]; *Datamation* [1979]; Sedmak and Liebergot [1978]; Steward [1977, 1978].

A Fault-Tolerant Computing System

James A. Katzman

Abstract

A fault-tolerant computer architecture is examined that is commercially available today and installed in many industries. The hardware is examined in this paper and the software is examined in a companion paper [Bartlett, 1978; also excerpted in the second half of this chapter]. References for both papers are at the end of the chapter.

INTRODUCTION

The increasing need for businesses to go on-line is stimulating a requirement for cost effective computer systems having continuous availability [Tandem Computers, Inc., 1976; Katzman, 1977a]. Certain applications such as automatic toll billing for telephone systems lose money each minute the system is down and the losses are irrecoverable. Systems commercially available today have met a necessary requirement of multiprocessing but not the sufficient conditons for fault-tolerant computing.

The greatest dollar volume spent on systems needing these fault-tolerant capabilities are in the commercial on-line, data base transaction, and terminal oriented applications. The design of the Tandem 16 NonStop* system was directed toward offering the commercial market an off-the-shelf, general purpose system with at least an order of magnitude better availability than existing off-the-shelf systems without charging a premium. This was accomplished by using a top down system design approach, thus avoiding the shortcomings of the systems currently addressing the fault-tolerant market.

Except for some very expensive special systems developed by the military, universities, and some computer manufacturers in limited quantities, no commercially available systems have been designed for continuous availability. Some systems such as the ones designed by ROLM have been designed for high MTBF by "ruggedizing," but typically computers have been designed to be in a monolithic, single processor environment. As certain applications demanded continuous availability, manufacturers recognized that a multiprocessor system was necessary to meet the demands for availability. In order to preserve previous development effort and compatibility, manufacturers invented awkward devices such as I/O channel switches and interprocessor communication adapters to retrofit existing hardware. The basic flaw in this effort is

that only multiprocessing was achieved. While that is necessary for continuously available systems, it is far from sufficient.

Single points of failure flourish in these past architectures (Figure 11-1). A power supply failure in the I/O bus switch or a single integrated circuit (IC) package failure in any I/O controller on the I/O channel emanating from the I/O bus switch will cause the entire system to fail. Other architectures have used a common memory for interprocessor communications, creating another single point of failure. Typically such systems have not even approached the problem of on-line maintenance, redundant cooling, or a power distribution system that allows for brownout conditions. In today's marketplace, many of the applications of fault-tolerant systems do not allow any down time for repair.

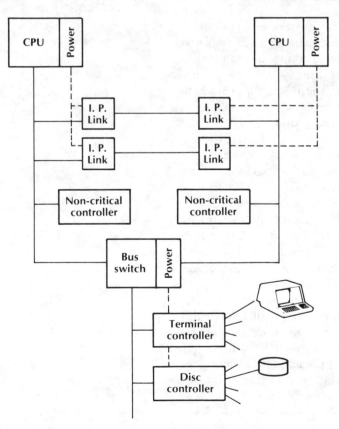

Figure 11–1. Example of previous fault-tolerant systems.

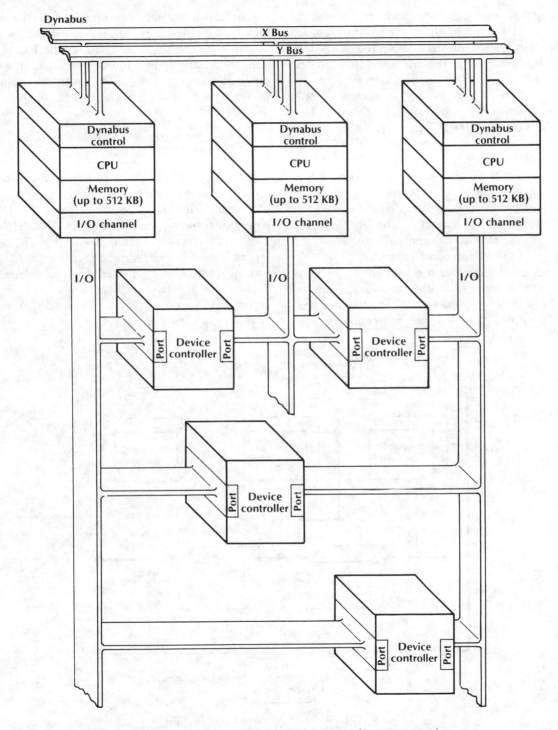

Figure 11–2. Tandem 16 system architecture. (See page 438.)

Expansion of a system such as the one in Figure 11-1 is prohibitively expensive. A three processor system, strongly connected in a redundant fashion, would require twelve interprocessor links on the I/O channels; five processors would need forty links; for n processors, $2n \times (n - 1)$ links are required. These links often consist of 100–200 IC packages and require entire circuit boards priced between \$6,000 and \$10,000 each. Using the I/O channel in this manner limits the I/O capabilities as a further undesirable side effect. The resulting hardware changes for expansion, if undertaken, are typically dwarfed in magnitude by the software changes needed when applications are to be geographically changed or expanded.

This paper describes the Tandem 16 architecture at the lowest level (the hardware). The first section deals with the overall system organization and packaging. The second section explains the processor module organization and its attachment to the interprocessor communications system. The third section discusses the I/O system organization. The fourth section discusses power, packaging, and on-line maintenance aspects that are not covered elsewhere in the paper.

SYSTEM ORGANIZATION

The Tandem 16 NonStop system is organized around three basic elements: the processor module, dual-ported I/O controllers, and the DC power distribution system (Figures 11-2, 11-3). The processors are interconnected by a dual-interprocessor bus system: the Dynabus; the I/O controllers are each connected with two independent I/O channels, one to each port; and the power distribution system is integrated with the modular packaging of the system.

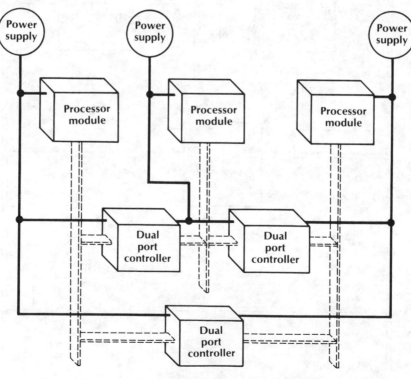

Figure 11–3. Tandem 16 power distribution.

The system design goal is twofold: (1) to continue operation of the system through any single failure, and (2) to be able to repair that failure without affecting the rest of the system. The on-line maintenance aspects were a key factor in the design of the physical packaging and the power-distribution of the system.

System Packaging

The cabinet (Figure 11-4) is divided into 4 sections: the upper card cage, the lower card cage, cooling, and power supplies. The upper card cage contains up to 4 processors, each with up to 512K bytes of independent main memory. The lower card cage contains up to 32 I/O controller printed circuit (PC) cards, where each controller consists of one to three PC cards. The cooling section consists of 4 fans and a plenum chamber that forces laminar air flow through the

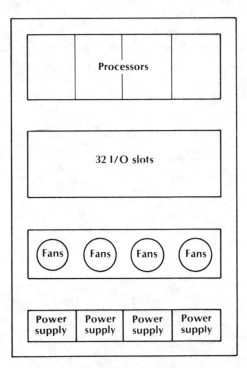

Figure 11–4.   Tandem 16 physical cabinet.

card cages. The power supply section contains up to 4 power supply modules. Multiple cabinets may be bolted together and the system has the capability to accommodate a maximum of 16 processors.

Each processor module, consisting of a CPU, memory, Dynabus control, and I/O channel, is powered by an associated power supply. If a failed module is to be replaced in this section its associated power supply is shut off, the module is replaced, and the power supply is turned on. Each card cage slot in the I/O card cage is powered by two different power supplies. Each of the I/O controllers is connected via its dual-port arrangement to two processors. Each of those processors has its own power supply; usually, but not necessarily, those two supplies are the ones that power the I/O controller (Figure 11-3). Each slot in the I/O card cage can be powered down by a corresponding switch disconnecting power from the slot from both supplies without affecting power to the remainder of the system. Therefore, if a power supply fails, or if one is shut down to repair a processor, no I/O controllers are affected.

The dual-power sourcing to the I/O controllers was originally designed using relay switching. This plan was abandoned for several reasons: a) to contend with relay failure modes is difficult; b) the number of contact bounces on a switch-over is neither uniform nor predictable making it difficult for the operating system to handle power-on interrupts from the I/O controllers; and c) during the switch-over, controllers do lose power, and while most controllers are software-restartable, communications controllers hang up their communications lines. We therefore devised a diode current sharing scheme whereby I/O controllers are constantly drawing current from two supplies simultaneously. If a power supply fails, all the current for a given controller is supplied by the second power supply. There is also circuitry to provide for a controlled ramping of current draw on turn-on and turn-off so there are no instantaneous power demands from a given supply causing a potential momentary dip in supply voltage.

Both fans and power supplies are electrically connected using quick disconnect connectors to speed replacement upon failure. No tools are required to replace a power supply. A screwdriver is all that is needed to replace a fan. Both replacements take less than 5 minutes.

Interconnections

Physical interconnection is done both using front edge connectors and backplanes. Communication within a processor module (e.g., between the CPU and main memory) takes place over four 50 pin front edge connectors using flat ribbon cable. Interprocessor communication takes place over the Dynabus on the backplane also utilizing ribbon cable. The I/O controllers use etch trace on the backplane for communication among PC cards of a multicard controller. The I/O channels are backplane ribbon cable connections between the processors and the I/O controllers.

Peripheral I/O devices are connected via shielded round cable either to a bulk-head patch panel or directly to the front edge connectors of the I/O controllers. If a patch panel is used, then there is a connection using round cables between the patch panel and the front edge connectors of the I/O controllers.

Power is distributed using a DC power distribution scheme. Physically, AC is brought in through a filtering and phase splitting distribution box. Pigtails connect the AC distribution box to one of the input connectors of a power supply. The DC power from the supply is routed through a cable harness to a laminated bus bar arrangement which distributes power on the backplanes to both processors and I/O controllers.

PROCESSOR MODULE ORGANIZATION

The processor (Figure 11-5) includes a 16-bit CPU, main memory, the Dynabus interface control, and an I/O channel. Physically the CPU, I/O channel and Dynabus control consist of two PC boards 16 inches by 18 inches, each containing approximately 300 IC packages. Schottky TTL circuitry is used. Up to 512K bytes of main memory are available utilizing core or semiconductor technology. Core memory boards hold 32K 17-bit words and each occupies two card

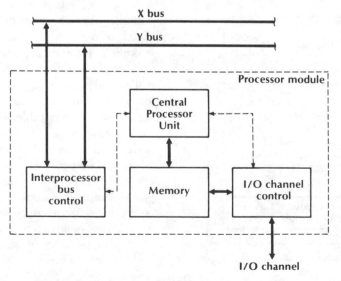

Figure 11-5. Tandem 16 processor organization.

slots because of the height of the core stack. Semiconductor memory is currently implemented utilizing 16-pin, 4K dynamic RAMs. These memory boards contain 48K 22-bit words per board and occupy only one card slot and are therefore three times denser than core.

The processor module is viewed by the user as a 16-bit, stack-oriented processor, with a demand paging, virtual memory system capable of supporting multiprogramming.

The CPU

The CPU is a microprogrammed processor consisting of a bank of 8 registers which can be used as general purpose registers, as a LIFO register stack, or for indexing; an ALU; a shifter; two memory stack management registers; program control registers (e.g., program counter, instruction register, environment or status register, and a next instruction register for instruction prefetching); scratch pad registers available only to the microprogrammer; and several other miscellaneous flags and counters for the microprogrammer.

The microprogram is stored in read-only memory and is organized in 512-word sectors of 32-bit words. The microinstruction has different formats for branching, sequential functions, and immediate operand operations. The Tandem 16 instruction set occupies 512 words with the decimal arithmetic option occupying another 512 words. The address space for the microprogram is 2K words.

The microprocessor has a 100 ns cycle time and is a two stage pipelined microprocessor, i.e., all microinstructions take two cycles to execute but one completes each cycle. In the first stage of the pipeline any two operands are selected by two source fields in the microinstruction for loading into the ALU input registers. In the second stage of the pipeline the ALU performs a primitive operation on the operands placed in the ALU input registers during the previous cycle and performs a shift operation on the results. In parallel, a miscellaneous operation

such as a condition code setting or a counter increment can be done, the result can be stored in any CPU register or dispatched to the memory system or I/O channel, and a condition test made on the results. Each of these parallel operations is controlled by a separate control field in the microinstruction.

The basic set of 123 machine instructions includes arithmetic operations (add, subtract, etc.), logical operations (and, or, exclusive or), bit deposit, block (multiple element) moves/compares/scans, procedure calls and exits, interprocessor SENDs, and I/O operations. All instructions are 16 bits in length. The decimal instruction set provides an additional 20 instructions dealing with four-word operands.

The interrupt system has 16 major interrupt levels which include interprocessor bus data received, I/O transfer completion, memory error, interval timer, page fault, privileged instruction violation, etc.

Provision is made for several events to cause microinterrupts. They are entirely handled by the CPU's microprocessor without causing an interrupt to the operating system. One event for example, is the receipt of a 16-word packet over the Dynabus. A packet is the primitive unit of data which is transferred over the Dynabus for interprocessor communication. The microprocessor puts the information in a predetermined area of memory and does not cause a system interrupt until the entire message is received.

The register stack is used for most arithmetic operations and for holding parameters for block instructions (moves/compares/scans) which need the parameters updated dynamically so that the instructions may be interruptable and restarted. The 8-register stack is a "wraparound" stack and is not logically connected to the memory stack.

Main Memory

Main memory is organized in physical pages of 1K words of 16 bits/word. Up to 256K words of memory may be attached to a processor. In the core memory systems there is a parity bit for single error detection, and in semiconductor memory systems there are 6 check bits/word to provide single error correction and double error detection. Due to the relative reliability of these two technologies, we have found that semiconductor memory, without error corrrection, is much less reliable than core, and that with error correction, it is somewhat more reliable than core. Battery backup provides short term nonvolatility to the semiconductor memory system for utility power outage considerations.

It might be noted that there are some memory systems using a 21-bit error correction scheme (5 check bits on a 16-bit data word instead of 6). While 5 bits are enough to correct all single bit errors, it does not detect approximately 1/3 of the possible double bit error combinations. In these conditions, this 5 check bit scheme will incorrectly deduce that some bit (neither of the bits actually in error) is incorrect and correctable. The scheme will then correct this bit (actually causing 3 bits to be in error), and deliver it to the system as "good," reporting a correctable memory error.

Memory is logically divided into 4 address

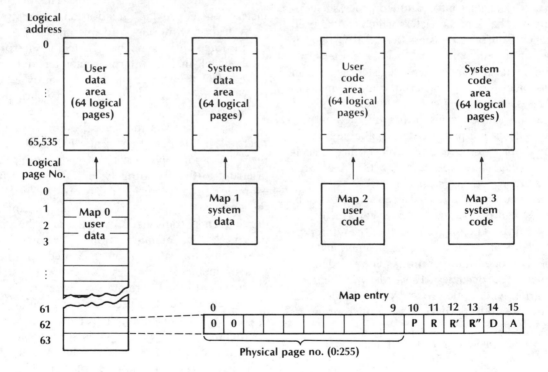

P = Parity

R,R',R" = Reference bits—used by operating system to select a page for overlay

D = Dirty bit—set whenever a write access is made to the page

A = Absent—"1" indicates that the page is not present in physical memory

Figure 11–6. Tandem 16 logical memory address spaces.

spaces (Figure 11-6). These are the virtual address spaces of the machine; both the system and the user have a code space and a data space. The code space is unmodifiable and the data space can be viewed either as a stack or a random access memory, depending on the addressing mode used. Each of these virtual address spaces are 64K words long addressed by a 16-bit virtual address.

The physical memory address is 16 bits with conversion from the virtual address to physical address accomplished through a mapping scheme. Four maps are provided, one for each logical address space; each map consists of 64 entries, one for each page in the virtual address space. The maps are implemented in 50 ns access bipolar static RAM. The map access and main memory error correction is included in the 500 nsec cycle time for semiconductor memory systems.

The unmodifiable code area provides reentrant, recursive, and sharable code. The data space (Figure 11-7) can be referenced relative to address 0 (global data or G+ addressing), or relative to the memory stack management registers in the CPU.

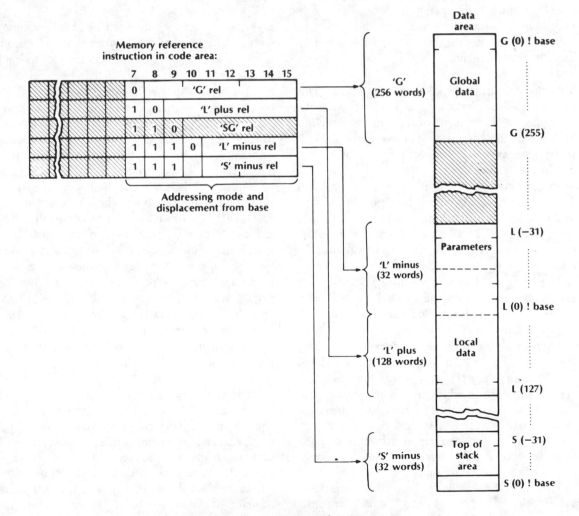

Figure 11–7. Tandem 16 data space.

The lowest level language provided on the Tandem 16 system is T/TAL, a high-level, block-structured, ALGOL-like language which provides structures to get at the more efficient machine instructions. The basic program unit in T/TAL is the PROCEDURE. Unlike ALGOL, there is no outer block, but rather a main PROCEDURE. T/TAL has the ability to declare certain variables as global. PROCEDURES cannot be nested in T/TAL, but a SUBPROCEDURE can be nested in a PROCEDURE and only in a PROCEDURE. A SUBPROCEDURE is limited in local variable access capabilities.

The memory stack, defined by two registers in the CPU, is used for efficient linkage to and from procedures, parameter passing, and dynamic storage allocation and deallocation for variables local to the procedure.

The L register (Local variables) points to the last stack marker placed on the stack. This marker contains return information about the caller such as the return address and the previous location of the L register. The contents of the L register are primarily changed by the procedure call and exit instructions.

Addressing relative to the L register provides access to parameters passed to a procedure (L−) and local variables of the procedure (L+). Parameters may be passed either by value (using direct addressing) or by reference (using indirect addressing).

The S register (stack top pointer) points to the last element placed on the stack. It is used for a SUBPROCEDURE's sublocal data area when S relative addressing (S−) is used.

There is a special mode of addressing used by the operating system, called System Global (SG+) addressing. It is used by the operating system while it is working in a user's virtual data space (on his behalf) and needs to address the system data space. The system data space contains many resource tables and buffers and the need to access them quickly justifies the existence of this addressing mode.

There are three tables known to the operating system, the microprogram and the hardware: the system interrupt vector (SIV), the I/O Control (IOC) table, and the Bus Receive Table (BRT). These tables will be explained in later sections as appropriate.

The Dynabus

The Dynabus is a set of two independent interprocessor buses. Bus access is determined by two independent interprocessor bus controllers. Each of these controllers is dual-powered, in the same manner as an I/O controller. The Dynabus controllers are very small, approximately 30 IC packages, and are not associated with, nor physically a part of any processor. Each bus has a two-byte data path and control lines associated with it. There are two sets of radial connections from each interprocessor bus controller to each processor module. They distribute clocks for synchronous transmission over the bus and for transmission enable. Therefore, no failed processor can independently dominate Dynabus utilization upon failure since in order to electrically transmit onto the bus, the bus controller must agree that a given processor has the right to transmit. Each bus has a clock associated with it, running independently of the processor clocks and located on the associated bus controller. The clock rate is 150 ns on two to eight processor systems. The clock does need to be slowed down for the longer interprocessor buses of greater than eight processors. Therefore each bus on small systems transfers at the rate of 13.3M bytes/second and on the larger systems at 10M bytes/second. Performance measurements have shown that under worst case test conditions the Dynabus is only 15% utilized in a ten processor system.

Each processor in the system attaches to both interprocessor buses. The Dynabus interface control section (Figure 11-8) consists of 3 high speed caches: an incoming queue associated with each interprocessor bus, and a single outgoing queue that can be switched to either of the buses. All caches are 16 words in length and all bus transfers are cache to cache. All components that

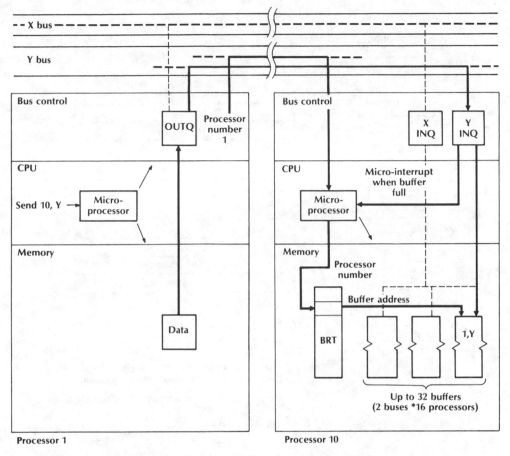

Figure 11–8.   Tandem 16 Dynabus interface and control.

attach to either of the buses are kept physically distinct, so that no single component failure can contaminate both buses simultaneously. Also in this section are clock synchronization and interlock circuitry. All processors communicate in a point to point manner using this redundant direct shared bus (DSB) configuration [Anderson and Jensen, 1975].

For any given interprocessor data transfer, one processor is the sender and the other the receiver. Before a processor can receive data over an interprocessor bus, the operating system must configure an entry in a table (Figure 11-9) known as the Bus Receive Table (BRT). Each BRT entry contains the address where the in-

coming data is to be stored and the number of words expected. To transfer data over a bus, a SEND instruction is executed in the sending processor, which specifies the bus to be used, the intended receiver, and the number of words to be sent. The sending processor's CPU stays in the SEND instruction until the data transfer is completed. Up to 65,535 words can be sent in a single SEND instruction. While the sending processor is executing the SEND instruction, the Dynabus interface control logic in the receiving processor is storing the data away according to the appropriate BRT entry. In the receiving processor this occurs simultaneously with program execution.

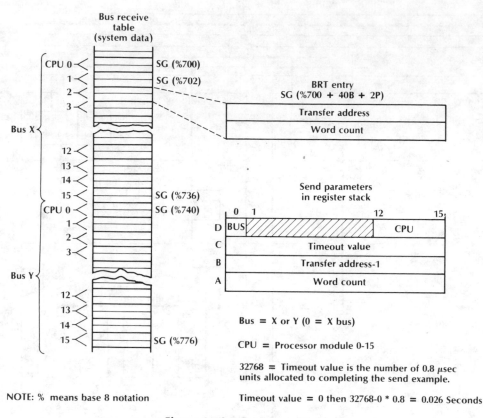

NOTE: % means base 8 notation

Figure 11–9. Bus receive table.

The message is divided into packets of 15 information words and an LRC check word. The sending processor first fills its outgoing queue with these packets, requests a bus transfer, and transmits upon grant of the bus by the interprocessor bus controller. The receiving processor fills the incoming queue associated with the bus over which the packet is received, and issues a microinterrupt to its own CPU. The microprocessor of the CPU checks the BRT entry, stores the packet away, verifies the LRC check word, and updates the BRT entry accordingly. If the count is exhausted the currently executing program is interrupted; otherwise program execution continues.

The BRT entries are two words that include a transfer count and buffer address. The SEND instruction has as parameters the designation of the bus to be used, the intended receiver, the data buffer address in the system data space, the word count to be transferred, and a timeout value. Error recovery action is to be taken in case the transfer is not completed within the timeout interval. These parameters are placed on the register stack and are dynamically updated so that the SEND instruction is interruptible on packet boundaries.

There are several levels of protocol, beyond the scope of this paper, dealing with the interprocessor bus that exist in software [Bartlett, 1978 and the second half of this paper], to assure that valid data are transferred. The philosophy for the hardware/software partitioning was to leave the more esoteric decisions to the software, e.g., alternate path routing, and error recovery procedures, with fault detection and reporting implemented in the hardware. Fault detection was designed in those areas having the highest anticipated probability of error.

The Input/Output Channel

The heart of the Tandem 16 I/O System is the I/O channel. All I/O is done on a direct memory access (DMA) basis. The channel is a microprogrammed, block multiplexed channel with the block size determined by the individual controllers. All the controllers are buffered to some degree so that all transfers over the I/O channel are at memory speed (4M Bytes/Second) and never wait for mechanical motion since the transfers always come from a buffer in the controller, rather than from the actual I/O device.

There exists a table in the system data space of each processor called the IOC (I/O Control) table that contains a two-word entry (Figure 11-10) for each of the 256 possible I/O devices attached to the I/O channel. These entries contain a byte count and virtual address in the system data space for data transfers from the I/O system.

The I/O channel moves the IOC entry to active registers during connection of an I/O controller and restores the updated values to the IOC upon disconnection. The I/O channel alerts the I/O controller when the count has been exhausted and that causes the controller to interrupt the processor.

The channel does not execute channel programs as on many systems but it does do data transfer in parallel with program execution. The memory system priority always permits I/O accesses to be handled before CPU or Dynabus accesses (in an on-line, transaction oriented environment, it is rare that a system is not I/O bound). The maximum I/O transfer is 4K bytes.

I/O SYSTEM ORGANIZATION

The I/O system had a design goal of being very efficient in a transaction, on-line oriented environment. This environment has constraints different from those of a batch environment. The figure of merit in an on-line system is the number of transactions/second/dollar that can be handled by the system. We also wanted an I/O system that had low overhead, fast transfer rates, no overruns, and no interrupts to the system until a logical entity of work was completed (i.e., no character by character interrupts from the terminals). The resulting design satisfied these goals by implementing an I/O system that was extremely simple.

I/O controllers reconnect to the channel when their buffers are stressed past a configurable threshold, transfer data in a burst mode until their buffer stress is zero (buffer empty on input operations, full on output operations), and disconnect from the channel. When the transfer terminates, the I/O controller interrupts the processor. Controllers may interrupt for other reasons than an exhausted byte count, e.g., a terminal controller receiving an end-of-page character from a page mode terminal, or I/O channel error condition, or a disc pack being mounted.

Dual-Port Controllers

The dual-ported I/O device controllers provide the interface between the Tandem 16 standard I/O channel and a variety of peripheral devices using distinct interfaces. While the I/O controllers are vastly different, there is a commonality among them that folds them into the Tandem 16 NonStop architecture.

Each controller contains two independent I/O channel ports implemented by IC packages which are physically separate from each other so that no interface chip can simultaneously cause failure of both ports. Each port of each controller has a 5-bit configurable controller number, and interrupt priority setting. These settings can

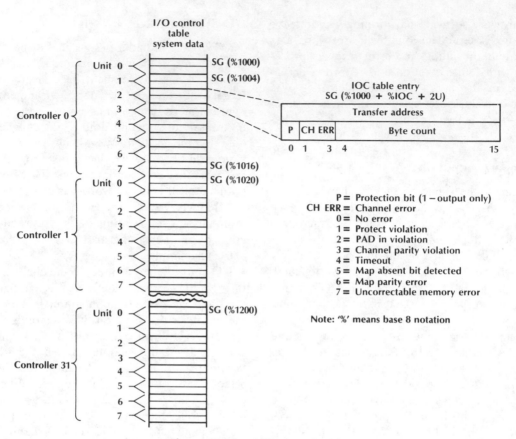

Figure 11–10. I/O control table.

be different on each port. The only requirement is that each port attached to an I/O channel must be assigned a controller number and priority distinct from controller numbers and priorities of other ports attached to the same I/O channel.

Each controller has a PON (power-on) circuit which clamps its output to ground whenever the controller's DC supply voltage is not within regulation. The PON circuit has hysteresis in it so that it will not oscillate if the power should hover near the limit of regulation. When the power is within regulation, the output of the PON circuit is at a TTL "1" level. A power-on condition causes a controller reset and also gives an interrupt to one of the two processors to which it is attached. The output of the PON circuit is also used to enable all the I/O channel

bus transceivers so that a controller being powered down will not cause interference on the I/O channels during the power transient. This is possible because the PON circuit operates with the supply voltage as low as .2 volts and special transceivers are used which correctly stay in a high impedance state as long as the control enable is at a logical "0."

Logically only one of the two ports of an I/O controller is active and the other port is utilized only in the event of a path failure to the primary port. There is an "ownership" bit (Figure 11-11) indicating to each port if it is the primary port or the alternate. Ownership is changed only by the operating system issuing a TAKE OWNERSHIP I/O command. Executing this special command causes the I/O controller to swap its primary and alternate port designation and to do a controller

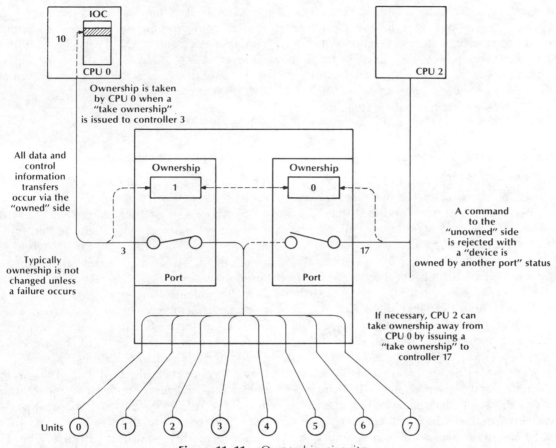

Figure 11–11. Ownership circuitry.

reset. Any attempt to use a controller which is not owned by a given processor will result in an ownership violation. If a processor determines that a given controller is malfunctioning on its I/O channel, it can issue a DISABLE PORT command that logically disconnects the port from that I/O controller. This does not affect the ownership status. That way, if the problem is within the port, the alternate path can be used, but if the problem is in the common portion of the controller, ownership is not forced upon the other processor.

A controller signals an interrupt on the I/O channel if the channel has indicated an exhausted transfer count, if the controller terminates the transfer prematurely, or for attention purposes.

When simultaneous interrupts occur on an I/O channel, a priority scheme determines which interrupt is handled first. There are two levels of priorities, designated "rank 0" and "rank 1." Each rank has up to 16 controllers assigned to it. Jumper wires on each controller determine the rank and position within the rank (positions 0 to 15). The I/O channel issues a rank 0 interrupt poll cycle and each controller assigned to rank 0 can place an interrupt request, if it needs service, on a dedicated data bit of the I/O channel determined by the jumper wires. If there are no controllers on rank 0 requiring service, the I/O channel issues the interrupt poll cycle for rank 1. Note, only 32 controllers can be assigned to a given channel and each one has a unique rank and position designation. The highest priority controller is granted access to the interrupt system. Thus a radial polling technique allows the processor to resolve 32 different controller priorities in just two poll cycles. Each port of a controller has a separate set of configuration jumpers so that a controller can have different priorities on its primary and alternate path.

Controller Buffer Considerations

In the design of the Tandem 16 I/O system, a lot of attention was paid to the overrun problem. While overruns are possible on this system, they have been made a rare occurrence. Each I/O controller has 3 configurable settings: the I/O controller number, the interrupt priority, and buffer stress threshold reconnect setting.

Each I/O controller is buffered to some extent. The asynchronous terminal controller has 2 bytes of buffering, while the disc controller has 4K bytes of buffering. Considerations of device transfer rate, channel transfer rate, the individual controller's buffer depth, the controller's reconnect priority, and a given channel's I/O complement can be used to determine the buffer's depth (stress threshold) at which a reconnect request should be made to the channel to minimize the chance of overrun. Each controller with a significant buffering (more than 32 bytes) has a configurable stress threshold. Buffer stress is defined as the number of cells full on an input operation, and the number of cells empty on output operations. In general, the I/O channel relieves stress while the I/O device generates more stress. Therefore the higher the stress, the more the buffer needs relief from the I/O channel, regardless of the direction of data transfer.

Tandem has developed a program which takes a system configuration and determines the appropriate stress threshold settings needed to guarantee no data overruns. Since reconnect overhead time is known, and all transfers on the I/O bus take place at memory speed, and the upper bound of the block length is known for each type of controller, it is a deterministic function as to whether or not an overrun is possible. If it is impossible to generate a no-overrun configuration, the program will output a minimum-overrun threshold setting. Most times, however, it is possible to iterate on the configuration until threshold settings can be determined that prevent overruns.

Disc Controller Considerations

The greatest fear that an on-line system user has is that "the data base is down" [Dolotta et al., 1976]. Many of these users are willing to pay the premium of having duplicated or "mirrored" data bases in case a disc drive fails. To meet this requirement, Tandem provides automatic mirroring of data bases.

A disc volume is a set of data contained on one spindle or one removable disc pack. A user may declare any of the disc volumes as mirrored pairs at system generation time (Figure 11-12). The system then maintains these pairs so that they always contain identical data. Thus protection is achieved for a single drive failure. Each disc drive in the system may be dual-ported. Each port of a disc drive is connected to an independent disc controller. Each of the disc controllers is also dual-ported and connected between two processors. A string of up to 8 drives (4 mirrored pairs) can be supported by a pair of controllers in this manner.

Note that in this configuration there are many paths to any given data and that data can be retrieved regardless of any single disc drive failure, disc controller failure, power supply failure, processor failure, or I/O channel failure.

The disc controller is buffered for a maximum length record which provides several features important in an on-line system. First, the disc controller is absolutely immune to overruns. Second, data to be written on two drives need be transferred over the I/O channel only once. The data may then be posted twice from the controller's internal buffer. Thus the channel's data transfer capacity is little impaired by mirrored volumes.

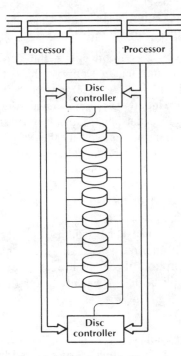

Figure 11–12. Tandem 16 disc subsystem organization.

This disc controller uses a Fire code [Peterson, 1961] for burst error correction and detection. It can correct 11 bit bursts in the controller's buffer before transmission to the channel. Since overlapped seeks are allowed by the controller, when data are to be read from a mirrored pair they can be read from the drive which has its arm closest to the data cylinder. It is interesting to note that since the majority of transactions in an on-line system are reads, mirrored volumes actually can increase performance.

NonStop I/O System Considerations

The I/O channel interface consists of a two-byte data bus and control signals. All data transferred over the bus are parity checked in both directions, and errors are reported via the interrupt system. A watchdog timer in the I/O channel detects if a nonexistent I/O controller has been addressed, or if a controller stops responding during an I/O sequence.

The data transfer byte count word in the IOC entry contains four status bits including a protect bit. When this bit is set to "1" only output transfers are permitted to this device.

Because I/O controllers are connected between two independent I/O channels, it is very important that word count, buffer address, and direction of transfer are controlled by the processor instead of within the controller. If that information were to be kept in the controller, a single failure could cause both processors to which it was attached to fail. Consider what would happen if a byte count register was located in the controller and was stuck in such a situation such that the count could not decrement to zero on an input transfer. It would be possible to overwrite the buffer and cause system tables to become meaningless. The error would propagate to the other processor upon discovery that the first processor was no longer operating.

Other error conditions that the channel checks for are violations of I/O protocol, attempts to transfer to absent pages (it is the operating system's responsibility to "tack down" the virtual pages used for I/O buffering), uncorrectable memory errors, and map parity errors.

POWER, PACKAGING, ON-LINE MAINTENANCE

The Tandem 16 power supply has 3 sections: a 5 volt interruptible section, a 5 volt uninterruptible section, and a 12–15 volt uninterruptible section. The interruptible section will stop supplying DC power when AC is lost while the uninterruptible sections will continue to supply DC power. The interruptible section powers I/O controllers and that portion of a processor which is not related to memory refresh operation. The uninterruptible sections provide power for the memory array and refresh circuitry. The 5 volt sections are switching regulated supplies while the 12–15 volt section is linearly regulated. The uninterruptible sections have a provision for a battery attachment so that in case of utility power failure, memory contents are kept for 1.5 to 4 hours, depending on the amount of memory attached to the supply.

The power supply accepts AC input of 110 or 220 volts ±20% to provide brownout insensitivity. At nominal line conditions, over 30 msec of ride through is provided by storage capacitors. A power-fail warning signal is provided when there is at least 5 msec of regulated power remaining so that the processor can go through an orderly shutdown. Some users must remain operational through utility power failure and have generator systems which provide continuous AC power for the entire system, including peripheral devices.

The power-fail warning scheme in the Tandem 16 power supply monitors charge in the storage capacitors rather than monitoring loss of AC peaks as is conventionally done. This has the advantage that the 5 msec to do a power shutdown sequence in the processor is guaranteed even if it occurs after a brownout period.

The power supply provides all other prudent features required in a computer system, such as over voltage and over current protection, and over temperature protection.

The power-up sequencing on disc drives has been implemented with independent rather than daisy chained circuits. In the daisy chained approach, one bad sequencer circuit can cause the remaining drives in the chain not to sequence up after a power failure.

Further Packaging and On-line Maintenance Considerations

Modularity is a key concept in the Tandem 16 system. The maintenance philosophy is to make all repair by module replacement at the user site without making the system unavailable to the user. Therefore the backplanes, power supplies, fans, I/O channels, as well as the PC cards are modular and easily replaceable. Thumb screws are used when they can be so that a minimum of tools are needed for repair. The package is designed so that there is easy access to all modules.

Processors and I/O controllers not only can be replaced on-line, but added on-line without system interruption if expansion is planned, all without application software being changed.

SUMMARY

The contribution of the Tandem 16 system lies in the synthesis of a system to directly address the need of the NonStop application marketplace. By avoiding the "onus of compatibility" to any previous system, an architecture could be designed from "scratch" that was "clean" and efficient.

The system goals have been met to a large degree. Systems have been shipped containing 2 to 10 processors. Many application programs are on-line and running. They recover from failures, and stay up continuously.

A "NonStop" Operating System

Joel F. Bartlett

Abstract

The Tandem 16 computer system is an attempt at providing a general-purpose, multiple-computer system which is at least one order of magnitude more reliable than conventional commercial offerings. Through software abstractions a multiple-computer structure, desirable for failure tolerance, is transformed into something approaching a symmetric multiprocessor, desirable for programming ease. The first section of this paper provides an overview of the hardware structure. In the second section are found the design goals for the operating system, "Guardian." The third section provides a bottom-up view of Guardian.

Background

On-line computer processing has become a way of life for many businesses. As they make the transition from manual or batch methods to on-line systems, they become increasingly vulnerable to computer failures. Whereas in a batch system the direct costs of a failure might simply be increased overtime for the operations staff, a failure of an on-line system results in immediate business losses.

System Overview

The Tandem 16 [Tandem Computers, Inc., 1976; Katzman, 1977a] was designed to provide a system for on-line applications that would be

significantly more reliable than currently available commercial computer systems. The hardware structure consists of multiple processor modules interconnected by redundant interprocessor buses. A PMS [Bell and Newell, 1971] definition of the hardware is found in Figure 11-13.

Each processor has its own power supply, memory, and I/O channel and is connected to all other processors by redundant interprocessor buses. Each I/O controller is redundantly powered and connected to two different I/O channels. As a result, any interprocessor bus failure does not affect the ability of a processor to communicate with any other processor. The failure of an I/O channel or of a processor does not cause the loss of an I/O device. Likewise, the failure of a module (processor or I/O controller) does not disable any other module or disable any inter-module communication. Finally, certain I/O devices such as disc drives may be connected to two different I/O controllers, and disc drives may in turn be duplicated such that the failure of an I/O controller or disc drive will not result in loss of data.

The system is not a true multiprocessor [Enslow, 1977], but rather a "multiple computer" system. The multiple computer approach is preferable for several reasons. First, since no module is shared by the entire system, it increases the system's reliability. Second, a multiple computer system does not require the complex hardware needed to handle multiple access paths to a common memory. In smaller systems, the cost of such a multiported memory is undesirable; and

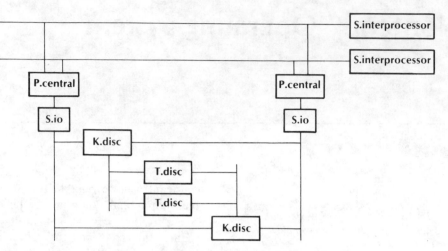

Figure 11–13. Hardware structure.

in larger systems, performance suffers because of memory access interference.

On-line repair is as necessary as reliability in assuring system availability. The modular structure of the Tandem 16 system allows processors, I/O controllers, or buses to be repaired or replaced while the rest of the system continues to operate. Once repaired, they may then be reintegrated into the system.

The system structure allows a wide range of system sizes to be supported. As many as sixteen processors, each with up to 512K bytes of memory, may be connected into one system. Each processor may also have up to 256 I/O devices connected to it. This provides for tremendous growth of application programs and processing loads without the requirement that the application be reimplemented on a larger system with a different architecture.

Finally, the system is meant to provide a general solution to the problem of providing a failure-tolerant, on-line environment suitable for commercial use. As such, the system supports conventional programming languages and peripherals and is oriented toward providing large numbers of terminals with access to large data bases.

SYSTEM DESIGN GOALS

Integrated Hardware/Software Design

The Tandem 16 system was designed to solve a specific problem. This problem was not stated in terms of hardware and software requirements, but rather in terms of system requirements. The hardware and software designs then proceeded in tandem to provide a unified solution. The hardware design concerned itself with the contents of each module, their interconnections to the common buses, and error detection and correction within modules and on the communication paths. The software design was given the problem of control; that is, selection of which modules to use and which buses to use to communicate with them. Furthermore, as errors are detected, it was the responsibility of the software to control recovery actions.

Operating System Design Goals

The first and foremost goal of the operating system, Guardian, was to provide a failure-tolerant system. This translated into the following design "axioms":

- The operating system should be able to remain operational after any single detected module or bus failure.
- The operating system should allow any module or bus to be repaired on-line and then reintegrated into the system.
- The operating system should be implemented in a reliable manner. Increased reliability provided by the hardware architecture must not be negated by software problems.

A second set of requirements came from the great numbers and sizes of hardware configurations that are possible:

- The operating system should support all possible hardware configurations, ranging from a two-processor, discless system through a sixteen-processor system with billions of bytes of disc storage.
- The operating system should hide the physical configuration as much as possible such that applications could be written to run on a great variety of system configurations.

OPERATING SYSTEM STRUCTURE

To satisfy these requirements, the operating system was designed to have the appearance of a true multiprocessor at the user level. The design of the system was strongly influenced by Dijkstra's work on the "THE" system [1968], and Brinch Hansen's implementation of an operating system nucleus for a single-processor system [1970]. The primary abstractions are processes, which do work, and messages, which allow interprocess communication.

Processes

At the lowest level of the system is the basic hardware as earlier described. It provides the capability for redundant modules, i.e., I/O controllers, I/O devices, and processor modules consisting of a processor, memory, and a power supply. These redundant modules are in turn interconnected by redundant buses. Error detection is provided on all communication paths and error correction is provided within each processor's memory. The hardware does not concern itself with the selection of communication paths or the assignment of tasks to specific modules.

The first abstraction provided is that of the process. Each processor module may have one or more processes residing in it. A process is initially created in a specific processor and may not execute in another processor. Each process has an execution priority assigned to it. Processor time is allocated on a strict priority basis to the highest priority ready process.

Process synchronization primitives include "counting semaphores" and process local "event" flags. Semaphore operations are performed via the functions PSEM and VSEM, corresponding to Dijkstra's P and V operations. Semaphores may only be used for synchronization between processes within the same processor. They are typically used to control access to resources such as resident memory buffers, message control blocks, and I/O controllers.

When certain low-level actions such as device interrupts, processor power-on, message completion or message arrival occur, they result in "event" flags being set for the appropriate process. A process may wait for one or more events to occur via the function WAIT. The process is activated as soon as the first WAITed for event occurs. Events are signaled via the function AWAKE. Event signals are queued using a "wake up waiting" mechanism so that they are not lost if the event is signaled when the process is not waiting on it. Like semaphores, event signals may not be passed between processors. Event flags are predefined for eight different events and may not be redefined.

When a process blocks itself to wait for some event to occur or for a semaphore to be allocated to it, it may specify a maximum time to block. If the time limit expires and the event has not occurred or the resource has not been obtained, then the process will continue execution but an error condition will be returned to it. This time-out allows "watch dog" timers to be easily placed on device interrupts or on resource allocations where a failure may occur.

Each process in the system has a unique identifier or "processid" in the form: < cpu #, process # >, which allows it to be referenced on a system-wide basis. This leads to the next abstraction, the message system, which provides a processor-independent, failure-tolerant method for interprocess communication.

Messages

The message system provides five primitive operations which can be illustrated in the context of a process making a request to some server process, Figure 11-14. The process's request for service will send a message to the appropriate server process via the procedure LINK. The message will consist of parameters denoting the type of request and any needed data. The message will be queued for the server process, setting an event flag, and then the requester process may continue executing.

When the server process wishes to check for any messages, it calls LISTEN. LISTEN returns the first message queued or an indication that no messages are queued. The server process will then obtain a copy of the requester's data by calling the procedure READLINK.

Next, the server process will process the request. The status of the operation and any result will then be returned by the WRITELINK procedure, which will signal the requester process via another event flag. Finally, the requester process will complete its end of the transaction by calling BREAKLINK.

A communications protocol was defined for the interprocessor buses that would tolerate any single bus error during the execution of any message system primitive. This design assures that a communications failure will occur if and only if the sender or receiver processes or their processors fail. Any bus errors which occur during a message system operation will be automatically corrected in a manner transparent to

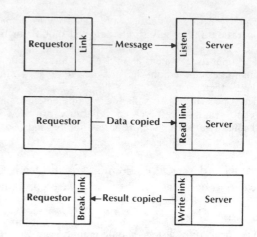

Figure 11–14.   Message system primitive operations.

the communicating processes and logged on the system console. The interprocessor buses are not used for communication between processes in the same processor, which can be done faster in memory. However, the processes involved in the message transfer are unable to detect this difference.

The message system is designed such that resources needed for message transmission (control blocks) are obtained at the start of a message transfer request. Once LINK has been successfully completed, both processes are assured that sufficient resources are in hand to be able to complete the message transfer. Furthermore, a process may reserve control blocks to guarantee that it will always be able to send messages to process a request that it picks up from its message queue. Such resource controls assure that deadlocks can be prevented in complex producer/consumer interactions, if the programmer correctly analyzes and anticipates potential deadlocks within the application.

Process-Pairs

With the implementation of processes and messages, the system is no longer seen as separate modules. Instead, the system can be viewed as a

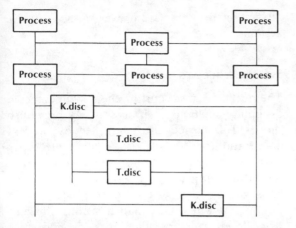

Figure 11–15. System structure after the addition of processes and messages.

set of processes which may interact via messages in any arbitrary manner, as shown in Figure 11-15.

By defining messages as the only legitimate method for process-to-process interaction, inter-process communication is not limited by the multiple-computer organization of the system. The system then starts to take on the appearance of a true multiprocessor. Processor boundaries have been blurred, but I/O devices are still not accessible to all processes.

System-wide access to I/O devices is provided by the mechanism of "process-pairs." An I/O process-pair consists of two cooperating processes located in two different processors that control a particular I/O device. One of the processes will

be considered the "primary" and one will be considered the "backup." The primary process handles requests sent to it and controls the I/O device. When a request for an operation such as a file open or close occurs, the primary will send this information to the backup process via the message system. These "checkpoints" assure that the backup process will have all information needed to take over control of the device in the event of an I/O channel error or a failure of the primary process' processor. A process-pair for a redundantly recorded disc volume is illustrated in Figure 11-16.

Because of the distributed nature of the system, it is not possible to provide a block of "driver" code that could be called directly to access the device. While potentially more efficient, such an approach would preclude access to every device in the system by every process in the system.

The I/O process-pair and associated I/O device(s) are known by a logical device name such as "SDISC1" or by a logical device number rather than by the processid of either process. I/O device names are mapped to the appropriate processes via the logical device table (LDT) in every processor, which supplies two processids for each device. A message request made on the basis of a device name or number results in the message's being sent to the first process in the table. If the message cannot be sent or if the message is sent to the backup process, an error indication will be returned. The processid entries

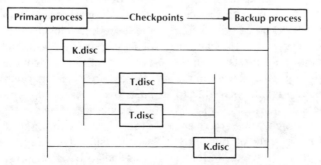

Figure 11–16. Process-pair for a redundantly recorded disc volume.

in the LDT will then be reversed and the message re-sent. Note two things: first, the error recovery can be done in an automatic manner; and second, the requester is not concerned with what process actually handled the request. Error recovery cannot always be done automatically. For example, the primary process of a pair controlling a line printer fails while handling a request to print a line on a check. The application process would prefer to see the process failure as an error rather than have the request automatically retried, which might result in two checks being printed.

The two primitives, processes and messages, blur the boundaries between processors and provide a failure-tolerant method for interprocess communication. By defining a method of grouping processes (process-pairs), a mechanism for uniform access to an I/O device or other system-wide resource is provided. This access method is independent of the functions performed within the processes, their locations, or their implementations. Within the process-pair, the message system is used to checkpoint state changes so that the backup process may take over in the event of a failure. This checkpoint mechanism is in turn independent of all other processes and messages in the system.

The system structure can be summarized as follows. Guardian is constructed of processes which communicate using messages. Fault tolerance is provided by duplication of components in both the hardware and the software. Access to I/O devices is provided by process-pairs consisting of a primary process and a backup process. The primary process must checkpoint state information to the backup process so that the backup may take over on a failure. Requests to these devices are routed using the logical device name or number so that the request is always routed to the current primary process. The result is a set of primitives and protocols which allow recovery and continued processing in spite of bus, processor, I/O controller, or I/O device failures. Furthermore, these primitives provide access to all system resources from every process in the system.

System Processes

The next step in structuring the system comes in assigning functions to processes. As previously shown, I/O devices are controlled by process-pairs. Another process-pair known as the "operator" is present in the system. This pair is responsible for formatting and printing error messages on the system console. Here is an example of where Guardian has not followed a strict level structure. The operator makes requests to a terminal process to print the messages, yet the terminal process wishes to send messages to the operator to report I/O channel errors. An infinite cycle is prevented by having the terminal process not send messages for errors on the operator terminal and having I/O processes never wait for message completions when sending errors to the operator. While it may be preferable to prevent cycles of any type in system design, they have been allowed in Guardian when it can be shown that they will terminate. The ability to reserve message control blocks assures that no cycle will be blocked because of resource problems.

Each processor has a "system monitor" process which handles such functions as process creation and deletion, setting time of day, and processor failure and reload cleanup operations.

A memory management process is also resident in each processor. This process is responsible for allocating a page of physical memory and then sending messages to the appropriate disc processes to do the actual disc I/O. Pages are brought in on a demand basis, and pages to overlay are selected on a "least recently used" basis over the entire memory of the processor.

The choice of relatively unsophisticated algorithms for scheduling and memory management was a result of the fact that the system was not intended to be a general-purpose timeshare system. Rather, it was to be a system which supported multiple processes and terminals in an extremely flexible manner.

Application Process Interface

Above the process and communication structure there exists a library of procedures which are used to access system resources. These procedures run in the calling process's environment and may or may not send messages to other processes in the system. For example, the file system procedures do not do the actual I/O operations. Instead, they check the caller's parameters, and if all is in order a message is sent to the appropriate I/O process-pair. Likewise, process creation is seen as a procedure call to NEWPROCESS, which does nothing but check the caller's parameters and then send a message to the system monitor process in the processor where the process is to be created. On the other hand, a procedure such as TIME which returns the current time of day does not send any messages. In either case, the access to system resources appears simply as procedure calls, effectively hiding the process structure, message system, hardware organization, and associated failure recovery mechanisms.

Initialization and Processor Reload

System initialization starts with one processor being cold loaded from some disc on the system. The load file contains a memory image of the operating system resident code and data, with all system processes in existence and at their initial states. The system monitor process then creates a command interpreter process.

Guardian may be brought up even though a processor or peripheral device is down. This is possible because operating system disc images may be kept on multiple disc drives, I/O controllers may be accessed by two different processors, and the terminal that has the initial command interpreter on it is selected by using the processor's switch register.

After a cold load, the system logically consists of one processor and any peripherals attached to it. More processors and peripherals may be added to the system via the command interpreter command:

: RELOAD 1, SDISC

This command will read the disc image for processor 1 from the disc SDISC and send it over either interprocessor bus to processor 1. Once it is loaded, all processes residing in other processors in the system will be notified that processor 1 is up.

This command is also used to reload a processor after it has been repaired. Guardian does not differentiate between an initial load of a processor and a later reload. In each case, resources are being logically added to the system and processes must be notified so that they may make use of them.

The previous example of a reload message being sent to all processes is an example of how functions are split in Guardian. A mechanism is provided for informing a process of a system status change. It may then take some unspecified action (including doing nothing). Similarly, a system power-on simply sets the PON event flag for all processes. The operating system kernel must only insure that the process structure and message system are correctly saved and restored. It is then the responsibility of individual processes to do such things as reinitialize their I/O controllers.

Operating System Error Detection

Besides the hardware-provided single error detection and correction on memory, and single error detection on the interprocessor and I/O buses, additional software error checks are provided. The first of these is the detection of a down processor. Every second, each processor in the system sends a special "I'm alive" message over each bus to all processors in the system. Every two seconds, each processor checks to see that it has received one of these messages from each processor. If a message has not been received, then it assumes that that processor is down.

Additionally, the operating system makes checks on the correctness of data structures such as linked lists when operations are done on them. Any processor detecting such an error will halt.

All I/O interrupts are bracketed by a "watch dog" timer such that the system will not hang up if an I/O operation does not complete with the expected interrupt. If an I/O bus error occurs, then the backup process will take over control of the device using the second I/O bus.

As previously noted, the interprocessor bus protocol is designed to correct single bus errors. In addition to this, extensive checks are made on the control information received over the buses to verify that it is consistent with the state of the receiving processor.

Power-fail/automatic restart is provided within each processor. A power failure is detected independently by each processor module and as a result is not a system-wide, synchronous event. The system was designed to recover from either a complete system power-fail, or a transient which will cause some of the processors to power-fail and then immediately restart.

The innovative aspects of Guardian lie not in any new concepts introduced, but rather in the synthesis of pre-existing ideas. Of particular note are the low-level abstractions, process and message. By using these, all processor boundaries can be hidden from both the application programs and most of the operating system. These initial abstractions are the key to the system's ability to tolerate failures. They also provide the configuration independence that is necessary in order for the system and applications to run over a wide range of system sizes.

Guardian provides the application programmer with extremely general approaches to process structuring, interprocess communication, and failure tolerance. Much has been said about structuring programs using multiple communicating processes, but few operating systems are able to support such structures.

Finally, the design goals of the system have been met to a large degree. Systems with between two and ten processors have been installed and are running on-line applications. They are recovering from failures and failures are being repaired on-line.

ACKNOWLEDGMENTS

An operating system is the work of many people. In particular I would like to acknowledge the contributions of Dennis McEvoy, Dave Hinders, Jerry Held, and Robert Shaw in its design, implementation, and testing.

REFERENCES

Anderson and Jensen [1975]; Bartlett [1978]; Bell and Newell [1971]; Brinch Hansen [1970]; Dijkstra [1968]; Dolotta et al. [1976]; Enslow [1977]; Katzman [1977]; Peterson [1961]; Tandem Computers, Inc. [1976].

Fault-Tolerant Design of Local ESS Processors

W. N. Toy

Abstract

The stored program control of Bell System Electronic Switching Systems (ESS) has been under development since 1953. During this period, the No. 1 ESS, the No. 2 ESS, and the No. 3 ESS have been developed and used extensively by Bell System operating companies to provide commercial telephone service. These systems serve all types of telephone offices: The large-capacity No. 1 ESS serves metropolitan offices, the medium-capacity No. 2 ESS was designed for suburban offices, and the No. 3 can be found in many small rural offices. The fault tolerant design of ESS processors provides the same highly dependable telephone service established by the previous electromechanical systems. Pertinent processor architecture features used to achieve ESS reliability objectives are discussed. A detailed discussion of the maintenance design of the 3A Processor is also included.

INTRODUCTION

Next to computer systems used in space-borne vehicles and U.S. defense installations, no other application has a higher availability requirement than a Bell System Electronic Switching System (ESS). These systems have been designed to be out of service no more than a few minutes per year. Furthermore, design objectives permit no more than 0.01 percent of the telephone calls to be processed incorrectly [Downing, Nowak, and Tuomenoksa, 1964]. For example, when a fault occurs in a system, few calls in progress may be handled incorrectly during the recovery process.

At the core of every ESS is a single high-speed central processor [Hart, Taylor, and Ulrich, 1969; Brown et al., 1969; Staehler, 1977]. To establish an ultrareliable switching environment, redundancy of system components and duplication of the processor itself has been the approach taken to compensate for potential machine faults. Without this redundancy, a single component failure in the processor might cause a complete failure of the entire system. With duplication, a standby processor takes over control and provides continuous telephone service.

When the system fails, the fault must be quickly detected and isolated. Meanwhile, a rapid recovery of the call processing functions (by the redundant component(s) and/or processor) is necessary to maintain the system's high availability. Next, the fault must be diagnosed and the defective unit repaired or replaced. The failure rate and repair time must be such that the probability is very small for a failure to occur in the duplicated unit before the first one is repaired.

ALLOCATION AND CAUSES OF SYSTEM DOWNTIME

The outage of a telephone (switching) office can be caused by facilities other than the processor. While a hardware fault in one of the peripheral units generally results in only a partial loss of service, it *is* possible for a fault in this area to bring the system down. By design, the processor has been allocated two-thirds of the system downtime. The other one-third is allocated to the remaining equipment in the system.

Field experience indicates that system outages due to the processor may be assigned to one of four categories shown in Figure 12-1 [Staehler and Watters, 1976]. The percentages in this figure represent the fraction of total downtime attributable to each cause. The four categories are as follows:

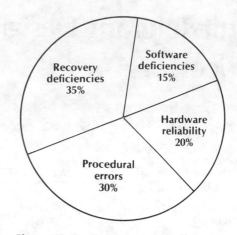

Figure 12–1. System outage allocation.

Hardware Reliability

Before the accumulation of large amounts of field data, total system downtime was usually assigned to hardware. We now know that the situation is more complex. Processor hardware actually accounts for only 20 percent of the downtime. With growing use of stored program control, it has become increasingly important to make such systems more reliable. Redundancy is designed into all subsystems so that the system can go down *only* when hardware failures occur simultaneously in duplicated units. However, the data now show that good diagnostic and trouble location programs are very critical parts of the total system reliability performance.

Software Deficiencies

Software deficiencies include all software errors that cause memory mutilation, and program loops that can only be cleared by major reinitialization. Software faults are the result of improper translation or implementation of the original algorithm. In some cases, the original algorithm may have been incorrectly specified. Program changes and feature additions are continuously incorporated into working offices. Software account for 15 percent of the downtime.

Recovery Deficiencies

Recovery is the system's most complex and difficult function. Deficiencies may include the shortcomings of either hardware or software design to detect faults when they occur. When the faults go undetected, the system remains extensively impaired until the trouble is recognized. Another kind of recovery problem can occur if the system is unable to properly isolate a faulty subsystem and configure a working system around it.

The many possible system states which may arise under trouble conditions make recovery a complicated process. Besides those already mentioned, unforeseen difficulties may be encountered in the field, and lead to inadequate recovery. Because of the large number of variables involved and because the recovery function is so strongly related to all other components of maintenance, recovery deficiencies account for 35 percent of the downtime.

Procedural Errors

Human error on the part of maintenance personnel or office administrators can also cause the system to go down. For example, someone in maintenance may mistakenly pull a circuit pack from the on-line processor while repairing a defective standby processor. Inadequate and incorrect documentation (e.g., users' manuals) may also be classified as human error. Obviously, the number of manual operations must be reduced if procedural errors are to be minimized. Procedural errors account for about 30 percent of the downtime.

The shortcomings and deficiencies of current systems are being continually corrected to improve system reliability.

DUPLEX ARCHITECTURE

When a fault occurs in a nonredundant single processor, the system will remain down until the processor is repaired. In order to meet the ESS reliability requirement, *redundancy* is included in the system design; continuous and correct operation is maintained by duplicating all functional units within the processor. If one of the units fails, the duplicated unit is switched in, maintaining continuous operation. Meanwhile, the defective unit is repaired. Should a fault occur in the duplicated unit during the repair interval, the system will, of course, go down. If the repair interval is relatively short, the probability of simultaneous faults occurring in two identical units is quite small. This technique of redundancy has been used throughout each ESS.

The first-generation ESS processor structure consists of two store communities: program store (PS) and call store (CS). The program store is a read-only memory (ROM) containing the call processing, maintenance, and administration programs; it also contains long-term translation and system parameters. The call store contains the transient data related to telephone calls in progress. The memory is electrically alterable to allow its data to be changed frequently. In one

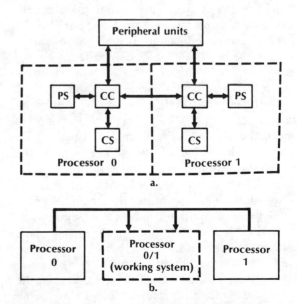

Figure 12–2. Single-unit duplex configuration. a.) Processor structure. b.) Two possible configurations.

particular arrangement, shown in Figure 12-2, the complete processor is treated as a single functional block and is duplicated. This type of single-unit duplex system has two possible configurations: Either Processor 0 or Processor 1 can be assigned as the on-line working system, while the other unit serves as standby backup. The mean-time-to-failure (MTTF), a measure of reliability, is given by the following expression [Smith, 1972]:

$$MTTF = \mu/2\lambda^2$$

where μ is the repair rate (reciprocal of the repair time), and λ is the failure rate.

The failure rate (λ) of one unit is the summation of failure rates of all components within the unit. For medium and small ESS processors, Figure 12-2 shows a system structure containing several functional units which are treated as a single entity, with λ still sufficiently small to meet the reliability requirement. The single-unit duplex configuration has the merit of being very simple in terms of the number of switching blocks in the system. This configuration simplifies not only the recovery program but also the hardware interconnection. It does this by eliminating the additional access required to make each duplicated block capable of switching independently into the on-line system configuration.

In the large No. 1 ESS, which contains many components, the MTTF becomes too low to meet the reliability requirement. In order to increase the value of the MTTF, either the number of components (failure rate) or the repair time must be reduced. Alternatively, the single-unit duplex configuration can be partitioned into a multiunit duplex configuration as shown in Figure 12-3. In this arrangement, each subunit contains a small number of components and is able to be switched into a working system. The system will fail only if a fault occurs in the redundant subunit while the original is being repaired. Since each subunit contains fewer components, the probability of two simultaneous

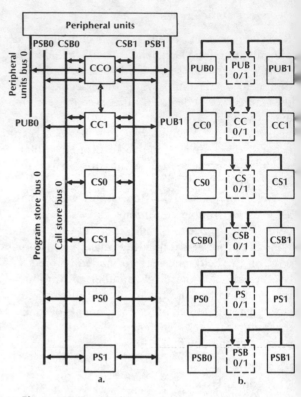

Figure 12–3. Multiunit duplex configuration. a.) Processor structure. b.) 64 possible configurations.

faults occurring in a duplicated pair of subunits is reduced. The MTTF of the multiunit duplex configuration can be computed by taking into consideration the conditional probability of a subunit failing during the repair time of the original subunit.

An example of a multiunit duplex configuration is shown in Figure 12-3. A working system is configured with a fault-free CCx-CSx-CSBx-PSx-PSBx-PUBx arrangement, where x is either Subunit 0 or Subunit 1. This means there are 2^6, or 64, possible combinations of system configurations. The MTTF is given by the following expression:

$$MTTF = \frac{r\mu}{2\lambda^2} \qquad (1)$$

where

$$r = 1/\{(\lambda_{CC}/\lambda)^2 + (\lambda_{CS}/\lambda)^2 + (\lambda_{CSB}/\lambda)^2$$
$$+ (\lambda_{PS}/\lambda)^2 + (\lambda_{PSB}/\lambda)^2 + (\lambda_{PUB}/\lambda)^2\} \quad (2)$$

The factor r is at a maximum when the failure rate (λ_i) for each subunit is the same. In this case

$$\lambda_{CC} = \lambda_{CS} = \lambda_{CSB} = \lambda_{PS} = \lambda_{PSB}$$
$$= \lambda_{PUB} = \lambda_i \quad (3)$$

or

$$\lambda_i = \frac{\lambda}{s} \quad (4)$$

where

$s =$ number of subunits in (2),
$s = 6$, and
$r = s$.

At best, the MTTF is improved by a factor corresponding to the number of partitioned subunits. This improvement is not fully realized since equipment must be added to provide additional access and to select subunits. The partitioning of the subsystem into subunits as shown in Figure 12-3 results in subunits of different sizes. Again, the failure rate for each individual subunit will not be the same; hence, the r-factor will be smaller than 6. Because of the relatively large number of components used in implementing the No. 1 ESS, the system is arranged in the multiunit duplex configuration in order to meet the reliability requirement.

Reliability calculation is a process of predicting, from available failure rate data, the achievable reliability of a system and the probability of meeting the reliability objectives for ESS applications. These calculations are most useful and beneficial during the early stages of design in order to assess various types of redundancy and determine the system's organization. In the small and medium ESS's, the calculations have supported the use of single-unit duplex structures. For large ESS's, it was necessary to partition the system into a multiunit duplex configuration.

FAULT SIMULATION TECHNIQUES

One of the more difficult tasks of maintenance design is fault diagnosis. Its effectiveness in diagnostic resolution can be determined by simulation of the system's behavior in the presence of a specific fault. By means of simulation, design deficiencies can be identified and corrected prior to any system being deployed in the field. It is necessary to evaluate the system's ability to detect faults, to recover automatically back into a working system, and to provide diagnostics information where the fault is within a few replaceable circuit packs. Fault simulation, therefore, is an important aspect of maintenance design.

There are essentially two techniques used for simulating faults of digital systems; physical simulation or digital simulation. Physical simulation is a process of inserting faults into a physical working model. This method produces more realistic behavior under fault conditions. A wider class of faults can be applied to the system, such as a blown fuse or shorted backplane interconnection. However, fault simulation cannot begin until the design has been completed and the equipment is fully operational. Also, it is not possible to insert faults interior to an integrated circuit.

Digital fault simulation is a means of predicting the behavior under failure of a processor modeled in a computer program. The computer used to execute the program (the host) is generally different from the processor being simulated (the object). Digital fault simulation gives a high degree of automation and excellent access to interior points of logic to monitor the signal flow. It allows diagnostic test development and evaluation to proceed well in advance of unit fabrication. The cost of computer simulation can be quite high for a large, complex system.

The physical fault simulation method was first employed to generate diagnostic data for the Morris Electronic Switching System [Tsiang and Ulrich, 1962]. Over 50,000 known faults were purposely introduced into the central control to be diagnosed by its diagnostic program. Test results associated with each fault were recorded. They were then sorted and printed in dictionary format to formulate a trouble locating manual (TLM). Under trouble conditions, by consulting the TLM, it was possible to determine a set of several suspected circuit packs which might contain the defective component. Using the dictionary technique at the Morris system, the average repair time was kept low and maintenance was made much easier.

The experience gained in the physical fault simulation was applied and extended in the No. 1 ESS development [Downing, Nowak, and Tuomenoksa, 1964]. Each plug-in circuit pack was replaced by a fault simulator which introduced every possible type of single fault on the replaced package one at a time and then recorded the system reaction on magnetic tape. This was done for all circuits packs in the system. In addition to diagnostic data for dictionaries, additional data were collected to determine the adequacy of hardware and software in fault detection and system recovery. Deficiencies were corrected to improve the overall maintenance of the system.

A digital logic simulator called LAMP [Chang, Smith, and Walford, 1974] was developed for the No. 1A ESS development. It played an important role in the hardware and diagnostic development of the No. 1A Processor. The simulator is capable of simulating subsystem with as many as 65,000 logic gates. All classical faults for standard logic gates are simulatable with logic nodes stuck at "0" or stuck at "1." Before physical units are available, digital simulation can be very effective in verifying the design, evaluating diagnostic access, and developing tests. Physical fault simulation has been demonstrated in the No. 1 ESS to give a very realistic behavior under fault conditions. The integration of both techniques was employed in the development of the No. 1A Processor to take advantage of both processes. The use of complementary simulation allows

faults to be simulated physically (in the system laboratory) and logically (on a computer). Most of the deficiencies of one simulation process are compensated for by the other. The complementary method provided both a convenient method for validating the results and more extensive fault simulation data than would have been normally if either process were used individually. Figure 12-4 shows the complementary process of fault simulation used in the No. 1A Processor development [Bowman et al., 1977; Goetz, 1974]. Maximum diagnostic performance was achieved from an integrated use of both simulation methods.

FIRST GENERATION ESS PROCESSORS

The world's first ESS provided commercial telephone service at Morris, Illinois, in 1959 for about a year on a field trial basis [Keister, Ketchledge, and Lovell, 1960]. The system demonstrated the use of stored program control and the basic maintenance philosophy of providing continuous and reliable telephone service. The trial established valuable guides for designing a successor, the No. 1 ESS.

No. 1 ESS Processor

The No. 1 ESS was designed to serve large metropolitan telephone offices, ranging from several thousand to 65,000 lines [Keister, Ketchledge, and Vaughan, 1964]. As in most large switching systems, the processor represents only a small percentage of the total system cost. Therefore, performance and reliability were of primary importance in the design of the No. 1 Processor; cost was secondary. In order to meet the reliability standards established by electromechanical systems, all units essential to proper operation of the office are duplicated (see Figure 12-3). The multiunit duplex configuration was necessary to increase the MTTF of the processor

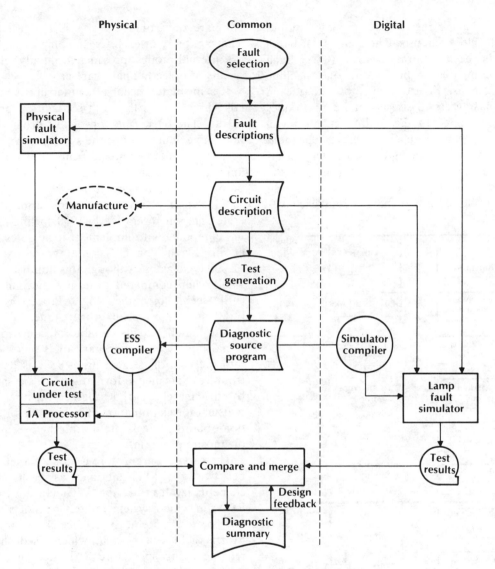

Figure 12–4. Complementary fault-simulation system.

because of the large number of components in each of the functional blocks.

Even with duplication, troubles must be found and corrected quickly to minimize exposure to system failure due to multiple troubles. All units are monitored continually so that troubles in the standby units are found just as quickly as those in the on-line units. This is accomplished by running the on-line and standby units in the synchronous and match mode of operation [Downing, Nowak, and Tuomenoksa, 1964]. Synchronization requires that clock timing signals be in close tolerance so that every operation in both halves is performed in step, and key outputs are compared for error detection. The synchronization of duplicated units is accomplished by having the on-line oscillator output drive both clock circuits. There are two match circuits in each central control (CC). Each matcher compares 24 bits within one machine cycle of 5.5 μs. Figure 12-5 shows that each matcher has access to six sets of internal nodes (24 bits per node). In the routine match mode, the points matched in each cycle are dependent upon the instruction being executed. The selected match points are those most pertinent to the data processing steps occurring during a given machine cycle. The two matchers in each CC

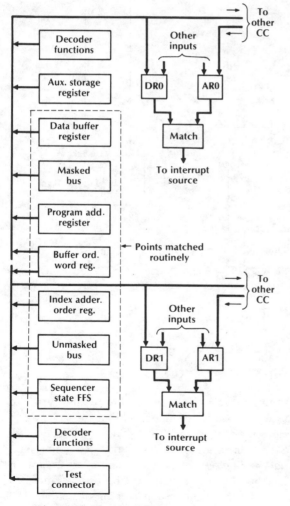

Figure 12–5. No. 1 CC match access.

compare the same sets of selected test points. The capability of each CC to compare a number of internal nodes provides a highly effective means of detecting hardware errors.

If a mismatch occurs, an interrupt is generated, which causes the fault-recognition program to run. The basic function of this program is to determine which half of the system is faulty. The suspected unit is removed from service and the appropriate diagnostic program is run to pinpoint the defective circuit pack.

The No. 1 ESS was designed during the discrete component era (early 1960s) using individual components to implement logic gates [Cagle et al., 1964]. The CC contains approximately 12,000 logic gates. Although this number appears small when compared to large-scale integration (LSI) technology, the No. 1 Processor was a physically large machine for its time.

The match circuits capable of comparing internal nodes are the primary tools incorporated into the CC for diagnosing as well as detecting troubles. Specified information can be sampled by the matchers and retained in the match registers for examination. This module of operation obtains critical data during the execution of diagnostic programs.

The early program store used permanent magnet twister (PMT) modules as basic storage elements [Ault et al., 1964]. They are a form of ROM in which system failures cannot alter the information content. Experience gained from the Morris field test system, which used the less reliable flying spot store, indicated that Hamming correction code was highly effective in providing continuous operation. At the time of development, it was felt that PMT modules might not be reliable enough. Consequently, the program store word included additional check bits for single-bit error correction (Hamming code). In addition, an overall parity check bit which covers both the data and their address is included in the word. The word size consists of 37 bits of information and seven check bits. When an error is corrected during normal operation, it is logged in an error counter. Also, detection of a single error in the address or a double error in the word will cause an automatic retry.

The call store is the temporary read and write memory for storing transient data associated with call processing. Ferrite sheet memory modules are the basic storage elements used in implementing the call store in the No. 1 ESS [Genke, Harding, and Staehler, 1964]. The call store used in most No. 1 offices is smaller than the program store. (At the time of design, the cost per bit of call store was considerably higher than that of program store.) Also, ferrite sheet memory modules were considered to be very reliable devices. Consequently, single-bit error detection rather than Hamming correction code was provided in the call store.

There are two parity check bits: one over both the address and data, and the other over the address only. Again, as in the program store, automatic retry is performed whenever an error is detected, and the event is logged in an error counter for diagnostic use.

Troubles are normally detected by fault-detection circuits, and error-free system operation is recovered by fault recognition programs [Downing, Nowak, and Tuomenoksa, 1964]. This requires the on-line processor to be capable of making a proper decision. If this is not possible, an emergency action timer will "time out" and activate special circuits to establish various combinations of subsystems into a system configuration. A special program which is used to determine whether or not the assembled processor is sane takes the processor through a series of tests arranged in a maze. Only one correct path through the maze exists. If the processor passes through successfully, the timer will be reset, and recovery is successful. If recovery is unsuccessful, the timer will time out again, and the rearrangement of subsystems will be tried one at a time (e.g., combination of CC, program store, and program store bus systems). For each selected combination, the special sanity program is

started and the sanity timer is activated. This procedure is repeated until a working configuration is found. The sanity program and sanity timer determine if the on-line CC is functioning properly. The active CC includes the program store and the program store bus.

Operational Results of No. 1 ESS

The No. 1 ESS has been in commercial operation since 1965. Over 1,000 systems are providing telephone service to more than 15 million subscribers. The performance of the No. 1 ESS has continually improved over a decade of continued effort to improve all phases of software and hardware.

Figure 12-6 shows the result of field data accumulated over many machine operating hours. This curve was derived from data in a paper [Fleckenstein, 1974] presented at the 1974 International Switching Symposium in Munich, Germany, and data supplied by W. C. Jones of Bell Laboratories.

When the No. 1 ESS was first cut into commercial service, many outages occurred because of software and hardware inadequacies that could only be weeded out with field experience. The inexperience of maintenance personnel also contributed heavily towards system outages. Most hardware and software bugs were corrected during the early years of operation. However, deficiencies still exist, and designs are continually upgraded in working systems. Continual improvements include better diagnostic access, more complete fault recognition and isolation programs, and more effective system recovery.

Improved diagnostic capability reduces repair time and human errors by decreasing the amount of human interaction required by the machine. Better maintenance procedures and more experienced craftpersonnel also contribute to improved system performance. The curve in Figure 12-6 shows that the outage rate improved as machine design and operating personnel matured.

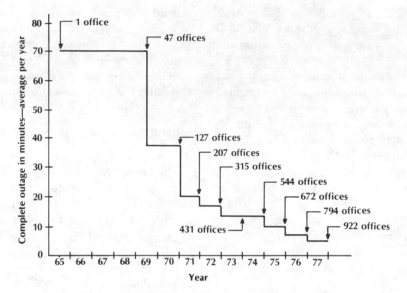

Figure 12–6. No. 1 ESS service performance.

No. 2 ESS Processor

The No. 2 ESS processor was developed during the mid-1960s [Spencer and Vigilante, 1969]. This system was designed for medium-sized offices ranging from 1,000 to 10,000 lines. The processor's design was derived from experience with the common stored program of a private branch exchange (PBX), the No. 101 ESS [Seley and Vigilante, 1964]. Since the capacity requirement of the No. 2 ESS was to be less than that of the No. 1 ESS, cost became one of the more important design considerations. (Reliability is equally important in all systems.) The No. 2 ESS contains much less hardware than the No. 1 ESS. Understandably, its component failure rate is also substantially less. Its CC contains approximately 5,000 gates (discrete components). To reduce cost and increase reliability, resistor-transistor logic (RTL) gates were chosen for the No. 2's processor since resistors are less expensive and more reliable than diodes [the No. 1 Processor used diode-transistor logic (DTL)].

Because the No. 2's CC, program store, and call store are smaller, they are grouped together

as a single switchable block in the single-unit duplex configuration shown in Figure 12-2. Calculations indicate that its MTTF is approximately the same as the No. 1 multiunit duplex structure, with each of the functional blocks and associated store buses grouped together as a switchable block. The use of only two subsystem configurations reduces considerably the amount of hardware needed to provide gating paths and control for each functional unit. Moreover, the recovery program is simplified, and the reliability of the system is improved.

The No. 2 Processor runs in the synchronous and match mode of operation [Beuscher et al., 1969]. The on-line oscillator output drives both clock circuits in order to keep the timing synchronized. The match operation is not as extensive as it is in the No. 1 ESS. For simplicity, there is only one matcher in the No. 2 ESS; it is located in the nonduplicated maintenance center (see Figure 12-7). The matcher always compares the call store input registers in the two CC's when call store operations are performed synchronously. A fault in almost any part of either CC quickly results in a call store input register mismatch. This occurs because almost all data manipulation performed in both the program control and the input-output (I/O) control involves processed data returning to the call store. The call store input is the central point whereby data eventually funnel through to the call store. By matching the call store inputs, an effective check of the system equipment is provided. Compared to the more complex matching of the No. 1 Processor, error detection in the No. 2 Processor may not be as instantaneous since only one crucial node in the processor is matched. Certain faults in the No. 2 Processor will go undetected until the errors propagate into the call store. This interval is probably no more than tens or hundreds of microseconds. During such a short interval, the fault would affect only a single call.

The No. 2 ESS matcher is not used as a diagnostic tool as is the matcher in the No. 1 Processor. Therefore, additional detection hardware is designed into the No. 2 Processor to help diagnose as well as detect faults.

When a mismatch occurs, the detection program is run in the on-line CC to determine if it contains the fault. This is done while the standby processor is disabled. If a solid fault in the on-

line processor is detected by the mismatch detection program, the control is automatically passed to the standby processor, causing it to become the on-line processor. The faulty processor is disabled and diagnostic tests are called in to pinpoint the defective circuit pack.

The program store also uses PMT modules as basic storage elements, with a word size of 22 bits, half the width of the No. 1's word size. Experience gained in the design and operation of the No. 101 ESS (PBX) showed that PMT stores were very reliable. The additional protection provided in the No. 1 Processor against memory faults by error correction was not considered to be as essential in the No. 2 Processor. This and the need to keep the cost down led to the choice of error detection *only* instead of the more sophisticated Hamming correction code.

Error detection works as follows: one of the 22 bits in a word is allocated as a parity check bit. The program store contains both program and translation data. Additional protection is provided by using odd parity for program words and even parity for translation data. This detects the possibility of accessing the translation data area of memory as instruction words. For example, a software error may cause the program to branch into the data section of the memory and execute the data words as instruction words. The parity check would detect this problem immediately. The program store includes checking circuits to detect multiple-word access. Under program control, the sense amplifier threshold voltage can be varied in two discrete amounts from its nominal value to obtain a measure of the operating margin. The use of parity check was the proper choice for the No. 2 ESS in view of the high reliability of these memory devices.

The No. 2 Processor call store uses the same ferrite sheet memory modules as the No. 1 Processor. However, the No. 2's data word is 16 bits wide instead of 24. Fault detection depends heavily upon the matching of the call store inputs when the duplex processors run in the synchronous mode. Within the call store circuit,

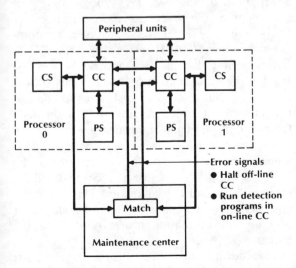

Figure 12–7. No. 2 CC match access.

the access circuitry is checked to see that access currents flow in the right direction at the correct time and that only two access switches are selected in any store operation. This ensures that only one word is accessed in the memory operation. Similarly, threshold voltages of the sense amplifiers may be varied under program control to evaluate the operating margins of the store. No parity check bit is provided in the call store.

Each processor contains a program timer which is designed to back up other detection methods. Normally, the on-line processor clears the timer in both processors at prescribed intervals if the basic call processing program cycles correctly. If, however, a hardware or software trouble condition exists (e.g., a program may go astray or a long program loop may prevent the timer from being cleared), the timer will time out and automatically produce a switch. The new on-line processor is automatically forced to run an initialization restart program which attempts to establish a working system. System recovery is simplified by using two possible system configurations rather than the multiunit duplex system.

SECOND GENERATION OF ESS PROCESSORS

The advent of silicon integrated circuits (IC's) in the mid-1960's provided the technological climate for dramatic miniaturization, improved performance, and cost-reduced hardware. "1A technology" refers to the standard set of (IC) devices, apparatus, and design tools that were used to design the No. 1A Processor and the No. 3A Processor [Becker et al., 1977]. The choice of technology and the scale of integration level was dictated by the technological advances made between 1968 and 1970. Small-scale integration (SSI), made possible by bipolar technology, was capable of high yield production. Because of the processor cycle time, high-speed logic gates with propagation delays from 5 to 10 ns were designed and developed concurrent with the No. 1A Processor.

No. 1A Processor

The No. 1A Processor, successor to the No. 1 Processor, was designed primarily for the control of large local and toll ESS with high processing capabilities (the No. 1A ESS and No. 4 ESS, respectively) [Budlong et al., 1977]. An important objective in developing the No. 1A ESS was to maintain commonality with the No. 1 ESS. High capacity was achieved by implementing the new No. 1A integrated technology and a newly designed system structure. These changes made possible an instruction execution rate that is four to eight times faster than the No. 1 Processor. Compatibility with the No. 1 ESS also allows the No. 1A Processor to be retrofitted into an in-service No. 1 ESS, replacing the No. 1 Processor when additional capacity is needed. The first 1A Processor was put into service in January 1976, as control for a No. 4 ESS in Chicago. Less than one year later, the first No. 1A ESS was put into commercial operation. By 1980, several hundred will be in service [Nowak, 1976].

The No. 1A Processor architecture is similar to its predecessor in that all of its subsystems have redundant units and are connected to the basic CC via redundant bus systems [Bowman et al., 1977]. One of the No. 1A Processor's major architectural differences is its program store [Ault et al., 1977]. It has a writable random-access memory (RAM) instead of PMT ROM. By combining disk memory and RAM, the system has the same amount of memory as a system with PMT, but at a lower cost. Backup copy of program and translation data is kept on disk. Other programs (e.g., diagnostics) are brought to RAM as needed; the same RAM spare is shared among different programs. More important is the system's ability to change the content of the store quickly and automatically. This simplifies considerably the administration and updating of program and translation information in working offices.

The additional disk (file store) subsystem adds flexibility to the No. 1A Processor [Ault et al.,

1977], but it also increases the complexity of system recovery. Figure 12-8 shows the multi-unit duplex 1A Processor. This configuration is similar to the No. 1 Processor arrangement (see Figure 12-3) with a duplicated file store included. The file store communicates with the program store or call store via the CC and the auxiliary unit bus. This allows direct memory access between the file store and the program store or the call store. The disk file and the auxiliary unit bus are grouped together as a switchable entity.

Error detection is achieved by the duplicated and matched synchronous mode of operation, as in the No. 1 Processor. Both CC's operate in step and perform identical operations. The matching

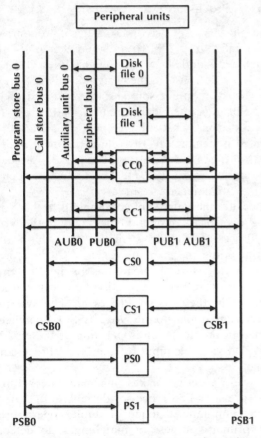

Figure 12–8. No. 1A processor configuration.

is done more extensively in the 1A to obtain as complete a check as possible. There are two match circuits in each processor. Each matcher has the ability to compare 24 internal bits to 24 bits in its mate once every machine cycle. (A machine cycle is 700 ns.) Any one of 16 different 24-bit internal nodes can be selected for comparison. The choice is determined by the type of instruction being executed. Rather than compare the same nodes in both CC's, the on-line and the standby CC's are arranged to match different sets of data. Four distinct internal groups are matched in the same machine cycle. This ensures the correct execution of any instruction.

The No. 1A Processor design is an improvement of the No. 1 Processor design. The No. 1A Processor incorporates much more checking hardware throughout various functional units in addition to matching hardware. Checking hardware speeds up fault detection and also aids the fault recovery process by providing indications that help isolate the faulty unit. The matching is used in various modes for maintenance purposes. This capability provides powerful diagnostic tools in isolating faults.

The program store and call store use the same hardware technology. The CC contains approximately 50,000 logic gates. While the initial design of the stores called for core memories, they have been replaced with semiconductor dynamic MOS memories. The word size is 26 bits; 24 data bits and 2 parity check bits. In the No. 1 Processor, the program store and the call store are fully duplicated. Because of their size, duplication requires a considerable amount of hardware, resulting in higher cost and increased component failures. To reduce the amount of hardware in the No. 1A Processor's store community, the memory is partitioned into blocks of 64K words, as shown in Figure 12-9. Two additional store blocks are provided as roving spares. If one of the program stores fails, a roving program store spare is substituted and a copy of the program in the file store is transferred to the program store replacement. This type of redun-

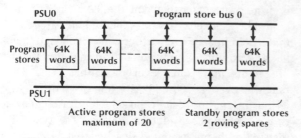

Figure 12–9. No. 1A program store structure.

dancy has been made possible by the ability to regenerate data stored in a failing unit. Since a program store can be reloaded from the file store in less than a second, a roving spare redundancy plan is sufficient to meet the reliability requirement. As a result, Hamming correction code was not adopted in the No. 1A program store. However, it is essential that an error be detected quickly. Two parity check bits are generated over a partially overlapped, interleaved set of data bits and address. This overlapping is arranged to cope with particular memory circuit failures which may affect more than one bit of a word.

The 1A call stores contain both translation data backed up on the file stores and call-related transient data which are difficult to regenerate. The roving spare concept is expanded for the call stores to include sufficient spares to provide full duplication of transient data. If a fault occurs in a store that contains translation data, one of the duplicated stores containing transient call data is preempted and loaded with the necessary translation data from the duplicated copy in the file store. A parity check is done in the same manner as in the program store, using two check bits.

The combination of writable program store and file store provides a very effective and flexible system architecture for administrating and implementing a wide variety of features which are difficult to obtain in the No. 1 ESS. However, this architecture also complicates the process of fault recognition and recovery. Reconfiguration into a working system under trouble conditions

is an extensive task, depending on the severity of the fault. (For example, it is possible for the processor to lose its sanity or ability to make proper decisions.) An autonomous hardware processor configuration (PC) circuit is provided in each CC to assist in assembling a working system. The PC circuit consists of various timers which ensure that the operational, fault recovery, and configuration programs are successfully executed. If these programs *are not* executed, the PC circuit controls the CC-to-program memory configuration, reloading program memory from file store when required, and isolating various subsystems from the CC until a working system is obtained.

No. 3A Processor

The No. 3A Processor was designed to control the small No. 3 ESS [Irland and Stagg, 1974], which can handle from 500 to 5,000 lines. One of the major concerns in the design of this ESS was the cost of its processor. The low cost and high speed of integrated logic circuitry made it possible to design a cost-effective processor that performed better than its discrete component predecessor, the No. 2 Processor. The No. 3A project was started in early 1971. The first system cut into commercial service in late 1975.

Because the number of components in the No. 3A Processor is considerably less than in the No. 1A Processor, all subsystems are fully duplicated, including the main store. The CC, the store bus, and the store are treated as a single switchable entity rather than individual switchable units as in the No. 1A Processor. The system structure is similar to the No. 2 ESS. Experience gained in the design and operation of the No. 2 provided valuable input for the No. 3 Processor design.

The 3A's design makes one major departure from previous ESS processor designs: it operates in the nonmatched mode of duplex operation. The primary purpose of matching is to detect errors. A mismatch, however, does not indicate *where* (which one of the processors) the fault has occurred. A diagnostic fault-location program must be run to localize the trouble so that the defective unit can be taken off-line. For this reason, the No. 3A Processor was designed to be self-checking, with detection circuitry incorporated as an integral part of the processor. Faults occurring during normal operation are discovered quickly by detecting hardware. This eliminates the need to run the standby system in the synchronous and match mode of operation, or the need to run the fault recognition program to identify the defective unit when a mismatch occurs.

The synchronous and match mode arrangement of the No. 1 Processor and the No. 2 ESS provides excellent detection and coverage of faults. However, there are many instances (e.g., periodic diagnostics, administration changes, recent change updates, etc.) when the system is not run in the normal match mode. Consequently, during these periods, the system is vulnerable to faults which may go undetected. The rapid advances in integrated circuit technology make possible the implementation of self-checking circuits in a cost-effective manner. This eliminates the need for the synchronous and match mode of operation. Self-checking design is covered in more detail in the next section.

Another new feature in ESS processor design is the application of microprogram technique in the No. 3A [Storey, 1976]. This technique provides a regular procedure of implementing the control logic. Standard error detection is made part of the hardware to achieve a high degree of checkability. Sequential logic, which is difficult to check, is easily implemented as a sequence of microprogram steps. Microprogramming offers many attractive features: it is simple, flexible, easy to maintain, and easy to expand.

The No. 3A Processor paralleled the design of the No. 1A Processor in its use of an electrically alterable (writable) memory. However, great strides in semiconductor memory technology after the No. 1A became operational permitted the use of semiconductor memory in the 3A rather than the core memory.

The 3A's call store and program store are consolidated into a single store system. This reduces cost by eliminating buses, drivers, registers, and controls. A single store system no longer allows concurrent access of call store and program store. However, this disadvantage is more than compensated for by the much faster semiconductor memory. Its access time is 1 μs (the earlier PMT stores had an access time of 6 μs).

Normal operation requires the on-line processor to run and process calls while the standby processor is in the halt state, with its memory updated for each write operation. For the read operation, only the on-line memory is read, *except* when a parity error occurs during a memory read. This results in a microprogram interrupt, which reads the word from the standby store in an attempt to bypass the error.

As discussed previously, the No. 2 Processor (first generation) is used in the No. 2 ESS for medium-size offices. It covers approximately 4,000 to 12,000 lines, with a call handling capability of 19,000 busy-hour calls. (The number of calls is related to the calling rate of lines during the busy hour.) The microprogram technique used in the No. 3A Processor design allows the No. 2 Processor's instruction set to be emulated. This enables programs written in the No. 2 assembly language to be directly portable to the No. 3A Processor. The ability to preserve the call processing programs permits the No. 2 ESS to be updated with the No. 3A Processor without having to undergo a complete, new program development.

The combination of the No. 3A Processor and the peripheral equipment of the No. 2 ESS is designated as the No. 2B ESS. It is capable of handling 38,000 busy-hour calls, twice the capability of the No. 2 ESS [Mandigo, 1976]. The No. 2B ESS can be expanded to cover about 20,000 lines. Furthermore, when an existing No. 2 ESS system in the field exceeds its real-time capacity, the No. 2 Processor can be taken out and replaced with the No. 3A Processor. The retrofit operation has been carried out successfully in working offices without disturbing telephone service.

MAINTENANCE DESIGN OF NO. 3A PROCESSOR

The 3A Processor is the most recent Bell System ESS processor. Self-checking hardware has been integrated into the design to detect faults during normal system operation. This simplified fault recognition technique is required to identify a subsystem unit when it becomes defective. Reconfiguration into a working system is immediate, without extensive diagnostic programs to

determine which subsystem unit contains the fault. The problem of synchronization, in a much shorter machine cycle (150 ns), is eliminated by not having to run both processors in step. The No. 3A Processor uses low-cost IC's to realize its highly reliable and flexible design.

General Systems Description

The general system block diagram of the No. 3A Processor is shown in Figure 12-10. The CC, the main store, and the cartridge tape unit are duplicated for reliability. These units are grouped as a single switchable entity rather than individual switchable units. The quantity of equipment within the switchable block is small enough to meet the reliability requirement; therefore, the

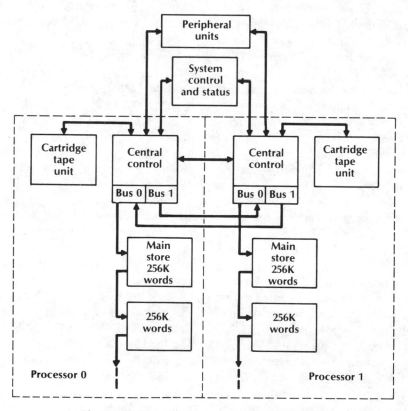

Figure 12–10.   No. 3A processor organization.

expense and complexity of providing communication paths and control for switchable units within the system are avoided. Each functional unit was designed to be as autonomous as possible, with a minimum number of output signal leads. This provides the flexibility necessary to expand the system and make changes easily.

As shown in Figure 12-10, the standard program store and call store are combined as a single storage unit to reduce cost. Although the processors are not run in the synchronous and match mode of operation, both stores (on-line and standby) are kept up to date. This is achieved by having the on-line processor write into both stores simultaneously when call store data are written or changed. Because of the volatile nature of a writable memory, low-cost bulk storage backup (cartridge tape) is required to reload the program and translation data when the latter are lost due to a store failure. The pump-up mechanism or store loader uses the microprogram control in conjunction with an (I/O) serial channel to transfer data between the cartridge tape unit and the main store. Other deferrable, infrequently used programs (i.e., diagnostics or growth programs) are stored on tape and paged in as needed.

The system control and status panel, a nonduplicated block, provides a common point for the display of overall system status and alarms. Included in this unit is the emergency action circuitry which allows the maintenance personnel to initialize the system or force and lock the system into a fixed configuration. Communication with the processor takes place via the I/O serial channel.

General Processor Description

Figure 12-11 shows a detailed block diagram of the CC. It is organized to process input data and handle call processing functions efficiently. The processor's design is based on the register type of architecture. Fast-access storage in the form of flip-flop registers provides short-term storage for information being used in current data processing operations. Sixteen general-purpose registers (GPRs) are provided as integral parts of the structure.

Microprogram control is the heart of the No. 3A Processor. It provides nearly all of the complex control and sequencing operations required for implementing the instruction set. Other complicated sequencing functions are also stored in the microprogram memory. Examples:

1. the bootstrap operation of reloading the program from the backup tape unit
2. the initializing sequence to restart the system under trouble conditions
3. the interrupt priority control and saving of essential registers
4. the emergency action timer and processor switching operation
5. the craft-to-machine functions

The regular structure of the microprogram memory makes error detection easier. The microprogram method of implementation also offers flexibility in changing control functions.

The data manipulation instructions are designed specifically for implementing the call processing programs. These instructions are concerned with logical and bit manipulation rather than with arithmetical operations. However, a binary ADD is included in the instruction repertoire for adding two binary numbers and for indexing. This allows other arithmetical operations to be implemented conveniently by the software combination of addition and logical operations, or by a microprogram sequence if higher speed is essential. The data manipulation logic contains rotation, Boolean function of two variables, first zero detection, and fast binary ADD.

The remaining functional blocks in Figure 12-11 deal with external interfaces. The 20 main I/O channels, each with 20 subchannels, allow the processor to control and access up to 400 peripheral units by means of 21-bit (16 data, 2 parity, and 3 start code bits) serial 6.67-MHz messages. The system is expandable in modules

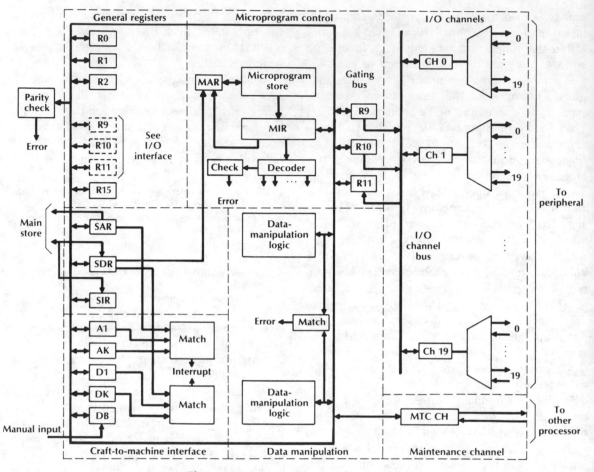

Figure 12–11. No. 3A central control.

of one main channel (20 subchannels). The I/O structure allows up to 20 subchannels (one from each main channel) to be active simultaneously. In addition, the craft-to-machine interface, with displays and manual inputs, is integrated into the processor. This interface contains many of the manual functions which will assist in hardware and software debugging. The control logic associated with this part of the processor is incorporated as part of the microprogram control. Lastly, the maintenance channel enables the on-line processor to control and diagnose the standby processor. The use of a serial channel reduces the number of leads interconnecting the two processors and causes them to be "loosely coupled." This facilitates the split mode or stand-alone configuration for factory test or system test.

Detection Techniques

Control Circuitry

The major feature of the No. 3A Processor's control logic is that it is microprogrammed. Microprogramming provides a more regular approach than the conventional technique to the

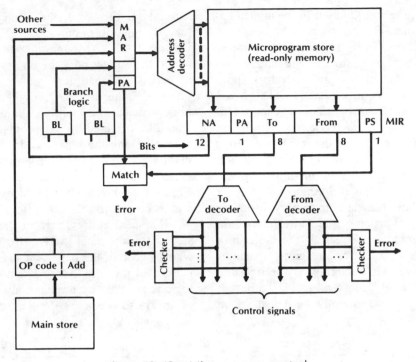

Figure 12–12. Microprogram control.

design of control logic. It also permits checking techniques to be applied more readily. The simplified microprogrammed structure of the system is shown in Figure 12-12. Each microprogram store word contains the address of the next instruction and a FROM and TO control field which specifies the source and destination for a data transfer operation. The store word may also specify some other types of operation. The microprogram address register (MAR) receives its contents from either the OPCODE of the main machine instruction to be executed (this forms the initial address of the microprogram which performs the instruction) or the last microprogram store word. One instruction from the main store results in the execution of a sequence of microinstructions. System operation consists of continually reading instructions from the main store and executing the specified sequences of microinstructions.

In designing the hardware check for the microprogram control, it is essential to recognize the types of failures which are most probable. Matching the checking techniques with the type of faults that actually occur yields the best results with the least amount of hardware. The microprogram control is constructed from integrated circuits: LSI for the memory and SSI for the associated control logic. Because of the method of isolating components and because of the physical proximity of devices on an integrated circuit chip, multiple faults within a chip have been analyzed and found to be of the type which would tend to affect the bits in the unidirectional manner: it affects adjacent bits, rather than nonadjacent bits in the word [Cook et al, 1973]. Unidirectional error refers to a fault which causes a data bit(s) to assume a wrong value of one type: 0 or 1, but not both simultaneously. (For example, 01100 to 01111, not to 01010.)

The checking technique used in the implementation of the microprogram control takes advantage of the error characteristics mentioned above. The microprogram store contains two types of data: control and address information. The control fields are immediately decoded and checked to provide control signals. A more efficient nonsystematic check code, such as the m-out-of-$2m$ code, would give the maximum detectability at the least possible cost in hardware. This code can detect all multiple-unidirectional errors. However, for the address field, it is desirable to maintain the data in binary form for addressing and to provide immediate binary data to several sources. Consequently, the choice of a systematic check code for the address field is essential to give this flexibility. By recognizing that the multiple-bit faults tend to affect adjacent bits rather than randomly disperse them

throughout the word, the binary field is interleaved with the m-out-of-$2m$ code as shown in Figure 12-13. Any multiple-adjacent-bit fault would then affect both the binary and the m-out-of-$2m$ code. Consequently, a single parity check bit is adequate to detect single-bit faults in the binary field, and multiple adjacent bit faults would be detected by the m-out-of-$2m$ check.

In checking the binary address field, parity is maintained on the address in the MAR and checked by 1) storing the correct parity (see Figure 12-12) in the word addressed in memory, and 2) comparing the two after the word is read out. The next address field in the microprogram store output register (MIR) also has a parity bit which becomes the parity bit of the MAR when it is gated into the MAR. The condition branch logic is checked by duplication. A match is not necessary to check the duplicated logic since its

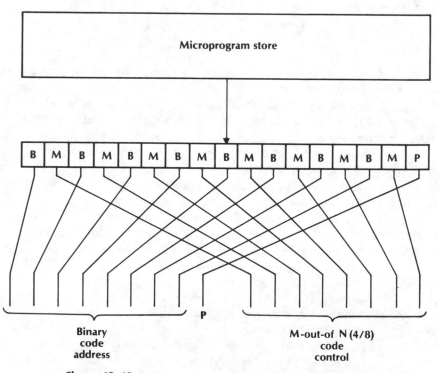

Figure 12–13. Microprogram store coding techniques.

output must change both the low-order bit and the parity bit of the MAR. One of the branch logic circuits feeds the low-order bit, and the other feeds the parity bit P_A (see Figure 12-12) so that branch logic failure is detected because of the resultant bad parity of the MAR.

The checking techniques (such as m-out-of-$2m$, interleaves parity, and duplication) are integrated into the No. 3A's design to detect the failures that may occur in the microprogram control. These types of checks are provided to detect the multiple-unidirectional type of faults that are possible with the integrated technology.

4-out-of-8 Decoder and Check

The TO and FROM control fields are each eight bits wide and encoded as a 4-out-of-8 code. There are 70 valid combinations in an 8-bit field; each combination has four 1's and four 0's. The fields, which are decoded to drive the control points of the processor, are checked by a self-checking checker which detects faults in the decoder and the input codes [Anderson, 1971].

Because of the large number of output leads in a fully decoded 4-out-of-8 code to 70 outputs, the decoder circuitry is divided into two groups. A control function is represented by two outputs, one from each group. Figure 12-14 shows the decoding arrangement whereby each group is sorted into five logic subgroups with 4, 3, 2, 1, and 0 inputs and designated as 4(1), 3(1), 2(1), 1(1), and 0(1), respectively. The numbers of gates belonging to the respective subgroups are 1, 4, 6, 4, and 1, as shown in the figure. Similarly, the second four bits in the 4-out-of-8 code are decoded and divided into the same subgrouping. The A subgroupings are paired with the B subgroups to obtain the 70 possible 4-out-of-8 code combinations. The $4_a(1)$ group pairs with the $0_b(1)$ group to give one combination; the $3_a(1)$ group pairs with the $1_b(1)$ group to give 16 combinations; and so on, as indicated in Figure 12-14. The 0(1) subgroup is redundant, and, therefore, it is not used.

The total number of decoder outputs from each group is 15 instead of 16. Within a decoder group, more than one output may be active simultaneously. For example, the 1111 input code can cause all gates to be active. This is entirely satisfactory since only the gate in the corresponding subgroup of the second decoder (in this case the 0(1) subgroup) would be active; gates in the other subgroups would *not* be active. Hence, one and only one pair of decoder outputs is active. This condition uniquely defines one of the possible 70 combinations in the 4-out-of-8 codes.

The decoder design provides the proper outputs which facilitate the implementation of the self-checking 4-out-of-8 checker. The self-checking circuit is realized by subdividing the checker into two separate independent subcircuits. Each subcircuit generates a single output whose values are arranged to be complementary for normal 4-out-of-8 input codes. For any errors in the input code, decoder, or check logic, the two outputs are alike (00 or 11).

A totally self-checking checker has the advantage of not requiring periodic tests in order to ensure that any faults occurring in the functional circuits will be detected immediately. The check scheme involves pairing the subgroups, corresponding to exactly four 1's, as follows: $0_a(1) - 4_b(1)$, $1_a(1) - 3_b(1)$, $2_a(1) - 2_b(1)$, $3_a(1) - 1_b(1)$, $4_a(1) - 0_b(1)$. An output is generated for each pairing. The alternating pairs are divided into separate groups, f and g, as indicated in Figure 12-15. Since only one pair will be active for a correct 4-out-of-8 input, the response from f and g will be 10 or 01 for the normal operating condition. If the input is other than a 4-out-of-8 code, the f and g outputs will be 11 or 00. For example, if the input is 11100011, the $3_a(1)$, $2_a(1)$, $1_a(1)$, and $0_a(1)$ from the A group and the $2_b(1)$, $1_b(1)$, and $0_b(1)$ from the B group will be active. This means two pairs of subgroups will be active: $3_a(1) - 1_b(1)$ in the f group and $2_a(1) - 2_b(1)$ in the g group. The alternating pairs are chosen to be in separate groups to ensure that

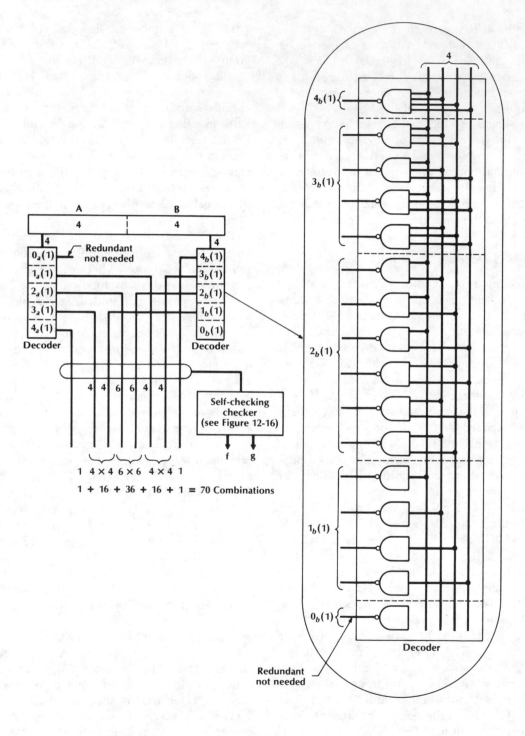

Figure 12–14.   4-out-of-8 decoding arrangement.

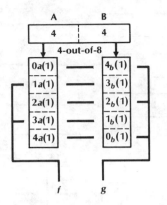

Figure 12–15. General diagram of 4-out-of-8 checker.

when there is more than one pair active, the resultant fg output is 11, representing an input with more than four 1's. If the input contains less than four 1's, none of the four pairs will be active. For example, if the input is 01110000, the $3_a(1)$, $2_a(1)$, $1_a(1)$, and $0_a(1)$ of the A group and the $0_b(1)$ of the B group will be active. These are outputs from each group, but none of them belong to a pair, hence, the fg output is 00, corresponding to an input combination with less than four 1's. The logic implementation of the 4-out-of-8 checker is shown in Figure 12-16.

The 0 (1) subgroup represents the condition of 1 or any number of 1's in the 4-bit input. This means the 0(1) gate is always active and redundant. The pairing of $4_a(1) - 0_b(1)$ does not need to include the $0_b(1)$ subgroup at all. Its gate and output is ignored in the implementation.

The FROM and TO decoder outputs fan out to various functional units for controlling logical operations or data transfers within the CC. Those that go to the data transfer logic control the gating of data from one register to another via the data bus. The circuitry of this functional block is partitioned on a 2-bit slice; all logic gates associated with the two bits are contained on a single circuit board. Since the decoder outputs fan out to 2 bits, any malfunction of the control within a circuit board would affect only those 2 bits of data. When the word is used at a later time, the error will be detected by the parity

check on the data. Consequently, it is sufficient to check the control signals prior to entering the data transfer block. This is also true for the data manipulation block since the circuitry is duplicated.

A number of microoperations consist of setting or clearing individual flip-flops or enabling dedicated paths where the use of a single TO or FROM field crosspoint would be inefficient. A miscellaneous decoder is provided; it takes inputs from both the TO and FROM fields. In this way, a 10×10 matrix (100 crosspoints) is generated by assigning only 10 of the 70 combinations from each of the TO and FROM fields. Most of these types of crosspoints control duplicated circuitry; hence, the decoding gate itself is duplicated. A fault in this area will result in an error in the data path and will be detected by a parity check.

Data Registers

There are two types of internal data registers: general purpose and special purpose. The latter type is dedicated to specific functions. Examples are the interrupt status register (IS) and the error register (ER). The general-purpose registers are

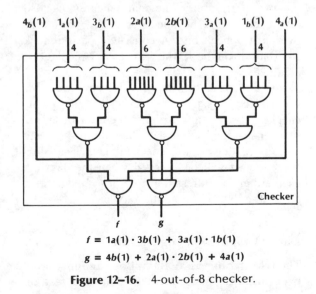

$$f = 1a(1) \cdot 3b(1) + 3a(1) \cdot 1b(1)$$
$$g = 4b(1) + 2a(1) \cdot 2b(1) + 4a(1)$$

Figure 12–16. 4-out-of-8 checker.

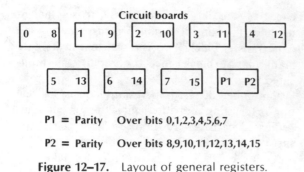

P1 = Parity   Over bits 0,1,2,3,4,5,6,7

P2 = Parity   Over bits 8,9,10,11,12,13,14,15

Figure 12–17. Layout of general registers.

involved with the handling of data associated directly with the instructions. The checking of the data transfer logic is done by partitioning two bits of the register on a single circuit board and then carrying two parity bits. This partitioning and the definition of the parity bits is illustrated in Figure 12-17, with the first circuit board containing two bits of every general-purpose register. Partitioning the registers in this way ensures that any fault on a circuit board will not affect more than two bits of any register. This also ensures that the fault will be detected by the two parity bits. If all of one register's bits were grouped on a single board, a catastrophic failure of that board could affect all of the bits, and the failure would not necessarily be detectable by the two parity bits. The main memory is also organized as a 2-bit slice per circuit pack plus two parity check bits. A consistent parity check is done throughout the entire system; I/O is included.

For any data transfer, the information from the source register is checked by the parity checker at a common point: the data bus. In a register-to-register transfer, the data in the destination register are not checked. This is satisfactory since it will be checked when the data are used either to address the store or to be operated on by the data manipulation logic.

Data Manipulation Logic (DML)

The DML contains rotation, Boolean function of two variables, first zero detection, and fast bi-

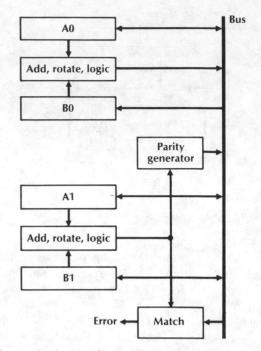

Figure 12–18. Duplicated data manipulation logic.

nary ADD. The DML is duplicated and matched to allow full checking in this area. Other coding techniques, such as parity prediction and residue coding, are available for arithmetical functions. However, for all logical functions of two variables, duplication is the simplest method of checking. Duplication eliminates the need for checking if the data arrived at the modification logic correctly.

As shown in Figure 12-18, a match circuit detects faults, and a parity generation circuit supplies parity on the DML output to interface with the rest of the system.

I/O Channels

The 20 I/O channels are 6.67-MHz serial channels. Each channel has 20 subchannels. Figure 12-19 shows the data flow from the processor to the I/O buffers. Three of the general-purpose registers, R9 through R11, are used; R9 loads the control buffer (IOS), R10 loads the data buffer (IOD), and R11 receives data from the I/O

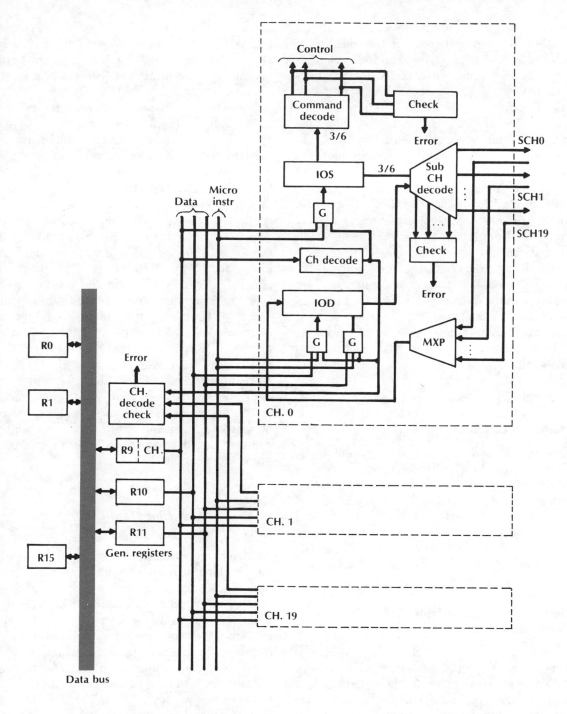

Figure 12–19. I/O channel structure.

channel. All command and selection signals are encoded in 3-out-of-6 codes and decoded to 1-out-of-20 codes. The channel address stored in R9 is used to direct the data and microinstructions to one of the 20 specified main channels. The decoding of the enable address is done individually in each main channel, with the output returning to a common point for checking. This is done to ensure that only the right channel is enabled. The command decoding and subchannel selector within each channel are similarly checked for proper decoding of 3-out-of-6 codes. The data messsage containing two parity check bits from R10 is transmitted by the channel and checked by the peripheral unit. In addition, prior to transmission of the message, the data are brought back by the microprogram sequence to the data manipultion logic and compared with the content of R10 to ensure that the data have been loaded properly. Messages received from the peripheral unit also have two parity bits, which are checked when they are placed on the bus.

Maintenance Channel (MCH)

The MCH is used for interprocessor communication, as well as for the diagnosis of one processor by the other processor. The MCH's structure is similar to the I/O channel and, therefore, the checking technique is the same. The data field uses the standard 2-bit parity in order to remain consistent with the rest of the processor. The command field is encoded in 3-out-of-6 codes.

Method of Checking Error Detection Circuits

Any circuitry used for checking purposes is incorporated as part of the system. Such circuitry should be as fail-safe as possible so that a failure in the system will cause a failure alarm. It has been shown that such a check circuit can be realized if the output is in the form of a 1-out-of-2 code, with 01 or 10 for the normal operation and 00 or 11 for the error condition [Carter, Duke, and Jessep, 1971]. Ultimately, these two outputs must be monitored to generate a single error output.

The final gate is not completely fail-safe. A failure in this gate will prevent the circuitry from giving any error indication, and faults normally detected will be ignored. A good design allows only a small portion of the detection hardware to be non-fail-safe. The checking of the non-fail-safe portion of the check logic is essential to guarantee reliable operation of these circuits. This is accomplished by a combination of hardware and software. This approach has been proved to be very effective in checking the check circuits, with both hardware and software costs kept to a minimum. The hardware provides the means of simulating test conditions or circuit faults which are extremely difficult or awkward to set up normally in the system. A flip-flop register, called the maintenance state (MS) register, is used for this purpose. Each bit represents an error or test condition. By appropriately setting up the MS register and applying a well designed test sequence, the detection circuitry can be checked on a periodic basis to ensure its proper application.

Method of Detecting Hard-Core Circuit Faults

Although the system is designed to be nearly self-checking, it contains a small hard-core portion which must be operating properly prior to running a program sequence. The circuitry usually includes the sequencing logic of the microprogram control and the addressing and fetching of instructions from the main store. For example, if the control to advance the program counter (PC) cannot be activated, the PC remains in one particular state. The same address is used at each reading, resulting in the same outputs from the store. The program, therefore, is stuck at one location, executing the same instruction repetitively, with no means of advancing through the program sequence to produce any useful work. The amount of hard-core circuitry is strongly dependent upon the system design and is difficult to eliminate. In a duplicated and matched system, when both processors are running in a synchronous mode with important outputs being matched continuously, any error in the hard-core circuitry will be detected instantaneously.

In the nearly self-checking design, the system does not run in a synchronous and match mode. This is done to reduce the complexity of software, thereby increasing reliability. A hardware timer is used to detect faults in the hard-core circuitry and also as a backup to protect the system from control by an insane CC due to either hardware or software troubles. The use of a timer depends upon the program meeting an obstacle or a series of tests arranged in a maze. If the program is successfully completed through the maze, the timer is reset by the maintenance control program. On the other hand, if the program strays off course, the timer will time out and the emergency action circuit will select a new configuration. The sanity test is repeated to verify a fault-free system.

The telephone processing program is cyclic in nature. It returns to the starting point at each scan upon completion of a series of tasks required by the call processing [Andrews et al., 1969]. Although the scan time may vary from scan to scan, depending on the amount of work required of the program, the maximum time can be easily determined.

The use of a hardware timer is closely tied with the system program. It is arranged so that a reset is generated for the timer only if the program proceeds through the scan correctly within the prescribed period. If the program deviates from the normal course, no reset will occur. In this case, the timer automatically times out, stops processing, and switches to the standby system.

There are two timers, one located in each processor; both are active at all times. Duplication is necessary in order to guarantee that the system be capable of recovery. It is possible that a single fault can disable one processor and its timer, thus necessitating the standby to perform the function. The timers are periodically reset by the on-line program. If they are not reset, the on-line timers will time out first. If the on-line timer does not work, the off-line timer will perform the task at a later time.

Recovery Techniques

Fault detection is the first and most important step in realizing a highly reliable system. Two other functions of equal importance are: 1) rapid recovery of the system to process calls, and 2) the protection of calls in progress in face of either hardware or software difficulties. This means the mechanism for switching controls must be highly reliable. Proper steps have been taken to give a smooth transition in the transfer of controls. In the design of the system, the combination of hardware and software is so intertwined as to provide the utmost protection against an insane CC from taking control of the system. A rapid and successful recovery is achieved by a combination of hardware and software so that continuity is maintained [Kennedy and Quinn, 1972].

Automatic Recovery

When an error is recognized in the on-line processor, several things may happen depending on the type of error. Error signals are buffered in the error register (ER) for diagnostic purposes. In addition, the error signals are sorted out and divided into three groups, with each group causing a different set of system actions. The least severe of the three are the errors associated with the I/O or MCH. These errors will cause an interrupt in which the processor has complete control in determining the exact cause of the trouble. If the error is a transient fault, it will be recorded and compiled for later analysis. If the error is determined to be a hardware fault within the switchable block of the processor, the interrupt program will initiate a reconfiguration to the standby machine by means of the MCH. This would be an orderly switch to the other processor; there would be no detrimental effect on the system.

The second type of error involves faults occurring in the standby portion of the system. These faults directly influence the on-line operation. For example, the system is organized to operate both stores asynchronously. Whenever data are written into the on-line store, they are written into the off-line store simultaneously. The processor waits for a store completion signal from both stores before proceeding with the next operation. If a response signal originates only from the on-line store, there is a $32\text{-}\mu s$ pause, and then a special timer times out and generates an error signal, indicating trouble in the off-line store. Under this condition, the processor is interrupted at the microinstruction level and appropriate action is taken to continue call processing with the standby store isolated.

The third type of error involves hardware faults within the on-line processor. An extension of the previous discussion will serve as a good example: If the store completion signal is received from the standby store and *not* from the on-line store, this error signal causes the system to switch to the standby configuration. In this situation, the system momentarily "hangs up." A restart in the standby machine would initialize the processor and continue with call processing, affecting, perhaps, only one call in the transient state.

Numerous check circuits are designed and integrated into the system. As soon as an error is detected, immediate action takes place to reconfigure the system into an error-free working system. In addition, duplicated hardware timers are provided to back up undetected hardware faults or software bugs which cause the program

to go astray. The recovery process involves two steps:

Step 1:   Reconfiguration
Step 2:   Restart or initialization—to enable the new processor configuration a smooth transition into full control of the system.

When a switch to the standby processor occurs, it must be initialized to a known state in order to start smoothly. This operation is divided into three stages, or levels. The first stage involves the elementary control of the microprogram store, ensuring that it can start and execute a sequence of microinstructions properly at a predetermined store location. This is done by hardware before the first microcycle. The operation consists of:

1. Setting the MAR to a predetermined address
2. Setting clock circuitry to a well-defined state
3. Setting the block hardware check (BHC) flip-flop to inhibit detection hardware from possibly generating an error signal, thus initiating a switch operation
4. Resetting various control flip-flops (e.g., STOP, FREEZE) which would directly affect the running of the microprogram control.

The second stage of initialization is done by microprogram. The primary function of the microprogram initialization is to set the various control bits or registers which have direct influence on running the main program sequence. For example:

1. Set the block interrupt (BIN) flip-flop to inhibit the external interrupt from interfering with the initializing program.
2. Reset the update (UPD) flip-flop to inhibit the standby store from being updated.
3. Set the isolate (ISO) flip-flop to prevent the off-line store operation from interfering with the on-line operation.
4. Reset the hardware timer to prevent it from timing out.

In addition, the microprogram decides whether or not the main store contains valid program data. If it does not, the alternative would be to switch the processor and try the other configuration since the program data are duplicated, with a copy in each store. The objective is to try to use each of the two copies before resorting to the use of a tape unit as a final backup. The sanity of the machine depends very heavily on the memory content. As a result, an arrangement (shown in Figure 12-20) has been implemented to allow a systematic way of recovering from system errors. The scheme uses two initialization sanity check bits (ISC1 and ISC2) as markers. They are part of the system status (SS) register. Normally, these two bits are in the 00 state. During the first time through the microprogram level of initialization (ISC1 = 0), this ISC1 bit is set to the 1 condition as a marker for subsequent initialization. The system then proceeds to the main program initialization. If the store contains correct program data, and if the system is fully recovered from the initialization, this marker bit will be reset. However, if the program data have been badly mutilated, the main program may wander aimlessly, executing bad programs.

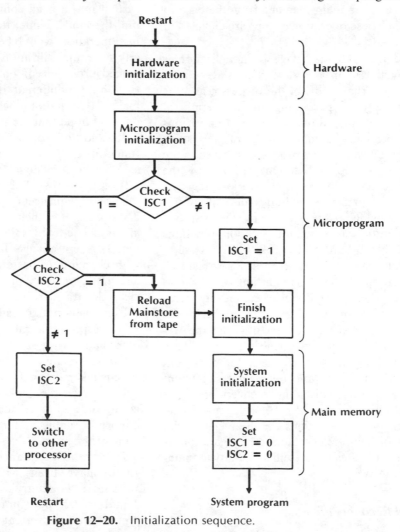

Figure 12–20.   Initialization sequence.

When a second initialization occurs within the same CC and the first marker bit is set to the 1 state, the initialization at the microprogram level will set the second marker bit to 1. It then directs the control to be passed on to the other processor with the expectation that its main memory and the rest of the hardware are in good working condition. Otherwise, it will switch back to the original processor and try to initialize for the third time. Now, with both marker bits set to 11, the microprogram initialization sequence will recognize this condition and take the drastic step of reloading the main memory from the backup tape unit. These operational steps are depicted in Figure 12-20.

The third and final stage of initialization is done by the main program. This stage covers both the internal status of the processor and the main store data pertaining to the peripheral equipment status, transient data, and various data associated with maintenance of the system. The internal state of the processor is saved in the main memory for subsequent analysis by the diagnostic program. Next, the various registers are set to a prescribed initial state. All control flip-flops, which were set up by the first two levels of initialization to inhibit various functions (such as block hardware check, block interrupt, and inhibit store update, etc.) are now restored to normal operation. This handling of the memory data, which have direct effect on the operation of the system, depends on the ability of the main program to run successfully and the frequency of initialization. Audit programs are called in to validate and check for consistent data in the memory and peripheral equipment status. The initialization and recovery programs clear selective portions of memory data and take increasingly severe actions on the memory, depending on the rate of system reconfiguration. A high rate indicates the system's inability to maintain its sanity.

Manual Recovery

Although the system is designed to recover automatically under trouble conditions, it is conceiv-

able for the system to be unable to reconfigure into a working mode. This can be caused by software bugs, hardware faults, or a combination of both. The processor may be switching continuously, spending all of its available time repeating initialization work. In other words, the control unit has gone insane and is incapable of making any rational decisions. In this case, the ultimate control of the system must be left to the judgment of qualified maintenance personnel. Hardware has been provided to give maintenance personnel the capability of forcing the system into a fixed configuration and locking it into the mode. Under this condition, the switching operation would be made inoperative and any system initialization would be directed to the locked processor. If both processors are defective, but to different degrees, manual control makes it possible to lock out the most defective one and hope that the system will limp along.

In addition to the manual force and lock functions of the emergency action panel, provision has been made to manually generate initialization and cause different categories of data in the nonwrite protect area of the store be cleaned. These categories include: 1) transient data which are associated with calls in a stable talking state, and 2) recent change data which are associated with changing of customer telephone lines. The automatic recovery program is only allowed to clear the transient data which affect telephone calls in the nontalking state. If an incomplete call is interrupted, the caller must try again. On the other hand, if the stable data are cleared, calls in the talking state are interrupted and the talking state is taken down. Hence, maintenance personnel are given the final control over recovery by taking the additional action of clearing the more important stable and recent change data portions of the store.

Due to the importance of these controls, safeguards have been designed into the manual switches and circuitry to protect against an accidental switch operation. This is necessary to prevent any inadvertent actions which may have severe effects on the system. Emergency controls are grouped together with system alarms and status indicators at the common system control panel, which is readily available to maintenance personnel. Additional redundancy has been designed into the system so that if both processors are down a positive indication must be given to maintenance personnel before the appropriate action can be taken. This is done by another hardware timer in the common system control panel. While the on-line program is progressing through the programs correctly, it must periodically reset this timer. If the on-line processor does not reset the timer, it will time out and set the alarm circuit, immediately bringing the situation to the attention of the craftperson.

Diagnostic Hardware

Fault detection determines whether or not a circuit is operating correctly, whereas fault diagnosis localizes the failure to a few replaceable circuit packs. Hardware has been integrated into the design of this system to allow a systematic approach for identifying failures via software. The most commonly used procedure in fault diagnosis [Bashkow, Friets, and Karson, 1963; Agnew, Forbes, and Stieglitz, 1967] is based upon the bootstrap technique. The hard-core portion of the machine can apply test sequences to itself. With a duplicated processor, the fault-free machine is used to check or diagnose the hard-core portion of the defective machine. Once the hard-core portion has been checked and found to be fault-free, it is used to start the diagnostic test of another portion of the processor. Therefore, subunits are tested before being used to check other subunits. This procedure continues until the fault is pinpointed.

In order to facilitate this diagnostic procedure, several important designs have been incorporated into the system. One is the MCH and its associated circuitry. Its primary function is the diagnosis of one processor by the other. The MCH is an autonomous portion of the processor which, under control of the other processor, can provide information about the state of the machine and exercise the machine at its most basic level by direct access to the microprogram control. Another hardware feature is the maintenance instruction, which provides complete access to the system at the most elementary level of hardware.

Maintenance Channel Facilities

The MCH interconnects and provides the main source of communication between the two processors. As shown in Figure 12-21, the MCH is a high-speed (6.67 MHz), serial, full duplex channel. This method of communication reduces the number of leads at the expense of additional hardware, making the interface easier to maintain. Since there are so few leads, the processors can be said to be "loosely interconnected"; they are isolated from each other in terms of hardware faults. That is, a fault in one processor will not affect the operation of the other processor.

The basic structure of the MCH shown in Figure 12-21 consists of a transmit-receive register (MCHTR), a command register (MCHC), and a buffer register (MCHB). The format of a MCH message is 20 bits of data, 2 parity check bits, and 8 bits of command. Although the processor is essentially a 16-bit machine, there are several 20-bit registers for store addressing. Consequently, the MCH message is dictated by the widest data word. For 16-bit data fields, the high four bits are not used. The commands are coded in 4-out-of-8 codes for ease in decoding and checking. The decoded outputs are used to control the primitive functions of the processor so that elementary operations can be observed by the on-line machine. For example, under MCH control, the clock can be stopped and stepped along one clock phase at a time. In between steps, the state of each phase is transmitted back to the other processor for analysis. In this way, the very hard-core is exercised to permit a systematic check of the clock circuitry.

Another basic operation involves transmitting microinstructions over the main channel and executing them one at a time. This is done by gating the received data in the MCHTR directly into the MIR: The command part of the message provides control for gating and executing the

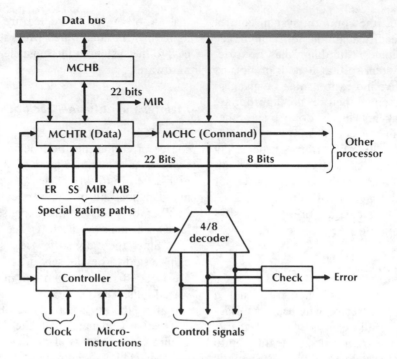

Figure 12–21. Maintenance channel.

microinstruction. This operation allows the on-line processor to step the off-line machine along one microinstruction at a time, thereby gaining access to the entire machine at the most elementary level for fault diagnosis.

The MCHB is used to temporarily store the data transmitted over the MCH. This data source can be used for a variety of operations. For example, in a READ-STORE operation, assume a 20-bit address has been received and buffered in the MCHB at the receiving end. When executed, the maintenance messages which follow (containing microinstructions) will gate the content of MCHB to the store address register (SAR) and read store at that address. In order to bring the store output back into the on-line processor, two more maintenance messages must be sent. The first message gates the store output to the MCHB, and the second message gates the content of the MCHB to the MCHTR and is then transmitted back to the on-line processor. Similarly, the data stored in the MCHB can also be used to write into the store. These operations

allow the on-line processor to check the off-line store control circuitry. The MCHB, in addition to buffering the incoming data which are to be directed to any internal register within the processor, may also be used to buffer data which are to be returned to the transmitting processor (on-line processor).

The MCH registers are connected to the common data bus to permit data transfer to any of the internal registers. Also, there are dedicated paths, as shown in Figure 12-21, to allow special registers (such as the error register, system status register, etc.) to be fetched directly without the aid of microinstructions. Some of these registers, particularly in the error register and the system status register, contain information which may be helpful to the diagnostic program, and, hence, must be saved prior to any diagnostic procedure.

Finally, the controller block, as shown in Figure 12-21, provides all of the necessary timing and sequencing operations that the MCH needs to transmit and receive messages. The off-line processor must be able to derive timing signals directly from the incoming serial data stream since the processor's clock may be stopped. Therefore, the MCH circuitry, which is closely integrated into the processor, is really an extension of the other processor since the two are connected by means of an "umbilical" cord.

Microdiagnostic Techniques

After the circuits associated with the microprogram control and the main store operation have been checked and verified to be operational, the off-line processor can execute instructions and initiate diagnostic procedures by itself. The microinstruction, being the most elementary operation, provides the best possible access to pinpoint faults within the machine. Therefore, if the diagnosis is performed at the microprogram level, isolating faults to a few replaceable circuit packs becomes a more efficient and effective process. The ideal situation would be to store the diagnostic routines on low-cost units and then page them into a writable microprogram store as needed [Bartow and McGuire, 1970]. However, in this system, the microprogram store is entirely ROM. This is necessary for reasons of cost and reliability. Therefore, it is not practical to store the diagnostic in the ROM because of the increase in the size and cost of the microprogram store.

In order to achieve equivalent microdiagnostic capability, a special microinterrupt (MI) instruction has been incorporated into the design to allow the machine to be exercised at the microprogram level. This is done by allowing the microsequences to be stored in the main memory. The MI instruction simply puts the processor in the interpret mode. While in this mode, the processor stops using the outputs from the microprogram memory and fetches microinstructions from successive main memory words. Any number of microinstructions may now be executed from main memory until the microinstruction, which turns off the intrepret mode, is given.

There are several advantages to the microinterpret technique. First, it will allow maintenance routines to be stored in low-cost tape units and paged into main memory as needed at a considerable cost reduction. Since the microprogram memory is a ROM, the microprograms stored in main memory can be changed much more easily than if they were stored in microprogram memory. Secondly, the interpret mode will allow microprogram sequences to be checked out before they are encoded in ROM. Lastly, and most importantly, the maintenance programmer has complete access to every control signal that exists within the machine.

Microprogram sequences in the interpret mode do run slower than the native mode since the main memory is slower than the microprogram memory. This is not an important disadvantage since diagnostic programs are normally run in the standby machine. However, the microinstructions are executed at the same speed.

Repair

When the fault has been diagnosed and located to within a few circuit packs, maintenance personnel must replace the packs one at a time until the defective one has been found. In pack replacement, the power must be turned off to avoid the harmful effects of breaking current on the connector. Since there are a number of leads from the processor to various functional units, power must be turned off "gracefully" so as not to cause any disturbance to the working system. Consequently, the operation is arranged in a sequence to ensure that no harmful transient signals are generated in the process. Similarly, the same protection is given in turning power on.

During the repair process, the working system is manually locked into a selected configuration. This is done to avoid any error conditions which may cause the system to switch control to the machine under repair. Since it is under repair, the machine is without power. Therefore, if an error occurs in the working system, it would be better to restart and attempt to run again with the same configuration. The hardware required to prevent any interaction from the machine under repair is minimal, but it must be integrated into the design at the beginning.

Hardware Implementation

Maintenance has been made an integral part of the 3A CC design. It uses the standard No. 1A ESS logic family with its associated packaging technology [Becker et al., 1977]. Up to 52 silicon integrated circuit chips (SIC's), each containing from 4 to 10 logic gates, can be packed on a 3.25 by 4.00-in. 1A ceramic substrate. The substrate is mounted on a 3.67 by 7-in. circuit board with an 82-pin connector for backplane interconnections. In the 3A CC, the 53 1A logic circuit packs average about 44 SIC's, resulting in an average of 308 gates per circuit pack, or a total of 16,482 gates. Figure 12-22 shows a detailed functional diagram of the 3A CC and the percentage of logic gates used in each functional unit.

Another insight into how the gates are used in the 3A is shown in Figure 12-23. The figure shows the relationship between working gates, maintenance access gates, and self-checking logic. The working gates are the portion which contribute to the data processing functions, while the maintenance access gates provide the

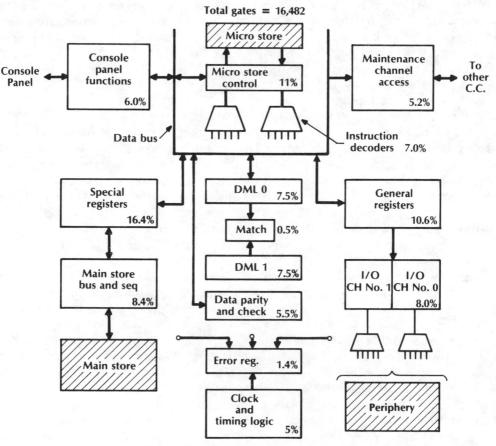

Figure 12–22.   No. 3A CC gate count.

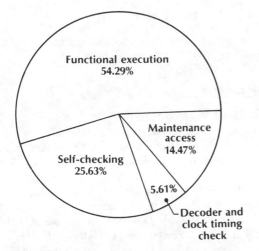

Figure 12–23. Logic gates in No. 3A CC. Total gates = 16,482.

necessary access to make the CC maintainable (i.e., maintenance channel and control panel). The self-checking gates are required to implement the parity bits, the check circuits, and the duplicate circuits that make the CC self-checking. As indicated, about 30 percent of the logic is used for checking. The design covers a high degree of component failures. It is estimated about 90 to 95 percent of the faults would be detected by hardware error detection logic. Certain portions of the checkers, timers, and interrupt logic are not checked. These circuits are periodically exercised under program control to ensure that they are fault-free.

SUMMARY

In order to achieve the reliability requirements, all ESS subsystem units are duplicated. When a hardware failure occurs in any of the subunits, the processor is reconfigured into a working system around the defective unit. The partitioning of subsystem units into switching blocks varies with the size of the ESS processors. For the medium- or small-size processors such as the No. 2 or the No. 3, the central control, the main memory, the bulk memory, and the store bus are grouped as a single switchable entity. A failure in one of the subunits is considered a failure in the switchable block. Since the number of components within a switchable block is sufficiently small, this type of single-unit duplex configuration meets the reliability requirement. For larger processors such as the No. 1 or the No. 1A, the central control, the program store, the call store, the store buses, and the bulk file store are treated individually as switchable blocks. This multi-unit duplex configuration allows a considerable number of combinations in which a working system can be assembled. The system is down only when two simultaneous failures occur, one in the subunit and the other in the duplicated subunit. A greater fault tolerance is possible with this configuration. This type of configuration is necessary for the large processor because each subunit contains a larger number of components.

The first generation of ESS processors, which includes the No. 1 and the No. 2, have provided commercial service since 1965 and 1969, respectively. The No. 1 ESS serves large telephone offices (metropolitan); the No. 2 is used in medium-size offices (suburban). Their reliability requirements are the same. Both processors depend on integrated maintenance software, with hardware that must 1) quickly detect a system failure condition, 2) isolate and configure a working system around the faulty subunit, 3) diagnose the faulty unit, and 4) assist the maintenance personnel in repairing the unit. The primary detection technique is the synchronous and match mode of operation of both central controls. Matching is done more extensively in the No. 1 than in the No. 2 since cost is one of major considerations in the design of the No. 2 Processor. In addition to matching, coding techniques, diagnostic access, and other check logic have been incorporated into the basic design of these processors to realize the reliability objectives.

The widespread acceptance of the No. 1 ESS and the No. 2 ESS has created the need for a second generation of ESS processors: the No. 1A and the No. 3A. They offer greater capability and are also more cost-effective. Both processors use the same integrated technology. The 1A Processor extends its performance range by a factor of four to eight times over the No. 1 Processor by using faster logic and faster memory. The 1A design takes advantage of the experience gained in the design and operation of the No. 1 ESS. The No. 1A Processor provides considerably more hardware for error detection and more extensive matching of a large number of internal nodes within the central control. The design of the No. 3A Processor has benefited by the experience gained from the No. 2 ESS. A major departure in the design of the 3A Processor from the design of other ESS processors is the nonsynchronous and the nonmatch mode of operation. The No. 3A Processor uses self-checking as primary means of error detection. Another departure is in the design of the No. 3A Processor's control section; it is microprogrammed. The No. 3A Processor's flexibility permits emulation of the No. 2 Processor quite easily.

ACKNOWLEDGMENT

The author would like to acknowledge the kind assistance of Pat Loprete, Jr.

REFERENCES

Agnew, Forbes, and Stieglitz [1967]; Anderson [1971]; Andrews et al. [1969]; Ault et al. [1964, 1977]; Bartow and McGuire [1970]; Bashkow, Friets, and Karson [1963]; Becker et al. [1977]; Beuscher et al. [1969]; Bowman et al. [1977]; Browne et al. [1969]; Budlong et al. [1977]; Cagle et al. [1964]; Carter, Duke, and Jessep [1971]; Chang, Smith, and Walford [1974]; Cook et al. [1973]; Downing, Nowak, and Tuomenoksa [1964]; Fleckenstein [1974]; Genke, Harding, and Staehler [1964]; Goetz [1974]; Harr, Taylor, and Ulrich [1969]; Irland and Stagg [1974]; Keister, Ketchledge, and Lovell [1960]; Keister, Ketchledge, and Vaughan [1964]; Kennedy and Quinn [1972]; Mandigo [1976]; Nowak [1976]; Seley and Vigilante [1964]; Smith [1972]; Spencer and Vigilante [1969]; Staehler [1977]; Staehler and Watters [1976]; Storey [1976]; Tsiang and Ulrich [1962].

Pluribus—An Operational Fault-Tolerant Multiprocessor

David Katsuki   Eric S. Elsam   William F. Mann   Eric S. Roberts

John G. Robinson   F. Stanley Skowronski   Eric W. Wolf

Abstract

The authors describe the Pluribus multiprocessor system, outline several techniques used to achieve fault-tolerance, describe their field experience to date, and mention some potential applications. The Pluribus system places the major responsibility for recovery from failures on the software. Failing hardware modules are removed from the system, spare modules are substituted where available, and appropriate initialization is performed. In applications where the goal is maximum availability rather than totally fault-free operation, this approach represents a considerable savings in complexity and cost over traditional implementations. The software-based reliability approach has been extended to provide error-handling and recovery mechanisms for the system software structures as well. A number of Pluribus systems have been built and are currently in operation. Experience with these sytems has given us confidence in their performance and maintainability, and leads us to suggest other applications that might benefit from this approach.

INTRODUCTION

The multiprocessor discussed in this paper had its beginnings in 1972 when the need for a second-generation interface message processor (IMP) [Heart et al., 1970] for the ARPA network (ARPANET) [Roberts and Wessler, 1970; Wolf, 1973b; Heart, 1975] became apparent. At that time, the IMP's Bolt Beranek and Newman (BBN) already installed at more than thirty-five

ARPANET sites, were Honeywell 316 and 516 minicomputers. The network was growing rapidly in several dimensions: number of nodes, hosts, and terminals; volume of traffic; and geographic coverage (including plans, now realized, for satellite extensions to Europe and Hawaii). A goal was established to design a modular machine which, at its lower end, would be smaller and less expensive than the 316's and 516's while being expandable in capacity to provide ten times the bandwidth of, and capable of servicing five times as many input-output (I/O) devices as, the 516 [Heart et al., 1973]. Related goals included greater memory addressing capability and increased reliability.

We decided on a multiprocessor approach because of its promising potential for modularity, for cost per performance advantages, for reliability, and because the IMP algorithm was clearly suitable for parallel processing by independent processors.

The IMP's communicate with host computers and with asynchronous terminals (IMP's with terminals attached are called TIP's [Ornstein et al., 1972].) Hosts use the network of IMP's and lines to communicate data messages of up to about 8,000 bits; the IMP's divide these messages into packets up to about 1,000 bits long. The functions performed by the IMP are those of a communications processor; they include storing and forwarding packets, generating headers, routing, retransmission, error checking, packet and message acknowledgment, message assembly and sequencing, flow control, line error detection, host and line status monitoring, and related housekeeping functions. The IMP's also send status and performance data to a network control center (NCC) which monitors and controls network operations [McKenzie et al., 1972; Ornstein and Walden, 1975]. The ARPANET IMP's operate 24 hours a day, often in unattended locations.

In applications of this sort, reliability requirements differ from those commonly found in other real-time systems. The IMP network forms only a part of a larger system; even a perfectly operating network is not sufficient to guarantee perfect overall system performance. Failures in the host, or in the interface between the host and IMP, may still introduce errors. What this means is that some sort of host-process to host-process error control is required for critical applications; the best that the IMP network can provide is a good environment for host-level error recovery processes. These processes need a network which rarely makes errors and which, when such errors do occur, can effectively process host-to-host retransmissions. In other words, occasional dropped messages and brief outages are acceptable; outages of more than a few minutes are undesirable even if scheduled in advance.

Once we realized that what was needed was not so much reliability as the ability to recover gracefully from failures, we began to see ways to provide a much more robust network by coding this type of fault-tolerance into our operating system and application algorithms, and by including special mechanisms for bypassing and localizing faults in our already-modular hardware designs. The machine that emerged [Heart et al., 1973, 1976; Bressler, Kraley, and Michel, 1975; Ornstein and Walden, 1975; Ornstein et al., 1975] we call the Pluribus (Figure 13-1 shows a typical Pluribus installation). It provides simple checking procedures such as parity, amputation features which allow failing equipment to be isolated and, optionally, redundant components. The software uses these features to detect, report, and isolate hardware failures. Since the symptoms of many subtle software failures are similar to those of intermittent hardware errors, fault-tolerant procedures which adequately recover from one can also recover from the other.

There is a spectrum of fault-tolerant approaches which are appropriate in various applications [Avizienis, 1975, 1976]; our approach opts for a relatively inexpensive system which can quickly reinitialize itself, omitting troublesome components. This approach is especially suitable for applications in which brief outages

Figure 13–1. The Pluribus front-end processor at Bolt Beranek and Newman's Research Computer Center.

can be tolerated and where overall correctness can be ensured by other techniques.

PLURIBUS SYSTEM ARCHITECTURE

The Pluribus may be characterized as a symmetric, tightly coupled multiprocessor, designed to be flexible and highly modular. Modules are physically isolated to protect against common failures, and a form of distributed switch is employed for intermodule communications. In this section, we discuss these characteristics and describe the hardware architecture of the Pluribus.

Major Design Decisions

In order to make the basic operation of the Pluribus clearer, it is useful to examine some of the major design decisions that have directed its development, and to consider those decisions in the context of other options for multiprocessor system design. We have identified three areas which we believe are key aspects of the Pluribus

approach to multiprocessing, each of which is considered in greater detail below.

Processor Symmetry

One dimension of multiprocessing involves the degree of inter-processor symmetry within the system [Enslow, 1974, p. 83]. In this dimension, one extreme might be a typical general purpose computer system, including a central processor, a front-end processor, and perhaps one or more channel processors. Such an asymmetric system is relatively inflexible in power since increasing its central processing capacity requires the introduction of a more powerful central processor. Building redundancy into an asymmetric system can be expensive, since replication of all critical resources involves duplicating virtually the whole machine.

At the other extreme are systems like the Pluribus in which all processors are identical. In such systems, the advantages of redundancy and flexibility are much easier to achieve since they include only one type of processing unit. Even without explicit redundancy, a symmetric system can provide graceful degradation of throughput when a processing element fails. Pluribus systems which are sized for fully redundant operation include just one extra processing module; thus the degradation which results from failure of any processing module consists only of a loss of excess throughput capacity.

Processor Coupling

Another multiprocessing dimension is the level at which processors cooperate to accomplish overall system requirements. At one extreme the processors might run totally separate programs under the direction of a supervisor program, communicating only at arm's length. Such processors may be described as "loosely coupled" [Enslow, 1974, p. 15]. At the other extreme, which is characterized by array processors such as ILLIAC IV [Barnes et al., 1968], the processors run in lockstep, with a single program operating simultaneously on a number of data streams. The Pluribus lies between these extremes. Its processors are tightly coupled in the sense that all processors can access all system resources and perform all parts of the operation program; they operate independently except for necessary software interlocks on specific I/O devices and data structures.

Flexibility

Although one of the goals in the creation of the Pluribus was to develop a machine with high throughput, this goal was complemented by the need for a smaller, cheaper machine with relatively low throughput. Similarly, although the Pluribus was conceived as having at least two of every resource to permit recovery after failures, it was also clear that not all applications required or could afford a fully redundant system. Thus it was desirable for the architecture to be flexible in at least two ways: The size-flexibility goal was to smooth large incremental steps in the cost-performance curve by utilizing a highly modular design, which could provide processing capacity well beyond our anticipated needs. Flexibility in the area of fault-tolerance and fault-recovery was a related goal, since the need for fault-tolerance involves primarily economic considerations and we wanted to allow our customers to select fault-tolerance features independent of their throughput requirements. Also implied in each of these goals was the requirement for easy expansion to meet changing requirements.

System Overview

A central requirement in any multiprocessor is that processing elements be able to communicate both among themselves and with shared resources such as memories and I/O equipment. Ease of communication is always desirable and is vital in tightly coupled systems, since any

delays or unwieldiness would immediately impact system operation and reduce programmability. These considerations, together with a natural desire for symmetry and simplicity, led us to adopt a unified addressing structure in which all common memory and I/O devices share the same address space. The Pluribus development was strongly influenced by previous unified-bus architectures in which processing, memory, and I/O units share not only a common address structure but also a single, time-multiplexed bus (the DEC PDP-11 is perhaps the most familiar example of this). Although multiprocessors based on the unified bus are both extensible and conceptually simple structures, they are vulnerable to single failures anywhere along the bus. In addition, the maximum throughput of such multiprocessors is limited both by the design bandwidth of the bus as well as by contention for common resources. To avoid these problems we used a unified bus to create the functional modules which make up the system, but not to form the main connection structure. We defined three basic functional modules which share a common address space but have separate intermodule communications paths: processor *buses*, memory *buses*, and I/O *buses*. A simplified system diagram is shown in Figure 13-2.

(In the following sections we will often use the term *bus* to mean a logical and physical module, as in "processor *bus*," rather than just an interconnection system. All such usages will be italicized for clarity.)

The system for interconnecting these modules had several major requirements. It had to be easily extensible to support as many as eight memory or I/O *buses* (common *buses*) and eight or more processor *buses*. It had to permit the operating software to remove malfunctioning modules from the system and incorporate newly acquired or repaired modules. In addition, it had to impose minimal cost penalties for smaller systems, while scaling up smoothly to produce large systems. Finally, it had to have no common point of failure which could lead to total system failure.

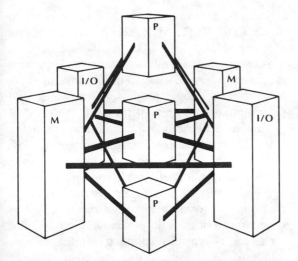

Figure 13–2. A simplified view of the functional modules in a typical Pluribus system showing their interconnectivity. No physical relationships are implied.

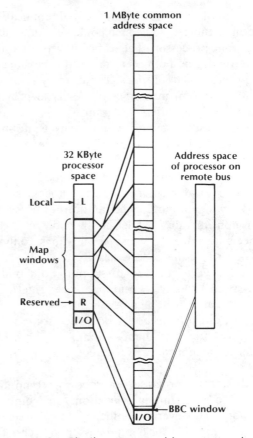

Figure 13–3. Pluribus system address space, showing the mapping of processor "local" address space into the system space. "Backwards bus-coupling" path from one processor bus through an I/O bus to another processor bus is shown on the right.

The approach we finally adopted is similar in function to a central crossbar switch although it differs greatly in implementation. The crossbar switch approach allows an extremely high-bandwidth interconnection scheme and has been used to advantage in several multiprocessors [Wulf and Bell, 1972]. However, the usual implementation techniques are vulnerable to single-point failures. To avoid these problems, we distributed the components of the switch among the various system modules in such a way that no single failure points remain. Switch elements are called bus couplers and consist of two circuit boards connected by a cable.

The bus couplers function by recognizing a range of addresses on processor or I/O *buses*, and initiating an access request on the appropriate common *bus* as a result. Since memory and I/O *buses* share a 20-bit address space, bus couplers must map 16-bit processor addresses into 20-bit system addresses under program control (see Figure 13-3). In addition to handling inter-*bus* communications, bus couplers perform several other functions which will be described later.

Modularity

Since the basic Pluribus was modular at several levels, an unusual degree of flexibility was available when we set out to define standard structures within the system. The three basic system modules described above have clear logical functions within the system, but their actual implementation depended on various tradeoffs between cost, throughput, and available physical components.

It was decided early that the goals of flexibility and symmetry could be achieved by segmenting the operational tasks into strips of code (task distribution routines, task-oriented application routines, timers, etc.) which could be run by any available processor. The concept was that the code should be both reentrant and accessible to all processors at all times. The primary function of the common memory modules is to provide space for data buffers, program work areas, and inter-processor communication areas. Code storage is divided into two parts: lightly used code is stored on common memory *buses* and is shared between processors; heavily used code is replicated in local memory on each processor *bus*. This strategy minimizes contention for access to common memory while holding down costs, especially since, in most applications, only a small part of the code is heavily used. The I/O modules were intended to support both polled low-speed I/O devices and high-speed interfaces capable of direct memory transfers. Couplers provide direct paths both from processor *buses* to I/O *buses* for control and polling, and from I/O *buses* to memory *buses* for direct memory transfers.

All normal processor-to-processor communication occurs through locations in common memory. However, to initialize the system, it must be possible for one processor to access the local memory and control registers of a processor on a different *bus*. To allow this, the bus couplers provide a limited reverse path through any common I/O *bus*.

In the following sections, we describe the physical implementation of these system modules and detail several support functions required by the architecture.

Physical System Structure

As mentioned in previous papers [Heart et al., 1973; Ornstein and Walden, 1975], we chose the Lockheed SUE minicomputer as the point of departure for our system. It is a 16-bit machine, generally similar to the DEC PDP-11, which incorporates a unified address structure and an asynchronous, time-multiplexed bus. It also permits the attachment of a flexible combination of

processors, memory, and I/O units. In contrast to the PDP-11, the SUE has its bus arbitration logic physically separated from the processor. This feature permits a bus to have one or several processors, or none at all. The Pluribus uses the bus, arbitration logic, processors, memories, and several minor I/O units of the SUE.

The basic Pluribus building block is the *bus* module. This module contains a modified SUE bus and card cage for up to twenty-four cards, together with completely self-contained cooling fans and power supply. Two *bus* modules can be connected to form an extended *bus*. A Pluribus system rack contains up to five *bus* modules, and each rack is typically supplied with a separate source of AC power. Systems sized to be fully redundant allow any *bus* module or any rack to be powered down for maintenance without affecting system availability (see Figure 13-4).

Bus Structure *(See Figure 13-5)*

A processor *bus* contains one or two processors and their associated local memory, a bus arbiter, and one bus coupler per logical path. Our current applications require 8 to 12K words of local memory for each processor. The flexibility of the processor *bus* allows us to easily vary this parameter as memory prices or the requirements of the application change.

The common memory *bus* contains an arbiter, bus coupler cards for all the connected paths, and enough memory modules to support the application. Up to 512K words of common memory can be supported in a system, although that amount of memory would probably not be concentrated on one memory *bus*. Typical Pluribus systems have from 32K to 80K words of memory on each *bus*, depending on the application.

In addition to the bus arbiter and bus coupler cards, an I/O *bus* also contains cards for each of the various types of I/O interfaces that are required, including interfaces for modems, terminals, host computers, etc., as well as interfaces for standard peripherals. The I/O *bus* also houses

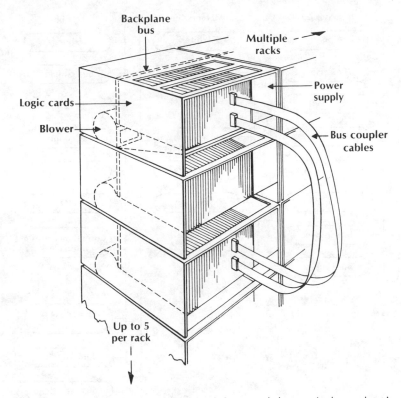

Figure 13–4. Physical organization of bus modules. Modules are independently supplied with power and cooling.

a number of special units, including 1) a real-time clock (RTC) which is used by the system for timing processes and communications links, 2) a special hardware task disbursing unit known as the pseudo-interrupt device (PID) discussed further below, and 3) a reload card which monitors up to eight communication lines, watching for (and processing) specially formatted reload messages from the outside world.

Inter-Bus Connection System

Since all processors in our system must be able to perform any system task, *buses* are connected so that all processors can access all shared memory and control the operation and sense the status of any I/O unit (see Figures 13-2 and 13-6).

To connect processors and common memory, one card of a bus coupler is installed on a common memory *bus*, and the other on a processor *bus*. Similar connections are made from every processor *bus* to every common I/O *bus*. Coupler cards are connected by cables which may be up to 30 ft. long, although most systems require a maximum of 10 ft.

The memory or I/O end of a bus coupler contains address-recognition circuitry and may be strapped to recognize and pass on to the memories or I/O devices any desired address range. When a processor makes a reference to common memory or I/O *buses*, the bus coupler cards on the processor *bus* all map the 16-bit address on the processor *bus* into a 20-bit system address and pass it to bus couplers at the other ends of the connecting cables. If the address is within the recognition range of a memory or I/O

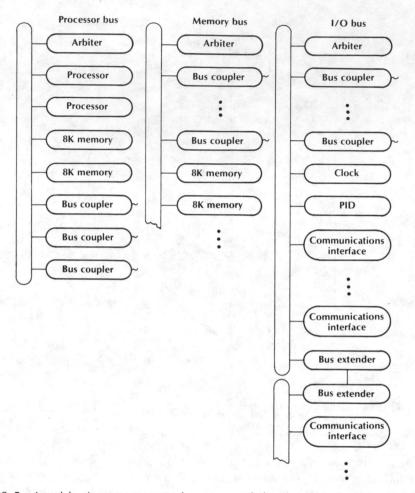

Figure 13–5. Local busing structure and contents of the three kinds of bus modules.

end bus coupler, it will request a service cycle on its *bus*. Data from the selected memory cell or device register are then passed back along the coupler path to the processor. This feature differentiates the system address space so that requests for memory or I/O *bus* access only cause service cycles on appropriate *buses*, thereby avoiding unnecessary contention.

Given a bus coupler connecting each processor *bus* to each common memory *bus*, all processors can access all common memory; I/O devices which do direct memory transfers must also access the common memories. These I/O devices are attached to as many I/O *buses* as are required to physically accommodate the number of devices and allow redundancy if necessary. Couplers connect each I/O *bus* to each memory *bus*. This coupler path is much like the processor-to-memory coupler path except that no address mapping needs to be done. I/O devices must respond to processor requests for action or information and in this respect the I/O devices act like memories. Bus couplers are also used to connect each processor *bus* to each I/O *bus*. Here

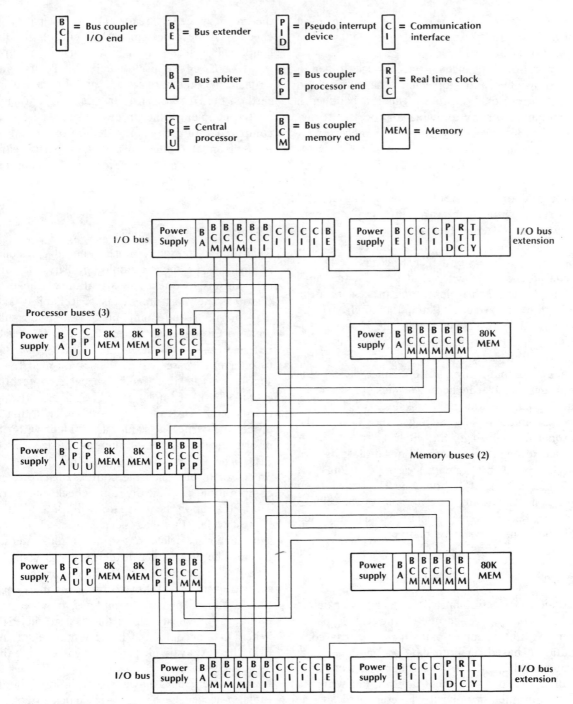

Figure 13–6.   Logical organization of a typical Pluribus system, showing inter-connections of the distributed switch (bus coupler) structure.

also, a mapping must be done between the 16-bit processor address space and the 20-bit system space (see Figure 13-3).

Processor *buses* need to access each other in order to start and stop each other and reload local memories. We provide this low bandwidth interconnection by allowing a processor to access another processor *bus* via its processor-to-I/O bus coupler. The coupler provides a small (4-word) mapping window from I/O space to each processor's space. A processor accesses another processor on a different *bus* by setting up and referencing this "backwards bus-coupling" window in the system I/O space.

The coupler paths that connect processor *buses* into memory and I/O *buses* have program-settable enabling switches at their far (memory and I/O) ends, thus permitting processors to be cut into and out of ("amputated" from) the system. The reverse paths in the processor-to-I/O couplers also have enabling switches; normally the forward paths are turned on and the backwards paths are shut off. Since these paths represent a hazard whereby a "sick" processor or device could damage the system, we have arranged that only by storing a password at the proper address can a switch be changed. A processor can neither enable nor disable its own access paths but one processor, deciding that another is sick and should be eliminated from the system, can amputate the *bus* of the offending processor. Reinstatement of an amputated *bus* happens in a similar manner.

Parity

To aid in detecting faulty bus couplers or defective memory, we compute and check parity across all bus coupler paths using a parity computation based on both data and address [U.S. Patent Office, 1977]. The scheme detects both "all zeros" and "all ones" failures. For writes to common memory, parity is computed at the processor or I/O end of the bus coupler and stored in the memory cell with the data. When the memory cell is read, the stored parity is checked at the processor or I/O end of the bus coupler. For access from processors to units on the I/O *buses* we use "feedback" parity; for writes to I/O the parity is computed by a special card on the I/O *bus*. The parity is then sent back up the coupler to the processor *bus* where it is compared with parity computed on that *bus*. For reads from I/O the special I/O parity card computes parity and compares it with recomputed parity on the processor *bus*.

Pseudo-Interrupt Devices

Real-time systems or, more generally, systems requiring fast response, employ priority interrupt mechanisms to direct the attention of the processor to the most urgent tasks. Reliability and load sharing requirements make it desirable that any processor be able to service any I/O device, but also raise such questions as which processor to interrupt for servicing. We have opted for a simple yet flexible method: each "interrupt event" (DMA completion, RTC tick, software events, etc.), instead of actually interrupting a processor, writes a value associated with its priority to a hardware queuing device called PID. The software is designed to allow each processor to put aside the context of its present computation periodically and check the PID. The PID, upon being read, will produce the highest value that has been stored in it and simultaneously delete that value from its internal queue. The processor can then use that value as an index to a table of tasks to be performed. The software uses the PID in a similar manner: each time a "strip" of code completes, it writes the number of the next strip in that task to the PID. When that becomes the highest number in the PID, the next available processor will execute the associated strip.

Our system does have two traditional interrupts, however. One is a 60-Hz clock interrupt. Each bus has its own 60-Hz clock, but conceptually this is an interrupt going to all processors;

its main function is to timeout locked data structures. The other classical interrupt is the power-fail/power-restore interrupt; each processor handles a power-fail interrupt from its own *bus* in the traditional way. Furthermore, bus couplers connected to processor *buses* will pass on any power-fail interrupt detected at their memory or I/O ends. A restoration of power causes first a *bus* master-reset and then a processor interrupt. We have adapted this interrupt mechanism to serve also as a *bus* activity watchdog timer. If any *bus* fails to show access activity for one second, a hardware timer fires, causing an artificial power-restore reset and interrupt. This provides recovery from some illegal hardware and software states.

Redundancy

To assure that a particular machine has enough redundant resources to allow survival in the face of component failures, we include at least one extra *bus* of each type so that a failure of any one resource, or the *bus* holding that resource, will not result in system failure. This approach also permits the system to survive many combinations of multiple failures. Thus if a system requires four processors to function at minimum acceptable throughput, six processors would be provided for reliability since the failure of any processor *bus* would disable two processors. Similarly, if a machine required at least 60K of memory to function, we would provide two *buses* each containing 60K of memory, or three *buses* each containing 30K of memory. It is important to note that redundant resources configured into a given machine are not idly standing by since they are used by the running machine to produce performance greater than the acceptable minimum.

I/O ports pose a special problem, since the devices and lines to which they are connected are frequently not doubled. For reliability, I/O interfaces can be doubled on separate I/O *buses*, but both interfaces must usually drive a single cable

leaving the machine. We allow this by constructing all of our I/O port drivers with circuits that present a high impedance while unpowered. In addition, each I/O interface has a watchdog timer which, if not held off by repeated processor accesses, will disconnect the driver circuits within a second. Thus the likelihood that malfunctioning or unpowered I/O interfaces will interfere with the signals put on the external cable by the backup I/O interface is kept to a minimum.

THE PLURIBUS OPERATING SYSTEM

Unlike most conventional systems, the principal responsibility for maintaining reliability in the Pluribus is placed on the system software rather than in the hardware structure. The Pluribus hardware was designed to provide an appropriate vehicle for software reliability mechanisms. Besides normal error checking and reporting in the hardware itself, programmed tests using known data patterns are run at intervals. When hardware errors are detected, system software exploits the redundancy of the hardware by forming a new logical system configuration which excludes the failing resource, using redundant counterparts in its place.

Pluribus systems also check the validity of their software structures. Redundant information is intentionally introduced into the data structures at various points and checked by processes operating upon those structures. An example of this technique applied to buffer structures is described in the next section. In addition, periodic background processes are used to recompute certain variables which are maintained by the operational system. If the recomputation uncovers a discrepancy, the variables are fixed directly or a more drastic recovery procedure is initiated.

In many cases, a failure is not detected at the exact time of occurrence but later when the software encounters some failure-induced discrepancy. By this time, the effects of the failure may be more widespread and the actual cause of the failure may be difficult to determine. In such cases, the system is not able to perform instantaneous recovery and seeks instead to restore normal operation as quickly as possible.

The remainder of this section discusses the organization of the Pluribus operating system and some of the techniques used for achieving coordination of multiple processors. These techniques are further explored below where two examples of Pluribus fault-tolerant software strategies are presented. One of these examines the Pluribus IMP buffer system in detail, and the other covers strategies for understanding failures when they occur and effecting necessary repairs.

General Responsibility of the Operating System

The software reliability mechanisms for a Pluribus system are coordinated by a small operating system (called STAGE) which performs the management of the system configuration and the recovery functions. The overall goal of the operating system is to maintain a reliable, current map of the available hardware and software resources. The map must include accurate information not only about the hardware structure of the machine, but also about variables and data structures associated with the processes that use the hardware. Moreover, the operating system must function correctly even after parts of the system hardware have ceased to be operational. New resources, as they are discovered, (e.g., because hardware has been added or repaired), should be incorporated as part of the ongoing operation of the application system.

Since any component of the system may fail at any time, the operating system must monitor its own behavior as well as that of the application system. It may not assume that any element of hardware or software is working properly—each must be tested before it is used and retested periodically to ensure that it continues to func-

tion correctly. The operating system must be skeptical of its current picture of the system configuration and continually check to see if the environment has changed.

Based on these considerations, the Pluribus operating system builds the map of its environment step by step. Each step tests and certifies the proper operation of some aspect of the environment, relying on those resources certified by previous steps as primitives. Early steps examine the operation of the local processor and its associated private resources. Subsequent steps look outward and begin to discover and test more global resources of the system, giving the checking process a layered appearance. In the Pluribus operating system, each processor begins by checking its own operation and by finding a clock for use as a time base. Once these resources have been verified, the processor can begin to coordinate with the other active processors to develop an accurate picture of the system.

At the same time, the system must balance the need for reliable primitives with the need to accomplish normal operation efficiently. When all the environment has been certified, the system should spend most of its processing power on advancing the operational algorithms and return only occasionally to the task of reverifying its primitives. When failures of the environment have been detected, however, the power of the system must be brought to bear on the task of reconfiguring to isolate the failure.

Hierarchical Structure of the STAGE System

The Pluribus operating system is organized as a sequence of stages which are polled by a central dispatcher. A processor starts with only the first stage enabled. As each stage succeeds in establishing a proper map of its segment of the system state, it enables the next stage to run. Each stage may use information guaranteed by earlier stages and thus may run only if the previous stage has successfully completed its checks. Once enabled, a stage will be polled periodically to verify that the conditions for successful completion of that stage continue to apply. The system applies most of its processing power to the last stage that is enabled but returns periodically to poll each earlier stage. The application system is the final stage in the sequence and may run only after the earlier stages have verified all the configuration information of the applications and the validity of the data structures.

Table 13-1 lists each stage of the Pluribus operating system, together with the aspects of the environment it guarantees. Many of the functions listed will not be discussed further but are provided to illustrate the layering of stages.

Since processors continue to perform each of the stages periodically, changes in the environment will eventually be noted. Any stage detecting a discrepancy in the configuration map will disable all later stages until the discrepancy is repaired. Then, all the later stages, which might depend on data verified by the disabling stage, will be forced to run all their checks, guaranteeing that they will make any further modifications to the configuration map necessitated by the first change. A serious failure, such as a nonexistent-memory interrupt, disables all but the first stage. In these cases, some reconfiguration might be needed, and all stages should perform all their checks before the application system is resumed.

Establishing Communication

So far, we have described the progress of one processor through the staged checking procedures of the operating system. All processors in the Pluribus perform the same checks, since it is important that they agree about the state of the system resources. Coordination of multiple processors with potentially different views of the hardware configuration requires two mechanisms: the processors must agree on an area of

Table 13–1. Pluribus operating system stages.

Stage	Function
0	Checksum local memory code (for stages 0, 1, 2). Initialize local interrupt vectors, and enable interrupts. Discover Processor *bus* I/O. Find some real-time clock for system timing.
1	Discover all usable common memory pages. Establish page for communication between processors.
2	Find and checksum common memory code (for stages 3, 4, 5). Checksum whole page ("reliability page").
3	Discover all common *buses*, PIDs, and real-time clocks.
4	Discover all processor *bus* couplers and processors.
5	Verify checksum (form stage 2) of reliability page code (for rest of stages plus perhaps some application routines). External reloading of missing code pages is possible once this stage is running.
6	Checksum all of local code.
7	Checksum common memory code. Maintain page allocation map.
8	Discover common I/O interfaces.
9	Poll application-dependent reliability and initialization routines. Periodically trigger restarts of halted processors.
10	Application system.

common memory in which to record the machine configuration map, and they must cooperate in their decisions to modify that map.

The first step in coordinating the multiple processors of a Pluribus is to agree on a page of memory through which to communicate. The procedure for initially establishing the page for communication is clearly delicate. Prior to establishing the page, the processors have no way to communicate about where it will be. The procedure must operate correctly in the face of failures which might leave some of the processors seeing a different set of common memory pages from the rest. Processors which are unable to see the communication area will attempt to use another memory page and must be prevented from interfering with the unaffected processors.

Any processor that is first starting up (or restarting after some massive failure) can assume nothing about the location of the communication page. Any page may be used, and therefore a small area for communication control variables is reserved on each page of common memory. Part of this area is used for a brief memory test, which must succeed before the page may be used at all. Every processor attempts to establish the lowest numbered (lowest address in memory space) page that it sees as the page through which to communicate. To be valid, any page must have a pointer to the current communication page, and the communication page must point to itself.

Each processor looks at the pointer on the lowest numbered page it can see. There are three possible states for the pointer. First, if it points to the page itself, the processor has found the communication page and may now proceed to interact with other processors about the common environment. If it points to a higher numbered page, the processor may just fix the pointer, as the requirement that the communication page be lowest makes this case inconsistent. If it points to a lower numbered page, the processor must attempt to check if the indicated communication page is active. It must assume that the data might simply be old or invalid and must time it out using a dedicated entry in a special array of timers which is allocated on each page. The processor increments the timer and, if it ever reaches a certain threshold, unilaterally fixes the communication pointer and starts to use this page for communication. The processor is prevented from doing this by any other processor which is successfully using the lower numbered

communication page; all such processors periodically zero all the timers on all memory pages in the system.

Consider what happens during various possible hardware failures. If the memory *bus* containing the communication page is lost, all processors will attempt to establish a new communication page on the other *bus*. Using their timers on the new lowest page (which initally points to the old one after the failure), they await the threshold. No one is holding the timers to zero, so the new page becomes the communication page when some processor's timer first runs out.

A processor blinded to the communication page by a *bus* or coupler failure will try to establish a higher numbered page for communication. From the point of view of the failing processor, this case is indistinguishable from the previous case, where the common *bus* failed. Since the rest of the processors are satisfied with the communication pointer, they will hold all timers to zero, and the failed processor will never be able to change the communication page pointer. If the processor sees a set of pages disjoint from the rest of the system, it behaves as if no other processors are running, but there is no memory where it may interfere and now we have two systems operating independently. In this case it is likely that the two systems will interfere over other resources; since multiple failures are required for this situation to occur in a Pluibus, we choose not to attempt recovery here.

The Consensus Mechanism

When configuration data must be updated, it is crucial to coordinate the Pluribus processors before making the modification. The mechanism to accomplish this goal we call consensus. Each stage has a consensus which is maintained as part of its environment. The first step in forming a consensus is to determine the set of processors that is executing the corresponding stage. This set has certified the primitives necessary to maintain successfully this stages's portion of the configuration map. In order for the system to respond to failures, the consensus must be kept current—new processors must be able to join rapidly and processors that may have halted or ceased to run the stage must be erased from the set.

Each processor, based on its hardware address in the Pluribus, is assigned a bit in three consensus arrays, called "next," "smoothed," and "fix-it." As part of the corresponding stage, every processor periodically sets its bit in the next consensus array to show that it wishes to participate in the consensus. After enough time has elapsed for each properly running processor to set its bit, this array is copied into the smoothed consensus and cleared. The set of processors in the smoothed array will then be used as a basis for decisions to reconfigure some portion of the resource map.

Any processor which wishes to modify some configuration information sets its bit in the appropriate fix-it array. Processors that agree with the configuration map clear their bits, and bits corresponding to processors not in the smoothed arrays are also cleared.

In effect, the bits in the fix-it array represent the votes of the individual processors in favor of a potential modification. In most cases, it is desirable that all processors agree before making the change. All processors wait until the fix-it array matches the smoothed array before implementing the fix. Other modifications might require only majority or two-thirds agreement. The choice of policy often depends on some tradeoff between resources (e.g., should we use more memory or more processors?). The Pluribus approach allows us to make this choice independently at each stage.

Since each processor in the Pluribus performs each stage of the checking code, the consensus mechanism provides the coordination needed to change the configuration map gracefully. When a stage detects a failure, the processor sets the appropriate fix-it bit and disables the following stages. When enough processors detect the failure they implement the fix to the configuration map. Now these processors can complete the later stages, devoting their attention to any further changes required by the failure. A processor which sees a different picture of the resources and cannot reach agreement with the rest of the system hangs forever at the point of detecting the discrepancy. This technique effectively prevents the processor from damaging the system.

Application-Dependent Checking

In general, it is desirable for the application system to perform its own checks before initiating or resuming normal operation. The last stage provides a mechanism which polls application-oriented processes to perform consensus-driven checks and repairs of their own data structures. This stage uses the results of the hardware (application-independent) discovery stages to certify its own data structures. For example, it could allocate or deallocate device parameter blocks as the I/O devices are discovered or disappear and initialize spare memory pages for use as data buffers as they become available. User-written reliability checks can be performed on any of the application data structures, and the appropriate reinitialization invoked to remedy failures.

Occasionally, it is possible for a processor checking application data structures to implement minor repairs to the data structures unilaterally. For major reconfigurations of the data structures, such as complete application system reinitialization, the checking routines must signal to the stage dispatcher that consensus is needed. The last concurring processor is then permitted to perform the reinitialization routine. Just as the early stages guarantee the hardware map, the application-dependent routines have the consensus mechanism at their disposal to validate the system data structures before entering the system. In addition, the application system data structures are rechecked periodically during normal system operation.

AN EXAMPLE OF APPLICATION RELIABILITY*

We use two general techniques to ensure the validity of data structures in the Pluribus. First, redundant information, where it exists, is checked for discrepancies, and appropriate action taken if they exist. Second, since detailed examination of all data for inconsistency is deemed impossible for any system of nontrivial complexity, we use watchdog timers to ensure the correct operation of the application system at various levels. As an example, we will discuss the buffer management strategy for the Pluribus IMP system.

Buffers in the Pluribus IMP circulate through the system from queue to queue; in some cases, they may be shared between two or more processes. Since a compromised queue structure may, in general, rapidly degrade the performance of the system, elaborate checking methods are built into the IMP program at various levels. In particular, we must be able to detect queues that are crossed or looped and buffers that have been lost (are on no queue at all.)

Associated with each buffer in the system is a set of use bits corresponding to various processes that consume buffers. Any process that enqueues a buffer for some other process first sets the use bit for that process. When a process dequeues a buffer, the appropriate use bit must be on or the buffer will not be processed. As a special case, buffers on the system free list must have all their bits turned off. The buffer-freeing routine only returns a buffer to the free list if the last remaining use bit is that of the freeing process.

This technique intentionally generates redundant information and continually validates it as a buffer circulates through the system. In other words, the existence of a buffer on a queue informs the system that some processing is de-

sired for that buffer. In principle, the use bit signals the same thing. Each buffer-processing routine could scan all the buffers in the system for those with its use bit set, but such strategy would clearly be inefficient. The redundancy check gives preference to neither the queue nor the use bit as an indication of need for service, but rather requires agreement between the two indicators. When they disagree, the system assumes that a failure has indeed occurred and attempts to correct it by forcing the queue to be empty, so that the effects of the failure can be contained as much as possible.

The use bits allow the prompt detection of looped and crossed queues. In addition, an improper buffer point will often lead to a failure of the use bit check.

We must also consider the case of a buffer which has been lost from all queues. This condition could arise due to a program bug or as a result of a queue being emptied after a use bit failure. We could employ a classical garbage-collection scheme for this purpose; unfortunately, the demand for buffers is often great in a high-speed communication system, and the requisite locking of the buffer resources during such a garbage collection would likely result in lost inputs.

The recovery scheme we have chosen is a watchdog timer mechanism. Each buffer has associated with it a flag set by normal activity of the buffer which, in this case, is defined to be the periodic appearance of that buffer on the free list. Whenever a buffer is freed, its flag is set. In addition, flags for all the buffers on the free list are set periodically. In the high-speed communications environment, where data passes through a network node very rapidly, each buffer must appear on the free list at least once every two minutes. Therefore, each buffer flag is checked every two minutes to be sure it is set, and then cleared. A zero flag indicates that the buffer has dropped out of normal activity, and the buffer is unilaterally freed and its use bits cleared. In this way, any lost buffer is detected within at most four minutes and returned to normal usage.

---

* Portions of the next two sections have appeared in J. G. Robinson and E. S. Roberts, "Software Fault-Tolerance in the Pluribus," *AFIPS Conference Proceedings*, vol. 47, copyright AFIPS Press, Montvale, N.J. Reproduced with permission.

ADVANTAGES OF THE PLURIBUS APPROACH TO FAULT-TOLERANCE

Two factors help to make our approach a cost-effective one. First, fault-tolerance is implemented primarily in software. This not only allows us to use unspecialized off-the-shelf hardware for much of our system, but also gives us considerable flexibility by allowing us to try new ideas as the product develops. When the time comes to upgrade machines in the field, a new software release is infinitely preferable to hardware modification. Implementing most fault detection in software also allows more complete error reporting than is characteristic of static-redundancy approaches.

The second factor is the modular nature of the Pluribus. Initially, the modular approach was chosen to permit easy expansion of the capabilities of a system to fit an application without being hampered by system-size boundaries. Our system expands by adding the same hardware modules as those which are duplicated to create a dynamic fault-tolerant system. Thus any system with more than the minimum number of processors for a given application both performs well and is fault-tolerant. A processor failure in such a system merely causes it to run a little slower. Since individual processors are relatively inexpensive, the percentage increase in system cost for processor redundancy is usually small, especially in large systems.

Sometimes the system requirements justify only limited fault-tolerance. An example is the large front-end processor which services the BBN Research Computer Center [Mann, Ornstein, and Kraley, 1976]. Here the bulk of the machine is fully redundant, but several of the host interfaces are used only occasionally for experimental systems, and their users can tolerate an occasional outage. Therefore, these interfaces are not duplicated, with a resultant savings in cost.

An additional factor contributing to cost-effectiveness is the relatively low percentage of processing power spent in explicit error detection (about 1 percent for current systems). We depend to a large extent on checks embedded in the operating program (such as code checksums) to detect errors, since the program is able to recover from failures whose effects are detected well after the fact. It is common practice for large software systems to include checks for some "impossible" software states and bad data structures. We have expanded checks to be comprehensive, including checks which catch many types of hardware errors as well as lingering software problems.

One interesting effect of our approach is to make even a minimal, nonredundant machine significantly more resilient to transient failures caused by either hardware or software. All of the fault-tolerant mechanisms which run in the large systems run also in the small ones, and there are many transient failures which cause only momentary confusion which is usually solved by some level of reset or reinitialization. Obviously, a solid failure of some critical component or destruction of the program cannot be resolved without redundant resources, but these are by no means the only possible failures.

One result of our modular approach is that in contrast to the usual state of affairs, we expect larger systems to be more reliable than smaller ones, since more resources are available to be redistributed in case of trouble.

RECENT FIELD EXPERIENCE

During the past [1977] year, we have had the opportunity to observe eight Pluribus IMP systems both under general operational conditions and in controlled field tests; the availability of these machines has been above 99.7 percent (by availability we mean uptime divided by scheduled uptime, excluding power and air-conditioning failures). Almost all the downtime was caused by program bugs which have been corrected since. Most recently, availability has been above 99.9 percent and we expect it to improve further as the machines reach maturity.

In evaluating this experience in terms of fault-tolerant performance, we feel that it is important to go beyond overall availability numbers and discuss the kinds of faults that the Pluribus system can report, the kinds we observed in the field, and the effects these faults had on system behavior.

The concepts of availability and fault-tolerance are complex when applied to a Pluribus since failure of a component generally results in a reduction in, rather than a complete loss of, performance. In many applications this is an advantage since extra capacity is useful during periods of peak load and reduced service is tolerable while repairing faults. For example, if an I/O interface or an entire I/O *bus* fails, the machine automatically substitutes a spare element with only a momentary (often unnoticeable) interruption of service and with no loss in performance. In the case of processors and memory, however, all resources are normally in use (none are in a standby mode) and the loss of any one (or several) of them forces a reduction in performance, but does not keep the system from running.

When used as an IMP, the principal measure of Pluribus performance is throughput. In the tests described below, the presence of program bugs (since corrected) resulted in somewhat lower availability than we had expected, but the three machines easily exceeded their contractual requirements and were able to deliver better than 92 percent of their rated throughput capacity 99.76 percent of the time and better than 50 percent of capacity 99.83 percent of the time.

Under normal operating conditions, it is possible to observe an IMP only by means of its reports to the NCC or by the reports of its neighbors in the network. Since IMP's often operate unattended, emphasis has been placed on the ability of each Pluribus to evaluate and report its internal hardware and software health. Three varieties of trouble-report messages are sent to the NCC.

Since the Pluribus continually evaluates the state of its hardware (see the discussion of the STAGE system), one type reports trouble in the hardware area. Examples of this are I/O errors, memory parity errors, power failures, and changes in configuration. The second type reflects the results of numerous interlocks and consistency checks which are made regarding tables, queues, variables, and other software entities. The third category concerns the Pluribus's role as part of the network. These reports monitor normal throughput statistics and temporary discontinuities in the IMP-IMP message handling protocols, and are normally not directly pertinent to the fault-tolerance of the Pluribus itself. In a few cases the reports are received some time after a fault has been detected and dealt with by the Pluribus, but most fault messages appear within a few seconds.

In the normal course of building and operating Pluribus systems during the past year [1977], we observed a number of unexpected hardware and software faults, but to verify our ideas and procedures we also wanted to observe a number of failure modes which would be expected to occur infrequently under normal operating conditions. To this end, we conducted an extensive series of tests over a three-month period using three four-processor Pluribus IMP's with redundant I/O interfaces, interconnected by high-speed terrestrial and satellite links. These tests demonstrated how the Pluribus handles many of the possible faults that might be encountered during the life of the equipment. We believe that the combination of the unexpected and planned faults we experienced constitutes a valid sample of the wide variety of intermittent failures in either hardware or software which such systems are likely to encounter. Examples of the types of fault recovery which were provoked or observed during these tests are discussed in the following sections.

Failures on the Processor Bus

We powered off various combinations of processor *buses* to demonstrate that the system would continue with traffic processing. We also tried placing bad instructions in various processors' local memories. In power failure situations, the remaining processors continued to operate without reinitialization. Data handled by the failed processor(s) was recovered by network protocols and a number of trouble-reports indicated this fact. Data structures which were "locked" by the failed processors were "unlocked" by a software watchdog timer. When power was restored, the processors were smoothly readmitted to the system. Processors with bad local memory either halted or looped, and were quickly reloaded by other processors and brought back into operation automatically.

Errors in or Loss of Common Memory

We created situations whereby the system suddenly saw common memory disappear. In some cases we powered off the memory *bus*; in others we "removed" memory from usability tables. We also observed some spontaneous parity errors. Since common memory pages are assigned specific roles at initialization time, loss of one or more pages caused a variety of reactions, depending on the role of the lost memory and the amount remaining. At one extreme, loss of all common memory prevented the system from continuing. At the other, loss of one of several pages of message buffers caused only a brief adjustment of memory assignments by the STAGE program. Most Pluribus systems are organized for fully redundant operation and have spare code and variable pages. Loss of a primary code or variables area caused a short transient in operations while the spare was initialized. As an example, loss of one-half of physical common memory (several pages of code, variables, and buffers) caused a reconfiguration lasting 15 s or less. During this period, all processors agreed on the reallocation of the remaining memory and reevaluated its usability. As a further test, we destroyed the integrity of various pages of common memory by storing random data in checksummed areas. The system

reacted by restoring the contents of the affected page from the backup copy. This process required about 10–12 s. We also created test conditions in which the system found that all copies of critical programs in common memory were unusable (their checksum was bad). At this time the system automatically requested that it be reloaded (from another of the Pluribus IMP's or the NCC). It should also be emphasized that the integrity of message buffers is also protected by software checksums; data harmed in any way is reported to the NCC, and the originator is notified so the retransmission can take place.

Loss of I/O Device

We both created and observed several situations wherein I/O devices were either removed or experienced errors. In these cases, the I/O device was eliminated from usability tables by all processors and a backup device substituted. The system continued to operate, although in some cases, depending on the configuration being used, reinitialization was required. Loss of an entire I/O *bus* was handled in much the same way.

Loss of Critical Hardware

We observed that redundantly configured Pluribus systems would survive the loss of the RTC and the PID by swapping to the backup. Very little time was lost before the system continued. Errors in PID and RTC operation also are checked for and reported.

Internal Software Errors

As previously mentioned, the STAGE system and the IMP code are designed to check on the internal consistency of various software structures. In addition, the system ensures that none of the asynchronous processors is allowed to remain in a waiting state or in a loop. On a very infrequent basis, we observed that a Pluribus will report that such a condition was detected and corrected. We also forced many of these situations to occur by destroying key data structures or by causing queues to be looped or crossed. The system detected these, reported the problem, and continued normally, reinitializing if necessary.

Artificial Pathological Conditions

We did not attempt to cause pathological behavior of Pluribus hardware components which would, for example, write zeros to portions of memory or amputate *buses* at random, although we simulated these conditions with the software. Our observations of pathological behavior in the field, although infrequent, convince us that many of these cases can be withstood by the fault-tolerant software. For example, during field tests we observed that some extraneous data appear occasionally in certain critical tables causing the Pluribus to reinitialize quickly or to suspend activity on a communications link briefly. The problem was traced to a special reloading device which was being improperly activated. This situation was eliminated by a minor program change.

We now have gained enough experience with the Pluribus fault-tolerant mechanisms to have confidence in their ability to detect and cope with failures. In the field, spontaneous failures have been of a relatively minor nature and have been successfully dealt with. Under test conditions, all the major and minor failures which occurred or which we created were well tolerated and the systems continued to function within their rated capacities.

PLURIBUS SYSTEM MAINTAINABILITY*

Most fault-tolerant systems are designed to be repaired, sooner or later, by humans. Maintain-

ability thus becomes a significant factor in long-term system performance. Since many systems are designed to recover from any single failure, but not from all multiple failures, the mean time to repair (MTTR) directly influences on-line spares requirements and hence the system cost for any given performance goal. To minimize MTTR, the system must provide accurate and unambiguous information about the nature of the detected fault and the automatic recovery process initiated. The environment in which the system operates is also important since the maintaining authority must be notified and must initiate the repair process as soon as possible.

The actual repair process may be carried out at several levels depending on the accuracy of the diagnostics and the obscurity of the failure symptoms. At the lowest level, the repair is accurately defined by the diagnostic and involves only the replacement of a faulty component. At the highest level, the failure may be caused by a design bug in either hardware or software. For the latter, the system must provide sufficient tools to permit overriding the operational recovery procedures. They must permit the repair personnel to reconfigure the system and run any required diagnostic procedures. The more powerful repair tools must be guarded to avoid operator-induced errors. Ideally this "fool-tolerance" [Goldberg, 1975, p. 32] should extend into all phases of repair. In practice we use only a two-level protection scheme that relies on experienced personnel not to make catastrophic errors.

Although we tend to think of hardware malfunctions as separate from software malfunctions, the symptoms of failure and the recovery procedures are frequently similar. In the Pluribus, the first detection of a fault is usually through failure of an embedded check in the main program, and frequently that is all that is required to initiate a correct recovery procedure. When the diagnostic value of an embedded check is insufficient to define a recovery proce-

---

* Portions of this section have appeared in J. G. Robinson and E. S. Roberts, "Software Fault-Tolerance in the Pluri-

bus," *AFIPS Conference Proceedings*, vol. 47, copyright AFIPS Press, Montvale, N.J. Reproduced with permission.

dure, various modular diagnostics may be run on the system. Thus in the case of a memory whose checksum is discovered to be wrong, the recovery action is to run a brief memory diagnostic and, if the memory appears usable, to restore the code from a spare copy.

Including a spare copy of some resource helps system recovery only if that spare resource works. Although it is traditional to run modular diagnostics on spare resources, our strategy has been to force the system to rotate use of resources from time to time. In some cases we use manual procedures, but the tendency has been to include automatic rotation procedures in the operational system software. This technique is clearly more appropriate to our application than it would be to a more traditional fault-tolerant requirement, since rotating faulty hardware into the operational system could cause a transient malfunction. On the other hand, it provides a better test of the hardware than modular diagnostics would provide.

One advantage of our reliance on embedded checks for failure detection is that we can detect that class of failure which is rarely caught by diagnostics. It is axiomatic that the operational program is the best program for certifying the hardware, but our operational program has also become the most comprehensive diagnostic for the hardware. In our experience, some of the most subtle hardware failures occur during operation of the application system, even though hardware diagnostic programs detect no errors. By augmenting the operational system with diagnostic capabilities, we have often been able to isolate even obscure or intermittent failures without interrupting normal operation.

Reporting Facilities

In the Pluribus IMP, the mechanism for reporting errors, recovery operations, and change-of-status information is the system trap (i.e., a supervisor call). Traps are reported locally on the system terminal and are also sent via trouble-reports to the network log at the NCC, where

they serve a variety of diagnostic purposes. Understanding the nature of a failure in the running system requires fairly accurate knowledge of the state of the machine at the instant of the failure. The initial implementation of the trap mechanism recorded only the code number of the trap, which set of processors had encountered it, and a total occurrence count. This proved inadequate for accurate diagnosis and we have augmented the original trap mechanism to allow for saving a large snapshot of the instantaneous state of the processor, including such information as the contents of general registers, the global system time, map register settings, the last value read from the PID, and other important local data. These snapshots allow us to examine diagnostic information about the failure after the recovery code has taken effect and normal operation of the system has resumed. In an operational IMP, the snapshot information is sent to a data collection program at the NCC, where it is both stored for future reference and printed out on a log terminal. The snapshot facility is usually only enabled for that set of traps which indicate system malfunctions of some kind, since there are many normal traps which indicate such things as network topology changes. The same data collection program also keeps track of the current configuration of each machine and reports any changes on the log terminal. Thus the reconfiguration resulting from some module failure is immediately apparent. Correlating a reconfiguration with preceding snapshot error messages is usually sufficient to isolate solid failures.

Remote Diagnosis and Repair

Where the failure is intermittent, or error indications are ambiguous, we can make further diagnosis from the NCC using the remote connection capabilities of the network. This allows personnel at the NCC to interact with a system at a remote site exactly as if they were using the system control terminal at the site. We have provided a command structure in the system which allows us to make either "soft" or "firm" overrides of the configuration control structure, loop communication links, and run a variety of special diagnostics, monitors, and traffic generators. This enables us to diagnose many problems from the NCC even before dispatching repair personnel to the site (this can be especially appropriate for diagnosing program bugs). The current software is best at diagnosing the solid failures typical of mature hardware and treats most long-term intermittents as unrelated transients. Although we plan to implement heuristics which can deal with this type of problem, the diagnosis of long-term intermittents currently requires human intervention. Fully redundant Pluribus systems may be thought of as networks of paths and *buses*, so by causing the system not to use a particular path or *bus* and watching the trap log, we are usually able to localize the source of a hardware intermittent. Partitioning the *bus* and using some subset of the modules on the *bus* further localizes an intermittent traced to a particular *bus*, and repairs can then proceed. The same tools for reconfiguration are, of course, also available to maintenance personnel on site through the system control terminal, and trap reports sent to the NCC are duplicated also.

Partitioning

In extreme cases, when all normal diagnostic approaches have been exhausted, it is also possible to partition a fully redundant machine into two separate machines and run the operation system in one half while running stand-alone diagnostics or another copy of the system in the other half. We originally expected to use this approach quite frequently, but experience has shown the technique to be less useful than we expected. Splitting a system is a combination of many "firm" overrides of the configuration control which are not currently protected against operator error (i.e., deleting the last copy of a resource from the use tables, or overlapping system resources across the partition). There is also the problem of identifying fault-free compo-

nents to include in the operational system half. In general, being able to identify a faulty module which is to be excluded from the operational system implies that we can fix the fault by replacing the module, which usually obviates the need for partitioning into two machines. And finally, once a machine has been split, any new failures are likely to cause fatal problems that the machine might have been able to cope with had it not been split. Our current feeling is that the risks of splitting an operational system usually outweigh the advantages.

Reloading and Down-Line Loading

An important facility provided by the Pluribus hardware allows us to load and start the machine with no onsite personnel. This is accomplished by special-format messages which trigger a simple reload device when received over the network. This device is used to load a software package capable of dumping or reloading the operating system and application code. The source of reload code may be either some other Pluribus IMP on the network, or a disk file at the network control center. These reloading facilities are also used for distributing software updates to the machines in the field. A Pluribus IMP which discovers all copies of some application code page to be compromised will attempt to get a down-line reload from a neighbor IMP. This request is reported to the NCC where an operator then sets up the reload source for the transfer. Its use enables an IMP without duplicated resources to recover quickly from transient failures caused by hardware or software.

Maintenance Experience

The prototype Pluribus systems performed their error recovery functions well in many cases. Minor problems were often bypassed so effectively that the users and maintenance personnel were never aware of the problem. Even following drastic failures, such as the loss of a common memory bus, normal system operation was restored within seconds. From our experience with these early systems, however, certain deficiencies in our original strategies have become clear.

In some failure cases, one repair would lead to another, until eventually a fairly major reinitialization would be performed, with obvious effects on the users of the system. Unfortunately, the massive recovery often destroyed evidence of the original failure, or masked evidence necessary for effective diagnosis. While the goal of restoring the system to normal operation was achieved, we were left without any idea of why the reinitialization was required. This was particularly frustrating when the frequency of occurrence was on the order of hours or days.

In other cases, normal operation seemed to continue while some hardware failure occurred undetected. Either the failure was covered by effective recovery at a fairly low level in the system or it occurred in a redundant portion of the hardware which was not being exercised. A second failure in conjunction with the first would remove the last copy of some critical resource, causing the system to fail.

These initial experiences led through several intermediate steps to the current set of maintenance tools and diagnostics. In the prototype systems, we were forced to remove the system software and run stand-alone diagnostics when trouble arose. Development of the original recovery algorithms into early versions of the current STAGE system allowed diagnosis and repair while running the operational system; however, system programmers were required to interpret the traps and wrestle the system into different configurations during repair. The usual repair team during this period included a system programmer (usually at the NCC) watching and interpreting the traps, with a maintenance technician on site replacing components.

At present, the tools and diagnostics are well enough defined and documented so that usually only maintenance personnel are required for a repair. Hardware and software staff at the NCC may offer suggestions when maintenance personnel are dispatched to a site and may still direct occasional repair efforts if a difficult problem or inexperienced personnel require it, but this is the exception rather than the rule.

OTHER APPLICATIONS AND EXTENSIONS

Since the Pluribus has evolved from a communications application where overall system availability rather than total fault-coverage is the goal, our approach is most obviously suitable for similar applications. We have opted for an approach which depends heavily upon reconfiguration and reinitialization when faults are detected, and which requires very little special hardware beyond that needed to implement our multiprocessor architecture. Our approach would not be suitable for applications where absolutely no downtime can be tolerated, where total computational context must be preserved over failures, or where overall correctness must be ensured. In these cases, traditional approaches involving some form of static redundancy or execution redundancy are indicated [Avizienis, 1975, 1976]. Techniques somewhat similar to ours, but for a redundant uniprocessor, are in use in the Bell System's latest Electronic Switching System [Myers et al., 1977]. Although we have not closely investigated applications outside the communications area, we believe our approach is suitable for many other tasks, and we discuss several of these briefly below.

Message Systems

We have made an extensive study of the possibility of using the Pluribus as the basis for a message system. By message system we mean not only traditional message-switching such as done in the Telex system, but also a system of mailboxes and files by which users can exchange and file messages without recourse to the U.S. Postal Service, secretaries, or filing cabinets, and which will permit complicated searches and sorts of message files. Such a system must have high availability but could easily tolerate brief outages after a failure.

Real-Time Signal Processing

We have already built one system which is the front-end and control processor for a seismic data collection network, and which performs some preprocessing of seismic data [Gudz, 1977]. We believe this application can be extended to other areas of real-time signal processing with requirements for high overall system availability. Since many signal processing tasks can be broken into parallel components, the multiprocessor architecture would be especially appropriate.

General-Purpose Timesharing Systems

It seems to us that explicit use of fault-tolerant techniques could benefit general-purpose time-sharing systems and large operating systems. These systems could operate continuously and are subject to minor hardware errors and subtle software bugs, but do not require totally uninterrupted operation. Although most large systems include some self-checking in the software, software fault-tolerance, to be truly effective, must be well integrated into the overall system.design, and into the special hardware features which are usually required.

One of the primary purposes of most large operating systems is to provide disk and tape handling features. In this context, reinitialization in response to faults is a much more serious problem than, for example, in the IMP. Various checkpointing procedures may be required to restore the overall system state to a point where restart is possible [Yourdon, 1972b, pp. 340–353]. Large operating systems often support a variety of checkpointing services since the best tech-

niques to use under these circumstances depend in part on the applications being serviced; in cases involving on-line database updates, the application programs themselves must be designed around their fault-tolerance requirements.

Reservation Systems

Airline, hotel, and car rental reservation systems provide good examples of on-line database systems which could benefit from well-designed software fault-tolerance systems. Once a reservation has been accepted, it must not be lost. Backup techniques such as dual updating of two copies of the database, perhaps located in different cities with independent central processors and telecommunications systems, may be worthwhile. On the other hand, minor problems (hardware or software) may be tolerated, especially if the problems can be resolved by reentering on-line transactions which were affected by the fault. Even with dual machines in remote locations, using a machine like the Pluribus would increase the reliability of each site separately, and provide substantial computing power in an expandable package. Further research will be required to understand fully the implications to the Pluribus of database integrity requirements for reservation systems.

Process Control

Our approach is clearly more appropriate to some areas of process than to others. We envision a typical application in the area of overall supervisory systems coordinating a number of subsidiary systems or controllers, and incorporating tasks such as inventory control and job scheduling. Processes that could afford to stop momentarily would be controlled directly. End-to-end error correction and fault-masking hardware would be used in the machine interface for applications needing overall fault-tolerance. As with the previous applications, some form of checkpointing would be built in to preserve context over restarts.

ACKNOWLEDGMENT

Much of the initial development of the Pluribus computer was supported by the Information Processing Techniques Office of the U.S. Defense Advanced Research Projects Agency, under Contract Numbers DAHC15-69-C-0179, F08606-73-C-0027, and F08606-75-C-0032, and by the Defense Communications Agency under Contract DCA200-C-616. Additionally, a number of the applications systems were developed under contracts from various branches of the U.S. Government.

Many people have contributed to the Pluribus project; Frank Heart has led the effort since its inception.

REFERENCES

Avizienis [1975, 1976]; Barnes et al. [1968]; Bressler, Kraley, and Michel [1975]; Enslow [1974]; Goldberg [1975]; Gudz [1977]; Heart [1975]; Heart et al. [1970, 1973, 1976]; Mann, Ornstein, and Kraley [1976]; McKenzie et al. [1972]; Myers et al. [1977]; Ornstein and Walden [1975]; Ornstein et al. [1972, 1975]; Roberts and Wessler [1970]; U.S. Patent Office [1977]; Wolf [1973b]; Wulf and Bell [1972]; Yourdon [1972b].

The STAR (Self-Testing And Repairing) Computer: An Investigation of the Theory and Practice of Fault-Tolerant Computer Design

Algirdas Avižienis   George C. Gilley   Francis P. Mathur

David A. Rennels   John A. Rohr   David K. Rubin

Abstract

This paper presents the results obtained in a continuing investigation of fault-tolerant computing which is being conducted at the Jet Propulsion Laboratory. Initial studies led to the decision to design and construct an experimental computer with dynamic (standby) redundancy, including replaceable subsystems and a program rollback provision to eliminate transient errors. This system, called the STAR computer, began operation in 1969. The following aspects of the STAR system are described: architecture, reliability analysis, software, automatic maintenance of peripheral systems, and adaptation to serve as the central computer of an outerplanet exploration spacecraft.

Index Terms—Fault-tolerant computers, replacement systems, self-repairing computers.

INTRODUCTION: CHRONOLOGY AND RATIONALE

This paper presents a summary of the theoretical results and design experience obtained in an investigation of fault-tolerant computing which is being conducted at the Jet Propulsion Laboratory (JPL). Initial studies (1961–1965) led to the conclusion that dynamic (also called standby) redundancy offered the greatest promise in the design of fault-tolerant digital computer systems [Avižienis, 1967c]. The *dynamic* redundancy [Short, 1968] approach requires a two-step procedure for the elimination of a fault: first, the presence of a fault is determined; second, a corrective action is taken (e.g., replacement of failed unit, repetition of program, reconfiguration of systems, etc.). The alternative to the dynamic approach is *static* (masking) redundancy [Short, 1968], which was already being utilized in existing component-redundant [Lewis, 1963; Kuehn, 1969] and triple-modular-redundant (TMR) [Lyons and Vanderkulk, 1962; Anderson and Macri, 1967; Kuehn, 1969] computers. Early analytic studies of dynamic redundancy with idealized series-parallel system models indicated that mean life gains of an order of magnitude and more over a nonredundant system could be expected from dynamically redundant systems with standby spares replacing failed units [Flehinger, 1958; Griesmer, Miller, and Roth, 1962; Reed and Brimley, 1962; Kruus, 1963]. This gain compared favorably with the mean life gain of less than two in the typical TMR systems. Other qualitative advantages of the dynamic over the static redundancy were: 1) greater isolation of catastrophic (nonindependent) faults which is especially important for densely packed microelectronic circuitry; 2) survival of system until all spares of one type are exhausted; 3) ability to eliminate errors which are caused by transient faults by the use of program rollback; 4) ready adjustability of the number and type of spare units; 5) utilization of the potentially lower failure rate of unpowered components in spare units; 6) avoidance of the circuit-related problems of static redundancy: increases in fan-out, fan-in, power requirements, and the need for isolation and synchronization of separate channels; and 7) facilitation of the checkout of spare units by means of standard diagnostic programs.

The attainment of the apparent advantages of a dynamically redundant system had been shown to depend very strongly on the successful execution of the detection and replacement operations [Flehinger, 1958; Griesmer, Miller, and Roth, 1962]: these observations have since been formalized as the concept of "coverage" [Bouricius, Carter, and Schneider, 1969a].

The second phase of the investigation (1965–1970) was focused on the identification and solution of the problems involved in the design of a general-purpose digital computer possessing the properties attributed to the abstract model of a dynamically redundant computing system. Three major areas of investigation were: 1) an investigation of fault-detection methods; 2) a study of computer architecture with emphasis on partitioning into subsystems with minimal interconnection requirements; and 3) a study of the "hardcore" problem, i.e., the alternate technologies and logic organizations for implementing the detection and switching functions. The choices among feasible alternatives in all three areas are strongly affected by assumptions on the available component technology and on the computing tasks to be required of the computer. In order to retain contact with the practice of computer design, it was decided to design and construct an experimental general-purpose digital computer which would incorporate dynamic redundancy (i.e., fault detection and replacement of failed subsystems) as integral parts of its structure. The design objectives have been carried out and the system, called the STAR (self-testing and repairing) computer, began operation in 1969. The modular nature of the STAR computer has allowed systematic expansion and modifications that are still being continued.

The first objective of the design is to study the class of problems which are encountered in transforming the theoretical model of a self-repairing system into a working computer. State-of-the-art integrated circuit and memory technology was employed in the design. The STAR computer characteristics were chosen to satisfy all predictable requirements of a spacecraft guidance, control, and data acquisition computer which would be used in the very long (ten years and more) unmanned missions exploring the outer planets of the solar system [Long, 1969]. The second objective was to provide a tool for laboratory studies of fault-tolerant computing, including the injection of transient as well as permanent faults of catastrophic nature. Very extensive displays of registers, manually controlled clocking, and provisions for convenient modification of subsystems were incorporated into the experimental STAR computer breadboard (Figure 14-1).

The STAR computer employs a balanced mixture of coding, monitoring, standby redundancy, replication with voting, component redundancy, and repetition in order to attain hardware-controlled self-repair and protection against transient faults. The principal goal of the design is to attain fault tolerance for a variety of faults: transient, permanent, random, and catastrophic. The actual construction (rather than simulation)

Figure 14–1. The STAR computer.

of the STAR breadboard has two significant advantages. First, the design process has uncovered interesting new hardware-related problems and led to numerous improvements. Second, the computer serves as a vehicle for further experimentation and refinement of the recovery techniques.

During the studies of fault-tolerant architecture and the design of the STAR computer, concurrent investigations were being conducted in other closely related areas of fault-tolerant computing, including studies of software, reliability prediction, and extension of dynamic redundancy to peripheral devices [Avižienis et al., 1969]. A complete redesign of the STAR computer is being performed to match the exact requirements of a control computer for the thermoelectric outer planet spacecraft (TOPS) [TOPS, 1970]. This effort led to the evaluation of additional fault-recovery techniques. The results of the efforts described above are summarized in the following sections of this paper.

ARCHITECTURE OF THE STAR COMPUTER

Methods of Fault Tolerance

The STAR computer is a replacement system that provides one standard configuration of functional subsystems with the required computing capacity. The standard computer is supplemented with one or more spares of each subsystem. The spares are unpowered and are used to replace operating units when permanent faults are discovered. The principal methods of error detection and recovery are the following.

1. All machine words (data and instructions) are encoded in error-detecting codes and fault detection occurs concurrently with the execution of the programs.
2. The computer is divided into a set of replaceable functional units containing their own instruction decoders and sequence generators. This decentralization allows simple fault location procedures and simplifies system interfaces.

3. Fault detection, recovery, and replacement are carried out by special-purpose hardware. In the case of memory damage, software augments the recovery hardware.
4. Transient faults are identified and their effects are corrected by the repetition of a segment of the current program; permanent faults are eliminated by the replacement of faulty functional units.
5. The replacement is implemented by power switching: units are removed by turning power off and connected by turning power on. The information lines of all units are permanently connected to the buses through isolating circuits; unpowered units produce only logic "zero" outputs.
6. The error-detecting codes are supplemented by monitoring circuits which serve to verify the proper synchronization and internal operation of the functional units.
7. The "hard core" test and repair processor (TARP) is protected by triplication and replacement of failed members of the triplet.

Hardware System Organization

The block diagram of the STAR computer is shown in Figure 14-2. Communication between the units is carred out on two four-wire buses: the memory-out (M-O) bus, and the memory-in (M-I) bus. The abbreviations designate the following units.

COP   Control processor, contains the location counter and index registers and performs modification of instruction addresses before execution.

LOP   Logic processor, performs logical operations on data words (two copies are powered).

MAP   Main arithmetic processor, performs arithmetic operations on data words.

ROM   READ-ONLY memory, 16,384 permanently stored words.

RWM   READ-WRITE memory unit with 4,096 words of storage (at least two copies powered; 12 units are directly addressable).

IOP   Input/output processor, contains I/O buffer registers.

IRP   Interrupt processor, handles interrupt requests.

TARP   Test and repair processor, monitors the operation of the computer and implements recovery (three copies are powered).

The functional units (processors and memories) of the STAR computer communicate by means of the M-I and M-O (four-wire) information buses. The 32-bit words are transmitted on these two buses as eight bytes of four bits each. Three control signals are sent from the TARP on the three-wire control bus to synchronize the operations of the functional units and to initiate recovery. Otherwise the functional units operate autonomously. Unless otherwise noted, one copy of each unit is powered at a given time. The decentralized organization allows a standard interface between each unit and the remainder of the computer. Each STAR unit interfaces with the computer by the means of 14 signal lines. Eleven lines, both in active and spare units, are

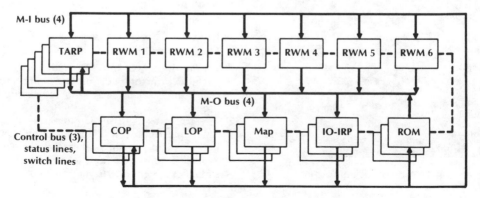

Figure 14–2. STAR computer organization.

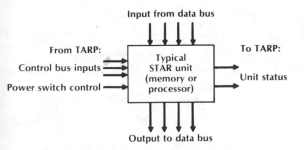

Figure 14–3. Functional unit of STAR computer.

permanently connected to the computer system buses, and three are connected to the TARP array. An unpowered unit cannot produce logic one outputs. The external connections of a STAR unit are shown in Figure 14-3.

The four input and four output lines are connected to the data M-I and M-O buses. They receive and send coded machine words in four-bit bytes. The power switch control input causes power to be applied to the unit. The three control bus input signals are: CLOCK, a basic timing input; SYNC, a periodic synchronization signal; and RESET, a signal that forces the unit into a standard initial state. Two unit status lines send information on the internal operation of the unit to the TARP. These lines carry multiplexed information which will be discussed in a following section. Each functional unit is autonomous and contains its own sequence generator as well as storage for the current operation code, operands, and results. The internal design of a unit may be altered without affecting other units as long as the interface specifications are observed.

It is to be noted that the IOP and IRP units are shown combined in Figure 14-2.

Standard Operation

The STAR computer has two modes of operation: the standard mode and the recovery mode (under TARP control). During the *standard mode* the stored programs are carried out. The TARP processor issues the principal CLOCK signal and SYNC signal which occurs when a new step is initiated in the execution of an instruction. Ten CLOCK periods form the basic time unit (cycle) of the computer. During the first period, a four-bit "step code" (in 2-out-of-4 encoding) is issued by the TARP to the M-O bus. The next eight periods are employed to transmit or manipulate one eight-byte machine word. During the tenth period a four-bit "condition-code" byte may be broadcast by one of the functional units. The ten-period cycle is needed because of the series-parallel organization of the computer.

One instruction is executed in two or three steps. In the first step, the address of the instruction is sent from the location counter in the COP to the memory (ROM and RWM) units. In the second step, the addressed memory unit broadcasts on the M-O bus the operation code and address of the instruction to all functional units. The address is indexed in the COP which transmits to the M-I bus if necessary. The appropriate units recognize the operation code, store the address, and initiate execution. In the third step the instruction is executed: an operand is placed on the appropriate bus and accepted by the destination unit. The first two steps require one cycle each; the duration of the third step depends on the instruction and requires 0, 1, or more cycles. Program interrupts begin without the first step. During the second step an instruction is broadcast by the interrupting unit (IO-IRP or TARP).

The instruction set consists of 180 single-address instructions, about one-third of which are indexable. It includes fixed-point arithmetic, maskable logic, and shift operations. Loop-facilitating and subroutine link register instructions are provided. There are 28 interrupts which can be masked out and tested under program control. A special class of instructions aids in fault tolerance. They include diagnostic instructions which exercise unit status messages and the fault-location logic in the TARP. Others perform updating of the "rollback" register in TARP units, name assignment and cancellation of RWM units, power control of spare units, duplexing of ROMs and processors, and absolute read or write operations in RWM units.

Computer Words: Formats and Encoding

There are two possible effects of logic faults upon the operation of a digital computer. First, a data word or an instruction word may be altered during storage, transmission, or processing. The effect is a *word error*. Second, during the execution of an instruction a processor or a memory module may act incorrectly, act out of turn, or fail to act at all. The effect is a *control error*. Both classes of errors are detected in the STAR computer. The present section considers coding techniques for word error detection; control errors are considered later.

Complete duplication offers the simplest word-error detection at the highest cost. Low-cost arithmetic error-detecting codes [Avižienis, 1967a] are attractive because they are preserved during arithmetic processing and mandatory duplication of an arithmetic processor is avoided. An intensive study of error codes led to the choice of modulo 15 arithmetic checking which is especially effective for a byte-organized computer with four-bit bytes [Avižienis, 1971; appears as Appendix B in this book].

All words in the STAR computer are encoded as shown in Figure 14-4. The 32-bit numeric operand word (Figure 14-4b) consists of the 28-bit binary number b, and a 4-bit check byte $c(b)$. The check byte is a binary number which has the value

$$c(b) = 15 - |b|_{15}$$

where $|b|_{15}$ means "the modulo 15 residue of b." This check byte causes the 32-bit word to be a multiple of 15. The checking algorithm casts out 15s, that is, it computes the modulo 15 residue of the entire coded word. A zero residue, represented by 1111, indicates a correct word: all other values of the residue indicate a fault. The casting out of 15s is implemented with a four-bit "end-around carry" adder and takes place concurrently with the transmission of a word on the bus.

The 32-bit instruction word (Figure 14-4a) consists of a 12-bit operation code and a 20-bit

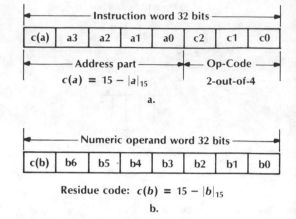

Figure 14-4. a.) STAR instruction word format. b.) STAR operand word format.

residue-coded address part. The 16-bit address is encoded in the same residue code as the operands, and the same checking algorithm is used. The operation code is divided into three bytes, and each byte is encoded in a 2-out-of-4 code. This code permits each byte to be checked individually. There are six valid forms of each byte, giving a total of 216 valid op-code variants. The structure of a bus checker circuit which performs word checking is shown in Figure 14-5. The single step-code and condition-code bytes also use the 2-out-of-4 code and are checked by the bus checker.

The initial choice of error codes in the STAR computer emphasized variety for the purpose of comparison and evaluation, and the arithmetic product (or AN) code was used for operands [Avižienis, 1967a]. Two reasons for the change to the present encoding of operands were: 1) the residue code is separable and allows the use of the more efficient two's complement algorithms for binary arithmetic, and 2) multiple precision and floating-point arithmetic is much more readily implemented with residue encoding. Residue encoding is also suitable for operation codes in STAR instructions. Its advantage is that an identical checking algorithm is applied to instructions and operands; an explicit identifica-

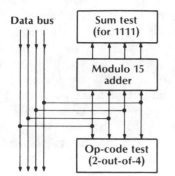

Figure 14–5.   The bus checker circuit.

tion is not required for checking, and loading of programs is facilitated. The drawback is that the bytes of the op-code cannot be checked individually as in the 2-out-of-4 encoding.

Control Error Detection

It has been observed that a large number of faults which cause control errors also cause word errors and are detectable by the use of error codes. Some critical control errors, however, do not fall into this category and require other methods of detection.

The principal method of control fault detection in the STAR computer is the validation that every unit is active at the proper time and that the proper algorithm is carried out within the unit. The initial design [Avižienis, 1968] used a four-wire status line for every replaceable unit to transmit one of six possible "2-out-of-4" coded status messages. Experience has shown that the diagnostic logic in the TARP is significantly simplified when status messages are conveyed to the TARP at predetermined clock times within each ten-unit cycle of operation. In the revised design, each status message is conveyed on two wires (in 1-out-of-2 encoding) and each message covers the time interval between two messages of the same type. The status-message originating circuits are duplicated in each unit to allow the detection of a fault in the status message.

The "output active" message indicates that the unit has produced a nonzero output to the bus in the preceding time interval. It serves to identify improperly active units which otherwise would destroy the information being transmitted on a bus, and make it impossible to locate the source of error. The absence of an expected active message is also a fault condition, since the all-zero word is not a validly coded operand or instruction. The checking of output activity is the most critical of all status monitoring functions.

The other status messages are multiplexed and sent over the same pair of wires as the output active messages because the activity information is not required continuously in the byte-serial machine structure. The status messages which are listed below aid in increasing the probability of immediate detection of incorrect operation.

The "disagree with bus" message is needed for duplex operation (discussed in the next section). Two identical units produce outputs to a bus which acts as an OR gate. Each unit compares the bus word to its internally held output word and records a disagree message if a mismatch occurs. The message is conveyed to the TARP at a specified time. The bus checker result together with disagree message permits a rapid identification of a faulty unit. In simplex operation this message helps to identify improper activity of another unit.

The "complete" message is essential for functional units which have variable-duration algorithms. Memory units issue "write complete" and "read complete" messages which are essential for immediate detection of incorrect storage events.

The "internal fault" message is produced by internal monitoring circuits within each unit. Its function is to indicate incorrect internal algorithms detected by duplication of critical signals, special test circuits, and "inverse microprogramming" in which an operation is deduced from active gating signals.

In addition to the above listed four types of messages, time is provided for a "special" status message which varies for different units. For example, the IO/IRP uses it to report to the TARP the arrival of an external interrupt request.

Properties of Functional Units

The main arithmetic processor (MAP) input consists of an operation code followed by a coded operand, and the output is a coded result followed by a condition-code byte, indicating either one of three singularities (sum overflow, quotient overflow, zero divisor) or the type of a good result (positive, zero, negative). The control processor (COP) stores the condition code and uses it to implement conditional branches instructions. The COP also contains the location counter LC, two index registers, and a four-bit adder to implement indexing of residue-coded addresses and incrementing the LC. The logic processor (LOP) performs the bit-by-bit logic operations and code conversions on input words. The arithmetic coding is removed from the operand before the operation, since error codes are not preserved during logic operations, and the final result is again encoded. The LOP operation is checked by operating two copies which issue disagree status messages when their outputs differ. The IO/interrupt processor (IO/IRP) receives external interrupt requests, initiates allowable interrupts, and carries out input/output buffering functions.

The READ-ONLY memory (ROM) contains the permanent programs and the associated constants. The present machine uses a "braid" assembly of transformers and wires for the permanent storage of 16,384 words. Complete replicas of the ROM are used as replacements. Each 4,096 word READ-WRITE memory (RWM) unit has two modes of operation. In the *absolute* mode a RWM unit recognizes its own wired-in absolute name. In the *relocated* mode a RWM unit responds to an assigned name. All relocated units with the same assigned name store and read out the same locations simultaneously. In case of a disagreement with the word on the M-O bus, the RWM unit sends a disagree status

message to the TARP. The relocated mode provides duplicate or triplicate storage for critical programs and data. When a RWM unit fails, its replacement unit can be assigned the same name, avoiding a discontinuity in addresses. Assignment and cancellation of assigned names is performed under program control; this provision allows selective redundancy of storage. A record of RWM name assignments is retained (in non-volatile storage) in all active TARP units. The accessing of storage locations within a RWM unit is checked by permanently storing the 4-bit check byte of its 12-bit internal address in every location. This byte is read out and checked against the contents of the address register during every read and write operation.

In the STAR computer only the logic processor and the RWM memory unit containing critical system programs are duplexed for normal operation. For experimentation, complete provisions have been made for optional duplex operation of all memory and processor units under program control. The combination of duplication and coding offers detection of all errors as well as a fast identification of one faulty unit. In order to permit duplex operation of processor and ROM units, active TARP units hold a record of units which are operating in duplex.

The Test and Repair Processor (TARP) and Recovery Mode

The "hard core" monitor of the STAR system is designated as TARP (test and repair processor) in Figure 14-2. The TARP monitors the operation of the STAR computer by two methods: 1) testing every word sent over the two data buses for validity of its code; and 2) checking the status messages from the functional units for predicted responses. An incorrect word or a deviation from predicted response causes an interruption of normal computing and an entry into the recovery mode of operation. The block diagram of one TARP is shown in Figure 14-6. It is functionally divided into two sections. One section provides standard mode machine control

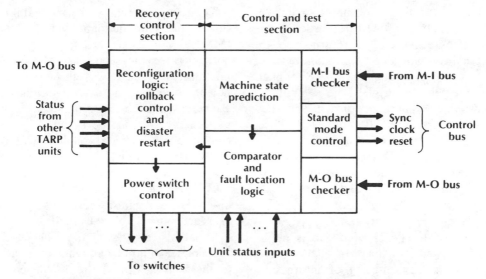

Figure 14–6. Test and repair processor (TARP) organization.

and fault location, and the other controls the recovery mode operation and effects the switching of replaceable units.

The Control and Test (*CAT*)

This section contains the standard mode control logic consisting of an op-code decoder, a clock, and a counter which generates the step-code signals for standard mode operation. The machine-state prediction logic uses the current instruction and step-code to predict which status messages should be received from each powered functional unit. It also predicts the information source and the type of encoding expected on each bus. The fault location compares the status and bus checker (Figure 14-5) results to the prediction. In most cases, it can localize an error to a particular functional unit. Upon detecting an error, the CAT section stops the machine and transfers its error information to the recovery control section.

Recovery Control (*REC*)

This section of the TARP contains a "rollback point" address register which specifies the location of the instruction at which normal operation is to be resumed after a recovery. This register is updated under program control. Before every updating, the contents of all processor registers needed for recovery is stored in duplexed memory units. Upon receipt of an error message from the CAT section, the REC section issues the "reset" signal which causes all powered units to be set to an initial state, and then broadcasts an unconditional jump instruction, which causes the program to be resumed at the "rollback" address. A repeated fault indication in the same unit leads to its replacement. The number of repetitions before replacement can be specified in the experimental TARP. To replace, power is turned off in the unit, a spare is turned on, and another reset (and jump) is issued. For cases of temporary power loss and other fault conditions which cannot be resolved by the fault location logic, the REC section contains a wired-in "disaster restart" procedure.

The TARP is the hard core of the system. Three fully powered copies of the TARP are operated at all times together with n standby spares ($n = 2$ in the present design). The outputs of the TARPs are decided by a 2-out-of-$(n + 3)$ threshold vote. When one powered TARP disagrees with the other two, the recovery mode is entered and an attempt is made to set the internal state of the disagreeing unit to match the other two units. If this TARP rollback attempt fails, the disagreeing unit is returned to the standby condition and one of the standby units receives power, goes through the TARP rollback, and joins the powered triplet. The computer is now restarted, a rollback performed, and standard operation continues. Because of the three unit requirement, design effort has been concentrated on reducing the TARP to the least possible complexity. Experience with the present model has led to several refinements of the design.

The replacement of faulty functional units is commanded by the TARP vote and is implemented by power switching. It offers several advantages over the switching of information lines which connect the units to the bus. The number of switches is reduced to one per unit, power is conserved, and strong isolation is provided for catastrophic failures. Magnetic power switches have been developed which are part of each unit's power supply and are designed to open for most internal failures. The threshold function is inherent in the control windings of the switch. The information lines of each unit are permanently connected to the buses through component-redundant isolation circuits. The signal on a bus is the logic OR of all inputs from the units, and unpowered units produce only logic zero outputs. The power switch and the buses utilize the component redundancy for protection against fatal "shorting" failures.

COMPARATIVE RELIABILITY ANALYSIS

This section considers the reliability (with respect to permanent failures) which can be expected for the STAR computer. The approach is to estimate the relative reliability with respect to an existing reference system. An absolute reliability prediction is not made because the failure rates for components which are being developed for a flight model are not yet adequately established.

The reference computer for reliability estimation is the nonredundant Mariner Mars 1969 (MM'69) computer, which was the on-board computer for the successful Mariner 6 and 7 missions to Mars. It was chosen because a detailed description and extensive failure rate data are readily available. With respect to computing performance it must be noted that the MM'69 computer is a bit-serial machine with a bit rate of 2.4 kHz and an instruction set of 16 op-codes, whereas the STAR is a byte-serial machine with a 0.5 MHz clock and an instruction set of 130 op-codes. This gain in performance is not used as a factor in reliability estimation.

Reliability models 1) the MM'69 computer, 2) a simplex computer equivalent in performance to the STAR, and 3) the STAR computer as shown in Figure 14-7. The MM'69 computer (Figure 14-7a) is assigned a complexity of unity. It is assumed that the simplex computer (Figure 14-7b) consisting of eight functional units is $8 \times CF$ times as complex as the MM'69 computer. The relative complexity factor CF is defined as the ratio of complexity (component count) of a single STAR unit to the complexity of the entire MM'69 computer. The value CF $= 1/3$ was established by detailed comparison and is used in the subsequent analysis. The comparison is made with respect to MM'69 technology, i.e., it is assumed that the simplex and the STAR computers employ the same components and packaging techniques as the MM'69 computer.

The STAR model (Figure 14-7c) consists of eight functional units plus the test and repair processor (TARP) array in series reliability. All units are considered to be of similar complexity and are allocated an equal number of spares. Results for $S = 2$ and $S = 3$ are presented. The reliability model applied to all units except the TARP is the standby-replacement redundancy model with dormant spares [Bouricius, Carter, and Schneider, 1969a; Mathur, 1971a]. The TARP was modeled as a hybrid-redundant $H(3, S)$ system [Mathur and Avižienis, 1970]. Details of the reliability models and measures

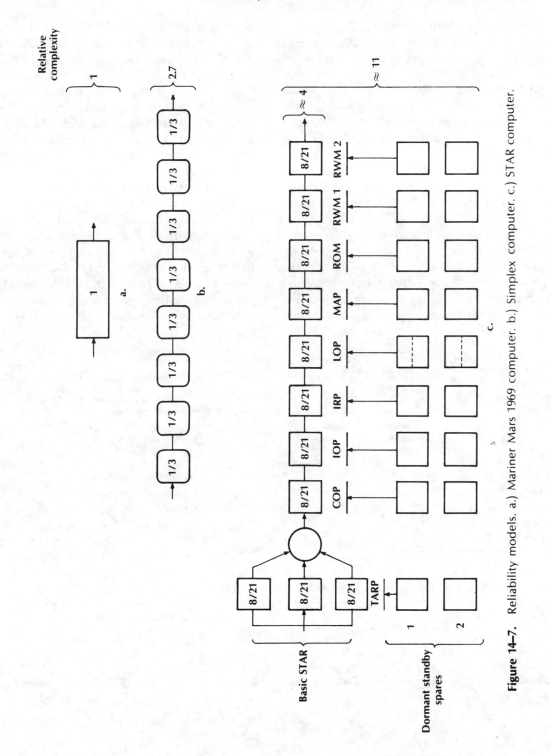

Figure 14-7. Reliability models. a.) Mariner Mars 1969 computer. b.) Simplex computer. c.) STAR computer.

are presented in Mathur [1971a]. The logic processor LOP is assumed to have an internal duplication of the circuits which are not protected by the error-detecting codes. Two sets of three RWM units each are shown; this is a pessimistic assumption, since the computer can function with only one of the six RWM units surviving.

The fault coverage factor [Bouricius, Carter, and Schneider, 1969] in the STAR model is taken into account in two ways: 1) by including the fault detector and recovery initiator as a separate processor (the TARP), and 2) by applying a self-testing factor (STF) to the relative complexities of the units. Note that the simplex computer (Figure 14-7b) does not contain a processor corresponding to the TARP in the STAR computer since the simplex computer is a computationally equivalent nonredundant machine without "test and repair" capabilities.

Since 4 bits of the 32-bit STAR word serve for error detection, a STF equal to 8/7 was chosen. The STF expresses the overhead due to the self-testing and repairing features within each STAR unit, that is, a STAR unit has 8/7 of the complexity of the same unit in the "simplex" computer. Applying CF = 1/3 and STF = 8/7 a STAR unit has the relative complexity of 8/21 with respect to the entire MM'69 computer.

Examples of reliability predictions based on the MM'69 data are shown in Tables 14-1 and 14-2 and Figures 14-8 and 14-9. The *lower bound* ($K = 1$) assumes equal failure rates of powered and spare units (K is the failure rate ratio). The *upper bound* ($K = \infty$) assumes a zero failure rate of spare units. Two-spare ($S = 2$) and three-spare ($S = 3$) STAR systems are considered. Table 14-1 and Figure 14-8 show the predicted reliability as a function of time. Table 14-2

Table 14-1. Reliability versus time for various configurations (CF = 1/3).

Mission Time (h)	MM'69 Computer	Simplex Computer	STAR Computer with S Spares			
			Upper Bound ($K = \infty$)		Lower Bound ($K = 1$)	
			S = 3	S = 2	S = 3	S = 2
4,368 (≈ 6 months)	0.928	0.82	0.9999998	0.99997	0.999995	0.99982
43,680 (≈ 5 years)	0.475	0.14	0.997	0.97	0.966	0.87
87,360 (≈ 10 years)	0.225	0.019	0.96	0.79	0.71	0.45

Table 14-2. Mission duration for specified reliability (CF = 1/3.)

Desired Mission Reliability	MM'69 Computer	Simplex Computer	Mission Duration in Years			
			STAR Computer with S Spares			
			Upper Bound		Lower Bound	
			S = 3	S = 2	S = 3	S = 2
0.9	0.7	0.3	12.5	7.5	6.7	4.5
0.8	1.5	0.6	16.0	9.7	8.5	6.0
0.7	2.4	0.9	18.5	11.7	10.0	7.0
0.6	3.5	1.3	20.5	13.5	11.3	8.3

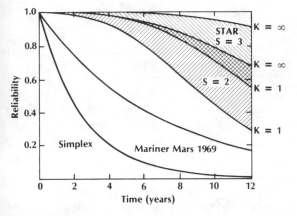

Figure 14–8. Reliability versus mission time MM'69, simplex, and STAR computers.

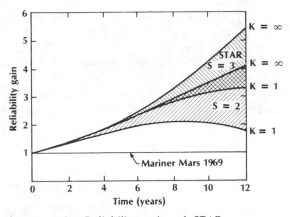

Figure 14–9. Reliability gain of STAR computer with respect to the MM'69 computer.

shows the time (in years) for which the reliability remains above a specified value. Figure 14-9 presents the predicted reliability gain, defined as the ratio STAR reliability/MM'69 reliability.

The computing operations for the foregoing analysis, the generation of tables, and the plotting of graphs was done with the aid of the computer-aided reliability estimation CARE program [Mathur, 1971b], which was developed as a design tool during the reliability study. CARE is a software package developed on the Univac 1108 computer system at JPL. CARE may be interactively accessed by a designer from a teletype console to calculate his reliability estimates. The input is in the form of a system configuration description followed by queries on the various reliability parameters of interest and their behavior with respect to mission time, fault coverage, failure rates, dormancy factors, allocated spares, and partitioning. The CARE program is extensible, and it may be updated to incorporate new reliablity models as they become available.

STAR COMPUTER SOFTWARE SYSTEM

Early in the design of the STAR computer it became evident that the fault-tolerant architecture would impose unconventional constraints on its software. The development of the software system for the STAR computer was initiated in 1968 and closely followed the hardware development. It is partitioned into two subsystems. The programming subsystem consists of three modules: an assembler, a loader, and a functional simulator. An executive program facilitates coordinated use of these modules. The operating subsystem consists of two modules: the resident executive module and the applications program module. The programming subsystem has been implemented on the Univac 1108 computer of the Scientific Computing Facility at JPL. The first version of a resident executive for the STAR computer is nearing completion.

SCAP (the STAR computer assembly program) is the first module of STAR software. Programs for the STAR computer are written in the assembly language SCAL. SCAP is a traditional two-pass assembler incorporating machine instructions, pseudo-operations, and macrofacilities. A unique feature of SCAP is the encoding of instruction and data words as required by the STAR computer. SCAP calculates the code required and generates the encoded value of the word. Another feature of SCAP is the COMPILE pseudo-operation which implements automatic compilation of simple arithmetic statements by the assembler.

The second module LOAD (the loader) reads the program into the simulated STAR computer memory. After all decks have been read, a

COMMON area is allocated, relocation is completed, and external linkage is accomplished. A map and cross-reference table are printed to aid in debugging and documenting the program. The third module of STAR software is the functional simulator, which is modular in nature and follows the latest STAR hardware configuration. Two special features are incorporated in the simulator. The first is the facility to simulate hardware errors in order to test the software aspects of error recovery. The second feature provides STAR register and memory dumps. An executive program facilitates the coordinated use of the assembler, loader, and simulator.

The modules of the operating subsystem of the STAR computer software system consist of the resident executive module and the applications programs module. The STAR resident executive augments the self-testing and repairing features of the hardware in addition to its normal functions. The standard features include interrupt control, input/output processing, and job scheduling. Novel features incorporated due to the fault-tolerant architecture of the STAR computer include a "cold start" capability, reconfiguration processing, rollback assistance, and diagnosis of faulty units. The cold start capability resets the hardware and software after a disaster restart as well as prior to an initial load. Reconfiguration processing is required for memory replacement, since software assistance is required to load a newly activated memory unit. All programs running on the STAR computer require rollback (recovery) points. The resident executive provides rollback status storage and controls events which are nonrepeatable, i.e., they may not occur more than once even if a rollback takes place. Finally, it implements diagnosis for faulty units to determine the cause and extent of failures for possible partial reuse. The present application programs module includes floating-point arithmetic subroutines, and test and demonstration programs. The applications programs which will be required for space missions are a part of the TOPS control computer subsystem project discussed later in this paper.

EXTENSION OF STAR TECHNIQUES TO PERIPHERAL SYSTEMS

The STAR techniques of fault tolerance can be systematically extended beyond the boundaries of the computer to effect automatic maintenance of various peripheral systems that communicate with the computer. The case which was investigated in connection with the STAR computer development is the implementation of automatic maintenance for a simplified model of the JPL thermoelectric outer planet spacecraft (TOPS) which is being proposed for the exploration of the outer planets [TOPS, 1970]. The potentially lower failure rates of unpowered spare units and the constant power demand of a replacement system are exceptionally important in missions requiring a ten-year survival of the spacecraft under very strict power constraints.

The methodology of extending the STAR techniques consists of several steps: 1) identification of the replaceable peripheral units; 2) selection of internal error detection functions which are economically feasible within the units themselves; 3) identification of possible functional redundancy, in which either another type of peripheral unit, or the computer itself can take over the function of a failed unit; 4) algorithmic description of the monitoring and recovery procedures to be performed for each unit by the computer; 5) development of fault-tolerant communication between the peripheral units and the I/O and interrupt processors of the computer; 6) translation of the monitoring and recovery procedures which have been assigned to the computer into computational requirements: speed, instruction set, storage size, input/output, and interrupt system complexity; and 7) estimation of reliability and mean life attainable for each peripheral unit. Several iterations of the design process lead to a system for which a balanced gain in the reliability has been attained by means of computer-controlled automatic maintenance. A detailed case study of the application of these techniques is presented in Gilley [1970].

The investigation has identified and quantized

the computing capability required from the STAR computer in order to effect the automatic maintenance of the TOPS spacecraft. Furthermore, the results have shown that: 1) the fully automatic maintenance of a complex long-life spacecraft is feasible through a systematic extension of STAR techniques, and 2) the automatic maintenance requirements of the spacecraft systems can be algorithmically described to the detail required to produce computer programs for their implementation. The results of the investigation have systematically extended dynamic redundancy to various peripheral subsystems of an information processing system. Beyond the specific example of a spacecraft, the methodology is applicable to computer-controlled automatic maintenance of other complex data processing, communication, and control systems.

DESIGN OF THE TOPS CONTROL COMPUTER

The most recent step in the development of the STAR computer concept has been the design of a control computer subsystem (CCS) for the thermoelectric outer planet spacecraft (TOPS) [TOPS, 1970]. After the TOPS requirements were quantified as described in the preceding section, the CCS design had still to meet four major externally-imposed constraints: 1) the weight of the subsystem was not to exceed 40 lbs.; 2) power consumption was not to be greater than 40 W; 3) probability of successfully completing a 100,000-hour mission was to be equal to or greater than 0.95 (using TOPS approved part failure rates; and 4) it could not, as a consequence of any single internal fault, result in a failure mode catastrophic to the mission.

Because of these constraints, it was not possible merely to "shrink" the STAR computer into a flight package. The STAR design was simplified by retaining only the capabilities needed to meet the TOPS functional requirements. The entire self-test and repair ability of the larger machine has been retained; in fact, the TOPS CCS has expanded failure detection and recovery capability. A variety of advances arising from the years of work on the STAR computer that preceded the TOPS effort have been incorporated into its design.

The CCS operates at a clock frequency of 500 kHz. The CCS word is the same length as the STAR word, 32 bits. The word-processing cycle, ten byte-times long in the STAR computer, has been reduced to nine in the CCS: eight for processing or transferring information and one (two in STAR) for the messages and decision making between words. The execution (including fetch) of an instruction requires one to three cycles. The STAR instruction set with over 200 variants has been reduced to less than 100. To detect word errors, the CCS uses the same residue code as the STAR computer. Unlike the STAR, however, the CCS employs the residue encoding also for operation codes of instructions. In addition to these failure detection measures, the CCS incorporates dual control logic and clocking, memory address checking simultaneous with all memory accesses, and a nondestructive read-after-write option on all store instructions.

The CCS consists of the seven STAR computer functional units designated the COP, LOP, IOP, IRP, ROM, RWM, and TARP (Figure 14-2). The IO/IRP has been split into independent IOP and IRP units in order to improve failure detection and isolation in a completely unattended environment. The MAP is deleted because software multiplication and division are sufficient, while addition and subtraction are done in the LOP. Simplifications in the instruction set have resulted in reduced hardware in the COP, LOP, IOP, and IRP. Conversely, there is increased hardware in the RWM and TARP for added failure detection. A 4,096-word ROM and two 4,096-word RWM units constitute the program storage capability of the CCS. In addition, another 4,096-word RWM (designated SHM) is shared (by use of two independent ports) by the CCS and measurement processor subsystem (MPS). All the CCS RWM units are identical; any one of them can be assigned either as a CCS internal memory or as the SHM. The SHM contains the MPS operating program and the most recent samples of spacecraft variables gathered by the MPS. Because the SHM is available to the CCS as part of its own memory, these samples are conveniently available to it for fault diagnosis and monitoring of spacecraft activity [Gilley, 1970].

CURRENT RESEARCH

The research and development program which led to the STAR computer is continuing in several directions. The design of several improved second-generation STAR functional units is under way, including a new arithmetic processor, a control processor for medium-scale integrated-circuit implementation, and the shared READ-WRITE memory unit for the storage of automatic maintenance information from the spacecraft telemetry system. Analysis of automatic maintenance algorithms and design of a command/data bus for their implementation are under intensive study. Other current investigations are concerned with the following areas: 1) hardware-software interaction in a fault-tolerant system with recovery, especially the interaction of the TARP and the operating system; 2) studies of advanced recovery techniques, i.e., post-catastrophic restart, TARP replacement schemes, recovery from massive interference, partial utilization of failed units; 3) advanced component technology, especially methods to attain bus and power switch (i.e., hard core) immunity to faults; 4) heuristic studies of fault tolerance by interpretation of extensive experiments with the STAR breadboard as the instrument; 5) design of a second-generation STAR-type computer with universal processor and storage modules, and their implementation by large-scale integration; 6) computational utilization of the spare units for supplemental tasks in a multiprocessing mode.

At the present time it is evident that the STAR computer design and construction effort has led to valuable new insights into the problem of fault-tolerant computing; further results in this field are expected from the research program in the future.

ACKNOWLEDGMENT

The research and development of the STAR computer has been performed in the Spacecraft Computers Section of the JPL Astrionics Division, and recognition is due to most of the Section's members for support in their respective specialties. The STAR concept of computer architecture is due to A. Avižienis, who has directed the overall research effort. The hardware design is directed by D. A. Rennels, the software effort by J. A. Rohr, reliability analysis by F. P. Mathur, and the implementation of peripheral automatic maintenance by G. C. Gilley. Technical contributions to the design have been made by P. H. Sobel and A. D. Weeks, and consultation has been contributed by R. K. Caplette, E. Greenberg, G. R. Hansen, E. H. Imlay, G. R. Kunstmann, J. Nievergelt, J. J. Wedel, and L. J. Zottarelli. The STAR effort has been administered by J. R. Scull, W. F. Scott, and J. J. Wedel. The power switch has been developed by the Stanford Research Institute, Menlo Park, Calif., and a fault-tolerant READ-ONLY memory has been designed by the M.I.T. Instrumentation Laboratory, Cambridge, Mass., under subcontracts from JPL. Construction of the computer was performed by J. Buchok, J. L. Cline, N. B. Funsten, J. C. Schooler, and B. Stall. The design of the TOPS Control Computer is due to D. K. Rubin, with technical contributions by N. Deo, G. Milligan, and M. Vineberg. A special acknowledgment is due to R. V. Powell of the JPL Research and Advanced Development Program Office, and F. J. Sullivan, Director, Electronics and Control, J. L. East, J. I. Kanter, T. S. Michaels, and G. A. Vacca of the NASA Office of Advanced Research and Technology, Washington, D.C., for their continued support and encouragement of the STAR computer effort.

REFERENCES

Anderson and Macri [1967]; Avižienis [1967a, 1967c, 1968, 1971]; Avižienis et al. [1969]; Bouricius, Carter, and Schneider [1969a]; Flehinger [1958]; Gilley [1970]; Griesmer, Miller, and Roth [1962]; Kruus [1963]; Kuehn [1969]; Lewis [1963]; Long [1969]; Lyons and Vanderkulk [1962]; Mathur [1971a, 1971b]; Mathur and Avižienis [1970]; Reed and Brimley [1962]; Short [1968]; TOPS [1970].

Automatic Fault Protection in the Voyager Spacecraft

C. P. Jones

Abstract

Due to reliability requirements placed on the Voyager spacecraft design and a mission resulting in long two-way light time communication links, on-board automatic fault detection and correction capabilities are a significant feature of that spacecraft's design. Most of the protection to otherwise mission-catastrophic failures is implemented in the software of the Voyager's central computer, while some resides in an attribute control-dedicated processor. This paper will present the role that automatic fault protection plays in achieving Voyager's overall reliability, its design evolution, and how its design was validated during system testing. In-flight experience will also be described, and from the lessons learned therein, conclusions and recommendations will be drawn for the benefit of future designs.

INTRODUCTION

The Mission

In August and September of 1977, two Voyager spacecraft were launched on four-year-long missions to investigate Jupiter and Saturn, their many satellites, and the traversed interplanetary environment. Voyager 2 is targeted by navigators to eventually rendezvous with Uranus some additional four years after its encounter with Saturn. The planetary encounter phases are each 100 days long and are marked by a 30-day "observatory" phase during which regular, peri-

Jones, C.P., "Automatic Fault Protection in the Voyager Spacecraft," AIAA Paper No. 79–1919, American Institute of Aeronautics and Astronautics.

odic observations are made of the planetary system. The next 30 days, or "far-encounter" phase, include increased observations of the planet's satellites and spacecraft reorientation maneuvers for the purpose of calibrating the various fields and particles instruments. The "near-encounter" phase, typically five days in length, provides the most intense data gathering during the encounter. Experiments utilizing Sun and Earth occulations by the planet are conducted as well as high-resolution observations by the spacecraft's remote sensing instruments. A 30-day "post-encounter" phase follows during which the activity pace drops to that of the earlier far-encounter phase.

Between encounters, each spacecraft conducts the necessary calibration exercises to ready itself for the next encounter while the "cruise science" instruments (typically fields and particles) gather information about the interplanetary medium.

The Spacecraft

The Voyager spacecraft design is a product of (1) the early (pre-1970) Thermoelectric Outer Planets Spacecraft (TOPS) concept, characterized by substantial redundancy, and a Self-Test and Repair (STAR) computer; (2) hard fiscal constraints of the 1970s; and, to some extent, (3) the recognition that earlier Mariner and Viking-class spacecraft designs, while not boasting the autonomy or operational flexibility of the TOPS design, could, in fact, meet the mission requirements provided that concerns about their long lifetime reliability could be allayed.

At launch, the Voyager spacecraft consisted of a Mission Module and a Propulsion Module. The Propulsion Module was jettisoned approximately one hour after launch following its 45-second thrust period that placed the spacecraft on its interplanetary trajectory. The Mission Module (henceforth referred to as the spacecraft), shown in Figure 15-1, differs markedly in appearance from its Mariner and Viking predecessors. Its configuration is dominated by a 3.7-m

diameter high-gain antenna (HGA), used for transmitting the spacecraft's S-band and X-band data links and for receiving the S-band uplink. Power is provided by three radioisotopic thermal generators (RTGs) that, in combination, output approximately 430 watts at Jupiter and 400 watts at Saturn. The majority of the spacecraft's electronics are mounted within the 10-sided bus structure behind the HGA. Fields and particles science instruments are fixed-mounted on either the bus structure or on booms extending from it, while remote sensing instruments are mounted on a 2-degree-of-freedom articulable "scan platform."

ACHIEVING RELIABILITY

The task of maximizing total Voyager spacecraft system reliability within the constraints of mission return, cost, and scheduling was distributed among design analysis, design and fabrication practices, fault-tolerance design requirements, testing, and conservative in-flight operational practices.

The traditional failure modes, effects, and criticality analysis (FMECA) was performed on the engineering subsystem designs to help identify design weaknesses and access vulnerability to random part failures. Additionally, the radiation environment at Jupiter prompted further analysis of the radiation and electrostatic discharge susceptibility of the spacecraft design. These activities led to a modest amount of circuit redesign, a parts hardening and component shielding effort, and to the goal of achieving an "equipotential" spacecraft through surface-to-surface grounding. Finally, electronic components and structural elements were analytically tested to determine if they operated within specification over environmental (thermal, acoustic, vibration, and radio frequency interference) limits, and in the case of electronic components, over electrical interface operating margins (input voltage variations, conducted interface noise, etc.).

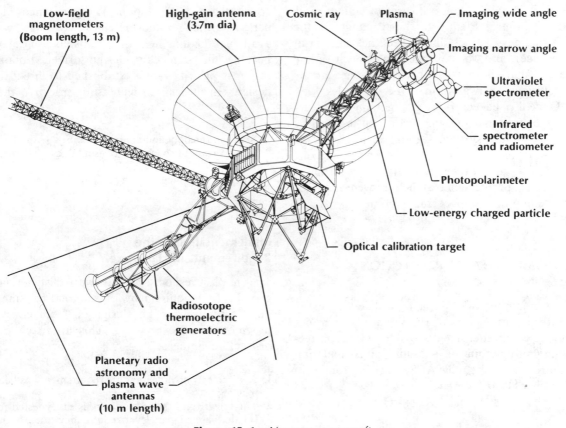

Figure 15–1. Voyager spacecraft.

Parts selection and screening, reliance on flight-proven designs where practical, a quality assurance program monitoring fabrication and assembly processes, and an underlying desire to "keep it simple" were significant aspects of the Voyager spacecraft reliability program.

Fault-tolerance, as a characteristic of the spacecraft system design, came about as a result of top-level design requirements on the system that were intended to (1) assure maximum fault-tolerance during mission-critical activities (during post-launch injection, at planetary closest approach, during off-Earth point maneuvers, etc.); (2) provide spacecraft safing in response to faults during unattended (nontracked) cruise; and (3) minimize the required ground support in the event of an on-board fault. The requirements

and their implementation had a profound effect on the spacecraft's hardware configuration and software design.

A comprehensive test program was conducted to validate the hardware and software designs. Each subsystem was first tested (in ambient conditions, then in a solar-thermal vacuum) to verify its performance and interface integrity. Next, each subsystem was integrated into the system, again with extensive validation of interface performance. Once the spacecraft was fully assembled and functionally validated, it was subjected to a rigorous set of environmental tests. Finally, the system, back in ambient conditions, performed operational sequences that demonstrated its mission readiness. The test program provided operating time on electronic systems, thereby weeding out cases of "infant mortality" failure, identified shortcomings in the software design (including that dedicated to fault tolerance), and substantiated that much of the design analysis that had been performed at the subsystem level was valid at the system level.

Once the spacecraft are in flight, only conservative operational practices can help protect the lifetime of the system. Careful management of consumables, a minimization of unit power on/off and thermal cycles, and strict monitoring of spacecraft performance all help prevent the foreshortening of the spacecraft lifetime.

AUTOMATIC FAULT PROTECTION DESIGN

The remainder of this paper will focus on the fault-tolerant aspects of the Voyager system design. A comprehensive discussion of fault protection wholly within the Attitude and Articulation Control Subsystem (AACS) can be found in Fleischer [1977].

Requirements

The top-level requirements referred to earlier include one whose intent was to eliminate from the design "all single-point failures" whose occurrence would result in the loss of all engineering data or the data from more than one science instrument. Any such failure prior to the spacecraft's Saturn encounter would be unacceptable. Obviously, the requirement had to be waived when considering primary structure, the HGA, the major elements of the Propulsion Module, and so on; but for electronic subassemblies the requirement was to be strictly adhered to. A second requirement dictated that whatever protection was to be provided had to be consistent with periods of unattended cruise, lasting up to 24 hours. This requirement applied primarily to

cruise phase safing responses; during encounter periods, when round-the-clock coverage was available, the long light time transmission delays became the significant design driver. Finally, response priorities were established to direct the design. In order of decreasing priority, they were:

1. Spacecraft safety and commandability
2. Preservation of spacecraft consumables
3. Downlink telemetry visibility
4. Ongoing sequence integrity

Implementation of the Requirements in Hardware

The simplest response the hardware designer can give to the requirement of eliminating single point failures from his design is to, of course, provide two of everything. This approach has distinct advantages:

1. It is patently obvious that the requirement has been met.
2. The integrity of the redundancy is easily tested for (in the case of part-level redundancy, there is no visibility beyond board-level testing).
3. Circuit designs are kept simple.
4. Where inherited designs are to be taken advantage of, it is considerably cheaper than adding part-level redundancy.

It was clear from the outset that the Voyager spacecraft would employ considerable redundancy. Of course, other steps were taken to achieve the same result. Designs were made to be as operationally independent as possible (e.g., subsystems were provided dedicated on/off relay interfaces with the power subsystem, and electrical interfaces between block redundant elements of two subsystems were cross-strapped, where practical, so that a failure in one subsystem did not require reconfiguration of another). Where critical decisions were to be made by hardware, majority logic was employed.

Implementation of the Requirements in Software

In most cases, adding redundant hardware doesn't provide fault tolerance. As a rule, redundant units are held in a de-energized, standby state and need to be powered on and, in some cases, initialized before they can perform their task of replacing a failed counterpart. One of the primary functions of the fault protection software then, is to manage the spacecraft's redundant elements. This management function includes determining if evidence of a problem exists, making the decision as to the appropriate action to be taken, and then affecting the action (executing the response). Table 15-1 itemizes those functions or subassemblies in which anomalous performance can trigger an automatic fault response. The table also shows the roles that hardware and software play in the detection-decision-action process of the various fault routines.

Table 15–1.   On-board redundancy and fault protection.

Function or Subassembly		Fault Protection			
		Detection	Decision	Action	Routine
RFS	Receiver	S/W	S/W	H/W	1
	S-band exciter	H/W	S/W	H/W	1,2
	S-band transmitter	H/W	S/W	H/W	1,2
	X-band exciter	H/W	S/W	H/W	1,2
	X-band transmitter	H/W	S/W	H/W	1,2
	Downlink frequency source	H/W	S/W	H/W	1,2
	Antenna control	S/W	S/W	H/W	1
MDS	Command detector unit	S/W	S/W	H/W	1
PWR	2.4 kHz inverter	H/W	H/W*	H/W & S/W	3
	System low voltage	H/W	H/W*	H/W & S/W	3
CCS	AACS PWR code response	S/W	S/W	S/W	5
	Processor	H/W & S/W	H/W & S/W	S/W	6
	Output unit	H/W & S/W	H/W & S/W	S/W	6
	Event timing	S/W	S/W	S/W	7
	Sequence abort	S/W	S/W	S/W	7
AACS	AACS processor	S/W	S/W	H/W & S/W	5
	AACS electronics	S/W	S/W	H/W & S/W	5
	Sun sensor	S/W	S/W	H/W & S/W	5
	Star tracker	S/W	S/W	H/W & S/W	5
	Attitude control thrusters	S/W	S/W	H/W & S/W	5**
	Gyros	S/W	S/W	H/W & S/W	5**
	Platform slewing	S/W	S/W	H/W & S/W	5
	CCS response to power codes	S/W	S/W	S/W	5
IRIS	IRIS standby heater units	H/W	S/W	H/W & S/W	4

* Majority voting circuits
**See Fleischer [1977].

Routine Name	Identifier	Routine Name	Identifier
CMDLOS	1	AACSIN	5
RFLOSS	2	ERROR	6
PWRCHK	3	TRNSUP	7
IRSPWR	4		

Before describing the fault routines, it is appropriate to establish an understanding of the hardware environment in which they operate.

COMMAND COMPUTER SUBSYSTEM FUNCTIONAL DESCRIPTION

The Command Computer Subsystem (CCS) serves as the central controller of the Voyager spacecraft. It is composed of two computers, each of which is used as an interrupt processor, reacting to periodic timing interrupts (hours, seconds, centiseconds, science data frame timing, command bit sync, etc.), and external level interrupts from other subsystems which are typically used to indicate external failures elsewhere in the spacecraft. Both processors have an 18-bit, plated-wire (hence nonvolatile) memory containing 4,096 words, half of which are "write protected" such that a "key" must be employed anytime this part of memory is to be altered. Fixed routines for command decoding and failure detection and correction are typical of the functions located in write-protected memory. The remaining half of the memory is used to load sequences which control the spacecraft's engineering and science subsystems during trajectory correction maneuvers, science data acquisition and transmittal, and various calibration exercises. Key system interfaces with CCS are shown in the block diagram in Figure 15-2.

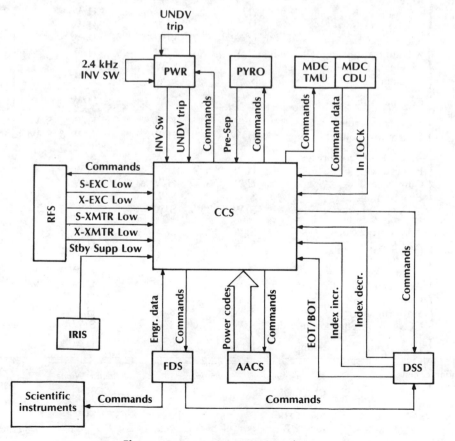

Figure 15–2.   CCS system interfaces.

CCS Routine Structure

The routine structure of the CCS has five essential parts.

1. Hardware receives levels and timing interrupts from other subsystems on the spacecraft.
2. Software preprocesses this data as *input*.
3. Software performs *intermediate processing*.
4. Software generates commands to other subsystems and telemetry as *output*.
5. Hardware generates switch closures or data patterns to other subsystems on the spacecraft.

The block diagram in Figure 15-3 depicts this structure. When a timing or level interrupt occurs, an element of sequence code (e.g., a command to be issued to another subsystem) or a fixed routine is executed. Following execution, the software returns to a "wait" state. During normal sequencing activity, the CCS is active (executing code) only a small percentage of the time.

FAULT-PROTECTION SOFTWARE

The Voyager fault-protection software exists within two subsystems; the CCS and the AACS. In the former, fault routines are initiated by interrupts received from external sources, and followed by the preprogrammed response. In AACS, however, fault routines are periodically executed and are always comparing current performance indicators against preprogrammed "norms." When an unfavorable comparison occurs, action is taken (see Fleischer [1977]).

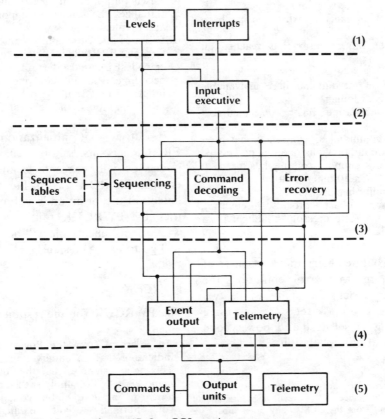

Figure 15–3. CCS routine structure.

Fault Protection in CCS

The fault routines resident in CCS are: ERROR, PWRCHK, RFLOSS, CMDLOS, IRSPWR, AACSIN, and TRNSUP.

Error

Whenever an abnormal condition (hardware or software) exists within the CCS, the ERROR routine is entered. The response generally is to place the CCS in a known, quiescent state. Reasons for ERROR entry are:

1. Hardware
   a. A low voltage condition exists.
   b. A primary command bit sync signal has been received before the previous one was processed.
   c. An attempt to write into protected memory without a memory-protect override has occurred.
   d. An execute of an execute instruction has been attempted.
   e. The processor bit generator has reached an illegal state.
2. Software
   a. The primary output unit has been unavailable for 14 seconds or longer.
   b. The self-test subroutine* has not executed correctly.
   c. A secondary command bit sync signal has been received before the previous one was processed.
   d. The sequencing support routine has been to activate more than 30 time/event tables.
   e. The output buffer has overflowed.
   f. During the launch phase a processor is counting relative to the other processor and Flight Data Subsystem (FDS).

Upon entry, the routine determines the source of the error and stores that error condition, the value of its hours clock, the status of its two interrupt registers, two mask registers, and three indicators relating to self-test and power code activity, and output unit availability.

---

* The self-test routine is primarily a software test of the hardware. It must be successfully executed before any commands are output from the CCS to any other subsystem.

If the rollback feature is enabled (rollback refers to the capability of *restarting* a predesignated portion of the sequence), then its particular time/event region is flagged to be restarted if and when the PWRCHK routine requests it. Next the ERROR routine:

1. Clamps the other processor and disables output units.
2. Terminates the following activities: command decoding; memory readout; sequence activity (except rollback); FDS/AACS memory load; power code processing (momentarily); and Data Storage Subsystem (DSS) tape positioning.
3. Clears the following: data received from the other CCS processor; output buffer data and not-available time counters; sequence support routine time and block schedules; FDS/AACS memory load pointers; power code processing and DSS tape positioning/active indicators; and, power low-voltage response enable.
4. Resets output and telemetry buffer pointers.
5. Initializes the sequence support routine counters and pointers.
6. Disables interrupts and unmasks the following interrupts: ERROR; DDS tape recorder inputs; power codes; internal interrupt; checksum; command decoding; demand read; one pulse per hour clock input; RFLOSS inputs; power inverter switch and IRSPWR inputs; and self-test.

If output unit initialization is enabled and ERROR has successfully reenabled itself and the power low-voltage response, and if the reason for entering ERROR was, in fact, a CCS tolerance detection trip or an undervoltage trip indication, then the PWRCHK routine is entered. Otherwise, the rollback table will be disabled and CCS will go to a WAIT state.

PWRCHK

The PWRCHK routine responds to either:

- An interrupt from the Power Subsystem (PWR), indicating that an undervoltage trip has occurred. This action signifies that the spacecraft power demand exceeds the supply such that the PWR can no longer maintain a DC bus voltage greater than 29.3 volts (normally 30 volts), or an AC bus voltage of 47.5 volts rms (normally 50 volts rms). Upon detecting this condition, PWR disconnects all nonessential loads (those not needed for commanding or assuring attitude control) and waits for the CCS, via PWRCHK, to restore the loads safely; or

· A CCS tolerance detector trip indicating that the CCS input power has dropped below a level where the processor can reliably function.

If the latter is the case, the PWRCHK response is to:

1. Assume that all other spacecraft loads have experienced power-on resets and issue mission phase-dependent reconfiguration commands as required.
2. Reset the CCS hardware clock.
3. Initiate the special rollback table, if present.
4. Enable RFLOSS and IRSPWR and initiate their execution.
5. Enable the celestial reference loss response portions of AACSIN.

6. Restart a search for celestial references if one was in progress at the time of PWRCHK entry.
7. Initiate the sequence abort/safing sequence, if enabled (e.g., during a trajectory correction maneuver, TCM).

If the PWRCHK entry is caused by an undervoltage trip, the response will depend on two other factors:

· Whether the PWR standby 2.4 kHz inverter has been selected.
· If a return to a science acquisition spacecraft state is desired.

The matrix in Table 15-2 describes the basic responses of PWRCHK in terms of the spacecraft loads switched, and the initiating event and the option override variable. In general, the

Table 15–2.   PWRCHK response matrix.

	PWRCHK Entry/Variables				
Function	Standby Inverter Selected	Override Option Set*	Override Option Reset	Tolerance Detector Trip	Undervoltage Trip During Launch
Radio transmitters	Redundancy selected Low power mode	Redundancy selected Low power mode	Redundancy selected Low power mode X-band off	No change	Powered off
Science instruments	No change	No change	Powered off	No change	No change
Science replacement heaters	No change	No change	Powered off	No change	No change
Tolerance detector trip responses 1–3	Yes	Yes	No	Yes	Yes
Tolerance detector trip responses 4–7	Yes	Yes	Yes	Yes	Yes

* PWRCHK automatically resets this variable after it is tested.

option override is set during far-, near-, and post-encounter phases and reset during cruise. During launch, a second variable is used to force all PWRCHK entries to be treated as one caused by a tolerance detector trip, thereby minimizing CCS activity during that critical mission phase.

Each time a power undervoltage trip signal is detected by the CCS, PWRCHK will increment a special undervoltage trip counter; likewise, a tolerance detector trip counter is provided. In addition, a "master counter" whose value is telemetered each hour by CCS is incremented by each PWRCHK entry, regardless of the cause. These counters provide useful data for subsequent ground-based fault analyses.

RFLOSS

The RFLOSS routine is designed to restore either the S-band or X-band (or both) downlinks subsequent to a failure of either an exciter or transmitter. Diode detectors within the Radio Frequency Subsystem (RFS) monitor the output power of the exciters and transmitters. Whenever the output power drops below a preset level the detector closes a switch. Any one or more of the four interrupts will cause RFLOSS to be entered and during the execution of the routine all four interrupts will be systematically interrogated.

Upon entry, the routine will first disable itself from reentry, increment the master counter, and then wait five seconds before processing the exciter interrupts. (This delay permits the routine to be tolerant of exciter interrupts produced at turn-on.) Following the five-second delay, the RFLOSS counter (ex post facto diagnostic trace) is incremented and the S-band exciter is checked. If the level indicates a failure, a command is issued to decouple the exciter's input frequency reference from the ground-transmitted uplink. This will eliminate the radio's voltage-controlled oscillator as a possible failure source. One second later, the RFLOSS counter is incremented again and the S-band exciter level rechecked. If still present, the routine will disable future entry into the S-band exciter interrupt subroutine and

issue the command to select the backup unit. The routine will then wait five seconds, increment the RFLOSS counter, and check the remaining three interrupt levels. Also, one second after the exciter switch, the S-band exciter level input is checked for the last time. If it still indicates a failed unit, the ultra-stable oscillator is turned off, thereby removing it as the last possible source of failure. At this point, the radio's auxiliary oscillator becomes the downlink frequency source.

The next interrupt level to be processed is that of the X-band exciter. If this interrupt indicates a failure, the routine will disable future X-band exciter failure checks and issue the command to select the redundant X-band exciter. If the failure indicator is still present one second later, the backup S-band exciter (the frequency source for the X-band exciter) is selected; future S-band exciter checks are then disabled.

After processing the exciter level inputs, the routine moves on to check first the S-band, then the X-band transmitter level inputs. As with the exciters, a delay (of five minutes) is provided to assure tolerance to the transmitter's turn-on characteristics. Following the five minute delay, if the S-band transmitter failure is indicated and it is the first such indication, the routine will select the redundant transmitter and proceed to the X-band transmitter check. If it is not the first indication, then the transmitters have already been switched and the suspected cause becomes the transmitter's input source, the S-band exciter. If the S-band exciter has not yet been switched, it will be at this time, future exciter switches will be disabled, and the routine will be reentered back at the five-second delay point (beginning). If the S-band exciter has already been switched, then the routine will inhibit future checks of the S-band transmitter interrupt, turn off the failed transmitter, and turn on the transmitter bay heater. The routine will then continue by processing the remaining X-band transmitter level interrupt in a manner identical to that for the S-band transmitter. Following this the routine is re-enabled and exited.

CMDLOS

The purpose of the Command Loss (CMDLOS) routine is to provide a means for the Voyager spacecraft to autonomously correct for a failure which is preventing the receipt of ground commands. Such failures can exist in the spacecraft's receiver (RCVR), command detector unit (CDU) of the Modulation/Demodulation Subsystem (MDS), or the CCS itself (which must do the actual command decoding). Additionally, misorientation of the spacecraft and, therefore, the narrow beamwidth HGA can lead to an inability to receive commands. Finally, the remote, yet possible, instance in which the receiver locks up on an RF spur being generated elsewhere within the RFS (i.e., the RF exciters or transmitters) is also a failure which must be protected against. Since the loss of commandability generally precludes any ground-based corrective action, the spacecraft is on its own in providing the needed protection. The only exception to this is the case in which one of the CCS's is unable to process command data it receives from the CDU. Should this happen, the ground merely needs to reformat the command so that it is executed by the other CCS. By having both CCS's always on-line, receiving and decoding the commands (only command execution need to be specified), protection against a single failure resulting in a permanent loss of commandability is provided.

Entry into the CMDLOS routine occurs when the CCS (each half independently) determines that a valid command has not been received in the last N hours, where N (typically 192 hours) reflects the current mission activity level and reliance on commandability. N is decremented by one each hour, but reset to its initial value each time the CCS successfully receives a command. If it ever underflows, CMDLOS is entered.

At the start of the routine, commands are issued to:

1. Decouple the downlink frequency source from the uplink.

2. Turn off S- and X-band ranging receivers.
3. Select the backup RCVR and CDU.
4. Issue a sun search command.

These commands reduce the chances of having the receiver false lock (1 and 2), select those units that are most likely the cause of the problem (3), and initiate a reorientation back to the Earth-line in the event that the spacecraft has lost its celestial references (4). The routine then waits six hours, at the end of which it checks to determine if a valid command has been received. If so, the routine is exited. If not, the low-gain antenna is selected, and after an additional six hours with no commanding, the following events occur:

1. Both S- and X-band transmitters are commanded to their low-power modes.
2. The heater for the transmitter electronics bay is turned on.
3. Commands to turn on the S- and X-band transmitters are issued.

These commands initialize the transmitter power/heater configuration so that subsequent events issued by CMDLOS do not result in too high a power demand from the spacecraft power subsystem or the subcooling of the transmitter electronics bay. (The yaw thruster hydrazine line thermally coupled to the bay could freeze, which would result in a loss of attitude control.) The rest of the events issued by CMDLOS are functionally identified in Tables 15-3 and 15-4, as the downlink configuration events and uplink configuration events, respectively. These events are issued in the following manner. The routine issues the first event from the downlink table, waits six minutes, then issues each of the events from the uplink table on six-minute centers. When the routine completes the uplink table it selects the next entry from the downlink table and cycles through the uplink table for a second time. This process continues until all the uplink events have been issued for all the downlink events. Before each uplink event during the above process, CMDLOS checks to determine if

Table 15–3. CMDLOS downlink configuration events.

1. Select S-band exciter #1.*
2. Select S-band transmitter #2.
3. Select S-band transmitter #2.
4. Select S-band transmitter #1.
5. Turn off X-band transmitter and exciter, turn on transmitter bay heater.
6. Turn off S-band transmitter and exciter.
7. Turn on S-band transmitter and exciter.
8. Turn on X-band transmitter and exciter, turn off transmitter bay heater and ultra-stable oscillator.
9. Turn on ultra-stable oscillator.

* All devices except the transmitter bay heater and ultra-stable oscillator have redundant power relays.

Table 15–4. CMDLOS uplink configuration events.

1. Select CDU B.*
2. Select RCVR #2.*
3. Select CDU A.*
4. Select HGA.
5. Dummy command
6. Select CDU B.*
7. Select RCVR #1.*
8. Select CDU A.*
9. Select LGA.
10. Dummy command
11. Dummy command

* These functions have redundant power relays.

a command has been received; if so, the routine is exited and the spacecraft is left in a commandable state. If not, the routine continues.

If no ground command has been received, the routine restarts the cyclic tables. This time, commands are issued to redundant relays to preclude any relay failure from preventing the attainment of a commandable spacecraft state. The routine will execute endlessly in this manner (redundant relays are selected only on even numbered cycles) until a command is received.

IRSPWR

The Infrared Interferometer Spectrometer and Radiometer Subsystems (IRIS) includes a Casse-grain optical system and interferometer subassembly whose temperatures are actively maintained by redundant proportional thermal controllers. If the operating thermal controller should fail, its standby redundant counterpart must be energized within two hours or the optics will supercool and become permanently misaligned. The purpose of the IRSPWR routine is to provide on-board selection of the IRIS standby heater unit should the prime unit fail. This routine is by far the simplest of all the fault routines aboard Voyager. Upon sensing a change in a level interrupt provided to CCS by IRIS (which indicates either a "normal" or "low" IRIS heater power supply voltage condition), the routine disables reentry, waits 60 seconds, increments the "master counter," and then examines the absolute state of the level input. If it is low, the prime supply is turned off, its backup turned on and the routine is exited (without re-enabling itself). If the level input is high, the routine re-enables itself and exits.

AACSIN

AACS Power Code Processing (AACSIN) controls the CCS half of the CCS/AACS power code interface. Power codes are of two types: functional and informational. Functional power codes are requests by AACS to have CCS issue specific commands to the power subsystem. There is a one-to-one relationship between functional power codes and power commands, and no intermediate processing is required other than formatting the power command. Informational power codes are issued by AACS when certain events occur in AACS for which the CCS has a "need to know." Those related to fault conditions are:

- Heartbeat
- Omen
- Celestial reference loss/acquistion
- Power supply fail
- Memory refresh fail
- Thruster branch fail
- Gyro fail

- Scan slew abort
- Command parity error
- Command sequence error
- Bad/no echo response
- TCM burn abort
- Turn complete

Heartbeat. As its name implies, the Heartbeat is a periodic ($\approx$ 2 seconds) signal from AACS to CCS whose presence is an indication of a healthy AACS processor. If a fault occurs (hardware or software) which stops the Heartbeat, then the CCS is programmed to take corrective action. Every ten seconds CCS checks for the reception of *any* power code. If none have occurred, CCS issues two self-test commands to AACS and disables commanding through the AACS hardware loader (normally not used). If two such events occur in one hour, CCS will repeat the response above, then select and initialize the redundant AACS electronics and processor.

Omen. The Omen power code triggers the CCS to store the next three non-Heartbeat power codes for the purpose of post-failure analysis. AACS issues this power code just prior to issuing each of the next nine power codes discussed below. The error-indicating power codes referred to later in the discussion of the Tandem and Turn Support Routine (TRNSUP) are all preceded by the Omen power code.

Celestial Reference Loss/Acquisition. Losses of the Sun reference cause the CCS to select the low-gain antenna (for possible uplink commanding while mispointed), slewing the platform so that its sensitive instruments are safely pointed at the calibration target and cannot view the Sun. Next, the FDS is commanded to an engineering-only data mode so that science instruments are placed in safe operating modes (high voltage off, etc.). The CCS then commands the AACS to execute a set of maneuver turns which will result in a 4π steradian search for the Sun. If the search is unsuccessful, the backup AACS processor and electronics are selected and the search is repeated. Upon Sun acquisition, the search pattern

terminates and the scan platform is slewed to a "neutral position," from which subsequent slew commands in the sequence can reposition it for science data taking.

Loss of the star reference results in selection of the low-gain antenna. Reacquisition causes a switch back to the high-gain antenna.

Power Supply, Memory Refresh, Thruster Branch, and Gyro Fail. These power codes do not result in any special processing, but because they are preceded by the Omen power code, they are stored for subsequent diagnostics.

Scan Slew Abort. The Scan Slew Abort power code indicates the AACS has been unable to complete a platform slew within some preset value of time. The possible reasons for this include:

- The platform has run up against a mechanical obstruction.
- The electronics controlling the platform actuator have failed.
- The present value was specified too low for that particular slew.

The CCS response to the power code is a function of how many have been received in one hour's time. The response is summarized in the table below. "L" is the software constant controlling the response.

Number of Aborts per Hour	Scan Slew Abort Response
$<L$	In-sequence scans are inhibited while the platform is slewed to a "neutral position." In-sequence scans are then enabled.
$=L$	The AACS electronics are switched.
$>L$	The routine is disabled from future entry, in-sequence scanning is inhibited, and the platform is commanded first to a "neutral position," then a "safe position."

Command Parity Error and Command Sequence Error. These commands do not result in any special processing, but like others preceded by the Omen power code, they are stored by CCS for subsequent readout and ground-based analysis.

Bad/No Echo Response. A feature of the AACS/CCS interface design is that CCS (through *one* of its processors designated as "prime for power codes") echoes back to AACS all the power codes it receives, except the Heartbeat and NOP (all zeros). When AACS discovers a mismatch between a previously sent power code and its echo, it issues the Bad/No Echo Response power code. The CCS response to this is to designate the *other* CCS processor as "prime for power codes," then echo the Bad/No Echo Response power code. Like the preceding power codes, this one is preceded by an Omen.

TCM Burn Abort and Turn Complete. These two informational power codes are used by the CCS routine TRNSUP. They each set an indicator which is tested by TRNSUP at "turn window open" and "turn window close" times (see the description of TRNSUP that follows).

TRNSUP. The Tandem and Turn Support Routine (TRNSUP) is employed whenever a spacecraft sequence is to be executed that requires maneuvering away from celestial references or includes a trajectory correction propulsive event. TRNSUP is loaded with the sequence as a utility routine and is called by the executing sequence to perform the following functions:

1. To issue CCS "tandem" events.
2. To check key fault indicators as a go/no-go test for subsequent sequenced events.
3. To check for proper maneuver turn durations.

Tandem Events. Tandem events issued by the CCS require that *both* CCS processors agree on the timing (within 900 msec) and content of the command data bits to be issued to the receiving subsystem (usually AACS). If either criterion is not met, the command is not issued, the executing sequence is halted, and a safing sequence is called. The function of the safing sequence is to assure that subsequent recovery data are recorded on-board, and that the spacecraft reacquire its celestial references.

Checking Key Fault Indicators. Whenever it is desired to check the status of fault indicators stored in CCS prior to executing an event, TRNSUP offers the option for the sequence to test for (a) prior celestial reference loss, (b) CCS tolerance detector trip status, and (c) error-indicating power codes from AACS.

If a prior reference loss has occurred, the sequence is terminated. If either a tolerance detector trip indication or an error-indicating power code trace is present, the sequence is terminated and the safing sequence is executed.

Maneuver Turn Duration. One final capability that the TRNSUP affords is checking the duration of maneuver turns. The sequence can be designed to call TRNSUP with a "turn window open" and a "turn window close" event. If TRNSUP determines that the TURN COMPLETE power code from AACS has been received at the window open time (too short a turn) or has not been received at window close time (too long a turn), the sequence is terminated, a turn abort command is issued to AACS, and the general safing routine is executed.

DESIGN VALIDATION

From the outset, when requirements were first being transformed into design concepts, the design validation process was at work. At each stage in the design of the fault algorithms (prose description, top-level flow chart, detailed logic flow, and finally, assembly language listing), the routines were analyzed for their completeness, efficiency, and mutual compatibility. Design groups spent hours working with failure models to see if the designs were adequate. Project reviews were conducted to scrutinize the philosophy, requirements, and designs of the routines and, in the process, they matured. Subsystem-level testing demonstrated their compatibility with their respective computers. Most productive of all were the tests conducted at the systems level, where all the hardware was integrated and operating, and the spacecraft were subjected to simulated faults. The matrix in Table 15-5 identifies to test personnel the minimum number of required tests to validate the fault protection software design and determine its launch and mission readiness. For each test, a procedure was written specifying:

1. The required initial conditions (spacecraft and support equipment).
2. A detailed test script, defining event timing, and required reporting during the test.
3. The expected final conditions following the test.

The combination of "initiating events" and "mission modes," again referring to Table 15-5, was selected to place the greatest demand on computer processing time and concurrently select failure situations that were either most likely to occur (e.g., undervoltage trips during phases of lowest power margin), or present the greatest risk to the mission (e.g., attitude control failures during TCMs).

Most "failures" during system test were induced via support equipment interfaces by either biasing failure-detecting circuits (in the case of RFLOSS tests), reducing the operating power margin (for PWRCHK tests), or by loading data into CCS or AACS memory corresponding to software-sensed failures. Only two tests, that for IRSPWR and the CCS tolerance detector trip, required special test circuitry at the spacecraft.

Verification of the proper failure response depended heavily on support equipment visibility into CCS and AACS with secondary reliance on the "traces" built into the routines for ex post facto diagnosis. Normal engineering telemetry, at 40 bits/second, was much too slow to see the fast-acting routines. In addition to simply verify-

Table 15–5. System test fault protection validation.

		Mission Mode Being Tested			
Routine*	Initiating Event	Launch	Cruise	TCM	Encounter
	CCS tolerance detector trip				x
PWRCHK	Inverter switch				x
	Undervoltage trip	x		x	x
	S-exciter fail			x	
RFLOSS	S-transmitter fail			x	
	X-exciter fail				x
	X-transmitter fail				x
IRSPWR	IRIS standby heater		x		
	Sun loss		x		
AACSIN	Canopus loss		x		
	Scan slew abort				x
	AACS processor fail	x		x	
CMDLOS	Command loss		x		
	Tandem error			x	
TRNSUP	Reference loss			x	
	Undervoltage trip			x	
	Omen power code			x	

* The ERROR routine was validated during CCS subsystem-level testing.

ing proper event timing, it was also required to assure that fault routines which were designed to operate independently from ongoing sequences did not interfere with sequence execution (or vice versa) and that routines which were designed to interrupt ongoing sequences, either restarted them properly (e.g., the launch sequence) or aborted them and safely secured the spacecraft (e.g., TCMs).

The tests demonstrated that the routine structures were sound but that in a few cases, subtle timing problems would require modifications to the design. Each time a change was made to the software, the test was rerun. Additionally, as hardware or software design changes were made (for other reasons), the routines were reviewed for impact, revised if needed, and then retested.

IN-FLIGHT EXPERIENCE

As of this writing, there have been several occurrences of in-flight execution of Voyager's fault protection routines. The causes for these events fall into three categories:

- An on-board failure or degraded performance was sensed and the appropriate routine was triggered.
- Unanticipated environmental factors, not accounted for in the design or use of the fault routines, led to unexpected fault algorithm execution.
- An error was committed in the sequence design process or in the conduct of the mission's real-time activities wherein the spacecraft's resulting performance appeared to be abnormal, and thus activated a routine.

Failures and Degraded Performance

Two examples in this category are the "stuck" scan platform on Voyager 1 and the failed receiver on Voyager 2. In each case, the fault routines (the Scan Abort portion of AACSIN and CMDLOS, respectively) executed properly, providing the needed safing and corrective action.

Environmental Factors

The Voyager fault routines were designed to be compatible with a spacecraft specified by its full set of design requirements. Some departures of the "as built" spacecraft from the design concept were uncovered during the test program and were either corrected or the software was modified to make accomodations where necessary. In two instances, however, tolerable, out-of-specification performance didn't become evident until after the first spacecraft was launched.

The incidents occurred near Earth. The Dry Inertial Reference Unit (DRIRU) CHECK routine (described in Fleischer [1977]) monitoring the spacecraft gyro performance during the ascent phase treated noise spikes induced by launch vehicle events as symptoms of a failing gyro. This resulted in several gyro swaps during the launch of Voyager 2 (launched first). The routine was disabled for the second launch. The second near-Earth event occurred as Voyager was jettisoning its propulsion module and deploying its RTG and science booms. Large tipoff rates, coupled with a reaction control system degraded by unexpected structural plume impingement, resulted in a swap of AACS thrusters, electronics, and processors. The backup system acquired its celestial references as required. For the second launch, the thruster monitoring routine was not enabled until time had passed to damp out tipoff-induced rates and null the associated position errors.

Sequence Errors

As discussed earlier, maneuver turn durations are checked by TRNSUP so that turns that are too short or too long result in a sequence abort and general spacecraft safing. Early in the mission, a sequence was designed in which a spacecraft yaw turn of 10 complete revolutions was to be executed. The acceptable turn duration checked on-board was determined by ground software based on the latest measured gyro scale factors, hence turn rates. Unfortunately, the data in the ground software were of insufficient accuracy. The difference between the actual yaw scale factor and the measured yaw scale factor was great enough (over the course of 10 revolutions) to cause the turn to last too long and abort the sequence. Subsequent gyro scale factor calibrations prevented this problem from recurring.

CONCLUSIONS AND RECOMMENDATIONS

Fault protection software, the automatic management of spacecraft redundancy, is key to the achievement of a reliable, fault-tolerant system design. It forms the bridge between a hardware configuration that is driven by a desire to maintain its simplicity, and strict mission reliability requirements, which lead to a highly complex spacecraft autonomy.

Hardware and design practice inheritance do not permit the designer to have sufficient flexibility to perform a classical top-down system design, one that reflects the "right mix" of hardware and software fault tolerance functions. But constraints like these also help bound the problem solutions and can force the evolution of fault protection software techniques. Fault protection software design must be compatible with the *actual* hardware operating characteristics. A design based on performance *specifications* needs to permit reasonable deviations from those specifications. In addition, failure thresholds should be set so that unacceptable performance triggers routine initiation, not just anomalous performance.

If a routine is to be active during any given mission phase, then it must be tested at the system level for proper operation during that phase. It should be demonstrated during the test that reasonable spacecraft operation does not invoke the routine. At the same time, the test must properly characterize or simulate the expected environment.

ACKNOWLEDGMENT

This paper presents the result of one phase of research carried out at the Jet Propulsion Laboratory, California Institute of Technology, under Contract No. NAS7-100, sponsored by the National Aeronautics and Space Administration.

REFERENCE

Fleischer [1977].

SIFT: Design and Analysis of a Fault-Tolerant Computer for Aircraft Control

John H. Wensley   Leslie Lamport   Jack Goldberg

Milton W. Green   Karl N. Levitt   P. M. Melliar-Smith

Robert E. Shostak   Charles B. Weinstock

Abstract

SIFT (Software Implemented Fault Tolerance) is an ultrareliable computer for critical aircraft control applications that achieves fault tolerance by the replication of tasks among processing units. The main processing units are off-the-shelf minicomputers, with standard microcomputers serving as the interface to the I/O system. Fault isolation is achieved by using a specially designed redundant bus system to interconnect the processing units. Error detection and analysis and system reconfiguration are performed by software. Iterative tasks are redundantly executed, and the results of each iteration are voted upon before being used. Thus, any single failure in a processing unit or bus can be tolerated with triplication of tasks, and subsequent failures can be tolerated after reconfiguration. Independent execution by separate processors means that the processors need only be loosely synchronized, and a novel fault-tolerant synchronization method is described. The SIFT software is highly structured and is formally specified using the SRI-developed SPECIAL language. The correctness of SIFT is to be proved using a hierarchy of formal models. A Markov model is used both to analyze the reliability of the system and to serve as the formal requirement for the SIFT design. Axioms are given to characterize the high-level behavior of the system, from which a correctness statement has been proved. An engineering version of SIFT is currently being built.

INTRODUCTION

This paper describes ongoing research whose goal is to build an ultrareliable fault-tolerant computer system named SIFT (Software Implemented Fault Tolerance). In this introduction, we describe the motivation for SIFT and provide some background for our work. The remainder of the paper describes the actual design of the SIFT system. The second section gives an overview of the system and describes the approach to fault tolerance used in SIFT. The third and fourth sections describe the SIFT hardware and software, respectively. The fifth section discusses the proof of the correctness of SIFT.

Motivation

Modern commercial jet transports use computers to carry out many functions, such as navigation, stability augmentation, flight control, and system monitoring. Although these computers provide great benefits in the operation of the aircraft, they are not critical. If a computer fails, it is always possible for the aircrew to assume its function, or for the function to be abandoned. (This may require significant changes, such as diversion to an alternative destination.) NASA, in its Aircraft Energy Efficiency (ACEE) Program, is currently studying the design of new types of aircraft to reduce fuel consumption. Such aircraft will operate with greatly reduced stability margins, which means that the safety of the flight will depend upon active controls derived from computer outputs. Computers for this application must have a reliability that is comparable with other parts of the aircraft. The frequently quoted reliability requirement is that the probability of failure should be less than 10^{-9} per hour in a flight of ten hours duration. A good review of the reliability requirements associated with flight control computers appears in Murray, Hopkins, and Wensley [1977]. This reliability requirement is similar to that demanded for manned space-flight systems.

A highly reliable computer system can have applications in other areas as well. In the past, control systems in critical industrial applications have not relied solely on computers, but have used a combination of human and computer control. With the need for faster control loops, and with the increased complexity of modern industrial processes, computer reliability has become extremely important. A highly reliable computer system developed for aircraft control can be used in such applications as well. Our objective in designing SIFT is to achieve the reliability required by these applications in an economic manner. Moreover, we want the resulting system to be as flexible as possible, so it can be easily adapted to changes in the problem specification.

When failure rates are extremely small, it is impossible to determine their values by testing. Therefore, testing cannot be used to demonstrate that SIFT meets its reliability requirements. It is necessary to *prove* the reliability of SIFT by mathematical methods. The need for such a proof of reliability has been a major influence on the design of SIFT.

Background

Our work on SIFT began with a study of the requirements for computing in an advanced commercial transport aircraft [Ratner et al., 1973; Wensley et al., 1973]. We identified the computational and memory requirements for such an application and the reliability required for the safety of the aircraft. The basic concept of the SIFT system emerged from a study of computer architectures for meeting these requirements.

The second phase in the development of the SIFT system, which has just been completed, was the complete design of the hardware and software systems [Wensley, 1972; Wensley et al., 1976]. This design has been expressed formally by rigorous specifications that describe the functional intent of each part of the system. A major influence during this phase was the Hierarchical Design Methodology developed at SRI [Robinson et al., 1976]. A further influence has been the need to use formal program proving techniques to ensure the correctness of the software design.

The current phase of the development calls for the building of an engineering model and the carrying out of tests to demonstrate its fault-tolerant behavior. The engineering model is intended to be capable of carrying out the calculations required for the control of an advanced commercial transport aircraft. SRI is responsible for the overall design, the software, and the testing, while the detailed design and construction of the hardware is being done by Bendix Corporation. The engineering model is scheduled to be built by the middle of 1979, with testing to be completed by the end of that year. Work is also continuing at SRI on proving the correctness of the system.

The study of fault-tolerant computing has in the past concentrated on failure modes of components, most of which are no longer relevant. The prior work on permanent "stuck-at-one" or "stuck-at-zero" faults on single lines is not appropriate for considering the possible failure modes of modern LSI circuit components, which can be very complex and affect the performance of units in very subtle ways. Our design approach makes no assumptions about the failure modes. We distinguish only between failed and nonfailed units. Since our primary method for detecting errors is the corruption of data, the particular manner in which the data are corrupted is of no importance. This has important consequences for failure-modes-and-effects analysis (FMEA), which is only required at the interface between units. The rigorous, formal specification of interfaces enables us to deduce the effects on one unit of improper signals from a faulty unit.

Early work on fault-tolerant computer systems used fault detection and reconfiguration at the level of simple devices such as flip-flops and adders. Later work considered units such as registers or blocks of memory. With today's LSI units, it is no longer appropriate to be concerned with such small subunits. The unit of fault detection and of reconfiguration in SIFT is a processor/memory module or a bus.

Several low-level techniques for fault tolerance, such as error detection and correction codes in memory, are not included in the design of SIFT. Such techniques could be incorporated in SIFT, but would provide only a slight improvement in reliability.

SIFT CONCEPT OF FAULT TOLERANCE

System Overview

As the name "Software Implemented Fault Tolerance" implies, the central concept of SIFT is that fault tolerance is accomplished as much as possible by programs rather than hardware. This includes error detection and correction, diagnosis, reconfiguration, and the prevention of a faulty unit from having an adverse effect on the system as a whole.

The structure of SIFT hardware is shown in Figure 16-1. Computing is carried out by the main processors. Each processor's results are stored in a main memory that is uniquely associated with the processor. A processor and its memory are connected by a conventional high bandwidth connection. The I/O processors and memories are structurally similar to the main processors and memories, but are of much smaller computational and memory capacity. They connect to the input and output units of the system which, for this application, are the sensors and actuators of the aircraft.

Each processor and its associated memory form a *processing module*, and each of the modules is connected to a multiple bus system. A faulty module or bus is prevented from causing faulty behavior in a nonfaulty module by the fault isolation methods described in the next section.

The SIFT system executes a set of *tasks*, each of which consists of a sequence of *iterations*. The input data to each iteration of a task are the output data produced by the previous iteration of some collection of tasks (which may include the task itself). The input and output of the

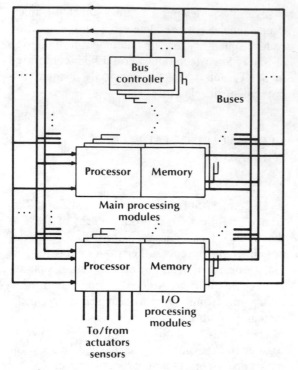

Figure 16–1. Structure of the SIFT system.

entire system is accomplished by tasks executed in the I/O processors. Reliability is achieved by having each iteration of a task independently executed by a number of modules. After executing the iteration, a processor places the iteration's output in the memory associated with the processor. A processor that uses the output of this iteration determines its value by examining the output generated by each processor which executed the iteration. Typically, the value is chosen by a "two out of three" vote. If all copies of the output are not identical, then an error has occurred. Such errors are recorded in the processor's memory, and these records are used by the executive system to determine which units are faulty.

SIFT uses the iterative nature of the tasks to economize on the amount of voting, by voting on the state data of the aircraft (or the computer system) only at the beginning of each iteration.

This produces less data flow along the buses than with schemes that vote on the results of all calculations performed by the program. It also has important implications for the problem of synchronizing the different processors. We must ensure only that the different processors allocated to a task are executing the same iteration. This means that the processors need be only loosely synchronized (e.g., to within 50 μs,), so we do not need tight synchronization to the instruction or clock interval.

An important benefit of this loose synchronization is that an iteration of a task can be scheduled for execution at slightly different times by different processors. Simultaneous transient failures of several processors will, therefore, be less likely to produce correlated failures in the replicated versions of a task.

The number of processors executing a task can vary with the task, and can be different for the same task at different times—e.g., if a task that is not critical at one time becomes critical at another time. The allocation of tasks to modules is in general different for each module. It is determined dynamically by a task called the global executive, which diagnoses errors to determine which modules and buses are faulty. When the global executive decides that a module has become faulty, it "reconfigures" the system by appropriately changing the allocation of tasks to modules. The global executive and its interaction with the individual processors is described in the fourth section.

Fault Isolation

An important property required in all fault-tolerant computers is that of fault isolation: preventing a faulty unit from causing incorrect behavior in a nonfaulty unit. Fault isolation is a more general concept than damage isolation. Damage isolation means preventing physical damage from spreading beyond carefully prescribed boundaries. Techniques for damage isolation include physical barriers to prevent propagation of mechanical and thermal effects and electrical barriers—e.g., high-impedance electrical connections and optical couplers. In SIFT, such damage isolation is provided at the boundaries between processing modules and buses.

Fault isolation in SIFT requires not only damage isolation, but also preventing a faulty unit from causing incorrect behavior either by corrupting the data of the nonfaulty unit, or by providing invalid control signals. The control signals include those that request service, grant service, effect timing synchronization between units, etc.

Protection against the corruption of data is provided by the way in which units can communicate. A processing module can read data from any processing module's memory, but it can write only into its own memory. Thus a faulty processor can corrupt the data only in its own memory, and not in that of any other processing modules. All faults within a module are treated as if they have the same effect: namely, that they produce bad data in that module's memory. The system does not attempt to distinguish the nature of a module fault. In particular, it does not distinguish between a faulty memory and a processor that puts bad data into an otherwise nonfaulty memory.

Note that a faulty processor can obtain bad data if those data are read from a faulty processing module or over a faulty bus. Preventing these bad data from causing the generation of incorrect results is discussed below in the section on Fault Masking.

Fault isolation also requires that invalid control signals not produce incorrect behavior in a nonfaulty unit. In general a faulty set of control signals can cause two types of faulty behavior in another unit.

- The unit carries out the wrong action (possibly by doing nothing).
- The unit does not provide service to other units.

In SIFT these two types of fault propagation are prevented by making each unit autonomous, with its own control. Improper control signals are ignored, and time-outs are used to prevent the unit from "hanging up" waiting for a signal that never arrives. The details of how this is done are discussed in the third section.

Fault Masking

Although a faulty unit cannot cause a nonfaulty processor to behave incorrectly, it can provide the processor with bad data. In order to completely mask the effects of the faulty unit, we must ensure that these bad data do not cause the processor to generate incorrect results. As we indicated above, this is accomplished by having the processor receive multiple copies of the data. Each copy is obtained from a different memory over a different bus, and the processor uses majority voting to obtain a correct version of the data. The most common case will be the one in which a processor obtains three copies of the data, providing protection from a single faulty unit.

After identifying the faulty unit, the system will be reconfigured to prevent that unit from having any further effect. If the faulty unit is a processing module, then the tasks that were assigned to it will be reassigned to other modules. If it is a bus, then processors will request their data over other buses. After reconfiguration, the system will be able to withstand a new failure—assuming that there are enough nonfaulty units remaining.

Because the number of processors executing a task can vary with the task and can be changed dynamically, SIFT has a flexibility not present in most fault tolerant systems. The particular application field—aircraft control—is one in which different computations are critical to different degrees, and the design takes advantage of this.

Scheduling

The aircraft control function places two types of timing requirements on the SIFT system.

- Output to the actuators must be generated with specified frequency.
- Transport delay—the delay between the reading of sensors and the generation of output to the actuators based upon those readings—must be kept below specified limits.

To fulfill these requirements, an iteration rate is specified for each task. The scheduling strategy must guarantee that the processing of each iteration of the task will be completed within the "time frame" of that iteration. It does not matter when the processing is performed, provided that it is completed by the end of the frame. Moreover, the time needed to execute an iteration of a task is highly predictable. The iteration rates required by different tasks differ, but they can be adjusted somewhat to simplify the scheduling.

Four scheduling strategies were considered for SIFT:

- fixed preplanned (nonpreemptive) scheduling;
- priority scheduling;
- deadline scheduling; and
- simply periodic scheduling.

Of these, fixed preplanned scheduling in which each iteration is run to completion, traditional in-flight control applications, was rejected because it does not allow sufficient flexibility.

The priority-scheduling strategy, commonly used in general-purpose systems, can meet the real-time requirements if the tasks with the fastest iteration rates are given the highest priorities. Under this condition, it is shown in Melliar-Smith [1977] that all tasks will be processed within their frames, for any pattern of iteration rates and processing times—provided the processing load does not exceed $\ln(2)$ of the capacity of the processor (up to about 70 percent loading is always safe).

The deadline-scheduling strategy always runs the task whose deadline is closest. It is shown in Melliar-Smith [1977] that all the tasks will be processed within their time frames provided the workload does not exceed the capacity of the processor (100 percent loading is permissible).

Unfortunately, for the brief tasks characteristic of flight-control applications, the scheduling overhead eliminates the advantages of this strategy.

The simply periodic strategy is similar to the priority strategy, but the iteration rates of the tasks are constrained so that each iteration rate is an integral multiple of the next smaller rate (and thus of all smaller rates). To comply with this requirement, it may be necessary to run some tasks more frequently than their optimum rate, but this is permissible in a flight control system. It is shown in Melliar-Smith [1977] that if the workload does not exceed the capacity of the processor (100 percent loading is possible), then simply periodic scheduling guarantees that all tasks will complete within their frames.

The scheduling strategy chosen for the SIFT system is a slight variant of the simply periodic method, illustrated by Figure 16-2. Each task is assigned to one of several priority levels. Each priority level corresponds to an iteration rate, and each iteration rate is an integral multiple of the next lower one. In order to provide very small transport delays for certain functions, and to allow rapid detection of any fault which causes a task not to terminate, the scheme illustrated in Figure 16-2 is modified as follows. The time frame corresponding to highest priority level (typically 20 ms) is divided into a number of subframes (typically 2 ms). The highest priority tasks are run in specific subframes, so that their results can be available to other tasks run in the next subframe, and they are required to complete within one subframe.

Processor Synchronization

The SIFT intertask and interprocessor communication mechanism allows a degree of asynchronism between processors and avoids the lockstep traditional in ultrareliable systems. Up to 50 μs of skew between processors can readily be accommodated, but even this margin cannot be assured over a ten-hour period with free-

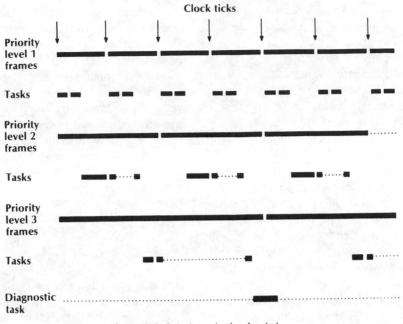

Figure 16–2. A typical schedule.

running clocks unless unreasonable requirements are imposed on the clocks. Thus, the processors must periodically resynchronize their clocks to ensure that no clock drifts too far from any other.

For reliability, the resynchronization procedure must be immune to the failure of any one clock or processor, and to a succession of failures over a period of time. In order to guarantee the high reliability required of SIFT, we cannot allow a system failure to be caused by any condition whose probability cannot be quantified, regardless of how implausible that condition may seem. This means that our synchronization procedure must be reliable in the face of the worst possible behavior of the failing component, even though that behavior may seem unrealistically malicious. We can only exclude behavior which we can *prove* to be sufficiently improbable.

The traditional clock resynchronization algorithm for reliable systems is the median clock algorithm, requiring at least three clocks. In this algorithm, each clock observes every other clock and sets itself to the median of the values that it sees. The justification for this algorithm is that, in the presence of only a single fault, the median value must either be the value of one of the valid clocks or else it must lie between a pair of valid clock values. In either case, the median is an acceptable value for resynchronization. The weakness of this argument is that the worst possible failure modes of the clock may cause other clocks to observe different values for the failing clock. Even if the clock is read by sensing the time of a pulse waveform, the effects of a highly degraded output pulse and the inevitable slight differences between detectors can result in detection of the pulse at different times.

In the presence of a fault that results in other clocks seeing different values for the failing clock, the median resynchronization algorithm can lead to a system failure. Consider a system of three clocks A, B, and C, of which C is faulty. Clock A runs slightly faster than clock B. The failure mode of clock C is such that clock A sees a value for clock C that is slightly earlier than its own value, while clock B sees a value for clock C that is slightly later than its own value. Clocks A and B both correctly observe that the value of clock A is earlier than the value of clock B. In this situation, clocks A and B will both see their own value as the median value, and therefore not change it. Both the good clocks A and B are therefore resynchronizing onto themselves, and they will slowly drift apart until the system fails.

It might be hoped that some relatively minor modification to the median algorithm could eliminate the possibility of such system failure modes. However, such hope is groundless. The type of behavior exhibited by clock C above will doom to failure any attempt to devise a reliable clock resynchronization algorithm for only three clocks. It can be proved that, if the failure-mode behavior is permitted to be arbitrary, then there cannot exist any reliable clock resynchronization algorithm for three clocks. The impossibility of obtaining exact synchronization with three clocks is proved in [Pease, Shostak, and Lamport, 1980]. The impossibility of obtaining even the approximate synchronization needed by SIFT has also been proved, but the proof is too complex to present here and will appear in a future paper. The result is quite general and applies not only to clocks, but to any type of integrator which is subject to minor perturbations as, for example, inertial navigation systems.

Although no algorithm exists for three clocks, we have devised an algorithm for four or more clocks which makes the system immune to the failure of a single clock. The algorithm has been generalized to allow the simultaneous failure of M out of N clocks when $N > 3M$. Here, we only describe the single-failure algorithm, without proving it correct. (Algorithms of this type often contain very subtle errors, and extremely rigorous proofs are needed to ensure their correctness.) The general algorithm, and the proof of its correctness, can be found in Pease, Shostak, and Lamport [1980].

The algorithm is carried out in two parts. In the first part, each clock* computes a vector of clock values, called the *interactive consistency vector*, having an entry for every clock. In the second part, each clock uses the interactive consistency vector to compute its new value.

A clock p computes its interactive consistency vector as follows. The entry of the vector corresponding to p itself is set equal to p's own clock value. The value for the entry corresponding to another processor q is obtained by p as follows.

1. Read q's value from q.
2. Obtain from each other clock r the value of q that r read from q.
3. If a majority of these values agree, then the majority value is used. Otherwise, the default value NIL (indicating that q is faulty) is used.

One can show that if at most one of the clocks is faulty, then: 1) each nonfaulty clock computes exactly the same interactive consistency vector; and 2) the component of this vector corresponding to any nonfaulty clock q is q's actual value.

Having computed the interactive consistency vector, each clock computes its new value as follows. Let δ be the maximum amount by which the values of nonfaulty processors may disagree. (The value of δ is known in advance, and depends upon the synchronization interval and the rate of clock drift.) Any component that is not within δ of at least two other components is ignored, and any NIL component is ignored. The clock then takes the median value of the remaining components as its new value.

Since each nonfaulty clock computes exactly the same interactive consistency vector, each will compute exactly the same median value. Moreover, this value must be within δ of the original value of each nonfaulty clock.

This is the basic algorithm that the SIFT processors will use to synchronize their clocks. Each SIFT processor reads the value of its own clock directly, and reads the value of another

---

* In the following discussion, a clock is assumed to be capable of logical operations. In SIFT, such a clock is actually a processor and its internal clock.

processor's clock over a bus. It obtains the value that processor r read for processor q's clock by reading from processor r's memory over a bus.

Reliability Prediction

A sufficiently catastrophic sequence of component failures will cause any system to fail. The SIFT system is designed to be immune to certain likely sequences of failures. To guarantee that SIFT meets its reliability goals, we must show that the probability of a more catastrophic sequence of failures is sufficiently small.

The reliability goal of the SIFT system is to achieve a high probability of survival for a short period of time—e.g., a ten-hour flight—rather than a large mean time before failure (MTBF). For a flight of duration T, survival will occur unless certain combinations of failure events occur within the interval T or have already occurred prior to the interval T and were undetected by the initial checkout of the system. Operationally, failures of the latter type are indistinguishable from faults that occur during the interval T.

To estimate the probability of system failure we use a finite-state Markov-like *reliability model* in which the state transitions are caused by the events of fault occurrence, fault detection, and fault "handling." The combined probability of all event sequences that lead to a failed state is the system failure probability. A design goal for SIFT is to achieve a failure rate of 10^{-9} per hour for a ten-hour period.

For the reliability model, we assume that hardware fault events and electrical transient fault events are uncorrelated and exponentially distributed in time (constant failure rates). These assumptions are believed to be accurate for hardware faults because the physical design of the system prevents fault propagation between functional units (processors and buses) and because a multiple fault within one functional unit is no more serious than a single fault. The model assumes that all failures are permanent (for the duration of the flight), so it does not consider transient errors. The effects of uncorrelated transient errors are masked by the executive system, which requires a unit to make multiple errors before it considers the unit to be faulty. It is believed that careful electrical design can prevent correlation of transient errors between functional units. The execution of critical tasks in "loose" synchronism also helps protect against correlation of fast transient errors. Failure rates for hardware have been estimated on the basis of active component counts, using typical reliability figures for similar hardware. For the main processors, we obtain the rate 10^{-4} per hour; for I/O processors and buses, we obtain 10^{-5} per hour.

For a SIFT system with about the same number of main processing modules, I/O processing modules, and buses, it can be shown that the large difference in failure rates between a main processing module and an I/O processing module or bus implies that we need only consider main processing module failures in our calculations. We can therefore let the state of the system be represented in the reliability model as a triple of integers (h, d, f) with $h \leqslant d \leqslant f$, where such a state represents a situation in which f failures of individual processors have occurred, d of those failures have been detected, and h of these detected failures have been "handled" by reconfiguration. There are three types of possible state transition.

- $(h, d, f) \rightarrow (h, d, f + 1)$, representing the failure of a processor
- $(h, d, f) \rightarrow (h, d + 1, f)$, $d < f$, representing the detection of a failure
- $(h, d, f) \rightarrow (h + 1, d, f)$, $h < d$, representing the handling of a detected failure

This is illustrated in Figure 16-3.

The first two types of transition—processor failure and failure detection, represented in Figure 16-3 by straight arrows—are assumed to have constant probabilities per unit time. However, the third type of transition—failure handling, represented in Figure 16-3 by wavy

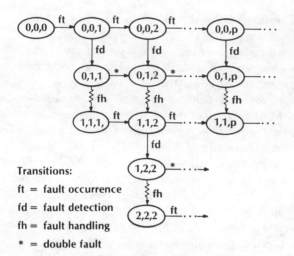

Transitions:
ft = fault occurrence
fd = fault detection
fh = fault handling
* = double fault

Figure 16–3. The reliability model.

arrows—represents the completion of a reallocation procedure. We assume that this transition must occur within some fixed length of time τ.

A state (h, d, f) with $h < d$ represents a situation in which the system is reconfiguring. To make the system immune to an additional failure while in this state is a difficult problem, since it means that the procedure to reconfigure around a failure must work despite an additional, undetected failure. Rather than assuming that this problem could be solved, we took the approach of trying to insure that the time τ that the system remains in such a state is small enough to make it highly unlikely for an additional failure to occur before reconfiguration is completed. We therefore made the pessimistic assumption that a processor failure which occurs while the system is reconfiguring will cause a system failure. Such

Table 16–1. Failure probabilities for a 5-processor system. ($T = 10$ hours.)

Failure Cause	Failure Probability
Exhaustion of spares	5×10^{-12}
Double fault ($\tau = 100$ ms.)	7×10^{-11}
Double fault ($\tau = 1$ sec.)	7×10^{-10}

failures are represented by the "double-fault" transitions indicated by asterisks in Figure 16-3. In our calculations, we assume that each of these transitions results in a system failure.

We have calculated the probability of system failure through a double fault transition, and also through reaching a state with fewer than two nonfaulty processors, for which we say that the system has failed because it has "run out of spares."* A brief summary of these failure probabilities for a five processor system is shown in Table 16-1.

THE SIFT HARDWARE

The SIFT system attempts to use standard units whenever possible. Special design is needed only in the bus system and in the interfaces between the buses and the processing modules.

The major parameters of the SIFT system are shown in Table 16-2. The column heading "Engineering Model" indicates the system intended for initial construction, integration, and testing. The column heading "Maximum" indicates the limits to which the engineering model can be expanded with only the procurement of additional equipment.

As described in the previous section, the fault-tolerant properties of SIFT are based on the interconnection system between units and upon the software system. The particular design of the processors and memories is irrelevant to our discussion of fault tolerance. We merely mention that the main processors and memories are based on the BD*micro*X computer—a modern, LSI-based 16-bit computer designed and manufactured by Bendix Corporation specifically for avionics or similar applications. The I/O processors are based upon the well-known 8080 microprocessor architecture.

To help the reader understand the operation

---

* The probability of system failure because of multiple *undetected* faults has not been computed precisely, but is expected to be comparable to the double fault values.

Table 16–2. Major parameters of the SIFT system, engineering model.

System Parameters	Engineering Model	Maximum
Main processors	5*	8
Main memories	5	8
I/O processors	5	8
I/O memories	5	8
Buses	5	8
External interfaces	5	8
Main processors		
Word length	16 bits	Same
Addressing capability	32K words	64K
Speed	500K IPS	Same
Arithmetic modes	Fixed point	Same
	Double length	
	Floating point	
Type	Bendix BDμ	Same
Main Memories		
Word length	16 bits	Same
Capacity	32K words	64K
Type	Semiconductor RAM**	Same
I/O Processors		
Word length	8 bits	Same
Type	Intel 8080	Same
I/O Memories		
Word length	8 bits	Same
Capacity	4K bytes	Same
Buses		
Speed	< 10 microsec. per word	Same
	Bit serial	
I/O Interfaces		
Type	1553A MILSTD	Same

* In addition, a spare unit of each type is to be built.
**Program memory would be read only memory (ROM) for actual flight use.

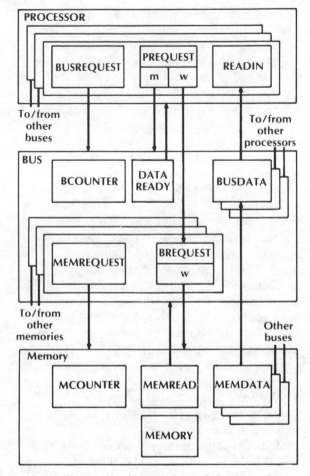

Figure 16–4. An abstract view of data transfers.

of the units and their interaction with one another, we describe the operation of the interconnection system in abstract terms. Figure 16-4 shows the connections among processors, buses, and memories. The varying replications of these connections are shown for each type of unit. Within each unit are shown a number of abstract registers that contain data or control information. Arrows that terminate at a register indicate the flow of data to the register. Arrows that terminate at the boundary of a unit indicate control signals for that unit.

We explain the operation of the interconnection system by describing how a processor *p* reads a word of data from location *w* of memory *m* via bus *b*. We assume normal operation, in which no errors or time-outs occur. Processor *p* initiates the READ operation by putting *m* and *w* into the register PREQUEST (p, b). Note that every processor has a separate PREQUEST register for each bus to which it is connected. When this register is loaded, a BUSREQUEST line is set to request attention from the appropriate bus. The processor must now wait until the requested bus and memory units have completed their part of the operation.

Each bus unit contains a counter-driven scanner that continuously scans the PREQUEST and BUSREQUEST lines from processors. When the scanner finds a processor that requires its attention (BUSREQUEST high), it stops and the bus is said to have been *seized* by that processor. The bus's counter then contains the identifying number of the processor that has seized it. When seized, the bus transfers the value *w* from the processor to a register connected to memory *m*. When this transfer has been completed, the MEMREQUEST line is raised calling for attention from the memory. The bus then waits for the memory to complete its actions.

Memory units contain counter-driven scanners that operate in the same manner as those in the bus units—i.e., they continuously scan all buses to determine which of them (if any) is requesting service. When a request is detected, the memory is said to be seized, and it reads the value *w* from the bus. The memory then reads the contents of its location *w* into MEMDATA register, and raises the MEMREAD line to inform the bus that the data are available. The memory leaves the state of MEMDATA and MEMREAD unchanged until it detects that the MEMREQUEST line from the bus has dropped, indicating that the bus has received the data from the MEMDATA register. The memory then drops the MEMREAD line and resumes scanning the buses for futher requests.

When the bus detects that the MEMREAD line from the memory is up, it transfers the data in the MEMDATA register to the BUSDATA register,

drops the MEMREQUEST line, and raises the DATAREADY line—indicating to the processor that the data are available. The bus leaves the state of the BUSDATA and DATAREADY lines unchanged until it detects that the BUSREQUEST line from the processor has dropped, indicating that the processor has received the data word. The bus then drops the DATAREADY line and resumes scanning the processors for further requests.

Meanwhile, the processor that made the original request has been waiting for the DATAREADY line to be raised by the bus, at which time it reads the data from the BUSDATA register. After completing this read, it drops the BUSREQUEST line and continues with other operations.

These actions have left the units in their original states. They are therefore ready to take part in other data transfer operations.

The precise behavior of the units can be described by abstract programs. Table 16-3 is an abstract program for the processor to bus interface unit.* It shows the unit's autonomous control, and the manner in which the unit requests service. Note how time-outs are used to prevent any kind of bus or memory failure from "hanging up" the unit. Abstract programs for the other units are similar.

The interconnection system units designed especially for the SIFT system are:

1. the processor-to-bus interfaces;
2. the buses;
3. the bus-to-memory interfaces.

These units all operate autonomously and contain their own control, which is implemented as a simple microprogrammed controller. For example, the bus control scanner that detects the processors' requests for service is controlled by a microprogram in a programmable read-only memory (PROM). The contents of this PROM are used for two purposes: first, part of the data is fed back to the PROM's address register to determine which word of the PROM is to be read next; second, part of the data is used as

---

* This program is only meant to illustrate the unit's main features; it does not accurately describe the true behavior of the unit.

Table 16–3. Abstract program for processor-to-bus interface unit.

Data:
  READIN(p,b)
  A set of registers, one for each bus b, that receive data read from another processor.

  PREQUEST(p,b)
  A set of registers, one for each bus b, that hold the parameters of a request to read one word from another module's memory over that bus.

  BUSREQUEST(p,b)
  A set of booleans that indicate a request from bus b.

  ———

  A constant that is the maximum time a processor will wait for a bus action.

  BUS FAIL(p,b)
  A boolean indicating that processor p timed-out before receiving data from bus b.

External Data (generated by other units):
  DATAREADY, BUSDATA from BUS module

Abstract Program:
  REQUEST(p,b) := m,w
  D := REALTIME
  WAIT ON (DATAREADY (b) OR REALTIME > (D + - - -))
  IF DATA READY (b)
    THEN BEGIN READIN(p,b) := BUSDATA(b)
              BUSREQUEST(p,b) := FALSE
              WAIT ON ((DATA READY = FALSE)
                  OR (REALTIME > (D + - - -))
    END
  ELSE BEGIN BUS REQUEST := FALSE
            BUSFAIL(p,b) := TRUE
    END

logic signals that control the operation of the unit in which the PROM resides. For example, this second part could contain data to open gates to allow the flow of information from one unit to another. Input signals to the controller are applied to some of the bits of the PROM's address register, thereby affecting which PROM words are read.

The interface units (items 1 and 3 above) consist mainly of a few registers, the controller, and the gates necessary to effect the data flow. The bus with its controller (item 2) contains a larger set of such gates, since each bus can allow data flow from every memory to every processor. We estimate that the complexity of a bus unit,

consisting of a bus together with all its interfaces, is about 10 percent of that of a main processing module. The logical structure is such that an LSI version of an entire bus unit will be practical for future versions of SIFT. However, the engineering model will be a mixture of LSI and MSI (medium scale integration) technology.

The design of the interfaces permits simultaneous operation of all units. For example, a processor can simultaneously read data from its memory and from another memory, while at the same time another processor is reading from the first processor's memory. Such simultaneous operation is limited only by contention at a memory unit. This contention is handled by conventional cycle-stealing techniques and causes little delay, since the memory cycle time is small (250 ns) compared to the time needed to transfer a full word through the bus (10 μs).

Since several processors may attempt to seize the same bus, or several buses may attempt to seize the same memory, a processor can have to wait for the completion of one or more other operations before receiving service. Such waiting should be insignificant because of the small amount of data that is transmitted over the buses.

THE SOFTWARE SYSTEM

The software of SIFT consists of the application software and the executive software. The application software performs the actual flight control computations. The executive software is responsible for the reliable execution of the application tasks, and implements the error detection and reconfiguration mechanisms discussed in the second section. Additional support software to be run on a large support computer is also provided.

From the point of view of the software, a processing module—with its processor, memory, and associated registers—is a single logical unit. We will therefore simply use the term "processor" to refer to a processing module for the rest of the paper.

The Application Software

The application software is structured as a set of iterative tasks. As described in the subsection on Scheduling, each task is run with a fixed iteration rate which depends upon its priority. The iteration rate of a higher priority task is an integral multiple of the iteration rate of any lower priority task. Every task's iteration rate is a simple fraction of the main clock frequency.

The fact that a task is executed by several processors is invisible to the application software. In each iteration, an application task obtains its inputs by executing calls to the executive

software. After computing its outputs, it makes them available as inputs to the next iteration of tasks by executing calls to the executive software. The input and output of a task iteration will consist of at most a few words of data.

The SIFT Executive Software

Formal specifications of the executive software have been written in a rigorous form using the SPECIAL language [Robinson and Roubine, 1977] developed at SRI. These formal specifications are needed for the proof of the correctness of the system discussed in the next section. Moreover, they are also intended to force the designer to produce a well-structured system. Good structuring is essential to the success of SIFT. A sample of these SPECIAL specifications is given in the Appendix. The complete formal specification is omitted from this paper. Instead, we informally describe the important aspects of the design.

The SIFT executive software performs the following functions:

1. run each task at the required iteration rate;
2. provide correct input values for each iteration of a critical task (masking any errors);
3. detect errors and diagnose their cause;
4. reconfigure the system to avoid the use of failed components.

To perform the last three functions, the executive software implements the techniques of redundant execution and majority voting described in the second section. The executive software is structured into three parts:

- the global executive task;
- the local executive;
- the local-global communicating tasks.

One global executive task is provided for the whole system. It is run just like a highly critical application task—being executed by several processors and using majority voting to obtain the output of each iteration. It diagnoses errors to decide which units have failed, and determines the appropriate allocation of tasks to processors.

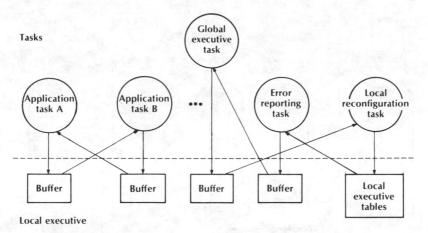

Figure 16–5. Logical structure of the SIFT software system.

Each processing module has its own local executive and local-global communicating tasks. The local-global communicating tasks are the error reporting task and the local reconfiguration task. Each of these tasks is regarded as a separate task executed on a single processor rather than as a replication of some more global task, so there are as many separate error reporting tasks and local reconfiguration tasks as there are processors.

Figure 16-5 shows the logical structure of the SIFT software system. The replication of tasks and their allocation to processors is not visible. Tasks communicate with one another through buffers maintained by the local executives. Note that the single global executive task is aware of (and communicates with) each of the local executives, but that the local executives communicate only with the single (replicated) global executive task and not with each other. In this logical picture, application tasks communicate with each other and with the global executive, but not with the local executives.

Figures 16-6 and 16-7 show where the logical components of Figure 16-5 actually reside within SIFT. Note how critical tasks are replicated on several processors. For the sake of clarity, many of the paths by which tasks read buffers have been eliminated from Figures 16-6 and 16-7.

The Local-Global Communicating Tasks

Each processor runs its local reconfiguration task and error reporting task at a specified frequency, just like any other task. These two tasks communicate with the global executive via buffers.

The local executive detects an error when it obtains different output values for the same task iteration from different processors.* It reports all such errors to the error reporting task. The error reporting task performs a preliminary analysis of these errors, and communicates its results to the global executive task. These results are also used by the local executive to detect possibly faulty units before the global executive has diagnosed the errors. For example, after several error reports involving a particular bus, the local executive will attempt to use other buses in preference to that one until the global executive has diagnosed the cause of the errors.

The local reconfiguration task maintains the tables used by the local executive to schedule the execution of tasks. It does this using information provided to it by the global executive.

The interaction of the global executive and the local-global communicating tasks is shown in Figure 16-8.

* It can also detect that a time-out occurred while reading from the memory of another processing module.

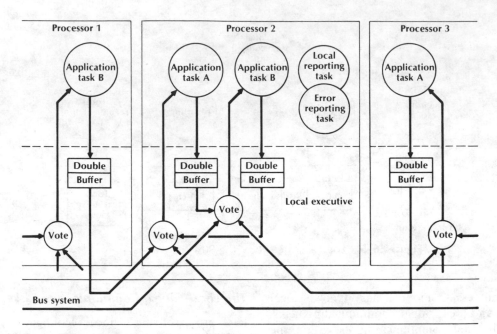

Figure 16–6. Arrangement of application tasks within SIFT configuration.

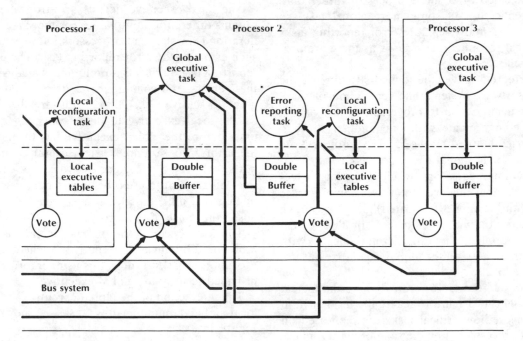

Figure 16–7. Arrangement of executive within SIFT configuration.

1. Error handler in each processor puts reports in error table.
2. Error reporter task in each processor reads error table and decides what conditions to report to the global executive. This report is put in a buffer.
3. Global executive (triplicated) reads each processor's buffer over three buses (to guard against bus errors) and votes for a plurality.
4. Global executive, using the diagnosis provided by the error reporter, determines what reconfiguration, if any, is necessary. If a reconfiguration is necessary, a report is put in a buffer.
5. Local reconfiguration task in each processor reads report from each of the global executive buffers and votes to determine plurality.
6. Local reconfiguration task changes the scheduling table to reflect the global executive's wishes.

Figure 16–8. Error reporting and reconfiguration.

The Global Executive Task

The global executive task uses the results of every processor's error task to determine which processing modules and buses are faulty. The problem of determining which units are faulty is discussed in the subsection on Fault Detection below. When the global executive decides that a component has failed, it initiates a reconfiguration by sending the appropriate information to the local reconfiguration task of each processor. The global executive may also reconfigure the system as a result of directives from the application tasks. For example, an application task may report a change of flight phase which changes the criticality of various tasks.

To permit rapid reconfiguration, we require that the program for executing a task must reside in a processor's memory before the task can be allocated to that processor. In the initial version of SIFT, there will be a static assignment of programs to memories. The program for a critical task will usually reside in all main processor memories, so the task can be executed by any main processor.

The Local Executive

The local executive is a collection of routines to perform the following functions: 1) run each task allocated to it at the task's specified iteration rate; 2) provide input values to, and receive output values from each task iteration, and 3) report errors to the local executive task.

A processor's local executive routine can be invoked from within that processor by a call from a running task, by a clock interrupt, or by a call from another local executive routine. There are four types of routines:

- error handler;
- scheduler;
- buffer interface routines;
- voter.

The *error handler routine* is invoked by the voter when an error condition is detected. It records the error in a *processor/bus error table*, which is used by the error reporting task described above.

The *scheduler routine* is responsible for scheduling the execution of tasks. Every task is run at a prespecified iteration rate that defines a sequence of time frames within which the task must be run. (For simplicity, we ignore the scheduling of the highest priority tasks in subframes that was mentioned in the subsection on Scheduling above.) A single iteration of the task is executed within each of its frames, but it may be executed at any time during that frame.

The scheduler is invoked by a clock interrupt or by the completion of a task. It always runs the highest priority task allocated to the processor that has not yet finished executing the iteration for its current time frame. Execution of a task may be interrupted by the clock, in which case its state is preserved until execution is resumed—possibly after the execution of a higher priority task. A task that has completed its current iteration is not executed again until after the start of its next time frame.

The *buffer interface routines* are invoked by a

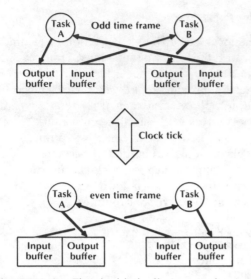

Figure 16–9. The double buffering mechanism.

task when it generates output for an iteration. These routines put the output into a buffer reserved for that task. These output values are used by the voter routines described below to obtain input for the tasks. Because a task may be run at any time during its time frame, the double-buffering scheme shown in Figure 16-9 is used. Each buffer consists of a double buffer. In any one time frame, one of the buffers is available for new data being generated by the task while the other contains the data generated last time frame. It is the latter values that are used to provide input to other tasks (and possibly to the same task). At the start of the next time frame, the buffers are switched around. Provision is also made for communication between processors operating at different frequencies.

The *voter routine* is invoked by a task to obtain the inputs for its current iteration. The task requests a particular output from the previous iteration of second task—which may be the same task. The voter uses tables provided by the local reconfiguration task to determine what processors contain copies of that output, and in which of their buffers. It reads the data from each of these buffers and performs a majority vote to obtain a single value. If all the values do

not agree, then an error has occurred, and the error reporter is called.

Fault Detection

Fault detection is the analysis of errors to determine which components are faulty. In SIFT, fault detection is based upon the processor/bus error table, an m by n matrix, where m is the number of processors and n the number of buses in time system. Each processor has its own processor/bus error table that is maintained by its local executive's error handler. An entry $Xp[i,j]$ in processor p's table represents the number of errors detected by processor p's local executive that involve processor i and bus j. Suppose that processor p is reading from processor q using bus r. There are five distinct kinds of errors that cause a matrix value to change:

1. the connection from bus r to processor q is faulty;
2. the connection from processor p to bus r is faulty;
3. bus r is faulty;
4. processor q is faulty;
5. processor p is faulty.

Processor p's error reporting task analyzes the processor/bus error table as follows to determine if any of these cases hold. Let $e > 0$ be a threshold of errors that will be tolerated for any processor/bus combination. It can deduce that case 1 holds if the following conditions all hold: (1) $Xp[q,r] > e$, (2) there exists a bus j such that $Xp[q,j] \leqslant e$, and (3) there exists a processor i such that $Xp[i,r] \leqslant e$. Either case 2 or 3 may hold if $Xp[i,r] > e$ for all active processors i. These two cases can only be distinguished by the global executive task, which has access to information from all the processors. (Case 3 holds if all active processors report bus r faulty; otherwise case 2 holds.) The error handler can deduce that case 4 holds if $Xp[q,j] > e$ for all active buses j. The error handler cannot be depended upon to diagnose case 5, since the failure of the processor executing it could cause the error handler to decide that any (or none) of the other four cases hold.

Once the error handler has performed this analysis, the appropriate action must be taken. In case 1, processor p will stop using bus r to talk to processor q. In cases 2 and 3, processor p will stop using bus r, and will report to the global executive that bus r is faulty. In case 4, processor p will report to the global executive that processor q is faulty.

The global executive task makes the final decision about which unit is faulty. To do this, it reads the faulty processor reports provided by the error reporting task. If two or more processors report that another processor is faulty, then the global executive decides that this other processor has indeed failed. If two or more processors report that a bus is faulty, then the global executive decides that the bus has failed.

The global executive may know that some unit produced errors, but be unable to determine which is the faulty unit. In that case, it must await further information. It can obtain such information by allocating the appropriate diagnostic tasks. If there is a faulty unit (and the error reports were not due to transient faults), then it should obtain the necessary information in a short time.

It can be shown that in the presence of a single fault, the above procedure cannot cause the global executive to declare a nonfaulty unit to be faulty. With the appropriately "malicious" behavior, a faulty unit may generate error reports without giving the global executive enough information to determine that it is faulty. For example, if processor p fails in such a way that it gives incorrect results only to processor q, then the global executive cannot decide whether it is p or q that is faulty. However, the majority voting technique will mask these errors and prevent a system failure.

The Simulator

An initial version of the SIFT system has been coded in PASCAL. Since the avionics computer is not available at this time, the executive is being debugged on an available general-purpose computer (a DEC PDP-10). To facilitate this, a simulator has been constructed. The simulator uses five asynchronous processes, each running a SIFT executive and a "toy" set of application tasks. The controlling process simulates the actions of the SIFT bus system and facilitates interprocess communications. Faults are injected, either at the processor or the bus levels, and a visual display of the system's behavior is provided. This gives us a means of testing software in the absence of the actual SIFT hardware.

THE PROOF OF CORRECTNESS

Concepts

Estimates of the reliability of SIFT are based upon the assumption that the software operates correctly. Since we know of no satisfactory way to estimate the probability that a piece of software is incorrect, we are forced to try to guarantee that the software is indeed correct. For an asynchronous multiprocess system such as SIFT, the only way to do this is to give a rigorous mathematical proof of its correctness.

A rigorous proof of correctness for a system requires a precise statement of what it means for the system to be correct. The correctness of SIFT must be expressed as a precise mathematical statement about its behavior. Since the SIFT system is composed of several processors and memories, such a statement must describe the behavior of many thousands of bits of information. We are thus faced with the problem that the statement of what it means for the SIFT software to be correct is too complicated to be humanly comprehensible.

The solution to this problem is to construct a higher level "view" of the SIFT system that is simpler than the actual system. Such a view is called a *model*. When stated in terms of the simple model, the requisite system properties can be made comprehensible. The proof of correctness is then performed in two steps: 1) we first prove that the model possesses the necessary correctness properties; and 2) we then prove that the model accurately describes the SIFT system [Shostak et al., 1977].

Actually, different aspects of correctness are best expressed in terms of different models. We use a hierarchy of models. The system itself may be viewed as the lowest level model. In order to prove that the models accurately describe the SIFT system, we prove that each model accurately describes the next lower-level one.

Models

We now make the concept of a model more precise. We define a model to consist of a set S of possible states, a subset S_0 of S consisting of the set of possible initial states, and a *transition relation* $\rightarrow$ on S. The relation $s \rightarrow s'$ means that a transition is possible from state s to state s'. It is possible for the relations $s \rightarrow s'$ and $s \rightarrow s''$ both to hold for two different states s' and s'', so we allow nondeterministic behavior. A *possible behavior* of the system consists of a sequence of states $s_0, s_1, \ldots$ such that s_0 is in S_0 and $s_i \rightarrow s_{i+1}$ for each i. Correctness properties are mathematical statements about the possible behaviors of the system.

Note that the behavior of a model consists of a linear sequence of transitions, even though concurrent operations occur in the SIFT system. Concurrent activity can be represented by transitions that change disjoint components of the state, so that the order in which they occur is irrelevant.

Each state of the model represents a collection of states in the real system. For example, in the reliability model discussed in the subsection on reliability prediction, the state is a triple of integers (h, d, f) which contains only the information that f processors have failed, d of those failures have been detected, and h of the detected failures have been handled. A single model state corresponds to all possible states the system could reach through any combination of f failures, d failure detections, and h reconfigurations.

We now consider what it means for one model to accurately describe a lower level one. Let S, S_0, and $\rightarrow$ be the set of states, set of initial states, and transition relation for the higher level model; and let S', S'_0, and $\rightarrow'$ be the corresponding quantities for the lower level model. Each state of the lower level model must represent some state of the higher level one, but different lower level states can represent the same higher level one. Thus there must be a mapping REP: $S' \rightarrow S$, where REP (s') denotes the higher-level state represented by s'.

Having defined a correspondence between the states of the two models, we can require that the two models exhibit corresponding behavior. Since the lower level model represents a more detailed description of the system, it may contain more transitions than the higher level one. Each transition in the lower level model should either correspond to a transition in the higher level one, or else should describe a change in the system that is invisible in the higher level model. This requirement is embodied in the following two conditions.

1. REP (S'_0) is a subset of S_0.
2. For all s', t' in S': if $s' \rightarrow t'$ then either:
   a. REP (s') = REP (t'); or
   b. REP $(s') \rightarrow$ REP (t').

If these conditions are satisfied, then we say that REP defines the lower level model to be a *refinement* of the higher level one.

If a model is a refinement of a higher level one, then any theorem about the possible behaviors of the higher level model yields a corresponding theorem about the possible behaviors of the lower level one. This is used to infer correctness of the lower level model (and ultimately, of the system itself) from the correctness of the higher level one.

A transition in the higher level model may represent a system action that is represented by a sequence of transitions in the lower level one. For example, the action of detecting a failure may be represented by a single transition in the higher level model. However, in a lower level model (such as the system itself), detecting a failure may involve a complex sequence of transitions. The second requirement means that in order to define REP, we must define some arbitrary point at which the lower level model is considered to have detected the failure. This problem of defining exactly when the higher level transition takes place in the lower level model turns out to be the major difficulty in constructing the mapping REP.

The Reliability Model

In the reliability model, the state consists of a triple (h, d, f) of integers with $h \leqslant d \leqslant f \leqslant p$, where p is the number of processors. The transition relation $\rightarrow$ is described in the subsection on Reliability Prediction above, as is the meaning of the quantities h, d, and f.

Associated with each value of h is an integer sf(h) called its *safety factor*, which has the following interpretation. If the system has reached a configuration in which h failures have been handled, then it can successfully cope with up to sf(h) additional (unhandled) failures. That is, the system should function correctly so long as $f - h$, the number of unhandled failures, is less than or equal to sf(h). The state (h, d, f) is called *safe* if $f - h \leqslant$ sf(h).

To demonstrate that SIFT meets its reliability requirements, we must show two things.

1. If the system remains in a safe state (one represented by a safe state in the reliability model), then it will behave correctly.
2. The probability of the system reaching an unsafe state is sufficiently small.

Property 2 was discussed in the subsection on Reliability Prediction. The remainder of this section describes our approach to proving 1.

The reliability model is introduced specifically to allow us to discuss property 2. The model does not reflect the fact that SIFT is performing any computations, so it cannot be used to state any correctness properties of the system. For that a lower level model is needed.

The Allocation Model

An Overview

SIFT performs a number of iterative tasks. In the *allocation model*, a single transition represents the execution of one complete iteration of all the tasks. As described in the subsection on Scheduling, most tasks are not actually executed every iteration cycle. For the allocation model, an unexecuted task is considered to perform a null calculation, producing the same result it produced during the previous iteration.

The input used by a task in its tth iteration is the output of the $(t - 1)$st iterations of some (possibly empty) set of tasks. Input to SIFT is modeled by a task executed on an I/O processor which produces output without requiring input from other tasks. The output which an I/O processor produces is simply the output of some task which it executes.

In the allocation model, we make no distinction between main processors and I/O processors. Bus errors are not represented in the model. SIFT's handling of them is invisible in the allocation model, and can be represented by a lower level model.

The fundamental correctness property of SIFT—property 1 above—is stated in terms of the allocation model as follows: if the system remains in a safe state, then each nonfaulty processor produces correct output for every critical task it executes. This implies the correctness of any critical output of SIFT generated by a nonfaulty I/O processor. (The possibility of faulty I/O processors must be handled by redundancy in the external environment.)

The allocation of processors to tasks is effected by the interaction of the global executive task, the local-global communicating tasks, and local executives, as described in the previous section. The output of the tth iteration of a local-global communicating task uses as input the output of the $(t - 1)$st iteration of the global executive. During the tth iteration cycle, the local executive determines what the processor should be doing during the $(t + 1)$st cycle—i.e., what tasks it should execute, and what processor memories contain the input values for each of these tasks. The processor executes a task by fetching each input from several processor memories, using a majority vote to determine the correct value, and then computing the task's output.* We assume that a nonfaulty processor will compute the correct output value for a task if majority voting obtains the correct value for each of the task's inputs.

The only part of the executive software that is explicitly represented in the allocation are the local-global communicating tasks. Although each processor's local-global communicating task is treated in SIFT as a separate task, it is more convenient to represent it in the allocation model as the execution on that processor of a single replicated task whose output determines the complete allocation of tasks to processors.

The States of the Allocation Model

We now describe the set of states of the allocation model. They are defined in terms of the primitive quantities listed below, which are themselves undefined. (To show that a lower level model is a refinement of the allocation model, we must define these primitive quantities in terms of the primitive quantities of that lower level model.) The descriptions of these quantities are given to help the reader understand the model: they have no formal significance.

P A set of processors. It represents the set of all processors in the system.

K A set of tasks. It represents the set of all (critical) tasks in the system.

LE An element of K. It is the single task that represents all the local-global communicating tasks, as described above.

e A mapping from the cross product of K and the set of nonnegative integers into some unspecified set of values. The value of $e(k, t)$ represents the correct output of the tth iteration cycle of task k. Thus, e describes what the SIFT tasks should compute. It is a primitive (i.e., undefined) quantity in the allocation model because we are not specifying the actual values the tasks should produce. (These values will, of course, depend upon the particular application tasks SIFT executes, and the inputs from the external environment.)

sf The safety factor function introduced in the reliability model. It remains a primitive quantity in the allocation model. It can be thought of as a goal the system is trying to achieve.

We define the allocation model state to consist of the following components.** (Again, the descriptions are to assist the reader and are irrelevant to the proof.)

t A nonnegative integer. It represents the number of iteration cycles that have been executed.

F A subset of P. It represents the set of all failed processors.

D A subset of F. It represents the set of all failed processors whose failure has been detected.

c A mapping from $P \times K$ into some unspecified set of values. The value $c(p, k)$ denotes the output of task k as computed by processor p. This value is presumably meaningless if p did not execute the tth iteration of task k.

The Axioms of the Model

We do not completely describe the set of initial states S_0 and the transition relation $\rightarrow$ for the allocation model. Instead, we give the following list of axioms about S_0 and $\rightarrow$. Rather than

---

* The fault diagnosis performed by the global executive is not represented in the allocation model.

** To simplify the discussion, one component of our actual model has been omitted.

giving their formal statement, we simply give here an informal description of the axioms. (Uninteresting axioms dealing with such matters as initialization are omitted.)

1. The value of $c(p, LE)$ during iteration cycle t, which represents the output of the tth iteration of processor p's local-global communicating task, specifies the tasks that p should execute during cycle $t + 1$ and the processors whose memories contain input values for each such task.
2. If a nonfaulty processor p executes a task k during iteration cycle t, and a majority of the copies of each input value to k received by p are correct, then the value $c(p, k)$ it computes will equal the correct value $e(k, t)$.
3. Certain natural assumptions are made about the allocation of tasks to processors specified by $e(LE, t)$. In particular, we assume that a) no critical tasks are assigned to a processor in D (the set of processors known to be faulty), and b) when reconfiguring, the reallocation of tasks to processors is done in such a way that the global executive never knowingly makes the system less tolerant of failure than it currently is.

To prove that a lower level model is a refinement of the allocation model, it will suffice to verify that these axioms are satisfied.

The Correspondence with the Reliability Model

In order to show that the allocation model is a refinement of the reliability model, we must define the quantities h, d, and f of the reliability model in terms of the state components of the allocation model—thereby defining the function REP.

The definitions of d and f are obvious; they are just the number of elements in the sets D and F, respectively. To define h, we must specify the precise point during the "execution" of the allocation model at which a detected failure is considered to be "handled." Basically, the value of h is increased to $h + 1$ when the reconfiguration has progressed to the point where it can

handle sf$(h + 1)$ *additional* errors. (The function sf appears in the definition.) We omit the details.

The Correctness Proof

Within the allocation model, we can define a predicate $CF(t)$ that expresses the condition that the system functions correctly during the tth iteration cycle. Intuitively, it is the statement that every nonfaulty processor produces the correct output for every task it executes. The predicate $CF(t)$ can be stated more precisely as follows.

If $e(LE, t - 1)$ indicates that p should execute a task k in K during the tth iteration cycle, and p is in $P - F$, then the value of $c(p, k)$ after the tth iteration equals $e(k, t)$.

(A precise statement of how $e(LE, t - 1)$ indicates that p should execute task k requires some additional notation, and is omitted.)

We can define the predicate SAFE(t) to mean that the system is in a safe state at time t. More precisely, SAFE(t) means that after the tth iteration cycle, sf$(h) \geqslant f - h$, where f and h are defined above as functions of the allocation model state. The basic correctness condition for SIFT can be stated as follows.

If SAFE (t') is true for all t' with $0 \leqslant t' \leqslant t$, then $CF(t)$ is true.

A rigorous proof of this theorem has been developed, based upon the axioms for the allocation model. The proof is too long and detailed to include here. It will appear in the final report to NASA at the conclusion of the current phase of the project.

Future Work

The basic correctness property of SIFT has been stated and proved for the allocation model. What remains to be done is to show that the actual system is a refinement of the allocation model. Current plans call for this to be done in terms of two lower level models. The first of these is the *operating-system model*. The allocation model represents all the computations in a given iteration cycle performed by all the processes as a single transition. The operating system model will represent the asynchrony of the actual computations. It will essentially be a high-level representation of the system that embodies the mechanisms used to synchronize the processors. The proof that the operating-system model is a refinement of the allocation model will be a proof of correctness of these synchronizing mechanisms.

The next lower level model will be the *program model*. It will essentially represent the PASCAL version of the software. We expect that proving the program model to be a refinement of the operating-system model will be done by the ordinary methods of program verification [Floyd, 1967].

Finally, we must verify that the system itself is a correct refinement of the program model. This requires verifying first that the PASCAL programs are compiled correctly, and second that the hardware correctly executes programs. (In particular, this involves verifying the fault-isolation properties of the hardware.) We have not yet decided how to address these tasks. Although most of this verification is theoretically straightforward, it presents a difficult problem in practice.

CONCLUSIONS

The SIFT computer development is an attempt to use modern methods of computer design and verification to achieve fault-tolerant behavior for real-time, critical control systems. We believe that the use of standard, mass-produced components helps to attain high reliability. Our basic approach, therefore, involves the replication of standard components, relying upon the software to detect and analyze errors and to dyamically reconfigure the system to bypass faulty units. Special hardware is needed only to isolate the

units from one another, so a faulty unit does not cause the failure of a nonfaulty one.

We have chosen processor/memory modules and bus modules as the basic units of fault detection and reconfiguration. These units are at a high enough level to make system reconfiguration easy, and are small and inexpensive enough to allow sufficient replication to achieve the desired reliability. Moreover, new advances in Large Scale Integration will further reduce their size and cost.

By using software to achieve fault-tolerance, SIFT allows considerable flexibility in the choice of error handling policies and mechanisms. For example, algorithms for fault masking and reconfiguration can be easily modified on the basis of operational experience. Novel approaches to the tolerance of programming errors, such as redundant programming and recovery blocks [Randell, 1975] can be incorporated. Moreover, it is fairly easy to enhance the performance of the system by adding more hardware.

While designing SIFT, we have been concerned with proving that it meets its stringent reliability requirements. We have constructed formal models with which to analyze the probability of system failure, and we intend to prove that these models accurately describe the behavior of the SIFT system. Our effort has included the use of formal specifications for functional modules. We hope to achieve a degree of system verification that has been unavailable in previous fault-tolerant architectures.

Although the design described in this paper has been oriented toward the needs of commercial air transports, the basic architectural approach has a wide applicability to critical real-time systems. Future work may extend this approach to the design of fault-tolerant software and more general fault-tolerant control systems.

APPENDIX: SAMPLE SPECIAL SPECIFICATION

This appendix contains an example of a formal specification extracted from the specifications of he SIFT executive software. The specification is written in a language called SPECIAL, a formally defined specification language. SPECIAL has been designed explicitly to permit the description of the results required from a computer program without constraining the programmer's decisions as to how to write the most efficient program.

The function that is specified here is the local executive's voter routine, described informally in the Software System section. This function is called to obtain a value from one of the buffers used to communicate between tasks. The value required is requested over the bus system from every replication of this buffer, and a consensus value that masks any errors is formed and returned to the calling program. Errors are reported and provision is made for buses that do not obtain a value (due to a nonresponding bus or memory) and for the possibility that there is no consensus.

The following notes are keyed to statements in the specification.

Notes

1. The function 'read_buffer' takes three arguments and returns a result. The buffer_name 'i' is the name of a logical buffer which may be replicated in several processors, while the address 'k' is the offset of the required word in the buffer and 'safe' is the value to be returned if no consensus can be obtained. The parameters 'a' and 't' need not be explicitly cited by the caller of this function but are deduced from the context.
2. Exception returns will be made if there are no active instances of the named buffer or if the offset is not within the buffer.
3. A response is obtained by interrogating a buffer in another processor. Each response is a record (also known as a "structure," containing a value field ("val") and flag field ("flag"), the latter set if no

```
OVFUN read_buffer (buffer_name i;address k;value safe)
                  [processor a;task t]
                  -> result r;                                      [1]

EXCEPTIONS                                                          [2]
     CARDINALITY(activated_buffers(a,i))=0;
     0>k OR k>=buffer_size(i);

EFFECTS
   EXISTS SET_OF response                                          [3]
        w=responses(a, activated_buffers(a,i),k):
     EXISTS SET_OF response
         z={response b|b INSET w AND b.flag} :

     IF(EXISTS value v;                                            [4]
            SET_OF response x|
            x = {response c|c INSET (w DIFF z)
                      AND c.val = v}:

        FORALL value u:                                            [5]
            SET_OF response y|
            y={response d|d INSET (w DIFF x DIFF z)
                      AND d.val=u:
         CARDINALITY (x) > CARDINALITY (y))

     THEN(EXISTS value v;                                          [6]
            SET_OF response x|
            x={response c|c INSET (w DIFF z)
                      AND c.val=v}:

        FORALL value u;                                            [6]
            SET_OF response y|
            y={response d|d INSET (w DIFF x DIFF z)
                      AND d.val=u}:
         CARDINALITY(x) > CARDINALITY(y);

        EFFECTS_OF errors(a, w DIFF x);                            [7]
        r=v)

     ELSE(EFFECTS_OF errors(a,w);                                  [8]
         r=safe);
```

response was obtained from the bus or store. The set 'w' of responses is the set obtained from all of the activated buffers known to processor 'a.' The set 'z' is the subset of no-response responses.

4. First we must check that a plurality opinion exists. This section hypothesises that there exists a consensus value 'v' together with the subset of responses 'x' that returned that value.

5. Here we consider all other values and establish for each of them that fewer responses contained this other value than contained the proposed consensus value.

6. Having established that a consensus value exists, we may now validly construct it, repeating the criteria of stages [4] and [5]. It is important to note that these are not programs but logical criteria. The actual implementations would not repeat the program.

7. This section requires that any responses not in the set 'x' (the set 'x' is the set reporting the consensus value) should be reported as errors, and the result is the consensus value 'v.' The expression

EFFECTS_ OF errors(a, w DIFF X))

indicates a state change in the module that contains the 0-function "errors." The specification indicates that an error report is loaded into a table associated with processor "a."

8. If there is no consensus value, as determined by stages [4] and [5], then all the responses must be reported as errors, and the safe value returned as the result.

ACKNOWLEDGMENT

The authors wish to acknowledge the help of other members of the Computer Science Laboratory who contributed to the development of SIFT. In particular, Dr. William H. Kautz helped in the formulation of the reliability model and with the diagnosis problem. Marshall Pease developed a proof showing that synchronization could not be achieved with three clocks. Lawrence Robinson indirectly aided the project by his creation of the hierarchical development methodology. We are indebted to numerous individuals of NASA-Langley Research Center: Nicholas D. Murray, the Project Monitor, has provided early and continuing guidance and encouragement; Billy Dove has provided inspiration and support within the context of a long-range NASA program of technology development for reliable aircraft control; Earl Migneault first alerted us to problems with the "obvious" solutions to the clock synchronization problem; Sal Bavuso has continually reviewed our work on reliability modeling; and Brian Lupton and Larry Spencer have provided considerable valuable comments during the course of the work.

REFERENCES

Floyd [1967]; Melliar-Smith [1977]; Murray, Hopkins, and Wensley [1977]; Pease, Shostak, and Lamport [1980]; Randell [1975]; Ratner et al. [1973]; Robinson and Roubine [1977]; Robinson et al. [1976]; Shostak et al. [1977]; Wensley [1972]; Wensley et al. [1973, 1976].

FTMP—A Highly Reliable Fault-Tolerant Multiprocessor for Aircraft

Albert L. Hopkins, Jr.   T. Basil Smith, III   Jaynarayan H. Lala

17

Abstract

FTMP is a digital computer architecture which has evolved over a ten-year period in connection with several life-critical aerospace applications. Most recently it has been proposed as a fault-tolerant central computer for civil transport aircraft applications. A working emulation has been operating for some time, and the first engineering prototype is scheduled to be completed in late 1979.

FTMP is designed to have a failure rate due to random causes of the order of 10^{-10} failures per hour, on ten-hour flights where no airborne maintenance is available. The preferred maintenance interval is of the order of hundreds of flight hours, and the probability that maintenance will be required earlier than the preferred interval is desired to be at most a few percent.

The design is based on independent processor-cache memory modules and common memory modules which communicate via redundant serial buses. All information processing and transmission is conducted in triplicate so that local voters in each module can correct errors. Modules can be retired and/or reassigned in any configuration. Reconfiguration is carried out routinely from second to second to search for latent faults in the voting and reconfiguration elements. Job assignments are all made on a floating basis, so that any processor triad is eligible to execute any job step. The core software in the FTMP will handle all fault detection, diagnosis, and recovery in such a way that applications programs do not need to be involved.

Failure-rate models and numerical results are described for both permanent and intermittent faults. A dispatch probability model is also presented. Experience with an experimental emulation is described.

INTRODUCTION

The FTMP (Fault-Tolerant Multiprocessor) is a computer architecture that has been studied, simulated, modeled, and emulated extensively over the past several years. It is scheduled to be implemented in an engineering prototype form within two years of this writing. The principal goal of FTMP is to be extraordinarily survivable without being difficult to program, operate, or maintain. It is presently predicted that the overall FTMP failure rate will be less than 10^{-9} failures per hour, provided that maintenance is available within no more than ten hours of dispatch. In most cases, however, it will not be necessary to maintain the FTMP at intervals of less than 200–300 hours.

The FTMP structure can be described as an arbitrary number of processor modules with local, or *cache*, memories, and an arbitrary number of memory modules, interconnected by redundant serial buses. Modules are associated into groups of three to perform triply redundant functions. All data is distributed synchronously and in triplicate, and every module contains a voting element to mask bus disagreements. All modules contain special circuits to create logical and physical boundaries to halt the propagation of faults from one module to another.

The FTMP is intended for use as one of at least two central computers in a redundant distributed digital system designed to serve as a highly survivable avionics system [Deyst and Hopkins, n.d.].

Background and Context

The development history of the FTMP dates to 1965, with a serial-bus multiprocessor concept for spaceborne control applications [Alonso, Hopkins, and Thaler, 1966, 1967]. Increasingly redundant versions were conceived, including one in 1969 intended to serve as a preliminary design baseline for a manned spacecraft, i.e., the space shuttle [Hopkins, 1971]. At that time, a concept was stated for the systematic design of a redundant, fault-tolerant vehicle, employing fault-tolerant "regional" computers, each of which was to be the master of an I/O bus connected to a number of dedicated (micro-) computers, local to each of a number of sensor and effector components or subsystems [Hopkins, 1970]. In the early 1970's, some of the basic concepts were tested by simulation in a laboratory multiprocessor arrangement called Cerberus. The National Science Foundation sponsored most of this testing effort.

There were two particularly significant outcomes of this work. One was a network I/O data communication structure to replace the topologically leaner, and therefore more vulnerable, I/O bus [Smith, 1975]. The second was a significant improvement in the redundancy management capability of the architecture [Hopkins and Smith, 1975, 1977a]. As a result of these developments the Draper Laboratory undertook the construction of breadboard emulations of the new multiprocessor and the network as independent Research and Development projects. Evaluations of various aspects of these emulations were sponsored by the National Science Foundation, the Office of Naval Research, the NASA Langley Research Center, and Draper itself.

The Draper study concerned itself with the design of a robust integrated avionics systems concept suitable for control-configured aircraft, and numerous other life-critical applications. This concept was to use a fault-tolerant central computer with a second remote identical computer available to take over in case of damage to the first. The concept also used the I/O network as a fault-tolerant and damage-tolerant medium for maintaining access to all surviving system elements. The third prong of the concept was a redundant sensor and effector architecture, with algorithms executed centrally to determine which, if any, of the sensors and effectors were malfunctioning [Deckert et al, 1977]. The entire system concept came to be called OSIRIS, (onboard, survivable, integrated, redundant information system [Hopkins and Smith, 1977b].)

Meanwhile, NASA Langley sponsorship further developed the fault-tolerant multiprocessor architecture in the direction of civil transport aircraft application, along with a competing architecture developed at SRI International, called SIFT [Murray, Hopkins, and Wensley, 1977] (see also Chapter 16 in this book). In 1977, a design specification was drawn up for an engineering prototype of the multiprocessor, to be built by a major avionics manufacturer. At this point, the name FTMP was adopted to signify this particular architecture and its derivatives.

The FTMP represents a major architectural advance beyond the contemporary practices of computer redundancy in aircraft systems. All too often, computers have been interconnected in the simplest possible way, leaving as a programming task the detection and isolation of each fault and the subsequent recovery. This approach has serious problems, including the means of granting authority to a valid module without granting it to an invalid one. It is also virtually impossible in such approaches to separate the redundancy management software from the applications programs, with the result that both are greatly complicated. Validation is a difficult problem in these systems.

The FTMP is quite different from some other fault-tolerant computers for different applications. A fault-tolerant spacecraft computer, for example, has a similar task, but a dissimilar survival requirement. Other fault-tolerant architectures are meant to serve general data processing tasks in a benign environment with maintenance available. The next subsection attempts to show how the architecture of the FTMP corresponds to the class of applications it is designed to serve.

Rationale of the FTMP Approach

The intended use of the FTMP is to support critical control functions in vehicles, process plants, life-support, or any similar application in which maintenance is available periodically or after a delay, and where loss of control leads with significant probability to high cost in terms of life or property. The failure rate at the system level must be remote. In civil transport aircraft this generally means the order of 10^{-9} failures per hour in flights of up to ten hours.

One can immediately rule out some of the classical approaches to redundant systems on the grounds that they do not permit the detection and location of faults concurrent with critical operation. Other approaches can be dismissed because of insufficient redundancy and fault coverage. Still others are unusable because they depend excessively on the applications software.

The approach must have the ability to mask, i.e., correct, errors without requiring program rollback. All resources, including those used only in case of malfunction, must be capable of being individually verified during system operation. The approach must further be capable of surviving a multiplicity of faults, although not necessarily all at the same time.

Apparently, the most efficient way to furnish the multiple fault tolerance and concurrent testing is in a multiprocessing or multicomputing structure. Moreover, in order to provide error masking, all critical transactions must be at least triplicated. This is the course that has been followed in both the FTMP and the SIFT architectures. The result is a variant of classical redundancy of the TMR-Hybrid type [Mathur, 1971a], in which spare elements are placed in a pool so that they can substitute for any element in any of several parallel TMR triads. We find it convenient to refer to this redundancy form as "parallel-hybrid" redundancy. Both FTMP and SIFT employ three times the resources nominally required by the application, plus an arbitrary level of spares, plus the hardware and software overhead necessary to manage the redundancy, i.e., fault detection and isolation, reconfiguration, and recovery. These two architectures employ graceful degradation as an important means of trading system cost against criticality. In projected aircraft, the flight critical functions account for a minority of the resource utilization. These functions are therefore supported with highest priority as resource pools diminish due to aggregated failures.

Beyond this point, FTMP and SIFT have gone separate ways. The FTMP has adopted a fully synchronous approach, which allows hardware-implemented bit-by-bit voting of all transactions. This in turn allows system management to be effected by majority rule, and means that the modules can be reassigned under executive control to different triads, or to spare status. Modules can be reconfigured in order to diagnose the location of a fault, to test the reconfiguration mechanisms, to activate spares for purposes of test and recovery, and to retire modules diagnosed as failed.

The next section discusses the theory of the FTMP architecture, and enlarges on several of the points that have been introduced here.

THEORY OF THE FTMP

Nominal Organization

Loosely defined, a multiprocessor is a computer with several processors and a single (possibly multiport) memory accessible to all processors. In the extreme, all instructions and data reside in a common memory available to any processor, so that processors are "anonymous." Given a suitable state vector, any processor can execute any procedure from any starting point. Motivations for multiprocessors are typically to increase productivity and availability at the same time, although these two purposes are competitive. At any rate, parallelism is intrinsic to the multiprocessor, as each processor is able to execute a different concurrent procedure subject to limitations imposed by resource sharing and sequential contraints on the procedures.

Memory Access

A "canonical form" of a multiprocessor is illustrated in Figure 17-1, which introduces the notion of memory private to each processor in addition to the common memory. The rationale for this private, or cache, memory stems from the limitations imposed on parallel operation by

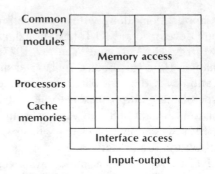

Figure 17–1. Multiprocessor functional form.

memory access constraints. In a multiprocessor with highly parallel memory access, memory conflicts would occur only when individual units of data are simultaneously requested, or are locked for sequential conflict resolution. This would be the optimum structure for parallelism, and the cache memory's role is reduced to a possible enhancement of processor execution speed.

In the FTMP, on the other hand, the memory access is highly serial, for reasons dictated by reliability and economy. This essentially means that the memory has a single port, and that the throughput of the multiprocessor is governed by the bandwidth of this memory port. In this case, the cache memory has a significant role in enhancing parallelism. The combination of processor and cache is a true computer, capable of performing elaborate operations on input data in response to terse commands. This means that the common memory can contain programs written in a language level higher than the processor's machine-language level, and that the processor-cache unit can interrupt the higher level statements during the time that other processor-cache units are accessing the common memory. In this mode of system operation, which is really a form of "virtual machine," a memory port of moderate bandwidth can support an instruction execution "bandwidth" that is, at least in principle, almost arbitrarily large.

The degree to which the instruction execution bandwidth can exceed the common memory port bandwidth depends on the parameters of the cache memory, the terseness of the higher level language, and the relative amount of input and output data for each independent procedure. Clearly, the enlargement of the cache memories tends toward a multicomputer organization. Indeed, at some point the total cache capacity becomes adequate to contain everything in common memory, and the usefulness of common memory is reduced to the buffering of interprocess data. Processor anonymity is significant to this application because of the frequent reconfigurations that need to take place in this computer for latent fault exposure. Anonymity also provides an intrinsic mechanism for dynamic load distribution among available processing resources. The cache memory, however, acts to reduce the anonymity of the processor. To put it another way, the degree of anonymity is determined by the ease of reloading the cache memory. With zero cache memory, anonymity is greatest. As cache memory is increased to support instruction bandwidth enhancement, the anonymity of the processor-cache units depends on the amount of cache memory whose contents are unique to one processor. Note that the incorporation of identical procedural and other constant data, or indeed identical variable data, in every cache memory has no adverse impact on anonymity.

The use of a cache memory in a sampled-data control application, such as the aircraft application considered here, is generally productive. The typical job step uses rather few data samples as input, and produces one data sample as output. The procedures used tend to lend themselves well to expression as macrooperations, i.e., higher level operations, such as floating point arithmetic, linear combination, elementary functions, vector and matrix operations, and so forth. The incorporation of procedures of this level as cache subroutines is reasonable and profitable in today's technology. The current high annual rate of memory density increase prompts one to observe that a fairly extensive set of procedures, and indeed a hierarchy of procedures, is increasingly appropriate for inclusion in cache memories.

The cache memory structure of the FTMP includes memories for data and procedures, partly read-write, partly read-only, designed to enhance instruction bandwidth with rather little loss of processor anonymity. The common memory, although highly modular, acts as a single-port paged memory, accessible to one processor at a time via a serial bus with a built-in contention mechanism.

Functional Resource Allocation

The programmer sees this multiprocessor as a machine for executing job steps, largely corresponding to periodic sampled-data updates. The magnitudes of these job steps will vary considerably from one control function to another, but will require something of the order of a few milliseconds, on the average, of processor time per job step. The procedure for each job step is written in a suitable language, and resides in common memory. Typically, each job step is scheduled to occur at a given time or following a given event. The relevant dispatch data for each scheduled job step is kept in a queue, where it is frequently examined to see if the job step is eligible to be run, or *invoked*. The frequent examinations are conducted by processors that have completed their earlier assignments, and are available to undertake new ones. When an available processor finds one or more eligible job steps, it selects one of them to invoke. In this way, job allocation is dynamic, and adjusts itself to the momentary load distribution and to module failures.

Input-output management in a multiprocessor can be more complex than it is in a single multiprogrammed computer, because as a single-port resource, it impinges on program parallelism. Depending on the statistics of external data traffic and of internal job steps, different access strategies may be appropriate. The most straightforward of these is to treat interface access as a single resource that is allocated to a single process for its exclusive use for the short period of time that a process requires access. Access may be granted on a priority basis or a first come first served basis. That is, when a processor needs interface access, it ascertains by means of flags in memory whether the interface is free. If not, the processor waits (with appropriate safeguards against lock-up) until it becomes free.

Redundant Organization

The physical organization of the FTMP is substantially more complex than the nominal organization outlined in the preceding section. A simplified module diagram of the computer is shown in Figure 17-2. Superficially, this diagram appears much the same as the nominal multiprocessor. The principal differences are that the buses for memory and interface access are redundant, and that the actual number of modules is three times the number of nominal modules plus some number of spares.

All activity is conducted by triads of modules and triads of buses. A module triad is formed by associating any three like modules with one another. This means that any module can serve as a spare for any triad. Such flexibility permits the best possible utilization of surviving modules. A single triad of bus lines is active at any one time for each of the memory and interface accesses. In other words, a three-member subset of N bus lines is chosen on a quasi-static basis to serve as a bus triad.

Every module of every kind is able to receive data from all incident bus lines, and contains a decision element to formulate a corrected version of bus data. It is necessary for each module to know which three bus lines are the active ones. These three lines are connected to a voter in each module, thus constituting a TMR element. The three active bus lines carry three independently generated versions of the data, each version coming from a different member of the triad that is transmitting the data. To accomplish this, it is necessary to assign each module to transmit on one specific bus line. Now if totally flexible module configuration is to be possible, it follows that the assignment of a module's transmission to a single bus line must be quasi-static and reconfigurable.

Bus Guardians

In addition to the redundancy described in the preceding few paragraphs, the redundant organization differs from the nominal one by virtue of the inclusion of independent submodules called bus guardian units in each processor, memory, and input-output access unit. Guardians are charged with governing the status of their associated modules. This includes power-on status, memory bus triad and transmission selection, and certain self-test configuration selections.

Each of the functions of the guardian has the characteristic that its failure modes have safe directions as well as unsafe ones. By biasing the failure modes toward the safe directions, it is possible to increase the probability of system survival. In general, the safe failure modes of a module are power-off, and bus transmission disconnected. To bias in this direction, one can employ redundant guardians in each module, and require agreement among them to establish power-on and bus transmission enable.

The connection of bus guardians is illustrated in Figure 17-3. It should first be noted that the guardian principle depends heavily on fault independence. Therefore, each guardian derives its power, its bus inputs, and its timing reference independently of all other guardians. It is moreover physically isolated from all other guardians and all modules. A particularly critical area from the isolation viewpoint is the control of the module's transmission interface onto the various bus lines. The bus isolation gates must be highly independent of one another, as must the guardian's enable signals to these gates. This is one of the crucial electrical and mechanical design aspects of the entire computer.

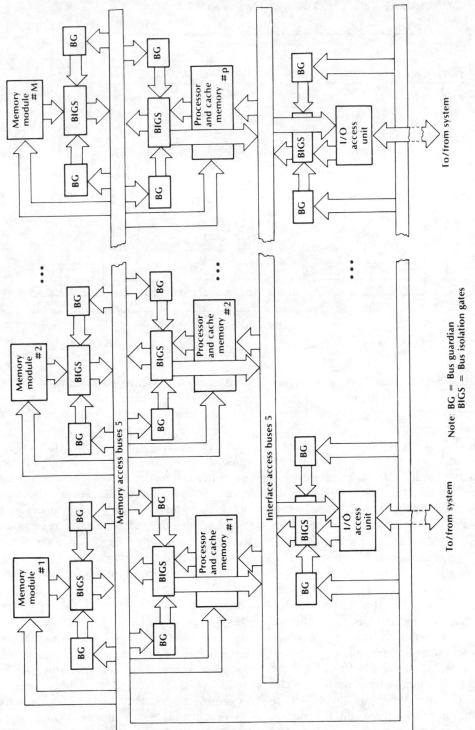

Figure 17-2. Simplified physical diagram of the FTMP.

Note: BG = Bus guardian
BIGS = Bus isolation gates

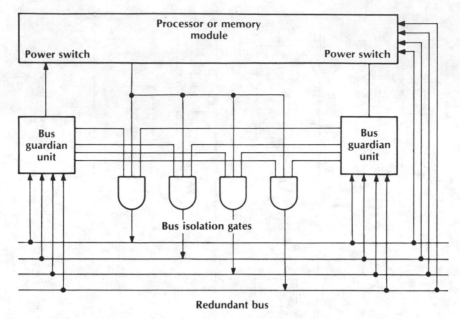

Figure 17–3.   Bus guardian connections.

Bus guardians are addressable as part of the common memory address space, and are capable of receiving messages from any processor triad via the active memory bus triad. A message to a guardian contains commands which are staticized by the guardian and applied to its outputs until superseded by a new command message. In this way, the probability is remote that a failed module can assert more than one erroneous data stream. As a result, correct data can be determined by the bus voters, and the malfunctioning module can be switched to a silent state. It is noted in passing that certain failures of a bus isolation gate can render a bus line useless, in which case the active bus triad must be reconfigured. However, most guardian failures are biased to appear as passive failures of the unit to which the particular guardian unit pertains.

Guardians are used as agents to convey the computer's configuration authority to all elements of the computer. They are highly secure against the random or willful malfunction of any single active transmitting module. They make possible the highly flexible reconfiguration on which the FTMP depends.

Processor and Memory Modules

All modules and buses are organized into triads. In the case of processors and memories, there can be numerous triads in existence at the same time, but only one memory bus triad and only one interface bus triad. Each processor triad acts as one functional processor, of which several can work in parallel. Each memory triad acts as a page of memory, of which several can exist at one time, but only one can communicate at a time with a processor triad.

When a processor fails, its triad will attempt to complete its current job step, which it will be able to do unless a second failure prevents it. The period of vulnerability to a second failure will be a fraction of a second. When the job step is complete, one of the other processor triads is assigned the task of reconfiguring the injured triad. When the erroneous module is identified, it is removed by commands to its guardians. If a spare is available, it is connected to the appropriate bus by its guardians, likewise upon command by the processor triad assigned to the reconfiguration. Triad identity will be assigned to the spare processor by a direct message. If no spares are available, the injured triad is retired. The resources of the multiprocessor are diminished by one processing unit, and the two unfailed members of the former triad are now available to be used as spares, should further failures occur.

The situation is much the same for memory modules. The principal difference is that memories are not anonymous. In fact, a read-only memory module is totally dedicated to its assigned function, and cannot be used as a spare. When a read-only memory triad is injured by the loss of a memory module, a read-write memory module can be used as a spare. It must be loaded to agree with the surviving triad members before a second failure occurs. If no spare is available, the triad is reduced to a dyad, which is vulnerable to the next failure, at which time one memory page is lost. This is a significant departure from the flexibility offered by the anonymous processor triads. The eventuality of read-only memory failure must clearly be covered by the inclusion of adequate spares, either read-write memories for flexible pooled use, or extra dedicated copies of read-only memory.

Input-Output Access

Figure 17-2 indicates the existence of input-output access modules connected to the internal interface bus and also the external environment.

The external interfaces of the computer can alternatively support dedicated, bused, or networked link structures to the sensor and effector components. The redundancy structure at this point depends on the redundancy desired in the external interface.

The simplest conceptual structure is a triple-redundant interface, such as a redundant external bus, where the triple modular redundancy structure is extended through to the component interfaces. Each external bus line can be dedicated to a different input-output access module, which in turn is assigned by its guardian units to transmit on one of the active interface bus lines. More complex variants are possible, in which each access module performs error correction by voting on incoming data from the external bus.

When an external interface is nonredundant, the strategy would be to assign it to a single access module, where the module would transmit on all three active interface bus lines. A malfunctioning access module could pollute the entire interface bus, but with suitable encoding and protocol there would be no serious consequences to the state of the system. The offending access module could be discovered and disconnected by bus guardian commands conducted over the memory bus, the major penalty being a time loss on the remainder of the input-output interface of the computer. For dedicated links, the loss of the link is noncritical by hypothesis. For a network, whose survival is assumed critical [Smith, 1975], the computer must interface with the network in several places via several distinct access modules. Each such interface would be simplex, but the system would survive the failure of all but one of them.

Synchronization

The employment of independent redundancy requires some form of synchronization among the independent data sources. Soft, or loose, synchronization involves such operations as buffering, comparing or voting, signaling consensus, and marking completed intervals. These can be done by program, given suitable intermodule data links. Hard, or tight, synchronization involves hardware comparison or voting, and a common time reference, whereas loose synchronization can employ separate time references.

Tight synchronization is employed in the FTMP. It provides the basis for solving some problems, and it presents some problems of its own. A common time reference, or clock, that supports hardware voting, allows instantaneous validation of internal data, configuration control, and, in some cases, interface data. In this way, it helps to make the redundant multiprocessor resemble the nominal one, which is advantageous to programmers at all levels.

The problems of common clocking stem primarily from the fact that it is critical to computer operation in the dynamic sense. The timing reference must be continuous and must remain within tolerances. A second consideration is that common clocking results in time-correlated data transfer, which is subject to correlated malfunction if subjected to external radiation of electromagnetic energy beyond the levels tolerated by shielding. The second problem is intrinsic to all synchronization, but is more severe for tight synchronization. The problem also exists in principle for any degree of shielding. When the statistics of such interference are known, the problem can be addressed in the time domain by encoding for error detection, rerun for recovery, or repetition for time independence.

The problem of maintaining a continuous timing reference is solved by a fault-tolerant redundant clocking arrangement, based on a majority logic algorithm described in Daly, Hopkins, and McKenna [1973]. A more recent embodiment, using voltage-controlled crystal oscillators, will be described in future reports. The basic principle of the system is shown in Figure 17-4, which shows a set of independent phase-locked oscillators arranged so that the failure of one of the oscillators does not destroy the phase lock of the survivors. The clock signal from each oscillator is distributed to every module and guardian, so that each can make an independent determination of clocking edges. These independent determinations are made by circuits called clock receivers, whose operational principles are closely similar to the clock receivers described in Daly, Hopkins, and McKenna [1973]. In normal, nonfailed operation, the outputs of all the clock receivers are in phase lock with each other and with all the oscillators. The same phase lock holds when an oscillator fails. The failure of a clock distribution line appears as an oscillator failure, and the failure of a clock receiver appears as a failure of the module or guardian that contains it. The approach is discussed further in the subsection on the Clock Generator below.

Malfunction Management

The unusually high level of dependability required in the FTMP makes it mandatory to consider all possible sources and effects of probable malfunctions. The probabilities associated with exposure to hazards are important here, as they are in any reliability analysis. The fact that reconfiguration and recovery are needed to meet reliability goals raises other issues of importance, having to do with the probabilities associated with the detection and identification of malfunctions, reconfiguration and recovery of the system, and the system status following a malfunction event. All those considerations relate both to the design and the evaluation of the system.

Malfunction Sources

A malfunction is a general term for anomalous behavior. Numerous kinds of malfunctions are distinguished, ranging from microscopic disorders in an integrated circuit to total aircraft impairment. Within the information processing segment of the total system, we are concerned about avoiding malfunctions that preclude the availability of viable contingencies. We can think of potential malfunctions as being infinitely rich in number and variety, and tractable solely because they can be treated as classes and subclasses.

The first class of malfunctions to be examined is that resulting from externally induced phenomena, such as physical penetration, radiation (atomic, electromagnetic), temperature extremes, or excursion of prime power. The common thread in these diverse physical environments is that their effects cannot be confined or localized to one or a few subportions of the information system. The entire system is vulnerable at one time, and for an arbitrarily high exposure it cannot be made otherwise. That is, the shielding, structure, environmental control, and prime power generation must all be designed to with-

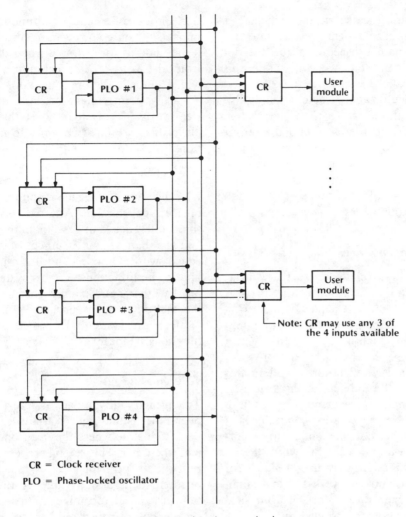

CR = Clock receiver
PLO = Phase-locked oscillator

Note: CR may use any 3 of
the 4 inputs available

Figure 17–4.   Fault-tolerant clock system.

stand stated levels of exposure to known hazards. Exposures in excess of these levels are
potentially catastrophic.

The second malfunction class is that of random malfunctions whose sources are internal to
the system. Typically, these result from circuit
failures. When idealized, such malfunctions are
permanent, isolated, unambiguous, visible, and
recoverable. Actual faults are apt to be marginal,
intermittent, correlated, hidden, uncovered, and/

or not perceived uniformly by multiple observ-
ers. This is the category of malfunctions that
redundancy addresses, although the nonideal
attributes of actual faults tend to undermine the
effectiveness of all redundant systems.

The third class of malfunction sources will
simply be denoted as "other sources." The first
two classes are broadly enough defined to be
stretched to cover everything, but it is useful to
emphasize certain sources separately. Thus we

include in this third category the deficiencies resulting from lapses in system specification, that is, where the domain of operation and the domain of design are not matched. Software in this sense is a specification. It specifies the sequential rules of hardware utilization. Logic design is also a specification in this sense, as are design factors related to the human interfaces and the sensor and effector interfaces. The architectural implications of this category are that the system must be tractable and understandable enough to reduce the probability of occurrence of such malfunctions to a negligible level.

Malfunction Consequences

It has been useful to characterize the various possible malfunctions according to the levels at which they affect the system [Avižienis, 1975]. There are *physical malfunctions* that occur within hardware elements, such as a short circuit in a transistor. These have been referred to by various writers as faults and failures, and in this paper the word "failure" refers to this category. A physical malfunction may or may not result in a *logic malfunction*, in which a logic variable is at some time or another complementary to its correct value. Where authors use the word "fault" for physical malfunction, they use "failure" for logic malfunction, and vice versa. A logic malfunction can occur in the absence of a physical malfunction, notably from induced sources.

A logic malfunction may or may not produce a *data malfunction*, often called an error. A data malfunction can occur in the absence of a logic malfunction, notably from specification lapses. A data malfunction, in turn, may or may not produce a *subsystem malfunction*, which in turn may or may not produce *system malfunction*.

We have portrayed a propagation chain from physical malfunctions to system malfunction, with some external entry points. Whether propagation takes place from one level to another depends on whether a causal link exists in the first place, and whether the phenomenon is masked by a redundancy. Thus a logic malfunc-

tion produces a data malfunction only if it impacts the outcome of an operation. Even then, it may not, as for example when the data results from the voting of three inputs, only one of which suffers a data malfunction.

A key point, often overlooked in simplistic treatments of redundancy, is that redundancy always has a limited capacity to mask malfunctions, and this capacity can degrade to zero without affecting the apparent behavior of the system. Therefore, a system designed to have tolerance may in fact have none at the inception of a critical mission. Alternatively it may have some tolerance, but less than the design level, and less than what is assumed. Masking is a two-edged sword. On one hand it is a mechanism for holding malfunctions at a low system level, while on the other hand it may obscure the fact that the malfunction has occurred and thereby has reduced the system's tolerance to future malfunctions [Hopkins, 1977].

Tolerance Renewal Principles

The primary advantage of hybrid redundancy over TMR is that injured triads are reconfigured back to a state where they can once again mask malfunctions. This is a process of tolerance renewal. In principle, the system failure rate is restored to its design value by the reconfiguration process. If reconfiguration were to fail, the system failure rate would increase, possibly by many orders of magnitude.

In practice, there are several ways in which an injured triad can fail to be reconfigured. These include exhaustion of spare modules, malfunction of the reconfiguration mechanism, failure to detect the need to reconfigure, and perhaps the use of a defective spare module. We can characterize the process of tolerance renewal as the detection and location of any physical malfunction, the removal of vulnerability from the triad containing the malfunction, the replacement, by spares, of functions thus removed, and the initialization of the reconstituted triad. All mechanisms involved in this process are subject to malfunction, of course, and such malfunctions constitute injury to their triads, and require that tolerance renewal be carried out on the appropriate modules.

The tolerance renewal mechanism in the FTMP is largely contained in the voters and the bus guardian units. Both the voters and the guardian units possess bus line interfaces, and therefore are both capable of degrading elements (i.e., bus lines) outside of their own modules (e.g., processor, memory, interface access). This by itself is not qualitatively different from a single malfunction. The important concern is that all guardians in a single module may fail in such a way as to enable that module to transmit on more than one bus line. Design steps are taken to minimize the probability of this eventuality, but the probability is finite that it will happen. A subsequent failure of the module in a malevolent state could cause an entire central computer to malfunction.

Fault Detection, Identification, and Recovery

The FTMP is designed to have a highly improbable loss of capability, with a total failure rate of less than 10^{-9} failures per hour in a flight of up to ten hours. This virtually rules out the use of ordinary triple modular redundancy, as the MTBF's achievable in large scale production have been consistently too low for such reliability without replacement of failed modules. Therefore some form of hybrid redundancy is needed. In a simplistic view, hybrid redundancy works by substituting a spare the first time the TMR voters disagree. This view has the shortcoming of not taking latency of faults into account. That is, the first fault may not result in any voter disagreements, whereas when combined with a second fault, it may frustrate recovery. A prerequisite for achieving highly improbable failure in a hybrid system is therefore to expose latent faults by systematic exercising, or "flexing" of all logic elements. The flexing period must be of the order of seconds for a reasonably

sized system with module MTBF's in the 10,000-hour range. Clearly, then, flexing cannot be relegated to preflight checkout, but must rather be conducted routinely in flight. An ordinary hybrid TMR system cannot routinely test itself when performing critical functions, as it is vulnerable during these times. A parallel hybrid TMR system can do this, however, and this becomes an integral part of the computer's architecture.

In the FTMP, an error correction mechanism exists in every module in the form of a voter. Each voter must be tested routinely to ensure that its error correcting capability is undiminished. Bus voters under normal conditions will correct single bus errors and will set error latches to indicate which of the buses was in disagreement. At this time the processor can record the identity of the nominal user of the bus for diagnostic purposes. A processor triad can flex its own voters during a test job step by having each triad member purposely utter independent bus data that causes all possible kinds of bus errors. To pass the test, all triad members must receive the same data, form the same corrected result, and indicate the same disagreement patterns in their error latches. This is a relatively simple test procedure, which can be conducted by a processor triad under test while other triads carry on normal functions. In a sense it qualifies the triad to conduct further testing, in which the triad's voters are the decision elements.

The remainder of the system testing function is carried out under the assumption that the processor voters and error latches are operational. The test process involves the conversion of every fault into an error, by making calculations whose results are sensitive to each logic variable. Each bus and module, including voters, guardians, isolation gates, clock receivers, oscillators, and data and power interfaces must be exercised in depth.

We might summarize the fault detection process as the arrival of disagreement errors at the voters of a processor triad, stimulated by normal or test activity. The detection of a fault initiates

the process of fault identification, which is the discovery of the module, bus, or other isolated element in which the failure resides. During the testing process for latent faults, there is relatively little ambiguity in the determination of faulty modules. In normal operation, however, an error on the bus can come from a number of sources. The identification of the faulty module generally requires the "rounding up of suspects," that is, the listing of elements that transmit on the disagreeing bus. If a module fault is permanent, the module can be found by moving it to another bus. If the bus is faulty, reconfiguration will not move the error to another bus.

Intermittent faults are less easy to identify. When the source of an error eludes detection by disappearing, all of the suspect elements are assigned one demerit, and a reconfiguration is then made to distribute the suspects evenly on different buses. Subsequent error occurrences and reconfigurations will cause a preponderance of demerits to accumulate in the name of the faulty module or bus.

The recovery process is one of assignment and initialization for modules, and voter and transmitter selection for buses. These are all accomplished by the bus guardian units upon receipt of commands from active triads executing system software. Recovery can take place even if single errors are present on the buses. In principle, therefore, an injured processor triad can reconfigure itself.

The use of program restart, or rollback, as a recovery mechanism is secondary, because it is neither sufficiently effective nor easy to implement. The first level of system defense is the masking of errors by the TMR method. The additional system failure rate reduction achievable by rollback cannot be measured, a priori, without an understanding of the applications software. It should be anticipated, however, that any event that defeats the TMR masking is apt to destroy the vehicle's state vector, which may or may not be catastrophic. In any event, some degree of program rerun should be included to support power-up initialization and to deal to some extent with the eventuality of uncovered errors. This will affect both system software and application software.

DESCRIPTION OF AN ENGINEERING PROTOTYPE OF THE FTMP

During the 1978 and 1979 time frame the Charles Stark Draper Laboratory is planning the construction, for NASA, of an engineering prototype of the FTMP. The hardware is to be built by a major avionics manufacturer using specifications provided by CSDL. CSDL will retain program responsibility, provide all system software, and will conduct the integration, test, and evaluation of the system. The project is being sponsored by the NASA Langley Research Center as a part of the Energy Efficient Aircraft Program. The implementation of the prototype is discussed in this section.

The proposed system is to be constructed of ten identical line replaceable units (LRU's) connected as indicated in Figure 17-5. Each LRU contains one processor/cache module, one memory module, one I/O port, one clock generator, and related peripheral support and control circuitry. Figure 17-6 shows how an LRU is divided into fault-containment regions. The principle region is detailed in Figure 17-7.

Up to three processor triads can be in operation simultaneously, utilizing nine of ten available processor/cache modules. The tenth module serves as a spare. With three triads operating simultaneously, the system is functioning as a three-processor multiprocessor.

Up to three memory triads can be formed from nine of the mass memory modules. The tenth module is a spare. Each memory triad is assigned to service a single 16K work region of the shared mass memory address space. With three memory triads operating simultaneously, 48K words of contiguous shared mass memory address space can be serviced.

The I/O ports use MIL-STD-1553 data formats and signaling protocols. MIL-STD-1553 is a United States Air Force standard for a bit serial, time multiplexed avionics data bus. A

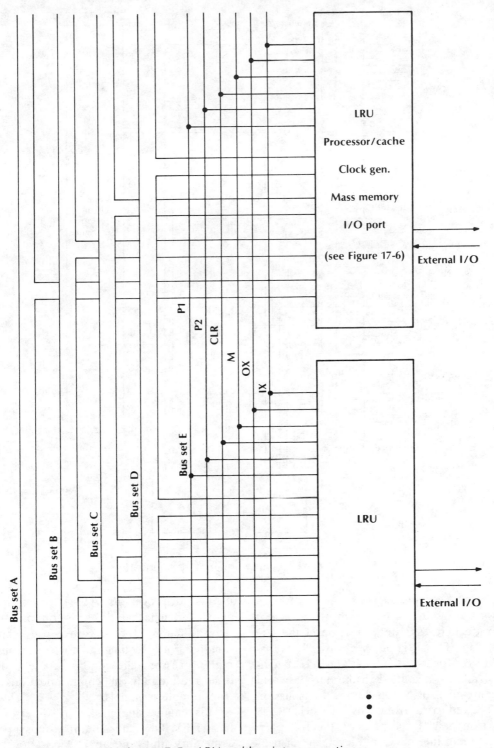

Figure 17–5. LRU and bus interconnections.

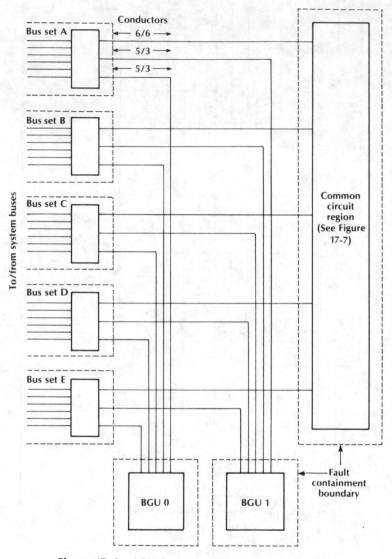

Figure 17–6. LRU fault containment boundaries.

single I/O port accepts the bit serial data from a processor triad, votes to mask any errors in that triad, and generates a single version of the I/O transmission. This version is electrically transformed to conform with MIL-STD-1553 specifications, and is transmitted to the outside world on one member of a full-duplex transmission pair. Received data from this MIL-STD-1553 transmission pair is accepted by the I/O port, converted to an internal signal level, and distrib-

uted to all processors. At least one port and its associated external transmission pair must remain functional for the system to remain operational. Error detection and correction outside the multiprocessor relies upon data encoding and time redundancy in communications to and from remote terminals.

This engineering prototype differs from the basic FTMP design in that it groups a processor, a memory unit, and an I/O port together in a

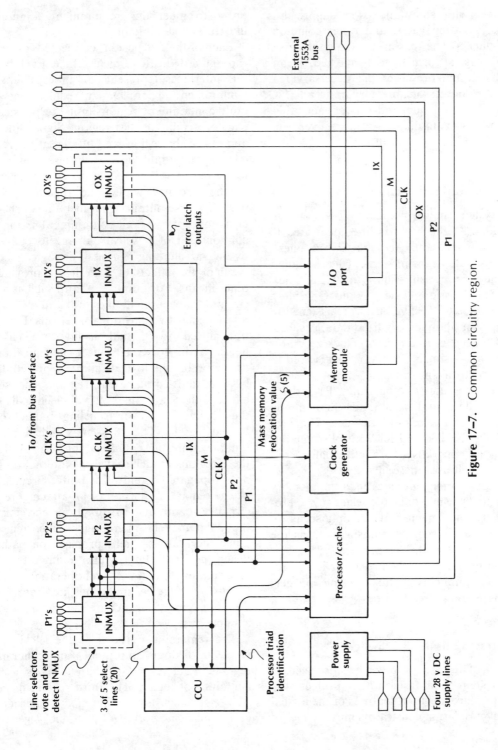

Figure 17-7. Common circuitry region.

single LRU with common power supply, bus guardians, isolation gates, and other common-failure elements. The reason for doing this arises from the physical form factors involved. Meanwhile, this design preserves the necessary features to allow processors, memory units, and I/O ports to be assigned independently of each other, and for the system to diagnose and recover from simultaneous failures of all three.

The Redundant Bus Structure

The bus system shown in Figure 17-5 is quintuple-redundant. Each bus has lines dedicated to processor transmission, (the two P bus lines); memory module transmissions, (the M line); clock generator transmission, (the CLK line); and I/O transmissions, (the IX and OX lines). Subsets of three of the five buses are assigned to carry processor and memory triad data. A subset of four of the five is used to carry clock generator transmissions. A single bus of the five is used to carry I/O port transmissions.

The processor uses two bus lines, P1 and P2, to transmit data and commands to common memory and status register devices. The processor triads also contend for control of the bus system via a cooperative, competitive allocation technique which uses these bus lines.

A triad of memory modules uses the memory bus lines to transmit data requested by a processor triad. Since memory triads only speak on command, there is no mechanism, such as the competitive poll used by the processors, to grant permission to transmit. The processor in control of the P bus implicitly grants transmission permission by issuing a read request.

LRU Interfacing to the Bus System

Each LRU of the system must be interfaced to the bus system in a fashion that protects the fault-tolerant architectural features of the logical design. Several design constraints must be met in

order to meet this requirement. Figure 17-6 illustrates a suitable interface.

Each of the five buses is connected to the LRU through a dedicated bus interface. Each of these bus interfaces represents an independent fault containment region. Design requirements for a fault containment region limit the physical impact of a fault in that region. Signal lines into and out of the region are buffered at the region's edge so that a fault on any of these lines external to the region will not affect the correct operation of the circuitry within the region, excepting possibly these output or input buffers. The principal concept of a fault-containment region is the containment of physical damage to one region by the surrounding regions. The logical containment of the effects of a fault are provided by other means. For example, a fault such as a short circuit to power on all lines into and out of a bus interface has two partitionable effects. First, data transmitted through that bus interface is likely to be received incorrectly. This is the logical impact of the fault. The logical failure is not contained by the fault-containment region. The second effect is physical. The fault will electrically stress the receiving and transmitting buffers of attached regions. This stress may induce physical faults within these buffers, but the design of these regions is such that these internal faults do not propagate beyond these buffer circuits.

The remaining portion of an attached region's circuitry continues to function correctly, although it may be operating on incorrect data. Since there are no fault propagation paths between regions, a fault within a single bus interface cannot affect the correct operation of another bus interface. A single bus interface failure, therefore, can at most cause the apparent loss of a single bus.

The remaining portions of the LRU are divided into three additional fault-containment regions. Each Bus Guardian Unit is a fault-containment region. The third region, or *principal region*, consists of common voters, processor/cache, mass memory, I/O port, clock generator, and power supply. The bus interface provides separately buffered copies of the P1, P2, and CLK lines to both bus guardians and the principal region. Since a fault within one of these attached regions cannot affect the separately buffered P1, P2, and CLK lines used by the other two regions, they each appear to have independent access to the bus system. In order for a bus interface to allow principal region transmissions onto a system bus line, it must have enabling signals from both bus guardians. Thus either guardian can block access to a particular bus line. Each of the guardians has what is effectively independent access to all incoming bus data. It can independently mask single bus errors via voting, and it processes incoming processor triad transmissions, responding only to write commands to its particular address location. The contents of these write commands alter the static enabling signals from the guardians. Each guardian provides an enable line to each bus interface for the P lines, M line, CLK line, and OX line.

The LRU interfacing is designed to protect the integrity of the bus system despite multiple sequential faults. A worst case bus interface failure can at most disable all of the lines of only one of the quintuple bus sets. The system can then be reconfigured to use the remaining lines of other buses. One element of a triad or the clock quad, if it fails, can impact at most one of the active bus sets. Again reconfiguration commands can isolate that faulty unit from the bus and assign a spare to replace it, thereby restoring system health. To cause a system failure, four of the five bus sets must fail, or two bus guardians within the same LRU must fail, enabling the principal region to access all bus lines, and in addition, the principal region must fail.

System Control Units

The bus guardian unit is a particular case of a generalized unit called a *system control unit*. Each LRU has four system control units. They are designated bus guardian unit 0 (BGU 0); bus guardian unit 1 (BGU 1); configuration control unit, (CCU); and the interprocessor triad communication unit, (IPC unit). The CCU and IPC units are part of the principal fault containment region. As previously stated, BGU 0 and BGU 1 are each a fault-containment region.

All of these system control unit types are similar and can be constructed from the same circuit. Figure 17-8 illustrates the functional requirements for such a common circuit. Essentially the circuit must take the serial processor command data, P1, P2, and CLK, pass it through error-correlation circuitry, if this data is in redundant form, and convert it to a parallel form. A system control unit only responds to a memory write command to its own particular memory address.

Register contents may be supplied as static enabling or data signals to circuitry external to the system control unit, or they may be used internally to control the error correction circuitry (if present).

A power monitoring circuit switches the register store to battery power when primary power to the unit is not within specification. When battery powered, the register contents are protected, and the enabling lines from the guardians are in the disable state. Total loss of all power to a guardian clears the register contents to the disable state.

The Principal Fault-Containment Region

All of the circuitry of an LRU is within the bounds of the principal fault-containment region excepting the two bus guardians and the bus interfaces.

The principal region can be viewed as being made up of seven subregions. These are: 1) input processing; 2) configuration control; 3) processor/cache; 4) memory; 5) I/O ports; 6) clock generator; and 7) power supply, as shown in Figure 17-7.

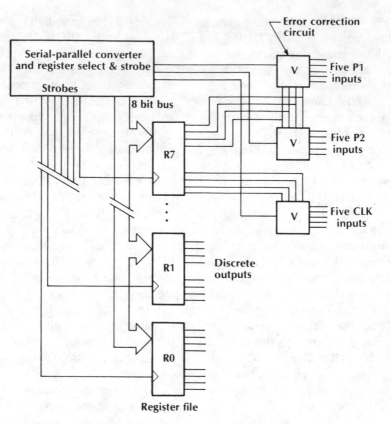

Figure 17–8.   System control unit.

Input Processing

All input to the principal region is from the bus interfaces, and is first processed by shared signal selectors, voters, and error detection circuits. The input circuitry generates a single version of the P1, P2, CLK, M, IX, and OX lines to be used by all modules within the region. This single version of each line is the appropriate majority function of the selected group of 3 out of 5 lines. Additionally, the voting circuitry detects and latches any error condition on the bus lines, and provides this information as input discretes to the processor. The selection of one of the ten possible groups of 3 out of 5 buses to be used by the majority circuitry or the selection of which IX line to be used, is made by selector discretes provided by the Configuration Control Unit.

Configuration Control Unit (CCU)

The Configuration Control Unit (CCU) is a system control unit. The CCU is used to control the INMUX circuitry, is used to assign the processor/cache unit to a processor triad and to start and stop the processor, and is used to assign the mass memory module to a memory triad.

Processor/ Cache Module

The processor/cache memory module is the most complex of the principal region. It can be partitioned into a number of submodules. These are: a) processor, b) cache memory, c) bus controller, d) IPC unit, and e) MIL-STD-1553 controller.

The Processor. The principal design requirements of the processor could be met using any of a large number of general purpose 16-bit minicomputer architectures. In order to support the projected computational requirements of an integrated avionics system, the basic processor has a raw instruction execution rate roughly equivalent to 500,000 16-bit fixed-point adds per second. A 16-bit fixed-point multiply has an execution time six times that of the fixed point add.

The instruction set of the processor is suitable for avionics applications and, in addition, provides for the following: 1) code is relocatable without modification; 2) code is read-only and reentrant; 3) the CALL and RETURN instructions support dynamic program loading efficiently; 4) memory protect is supported for a region of the cache RAM; and 5) privileged user modes of operation are provided to prevent the direct execution of I/O and mass memory access instructions by applications code.

The processor is adapted to use the output of the CLK generator as its time base and incorporates a microcode interlock with the bus controller which allows three processors to be synchronized by using particular bus events, such as bus grant.

Cache Memory. The cache memory is a 4K × 16 semiconductor RAM and 4K × 16 semiconductor PROM array. It interfaces to the processor over the processor's internal parallel bus. Access time for this memory is 400 ns. There is no requirement for nonvolatility in the RAM portion of this memory.

Bus Controller. The bus controller is responsible for the bit-by-bit control of the processor side of bus activity. On command of the processor, the bus controller conducts a competitive polling sequence to acquire control of the main memory bus. The controller then holds the bus until instructed to release it. It makes use of the triad identification provided by the CCU and a priority field provided by the processor during the polling sequence. While holding the bus, it performs memory reads and writes as requested by the processor. Data and memory address transfers between the processor and controller are handled in parallel. The controller performs the necessary timing, serial to parallel and parallel to serial conversions for the processor. The processor handles block transfers performing the necessary housekeeping, streaming parallel memory addresses, and accepting whole word data streams from the controller and storing them in cache memory, or streaming parallel addresses and data to the controller for storage in the common memory.

Interprocessor Triad Communication Unit. The Interprocessor Triad Communication Unit (IPC) is used by the executive for direct processor-triad to processor-triad communications. The IPC registers are available as discretes to the processor.

MIL-STD-1553 Controller. A MIL-STD-1553 controller interfaces to the processor over the processor's internal parallel bus. It conforms to the standard format, except that the outgoing and incoming data paths have been split so as to provide full-duplex transmission paths.

Memory Module

The memory module contains a 16K × 16 CMOS memory array with the appropriate control circuitry to respond to processor triad memory read and write commands.

Input to the memory control circuitry is the bit-serial quantity represented by the outputs of the P-INMUX outputs and CLK-INMUX. The most significant bits of the incoming address are compared to the relocation register provided by the CCU. If they match, a read or write operation is performed. If they do not match, the incoming command is ignored. Read responses are made using the M bus. Responses are clocked using the output of the CLK-INMUX.

I/O Port

The I/O port is principally a signal level shifter and data synchronizer. A single corrected version of I/O output data, OX, is accepted by the I/O port from the common input module, and is buffered to conform to MIL-STD-1553 specifications. The transmitting processor triad is responsible for formatting the OX lines signal to conform to the MIL-STD-1553 format.

The I/O port receives I/O input data, synchronizes it so that transitions do not occur near system clock edges, converts the signal levels to an internal standard, and transmits the signal on an IX line to all processors.

Clock Generator

As discussed in the subsection on Synchronization, the entire fault-tolerant multiprocessor rests on an assumption of synchronized operation based on a common timing reference. Each LRU includes a clock generator which can be synchronized to the common reference, and which, if gated by the BGU's onto a CLK bus, could serve as a contributing element to the common reference in the manner shown in Figure 17-4. The clock generation circuit of an LRU interacts with the CLK bus lines, the CLK-INMUX, and the other clock generators. To understand the function of the clocking system, it is necessary to discuss all of these components as they interrelate with one another.

The clock bus is a component part of the quintuple redundant busing system. Each of the five bus sets includes one clock bus line, CLK. Normally, four of the five CLK lines are active and one is inactive. Four clock generators are chosen as the clock sources, each being assigned to a different clock bus. Each transmits a clock signal which is phase-locked to the other three active clock generators. Thus the system has available at all points a quad-redundant time base. Each clock receiver listens to three of the four active clock buses and generates a derived clock which remains correct even if one of the

three input signals fails. It is therefore possible to tolerate a single failure of one of the elements of the clock quad without affecting the correctness of the derived clocks generated throughout the system.

Each bus guardian and each CLK-INMUX uses a clock receiver to generate its own corrected version of the system clock, despite single faults in the clock quad.

Each clock generator, whether active or in standby mode, phase locks its output to its CLK-INMUX output. Thus the clock generator outputs a clock which is in phase with the majority of three CLK buses. When active, the output of the clock generator is gated onto one of the four CLK buses, and its associated CLK-INMUX is adjusted to listen to the other three CLK buses. In this configuration the correctly functioning clock generators will produce multiple phase-locked clocks which will remain phase-locked despite any failure of a single clock element of the quad.

When a failure is detected, the system reconfigures, replacing the failed CLK bus or clock generator. Standby clock generators are already phase-locked to the corrected system clock, so that they can be switched in to replace a failed clock generator with minimal transients in clock frequency and with negligible risks. This restores the fault-tolerant character of the clocking system, positioning it to tolerate the next clocking component failure.

Power Supply

The power supply provides regulated power to the LRU. The power supply can draw power from any of the four primary 28-V DC power buses. A circuit breaker or fuse protects each of these buses from a short circuit within the LRU. The power supply must have adequate energy storage so that its output remains within regulation for the time it takes these protective devices to act and the bus voltages to return to normal after a short circuit within another LRU. The output of the power supply is overvoltage protected, possibly with serial redundant protection.

The bus interface devices will be designed to operate safely for all power supply voltages beneath the overvoltage protection limit; that is, the bus interface will present a high impedance load on the bus for all voltage levels if the corresponding enables from the BGU's are unasserted.

The BGU's will monitor power supply voltages. If out-of-regulation voltages are detected, the contents of the BGU registers will be frozen, and all enabling outputs will revert to the unasserted state.

A battery backup is used to provide power to the CMOS memory array, and to the BGU and CCU register files, when primary power is lost. If this battery power fails when primary power is down, the register files of the BGU's and CCU will be cleared.

Primary Power

Power is distributed to all LRU's of the system by means of four 28-V DC power buses. Four 400-Hz 110-V DC to 28-V DC power converters provide power to these buses. These power supplies are overvoltage and overcurrent protected. If an overcurrent condition arises, the 28-V DC output will current-limit but return to normal when the protective devices within the shorting LRU open. Energy storage with the power supply must be adequate to tolerate momentary power interruptions such as are typically caused by power switching in aircraft power distribution systems.

SURVIVAL AND DISPATCH PROBABILITY MODELS FOR THE FTMP

The FTMP has several different failure modes, each of which is amenable to a different mathematical tool. Specifically, the probability of failure due to exhaustion of spares can be adequately modeled using combinatorial methods, whereas Markov processes are better suited to modeling coverage-related problems. Fortunately, each of these failure modes predominates in a different time segment, and therefore can be modeled and analyzed independently.

Survival Probability Models

The computation of survival probability of the FTMP for random hard failures is divided into the following three phases:

- probability of failure due to the lack of perfect coverage using a Markov process model;
- probability of failure due to exhaustion of spares using a combinatorial model;
- probability of failure due to BGU failures in enable mode using a combinatorial model.

In the FTMP some time is required to detect, isolate, and recover from any failure. During this time a second failure may arrive in such a place as to be catastrophic. Therefore, the coverage [Bouricius et al., 1971] is imperfect. This phenomenon is most conveniently modeled using Markov processes, as each distinct failure or recovery moves the system into a state that is dependent only on the present state of the system. However, to limit the number of states to a reasonable level, it is necessary to make some approximations. The most effective of these approximations is to assume that recovery from a failure returns the system to a perfect state, which is the initial state of the system, rather than to a computationally degraded state. In effect, this implies an unlimited supply of spare units of each kind. The probability of failure due solely to exhaustion of equipment can be computed independently using combinatorial methods. The basic premise which allows one to decouple and model these two modes of failures separately is the predominance of each mode during a different time span. As will be shown in the following sections, in the short run (0–50 hr) it is the threat of near simultaneous failures which most affects system survivability, whereas in the long run (> 100 hr) the system is likely to fail due to a lack of equipment. In addition to these, there is a third failure mode peculiar to the FTMP architecture that has to be accounted for. This relates to two bus guardian units in an LRU failing so as to enable a failed unit (processor, memory, etc.) to transmit simultaneously on a number of buses. It will be shown that this mode does not affect the reliability since its probability is insignificant at all times.

The following three subsections describe the models and the results.

Lack of Coverage: Markov Model

Since all the information as well as all the computations in the FTMP computer are triply redundant, any single failure in the system is completely masked by the majority voters. Therefore, if the system starts out in a totally fault-free state, it takes at least two successive failures without recovery to produce a catastrophic system failure. However, not all double failures are catastrophic. In fact, most double failures can be tolerated by the FTMP without any problem. The following is a list of all the catastrophic double failure combinations:

- two processors in a triad fail;
- two memory modules in a triad fail;
- two active buses fail;
- one active bus fails and a processor or memory enabled on another active bus fails;
- two active oscillators fail;
- one active bus and an oscillator enabled on another bus fails;
- one LRU fails in common mode and an associated processor, memory, or bus fails;
- two associated LRU's fail in common mode.

The common mode LRU failure refers to a failure of any of the LRU components that are shared by the processor, memory, and I/O port in that LRU. These include the local power supply, the oscillator, the two BGU's, and the selectors and voters. A local power supply failure in an LRU, for example, will result in the simultaneous loss of the processor, memory, and I/O port in that LRU. The BGU failures include only the disable mode, since the enable mode is taken care of separately. Finally, the bus failure includes a failure of any of the five lines constituting a bus or a failure of any of the ten bus interface gates connected to that bus.

A Markov model of the FTMP computer reliability based on the above discussion is shown in Figure 17-9. The system is initially in a completely fault-free state or "ALL GOOD" state. It will be shown shortly that at time $t = 0$, such as a take-off time, the probability of having a latent failure in the system should be about 10^{-6} to achieve a system failure rate of 10^{-9} failures per hour. That is, one must be certain with a probability of about 0.999999 that the system is initially fault-free. In the following discussion, it is assumed that the system is initially fault-free. Some of the other assumptions used in developing the model are outlined below.

As explained earlier, it is assumed that reconfiguration around a failed unit returns the system to the perfect state. It is also assumed that all the failed buses are active and that all triple undetected faults cause system failure. These simplifying assumptions reduce the number of states in the model considerably without significantly altering the system failure probability. For example, contribution of triple faults to the system failure probability is found to be less than 2 percent.

A baseline set of failure and recovery rates, as shown in Table 17-1, was used to obtain a numerical solution of the Markov model. The values shown in Table 17-1 are the mean values. The model uses random values that are exponentially distributed around these means. One may argue about the fidelity of exponential distributions, although it is our contention that they represent the actual reconfiguration time distributions sufficiently well for this purpose [Laprie, 1975].

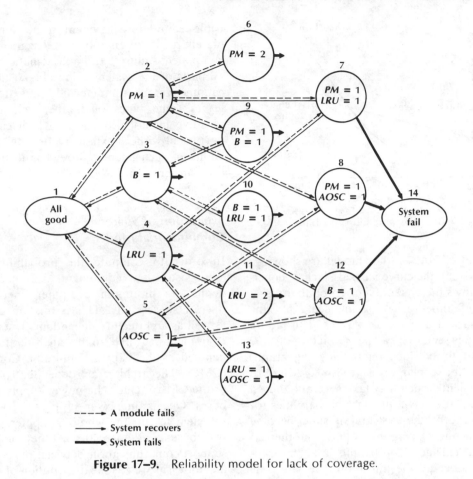

Figure 17–9. Reliability model for lack of coverage.

Table 17–1. Baseline parameter values.

System Configuration		CMC	Failure Rate (per hour)	MTBF (hrs)	Recovery Time (sec)
# Processors	10	5	2×10^{-4}	5,000	0.25
# Memory units	10	2	2×10^{-4}	5,000	0.25
# I/O units	10	1	5×10^{-5}	20,000	
# Buses	5	3	10^{-5}	100,000	0.25
# Main power Supply units	4	1	10^{-4}	10,000	
# BGUs	20		EN $= 10^{-6}$	1,000	
			DIS $= 10^{-5}$	100,000	
# LRUs	10		CMF $= 1.46 \times 10^{-4}$	7,000	0.25
# Oscillators	10	3	10^{-5}	100,000	1.0

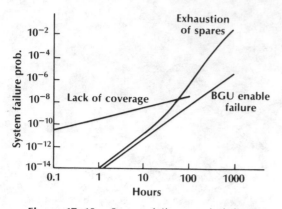

Figure 17–10.   System failure probability.

The results of the Markov model are shown in Figure 17-10 by the curve labeled "lack of coverage." It shows the system failure probability as a function of time on a log–log scale for the baseline hazard and recovery rates. The failure probability is seen to be a linear function of time (linear and unity slope on the log–log graph) which can be explained as follows. After an initial transient, which may take several hundred seconds to settle down, the state probabilities for all states except the system fail state become nearly constant. During this equilibrium there is a constant leakage of probability into the trapping state since all the transition rates are time invariant. Since the total leakage rate is only about 10^{-9} per hour, the state probabilities diminish extremely slowly, and a state of equilibrium would hold for hundreds of hours. For the baseline case, the system failure rate due to lack of coverage is found to be about 3×10^{-10} per hour.

The reason for having an initial latent-failure probability of 10^{-6} now becomes clear. This is the probability of the system being in states 2 through 5, that is, the single-undetected-failure states (see Figure 17-9). The transition rate from those four states into the system fail state or the probability of arrival of a second catastrophic failure is of the order of magnitude of 10^{-3} per hour. To prove that the system is initially fault-free with absolute certainty is not possible. The triple redundancy prevalent in the system immediately points to any obvious disagreements and component failures, and a systematic exercise of all parts of the system using diagnostic routines can uncover most undetected faults. But this still leaves some types of faults, such as pattern sensitive memory locations, which can not be uncovered without exhaustive testing. The probability of such latent failures has to be reduced to an insignificant level.

Exhaustion of Spares Combinatorial Model

In order to compute the probability of not having sufficient equipment, it is necessary to define the minimum equipment necessary to operate successfully. This is mission dependent as well as architecture dependent. The minimum equipment required to fly an aircraft shall be denoted as the Critical Minimum Complement (CMC). The architecture-dependent parameters of the CMC include the power supply units and buses. One main power supply unit is deemed sufficient to run the whole computer. Similarly, two buses are adequate at the minimum to support communication between processors and memories, as well as the distribution of the clock. However, for one pathological clock failure mode it would be necessary to have three buses. The minimum number of processors and memories required is mission dependent. The throughput of the FTMP computer in a fully operational state is estimated to be 500,000 operations per second and the minimum throughput necessary to support all flight-critical functions is estimated to be about 200,000 operations per second. Similarly, the total storage capacity of the computer is 48,000 words while the critical programs are estimated to be less than 16,000 words. Thus two processor triads and one memory triad have to be operational to support the critical functions. There are a number of ways of achieving this, one of which uses five processors and two memories. It is, of course, possible to lose another processor in the fully populated triad and still be operational, although the probability of such an event is only 3/5. The number of I/O ports necessary to interface with the I/O network is one. Table 17-1 lists the critical minimum complement based on the above discussion. This table lists the minimum number of oscillators as three, which is what is needed to generate a clock. However, this is dominated by a larger requirement of five or more oscillators necessary to operate five processors, two memories, and an I/O port, all of which may be in different LRU's.

Figure 17-10 shows the overall failure probability due to lack of equipment for a period of up to 1,000 hr. In the short run, the number of buses is critical, while in the long run it is the number of LRU's. The number of power supplies is adequate at all times.

Bus Guardian Unit Failures— Combinatorial Model

This section discusses the system failure probability due to BGU failures in the enable mode. Although this mode can be made about an order of magnitude less likely than the normal disable failure mode, it is nonetheless present and must be accounted for. As explained earlier, one single BGU may disable a unit from transmitting on a bus, while both BGU's in an LRU unit must agree before a unit is enabled on a bus. Under the normal circumstances, an active unit (processor, memory, etc.) will be enabled on a single bus. With two BGU's failed in the enable mode, a unit would be enabled on more than one bus. This by itself presents little, if any, problem since three members of a triad transmit in tight synchronism on three buses. However, if the unit enabled on multiple buses fails and does not transmit in synchronism, a number of buses immediately become useless, and this may result in a catastrophic system failure. Thus it takes at least three related failures in a single LRU for the system to fail. The BGU enable mode failures are nonrecoverable. That is, the system can

not be reconfigured around a failed BGU. The results for the baseline parameter values are shown in Figure 17-10. It is seen that the system failure probability due to this peculiarity of the architecture is at all times insignificant.

Unified Survival Probability Results

The following conclusions can be drawn from Figure 17-10.

1. During a typical commercial flight of one to ten hours the most likely threat of the FTMP computer failure is due to an arrival of two failures so close that system reconfiguration is not possible. The probability of this event, however, is acceptably low (about 3×10^{-10} per hour) because of high component MTBF's and fast reconfiguration times.
2. There is very little chance that the FTMP computer will run out of spares during a ten-hour flight, assuming that the system initially has all ten LRU's fully operational. In longer flights, however, failure would be quite possible as evidenced by the sharply rising failure probability curve after 50 hours. Lack of equipment is a critical item as far as the dispatch reliability of the computer is concerned, and is discussed in detail in the subsection on Dispatch Reliability below.
3. Finally, the system failure rate due to BGU enable mode failures is substantially lower than other system failure modes. Therefore it does not contribute significantly to the overall system failure probability.

The overall system failure probability due to all causes, up to about 50 hours, is dominated by the probability of failure due to near simultaneous failures. During this time the probability of exhaustion of spares is several orders of magnitude lower. Beyond 100 hours the opposite is true. Strictly speaking, the overall failure probability is a complex function of all the contributing failure probabilities. However, under certain circumstances, it can be approximated very closely by just the predominant failure probability.

Impact of Intermittent Faults

An intermittent fault in a digital computing system may be defined as a fault that persists only part of the time. Physically, this may correspond to a loose connection between components, a loose bond within a semiconductor device, a temperature sensitive device, etc. Since an intermittent fault manifests itself only a fraction of the time, it injects an additional level of latency to the problem of fault detection. This would lead to longer fault detection and isolation times, thereby reducing the system reliability. The actual extent to which the system reliability would be degraded due to intermittent faults would depend on the degree of latency of the fault. That is, the higher the percentage of time a fault stays in the good state, the higher the chance of it being undetected. With the presence of such a lurking fault in a triad, for example, a second fault in another member of the triad leads to a situation where two out of three members of the triad are at one time or another malfunctioning. If this situation is not redressed promptly by reconfiguration of faulty elements it can result in a catastrophic system failure. On the other hand, the presence of two intermittent faults in two members of a triad can be tolerated as long as one or both of them stay in the lurking mode. This apparently should result in an increased level of fault-tolerance. The following study was undertaken to analyze these contradictory impacts of intermittent faults on the FTMP reliability.

To incorporate intermittent faults in the FTMP survivability models, it is necessary first to define various states and their transition rates corresponding to intermittent faults. In the simplest form, an element with an intermittent fault may be represented by two states: a failed state and a pseudofailed state [Breuer, 1973]. In the first state the fault is actually present, that is, use of the element will produce an incorrect output. In the second state, the fault is in a benign mode, and use of the element will not corrupt the output. An intermittent fault will oscillate between these two states with a frequency that is

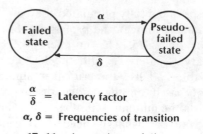

$$\frac{\alpha}{\delta} = \text{Latency factor}$$

α, δ = Frequencies of transition

Figure 17–11.   Intermittent failure model.

dependent upon the characteristics of the fault. In general, the transition rate from the failed to the pseudofailed state may not be the same as the rate in the other direction (see Figure 17-11). The ratio of transition rates, α/δ, is a measure of the additional latency due to the intermittent nature of the fault. The higher the ratio α/δ, the higher is the percent of time a fault stays in the pseudofailed state and is invisible a longer time. For $\alpha/\delta = 0$, the intermittent fault really becomes a hard fault since all the time is spent in the failed state.

Certain assumptions have been made regarding the use of this basic model to keep the overall models and the number of parameters tractable. For example, α and δ are assumed to be constant with respect to time. In addition, all faults are assumed to be intermittent with the same transition frequencies and duty cycles. In practice there will be faults with various frequencies which will most likely vary with time as the intermittent faults transition into hard faults. However, the present purpose is to get an insight into how an intermittent fault affects the system survivability. This is best done by simulating a situation where all the failures are intermittent and stay intermittent during the course of investigation.

A Markov process coverage model of a triple modular redundant (TMR) system incorporating the intermittent failure model was developed, as shown in Figure 17-12. The reasons for modeling a TMR before going to a full-fledged multiprocessor model are twofold. It involves fewer parameters, making it easier to establish a cause and effect relationship between reliability and

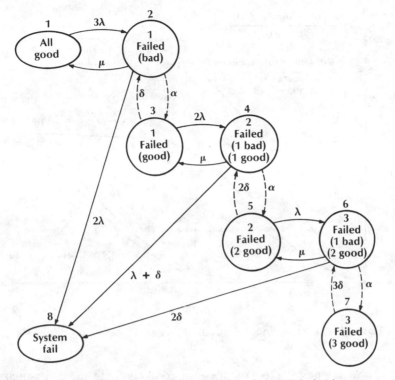

Figure 17–12.   Intermittent failure model of a TMR-hybrid system.

various parameters. It also involves fewer states and can be analyzed for a wider range of parameter values. Since the FTMP multiprocessor under investigation is a combination of a number of triads, the TMR results can generally lead to a good understanding of the FTMP reliability behavior.

Figure 17-12 shows three different ways in which a catastrophic system failure can result. The first is the occurrence of two simultaneous failures, that is, the failure of a second element before the first failure has been diagnosed and recovered from (transition 2–8). This is the only mode of failure in a TMR system if all the failures were hard failures. However, due to the intermittent nature of our assumed failures, the system can survive even in the presence of two failures as long as at least one of the faulty elements is in the pseudofailed state (states 4, 5, 6, 7). In such a case, the arrival of another failure in the third element (transition 4–8), or the

transition of an element from a pseudofailed to a failed state (transition 6–8), leads to a catastrophic system failure. The model was solved numerically for a number of different values of α, δ, λ, and μ. Some of the important results are shown graphically in Figure 17-13. It is found that the failure probability is not a monotonic function of α or δ. However, if the ratio α/δ is held constant, the failure probability increases with δ as shown in Figure 17-13. Similarly, for a constant δ, the failure probability generally increases with α/δ. In the steady state, the ratio of state probabilities P_3 to P_2 is given by α/δ. That is

$$\frac{P_3}{P_2} = \frac{\alpha}{\delta}.$$

This is assuming there is no leakage from state 2 to the system fail state 8. Physically, the ratio α/δ represents the relative time a fault stays in the lurking mode. That is, the higher the variable

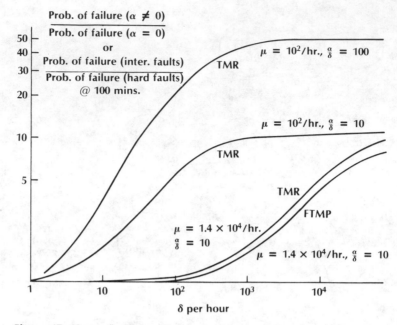

Figure 17–13. Influence of intermittency on the system failure rate.

α/δ, the higher is the latency factor of the intermittent fault. For a fixed ratio α/δ, increasing δ implies a higher leakage rate from state 4, resulting in a higher failure probability. In other words, since the ratio α/δ is fixed, the duty cycle between failed and pseudofailed states is a constant, and therefore, increasing the frequency of transition between these two states only increases the chance of a lurking fault suddenly crashing the system. It is evident from these results that the worst situation arises where the latency of intermittent faults is high (a high α/δ) and the frequency of transition from pseudofailed to failed state is high (a high δ).

The worst case system failure probability with intermittent faults, for the range of parameters investigated, is about fifty times higher than that due to hard failures (see Figure 17-13). The critical frequencies, that is, the worst case α and δ, depend upon the recovery time. The faster the recovery time, the higher these frequencies are. For example, for a recovery time of 36 s, the critical δ is 10^4 per hour or about 3 Hz, while for

a recovery time of a one-quarter second, it is about 30 Hz. Increasing the transition frequencies beyond the critical levels does not further deteriorate the reliability appreciably.

To extend these results to the FTMP computer, a 49-state Markov model was developed. This is basically an expanded version of the 14-state hard failure model described in the subsection on Lack of Coverage. All the assumptions of that model carry forward here. This model was solved for the base-line parameter values shown in Table 17-1. The FTMP reliability behavior with respect to α and δ was found to be in close agreement with that of the TMR-hybrid system qualitatively as well as quantitatively. As shown in Figure 17-13, the FTMP curve is remarkably close to the TMR curve with typical FTMP failure and recovery rates.

Finally, it should be noted that some of the high-frequency intermittent faults, which could do the most damage, may actually look like hard faults. A fault in a processor module, for example, may cause that module to go out of synchro-

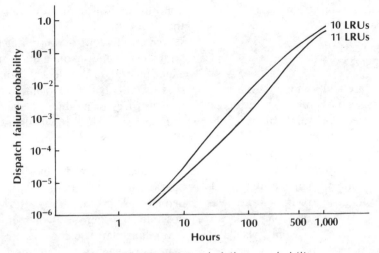

Figure 17–14. Dispatch failure probability.

nism with the other two triad members, thereby making its presence felt after it disappears. Therefore, the overall impact of the intermittent faults may not be as severe as suggested here.

Dispatch Reliability of the FTMP Computer

Availability of equipment, in general, is an important concern in the commercial air transport industry. Availability of avionics equipment, in particular, is economically more important since it tends to be at the heart of "Go/NoGo" decisions. A central computer with digital "fly-by-wire" authority certainly falls into this category. It is imperative, therefore, that the dispatch reliability of the FTMP computer be commensurate with its high survival probability. A preliminary estimate of the dispatch reliability is carried out in this section.

Let the "dispatch minimum complement" (DMC) denote the amount of equipment (processors, memories, etc.) necessary to be operational before take-off for the computer to survive through the flight with a given probability. Using a trial-and-error approach with the combinatorial models of the section on exhaustion of

spares, the DMC for the baseline case was found to be as follows:

Dispatch Minimum Complement:
    Processors   = 8
    Memories   = 6
    Buses   = 4
    Power Supplies = 3

The question to be answered at this point is, how long would it take an initially fully operational FTMP to degrade below the DMC and thereby fail the dispatch criteria? The probability of this event at time t, assuming no maintenance, is shown as a functon of time in Figure 17-14. It is seen from this figure that there is a 7 percent chance that the computer will be below the dispatch minimums if the maintenance is scheduled every 300 hours. The probability of requiring unscheduled maintenance can be reduced to just over two percent by carrying an extra LRU or by shortening the maintenance interval to 200 hours. This would seem to satisfy the needs of most airlines as far as the computer dispatch reliability is concerned. Beyond this, however, the dispatch reliability is bounded by the reliability of main power supply units. That is, the dispatch reliability can be improved only by modifying the architecture to include five or more main power supply units.

EXPERIMENTAL RESULTS

In order to demonstrate and validate as many of the design concepts as possible, a breadboard multiprocessor was used to emulate many of the design features of the proposed system. This demonstration was of an integrated nature in that the experimental setup duplicated much of the information environment which a final product of this nature might encounter, and was therefore able to verify not only the separate design pieces forming the whole, but was also able to confirm predicted interactions between disjoint pieces, and in some cases unearth unexpected interactions.

The basic experimental apparatus consisted of a fault-tolerant multiprocessor, modeled along the lines of the FTMP. The multiprocessor served as the control computer for a Boeing 707 aircraft simulation on a hybrid computer. The experimental fault-tolerant multiprocessor consists of 14 National Semiconductor IMP-16-based processor modules, seven common memory modules of 2K × 16 words, two I/O ports, and ten I/O nodes. The processor modules include 1K RAM/1K ROM cache memory storage. With the 14 processor modules it is possible to operate up to 4 triads of processors simultaneously. With the seven RAM modules it is possible to operate two memory triads. The redundant data busing system is triply redundant, and each attached module has two Bus Guardian Units associated with it for protecting the bus system. An I/O node remote from the multiprocessor and local to the hybrid computer

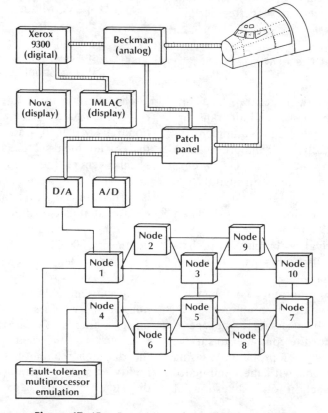

Figure 17–15. Experimental simulation system.

provides A/D and D/A interfacing to the simulated aircraft as shown in Figure 17-15. Figure 17-16 is a photograph of the multiprocessor emulation hardware.

Fault Diagnostic Capabilities

Each processor module of the experimental system includes special circuitry for noting and recording disagreements among the three copies of each bus line. All other modules or receiving elements have only error masking circuits. The error detection circuitry functions as expected. Most faults manifest themselves as bus errors, and are therefore easily detected. Certain classes of latent faults are detected by diagnostic programs which basically force bus errors if a latent fault exists. Records kept by diagnostic programs and fault isolation procedures enable the location of both transient and hard failures.

Most faults are detectable as one of a large class of faults. For example, all processor failures are detected at the bus without the aid of special diagnostic code to test the processor or knowledge of the fault mechanism. Some special attention to specific failure modes and effects was required to devise latent fault detection programs. While code was not written for unearthing all possible latent faults, sufficient latent testing code was written so as to establish considerable confidence in the method.

The bus isolation mechanism serves as intended and is able to isolate processor failures from the bus system.

This integrated system's demonstration illustrates all significant aspects of the FTMP architecture. It demonstrates the hardware capability to mask faulty unit outputs in the short run, and the capability to detect the fault, isolate the unit, and to reorganize so as to restore system health, all concurrent with normal program activity.

Software Experience

The software for the demonstration consists principally of executive or system software and applications software. Executive or system software was written and debugged by staff thoroughly familiar with the experimental hardware and design objectives. The applications software was provided by a team which was briefed only in general terms as to the nature of fault recovery mechanisms and the overall system architecture. The applications software team was provided with detailed explanations of the executive-to-applications interfaces and executive services, as well as a reasonably short list of programming constraints.

Multiprocessor Executive

The multiprocessor executive provides a simple task dispatch mechanism. Tasks awaiting their

Figure 17–16.   Multiprocessor emulation hardware.

time of execution are organized in a queue sorted by scheduled start time. As processor triads become free (having finished a previous task) they consult this list and take the next scheduled job. Jobs may be inserted into any relative position of the time queue as long as it remains properly sorted. Executive functions provide for the routine iterative scheduling of the same job step, as might be required for an autopilot iteration, for example. Alternatively, any job, by a call to the executive, can insert a job into the time queue. The executive also handles the removal of a job from the queue when it is taken up for execution.

In addition to the time queue, the executive handles an event queue. Jobs in the event queue have their execution blocked waiting for a particular event to occur. When the event does occur, the affected job is moved from the event queue to the top of the time queue. Jobs can be inserted into the event queue by any job, through a call to the executive. Events can be signaled by the executive or by another job through a call to the executive.

The executive also provides interfaces for all I/O traffic, common memory to/from cache data transfers, real-time clock, and for other relatively simple functions commonly thought of as executive-related.

Critical to the success of the demonstration are the executive functions which provide for automatic error logging and recovery. Executive functions perform all common memory to/from cache transfers, and all I/O. During these functions any errors that might occur will become visible. The executive handles the proper logging of the error, schedules recovery action, and, via voting, masks the error for the applications task which was using the executive function. Thus, to the applications task, error handling is completely invisible. Additionally, since hardware monitoring is used, error checking, error masking, and majority voting do not impact the applications execution speed.

The executive schedules error diagnostics, latent test routines, and error recovery routines using basically the same mechanisms used to schedule applications tasks. These executive tasks, running concurrently with the applications tasks, but in different processor triads, maintain the system, repairing faults, searching out latent failures, configuring processor triads and memory triads, and starting and stopping triads as required. Thus in the background, behind the system application, continuous activity is in progress to maintain the integrity of the system assuring faultless and error-free execution of applications of software.

An executive providing these functions was written for the experimental test hardware. Although it is not complete, in that only representative latent faults were tested, the executive does provide the basic facilities for providing error free execution of both executive and applications code. The software framework for latent test procedures is fully developed although it is only sparsely populated. Error detection and recovery from all classes of faults is demonstrated in the simulated environment without interfering with the applications tasks.

Cache Memory Management

The experimental hardware and the proposed future system both have a common memory shared by all processor triads and private cache memories which are part of the processor modules. Programs are executed exclusively out of a processor's cache memory. Clearly, the burden of program loading from common memory, program overlaying, and other functions associated with bringing sections of code from common memory to the cache for execution could not be placed on the applications coding.

In the experimental computer, a software cache-memory management system was provided as part of the executive. At the subroutine call interface, conventions were adopted that provided for the automatic loading of called routines.

A last used, first out algorithm clears space in the cache if unused space is not available. If a calling routine is dropped from the cache to make room for loading of the called routine, it is reloaded by the subroutine return interface.

The efficiency of this process of loading instructions into the cache before execution depends a great deal on the number of times an instruction is executed each time it is brought from common memory. Each word brought from common memory will take about $5\mu s$ in the FTMP. Thus one triad executing 190K instructions per second could completely fill the bus capacity. In the experimental system, it is found that the applications programs execute between 10 and 40 instructions for every instruction brought from common memory. If an overall average of 20 can be maintained in the proposed system, a processor triad now projected to have a raw computing power of 200K instructions per second would load the bus with 10K instruction fetches per second. With reasonable allowances made for data transfers and queuing overheads, this suggests a maximum capacity of 4 or 5 processor triads before saturating the memory bus.

CONCLUSION

Critical Areas of the FTMP Design

The following are areas where the FTMP has required, or will require, special care in conception, analysis, and/or design.

1. The phase-locked redundant clock has presented problems in latent fault exposure and in theoretical validation. Both of these are believed to be solved.
2. Mechanical and electrical design of bus guardians, bus isolation gates, and the buses themselves, must be done with care in order to prevent undesired fault propagation. The engineering prototype design to achieve this is partially complete at this writing.
3. Cold start capability requires the default formation of a triad or the equivalent. This has not yet been designed.

4. Self-test programs must be virtually complete, including perhaps attempts at finding pattern-sensitive failures over a period of time that is large compared to the basic test cycle. These programs will operate by producing bus errors as results of logic malfunctions. They do not need to diagnose the nature of the fault.
5. Mechanisms must be provided in hardware and software to screen or inhibit interferences caused by a lower priority procedure from impinging on a higher priority procedure. The opposite may or may not be possible.
6. Finally, validation must be made effective to a higher degree than ever before. Although some approaches are available, it remains to show how effective they will be.

Summary

The FTMP is a complex multiprocessor computer that employs a form of redundancy related to TMR-Hybrid redundancy, denoted here as Parallel-Hybrid redundancy, in which each major module can substitute for any other module of the same type. Despite the conceptual simplicity of the redundancy form, the implementation has many intricacies owing partly to the low target failure rate, and partly to the difficulty of eliminating single-fault vulnerability.

An extensive analysis of the computer through the use of such modeling techniques as Markov processes and combinatorial mathematics shows that for random hard faults the computer can meet its requirements. It was also shown that the maintenance scheduled at intervals of 200 hr or more can be adequate most of the time. The probability of requiring unscheduled maintenance during this time interval can be reduced to about 2 percent by carrying one or two spare LRU's.

A study of intermittent faults revealed that the longer a fault stays in a pseudofailed state the worse is the system failure probability. Furthermore, high frequency faults also tend to affect the system failure probability adversely. This places an obvious burden upon the computer design and production activities to limit the intermittent failure arrivals and/or their duty cycles and frequencies to values such that the overall failure criterion can be met.

ACKNOWLEDGMENTS

The authors would like to thank Dr. Jean-Claude Laprie of L.A.A.S., Toulouse, France, for his verification of the numerical results for intermittent faults. Dr. John M. Myers and Dr. Anatol Holt were responsible for an analytical validation of the phase-locked fault-tolerant clock.

REFERENCES

Alonso, Hopkins, and Thaler [1966, 1967]; Avižienis [1975]; Bouricius et al. [1971]; Breuer [1973]; Daly, Hopkins, and McKenna [1973]; Deckert et al. [1977]; Deyst and Hopkins [n.d.]; Hopkins [1970, 1971, 1977]; Hopkins and Smith [1975, 1977a, 1977b]; Lala and Hopkins [1978]; Laprie [1975]; Mathur [1971a]; Murray, Hopkins, and Wensley [1977]; Smith [1975].

A Design Methodology for High Reliability Systems: The Intel 432®

Daniel P. Siewiorek   David Johnson

After the presentation of numerous techniques and evaluation criteria, the question remains, how can these techniques be applied to produce a coherent, balanced system design? This chapter attempts to answer that question by proposing a top-down design methodology and illustrating its application in a detailed example, the Intel 432.

A DESIGN METHODOLOGY FOR A HIGH RELIABILITY SYSTEM

The methodology consists of eight steps:

1. Define system objectives.
2. Limit the scope.
3. Define the layers of fault handling.
4. Define reconfiguration and repair boundaries.
5. Design the fault-handling mechanisms.
6. Identify the hardcore.
7. Evaluate the design against the objectives.
8. Return to Step 3 and iterate the design if necessary.

Each of the first six steps is discussed in detail in the following subsections.

Define System Objectives

As illustrated in Chapter 5, there are multiple objectives in the design of computing systems: in particular, cost, performance, and reliability.

Published courtesy Intel Corporation.

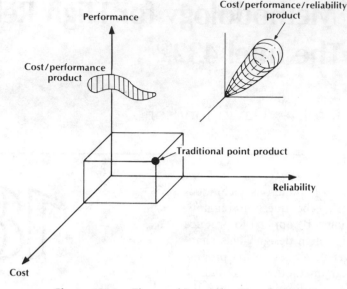

Figure 18–1. The product evaluation space.

The first decision in the design of a new system is where in the cost/performance/reliability space the system is to be positioned. Figure 18-1 depicts three generic system types in the evaluation space. The first is the traditional point product, which evaluates to a single cost/performance/reliability number. The second is a family of products that requires more resources (hence, cost) to deliver more performance. Examples include a computer family such as the IBM System/360-System/370 or the DEC PDP-11. It is nearly impossible to modify cost and performance without altering reliability. Generally, higher performance systems have lower reliability because of the extra components. Another technique for expanding the performance and reliability range is to add resources in a modular fashion. In the Tandem and Pluribus systems of Chapters 11 and 13, for example, processors, memory, and I/O can be replicated to enhance performance. These resources can also be utilized to enhance reliability (shadow computers in the case of Tandem and spare processor/memory/switch components in the case of Pluribus). Thus, there is a trend toward products that

occupy a volume in the evaluation space to which resources can be added to enhance performance or reliability or both.

Although the cost/performance design space is relatively well understood, the reliability dimension is not. However, it is possible to evaluate system reliability and fault-tolerant capabilities by using such key measures as:

· System availability
· Fault coverage (completeness of fault detection)
· Granularity of fault isolation
· Probability of system survival for a given period
· Extent of graceful degradation of service
· Range of applications covered by the design
· Division of fault-tolerant responsibilities among hardware, system software, and application programs

The definition of system objectives imposes the needs of the selected set of applications onto the key fault-tolerant metrics.

It is extremely important to establish the system objectives as early as possible. These objectives help to limit the overwhelming number of design alternatives by restricting the design

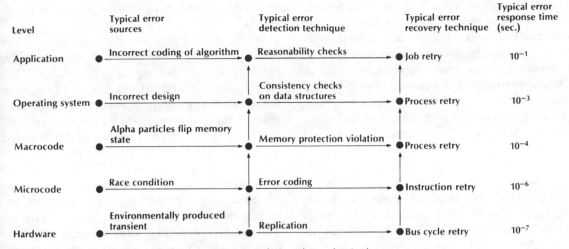

Level	Typical error sources	Typical error detection technique	Typical error recovery technique	Typical error response time (sec.)
Application	Incorrect coding of algorithm	Reasonability checks	Job retry	10^{-1}
Operating system	Incorrect design	Consistency checks on data structures	Process retry	10^{-3}
Macrocode	Alpha particles flip memory state	Memory protection violation	Process retry	10^{-4}
Microcode	Race condition	Error coding	Instruction retry	10^{-6}
Hardware	Environmentally produced transient	Replication	Bus cycle retry	10^{-7}

Figure 18–2. Levels in a hypothetical system.

space, and by providing the criteria for making design decisions. Without a well-defined set of objectives, the design process will fail to focus, and inconsistent design decisions may be made.

Limit the Scope

In order to make intelligent design trade-offs, the scope of the system objectives must be limited. Numerous environmental factors must be selected to refine the system objectives defined earlier. These environmental assumptions will intensify the focus of the design and limit the system development effort. Environmental factors include:

- What is the maintenance strategy? Is field repair possible? Is on-line repair required? What is acceptable as a field replaceable unit (component, module, subsystem)? What is the response time of the field service people?
- What parts of the system will the fault-tolerant design encompass (central system, I/O devices, power)?
- What are the relative failure rates for various parts of the system?
- What are the dominant failure modes in the system?
- What types of failures will be considered? Single or multiple concurrent faults? What is the ratio of

transient to permanent faults? What error sources are considered (external environment, hardware, software, operator)?

Define the Layers of Fault Handling

Systems are composed of a hierarchy of levels. Faults and errors may be generated at any of the levels in the hierarchy. Indeed, mechanisms for each of the ten stages in handling a fault (confinement, detection, masking, retry, diagnosis, reconfiguration, recovery, restart, repair, and reintegration) can be proposed at each level. Figure 18-2 is an incomplete example of a hypothetical system composed of five hierarchical levels. Typical errors, typical techniques for the detection and recovery stages of fault handling, and typical error response times are also given. If an error is not detected at the level in which it originated, the detection of the error is left to higher levels. Likewise, if the current level lacks the capacity to recover from a particular detected error, appropriate information about the detected error must be passed onto a higher level.

As an undetected error propagates up the levels in the hierarchy, it affects an increasing amount of system state and data structures. Longer response times to an error mean that the error manifestations have become more diverse. The error recovery becomes more complex. If left totally to software, error recovery routines may easily become more complex than the application software.

Error-detection techniques should be established at the various boundaries to ensure that the coverage holes from one level to the next do not align. Figure 18-3 graphically depicts several levels in a system, each with "holes" in its coverage. The existence of holes represents trade-offs between fault-tolerant design goals such as speed of recovery and granularity of fault isolation, and system constraints such as cost and available technology. However, awareness of the system's hierarchical structure allows the design to handle all faults, some immediately

and others after reflection to higher levels of the system.

When error correction is performed at the lower levels, a straightforward combinational recovery can be attempted. For example, the state affected by the current level can be double buffered, so that the prior state is released only upon successful completion of the operation at this level. If an error is detected, the buffered prior state can be used to retry. The higher this solution is applied in the system hierarchy, the more state that has to be buffered and the longer the time between checking for errors and the greater the opportunity for the error to interact with healthy activities, causing incorrect decisions. The longer an error, and hence a physical fault, goes undetected, the more data structures in the system may be polluted.

The situation is even more critical in a multi-

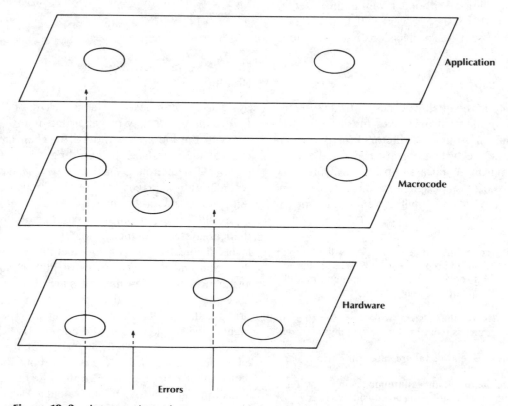

Figure 18–3. Interception of errors at multiple system levels due to imperfect coverage.

processor, where memory and data structures are shared by several concurrently executing processes. Errors can be multiplied by nonfailed components that make incorrect decisions or initiate incorrect operations based on the erroneous information.

Define Reconfiguration and Repair Boundaries

Next, conceptual and physical boundaries for error confinement and isolation must be specified. In order to produce a coherent design strategy, these boundaries must reflect the previously defined system objectives, such as modularity and maintenance/repair strategies. Ideally, boundaries drawn for each level in the hierarchy define nonoverlapping regions.

The percentage of faults detected is the single most important factor in successful recovery. An undetected error usually results in incorrect information's crossing system boundaries and ultimately to a system failure.

Once the confinement boundaries have been established, the repair and reconfiguration boundaries can be drawn. The repair and reconfiguration regions are placed to maximize the effectiveness of the recovery procedures. Before establishing the repair and reconfiguration regions it is important to review the general procedure for recovery.

The purpose of reconfiguration/recovery is to return the system to an operational state. This new operational state should have as many of the original hardware resources available as possible, and the transition to this new state should have minimal impact on normal system operation. Figure 18-4 depicts the generalized reconfiguration/recovery procedure employed at each level in the system hierarchy. After an error has been detected, the faulted operation is frozen (halted). This guarantees that corrupted information cannot leave the faulty reconfiguration/repair region. Next an attempt is made to reestablish the correct operation of the hardware. If the fault is

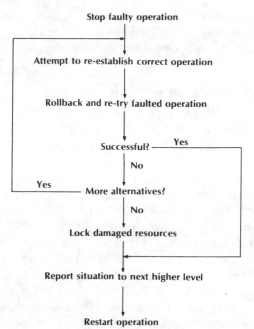

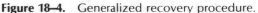

Figure 18–4. Generalized recovery procedure.

transient, correct operation can resume after the transient interference has subsided. If the fault is permanent, it may be possible to resume operation by reconfiguring around the faulty reconfiguration/repair region. Next the faulted operation is rolled back and the operation retried. The correction phase of recovery ends when either the operation has been successfully retried or there are no more alternatives for correcting the situation. If the faulted operation cannot be completed, any shared resources damaged or left in an inconsistent state are locked. Next the error is reported by signaling the next higher level in the hierarchy. The final step is restart. If recovery was successful, control moves to the next operation. Otherwise control passes up to the next higher level in the recovery hierarchy.

Typically, recovery takes one of two forms: retry (good for transient error correction and permanent failure detection) and standby-sparing/graceful degradation. In the latter case, the computation is moved to another part of the system and restarted. Enough information must be retained so that the restart can be executed cleanly without interference from the side effects of the partially completed first instantiation.

Design the Fault-Handling Mechanisms

Now mechanisms can be designed for each of the ten fault-handling stages at each of the system levels. The previous steps in the design methodology resulted in the definition of regions for fault isolation and subsequent recovery. The partitioning establishes the ideal recovery, reconfiguration, and repair regions in the system. It also describes the extent and the completeness of detection and recovery mechanisms at each level in the system. Hence, system partitioning will provide the higher-level guidelines during the design of the detection and recovery mechanisms, ensuring that the fault-handling mechanisms are applied in a unified manner in support of the system objectives.

The mechanisms are aimed at containing errors at the defined conceptual boundaries. Generally, smaller boundaries are more costly in terms of hardware or time but allow for more complete recovery. At the hardware levels the goal is to effect recovery without software intervention. At the software levels the goal is to prevent incorrect data from passing across boundaries.

Location and isolation of a failure can be achieved by analyzing the state of the system when the error was detected. The activity of the error-associated components should be stopped and their intermediate state frozen. A mechanism should be provided to notify some other components in the system of the stoppage. Some nonaffected intelligence can examine the state information, exercise the components, and initiate a recovery. Thus, at each conceptual boundary the object should be controllable and observable. If the fault cannot be resolved by the existing state, a diagnostic sequence can be initiated.

Identify the Hardcore

At this point in the design process it is very important to evaluate the effectiveness of the fault-tolerant mechanisms. This evaluation is based on three checkpoints:

- Are all the fault-handling mechanisms in the system exercised as part of normal operation?
- Do the detection mechanisms provide the desired level of fault coverage?
- Are there any common-mode failures (single-point dependencies) that undermine the detection and recovery mechanisms?

Failures are detected only when an erroneous piece of information is processed. If any portion of the system is not exercised as a part of normal operation, then latent faults may accumulate. The presence of these latent faults may violate the environmental assumptions (such as no concurrent multiple failures) made earlier in the design process. Two areas of a system where latent faults could occur are the detection and recovery mechanisms, and memory locations that are used only during software recovery. An evaluation of the system fault coverage is important because the detection and recovery circuits that were just added to the design may not be fault tolerant. Indeed, they may not be covered by the fault-detection mechanisms or they may have introduced common-mode failures. These circuits may need to be self-checking or covered by periodic testing.

THE IMPACT OF TECHNOLOGY

Ever since the introduction of integrated circuits (ICs), their complexity has been doubling every one to two years. With the advent of the fourth-generation microprocessors in 1978 (typified by the Intel 8086, Motorola 68000, and Zilog Z8000), LSI technology offers, in a small number of chips, capabilities that were reserved for room-size mainframe computers a scant 15 years before. VLSI technology provides the opportunity to devote hardware complexity to areas such as increased functionality, modularity, and reliability. Increased functionality can be achieved by implementing traditional software and operating system functions directly in hardware. Due to the exponential relationship between complexity and chip development costs, the number of chip types has to be kept small. Hardware complexity can be added to allow an orderly, modular expansion of system capabilities. Modularity also provides at least three cost advantages to the system user. First, high-volume production decreases the cost per chip. Second, the system capacity can be closely matched to the application. And third, the system can grow at the pace of the application demands—there is no need to abandon previous hardware acquisitions in order to increase capacity. Another opportunity is to devote hardware to error detection and recovery. In fact, the commercial marketplace is becoming increasingly concerned with system reliability. This concern is manifested by the large market demand for special chips (such as for CRC checks) and systems (such as Tandem) that offer enhanced reliability.

THE INTEL 432 DETECTION MECHANISMS

The Intel 432 system is used to illustrate the design methodology outlined above. After briefly discussing the first three steps (define system objectives, limit the scope, and define layers of fault handling) we will examine in detail the next three steps (define reconfiguration and repair boundaries, design the fault-handling mechanisms, and identify the hardcore) for the lowest fault-handling layer in the system hierarchy.

Define System Objectives

One of the primary objectives for the 432 Micromainframe™ system was to match the expanding needs of fault-tolerant applications with the

increasing capabilities of VLSI technology. Specifically, the Intel 432 detection mechanisms have the following objectives.

- Provide comprehensive and complete fault coverage
- Provide error confinement and isolation to small logic blocks
- Represent a *modular* option to the basic 432 system functionality

Limit the Scope

The objectives were further refined by three environmental assumptions. First, it is assumed that all fault occurrences are independent, and that two or more faults will not occur simultaneously; however, it will be possible for a second fault to occur while a latent fault is present in the system. Second, the design assumes that transients will be the dominant type of fault occurrence (see Chapter 2). The third assumption is that the field environment will allow access to the system for repair. Although this is not a very restrictive assumption, it serves to focus attention on repairable systems rather than on systems that must remain operational until every resource in the system has been exhausted.

From this set of objectives and environmental assumptions two design decisions were made.

- The propagation of errors between levels should be minimized.
- The detection and recovery mechanisms must address every level of the system.

The propagation of errors needs to be minimized to prevent information overload at higher levels in the system structure. If all failures are allowed to propagate to the top, the system loses its ability to react to the fault conditions. The complexity of the response to diverse failure manifestations at higher system levels may make implementation impossible, force a reduction in the completeness of fault coverage, or force a reduction in the generality of operation.

Placing detection and recovery at every level

of the system makes possible a more general and complete solution to the problems of handling system failures. This approach divides the responsibilities of fault tolerance, allowing faster, simpler, and more general solutions to fault detection and recovery. Each level need address only the set of faults that can be generated by that level. By controlling and reducing the number of errors propagated to the next level, parallel and independent development may proceed on different levels (hardware, system software, applications). The designers at one level can assume that lower levels will always provide consistent and correct operation.

Define Layers of Fault Handling

The goal of the 432 detection mechanisms is to prevent any hardware errors from propagating into higher levels of the system. Figure 18-5 shows the levels defined in the system hierarchy. The hardware is divided into two levels: memory array modules, and hardware system. At the module level, detection is provided for the RAM arrays inside memory modules. This isolates RAM failures from other types of failures (controller, bus drivers, and the like) in the memory module. All other internal errors are allowed to propagate to the next level. At the hardware system level (modules and their interconnection), comprehensive detection is present and the goal is to prevent any errors from propagating up into the software system. These detection mechanisms isolate the errors to a single module or a single section of the interconnect system.

Define Reconfiguration and Repair Boundaries

Two major principles guide the design of 432 detection mechanisms.

- The arrangement of the detection mechanisms to form confinement areas.
- The effective use of VLSI technology.

| Application software |
| Operating system software |
| Hardware system |
| Memory array modules |

Figure 18–5. Hierarchy of levels in the Intel 432.

The purpose of a confinement area is to limit damage by error propagation and to localize the faulty area for recovery and repair. A confinement area is defined as a module of the system that has a limited number of tightly controlled interfaces. Detection mechanisms are placed at every interface to ensure that no inconsistent data can leave the area and corrupt other confinement areas.

Confinement areas form a conceptual framework for the systematic and coherent placement and definition of the detection mechanisms at each system level. The confinement areas also provide a conceptual view of the system under fault conditions. This clarifies the external (software) view of the hardware and eliminates the need for diagnostic probing as a method of fault isolation.

The second principle is the effective use of VLSI technology. The cornerstone of this principle is that VLSI replication will be used to achieve the functionality required to implement the 432 mechanisms. Replication is used because it allows a wide range of products to be built from a small set of chip types. The same components provide modular expansion of performance, memory storage, and detection capabilities. This approach allows high-volume production for each of the components in the set.

An overview of the Intel 432 architecture will help to illustrate how the system responds to the remaining steps in the design methodology. We omit the numerous synthesis evaluation cycles inherent in any design process and present only the final system.

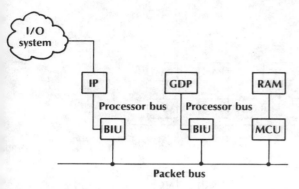

Key: **GDP** = **Generalized Data Processor**
      IP = **Interface Processor**
      BIU = **Bus Interface Unit**
      MCU = **Memory Control Unit**

Figure 18–6. Basic Intel 432 hardware organization.

Figure 18-6 shows the basic hardware organization of the 432. The central system is composed of three different module types: an Interface Processor (IP), a Generalized Data Processor (GDP), and a memory. These modules are connected via a Packet Bus. The GDP is the central processing unit in the machine. It provides the basic computation power of the 432 with a capability-based logical addressing structure to provide a secure software run-time environment. For a complete description of the processor architecture see Intel [1981]. The GDP module is composed of the processor and an interface (that is a Bus Interface Unit) between the local processor bus and the system-wide Packet Bus. The IP module provides an interface between an independent I/O system and the central 432 system. The IP is responsible for managing all I/O traffic and providing a protected, capability-based interface into the central system. The IP module contains the processor, the interface to the I/O system, and the interface between the local processor bus and the system-wide Packet Bus. The memory module provides control of a dynamic RAM memory array and an interface to the Packet Bus.

The Packet Bus provides a high-speed central system communications channel. The bus is a message based, multiprocessor bus, composed of 16 data, 3 control, and 3 arbitration lines. The bus supports not only processor-to-memory transfers but also transfers directly between modules (that is, processor to processor). The Packet Bus is the only intermodule communications channel. There are no interrupts or any other independent signals between modules.

The system is composed of five VLSI chip types, plus a minimum of TTL support logic for electrical buffering.

- The GDP is a two-chip processing unit.
- The IP is a single-chip processor.
- The bus interface unit (BIU) is a single chip that provides an interface between the local processor bus, which is internal to a processor module, and the packet bus, which provides system wide communication.
- The memory control unit (MCU) is a VLSI chip that manages the dynamic RAM array and provides an interface between the memory and the packet bus.

Figure 18-7 illustrates how a 432 system can be expanded to provide increasing processing and I/O power as well as increased memory space and communication bandwidth. This expansion is achieved solely through VLSI replication and is totally transparent to the software system. The multiple processors manage themselves by a cooperative hardware dispatching mechanism that provides transparent multiprocessing capabilities. The BIU and MCU provide interleaving and distributed control functions that act to balance the bus and memory loading without any software interaction.

Figure 18-8 shows the four types of confinement areas in a 432 system. There is a confinement area for each module type and for the Packet Bus. These confinement areas were chosen because they match the basic units of system expansion. When a module has its confinement mechanisms activated, it can be viewed as a self-checking module. The operation of a self-checking module is designed so that no inconsistent

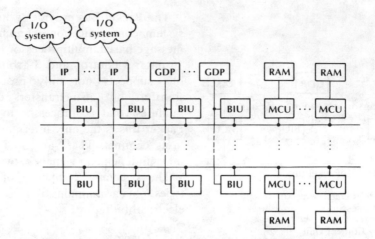

Figure 18–7. Expanded Intel 432 configuration.

data will be allowed to leave the module and corrupt another confinement area.

Design the Fault-Handling Mechanisms

The Intel 432's fault-handling mechanisms at all levels in the system hierarchy are beyond the scope of this book. We will focus on the confinement, detection, and isolation/reporting mechanisms at the two hardware levels (memory array modules and hardware system).

The detection mechanisms are separated into four distinct groups based on the type of operation they are designed to cover.

Transfer of Information

Information flow in the system is covered by two separate detection mechanisms: A two-bit odd/even interlaced parity scheme is used on the packet bus. This mechanism detects all single-bit errors, all double-bit errors on adjacent lines, an all-zero bus, and certain other combinations of multiple-bit errors (see Chapter 3). Duplication of signal paths (two physical signal lines for each logical signal) is used to detect errors in bus

arbitration lines. Duplication will detect any failure along a signal path.

Storage of Information

A Hamming code is used to detect and correct errors within the memory array. Seven check bits are appended to the four-byte storage array word. These check bits are computed from the data to be stored and the address of the storage location. Including the address bits in the ECC prevents inadvertent aliasing of one address for another. That is, even though two different memory locations contain the same data, the ECC bits will be different. This coding technique provides detection for all single, double, and multiple odd-bit errors either in the address sent to the array or in the data stored in the array; it also provides error correction for all single-bit errors in the data stored in the array.

Transformation of Information

Whenever data undergoes transformation in the 432 system, error detection is available by complete duplication of all circuitry. Additional circuitry (also duplicated) is used to compare the

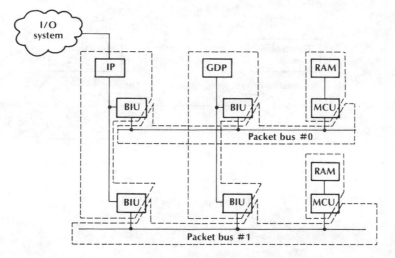

Figure 18–8. Multiprocessor configuration of the Intel 432 illustrating confinement areas.

results of the two operations. This detection mechanism (the comparison logic) is implemented totally in VLSI and is called Functional Redundancy Checking (FRC).

As discussed in Chapter 3, there are several advantages to duplication and matching, including:

- Systems that do not need high reliability are not penalized by the extra cost of error-detection mechanisms.
- Systems that evolve to higher reliability requirements can be upgraded without massive conceptual redesign.
- Fault detection coverage is very high.
- The number of VLSI component types does not increase.

To provide FRC, the hardware is divided into blocks of functionality that may include any number of components and interconnections. Each block is then duplicated and equipped with comparison logic in the VLSI component at the block's external interfaces. One of the pair is selected as the Master; the other functions as the Checker. The Master logic block is responsible for carrying out the normal operation of the block. The Checker disables its outputs and instead monitors the outputs of its Master. The

Checker is responsible for duplicating the operation of the Master and for using its comparison circuitry to detect any inconsistency between the two blocks. Figure 18-9 shows the general application of FRC to form a self-checking block of logic. Figure 18-10 provides a basic schematic for the FRC circuits. These circuits are all located inside the VLSI components.

This detection method detects any operational error occurring in either the Master or Checker blocks of functionality. The only circuitry that must be relied upon in the event of a failure is the comparison and fault reporting circuitry of the Checker. This circuitry is periodically tested to detect any latent faults that may reside in the detection or reporting logic (see the section below on Identify the Hardcore).

Protocols

There are two timeouts in the system to protect against errors in the bus protocols. One timeout is used for the local processor bus protocol; the other is used for the Packet Bus protocol. The BIU and MCU components continually monitor for incorrectly formed bus cycles. All requests

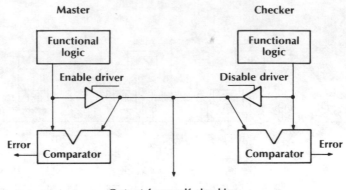

Figure 18–9. Functional redundancy checking.

must eventually be followed by the paired reply. If a set number of the bus time slots pass without the paired reply appearing, each BIU and MCU times out. The detection of any error in the system is reported via a network of error reporting lines.

These error-detection mechanisms are used to implement the previously defined confinement areas. The GDP confinement area, shown in Figure 18-11, consists of the GDP components, the local processor bus, the BIU components (except the Packet Bus arbitration logic), and any miscellaneous components used to support the GDP. FRC is the only detection mechanism used in this confinement area. The FRC detection is applied at the points where the module interfaces with the Packet Buses.

The IP confinement area, shown in Figure 18-12, contains the IP component, the local processor bus, the BIU components (except the Packet Bus arbitration logic), any miscellaneous components used to support the IP, and some of the support components in the interface between the IP and the I/O system. FRC is applied at the module interfaces to the Packet Buses and at the interface to the I/O subsystem.

The memory module confinement area, shown in Figure 18-13, covers the MCU component, the RAM components, the storage array bus, and the support logic between the MCU and the

RAM array. The memory confinement area is covered by two independent detection mechanisms. An ECC code provides coverage for failures in the RAM chips, the address lines, and the buffers/latches between the MCU and the array. The TTL circuits are covered only for faults that manifest themselves as a single- or double-bit data or address failure. FRC is applied at both the Packet Bus interface and the storage array interface to the MCU. This FRC detection completely covers the operation of the MCU (including array control signals). The MCU provides further array protection by implementing all write requests as a read-modify-write sequence. When this approach is combined with the ECC coverage of the address lines, it is assured that data will never be written into an incorrect memory location. The MCU performs the following sequence in response to a write request.

1. Generate array address.
2. Read data and ECC.
3. Check ECC for correct address and valid data.
4. Generate ECC check bits for new data.
5. Write the data into the array.

Figure 18-14 shows the packet bus confinement area. This confinement area covers the Packet Bus data, control, and arbitration lines, the TTL buffering at each node along the bus, and the arbitration logic inside the BIUs and

Logic included in each VLSI component

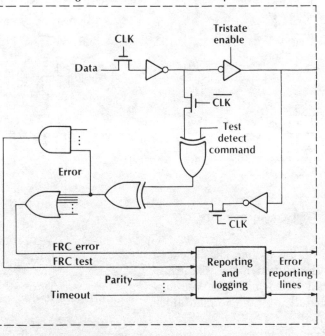

Figure 18–10.   Details for FRC circuitry.

MCUs. The two-bit interleaved parity scheme is used to provide fault coverage for the data and control lines plus their associated TTL buffers. Every node on the bus checks for correct parity on every bus cycle. This guarantees that parity errors during address transmission cycles will still be detected.

The three arbitration lines and their associated TTL buffers are covered by duplication. There is one arbitration network for Master modules, another network for Checker modules. The master modules drive both sets of lines (allowing FRC checking), but the master and checker sense the arbitration results independently. A failure in the arbitration network is detected by an FRC error in the node's use of the arbitration lines during the next arbitration cycle.

Figure 18-15 pictures a multiprocessor 432 system with resources dedicated to providing fault detection. A comparison of Figures 18-7 and 18-15 shows the flexibility of the 432 expansion. The replication of VLSI can be used to

increase performance, or fault-tolerant capabilities, or both.

Identify the Hardcore

The detection mechanisms described above provide fault coverage in the 432 central system. However, this coverage applies only to information being processed or to resources being used as a part of normal operation. Latent faults are faults that exist in those parts of the system that are not exercised in the course of normal operation. As long as part of the system remains dormant, a fault will have no opportunity to generate errors in the system. However, if a second fault occurs, the dormant part of the system may be activated (as part of recovery operation, for instance), causing the system to face a double-error condition. Thus, latent fault detection is desirable for all parts of the system not exercised during normal operation. The 432

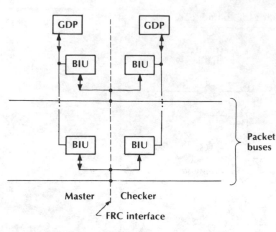

Figure 18–11.   GDP confinement area.

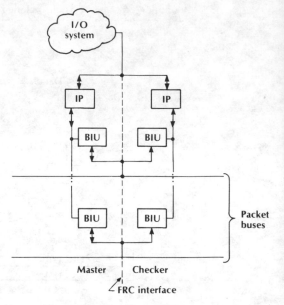

Figure 18–12.   IP confinement area.

system exposes latent faults by periodically exercising the parts of the system not used during normal system operation. Once a latent fault has been exposed, it is handled by the normal fault-handling mechanisms.

Two obvious areas of the machine where latent faults can occur are the detection mechanisms used in establishing the confinement areas, and memory locations not accessed during normal operation.

The system software is responsible for periodically exercising the detection mechanisms in the BIUs and MCUs. The FRC, parity, and ECC detection circuits can all be exercised via special commands available to the software. The FRC and parity circuits are exercised by a command that forces an internal disagreement at each FRC comparator input and in the two Packet Bus parity bits. The outputs from each FRC comparator and the two parity trees are checked to confirm that they are operating correctly. With different values placed in a test register, the complete parity tree and FRC circuits can be checked. This test of the detection circuits is done completely internally; no corrupt information propagates outside of the tested component.

The ECC circuits are checked by a second command, which allows software to write bad check bits into an ECC field. After writing in a bad check field, the periodic correction of every

memory location (the scrubbing mechanism discussed below) by the MCU will automatically exercise the ECC logic when it accesses that memory location.

The mechanism for periodically accessing all memory locations is called scrubbing. Scrubbing is tied in with the refresh mechanism to perform the function totally within the MCU without any additional performance degradation or software intervention. The MCU reads one location during every refresh access. The read data are checked and correctly re-stored in the array via the ECC mechanism. This guarantees access to every location approximately once every second. In this way, scrubbing virtually eliminates the probability of an access's encountering a word with a double-bit failure.

THE INTEL 432 ERROR ISOLATION AND REPORTING MECHANISMS

Error isolation is achieved by capturing all relevant information about the error and then re-

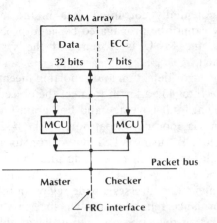

Figure 18–13. Memory confinement area.

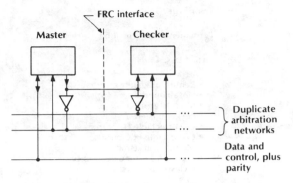

Figure 18–14. Packet bus confinement area.

porting the error information to all other modules in the system. This reporting procedure isolates the error to a single confinement area, allowing recovery to proceed without any diagnostic probing of the system. In addition to their normal data paths, all of the local processor buses and the system-wide Packet Buses have an additional signal for transmitting error report messages. The component detecting the error broadcasts an error report message to the other modules of the system over this network of error reporting lines.

The error report message has two fields: the first specifies the type of error detected, and the second identifies the location at which the error was detected. The type field assigns the fault to one of 16 possible classes. The location field uniquely identifies the BIU or MCU that detected the error by providing the packet bus ID and the module ID of the component that detected the error. A single-parity bit appended to the end of the message provides error detection in the error reporting mechanism.

Upon receiving the error report, each BIU and MCU independently determines whether the reported error is transient or permanent. An error is considered permanent if the same error is reported twice within a software-specified time

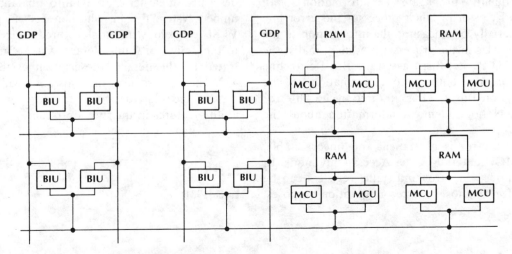

Figure 18–15. Multiprocessor system with detection.

Error Type: 5 bits

Permanent/transient: 1 bit

Error Class: 4 bits

- • Report line parity error
- • Unsafe module
- • Module error
- • Packet bus error
- • Uncorrectable ECC error
- • Correctable ECC error
- • Module/bus error
- • Successful error detection test
- • 8 classes reserved

Error Location: 9 bits

Packet bus ID: 3 bits (0-7)

Module ID: 6 bits (0-62)

Figure 18–16.   Error log content.

window. The error report message is recorded in the error report logs of each BIU and MCU component, where is it accessible to the software system. Figure 18-16 shows the organization of the error report log.

Consider an example in which an MCU on Packet Bus 0 in Figure 18-8 detects an ECC error. The MCU serially broadcasts an error report message on the Bus 0 error report lines. The error message is received by all BIUs and MCUs on Bus 0. The BIUs on Packet Bus 0 subsequently propagate the information to all BIUs by asserting their processor bus error line and serially broadcasting the information to the other BIUs in the processor module. Finally, the BIUs on Packet Bus 1 assert the Bus 1 error line and broadcast the error information to the MCUs on Bus 1. Thus, in three cycles all error registers hold identical information about the error.

If the error is permanent and uncorrectable, the MCU enters Register-Access-Only mode. In this mode, the error and status registers can be read for diagnosis and reconfiguration purposes, but potentially corrupted data in the memory array cannot be propagated by good processors. Thus, the MCU is frozen and the system is notified.

The error-detection and reporting mechanisms of the Intel 432 allow it to meet the objectives of excellent fault coverage and fine-grain fault isolation via modular expansion of the 432 functionality. By using VLSI replication to achieve modular growth in processing and interconnection power as well as fault-tolerant functionality, the Intel 432 addresses a wide region in the cost/performance/reliability design space. Although these error-detection and reporting mechanisms may be costly to implement in conventional logic, the advent of VLSI minimizes the cost of the fault-tolerant functionality.

SUMMARY

The trend in applications is toward an expanding and diversifying set of fault-tolerant needs. The systematic methodology introduced in this chapter provides a method for future designers to meet the expanding needs for fault tolerance in systems with increasingly complex applications. This design strategy provides a top-down methodology for combining the numerous techniques described in earlier chapters into a balanced and unified system design. The benefits of applying VLSI technology and a structured methodology to the design of fault-tolerant systems are illustrated by the detailed description of the Intel 432. The authors hope that this book will inspire system and chip designers to incorporate reliability features in their next product.

REFERENCE

Intel [1981]

Appendixes

Coding for Error Control

D. T. Tang   R. T. Chien

Abstract

Tutorially presented are theoretical and practical concepts that underlie error-control coding for data computing, storage, and transmission systems.

Emphasis is on cyclic codes, the most deeply studied and widely used of the many available codes. Operations of typical binary shift registers illustrate the encoding and decoding processes.

Strategic considerations for applying coding to computer-communication systems are discussed. Actual applications further exemplify the basis for code selection.

Error rates associated with current digital systems are usually extremely low in spite of the increasingly high speed of processing and transmission. Recent developments in error-correcting codes have contributed toward achieving the high reliability required by today's digital systems, and it is evident that the use of coding methods for error control has become an integral part in the design of modern computers and communications systems.

This paper is intended as an introduction to the theory and applications of error-control codes, involving both error detection and error correction. The first two parts of this paper are concerned with fundamental definitions in coding and digital data channels. In the following sections, concepts of errors, code structures for error control, and some general properties of shift-register circuits are introduced. Methods of implementing encoders and decoders as well as the functional classes of error-control codes are also described. The last two sections deal with coding strategy and applications of error-control

Reprinted by permission from *IBM Systems Journal,* Vol. 8, No. 1, 1969, pp. 48–86. © 1969 by International Business Machines Corporation.

schemes in existing data-transmission and storage systems.

BASIC DEFINITIONS

Coding is the representation of information (signals, numbers, messages, etc.) by code symbols or sequences of code symbols (often called *code words*). The set of code words and their mapping, which determines the set, characterize a *code*. Information is said to be placed into code form by *encoding* and extracted from code form by *decoding*. Certain codes may have a larger average code length than others. Such codes are said to contain "redundancy," which can be used to advantage for error control.

Redundancy

The development of redundancy schemes, in the form of coding suitable for modern digital systems, took place after the inspiration of Shannon's basic theorem in 1948 [Shannon, 1948]. Among other things, Shannon showed that even in a noisy channel, errors in data transmission can be reduced to any desired level if a certain minimum percentage of redundancy is maintained by means of proper encoding and decoding of the data. Although Shannon's theorem does not suggest any procedure for constructing such codes, the work of Golay [1949], Hamming [1950], Slepian [1956], Prange [1957], and many others has contributed a whole body of new knowledge—coding theory [Peterson, 1961; Lucky, Salz, and Weldon, 1968]. Mathematical structures have been used to construct codes with various types of error control, and these structures provide means of analysis as well as sophisticated encoding and decoding procedures.

Source Codes

Since encoding is no more than the digital representation of information, a code does not necessarily have error-control capability. *Source codes*, for example, are designed to represent information with sequences of code symbols in the most efficient way, i.e., using the smallest possible number of code symbols on the average [Huffman, 1952]. Therefore, source codes usually contain negligible redundancy and should not be confused with the error-control *channel codes* used under noisy situations. Typically, a source code is first used to represent the output of an information source. Then an error-control coding scheme is implemented to cope with the noisy condition in which the resulting code sequence is to be transmitted or stored.

Block Codes

An important class of error-control codes is that of *block codes*. A block code consists of "code words," which are sequences of code symbols of fixed length n, often referred to as *n-tuples* or *n-vectors*. In most cases, the information sequence to be encoded contains k digits, which are encoded as an n-tuple code word. The *redundancy* (normalized) is $(n - k)/n$, or r/n, where $r = n - k$. Such a block code is often denoted as an (n, k) code.

Binary Codes

Because of their applications in digital data transmission, storage, and processing systems, *binary codes* are by far the most important codes used. The simplicity of the binary representation of information lends itself conveniently to mathematical treatments, and as a result, we now know much more about binary codes than others. We deal almost exclusively with binary codes in this paper. Although familiarity with basic matrix operations is assumed, other concepts of modern algebra are described as they are used.

ERRORS IN DIGITAL DATA CHANNELS

Transmission and Storage

The transmission and storage of digital data have much in common. They both accomplish the transfer of digital data from a source to a destination. For transmission, the source and destination are mainly separated in space, and for storage, they are mainly separated in time. Transmitting lunar photographs from a distant satellite back to earth, transferring data from one computer component to another only inches away, and writing and reading data on magnetic tape can all be described by the same general process consisting of the steps shown in the block diagram in Figure A-1.

Source Encoding

The purpose of the source encoder is to produce the best digital representation of data originating at the information source. Source encoding often requires redundancy removal. When the information at the source is in analog form, the quantization of analog signals must also be performed. This part of the system is normally independent of the channel characteristics or noise statistics. After the error-control encoder (or channel encoder) adds the appropriate amount of redundancy, the modulator then transforms the digital code symbols into physical signals, such as voltage waveforms, ready for

transmission or storage via the noisy channel. On the other end of the channel, the exact reversal of the above procedure is performed in complementary steps.

Modulation and Demodulation

Both the modulator and demodulator must be considered as parts of the digital data channel, since an error-control code can only protect against errors corresponding to the wrong identifications of digital symbols. Modulation and demodulation techniques designed to produce the fewest possible errors are usually analog in nature.

Although the analyses of modulation-demodulation techniques are basically communications problems, which are not discussed in this paper, several related facts are mentioned here. In order to demodulate properly, the demodulation must be able to establish the synchronization of received signals so that the detection of a digital symbol is based on the proper portion of the detected waveform. Any small change in detection threshold level or sampling delay would, strictly speaking, result in a different digital data channel. However, we may assume that the

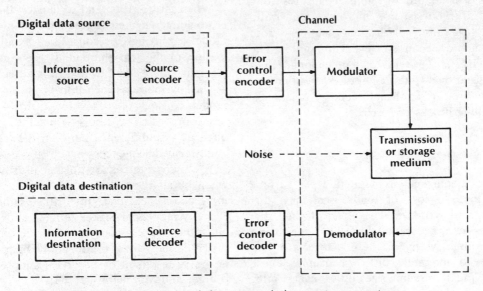

Figure A-1. Generalized data transmission or storage system.

system parameters do not change greatly during a typical operating period. All temporary effects of changes can be regarded as noise and included in the error statistics. In the final analysis, the error statistics of the demodulated signals characterize the digital data channel.

ERROR SOURCES

Error Statistics

The distribution of error statistics depends heavily on the following sources of errors:

- *Modulator and demodulator circuit noise* is predominantly thermal in origin and results mostly in uncorrelated errors.
- *Physical disturbances in terminal components* include changing air gap and changing surface velocity in magnetic surface recording. Errors caused by physical disturbances are highly correlated and tend to cluster in bursts.
- *Physical disturbances in transmission or storage media* are usually sources of bust errors.

The first two error sources are self-explanatory, but there are many causes of transmission and storage disturbances. The most common cause of errors in telephone lines, for example, is switching-impulse noise. The duration of such impulses is in the order of milliseconds, resulting in short error bursts. For microwave and radio links, typical fading or dropouts may last from milliseconds to seconds or even to minutes. The resulting bursts thus tend to be much longer than those caused by switching impulses, and they are often difficult to control by codes, unless extremely long blocks are used.

Storage

In storage media, such as magnetic tapes, surface defects include loss of oxide, scratches, dirt particles, and wrinkles. The effect of such disturbances can accumulate until a tape is no longer usable. Many of these defects are also common to magnetic disks or drums. These defects typically assume sizes up to several mils,

resulting again in short bursts of errors. Core storage arrays usually remain reliable after they are tested, although breakage or other accidental defects may later cause independent errors. Generally speaking, burst errors are much more likely to be caused by physical disturbances. Background noises do exist, but become significant only in special cases such as space communications.

Channel Models

A digital data channel is characterized by the error statistics associated with the input and output alphabets of the channel. Therefore, it is often desirable to represent the error statistics in terms of a certain simple mathematical model. List all the conditional probabilities of receiving the symbols in the output alphabet, for all possible transmitted symbols in the input alphabet. If these probabilities are independent of the locations of symbols, then we have a model completely characterizing a digital *memoryless channel* [Shannon, 1948]. In such a channel, probabilities of erroneous symbols are independent of the neighboring transmitted or received sequences of symbols.

When most errors tend to cluster, the channel is no longer a memoryless one. A memoryless model can at best be considered as an approximation of the real channel. If the clustering of errors is independent of the transmitted symbols, a Markov model is the appropriate one. Such a model consists of states identified by one or more preceding symbols from the "error sequence" (the difference between the transmitted and received sequences).

When error bursts are not necessarily solid, or when bursts themselves tend to cluster, such as in a fading channel, one must either go to Markov models of higher orders or use a different model, such as one in which the probability distribution of the number of digits between errors is described by a certain simple function [Berger and Mandelbrot, 1963].

MATHEMATICAL STRUCTURES IN CODING

Some basic concepts of code structure and requirements of error-control are now discussed. We choose a subset from the set of all n-tuples to form a code set. This code set has some error-control capability, since the receiver can detect the occurrence of an error when the received n-tuple is not in the chosen code set. For errors to be corrected, we must also have a decoding procedure that determines the supposedly transmitted code word when an unacceptable n-tuple is received. This can be done by a table lookup procedure at the receiving end.

A mathematical treatment of the encoding-decoding process is needed to (1) select a set of n-tuple code words with a specified error-control capability, and (2) build a structure so that the code set can be decoded systematically without table lookup (which is clearly impractical for large code sets). Such structures yield properties of code sets that facilitate analysis and simplification of the encoding-decoding procedure.

Linear Separable Codes

It is desirable to divide a code word into an information part and a redundant checking part. A code with this feature is a *separable code*. In the case of the *linear separable codes*, each of the check symbols is a certain linear combination of the information symbols. For example, a binary information 4-tuple (i_1, i_2, i_3, i_4) can be coded as a binary 7-tuple with three binary check symbols (c_1, c_2, c_3). Here, a 7-tuple code word may take the general form $(i_1, i_2, i_3, i_4, c_1, c_2, c_3)$, with

$$c_1 = i_1 + i_2 + i_3, \quad c_2 = i_2 + i_3 + i_4,$$
$$c_3 = i_1 + i_2 + i_4$$

where additions are binary operations.* The

---

* The addition (+) and the multiplication (·) in a binary field are defined by the following equations: $0 + 0 = 0$, $0 + 1 = 1 + 0 = 1$, $1 + 1 = 0$, $0 \cdot 0 = 0 \cdot 1 = 1 \cdot 0 = 0$, and $1 \cdot 1 = 1$.

relationship can be conveniently illustrated by an example expressed in matrix form as shown in Equation 1. A code word vector results when a binary information 4-tuple operates on the code generator matrix. The configuration of the generator matrix is obtained from coefficients of the corresponding simultaneous equations, which depend upon the nature of the code selected.

$$[i_1, i_2, i_3, i_4] \begin{bmatrix} 1 & 0 & 0 & 0 & 1 & 0 & 1 \\ 0 & 1 & 0 & 0 & 1 & 1 & 1 \\ 0 & 0 & 1 & 0 & 1 & 1 & 0 \\ 0 & 0 & 0 & 1 & 0 & 1 & 1 \end{bmatrix} \quad (1)$$
$$= [v_1, v_3, \ldots, v_7]$$

An equivalent way to characterize a linear code is to specify a set of simultaneous *parity equations* that must be satisfied by the code symbols. Using the example in Equation 1, the following three equations must be satisfied by all the code words that take the form $(v_1, v_2, \ldots, v_7)$:

$$v_1 + v_2 + v_3 + v_5 = 0$$
$$v_2 + v_3 + v_4 + v_6 = 0$$
$$v_1 + v_2 + v_4 + v_7 = 0$$

Again, this set of linear simultaneous equations can be conveniently written in matrix form as follows:

$$[v_1, v_2, \ldots, v_7] \begin{bmatrix} 1 & 0 & 1 \\ 1 & 1 & 1 \\ 1 & 1 & 0 \\ 0 & 1 & 1 \\ 1 & 0 & 0 \\ 0 & 1 & 0 \\ 0 & 0 & 1 \end{bmatrix} = 0$$

In general, a k-tuple information part can be coded into an n-tuple code word according to the equation

$$\mathbf{iG} = \mathbf{v}$$

where the matrix $\mathbf{i}$ is 1 by k, $\mathbf{G}$ is k by n, and $\mathbf{v}$ is

1 by n. The matrix $\mathbf{G}$ is called the *generator matrix* of the code. Alternatively, the parity equations may be written in the form

$$\mathbf{v}\mathbf{H}^{\mathrm{T}} = \mathbf{0}$$

where $\mathbf{v}$ is 1 by n, $\mathbf{H}^{\mathrm{T}}$ is n by $r(= n - k)$, and $\mathbf{0}$ is 1 by r. $\mathbf{H}^{\mathrm{T}}$ is the transpose of $\mathbf{H}$, which is called the *parity-check matrix* of the code. For some basic structural features of linear codes, see Appendix 1.*

Polynomial Cyclic Codes

One way to represent an n-tuple is to consider the symbols of the n-tuple to be coefficients of a polynomial of degree $n - 1$ or less. Specifically, an n-tuple $(a_1, a_2, \ldots, a_n)$ gives rise to a polynomial representation

$$a_1 x^{n-1} + a_2 x^{n-2} + \cdots + a_n.$$

When the addition and multiplication are both defined on the symbols used as the coefficients of polynomials, the addition and multiplication of polynomials can be carried out in the ordinary manner. The addition of two polynomials of degree $n - 1$ or less does not differ from the addition of corresponding n-tuples. The product of two polynomials $a(x)$ and $b(x)$ of degree $n - 1$ or less can be defined as another polynomial $c(x)$, also of degree $n - 1$ or less, which is the residue of the usual product when divided by $x^n + 1$. This operation is written in the form

$$a(x)b(x) \equiv c(x)\,\mathrm{modulo}\,(x^n + 1)$$

We use the symbol $\equiv$ in this paper to mean "is congruent to."

Any binary polynomial $g(x)$ must divide $x^n + 1$ for some positive integer n. The set of all polynomials that are distinct multiples of $g(x)$ · modulo $x^n + 1$ constitutes a *cyclic (polynomial) code* in the sense that if $a(x)$ and $b(x)$ are code polynomials then $a(x) + b(x)$ is also a code polynomial.

* All references are to appendixes at the end of this paper, pages 656-669.

Furthermore, any cyclic (end-around) shift of a code word is also a code word, since a cyclic shift of a code word is equivalent to the multiplication of x^i by the code polynomial modulo $(x^n + 1)$, resulting in another polynomial in the code set. The polynomial $g(x)$ is called the *generator polynomial* of the code, and such a polynomial uniquely characterizes a cyclic code. The polynomial $h(x) = (x^n + 1)/g(x)$ is called the *recursive polynomial* of the same code.

If the degree of $g(x)$ is r, then there are 2^k distinct multiples of $g(x)$ of degree $n - 1$ or less, where $k = n - r$ is also the degree of $h(x)$. Some basic structural features of polynomial codes are included in Appendix 2.

GENERAL REQUIREMENTS FOR ENCODING AND DECODING

Thus far we have discussed the generation of linear separable and cyclic codes and have appended some basic structural features of these codes. Now, we briefly discuss certain general requirements of linear and cyclic codes. It was stated that the encoding procedure consists of essentially the selection of an n-tuple code word, given any number of information symbols. At the same time, the decoding procedure essentially consists of determining what these information symbols should be when receiving any n-tuple. Without any code structure, decoding can only be done by table lookup.

Error Syndromes

When linear codes are used, however, the correctable error patterns become separable from the code words and can thus be identified independently of the code words transmitted. To show this, let $\mathbf{v}$ be a code word, and $\mathbf{H}$ be a parity-check matrix. If the error is e (an n-tuple), then the received n-tuple is $\mathbf{v}' = \mathbf{v} + \mathbf{e}$. If we calculate the *syndrome*, defined as

$$\mathbf{S} = \mathbf{v}'\mathbf{H}^{\mathrm{T}} = (\mathbf{v} + \mathbf{e})\mathbf{H}^{\mathrm{T}} = \mathbf{v}\mathbf{H}^{\mathrm{T}} + \mathbf{e}\mathbf{H}^{\mathrm{T}} = \mathbf{e}\mathbf{H}^{\mathrm{T}}$$

we see that it is an r-tuple independent of the code word $\mathbf{v}$. The syndrome $\mathbf{S}$ contains all the information regarding the error that has been added to the code word during the transmission. For a deterministic correction scheme, each syndrome must be identified with a unique error n-tuple. Since the zero syndrome always means "no error," a nonzero syndrome is necessary for the detection of any error n-tuple.

The following observation can now be made for a binary code. Since the syndromes are r-tuples, there are 2^r distinct forms. Clearly, we cannot expect the code to correct more than 2^r distinct errors (including no error). Furthermore, if two errors result in the same syndrome, at most one of them can be corrected. A condition for a set of errors to be correctable is for any two errors $\mathbf{e}_1$ and $\mathbf{e}_2$ from the set to satisfy

$$\mathbf{e}_1 \mathbf{H}^\mathsf{T} - \mathbf{e}_2 \mathbf{H}^\mathsf{T} = (\mathbf{e}_1 - \mathbf{e}_2)\mathbf{H}^\mathsf{T} \neq \mathbf{0}$$

In terms of polynomials, the condition becomes

$$e_1(x) = e_2(x) \neq 0 \text{ modulo } g(x)$$

where $e_1(x)$ and $e_2(x)$ are any two correctable error polynomials. In particular, if an error takes the same form as a code word, then it cannot be distinguished from zero error.

For a cyclic code, the syndrome of an error $e(x)$ usually means the residue of $e(x)$ · modulo $g(x)$, the generator polynomial. However, depending on the specific decoding procedure chosen, the syndrome may take other forms such as the residue of $x^r e(x)$ modulo $g(x)$.

Conditional Maximum Likelihood Decoding

It should be noted that the performance of a decoding scheme depends on the characteristics of the information source and the channel, as well as that of the code used. Generally speaking, if we want to minimize the decoding error with a specific code, the *conditional maximum likelihood* decision scheme should be used. With this scheme, a code word $\mathbf{v}_i$ is selected as the decoded message upon receiving $\mathbf{v}'$, such that the conditional probability $P(\mathbf{v}_i|\mathbf{v}')$ is maximum for all $\mathbf{v}_i$. In evaluating these conditional probabilities, accurate source statistics must be used. This introduces an immediate difficulty since such detailed source statistics are usually not available. Furthermore, the calculation of $P(\mathbf{v}_i|\mathbf{v}')$ for all $\mathbf{v}_i$ is impractical for most cases.

Maximum Likelihood Decoding

An alternative method of decoding is to use the *maximum likelihood* decision rule, which selects a code word $\mathbf{v}_i$, upon receiving $\mathbf{v}'$, such that conditional probability $P(\mathbf{v}'|\mathbf{v}_i)$ is maximum for all possible code words. The calculation of conditional probabilities $P(\mathbf{v}'|\mathbf{v}_i)$ no longer depends on the source statistics. This rule is equivalent to the conditional maximum likelihood decision rule when all source symbols are equally likely. For linear codes, this decoding method requires that, among all error n-tuples resulting in the syndrome calculated, the one with the highest probability of occurrence should be taken as the error that occurred. Note that the error can be identified independently of the code transmitted.

Minimum Distance Decoding

We may consider all possible n-tuples to be points in an n-dimensional space, and define a *distance function* $D(\mathbf{x}, \mathbf{y})$ between two points (n-tuples) $\mathbf{x}$ and $\mathbf{y}$ to be the number of places where the two n-tuples differ. (In binary cases, this is usually called the "Hamming distance.") We may then use the following *minimum distance* decoding scheme: upon receiving $\mathbf{v}'$, select a code word $\mathbf{v}_i$ that minimizes $D(\mathbf{v}', \mathbf{v}_i)$ among all code words. Minimum distance decoding is equivalent to that obtained by using the maximum likelihood decision rule, provided that the errors are independent. This geometrical interpretation of the coding and decoding procedure is often very useful.

The distance function previously defined has

the following "triangular" property: for any three points $\mathbf{x}$, $\mathbf{y}$, and $\mathbf{z}$, then $D(\mathbf{x},\mathbf{y}) + D(\mathbf{y},\mathbf{z}) \geqslant D(\mathbf{x},\mathbf{z})$. From this property, one can show that, if for a given code the minimum distance between any pair of code words is D_m, then this code is capable of correcting t errors and simultaneously detecting d errors $(d > t)$ as long as $d + t < D_m$. On the other hand, if t-error correction is desired, then $D_m \geqslant 2t + 1$.

LINEAR SWITCHING CIRCUITS AND SHIFT REGISTERS

A properly designed electronic linear switching circuit is capable of storing and manipulating a given digital message sequence algebraically, and hence can be used for encoding or decoding purposes. The basic elements of a linear switching circuit are: delay units, adders, and multipliers. In binary cases, no multipliers are necessary because the multiplication of 1 implies a direct connection, and the multiplication of 0 implies no connection. A switching circuit with modulo 2 adders and delay units (or registers) is referred to as a shift-register circuit.

The relationship between input and output sequences of a linear switching circuit depends upon the connections among the basic elements previously described. With respect to a pair of input/output points, the behavior of such a circuit can be described by its unit response. This response is the output sequence caused by an input sequence wherein the first symbol is 1, and all the following symbols are 0. (The initial contents of all delay units must be 0.)

Polynomials in Delay Operator D

We may denote a sequence $s = (s_1, s_2, \ldots)$ in terms of its transform [Huffman, 1956], which is a power series in the delay operator D

$$s(D) = s_1 + s_2 D + s_3 D^2 + \cdots$$

For ease of algebraic manipulation, a code polynomial $A(x)$ representing an n-tuple is usually

transmitted with the higher-order-first convention. Writing

$$A(x) = a_1 x^{n-1} + a_2 x^{n-2} + \cdots + a_{n-1} x + a_n$$
$$= x^{n-1}(a_1 + a_2 x^{-1} + \cdots + a_{n-1} x^{2-n} + a_n x^{1-n})$$

we see that, in a sense, x^{-1} becomes equivalent to the delay operator D.

Consider the binary shift-register circuits as shown in Figure A-2a and b. If $s(D) = 1$, one can see from the paths directed from the input to the output that, in both cases,

$$t(D)|_{s(D)=1} = T(D) = 1 + D^2 + D^3$$

If we let $D = x^{-1}$ in $T(D)$, we have

$$T(1/x) = 1 + x^{-2} + x^{-3}$$

or

$$x^3 T(1/x) = x^3 + x + 1 = T^*(x)$$

Here, $T^*(x)$ denotes the reciprocal of $T(x)$ and is obtained by reversing the order of coefficients in $T(x)$. Thus, in terms of polynomials in x, the circuits in Figure A-2 are both circuits for multiplying the input polynomial by the polynomial $x^3 + x + 1$. The coefficient of the highest degree term in the product is obtained at the output without any delay.

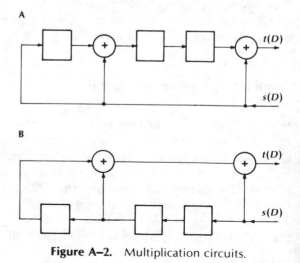

Figure A–2. Multiplication circuits.

A

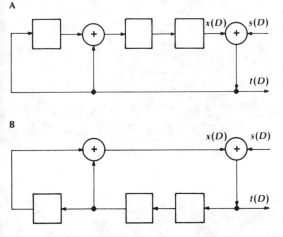

A

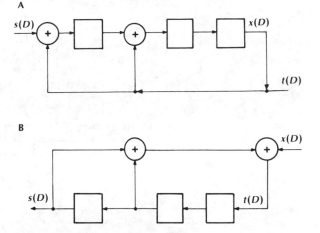

B

B

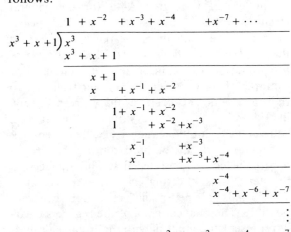

Figure A–3. Division circuits.

Figure A–4. Division circuits that produce residues.

Figure A-3a and b shows two division circuits whose functions can be easily analyzed by first observing that the following relationships hold in both circuits

$$x(D) = (D^3 + D^2)t(D)$$

and

$$x(D) + s(D) = t(D)$$

Combining the above two equations, we have

$$s(D) = (D^3 + D^2 + 1)t(D)$$

or

$$T(D) = \frac{t(D)}{s(D)} = \frac{1}{D^3 + D^2 + 1}$$

Similarly, for both circuits in Figure A-4,

$$\frac{t(D)}{s(D)} = \frac{D^3}{D^3 + D^2 + 1}$$

In terms of polynomial representations, all circuits in Figures A-3 and A-4 are circuits for dividing the input polynomial by the polynomial $x^3 + x + 1$. The first bit of the quotient (coefficient of the highest degree term) is obtained at the output without any delay or after three units· of delay depending upon whether 1 or D^3 appears in the numerator of the transfer function.

Figure A-5 shows circuits for respectively mul-

tiplying and dividing the input polynomial by an arbitrary polynomial of degree m,

$$A(x) = x^m + a_{m-1}x^{m-1} + \cdots + a_1 x_1 + a_0$$

The division circuits described perform essentially the long division process. Thus, if the input polynomial is a multiple of the dividing polynomial, the output sequence is the quotient followed by zeros. Otherwise, the output sequence is the infinite sequence corresponding exactly to what one obtains in the long division process. For example, if we divide x^3 by $x^3 + x + 1$ as follows:

$$
\begin{array}{r}
1 + x^{-2} + x^{-3} + x^{-4} \qquad + x^{-7} + \cdots \\
\hline
x^3 + x + 1 \,) \, x^3 \\
x^3 + x + 1 \\
\hline
x + 1 \\
x \quad + x^{-1} + x^{-2} \\
\hline
1 + x^{-1} + x^{-2} \\
1 \quad + x^{-2} + x^{-3} \\
\hline
x^{-1} \quad + x^{-3} \\
x^{-1} \quad + x^{-3} + x^{-4} \\
\hline
x^{-4} \\
x^{-4} + x^{-6} + x^{-7} \\
\hline
\vdots
\end{array}
$$

The outcome is $1 + x^{-2} + x^{-3} + x^{-4} + x^{-7} + \cdots$. The division circuit of Figure A-3a or

A

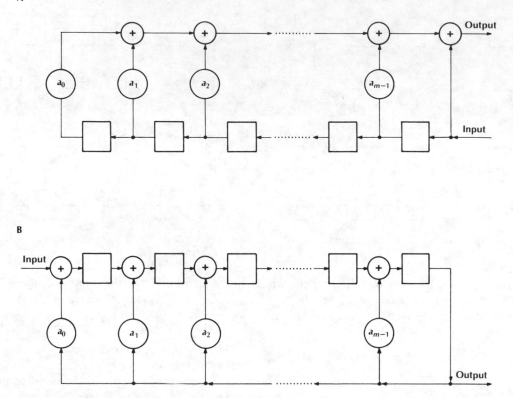

Figure A–5. Generalized multiplication and division circuits.

A-3b, on the other hand, gives a corresponding output sequence $1 + D^2 + D^3 + D^4 + D^7 + \cdots$.

The circuit in Figure A-4a (or the general circuit of Figure A-5b) has the following special property. The contents of the registers represent the residue of the division after the last term of the input polynomial has entered the circuit. For example, if we consider the register from left to right as coefficients of 1, x, and x^2, respectively, in Figure A-4a, then a shift to the right is equivalent to multiplication by x. The feedback connections add the output from the third register to the contents of the first and the second registers, thus effecting $x^3 = 1 + x$ (or $x^3 + x + 1 = 0$) whenever this reduction becomes possible. The final contents of the registers clearly represent the input polynomial minus all mul-

tiples of $x^3 + x + 1$, that is, the residue of the input polynomial modulo $x^3 + x + 1$.

The shift-register contents of other types of division circuits do not necessarily correspond to residues. For example, the shift-register contents of the circuit in Figure A-3a represent the residue of the input polynomial multiplied by $x^3 \cdot$ modulo $x^3 + x + 1$. In general, register contents represent linear transforms of the residue coefficients described above.

ENCODERS AND DECODERS

An encoder for an (n, k) linear code produces an n-tuple code word when an information k-tuple is given. This fact is illustrated by writing the symbols in the n-tuple code word as functions of

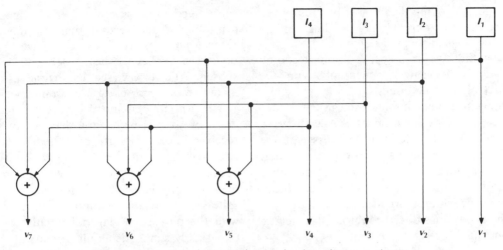

Figure A–6. Combinatorial encoder for a linear code.

the given k-tuple and implementing each of these functions (as Boolean functions) with logic circuits. For example, the linear code specified by Equation 1 may be implemented by the circuit in Figure A-6. Note that the information symbols remain unchanged; thus, the code obtained is separable.

When a cyclic polynomial code is used, it is convenient to generate the code polynomials in a sequential manner. The binary cyclic code with generator polynomial $g(x) = x^3 + x + 1$, for example, may be encoded with the shift-register (multiplication) circuits in Figure A-2 yielding a nonseparable code structure. When the code is separable, a division circuit capable of producing the residue of the input polynomial modulo $g(x)$ can be used to produce the check symbols. Figure A-7 shows such an encoder. During the transmission of the first k bits, information symbols are fed into the encoders shown in Figure A-7. The switch K is in the 0 position, allowing the same symbols to appear unchanged at the output. At the end of k bits, the desired residue has formed in the registers and is obtained by throwing the switch K to the 1 position. Since the feedback of the division circuit is now nullified, the register contents will next appear at the output.

The cyclic code generated by the polynomial $g(x) = x^3 + x + 1$ is identical to the linear code described by the generator matrix of Equation 1. Encoders shown in Figures A-6 and A-7, therefore, yield the same code words when fed with the same k-tuple input.

The basic function of a decoder is to establish mapping from the syndrome (r-tuple) of the received message to an error n-tuple. By subtracting the error from the received message, one obtains the transmitted code word which, in the case of separable codes, contains the original information k-tuple.

Since the mapping being implemented can be completely specified by a table, an immediate approach to the design of a decoder is via a logic circuit that implements the table lookup proce-

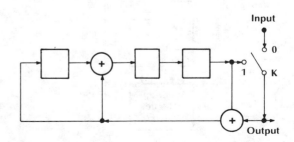

Figure A–7. Sequential encoder for a linear code.

dure. When decoding delay must be minimized, the logic circuit approach in decoding can be quite attractive. The obvious limit to this approach is that the complexity of the decoding circuit tends to grow exponentially with the capability of the code used.

With cyclic codes, simplification in the decoding circuitry is possible. Figure A-8 shows a general-purpose decoder which consists of the following components: a division circuit that serves as a syndrome generator, an n-stage buffer storage that retains the message received, and a syndrome recognition circuit that usually recognizes the syndromes of error vectors that include an erroneous highest-degree digit.

To see how this decoder works, let $a_1 x^{n-1} + \cdots + a_{n-1} x + a_n$ be the code polynomial and let $a'(s) = a(x) + e(x)$ be the received polynomial, where $e(x)$ represents the error. As mentioned earlier, the syndrome of $a'(x)$ generated here by a division circuit of $g(x)$ is independent of $a(x)$. The syndrome is obtained when the last digit of the code word, a_n, has entered the decoder. If the first digit is not in error, the syndrome detection circuit maintains a zero output and the highest order bit is obtained unaltered at the output. After a shift, the transformed syndrome corresponds to $xe(x)$, which is the original error with the coefficients advanced one position toward the high-degree end. The syndrome recognition circuit then recognizes the syndrome if the second digit in the original received message is in error. Since the same argument applies to the subsequent shifts and subsequent errors, we see that erroneous digits of a correctable error pattern can all be corrected.

The decoding circuit of Figure A-8 requires a delay of n digits before the decoded message is received. The errors are corrected sequentially. Although generally applicable to all types of cyclic codes, the syndrome recognition circuit may in many cases still be too complicated (in spite of the relative simplicity in comparison with the pure combinatorial circuit). However, remarkably simple decoding circuits of this type are possible with cyclic burst-error-correcting codes (including the Hamming codes).

If a code is used for error detection only, one merely needs a recognition circuit to determine whether the residue is zero. A nonzero indicates that an error has been detected.

FUNCTIONAL CLASSES OF ERROR-CONTROL CODES

Several functional classes of cyclic polynomial codes have been found:

- *Singe-Error-Correcting Codes.* A single-error-correcting code of length n is capable of correcting any error affecting no more than one symbol in a code block of n symbols.
- *Burst-Error-Correcting Codes.* A burst-error-correcting code of length n is one that can correct any span of errors of fixed length b or less in a code block of n symbols.
- *Independent-Error-Correcting Codes.* An independent- (or multiple-) error-correcting code is a code of length n that is capable of correcting up to a multiple of t errors within a code block of length n.
- *Multiple-Character-Correcting Codes.* A multiple-character-correcting code is a code of length n characters, where a character is a group of bits with fixed length. Any combination up to a fixed number of character errors within a block may be corrected.

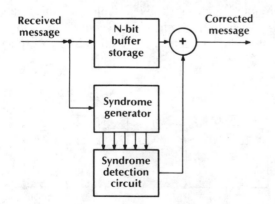

Figure A–8. General-purpose decoder for cyclic code.

Depending upon channel characteristics, members of these code classes may be selected.

Methods for finding generator polynomials for these codes are given in Appendix 3.

Certain specialized codes are modifications of some members of previously mentioned functional classes of codes. Interleaved codes, N-dimensional codes, and shortened codes, for example, are methods of constructing stronger codes based on weaker ones. Self-orthogonal codes are characterized by their threshold logic decodability, which leads to simple decoding circuits. Synchronization codes add framing capability to error control. Convolution codes form a class of nonblock codes with various possible error-control capabilities and are often used in conjunction with the sequential decoding technique. Constant-weight codes are useful in channels with some special properties. Arithmetic codes are based on arithmetic operations and are useful in channels which include arithmetic processors. Certain basic properties of such specialized codes are included in Appendix 4.

CODING STRATEGY

When an error-control code is considered in a digital transmission or storage system, one should ask not only what can this code do, but also what is needed to achieve the capability of the code.

Generally speaking, the longer the block length (i.e., larger n), the more storage the decoder requires, and the greater the minimum decoding delay. It is also generally true that the longer the code block the larger the class of errors to be corrected, hence the more complicated the decoding circuits. However, the distribution of errors in longer code blocks becomes much more predictable, thereby permitting the use of codes with smaller redundancy while maintaining the same reliability.

The data flow in a complex computer system may take different forms at different levels corresponding to the channels described previously. Therefore, basic requirements for error-control codes may also change in emphasis from one case to another. For example, intermachine data transmission may go through many conventional communications channels. The primary requirements of the preferred error-control scheme are high reliability and high information rate. Since decoding delay does not reduce throughput, one would tend to use longer codes with lower redundancy even though they require more decoding complexity.

For intramachine transmission, such as going in and out of an internal random-access storage, the primary coding requirements are high reliability and speed. Thus, simple decoding by circuitry is essential in keeping storage access-time small. Another feature of the codes used for intramachine transmission is that an error-control code is often used in the detecting mode, since retransmission can usually be effected by simple instructions based on the outcome of error detection. There are exceptions to such general rules. An optimum coding strategy can be achieved, and the best code obtained, only after a design engineer evaluates several alternatives.

We now outline several different courses of action he may prefer as an alternative of forward-acting full-power correction with block codes.

Error Detection

The main advantage of error detection is the simplicity of its implementation. An error is detected if the received message yields a nonzero syndrome. For cyclic codes, a division circuit plus a test for zero constitute a complete decoder.

The detection capability of a code is closely related to its correction capability. If a code is capable of correcting a set $\{e_i\}$ of error n-tuples, then the syndromes of any two errors, e_i and e_j from the set must be distinct. This implies that any error of the form $e_i + e_j$ must be detectable. It should be pointed out that the code also detects many other errors. Any error of the form

$e_i + e_j + v$ is clearly detectable if v is a code vector (and $vH^T = 0$). This often results in a significant reduction in the undetected and uncorrected error rate.

From the preceding, we observe that a t-error-correcting code is capable of detecting all combinations of $2t$ errors, and a burst-b-correcting code is capable of detecting any two bursts of length b or less. A Fire code generated by $g(x) = (x^c + 1)p(x)$—as described in Appendix 3—when used for detection only, is capable of detecting any combination of two bursts of which the length of the shorter burst is no greater than the degree of $p(x)$. Any cyclic code of degree r is capable of detecting all single bursts of length up to r.

Error detection is an attractive means of error control provided it is possible to effect retransmission. In the case of data transmission, this implies the existence of a reliable feedback channel, which is used to relay the request-for-retransmission message back to the sender [Shannon, 1959; Turin, 1965; Schalkwijk and Kailath, 1966]. Many data links within a computer system have the ability to regenerate a message at the sending end when it is not cleared at the receiving end. On the other hand, an error detected during a readback process from storage may not be successfully avoided by rereading the same message when the error is due to permanent damage in the storage medium or when the error occurred during the writing process.

When a feedback channel is available, one should calculate, from available statistics, the probability of requests for retransmission and the average time the system is tied up because of the requests. Performance of the detection-retransmission method can then be evaluated within the context of given system parameters [Frey and Benice, 1964]. In general, detection and retransmission is effective against highly clustered errors. For random errors or for a combination of random and burst errors, some error will tend to appear regularly in every block. In such cases, some forward-acting error correction

is necessary to maintain the performance of the transmission system.

Partial Correction

We have seen that, even where a feedback channel is available, some forward error correction is often needed to combat random errors. For most codes, there is a trade-off between the numbers of correctable and detectable errors. A multiple-error-correcting code is capable of correcting t errors and simultaneously detecting d errors as long as the minimum distance of this code is at least $t + d + 1$. A fire code generated by $g(x) = (x^c - 1)g(x)$ is capable of correcting a burst of length up to b and simultaneously detecting any other burst of length up to $dc \geqslant b$ as long as $b + d - 1 \leqslant c$ and $b \leqslant m$, the degree of $p(x)$. See Appendix 3.

Aside from the need to use partial correction in conjuction with the detection-retransmission method, there may be other reasons for the use of partial correction in the overall error-control scheme, namely, to minimize the decoding complexity. We mention here two situations wherein partial correction may prove useful.

1. In the case of multiple-error correction, decoding complexity grows exponentially with the number of errors corrected. Thus, even if a given code can correct $t > 1$ errors, one may still want to go through a single-error-correction procedure and test the syndrome for possible erroneous correction. If single errors account for a large portion of the overall error rate, considerable reduction in average decoding delay can thereby be achieved. Success of single-error correction eliminates the need to go through the more complicated t-error-correction. If two or more errors occur, the single-error-correction procedure may make an erroneous correction in some cases. However, due to the minimum distance of the code, the result is still a detectable error. The correction algorithm specifies returning to the original message received and trying a more powerful correction procedure. A similar approach also applies to the partial correction of multiple errors up to the maximum number of correctable errors.

2. For certain classes of multiple-error-correcting codes, simple circuit implementation is possible for correcting a small number of errors. Since threshold-logic decoding has error detection and correction capabilities approaching those of multiple-error correcting codes, the combination of partial correction by logic circuitry and detection may prove very useful.

Erasures

Erasures usually correspond to detected signals that are considered to be in a certain "no-confidence zone." In the case of binary level detection, the erasure zone is intermediate between the 1- and the 0-zone. In general, an erasure implies an unknown symbol (or character) at a known location.

In a pure erasure channel, locations of errors are always known. The error-correction capability of a code in an erasure channel is similar to its detection capability in a nonerasure channel. An erasure pattern is correctable if (and only if), by substituting all possible combinations of symbols at these erased digits, only one results in a code word. With a t-error-correcting code, any pattern of $2t$ erasures is correctable. This follows immediately from the fact that, with $2t$ erasures, any two n-tuples resulting from different substitutions can differ at most at $2t$ digits. However, a t-error-correcting code must have a minimum distance of at least $2t + 1$, which means these two n-tuples cannot both be code words. Similarly, with a burst-b-correcting code, any pattern consisting of two erasure bursts of length b or less is correctable.

In more realistic channels, erasures are often compounded with nonerasure errors. Again, there is a trade-off between the numbers of correctable errors and erasures. For example, a multiple-error-correcting code is capable of correcting any combination of t errors and e erasures as long as the minimum distance of the code is at least $2t + e + 1$.

Generally speaking, the use of erasures tends to reduce the uncorrectable-error rate. The amount of improvement is a function of the detailed statistics of the detected signals and of the thresholds that define the erasures. The price of improvement here is a probable increase in decoding complexity. When correcting combinations of errors and erasures with a multiple-error-correcting code, one must perform the additional step of transforming the error syndromes in order to separate the erasures from nonerasures before the ordinary decoding procedures can be applied [Forney, 1965]. At least part of this added effort is compensated by a reduction in the number of errors to be corrected, as compared with forcing all erasures into decisions of code symbols. The erasure concept can be generalized as an increased number of levels at the detector output whereby further gain in reliability is possible [Forney, 1966].

Adaptive Coding Schemes

If the noise characteristics of a digital data channel tend to change from time to time, an adaptive coding scheme may be desirable. In the method of detection and retransmission, certain forward-acting partial correction becomes necessary if a small number of errors tend to occur regularly. The amount of partial correction can be monitored at the receiving end to cope with the varying error rate. Recently, an interesting method of adaptive decoding without feedback has been developed [Frey, 1967]. With this method, a received message is analyzed to determine whether the burst-error correction or the independent-error correction should be performed. Methods have been studied for changing the code used (as well as the decoding algorithm) in such a way as to minimize implementation complexity [Tang, 1965; Tang and Chien, 1966].

Sequential Decoding

Although sequential decoding has been successfully applied to space communications, its use in computer systems is still in an exploratory stage. Quantitative performance evaluation of a sequential decoding algorithm is difficult without actual implementation and testing. As we have indicated previously, since the decoding algorithm can only be implemented by a computer, sequential decoding is not applicable where sufficient processing capability is not provided. Another factor that may limit the use of sequential decoding is that decoding effort is a random variable without an upper bound. However, the sequential decoding algorithm is applicable to a wide range of conditions, including those in which other block coding schemes do not perform satisfactorily. Such conditions exist, for example, where the initial error rate is high, or where high reliability is required at a high information rate.

SOME ERROR-CONTROL APPLICATIONS

Data Communications

Many IBM terminals use cyclic codes for error detection. Because of their relatively low error rates, the codes are mostly burst-detecting codes that usually have very little redundancy.

The IBM 1050 data communication system uses an interleaved code, generated by $g(x) = (x^6 + 1)$, in which six check digits form a character at the end of each message. Single burst-errors of length up to six are detectable, as are many other error patterns.

The Binary Synchronous Communication (BSC) [Eisenbies, 1967] convention uses a burst-2-correcting code generated by $g(x) = (x + 1)p(x)$, where $p(x)$ is a primitive polynomial of degree 15. The BSC code is capable of detect-

ing two bursts of length two. Also, because the minimum distance is four, BSC can detect any three or fewer independent errors in messages up to a length of $2^{15} - 1$.

Although errors on microwave links used for voice-grade channels are effectively eliminated by the use of pulse code modulation and repeaters, encoders and decoders for additional error control are provided. For example, private lines are available with additional coding equipment, wherein the code used is a shortened (200, 175) BCH type with a minimum distance equal to eight. The generator polynomial of this code is of the form $g(x) = (x + 1)m_1(x)m_3(x)m_5(x)$, where $m_1(x)$, $m_3(x)$, and $m_5(x)$ are polynomials of degree eight. The (200, 175) code is obtained by shortening a full-length (255, 230) code. This code is capable of correcting three independent errors and, in addition, detecting four errors. Retransmission is requested if an uncorrectable error is detected. The use of a convolutional code with one-sixth redundancy is also an option with the direct-distance-dialing switched network.

Data Storage

Although magnetic cores are highly reliable, such storage elements as drivers, sense amplifiers, and read-write gates, which control the storage operation, are subject to occasional failures. The use of an error-control code in the CPU of a computing system not only helps to locate failures, but also keeps the CPU in operation when the effect of a failure is within the correction capability of the code used.

The IBM 650 central processing unit uses a "bi-quinary" code, which encodes a decimal digit into seven binary digits with two 1's. This code, like the four-of-eight code, detects all odd numbers of errors.

The IBM 7030 (STRETCH) computer uses a single-error-correcting double-error-detecting code with 64 data bits and eight check bits. The encoding and decoding are implemented by logic circuits.

The IBM 7070 data processing system uses a "two-of-five" code with an addtional overall parity check. Many other CPU's, including SYSTEM/360, use single parity checks for error detection.

Auxiliary Storage

Disk files, like other magnetic surface-recording systems, are vulnerable to surface irregularities. Therefore, protection against burst error is usually needed. As the recording density increases, more powerful coding schemes are needed. The IBM 1300-series disk storage uses a cyclic code for burst detection, in which there are 13 check digits at the end of every record. The IBM 2301 drum storage unit also uses a cyclic code with 19 check digits for error detection. Most of the other disk files use similar cyclic codes for error detection.

Magnetic tape units used today contain several tracks, and a character or a byte is obtained by reading one bit from each track. Error control is necessary since tapes are relatively less reliable than magnetic cores. Control can be achieved in a number of ways. The tractor tape unit has 22 tracks, 16 of which are information bits and six are check bits. Each character is a (22, 16) code obtained by shortening a (31, 25) BCH code with minimum distance of four. The IBM 727 and 729-series magnetic tape units use a two-dimensional coding scheme. One track, which provides a *vertical redundancy check* (VRC), is used for an overall check on each character. Also, one character at the end of each record is used for an overall check on each track and is known as the *longitudinal redundancy check* (LRC). The overall code detects errors in a single track, plus many other errors.

The IBM 2400-series magnetic tape units use a coding scheme involving another character next to LRC as a check based on a cyclic code, in addition to the VRC and LRC already described. This check is called *cyclic redundancy check* (CRC) and is discussed in greater detail in Appendix 5.

Digital Cypress Error Control

The photo-digital storage for the IBM 1360 computer, known as Digital Cypress [Oldham, Chien, and Tang, 1968], uses a (366, 300) Reed-Solomon code, which is one of the most sophisticated codes ever used for storage. With six bits in each character, this code is a multiple-character-error-correcting code with a minimum distance (on the character basis) equal to 12, which requires 11 check characters (66 bits). The full length of the code is $2^6 - 1$ characters (i.e., 63 characters or 378 bits). There are 300 bits (or 50 characters) of data plus two characters for line number and 11 check characters. The code is capable of correcting any combination of independent and burst errors representable by five characters. A sixth character error, plus many others, can be detected.

Except for the encoder and the syndrome-generating circuit, the Digital Cypress decoding procedure is implemented by programming, the strategy for which may be outlined as follows. When a nonzero syndrome is detected, a rescan is called for first. If the error is still present, the program goes to a single-error partial-correction subroutine. If that procedure is unsuccessful in correcting the error, a two-error partial-correction subroutine is called. The full-power correction routine is used only when both the single-error- and the double-error-correction subroutines are unsuccessful.

CONCLUDING REMARKS

We have developed basic concepts of error-control coding, with emphasis on the use of cyclic codes, which form a subclass of linear block codes. The use of an error-control scheme should be an integral part of the overall system design, rather than a "remedy" or a "bonus" for a system with unsatisfactory reliability. To achieve a proper error-control scheme, a systems engineer needs an extensive knowledge of existing coding methods and their implementations. Since this paper is not intended to give a full treatment of the theory and applications of all types of codes, the aim has been to expose some of the underlying principles involved in selecting an error-control coding scheme for a realistic computer or communication system.

The demands on overall data-processing and communications capacities have been increasing and are expected to grow. This implies a prevailing need to fully utilize every communication or memory channel available. One approach is by way of error-control coding. With advances in integrated circuit technology, costs of logic and storage elements are declining in comparison with increasing rates of data-processing. Thus, circuit-implemented error-control schemes are expected to become increasingly attractive. One objective of system designers is to achieve "ultra reliable" components, in which error-control capabilities are an integral part of the monolitic circuit design.

As applications of more sophisticated error-control coding schemes for computer and communications systems become more extensive, one may expect coding principles to be applied to other types of problems. For example, algebraic procedures typical of encoding and decoding can be used to obtain solutions in such problem areas as file organization and document retrieval [Chien and Frazer, 1966; Abraham, Ghosh, and Ray-Chaudhuri, 1968]. Since a document in a file is usually characterized by a list of "descriptors" contained in a "dictionary," a binary n-vector can identify a document, wherein each position of the n-vector represents a descriptor. Storage required for such a dictionary becomes too large to be practical in most cases. However, if we regard the n-vectors as errors, the vectors can be transformed into r-tuples (syndromes) appropriate to the code selected. The r-tuples can then be used to identify documents in the file. Requests for retrieval can be handled with the help of the corresponding decoding algorithm.

The design of matrix switches, such as those used in main storage arrays, is another example.

It has been shown that certain codes can be used to determine selection patterns in a matrix switch so that all driving power is channeled to the selected output only [Constantine, 1958; Chien, 1960].

Coding concepts and techniques are also potentially useful in such other areas as signal design, digital modulation, pattern recognition, fault diagnosis, image processing, and cryptography.

APPENDIX 1: STRUCTURE OF LINEAR CODES

The first four columns of the four-by-seven coefficient matrix in Equation 1 form an identity submatrix. In general, the generator matrix of a separable code is a k by n matrix containing a k by k identity submatrix. The columns of the submatrix correspond to information positions.

A fundamental property of a linear code is that if $\mathbf{v}_i$ and $\mathbf{v}_j$ are two code words, then $\mathbf{v}_k (= \mathbf{v}_i + \mathbf{v}_j)$ must also be a code word, since

$$\mathbf{v}_i + \mathbf{v}_j = \mathbf{x}_i \mathbf{G} + \mathbf{x}_j \mathbf{G} = (\mathbf{x}_i + \mathbf{x}_j)\mathbf{G} = \mathbf{x}_k \mathbf{G}$$
$$= \mathbf{v}_k$$

The use of a generator matrix to represent a code eliminates the need to list all the n-tuples in the code set. In the binary case, a k by n generator matrix uniquely specifies the code set containing 2^k n-tuples.

With respect to every linear code set V, it is possible to find a set U of n-tuples such that U and V are "orthogonal" in the sense that for any n-tuple code word $\mathbf{v}$ in V and any n-tuple code word $\mathbf{u}$ in U,

$$\mathbf{v}\mathbf{u}^T = \mathbf{0}$$

Here, $\mathbf{v}$ and $\mathbf{u}$ are row matrices, and $\mathbf{u}^T$ denotes the transpose of $\mathbf{u}$. The set U is obtained by summing all possible combinations of rows of an r by n parity-check matrix. The orthogonality requirement can, therefore, be written as

$$\mathbf{GH}^T = \mathbf{0}$$

Given the code word $\mathbf{v} = (v_1, v_2, \ldots, v_n)$ in V that satisfies the equation

$$\mathbf{vH}^T = [v_1, \ldots, v_n]\begin{bmatrix} h_{11} & h_{21} & \cdots & h_{r1} \\ h_{12} & h_{22} & \cdots & h_{r2} \\ \vdots & \vdots & & \vdots \\ h_{1n} & h_{2n} & \cdots & h_{rn} \end{bmatrix} = \mathbf{0}$$

then the following set of linear simultaneous equations is obtained:

$$h_{11}v_1 + h_{12}v_2 + \cdots + h_{1n}v_n = 0$$
$$\vdots \qquad \vdots \qquad \qquad \vdots$$
$$h_{r1}v_1 + h_{r2}v_2 + \cdots + h_{rn}v_n = 0$$

A parity-check matrix $\mathbf{H}$ specifies r linear simultaneous parity-check equations that must be satisfied by the symbols of every code word from V.

To obtain the parity-check matrix, we can write the generator matrix in the standard form $\mathbf{G} = [\mathbf{I}_k \mathbf{P}]$, where $\mathbf{I}_k$ is a k by k identity submatrix and $\mathbf{P}$ is a k by r submatrix that describes the interdependence between information and parity-check symbols. The parity-check matrix can then be written as $\mathbf{H} = [\mathbf{P}^T \mathbf{I}_r]$. One can check to see that

$$\mathbf{GH}^T = [\mathbf{I}_k \mathbf{P}]\begin{bmatrix} \mathbf{P} \\ \mathbf{I}_r \end{bmatrix} = \mathbf{0}$$

Although the specification of either a generator matrix or a parity-check matrix uniquely determines a linear code, neither the generator matrix nor the parity-check matrix is unique. In general, different generator or parity-check matrices for the same code are obtainable from one another by means of nonsingular linear transformations.

APPENDIX 2: STRUCTURE OF POLYNOMIAL CODES

Given a generator of polynomial $g(x)$ of a cyclic code, a corresponding generator matrix $\mathbf{G}$ can be written by listing k n-tuples (corresponding to k code polynomials), none of which can be obtained by a linear combination of the others. For example, n-tuples corresponding to $x^i g(x)$, $i = k-1, k-2, \ldots, 0$ constitute k rows of a generator matrix of the same code. The generator matrix of the specific form $\mathbf{G} = [\mathbf{I}_k \mathbf{P}]$ can be determined as follows. For each x^i, where $i = n-1, n-2, \ldots, r$, find the residue $p_i(x) \equiv x^i$, modulo $g(x)$. The k polynomials

$$x^i + p_i(x) \qquad (\text{where } i = n-1, n-2, \ldots, r)$$

are multiples of $g(x)$ and are, therefore, code words. Also, by writing the corresponding n-tuple as rows, the result is a generator matrix of the form

$$\mathbf{G} = [\mathbf{I}_k \mathbf{P}]$$

To obtain a *parity-check matrix* $\mathbf{H}$, simply write each n-tuple corresponding to $x^i h(x)$, $i = 0, 1, \ldots, r-1$ in the reverse order. The r rows thus obtained form a parity-check matrix. This procedure can be checked by identifying the product of any row of $\mathbf{G}$ corresponding to $x^i g(x)$, where $0 \le i \le k-1$, and any row of the previously mentioned $\mathbf{H}$ to be identical to one of the missing coefficients in the equation $g(x)h(x) = x^n + 1$. To obtain the specific form $\mathbf{H} = [\mathbf{P}^T \mathbf{I}_r]$, we find the residue $q_i(x) \equiv x^i$, modulo $h(x)$, for each x^i, where $i = k, k+1, \ldots, n$. The reversal of each n-tuple corresponding to the polynomials $x^i + q_i(x)$, where $i = k, k+1, \ldots, n$, which are all multiples of $h(x)$, gives the r rows of the parity-check matrix in the desired form $\mathbf{H} = [\mathbf{P}^T \mathbf{I}_r]$.

For example, consider the primitive polynomial $g(x) = x^3 + x + 1$, which as a generator polynomial, generates a code of length $2^3 - 1 = 7$. To write the corresponding generator matrix, calculate the residues of x^i as follows:

$p_3(x) \equiv x^3 \equiv x + 1, p_4(x) \equiv x^4 \equiv x^2 + x,$

$p_5(x) \equiv x^5 \equiv x^3 + x^2 \equiv x^2 + x + 1,$

$p_6(x) \equiv x^6 \equiv x^3 + x^2 + x \equiv x^2 + 1,$

$$\text{modulo } (x^3 + x + 1)$$

The following generator matrix contains rows corresponding to the vector representation of polynomials $x^i + p_i(x)$, $i = 6, 5, 4, 3$:

$$G = \begin{bmatrix} 1 & 0 & 0 & 0 & 1 & 0 & 1 \\ 0 & 1 & 0 & 0 & 1 & 1 & 1 \\ 0 & 0 & 1 & 0 & 1 & 1 & 0 \\ 0 & 0 & 0 & 1 & 0 & 1 & 1 \end{bmatrix}$$

To write the parity-check matrix, first calculate $h(x) = (x^7 + 1)/(x^3 + x + 1)$ as follows:

$$
\begin{array}{r}
x^4 + x^2 + x + 1 \\
x^3 + x + 1 \overline{)x^7 \qquad\qquad\qquad + 1} \\
\underline{x^7 + x^5 + x^4} \\
x^5 + x^4 \qquad\qquad + 1 \\
\underline{x^5 \qquad + x^3 + x^2} \\
x^4 + x^3 + x^2 \qquad + 1 \\
\underline{x^4 \qquad + x^2 + x} \\
x^3 \qquad + x + 1 \\
\underline{x^3 \qquad + x + 1} \\
0
\end{array}
$$

Thus, $h(x) = x^4 + x^2 + x + 1$, and

$q_4(x) \equiv x^4 \equiv x^2 + x + 1,$

$q_5(x) \equiv x^5 \equiv x^3 + x^2 + x,$

$q_6(x) \equiv x^6 \equiv x^4 + x^3 + x^2 \equiv x^3 + x + 1,$

$$\text{modulo } (x^4 + x^2 + x + 1)$$

Writing, in reverse order, the vector representation of polynomials $x^i + q_i(x)$, where $i = 4, 5, 6$, we have the parity-check matrix

$$H = \begin{bmatrix} 1 & 1 & 1 & 0 & 1 & 0 & 0 \\ 0 & 1 & 1 & 1 & 0 & 1 & 0 \\ 1 & 1 & 0 & 1 & 0 & 0 & 1 \end{bmatrix}$$

It can be seen that the cyclic code in this example is identical to the linear code of the last example.

APPENDIX 3: METHODS FOR FINDING GENERATOR POLYNOMIALS

Single-Error-Correcting Codes

Single-error-correcting codes are often referred to as Hamming codes [Hamming, 1950]. In such a code, any two distinct single errors x^i and x^j must yield distinct syndromes. Let $\mathbf{e}_i$ and $\mathbf{e}_j$ be row vectors corresponding to x^i and x^j respectively.

$$\mathbf{e}_i \mathbf{H}^T \neq \mathbf{e}_j \mathbf{H}^T$$

or

$$(\mathbf{e}_i + \mathbf{e}_j)\mathbf{H}^T \neq \mathbf{0}$$

Thus, the generator polynomial $g(x)$ never divides $x^i + x^j$ for any i and j. This condition can be satisfied if we choose the code length n to be e, where e is the *period* of $g(x)$. The period e is the smallest integer such that $g(x)$ divides $x^e + 1$. With i and j both smaller than n, $g(x)$ can never divide $(x^i + x^j) = x^j(x^{i-j} + 1)$. In particular, if an rth degree $g(x)$ is *irreducible* (i.e., not divisible by any other polynomial except 1), then the period of $g(x)$ divides $2^r - 1$. Then, if the period of $g(x)$ is $2^r - 1$, $g(x)$ is said to be *primitive*. A single-error-correcting code generated by a primitive polynomial is "close-packed" in the sense that all 2^r syndromes are used for the prescribed correctable errors, $2^r - 1$ single errors and one zero error. Since primitive polynomials are known to exist for all degrees, Hamming codes of length $2^r - 1$ exist for all r.

Burst-Error-Correcting Codes

One way to generalize the class of single-error-correcting codes is to obtain codes to correct any error burst within a span of b digits. Such codes are called burst-b correcting codes [Abramson, 1959; Fire, 1959] and are suitable for channels with occasional error bursts.

A class of burst-correcting codes, known as *Fire codes* [Fire, 1959], is best defined as the class of cyclic codes wherein the generator polynomials take the form

$$g(x) = (x^c + 1)p(x)$$

Here, $c \geqslant 2b + 1$, the length of the code is the least common multiple (LCM) of c and the period of $p(x)$, and the degree of $p(x)$ is at least b. When these conditions are satisfied, the resulting code is capable of distinguishing syndromes resulting from any two burst errors each of length no greater than b.

There are burst-error-correcting codes other than the class of Fire codes; many are optimum codes, which are more efficient than the Fire codes of the same length and maximum correctable bursts [Elspas and Short, 1962].

Independent-Error-Correcting Codes

It was pointed out earlier that an irreducible polynomial $p(x)$ can be used to generate a single-error-correcting code of a length equal to the period e of the polynomial $p(x)$, where e is the smallest integer such that $p(x)$ divides $x^e + 1$. If we properly combine several irreducible factors of $x^e + 1$, we can obtain the generator polynomial of an independent (or multiple)-error-correcting code. Given that some α is a root of $m_1(x) = p(x)$, i.e., $p(\alpha) = 0$. Then for any i, only one among these factors, denoted by $m_i(x)$, satisfies $m_i(\alpha^i) = 0$. These $m_i(x)$, called the *minimum polynomials* of x^i, are not necessarily distinct for different i's.

BCH Codes

The binary BCH (Bose-Chaudhuri-Hocquenghem) codes form a class of multiple-error-correcting codes [Hocquenghem, 1959; Bose and Ray-Chaudhuri, 1960a, 1960b; Peterson, 1961] that can be described in terms of the minimum polynomials $m_i(x)$ as follows. Let the generator polynomial be defined as

$$g(x) = \text{LCM} \, [m_1(x), m_3(x), \ldots, m_{2t-1}(x)] \quad (2)$$

then the code generated by $g(x)$ is a t-error correcting code with a minimum distance at least $2t + 1$ and a length $n = e_1$, where e_1 is the period of $m_1(x)$.

If the generator polynomial is

$$g(x) = \text{LCM} \, [m_0(x), m_1(x), m_3(x), \ldots, m_{2t-1}(x)] \quad (3)$$

the corresponding code has a minimum distance of at least $2t + 2$. The length of this code is again $n = e_1$ for $t \geqslant 1$. For $t = 0$, $g(x) = m_0(x) = x + 1$. The code generated by $g(x) = x + 1$ has a minimum distance of 2. This is a code with a single parity digit, and the code length can be arbitrary.

Given any $m_1(x)$, one could obtain $m_i(x)$ for any i by using algebraic procedures [Albert, 1956; Peterson, 1961, pp. 141–142]. However, this is generally time consuming and unnecessary since tables of binary minimum polynomials are available [Peterson, 1961, pp. 254–70].

Examples

As an example, assume that we are generating a binary double-error-correcting code of length $n = 2^6 - 1 = 63$. Since a primitive polynomial of degree six has a period equal to 63, we select $m_1(x)$ as a primitive polynomial. From Peterson [1961, pp. 254–270], if the primitive polynomial $x^6 + x + 1$ is chosen as $m_1(x)$, then $m_3(x) = x^6 + x^4 + x^2 + x + 1$. From Equation 3, the generator polynomial

$$g(x) = \text{LCM} \, [m_1(x), m_3(x)] = m_1(x)m_3(x)$$
$$= (x^6 + x + 1)(x^6 + x^4 + x^2 + x + 1)$$
$$= x^{12} + x^{10} + x^8 + x^5 + x^4 + x^3 + 1$$

generates a (63, 51) code with a minimum distance at least 5, good for double independent-error correction. Note that the coefficients in the product can be obtained by first writing the product in the ordinary fashion. Then all even coefficients are transformed to 0's and all the odd ones to 1's.

The period of $m_i(x)$ may be smaller than that of $m_1(x)$; the degree of $m_i(x)$ may also be smaller than that of $m_1(x)$. Such properties are sometimes useful, as shown in the following example.

With the same $m_i(x)$ as used in the last example, if we let $m'_1(x) = m_3(x)$ and $\beta = \alpha^3$, such that $m'_1(\beta) = m_3(\alpha^3) = 0$, then $m'_3(x) = m_9(x)$, where $m'_3(x)(\beta^3) = m_9(\alpha^9) = 0$. From Peterson [1961, pp. 254–270] we find that $m_9(x) = x^3 + x^2 + 1$. From Equation 3, the generator polynomial is

$$g(x) = (x + 1)(x^6 + x^4 + x^2 + x + 1)$$

$$\cdot\ (x^3 + x^2 + 1) \tag{4}$$

$$= x^{10} + x^7 + x^6 + x^4 + x^2 + 1$$

which generates a (21, 11) code with a minimum distance of 6.

It should be pointed out that the minimum distance d guaranteed by the BCH code in Equation 2 is just a lower bound to the actual minimum distance of the code. For example, the primitive binary polynomial $m_1(x) = x^{11} + x^2 + 1$ has a period $2^{11} - 1 = 89 \times 23$. The polynomial $m_{89}(x) = x^{11} + x^9 + x^7 + x^6 + x^5 + x + 1$ has a period of 23. Assuming $\beta = \alpha^{89}$ and $m'_1(x) = m_{89}(x)$, then the roots of $m'_1(x)$ are $\beta, \beta^2, \beta^4, \beta^8, \beta^{16}, (\beta^{32} = \beta^9), \beta^{18}, (\beta^{36} = \beta^{13}), (\beta^{26} = \beta^3), \beta^6, \beta^{12}$. Since $m'_1(x) = m'_2(x) = m'_3(x) = m'_4(x)$, as a BCH code, $m_1(x)$ generates a (23, 12) code of minimum distance at least 5. However, the (23, 12) code is equivalent to the Golay code [1958] with a minimum distance equal to 7. Other BCH codes have also been found to have actual minimum distances exceeding those guaranteed by the theory of BCH codes [Lum, 1966].

Error-correction procedures of BCH codes are rather complicated. They generally involve solving the roots of a t-degree polynomial and a set of t simultaneous equations, where t is the number of correctable errors. The number of operations needed to perform these procedures grows exponentially with respect to t. Recent research suggests ways of significantly reducing the decoding complexity of BCH codes [Chien, 1964; Berlekamp, 1968; Massey, 1969]. Perhaps decoding complexity will eventually increase only linearly with t.

For many applications where the number of errors to be corrected in a code block is small, logic implementation of table lookup is a practical solution to the decoding of BCH codes. Another attractive method of implementation by means of majority gates can be used for a class called "self-orthogonal" codes, which includes certain BCH codes. This subject is covered later in Appendix 4.

Another well-known class of multiple-error-correcting code is the class of Reed-Muller codes [Muller, 1954; Reed, 1954]. Although not originally formulated in terms of cyclic codes, Reed-Muller codes have been shown to be obtainable from a special class of BCH codes [Kasami, Lin, and Peterson, 1968; Weldon, 1968].

Multiple-Burst-Correcting Codes

The BCH codes described earlier exist in other than binary cases. A q-nary BCH code can be generated by a q-nary polynomial (a polynomial with q-nary coefficients), provided the q symbols can be identified as elements in a field.* A character (or a byte) consisting of a binary m-tuple, for example, may be considered as belonging to a field of 2^m elements.

---

* There are two operations defined in a field, addition and multiplication. If 2^m binary m-tuples are represented by corresponding polynomials, the addition and multiplication of binary polynomials can be taken as field operations, provided that we always reduce a product polynomial of degree m or higher to its residue modulo, a fixed, irreducible polynomial of degree m. For a rigorous treatment on the theory of finite fields, see Chapter 6 in Peterson [1961].

Reed-Solomon Codes

Reed-Solomon codes are a special class of BCH codes where the message symbols are m-tuples [Reed and Solomon, 1960]. When used for binary messages, binary symbols must be grouped as m-tuples (or characters). A generator polynomial taking the form

$$g(x) = (x - \alpha)(x - \alpha^2) \cdots (x - \alpha^{d-1}) \quad \textbf{(5)}$$

generates a code with minimum distance of at least d. Note that the coefficients of the generator polynomial and code polynomials are now m-tuples and the distance between two code words is the number of places wherein corresponding m-tuples differ. The length of this code is $e = 2^m - 1$ characters, or $m(2^m - 1)$ binary digits.

Because of their independent-character-error-correcting capability, Reed-Solomon codes are effective against multiple bursts of error if they occur within a code block. The decoding procedure is rather complex and usually requires program implementation. The code efficiency is usually attractive when compared with the efficiency of competitive schemes, such as the use of interleaved codes. A Reed-Solomon code with a minimum distance equal to 12 has been used in Digital Cypress [Oldman, Chien, and Tang, 1968].

Example Decoders

We indicated previously that burst-error-correcting codes can easily be implemented. This is illustrated in the following example. A binary code having as its generator polynomial

$$g(x) = (x + 1)(x^4 + x + 1)$$
$$= x^5 + x^4 + x^2 + 1$$

is a burst-2 correcting code of length 15, a decoder for which is shown in Figure A-9. The registers in the division circuit contain the residue of $x^3 e(x)$ modulo $g(x)$, where $e(x)$ is the error polynomial. Since the syndrome detection circuit must recognize the syndrome when the error burst is located at the high-degree end, we may write the corresponding error polynomial as

$$e(x) = x^{15-2} b(x)$$

where $b(x)$ is the error-burst polynomial of degree $b - 1 = 1$. The syndrome of this $e(x)$ is the residue of $x^{15-2+5} b(x)$ modulo $(x^5 + x^4 + x^2 + 1)$, which is simply $x^3 b(x)$. The existence of

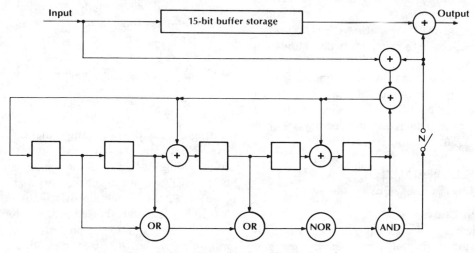

Figure A–9.   Decoder for a burst-2 code.

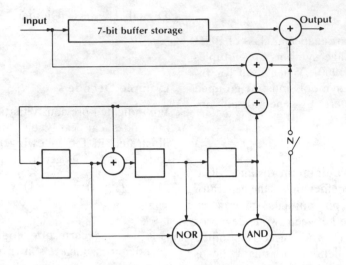

Figure A–10. Decoder for a single-error-correcting code.

three zeros in this syndrome is taken as the basis of syndrome detection as shown in Figure A-9. Once the burst location is determined, feedbacks in the division circuit can be cut off or, as shown in Figure A-9, nullified by establishing an additional feedback path. The detected error pattern (including no error) is then gated through and removed from the received message coming out of the 15-bit buffer storage. Switch N is closed only during the second n-bit cycle.

Another example is the single-error-correcting code generated by $g(x) = x^3 + x + 1$, a decoder for which is shown in Figure A-10. The operation of this decoder is similar to that shown in Figure A-9.

In some applications, the input message may not be in the exact serial form. Combinatorial decoders or decoders that combine serial and parallel operations then become distinct possibilities [Gill, 1966; Sih and Hsiao, 1966].

APPENDIX 4: SPECIALIZED ERROR-CONTROL CODES

Interleaved Codes

The interleaving of codes is just like the time-division multiplexing of a number of messages.

Each "subcode" consists of symbols separated periodically by m digits; there are m such subcodes. Usually all m subcodes are generated by the same polynomial $g'(x)$. Clearly, if the length of the subcode is n', the overall code length is $n = mn'$. The generator polynomial of the interleaved code can be shown to be

$$g(x) = g'(x^m)$$

where $g'(x)$ is the generator polynomial of individual subcodes.

Interleaved codes tend to break up error bursts, and subcodes interpret them as independent errors. Thus, one can use independent-error-correcting codes of acceptable decoding complexity against burst or multiple-burst errors, which might otherwise require a multiple-burst-correcting code with impractical decoding complexity. On the other hand, a single-burst-correcting code with simple implementation cannot handle long bursts (e.g., drop-outs) unless the code is long. In that case, long code words would be exposed to some additional errors not protected by the code. The main disadvantage of interleaved codes is that the redundancy requirement is relatively high in comparison with that of multiple-burst-error-correcting codes.

N-Dimensional Codes

The *N*-dimensional codes are, as the name suggests, best discussed in geometric terms. Figure A-11 shows a two-dimensional code format in which each row belongs to a subcode and each column belongs to another (not necessarily distinct) subcode.

If d_1 and d_2 are respectively the minimum distances of row and column subcodes, then the two-dimensional code has a minimum distance $d = d_1 d_2$. More dimensions can be added to the code to further strengthen the correction capability.

The above two-dimensional code is equivalent to a two-level interleaved code. Columns of information symbols can be considered as being interleaved with the row subcode, and *N* iterations of interleaving clearly result in an *N*-dimensional code. It is from this point of view that *N*-dimensional codes are often referred to as iterated codes [Birdsall and Ristenblatt, 1958]. The geometrical interpretation of *N*-dimensional codes also enables one to obtain simple implementations of such codes especially for such storage devices as tapes and core arrays whose geometrical configurations are ideal.

An *N*-dimensional code may also suffer from the high redundancy requirement when used in burst channels because of interleaving. Nevertheless, such a code has the attractive feature that as long as the error rate is reduced in each level of iteration, more and more iterations will, in theory, make the error rate diminish while keeping the information rate nonzero [Elias, 1954].

Shortened Codes

We have seen that in any cyclic code capable of correcting single errors, the code length should not exceed *e*, the period of the generator polynomial. However, an (n, k) code can be shortened to become an $(n - s, k - s)$ code by constraining the *s* high-degree digits of the code polynomial to be always zero. These *s* digits are then omitted from all code words. The linear sequential encoder of Figure A-7 can be used for shortened codes without change. However, if the decoding delay is to be $n' = n - s$ digits instead of *n* digits, the input of the division circuit in the decoder of Figure A-8 should be premultiplied by x^s. The same syndrome detection circuit can then be used [Peterson, 1961, pp. 194–195].

Shortened codes are often used because natural lengths may not be suitable in some applications. They can also be used to improve reliability, since with the reduced code length ($n - s$), the expected number of errors is reduced by a factor $(n - s)/n$. The most attractive feature of shortened codes, however, is that the maximum correctable errors may now exceed what was originally possible with full-length codes [Kasami, 1963]. This feature is particularly desirable with burst-error correcting codes, since the increased correcting capability presents no extra decoding complexity. In applications to variable length messages, codes that have increased capabilities at shorter lengths can achieve additional reduction in overall error rate.

Threshold-Logic-Decodable Codes

We have seen that decoding complexity is a severe limitation to the application of powerful BCH codes. It is, therefore, desirable to find new classes of codes with structures that enable one

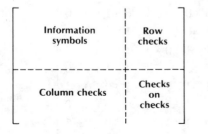

Figure A–11.   Two-dimensional code format.

to use simple decoding procedure. Codes obtained from projective and Euclidean geometries have recently been shown to be decodable by threshold logic [Rudolph, 1967]. We shall illustrate the basic concept with a special class of binary "self-orthogonal" codes [Massey, 1963].

Self-orthogonality is defined on the parity-check matrix as follows: the set of rows $(h_1, h_2, \ldots, h_J)$ in a parity-check matrix H with 1's in a particular column i are self-orthogonal on the ith column if, in this set (considered as a submatrix), no other column contains two or more 1's. To decode the digit corresponding to the ith column of H, we first assume that the error at this digit is unknown, and that each of the J parity equations from the set gives an "estimate" of this error. The majority determines the final error value. Since an error corresponding to the ith column has J votes, while an error at any other position has at most one vote (because of the self-orthogonality), the majority decision must be correct as long as the total number of errors does not exceed $J/2$. If the self-orthogonality condition can be established for every digit (not necessarily with the same parity-check matrix), the code is threshold decodable with a miminum distance at least $J + 1$.

The most interesting case occurs when the code is cyclic, because a decoder with the general form shown in Figure A-8 can be used. The syndrome detection circuit, in this case, contains majority logic with inputs from J modulo-2

adders performing the set of J parity checks found to be self-orthogonal on the highest-degree digit. We now demonstrate this with an example.

Self-Orthogonal Decoding Example

The code generated by $g(x) = x^{10} + x^7 + x^6 + x^4 + x^2 + 1$ of Equation 4 was shown to be a (21, 11)-code with minimum distance equal to six. Using the division circuit of Figure A-4a in the decoder of Figure A-8, the contents of the shift-registers (considered as an r-tuple) give the syndrome of the error, which, in this case, is the residue of the received polynomial modulo $g(x)$. The ith column of the parity-check matrix can be written as the residue of x^{i-1} modulo $g(x)$ as in Equation 6.

This matrix does not satisfy the desired "self-orthogonality" condition. However, an equivalent parity-check matrix can be obtained by cyclically shifting the first row of $\mathbf{H}$ in Equation 6. There are five such cyclic shifts with a 1 in the right-most column (because the row has five 1's) as shown in Equation 7.

The five rows of $\mathbf{H}'$ are self-orthogonal on the right-most column, since no other column contains two 1's. The minimum distance is 6. Any row of $\mathbf{H}'$, denoted by $\mathbf{h}_i$, is a linear combination of a unique collection of rows in $\mathbf{H}$ and can be

$$\mathbf{H} = \begin{bmatrix} 0 & 0 & & \cdot & \cdot & \cdot & & 0 & 1 & 0 & 0 & 1 & 1 & 0 & 0 & 0 & 0 & 1 & 0 & 1 \\ 0 & & & & & & & 1 & 0 & 0 & 1 & 1 & 0 & 0 & 0 & 0 & 1 & 0 & 1 & 0 \\ & & & & & & 1 & & & 1 & 1 & 0 & 0 & 0 & 0 & 1 & 0 & 1 & 0 & 0 \\ & \cdot & & & & 1 & & \cdot & 1 & 0 & 1 & 1 & 0 & 1 & 0 & 1 & 1 & 0 & 1 \\ & \cdot & & & 1 & & & \cdot & 0 & 1 & 0 & 1 & 1 & 0 & 1 & 1 & 1 & 1 & 1 \\ & \cdot & & 1 & & & & \cdot & 1 & 0 & 1 & 1 & 0 & 1 & 1 & 1 & 1 & 1 & 0 \\ & & 1 & & & & & & 0 & 1 & 0 & 1 & 1 & 1 & 1 & 1 & 0 & 0 & 1 \\ & 1 & & & & & & & 1 & 0 & 1 & 1 & 1 & 1 & 1 & 0 & 0 & 1 & 0 \\ 0 & 1 & & & & & 0 & 0 & 1 & 0 & 0 & 1 & 1 & 0 & 0 & 0 & 0 & 1 \\ 1 & 0 & & \cdot & \cdot & \cdot & & 0 & 0 & 1 & 0 & 0 & 1 & 1 & 0 & 0 & 0 & 0 & 1 & 0 \end{bmatrix} \tag{6}$$

$$\mathbf{H'} = \begin{bmatrix} 0 & 0 & 0 & 0 & 0 & 0 & 0 & 0 & 0 & 1 & 0 & 0 & 1 & 1 & 0 & 0 & 0 & 0 & 1 & 0 & 1 \\ 0 & 1 & 0 & 0 & 0 & 0 & 0 & 0 & 0 & 0 & 0 & 1 & 0 & 0 & 1 & 1 & 0 & 0 & 0 & 0 & 1 \\ 0 & 0 & 0 & 0 & 1 & 0 & 1 & 0 & 0 & 0 & 0 & 0 & 0 & 0 & 0 & 0 & 1 & 0 & 0 & 1 & 1 \\ 1 & 0 & 0 & 0 & 0 & 1 & 0 & 1 & 0 & 0 & 0 & 0 & 0 & 0 & 0 & 0 & 0 & 1 & 0 & 0 & 1 \\ 0 & 0 & 1 & 1 & 0 & 0 & 0 & 0 & 1 & 0 & 1 & 0 & 0 & 0 & 0 & 0 & 0 & 0 & 0 & 0 & 1 \end{bmatrix} \qquad (7)$$

"synthesized" from the 10 left-most digits by adding rows of $\mathbf{H}$ (or Equation 6) with 1's at the desired position. These sums are equivalent to modulo-2 additions of the contents of the corresponding shift-registers. A complete implementation of the decoder is shown in Figure A-12.

Self-orthogonal codes, such as the one just discussed, belong to a general class of threshold-logic decodable codes, which are derived from finite geometries. For more details regarding the recent developments in threshold decodable codes, see Weldon [1966] and Chow [n.d.].

Synchronization Codes

The error-control codes discussed thus far deal with additive errors, and we assume that there is no misidentification of locations of symbols. In real transmission or storage systems, however, synchronization errors can occur at a bit level, character level, and even at a higher level, where the framing of code words is involved. Various methods of controlling synchronization errors have been suggested. The use of a synchronization sequence with a sharp autocorrelation function [Barker, 1953] sets up the word-framing. To avoid subsequent loss of word synchronization due to the possible loss of bit synchronization, such special sequences may be inserted before each code word, or periodically at longer intervals to avoid the need for excessive redundancy.

When a cyclic code is to be used for error control, it is possible to incorporate synchronization-error control in the code capability. Since, in that case, a cyclic shift of a code word is also a code word, ordinary coding schemes must be modified if a slip in word framing is to be controlled within the context of a code. There are three possibilities:

- Add a fixed n-tuple, with a special synchronization property, to every code word. (Such a code is known as a "coset code.") The same n-tuple is subtracted from the received message after the word-framing is established [Tong, 1966].
- Use a shortened cyclic code to control word-framing [Tong, 1966].
- Use an extended cyclic code for the same purpose [Bose and Caldwell, 1967; Weldon, 1967].

Recovering errors due to the loss or insertion of bits within a code block is a different problem and has yielded relatively few results [Sellers, 1962; Ullman, 1966]. A more practical method is the detection of this type of errors accompanied by a possible request for retransmission.

Convolutional Codes

The relationship between information symbols and code symbols need not be confined to disjoint blocks. In a *convolutional* (or *recurrent*) *code*, check digits in a given block check some of the information digits in other blocks as well. One may describe a convolutional code as one that has overlapping blocks. In a separable linear code, the generator matrix may be written in the standard form $\mathbf{G} = [\mathbf{I}_k \mathbf{P}]$. Similarly, we may write the generator matrix for a truncated convolutional code of length $n' = m(k + r)$ as

$$\mathbf{G} = \begin{bmatrix} \mathbf{I}_k & \mathbf{P_0} & 0 & \mathbf{P_1} & \cdots & 0 & \mathbf{P_{m-1}} \\ 0 & 0 & \mathbf{I}_k & \mathbf{P_0} & \cdots & 0 & \mathbf{P_{m-2}} \\ & & & \cdot & & & \\ & & & & \cdot & & \\ & & & & & \mathbf{I}_k & \mathbf{P_0} \end{bmatrix}$$

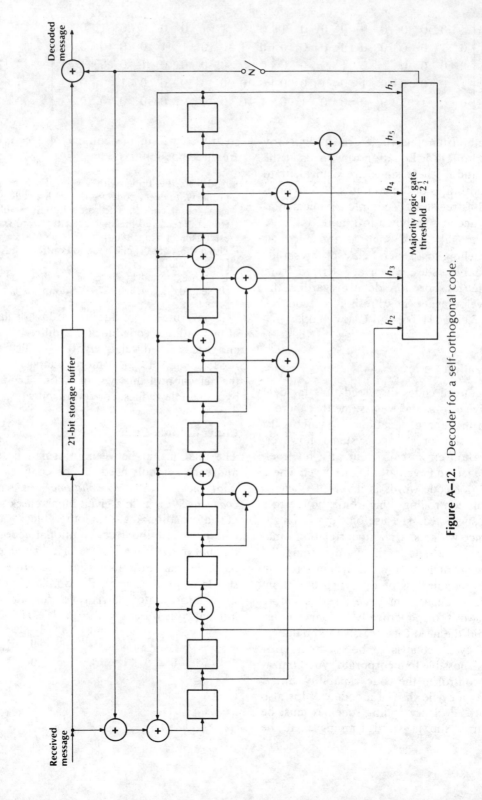

Figure A–12. Decoder for a self-orthogonal code.

Here, the first k information digits are related to the r following check digits in the same block by $\mathbf{P_0}$ and are related to the check digits in the $m-1$ following blocks by $\mathbf{P_1}, \ldots, \mathbf{P_{m-1}}$. The corresponding parity-check matrix is the following:

$$
\mathbf{H} = \begin{bmatrix}
\mathbf{P_0^T} & \mathbf{I_r} & 0 & 0 & & \\
\mathbf{P_1^T} & 0 & \mathbf{P_0^T} & \mathbf{I_r} & & \\
\vdots & \vdots & \vdots & \vdots & \ddots & \\
\mathbf{P_{m-1}^T} & 0 & \mathbf{P_{m-2}^T} & 0 & \mathbf{P_0^T} & \mathbf{I_r}
\end{bmatrix}
$$

Although convolutional codes for correcting burst errors [Hagelbarger, 1959; Wyner and Ash, 1963; Berlekamp, 1964] and independent errors [Bussgang, 1965; Robinson, 1965] have been studied, at present they are not as well understood as block codes. As far as theoretical error-control capability is concerned, there appears to be no significant difference between block codes and convolutional codes [Freiman and Robinson, 1965].

There are two different approaches in decoding a convolutional code. The first is "deterministic decoding," in which syndromes are calculated and algebraic procedures are carried out to determine the error sequence, similar to the decoding of block codes. However, if the decoding results of previous blocks are fed back to modify syndromes that determine the following blocks, any decoding error may "propagate" to succeeding blocks. Although the error propagation problem may not be serious, it must be analyzed and evaluated when convolutional codes are used.

Another method of decoding a convolutional code is known as the "sequential decoding" technique [Wozencraft, 1957; Fano, 1963; Jelinek, 1968]. With sequential decoding, one evaluates the accumulated likelihood of correct decisions at each digit and accepts a digit only after a certain number of succeeding digits tend to confirm (in terms of accumulated likelihood measure) that the first digit is correct. If succeeding digits indicate that the first digit is in error, a search through the code tree, based on a predetermined algorithm follows, with corresponding likelihood evaluated, until a satisfactory decoding of the digit is found.

The following can be said about sequential decoding in general:

- The decoding algorithm is usually flexible enough to be used on a variety of channels.
- Randomly chosen convolutional codes can be used.
- A computer with large storage is required.
- In theory, given sufficient redundancy, the decoding error decreases exponentially with the constraint length n'.
- The decoding effort (in terms of computations or storage required) is a random variable without an upper bound, although the expected decoding effort is bounded.

Constant-Weight Codes

A constant-weight code consists of all n-vectors of a certain fixed weight (number of 1's) w. Since two n-vectors of weight w do not always result in a vector sum of the same weight, such codes are generally not linear codes. Constant-weight codes are useful in asymmetric channels in which errors of one polarity dominate, since such errors always change the weight of the code vectors and, thus, can be detected [Berger, 1961; Freiman, 1961]. The minimum Hamming distance between any two code vectors is two. Therefore, any combination of an odd number of errors can also be detected. When $n = 2w$, the code vectors can be used directly to specify the exact bipolar signal sequences to be used in the channel. Such signals would contain no dc component. This is a desirable feature, since it is common for a channel frequency characteristic to assume a zero at the zero frequency.

Arithmetic Codes

Arithmetic codes have been proposed for use with computers to control errors that occur in arithmetic operations as well as in transmission and storage [Brown, 1960]. Code words are considered integer numbers, and ordinary arithmetic operations apply. There is a generator A, similar to that of cyclic polynomial codes, and the code words are all integer multiples of A, within a certain range of n digits. For binary arithmetic codes, the number of redundant digits is the smallest integer $r \geqslant \log_2 A$. Such a code is linear with respect to arithmetic operations, i.e., $AN_1 + AN_2 = A(N_1 + N_2) = AN_3$.

An error in arithmetic code is defined by subtracting the transmitted code "number" from the received number arithmetically. Because of carries, a "single" arithmetic error may appear as a burst of errors in the vector representation.

A single-error-detecting arithmetic code can be obtained by letting $A = 3$. Since a single error must assume a magnitude of the form $\pm 2^i$, no single error can change one code number to another because code numbers must differ by a multiple of · three. Such a multiple can never assume the form $\pm 2^i$. The arithmetic code length can be arbitrary.

For single-error correction, the residues of $\pm 2^i$ $(i = 0, \ldots, n - 1)$ modulo A (which are similar to the syndromes in polynomial codes) must be distinct. For example, with $A = 19$, we have the following residues:

$$
\left.
\begin{aligned}
&2^0 \equiv 1, 2^1 \equiv 2, 2^2 \equiv 4, 2^3 \equiv 8, 2^4 \equiv 16, \\
&2^5 \equiv 13, 2^6 \equiv 7, 2^7 \equiv 14, 2^8 \equiv 9, -2^0 \equiv 18 \\
&-2^1 \equiv 17, -2^2 \equiv 15, -2^3 \equiv 11, -2^4 \equiv 3, \\
&-2^5 \equiv 6, -2^6 \equiv 12, -2^7 \equiv 5, -2^8 \equiv 10
\end{aligned}
\right\} \text{modulo 19}
$$

The code length is nine digits with five redundancy digits. Despite their attractive features for error control in computer-communication systems, there are few known classes of arithmetic codes. However, some encouraging results in the theory of arithmetic codes for multiple-error correction have recently been obtained [Chien, Hong, and Preparata, 1968].

APPENDIX 5: CYCLIC REDUNDANCY CHECKING

Operation of the CRC in IBM 2400-series magnetic tapes is now illustrated. If $a_i(x)$, $i = 0, \ldots, 8$, indicates the message polynomials on the ith track, then the CRC character contains the residue

$$
\begin{aligned}
c(x) &= c_0 + c_1 x + \cdots + c_8 x^8 \\
&\equiv \sum_{i=0}^{8} x^{i+1} a_i(x) \text{ modulo } g(x)
\end{aligned}
$$

where

$$
g(x) = x^9 + x^6 + x^5 + x^4 + x^3 + 1
$$

The residue $c(x)$ can be obtained from the division circuit shown in Figure A-13. Comparing Figure A-13 with Figure A-4a, it is clear that the contribution of $xa_0(x)$ in the residue $c(x)$ is $c^{(0)}(x) \equiv xa_0(x)$ modulo $g(x)$. Similarly, because of the successively advanced input points, the contribution of $xa_i(x)$ in $c(x)$ is $c^{(i)}(x) \equiv x^{i+1} a_i(x)$ modulo $g(x)$. The complete residue is $\sum_{i=0}^{8} c^{(i)}(x) = c(x)$.

The effect of the premultiplication by x at all inputs is equivalent to an additional shift after the last digits in $a_i(x)$ are in the division circuit. The CRC-coded message in the ith track is $m_i(x) = xa_i(x) + c_i$. When the error-free coded messages in nine tracks are fed into the division circuit of Figure A-13, the shift-register contents correspond to the residue of

$$
\begin{aligned}
\sum_{i=0}^{8} x^i m_i(x) &= \sum_{i=0}^{8} x^{i+1} a_i(x) + \sum_{i=0}^{8} x^i c_i \\
&\equiv c(x) + c(x) = 0 \qquad \text{modulo } g(x)
\end{aligned}
$$

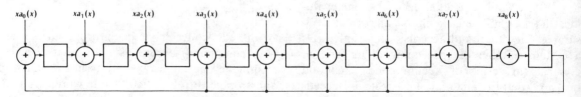

Figure A–13.   Nine-bit division circuit.

If an error $e_i(x)$ occurs in the ith track, then the register contents correspond to

$$s(x) \equiv x^i e_i(x) \qquad \text{modulo } g(x) \qquad \textbf{(8)}$$

which is not zero if $g(x)$ does not divide $e_i(x)$.

To determine the track i, feed the VRC error sequence into a second division circuit similar to the one shown in Figure A-13, but with the input point corresponding to that of the eighth track. An error appears in the VRC sequence when $e(x)$ occurs in any single track. Therefore, the register contents of the second division circuit correspond to

$$s'(x) \equiv x^8 e_i(x) \text{ modulo } g(x)$$

Making $8 - i$ additional shifts in the original divider after $s(x)$ is obtained (and referring to Equation 8), the register contents are

$$x^{8-i} s(x) = x^{8-i} x^i e_i(x) \equiv s'(x) \text{ modulo } g(x)$$

matching the register contents of the second divider. After the error track is determined by shifting and matching the divider register contents, the track is reread with the VRC error sequence added to the message. Many errors not correctable by the above procedure, including any single-track error $e_i(x)$ that is divisible by $g(x)$ and any combination of odd numbers of bit errors, are still detectable.

REFERENCES

Abraham, Ghosh, and Ray-Chaudhuri [1968]; Abramson [1959]; Albert [1956]; Barker [1953]; Berger [1961]; Berger and Mandelbrot [1963]; Berlekamp [1964, 1968]; Birdsall and Ristenblatt [1958]; Bose and Caldwell [1967]; Bose and Ray-Chaudhuri [1960a, 1960b]; Brown [1960]; Bussgang [1965]; Chien [1960, 1964]; Chien and Frazer [1966]; Chien, Hong, and Preparata [1968]; Chow [n.d.]; Constantine [1958]; Eisenbies [1967]; Elias [1954]; Elspas and Short [1962]; Fano [1963]; Fire [1959]; Forney [1965, 1966]; Freiman [1961]; Freiman and Robinson [1965]; Frey [1967]; Frey and Benice [1964]; Gill [1966]; Golay [1949, 1958]; Hagelbarger [1959]; Hamming [1950]; Hocquenghem [1959]; Huffman [1952, 1956]; Jelinek [1968]; Kasami [1963]; Kasami, Lin, and Peterson [1968]; Lucky, Salz, and Weldon [1968]; Lum [1966]; Massey [1963, 1969]; Muller [1954]; Oldham, Chien, and Tang [1968]; Peterson [1961]; Prange [1957]; Reed [1954]; Reed and Solomon [1960]; Robinson [1965]; Rudolph [1967]; Schalkwijk and Kailath [1966]; Sellers [1962]; Shannon [1948, 1959]; Sih and Hsiao [1966]; Slepian [1956]; Tang [1965]; Tang and Chien [1966]; Tong [1966]; Turin [1965]; Ullman [1966]; Weldon [1966, 1967, 1968]; Wozencraft [1957]; Wyner and Ash [1963].

Arithmetic Error Codes: Cost and Effectiveness Studies for Application in Digital System Design

Algirdas Avižienis

Abstract

The application of error-detecting or error-correcting codes in digital computer design requires studies of cost and effectiveness tradeoffs to supplement the knowledge of their theoretical properties. General criteria for cost and effectiveness studies of error codes are developed, and results are presented for arithmetic error codes with the low-cost check modulus $2^n - 1$. Both separate (residue) and nonseparate (AN) codes are considered. The class of multiple arithmetic error codes is developed as an extension of low-cost single codes.

METHODOLOGY OF CODE EVALUATION

Scope of the Problem

In this paper the name *arithmetic error codes* identifies the class of error-detecting and error-correcting codes which are preserved during arithmetic operations. Given the digital number representations, x, y, an arithmetic operation $*$, and an encoding $f: x \rightarrow x'$, we say that f is an arithmetic-error code with respect to $*$ if and only if there exists an algorithm $A*$ for coded operands to implement the operation $*$ such that

$$A * (x', y') \equiv (x * y)'.$$

The definition applies to single-operand operations and multioperand operations as well, i.e.,

$$A * (x') \equiv (* x)'$$

and

$$A * (x'_1, x'_2, \ldots, x'_n) \equiv (x_1 * x_2 * \cdots * x_n)',$$

must be satisfied in those cases.

Arithmetic error codes are of special interest in the design of fault-tolerant computer systems, since they serve to detect (or correct) errors in the results produced by arithmetic processors as well as the errors which have been caused by faulty transmission or storage. The same encoding is applicable throughout the entire computing system to provide *concurrent diagnosis*, i.e., error detection which occurs concurrently with the operation of the computer. Real-time detection of transient and permanent faults is obtained without a duplication of arithmetic processors.

The economic feasibility of arithmetic error codes in a computer system depends on their cost and effectiveness with respect to the set of arithmetic algorithms and their speed requirements. The choice of a specific code from the available alternatives further depends on their relative cost and effectiveness values. This paper presents the results of an investigation of the cost and effectiveness of arithmetic error codes in digital system design. Other new results include several classes of multiple arithmetic error codes. The investigation was stimulated by the need for low-cost real-time fault detection in the fault-tolerant STAR computer [Avižienis, 1968; Avižienis et al., 1971]. Favorable results led to the choice of arithmetic encoding of both data words and instruction addresses in this machine. Preliminary reports on parts of the results have been made on several occasions previously [Avižienis, 1964, 1965, 1966a, 1966b, 1967a, 1967b, 1969].

The Criteria of Cost

For the purposes of this paper a "perfect" computer is a reference computer in which logic faults do not occur. The specified set of arithmetic algorithms is carried out with prescribed speed and without errors. For a given algorithm, word length, and number representation system of the perfect computer the introduction of any error code will result in changes that represent the *cost* of the code. The components of the cost are discussed below in general terms applicable to all arithmetic error codes.

Word Length

The encoding introduces redundant bits in the number representation. A proportional hardware increase takes place in storage arrays, data paths, and processor units. The increase is expressed as a percentage of the perfect design. "Complete duplication" (100 percent increase) is the encoding which serves as the limiting case.

The Checking Algorithm

This tests the code validity of every incoming operand and every result of an instruction. A correcting operation follows when an error-correcting code is used. The cost of the checking algorithm has two interrelated components: the hardware complexity and the time required by checking. The complete duplication case requires only bit-by-bit comparison; other codes require more hardware and time. Provisions for fault detection in the checking hardware itself are needed and add to the cost.

The Arithmetic Algorithms

An encoding usually requires a more complex algorithm for the same arithmetic operation than the perfect computer. This cost is expressed by the incremental time and hardware required by the new algorithm. The reference case of complete duplication does not add any cost of this type (the algorithms are not changed, but they are performed in two separate processors). The set of arithmetic algorithms which is usually provided in a general-purpose processor is discussed in the section on Fault Effects in Binary Arithmetic Processors.

The Criteria of Effectiveness

An *arithmetic error* occurs when a logic fault causes the change of one or more digits in the result of an algorithm. A *logic fault* is defined to be the deviation of one or more logic variables from the values specified in the perfect design. Logic faults differ in their duration, extent, and nature of the deviation from perfect values. The effectiveness of an arithmetic error code in a computer may be expressed in two forms: as a direct *value effectiveness*, and as a design-dependent *fault effectiveness*.

Value Effectiveness

The most direct measure of effectiveness is the listing of the error values that will be detected or corrected when the code is used. These values are determined by the properties of the code and are independent of the logic structure of the computer in which the code will be used. Value effectiveness for 100 percent detection (or correction) of some class of error values has been the main measure of arithmetic codes. For example, *single* error detection (or correction) is said to occur when *all* (100 percent) errors of value

$$\pm cr^i \qquad 0 < c < r \qquad 0 < i < n - 1$$

are detected (or corrected) in an n-digit, radix-r number [Brown, 1960; Peterson, 1961, pp. 236–244]. There is no direct reference for algorithms or their implementation. The present study considers value effectiveness with less than 100 percent detection. Such codes may be useful when their cost is low and when other means of fault tolerance supplement the codes in a computer.

Fault Effectiveness

The purpose of arithmetic error codes in digital systems is to detect the occurrence of logic faults. The detection enables the system to initiate corrective action (error correction, diagnosis, program restart, etc.). In order to assess the effectiveness of fault detection, the value effectiveness of a code must be translated into a measure of *fault effectiveness* for one or more specified types of logic faults. The translation is performed separately for every algorithm and requires an *error table* for every type of fault. The error table is generated from the description of the logic implementation of the algorithm α. The specified fault ϕ is applied to every logic circuit which is used by the algorithm. Every application yields an *error value* E (or a *set* of error values $\{E\}$) by which the fault will change the perfect value S of the result to the actual (incorrect) value $S* = S + E$. The error table $T(\alpha, \phi)$ lists all error values together with their relative frequencies of occurrence during the compilation of $T(\alpha, \phi)$. A comparison of $T(\alpha, \phi)$ with the detectable error values of the given code f shows which entries of the error table are not detectable. The fault effectiveness of f with respect to (α, ϕ) is the *percentage* of all occurrences of ϕ which will be detected (or corrected) when f is employed. Less than 100 percent fault-effective codes are of interest when their cost is low, because other methods of fault tolerance (especially program restarts) can be used to reinforce the codes [Avižienis, 1968; Avižienis et al., 1971]. If the fault effectiveness for (α, ϕ) is not sufficient, it may be improved by redesigning the implementation of α to eliminate some or all of the undetectable entries of $T(\alpha, \phi)$.

During the compilation of the error table $T(\alpha, \phi)$ an application of the fault ϕ to a logic circuit changes the radix-r, n-digit perfect result $s \equiv (s_{n-1}, \ldots, s_1, s_0)$ to an "actual" (incorrect) result $s*$ which differs from the s in at least one digit. The digit changes which have taken place are described by the error number $e \equiv (e_{n-1}, \ldots, e_1, e_0)$ defined digitwise as

$$e_i = s*_i - s_i \qquad \text{for } 0 \le i \le n - 1.$$

The digits of e are in the range $-r + 1 \le e_i \le r - 1$, and e itself represents the error value E in the range

$$-(r^n - 1) \le E \le r^n - 1.$$

When e is recoded to have the minimum number of nonzero digits, this minimum number is defined to be the *arithmetic distance* between s and $s*$, as well as the *arithmetic weight* of e [Peterson, 1961, pp. 236–244]. The weight of an error value has been employed to indicate its relative probability (single, double, etc.) The results of following sections show that the weight of an error number is data dependent in some algorithms and therefore not suitable as a general criterion of fault effectiveness.

Classes of Logic Faults

Single Faults

A single logic fault is the deviation of one logic variable from the design value. During an interval of time ΔT_i (to be called a *use*) it has two possible forms: a) the logic variable is "stuck-on-zero" (abbreviated S0) when it assumes the actual value 0 instead of the design value 1; and b) the logic variable is "stuck-on-1" (abbreviated S1) when it assumes the actual value 1 instead of the design value 0.

The circuits that are used to store, transmit, or generate digit values during an algorithm will be called *digit circuits*. A single fault is said to be *local* if its immediate effect changes the value of only one digit, i.e., the local fault in position $i(0 \le i \le n - 1)$ of a radix-r operand adds the value

$$cr^i, \qquad -r + 1 \le c \le r - 1$$

to the affected number. The value of the error number is either cr^i, or an arithmetic function of cr^i, determined by the location of the fault and the microprogram of the algorithm. A single fault which immediately affects more than one digit is *distributed*. Its effect is expressed as the cumulative effect of two or more local faults.

One-Use and Repeated-Use Faults

With respect to the microprogram of the algorithm, there are one-use and repeated-use faults. The fault is a *one-use* fault when the faulty digit circuit is used only once before the checking algorithm is performed. Iterative algorithms (multiplication, division, byte-serial addition, etc.) employ the same digit circuits repeatedly in order to generate the result; if one of these circuits is faulty, a *repeated-use* fault results. Repeated-use faults differ according to their one-use effectiveness, duration, and determinancy. The fault is ineffective during the use ΔT_i if the fault-induced value is identical to the design value. The fault is *transient* if it does not exist during one or more of the uses: otherwise it is *permanent*. A transient fault is equivalent to a permanent fault that is ineffective during some uses; consequently, transient faults are a subset of permanent faults. Some types of failures cause the logic value at a point to become uncertain, and it is interpreted randomly as either one or zero during the repeated uses of the faulty circuit. In these cases neither a constant S0 nor a constant S1 fault exists for all uses; the fault is *indeterminate* and is called "stuck-on-X," abbreviated SX. An indeterminate fault has the combined effect of two transient faults (one S0, the other S1) affecting the same variable.

Cumulative Fault Effects

A multiple (double, triple, etc.) fault occurs when two or more faulty logic variables exist during the same algorithm. Its effect is expressed as the cumulative effect of two or more single faults. A review of the fault model shows that the effect of any fault is equivalent to the cumulative effect of a set of local one-use faults. The *basic fault* is defined to be a local one-use fault (either S0 or S1 at ΔT_i). In the study of fault effectiveness, the effect of a basic fault is determined for every digit circuit and every algorithm of a processor or storage array. The effect of any other fault is then determined in two steps: *a*) identify the set of basic faults which corresponds to the given fault; and *b*) determine the effect (error value, or set of possible error values) of the given fault by applying sequentially the basic faults identified in step *a*.

The classification of faults is summarized in Figure B-1.

FAULT EFFECTS IN BINARY ARITHMETIC PROCESSORS

Basic Faults in Parallel Arithmetic

The set of arithmetic algorithms which is provided in a general-purpose processor includes at least the eight algorithms listed in Table B-1 either separately or as parts of composite algorithms, multiplication, and division. In this section we determine the error magnitudes due to the existence of a basic (local, one-use) fault in a digit circuit of a radix-2 processor. A parallel design is assumed, in which the algorithms of Table B-1 use the digit circuits of the processor

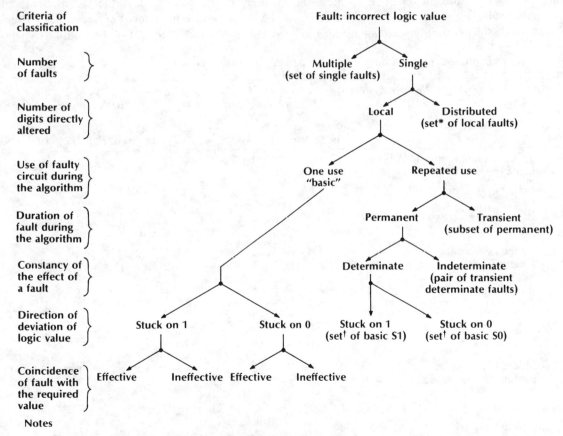

Notes

* Membership of set determined by logical design of the net and by the nature of the fault
† Membership of set determined by algorithm being implemented

Figure B–1.   Classification of logic faults.

only once, and the faults are single-use faults. The error magnitudes $|E|$ which can be generated by a basic fault and their arithmetic weights are presented in Table B-1. The radix-2 operands are n binary digits long ($0 \leq i \leq n - 1$). Two systems for the representation of negative numbers are considered: complements with respect to $N_1 = 2^n - 1$ (one's complements), and complements with respect to $N_2 = 2^n$ (two's complements). All operands and results are treated as unsigned integer values for checking purposes. The transfer (A1) is included in every other algorithm; thus the $|E| = 2^i$ of a transfer may occur in every case. If the same register is used to hold an operand and the result, a repeated-use fault may result.

Table B-1 shows that error magnitudes of weights greater than one occur for a single basic fault. In (A2)–(A5) they assume the form $c2^j$, with $1 \leq c \leq 2^{k+1} - 1$; that is, the nonzero digits in the error number are contained in at most $k + 1$ adjacent positions. In modulo N addition and subtraction, every $|E| = 2^i$ with weight 1 has an associated $|E| = N - 2^i$, usually with weights 2 or 3. The origins of error values with weights greater than 1 are discussed next.

Arithmetic Shifts (A2, A3)

These are subject to basic faults that affect the values of the end digits. In the k-digit right shift (A3) for both complement systems, the left-end digit x_{n-1} is replicated k times. A fault in x_{n-1} or

Table B–1. Magnitudes due to a basic fault in a parallel binary processor.

Algorithm	Number System	$N_1 = 2^n - 1$ (one's complement) Error Magnitude $|E|$	Weight W	$N_2 = 2^n$ (two's complement) Error Magnitude $|E|$	Weight W
A1	Transfer (applies also to A2–A7 below)	2^i	1	2^i	1
A2	Left shift, k digits	$2^k - 1$	2	$2^k - 1$	2
A3	Right shift, k digits	$2^{n-1-k}(2^{k+1} - 1)$	2	$2^{n-1-k}(2^{k+1} - 1)$	2
A4	Range extension, k digits	$2^{n-1}(2^{k+1} - 1)$ $2^n(2^k - 1)$	2 2	$2^{n-1}(2^{k+1} - 1)$ $2^n(2^k - 1)$	2 2
A5	Range contraction, k digits ($1 \leq c \leq 2^k - 1$)	$c2^{n-k}$ $2^{n-1-k}(2^{k+1} - 1)$	$1 \leq w \leq \lfloor k/2 + 1 \rfloor$ 2	$c2^{n-k}$ $2^{n-1-k}(2^{k+1} - 1)$	$1 \leq w/2 \leq \lfloor k/2 + 1 \rfloor$ 2
A6	Modulo N addition or modulo N subtraction	$2^n - 1 - 2^i$	2, ($i = 0$, $n - 1$) 3, ($1 \leq i \leq n - 2$)	$2^n - 2^i$	1, ($i = n - 1$) 2, ($0 \leq i \leq n - 2$)
A7	Additive inverse (complementation)	2^i	1	2^i Also see (A6)	1
A8	Roundoff, k digits Also see (A6) for case (a)	2^k	1	2^k	1

the setting circuit affects $k + 1$ left-end digits of the results, giving

$$|E| = \sum_{n-1-k}^{n-1} 2^i.$$

In the k-digit left shift (A2), k new digits are filled in at the right end. They are equal to x_{n-1} for $N_1 = 2^n - 1$, and they are zero for $N_2 = 2^n$. In both cases, a fault will generate

$$|E| = \sum_{0}^{k-1} 2^i.$$

Range Extension and Contraction

In the k-digit range extension (A4), k identical digits equal to x_{n-1} are attached at the left end. An incorrect value of x_{n-1} will give

$$|E| = \sum_{n-1}^{n-1+k} 2^i.$$

A fault in the sensing circuit will give

$$|E| = \sum_{n}^{n-1+k} 2^i.$$

The value $|E| = 2^i (n \le i \le n + k - 1)$ occurs when one of the new digits is altered by a fault. The k-digit range contraction (A5) is the inverse operation, in which k identical digits $(x_{n-1}, \ldots, x_{n-k})$ are removed at the left end when they are equal to the leftmost remaining digit x_{n-k-1}. An incorrect removal gives $|E| = c2^{n-k}$, with $1 \le c \le 2^k - 1$. An incorrect value of x_{n-k-1} (e.g., 1 instead of 0) causes the removal of k identical digits (e.g., all 1s), giving

$$|E| = \sum_{n-k-1}^{n-1} 2^i.$$

Modulo N Addition or Subtraction(A6)

This requires the "casting out" of N or of $-N$ from the sum or difference, respectively. A basic fault which locally generates $|E| = 2^i$ may cause an error in the "casting out," either by causing it unnecessarily, or by inhibiting it when it should take place. In both cases $|E| = N - 2^i$ occurs; its weight is 1, 2, or 3, depending on N and i.

The Additive Inverse (A7)

This is the fixed subtraction $N - X$, called "complementation." For $N_1 = 2^n - 1$ it is the digitwise negation of x. For $N_2 = 2^n$, the negation of x is followed by the addition of 1 to the least significant digit, and the addition errors of (A6) may also occur.

Roundoff (A8)

The roundoff of k digits $(i = 0, \ldots, k - 1)$ is implemented by one of three methods: *a*) range test of $x_{k-1}, \ldots, x_0$ followed by the addition of 0 or 1 to x_k; *b*) always setting x_k to 1; and *c*) truncation (without arithmetic). Cases *a* and *b* both may have $|E| = 2^k$; case *a* is also subject to the addition error of (A6).

Repeated-Use Faults in Binary Processors

Two classes of algorithms are subject to repeated-use faults: algorithms (A1)–(A8) of Table B-1 in a byte-serial arithmetic processor, and multiplication and division in a parallel processor.

In a byte-serial processor, the kb digits long operands enter the processor in a sequence of k bytes, and the digit circuits are used k times. The length of each byte is $b > 1$ digits. The value of k is variable in some processors. A permanent local fault will affect the same relative position $h(0 \le h \le b - 1)$ within each byte. The fault may be ineffective during some of the k uses.

Of the algorithms in Table B-1, byte-serial processing directly affects (A1)–(A3), (A6), and (A7). The error magnitudes 2^i and $N - 2^i$ are replaced by the sets of possible error magnitudes $\{|E_c|\}$ and $\{N - |E_c|\}$, with

$$E_c = \sum_{j=0}^{k-1} d_j 2^{bj+h}$$

where $d_j = 0$ if the fault is ineffective for the jth byte, $d_j = 1$ for an effective S1, and $d_j = -1$ for an effective S0. There are $2^k - 1$ nonzero magnitudes $|E_c|$ for a determinate (S0 or S1) local fault, and $(3^k - 1)/2$ nonzero magnitudes $|E_c|$ for an indeterminate (SX) local fault. Which one of the $2^k - 1$ or $3^k - 1$ nonzero sets of the coefficients d_j occurs is determined by the digit values of the operand or operands. An equal frequency of occurrence is assumed here. The arithmetic weights W are in the following ranges: 1) for $|E_c|$: $1 \le W \le k$; 2) for $2^n - |E_c|$: $2 \le W \le k + 1$; and 3) for $(2^n - 1) - |E_c|$: $2 \le W \le k + 2$. The end-condition errors of the shifts (A2) and (A3), the range algorithms (A4) and (A5), and the roundoff (A8) do not differ from the parallel case ($k = 1, b = n - 1$) and the results of Table B-1 apply.

Parallel multiplication and division may be intolerably slowed down by the checking of individual additions and shifts, therefore, the repeated-use error magnitudes are of interest. It is assumed that the partial products or partial remainders are not checked, but returned to the accumulator as operands for the next step. The effect of a local fault in the digit circuits is cumulative, and different positions of the results are affected by successive steps because of the shifting. The set of expected error magnitudes is determined by the details of the algorithm.

Most readily susceptible to analysis are algorithms that employ fixed shifts of b bits. In this case the error numbers caused by a local fault in the digit circuits are the same as those developed during an addition or shift in a byte-serial processor with byte length b. End-condition setting in shifts, multiplier digit recoding, and quotient digit selection may contribute additional error values. More error values are also contributed by the multiple-forming circuits which shift the multiplicand (or divisor) left to obtain the multiples 2, 4, 8, etc. For example, a fault in the multiplicand register with provisions to add $c_j = 0, \pm 1, \pm 2$ times the operand to the partial product during the jth step affects one of two adjacent positions $(i, i + 1)$ of the sum. The sets of possible error magnitudes are $\{|E|\}$ and $\{N - |E|\}$, with

$$E = \sum_{j=0}^{k-1} c_j d_j 2^{bj}$$

where b is the length of one right shift. The set of error magnitudes for any given variation of an algorithm and logic structure of the processor is obtained as the cumulative effect (sum) of appropriately shifted contributions of the error magnitudes in Table B-1.

LOW-COST RADIX-2 ARITHMETIC CODES

Implementation of Arithmetic Error Codes

Arithmetic error codes are classified into separate and nonseparate codes [Garner, 1966]. Both classes possess many common properties, but differ significantly in their implementation. The nonseparate code considered is the AN code [Brown, 1960; Peterson, 1961], which is formed when an uncoded operand x is multiplied by the *check modulus* A to give the coded operand Ax. The separate codes are the *residue code* [Peterson, 1958], and the *inverse residue* code [Avižienis, 1967a, 1969], which is a previously unexplored variant of the residue code. The inverse residue code has significant advantages in fault detection of repeated-use faults. The modulo A inverse residue encoding for a number x attaches a check symbol x'' to form the pair (x, x''). The value of x'' is X'':

$$X'' = A - (A|X) = A - X'$$

where $A|X$ designates the modulo A residue of X.

$A|X$ is the value X' of the check symbol x' employed in modulo A residue encoding (x, x'). The inverse residue code is a separate code, since it has no arithmetic interaction between x and x'' [Garner, 1966], and should not be confused with the nonseparate systematic subcodes of AN codes [Henderson, 1961; Garner, 1966].

The set of undetectable error magnitudes $|E_m|$ (called *misses* in the subsequent discussion) for both AN and residue codes consists of all multiples of the check modulus A:

$$|E_m| = KA, \qquad K = 1, 2, \ldots, \lfloor (r^n - 1)/A \rfloor$$

for n-digit radix-r operands. The effectiveness and the cost of arithmetic checking depends very strongly on the choice of the check modulus A. The *checking algorithm* which establishes whether a detectable (or correctable) error exists in the result z for both classes of codes computes the modulo A residue $A|Z$, where Z is the unsigned integer value of z. The increase in word length is the same for both classes of codes. For radix-2 it is $\lceil \log_2 A \rceil$ bits.

The most significant differences of implementation are caused by the property of separateness. For residue codes, the operands x, y and their check symbols x', y' enter separate (*main* and *check*) processors which produce the main result z (value Z) and the check result z' (value Z'). The checking algorithm computes $A|Z$ and compares it to Z'. If the values are equal, either the correct result has been obtained, or a miss has occurred. Disagreement indicates a fault in either the main or the check processor; the uncertainty precludes fault location and error correction without supplementary procedures. An exception in the check procedure occurs for division $X \div Y$ which produces the quotient Q and the remainder P. The checking algorithm computes both $A|Q$ and $A|P$. The check processor computes the value $(A|Q) \cdot Y' + (A|P)$ which is compared to X' for equality [Garner, 1958]. The *inverse residue code* differs from the residue code in only one respect: the check result

has the value $Z'' = A - (A|Z)$ when an error has not occurred. The checking algorithm computes $A|Z$ and forms the check sum $F = A|[(A|Z) + Z'']$, where $F = 0$ indicates that either the result is correct, or a miss has occurred.

For the nonseparate AN code the checking algorithm computes $A|Z$, where Z is the value of a result. $A|Z = 0$ indicates either a correct result or a miss. A nonzero $A|Z$ indicates a fault: for certain choices of A the value $A|Z$ indicates the error value E for error correction [Brown, 1960; Peterson, 1961; Garner, 1966]. The algorithms of the processor are designed to compute with product-coded numbers [Avižienis, 1966b]. All intermediate steps of the algorithms must preserve product coding in order to retain the error-checking properties in the result. The hardware cost of AN codes is in the greater complexity of the main processor, while for residue codes it is in the separate check processor.

The Low-Cost Checking Algorithm

A practical checking method must satisfy both cost and effectiveness constraints. For radix-2 numbers, every odd integer $A > 1$ will detect weight 1 error magnitudes. The search for values of A which have a low-cost checking algorithm identified the class of *low-cost* arithmetic codes [Avižienis, 1964] which employ check moduli of the form

$$A = 2^a - 1, \qquad \text{with integer } a > 1.$$

The parameter a is called the *group length* of the code. Since division is a complex algorithm, the checking algorithms for most odd $A > 1$ are relatively costly and slow. The check modulus $2^a - 1$ is an exception because the congruence

$$K_i r^i \equiv K_i \text{ modulo } (r - 1), \qquad r = 2^a$$

allows the use of modulo $2^a - 1$ summation of the k groups (a-bit segments of value K_i, with $0 \leq K_i \leq 2^a - 1$) that compose the ka-bit number Z to compute the *check sum* $(2^a - 1)|Z$. Division by A is replaced by an "end-around carry" addition algorithm, which "casts out $2^a - 1$'s" in a byte-serial or parallel implementation.

It is also important to note that the low-cost check moduli $2^a - 1$ are exceptionally compatible with binary arithmetic. A complete set of algorithms has been devised for AN-coded operands [Avižienis, 1964, 1967a], and an experimental byte-serial processor with four-bit bytes, $ka = 32$, $a = 4$, and $A = 15$ has been constructed for the STAR computer [Avižienis, 1966b, 1968]. While AN codes are limited to one's complement $(N = 2^n - 1)$ algorithms, the two's complement $(N = 2^n)$ algorithms can be carried out as well with the separate residue and inverse residue codes, which also display implementation advantages for multiple-precision algorithms. A set of algorithms for a two's complement inverse residue code processor (including multiple precision) has been developed to replace the AN code processor of the STAR computer [Avižienis et al., 1971].

Fault Effectiveness: One-Use Faults

It was already noted that the check moduli $2^a - 1$, with $a > 1$, will detect all weight 1 error magnitudes 2^j, with $0 \le j \le ka - 1$. Furthermore, all error values which can be confined within $a - 1$ adjacent bits of the error number (bursts of length $a - 1$ or less) will be detected, since their error magnitudes are $g2^j$, with g in the range $1 \le g \le 2^{a-1} - 1$. Only one error magnitude (out of $2^a - 1$ possibilities) confined within a adjacent bits is undetectable (that described by a adjacent 1's). This is important with respect to algorithms (A1)–(A5) of Table B-1, which contains error magnitudes of the forms $(2^k - 1)2^j$ and $(2^{k+1} - 1)2^j$ The choice of $a \ge k + 2$ will guarantee complete fault detection for these algorithms.

For operands of length $n = ka$ bits, the check

modulus $2^a - 1$ will detect the one's complements $(2^{ka} - 1) - |E|$ of all detectable error magnitudes $|E|$. Some weight 2 error magnitudes will not be detected: the undetectable error numbers are caused by one S1 and one S0 basic fault with a certain separation. The fraction f_2 of undetected weight 2 error magnitudes for $a > 2$ is

$$f_2 = (k - 1)a/[2a(ka - 3) + 6/k].$$

For $a > 2$, $f_2 < 1/2a$ holds [Avižienis, 1964]. For example, given $ka = 24$, $a = 3$ yields $f_2 = 0.166$, $a = 4$ yields $f_2 = 0.118$, and $a = 6$ yields $f_2 = 0.071$. The case of $a = 2$ is an unfavorable exception, yielding $f_2 \cong 0.5$ for any value of k. The analysis may be continued for higher weights, due to several independent basic faults; however, errors due to repeated use of a single faulty circuit are of more immediate interest.

Fault Effectiveness: Determinate Repeated-Use Faults

For the case of a determinate local repeated-use fault discussed earlier in the section on Repeated-Use Faults in Binary Processes above, which considers kb bits long operands processed in k bytes of b bits each, an analytic solution indicates very effective fault detection for the choice $b = a$ [Avižienis, 1965]. All possible $2^k - 1$ error magnitudes (and their one's complements) are detected by the check modulus $2^a - 1$ for $k < 2^a - 1$. Only one miss (undetectable error) occurs when $k = 2^a - 1$; the count of misses ϵ for $k \ge 2^a - 1$ is given by the expression

$$\epsilon = \sum_{j=1}^{\lfloor k/(2^a-1)\rfloor} k!/[j(2^a - 1)]! \, [k - j(2^a - 1)]! \, .$$

For example, the check modulus $\alpha = 15$ with byte length $b = 4$ allows no misses for words up to $n = 56$ bits, and $\alpha = 31$ with $b = 5$ up to $n = 150$ bits. The expressions for the miss count ϵ

are derived by considering all possible ways in which result value $2^a - 1$ consisting of all ones can be generated by modulo $2^a - 1$ summation of k contributions of either 0 or 2^h, with $0 \leq h \leq a - 1$.

For any choice of the pair (a, b) and the word length $n = kb = ca$, it has been shown that the first miss occurs when the word length reaches the value

$$n' = c'a(2^{a/k'} - 1)$$

where $c'a = k'b$ is the least common multiple of a and b [Aviẑienis, 1965]. Consequently, the maximum value of n' results when $k' = 1$, giving $b = c'a$, and

$$n'_{max} = c'a(2^a - 1) = b(2^a - 1).$$

The choice of $b = 2a$ will double the "safe length"; for example, $\alpha = 15$ and $b = 8$ allows no misses for words up to 112 bits, and $\alpha = 7$ and $b = 6$ up to 36 bits. The minimum value of n' is obtained when a and b are relatively prime: in this case we have $n'_{min} = ab$.

The effectiveness of any choice of the pair (a, b) can be expressed in terms of the percentage of misses among all possible $2^k - 1$ error magnitudes which can be caused by a local determinate fault. Given a miss count ϵ, the *miss percentage* is obtained as $100\epsilon/(2^k - 1)$, where $n = kb$ is the word length of the operands. The miss percentages for various word lengths are obtained using a computer program which tabulated all misses for word lengths up to $k = 18$ bytes, check lengths $2 \leq a \leq 12$, and byte lengths $2 \leq b \leq 10$ and $b = 12$ [Aviẑienis, 1965]. The maximum word length of 18 bytes results in a total of $2^{18} - 1 = 262,143$ possible nonzero error magnitudes. In selected cases the maximum word length was extended to 20 bytes, i.e., $2^{20} - 1 = 1,048,575$ possible nonzero error magnitudes. The miss percentages (for the same values of b) were also tabulated for 11 moduli A which detect all weight 2 and 5 check moduli which detect all weight 2 and 3 error magnitudes

[Peterson, 1961, pp. 236-44]. The word lengths used were n, with the requirement that $2^n - 1$ should be divisible by A.

The results of the tabulation (available in Aviẑienis [1965]) show that for a and b relatively prime, the percentage of misses rapidly becomes $100/(2^a - 1)$ after the first miss which occurs at word length $n' = ab$ (the minimal case). For other pairs (a, b), the miss percentages beyond the word length n' tend to overshoot $100/(2^a - 1)$ and then go below $100/(2^a - 1)$ with increasing word length. The weight 2 and weight 2, 3 detecting check moduli A display miss percentages which are comparable to those of relatively prime (a, b).

Fault Effectiveness: Indeterminate Repeated-Use Faults

A local indeterminate fault (used m times) will contribute to the error magnitude in one of 3^m possible ways. During each use the contribution will be 0, 2^i, or -2^i with various values of i. For the same repeated-use model as used in the preceding section, the choice $b = a$, and the word length ka, the number of misses ϵ' due to the indeterminate fault (excluding the determinate subset) is given by the expression

$$\epsilon' = \sum_{j=1}^{\lfloor k/2 \rfloor} k!/2[(k - 2j)!](j!)^2.$$

The total count of possible nonzero error magnitudes is $(3^k - 1)/2$. The miss percentage $100\epsilon'/2(3^k - 1)$ is highest for $k = 2$ and gradually decreases with increasing k. For values $k \geq 2^a - 1$ the determinate subset contributes the miss count ϵ, and the total number of misses is $\epsilon + \epsilon'$. We also note that the value of ϵ' is independent of a. Table B-2 lists the miss percentages (excluding the determinate subset) for the byte counts $2 \leq k \leq 12$.

Given any pair (a, b), the first miss due to an indeterminate fault (excluding the determinate

Table B–2. Miss percentages for byte counts $2 \leqslant k \leqslant 12$.

k	$(3^k - 1)/2$	ϵ'	Miss %
2	4	1	25.00
3	13	3	23.08
4	40	9	22.50
5	121	25	20.66
6	364	70	19.23
7	1093	196	17.93
8	3280	553	16.86
9	9841	1569	15.94
10	29524	4476	15.16
11	88573	12826	14.48
12	265720	36894	13.88

subset) occurs when the word length exceeds the least common multiple of a and b, that is, the first miss occurs for the word length n'', where

$$n'' > c'a$$

where $c'a = k'b$ is the least common multiple. Consequently, the maximum safe length n is attained for a and b relatively prime, with $n''_{max} > ab$. In this case the first miss is due to the determinate subset and occurs for $n'' = ab$. For other choices of the pair (a, b) we observe

$$n''_{max} < n'_{max}.$$

The total miss percentages $100(\epsilon' + \epsilon)/2(3^k - 1)$ are of interest in the cases $b \neq a$ as well. An exhaustive tabulation by means of a computer program was performed for word lengths up to $k = 12$ bytes; that is, $(3^{12} - 1)/2 = 265,720$ nonzero error magnitudes were considered. The check lengths were again $2 \leq a \leq 12$, and the byte lengths were $2 \leq b \leq 10$ and $b = 12$. It was observed that for relatively prime pairs (a, b) the miss percentages were close to $100/(2^a - 1)$, becoming greater for pairs with common divisors, and reaching the

maximal values of Table B-2 for $b = a$ and $b = c'a$. Complete results of the tabulation are presented in [Avižienis 1965].

It is noted that the most favorable choices of pairs (a, b) in the determinate faults are the least desirable choices for indeterminate faults, and vice versa. The choice of the most suitable values therefore depends on the relative frequencies of these two types of faults.

Repeated-Use Faults in Residue Codes

The results of the preceding sections on repeated-use faults apply directly to the fault effectiveness of the low-cost AN codes $(2^a - 1)X$. The low-cost residue codes in the byte-serial processor suffer a serious disadvantage because of a new variety of an undetectable repeated-use determinate fault. The miss occurs when the check symbol x' of value $(2^a - 1)|X$ uses the same digit circuits as the operand x. In this case, the fault affects the relative position $h(0 \leq h \leq b - 1)$ in x' as well as in every byte of x, and a compensating error may occur. In the preferred choice $b = a$, the miss will occur whenever the position h in x' and *exactly one* position in x are altered by an S0 or S1 fault. For example, consider the modulo 15 residue encoding

$$x = 0010, 0011, 0101, \qquad x' = 1010.$$

An S1 fault sets the rightmost ($h = 0$) bit to 1 in every byte of x and in x' (boldface indicates changed bits) to give $x*$, $x'*$:

$$x* = 001\mathbf{1}, 0011, 0101, \qquad x'* = 101\mathbf{1}.$$

The checking algorithm yields $15|X* = 1011$ which is equal to $X'*$, and a "compensating miss" occurs which is independent of the length of x as long as only one byte in x is affected.

The compensating miss is eliminated by the use of the *inverse* residue code in which $X'' = (2^a - 1) - X'$ is substituted for X'. Consider the preceding example with the inverse residue $X'' = 1111 - 1010 = 0101$ replacing X'. The same S1 fault causes

$$x* = 00\mathbf{1}1, 0011, 0101, \qquad x''* = 0101.$$

The check yields $15|X* = 1011$: adding $X''*$ modulo 15 gives the result 0001 which indicates an error, since it is not equal to 1111.

The fault remains detectable even when one change each occurs in x and x'. Consider the previous example with a new operand y and its inverse residue y'':

$$y = 1000, 1101, 0101, \qquad y'' = 0100.$$

The check gives $15|Y = 1011$, and $15|Y + Y'' = 1111$, i.e., no error. The previous S1 fault causes

$$y* = 100\mathbf{1}, 1101, 0101, \qquad y''* = 0101.$$

The check gives $15|Y* = 1100$ and $15|Y* + Y''* = 0010$, indicating an error.

The compensating miss does not occur because the change $0 \rightarrow 1$ in y'' corresponds to the change $1 \rightarrow 0$ in y'. The first miss will occur when $y*$ consists of 14 bytes, each containing a zero in the rightmost position $n = 0$, and y'' also has a zero in $h = 0$. All results of the determinate fault effectiveness study are directly applicable to the low-cost inverse residue codes. This result led to the choice of modulo 15 inverse residue codes for both data words and address parts of instructions in the fault-tolerant STAR computer [Avižienis et al., 1971].

MULTIPLE ARITHMETIC ERROR CODES

Multiple Low-Cost Codes

The preceding section treated *single* codes which use only one check modulus. A study of fault-locating properties of the low-cost codes led to the observation that the use of *multiple* codes with two or more check moduli could provide complete fault location, corresponding to error correction [Avižienis, 1965, 1967a]. Continued study of multiple encodings has led to the development of several new varieties of arithmetic error codes, first discussed in [Avižienis 1969].*

First it is shown that a single low-cost check modulus $2^a - 1$ has partial error-location properties in both AN and residues codes. Consider the error value pairs $(0 \le i \le ka - 1)$:

$$\{2^i; -(2^{ka} - 1) + 2^i\} \qquad \text{and}$$
$$\{-2^i; (2^{ka} - 1) - 2^i\}$$

that may be caused by a basic fault during a transfer or one's complement additive inverse, shift, or addition (the operand is ka bits long). Writing the value of 2^i as a radix-2^a number, we have

$$2^i = 2^h 2^{ja}, \qquad h = i - ja.$$

The index $h = i - ja$ is called the *intra-group index* and j is called the *group index*. Their ranges are

$$0 \le h \le a - 1 \qquad \text{and} \qquad 0 \le j \le k - 1.$$

It is evident that

$$2^a | 2^h 2^{ja} = 2^a | [-(2^{ka} - 1) + 2^h 2^{ja}] = 2^h$$
$$2^a | (-2^h 2^{ja}) = 2^a | [(2^{ka} - 1) - 2^h 2^{ja}]$$
$$= (2^a - 1) - 2^h.$$

The sign and the intra-group index h are uniquely identified for the error values $\pm 2^i$, even if the value of the end-around carry is incorrect due to the addition of $\pm 2^i$. The a-bit residue 2^h has a single 1 digit, and $(2^a - 1) - 2^h$ has a single 0 digit. For example, (with $h = 3$, $a = 4$) the

---

* Multiple arithmetic encodings have been recently described in Rao [1970] and Rao and Garcia [1971]. It must be noted that the use of multiple check moduli for single-error correction was first described in Avižienis [1965, pp. 12-13] and [1967a, pp. 36-37], and details were presented in Avižienis [1969], considerably prior to Rao [1970] and Rao and Garcia [1971]. Papers by Avižienis [1965, 1967a] and additional communication on the topic were supplied to Garcia at a UCLA short course in April 1968.

residue is 1000 for the error 2^{3+4j}, and 0111 for -2^{3+4j}.

In the case of AN low-cost codes, the modulo $2^a - 1$ checking algorithm directly yields the check sum residues described above. In the case of residue low-cost codes, the main result X and the check result X' are computed. The checking algorithm must compute the a-bit check sum F:

$$F = (2^a - 1)|[(2^a - 1)|X + (2^a - 1) - X'].$$

A correct result (X, X') will yield the all ones form of $F = 0$. It is readily shown that an erroneous main result $X \pm 2^i$ yields $F = (2^a - 1)|(\pm 2^h)$, identical to the check sums of the AN code. An erroneous check result $(2^a - 1)$ $|(X' \pm 2^h)$ yields $F = (2^a - 1)|(\mp 2^h)$, and the sign information becomes ambiguous: 1000 indicates the error $+2^{3+4j}$ in the main result, or the error -2^3 in the check result. The ambiguity is eliminated by the inverse residue codes which use $X'' = (2^a - 1) - X'$ as the check result. The check sum for the inverse residue code is

$$G = (2^a - 1)|[(2^a - 1)|X + X''].$$

When X'' is correct, $G = 0$ is represented by the all ones form. An error in the main result X gives the same check sum as for the residue code. An erroneous check result has the value $(2^a - 1)$ $|(X'' \pm 2^h)$, which replaces X'' and yields the check sum $G = (2^a - 1)|(\pm 2^h)$. Both the sign and the intra-group index h are known. The group index j remains unknown; it is also not known whether the check result or the main result is in error.

The preceding result has two applications. First, it has been used to derive the miss percentage equations for repeated-use faults in the section above on Low-Cost Radix-2 Arithmetic Codes. Second, it has led to the observation that the use of more than one low-cost check modulus will permit the unique identification of the bit index i of the error values $\pm 2^i$, and subsequent error correction, while using only the low-cost check moduli $2^{a_1} - 1$, $2^{a_2} - 1$, etc. [Avižienis, 1965, 1967a].

The check modulus $A^i = 2^{a_i} - 1$ has the group length of a_i bits. Given the pair (a_1, a_2) with GCD $(a_1, a_2) = 1$, there will be $a_1 a_2$ distinct pairs of intra-group indices

$$\{h_1, h_2\}, \qquad 0 \le h_1 \le a_1 - 1,$$
$$0 \le h_2 \le a_2 - 1.$$

For example, $a_1 = 3$ and $a_2 = 4$ yield twelve pairs of indices:

$$h_1 = |2, 1, 0|2, 1, 0|2, 1, 0|2, 1, 0|$$
$$h_2 = |3, 2, 1, 0|3, 2, 1, 0|3, 2, 1, 0|.$$

The same observation applies to sets of three or more group lengths $\{a_1, a_2, \ldots, a_m\}$ which are pairwise prime. The length of the binary number for which distinct sets of intra-group indices $\{h_1, h_2, \ldots, h_m\}$ exist is p bits, while the encoding requires s bits, with

$$p = \prod_{i=1}^{m} a_i \qquad \text{and} \qquad s = \sum_{i=1}^{m} a_i.$$

For example, the choice of $a_1 = 3$, $a_2 = 4$, $a_3 = 5$ will give $p = 3 \cdot 4 \cdot 5 = 60$ distinct sets of three intra-group indices with $s = 3 + 4 + 5 = 12$ bits used for encoding [Avižienis, 1965, 1967a].

The effect of the m-tuple low-cost code with m pairwise prime group lengths $\{a_1, a_2, \ldots, a_m\}$ is the same as the effect of a code with a single check modulus $2^p - 1$ with respect to single-error correction and double-error detection for error values $\pm 2^i$ and $\mp (2^p - 1 - 2^i)$ over $0 \le i \le p - 1$. Burst-error detection is 100 percent effective for all bursts up to and including $s - 1$ adjacent positions. Most important, the m separate low-cost checking algorithms are retained by an m-tuple low-cost code. One low-cost check is sufficient to detect the error values for which correction is possible; the other checks need to be performed only when an error is indicated and may share the same hardware.

Both AN and residue codes are suitable for multiple low-cost encoding. In the case of ordinary and inverse residue codes, the use of more than one check modulus resolves whether the error is in the main or in the check result: if only one check result indicates an error, it is incorrect; if all check results indicate an error, then it is traced to the bit i in the main result by the set of intra-group indices. The sign ambiguity of single residue codes is eliminated, and correction takes place either in the main result, or in the incorrect residue. An important difference between multiple low-cost residue and AN codes is the length of the uncoded information word. The nonseparate AN codes allow $p - s$ information bits, while the separate residue codes allow p information bits, with the s check bits added on as separate check symbols. Residue codes with the same number of check bits provide the same performance for a longer information word. The separateness of residue codes leads to a simpler design of the main processor which deals with uncoded operands, rather than with multiples of the check moduli which are used in the AN code processor.

The use of two or more low-cost check moduli permits multiple "mixed" low-cost encodings. A *mixed low-cost code* is a single or multiple low-cost AN code (p bits long) with a low-cost residue encoding (single or multiple) of the AN-coded words. Given the moduli $\{A_1, \ldots, A_m\}$, the mixed codes possess the same error-location properties as the corresponding *uniform* (AN or residue) multiple codes. For an example, consider the moduli $\{7, 15, 31\}$, with $a_1 = 3$, $a_2 = 4$, $a_3 = 5$. The uniform residue code has $p = 3 \cdot 4 \cdot 5 = 60$ information bits and $s = 3 + 4 + 5 = 12$ check bits. The uniform AN code has $p - s = 48$ information bits encoded with $A = 7 \cdot 15 \cdot 31 = 3255$; however, the checking algorithms remain separate modulo 7, 15, 31 low-cost checks. Six versions of the mixed code are available:

three with double-residue encoding: (7, 15), (7, 31), (15, 31); and three with single-residue encoding: (7), (15), (31). In all six cases the AN-coded word must remain $p = 60$ bits long; e.g., the AN code with $A_3 = 31$ has 55 information bits and 5 check bits, plus the 7 check bits of the double residue code with $A_1 = 7$, $A_2 = 15$. The error location algorithm uses the intra-group indices as in the uniform codes; an error in the main result is identified by the AN code check.

"Hybrid-Cost" Forms of Multiple Codes

In this section it is shown that the partial error-location property of the low-cost codes provides a low-cost extension of the range of other (non-low-cost) error-correcting codes. *Hybrid-cost* arithmetic error codes are multiple codes with a set of moduli $\{A_1, A_2, \ldots, A_m\}$ which includes one or more low-cost check moduli A_i, as well as one or more non-low-cost check moduli A'_j with the properties of error correction [Brown, 1960; Peterson, 1961, pp. 236-44; Henderson, 1961; Garner, 1966].

A hybrid-cost code (for example, the double code with moduli A, A'), offers two advantages over one error-correcting check modulus A'. First, the low-cost code (modulo $2^a - 1$) checking algorithm alone is sufficient to detect errors which are corrected by A'. Second, suitable choices of the pairs (A, A') permit the use of the intra-group index h of the low-cost code ($h = 0, 1, \ldots, a - 1$) to extend the range covered by A'. Given a single-error-correcting check modulus A' with the period of g bits, and the low-cost check modulus $A = 2^a - 1$ such that GCD $(g, a) = 1$, it is evident that the intra-group index h extends the range of the hybrid-cost code to $p' = g \cdot a$ bits. For example, $A' = 23$ gives distinct values of the residue $23|(\pm 2^i)$ for $0 \le i \le 10, 11 < i < 21$, etc., identifying uniquely the index i and the sign of $\pm 2^i$ for an 11-bit operand [Brown, 1960]. Together with $A = 2^a$

− 1, the length for unique identification of the index and sign is $11a$ bits as long as GCD $(11, a)$ = 1 [Avižienis, 1969]. The use of $f \leq 2$ low-cost check moduli $(A_1, \ldots, A_f)$ with some A' will give the combined effect of the f-tuple low-cost code with the error-correcting properties of A', as long as the check moduli have pairwise GCD = 1.

Three distinct classes of f-tuple hybrid-cost codes (with $f \geq 2$) can be identified: 1) uniform AN codes; 2) uniform residue codes; and 3) mixed (AN + residue) codes. The codes are similar to low-cost multiple codes described previously with the exception that one or more check moduli A'_j are non-low-cost. Differences between the three classes of codes appear in their implementation. The hybrid-cost AN codes $AA'X$ have the disadvantage of a costlier and slower implementation of arithmetic algorithms, since A' is not a low-cost check modulus. The hybrid-cost residue codes avoid these difficulties because they are separate. The use of more than one check modulus resolves the question whether the error is in the main or in the check result. In a double hybrid-cost residue code with the check moduli (A, A') the low-cost modulo A check is carried out each time for error detection. An error indication initiates the modulo A' check. If the latter does not indicate an error, then the modulo A check result is incorrect, and correction of the check result follows. If the modulo A' check result also indicates an error, then the main result is corrected, using both check results.

The mixed hybrid-cost codes have two major variants: 1) low-cost AN code with modulo A' residue encoding; 2) error-correcting $A'X$ code with modulo-A low-cost residue encoding. The first variant gives simple algorithms in the main processor, but must resolve the problem (existing also for hybrid-cost residue codes) of checking the error-correcting modulo A' residue if the modulo A' check is used only after detection using low-cost A. The second variant (preferably with inverse residue code) gives simple residue checking for error detection, but requires complex algorithms in the main processor which operates on multiples of the non-low-cost check modulus A'. Other minor variants of mixed hybrid-cost codes are created when two or more check moduli are used for the AN part and/or the residue part. Each part, in turn, can be low cost or hybrid cost.

In conclusion it is noted that the use of multiple low-cost and hybrid-cost arithmetic encodings offers a variety of implementations. Fault location and error correction by means of multiple encodings employs the low-cost codes alone as well as to extend the range covered by error-correcting codes. It is also important to observe that multiple encodings permit the use of residue codes for error correction, since they distinguish whether the error is in the main result or in one of the check results. This information is not available with one residue and the generally less convenient nonseparate AN codes have to be used in single encodings. Detailed consideration of multiple encodings is presented in Avižienis [1969]. Finally, it should be noted that the concepts of multiple encoding (AN, residue, and mixed) are applicable to multiple non-low-cost check moduli as well.

ACKNOWLEDGMENT

The author wishes to acknowledge stimulating discussions with D. A. Rennels, D. K. Rubin, J. J.. Wedel, and A. D. Weeks of the Jet Propulsion Laboratory, Pasadena, Calif.

REFERENCES

Avižienis [1964, 1965, 1966a, 1966b, 1967a, 1967b, 1968, 1969]; Avižienis et al. [1971]; Brown [1960]; Garner [1958, 1966]; Henderson [1961]; Peterson [1958, 1961]; Rao [1970]; Rao and Garcia [1971].

Recent Developments in the Theory and Practice of Testable Logic Design

R. G. Bennetts   R. V. Scott

Abstract

This paper surveys and summarizes the major contributions to the theory and practice of testable logic design. The first part, dealing with the theoretical procedures, discusses the design of easily testable combinational, sequential, and iterative networks, illustrating major techniques with common running examples. The second part comments on the more practical aspects such as board layout, test point siting, and other facilities for easing the problems associated with testing.

C

INTRODUCTION

Interest has been focussed recently on the problems of designing and implementing logic circuits that are "easily testable" (a term we will define later). This paper is a natural extension to the large amount of research effort that has been devoted to the generation of test sequences for logic circuits [Bennetts and Lewin, 1971] and constitutes an attempt to present some of the major considerations and techniques that have been described in the literature. It has the dual objective of both reviewing the literature and discussing the concepts of some of the design algorithms contained therein. In most cases, detailed descriptions of the algorithms are omitted, but their effect on the design of an actual circuit is shown, hopefully enabling the reader to make some assessment of their value.

The paper divides into two main sections. The first discusses techniques for constraining the logic design itself—the end product being a logic circuit schematic—whereas the second relates to the more practical aspects of implementation: board layout, single-shot facilities, test point siting, etc.

The paper as a whole, therefore, attempts to show what effect "testability" can have on digital circuit engineering, and this reflects the shortcomings of test sequence generation algorithms. These shortcomings, which have been discussed more fully elsewhere [Bennetts, 1974] by one of the authors, are due to such factors as circuit complexity and size, computational limitations, shortcomings of the algorithms and the stuck-at-model upon which they are based, limitations of the testing system, etc. Although considerable research effort is being devoted to overcome these limitations, it has long been recognized that constraints must eventually be placed on the actual design, in order to produce logic circuit designs that are "easily testable." Reddy [1974] has defined an easily testable network as one having the following properties: (1) small test set; (2) contains no logical redundancy; (3) test set can be derived without much extra work, either during the design phase or after the network is defined; (4) structure of the test set is such that it is both easy to generate and interpret the results; (5) faults locatable to the desired degree.

This list is qualitative only, but for the purpose of this paper it will serve as a working definition for "easily testable" circuits. Various other properties may also be desirable and can be added to the list—e.g.: (6) final gate-count should not be excessively high compared with a "normal" implementation; (7) minimum number of additional primary control inputs and observable outputs used to enhance testability.

THEORETICAL DEVELOPMENTS

This section discusses design algorithms for combinational and sequential logic and comments briefly on the design of easily tested iterative arrays.

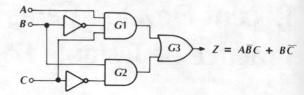

Figure C–1. Simple combinational circuit example.

Combinational Circuits

The various procedures to be introduced will be illustrated where possible by the following simple Boolean function:

$$z = f(ABC) = A\bar{B}C + B\bar{C} \tag{1}$$

A normal AND-OR-INVERT implementation of this function is shown in Figure C-1; a minimal test set to detect any single stuck-at-1 or stuck-at-0 (s-a-1, s-a-0) fault on either the primary inputs, primary input fanout branches, or gate outputs is given by:

$$T = \{A\bar{B}C/\bar{Z}, \bar{A}\,\bar{B}C/\bar{Z}, A\bar{B}C/Z, \bar{A}\,B\bar{C}/Z,$$
$$ABC/\bar{Z}\} \tag{2}$$

(This result is obtained using the Boolean difference approach [Bennets, 1972] and incorporating the concept of pseudo-primary inputs [Bennetts, 1973] to generate specific tests, if they exist, for primary input fanout branches.)

The Reed-Muller Expansion Technique (Reddy)

In the paper by Reddy already mentioned [1974], a design technique is presented for realizing any arbitrary n-variable logic function using AND and EOR (exclusive-OR) gates only, and having the following properties:

1. If the primary input leads are fault-free, then a fault-detection test set of only $(n + 4)$ tests exists.
2. If the primary inputs themselves could also be faulty, then the number of fault-detecting tests is increased by $2n_e$ (defined later). It is also shown

that this can be reduced back to $(n + 4)$ by the addition of one extra AND gate whose output is observable.

The basis of the technique is to determine the *Reed-Muller* expansion [Mukhopadhyay and Schmitz, 1970] of the function and to implement this directly. The Reed-Muller expansion is a special case of the more general *ring-sum expansion* of a logic function—the latter being defined in the following manner:

$$f(x_1 x_2 \cdots x_n) = c_0 \oplus c_1 \dot{x}_1 \oplus c_2 \dot{x}_2 \oplus \cdots$$
$$\oplus c_n \dot{x}_n \oplus c_{n+1} \dot{x}_1 \dot{x}_2 \oplus c_{n+2} \dot{x}_1 \dot{x}_3 \oplus \cdots \quad \textbf{(3)}$$
$$\oplus c_{2^n-1} \dot{x}_1 \dot{x}_2 \cdots \dot{x}_n$$

where $\dot{x}_i$ is either x_i or $\bar{x}_i$ and c_j a binary constant 0 or 1. Note that in the full expression, x_i can either take its true (x_i) or complemented ($\bar{x}_i$) value, but not both. If all x_i's take their true (uncomplemented) value, then this special case is known as the Reed-Muller expansion or, alternatively, complement-free ring sum expansion of the logic function.

The Reed-Muller expansion for a function can be formed in two distinct stages. The first uses the fact that the OR operators in an s-o-p expression can be directly replaced by exclusive -OR operators if all the terms are originally disjoint—i.e., mutually exclusive. (Bennetts [1975], describes a simple test and modification procedure for converting any s-o-p to an equivalent sum of mutually-exclusive products.) Full conversion to a complement-free Reed-Muller form makes use of the identity

$$\bar{x}_i \equiv x_i \oplus 1$$

to replace all complemented literals present in any term. Two other identities are used:

$$x_i(x_j \oplus x_k) \equiv x_i x_j \oplus x_i x_k$$

and

$$0 \oplus f(X) \equiv f(X).$$

Applying these to $f(ABC)$ in (1) has the following result:

$$f(ABC) = A\bar{B}C + B\bar{C} \quad \text{(already disjoint)}$$
$$= A\bar{B}C \oplus B\bar{C}$$
$$= AC(B \oplus 1) \oplus B(C \oplus 1) \quad \textbf{(4)}$$
$$= ABC \oplus AC \oplus BC \oplus B$$
$$= 0 \oplus B \oplus AC \oplus BC \oplus ABC$$

A direct implementation of (4) is shown in Figure C-2; the dotted output will be explained later.

Kautz [1971] has shown that to detect a single faulty EOR gate in such an array, it is sufficient to supply a set of test inputs which will apply all possible input combinations to each cell. For the type of array shown in Figure C-2, such a test set T_1 is given by:

$$T_1 = \begin{array}{cccc} D & A & B & C \\ 0 & 0 & 0 & 0 \\ 0 & 1 & 1 & 1 \\ 1 & 0 & 0 & 0 \\ 1 & 1 & 1 & 1 \end{array} \quad \text{four input vectors} \quad \textbf{(5)}$$

The form of the T_1 test set is always the same independent of the number of input variables n, and constitutes four tests only. In addition to the EOR gate fault-cover, Reddy demonstrates that this test set will also detect (1) any s-a-0 fault on an AND gate input or output (tests 0111, 1111) and (2) any s-a-1 fault on the output of any AND gate (tests 0000, 1000).

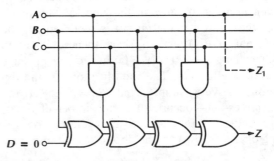

Figure C-2. Reed-Muller implementation for $f(ABC)$.

It remains therefore to provide a test set T_2 to detect s-a-1 faults on the AND gate inputs. This is achieved by observing that to test an AND gate input s-a-1, it is necessary to set that input to 0 with all other inputs to 1. The fault-free output is then 0 changing to 1 if the s-a-1 fault exists, and this fault-effect is then further propagated through the EOR gates to the primary output. A systematic way of checking for all AND gate inputs s-a-1, therefore, is to successively set one primary input to 0 and all others to 1. For example, T_2 is given by:

$$T_2 = \begin{array}{cccc} D & A & B & C \\ x & 0 & 1 & 1 \\ x & 1 & 0 & 1 \\ x & 1 & 1 & 0 \end{array} \quad n \text{ input vectors} \tag{6}$$

$$(x \text{ is ``don't care''})$$

Thus, for an n-variable function, T_2 will contain n tests and the full test set $T(= T_1 + T_2)$ will contain $(n + 4)$ tests.

This result is based on the primary inputs themselves being fault-free; i.e., single s-a-1, s-a-0 faults are assumed to occur only on the fanout branches to the AND gates. If this restriction is lifted, the paper shows that the number of tests is increased by a factor $2n_e$ where n_e is the number of input variables that appear an *even* number of times in the product terms of the Reed-Muller expansion—i.e., $n_e = 1$ (input A) in (4). Reddy also demonstrates how this additional set of $2n_e$ tests is removed by an extra AND gate with its output made observable. The inputs to this AND gate are those appearing an even number of times in the Reed-Muller product terms, and if the circuit is modified so, the original $(n + 4)$ tests in T are then sufficient to detect single s-a-0, s-a-1 faults on the primary inputs themselves. The modification for the example is very simple since only one of the variables—A—occurs an even number of times. It is sufficient, therefore, to allow direct monitoring of A as shown by the dotted output in Figure C-2.

A later extension to this work has been reported by Kodandapani [1974] in which he notes that one of the test vectors in the 4-vector test set T_1 can be removed by assigning the don't-care variable D in the test set T_2 in a specific manner.

The input combinations 00, 01, and 11 are applied to each EOR gate by the 0000, 0111, and 1111 vectors of T_1 respectively. Kodandapani observes that it is possible to apply the remaining 10 input by assigning values to the don't-care variable in T_2 rather than by using the 1000 vector in T_1.

The algorithm is based on a re-ordering of the terms in the Reed-Muller expansion with identification of certain subsets of product terms containing x_1, $x_1 x_2$, $x_1 x_2 x_3$, etc. Each subset is then ANDed with an appropriate vector of the T_2 test set, and the result produces the complement of the assignment to be given to the don't-care variable for that particular vector. The validity of the procedure and a description of the algorithm are presented in the paper; the result, in this case, is given by:

$$T_1 = \begin{array}{cccc} D & A & B & C \\ 0 & 0 & 0 & 0 \\ 0 & 1 & 1 & 1 \\ 1 & 1 & 1 & 1 \end{array} \quad \text{three input vectors} \tag{7}$$

and

$$T_2 = \begin{array}{cccc} D & A & B & C \\ 1 & 0 & 1 & 1 \\ 0 & 1 & 0 & 1 \\ 0 & 1 & 1 & 0 \end{array} \quad n \text{ input vectors} \tag{8}$$

The two major objections to the Reed Muller technique are (1) the prohibitive cost of implementation (each multi-literal term in the Reed-Muller expansion implies one EOR gate and at least one AND gate) and (2) the corresponding excessive propagation delay.

Reddy comments on the second point in the 1974 paper. The following section describes an alternative technique, again by Reddy, that always results in a three-level implementation.

Three Level OR-AND-OR Technique (Reddy)

This technique [Reddy, 1972b] is a combinational circuit design procedure in which any single s-a-1 or s-a-0 fault is locatable within certain fault indistinguishability constraints and which results in networks having up to three levels and employing only AND and OR gates. The application of the procedure is restricted to positive unate logic functions* and produces three level OR-AND-OR implementations in which every distinguishable fault is locatable. The process commences with the design of an irredundant three-level OR-AND-OR *prime tree*. The definition and synthesis of prime trees have been presented by Dandapani and Reddy [1974]. Briefly, a prime tree is defined as the following:

- A *restricted tree network* consists of AND, OR, and NOT gates only and has the restriction that any input to a NOT gate is a primary input.
- A *restricted prime tree* is a restricted tree network implementing a function f and satisfying the following conditions:
  - If the primary output gate is an OR type and if $f = T_1 + T_2 + \cdots + T_p$ where T_i is a product of literals then T_i is a prime implicant of f, $1 \leqslant i \leqslant p$.
  - If the primary output gate is an AND type, and if $f = U_1 \cdot U_2 \cdots U_q$ where U_i is a sum of literals, then U_i is a prime implicate of f, $1 \leqslant i \leqslant q$. (Examples of restricted prime trees are given in Dandapani and Reddy [1974], Figure 5.)
- A *prime tree* is a tree network containing AND, OR, NAND, NOR, or NOT gates which is either a restricted prime tree in its own right, or whose test-equivalent network [Kohavi and Kohavi, 1972] is a restricted prime tree.

The procedure presented in Reddy [1972b] commences with a prime tree implementation of the original unate function and then applies certain network modification procedures aimed

* A logic function $f(x_1 x_2 \cdots x_n)$ is unate if and only if it is representable as a sum-of-product or product-of-sum expression in which no literal x_i appears in both its complemented and uncomplemented form. A positive unate function is one in which all x_i's are uncomplemented.

at enhancing the fault distinguishability properties of the tree.

In reality, of course, many functions are not unate, but Reddy suggests that if true and complemented versions of primary inputs were available from independent sources, the function could be converted to a positive unate form by considering the complemented variables to be independent. For example, $f(ABC)$ in (1) is not unate, but could be converted to such if $\overline{B}$ and $\overline{C}$ are considered to be independent variables α and β respectively. This would modify the function to:

$$f(ABC) = A\alpha C + B\beta \qquad (9)$$

The prime tree realization of (9) is, unfortunately, a trivial network (it results in a two-level rather than three-level network) and does not really illustrate the technique. To convey something of the application of the process, however, Figure C-3 is borrowed from Reddy [1972b] and demonstrates the totally fault-locatable implementation for the logic function given by:

$$f(AB, \ldots, K) = ACEF + BCEF + ADEF$$
$$+ BDEF + GCH + DGH \quad (10)$$
$$+ AIF + BIJ + KIJ$$

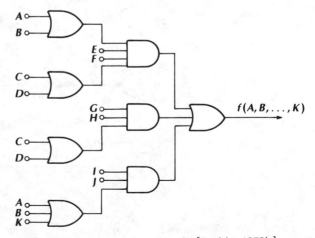

Figure C–3. Prime tree example [Reddy, 1972b].

Use of Additional Control Logic (*Hayes*)

Both techniques discussed so far have attempted to minimize the number of additional control inputs or observable output requirements. A procedure by Hayes [1974], however, discusses the addition of control logic to increase the diagnosability of the circuit—either by rendering observable internal conditions that are not normally so (extra primary outputs) or by allowing external control of internal conditions not normally directly controllable (extra primary inputs). The paper examines the systematic use of control logic to reduce the number of tests assuming that any additional control logic must itself be testable if it is to serve any useful purpose.

The main aim is to improve the circuit's "controllability," defined as the extent to which internal conditions can be controlled by applying signals to the primary inputs, by the addition of extra control inputs and gates. In this case, the gates used are the EOR type, and the first stage

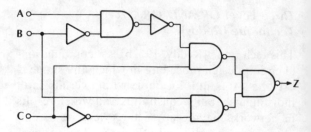

Figure C–4. Two-input NAND + INVERTER implementation of $f(ABC)$.

is to produce a design based solely on 2-input NAND gates and inverters. The inverters are then replaced by EOR gates and additional EOR gates inserted in all other NAND gate input lines not containing an EOR gate. The application of these two stages to the running example is shown in Figures C-4 and C-5. Note that the other inputs to the EOR gates are brought out as primary inputs and for normal operation assigned 1 if the particular EOR gate replaced an inverter and 0 otherwise.

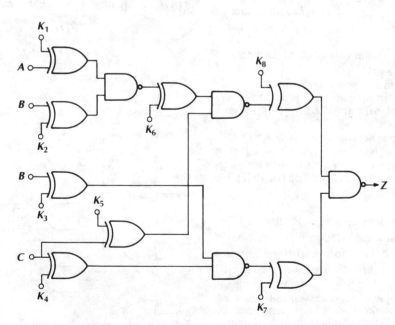

Figure C–5. Fully modified testable network with control lines K_1 to K_8.

With regard to the generation of tests for such a circuit, consider the basic module shown in Figure C-6a. In order to fully test such a module, it is necessary in the first instance to apply all four input combinations to each EOR gate and ensure that their outputs produce the four different input combinations to the following NAND gate. One way of doing this with four tests is shown in Figure C-6b—ignoring the additional test shown below the dotted line for the moment.

If x_k becomes an input to a following EOR gate, however, it is necessary to generate an additional 0 on x_k to satisfy the following EOR input requirement of two 1's and two 0's. The extra test shown beneath the dotted line will achieve this, and each module now requires a minimum of five tests. These tests will (1) ensure full fault-cover (Hayes comments that the fault cover includes all multiple fault situations as well as the single fault ones) and (2) enable all the necessary input conditions to be generated for successor modules.

The main problem now is to specify five-bit sequences on all primary and control lines so that module outputs and successor module inputs are compatible. Hayes offers an algorithm for doing this based on the observation that each five-bit sequence on the primary and NAND gate inputs in the module must be a permutation of the sequence 00111.

There are only ten such sequences, denoted by the set $P = \{X_0, X_1, \ldots, X_9\}$ where $X_0 = 00111$, $X_1 = 01011$, etc., and two sequences are *compatible* if their NAND product, on a bit-for-bit basis, produces a result that is also in P, e.g., $\overline{X_0 X_1} = 11100(X_9)$; therefore X_0 is compatible with X_1. Note however that $\overline{X_0 X_9} = 11011$, and this is not a permutation of 00111: X_0 and X_9 are therefore *incompatible*.

The procedure itself, then, is to arbitrarily assign sequences from P to the primary inputs and then derive sequences on the control inputs to the first set of EOR gates to produce a compatible pair of sequences on the following NAND gate inputs. The NAND gate outputs must themselves be sequences from P (because the inputs were compatible), and these become the inputs to the next set of EOR gates. So the process repeats itself until the primary outputs are reached. Applying this to Figure C-5 produces the following possible test set:

A	B	C	K_1	K_2	K_3	K_4	K_5	K_6	K_7	K_8	Z
0	0	0	0	0	0	0	0	1	1	1	1
0	0	0	1	1	1	1	1	0	0	0	1
1	1	1	1	0	1	0	1	0	0	1	1
1	1	1	0	1	0	1	0	0	0	1	0
1	1	1	0	0	0	0	0	1	1	1	0

Hayes also comments on the application of this approach to sequential circuits defined by the standard Huffman model—i.e., a delay-free combinational network and a set of feedback lines each containing a unit delay element.

The procedure here is to convert the combinational network into a two-input NAND gate version with additional EOR gates as before, but the sequential nature of the circuit introduces two additional problems: the first is that the

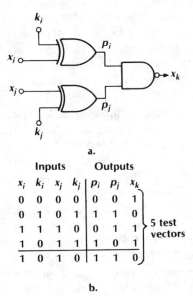

a.

Inputs | **Outputs**

x_i	k_i	x_j	k_j	p_i	p_j	x_k
0	0	0	0	0	0	1
0	1	0	1	1	1	0
1	1	1	0	0	1	1
1	0	1	1	1	0	1
1	0	1	0	1	1	0

5 test vectors

b.

Figure C–6. Basic logic module and possible test vectors.

initial value of the feedback lines must be determined and be compatible with the sequence assigned to the primary inputs. The second problem is similar: the sequences assigned to the delay element input must be related to those assigned to the delay element outputs both from the viewpoint of compatibility and from the unit delay property. Both these problems are overcome by introducing the concept of *sequence rotation*. If the ith sequence in P is defined by $X_i = c_1 c_2 c_3 c_4 c_5$ where c_1, c_2, etc., are binary constants 0 or 1, then the rotation of X_i, denoted by $r(X_i)$, is given by the sequence $c_2 c_3 c_4 c_5 c_1$ and is itself a sequence in P. The problems are then solved by assigning sequences to the feedback line inputs to the combinational circuit so that if X_i is assigned to one of the feedback lines—i.e., delay element output—this implies the sequence $r(X_i)$ on the delay line input. The problem now is to find a set of sequences through the combinational circuit that finally match at the inputs. In some cases, this results in unresolvable conflicts. Hayes demonstrates how these may be overcome by the insertion into the module of yet another pair of EOR gates—between the existing pair and the NAND gate—and he concludes therefore that the approach is quite general.

He does note, however, that the cost of improving the diagnosability of the network is a large increase in the number of gates and additional inputs and outputs (it is suggested that, for maximum diagnosability, each EOR gate output should be directly observable) and comments that, in practice, there may be quite severe limitations—e.g., restrictions due to the physical size, reliability requirements, number of available input/output lines, propagation delay constraints, and length of test vectors. Some of the additional EOR gates can be removed—for instance, if they are not needed for normal inversion purposes and if their removal does not violate the compatibility constraint. This can be applied to Figure C-5 and removes the EOR gates with control inputs K_1, K_3 and K_5. This causes a modification to the previous test set and

a possible reduced sequence is now given by:

A	B	C	K_2	K_4	K_6	K_7	K_8	Z
0	0	0	0	0	1	0	1	1
1	0	1	1	1	0	0	0	1
0	1	0	0	1	0	1	1	1
1	1	1	1	0	0	1	1	0
1	1	1	0	1	1	1	1	0

Minimally Tested Logic Networks (*Saluja and Reddy*)

The previous technique by Hayes utilizing extra control logic and producing combinational logic designs that are fully tested by five tests provoked further investigation into minimally tested networks. A paper by Saluja and Reddy [1974] presents a design process that produces circuit designs that are fully tested by three tests. Their procedure is based on the fact that any n-input 1-output gate of the AND, OR, NAND, NOR variety is fully tested for single or multiple stuck-at fault conditions on its inputs or output by $(n + 1)$ tests. Therefore, if the circuit utilizes two-input gates throughout, then each gate is tested by three tests only. The addition of certain control inputs and observable outputs allows this idea to be extended to the whole circuit. The procedure is illustrated below.

Consider first the three input AND gate shown in Figure C-7a. By replacing the gate with a three-level AND-OR-AND using two input gates as shown in Figure C-7b, one may derive a version that is fully tested by three sets of input combinations. These are shown in the figure and rely on the provision of an extra control input K_1 and observable outputs 0_1 and 0_2.

Similar circuits exist for three-input OR, NAND, and NOR gates, and obvious extensions can be made for n-input gates where $n > 3$.

The first step in the procedure, therefore, is to replace any n-input AND or OR gates, for which $n > 2$, with cascaded two-input gates—omitting

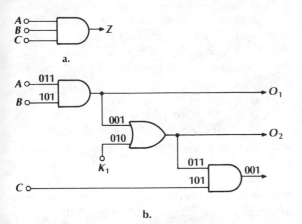

Figure C–7. Minimally-tested 3-input AND module.

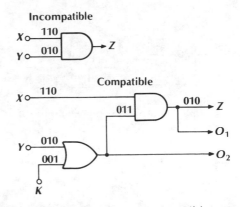

Figure C–9. Example of an incompatible set of gate input sequences and the necessary modifications.

for the time being any intermediate control gates such as the OR gate in Figure C-7b. This is demonstrated in Figure C-8.

The next step is to assign test sequences to the first level gates (those nearest the primary inputs) by selecting any two sequences from the following sets S_1 and S_2, depending on whether the gate is AND or OR:

$$\text{AND gate: } S_1 = \{011, 101, 110\}$$

$$\text{OR gate: } S_2 = \{100, 010, 001\}$$

It can be seen that the application of any two sequences from S_1 will apply the combinations 01, 10, and 11 to the AND gate inputs, and that this is a necessary and sufficient set to test for any single or multiple s-a-1, s-a-0 fault set on the gate inputs and output. A similar result holds for the S_2 set in relation to the OR gate—the combinations in this case being 01, 10, and 00.

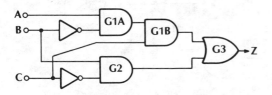

Figure C–8. Two-input gate version of $f(ABC)$.

The outputs from the first level gates will either be a correct part of the necessary test sequences for their successor gates, or not. In the event of a gate output being incompatible* with the the requirements of a successor gate, the successor gate is suitably modified by introducing extra gates with additional control inputs and observable outputs.

There are many possibilities here; one of them is illustrated in Figure C-9. Here, the two-input AND gate to the left is assumed to have the input sequences shown—these being the outputs generated by predecessor gates. Although one of these sequences (on x) comes from S_1, the other on y comes from S_2, and the gate must be replaced by the OR-AND circuit shown.

Figure C-10 shows the compatible/incompatible conditions for a certain set of sequences applied to the circuits' primary inputs, and Figure C-11 presents the final circuit showing the modifications due to the incompatibilities. This circuit has an additional five control inputs and seven observable outputs.

Saluja and Reddy note that the number of extra control inputs cannot exceed six since only six different sequences will ever be required (in

---
* The terms *compatible* and *incompatible* are used in the same sense as in the discussion above.

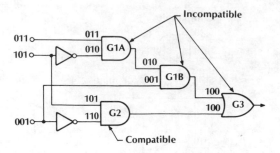

Figure C–10. Compatible and incompatible gate conditions.

the example K_1, K_2 and K_3 are the same and could be joined), and that the additional observable outputs enable fault location to be made right down to single gates.

They also point out that the extension of the procedure to cover the combinational section of sequential networks is similar to the procedure outlined by Hayes [1974].

Sequential Circuits

Apart from the extension to easily tested combinational circuit design procedures already mentioned, most research workers have concentrated on improving the testability of sequential networks by modifying the initial reduced state-table description. The underlying objectives here stem from the ideas contained in Hennie's paper [1964] regarding the derivation of a *checking experiment* from an analysis of the state table. (A checking experiment on a sequential machine is the application of input sequences to the input terminals with observations of the output sequences at the output terminals to determine whether or not the machine is operating correctly.)

In his paper, Hennie defines certain types of input/output sequences and shows how, subject to limitations in the structure and faulty behavior of the sequential machine, they could be used to assist in the derivation of a checking experiment capable of demonstrating (a) that all the states exist and (b) that all defined transitions between the states could be made.

Foremost among these sequences is the *distinguishing sequence*—an input sequence whose output response enables unique identification of the starting state. Hennie shows how distinguishing sequences can be used to reduce considerably the total length of the checking experiment. Unfortunately, not all state-tables possess distinguishing sequences, and although this does not inhibit the derivation of a checking experiment, it does cause the derivation to be more complicated. A significant paper by Kohavi and Lavallee [1967] demonstrates how state-tables not pos-

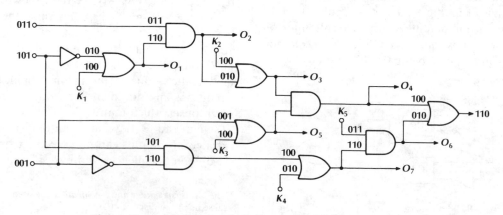

Figure C–11. Fully modified circuit tested by three tests.

Table C–1. State table for synchronous 110 pattern recognizer.

Present State	Next State/Output z_1	
	$x_1 = 0$	$x_1 = 1$
A (00)	A/0	B/0
B (11)	A/0	C/0
C (10)	A/1	C/0

sessing distinguishing sequences could be modified by the provision of extra outputs.

They go on to show how a checking experiment could be derived. Before demonstrating their procedure, we will again introduce a relatively simple example to be used as a running example.

Table C-1 represents the behavior of a synchronous pattern recognizer whose output z_1 goes to 1 only when the input pattern $x_1 = 110$ has occurred. This state-table does not possess a distinguishing sequence (any sequence beginning with 0 would not be able to differentiate between a state of A or B, and any beginning with 1 between B or C) and a checking experiment would have to be based on identification of a *characterizing set* with the associated *locating sequences* [Hennie, 1964]. For this state-table therefore, using the following locating sequences (with the simplifications suggested by Hennie),

- State A: $L_A = 0\,0\,0\,1\,0$ (terminating in state A);
- State B: $L_B = 0\,0\,0\,0\,0\,0\,1\,0$ (terminating in state A); and
- State C: $L_C = 0\,1\,1\,0\,1\,1\,0\,1\,1\,1\,0$ (terminating in state A);

and the *synchronizing sequence* 0 (synchronizing to state A), a suitable input sequence for a checking experiment is given by

$$| 0 | L_A \; 1 \; L_B \; 1 \; 1 \; L_C \; | 0 \; 0 \; L_A \; 0 \; 1 \; 0 \, |$$
$$1 \; 0 \; L_A \; 1 \; 1 \; 0 \, | 1 \; 0 \; 0 \; L_A \; 1 \; 0 \; 1 \; 0 \, |$$
$$1 \; 1 \; 0 \; L_A \; 1 \; 1 \; 1 \; 0 \, | 1 \; 1 \; 0 \; 0 \; L_A \; 1 \; 1 \; 0 \; 1 \; 0 \, | \quad \textbf{(11)}$$
$$1 \; 1 \; 1 \; 0 \; L_A \; 1 \; 1 \; 1 \; 1 \; 0 \, |$$

(100 symbols)

This has been derived using the procedure in Hennie's paper, and it should be recognized that other checking experiments could be derived that are possibly shorter in length. This is not too important, however, since the decrease in length would only be marginal and the purpose of defining the experiment is for comparison only.

To complete the picture for this example, Figure C-12 illustrates a possible implementation using D-type bistables (the dotted output z_2 can be ignored for the moment). This and other implementations shown later were produced by a computer assisted logic design (CALD) suite of programs [Lewin, Purslow, and Bennetts, 1972].

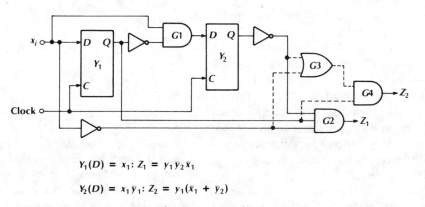

$$Y_1(D) = x_1 : Z_1 = y_1 \bar{y}_2 \bar{x}_1$$

$$Y_2(D) = x_1 \bar{y}_1 : Z_2 = y_1 (\bar{x}_1 + \bar{y}_2)$$

Figure C–12. *D*-type implementation of 110 pattern recognizer.

Additional Outputs to Produce Distinguishing Sequences (Kohavi and Lavallee)

Kohavi and Lavallee's paper [1967] is but one of a number of papers that have appeared since the original paper by Hennie and that seek to reduce the length of the checking experiment either by using special sequences or by optimizing the order in which states and transitions are checked, or both. This aspect of state-table analysis is not discussed further here except to say that many efficient algorithms are now available. The interested reader is referred either to the bibliography in Bennetts and Lewin [1971] or to more recent publications of which Hsieh [1971], Farmer [1973], and Kohavi, Rivierre, and Kohavi [1973] are representative.

The contribution of interest, however, is the procedure in Kohavi and Lavallee's paper for modifying a state-table to possess a distinguishing sequence if it does not already do so. This can be regarded as a design constraint for testability and is based on the provision of extra output variables.

The procedure is based on identifying present state pairs whose next states are identical for the same input condition and output results. Such state pairs, called *repeated states*, are illustrated by states (AB) and (BC) in Table C-1. The procedure also identifies any present state pairs whose implied entry derivations eventually loop back to a predecessor pair. An implied entry for any present state pair is the next state pair under the same input condition that has the same output value. In Table C-1, for instance, the present state pair (AB) implies (BC) for $x_1 = 1$ and (BC) then implies (CC) under $x_1 = 1$. These implications can be chained together to form a *testing graph*. It is shown that if the testing graph ever loops back on itself, the input sequence that causes this cannot be a distinguishing sequence. (This looping feature is not present in the testing graph for the example in Table C-1.)

The procedure therefore seeks to eliminate all repeated states and testing graph loops by selec-

tive addition of extra output variables and, in the case of Table C-1, a single output z_2 is sufficient to break the repeated state pairs (AB) and (BC). Shown in Table C-2, this version now possesses the very simple distinguishing sequence $x_1 = 0$. Application of Kohavi and Lavallee's algorithm for deriving checking experiments produces the following much reduced input sequence:

$$0\ 0\ 0\ 1\ 0\ 1\ 1\ 0\ 1\ 1\ 1\ 0 \text{ (12 symbols).} \quad (12)$$

The modification involves the addition of gates G3 and G4 shown in Figure C-12 to produce the extra output z_2 (shown dotted).

Additional Inputs to Improve Testability (Murakami, Kinoshita, and Ozaki)

As in easily tested combinational circuit procedures, an alternative approach to improve sequential machine testability is to add extra control input variables rather than observable output functions. This is considered by Murakami, Kinoshita, and Ozaki [1970], who introduce the concept of a *counter cycle* C_1 defined in the following way:

A counter cycle C_1 for an n-state sequential machine of the Mealy type is an alternating sequence of states s_i and input symbol I such that

$$C_1 = s_1\, I s_2\, I s_3\, I \cdots s_n\, I s_1$$

where

$$\delta(s_i, I) = s_{i+1} \text{ and } \lambda(s_i, I) = 0$$
$$1 \leqslant i \leqslant n - 1$$

and

$$\delta(s_n, I) = s_1 \text{ and } \lambda(s_n, I) = 1$$

where $\delta(s_i, I)$ and $\lambda(s_i, I)$ are the next state and output functions, respectively.

An application of n consecutive input symbols I to the sequential machine will produce an output sequence of $(n - 1)$ 0's and one 1. The

Table C–2. State table with additional output z_2.

| Present State | Next State/Output $z_1 z_2$ | |
	$x_1 = 0$	$x_1 = 1$
A (00)	A/00	B/00
B (11)	A/01	C/00
C (10)	A/11	C/01

Table C–3. State table with additional input x_2.

| Present State | Next State/Output z_1 | | |
	$x_1 x_2 =$ 00(α)	$x_1 x_2 =$ 10(β)	$x_1 x_2 =$ 01(ϵ)
A (00)	A/0	B/0	B/0
B (11)	A/0	C/0	C/0
C (10)	A/1	C/0	A/1

relative position of the 1 in the output sequence will vary with the initial starting state and will uniquely identify it: e.g., an output response of 00 . . . 01 will identify s_1 as the start state; 00 . . . 010 will identify s_2, and so on. Such an input sequence therefore is a distinguishing sequence, and the authors show that if the sequential machine contains a counter cycle (called a *CC machine*), then reduced checking experiments are easily derived.

They also demonstrate how non-CC machines may be converted into CC machines by the addition of an extra symbol ϵ so that

$$\delta(s_i, \epsilon) = s_{i+1} \text{ and } \lambda(s_i, \epsilon) = 0$$

$$1 \leqslant i \leqslant n - 1$$

and

$$\delta(s_n, \epsilon) = s_1 \text{ and } \lambda(s_n, \epsilon) = 1.$$

It can be seen that the basic state-table (Table C-1) is non-CC and Table C-3 shows a suitable CC version. Note that the extra input symbol ϵ has been coded 01 and an extra input variable x_2 introduced so that $x_2 = 0$ for normal operation.

Denoting $x_1 x_2 = 00$ by α, $x_1 x_2 = 10$ by β, and $x_1 x_2 = 01$ by ϵ, a suitable checking experiment for Table C-3, using Murakami's procedure, is given by:

Input	$\epsilon\epsilon\epsilon\epsilon\epsilon\epsilon$	$\alpha\epsilon\epsilon\epsilon$	$\beta\epsilon\epsilon$	$\epsilon\alpha\epsilon\epsilon\epsilon$
Output	001001	0001	001	00001

$$\text{(31 symbols)} \qquad \textbf{(13)}$$

$$\begin{matrix} \epsilon\beta\epsilon & \epsilon\epsilon\alpha\epsilon\epsilon\epsilon & \epsilon\epsilon\beta\epsilon \\ 001 & 001001 & 0001. \end{matrix}$$

A D-type implementation is shown in Figure C-13.

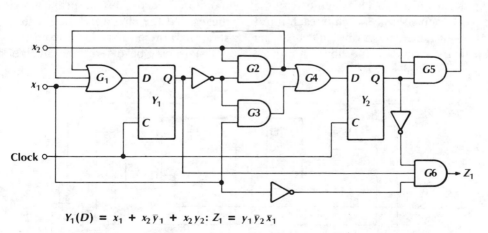

$$Y_1(D) = x_1 + x_2\bar{y}_1 + x_2 y_2 : Z_1 = y_1\bar{y}_2\bar{x}_1$$

$$Y_2(D) = x_1\bar{y}_1 + x_2\bar{y}_1$$

Figure C–13. *D*-type implementation of counter cycle version.

This work has been extended by Holborow [1972], who has shown that the length of the checking experiment can be significantly reduced by ordering the states according to the number of transitions into them (number of times they appear in the state-table) before assigning the next state/output values under the ϵ input symbol. This characteristic has been included in the derivation of Table C-3.

Shift Register Modifications for Synchronous Circuits (*Williams and Angell*)

The paper by Williams and Angell [1973] suggests that most problems in sequential circuit testing can be overcome if (1) the circuit can easily be set to any desired internal state, and (2) it is easy to find a sequence of input patterns such that the resulting output sequence will indicate whether the circuit was in a given state.

The second property is, of course, the distinguishing sequence requirement and, unlike previous authors, Williams and Angell base their modifications on the implementation itself rather than on the state-table. The suggestion is that bistables in the circuit can, under the control of a signal p, be connected together in a chain to behave as a shift-register. This facility can be modeled by a double-throw switch in each input lead of every bistable and in one or two of the circuit's primary output connections. All these

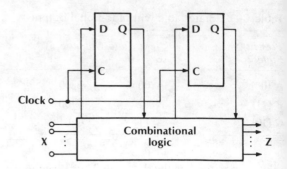

Figure C–14. Standard model for a synchronous sequential circuit.

switches are ganged together, and the circuit can operate either in its "normal" mode or "shift-register" mode. The principle is illustrated in Figures C-14 and C-15 where, for simplicity, two D-type bistables have been assumed. For JK and other two-input, two-output bistables, the number of switches would be doubled. Figure C-16 describes the characteristics of the switch and shows a suitable implementation (a two-input multiplexer in fact).

In the shift-register mode, the first bistable can be set directly from one of the primary inputs, and the output of the last bistable can be directly monitored on one of the primary outputs. This means that the circuit can be set to any desired state from the primary inputs and that the internal state can be determined by the signal se-

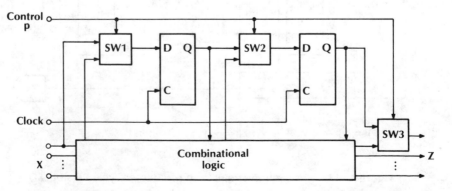

Figure C–15. Modified circuit model: includes double-throw switches.

quence appearing on the primary outputs. The procedure for testing the circuit therefore is as follows:

Step 1. Switch to shift register mode and check the shift-register operation.
Step 2. Set the initial state into the shift-register.
Step 3. Return to normal mode and apply the test input pattern.
Step 4. Switch to shift-register mode and shift out the final state while setting the starting state for the next test. Return to Step 3.

To demonstrate the approach on the pattern recognizer, Figure C-17 shows a reconfigured version of Figure C-12 that includes the additional switches, and Figure C-18 shows the "combinational" circuit to be tested, with inputs x (the original circuit input), y_1 and y_2 (the bistable outputs), and p (the mode control input), and outputs z_1 (the original circuit output), and d_1 and d_2 (the bistable inputs). A suitable test sequence can be derived using any suitable combinational circuit test sequence generation procedure such as has been described by Bennetts

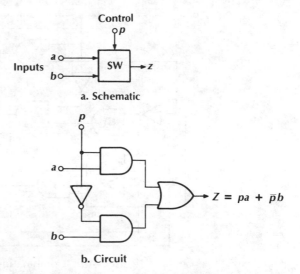

Figure C–16. Schematic and circuit for double-throw switch.

[1972, 1973], and can be applied using the four-step procedure outlined above.

Obviously, the length of the shift register will determine the time spent in Step 4, and this may

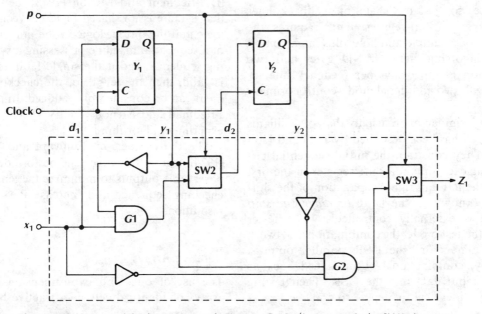

Figure C–17. Modified version of Figure C-12 (input switch SW1 is not required for this example).

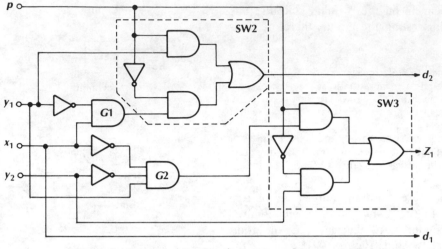

Figure C–18.   Combinational segment of Figure C-17.

represent an excessive proportion of the total testing time. The authors offer suggestions as to how this time may de decreased by forming several shorter shift-registers with the accompanying more complex switches. The paper also discusses the application of the approach to asynchronous logic. In this case, the strategy is to use one feedback line to control the next in sequence, so that the chain of feedback lines behaves as a shift-register. This requires the addition of a sample-and-hold plus latch combination involving eight NAND gates and two extra propagation delays per feedback line together with two additional mode-control primary inputs.

A very similar approach to that of Williams and Angell has been described by Toth and Holt [1974]. They constrain the initial sequential circuit design to contain a shift register in the first place. The left and right propagation of the shift register (known as the DSR or *diagnostic shift register*) is externally controlled by the tester and, in the test mode, the combinational network inputs come from the DSR parallel outputs. Similarly, combinational outputs feed back as parallel input data into the DSR. Their testing strategy is identical to Steps 1 to 4 above.

Other Sequential Circuit Procedures

This section draws attention to three other relatively academic papers of relevance to sequential machine testability. The first, by Meyer and Yeh [1971], discusses the design of sequential circuits possessing distinguishing sequences. The second, by Friedman and Menon [1973], demonstrates that if there is no shared logic between the state logic and the output logic in the implementation of a sequential machine possessing a synchronizing sequence, and if the single fault assumption is valid, then the length of the checking experiment can be considerably reduced. In particular, Friedman and Menon modify Hsieh's checking experiment algorithm [1971].

The third paper, by Fujiwara and Kinoshita [1974], is an alternative scheme for adding extra observable outputs to minimize the length of the checking sequence and increase the diagnostic resolution.

Iterative Arrays

The use of one- and two-dimensional iterative arrays of identical cells is attractive because of he advantages of design regularity and ease of abrication. If they are to realize their full potenial, however, they must also be easily tested. Several authors have studied this. In particular, Landgraff and Yau [1971] have considered the design and testing of arrays based on combinational cells and have specified the following conditions for which the array is testable:

- It must be possible to initialize the inputs of each cell of the array to all possible input values using the array's external inputs only.
- It must be possible to sensitize a path from the outputs of the cell to the outputs of the array to enable the propagation of a cell fault-effect.

The paper shows how the design of an array that is not initially testable, as defined above, can be modified by additional logic and input/output terminals. This is achieved by inserting test points monitored at the external outputs, or by modifying to ensure that each cell can be set into a known state. Rendering the array testable results in a reduction in the number of tests, and the paper includes appropriate test derivation algorithms.

Two other papers of interest are those by Friedman [1973] and Reddy and Wilson [1974]. Friedman, who has extended some previous work [Menon and Friedman, 1971], considers the properties of unilateral combinational arrays that enable them to be tested with a fixed constant number of tests independent of the number of cells. Referring to such systems as *C-testable*, he shows how a non C-testable array can be made C-testable by augmenting the state-table describing the basic cell.* At the most, for an arbitrary N-state cell, this involves the addi-

---

* The behavior of a two-dimensional combinational cell with x (horizontal) and z (vertical) inputs and corresponding $\hat{x}$ and $\hat{z}$ outputs is usually defined by a table which has a row for each x input and a column for each z input. Each row is referred to as the state, and the entries in the table consist of the corresponding $(\hat{x}, \hat{z})$ pair outputs for each (x, z) combination of cell inputs.

tion of one more row and less than $(\log_2 N)^2$ columns. These additions may make use of unassigned input/output values or may require further inputs or outputs.

Reddy and Wilson [1974] discuss the design of two-dimensional iterative arrays to realize all n-variable symmetric and elementary threshold functions that require, at the most, $2n$ tests to detect all possible permanent stuck-at-faults.

PRACTICAL ASPECTS OF TESTABLE LOGIC DESIGN

This section is primarily based on two papers [Boswell, 1972; Schneider, 1974]. The first, by Boswell, suggests (quite rightly) that the efficiency of practical automatic test systems could be considerably enhanced if the logic designer included testability among his design criteria. Boswell presents eight empirical guidelines "that have proved highly successful" in practice. The present authors make no apology in repeating these guidelines here and, in some cases, have enlarged upon the comments made by Boswell. (A similar set of guidelines has been discussed in a General Radio Systems pamphlet [n.d.].)

Guideline 1: Give the tester access to internal circuit board nodes

Boswell suggests that this can be achieved either by using spare edge connector pins or by providing a separate edge connector specifically for test purposes. This guideline, which relates to the problem of strategic test point siting, has been studied by Russell and Kime [1971] and Hayes and Friedman [1974]. Their contributions are discussed in the following subsection, but before this, it is worthwhile summarizing Schneider's comments on accessibility. He suggests that the outputs of all memory units (bistables) should be directly observable and that, furthermore, access to the dc set or reset inputs should be available, enabling individual control of each bistable. This would obviously take up many extra connector positions, but nevertheless is a constraint imposed on the design layout of boards tested by the system described by Adshead, Jain, and Knowles [1972].

Schneider demonstrates how the extra facility of resetting (or setting) a bistable can be tied in with existing reset logic, if it exists, either by using an additional gate or by simply using wired-OR if the particular logic family permits it. Alternatively, if additional edge connector inputs are not available, a power-up reset that momentarily remains low as power is applied can be used to at least ensure that the initial start state is known. This is simply a CR network between the power line and ground whose output is attached to the DC reset input of the bistable. Such a facility would not be accessible by the tester; however, by switching the power off and on, a crude method of re-initialization could be effected. (The authors hasten to add that this is not suggested by Schneider and there are other obvious considerations in doing this of course!) These three techniques are illustrated in Figure C-19.

Strategic Test Point Siting (*Russell and Kime, Hayes and Friedman*)

Russell and Kime [1971] analyze the fault detectability and diagnosability of a combinational network by considering it from a purely structural viewpoint—i.e., the logical function of each gate is disregarded and is merely considered to be a node. This is thought to (1) provide insight into the contribution of network structure to the diagnosis process, and (2) be useful for purely structural problems such as identifying strategic sites for test point placement.

The authors make use of two directed graph models for the circuit—the basic and detailed models—and, using the mathematical techniques of graph theory, they discuss such topics as (1) fan-in, fan-out, and the effects of reconvergence

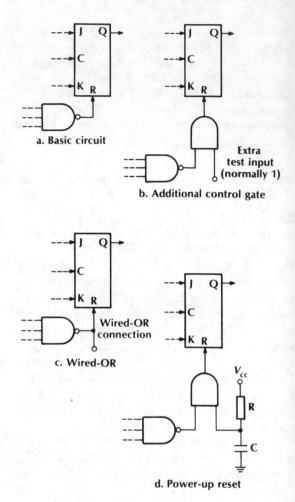

a. Basic circuit

b. Additional control gate

c. Wired-OR

d. Power-up reset

Figure C–19. Techniques for overriding internal reset conditions.

on fault detectability; (2) fault-equivalence for graph condensation purposes; and (3) criteria for optimizing the increased diagnostic resolution afforded by additional test points.

Hayes and Friedman [1974] describe an alternative scheme for fan-out free and restricted fan-out combinational networks which does make use of the individual gate functions. They present a method for labeling the connections within the circuit so that a minimal set of tests can be derived corresponding to a minimal labeling. The labeling is derived from the minimum number of essential 0's and 1's that must be placed on each input to an n-input gate to provide complete stuck-at fault detection cover. Thus the label for c_i, the output line of an n-input NAND gate G_i, would be given by $(1, n)$, a logical zero corresponding to the any-or-all inputs s-a-0 test and n logical ones corresponding to the n separate tests for inputs s-a-1. If the test set for the circuit is known, and corresponding line vectors calculated—as in Figure C-7b for instance—then some of the 0's and 1's in each vector may not be essential. This is incorporated into the labeling and serves to indicate where test points would be helpful. This idea can then be turned around the other way and a minimal test set derived from a corresponding minimal labeling.

These concepts form the basis for a branch-and-bound algorithm for selecting an optimal or near-optimal set of q test points, where $1 < q <$ the maximum number of permissible test points determined by the number of available spare pins.

Schneider also discusses test point siting, from a more intuitive point of view, suggesting that the junctions of large fan-in and fan-out are "ideal"—either for logic level monitoring or insertion. Other good candidates are important lines such as master clocks or reset lines, and logically redundant lines (discussed in the next section).

Guideline 2: As a general rule, avoid logically redundant circuits

A connection in a circuit is logically redundant if the output function is independent of the binary value on the connection for all input combinations. Any fault on such a connection is therefore undetectable. This is of no direct consequence to the operation of the circuit, but it can mask the detection of other stuck-at faults that would normally be detected by a particular test set. This phenomenon was initially reported by Friedman [1967] and has been considerably extended by Dandapani, Reddy, and Robinson

[1970]. Examples are given in Friedman and Menon's book [1971].

Unfortunately, redundancy is often essential to maintain the correct operation of the final circuit—the inclusion of bridging terms to remove static hazards in combinational logic for instance—and although the guideline is sound, it is not always possible to follow it.

Guideline 3: Make faults as easy to locate as possible

The diagnostic resolution of any test set is always limited by the indistinguishable fault set (IFS) grouping [Schertz and Metze, 1972] relative to the particular implementation of the function. Reference to some theoretical work in this area has already been made [Reddy, 1972], but Boswell demonstrates how, in some cases, locational uncertainty can be removed if connections in the same IFS group are arranged to go to the same gate rather than to two or more different gates. This would not remove the indistinguishability but would make the fault group locatable to the single gate alone.

Schneider also makes a number of practical suggestions regarding the layout and packaging of printed circuit boards to assist the location of faults. These are summarized below:

- Keep analog and digital subsystems physically apart if possible because of the different testing strategies and test equipment required.
- If a board contains more than one independent sub-circuit, try to keep them physically separate—i.e., partition the board.
- In conjunction with this, separate power lines assist circuit isolation. Tri-state logic is also useful.
- Employ a uniform layout for integrated circuits (relative position and pin orientation) and board edge connectors (same number pin for power input, ground, etc.)
- For easy removal and testing, mount MSI/LSI chips in sockets rather than solder directly to the board.

The reader should note that this list is not complete. These and other practical suggestions regarding layout are covered in Boswell [1972] and Schneider [1974]. The General Radio Systems pamphlet [n.d.] is also recommended.

Guideline 4: Use synchronous (clocked) circuitry whenever possible

Boswell's main point here is that every tester possesses a latency period (the time lapse between the tester applying the test and sampling the response), which could result in undetected output changes if they occurred within this period. He suggests therefore that asynchronous logic should be avoided.

There are other complications in the testing of asynchronous logic apart from those introduced by the speed of response. These stem from (1) the non-deterministic behavior of asynchronous circuits under certain fault conditions, especially those that re-introduce critical race possibilities, and (2) the fact that repetition of the same input value is not recognized by the circuit. This obviously inhibits the allowable test sequence and generally complicates the state-table analysis approach to checking experiment derivation.

Guideline 5: Take precautions to isolate the clock from the logic

The test application rate of the tester, determined by the test setup plus latency periods, may be less than the operating speed of the logic. It makes sense, therefore, to enable the internal high-speed clock to be replaced by an external lower speed one, including a single-shot facility.

Guideline 6: Make it possible to initialize sequential circuits prior to testing

The reasons for doing this have already been discussed in previous sections. Boswell com-

ments on the alternative procedures of either applying a synchronizing sequence [Hennie 1964] or providing a master reset. He claims that, of the two, the second is preferable since it does not imply a decision-making capability within the tester itself. This is not strictly true because the presence of a fault prior to initialization may inhibit correct initialization irrespective of the means to achieve it. In either case, therefore, the test equipment needs to assess the status of the circuit and act accordingly—i.e., it must possess decision-making capabilities.

Guideline 7: Take into account the operational characteristics of the tester to be used for a particular board

Boswell describes the various ways by which testers change the binary values of the input patterns to the circuit-under-test. This may be done simultaneously (parallel), in fixed n-bit groups (quasi-parallel), or singly (serial), and it is possible for the latter two to have an adverse effect on the circuit's operation. In particular, it may introduce critical race conditions into asynchronous sequential circuits that would not occur under normal operating conditions. Knowledge of the tester characteristics, therefore, may act as a constraint on the ordering of tests in a testing sequence to prevent the possible rejection of a fault-free board.

Guideline 8: Take test economics into consideration when developing a new logic design

The physical characteristics and limitations of the tester, its voltage level output and interface specifications, test application rate, and other such factors should all be taken into consideration before embarking upon a new logic design exercise. In a way, the economics of testing is one of the most unstable cost factors in the total cost of design and production of a logic board. It varies tremendously with the logic circuit type and complexity, the degree of confidence to be placed in the final board or chip, who is doing the testing (manufacturer or user), whether standard test generation algorithms are suitable or whether intuitive procedures must be employed, and a host of other factors. What it really comes down to in the end is that you only get what you pay for, and since integrated circuit technology and digital systems based on it always seem to be one step ahead of the procedure for testable design and test sequence generation, nobody is really sure of what they're getting. Certainly, MOS memory arrays seem to be offering new challenges from a testability viewpoint [Chiang and Standridge, 1975; Hnatek, 1975] and many research workers, including the authors [Bennetts et al., 1975], are still seeking test sequence generation algorithms for sequential circuits containing 1,000 or more gates and bistables—this being the size of large-scale integrated circuit designs to come. Although test economics is important, therefore, it is very difficult to accurately predict at the moment. All that one can say is that it will be relatively expensive.

CONCLUDING REMARKS

This paper has described some of the more important procedures for designing testability into logic networks, and it has been shown that this almost always results in additional logic with varying requirements for additional inputs and outputs. One of the authors has recently evaluated [Bennetts, 1976] the effect of applying three of the combinational circuit techniques to sixteen circuits taken from the series 74 TTL logic family and has produced graphs showing the distribution of percentage increase of a number of circuit parameters. In particular, the graphs show the distribution of percentage increases in the number of primary inputs, number of primary outputs, number of basic gates, propagation delay, and failure rate, and in some cases the percentage increases can be very considerable (see graphs 1-10 in Bennetts [1976] for more detail).

These increases are inevitable, but the consolidation of microelectronic technology has caused a shift in design emphasis from fully minimized implementations to those possessing a high reliability and integrity, and the ability to fully test the final product is an essential feature of this. As always, practical solutions will be a compromise between the costs of design, production, and testing on the one hand and the specification on the other. It is therefore very necessary that the design engineers appreciate the concepts and implications of the procedures for including or improving testability. We have attempted to provide the basis for this.

Finally, the paper has dealt specifically with those design constraints that improve the testability properties of the final circuit. The authors would like to point out, however, that other closely allied constraints may also be imposed on the circuit design. These constraints arise from general considerations of fault-tolerant design to achieve high reliability, and they may well be at variance with testability constraints. For this reason, therefore, they are drawn to the reader's attention. The reference set that is included in these lists is a representative selection of recent papers and should not be regarded as a complete survey: (1) fail-safe logic circuit/system design [*IEEE Trans. Computers*, 1971, pp. 536–542; 1972, pp. 1189–1196; 1974, pp. 41–47, 113–118, 369–374, 1149–1154]; (2) sequential machine assignment procedures for achieving fault-tolerance [*IEEE Trans. Computers*, 1971, pp. 1270–1275; 1972, pp. 492–495, 1973, pp. 239–249, 662–669; 1974, pp. 494–500, 651–657, 736–739]; and (3) design of self-testing, self-diagnostic logic circuits [*IEEE Trans. Computers*, 1971, pp. 1413–1414; 1973, pp. 263–269, 298–306; 1974, pp. 1100–1102].

These and other topics associated with the

general area of fault-tolerant hardware and software design are also discussed in *Proceedings of the International Symposium on Fault-Tolerant Computing, IEEE Computer Society* [1971–1975].

ACKNOWLEDGMENT

One of the authors, Mr. R. V. Scott, would like to acknowledge the financial assistance of a Science Research Council research studentship.

REFERENCES

Adshead, Jain, and Knowles [1972]; Bennetts [1972, 1973, 1974, 1975, 1976]; Bennetts and Lewin [1971]; Bennetts et al. [1975]; Boswell [1972]; Chiang and Standridge [1975]; Dandapani and Reddy [1974]; Dandapani, Reddy, and Robinson [1970]; Farmer [1973]; Friedman [1967, 1973]; Friedman and Menon [1971, 1973]; Fujiwara and Kinoshita [1974]; General Radio Systems [n.d.]; Hayes [1974]; Hayes and Friedman [1974]; Hennie [1964]; Hnatek [1975]; Holborrow [1972]; Hsieh [1971]; Kautz [1971]; Kodandapani [1974]; Kohavi and Kohavi [1972]; Kohavi and Lavallee [1967]; Kohavi, Rivierre, and Kohavi [1973]; Landgraff and Yau [1971]; Lewin, Purslow, and Bennetts [1972]; Menon and Friedman [1971]; Meyer and Yeh [1971]; Mukhopadhyay and Schmitz [1970]; Murakami, Kinoshita, and Ozaki [1970]; Reddy [1972b, 1974]; Reddy and Wilson [1974]; Russell and Kime [1971]; Saluja and Reddy [1974]; Schertz and Metze [1972]; Schneider [1974]; Toth and Holt [1974]; Williams and Angell [1973].

Summary of MIL-HDBK-217B Reliability Model

Experience has shown that 90 percent or more of the failure rate of a typical digital print circuit board is accounted for by the integrated circuit chips. To a first approximation the failure rates of the printed circuit board, capacitors, and resistors can be ignored in design studies. Hence, this appendix only summarizes the MIL-HDBK-217B model for integrated circuit chips. For boards populated primarily by discrete devices, or for nonelectronic components, the reader is referred to U.S. Department of Defense [1976].

The failure rate, λ, in failures per million hours for monolithic MOS and bipolar chips takes the form of:

$$\lambda = \pi_L \pi_Q (C_1 \pi_T + C_2 \pi_E) \pi_P$$

Values of each factor will be discussed in turn.

π_L

The learning factor has a value of 10 if the device is new, if there are major changes in the fabrication process, or if the fabrication process is being restarted after an extended interruption. Otherwise the value of π_L is 1.0.

π_Q

The quality factor is a function of the amount of device screening. Table D-1 lists the values of π_Q. Whereas most commercial parts are not subject-

From U.S. Department of Defense, "Military Standardization Handbook: Reliability Prediction of Electronic Equipment," MIL-HDBK-217B (Washington, D.C., 1976).

Table D–1. Quality factors.

Quality Level	Screening Standard	π_Q
A	Mil-M-38510 Class A	1
B	Mil-M-38510 Class B	2
B-1	Mil-Std-883, Method 5004, Class B	5
B-2	Same as B-1 with some tests waived	10
C	Mil-M-38510 Class C	16
C-1	Mil-Std-883, Method 5004, Class C	90
D	Commercial, hermetically sealed	150
D-1	Commercial, organic seal	300

ed to Class C screening requirements, their operational environment does not expose the devices to the failure modes that Class C screening is designed to stress. The Class C quality factor seems the most appropriate for devices used in computers built by reputable manufacturers.

π_T

The temperature acceleration factor is a function of device technology. If T_j is the worst case junction temperature (°C), then:
For linear (bipolar and MOS), MOS, ECL, bipolar beam lead:

$$\pi_T = 0.1e^{(-8121[1/(T_j+273)-1/298])}$$

For other bipolar (especially TTL):

$$\pi_T = 0.1e^{(-4794[1/(T_j+273)-1/298])}$$

If T_j is unknown, it may be approximated as follows.

• Low power TTL, MOS:

$$T_j = \text{ambient } T(°C) + K(°C)$$

where K is 13 (°C) if there are more than 30 gates or 120 linear transistors or the device is a memory. Otherwise K is 5 (°C).
• All others:

$$T_j = \text{ambient } T(°C) + L(°C)$$

where L is 25 (°C) if there are more than 30 gates or 120 linear transistors or the device is a memory. Otherwise L is 10 (°C).

Table D-2 gives useful values of π_T.

π_E

The application environment factor depends on the operational environment, as indicated in Table D-3.

π_P

The pin multiplier is a function of technology as depicted in Table D-4.

C_1, C_2

The complexity factors are a function of density and function as given in Table D-5.

For initial design evaluations it is convenient to have the equations for λ available on a

Table D–2. Some useful values of π_T.

Ambient Temperature	Low Power TTL		MOS		TTL		ECL	
	Small	Large	Small	Large	Small	Large	Small	Large
25 (°C)	0.13	0.20	0.16	0.31	0.17	0.35	0.24	0.82
40 (°C)	0.28	0.40	0.56	1.0	0.35	0.67	.82	2.5

Table D–3. Environmental factor, π_E.

Environment	Example	π_E
Ground, benign	Computer room	0.2
Space flight	Satellite	0.2
Ground, fixed	Factory floor	1.0
Airborne, inhabited	Cockpit	4.0
Naval, sheltered	Bridge of a surface ship	4.0
Ground, mobile	Jeep	4.0
Airborne, uninhabited	Aircraft equipment bay	6.0
Naval, unsheltered	Engine room of a surface ship	5.0
Missile, launch	Missile	10.0

Table D–4. Pin multiplier π_P.

Number of Pins	SSI/MSI	LSI	Memories
1–23	1.0	1.0	1.0
24	1.1	1.0	1.0
25	1.1	1.0	1.1
26–41	1.1	1.1	1.1
42–64	1.2	1.1	1.1
> 64	1.3	1.2	1.1

Table D–5. Complexity factors C_1, C_2.

Density/Function	C_1	C_2
SSI/MSI	$1.29\,(10)^{-3}(N_G)^{0.677}$	$3.89\,(10)^{-3}\,(N_G)^{0.359}$
Linear	$.56\,(10)^{-3}(N_T)^{0.763}$	$2.6\,(10)^{-3}(N_T)^{0.547}$
LSI $(100 < N_G < 1300)$	$18.7\,(10)^{-3}\,e^{[.00471\,N_G]}$	$13(10)^{-3}e^{[.00423\,N_G]}$
ROM memory	$1.14\,(10)^{-3}(B)^{0.603}$	$.32\,(10)^{-3}(B)^{0.646}$
RAM memory	$1.99\,(10)^{-3}(B)^{0.603}$	$.56\,(10)^{-3}(B)^{0.644}$

Key: N_G is the number of gates
$\quad N_T$ is the number of transistors
$\quad B$ is the number of bits

programmable calculator or a time-sharing system. Tables D-6 through D-10 were produced by a BASIC program and have proved helpful when programs such as AUTOFAIL and FAIL [Elkind, 1980a] are not available. Reliability calculations and design trade-offs are tedious and time-consuming and are best handled by AUTO-FAIL or FAIL. However, the user must be fully aware of the model parameters, the significance of the parameters, and the model's sensitivity to the parameters. Otherwise, the model will not produce meaningful, calibratable predictions.

Table D–6. Failure per million hours for TTL and MOS as a function of gate complexity.

Gates/ Chip	Bipolar Lambda	MOS Lambda
1	0.069409	0.079252
2	0.091287	0.107024
3	0.107416	0.128123
4	0.120704	0.145864
5	0.132232	0.161495
6	0.142535	0.175642
7	0.151925	0.188674
8	0.160604	0.200830
9	0.168707	0.212272
10	0.176333	0.223119
15	0.209387	0.270951
20	0.236932	0.311733
25	0.261034	0.348033
30	0.282729	0.381158
35	0.302623	0.411880
40	0.321105	0.440699
45	0.338442	0.467963
50	0.354827	0.493923
60	0.385285	0.542655
70	0.413295	0.587975
80	0.439380	0.630587
90	0.463902	0.670980
100	0.483965	0.712481
150	0.602949	0.892145
200	0.751283	1.117273
250	0.936233	1.399409
300	1.166869	1.753037
350	1.454514	2.196335
400	1.813312	2.752117
450	2.260923	3.449020
500	2.819410	4.322995
600	4.386130	6.794265
700	6.827237	10.684093
800	10.632875	16.809997
900	16.569166	26.462414
1000	25.834288	41.679265
1100	40.303211	65.680445
1200	62.911668	103.55572
1300	98.258928	163.35424

Note: $\pi_Q = 16$, $\pi_L = 1$, $\pi_E = 1$, $T_j = 50°C$.

Table D–7. Failures per million hours for bipolar ROM as a function of bit complexity.

Bits/Chip	Lambda
2	0.017635
4	0.027153
8	0.041818
16	0.064418
32	0.099253
64	0.152961
128	0.235782
256	0.363528
512	0.560611
1,024	0.864732
2,048	1.33413
4,096	2.05878
8,192	3.17774
16,384	4.90595
32,768	7.57570
65,536	11.7009

Note: $\pi_Q = 16$, $\pi_L = 1$, $\pi_E = 1$, $T_j = 50°C$.

Table D–8. Failures per million hours for bipolar RAM as a function of bit complexity.

Bits/Chip	Lambda
2	0.030799
4	0.047393
8	0.072942
16	0.112287
32	0.172888
64	0.266250
128	0.410112
256	0.631833
512	0.973623
1,024	1.500606
2,048	2.313288
4,096	3.566814
8,192	5.500706
16,384	8.484838
32,768	13.090480
65,536	20.200135

Note: $\pi_Q = 16$, $\pi_L = 1$, $\pi_E = 1$, $T_j = 50°C$.

Table D–9. Failures per million hours for MOS ROM as a function of bit complexity.

Bits/Chip	Lambda
2	0.030846
4	0.047220
8	0.072297
16	0.110711
32	0.169566
64	0.259757
128	0.397991
256	0.609903
512	0.934823
1,024	1.43311
2,048	2.19743
4,096	3.37002
8,192	5.16935
16,384	7.93094
32,768	12.1703
65,536	18.6794

Note: $\pi_Q = 16$, $\pi_L = 1$, $\pi_E = 1$, $T_j = 50°C$.

Table D–10. Failures per million hours for MOS RAM as a function of bit complexity.

Bits/Chip	Lambda
2	0.053861
4	0.082421
8	0.126145
16	0.193096
32	0.295627
64	0.452675
128	0.693267
256	1.061909
512	1.626853
1,024	2.492778
2,048	3.820270
4,096	5.855726
8,192	8.977270
16,384	13.765292
32,768	21.110812
65,536	32.381991

Note: $\pi_Q = 16$, $\pi_L = 1$, $\pi_E = 1$, $T_j = 50°C$.

REFERENCE

Elkind [1980a]; U.S. Department of Defense [1976].

Summary of MIL-HDBK-217C Reliability Model

When first released in April 1979, MIL-HDBK-217C [U.S. Department of Defense, 1979] followed the same general form as 217B. Subsequently an update was released in May 1980, known as MIL-HDBK-217C Notice 1. Notice 1 was subsequently different from 217C, primarily in the addition of power dissipation and package type in the calculation of junction temperature. The failure rate model for monolithic devices is summarized for both 217C and 217C Notice 1.

217C MODEL

The MIL-HDBK-217C is very similar to the 217B model. Hence, only the differences from MIL-HDBK-217B will be presented. If not stated otherwise, the same equations and parameters are used for MIL-HDBK-217C that were specified for MIL-HDBK-217B.

π_E

The Airborne Inhabited and Airborne Uninhabited environment classes were expanded into four classes, as indicated in Table E-1.

π_T

The junction temperature equation for TTL also covers Schottky TTL and low power Schottky TTL.

C_1, C_2

The complexity factors for LSI, ROM, and RAM were changed as follows:

LSI
$N_G < 1,000$ gates
same as SSI/MSI

$N_G > 1,000$ gates
$C_1 = 0.051 \ e^{(.001 N_G)}$
$C_2 = 0.0171 \ e^{(.001 N_G)}$

Table E–1. Additional environmental classes in MIL-HDBK-217C.

Class	Example	Value
Airborne, inhabited, transport	Cockpit of long-mission aircraft	2.8
Airborne, inhabited, fighter	Cockpit of high-performance aircraft	5.6
Airborne, uninhabited, transport	Equipment bay of long-mission aircraft	4.2
Airborne, uninhabited, fighter	Equipment bay of high-performance aircraft	8.4

ROM

$$C_1 = .285 \ (10)^{-3}(B)^{0.603}$$
$$C_2 = .08 \ (10)^{-3}(B)^{0.646}$$

RAM

$$C_1 = .995 \ (10)^{-3}(B)^{0.603}$$
$$C_2 = .28 \ (10)^{-3}(B)^{0.644}$$

for $B \leqslant 16,384$.

In the case of LSI devices, the coefficient of N_G in the exponent decreased by a factor of four from MIL-HDBK-217B. C_1 and C_2 decreased by a factor of four for ROMs and a factor of two for RAMs. These decreases reflect the increased reliability of semiconductor components as fabrication experience grows.

217C NOTICE 1 MODEL

The failure rate, λ, in failures per million hours for monolithic MOS and bipolar chips takes the form of:

$$\lambda = \pi_L \pi_Q [C_1 \pi_T \pi_V \pi_{PT} + (C_2 + C_3)\pi_E]$$

Values for each factor will be discussed in turn.

π_L

The learning factor has a value of 10 if the device is new, if there are major changes in the fabrication process, or if the fabrication process is being restarted after an extended interruption. Otherwise the value of π_L is 1.0.

π_Q

The quality factor is a function of the amount of device screening. Table E-2 lists the values of π_Q. Note the decreases in π_Q (ranging from a factor of 1.5 to 8.5 lower) over the values, for the same classes, in MIL-HDBK-217B.

π_T

The temperature acceleration factor is a function of device technology, package type, case temper-

Table E–2. Quality factors for MIL 217C notice 1.

Quality Level	Screening Standard	π_Q
S	MIL-M-38510, Class S	0.5
B	MIL-M-38510, Class B	1.0
B-1	MIL-STD-883, Method 5004, Class B	3
B-2	Same as B-1 with some tests waived	6.5
C	MIL-M-38510, Class C	8.0
C-1	MIL-STD-883, Method 5004, Class C	13.0
D	Commercial, hermetically sealed	17.5
D-1	Commercial	35.0

ature, and power dissipation.

$$\pi_T = 0.1 e^{(-A[(1/(T_j+273))-(1/298)])}$$

where A is a function of technology and package type as given in Table E-3 and T_j is the worst-case junction temperature. T_j is given by:

$$T_j = T_C + \Theta_{JC} P$$

where:

T_C is the case temperature (°C)

Θ_{JC} is the junction to case thermal resistance (°C/watt) for a device soldered onto a printed circuit board.

P   is the worst-case power dissipation.

If Θ_{JC} is unknown, the values in Table E-4 may be used. Some useful values of π_T are given in Table E-5. Early experience suggests that 217C Notice 1 is very sensitive to the junction temperature calculation. In particular, the default values for Θ_{JC} lead to questionably large values for T_j, especially in the case of nonhermetic packages.

π_V

The voltage stress factor, π_V, is 1.0 for all technologies other than CMOS. π_V is also 1.0 for CMOS with $V_{DD} = 5$ volts. For supply voltage between 12 and 15.5 volts:

$$\pi_V = 0.11 e^x$$

Table E–3. Technology and package parameter, A, used in calculation of π_T.

Technology	Package Type	A
TTL, ECL	Hermetic	4635
TTL, ECL	Nonhermetic	5214
Schottky TTL	Hermetic	5214
Schottky TTL	Nonhermetic	5794
Low Power Schottky TTL, PMOS	Hermetic	5794
Low Power Schottky TTL	Nonhermetic	6373
PMOS	Nonhermetic	8111
NMOS	Hermetic	6373
NMOS	Nonhermetic	9270
CMOS, Linear	Hermetic	7532
CMOS, Linear	Nonhermetic	10429

Table E–4. Default values for thermal resistance, θ_{JC}.

Package Type	Number of Pins	θ_{JC}
Hermetic DIP	≤ 22	30
Hermetic DIP	> 22	25
Nonhermetic DIP	≤ 22	125
Nonhermetic DIP	> 22	100

Table E–5. Some useful values of π_T.

Junction Temperature	Low-Power TTL		NMOS		TTL	
	Hermetic	Nonhermetic	Hermetic	Nonhermetic	Hermetic	Nonhermetic
25 (°C)	0.1	0.1	0.1	0.1	0.1	0.1
40 (°C)	0.26	0.28	0.28	0.44	0.21	0.26
70 (°C)	1.3	1.7	1.7	5.9	0.77	1.0
90 (°C)	3.25	4.6	4.6	26.2	1.6	2.3

where:

$$x = \frac{0.168 V_s (T_j + 273)}{298}$$

with V_s the supply voltage.

π_{PT}

π_{PT} is the PROM programming technique factor. π_{PT} is 1.0 for all devices except PROMs. For bipolar PROMs:

$$\pi_{PT} = 0.985 + 9.5 \times 10^{-5}(B)$$

where B is the number of bits. For MOS PROMs:

$$\pi_{PT} = 0.95 + 7.5 \times 10^{-5}(B)$$

π_E

The application environment factor depends on the operational environment as indicated in Table E-6.

Table E–6. Environmental factor, π_E.

Environment	Example	π_E
Ground, benign	Computer room	1.0
Space flight	Satellite	1.0
Ground, fixed	Factory floor	2.5
Airborne, inhabited, transport	Cockpit of long-mission aircraft	3.5
Airborne, inhabited, fighter	Cockpit of high-performance aircraft	7.0
Naval, sheltered	Bridge of a surface ship	4.0
Ground, mobile	Jeep	4.0
Airborne, uninhabited, transport	Equipment bay of long-mission aircraft	4.0
Airborne, uninhabited, fighter	Equipment bay of high-performance aircraft	8.0
Naval, unsheltered	Engine room of a surface ship	5.0
Missile, launch	Missile	10.0

Table E–7. MIL-HDBK-217C, notice 1 complexity factors.

Density/Function	C_1	C_2
Bipolar SSI/MSI	$7.48 (10)^{-4}(N_G)^{0.654}$	$2.19 (10)^{-4} \cdot (N_G)^{0.364}$
MOS SSI/MSI	$2.17 (10)^{-3}(N_G)^{0.357}$	$3.11 (10)^{-4} \cdot (N_G)^{0.178}$
Linear	$1.57 (10)^{-3}(N_T)^{0.780}$	$8(10)^{-4}(N_T)^{0.535}$
Bipolar LSI $(100 < N_G < 20,000)$	$1.48 (10)^{-3}(N_G)^{0.506}$	$3.2 (10)^{-4}(N_G)^{0.279}$
MOS LSI $(100 < N_G < 20,000)$	$1.75 (10)^{-3}(N_G)^{0.4}$	$2.52 (10)^{-4} \cdot (N_G)^{0.226}$
Bipolar RAM $(B \leqslant 16,384)$	$2.2 (10)^{-3}(B)^{0.576}$	$4(10)^{-5}(B)^{0.554}$
Dynamic MOS RAM $(B \leqslant 65,536)$	$5(10)^{-4}(B)^{0.610}$	$3(10)^{-5}(B)^{0.585}$

(Table continues on next page)

Table E–7 —*Continued*

Density/Function	C_1	C_2
Static MOS RAM $(B \leqslant 65,536)$	$6(10)^{-4}(B)^{0.653}$	$4(10)^{-5}(B)^{0.609}$
Bipolar ROM, PROM $(B \leqslant 65,536)$	$8.8\,(10)^{-4}(B)^{0.388}$	$4.5\,(10)^{-5}(B)^{0.378}$
MOS ROM, PROM $(B \leqslant 65,536)$	$1.2\,(10)^{-3}(B)^{0.425}$	$6.6\,(10)^{-5}(B)^{0.399}$

Key: N_G is the number of gates
N_T is the number of transistors
B is the number of bits

C_1, C_2

C_1 and C_2 are a function of the device complexity and the device function as given in Table E-7.

C_3

C_3 is a function of package complexity as given in Table E-8.

REFERENCE

U.S. Department of Defense [1979, 1980].

Table E–8. MIL-HDBK-217C, notice 1 package complexity.

Package Type	C_3
Hermetic DIPs with solder or weld seals	$2.8\,(10)^{-4}(N_P)^{1.08}$
Hermetic DIPs with glass seals	$9(10)^{-5}(N_P)^{1.51}$
Nonhermetic DIPs	$2(10)^{-4}(N_P)^{1.23}$
Hermetic Flatpacks	$3(10)^{-5}(N_P)^{1.82}$
Hermetic Cans	$3(10)^{-5}(N_P)^{2.01}$

Note: N_P is the number of pins on the package connected to the device substrate.

References

[Abraham, 1975]
Abraham, J. A. "A Combinatorial Solution to the Reliability of Interwoven Redundant Logic Networks." *IEEE Trans. Comp.* C-24 (May 1975): 578–584.

[Abraham, Gosh, and Ray-Chaudhuri, 1968]
Abraham, C. T.; S. P. Ghosh; and D. K. Ray-Chaudhuri. "File Organization Schemes Based on Finite Geometries. *Information and Control* 12, no. 2 (February 1968): 143–163.

[Abraham and Siewiorek, 1974]
Abraham, J. A., and D. P. Siewiorek. "An Algorithm for the Accurate Reliability Evaluation of Triple Modular Redundancy Networks." *IEEE Trans. Comp.* C-23 (July 1974): 682–692.

[Abramson, 1959]
Abramson, N. M. "A Class of Systematic Codes for Non-Independent Errors." *IRE Trans. Information Theory* IT-5, no. 4 (December 1959): 150–157.

[Adshead, Jain, and Knowles, 1972]
Adshead, H. G.; G. C. Jain; and A. J. Knowles. "New Dimensions in Automatic Logic Testing and Diagnostics." In *Proceedings International Conference on Computer Aided Design,* Institute of Electrical Engineers, 1972, pp. 112–118.

[Aggarwal and Rai, 1978]
Aggarwal, K. K., and S. Rai. "Symbolic Reliability Evaluation Using Logical Signal Relations." *IEEE Trans. Reliability* R-27, no. 3 (August 1978): 202–205.

[Agnew, Forbes, and Stieglitz, 1967]
Agnew, P. W.; R. E. Forbes; and C. B. Stieglitz. "An Approach to Self-Repairing Computers." In *Digest 1st Annual IEEE Computer Conf.,* Chicago, 1967 60–64.

[Albert, 1956]
Albert, A. A. *Fundamental Concepts of Higher Algebra.* Chicago: University of Chicago Press, 1956.

[Almassy, 1979]
Almassy, G. "Limits of Models in Reliability Engineering." In *Proc. Annual Reliability and Maintainability Symposium, 1979,* IEEE Reliability Society, 1979, pp. 364–367.

[Alonso, Hopkins, and Thaler, 1966]
Alonso, R. L.; A. L. Hopkins, Jr.; and H. A. Thaler. "Design Criteria for a Spacecraft Computer," In *Proc. Seminar on Spaceborne Multiprocessors,* Boston, 1966. pp. 21–28

[Alonso, Hopkins, and Thaler, 1967]
Alonso, R. L.; A. L. Hopkins, Jr.; and H. A. Thaler. "A Multiprocessing Structure." In *Digest 1st IEEE Computer Conf.,* Chicago, 1967. pp. 56–60

[Anderson, 1971]
Anderson, D. A. "Design of Self-Checking Digital Networks Using Code Techniques." Ph.D. diss., University of Illinois, 1971.

[Anderson and Jensen, 1975]
Anderson, G. A., and E. D. Jensen. "Computer Interconnection Structures: Taxonomy Characteristics and Examples." *ACM Computing Surveys,* 7, no. 4 (December 1975): 197–215.

[Anderson and Lee, 1979]
Anderson, T., and P. A. Lee. "The Provision of Recoverable Interfaces." In *Proceedings 9th International Fault Tolerant Computing Symposium, IEEE Computer Society, Madison, WI* 1979, pp. 87–94.

[Anderson and Macri, 1967]
Anderson, J. E., and F. J. Macri. "Multiple Redundancy Applications in a Computer." In *Proc. Annual Symp. Rel.,* Washington, DC, 1967. pp. 553–562

[Anderson and Metze, 1973]
Anderson, D. A., and G. Metze. "Design of Totally Self-Checking Check Circuits for m-out-of-n Codes." *IEEE Trans. Comp.* C-22 (March 1973): 263–269.

[Andrews et al., 1969]
Andrews, R. J.; J. J. Driscoll; J. A. Herndon; P. C. Richards; and L. R. Roberts. "Service Features and Call Processing Plan." *Bell Systems Tech. Journal,* 48, no. 8 (October 1969): pp. 2713–2764.

[ARINC, 1964]
ARINC Research Corporation. *Reliability Engineering.* Englewood Cliffs, NJ: Prentice-Hall, 1964.

[Armstrong, 1961]
Armstrong, D. B. "A General Method of Applying Error Correction to Synchronous Digital Systems." *Bell System Tech. Journal* 40 (March 1961): 577–593.

[Arulpragasm and Swarz, 1980]
Arulpragasm, J. A., and R. S. Swarz. "A Design for Process State Preservation on Storage Unit Failure." In *Digest of 10th*

International Fault Tolerant Computing Symposium, IEEE Computer Society, Kyoto, Japan, pp. 47–52.

[Ashjaee and Reddy, 1976]
Ashjaee, and S. M. Reddy. "On Totally Self-Checking Checkers for Separable Codes." In *Proceedings 6th International Fault Tolerant Computing Symposium,* IEEE Computer Society, Pittsburgh, PA, 1976, pp. 151–156

[Ault et al., 1964]
Ault, C. F.; L. E. Gallaher; T. S. Greenwood; and D. C. Koehler. "No. 1 ESS Program Store." *Bell System Tech. Journal* 43 (September 1964): 2097–2146.

[Ault, et al., 1977]
Ault, C. F.; J. H. Brewster; T. S. Greenwood; R. E. Haglund; W. A. Read, and M. W. Rolund, "1A Processor-Memory Systems." *Bell System Tech. Journal,* vol. 56, no. 2 (February 1977): 181–205.

[Avizienis, 1964]
Avizienis, A. "A Set of Algorithms for a Diagnosable Arithmetic Unit." Jet Propulsion Lab 34–546. Pasadena, CA, 1964.

[Avizienis, 1965]
Avizienis, A. "A Study of the Effectiveness of Fault-Detecting Codes for Binary Arithmetic." Jet Propulsion Lab 32–711. Pasadena, CA, 1965.

[Avizienis, 1966a]
Avizienis, A. "Codes for Fault Detection in Digital Arithmetic Processors." In W. A. Kalenich, ed., *Information Processing 1965: Proc. IFIP Congress,* vol. 2, Washington, DC: Spartan Books, 1966, p. 634.

[Avizienis, 1966b]
Avizienis, A. "The Diagnosable Arithmetic Processor." In *Space Programs Summary.* Pasadena, CA: Jet Propulsion Lab, 1966, pp. 76–80.

[Avizienis, 1967a]
Avizienis, A. "Concurrent Diagnosis of Arithmetic Processors." In *Digest 1st Annual IEEE Computer Conf.,* 1967, pp. 34–37.

[Avizienis, 1967b]
Avizienis, A. "Application of Codes in Digital Computer Systems." In *International Conference on Information Theory,* San Remo, Italy, 1967.

[Avizienis, 1967c]
Avizienis,, A. "Design of Fault-Tolerant Computers." In *FJCC, AFIPS Conf. Proc.,* vol. 31, Washington, DC: Thompson, 1967, pp. 733–743.

[Avizienis, 1968]
Avizienis, A. "An Experimental Self-Repairing Computer." In A. J. H. Morrell, ed., *Information Processing 1968, Proc. IFIP Congress,* vol. 2, North Holland, 1968, pp. 872–877.

[Avizienis, 1969]
Avizienis, A. "Digital Fault Diagnosis by Low-Cost Arithmetical Coding Techniques." In *Proc. Purdue Centennial Year Symposium Information Processing,* vol. 1, Lafayette, IN, 1969. pp. 81–91.

[Avizienis, 1971]
Avizienis, A. "Arithmetic Error Codes: Cost and Effectiveness Studies for Application in Digital System Design." *IEEE Trans. Comp.* C-20 (November 1971): 1322–1331.

[Avizienis, 1973]
Avizienis, A. "Arithmetic Algorithms for Error-Coded Operands." *IEEE Trans. Comp.* C-22 (June 1973): 566–572.

[Avizienis, 1975]
Avizienis, A. "Architecture of Fault-Tolerant Computing Systems." In *Digest Fifth Int. Symp. Fault-Tolerant Computing,* IEEE Computer Society, Paris, France, 1975, pp. 3–16.

[Avizienis, 1976]
Avizienis, A. "Approaches to Computer Reliability—Then and Now." In *AFIPS Conf. Proc.* vol. 45, Montvale, NJ, AFIPS Press, 1976, pp. 401–411

[Avizienis, 1977]
Avizienis, A. "Fault-Tolerant Computing—Progress, Problems, and Prospects." In *Proceedings IFIP Congress,* North Holland, 1977, pp. 405–420.

[Avizienis, 1978]
Avizienis, A. "Fault-Tolerance: The Survival Attribute of Digital Systems." *Proceedings of the IEEE,* vol. 66 (October 1978): 1109–1125.

[Avizienis, et al., 1969]
Avizienis, A.; F. P. Mathur; D. A. Rennels; and J. A. Rohr. "Automatic Maintenance of Aerospace Computers and Spacecraft Information and Control Systems." In *Proc. AIAA Aerosp. Comput. Syst. Conf.,* AIAA Paper 69-966, 1969.

[Avizienis, et al., 1971]
Avizienis, A.; G. C. Gilley; F. P. Mathur; D. A. Rennels; J. A. Rohr; and D. K. Rubin. "The STAR (Self-Testing and Repairing) Computer: An Investigation on the Theory and Practice of Fault-Tolerant Computer Design." *IEEE Trans. Comp.* C-20 (October 1971): 1312–1321.

[AWST, 1981]
"Velocity, Altitude Regimes to Push Computer Limits." *Aviation Week & Space Technology,* 6 April 1981, pp. 49–51.

[Ball, 1980]
Ball, M. O. "Complexity of Network Reliability Computations." *Networks* 10 (1980): 153–5.

[Ball and Hardie, 1967]
Ball, M. O. and F. Hardie. "Effects and Detection of Intermittent Failures in Digital Systems." IBM 67-825-2137. 1967.

[Barker, 1953]
Barker, R. H. "Group Synchronizing of Binary Digital Systems." In W. Jackson, ed., Communication Theory, vol. 4. New York: Academic Press, 1953, pp. 273–287.

[Barlow, 1965]
Barlow, R. E., and F. Proschan. Mathematical Theory of Reliability. New York: Wiley, 1965.

[Barlow, 1975]
Barlow, R. E., and F. Proschan. Statistical Theory of Reliability and Life Testing: Probability Models. New York: Holt, Rinehart and Winston, 1975.

[Barnes et al, 1968]
Barnes, G. H., R. M. Brown, M. Kato, D. J. Kuch, D. L. Skotnick, and R. A. Stokes. "The Illiac IV Computer." IEEE Trans. Comp. C-17 (August 1968): 746–757.

[Barsi and Maestrini, 1973]
Barsi, F., and R. Maestrini. "Error Correcting Properties of Redundant Residue Number Systems." IEEE Trans. Comp. C-22 (March 1973): 307–924.

[Barsi and Maestrini, 1974]
Barsi, F., and P. Maestrini. "Error Detection and Correction by Product Codes in Residue Number Systems." IEEE Trans. Comp. C-23 (September 1974): 915–924.

[Bartlett, 1978]
Bartlett, J. F. " A 'NonStop' Operating System." In Proceedings Hawaii Int. Conf. of System Sciences. Honolulu, HI 1978, pp. 103–119

[Bartow and McGuire, 1970]
Bartow, N. and R. McGuire. "System/360 Model 85 Microdiagnostics," SJCC AFIPS Conf. Proc., Vol. 36. Montvale, NJ: AFIPS Press, 1970, pp. 191–197.

[Bashkow, Friets, and Karson, 1963]
Bashkow, T. R.; J. Friets; and A. Karson. "A Programming System for Detection and Diagnosis of Machine Malfunctions." IEEE Trans. Elec. Comp. EC-12, no. 1 (February 1963): pp. 10-17.

[Baskin, Borgerson, and Roberts, 1972]
Baskin, H. B.; B. R. Borgerson; and R. Roberts. "PRIME–A Modular Architecture for Terminal Oriented Systems." In Conf. Proc., vol. 40, AFIPS Press, Montvale, NJ: 1972, pp. 431–437.

[Beaudry, 1978]
Beaudry, M. D. "Performance Related Reliability Measures for Computing Systems," IEEE Trans. Comp. C-27 (June 1978): 540–547.

[Becker, et al., 1978]
Becker, J. O.; J. G. Cheoalier; R. K. Eisenhart; J. H. Forster; A. W. Fulton; W. L. Harrod. "1A Processor—Technology and Physical Design." Bell System Tech. Journal 56 (February 1977): 207–236.

[Beister, 1968]
Beister, J. "On the Implementation of Failure-Tolerant Counters." IEEE Trans. Comp. C-17 (September 1968): 885–886.

[Bell and Newell, 1971]
Bell, C. G., and A. Newell. Computer Structures: Readings and Examples, New York: McGraw-Hill, 1971.

[Bell and Strecker, 1976]
Bell, C. G., and W. D. Strecker. "Computer Structures: What Have We Learned from the PDP-11?" Proc. Third Ann. Symp. on Comp Architecture, Clearwater FL 1976 (IEEE/ACM) pp. 1-14..

[Bell et al., 1970]
Bell, C .G.; R. Cady; H. McFarland; B. Delaji; J. O'Loughlin; R. Noonan; and W. Wulf. "A New Architecture for Mini-Computers: The DEC PDP-11." SJCC, AFIPS conf. Proc, vol. 36, 1970, pp. 657–675.

[Bell et al., 1978]
Bell, C. G.; A. Kotok; T. N. Hastings; and R. Hill. "The Evolution of the DECsystem 10." Comm. ACM. 21 (January 1978): 44–63.

[Bellis, 1978]
Bellis, H. "Comparing Analytical Reliability Models to Hard and Transient Failure Data." Master's thesis, Carnegie-Mellon University Department of Electrical Engineering, 1987.

[Bennetts, 1972]
Bennetts, R. G. "A Realistic Approach to Fault Detection Test Set Generation for Combinational Logic Circuits," BCS Computer Journal 15, no. 3 (1972): 238–246.

[Bennetts, 1973]
Bennetts, R. G. "A Contribution to the Boolean Difference Procedure for Generating Tests for Combinational Logic Circuits." In BCS Datafair Conf. Proc., vol. 2, 1973, pp. 431–436.

[Bennetts, 1974]
Bennetts, R. G. "Automatic Test Sequence Generation for Complex Digital Networks." in Proc. Automatic Testing, 1974 Conference, 1974, pp. 27–36.

[Bennetts, 1975]
Bennetts, R. G. "On the Analysis of Fault Trees" IEEE Trans. Reliability R-24, (August 1975): 175–185.

[Bennetts, 1976]
Bennetts, R. G. "An Evaluation of Techniques for Designing Easily-Tested Combinational Logic Circuits." In Proc. Automatic Testing, 1976 Conference, 1976 pp. 94–106.

[Bennetts and Lewin, 1971]
Bennetts, R. G., and D. W. Lewing "Fault Diagnosis of Digital Systems—A Review." *Computer* Vol. 4, no. 4 (July/August 1971): 12–20.

[Bennetts and Scott, 1976]
Bennetts, R. B., and R. V. Scott. "Recent Developments in the Theory and Practice of Testable Logic Design." *Computer* vol. 9, no. 6 (June 1976): pp. 47–62.

[Bennetts et al., 1975]
Bennetts, R. G.; D. C. Brittle; A. C. Prior; and J. L. Washington. "A Modular Approach to Test Sequence Generation for Large Digital Networks." *Digital Processes* 1, no. 1 (1975): pp. 3–24.

[Berger, 1961]
Berger, J. M. "A Note on Burst Error Detection Codes for Asymmetric Channels." *Information and Control* 4, no. 3 (March 1961): pp. 68–73

[Berger and Lawrence, 1974]
Berger, R. W.; and K. Lawrence. "Estimating Weibull Parameters by Linear and Nonlinear Regression." *Technometrics,* 16, no. 4 (November 1974): 617–619.

[Berger and Mandelbrot, 1963]
Berger, J. M., and B. Mandelbrot. "A New Model for Error Clustering in Telephone Circuits." *IBM J. Res. and Dev.* 7, no. 3 (July 1963): 224–236.

[Berlekamp, 1964]
Berlekamp, E. R. "Note on Recurrent Codes." *IEEE Trans. Info. Theory* IT-10, no. 3 (July 1964): 257–259.

[Berlekamp, 1968]
Berlekamp, E. R. *Algebraic Coding Theory.* New York: McGraw-Hill, 1968.

[Beuscher et al., 1969]
Beusher, H. J.; G. E. Fessler; D. W. Huffman; P. J. Kennedy; and E. Nussbaum. "Administration and Maintenance Plan." *Bell System Tech. Journal* 48, no. 8 (October 1969): 2765–2815.

[Bhatt and Kinney, 1978]
Bhatt, A. K., and L. L. Kinney. "A High Speed Parallel Encoder/Decoder for b-Adjacent Error-Checking Codes." In *Proc. Third USA–Japan Computer Conf.* AFIPS, 1978, pp. 203–207.

[Birdsall and Ristenblatt, 1958]
Birdsall, T. G., and M. P. Ristenblatt. "Introduction to Linear Shift-Register Generated Sequences." Ann Arbor: University of Michigan Research Institute, 1958.

[Black, Sundberg, and Walker, 1977]
Black, C. J.: C. E. Sundberg; and W. K. S. Walker. "Development of a Spaceborne Memory with a Single Error and Era-
sure Correction Scheme," In *Digest of Seventh International Fault Tolerant Computing Symposium,* IEEE Computer Society, Los Angeles, CA, 1977, pp. 50–55.

[Boone, Liebergot, and Sedmak, 1980]
Boone, L. A.; H. L. Liebergot; and R. M. Sedmak. "Availability, Reliability, and Maintainability Aspects of the Sperry Univac 1100/60." In *Digest of Ten International Fault-Tolerant Computing Symposium,* Kyoto, Japan, IEEE Computer Society, 1980, pp. 3–8.

[Borgerson and Freitas, 1975]
Borgerson, B. R., and R. F. Freitas. "A Reliability Model for Gracefully Degrading and Standby-Sparing Systems." *IEEE Trans. Comp.* (May 1975): 517–525.

[Borgerson, Hanson, and Hartley, 1978]
Borgerson, B. R.; M. L. Hanson; and P. A. Hartley. "The Evolution of the Sperry Univac 1100 Series: A History, Analysis and Projection." *Comm. ACM* 1 (January 1978): 25–43.

[Borgerson et al., 1979]
Borgerson, B. R.; M. D. Godfrey; P. E. Hagerty; and T. R. Rykkem. "The Architecture of Sperry Univac 1100 Series Systems." In *Digest, Sixth Ann. Int. Symp. on Computer Architecture,* Philadelphia, PA: IEEE/ACM, 1979, pp. 137–146.

[Bose and Caldwell, 1967]
Bose, R. C., and J. G. Caldwell. "Synchronizable Error-Correcting Codes." *Information and Control* 10, no 6 (June 1967): 616–630.

[Bose and Ray-Chaudhuri, 1960a]
Bose, R. C., and D. K. Ray-Chaudhuri. "On a Class of Error Correcting Binary Group Codes." *Information and Control* 3, no. 1 (March 1960): 68–79.

[Bose and Ray-Chaudhuri, 1960b]
Bose, R. C., and D. K. Ray-Chaudhuri. "Further Results on Error-Correcting Binary Group Codes." *Information and Control* 3, no. 3 (September 1960): 279–290.

[Bossen, 1970]
Bossen, D. C. "b-Adjacent Error Correction." *IBM J. Res. and Dev.* 14, no. 4 (July 1970): 402–408.

[Bossen and Hong, 1971]
Bossen, D. C., and S. J. Hong. "Cause and Effect Analysis for Multiple Fault Detection in Combinational Networks." *IEEE Trans. Comp.* C-20, (November 1971): 1252–1257.

[Boswell, 1972]
Boswell, F. R. "Designing Testability into Complex Logic Boards." *Electronics International* 45, no. 17 (14 August 1972): 116–119.

[Bouricius, Carter, and Schneider, 1969a]
Bouricius, W. G.; W. C. Carter; and P. R. Schneider. "Reli-

ability Modeling Techniques for Self-Repairing Computer Systems." In *Proc. 24th National Conference of the ACM*, ACM, 1969, pp. 295–309.

[Bouricius, Carter, and Schneider, 1969b]
Bouricius, W. G.; W. C. Carter; and P. R. Schneider. "Reliability Modeling Techniques and Trade-Off Studies for Self-Repairing Computers." IBM RC2378, 1969.

[Bouricius et al., 1971]
Bouricius, W. G.; W. C. Carter; D. C. Jessep; P. R. Schneider; and A. B. Wadia. "Reliability Modeling for Fault-Tolerant Computers." *IEEE Trans. Comp.* C-20 (November 1971): 1306–1311.

[Bowman et al. 1977]
Bowman, P. W.; M. R. Diebman; F. M. Gaety; R. F. Kranzmann; E. H. Stredde; and R. J. Watters. "1A Processor—Maintenance Software." *Bell System Tech. Journal*, 56 (February 1977) pp. 225–287.

[Bozorgui-Nesbat and McCluskey, 1980]
Bozorgui-Nesbat, S., and E. J. McCluskey. "Structured Design for Testability to Eliminate Test Pattern Generation." In *Digest of Tenth International Fault Tolerant Computing Symposium*, IEEE Computer Society, 1980, pp. 158–163.

[Bressler, Kraley, and Michel, 1975]
Bressler, R. D.; M. F. Kraley; and A. Michel. "Pluribus: A Multiprocessor for Comminications Networks." In *14th Annual ACM/NBS Technical Symp.--Computing in the Mid-70s: An Assessment*, 1975, pp. 13–19.

[Breuer, 1973]
Breuer, M. A. "Testing for Intermittent Faults in Digital Circuits." *IEEE Trans. Comp.* C-22 (March 1973): 241–246.

[Breuer and Friedman, 1976]
Breuer, M. A., and A. D. Friedman.*Diagnosis and Reliable Design of Digital Systems*. Potomac, MD: Computer Science Press, 1976.

[Breuer and Friedman, 1980]
Breuer, M. A., and A. D. Friedman. "Functional Level Primitives in Test Generation."*IEEE Trans. Comp* C-29 (March 1980): 223–235.

[Brinch Hansen, 1970]
Brinch Hansen, P. "The Nucleus of a Multi-programming System." *Comm. ACM.* 13 (April 1970): 238–241.

[Brodsky, 1980]
Brodsky, M. "Hardening RAMs Against Soft Errors." *Electronics*, Vol. 53, April 24, 1980. McGraw-Hill.

[Brown, 1960]
Brown, D. T. "Error Detecting and Correcting Binary Codes for Arithmetic Operations." *IRE Trans. Elec. Comp.* EC-9, no. 3 (September 1960): 333–337.

[Brown, Tierney, and Wasserman, 1961]
Brown, W. G.; J. Tierney; and R. Wasserman. "Improvement of Electronic-Computer Reliability Through the Use of Redundancy." *IRE Trans. Elec. Comp.* EC-10, no. 3 (September 1961): 407–416.

[Browne, et al., 1969]
Browne, T. E.; T. M. Quinn; W. N. Toy; and J. E. Yates. "No. 2 ESS Control Unit System." *Bell System Tech. Journal*, 48, no. 2 (October 1969): 443–476.

[Brule, Johnson, and Kletsky, 1960]
Brule, J. D.; R. A. Johnson; and E.J. Kletsky. "Diagnosis of Equipment Failures." *IRE Trans. Reliability and Quality Control* RQC-9 (April 1960): 23–24.

[Budlong, et al. 1977]
Budlong, A. H.; B. G. DeLiegish; I. M. Neville; J. S. Nowak; J. L. Quinn; and F. W. Wendloud. "1A Processor—Control System." *Bell System Tech. Journal* 56, no. 2 (February 1977): 135–179.

[Bussgang, 1965]
Bussgang, J. J. "Some Properties of Binary Convolutional Code Generators." *IEEE Trans. Info Theory* IT-11, no. 1 (January 1965): 90–100.

[Butner and Iyer, 1980]
Butner, S. E., and R. K. Iyer. "A Statistical Study of Reliability and System Load at SLAC." Center for Reliable Computing, Stanford University, 1980.

[Cagle, et al., 1964]
Cagle, W. B.; R. S. Menne; R. S. Skinner; R. E. Staehler; and M. D. Underwood. "No 1 ESS Logic Circuits and Their Application to the Design of the Central Control." *Bell System Tech. Journal* 43, no. 5, Part 1 (September 1964): 2055–2095.

[Carter, Duke, and Jessep, 1971]
Carter, W. C.; K. A. Duke; and D. C. Jessep. "A Simple Self-Testing Decoder Checking Circuit." *IEEE Trans. Comp.* C-20 (November 1971): 1413–1414.

[Carter, Duke, and Jessep, 1973]
Carter, W. C.; K. A. Duke; and D. C. Jessup. "Lookaside Techniques for Minimum Circuit Memory Translators." *IEEE Trans. Comp.* C-20 (March 1973): 283–289.

[Carter and McCarthy, 1976]
Carter, W. C.; and C. E. McCarthy. "Implementation of an Experimental Fault-Tolerant Memory System." *IEEE Trans. Comp.* C-25 (June 1976): 557–568.

[Carter et al., 1964]
Carter, W. C., H. C., Montgomery, R. J. Preiss, and H. J. Reinheimer. "Design of Serviceability Features for the IBM System/360," *IBM Journal of Research and Development*, vol. 8, no. 2, April 1964, pp. 115–126.

[Carter and Schneider, 1968]
Carter, W. C.; and P. R. Schneider. "Design of Dynamically Checked Computers." In *Proceedings IFIP Congress,* vol. 2. North-Holland Publ. Co. 1968, pp. 878–883.

[Carter and Wadia, 1980]
Carter, W. C.; and A. B. Wadia. "Design and Analysis of Codes and Their Self-Checking Circuit Implementations for Correction and Detection of Multiple b-Adjacent Errors." In *Digest of Tenth International Fault-Tolerant Computing Symposium,* IEEE Computer Society, Kyoto Japan 1980, pp. 35–40.

[Carter, Wadia, and Jessep, 1972]
Carter, W. C.; A. B. Wadia; and D. C. Jessep, Jr. "Computer Error Control by Testable Morphic Boolean Functions—A Way of Removing Hardcore." In *Digest of Second Int. Symp. on Fault-Tolerant Computing,* IEEE Computer Society, Boston, MA 1972, pp. 154–159.

[Castillo, 1980]
Castillo, X. "Workload, Performance, and Reliability of Digital Computing Systems." Carnegie-Mellon University Technical Report, Computer Science Department, 1980.

[Castillo and Siewiorek, 1980]
Castillo, X., and D. P. Siewiorek. "A Performance-Reliability Model for Computing Systems." *Digest Tenth Int. Fault-Tolerant Computing Symposium,* Kyoto, Japan. 1980, pp. 187–192.

[Chandy and Ramamoorthy, 1972]
Chandy, K. M., and C. V. Ramamoorthy. "Rollback and Recovery Strategies for Computer Programs." *IEEE Trans. Comp.* C-21 (June 1972): 546–556.

[Chaney, Ornstein, and Littlefield, 1972]
Chaney, T. J.; S. M. Ornstein; and W. M. Littlefield. "Beware the Synchronizer." *CompCon,* 1972, pp. 317–319.

[Chang, 1965]
Chang, H. Y. "An Algorithm for Selecting an Optimum Set of Diagnostic Tests." *IEEE Trans. Elec. Comp.* EC-14 (October 1965): 705–711.

[Chang, 1968]
Chang, H. Y. "A Distinguishability Criterion for Selecting Efficient Diagnostic Tests." In *SJCC, AFIPS Conf. Proc.* vol. 32, Washington, DC: Thompson, 1968, pp. 529–534.

[Chang, Manning, and Metze, 1970]
Chang, H. Y.; E. G. Manning; and G. Metze. *Fault Diagnosis of Digital Systems.* New York: Wiley Interscience, 1970.

[Chang, Smith, and Walford, 1974]
Chang, H. Y.; G. W. Smith, Jr.; and R. B. Walford. "LAMP: System Description." *Bell System Tech. Journal* 53 (October 1974): 1431–1449.

[Chen and Avizienis, 1978]
Chen, L., and A. Avizienis. "N-Version Programming: A Fault-Tolerance Approach to Reliability of Software Opera-

tion." In *Digest of Eighth International Fault-Tolerant Computing Symposium,* IEEE Computer Society, Toulouse. France, 1978, pp. 3–9.

[Cheung, 1980]
Cheung, R. C. "A User-Oriented Software Reliability Model," *IEEE Trans. Soft. Eng.* SE-6, no. 6 (March 1980) 118–125.

[Cheung and Ramamoorthy, 1975]
Cheung, R. C., and C. V. Ramamoorthy. "Optimal Measurement of Program Path Frequencies and its Applications." In *Proc. Int. Federation Automatic Control Congress* 1975.

[Chiang and Standridge, 1975]
Chiang, A. C. L., and R. Standridge. "Pattern Sensitivity on 4K RAM Devices." *Computer Design* 14, no. 2 (February 1975): 88–91.

[Chien, 1960]
Chien, R. T. "A Class of Optimal Noiseless Load-Sharing Matrix Switches." *IBM J. Res. and Dev.* 4, no. 4 (October 1960): 414–417.

[Chien, 1964]
Chien, R. T. "Cyclic Decoding Procedures for Bose-Chaudhuri-Hocquenghem Codes." *IEEE Trans. Info. Theory* IT-10, no. 4 (October 1964): 357–363.

[Chien and Frazer, 1966]
Chien, R. T., and D. Frazer. "An Application of Coding Theory to Document Retrieval." *IEEE Trans. Info. Theory* IT-12, no. 2 (April 1966): 92–96.

[Chien, Hong, and Preparata, 1968]
Chien, R. T.; S. J. Hong; and F. P. Preparata. "Some Contributions to the Theory of Arithmetic Codes." In *Proc. Hawaii Int. Conf. on Systems Sciences,* University of Hawaii Press, Honolulu, Hawaii, 1968, pp. 460–462.

[Chinal, 1977]
Chinal, J. P. "High Speed Parity Prediction for Binary Adders." In *Digest Seventh International Fault-Tolerant Computing Symposium,* IEEE Computer Society, Los Angeles, CA, 1977, p. 190.

[Chou and Abraham, 1980]
Chou, T. C. K., and J. A. Abraham. "Performance/Availability Model of Shared Resource Multiprocessors." *IEEE Trans. Reliability* R-29, no. 1 (April 1980): 70–74.

[Chow, n.d.]
Chow, D. K. "A Geometric Approach to Coding Theory with Application to Information Retrieval." University of Illinois Report R-368. Urbana, IL, n.d.

[Constantine, 1958]
Constantine, G., Jr. "A Load-Sharing Matrix Switch." *IBM J. Res. and Dev.* 2, no. 3 (July 1958): 204–211.

[Cook et al., 1973]
Cook, R. W.; W. H. Sisson; T. F. Storey; and W. N. Toy. "De-

sign of a Self-Checking Microprogram Control." *IEEE Trans. Comp.* C-22 (March 1973): 255–262.

[Cooper and Chow, 1976]
Cooper, A. E., and W. T. Chow. "Development of On-Board Space Computer Systems." *IBM J. Res. and Dev.* 20, no. 1 (January 1976): 5–19.

[Cornell and Halstead, 1976]
Cornell, L., and M. H. Halstead. "Predicting the Number of Bugs Expected in a Program Module." Purdue University CSD-TR-20r. 1976.

[Costes, Landrault, and Laprie, 1978]
Costes, A.; C. Landrault; and J. C. Laprie. "Reliability and Availability Models for Maintained Systems Featuring Hardware Failures and Design Faults." *IEEE Trans. Comp.* C-27 (June 1978): 548–560.

[Craig, 1964]
Craig, E. J. *Laplace and Fourier Transforms for Electrical Engineers.* New York; Holt, Rinehart and Winston, 1964.

[Craig, 1980]
Craig, S. R. "Incoming Inspection and Test Programs." *Electronics Test,* October 1980, pp. 58–73.

[Crouzet and Landrault, 1980]
Crouzet, Y., and C. Landrault. "Design of Self-Checking MOS LSI Circuits, Application to a Four-Bit Microprocessor." *IEEE Trans. Comp.* C-29 (June 1980): 532–537.

[Daly, Hopkins, and McKenna, 1973]
Daly, W. M.; A.L. Hopkins, Jr.; and J. F. McKenna Jr. "A Fault-Tolerant Clocking System." In *Dig. Third Int. Symp. Fault-Tolerant Computing,* IEEE Computer Society, 1973.

[Dandapani and Reddy, 1974]
Dandapani, R., and S. M. Reddy. "On the Design of Logic Networks with Redundancy and Testability Considerations." *IEEE Trans. Comp.* C-23 (November 1974): 1139–1149.

[Dandapani, Reddy, and Robinson, 1970]
Dandapani, R.; S. M. Reddy; and J. P. Robinson. "An Investigation into Redundancy and Testability of Combinational Logic Networks." AD 174-157, 1970.

[Datamation, 1979]
"The Microarchitecture of Univac's 1100/60." *Datamation,* July 1979, pp. 173-178.

[Davies and Wakerly, 1978]
Davies, D.; and J. F. Wakerly. "Synchronization and Matching in Redundant Systems." *IEEE Trans. Comp.* C-27 (June 1978): 531–539.

[DeAngelis and Lauro, 1976]
DeAngelis, D., and J. A. Lauro. "Software Recovery in the Fault-Tolerant Spaceborne Computer." In *Digest Sixth International Fault Tolerant Computing Symposium,* IEEE Computer Society, Pittsburgh, PA, 1976, pp. 143–148.

[DEC, 1971]
Digital Equipment Corporation. *PDP-8/e Engineering Circuit Diagrams.* Bedford, MA, 1971.

[DEC, 1972]
Digital Equipment Corporation. *PDP-8/e Maintenance Manual.* DEC-8E-HR1B-D. Bedford, MA, 1972.

[DEC, 1975a]
Digital Equipment Corporation. *LSI-11 PDP-11/03 User's Manual.* Bedford, MA, 1975.

[DEC, 1975b]
Digital Equipment Corporation. *RXV-11 User's Manual.* Bedford, MA, 1975.

[DEC, 1975c]
Digital Equipment Corporation. "A Reliability Report. " Bedford, MA, 1975.

[DEC, 1977]
Digital Equipment Corporation. *VAX-11/780 Architecture Handbook.* Bedford, MA, 1977.

[DEC, 1978]
Digital Equipment Corporation *TOPS-10 and TOPS-20 SYSERR Manual.* Bedford, MA, 1978.

[DEC, 1979]
Digital Equipment Corporation. *PDP-11 Bus Handbook.* Bedford, MA, 1979.

[Deckert et al., 1977]
Deckert, J. C.; M. N. Desai; J. J. Deyst; and A. J. Willsky. "F8-DFBW Sensor Failure Identification Using Analytic Redundancy." *IEEE Trans. Autom. Contr.* AC-22, no. 5 (October 1977): 795–803.

[DeGroot, 1975]
DeGroot, M. H. *Probability and Statistics.* Reading, MA: Addison-Wesley, 1975.

[Dennis, 1974]
Dennis, N. G. "Ultrareliable Voter Switches, with a Bibliography of Mechanization." *Microelectronics and Reliability,* August 1974, pp. 299–308.

[DeSousa and Mathur, 1978]
De Sousa, P. T.; and F. P. Mathur. "Sift-Out Modular Redundancy." *IEEE Trans. Comp.* C-27 (July 1978): 624–627.

[Deyst and Hopkins]
Deyst, J. J., Jr., and A. L. Hopkins, Jr. "Highly Survivable Integrated Avionics." *Astronautics and Aeronautics,* forthcoming.

[Diaz, Azema, and Ayache, 1979]
Dias; M.; P. Azema; and J. M. Ayache. "Unified Design of Self-Checking and Fail-Safe Combinational Circuits and Sequential Machines." *IEEE Trans. Comp.* C-28 (March 1979): 276–281.

[Diaz, Geffroy, and Courvoisier, 1974]
Diaz, M.; J. C. Geffroy; and M. Courvoisier. "On-Set Realization of Fail-Safe Sequential Machines." *IEEE Trans. Comp.* C-23 (February 1974): 133–138.

[Dickinson, Jackson, and Randa, 1964]
Dickinson, M. M.; J. B. Jackson; and G. C. Randa. "Saturn V Launch Vehicle Digital Computer and Data Adapter." In *FJCC. AFIPS Conf. Proc.* Vol. 26, 1964, pp. 501–516.

[Dijkstra, 1968]
Dijkstra, E. W. "The Structure of the 'THE' Multiprogramming System." *Comm ACM.* 11 (1968): 341–346.

[Dolotta et al., 1976]
Dolotta, T. A.; M. I. Bernstein; R. S. Dickson, Jr.; N. A. France; B. A. Rosenblatt; D. M. Smith; and T. B. Steel, Jr. *Data Processing in 1980–1985.* New York: Wiley, 1976.

[Downing, Nowak, and Tuomenoksa, 1964]
Downing, R. W.; J. S. Nowak; and L. S. Tuomenoksa. "No 1 ESS Maintenance Plan." *Bell System Tech. Journal* Vol. 43 no. 5, Part 1, (September 1964): pp. 1961–2019.

[Droulette, 1971]
Droulette, D. L. "Recovery through Programming System/360–System/370." In *SJCC AFIPS Conf. Proc.* Vol. 38, AFIPS Press, Montvale, NJ, 1971, pp. 467–476.

[Eames and Spann, 1977]
Eames, S., and A. Spann. "Life Cycle Cost Analysis Utilizing Generalized Data Elements." In *Proc. 15th Annual Spring Reliability Seminar,* IEEE Boston Section, 1977, pp. 12–39.

[Eisenbies, 1967]
Eisenbies, J. L. "Conventions for Digital Data Communication Design." *IBM Syst. J.* 6, no. 4 (1967): 267–302.

[Elias, 1954]
Elias, P. "Error-Free Coding." *IRE Trans. Professional Group on Information Theory* PGIT-4 (1954): 29–37.

[Elkind, 1980a]
Elkind, S. A. "Fail Users Manual." Carnegie-Mellon University Department of Electrical Engineering, 1980.

[Elkind, 1980b]
Elkind, S. A. "Towards Automatic Design of Reliable Systems." PhD. Diss. proposal, Carnegie-Mellon University Department of Electrical Engineering, 1980.

[Elkind and Siewiorek, 1978]
Elkind, S. A., and D. P. Siewiorek: "Reliability and Performance Models for Error Correcting Memory and Register Arrays." Carnegie-Mellon University CMU-CS-78-118, 1978.

[Elkind and Siewiorek, 1980]
Elkind, S. A., and D. P. Siewiorek. "Reliability and Performance of Error-Correcting Memory and Register Arrays." *IEEE Trans. Comp.* C-29 (October 1980): 920–927.

[Elspas and Short, 1962]
Elspas, B., and R. A. Short. "A Note on Optimum Burst-Error-Correcting Codes." *IRE Trans. Information Theory* IT-8, no. 1 (January 1962): 39–42.

[Enslow, 1974]
Enslow, P. H., Jr., ed. *Multiprocessors and Parallel Processing.* New York: Wiley, 1974.

[Enslow, 1977]
Enslow, P. H., Jr. "Multiprocessor Organization—A Survey." ACM *Computing Surveys* 9 (March 1977): 103–129.

[Esary and Proschan, 1962]
Esary, J. D., and F. Proschan. "The Reliability of Coherent Systems." In Wilcox and Mann, eds., *Redundancy Techniques for Computing Systems,* Washington, DC: Spartan Books, 1962, pp. 47–61.

[Fano, 1963]
Fano, R. M. "A Heuristic Discussion of Probabilistic Decoding." *IEEE Trans. Info. Theory* IT-9, no. 2 (January 1963): 64–74.

[Farmer, 1973]
Farmer, D. E. "Algorithms for Designing Fault-Detection Experiments for Sequential Machines." *IEEE Trans. Comp.* C-22 (February 1973): 159–167.

[Ferdinand, 1974]
Ferdinand, A. E. "A Theory of Systems Complexity." *Int. J. Gen. Syst.* 1 (1974): 19–33.

[Finkelstein, 1970]
Finkelstein, H. A. "An Investigation into the Extension of Redundancy Techniques." Coordinated Science Laboratory, University of Illinois R-455. Urbana, IL, 1970.

[Fire, 1959]
Fire, P. "A Class of Multiple-Error-Correcting Binary Codes for Non-Independent Errors." Sylvania Reconnaissance Systems Laboratory RSL-E-2. Mountain View, CA, 1959.

[Fitzsimmons and Love, 1978]
Fitzsimmons, A., and T. Love. "A Review and Evaluation of Software Science." *ACM Computing Surveys* 10 (March 1978): 3–18.

[Fleckenstein, 1974]
Fleckenstein, W. O. "Bell System ESS Family—Present and Future." In *ISS Record,* Munich, Germany, 1974.

[Flehinger, 1958]
Flehinger, B. J. "Reliability Improvement through Redundancy at Various Systems Levels." *IBM J. Res. and Dev.* no. 2, (April 1958): 148–158.

[Fleischer, 1977]
Fleischer, G. E. "Voyager Altitude Control Flight Software Techniques for Fault Detection/Correction." AIAA Paper

No. 77-1058, presented at the Guidance and Control Conference, Hollywood, FL, August 1977.

[Floyd, 1967]
Floyd, R. W. "Assigning Meanings to Programs." In J. T. Schwartz, ed., *Mathematical Aspects of Computer Science,* Providence, RI. American Mathematical Society, 1967, pp. 19–32.

[Foley, 1979]
Foley, E. "The Effects of the Microelectronics Revolution on the Systems and Board Test." *Computer* 12, no. 10 (October 1979): 32–38.

[Forney, 1965]
Forney, G. D., "On Decoding BCH Codes." *IEEE Trans. Info. Theory* IT-11, no. 4 (October 1965): 549–557.

[Forney, 1966]
Forney, G. D. "Generalized Minimum Distance Coding." *IEEE Trans. Info. Theory* IT-12, no. 2 (April 1966): 125–131.

[Frank and Frisch, 1970]
Frank, H., and I. T. Frisch. "Analysis and Design of Survivable Networks." *IEEE Trans. Comm. Tech.* COM-18 (May 1970): 501–519.

[Frank and Yau, 1966]
Frank, H., and S. S. Yau. "Improving Reliability of a Sequential Machine by Error-Correcting State Assignments." *IEEE Trans. Elec. Comp.* 15 (February 1966): 111–113.

[Frechette and Tanner, 1979]
Frechette, T. J., and F. Tanner. "Support Processor Analyzer Errors Caught by Latches." *Electronics* 52, no. 23 (November 1979): McGraw-Hill, 116–118.

[Freeman and Metze, 1972]
Freeman, H. A., and G. Metze. "Fault Tolerant Computers Using 'Dotted Logic' Redundancy Techniques." *IEEE Trans. Comp.* C-21 (August 1972): 867–871.

[Freiman, 1962]
Freiman, C. V. "Optimal Error Detection Codes for Completely Asymmetric Binary Chanels." *Information and Control* 5, no. 1 (March 1962): 64–71.

[Freiman and Robinson, 1965]
Freiman, C. V., and J. P. Robinson. "A Comparison of Block and Recurrent Codes For The Correction of Independent Errors." *IEEE Trans. Info. Theory* IT-11, no. 3 (July 1965): 445–449.

[Frey, 1967]
Frey, A. H., Jr. "Adaptive Decoding without Feedback." In *Proc. Int. Symp. on Information Theory,* Athens, 1967.

[Frey and Benice, 1964]
Frey, A. H., Jr., and R. J. Benice. "An Analysis of Retransmission Systems." *IEEE Trans. Comm. Tech.* COM-12 (December 1964): 135–146.

[Friedman, 1967]
Friedman, A. D. "Fault Detection in Redundant Circuits." *IEEE Trans. Elec. Comp.* EC-16 (February 1967): 99–100.

[Friedman, 1973]
Friedman, A. D. "Easily Testable Iterative Systems." *IEEE Trans. Comp.* C-22 (December 1973): 1061–1064.

[Friedman and Menon, 1971]
Friedman, A. D., and P. R. Menon. *Fault Detection in Digital Circuits.* Englewood Cliffs, NJ: Prentice-Hall, 1971.

[Friedman and Menon, 1973]
Friedman, A. D., and P. R. Menon. "Restricted Checking Sequences for Sequential Machines." *IEEE Trans. Comp.* C-22 (April 1973): 397–399.

[FTSC, 1976]
"The Fault-Tolerant Spaceborne Computer." In *Digest Sixth International Symp. on Fault-Tolerant Computing,* IEEE Computer Society, Pittsburgh, PA, 1976, pp. 129–147.

[Fujiwara and Kawakami, 1977]
Fujiwara, E., and T. Kawakami. "Modularized b-Adjacent Error Correction." In *Direct Seventh International Fault-Tolerant Computing Symposium* IEEE Computer Society, Los Angeles, CA, 1977, p. 199.

[Fujiwara and Kinoshita, 1974]
Fujiwara, H., and K. Kinoshita. "Design of Diagnosable Sequential Machines Utilizing Extra Outputs." *IEEE Trans. Comp.* C-23 (February 1974): 138–145.

[Funami and Halstead, 1975]
Funami, Y., and M. H. Halstead. "A Software Physics Analysis of Akiyama's Debugging Data." Purdue University CSD-TR-144. 1975.

[Gandhi, Knoue, and Henley, 1972]
Gandhi, S. L.; K. Knoue; and E. J. Henley. "Computer Aided System Reliability Analysis and Optimization." In *Proc. IFIP Working Conference on Principles of Computer-Aided Design,* Eindhoven, 1972, pp. 283–308.

[Garner, 1958]
Garner, H. L. "Generalized Parity Checking." *IRE Trans. Elec. Comp.* EC-7 (September 1958): 207–213.

[Garner, 1966]
Garner, H. L. "Error Codes for Arithmetic Operations." *IEEE Trans. Elec. Comp.* EC-15 (October 1966): 763–769.

[Gavrilov, 1960]
Gavrilov, M. A. "Structural Redundancy and Reliability of Relay Circuits." In *Proceedings International Federation of Automatic Control Congress,* 1960, pp. 838–844.

[Gay and Ketelsen, 1979]
Gay, F. A., and M. L. Ketelsen. "Performance Evaluation for Gracefully Degrading Systems." In *Digest Ninth Int. Conf. Fault-Tolerant Computing Symposium,* IEEE, Madison, WI, 1979, pp. 51–58.

[Gear, 1976]
Gear, G. "Intel 2708 8K UV Erasable PROM." Intel Corporation RR-12. Santa Clara, CA, 1976, pp. 51–58.

[Geilhufe, 1979]
Geilhufe, M. "Soft Errors in Semiconductor Memories." In *Digest of Papers Spring CompCon,* IEEE Computer Society, 1979, pp. 210–216.

[General Radio, n.d.]
General Radio Co. Ltd., Systems Division. *How to Design Logic Boards for Easier Automatic Testing and Troubleshooting,* n.d.

[Genke, Harding, and Staehler, 1964]
Genke, R. M.; P. A. Harding; and R. E. Staehler. "No. 1 ESS Call Store–A-AO, 2-Megabit Ferrite Sheet Memory." *Bell System Tech. Journal* 43, no. 5, part 1, (September 1964): 2147–2191.

[Gill, 1966]
Gill, A. " On the Series-to-Paralles Transformations of Linear Sequential Circuits." *IEEE Trans. Elec. Comp.* EC-15 (February 1966): 107–108.

[Gilley, 1970]
Gilley, G. C., *Automatic Maintenance of Spacecraft Systems for Long-Life Deep-Space Missions.* Ph.D. diss., University of California, Department of Computer Science, Los Angeles, 1970.

[Goetz, 1974]
Goetz F. M. "Complementary Fault Simulation." In *Proc. 3rd Annual Texas Conf. Computing Systems,* Austin, Texas 1974.

[Golay, 1949]
Golay, M. J. E.; "Notes on Digital Coding." In *Proceedings of the IRE* 37 (1949): 657.

[Golay, 1958]
Golay, M. J. E.; "Notes on the Penny-Weighing Problem, Lossless Symbol Coding with Nonprimes, etc." *IRE Trans. Information Theory* IT-4, no. 3 (September 1958): 103–109.

[Goldberg, 1975]
Goldberg, J. "New Problems in Fault-Tolerant Computing." In *Int. Digest Fifth IEEEE Fault-Tolerant Computing Symposium,* Computer Society, Paris, France, 1975.

[Goldberg, Levitt, and Short, 1966]
Goldberg, J.; K. N. Levitt; and R. A. Short. "Techniques for the Realization of Ultra-Reliable Spaceborne Computers." Menlo Park, CA: Stanford Research Institute, 1966.

[Golberg, Levitt, and Wensley, 1974]
Goldberg, J.; K. N. Levitt; and J. H. Wensley. "An Organization for a Highly Reliable Memory." *IEEE Trans. Comp.* C-23 (July 1974): 693–705.

[Grason and Nagle, 1980]
Grason, J. and A. Nagle. "Digital Test Generation and Design for Testability." In *Proc. 17th Annual Design Automation Conference.* IEEE/ACM 1980, pp. 175–189.

[Griesmer, Miller, and Roth, 1962]
Griesmer, J. E.; R. E. Miller; and J. P. Roth. "The Design of Digital Circuits to Eliminate Catastrophic Failures." In *Redundancy Techniques for Computing Systems.* Wilcox and Mann (Eds). Washington, DC: Spartan Books, 1962, pp. 328–348.

[Gudz, 1977]
Gudz, R. T. "Application of the Pluribus Multiprocessor in a Distributed. Data Collection and Processing Network." In *Conf. Rec. OCEANS 77,* 1977.

[Gupta, Porter, and Lathrop, 1974]
Gupta, A.; W. A. Porter; and J. W. Lathrop. "Defect Analysis and Yield Degradation of Integrated Circuits." *IEEE J. Solid-State Circuits* SC-9 (June 1974): 96–103.

[Gurzi, 1965]
Gurzi, K. J. "Estimates for the Best Placement of Voters in a Triplicated Logic Network." *IEEE Trans. Elec. Comp.* EC-14 (October 1965): 711–717.

[Hagelbarger, 1959]
Hagelbarger, D. W. "Recurrent Codes: Easily Mechanized, Burst-Correcting Binary Codes." *Bell System Tech. Journal* 38 no. 4 (July 1959): 969–984.

[Halstead, 1979]
"Commemorative issue in honor of Dr. Maurice H. Halstead." Special issue of *IEEE Trans. Soft. Eng.* SE-5, no. 2 (March 1979).

[Hamming, 1950]
Hamming, W. R. "Error Detecting and Error Correcting Codes." *Bell System Tech. Journal* 29, no. 2 (April 1950): 147–160.

[Hampel and Winder, 1971]
Hampel, D., and R. O. Winder. "Threshold Logic" *IEEE Spectrum* (May 1971): 32–39.

[Harr, Taylor, and Ulrich, 1969]
Harr, J. A.; F. F. Taylor; and W. Ulrich. "Organization of the No. 1 ESS Central Processor." *Bell System Tech. Journal* 48 (September 1969).

[Harrahy, 1977]
Harrahy, J. J. "Assessment of Plastic, Commercial Grade IC Failure Rates Achieved in Field Operation." In *Proc. 15th*

Annual Spring Reliability Seminar, IEEE Boston Section, 1977, pp. 144–172.

[Hayes, 1974]
Hayes, J. P. "On Modifying Logic Networks to Improve Their Diagnosability." *IEEE Trans. Comp.* C-23 (January 1974): 56–62.

[Hayes and Friedman, 1974]
Hayes, J. P., and A. D. Friedman. "Test Point Placement to Simplify Fault Detection." *IEEE Trans. Comp.* C-23 (July 1974): 727–735.

[Heart, 1975]
Heart, F. E. "The ARPA Network." In R. L. Grimsdale and F. F. Kuo, eds., *Communication Networks: Proc NATO Advanced Study Institute of September 1973,* Leyden: Noordhoff, 1975, pp. 19–33.

[Heart et al., 1970]
Heart, F. E.; R. E. Hahn; S. M. Ornstein; W. R. Crowther; and D. C. Walden. "The Interface Message Processor for the ARPA Computer Network." In *AFIPS Conf. Proc.,* vol. 36, Montvale, NJ. AFIPS Press, 1970. pp. 551–567.

[Heart et al., 1973]
Heart, F. E.; S. M. Ornstein; W. R. Crowther; and W. B. Barker. "A New Minicomputer/Multiprocessor for the ARPA Network." In *AFIPS Conf. Proc.,* vol. 42, Montvale, NJ: AFIPS Press, 1973, pp. 529–537.

[Heart et al., 1976]
Heart, F. E.; S. M. Ornstein; W. R. Crowther; W. B. Barker; M. F. Kraley; R. D. Bressler; and A. Michel. "The Pluribus Multiprocessor System." In *Multiprocessor Systems: Infotech State of the Art Report,* Maidenhead, England: Infotech International Ltd., 1976, pp. 307–330.

[Hecht, 1976]
Hecht, H. "Fault-Tolerant Software for Real-Time Applications." *ACM Computing Surveys* 8 (December 1976): 391–407.

[Henderson, 1961]
Henderson D. S. "Residue Class Error Checking Codes." In *Preprints Papers 16th Natl. Meet. Ass. Comput. Mach.,* ACM, 1961.

[Hennie, 1964]
Hennie, F. C. "Fault Detecting Experiments for Sequential Circuits." In *Proc. 5th Annual Symp. on Switching Theory and Logic Design,* IEEE 1964, pp. 95–110.

[Hennie, 1968]
Hennie, F. C. *Finite State Models for Logical Machines.* New York: Wiley 1968.

[Hewlett, 1973]
Hewlett-Packard Journal, 25, no. 4, (January 1973).

[Hnatek, 1975]
Hnatek, E. R. "4-Kilobit Memories Present a Challenge to Testing." *Computer Design* 14, no. 5 (May 1975): 117–125.

[Hocquenghem, 1959]
Hocquenghem, A. "Codes Correcteurs d'Erreurs." *Chiffres* 2 (1959): 147–156.

[Holborow, 1972]
Holborow, C. E. "An Improved Bound on the Length of Checking Experiments for Sequential Machines with Counter Cycles." *IEEE Trans. Comp.* C-21 (June 1972): 597–598.

[Hong and Patel, 1972]
Hong, S. J., and A. M. Patel. "A General Class of Maximal Codes for Computer Applications." *IEEE Trans. Comp.* C-21 (December 1972): 1322–1331.

[Hopkins, 1970]
Hopkins, A. L., Jr. "A New Standard for Information Processing Systems for Manned Space Flight." In *Proceedings IFAC 3rd Symp. Control Systems in Space,* Toulouse, France 1970.

[Hopkins, 1971]
Hopkins, A. L., Jr. "A Fault-Tolerant Information Processing Concept for Space Vehicles." *IEEE Trans. Comp.* C-20, no. 11, (November 1971): 1394–1403.

[Hopkins, 1977]
Hopkins, A. L., Jr. "Design Foundations for Survivable Integrated On-Board Computation and Control." In *Proc. Joint Automatic Control Conf.,* 1977, pp. 232–237.

[Hopkins and Smith, 1975]
Hopkins, A. L., Jr., and T. B. Smith, III. "The Architectural Elements of a Symmetric Fault Tolerant Multiprocessor." *IEEE Trans. Comp.* C-24 (May 1975): 498–505.

[Hopkins and Smith, 1977a]
Hopkins, A. L., Jr., and T. B. Smith, III. "OSIRIS—A Distributed Fault-Tolerant Control System," In *Digest 14th IEEE Computer Society Int. Conf.,* IEEE, 1977.

[Hopkins and Smith, 1977b]
Hopkins, A. L. Jr., and T. B. Smith III, United States Patent No. 4,015,246 Synchronous Fault-Tolerant Multiprocessor System, March 29, 1977.

[Hopkins, Smith, and Lala, 1978]
Hopkins, A. L., Jr.; T. B. Smith, III; and J. H. Lala. "FTMP—A Highly Reliable Fault-Tolerant Multiprocessor for Aircraft." *Proceedings of the IEEE* 66 (October 1978): 1221–39.

[Horowitz, 1975]
Horowitz, E. *Practical Strategies for Developing Large Scale Systems.* Reading, MA: Addison-Wesley, 1975.

[Hotchkiss, 1979]
Hotchkiss, J. "The Roles of In-Circuit and Functional Board Test in the Manufacturing Process." *Electronic Packaging and Production* 19 (January 1979): 47–66.

[Howard, 1971]
Howard, R. A. *Dynamic Probabilistic Systems.* New York: Wiley, 1971.

[Howard and Nahourai, 1978]
Howard, J. S., and J. Nahourai. "Improvement in LSI Production Using an Automated Parametric Test System." *Solid State Technology* 21 (July 1978).

[Hsiao, 1970]
Hsiao, M. Y. "A Class of Optimal Minimum Odd-Weight-Column SEC-DED Codes." *IBM J. Res. and Dev.* 14, no. 4, (July 1970): 395–401.

[Hsiao and Bossen, 1975]
Hsiao, M. Y., and D. C. Bossen. "Orthogonal Latin Square Configuration for LSI Yield and Reliability Enhancement." *IEEE Trans. Comp.* C-24 (May 1975): 512–516.

[Hsiao, Bossen, and Chien, 1970]
Hsaio, M. Y.; D. C. Bossen; and R. T. Chien. "Orthogonal Latin Square Codes." *IBM J. Res. and Dev.* 14, 4 (July 1970).

[Hsieh, 1971]
Hsieh, E. P. "Checking Experiments for Sequential Machines." *IEEE Trans. Comp.* C-20 (October 1971): 1152–66.

[Huffman, 1952]
Huffman, D. A. "A Method for the Construction of Minimum-Redundancy Codes." In *Proceedings of the IRE* 40 (1952): 1098–1101.

[Huffman, 1956]
Huffman, D. A. "The Synthesis of Linear Sequential Coding Networks." In *Information Theory,* New York: Academic Press, 1956, pp. 77–95.

[IBM]
International Business Machines. *I/O Supervisor—IBM System/360 Operating System Program Logic Manuals.* GY28–6616.

[IBM]
International Business Machines. *MVT Job Management —IBM System/360 Operating System. Program Logic Manuals.* GY28–6660.

[IBM]
International Business Machines. *MCH for Model 65—IBM System/360 Operating System. Program Logic Manuals.* GY27–7155.

[IBM]
International Business Machines. *MCH for Model 85—IBM System/360 Operating System. Program Logic Manuals.* GY27–7184.

[IBM]
International Business Machines. *Concepts and Facilities —IBM System/360 Operating System. System Reference Library.* GC28–6535.

[IBM]
International Business Machines. *Operator's Reference—IBM System/360 Operating System. System Reference Library.* GC28–6691.

[IBM]
International Business Machines. *MVT Guide—IBM System/360 Operating System. System Reference Library.* GC28–6720.

[IBM]
International Business Machines. *MFT Guide—IBM System/360 Operating System. System Reference Library.* GC27–6939.

[IBM]
International Business Machines. *Machine Check Handler for the IBM System/370 Models 155 and 165. Systems Logic.* GY27–7198.

[IBM]
International Business Machines. "IBM SDLC General Information."

[IEEE, 1971a]
IEEE Trans. Comp. C-20 (1971): 536–542, 1270–1275, 1413–1414.

[IEEE, 1971b]
IEEE Computer Society. *Proc. Int. Symp. Fault-Tolerant Computing,* 1971.

[IEEE, 1972a]
IEEE Trans. Comp. C-21 (1972): 492–495, 1189–1196.

[IEEE, 1972b]
IEEE Computer Society. *Digest Second Int. Symp. Fault-Tolerant Computing.* 1972.

[IEEE, 1973a]
IEEE Trans. Comp. C-22 (1973): 239–249, 263–269, 298–306, 662–669.

[IEEE, 1973b]
IEEE Computer Society. *Digest Third Int. Symp. Fault-Tolerant Computing.* 1973.

[IEEE, 1974a]
IEEE Trans. Comp. C-23 (1974): 41–47, 113–118, 369–374, 494–500, 651–657, 736–739, 1100–1102, 1149–1154.

[IEEE, 1974b]
IEEE Computer Society. *Digest Fourth Int. Symp. Fault-Tolerant Computing,* 1974.

[IEEE, 1975]
IEEE Computer Society. *Digest Fifth Int. Symp. Fault-Tolerant Computing,* 1975.

[IEEE, 1977]
IEEE, Boston Section. Annual Spring Reliability Seminar, April 1977.

[Ihara, et al., 1978]
Ihara, H.; K. Fukuoka; Y. Kubo; and S. Yokota. "Fault-Tolerant Computer System with Three Symmetric Computers." *Proceedings of the IEEE* 66 (October 1978): 1160–1177.

[Ingle and Siewiorek, 1973a]
Ingle, A. D., and D. P. Siewiorek. "Extending the Error Correction Capability of Linear Codes." Carnegie-Mellon University Technical Report, Department of Computer Science, 1973.

[Ingle and Siewiorek, 1973b]
Ingle, A. D., and D. P. Siewiorek. "A Reliability Model for Various Switch Designs in Hybrid Redundancy." Technical Report, Carnegie-Mellon University Department of Computer Science, 1973.

[Ingle and Siewiorek, 1976]
Ingle, A. D., and D. P. Siewiorek. "A Reliability Model for Various Switch Designs in Hybrid Redundancy." *IEEE Trans. Comp.* C-25 (February 1976): 115–133.

[Intel, 1981]
"The Intel 432 System Summary," Intel Corp., Aloha, Oregon, 1981.

[Interdata, 1975]
Interdata, Inc. *Model 8/32 Processor User's Manual.* 1975.

[Irland and Stagg, 1974]
Irland, E. A., and U. K. Stagg. "New Developments in Suburban and Rural ESS (No. 2 and No. 3 ESS)." In *ISS Record,* Munich, Germany, 1974.

[Jack, Kinney, and Berg, 1977]
Jack, L. A.; L. L. Kinney; and R. O. Berg. "Comparison of Alternative Self-Check Techniques in Semiconductor Memories." In *Proc. Spring CompCon,* Vol. 14, IEEE Computer Society, Long Beach, CA, 1977, pp. 170–173.

[Jack, et al., 1975]
Jack, L. A.; R. O. Berg; L. L. Kinney; and G. J. Prom. "Coverage Analysis of Self Test Techniques for Semiconductor Memories." Honeywell Corporation Technical Report, MR12399. Minneapolis, MN, 1975.

[Jelinek, 1968]
Jelinek, F. *Probabilistic Information Theory: Discrete and Memoryless Models.* New York: McGraw-Hill, 1968.

[Jelinsky and Moranda, 1973]
Jelinsky, Z., and P. B. Moranda. "Applications of a Probability Based Method to a Code Heading Experiment." In *Proc.*

IEEE Symp. Computer Software Reliability, IEEE, 1973, p. 78.

[Jensen, 1963]
Jensen, P. A. "Quadded NOR Logic." *IEEE Trans. Reliability* R-12, no. 3 (September 1963): 22–31.

[Jensen, 1964]
Jensen, P. A. "The Reliability of Redundant Multiple-Line Networks." *IEEE Trans. Reliability* R-13, no. 1 (March 1964). 23–33.

[Jones, 1979]
Jones, C. P. "Automatic Fault Protection in the Voyager Spacecraft." Jet Propulsion Laboratory, California Institute of Technology AIAA Paper No. 79-1919. Pasadena, CA, 1979.

[Kamal, 1975]
Kamal, S. "An Approach to the Diagnosis of Intermittent Faults." *IEEE Trans. Comp.* C-24 (May 1975): 461–467

[Kamal and Page, 1974]
Kamal, S., and C. V. Page. "Intermittent Faults: A Model and Detection Procedure." *IEEE Trans. Comp.* C-23 (July 1974): 173–179

[Kaneda and Fujiwara, 1980]
Kaneda, S., and E. Fujiwara. "Single Byte Error Correcting—Double Byte Error Detecting Codes for Memory Systems." In *Digest Tenth International Fault-Tolerant Computing Symposium,* IEEE Computer Society, Kyoto, Japan, 1980, pp. 41–46.

[Kasami, 1963]
Kasami, T. "Optimum Shortened Cyclic Codes for Burst-Error-Correction." *IEEE Trans. Info. Theory* IT-9, no. 2 (April 1963): 105–109.

[Kasami, Lin, and Peterson, 1968]
Kasami, T.; S. Lin; and W. Peterson. "New Generalizations of the Reed-Muller Codes Part I: Primitive Codes." *IEEE Trans. Info. Theory* IT-14, no. 2 (March 1968): 189–199.

[Katsuki et al., 1978]
Katsuki, D.; E. S. Elsam; W. F. Mann; E. S. Roberts; J. F. Robinson; R. S. Skowronski; and E. W. Wolf. "Pluribus—An Operational Fault-Tolerant Multiprocessor." *Proceedings of the IEEE* 66 (October 1978): 1146–1159.

[Katzman, 1977a]
Katzman, J. A. "System Architecture for NonStop Computing." *CompCon,* 1977, p. 77–80.

[Katzman, 1977b]
Katzman, J. A. "A Fault-Tolerant Computing System." Tandem Computers, Inc., Cupertino, CA, 1977.

[Kautz, 1962]
Kautz, W. H. "Codes and Coding Circuitry for Automatic Error Correction within Digital System." In R. H. Wilcox and

W. C. Mann, eds., *Redundancy Techniques for Computing Systems,* Washington, DC: Spartan Books, 1962, pp. 152–195.

[Kautz, 1968]
Kautz, W. H. "Fault Testing and Diagnosis in Combination Digital Circuits." *IEEE Trans. Comp.* C-17 (April 1968): 352–366.

[Kautz, 1971]
Kautz, W. H. "Testing Faults in Combinational Cellular Logic Arrays." In *Proc. 8th Annual Symposium on Switching and Automata Theory,* IEEE 1971, pp. 161–174.

[Kautz, Levitt, and Waksman, 1968]
Kautz, W. H.; K. N. Levitt; and A. Waksman. "Cellular Interconnection Arrays." *IEEE Trans. Comp.* C-17 (May 1968): 443–451.

[Keister, Ketchledge, and Lovell, 1960]
Keister, W.; R. W. Ketchledge; and C. A. Lovell. "Morris Electronic Telephone Exchange." *Proc. Inst. Elec. Eng.* 107, no. 20 (1960): 257–263.

[Keister, Ketchledge, and Vaughan, 1964]
Keister, W.; R. W. Ketchledge; and H. E. Vaughan. "No. 1 ESS: System Organization and Objectives." *Bell System Tech. Journal* 43, no. 5, part 1, (September 1964): 1831–1844.

[Keller, 1976]
Keller, T. W. "CRAY-1 Evaluation Final Report." :Los Alamos Scientific Laboratory, 1976.

[Kennedy and Quinn, 1972]
Kennedy, P. J., and T. M. Quinn. "Recovery Strategies in the No. 2 ESS." In *Digest Second International Fault-Tolerant Computing Symposium,* IEEE Boston, MA, 1972.

[Khodadad-Mostashiry, 1979]
Khodadad-Mostashiry, B. "Parity Prediction in Combination Circuits." In *Digest Ninth International Fault-Tolerant Computing Symposium,* IEEE Computer Society, Madison, WI, 1979.

[Kime, 1970]
Kime, C. R. "An Analysis Model for Digital System Diagnosis." *IEEE Trans. Comp.* C-19 (November 1970): 1063–1073.

[Kini, 1981]
Kini, V. "Automatic Synthesis of Symbolic Reliability Functions for Processor-Memory-Switch Structures." Ph.D. diss., Electrical Engineering Department Carnegie-Mellon University, 1981.

[Klaassen and Van Peppen, 1977a]
Klaassen, K. B., and J. C. L. Van Peppen. "Majority and Similarity Voting in Analogue Redundant Systems." *Microelectronics and Reliability,* 1977, pp. 47–54.

[Klaassen and Van Peppen, 1977b]
Klaassen, K. B., and J. C. L. Van Peppen. "Reliability Improvement by Redundancy Voting in Analogue Electronic Systems." *Microelectronics and Reliability,* 1977, pp. 593–600.

[Klaschka, 1969]
Klaschka, T. F. "Reliability Improvement by Redundancy in Electronic Systems, II: An Efficient New Redundancy Scheme—Radial Logic." Royal Aircraft Establishment, Ministry of Technology 69045. Farnborough. U.K., 1969.

[Klaschka, 1971]
Klaschka, F. "A Method for Redundancy Scheme Performance Assessment." In *Digest First International Fault Tolerant Computing Symposium,* IEEE Computer Society, Pasadena, CA, 1971. pp. 69–73.

[Klein, 1976]
Klein, M. R. "Microcircuit Device Reliability, Digital Detailed Data." Reliability Analysis Center RADC MDR-4. Griffiss AFB, Rome, NY, 1976.

[Kleinrock and Naylor, 1974]
Kleinrock, L., and W. F. Naylor. "On Measured Behavior of the ARPA Network." *Proc. AFIPS NCC* 43 (1974): 767–778.

[Knuth, 1969]
Knuth, D. E. *The Art of Computer Programming. Volume 2: Seminumerical Algorithms.* Reading, MA: Addison-Wesley, 1969.

[Kodandapani, 1974]
Kodandapani, K. L. "A Note on Easily Testable Realizations for Logic Functions." *IEEE Trans. Comp.* C-23 (March 1974): 332–333.

[Kohavi and Kohavi, 1972]
Kohavi, I., and Z. Kohavi. "Detection of Multiple Faults in Combinational Logic Networks." *IEEE. Trans. Comp* C-21 (June 1972): 556–558.

[Kohavi and Lavellee, 1967]
Kohavi, Z., and P. Lavellee. "Design of Sequential Machines with Fault Detection Capabilities." *IEEE Trans. Comp.* C-16 (August 1967): 473–484.

[Kohavi, Rivierre, and Kohavi, 1973]
Kohavi, Z.; J. A. Rivierre; and I. Kohavi. "Machine Distinguishing Experiments." *BCS Computer Journal* 16, no. 2 (1973): 141–147.

[Kole, 1980]
Kole, R. S. "An Advanced Telecommunications Protocol Controller." *Fairchild Journal of Semiconductor Progress,* January/February 1980, pp. 4–8.

[Kruus, 1963]
Kruus, J. "Upper Bounds for the Mean Life of Self-Repairing Systems." University of Illinois R-172, AD-418. Urbana, IL, 1963.

[Kuehn, 1969]
Kuehn, E. "Computer Redundancy: Design, Performance, and Future." *IEEE Trans. Reliability* R-18, no. 1 (February 1969): 3–11.

[Kulzer, 1977]
Kulzer, J. J. "Systems Reliability: A Case Study of No. 4 ESS." In *System Security and Reliability,* Maidenhead, Berkshire, England: Infotech, 1977, pp. 186–188.

[Kunshier and Mueller, 1980]
Kunshier, D. J., and D. R. Mueller. "Support Processor Based System Fault Recovery." In *Proc. Tenth Int. Symp. Fault Tolerant Computing,* IEEE Computer Society, Kyoto, Japan, 1980, pp. 197–301.

[Lala and Hopkins, 1978]
Lala, J. H., and A. L. Hopkins, Jr. "Survival and Dispatch Probability Models for the FTMP Computer." In *Dig. Eighth Int. Fault-Tolerant Computing Symp.,* IEEE Computer Society: Toulouse, France, 1978, pp. 37-43.

[Lampson, 1979]
Lampson, B. W. "Bravo." In Xerox Corporation, *Alto User's Handbook,* Xerox Palo Alto Research Center, Palo Alto, CA, 1978

[Landgraff and Yau, 1971]
Landgraff, R. W., and S. S. Yau. "Design and Diagnosable Iterative Arrays." *IEEE Trans. Comp.* C-20 (August 1971): 867–877.

[Lapp and Powers, 1977]
Lapp, S., and G. Powers. "Computer-Aided Synthesis of Fault-Trees." *IEEE Trans. Reliability* R-26, no. 1 (April 1977): 2.

[Laprie, 1975]
Laprie, J.-C. "Reliability and Availability of Repairable Structures." In *Dig. Fifth Int. Fault-Tolerant Computing Symp.,* IEEE Computer Society, Paris, France, 1975, pp 87–92.

[Larsen and Reed, 1972]
Larsen, R. W., and I. S. Reed. "Redundancy by Coding Versus Redundancy by Replication of Failure-Tolerant Sequential Circuits." *IEEE Trans. Comp* C-21 (February 1972): 130–137.

[Lee, Ghani, and Heron, 1980]
Lee, P. A.; N. Ghani; and K. Heron. "A Recovery Cache for the PDP-11." *IEEE Trans. Comp.* C-29 (June 1980): 546–549.

[Lesser and Shedletsky, 1980]
Lesser, J. D., and J. J. Shedletsky. "An Experimental Delay Test Generator for LSI Logic." *IEEE Trans. Comp.* C-29 (March 1980): 235–248.

[Levine and Meyers, 1976]
Levine, L., and W. Meyers. "Semiconductor Memory Reliability with Error Detecting and Correcting Codes." *Computer* 9, no. 10 (October 1976): 43–50.

[Levitt, Green, and Goldberg, 1968]
Levitt, K. N.; M. W. Green; and J. Goldberg. "A Study of the Data Commutation Problems in a Self-Repairable Multiprocessor." In *SJCC, AFIPS, Conf. Proc.,* vol. 32, Thompson Books, Washington, DC, 1968, pp. 515–527.

[Lewin, Purslow, and Bennetts, 1972]
Lewin, D. W.; E. Purslow; and R. G. Bennetts. "Computer Assisted Logic Design—the CALD System." In *IEEE Conference Publication CAD Conference,* 1972, pp. 343–351.

[Lewis, 1963]
Lewis, T. B. "Primary Processor and Data Storage Equipment for Orbiting Astronomical Observatory." *IEEE Trans. Elec. Comp.* EC-12 (December 1963): 677–686.

[Lewis, 1979]
Lewis, D. W. "A Fault-Tolerant Clock Using Standby Sparing." In *Digest Ninth International Fault-Tolerant Computing Symposium,* IEEE Computer Society, Madison, WI, 1979, pp. 33–40.

[Lilliefors, 1969]
Lilliefors, H. W. "On the Kolmogorov-Smirnov Test for the Exponential Distribution with Mean Unknown," *J. Amer. Statis. Assoc.* 64 (1964): 387–389.

[Lin, 1970]
Lin, S. *An Introduction to Error-Correcting Codes.* Englewood Cliffs, NJ: Prentice-Hall, 1970.

[Littlewood, 1975]
Littlewood, B. "A Reliability Model for Markov Structured Software." In *IEEE Conf. Reliable Software,* 1975, pp. 204–207.

[Littlewood, 1979]
Littlewood, B. "How to Measure Software Reliability and How Not To." *IEEE Trans. Soft. Eng.* SE-5, no. 2, (June 1979): 103–110.

[Locks, 1973]
Locks, M. O. *Reliability, Maintainability, and Availability Assessment.* Washington, DC: Spartan Books/Hayden Book Company, 1973.

[Long, 1969]
Long, J. E. "To the Outer Planets." *Astronautics and Aeronautics* 7 (June 1969): 32–47.

[Longden, Page, and Scantlebury, 1966]
Longden, M.; L. J. Page; and R. A. Scantlebury. "An Assessment of the Value of Triplicated Redundancy in Digital Systems." In *Microelectronics and Reliability,* Vol. 5, Elmsford, NY: Pergamon Press, 1966, pp. 39–55.

[Losq, 1975a]
Losq, J. "Influence of Fault-Detection and Switching Mechanisms on the Reliability of Stand-by Systems." In *Digest Fifth Int. Fault-Tolerant Computing Symposium* IEEE Computer Society: Paris, France, 1975, pp. 81–86.

[Losq, 1975b]
Losq, J. "A Highly Efficient Redundancy Scheme: Self-

Purging Redundancy." Digital Systems Laboratory, Stanford University Tech. Report No. 62. Stanford, CA, 1975.

[Losq, 1976]
Losq, J. "A Highly Efficient Redundancy Scheme; Self-Purging Redundancy." *IEEE Trans. Comp.* C-25 (June 1976): 569–578.

[Losq, 1977]
Losq, J. "Effects of Failures on Gracefully Degraded Systems." In *Digest Seventh International Fault Tolerant Computing Symposium,* IEEE Computer Society, Los Angeles, CA, 1977, pp. 29–34.

[Losq, 1978]
Losq, J. "Testing for Intermittent Failures in Combinational Circuits." In *Proc. Third USA–Japan Computer Conf.* AFIPS and IPSJ, 1978, pp. 165–170.

[Lucky, Salz, and Weldon, 1968]
Lucky, R. W.; J. Salz; and E. J. Weldon, Jr. *Principles of Data Communication.* New York: McGraw-Hill, 1968

[Lum, 1966]
Lum, V. Y. "On Bose-Chaudhuri-Hocquenghem Codes Over GF(q)." University of Illinois R-306. Urbana, IL, 1966.

[Lunde, 1977]
Lunde, A. "Empirical Evaluation of Instruction Set Processor Architecture." *Comm. ACM* 20, no. 3 (March 1977): 143–153.

[Lynch, Wagner, and Schwartz, 1975]
Lynch, W. C.; W. Wagner; and M. S. Schwartz. "Reliability Experience with Chi/OS." *IEEE Trans. Soft. Eng.* SE-1, no. 2 (June 1975): 253–257

[Lyons and Vanderkulk, 1962]
Lyons, R. E., and W. Vanderkulk. "The Use of Triple-Modular Redundancy to Improve Computer Reliability." *IBM J. Res. and Dev.* 6, no. 2 (April 1962): 200–209

[MacWilliams and Sloan, 1978]
MacWilliams, F. J., and N. J. A. Sloane. *The Theory of Error-Correcting Codes.* New York: North-Holland, 1978.

[Maison, 1971]
Maison, F. P. "THE MECRA: A Self-Reconfigurable Computer for Highly Reliable Process." *IEEE Trans. Comp.* C-20 (November 1971): 1382–1388.

[Mandelbaum, 1972a]
Mandelbaum, D. "On Error Control in Sequential Machines." *IEEE Trans. Comp.* C-21 (May 1972): 492–495.

[Mandelbaum, 1972b]
Mandelbaum, D. "Error Correction in Residue Arithmetic." *IEEE Trans. Comp.* C-21 (June 1972): 538–545.

[Mandigo, 1976]
Mandigo, P. D. "No. 2B ESS: New Features for a More Effi-

cient Processor." *Bell Labs Rec.* 54, no.11, (December 1976): 304–309.

[Mann, Ornstein, and Kraley, 1976]
Mann, W. F.; S. M. Ornstein; and M. F. Kraley. "A Network-Oriented Multiprocessor Front-End Handling Many Hosts and Hundreds of Terminals." In *AFIPS Conf. Proc.,* Vol. 45. Montvale, NJ: AFIPS Press, 1976, 533–540.

[Marouf and Friedman, 1977]
Marouf M. A., and A. D. Friedman. "Efficient Design of Self-Checking Checkers for m-out-of-n Codes." In *Digest Seventh International Fault-Tolerant Computing Symposium,* IEEE Computer Society, Los Angeles, CA, pp. 134–149.

[Marouf and Friedman, 1978]
Marouf, M. A., and A. D. Friedman. "Design of Self-Checking Checkers for Berger Codes." In *Digest Eighth International Fault Tolerant Computing Symposium,* IEEE Computer Society, Toulouse, France, 1978, pp. 179–184.

[Massey, 1963]
Massey, J. *Threshold Decoding,* Cambridge, MA: MIT Press, 1963.

[Massey, 1969]
Massey, J. L. "Feedback Shift-Register Synthesis and BCH Decoding." *IEEE Trans. Info. Theory.* Vol. IT-15, Jan. 1969, pp. 122–127.

[Mathur, 1971a]
Mathur, F. P. "Reliability Estimation Procedures and CARE: The Computer Aided Reliability Estimation Program." *Jet Propulsion Laboratory Quarterly Tech. Review* 1 (October 1971).

[Mathur, 1971b]
Mathur, F. P. "On Reliability Modeling and Analysis of Ultra-Reliable Fault-Tolerant Digital Systems." *IEEE Trans. Comp.* C-20 (November 1971): 1376–1382.

[Mathur and Avizienis, 1970]
Mathur, F. P., and A. Avizienis. "Reliability Analysis and Architecture of a Hybrid-Redundant Digital System: Generalized Triple Modular Redundancy with Self-Repair." In *SJCC, AFIPS Conf. Proc.,* Vol. 36, Montvale, NJ: AFIPS Press, 1970, pp. 375–383.

[Mathur and De Sousa, 1975]
Mathur, F. P. and P. De Sousa. "Reliability Modeling and Analysis of General Modular Redundant Systems." *IEEE Trans. Reliability* R-24, no. 5 (December 1975): 296–299.

[McCluskey and Clegg, 1971]
McCluskey, E. J., and F. W. Clegg. "Fault Equivalence in Combinational Logic Networks." *IEEE Trans. Comp.* C-20 (November 1971): 1286–1293.

[McCluskey and Ogus, 1977]
McCluskey, E. J., and R. C. Ogus. "Comparative Architecture of High-Availability Computer Systems." In *Proc. Comp Con,* IEEE 1977, pp. 288–293.

[McConnel, 1981]
McConnel, S. R. "Analysis and Modeling of Transient Errors in Digital Computers." PhD. diss, Carnegie-Mellon University Department of Electrical Engineering, 1981.

[McConnel and Siewiorek, 1981]
McConnel, S. R., and D. P. Siewiorek. "Synchronization and Voting." *IEEE Trans. Comp.* C-30 (February 1981): 161–164.

[McConnel, Siewiorek, and Tsao, 1979a]
McConnel, S. R.; D. P. Siewiorek; and M. M. Tsao. "The Measurement and Analysis of Transient Errors in Digital Computer Systems." In *Digest Ninth Int. Fault-Tolerant Computing Symposium,* IEEE Computer Society, Madison, Wisconsin 1979, pp. 67–70.

[McConnel, Siewiorek, and Tsao, 1979b]
McConnel, S. R.; D. P. Siewiorek; and M. M. Tsao. "Transient Error Data Analysis." Technical Report, Carnegie-Mellon University Department of Computer Science 1979.

[McDonald, 1976]
McDonald, J. C. "Testing for High Reliability: A Case Study." *Computer* 9, no. 2 (February 1976): 18–21.

[McDonald and McCracken, 1977]
McDonald, J. C., and P. T. McCracken. "Testing for High Reliability." In *Proc. CompCon,* IEEE 1977, pp. 190-191.

[McKenzie et al., 1972]
McKenzie, A. A.; B. P. Cosell; J. M. McQuillan; and M. J. Thrope. "The Network Control Center for the ARPA Network." In *Proc. 1st Int. Conf. Computer Communication,* 1972, pp. 185–191.

[McKevitt, 1972]
McKevitt, J. F. "Parity Fault Detection in Semiconductor Memories." *Computer Design* 11, no. 7 (July 1972): 67–73.

[McNamara, 1977]
McNamara, J. E. *Technical Aspects of Data Communications.* Bedford, MA: Digital Press, 1977.

[Mei, 1970]
Mei, K. C. Y. "Fault Dominance in Combinational Circuits." Digital Systems Lab, Stanford University Technician Note 2. Stanford, CA, 1970.

[Mei, 1974]
Mei, K. C. Y. "Bridging and Stuck-At-Faults." *IEEE Trans. Comp.* C-23 (July 1974): 720–727.

[Melliar-Smith, 1977]
Melliar-Smith, P. M. "Permissible Processor Loadings for Various Scheduling Algorithms." Menlo Park, CA: SRI International, 1977.

[Melsa and Cohen, 1978]
Melsa, J. L., and D. L. Cohen. *Decision and Estimation Theory.* New York: McGraw-Hill, 1978.

[Menon and Friedman, 1971]
Menon, P. R., and A. D. Friedman. "Fault Detection in Iterative Logic Arrays." *IEEE Trans. Comp.* C-20 (May 1971): 524–535.

[Meraud, Browaeys, and Germain, 1976]
Meraud, C.; F. Browaeys; and G. Germain. "Automatic Roll-back Techniques of the COPRA Computer." *Digest Sixth International Fault-Tolerant Computing Symposium,* IEEE Computer Society, Pittsburgh, PA, pp. 23–31.

[Meraud et al., 1979]
Meraud, C.; F. Browaeys; J. P. Queille; and G. Germain. "Hardware and Software Design of the Fault-Tolerant Computer COPRA." *Digest Ninth International Fault-Tolerant Computing Symposium,* IEEE Computing Society, Madison, WI, p. 167.

[Meyer, 1971]
Meyer, J. F. "Fault Tolerant Sequential Machines." *IEEE Trans. Comp.* C-20 (October 1971): 1167–1177.

[Meyer, 1978]
Meyer, J. F. "On Evaluating the Performability of Degradable Computing Systems." In *Digest Eighth International Fault-Tolerant Computing Symposium,* IEEE Computer Society, Toulouse, France, 1978, pp. 44–49.

[Meyer, Furchgott, and Wu, 1979]
Meyer, J. F.; D. G. Furchgott; and L. T. Wu. "Performability Evaluation of the SIFT Computer." In *Digest Ninth Int. Fault-Tolerant Computing Symposium,* IEEE Computer Society, Madison WI, 1979, pp. 43–50.

[Meyer, Furchgott, and Wu, 1979]
Meyer, J. F.; D. G. Furchgott; and L. T. Wu. "Performability Evaluation of the SIFT Computer." In *IEEE Trans. Comp.* C-29 (June 1980): 501–509.

[Meyer and Yeh, 1971]
Meyer, J. F., and K. Yeh. "Diagnosable Machine Realizations of Sequential Behavior." In *Digest First International Fault-Tolerant Computing Symposium,* IEEE Computer Society, Boston, MA, 1971.

[Miller and Freund, 1965]
Miller, I., and J. Freund. *Probability and Statistics for Engineers.* Englewood Cliffs, NJ: Prentice-Hall, 1965.

[Mine and Hatayama, 1979]
Mine, H., and K. Hatayama. "Performance Evaluation of a Fault-Tolerant Computing System." In *Digest Ninth International Fault Tolerant Computing Symposium,* IEEE Computer Society, Madison, WI, 1979, pp. 59–62.

[Mine and Koga, 1967]
Mine, H., and Y. Koga. "Basic Properties and a Construction Method for Fail-Safe Logical Systems." *IEEE Trans. Elec. Comp.* EC-16 (June 1967): 282–289.

[Misra, 1970]
Misra, K. B. "An Algorithm for the Reliability Evaluation of Redundant Networks." *IEEE Trans. Reliability* R-19 no. 4 (November 1970): pp. 146–151.

[Miyamoto, 1975]
Miyamoto, I. "Software Reliability in Online Real Time Environment." In *Proc. Int. Conf. Reliable Software,* IEEE 1975, pp. 518–527.

[Mohanly, 1973]
Mohanly, S. N. "Models and Measurements for Quality Assessment of Software." *ACM Computer Surveys* 11 (September 1973), pp. 250–275.

[Moore and Shannon, 1956]
Moore, E. F., and C. E. Shannon. "Reliable Circuits Using Less Reliable Relays." *J. Franklin Inst.* 262 (September 1956): 191–208.

[Morganti, 1978]
Morganti, M. Personal communication to authors, 1978.

[Morganti, Coppadoro, and Ceru, 1978]
Morganti, M.; G. Coppadoro; and S. Ceru. "UDET 7116—Common Control for PCM Telephone Exchange: Diagnostic Software Design and Availability Evaluation." In *Digest Eighth Int. Fault-Tolerant Computing Symposium.* IEEE Computer Society, Toulouse, France, 1978, pp. 16–23.

[Muehldorf, 1975]
Muehldorf, E. I. "Fault Clustering: Modeling and Observation of Experimental LSI Chips." *IEEE J. Solid-State Circuits* SC-10 (August 1975): 237–244.

[Mukai and Tohma, 1974]
Mukai, Y., and Y. Tohma. "A Method for the Realization of Fail-Safe Asynchronous Sequential Circuits." *IEEE Trans. Comp.* C-23 (July 1974): 736–739.

[Mukhopadhyay and Schmitz, 1970]
Mukhopadhyay, A., and G. Schmitz. "Minimization of EXCLUSIVE OR and LOGICAL EQUIVALENCE Switching Circuits." *IEEE Trans. Comp.* C-19 (February 1970): 132–140.

[Muller, 1954]
Muller, D. E. "Application of Boolean Algebra to Switching Circuit Design and to Error Detection." *IRE Trans. Elec. Comp.* ED-3 (September 1954): 6–12.

[Murakami, Kinoshita, and Ozaki, 1970]
Murakami, S.; K. Kinoshita; and H. Ozaki. "Sequential Machines Capable of Fault Diagnosis." *IEEE Trans. Comp.* C-19 (November 1970): 1079–1085.

[Murphy, 1964]
Murphy, B. T. "Cost-Size Optima of Monolithic Integrated Circuits." *Proceedings of the IEEE* 52 (December 1964): 1537–1545.

[Murray, Hopkins, and Wensley, 1977]
Murray, N. D.; A. L. Hopkins, Jr.; and J. H. Wensley. "Highly Reliable Multiprocessors." In P. Kurzhals, ed., *Integrity in Electronic Flight Control Systems,* Neuilly-sur-Seine, France: AGARD–NATO, 1977, pp. 17.1–17.16.

[Musa, 1975]
Musa, J. D. "A Theory of Software Reliability and Its Applications." *IEEE Trans. Soft. Eng* SE-1, no. 3 (September 1975): 312–327.

[Myers et al., 1977]
Myers, M. N.; W. A. Route, and K. W. Yoder. "Maintenance Software." *Bell System Tech. Journal* 56 no. 7 (September 1977): 1139–1167.

[Nadig, 1977]
Nadig, H. J. "Signature Analysis—Concepts, Examples and Guidelines." *Hewlett-Packard Journal,* May 1977, pp. 15–21.

[Nakagawa and Osaki, 1975]
Nakagawa, T., and S. Osaki. "The Discrete Weibull Distribution." *IEEE Trans. Reliability* R-24, no. 5 (December 1975): 300–301.

[Nelson, 1973]
Nelson, E. C. "A Statistical Basis for Software Reliability Assessment." TRW, 1973.

[Neumann and Rao, 1975]
Neumann, P. G., and T. R. N. Rao. "Error-Correcting Codes for Byte-Organized Arithmetic Processors." *IEEE Trans. Comp.* C-24 (March 1975): 226–232.

[Ng and Avizienis, 1980]
Ng, Y. W., and A. Avizienis. "A Unified Reliability Model for Fault-Tolerant Computers." *IEEE Trans. Comp.* C-29 (November 1980): 1002–1011.

[Nicholls, 1979]
Nicholls, D. B. "Microcircuit Device Reliability, Digital Failure Rate Data." Reliability Analysis Center RADC MDR-12. Griffiss AFB, Rome, New York, 1979.

[Nowak, 1976]
Nowak, J. S. "No 1A ESS--A New High Capacity Switching System." In *Int. Switching Symp. Record,* Japan, 1976.

[O'Brien, 1976]
O'Brien, F. J. "Rollback Point Insertion Strategies." In *Digest Sixth International Fault Tolerant Computing Symposium,* IEEE Computer Society, Pittsburgh, PA, 1976, pp. 138–142.

[Ogus, 1973]
Ogus, R. C. "Fault-Tolerance of the Iterative Cell Array Switch for Hybrid Redundancy Through the Use of Failsafe Logic." Digital Systems Lab, Stanford University Departments of Electrical Engineering and Computer Science. Stanford, CA, 1973.

[Ogus, 1974]
Ogus, R. C. "Fault-Tolerance of the Iterative Cell Array Switch for Hybrid Redundancy." *IEEE Trans. Comp.* C-23 (July 1974): 667–681.

[Ohm, 1979]
Ohm, V. J. "Reliability Considerations for Semiconductor Memories." In *Spring Digest of Papers, CompCon* IEEE Computer Society, 1979, pp. 207–209.

[Oldham, Chien, and Tang, 1968]
Oldham, I. B.; R. T. Chien; and D. T. Tang. "Error Detection and Correction in a Photo-Digital Memory System." *IBM J. Res. and Dev.* 12, no. 6 (November 1968): 422–430.

[Ornstein and Walden, 1975]
Ornstein, S. M., and D. C. Walden. "The Evolution of a High Performance Modular Packet-Switch." In *Proc. Int. Conf. Communications,* Vol. 1, 1975, pp. 6-17–6-21.

[Ornstein et al., 1972]
Ornstein, S. M.; F. E. Heart; W. R. Crowther; S. B. Russell; H. K. Rising; and A. Michel. "The Terminal IMP for the ARPA Computer Network." *AFIPS Conf. Proc.,* Vol. 40, Montvale, NJ: AFIPS Press, 1972, pp. 243–254.

[Ornstein, et al., 1975]
Ornstein, S. M.; W. R. Crowther; M. F. Kraley; R. D. Bressler; A. Michel; and F. E. Heart. "Pluribus—A Reliable Multiprocessor." In *AFIPS Conf. Proc.,* Vol. 44, AFIPS Press, Montvale, NJ: 1975, pp. 551–559.

[Osman and Weiss, 1973]
Osman, M. Y., and C. D. Weiss. "Shared Logic Realizations of Dynamically Self-Checked and Fault-Tolerant Logic." *IEEE Trans. Comp.* C-22 (March 1973): 298–306.

[Ossfeldt and Jonsson, 1980]
Ossfeldt, B. E., and I. Jonsson. "Recovery and Diagnostics in the Central Control of the AXE Switching System." *IEEE Trans. Comp.* C-29 (June 1980): 482–491.

[Ozgunner, 1977]
Ozgunner, F. "Design of Totally Self-Checking Asynchronous and Synchronous Sequential Machines." In *Digest Seventh International Fault Tolerant Computing Symposium,* Los Angeles, CA: IEEE Computer Society, 1977, pp. 124–129.

[Pascoe, 1975]
Pascoe, W. "2107A/2107B N-Channel Silicon Gate MOS 4K RAMS." Santa Clara, CA: Intel Corporation RR-7, 1975.

[Patterson and Metze, 1974]
Patterson, W. W., and G. Metze. "A Fail-Safe Asynchronous Sequential Machine." *IEEE Trans. Comp.* C-23 (April 1974): 369–374.

[Pearson and Hartley, 1954]
Pearson, E. S., and H. O. Hartley, eds., *Biometriva Tables for Statisticians,* Vol. 1. Cambridge University Press, 1954.

[Pease, Shostak, and Lamport, 1980]
Pease, M.; R. Shostak; and L. Lamport. "Reaching Agreement in the Presence of Faults." *Journal of the Association for Computing Machinery,* vol. 27, no. 2 (April 1980): 228–234.

[Peterson, 1958]
Peterson, W. W. "On Checking an Adder." *IBM J. Res. and Dev.* 2 no. 2 (April 1958): 166–168.

[Peterson, 1961]
Peterson, W. W. *Error-Correcting Codes.* Cambridge, MA: MIT Press, 1961.

[Peterson and Weldon, 1972]
Peterson, W. W., and E. J. Weldon, Jr. *Error-Correcting Codes.* 2nd ed. Cambridge MA: MIT Press, 1972.

[Phister, 1979]
Phister, M., Jr. *Data Processing Technology and Economics.* Bedford, MA: Digital Press, 1979.

[Pierce, 1977]
Pierce, R. "Service Economic Model Simulator," *Electro,* November 2, 1977.

[Pierce, 1962]
Pierce, W. H. "Adaptive Vote-Takers Improve the Use of Redundancy." In R. H. Wilcox and W. C. Mann, eds., *Redundancy Techniques for Computing Systems.* Washington, DC: Spartan Books, 1962, pp. 229–250.

[Pierce, 1965]
Pierce, W. H. *Failure Tolerant Design.* New York: Academic Press, 1965.

[Platteter, 1980]
Platteter, D. G. "Transparent Protection of Untestable LSI Microprocessors." In *Digest Tenth International Fault Tolerant Computing Symposium.* Kyoto Japan: IEEE Computer Society, 1980, pp. 345–347.

[Posa, 1980]
Posa, J. G. "Memory Makers Turn to Redundancy." *Electronics* 53, McGraw-Hill (December 1980): 108–110.

[Pradhan, 1978a]
Pradhan, D. K. "Asynchronous State Assignments with Unateness Properties and Fault-Secure Design." *IEEE Trans. Comp.* C-27 (May 1978): 396–404.

[Pradhan, 1978b]
Pradhan, D. K. "Fault-Tolerant Asynchronous Networks Using Read-Only Memories." *IEEE Trans. Comp.* C-27 (July 1978): 674–679.

[Pradhan, 1980]
Pradhan, D. K. "A New Class of Error-Correcting/Detecting Codes for Fault-Tolerant Computer Applications." *IEEE Trans. Comp.* C-29 (June 1980): 471–481.

[Pradhan and Reddy, 1974a]
Pradhan, D. K., and S. M. Reddy. "Design of Two-Level Fault-Tolerant Networks." *IEEE Trans. Comp.* C-23 (January 1974): 41–47.

[Pradhan and Reddy, 1974b]
Pradhan, D. K., and S. M. Reddy. "Fault-Tolerant Asynchronous Networks." *IEEE Trans. Comp.* C-23 (January 1974): 651–658.

[Pradhan and Stiffler, 1980]
Pradhan, D. K., and J. J. Stiffler. "Error-Correcting Codes and Self-Check Circuits." *Computer* 13, no. 3 (March 1980): 27–37.

[Prange, 1957]
Prange, E. "Cyclic Error Correcting Codes in Two Symbols." U.S. Air Force Cambridge Research Center AFCRC-TN-58-156, Bedford, MA; 1957.

[Preparata, Metze, and Chien, 1967]
Preparata, F. P.; G. Metze, and R. T. Chien. "On the Connection Assignment Problem of Diagnosable System." *IEEE Trans. Elec. Comp.* EC-16 (December 1967): 848–854.

[Queyssac, 1979]
Queyssac, D. "Projecting VLSI's Impact on Microprocessors." *IEEE Spectrum* 16, no. 5 (1979): 38–41.

[Ramamoorthy and Han, 1973]
Ramamoorthy, C. V., and Y. W. Han. "Reliability Analysis of Systems with Concurrent Error Detection." University of California at Berkeley, Departments of Electrical Engineering and Computer Science, 1973.

[Randell, 1975]
Randell, B. "System Structure for Software Fault Tolerance." *IEEE Trans. Soft. Eng.* SE-1, no. 2 (June 1975): 220–232.

[Randell, Lee, and Treleaven, 1978]
Randell, B.; P. A. Lee; and P. C. Treleaven. "Reliability Issues in Computing System Design. *Computing Surveys* 10, no. 2 (June 1978): 123–165

[Rao, 1970]
Rao, T. R. N. "Biresidue Error-Correcting Codes for Computer Arithmetic." *IEEE Trans. Comp.* C-19 (May 1970): 398–402.

[Rao, 1972]
Rao, T. R. N. "Error Correction in Adders Using Systematic Subcodes." *IEEE Trans. Comp.* C-21 (March 1972): 254–259.

[Rao, 1974]
Rao, T. R. N. *Error Coding for Arithmetic Processors.* New York: Academic Press, 1974.

[Rao and Garcia, 1971]
Rao, T. R. N., and O. N. Garcia. "Cyclic and Multiresidue Codes for Arithmetic Operations." *IEEE Trans. Info. Theory* IT-17 No. 1 (January 1971): 85–91.

[Ratner et al., 1973]
Ratner, R. S.; "Computational Requirements and Technology." Menlo Park, CA: SRI International, 1973.

[Ray-Chaudhuri, 1961]
Ray-Chaudhuri, D. K. "On the Construction of Minimally Redundant Reliable Systems Design." *Bell System Techn. Journal* 40, no. 2 (March 1961): 595–611.

[Raytheon, 1974]
Raytheon Company. *Reliability Model Derivation of a Fault-Tolerant, Dual, Spare-Switching Digital Computer System.* NASA CR-132441. Sudbury, MA: 1974.

[Raytheon, 1976]
Raytheon Company. *An Engineering Treatise on the CARE II Dual Mode and Coverage Models.* NASA CR-144993. Sudbury, MA: 1976.

[Reddy, 1972a]
Reddy, S. M. "Easily Testable Realization for Logic Functions." *IEEE Trans. Comp.* C-21 (November 1972): 1183–1188.

[Reddy, 1972b]
Reddy, S. M. "A Design Procedure for Fault-Locatable Switching Circuits." *IEEE Trans. Comp.* C-21 (December 1972): 1421–1426.

[Reddy, 1978]
Reddy, S. M. "A Class of Linear Codes for Error Control in Byte-per-Card Organized Digital Systems." *IEEE Trans. Comp.* C-27 (May 1978): 455–459

[Reddy and Wilson, 1974]
Reddy, S. M., and J. R. Wilson. "Easily Testable Cellular Realizations for (exactly p)-out-of-n and (p or more)-out-of-n Logic Functions." *IEEE Trans. Comp.* C-23 (January 1974): 98–100.

[Reed, 1954]
Reed, I. S. "A Class of Multiple-Error-Correcting Codes and the Decoding Scheme." *IRE Trans. Professional Group on Information Theory* PGIT-4 (September 1954): 38–49.

[Reed and Brimley, 1962]
Reed, I. S., and D. E. Brimley. "On Increasing the Operating Life of Unattended Machines." RAND Corporation RM-3338-PR. Santa Monica, CA, 1962.

[Reed and Chiang, 1970]
Reed, I. S., and A. C. L. Chiang. "Coding Techniques for Failure-Tolerant Counters." *IEEE Trans. Comp.* C-19 (November 1970): 1035–1038.

[Reed and Soloman, 1960]
Reed, I. S., and G. Soloman. "Polynomial Codes over Certain

Finite Fields." *Journal of the Society for Industrial and Applied Mathematics* 8, no. 2 (1960): 300–304.

[Reliability, 1976a]
Reliability Analysis Center. *Microcircuit Device Reliability: Memory/LSI Data.* MDR-3. Griffiss AFB, Rome, New York 1976.

[Reliability, 1976b]
Reliability Analysis Center. *Microcircuit Device Reliability: Digital Detailed Data.* MDR-4. Griffiss AFB, Rome, New York 1976.

[Reliability, 1979a]
Reliability Analysis Center. *Digital Failure Rate Data.* MDR-12. Griffiss AFB, Rome, NY, 1979.

[Reliability, 1979b]
Reliability Analysis Center. *Memory/LSI Data.* MDR-13. Griffiss AFB, Rome, NY, 1979.

[Rennels, 1980]
Rennels, D. A. "Distributed Fault-Tolerant Computer Systems." *Computer* 13, no. 3 (March 1980): 55–65.

[Reynolds and Kinsbergen, 1975]
Reynolds, C. H., and J. E. Kinsbergen. "Tracking Reliability and Availability." *Datamation* 21, no. 11 (November 1975): 106–116.

[Rhodes, 1964]
Rhodes, L. J. "Effects of Failure Modes on Redundancy." In *Proc. 10th National Symp. Reliability and Quality Control,* Washington, DC, 1964, pp. 360–364.

[Rickers, 1975/76]
Rickers, H. C. "Microcircuit Device Reliability Memory/LSI Data." Reliability Analysis Center, RADC/RBRAC MDR-3. Griffiss AFB, Rome, NY, 1975–1976.

[Roberts, 1965]
Roberts, N. H. *Mathematical Methods in Reliability Engineering.* New York: McGraw-Hill, 1965.

[Roberts and Wessler, 1970]
Roberts, L. G., and B. D. Wessler. "Computer Network Development to Achieve Resource Sharing." In *AFIPS Conf. Proc.,* Vol. 36, Montvale, NJ: AFIPS Press, 1970, pp. 543–549.

[Robinson, 1965]
Robinson, J. P. "An Upper Bound on Minimal Distance of Convolutional Code." *IEEE Trans. Info. Theory* IT-11, no. 4 (October 1965): 567–571.

[Robinson and Roubine, 1977]
Robinson, L., and O. Roubine. "SECIAL—A Specification and Assertion Language." Menlo Park, CA: SRI International, 1977.

[Robinson et al, 1976]
Robinson, L.; K. N. Levitt; P. G. Neuman; and A. K. Saxena. "A Formal Methodology for the Design of Operating System Software." In R. T. Yeh, ed., *Current Trends in Programming Methodology,* Vol. 1. Englewood Cliffs, NJ: Prentice-Hall, 1976, pp. 61–110.

[Romano, 1977]
Romano, A. *Applied Statistics for Science and Industry.* Boston: Allyn and Bacon, 1977.

[Rosenthal, 1977]
Rosenthal, A. "Computing the Reliability of Complex Networks." *SIAM J. Appl. Math.* 32, no. 2 (March 1977): 384–393.

[Ross, 1972]
Ross, S. M. *Introduction to Probability Models.* New York: Academic Press, 1972.

[Roth, 1966]
Roth, J. P. "Diagnosis of Automata Failures: A Calculus and a Method." *IBM J. Res. and Dev.* 10, no. 4, (July 1966): 278–281.

[Roth, Bouricius, and Schneider, 1967]
Roth, J. P., W. G. Bouricius, and P. R. Schneider. "Programmed Algorithms to Compute Tests to Detect and Distinguish between Failures in Logic Circuits." *IEEE Trans. Elec. Comp.* EC-16 (October 1967): 567–580.

[Roth et al., 1967]
Roth, J. P.; W. G. Bouricius; W. C. Carter; and P. R. Schneider. "Phase II of an Architectural Study for a Self-Repairing Computer." SAMSO-TR-67-106. U.S. Air Force Space and Missile Division, El Segundo, CA.

[Rubin, 1967]
Rubin, D. K. "The Approximate Reliability of Triply Redundant Majority-Voted Systems." *Digest, First Annual IEEE Comput. Conf.* Chicago: IEEE Publications, 1967, pp. 46–49.

[Rudolph, 1967]
Roudolph, L. D. "A Class of Majority Logic Decodable Codes," *IEEE Trans. Info. Theory* IT-13, no. 12 (April 1967): 305–306.

[Russel, 1978]
Russel, R. M. "The CRAY-1 Computer System." *Comm. ACM* 21 (January 1978): 63–72.

[Russel, 1980]
Russel, S. C. "Incoming Inspection and Test Programs," *Electronic Test,* October 1980, pp. 46–57.

[Russell and Kime, 1971]
Russell, J. D., and C. R. Kime. "Structural Factors in the Fault Diagnosis of Combinational Networks." *IEEE Trans. Comp.* C-20 (November 1971): 1276–1285.

[Russell and Tiedeman, 1979]
Russell, D. L., and M. J. Tiedeman. "Multiprocess Recovery Using Conversations." In *Digest Ninth International Fault Tolerant Computing Symposium,* IEEE Computer Society, Madison, WI, 1979, pp. 106–110.

[Russo, 1965]
Russo, R. L. "Synthesis of Error-Tolerant Counters Using Minimum Distance Three State Assignments." *IEEE Trans. Elec. Comp.* EC-14 (June 1965): 359–366.

[Saluja and Reddy, 1974]
Saluja, K. K., and S. M. Reddy. "On Minimally Testable Logic Networks." *IEEE Trans. Comp.* C-23 (November 1974): 552–554.

[Satyanarayana and Prabhakar, 1978]
Satyanarayana, A., and A. Prabhakar. "New Topological Formula and Rapid Algorithm for Reliability Analysis of Complex Networks." *IEEE Trans. Reliability* R-27, no. 2 (June 1978): 82–100.

[Savir, 1978]
Savir, J. "Testing for Intermittent Failures in Combinational Circuits by Minimizing the Mean Testing Time for a Given Test Quality." In *Proc. Third USA—Japan Computer Conf.* AFIPS and IPSJ, 1978, pp. 155–161.

[Sawin, 1975]
Sawin, D. H. "Design of Reliable Synchronous Sequential Circuits." *IEEE Trans Comp.* C-24 (May 1975): 567–570.

[Schalkwijk and Kailath, 1966]
Schalkwijk, J. P., and T. Kailath. "A Coding Scheme for Additive Noise Channels with Feedback—Part I: No Bandwidth Constraint." *IEEE Trans. Info. Theory* IT-12, no. 4 (April 1966): 172–188.

[Schertz and Metze, 1972]
Schertz, D. R., and G. Metze. "A New Representation for Faults in Combinational Digital Circuits." *IEEE Trans. Comp.* C-21 (August 1972): 858–866.

[Schick and Wolverton, 1978]
Schick, G. J., and R. W. Wolverton. "An Analysis of Computing Software Reliability Models." *IEEE Trans. Soft. Eng.* SE-4, no. 2 (March 1978): 104–120.

[Schneider, 1974]
Schneider, D. "Designing Logic Boards for Automatic Testing." *Electronics International* 47, no. 15 (July 1974).

[Schneidewind, 1975]
Schneidewind, N. F. "Analysis of Error Processes in Computer Software." In *Proc. Int. Conf. Reliable Software,* IEEE, 1975, pp. 337–346.

[Sedmak and Liebergot, 1978]
Sedmak, R. M., and H. L. Liebergot. "Fault Tolerance of a General Purpose Computer Implemented by Very Large Scale Integrating." In *Digest Eight International Fault Tolerant Computing Symposium,* IEEE Computer Society, Toulouse, France 1978, pp. 137–143.

[Sedmak and Liebergot, 1980]
Sedmak, R. M., and H. L. Liebergot. "Fault Tolerance of a General Purpose Computer Implemented by Very Large Scale Integrating." *IEEE Trans. Comp.* C-29 (June 1980): 492–500.

[Seley and Vigilante, 1964]
Seley, E. L., and F. S. Vigilante. "Common Control—For an Electronic Private Branch Exchange." *IEEE Trans. Comm. Electron.* 83, no. 73, (July 1964): 321–329.

[Sellers, 1962]
Sellers, E. F. "Bit Loss and Gain Correction Code." *IEEE Trans. Info. Theory* IT-8, no. 1 (January 1962): 36–38.

[Sellers, Hsiao, and Bearnson, 1968a]
Sellers, E. F.; M. Y. Hsiao; and L. W. Bearnson. "Analyzing Errors with the Boolean Difference." *IEEE Trans. Comp.* C-17 (July 1968): 676–683.

[Sellers, Hsiao, and Bearnson, 1968b]
Sellers, E. F.; M. Y. Hsiao; and L. W. Bearnson. *Error Detecting Logic for Digital Computers.* New York: McGraw-Hill, 1968.

[Seshu and Freeman, 1962]
Seshu, S., and D. N. Freeman. "The Diagnosis of Asynchronous Sequential Switching Systems." *IRE Trans. Elec. Comp.* EC-11, no. 8 (August 1962): 459–465.

[Shannon, 1948]
Shannon, C. E. "A Mathematical Theory of Communications." *Bell System Tech. Journal* 27 no. 3 (July 1948): 379–423, 623–656.

[Shannon, 1959]
Shannon, C. E. "Probability of Error for Optimal Codes in a Gaussian Channel." *Bell System Tech. Journal* 38 (May 1959): 611–656.

[Shedletsky, 1978a]
Shedletsky, J. J. "Error Correction by Alternative Data Retry." *IEEE Trans. Comp.* C-27 (February 1978): 106–112.

[Shedletsky, 1978b]
Shedletsky, J. J. "A Rollback Interval for Networks with an Imperfect Self Checking Property." *IEEE Trans. Comp.* C-27 (June 1978): 500–508.

[Shedletsky and McCluskey, 1975]
Shedletsky, J. J.; and E. J. McCluskey. "The Error Latency of a Fault in a Combinatorial, Digital Circuit." In *Digest Fifth International Fault Tolerant Computing Symposium,* IEEE Computer Society, Paris, France, 1975, pp. 210–314.

[Shedletsky and McCluskey, 1976]
Shedletsky, J. J.; and E. J. McCluskey. "The Error Latency of a Fault in a Sequential Circuit." *IEEE Trans. Comp.* C-25 (June 1976): 655–659.

[Shen and Hayes, 1980]
Shen, J. P., and J. P. Hayes. "Fault Tolerance of a Class of Connecting Architecture." In *Proc. Seventh Ann. Symp. on Computer Architecture,* La Boule, France: IEEE Press, 1980, pp. 61–71.

[Shooman, 1968]
Shooman, M. L. *Probabilistic Reliability: An Engineering Approach.* New York: McGraw-Hill, 1968.

[Shooman, 1970]
Shooman, M. L. "The Equivalence of Reliability Diagrams and Fault-Tree Analysis." *IEEE Trans. Reliability* R-19, no. 2 (May 1970): 74–75.

[Shooman, 1973]
Shooman, M. L. "Operational Testing and Software Reliability Estimation During Program Development." In *Record, IEEE Symposium on Computer Software Reliability,* 1973, pp. 51–57.

[Short, 1968]
Short, R. A. "The Attainment of Reliable Digital Systems through the Use of Redundancy: A Survey." *IEEE Computer Group News* 2 (March 1968): 2–17.

[Shostak et al., 1977]
Shostak, R. E.; "Proving the Reliability of a Fault-Tolerant Computer System." In *Proc. 14th IEEE Comput. Soc. Int. Conf.,* 1977.

[Shrivastava and Akinpelu, 1978]
Shrivastava, S. K., and Akinpelu, A. A. "Fault-Tolerant Sequential Programming Using Recovery Blocks." In *Digest Eight International Fault Tolerant Computing Symposium,* IEEE Computer Society, Toulouse, France, 1978, p. 207.

[Siewiorek, 1975]
Siewiorek, D. P. "Reliability Modeling of Compensating Module Failures in Majority Voted Redundancy." *IEEE Trans. Comp.* C-24 (May 1975): 525–533.

[Siewiorek, 1977]
Siewiorek, D. P. "Multiprocessors: Reliability Modeling and Graceful Degradation." In *Infotech State of Art Conference on System Reliability,* London: Infotech International Ltd. 1977, pp.48–73.

[Siewiorek, Bell, and Newell, 1982]
Siewiorek, D. P.; C. G. Bell; and A. Newell, *Computer Structures: Principles and Examples.* New York: McGraw-Hill, 1982.

[Siewiorek, Canepa, and Clark, 1976]
Siewiorek, D. P.; M. Canepa; and S. Clark. "C.vmp: The Analysis, Architecture, and Implementation of a Fault Tolerant Multiprocessor." Technical Report Carnegie-Mellon University Departments of Electrical Engineering and Computer Science, Pittsburgh, PA.

[Siewiorek, Canepa, and Clark, 1977]
Siewiorek, D. P.; M. Canepa; and S. Clark. "C.vmp: The Architecture and Implementation of a Fault-Tolerant Multiprocessor." In *Proc. Seventh Annual Int. Symp. Fault-Tolerant Computing,* IEEE Computer Society, Los Angeles, CA, 1977, pp. 37–43.

[Siewiorek and McCluskey, 1973a]
Siewiorek, D. P., and E. J. McCluskey. "Switch Complexity in Systems with Hybrid Redundancy." *IEEE Trans. Comp.* C-22 (March 1973): 276–282.

[Siewiorek and McCluskey, 1973b]
Siewiorek, D. P., and E. J. McCluskey. "An Iterative Cell Switch Design for Hybrid Redundancy." *IEEE Trans. Comp.* C-22 (March 1973): 290–297.

[Siewiorek and Rennels, 1980]
Siewiorek, D. P., and D. Rennels. "Workshop Report: Fault-Tolerant VLSI Deisgn." *Computer,* December 1980, pp. 51–53.

[Siewiorek, et al., 1978a]
Siewiorek, D. P.; V. Kini; H. Mashburn; S. R. McConnel; and M. M. Tsao. "A Case Study of C.mmp, Cm*, and C.vmp: Part I—Experiences with Fault Tolerance in Multiprocessor Systems." In *Proceedings of the IEEE* 66 (October 1978): 1178–1199.

[Siewiorek, et al. 1978b]
Siewiorek, D. P.; V. Kini; R. Joobbani; and H. Bellis. "A Case Study of C.mmp, Cm*, and C.vmp: Part II—Predicting and Calibrating Reliability of Multiprocessor Systems." *Proceedings of the IEEE,* 66 (October 1978): 1200–1220.

[Signetics, 1975]
Signetics Product Reliability Report R363, June 1975, Signetics Corporation, Sunnyvale, CA.

[Sih and Hsiao, 1966]
Sih, K. Y., and M. Y. Hsiao. "Cyclic Codes in Multiple Channel Parallel Systems." *IEEE Trans. Elec. Comp.* EC-15 (December 1966): 927–930.

[Sklaroff, 1976]
Sklaroff, J. R. "Redundancy Management Technique for Space Shuttle Computers." *IBM J. Res. and Dev.* 20, no. 1 (January 1976): 20–28.

[Slepian, 1956]
Slepian, D. "A Class of Binary Signalling Alphabets." *Bell System Tech. Journal* 35 (January 1956): 203–234.

[Smith, 1972]
Smith, D. J. *Reliability Engineering* New York: Barnes and Noble, 1972.

[Smith, 1975]
Smith, T. B., III. "A Damage- and Fault-Tolerant Input/Output Network." *IEEE Trans. Comp.* C-24 (May 1975): 506–512.

[Smith and Hopkins, 1978]
Smith, T. B., III and A. L. Hopkins, Jr. "Architectural Description of a Fault-Tolerant Multiprocessor Engineering Prototype." In *Digest Eighth International Fault Tolerant Computing Symposium,* p. 194. IEEE Computer Society, Toulouse, France, 1978.

[Smith and Metze, 1978]
Smith, J. E., and G. Metze. "Strongly Fault Secure Logic Networks." *IEEE Trans. Comp.* C-27 (June 1978): 491–499.

[Snow and Siewiorek, 1978]
Snow, E. and D. P. Siewiorek. "Impact of Implementation Design Tradeoffs on Performance: The PDP-11, A Case Study." In C. G. Bell, J. C. Mudge, and J. E. McNamara, eds., *Computer Engineering: A DEC View of Hardware Design.* Bedford, MA: Digital Press, 1978, pp. 327–364.

[Snyder, 1975]
Snyder, D. L. *Random Point Processes.* New York: Wiley, 1975.

[Spencer and Vigilante, 1969]
Spencer, A. E., and F. S. Vigilante. "No. 2 ESS—System Organization and Objectives." *Bell System Tech. Journal* 48 (October 1969): 2607–2618.

[Sperry, 1979]
Sperry Univac Corporation. "The Microarchitecture of Univac's 1100/60," *Datamation,* July 1979, pp. 173–178.

[Spillman, 1977]
Spillman, R. J. "A Markov Model of Intermittent Faults in Digital Systems." In *Seventh Int. Fault-Tolerant Computing Symp.* Los Angeles, CA: IEEE Computer Society, 1977, pp. 157–161.

[Srinivasan, 1971a]
Srinivasan, C. V. "Codes for Error Correction in High-Speed Memory Systems, Part I: Correction of Cell Defects in Integrated Memories." *IEEE Trans. Comp.* C-20 (August 1971): 882–888.

[Srinivasan, 1971b]
Srinivasan, C. V. "Codes for Error Correction in High-Speed Memory Systems, Part II: Correction of Temporary and Catastrophic Errors." *IEEE Trans. Comp.* C-20 (December 1971): 1514–1520.

[Staehler, 1977]
Staehler, R. E. "1A Processor—Organizations and Objectives." *Bell System Tech. Journal* 56, no. 2 (February 1977): 119–134.

[Staehler and Watters, 1976]
Staehler, R. E. and R. J. Watters. "1A Processor—An Ultra-Dependable Common Control." In *Int. Switching Symp. Record,* Japan, 1976.

[Stapper, 1973]
Stapper, C. H. "Defect Density Distribution for LSI Yield Calculations." *IEEE Trans. Elec. Devices* ED-20 (July 1973): 655–657.

[Stewart, 1977]
Stewart, J. H. "Future Testing of Large LSI Circuit Cards." In *IEEE, Digest of Papers, 1977 Semiconductor Test Symposium.* Cherry Hill, NJ, 1977, pp. 6–15.

[Stewart, 1978]
Stewart, J. H. "Application of Scan Set for Error Detection and Diagnostics." In *IEEE Digest of Papers, 1978 Semiconductor Test Conference.* Cherry Hill, NJ, 1978, pp. 152–158.

[Stiffler, 1976]
Stiffler, J. J. "Architectural Design for Near-100% Fault Coverage." In *Digest Sixth International Fault Tolerant Computing Symposium,* IEEE Computer Society, Pittsburgh, PA, 1976.

[Stiffler, 1978]
Stiffler, J. J. "Coding for Random-Access Memories." *IEEE Trans. Comp.* C-27 (June 1978): 526–531.

[Stiffler, Bryant, and Guccione, 1979]
Stiffler, J. J.; L. A. Bryant; and L. Guccione. "CARE III Final Report: Phase One." NASA Langley Research Center NASA Contractor Report 159122. Langley, VI: 1979.

[Storey, 1976]
Storey, T. F. "Design of a Microprogram Control for a Processor in an Electronic Switching System," *Bell System Tech. Journal* no. 2 (February 1976): 183–232.

[Strecker, 1978]
Strecker, W. D. "VAX-11/780—A Virtual Address Extension to the DEC PDP-11 Family," NCC AFIPS Proceedings, vol. 47. Montvale, NJ: AFIPS Press, 1978, pp. 967–980.

[Sturges, 1926]
Sturges, "The Choice of a Class Interval." *J. Amer. Statistical Association.* 21 (1926): 65–66.

[Su, Koren, and Malaiya, 1978]
Su. S. Y. H.; I. Koren; and Y. K. Malaiya. "A Continuous-Parameter Markov Model and Detection Procedures for Intermittent Faults," *IEEE Trans. Comp.* C-27 (June 1978): 567–570.

[Susskind, 1972]
Susskind, A. K. "Additional Applications of the Boolean Dif-

ference to Fault Detection and Diagnosis." In *Digest Second Int. Fault-Tolerant Computing Symposium,* IEEE Computer Society, Boston, MA, 1972, pp. 58–61.

[Swan, 1977]
Swan, R. J. "The Switching Structure and Addressing Architecture of an Extensible Multiprocessor: The Cm*." Ph.D. diss., Carnegie-Mellon University, 1977.

[Swan, Fuller, and Siewiorek, 1977]
Swan, R. J.; S. H. Fuller; and D. P. Siewiorek. "Cm*—A Modular Multi-Microprocessor." In *AFIPS Conf. Proc.,* vol. 46. Montvale, NJ: AFIPS Press, 1977, pp. 637–644.

[Tammaru and Angell, 1967]
Tammaru, E., and J. B. Angell. "Redundancy for LSI Yield Enhancement." *IEEE J. Solid-State Circuits* SC-2 (December 1967): 172–182.

[Tandem, 1976]
Tandem Computers. *Tandem/16 System Description.* Cupertino, CA, 1976.

[Tang, 1965]
Tang, D. T. "Dual Codes are Variable Redundancy Codes." In *IEEE International Convention Record* 13, (1965): 220–226.

[Tang and Chien, 1966]
Tang, D. T., and R. T. Chien. "Cyclic Product Codes and Their Implementation." *Information and Control* 9, no. 2 (April 1966): pp. 196–209.

[Tang and Chien, 1969]
Tang, D. T., and R. T. Chien. "Coding for Error Control." *IBM Syst. J.* 8 no. 1 (1969): 48–85.

[Tasar and Tasar, 1977]
Tasar, O., and V. Tasar. "A Study of Intermittent Faults in Digital Computers." In *AFIPS Conf. Proc.* vol. 46. Montvale, NJ: AFIPS Press, 1977, pp. 807–811.

[Teoste, 1962]
Teoste, R. "Design of a Repairable Redundant Computer." *IRE Trans. Elec. Comp.* C-11 (October 1962): 643–649.

[Teoste, 1964]
Teoste, R. "Digital Circuit Redundancy." *IEEE Trans. Reliability* R-13, no. 3 (June 1964): 42–61.

[Texas, 1976]
Texas Instruments. *The TTL Data Book for Design Engineers.* 2d. ed. Dallas, Texas 1976.

[Texas, n.d.]
Texas, Instruments. *Preliminary Reliability Report for TI Series TMS4030, TMS4050, TMS4060 4K RAMS.* Bulletin CR-112. Dallas, TX, n.d.

[Thatte and Abraham, 1978]
Thatte, S. M., and J. A. Abraham. "A Methodology for Functional Level Testing of Microprocessors." In *Digest Eighth Int. Fault-Tolerant Computing Symposium* IEEE Computer Society, Toulouse, France, 1978, pp. 90–95.

[Thayer, Lipow, and Nelson, 1978]
Thayer, T. A.; M. Lipow; and E. C. Nelson. *Software Reliability.* New York: North-Holland, 1978.

[Thoman, Bain, and Antle, 1969]
Thoman, D. R.; L. J. Bain; and C. E. Antle. "Inferences on the Parameters of the Weibul Distribution." *Technometrics* 11, no. 3 (August 1969): 445–460.

[Thompson and Ritchie, 1974]
Thompson, K., and D. M. Ritchie. "The UNIX Time-Sharing System." *Comm. ACM* 17 (July 1974): 365–375.

[Tohma, 1974]
Tohma, Y. "Design Technique of Fail-Safe Sequential Circuits Using Flip-Flops for Internal Memory." *IEEE Trans. Comp.* C-23 (November 1974): 1149–1154.

[Tohma and Aoyagi, 1968]
Tohma, Y., and S. Aoyagi. "Failure-Tolerant Sequential Machines Using Past Information." *Electronics and Communications in Japan* 51-C, no. 11 (1968): 95–101. Also *IEEE Trans. Comp.* C-20 (April 1971): 392–396.

[Tohma and Aoyagi, 1971]
Thoma, Y., and S. Aoyagi. "Failure-Tolerant Sequential Machines with Past Information." *IEEE Trans. Comp.* C-20 (April 1971): 392–396.

[Tohma, Ohyama, and Sakai, 1971]
Tohma, Y.; Y. Ohyama; and R. Sakai. "Realization of Fail-Safe Sequential Machines Using a k-out-of-n Code." *IEEE Trans. Comp.* C-20 (November 1971): 1270–1275.

[Tokura, Kasami, and Hashimoto, 1971]
Tokura, N.; T. Kasami; and A. Hashimoto. "Fail-Safe Logic Nets," *IEEE Trans. Comp.* C-20 (March 1971): 323–330.

[Tong, 1966]
Tong, S. Y. "Synchronization Recovery Techniques for Binary Cyclic Codes." *Bell System Tech. Journal* 45 (April 1966): 561–596.

[TOPS, 1970]
"TOPS Outer Planet Spacecraft." *Astronautics and Aeronautics* 8 (September 1970).

[Torng, 1972]
Torng, H. C. *Switching Circuits: Theory and Logic Design.* Reading, MA: Addison-Wesley, 1972.

[Toth and Holt, 1974]
Toth, A., and C. Holt. "Automated Data-Based Driven Digital Testing." *Computer,* January 1974, pp. 13–19.

[Toy, 1978]
Toy, W. N. "Fault-Tolerant Design of Local ESS Processors." *Proceedings of the IEEE* 66 (October 1978): 1126–1145.

[Trivedi and Shooman, 1975]
Trivedi, A. K, and M. L. Shooman. "A Many-State Markov Model for the Estimation and Prediction of Computer Software Performance." In *Proc. Int. Conf. on Reliable Software,* IEEE Computer Society, Los Angeles, CA, 1975, pp. 208–220.

[Troy, 1977]
Troy, R. "Dynamic Reconfiguration: An Algorithm and Its Efficiency Evaluation." In *Digest Seventh International Symposium on Fault Tolerant Computing* IEEE Computer Society, Los Angeles, CA, 1977, pp. 44–49.

[Troy, 1978]
Troy, R. "Rollback Model for Interactive Processes." In *Digest Eighth International Symposium on Fault Tolerant Computing* IEEE Computer Society, Toulouse, France, 1978.

[Tryon, 1962]
Tryon, J. G. "Quadded Logic." In Wilcox and W. C. Mann, eds., *Redundancy Techniques for Computing Systems,* Washington, DC: Spartan Books, 1962, pp. 205–228.

[Tsao, 1978]
Tsao, M. M. "A Study of Transient Errors on Cm*." Master's report, Carnegie-Mellon University, 1978.

[Tsao, 1982]
Tsao, M. M. "A PDP-8 Implementation AMO Bit-Sized Microprocessors." In D. P. Siewiorek; C. G. Bell; and A. Newell, *Computer Structures: Principles and Examples,* New York: McGraw-Hill, 1982, pp. 219–226.

[Tsiang and Ulrich, 1962]
Tsiang, S. H., and W. Ulrich. "Automatic Trouble Diagnosis of Complex Logic Circuits." *Bell System Tech. Journal* (July 1962).

[Turin, 1965]
Turin, G. L. "Signal Design for Sequential Detection Systems with Feedback." *IEEE Trans. Info. Theory* IT-11, no. 7 (July 1965): 401–408.

[Ullman, 1966]
Ullman, J. D. "Near-Optional, Single-Synchronization-Error-Correcting Code." *IEEE Trans. Info. Theory* IT-12, no. 4 (October 1966): 418–425.

[U.S., 1965]
U.S. Department of Defense. *Military Standardization Handbook: Reliability Prediction of Electronic Equipment.* MIL-HDBK-217. 1965.

[U.S., 1974]
U.S. Department of Defense. *Military Standardization Handbook: Reliability Prediction of Electronic Equipment.* MIL-HDBK-217B. 1974.

[U.S., 1976]
U.S. Department of Defense. *Military Standardization Handbook: Reliability Prediction of Electronic Equipment.* MIL-STD-HDBK-217B. Notice 1, 1976.

[U.S., 1979]
U.S. Department of Defense. *Military Standardization Handbook: Reliability Prediction of Electronic Equipment.* MIL-HDBK-217C. 1979.

[U.S., 1980]
U.S. Department of Defense. *Military Standardization Handbook: Reliability Prediction of Electronic Equipment.* MIL-HDBK-217C. Notice 1, 1980.

[Usas, 1978]
Usas, A. M. "Checksum Versus Residue Codes for Multiple Error Detection." In *Digest Eighth International Fault Tolerant Computing Symposium,* 1978. IEEE Computer Society, Toulouse, France, p. 224.

[U.S. Patent, 1977a]
U.S. Patent No. 4 015 246. "Synchronous Fault-Tolerant Multiprocessor System." Washington, DC, 1977.

[U.S. Patent, 1977b]
U.S. Patent No. 4 035 766. Washington, DC, 1977.

[von Alven, 1964]
von Alven, W. H. (Ed). *Reliability Engineering.* Englewood Cliffs, NJ: Prentice-Hall, 1964.

[von Neumann, 1956]
von Neumann, J. "Probabilistic Logics and the Synthesis of Reliable Organisms from Unreliable Components." In C. E. Shannon and J. McCarthy, eds., *Automata Studies,* Princeton: Princeton University Press, 1956, pp. 43–98.

[Wachter, 1975]
Wachter, W. J. "System Malfunction Detection and Correction." In *Digest Fifth International Fault Tolerant Computing Symposium* IEEE Computer Society, Paris France, 1975, pp. 196–201.

[Wakerly, 1974]
Wakerly, J. "Partially Self-Checking Circuits and Their Use in Performing Logical Operations." *IEEE Trans. Comp.* C-23 (July 1974): 658–666.

[Wakerly, 1976]
Wakerly, J. "Microcomputer Reliability Improvement Using Triple-Modular Redundancy." In *Proceedings of the IEEE.* 64 (June 1976): 889–895.

[Wakerly, 1978]
Wakerly, J. *Error Detecting Codes. Self-Checking Circuits and Applications.* New York: North-Holland, 1978.

[Waksman, 1968]
Waksman, A. "A Permutation Network." *J. ACM,* 15, no. 1 (January 1968): 159–163.

[Wang and Lovelace, 1977]
Wang, S. D., and K. Lovelace. "Improvement of Memory Reliability by Single-Bit-Error Correction." Long Beach, CA: IEEE Press, 1977

[Warner, 1974]
Warner, R. M., Jr. "Applying a Composite Model to the IC Yield Problem." *IEEE J. Solid-State Circuits.* SC-9, no. 6 (June 1974): 86–95.

[Watson and Hastings, 1966]
Watson, R. W., and C. W. Hastings. "Self-Checked Computation Using Residue Arithmetic." *Proceedings of the IEEE* 54 (December 1966): 1920–1931.

[Weissberger, 1980]
Weissberger, A. J. "An LSI Implementation of an Intelligent CRC Computer and Programmable Character Comparator." *IEEE Trans. Comp.* C-29 (February 1980): 116–124.

[Weldon, 1966]
Weldon, E. J. "Difference-Set Cyclic Codes." *Bell System Tech. Journal.* 45 (September 1966): 1045–1057.

[Weldon, 1967]
Weldon, E. J. "A Note on Synchronization Recovery with Extended Cyclic Codes." In *Proc. First Annual Princeton Conference on Information Sciences and Systems,* Princeton, NJ, 1967. p. 233.

[Weldon, 1968]
Weldon, E. J. "New Generalizations of the Reed-Muller Codes Part II: Nonprimitive Codes." *IEEE Trans. Info. Theory* IT-14, no. 2 (March 1968): 199–205.

[Wensley, 1972]
Wensley, J. H. "SIFT Software Implemented Fault Tolerance." In *FJCC,* AFIPS Conf. Proc. Vol. 41, pp. 243–253. Montvale, NJ: AFIPS Press, 1972.

[Wensley et al., 1973]
Wensley, J. H. et al.: "Architecture." Menlo Park, CA: SRI International, 1973.

[Wensley et al., 1976]
Wensley, J. H.: M. W. Green; K. N. Levitt; and R. E. Shostak. "The Design, Analysis, and Verification of the SIFT Fault Tolerant System." In *Proc. 2nd Int. Conf. Software Engineering,* Long Beach, CA: IEEE Computer Society, 1976, pp. 458–469.

[Wensley et al., 1978]
Wensley, J. H.; L. Lamport; J. Goldberg; M. W. Green: K. N. Levitt; P. M. Melliar-Smith; R. E. Shostak; and C. B. Weinstock. "SIFT; Design and Analysis of a Fault-Tolerant Computer for Aircraft Control." *Proceedings of the IEEE* 66 (October 1978): 1240–1255.

[Wilcox and Mann, 1962]
Wilcox, R. H. and W. C. Mann. *Redundancy Techniques for Computer Systems,* Spartan Books, 1962.

[Wilkov, 1972]
Wilkov, R. "Analysis and Design of Reliable Computer Networks." *IEEE Trans. Communication* COM-20, no. 3 (1972): 660.

[Williams and Angell, 1973]
Williams, M. J., and J. B. Angell. "Enhancing Testability of LSI Circuits via Test Points and Additional Logic." *IEEE Trans. Comp.* C-22 (January 1973): 46–60.

[Williams and Parker, 1979]
Williams, T. W., and K. P. Parker. "Testing Logic Networks and Designing for Testability." *Computer* 12, no. 10 (October 1979): 9–21.

[E. W. Wolf, 1973]
Wolf, E. W. "An Advanced Computer Communication Network." In *AIAA Computer Network Systems Conf. Record,* 1973.

[J. K. Wolf, 1973]
Wolf, J. K. "A Survey of Coding Theory: 1967–1972." *IEEE Trans. Info. Theory* IT-19, no. 4 (July 1973): 381–389.

[Wolverton and Shick, 1974]
Wolverton, R. W., and G. J. Shick. "Assessment of Software Reliability." TRW-SS-73-04. Los Angeles, CA, 1974.

[Wozencraft, 1957]
Wozencraft, J. M. "Sequential Decoding for Reliable Communicating." Research Laboratory for Electronics, MIT TR325. Boston, MA, 1957.

[Wulf and Bell, 1972]
Wulf, W. A., and C. G. Bell. "C.mmp—A Multi-Mini-Processor." In *AFIPS Conf. Proc.,* vol. 41, Montvale, NJ: AFIPS Press, 1972, pp. 765–777.

[Wyle and Burnett, 1967]
Wyle, H., and G. J. Burnett. "Some Relationships between Failure Detection Probability and Computer System Reliability." *FJCC, AFIPS Conf. Proc.,* vol. 31, Montvale, NJ: Academic Press, 1967, pp. 745–756.

[Wyner and Ash, 1963]
Wyner, A. D. and R. B. Ash, "Analysis of Recurrent Codes," *IEEE Trans. Inform. Th.,* IT-11, no. 3 (July 1963): 148–156.

[Yakowitz, 1977]
Yakowitz, S. J., *Computational Probability and Simulation,* Reading, MA : Addison-Wesley, 1977.

[Yourdon, 1972a]
Yourdon, E., "Reliability Measurements for Third Generation Systems." In *Proceedings of the Annual Reliability and Maintainability Symposium,* IEEE Computer Society, 1972, pp. 174–182.

[Yourdan, 1972b]
Yourdan, E., *Design of On-Line Computing Systems.* Englewood Cliffs, NJ: Prentice-Hall, 1972.

CONTRIBUTING AUTHORS

At the time of original publication of the reprinted articles included in this volume, the following were the authors' affiliations:

Chapter 9

Donald L. Droulette: IBM Corporation

Chapter 10

L. A. Boone, H. L. Liebergot, and R. M. Sedmak: Sperry Univac

Chapter 11

James A. Katzman: Tandem Computers

Joel F. Bartlett: Tandem Computers

Chapter 12

W. N. Toy: Processor Design Group, Bell Laboratories

Chapter 13

David Katzuki, Eric S. Elsam, William F. Mann, Eric S. Roberts, John G. Robinson, F. Stanley Skowronski, and Eric W. Wolf: Bolt, Beranek and Newman, Inc.

Chapter 14

Algirdas Avizienis and George C. Gilley: Jet Propulsion Laboratory, California Institute of Technology, and the Department of Computer Science, University of California at Los Angeles

Francis P. Mathur, David A. Rennels, John A. Rohr, and David K. Rubin: Jet Propulsion Laboratory, California Institute of Technology

Chapter 15

C. P. Jones: Systems Design and Engineering Section, Jet Propulsion Laboratory, California Institute of Technology

Chapter 16

John H. Wensley, Leslie Lamport, Jack Goldberg, Milton W. Green, Karl N. Levitt, P. M. Melliar-Smith, Robert E. Shostak, and Charles B. Weinstock: SRI International

Chapter 17

Albert L. Hopkins, Jr., T. Basil Smith, III, and Jaynarayan H. Lala: Charles Stark Draper Laboratory, Inc.

Appendix B

Algirdas Avizienis: Jet Propulsion Laboratory, California Institute of Technology

Appendix C

R. G. Bennetts and R. V. Scott: Southampton University, Southampton, England

---

TRADEMARKS

Figures II–3, II–4

Michael Marshall and G. David Low (Jet Propulsion Laboratory, California Institute of Technology), "Report of the Autonomous Spacecraft Maintenance Study Group Interim Draft Report," (July 28, 1980). Reprinted by permission.

Tables II–10, II–11, II–12, II–13, II–14

Abstracted from Michael Marshall and G. David Low (Jet Propulsion Laboratory, California Institute of Technology), "Report of the Autonomous Spacecraft Maintenance Study Group Interim Draft Report," (July 28, 1980). Reprinted by permission.

Tables 5–14, 5–15

Xavier Castillo, "Workload Performance and Reliability of Digital Computing Systems," Carnegie-Mellon University, Department of Electrical Engineering (December 1980). Reprinted by permission.

Figures 5–51, 5–52

Xavier Castillo and D. P. Siewiorek, "A Performance-Reliability Model for Computing Systems," IEEE PROCEEDINGS 10th INTERNATIONAL SYMPOSIUM ON FAULT-TOLERANT COMPUTING (1980). Copyright © 1980 IEEE. Reprinted by permission. (Originally published by Carnegie-Mellon University, Department of Computer Science, 1980.)

Figures 1–4, 1–6

S. Russell Craig, "Incoming Inspection and Test Programs," ELECTRONICS TEST (October 1980). Reprinted by permission.

Figures 3–54

N.G. Dennis, "Ultrareliable Voter Switches, with a Bibliography on Mechanization," MICROELECTRONICS AND RELIABILITY (August 1974). Copyright © 1974 Pergamon Press, Ltd. Reprinted by permission.

Figures 5–59 through 5–73

Steven Elkind, "Towards Automatic Design of Reliable Systems," Ph.D. thesis proposal, Carnegie-Mellon University, Department of Electrical Engineering (January 16, 1980). Reprinted by permission.

Figures 5–16 through 5–19, 5–57, 5–58; Tables 5–6, 5–7, 5–16, 5–17, 5–18

Steven Elkind and Daniel P. Siewiorek, "Reliability and Performance Models for Error Correcting Memory and Register Arrays," IEEE TRANSACTIONS ON COMPUTERS, vol. C-29, no. 10 (October 1980). Copyright © 1980 IEEE. Reprinted by permission. (Originally published by Carnegie-Mellon University, 1978.)

Figures 1–3, 4–2

Eugene Foley, "The Effects of Microelectronics Revolution on Systems and Board Test," COMPUTERS, vol. 12, no. 10 (October 1979). Copyright © 1979 IEEE. Reprinted by permission.

Figure 4–8

Adapted from, T. J. Frechette and F. Tanner, "Support Processor Analyzes Error Caught by Latches," ELECTRONICS (November 8, 1979). Copyright McGraw-Hill, Inc. 1979. All rights reserved. Reprinted by permission.

Figure 2–2

Michael Geilhufe, "Soft Errors in Semiconductor Memories," DIGEST OF PAPERS, COMPCON SPRING 1979, IEEE (1979). Copyright © 1979 IEEE. Reprinted by permission.

Tables 4–7, 4–8, 4–9

Adapted from, J. Grason and A. Nagle, "Digital Test Generation Design for Testability," PROCEEDINGS OF 17th ANNUAL DESIGN AUTOMATION CONFERENCE (1980). Copyright © 1980 IEEE. Reprinted by permission.

Figures 3–47, 3–48

K. J. Gurzi, "Estimates for the Best Placement of Voters in a Triplicated Logic Network," IEEE TRANSACTIONS ON ELECTRONIC COMPUTERS, vol. EC-14 (October 1965). Copyright © 1965 IEEE. Reprinted by permission.

Figure 3–60

M. Y. Hsiao, D. C. Bossen, R. T. Chen, "Orthogonal Latin Square Codes," IBM JOURNAL OF RESEARCH AND DEVELOPMENT, vol. 14, no. 4 (July 1970). Copyright © 1970 by International Business Machines Corporation. Reprinted by permission.

Figures 5–7, 5–8, 5–9, 5–10

Ashok Ingle and Daniel Siewiorek, "A Reliability Model for Various Switch Designs in Hybrid Redundancy," IEEE TRANSACTIONS ON COMPUTERS, vol. C-25, no. 2 (February 1976). Copyright © 1976 IEEE. Reprinted by permission. (Originally published by Carnegie-Mellon University, Department of Computer Science, October 1973.)

Figure II–2

J. J. Kulzer, "Systems and Reliability: A Case Study of No. 4 ESS," Infotech State of the Art Report SYSTEM RELIABILITY AND INTEGRITY, Pergamon Infotech Limited, Maidenhead (UK), 1978. Reprinted by permission.

Figures 3–88, 3–90

K. N. Levitt, M. W. Green, J. Goldberg, "A Study of the Data Communication Problems in a Self-Repairable Multiprocessor," AFIPS CONFERENCE PROCEEDINGS, vol. 32 (1968), Spring Joint Computer Conference. Reprinted by per-

Index

753